CONSUMER
BEHAVIOUR

A European Perspective

Fifth Edition

CONSUMER BEHAVIOUR
A European Perspective

Michael Solomon
Gary Bamossy
Søren Askegaard
Margaret K. Hogg

Harlow, England • London • New York • Boston • San Francisco • Toronto • Sydney
Auckland • Singapore • Hong Kong • Tokyo • Seoul • Taipei • New Delhi
Cape Town • São Paulo • Mexico City • Madrid • Amsterdam • Munich • Paris • Milan

Pearson Education Limited
Edinburgh Gate
Harlow
Essex CM20 2JE
England

and Associated Companies throughout the world

Visit us on the World Wide Web at:
www.pearson.com/uk

First published by Prentice Hall Europe 1999
Second edition published 2002
Third edition published 2006
Fourth edition published 2010
Fifth edition published 2013

ISBN: 978-0-273-77272-9 (print)
     978-0-273-77275-0 (PDF)
     978-0-273-78108-0 (eText)

British Library Cataloguing-in-Publication Data
A catalogue record for this book is available from the British Library

Library of Congress Cataloging-in-Publication Data
Solomon, Michael R.
   Consumer behaviour : a European perspective / Michael Solomon, Gary Bamossy,
Søren Askegaard. -- 5 Edition.
     pages cm
   Includes bibliographical references and index.
   ISBN 978-0-273-77272-9
   1. Consumer behavior--Europe.   I. Bamossy, Gary J., 1949-   II. Askegaard, Søren.   III. Title.
   HF5415.33.E85S65 2013
   658.8'342094--dc23

                                                        2013008564

10 9 8 7 6 5 4 3 2 1
17 16 15 14 13

Typeset in 9.25/12.5pt ITC Giovanni Std by 35
Printed and bound by L.E.G.O. S.p.A., Italy

BRIEF CONTENTS

CONTENTS

Part A
CONSUMERS IN THE MARKETPLACE

Chapter 1
AN INTRODUCTION TO CONSUMER BEHAVIOUR

Chapter 2
A CONSUMER SOCIETY

Chapter 3
SHOPPING, BUYING AND EVALUATING

Part B
HOW CONSUMERS SEE THE WORLD AND THEMSELVES

Chapter 4
PERCEPTION

Chapter 5
THE SELF

Part C
CONSUMERS AS DECISION-MAKERS

Part D
EUROPEAN CONSUMERS AND THEIR SOCIAL GROUPS

Part E
CULTURE AND EUROPEAN CONSUMERS

Companion Website

For open-access student resources specifically written to complement this textbook and support your learning, please visit www.pearsoned.co.uk/solomon

ON THE WEBSITE

Lecturer Resources

For password-protected online resources tailored to support the use of this textbook in teaching, please visit www.pearsoned.co.uk/solomon

We wrote this book because we're fascinated by the everyday activities of people. The field of consumer behaviour is, to us, the study of how the world is in large part influenced by the action of marketers. We're fortunate enough to be teachers and researchers (and occasionally consultants) whose work allows us to study consumers. Given that we're also consumers, we can find both professional and personal interest in learning more about how this process works. As consumers and future managers, we hope you find this study to be fascinating as well. Whether you're a student, manager or professor, we're sure you can relate to the trials and tribulations associated with last-minute shopping, preparing for a big night out, agonizing over a purchase decision, fantasizing about a week skiing in the Swiss Alps, celebrating a holiday on the Cote d'Azur or commemorating a landmark event, such as graduating from university, getting a driver's licence or (dreaming about) winning the lottery.

Buying, having and being

Our understanding of this field goes beyond looking at the act of *buying* only, but extends to both *having* and *being* as well. Consumer behaviour is about much more than just buying things; it also embraces the study about how having (or not having) things affects our lives, and how our possessions influence the way we feel about ourselves and about each other – our state of being. In addition to understanding why people buy things, we also try to appreciate how products, services and consumption activities contribute to the broader social world we experience. Whether shopping, cooking, cleaning, playing football or hockey, lying on the beach, emailing or texting friends, or even looking at ourselves in the mirror, our lives are touched by the marketing system.

The field of consumer behaviour is young, dynamic and in flux. It is constantly being cross-fertilized by perspectives from many different disciplines. We have tried to express the field's staggering diversity in this text. Consumer researchers represent virtually every social science discipline, plus a few represent the physical sciences and the arts for good measure. From this melting pot has come a healthy debate among research perspectives, viewpoints regarding appropriate research methods, and even deeply held beliefs about what are and what are not appropriate issues for consumer researchers to study in the first place.

A European perspective on consumers and marketing strategy

The main objective for this new, fifth edition has been to significantly increase its relevance for European students and scholars, while retaining the accessibility, contemporary approach, and the level of excellence in the discussions of consumer behaviour theory and applications established over the last ten editions of Michael Solomon's *Consumer Behavior*. Based on the tenth American edition, we have tried to satisfy the need for a comprehensive consumer behaviour textbook with a significant European content. Hence, we have added illustrative examples and cases which are analysed and discussed in a European consumer context, as well as numerous European scholarly references, including essays on the future of the field written by leading European consumer behaviour scholars. The text also includes a number of advertisements of European origin so that the reader can visualize various elements in the marketing applications of consumer behaviour theory.

These changes, which focus on European consumers and research, have been made throughout the book. However, the most substantial changes relevant to the field of consumer research have been the economic recession and budgetary crisis that has followed the financial crisis, and the proliferation of new social media interactivity. These two developments are featured in a number of examples throughout the book. The new edition also offers many examples of the new opportunities and challenges in this marketplace, as well as discussing the implications and challenges of carrying out business strategies and developing tactics.

The internationalization of market structures makes it increasingly necessary for business people to acquire a clear perspective and understanding of cultural differences and similarities among consumers from various countries. One of the challenges of writing this book has been to develop materials which illustrate *local* as well as *pan-European* and *global* aspects of consumer behaviour. In this spirit, we have kept a number of American and other non-European examples to illustrate various similarities and differences on the global consumer scene. The book also emphasizes the importance of understanding consumers in formulating marketing strategy. Many (if not most) of the fundamental concepts of marketing are based on the practitioner's ability to understand people. To illustrate the potential of consumer research to inform marketing strategy, the text contains numerous examples of specific applications of consumer behaviour concepts by marketing practitioners.

Digital consumer behaviour

As more of us go online every day, there's no doubt the world is changing – and consumer behaviour is constantly evolving in response to the web and social media (e.g. Facebook, Twitter). The fifth edition seeks to highlight the new world of the digital consumer. Today, consumers and producers come together electronically in ways we have never known before. Rapid transmission of information alters the speed at which new trends develop and the direction in which they travel, especially because the virtual world lets consumers participate in the creation and dissemination of new products.

One of the most exciting aspects of the new digital world is that consumers can interact directly with other people who live just down the street or half way across the world. As a result, we are having to radically redefine the meaning of community. It's no longer enough to acknowledge that consumers like to talk to each other about products. Now we share opinions and get the up-to-date information about new films, CDs, cars, clothes, in electronic communities that might include a young parent from Aalborg or Aachen, a senior citizen from Stockholm or Les Moutiers, or a teenager from Amsterdam or Istanbul. And many of us meet up in computer-mediated environments (CMEs) such as Facebook or Twitter. We have started to thread material and examples about these new emerging consumer playgrounds throughout the text.

We have just begun to explore the ramifications for consumer behaviour when a web surfer can project her own picture onto a website to get a virtual makeover or a corporate purchasing agent can solicit bids for a new piece of equipment from vendors around the world in minutes. These new ways of interacting in the marketplace create bountiful opportunities for marketing managers and consumers alike.

However, is the digital world always a rosy place? Unfortunately just as in the 'real world' the answer is no, as recent experiences in the UK with Twitter indicate (e.g. trolling). In addition to insulting consumers, the potential to exploit them, whether by invading their privacy, preying on the curiosity of children, or simply providing false product information, is always there. So inevitably the digital world comes with its own warnings. That said, it is difficult to imagine going back to a world without the web, and it is changing the field of consumer behaviour all the time – so watch this space.

Pedagogical features

Throughout the text there are numerous boxed illustrative examples which highlight particular aspects of the impact and informing role that consumer behaviour has on marketing activities. These colour-coded boxes are entitled:

- **Multicultural dimensions**,
- **Marketing opportunity**,
- **Marketing pitfall**, and
- **Consumer behaviour as I see it . . .** ,

and represent examples from several European and global markets. There are several other features within each chapter to assist you in learning and reviewing this text, and to check and critically evaluate your understanding of topics; these include:

- chapter **objectives**,
- an opening illustrative **vignette**,
- highlighted **key terms**,
- a **chapter summary**, and
- **Consumer behaviour challenge** questions.

To familiarize yourself with these features and how they will benefit your study from this text, they are reproduced and described in the Guided Tour on pages xix–xxi.

Case study problems

The fifth edition has seven new cases alongside nine cases retained from the fourth edition, so 16 teaching cases in all! These cases were written by our European colleagues who teach and research consumer behaviour. The case material covers various companies (e.g. IKEA; Dodge; BMW and the Mini car), industries (e.g. the Turkish leisure industry, the Swedish furniture retailing industry; the Austrian retail industry; and the UK telecommunications and funeral industries) and countries (e.g. Austria, Denmark, Finland, Greece, Sweden, Spain, Turkey and the UK). The cases integrate the topics covered in the preceding chapters, and appear at the end of each Part of the book. The questions at the end of each case study are designed to allow you to apply your understanding to real-life events and consumer behaviour activities; to develop your analytical skills; and to facilitate understanding of the different markets and cultural contexts across Europe. The questions often invite you to draw cross-cultural comparisons with your own consumer society.

Structure of the text

The structure of this textbook is simple: **Part A** opens with an overview chapter of the book and the discipline of consumer behaviour, and then provides chapters which place *you* in our contemporary culture of consuming (Chapter 2). The third chapter in this introductory section becomes more specific about you and your consumer behaviours, and describes how you navigate the retail world in which you make so many decisions on a daily basis. In short, this opening section of the book is designed to give you a context of 'what is CB, what is consumer culture, and how do I fit into it?' The book's remaining 12 chapters move through a micro to a macro perspective on theory and applications of consumer behaviour. Think of the book as a sort of photograph album of consumer behaviour: each chapter provides a 'snapshot' of consumers, but the lens used to take each picture grows successively wider. The book begins with issues related to the individual consumer and expands its focus until it eventually

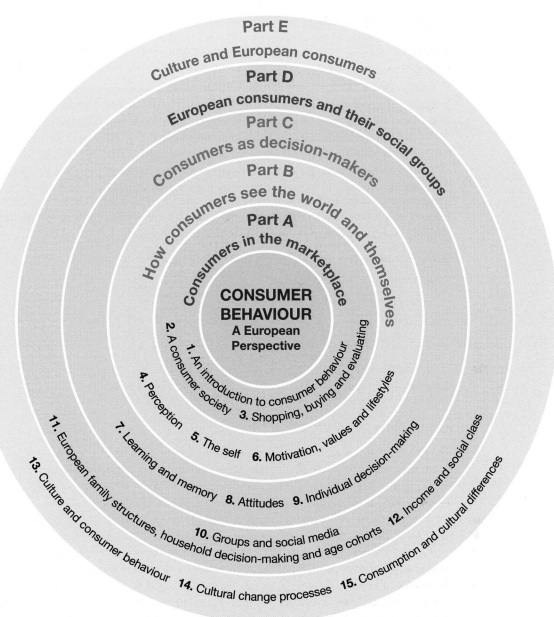

The wheel of consumer behaviour

considers the behaviours of large groups of people in their social settings. The topics covered correspond to the Wheel of Consumer Behaviour presented in the figure opposite.

Following the three introductory chapters, **Part B**, 'How consumers see the world and themselves' considers the consumer at the most micro level. It examines how the individual *perceives and receives* information from their immediate environment, how we use consumption as a tool in our life-long identity project of representing our *self*, and what *motives* are about (e.g. emerging new values around sustainability), and how we combine perceptions, sense of self, and motives to shape our *lifestyle(s)*.

Part C, 'Consumers as decision-makers', explores the ways in which consumers use the information they have acquired to learn and rely on memory, and to make decisions about consumption activities, both as individuals and as group members.

Part D, 'European consumers and their social groups', further expands the focus by considering how the consumer functions as a part of a larger social structure. No other consumer behaviour textbook offers as complete and up-to-date set of materials on the consumers of the EU27 as appear in this section (and the next). This structure includes the influence of different social groups to which the consumer belongs and/or identifies with, featuring social class, family and age groups.

Finally, **Part E**, 'Culture and European consumers', completes the picture as it examines marketing's impact on mass culture. This discussion focuses on the relationship of marketing to the expression of cultural values and lifestyles, how products and services are related to rituals and cultural myths, and the interface between marketing efforts and the creation of art, music, and other forms of popular culture that are so much a part of our daily lives. It also includes a section on major cultural change processes, analysed from the perspectives of globalization and postmodernism, and concludes by sketching in consumers' lives in the wider Europe.

GUIDED TOUR

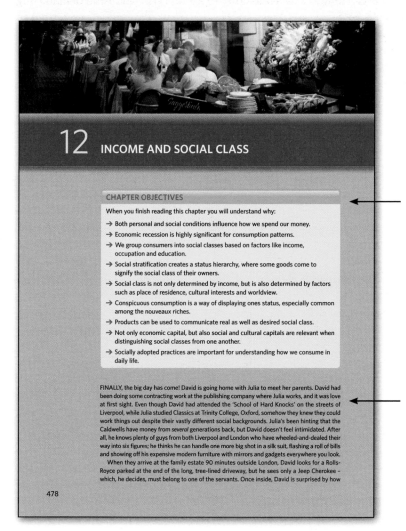

Chapter objectives let you know from the beginning what the chapter has to offer you, and referring back to them will help you ensure you're gathering all you need from your reading.

Opening vignettes introduce each chapter with a short, country-specific illustrative scenario highlighting the consumer behaviour issues that come up in everyday life.

Consumer behaviour as I see it features ask leading academics to comment on key consumer behaviour theories, giving you a fresh perspective on the chapter material.

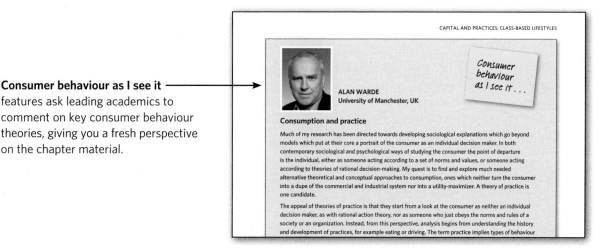

Marketing opportunity boxes show how consumer research informs marketing strategy.

MARKETING OPPORTUNITY ✓

Second-hand stores – the new in-place for consumers?

With the financial crisis turning into an economic crisis, new market opportunities replace the ones that went away with the carefree years that opened the twenty-first century. Second-hand shops are experiencing a boom in many European countries, not only for reasons of frugality, but also because many consumers consider this type of recycling a more ethical approach to consumption than the use-and-throw-away logic of former days. In the UK, Oxfam has experienced a boom in demand as soon as the economic crisis began[25] and has continued to grow. A sure sign of crisis is that in the same period, donations have gone down: 'Recession bites'.[26] In Denmark, second-hand shopping has also soared, and growth rates in some online second-hand services have exceeded 40 per cent over the last couple of years. This can hardly be explained by the crisis alone

– it probably also reflects a changed attitude towards second-hand consumption. Old stuff both makes it easier to feel unique through one's finds, there may be more stories attached to the old things, and finally – in contemporary consumer society of relative affluence, it might no longer be seen as socially downgrading to shop for recycled things, since it might be a sign of smartness and ability to locate 'good stuff' rather than lack of means.[27] Finally, second-hand is not just in order to get a cheap bargain. So called commission stores have sprung up, where consumers ready to make a bit of a change in their wardrobe put their designer clothes and accessories up for sale. A price is agreed between store owner and seller, and once the Louis Vuitton bag is sold, they split the amount often fifty-fifty.[28]

Social class

All societies can be roughly divided into the haves and the have-nots (though sometimes 'having' is a question of degree). While social equality is a widely held value throughout Europe, the fact remains that some people seem to be more equal than others. As David's encounter with the Caldwells suggests, a consumer's standing in society, or social class, is determined by a complex set of variables, including income, family background and occupation.

485

MARKETING PITFALL ✗

Steinar gazes over the expansive new verandah of his summer cottage on a tranquil island off Norway's south-eastern coast, chatting on his cell phone. The 50-year-old Oslo accountant recently added a host of amenities such as hot running water to his *hytte*, as Norwegians call their rustic summer cabins. Now he plans to put in a paved road to his front door and a swimming pool in the garden. 'There's nothing wrong with a little comfort', says Steinar. Well, maybe not in other summer playgrounds such as France's Côte d'Azur, but here in austere Norway, the words 'comfort' and 'vacation' are not synonymous. Thanks to the recent oil boom, many Norwegians are spending their new-found wealth upgrading spartan summer chalets with tennis courts, jacuzzis and even helipads. But in a country where simplicity and frugality are cherished virtues, and egalitarianism is strong, the display of wealth and money is suspect. Some politicians have suggested bulldozing the houses of the wealthy if they block access to the sea, and trade union leaders have blasted a new breed of Norwegians who favour showy yachts and life in the fast lane, and who build fences around private property.

'The rich can be quite vulgar', grumbles Steinar's neighbour Brit, who demanded that he trim a metre or so off his verandah because she and her husband, Gustav, could see it from their cabin lower down the hill. Both teachers, Brit and Gustav are nearing retirement, and have a more traditional Norwegian view of how to spend their summer, and how to spend their money. At stake, many say, are Norwegian ideals of equality and social democracy. These dictate that all Norwegians should have the same quality of life and share the national wealth equally. Norwegians champion austerity because they haven't always been prosperous. Before oil was discovered about 35 years ago, only a few families were considered wealthy. This frugality is obvious even in the capital, Oslo. For all the new oil money, plus low inflation, the city isn't a brash 'Kuwait of the North'.

Summer chalets should reflect the spartan mood, die-hards say, and vacation activities must be limited. Scraping down paint is popular, as is hammering down loose floorboards. So is swimming in lakes, fishing for supper and chopping wood. But not much else. As another neighbour, Aase, puts it: 'We like to, uh, sit here. I'd like the rich to stay away from here. They would ruin the neighbourhood.'[33]

487

The importance of cultural knowledge, and the dangers of ignoring it, are made clear in **Marketing pitfall** boxes.

Multicultural dimensions boxes highlight behavioural differences across countries and continents to help you understand the full diversity of global consumer behaviour.

MULTICULTURAL DIMENSIONS ✥

Anyone mingling with the crowd when India plays cricket at the Oval or shopping in areas with a large Asian population, such as Harrow or Slough or Wolverhampton, would find ample evidence of the material aspirations of young British Asians.

Asians as a group seem an attractive target for businesses. They are increasing in numbers (growing from 2.3m, according to the 2001 census); younger than the white population overall; more likely to be found in big cities; and making important economic advances. Indeed, most of the Asian population is British-born and one, two or even three, generations removed from their countries of ancestral origin. While the first generation had to save money and establish themselves, their children and grandchildren have British roots and are subject to tensions between their cultural upbringing and their degree of Britishness (remember *Bend it like*

Beckham?). One study concluded that 'the resulting bi-cultural self is one of both joy and frustration but above all it is one of continual negotiation and compromise'.[64]

Yet, communications professionals have tended to put them in a niche or ignore them. In January 2003, just 2 per cent of advertising campaigns featured actors from ethnic minorities – despite blacks and Asians making up 8 per cent of the population. In an effort to correct this imbalance, marketing consultant Anjna Raheja coined the term 'brown pound'. 'It was intended', she says, 'to draw attention to the growing economic power of Asian – and black – consumers.[65] In 2009, the first TV channel oriented specifically towards young Asians in the UK, Brit Asia TV, opened with a focus on the British Asian music scene and youth culture, yet another example of the proliferation of specialized media in the digital age.[66]

Class structure around the world

Every society has some type of hierarchical class structure, where people's access to products and services is determined by their resources and social standing. Of course, the specific

Chapter summaries provide a clear and concise way to look back over the key concepts and issues.

Each chapter ends with a **Consumer Behaviour Challenge** section. Here you'll find short, discursive questions designed to encourage critical examination of the topics and issues raised in the chapter.

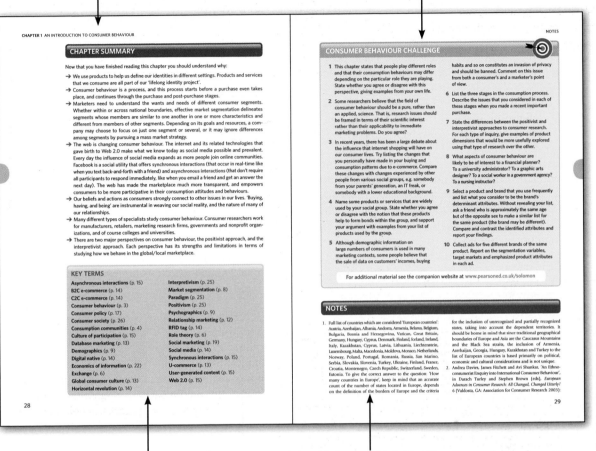

Key terms are given at the end of each chapter with page references so you can easily find their definitions in the text.

Notes provide you with a thorough list of sources for further reading, and are an ideal place to start building a bibliography for a research project.

Detailed **Case studies** end each part of the book. Covering various companies, industries and countries, they integrate topics from the preceding chapters and encourage you to think about how what you've learned applies in the real world.

CASE STUDY 10

Good child, bad child: observing experiences of consumer socialization in a twenty-first century family

BEN KERRANE, Manchester Business School, University of Manchester, UK

Context

Families play a large part in our lives. Indeed many decisions and purchases which we make in our adult lives are likely to be shaped and informed by our childhood experiences,

The Baldwin family story

Carole and Ray Baldwin got married two years ago. Before this they had spent several years cohabiting. They met following the death of Carole's first husband and the breakdown

Her requests are regularly granted with minimal parental resistance. Ray, in particular, often buys Nina expensive products much to her half sister's annoyance. Indeed Nina's parents often anticipate Nina's desire for products, and purchase items for her without Nina having to instigate the process. For instance, Carole and Ray recently purchased a new mobile phone for Nina even though Jessica had been constantly asking for one for weeks before. Nina did not even ask to be bought a mobile phone. As Ray commented: 'No, Nina didn't ask for it, it was our treat. Jessica had been on at me for ages to get her one, but she goes about asking for things the wrong way. Nina just doesn't ask for things, but Jessica's like a dripping tap, and she goes on and on at you'.

their parents as it is rather un-cool to be too closely associated with one's family's opinions and views as a teenager.

QUESTIONS

1 Jessica and Nina experience different environments within the family home. How and why? Identify and evaluate the features which distinguish the two environments experienced by Jessica and Nina.

2 How did the different treatment of Jessica and Nina affect their success in deploying influence strategies? How might their different experiences affect their consumer socialization?

ABOUT THE AUTHORS

Michael R. Solomon, PhD, joined the Haub School of Business at Saint Joseph's University in Philadelphia as Professor of Marketing in 2006, where he also serves as Director of the Center for Consumer Research. From 1995 to 2006, he was the Human Sciences Professor of Consumer Behavior at Auburn University. Prior to joining Auburn he was Chairman of the Department of Marketing in the School of Business at Rutgers University, New Brunswick, New Jersey.

Professor Solomon's primary research interests include consumer behaviour and lifestyle issues, branding strategy, the symbolic aspects of products, the psychology of fashion, decoration and image, services marketing, and the development of visually oriented online research methodologies. He currently sits on the Editorial Boards of the *Journal of Consumer Behaviour*, the *European Business Review*, and the *Journal of Retailing*, and he recently completed a six-year term on the Board of Governors of the Academy of Marketing Science.

In addition to this book, he is also the co-author of the widely used textbook *Marketing: Real People, Real Decisions*. Professor Solomon frequently appears on television and radio shows such as *The Today Show*, *Good Morning America*, Channel One, The Wall Street Journal Radio Network, and National Public Radio to comment on consumer behaviour and marketing issues.

Gary J. Bamossy, PhD, is Professor of Marketing at the McDonough School of Business, Georgetown University, in Washington DC, and Visiting Professor at the Olayan School of Business, American University of Beirut. From 1985 to 1999 he was on the Faculty of Business and Economics at the Vrije Universiteit, Amsterdam, as *Hoogleraar*, *Marktkunde* (Professor of Marketing), and Director of Business Research for the VU's participation at the Tinbergen Research Institute. Prior to his appointment at Georgetown, he was Director of the Global Business Program and a member of the marketing faculty at the University of Utah (1999–2005).

Professor Bamossy's primary research interests are on the global diffusion of material culture, and on sustainable consumption. He has published numerous articles on these and related topics in academic journals and as chapters in research books. He has given invited lectures on materialism and sustainable consumption issues at universities, companies and government agencies in North America, Europe and Asia, and his work has been funded by the Dutch Science Foundation (KNAW), the Marketing Science Institute, the Davidson Institute (University of Michigan) and the Anglo-Dutch Scholar Forum. Together with Professor W.F. van Raaij, Dr Bamossy co-chaired the first European conference for the Association for Consumer Research, in Amsterdam. For the past several years, Dr Bamossy has served as an Invited Member by The Bank of Sweden, to nominate a candidate for the Nobel Memorial Prize in Economic Sciences.

Professor Bamossy is a frequent contributor to the mass media. His research has been quoted or written about in the *Wall Street Journal Europe*, *The Washington Post*, *The Los Angeles Times*, *The Atlanta Journal Constitution*, The Associated Press, National Public Radio, CBS Television, *Fox News* and CBS Radio.

Søren Askegaard entered the atmosphere the same year as Yuri Gagarin left it. After wanting to be a postman for most of his childhood, he is now Professor of Marketing at the University of Southern Denmark. He has a post-graduate Diploma in Communication Studies from the Sorbonne University, Paris and PhD in Business Studies from Odense University, 1993.

Professor Askegaard's research interests generally are in the field of consumer culture theory and commercial symbolism. He is generally interested in debunking what is known as 'common sense', and he likes to act as a 'Martian' in his own society (as well as other societies), in order to catch a glimpse of all the funny, little – and not-so-little – things we do (and consume!), while thinking that it is 'perfectly normal'.

Professor Askegaard has given invited lectures at universities in Europe, North America, Asia and Latin America. He has served on a dozen programme committees for scientific conferences and is, among other things, co-organizer of the 2012 Consumer Culture Theory conference at Oxford University. He has been a visiting professor at universities in France, Sweden, Turkey and the USA.

Professor Askegaard is currently associate editor at *The Journal of Consumer Research*, the leading scientific journal for research in consumer behaviour. He also serves on the editorial boards for four other journals. His research has been published in numerous international journals and anthologies. For his research accomplishment he has received three research awards, including the Danish Marketing Association's Research Award. In 2008, he received the Danish Academy for Business Research Award for making his and his colleagues' research beneficial to the business community in Denmark. He also serves as the honorary consul of France in Odense, Denmark.

His research has been widely quoted by the mass media in Denmark, where he is a frequent commentator on consumer and market issues. His research has also been featured in the Swedish media and on BBC 4.

Margaret K. Hogg holds the Fulgoni Chair of Consumer Behaviour and Marketing in the Department of Marketing at Lancaster University Management School (LUMS). She read for an MA (Hons) in Politics and Modern History at Edinburgh University; postgraduate studies in History at the Vrije Universiteit, Amsterdam; an MA in Business Analysis at Lancaster University; and a PhD in Consumer Behaviour and Retailing at Manchester Business School. She worked for six years in marketing with 'K Shoes' in Kendal. She spent eight years at Manchester School of Management (MSM), UMIST before moving to LUMS in May 2004.

Professor Hogg's main areas of research interests are around the issues of identity, self and consumption within consumer behaviour. Her work has appeared in refereed journals including the *Journal of Advertising, Journal of Business Research, Journal of Marketing Management, European Journal of Marketing, International Journal of Advertising, Journal of Services Marketing, Journal of Consumer Policy, Marketing Management Journal, Advances in Consumer Research* and *Consumption, Markets and Culture*. She edited six volumes of papers on Consumer Behaviour in the Sage Major Works series (2005 and 2006) and has co-authored numerous book chapters. Professor Hogg regularly presents papers at international conferences including European Marketing Academy (EMAC), US, European and Asia-Pacific meetings of the Association for Consumer Research (ACR), the Society for Consumer Psychology (SCP) and AMA Marketing and Public Policy. She has given numerous seminar papers as an invited speaker (e.g. in Australia, New Zealand and Europe). She is a regular reviewer for the UK Economic and Social Research Council (ESRC) and for the Social Sciences and Humanities Research Council of Canada, as well as for the *Journal of Consumer Culture, Journal of Consumer Research, European Journal of Marketing, The Journal of Marketing Management* and *Marketing Theory*. She has been on the conference programme committees for US and European meetings of the Association for Consumer Research (ACR).

Professor Hogg held an award under the French Agence Nationale de la Recherche (ANR/ Programme Blanc) for two studies as part of Professor Dominique Roux's (Paris XII) project on New Approaches to Consumer Resistance (NACRE). She has taught extensively on consumer behaviour at undergraduate and postgraduate level, and supervised and examined a wide range of PhD students.

ACKNOWLEDGEMENTS

Many of our colleagues from the business world as well as from universities throughout Europe and beyond have made significant contributions to previous editions of this book by helping us identify important issues, and helping us think through them more clearly. We are grateful for their support, enthusiasm and their willingness to share their knowledge with us. In addition, numerous colleagues developed European case materials and chapter-opening vignettes for this text, or provided valuable comments and feedback in the market research process and reviewing of manuscript drafts. To them, our special thanks:

Emma N. Banister, *University of Manchester, UK*

Carlos Ballesteros, *Universidad Pontificia Comillas, Madrid, Spain*

Suzanne C. Beckmann, *Copenhagen Business School, Denmark*

Kok Hoi Beh, *De Montfort University, Leicester, UK*

Russell W. Belk, *York University, Toronto, Canada*

Matthias Bode, *University of Southern Denmark, Denmark*

Carlos Brito, *University of Porto, Portugal*

Marylyn Carrigan, *Coventry University, UK*

Janeen Arnold Costa, *Emerita, University of Utah*

Teresa Davis, *University of Sydney, Australia*

Hanna-Kaisa Desavelle, *Tampere University of Technology, Finland*

Mandy Dixon, *Lancaster University, UK*

Julie Emontspool, *University of Southern Denmark, Denmark*

Basil Englis, *Berry College, Georgia, USA*

Burçak Ertimur, *University of California, Irvine, USA*

Jim Freund, *Lancaster University, UK*

Güliz Ger, *Bilkent University, Ankara, Turkey*

Lampros Gkiouzepas, *Technological Educational Institute of Thessaloniki, Greece*

Kent Grayson, *Northwestern University, USA*

Andrea Groeppel-Klein, *University of Saarland, Germany*

Minni Haanpää, *University of Lapland, Finland*

Patrick Hetzel, *University of Paris II, Panthéon-Assas, France*

Sally Hibbert, *Nottingham University Business School, UK*

Robert J.W. Hogg, *London, UK*

Katerina Karanika, *University of Exeter, UK*

Kalipso M. Karantinou, *Athens University of Economics and Business, Greece*

Kathy Keeling, *University of Manchester, UK*

Ben Kerrane, *University of Manchester, UK*

Dannie Kjeldgaard, *University of Southern Denmark, Denmark*

Ingeborg Astrid Kleppe, *Norwegian School of Economics, Bergen, Norway*

Gry Høngsmark Knudsen, *University of Southern Denmark, Denmark*

Marius K. Luedicke, *City University, UK*

Pauline Maclaran, *Royal Holloway College, University of London, UK*

Morven G. McEachern, *Salford University, UK*

Damien McLoughlin, *University College, Dublin, Ireland*

Ilona Mikkonen, *Helsinki School of Economics, Finland*

Johanna Moisander, *Helsinki School of Economics, Finland*

Susanna Molander, *Stockholm University School of Business, Sweden*

Gabriele Morello, *GMA-Gabriele Morello and Associates, Palermo, Italy*

Stephanie O'Donohoe, *University of Edinburgh, Scotland*

Şahver Ömeraki, *Bilkent University, Ankara, Turkey*

Stijn van Osselaer, *Erasmus University, The Netherlands*

Jacob Östberg, *Stockholm University, Sweden*

Julie Ozanne, *Virginia Tech, USA*

Connie Pechmann, *University of California, Irvine, USA*

Lisa Peñaloza, *EDHEC, France*

Maria G. Piacentini, *Lancaster University, UK*

Linda Price, *University of Arizona, USA*

Effi Raftopoulou, *Keele University, UK*

Diego Rinallo, *Kedge Business School, Marseille, France*

Joonas Rokka, *Helsinki School of Economics, Finland*

Dominique Roux, *Université Paris 12, France*

Özlem Sandikci, *Bilkent University, Ankara, Turkey*

Tanja Schneider, *Oxford University, UK*

Jonathan Schroeder, *Rochester Institute of Technology, NY, USA*

Laura Sierra, *Universidad Pontificia Comillas, Madrid, Spain*

Diana Storm, *University of Southern Denmark, Odense, Denmark*

Carolyn Strong, *University of Bath, UK*

Peter Svensson, *Lund University, Sweden*

Darach Turley, *Dublin City University, Ireland*

Sofia Ulver-Sneistrup, *Lund University, Sweden*

Anu Valtonen, *University of Lapland, Finland*

Carmelina Vela, *Universidad Pontificia Comillas, Madrid, Spain*

Alan Warde, *University of Manchester, UK*

Jonathan Wilson, *University of Greenwich, London, UK*

We would also like to express our sincere thanks to our students in Denmark, the Netherlands and the UK who have proved to be valuable sources of ideas and examples throughout our work on this text. Thanks also to our friends and colleagues at Syddansk Universitet, the Vrije Universiteit, Amsterdam, Georgetown University and Lancaster University Management School for their support and inspiration throughout this project.

Gary, Søren and Margaret want to offer a special and personal word of thanks to Mike Solomon. While we were busy getting together the materials for this fifth European edition, Mike was just completing the manuscript for the tenth edition of *Consumer Behavior*. He shared materials with us as soon as they were ready, providing us with a pace and structure which kept us focused and on schedule! Mike was the perfect senior author – there when we needed something from him, and otherwise a positive source of energy and enthusiasm, coming from a comfortable distance. Ultimately, a great deal of synergy developed in our work together. We ended up sharing new materials, sources of research and ideas in a mutual process of give and take. Thanks for giving us this opportunity to work with you, Mike.

Gary Bamossy would like to thank Anne Marie Parlevliet in Amsterdam for her excellent desk research on developments in The Netherlands and the EU, and Jerome West, for source work and critical discussions on the EU. Both of you have made my revision efforts enjoyable. A special thanks to Janeen, Joost, Lieke and Jason – whose world views and consumption practices continue to amaze, amuse, inspire and enlighten me. Søren Askegaard would like to thank Kira Strandby for her excellent support in finding new material for a variety of chapters and for her tutorials on social media. He would also like to thank Caroline, Steen and Niels, for their patience – you can get back the large-screened top-floor computer now, boys! Margaret Hogg would like to say a very sincere 'thank you' to her family, Daniel, Julietta, Zoe and Robert, and to her late husband, Richard, for their generous, unstinting and loving support since she started this project.

PUBLISHER'S ACKNOWLEDGEMENTS

We are grateful to the following for permission to reproduce copyright material:

Figures

Figure 2.1 adapted from 'Culture and consumption: A theoretical account of the structure and movement of the cultural meaning of consumer goods', *Journal of Consumer Research*, Vol. 13, p. 72 (McCracken, G. 1986), The Chicago University Press; Figure 2.2 from Venkatesh, A., Ethnoconsumerism: A New Paradigm to Study Cultural and Cross-Cultural Consumer Behavior, *Marketing in a Multicultural World* (Costa, J.A. and Bamossy, G. (eds) 1995), Sage, Copyright 1995 Reproduced with permission of SAGE PUBLICATIONS INC BOOKS in the format textbook and ebook via Copyright Clearance Center; Figure 3.6 from Cyber-marketscapes and consumer freedoms and identities, *European Journal of Marketing*, Vol. 32 (7/8), pp. 664–76 (Venkatesh, A. 1998), *European journal of marketing* by EMERALD GROUP PUBLISHING LIMITED. Reproduced with permission of EMERALD GROUP PUBLISHING LIMITED in the format reuse in a book/textbook via Copyright Clearance Center; Figure 5.1 from *OECD Health Statistics*, OECD Publishing (2011), OECD (2011), 'Overweight and obesity', in OECD Factbook 2011–2012: Economic, Environmental and Social Statistics, OECD Publishing. http://dx.doi.org/10.1787/factbook-2011-109-en; Figure 6.5 from Consumer purchase motives and product perceptions: a laddering study on vegetable oil in three countries, *Food Quality and Preference*, Vol. 9, No. 6, pp. 455–66 (Nielsen, N.A., Bech-Larsen, T. and Grunert, K.G. 1998), Elsevier, Food quality and preference by PERGAMON. Reproduced with permission of PERGAMON in the format reuse in a book/textbook via Copyright Clearance Center; Figure 6.8 from CCA, Paris, 1990; Figure 6.9 adapted from What about disposition? Reprinted with permission from *Journal of Marketing*, published by the American Marketing Association, Jacoby, J., Berning, C.K. and Dietvorst, T.F., April 1977, Vol. 14, No. 23; Figure 6.10 adapted from *The Why of Consumption*, Routledge (Ratneshwar, S., Mick, D.G. and Huffman, C. (eds) 2000) pp. 1–8; Figures Case Study 7, pp. 383–4 from British Telecom; Figure 9.1 from Digital TV World Household Forecasts report by Simon Marsh, cited by Clarke in 'Digital TV homes to double within five years' Broadband TV News Correspondent inShare June 17, 2011 http://www.broadbandtvnews.com/2011/06/17/digital-tv-homes-to-double-within-five-years/ accessed 17 February 2012; Figure 10.1 adapted from Reference group influence on product and brand purchase decisions, *Journal of Consumer Research*, Vol. 9, September, p. 185 (Bearden, W.O. and Etzel, M.J. 1982), Reprinted with permission of The University of Chicago Press; Figure 10.4 from How Brand Community Practices Create Value, *Journal of Marketing*, Vol. 73, No. 5, September, pp. 30–51 (Schau, H.J., Muniz, A.M. and Arnould, E.J. 2009); Figure 10.6 adapted from The market maven: A diffuser of marketplace information. Reprinted with permission from *Journal of Marketing*, published by the American Marketing Association, Feick, L. and Price, L., January 1987, Vol. 51; Figure 10.7 adapted from Assessment of the psychometric properties of an opinion leadership scale, *Journal of Marketing Research*, Vol. 23, May, pp. 184–8

(Childers, T.L. 1986) and also adapted from The King and Summers opinion leadership scale: revision and refinement, *Journal of Business Research* Vol. 31, pp. 55–64 (Reinecke Flynn, L., Goldsmith, R.E. and Eastman, J.K. 1994), Journal of business research by UNIVERSITY OF GEORGIA. Reproduced with permission of ELSEVIER INC. in the format reuse in a book/textbook via Copyright Clearance Center and with the permission of Leisa Flynn; Figure 10.8 adapted from F.C. Bartlett, Remembering (Cambridge: Cambridge University Press, 1932), *Social psychology* by GERGEN, KENNETH J. p. 365, Copyright 1981 in the format Textbook via Copyright Clearance Center; Figure 12.3 from www.gfk-geomarketing.de/fileadmin/newsletter/pressrelease/purchasing-power-europe.html, © GfK GeoMarketing, study 'GfK Purchasing Power Europe 2012/2013'; Figure 12.5 from Kharas, H. (2010), 'The Emerging Middle Class in Developing Countries', OECD Development Centre Working Papers, No. 285, OECD Publishing. http://dx.doi.org/10.1787/5kmmp8lncrns-en; Figure 12.8 adapted from La sociologie de P. Bourdieu et son apport au marketing, *Recherches et Applications en Marketing*, Vol. VIII, No. 2, p. 123 (Moingeon, B. 1993); Figure 13.1 from Ethnoconsumerist Methodology for Cultural and Cross-Cultural Consumer Research, *Interpretive Consumer Research*, pp. 87–108 (Meamber, L. and Venkatesh, A. 2000), R. Elliott and S. Beckmann (eds), Copenhagen Business School Press; Figure 14.1 adapted from Building Up and Breaking Down: The Impact of Cultural Sorting on Symbolic Consumption, *Research in Consumer Behavior*, pp. 325–51 (Solomon, M.R. 1988), Sheth, J. and Hirschman, E.C. (eds), JAI Press, RESEARCH IN CONSUMER BEHAVIOR: A RESEARCH ANNUAL by Sheth, Jagdish N. Copyright 1988 Reproduced with permission of EMERALD GROUP PUBLISHING LIMITED in the format Republish in a textbook and 'other book' via Copyright Clearance Center; Figure 15.3 adapted from Atravesandofronteras/border crossings: A critical ethnographic exploration of the consumer acculturation of Mexican immigrants, *Journal of Consumer Research*, Vol. 21 (June), pp. 32–54 (Peñaloza, L. 1994); Figure 15.4 from Dominated Consumer Acculturation: The Social Construction of Migrant Women's Consumer Identity Projects in a Turkish Squatter, *Journal of Consumer Research*, Vol. 34 (June), p. 53 (Ustuner, T. and Holt, D.B. 2007), Fig. 2, The Journal of consumer research by AMERICAN ASSOCIATION FOR PUBLIC OPINION RESEARCH, reproduced with permission of UNIVERSITY OF CHICAGO PRESS in the format reuse in a book/textbook via Copyright Clearance Center; Figure 15.5 from The challenges of Islamic Branding: Navigating Emotions and Halal, *Journal of Islamic Marketing*, Vol. 2, No. 1, p. 34 (Bilal, J., Wilson, A.J. and Liu, J. 2011), Figure 4, Classification of Islamic Brands, Journal of Islamic Marketing by EMERALD GROUP PUBLISHING LTD. Reproduced with permission of EMERALD GROUP PUBLISHING LTD in the format reuse in a book/textbook via Copyright Clearance Center.

Screenshots

Screenshot p. 363, from www.ask.com; Screenshot p. 433 from © Threadless.com 2009; Screenshot p. 572 from LOOKK.com, Courtesy of LOOKK.

Tables

Table 1.4 adapted from Alternative ways of seeking knowledge in consumer research, *Journal of Consumer Research*, Vol. 14 (March), pp. 508–21 (Hudson, L.A. and Ozanne, J.L. 1988), Reprinted with the permission of The University of Chicago Press; Table 2.1 adapted from Trusting, complex, quality conscious or unprotected? Constructing the food consumer in different European national contexts, *Journal of Consumer Culture*, Vol. 7, No. 3, pp. 379–402 (Halkier, B. *et al.* 2007), copyright © 2007 by Sage. Reprinted by permission of SAGE Publications and Bente Halkier. This table builds on data from the project 'Consumer Trust in Food: A European Study of the Social and Institutional Conditions for the Production of Trust (TRUSTINFOOD 2002–4). The project was financed by the EU Commission's Quality of Life and Management of Living Resources Programme. The project included the following partners: Unni Kjaernes (coordinator), National Institute for Consumer Research (SIFO), Norway; Pedro Graca, University of Porto, Portugal; Bente Halkier, Roskilde University, Denmark; Mark Harvey, University of Manchester, UK; Lotte Holm, Copenhagen University, Denmark; Roberta Sassatelli, University of Bologna, Italy; Alan Warde, University of Manchester, UK; Corinna Willhöft, Federal Center for Nutrition and Food (BFEL), Karlsruhe, Germany; Table 3.1 from http://www.retail-index.com/HOMESEARCH/FoodRetailers/tabid/3496/Default.aspx accessed 16 February 2012, © 2011 Veraart Research; Table 3.2 adapted from *Welcome to Marketing.Com: The Brave New World of E-Commerce*, Prentice Hall (Solomon, M.R. and Stuart, E.W. 2001), Solomon, Michael R., E-COMMERCE SUPPLEMENT, 2nd Ed., © 2000. Reprinted and Electronically reproduced by permission of Pearson Education, Inc. Upper Saddle River, New Jersey; Table 6.1 adapted from Interpreting Dichter's Interpretations: An Analysis of Consumption Symbolism in The Handbook of Consumer Motivation', *Marketing and Semiotics: Selected Papers from the Copenhagen Symposium* (Durgee, J.F. 1991), Hartvig-Larsen, H., Mick, D.G. and Alsted, C. eds, Copenhagen Business School Press; Table 6.2 from Measuring the Cultural Values Manifest in Advertising, *Current Issues and Research in Advertising*, 6.1, pp. 71–92 (Pollay, R.W. 1983), Reprinted by permission, CtC Press All rights reserved, Current issues and research in advertising Copyright 1983 by TAYLOR & FRANCIS INFORMA UK LTD – JOURNALS. Reproduced with permission of TAYLOR & FRANCIS INFORMA UK LTD – JOURNALS in the format Republish in a textbook and 'other' book via Copyright Clearance Center; Table 8.1 adapted from Consumer Attitudes towards Sustainability Aspects of Food Production: Insights from Three Continents, *Journal of Marketing Management*, Vol. 28 (March), pp. 334–72 (Krystalis, A., Grunert, K.G., de Barcellos, M.D., Perrea, T. and Verbeke, W. 2012), Taylor and Francis, copyright © Westburn Publisher Limited, reprinted by permission of Taylor & Francis Ltd, www.tandf.com on behalf of the Westburn Publisher Limited. STM Licence and by permission of Professor Krystalis; Table 9.3 from On the psychology of loss aversion: Possession, valence, and reversals of the endowment effect, *Journal of Consumer Research*, Vol. 34 (October), p. 370 (Brenner, L., Rottenstreich, Y., Sood, S. and Bilgin, B. 2007), Table 1, The Journal of consumer research by AMERICAN ASSOCIATION FOR PUBLIC OPINION RESEARCH Reproduced with permission of UNIVERSITY OF CHICAGO PRESS in the format reuse in a book/textbook via Copyright Clearance Center; Table 9.6 from www.millwardbrown.com/libraries/optimor_brandz_files/2011_brandZ_top100_report.sflb.ashx; Table 10.1 adapted from 'Students and housewives: Differences in susceptibility to reference group influence', *Journal of Consumer Research* Vol. 4 (September), p. 102 (Whan Park, C. and Parker Lessig, V. 1977), Reprinted with permission of The University of Chicago Press; Table 13.1 from 'The ritual dimension of consumer behavior', *Journal of Consumer Research*, Vol. 12 (December), pp. 251–64 (Rook, D.W. 1985), Reprinted with permission of The University of Chicago Press, The Journal of consumer research by AMERICAN ASSOCIATION FOR PUBLIC OPINION RESEARCH Copyright 1985 Reproduced with permission of UNIVERSITY OF CHICAGO PRESS – JOURNALS in the format Textbook and 'other' book via Copyright Clearance Center; Table 13.2 adapted from 'Gift receipt and the reformulation of interpersonal relationships', *Journal of Consumer Research*, Vol. 25 (March), pp. 385–402 (Ruth, J.A., Otnes, C.C. and Brunel, F.F. 1999); Table 14.3 from *Signs in Contemporary Culture: An Introduction to Semiotics* New York: Longman (Berger, A.A. 1984) p. 86, Copyright © 1984. Reissued 1989 by Sheffield Publishing Company, Salem, WI. Reprinted with permission of the publisher; Table 14.5 from 'Cognitive style and personal involvement as explicators of innovative purchasing of health food brands', *European Journal of Marketing*, Vol. 27, No. 2, pp. 5–16 (Foxall, G.R. and Bhate, S. 1993), Used with permission, European journal of marketing by EMERALD GROUP PUBLISHING LIMITED. Reproduced with permission of EMERALD GROUP PUBLISHING LIMITED in the format reuse in a book/textbook via Copyright Clearance Center.

Text

Text p. 78 from John Lewis expands Collect and Click to Waitrose stores, *The Guardian* 31/08/2011 (Smithers, R.), http://www.guardian.co.uk/business/2011/aug/31/john-lewis-click-collect-waitrose?INTCMP=SRCH accessed Jan 24 2012, Marketing Opportunity, Copyright Guardian News & Media Ltd. 2011; Text p. 83 from Why pop-ups pop up everywhere, *The Guardian*, 12/10/2010 (Cochrane, K.), http://www.guardian.co.uk/lifeandstyle/2010/oct/12/pop-up-temporary-shops-restaurants accessed 24 Jan 2012, Marketing Opportunity, Copyright Guardian News & Media Ltd. 2010; Text p. 124 adapted from A New Market for Old Olive Trees, *The Wall Street Journal* (Snyder, W.R. 2008), http://online.wsj.com/article/SB120846638155724155.html, Marketing Opportunity, Wall Street journal Copyright 2008 by DOW JONES & COMPANY, INC. Reproduced with permission of DOW JONES & COMPANY, INC. in the format Republish in print and ebook via Copyright Clearance Center; Text pp. 137–8 adapted from A fresh look inside the shop freezer, *The Financial Times*, 24/03/2004 (Dowdy, C.), Marketing Opportunity, © The Financial Times Limited. All Rights Reserved; Text p. 151, from Ready for my video chat close up, *New York Times*, 19/04/2012 (Austin, C.), http://www.nytimes.com/2012/04/19/fashion/ready-for-my-video-chat-close-up.html?_r=1, Marketing Opportunity; Text p. 262 adapted from What's that Smell in the Movie Theatre? It's an Ad, *Adage* (Hall, E.), http://adage.com/article?article_id=129864, Marketing Opportunity, Text p. 281 adapted from Flavor of Nostalgia Grows More Appealing to Poles Brimming With Pride, *New York Times* (Berendt, J.), http://www.nytimes.com/2012/04/19/world/europe/flavor-of-nostalgia-grows-more-appealing-to-puffed-up-poles.html?_r=1, Marketing Opportunity; Text p. 299 from 'Advertisers' funny business', *Financial Times*, 17/02/2004 (Benady, A.), http://news.ft.com/servlet/ContentServer?pagename=FT.com/StoryFT/FullStory&c=StoryFT&cid=1075982574327&p=1012571727085, Marketing Pitfall, © The Financial Times Limited. All Rights Reserved; Text p. 350 adapted from 'CB As I See It', *Consumer Behaviour: Buying, Having, and Being, Global Edition*, 10 ed., (Fitzsimons, G. 2013), Solomon, M.R. (author), Pearson, with the permission of Professor G Fitzsimons; Text p. 361 adapted from Ad men use brain scanners to probe our emotional response, *The Guardian*, 14/01/2012 (Neate, R.), at http://www.guardian.co.uk/media/2012/jan/14/neuroscience-advertising-scanners?INTCMP=SRCH accessed

PUBLISHER'S ACKNOWLEDGEMENTS

January 27 2012, Marketing Opportunity, Copyright Guardian News & Media Ltd. 2012; Text, p. 462 adapted from http://www.csmonitor.com/The-Culture/2009/0126/poles-find-solidarity-in-milk-bars Hilary Heuler (2009), 'Poles Find Solidarity in Milk Bars', Christian Science Monitor, 26 January 2009; Text p. 487 from 'Cabin fever swirls around posh cottages on Norwegian coast', *Wall Street Journal Europe*, p. 1 (Beck, E.), Marketing Pitfall, Wall Street journal Europe Copyright 1997 by DOW JONES & COMPANY, INC. Reproduced with permission of DOW JONES & COMPANY, INC. in the format Republish in a textbook and ebook via Copyright Clearance Center.

Photographs
(Key: b-bottom; c-centre; l-left; r-right; t-top)

Alamy Images: Martin Dalton 409, Nick Turner 403, Stockfolio 236; **American Association of Advertising Agencies:** 21; **Apple, Inc:** 190; **Bianco Footwear:** 157; **BooneOakley Advertising:** 139; **British Heart Foundation:** 430b; **BT Image Library:** 355; **Caroline Penhoat:** 539; **Church & Dwight Co, Inc:** 344; **Corbis:** Arnd Wiegmann / Reuters 76r, Charles Jean Marc / Sygma 76l, Image Source 234t, James Marshall 81, Mark Peterson 608; **Courtesy of Procter & Gamble UK:** 127, 282r, 389; **D'Adda, Lorenzini.Vigorelli, BBDO:** Ilab Rubin 161; **DiMassimo Inc:** 210; **www.epa-photos.com:** Thomas Frey 579, 579r, **Eurorscg.com:** 134; **Gary Bamossy:** 205, 297, 445, 458; **Getty Images:** 169, 315, 404, AFP 125, 237, Bloomberg 48, Carl Schneider 414, Kevin Winter 552, Oli Scarff 82, Taxi / Gen Nishino 545;

Goretex: 66r; **H.J. Heinz Company Limited:** 71; **Hewlett Packard:** 72; **Image courtesy of The Advertising Archives:** 90, 142t, 188, 188c, 190b, 193b, 211b, 268, 282l, 282cr, 318b, 355b, 367b, 389b, 390b, 412b, 459, 502, 625; **iParty Corp:** 364; **iStockphoto:** dwphotos 209; **Jacek Wolowski:** 368; **Maidenform:** 591; **Marks and Spencer plc (company):** Jonty Davies 399, Rankin 233; **Courtesy: Mary Boone Gallery, New York.:** 63; **Pearson Education Ltd:** David Pu'u.Corbis.photolibrary.com 214, Imagemore Co., Ltd 281, Simon Marcus. Corbis. photolibrary.com 208; **Photo Researchers, Inc.:** Peter Byron 88; **Pirelli:** 188t; **Press Association Images:** Myung J Chun 67, Paul Mccarten / Landov 428; **Professor Robert Kozinets:** 221; **Reuters:** Darren Staples 78; **Saga Publishing Ltd:** 469; **Shutterstock.com:** 129, 400, Bikeworldtravel 333r, Songquan Deng 333l, Luc Ubaghs 450, Wayne Howes 488; **Soren Askegaard:** 42t; **Sunkist Growers:** 128; **The Absolut Company:** 596; **The Body Shop:** 53b, / Image courtesy of The Advertising Archives 173; **TopFoto:** Susan Goldman / The Image Works 428; **Barts and The London NHS Trust:** 402; **UNICEF/Thierry Delvigne-Jean:** Jan Burwick 18; **Unilever:** 42b, 171, 412; **Volkswagen Group:** 66b, 234b, 390; **WELT Kompakt:** 16; **Xin Zhao:** 154; **Y&R Dubai:** 318t.

Cover image: *Front:* **Alamy Images:** Ian Shaw.

In some instances we have been unable to trace the owners of copyright material, and we would appreciate any information that would enable us to do so.

Part A

CONSUMERS IN THE MARKETPLACE

This introductory part comprises three chapters. The first chapter previews much of what this book is about and gives an overview of the field of consumer behaviour. It examines how the field of marketing is influenced by the actions of consumers, and also how we as consumers are influenced by marketers. It also surveys consumer behaviour as a discipline of enquiry, and describes some of the different approaches that researchers use in order better to understand what makes consumers behave as they do. The second chapter takes a look at contemporary consumer culture and, more particularly, its globalization tendencies. It digs deeper into how marketing and culture are intertwined in contemporary societies and raises the important issue of the meaning of consumer goods for consumers. The third chapter offers a broad overview of the consumer in the marketplace, through its investigation of the modern ritual of the shopping process. It also looks at various contemporary retail environments, and the roles they play in consumers' social lives.

1 AN INTRODUCTION TO CONSUMER BEHAVIOUR

CHAPTER OBJECTIVES

When you finish reading this chapter you will understand why:

→ We use products to help us define our identities in different settings.

→ Consumer behaviour is a process.

→ Marketers need to understand the wants and needs of different consumer segments.

→ The web is changing consumer behaviour.

→ Our beliefs and actions as consumers strongly connect to other issues in our lives.

→ Many different types of specialists study consumer behaviour.

→ There are two major perspectives on consumer behaviour.

NATHALIE is working at her computer. It is early autumn and the beginning of a new term at her Danish university. Time for getting new books and study materials. As a second-year student, she is not surprised to find that several of the required books are still unavailable at the campus bookshop.

She goes online to check if she can get her books from one of the internet bookshops. She uses her favourite portal (**www.jubii.dk**) to check out the Scandinavian bookshops, which she thinks might be able to deliver the books faster than their international competitors. None of them have all of the books in stock that she needs, and she really feels that she should get all of the books from the same store. On an impulse, Nathalie visits a student shop which sells used books and provides search facilities for a number of online booksellers. She searches for a couple of the titles she is looking for, but the search facility does not seem to work. For a moment, she considers putting some of her used books up for sale, then decides not to let herself be distracted, and moves on to the UK version of **Amazon.com**. She has heard from friends that prices are a little steeper here (relative to the other internet bookshops), but she knows this site well by now. Besides, the books she wants are in stock and can be delivered in about a week, maybe less. Considering that the chances of the books she needs appearing in the campus bookshop on time seem pretty slim, Nathalie decides to go ahead and buy them online.

While she fills out the order form, she tries to plan where to go next. She and her friend are looking for an interesting topic for a course project and she wants to look at ideas for a relevant European project, clicking on CESSDA's website, (**http://www.cessda.org/**) for some inspiration. Also, she wants to visit a few of her favourite sites for news, music and travel. 'A little information update before meeting her friends this afternoon for coffee,' she thinks to herself. She clicks 'OK' to her order confirmation and is glad to have that out of the way. She navigates her way back to **http://www.cessda.org** and starts her search. All the while, she is thinking to herself that it would be nice to spend a little time checking out the latest in fashion and beauty tips; a little treat to herself while she still has some time on her hands. Suddenly Nathalie remembers that there were a couple of study plans to print out from the university website – and a few e-mails to answer. She checks her e-mail account and is a little surprised to see that she has received so much mail today – seems like everybody just realized that summer is over and wants to get started on new projects. It makes her feel joyful, even invigorated . . .

DIANA STORM, Copenhagen Business School

CONSUMPTION IN EUROPE? THE EUROPEAN CONSUMER?

This is a book about **consumer behaviour**, written from a European perspective. But what does that mean exactly? Obviously, to write about a 'European' consumer or a 'European's consumer behaviour' is problematic. For that matter, one might even ask 'What and where is Europe'? For it is a concept as well as a continent, and the borders of both oscillate wildly. The most common present-day usage of the term 'Europe', seems to be the shorthand for (and synonymous with) the European Union. The external borders of this supranational project are well-defined, and in some cases well-defended. But they remain movable, having consistently shifted outward over the last half century. From a core of six founding members in the continent's west, this 'Europe' has expanded to comprise 27 states, as far east as Cyprus. Where to draw Europe's Eastern border, and does it really have one?[1]

Some of the general theory about the psychological or sociological influences on consumer behaviour may be common to all Western cultures. On the one hand, some theories may be culturally specific. Certain groups of consumers do show similar kinds of behaviour across national borders, and research on consumers in Europe suggests that we even use our understanding of the consumption environment to make sense of the foreign cultures we are visiting.[2] On the other hand, the ways in which people live their consumption life vary greatly from one European country to another, and sometimes even within different regions of the same country. As a student of consumer behaviour, you might want to ask yourself: 'In which consumption situations do I seem to have a great deal in common with fellow students from other European countries? And in what ways do I seem to resemble more closely my compatriots? In what ways do subcultures in my country exert a strong influence on my consumption patterns, and how international are these subcultures?' To add to the complexity of all this, the EU continues to expand, adding new members. *Eurostat* officially reports on and offers rich data for 27 countries (EU27) and estimates the European population at roughly 503 million consumers.[3] These 'new' European consumers come from vastly different economic and political circumstances, and each has their own unique historical and cultural development. Much more on these consumers' aspirations and consumption behaviours will be reviewed in chapters in Parts D and E of this text which forms a portrait of European consumers.

This book is about consumer behaviour theory in general, and we will illustrate our points with examples from various European markets as well as from the United States and other countries. Each chapter features 'Multicultural dimensions' boxes which spotlight international aspects of consumer behaviour. From both a global and a pan-European perspective, these issues will be explored in depth in Chapters 2, 13, 14 and 15.

Consumer behaviour: people in the marketplace

You can probably relate to at least some general aspects of Nathalie's behaviour. This book is about people like Nathalie. It concerns the products and services they buy and use, and the ways these fit into their lives. This introductory chapter briefly describes some important aspects of the field of consumer behaviour, including the topics studied, who studies them, and some of the ways these issues are approached by consumer researchers.

But first, let's return to Nathalie: the sketch which started the chapter allows us to highlight some aspects of consumer behaviour that will be covered in the rest of the book.

- As a consumer, Nathalie can be described and compared to other individuals in a number of ways. For some purposes, marketers might find it useful to categorize Nathalie in terms of her age, gender, income or occupation. These are some examples of descriptive characteristics of a population, or *demographics*. In other cases, marketers would rather know something about Nathalie's interests in fashion or music, or the way she spends her leisure time. This sort of information often comes under the category *psychographics*, which refers to aspects of a person's lifestyle and personality. Knowledge of consumer characteristics plays an extremely important role in many marketing applications, such as defining the market for a product or deciding on the appropriate techniques to employ when targeting a certain group of consumers.

- Nathalie's purchase decisions are heavily influenced by the opinions and behaviours of her friends. A lot of product information, as well as recommendations to use or avoid particular brands, is picked up in conversations among real people, rather than by way of television commercials, magazines or advertising messages. The bonds among Nathalie's group of friends are in part cemented by the products they all use. The growth of the web has created thousands of online **consumption communities** where members share opinions and recommendations about anything from Barbie dolls to iPhone apps. Natalie forms bonds with fellow group members because they use the same products. There is also pressure on each group member to buy things that will meet with the group's approval, and often a price to pay in the form of group rejection or embarrassment when one does not conform to others' conceptions of what is good or bad, 'in' or 'out'.

- As a member of a large society, people share certain cultural values or strongly held beliefs about the way the world should be structured. Other values are shared by members of *subcultures*, or smaller groups within the culture, such as ethnic groups, teens, people from certain parts of the country, or even Lady Gaga's 'Little Monsters'. The people who matter to Nathalie – her *reference group* – value the idea that women in their early twenties should be innovative, style-conscious, independent and up front (at least a little). While many marketers focus on either very young targets or the thirty-somethings, some are recognizing that another segment which is attracting marketers' interest is the rapidly growing segment of older (50+) people.[4]

- When browsing through the websites, Nathalie is exposed to many competing 'brands'. Many offerings did not grab her attention at all; others were noticed but rejected because they did not fit the 'image' with which she identified or to which she aspired. The use of *market segmentation strategies* means targeting a brand only to specific groups of consumers rather than to everybody – even if that means that other consumers will not be interested or may choose to avoid that brand.

- Brands often have clearly defined *images* or 'personalities' created by product advertising, packaging, branding and other marketing strategies that focus on positioning a product a certain way or by certain groups of consumers adopting the product. One's leisure activities in particular are very much lifestyle statements: it says a lot about what a person is interested in, as well as something about the type of person they would like to be. People often choose a product offering, a service or a place, or subscribe to a particular idea, because they like its image, or because they feel its 'personality' somehow corresponds to their own. Moreover, a consumer may believe that by buying and using the product, its desirable qualities will somehow magically 'rub off'.

● When a product succeeds in satisfying a consumer's specific needs or desires, as **http://www.amazon.co.uk** did for Nathalie, it may be rewarded with many years of *brand* or *store loyalty*, a bond between product or outlet and consumer that may be very difficult for competitors to break. Often a change in one's life situation or self-concept is required to weaken this bond and thus create opportunities for competitors.

● Consumers' evaluations of products are affected by their appearance, taste, texture or smell. We may be influenced by the shape and colour of a package, as well as by more subtle factors, such as the symbolism used in a brand name, in an advertisement, or even in the choice of a cover model for a magazine. These judgements are affected by – and often reflect – how a society feels that people should define themselves at that point in time. Nathalie's choice of a new hairstyle, for example, says something about the type of image women like her want to project. If asked, Nathalie might not be able to say exactly why she considered some websites and rejected others. Many product meanings are hidden below the surface of the packaging, the design and advertising, and this book will discuss some of the methods used by marketers and social scientists to discover or apply these meanings.

● **Amazon.co.uk** has a combined American and international image that appeals to Nathalie. A product's image is often influenced by its *country of origin*, which helps to determine its 'brand personality'. In addition, our opinions and desires are increasingly shaped by input from around the world, thanks to rapid advancements in communications and transportation systems (witness the internet!). In today's global culture, consumers often prize products and services that 'transport' them to different locations and allow them to experience the diversity of other cultures. While the global/European recession has had an impact on many consumer behaviours,[5] young/single European consumers seem to be making use of the internet for another form of 'shopping', with online data websites reporting revenues of over half a billion euros! In the UK, the Office for National Statistics has added online dating as a category in its basket for measuring goods and services as a cost of living. As the financial analyst for online dating puts it: 'People don't cut back on hooking up, but meeting people online is cheaper – you get to sift through potential suitors.'[6]

The field of consumer behaviour covers a lot of ground: it is the study of the processes involved when individuals or groups select, purchase, use or dispose of products, services, ideas or experiences to satisfy needs and desires. Consumers take many forms, ranging from a 6-year-old child pleading with her mother for wine gums to an executive in a large corporation deciding on an extremely expensive computer system. The items that are consumed can include anything from tinned beans to a massage, democracy, rap music, and even other people (the images of rock stars, for example). Needs and desires to be satisfied range from hunger and thirst to love, status or even spiritual fulfilment. There is a growing interest in consumer behaviour, not only in the field of marketing but from the social sciences in general. This follows a growing awareness of the increasing importance of consumption in our daily lives, in our organization of daily activities, in our identity formation, in politics and economic development, and in the flows of global culture, where consumer culture seems to spread, albeit in new forms, from North America and Europe to other parts of the world. This spread of consumer culture via marketing is not always well received by social critics and consumers, as we shall see in subsequent chapters.[7] Indeed, consumption can be regarded as playing such an important role in our social, psychological, economic, political and cultural lives that today it has become the 'vanguard of history'.[8]

Consumers are actors on the marketplace stage

The perspective of **role theory**, which this book emphasizes, takes the view that much of consumer behaviour resembles actions in a play,[9] where each consumer has lines, props and costumes that are necessary to a good performance. Since people act out many different roles, they may modify their consumption decisions according to the particular 'play' they are in at the time. The criteria that they use to evaluate products and services in one of their roles may be quite different from those used in another role.

Another way of thinking about consumer roles is to consider the various 'plays' that the consumer may engage in. One classical role here is the consumer as a 'chooser' – somebody who, as we have seen with Nathalie, can choose between different alternatives and explores various criteria for making this choice. But the consumer can have many other things at stake than just 'making the right choice'. We are all involved in a communication system through our consumption activities, whereby we communicate our roles and statuses. We are also sometimes searching to construct our identity, our 'real selves', through various consumption activities. Or the main purpose of our consumption might be an exploration of a few of the many possibilities the market has to offer us, maybe in search of a 'real kick of pleasure'. On the more serious side, we might feel victimized by fraudulent or harmful offerings, and we may decide to take action against such risks from the marketplace by becoming active in consumer movements. Or we may react against the authority of the producers by co-opting their products, and turning them into something else, as when military boots all of a sudden became 'normal' footwear for peaceful women. We may decide to take action as 'political consumers' and boycott products from companies or countries whose behaviour does not meet our ethical or environmental standards. Hence, as consumers we can be choosers, communicators, identity-seekers, pleasure-seekers, victims, rebels and activists – sometimes simultaneously.[10]

Consumer behaviour is a process

In its early stages of development, the field was often referred to as *buyer behaviour*, reflecting an emphasis on the interaction between consumers and producers at the time of purchase. Marketers now recognize that consumer behaviour is an ongoing *process*, not merely what happens at the moment a consumer hands over money or a credit card and in turn receives some good or service.

The **exchange**, in which two or more organizations or people give and receive something of value, is an integral part of marketing.[11] While exchange remains an important part of consumer behaviour, the expanded view emphasizes the entire consumption process, which includes the issues that influence the consumer before, during and after a purchase. Figure 1.1 illustrates some of the issues that are addressed during each stage of the consumption process.

Consumer behaviour involves many different actors

A consumer is generally thought of as a person who identifies a need or desire, makes a purchase and then disposes of the product during the three stages in the consumption process. In many cases, however, different people may be involved in the process. The *purchaser* and *user* of a product may not be the same person, as when a parent chooses clothes for a teenager (and makes selections that can result in 'fashion suicide' from the teenager's point of view).

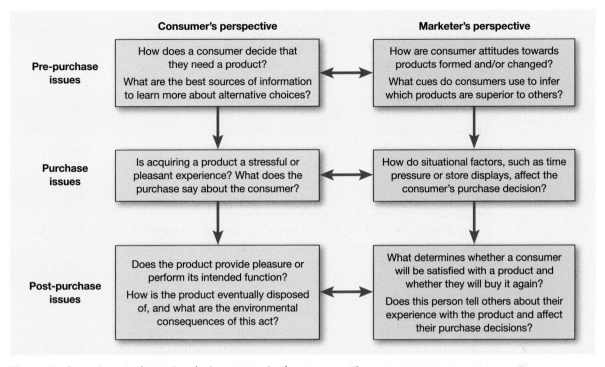

Figure 1.1 Some issues that arise during stages in the consumption process

In other cases, another person may act as an *influencer*, providing recommendations for (or against) certain products without actually buying or using them. For example, a friend, rather than a parent, accompanying a teenager on a shopping trip may pick out the clothes that they decide to purchase.

Finally, consumers may be organizations or groups in which one person may make the decisions involved in purchasing products that will be used by many, as when a purchasing agent orders the company's office supplies. In other organizational situations, purchase decisions may be made by a large group of people – for example, company accountants, designers, engineers, sales personnel and others – all of whom will have a say in the various stages of the consumption process. As we will see in Chapter 11, one important organization is the family, where different family members play pivotal roles in decision-making regarding products and services used by all.

CONSUMERS' IMPACT ON MARKETING STRATEGY

Surfing cool websites is a lot of fun. But, on the more serious side, why should managers, advertisers, and other marketing professionals bother to learn about consumer behaviour?

Very simply, *understanding consumer behaviour is good business*. The basic marketing concept states that firms exist to satisfy needs. Marketers can only satisfy these needs to the extent that they understand the people or organizations who will use the products and services they are trying to sell.

Consumer response is the ultimate test of whether a marketing strategy will succeed. Thus, a marketer should incorporate knowledge about consumers into every facet of a successful marketing plan. Data about consumers help organizations to define the market and identify threats to and opportunities for a brand. And, in the wild and wacky world of marketing, nothing is forever: this knowledge also helps to ensure that the product continues to appeal to its core market.

The Sony Walkman is a good example of a successful product that needed to update its image – especially since the company faced fierce competition from the incredibly popular Apple iPod. Although Sony revolutionized the mobile music experience and sold almost 300 million Walkmans in the process, today's teens see portable cassette players as dinosaurs (assuming they have even heard of cassettes!). The company's advertising agency followed 125 teens to see how they use products in their day-to-day lives. Based on this consumer research, Sony relaunched the product with a removable 'Memory Stick' instead of a cassette player so it works with MP3 files.[12]

Market segmentation: to whom are we marketing?

Whether within or across national boundaries, effective **market segmentation** delineates segments whose members are similar to one another in one or more characteristics and different from members of other segments. Depending on its goals and resources, a company may choose to focus on just one segment or several, or it may ignore differences among segments by pursuing a mass market strategy. In the internet-based market, **Amazon.com** tries to reach multiple segments at the same time. Alternatively, Meetic (the large European dating and chat site) offers a very similar product to all its customers – online dating services – but localizes its offerings for dozens of European countries by offering country sites in the local language . . . a key consideration for many when it comes to dating and chatting![13]

In many cases, it makes a lot of sense to target a number of market segments. The likelihood is that no one will fit any given segment description exactly, and the issue is whether or not consumers differ from our profile in ways that will affect the chances of their adopting the products we are offering.

Many segmentation variables form the basis for slicing up a larger market, and a great deal of this book is devoted to exploring the ways marketers describe and characterize different segments. The segmentation variables listed in Table 1.1 are grouped into four categories, which also indicate where in the book these categories are considered in more depth.

Table 1.1 Variables for market segmentation

Category	Variables	Location of discussion
Demographics	Age	Chapter 11
	Gender	Chapter 5
	Social class, occupation, income	Chapter 12
	Ethnic group, religion	Chapters 13, 15
	Stage in life	Chapter 11
	Purchaser *vs* user	Chapter 10
Geographic	Region	Chapters 13, 15
	Country differences	Chapters 2, 15
Psychographic	Self-concept, personality	Chapter 5
	Lifestyle	Chapters 6, 13, 14, 15
Behavioural	Brand loyalty, extent of usage	Chapter 8
	Usage situation	Chapter 9
	Benefits desired	Chapter 6

While consumers can be described in many ways, the segmentation process is valid only when the following criteria are met:

- Consumers within the segment are similar to one another in terms of product needs, and these needs are different from consumers in other segments.
- Important differences among segments can be identified.
- The segment is large enough to be profitable.
- Consumers in the segment can be reached by an appropriate marketing mix.
- The consumers in the segment will respond in the desired way to the marketing mix designed for them.

Demographics are statistics that measure observable aspects of a population, such as birth rate, age distribution or income. The national statistical agencies of European countries and pan-European agencies such as *EuroStat*[14] are major sources of demographic data on families, but many private firms gather additional data on specific population groups. The changes and trends revealed in demographic studies are of great interest to marketers, because the data can be used to locate and predict the size of markets for many products, ranging from mortgages to baby food to health care for senior aged consumers.

In this book, we will explore many of the important demographic variables that make consumers the same as, or different from, others. We'll also consider other important characteristics that are not so easy to measure, such as **psychographics** – differences in consumers' personalities and tastes which can't be measured objectively. For now, let's summarize a few of the most important demographic dimensions, each of which will be developed in more detail in later chapters. However, a word of caution is needed here. The last couple of decades have witnessed the growth of new consumer segments that are less dependent on demographics and more likely to borrow behavioural patterns and fashions across what were formerly more significant borders or barriers. It is now not so uncommon to see men and women, or grandmothers and granddaughters, having similar tastes. Hence, useful as they might be, marketers should beware of using only demographic variables to predict consumer tastes.

Age

Consumers in different age groups have very different needs and wants, and a better understanding of the ageing process of European consumers will continue to be of great importance to marketers as well as public policy decision-makers.[15] While people who belong to the same age group differ in many other ways, they do tend to share a set of values and common cultural experiences that they carry throughout life.[16] *Marie Claire*, the French magazine that is published in 25 editions and 14 languages, has noticed that its circulation and readership has fallen in past years, due primarily to not keeping pace with its younger readers and their reading habits. In the past, article length was typically nine to ten pages, and what is now desired is two to five pages. Rather than concentrating on serious articles on contemporary women's issues, the newer and younger readership is looking for something more fun and entertaining. Finding the balance of 'fun' (e.g. 'Four celebs' secrets to fabulous legs') and 'serious' (e.g. 'The role of the veil in Islamic dress') has been the challenge in bridging women readers of different age groups. While the print version of the magazine honours the magazine's long history, *Marie Claire* is now also available via your iPad app, and a full digital edition (for a fee) is available on the web – formats which also appeal to their youthful readers.[17]

Gender

Many products, from fragrances to footwear, are targeted at men or women. Differentiating by gender starts at a very early age – even nappies are sold in pink-trimmed versions for girls and blue for boys. As proof that consumers take these differences seriously, market research has revealed that many parents refuse to put baby boys in pink nappies![18]

One dimension that makes segmenting by gender so interesting is that the behaviours and tastes of men and women are constantly evolving. In the past most marketers assumed that men were the primary decision-makers for car purchases, but this perspective is changing with the times.

Sometimes, the gender segmentation can be an unintended product of an advertising strategy. Wranglers launched a European campaign featuring macho Wild West values such as rodeo riding, after an earlier campaign, featuring a supermodel, had made their sales of jeans to women grow 400 per cent but put men off their brand.[19]

MARKETING OPPORTUNITY

Websites for women

Segmenting by gender is alive and well in cyberspace.[20] In France, for example, a group of women started the country's first women's electronic magazine and web portal called **Newsfam.com**. These entrepreneurs are hoping to reproduce the success of American sites like **iVillage.com** and **Women.com**.[21] To underscore the idea that men and women differ in their tastes and preferences (the French would say *vive la différence!*), a website for high-tech products called **Hifi.com** opened a sister site just for women called **herhifi.com**. Within two years, **herhifi.com** was out of business, as the firm's notion that women would respond to a 'female' site for information on hi-fi equipment just did not seem to have any value to women. And if the demographic variable of gender segmentation is not nuanced enough for you in cyberspace, Meetic.com, Europe's largest online dating site, has now partnered with DatingDirect.com, a multi-country European site which targets individuals based on their sexual orientation, a lifestyle variable.[22]

Family structure

A person's family and marital status is yet another important demographic variable, since this has such a big effect on consumers' spending priorities. Young bachelors and newly-weds are the most likely to take exercise, go to wine bars and pubs, concerts and the cinema and to consume alcohol. Families with young children are big purchasers of health foods and fruit juices, while single-parent households and those with older children buy more junk food. Home maintenance services are most likely to be used by older couples and bachelors.[23] Chapter 11 provides an overview of European family structures, and the diversity of what constitutes 'family' and 'households' throughout Europe.

Social class and income

People in the same social class are approximately equal in terms of their incomes and social status. They work in roughly similar occupations and tend to have similar tastes in music, clothing and so on. They also tend to socialize with one another and share many ideas and values.[24] The distribution of wealth is of great interest to marketers, since it determines which groups have the greatest buying power and market potential.[25] As the number of member states of Europe continues to grow, the consumer behaviour implications of social class and income categories continues to grow as well! More on this dynamic construct of our European populace in Chapter 12.

Race and ethnicity

Immigrants from various countries in Africa and Asia are among the fastest-growing ethnic groups in Europe. As our societies grow increasingly multicultural, new opportunities develop

This Brazilian ad employs a novel message to encourage eye exams.

Source: Courtesy of Almap BBDO Communicacoes Ltda., photographer Alexandre Ermel.

to deliver specialized products to racial and ethnic groups, and to introduce other groups to these offerings.

Sometimes, this adaptation is a matter of putting an existing product or service into a different context. Turks in Berlin do not have to rely solely on the small immigrants' green-groceries and kiosks known from so many other European cities. A Turkish chain has opened the first department store in Berlin, carrying Turkish and Middle Eastern goods only, catering to both the large Turkish population as well as to other immigrant groups and Germans longing for culinary holiday memories. As one of the fastest growing segments in the European food market, halal foods now has its own ongoing marketing research organizations and media outlets for European managers and consumers.[26]

Geography

In Europe, most of the evidence points to the fact that cultural differences persist in playing a decisive role in forming our consumption patterns and our unique expressions of consumption. At the same time, global competition tends to have a homogenizing effect in some markets such as music, sports, clothing and entertainment, and multinational companies such as Sony, Pepsi, Nintendo, Nike and Levi Strauss continue to dominate or play important roles in shaping markets.[27] With the creation of the single European market, many companies have begun to consider even more the possibilities of standardized marketing across national boundaries in Europe. The increasing similarity of the brands and products available in Europe does not mean that the consumers are the same, however! Variables such as personal motivation, cultural context, family relation patterns and rhythms of everyday life, all vary substantially from country to country and from region to region. And consumption of various product categories is still very different.

To sum up, a European segmentation must be able to take into consideration:

● consumption which is common across cultures (the global or regional, trends, lifestyles and cultural patterns that cross borders); and

● consumption which is specific to different cultural groups (differences in values, lifestyles, behavioural patterns, etc. among different cultures and subcultures).

MARKETING OPPORTUNITY

New segments

Marketers have come up with so many ways to segment consumers – from the overweight to overachievers – that you might think they had run out of segments. Hardly. Changes in lifestyle and other characteristics of the population are constantly creating new opportunities. The following are some 'hot' market segments.

The gay community

In more and more societies, the gay minority is becoming increasingly visible. New media featuring homosexual lifestyles and the consumption patterns attached to them flourish and marketers claim that the gay community is as attractive a marketing niche as many other subcultures and that this group forms a 'hungry target'.[28] For example, in the marketing of Copenhagen as a tourist destination, the gay community has been explicitly chosen as one of the target markets. The gay segment tends to be economically upmarket and is frequently involved in travelling and short holidays to metropolitan areas. So the tourist board has tried to reach it through specific marketing activities targeted at gay environments in Europe. Recently, London has emerged as 'more than a destination' tourist spot for gays, based on the city's overall welcome to gays, which is not focused on just one specific area or neighbourhood. The government-funded 'visitbritain' website targets gay visitors, touting Britain as the 'United Queendom'.[29]

Single females

A worldwide study by Young and Rubicam has discovered a new and interesting market segment, that of well-educated, intelligent women who choose to stay single and pursue their life and career goals without husband or children. Furthermore, they represent heavy-spending consumers. They are reportedly brand-loyal and highly influenced by their friends in terms of consumption choices. The way to reach this attractive consumer group is to speak to their feelings of independence and self-respect.[30]

Disabled people

In the wake of legislation on the rights of disabled people, some marketers are starting to take notice of the estimated 10 to 15 per cent of the population who have some kind of disability. Initiatives include special phone numbers for hearing-impaired customers and assistance services for disabled people. IBM and Nissan have also used disabled actors in their advertising campaigns.[31] Mattel Inc., which produces Barbie, launched a sister doll, Becky, in a wheelchair – a reflection of the growing awareness of the disabled population in society.

Even then, the problem of specifying the relevant borders arises. Cultural borders do not always follow national borders. Although national borders are still very important for distinguishing between cultures, there may be important regional differences within a country, as well as cultural overlap between two countries.[32] Add to this the significant trends of immigration across Europe (mostly East to West) and the import of foreign (often American) cultural phenomena, and you begin to understand why it is very difficult to talk about European countries as being culturally homogeneous. For example, it is important to distinguish between, say, Dutch *society* with all its multicultural traits and debates and Dutch *culture*, which may be one, albeit dominant, cultural element in Dutch society. Furthermore, Dutch culture (as is the case with all cultures) is not a *static* but a *dynamic* phenomenon, which changes over time and from contact, interaction and integration with other cultures.

Relationship marketing: building bonds with consumers

Marketers are carefully defining customer segments and listening to people as never before. Many of them have realized that the key to success is building lifetime relationships between brands and customers. Marketers who believe in this philosophy – so-called **relationship marketing** – are making an effort to keep in touch with their customers on a regular basis, and are giving them reasons to maintain a bond with the company over time. Various types of membership of retail outlets, petrol companies and co-operative movements illustrate this. One co-operative chain offers reductions to its members on such diverse goods as travelling, clothing, home appliances, electronics and garden furniture.[33]

Some companies establish these ties by offering services that are appreciated by their customers. Many companies donate a small percentage of the purchase price to a charity such as the Red Cross or the World Wildlife Fund, or for the care of the poor and marginalized in society. This cements the relationship by giving customers an additional reason to continue buying the company's products year after year.

Another revolution in relationship building is being brought to us by courtesy of **database marketing**. This involves tracking consumers' buying habits by computer and crafting products and information tailored precisely to people's wants and needs.

Keeping close tabs on their customers allows database marketers to monitor their preferences and communicate with those who show an interest in their products or services. Information is passed to the appropriate division for follow-up. DVD online rental companies such as ScreenSelect in the UK and Web.DE in Germany are testing a system that makes recommendations based on a consumer's prior rentals and offers special promotions based on these choices.[34] However, some consumers feel threatened by this kind of surveillance and resist such marketing efforts. Hence, attempts have been made to ensure that database marketing conforms to the requirements of respondent confidentiality.[35]

MARKETING'S IMPACT ON CONSUMERS

For better or worse, we live in a world that is significantly influenced by marketers. We are surrounded by marketing stimuli in the form of advertisements, shops and products competing for our attention and our cash. Much of what we learn about the world is filtered by marketers, whether through conspicuous consumption depicted in glamorous magazine advertising or via the roles played by family figures in TV commercials. Ads show us how we ought to act with regard to recycling, alcohol consumption and even the types of house or car we aspire to. In many ways we are at the mercy of marketers, since we rely on them to sell us products that are safe and perform as promised, to tell us the truth about what they are selling, and to price and distribute these products fairly.

The global consumer

Since 2006, the majority of people on earth live in urban centres – the number of mega-cities, defined as urban centres of 10 million or more, is projected to grow to 26 in 2015.[36] One highly visible – and controversial – by-product of sophisticated marketing strategies is the movement towards a **global consumer culture**, in which people are united by their common devotion to brand-name consumer goods, film stars and rock stars.[37] Some products in particular have become so associated with an American/Western lifestyle that they are prized possessions around the world. In Chapters 2, 13 and 14 we will pay special attention to the good and bad aspects of this cultural homogenization.[38] On the other hand, popular culture continues to evolve as products and styles from different cultures mix and merge in new and interesting ways. For example, although superstars from the US and the UK dominate the worldwide music industry, there is a movement afoot to include more diverse styles and performers. In Europe, local music acts are grabbing a larger share of the market and pushing international (that is, English-speaking) acts down the charts. Revenue from Spanish-language music has quadrupled in five years.

We owe much of this interconnectedness and global consumer perspective to exciting new developments in technology that allow us to link with companies – and with each other – regardless of our physical locations. Indeed, our old model of sitting in front of a PC to surf the web will soon disappear like the horse and buggy. **U-commerce** is the use of *ubiquitous networks* that will slowly but surely become a part of us, whether in the form of wearable computers or customized advertisements beamed to us on our mobile phones ('Hey, you're walking by McDonald's. Come on in for today's burger special').[39]

Many products already carry a plastic **RFID tag** containing a computer chip and a tiny antenna that lets the chip communicate with a network. Grocery items will tell the store what needs to be restocked and which items are past their expiration dates, and your house will know when you're pulling into the driveway as it turns on the lights and starts your favourite music before you walk in the door.

Virtual consumption and the power of crowds

There is little doubt that the digital revolution is one of the most significant influences on consumer behaviour, and the impact of the web will continue to expand as more and more people around the world log on. Many of us are avid web surfers, and it is hard to imagine a time when texting, MP3 files, iPhones or BlackBerrys were not an accepted part of daily life.

And, it's not all about businesses selling to consumers (**B2C e-commerce**). The cyberspace explosion has created a revolution in consumer-to-consumer activity (**C2C e-commerce**): welcome to the new world of *virtual brand communities*. Just as e-consumers are not limited to local retail outlets in their shopping, they are not limited to their local communities when looking for friends or fellow fans of wine, hip-hop or skateboarding.

Picture a small group of local collectors who meet once a month at a local diner to discuss their shared interests over coffee. Now multiply that group by thousands, and include people from all over the world who are united by a shared passion for sports memorabilia, Barbie dolls, Harley-Davidson motorcycles, refrigerator magnets, or massively multiplayer online games (MMOGs) such as *World of Warcraft* and *Guild Wars 2*. The web also provides an easy way for consumers around the world to exchange information about their experiences with products, services, music, restaurants and movies. The Hollywood Stock Exchange (**hsx.com**) offers a simulated entertainment stock market where traders predict the four-week box office take for each film. The popularity of chat rooms where consumers can go to discuss various topics with like-minded 'Netizens' around the world grows every day, as do immersive virtual worlds such as Second Life, Habbo Hotel and Kaneva. News reports tell us of the sometimes wonderful and sometimes horrific romances that have begun on the internet as people check out potential mates on sites such as **Match.com** or **OKCupid**. In a recent month, one dating site (Plenty of Fish) alone had 122 million visits.[40]

If you're a typical student, you probably can't recall a time when the internet was just a static, one-way platform that transmitted text and a few sketchy images. And – believe it or not – in the last century even *that* crude technique didn't exist. You may have read about this in a history class. People actually hand-wrote letters to each other and waited for printed magazines to arrive in their mailboxes to learn about current events! The term **digital native** originated in a 2001 article to explain a new type of student who was starting to turn up on campus. These consumers grew up 'wired' in a highly networked, always-on world where digital technology had always existed.[41]

Fast forward a decade: today the internet is the backbone of our society. Widespread access to devices like personal computers, digital video and audio recorders, web cams, and smart phones ensures that consumers of practically any age and who live in virtually any part of the world can create and share content. But, information doesn't just flow from big companies or governments down to the people; today each of us can communicate with huge numbers of people by a click on a keypad, so information flows *across* people as well.

That's what we mean by a **horizontal revolution**. This horizontal revolution is characterized in part by the prevalence of social media. **Social media** are the online means of communication, conveyance, collaboration and cultivation among interconnected and interdependent networks of people, communities and organizations enhanced by technological capabilities and mobility.

Do you remember all those crazy Mentos/Diet Coke videos? At least 800 of them flooded YouTube after people discovered that when you drop the small sweets into bottles of Diet Coke you get a geyser that shoots 20 feet into the air. Needless to say (millions of views later!), Mentos got a gusher of free publicity out of the deal too.[42] **User-generated content**, where everyday people voice their opinions about products, brands, and companies on blogs, podcasts, and social networking sites such as Facebook and Twitter, and even film their own commercials that thousands view on sites such as YouTube, probably is the biggest marketing phenomenon of this decade. This important trend helps to define the era of **Web 2.0** – the rebirth of the internet as a social, interactive medium from its original roots as a form of one-way transmission from producers to consumers.

The internet and its related technologies that gave birth to Web 2.0 make what we know today as social media possible and prevalent. Every day the influence of social media expands as more people join online communities. Facebook, a social utility that offers **synchronous interactions** (that occur in real-time like when you text back and forth with a friend) and **asynchronous interactions** (that don't require all participants to respond immediately, as when you e-mail a friend and get an answer the next day), photo-sharing, games, applications, groups, e-retailing, and more, has as of the time of writing more than 600 million active users.[43] If Facebook were a country, it would be the third most populated in the world. People aren't just joining social communities. They are contributing too! YouTube users upload more than 35 hours of video every single minute of every day. That's roughly equivalent to 176,000 full-length movies uploaded weekly. In just 30 days on YouTube, more video is broadcast than in the last 60 years on CBS, NBC and ABC broadcasting networks combined.[44] Consider these mind-boggling social media stats:[45]

- If you were paid $1 for every time an article was posted on Wikipedia, you would earn $156.23 per hour.
- It took radio 38 years to reach 50 million listeners. TV took 13 years to reach 50 million users. The internet took four years to reach 50 million people. In under nine months, Facebook added 100 million users.
- About 70 per cent of Facebook users are outside the USA.
- Social media activity has overtaken porn as the number one online activity.
- One out of eight couples married last year met using a social media site.
- 80 per cent of companies use LinkedIn as their primary recruiting tool.
- 25 per cent of search results for the world's top 10 brands are to user-generated content.
- More than 1.5 billion pieces of content are shared on Facebook daily.
- 80 per cent of Twitter usage is from mobile devices, and 17 per cent have tweeted while in the toilet.

This is all exciting stuff, especially because social media platforms enable a **culture of participation**; a belief in democracy, the ability to freely interact with other people, companies and organization, open access to venues that allows users to share content from simple comments to reviews, ratings, photos, stories, and more, and the power to build on the content of others from your own unique point of view. Of course, just like democracy in the real world we have to take the bitter with the sweet. There are plenty of unsavory things going on in cyberspace, and the hours people spend on Facebook, in online gambling sites, or in virtual worlds like Second Life have led to divorce, bankruptcy or jail in the real world.

In the next chapter, we will take a look at the cultural dimensions of marketing and its impact on consumers. The relationship between marketing and consumption in a globalizing and increasingly unsustainable consumer society raises some real ethical issues. Right now, however, we will turn our attention to some of the more specifically ethical issues in the direct relationship between marketers and consumers.

The explosion of online communications changes the media landscape as traditional media platforms try to adapt. This German newspaper ad says, 'We sign-in our pets on Facebook. Are we ready for a new newspaper? *Welt Kompakt*. Concise. Different. Printed.'
Source: Courtesy of WELT KOMPAKT.

Marketing ethics

In business, conflicts often arise between the goal to succeed in the marketplace and the desire to conduct business honestly and maximize the well-being of consumers by providing them with safe and effective products and services. Some people argue that by the time people reach university, secondary school or are actually employed by companies, it is a little late to start teaching them ethics! Still, many universities and corporations are now focusing very intently on teaching and reinforcing ethical behaviour.

Prescribing ethical standards of conduct

Professional organizations often devise a code of ethics for their members. For example, European or national consumer protection laws or various national marketing associations' codes of ethics provide guidelines for conduct in many areas of marketing practice. These include:

● Disclosure of all substantial risks associated with a product or service.

● Identification of added features that will increase the cost.

● Avoidance of false or misleading advertising.

● Rejection of high-pressure or misleading sales tactics.

● Prohibition of selling or fund-raising under the guise of conducting market research.

Socially responsible behaviour

Whether intentionally or not, some marketers do violate their bond of trust with consumers. In some cases these actions are illegal, as when a manufacturer deliberately mislabels the contents of a package or a retailer adopts a 'bait-and-switch' selling strategy, whereby consumers are lured into the store with promises of inexpensive products with the sole intention of getting them to switch to higher-priced goods. A similar problematic issue of the luring of consumers is the case of misleading claims, for instance on food product labels.[46] For example, what about a label such as '100 per cent fat-free strawberry jam'?

In other cases, marketing practices have detrimental effects on society even though they are not explicitly illegal. The introduction of so-called alcopops, a mix of alcohol and soda or lemonade, targeted more or less explicitly at the teen market, has caused considerable debate in various European countries. Following negative press coverage, sales have gone down in Sweden and the UK, and the two largest retail chains in Denmark withdrew these drinks from their product range.[47] Others have run into difficulties by sponsoring commercials depicting groups of people in an unfavourable light to get the attention of a target market. One may recall the heated debate as to whether Benetton's advertising campaigns are attempts to sensitize consumers to the world's real problems, as the company contends, or to exploit unfortunate people – as in the ads depicting an AIDS victim, a dead Croat soldier or a ship packed with Albanian refugees – in order to sell more Benetton clothing.[48]

MARKETING PITFALL ⊗

Women for s@le!

The charge against abuse of marketing techniques has taken on new dimensions with the rise of the internet. Would you like to buy a Latvian girl for escort service? Or a Russian bride by mail order? The trade in women from Eastern Europe, Asia or Latin America has reached new heights with the easier contact made possible by the internet. Obvious problems are created by the difficulty of distinguishing between serious marriage bureaux or au pair agencies on the one side and organized traders of women for various kinds of prostitution services on the other. According to human rights organizations, many women who believe that they are going to marry the prince of their dreams end up as 'sexual services workers', sometimes under slavery-like conditions.[49]

Faced with the rising phenomenon of the 'political consumer' – a consumer who expresses their political and ethical viewpoints by selecting and avoiding products from companies which are antithetical to these viewpoints – the industry is increasingly coming to realize that ethical behaviour is also good business in the long run, since the trust and satisfaction of consumers translates into years of loyalty from customers. However, many problems remain. Throughout this book, ethical issues related to the practice of marketing are highlighted. Special boxes headed 'Marketing pitfall' feature dubious marketing practices or the possible adverse effects on consumers of certain marketing strategies.

Public policy and consumerism

Public concern for the welfare of consumers has been an issue since at least the beginning of the twentieth century. This is normally referred to as **consumer policy**. Partly as a result of consumers' efforts, many national and international agencies have been established to oversee consumer-related activities. Consumers themselves continue to have a lively interest in consumer-related issues, ranging from environmental concerns, such as pollution caused by oil spills or toxic waste, the use of additives and genetically manipulated material in food and so on, to excessive violence and sex on television.

Consumer research and consumer welfare

The field of consumer behaviour can play an important role in improving our lives as consumers.[50] Many researchers play a role in formulating or evaluating public policies, such as ensuring that products are labelled accurately, that people can comprehend important information presented in advertising, or that children are not exploited by programme-length toy commercials masquerading as television shows.

Of course, to a large degree consumers are dependent on their governments for regulation, police safety and environmental standards. The extent of supervision may depend on such factors as the national political and cultural climate. Debates within the EU concerning regulation of the use of pesticides and food additives are examples here. In addition, a country's traditions and beliefs may make it more sympathetic to one or the other point of view expressed by consumers or producers. For example, the cross-Atlantic debate concerning market acceptance of genetically modified food products has also given rise to research about consumers' attitudes towards the acceptability and labelling of such products. The consumer resistance to genetically modified food products in Europe has recently caused BASF, the German chemical concern, to stop developing these crops for Europe, and shift their research facilities to North America.[51]

Promoting consumers' rights, prosperity and well-being are core values of the European Union (EU), and this is reflected in its laws. Membership of the European Union ensures additional protection for consumers. Table 1.2 describes ten basic principles of how EU law protects you, as a consumer, no matter where you are in the EU. What is described is the minimum level of protection all EU countries should, according to EU law, give consumers. The details of exactly what your rights are – and how you can apply them – will vary from country to country depending on how they have implemented the EU rules in their national law. You should note that national consumer protection laws may – in some cases – give you a higher level of protection.

There is also a growing movement to develop knowledge about **social marketing**, which attempts to encourage such positive behaviours as increased literacy and to discourage negative activities such as drink-driving.[52] A project in Sweden aimed at curbing adolescent drinking illustrates social marketing at work. The Swedish Brewers' Association is investing 10 million Skr (about €1.16 million) in a co-operative effort with the Swedish Non-Violence Project to change teens' attitudes to alcohol consumption. Consumer researchers working on the project discovered that Swedish adolescents freely admit that they 'drink in order to get drunk' and enjoy the feeling of being intoxicated, so persuading them to give up alcohol is a formidable task. However, the teens reported that they are also afraid of losing control over

This German ad for Unicef makes a statement about the problem of child labour.

© German National Committee for UNICEF and Springer & Jacoby Fuenfte Werbeagentur GmbH & Co. KG. Photo: Jan Burwick.

Table 1.2 Ten principles of consumer protection in the EU

1 **Buy what you want, where you want.** Whether you physically go to a different EU country for shopping, or whether you order goods over the phone, via the internet, or by post, you should not have to pay customs duty or additional VAT on those purchases.

2 **If it doesn't work, send it back.** Under EU law, if a product you buy does not conform to the agreement you made with the seller at the time of purchase, you can take it back and have it repaired or replaced. Alternatively, you can ask for a price reduction, or a complete refund of your money. This applies for up to two years after you take delivery of the product.

3 **High safety standards for food and consumer goods.** Food safety is based on the principle that consumers need to look at the whole of the 'food chain' in order to ensure safety. EU food safety laws therefore regulate how farmers produce food (including what chemicals they use when growing plants and what they feed their animals), how food is processed, what colourings and additives can be used in it and how it is sold. The EU's safety laws on other consumer goods (toys, cosmetics, electrical equipment, etc.) are also strict.[53]

4 **Know what you are eating.** How can you find out what's in your food? Just look at the information on the package! EU laws on food labelling enable you to know what you are eating. Full details of the ingredients used to make a food product must be given on the label, along with details of any colouring, preservatives, sweeteners and other chemical additives used. EU food labelling laws regulate which products can be called 'organic' and the use of names associated with quality products from particular European regions – for example, if it is labelled *Prosciutto di Parma* you can be sure the ham comes from Parma, if it is labelled *Kalamata* you can be sure the olives are from Kalamata.

5 **Contracts should be fair to consumers.** EU law says that unfair contract terms are prohibited. Irrespective of which EU country you sign such a contract in, EU law protects you from unfair contract terms.

6 **Sometimes consumers can change their mind.** As a general principle, you can cancel a contract made by a doorstep salesperson within seven days. EU law also protects you, as a consumer, when you buy from mail order, internet or telesales companies and other 'distance sellers'.

7 **Making it easier to compare prices.** How do you compare the price of two different brands of breakfast cereal when one comes in a 375g box and the other in a 500g box? EU law requires supermarkets to give you the 'unit price' of products – for example, how much they cost per kilo or per litre – to help make it easier for you to decide which one is best value for money.

8 **Consumers should not be misled.** Advertising that misleads or deceives consumers is prohibited under EU law. In addition, when you are dealing with telesales, mail order or online retailers, sellers must be open and honest with you. EU law requires them to give you full details of who they are, what they are selling, how much it costs (including taxes and delivery charges) and how long it will take for them to deliver it.

9 **Protection while you are on holiday.** Package tour operators must have arrangements in place to get you home should they go bankrupt while you are on holiday. They must also offer you compensation if your holiday does not correspond to what they promised in their brochure. Last, but by no means least, EU law makes it easier for you to take your furry friends on holiday with you. Once your veterinarian has issued your cat, dog or ferret with one of the new 'pet passports' your pet can travel with you to any EU country.

10 **Effective redress for cross-border disputes.** Consumer interests should be promoted and defended, particularly in view of the increasing complexity of the markets in which they operate. The scope and size of markets has grown enormously over the last few years, not least due to the introduction of the euro, the development of e-commerce and increased intra-EU mobility. Recognising consumers as essential, responsible economic agents in the internal market is one of the key principles of European consumer policy. Consumers should be empowered to make informed choices about the goods and services that they purchase.

Source: Versions of the brochure are available in 20 European languages at: http://europa.eu.int/comm/consumers/cons_info/10principles_en.htm

their own behaviour, especially if there is a risk of their being exposed to violence. And while worries about the long-term health effects of drinking don't concern this group (after all, at this age many believe they will live forever), female adolescents reported a fear of becoming less attractive as a result of prolonged alcohol consumption.

Based on these findings, the group commissioned to execute this project decided to stress a more realistic message of 'Drink if you want to, but within a safe limit. Don't lose control, because if you do, you might get yourself into violent situations'. They made up the motto 'Alco-hole in your head' to stress the importance of knowing one's limits. This message is being emphasized along with strong visual images that appear on billboards, in video spots that depict situations involving young drinkers getting out of control, and in school presentations given by young people who will be credible role models for teens.[54]

DO MARKETERS MANIPULATE CONSUMERS?

One of the most common and stinging criticisms of marketing is that marketing techniques (especially advertising) are responsible for convincing consumers that they 'need' many material goods and that they will be unhappy and somehow inferior if they do not have these 'necessities'. The issue is complex, and one that is certainly worth considering: do marketers give people what they want, or do they tell people what they ought to want?

Philosophers have approached this issue when considering the concept of free will. It has been argued that in order to claim that consumers are acting autonomously in response to ads, the capacity for free will and free action must be present. That is, the consumer must be capable of deciding *independently* what to do, and not be prevented from carrying out that decision. This, it has been argued, is probably true for purely informative advertising, where only the product or store information required to make a rational decision is provided, whereas the case for advertising where imagery or underlying motivations are tapped is not as clear.[55] Such a view presupposes that informative advertising is somehow more objective than imagery-based advertising. But functionality and utility are also important images of a specific cultural context that uses references to our reason to seduce us.[56] Three issues related to the complex relationship between marketing practices and consumers' needs are considered here.

Do marketers create artificial needs?

The marketing system has come under fire from both ends of the political spectrum. On the one hand, some conservative traditionalists believe that advertising contributes to the moral breakdown of society by presenting images of hedonistic pleasure. On the other hand, some leftists argue that the same misleading promises of material pleasure function to buy off people who would otherwise be revolutionaries working to change the system.[57] Through advertising, then, the system creates demand that only its products can satisfy.

One possible response to such criticism is that a need is a basic biological motive, while a want represents one way that society has taught us that the need can be satisfied. For example, while thirst is biologically based, we are taught to want Coca-Cola to satisfy that thirst rather than, say, goat's milk. Thus, the need is already there: marketers simply recommend ways to satisfy it. A basic objective of advertising is to create awareness that these needs exist, rather than to create them.

However, marketers are important engineers of our environment. And beyond the level of banality, needs are always formed by the social environment. Thus, in a sense, needs are always 'artificial' because we are interested in needs only in their social form. Alternatively, needs are never artificial because they are always 'real' to the people who feel them. 'Needs'

DESPITE WHAT SOME PEOPLE THINK, ADVERTISING CAN'T MAKE YOU BUY SOMETHING YOU DON'T NEED.

Some people would have you believe that you are putty in the hands of every advertiser in the country.

They think that when advertising is put under your nose, your mind turns to oatmeal.

It's mass hypnosis. Subliminal seduction. Brain washing. Mind control. It's advertising.

And you are a pushover for it.

It explains why your kitchen cupboard is full of food you never eat.

Why your garage is full of cars you never drive.

Why your house is full of books you don't read, TV's you don't watch, beds you don't use, and clothes you don't wear.

You don't have a choice. You are forced to buy.

That's why this message is a cleverly disguised advertisement to get you to buy land in the tropics.

Got you again, didn't we? Send in your money.

ADVERTISING

ANOTHER WORD FOR FREEDOM OF CHOICE.

American Association of Advertising Agencies

This ad was created by the American Association of Advertising Agencies to counter charges that ads create artificial needs.

Source: American Association of Advertising Agencies.

are something we are socialized to have. In the case of the Coca-Cola *vs* goat's milk example, it should be remembered that we do not eat and drink solely to satisfy a biological need. We eat and drink for a number of reasons, all of them embedded in our cultural context. What is the need of a sofa? A TV? A car? A textbook on consumer behaviour? Thus, a better response would be that marketers do not create artificial needs, but they do contribute heavily to the socialization of people in contemporary society and thus to the establishment of the *social* system of needs. Consequently, marketers must take a share of responsibility for the development of society.

Is advertising necessary?

The social critic Vance Packard wrote more than 50 years ago, 'Large-scale efforts are being made, often with impressive success, to channel our unthinking habits, our purchasing decisions, and our thought processes by the use of insights gleaned from psychiatry and the social sciences.'[58] The economist John Kenneth Galbraith charged that radio and television are important tools to accomplish this manipulation of the masses. Because consumers do not need to be literate to use these media, repetitive and compelling communications can reach almost everyone. This criticism may even be more relevant to online communications, where a simple click delivers a world of information to us.

Many feel that marketers arbitrarily link products to desirable social attributes, fostering a materialistic society in which we are measured by what we own. One influential critic even argued that the problem is that we are not materialistic enough – that is, we do not suffi- ciently value goods for the utilitarian functions they deliver but instead focus on the irrational value of goods for what they symbolize. According to this view, for example, 'Beer would be enough for us, without the additional promise that in drinking it we show ourselves to be manly, young at heart, or neighbourly. A washing machine would be a useful machine to wash clothes, rather than an indication that we are forward-looking or an object of envy to our neighbors.'[59] One narrow response is to argue that 'Products are designed to meet existing needs, and advertising only helps to communicate their availability.'[60] According to the **economics of information** perspective, advertising is an important source of consumer information.[61] This view emphasizes the economic cost of the time spent searching for products. Accordingly, advertising is a service for which consumers are willing to pay because the information it provides reduces search time.

Such arguments seem somewhat outdated at the beginning of the twenty-first century, when advertising has been embraced as an art form in itself. Today, children are brought up to be both consumers and readers of advertising. A predominantly functional approach to consumption, as in the former planned economies of Eastern Europe, did not make people happier, nor did it prevent them from establishing mythologies about other goods, such as the scarce and expensive ones from the West. Advertisers, just like marketers, are important communicators. Their importance must be accompanied by a sense of responsibility concern- ing the social and individual effect of their messages.

Do marketers promise miracles?

Consumers are led to believe via advertising that products have magical properties; they will do special and mysterious things for them that will transform their lives. They will be beauti- ful, have power over others' feelings, be successful, be relieved of all ills, and so on. In this respect, advertising functions as mythology does in primitive societies: it provides simple, anxiety-reducing answers to complex problems. Is this a problem in itself?

Yes and no. The consumer is not an automaton that will react in a predefined way to cer- tain stimuli. On the other hand, we are all partly socialized by the market and its messages. So, whereas the manipulative effectiveness of advertising is often overstated, there is little doubt that advertising creates and changes patterns of consumption. This is especially so in the new market economies, where the population does not maintain the same distance from and critical attitude to advertising messages and imagery.

But the effect is in general more subtle than simple manipulative persuasion. In most cases, advertisers simply do not know enough about people to manipulate them directly. Consider that the failure rate for new products ranges from 40 to 80 per cent. The main effect of advert- ising may often be found on the more general level, in the promotion of the idea that your self and your personal relationships, your success and your image all depend on your con- sumer choices.

CONSUMER BEHAVIOUR AS A FIELD OF STUDY

Although people have been consumers for a very long time, it is only recently that consump- tion *per se* has been the focus of formal study. In fact, while many business schools now require that marketing students take a consumer behaviour course, most universities and business schools did not even offer such a course until the 1970s. Much of the impetus for the attention now being given to consumer behaviour was the realization by many business people that the consumer really *is* the boss.

Interdisciplinary influences on the study of consumer behaviour

Where do you find Consumer Researchers? Just about anywhere we find consumers. Consumer researchers work for manufacturers, retailers, marketing research firms, governments and nonprofit organizations, and, of course, colleges and universities. Professional groups, such as the Association for Consumer Research, have been formed since the mid-1970s, and European academics and practitioners are major contributors to the growing literature on consumer behaviour. To gain an idea of the diversity of interests of people who do consumer research, consider the list of professional associations that sponsor the field's major journal, the *Journal of Consumer Research*: the American Association of Family and Consumer Sciences, the Association for Consumer Research, the Society for Consumer Psychology, the International Communication Association, the American Sociological Association, the Institute of Management Sciences, the American Anthropological Association, the European Marketing Academy, the American Marketing Association, the Society for Personality and Social Psychology, ESOMAR (The European Society for Opinion and Market Research), and the American Economic Association. That's a pretty diverse group!

You'll find researchers doing sophisticated experiments in laboratories that involve advanced neural imaging machinery,[62] or interviewing shoppers in malls. They may conduct focus groups or run large-scale polling operations. For example, when the advertising agency began to work on a new campaign for retailer JCPenney (an American retailer, positioned in the market similar to Marks & Spenser, or H&M in Europe), it sent staffers to hang out with more than 50 women for several days. They wanted to really understand the respondents' lives, so they helped them to clean their houses, carpool, cook dinner and shop. As one of the account executives observed, 'If you want to understand how a lion hunts, you don't go to the zoo – you go to the jungle.'[63]

And, researchers work on many types of topics, from everyday household products and high-tech installations to professional services, museum exhibits and public policy issues such as the effect of advertising on children. Indeed, no consumer issue is too sacred: some intrepid investigators bravely explore 'delicate' categories like incontinence products and birth control devices. The marketing director for Trojan condoms notes that, 'Unlike laundry, where you can actually sit and watch people do their laundry, we can't sit and watch them use our product.' For this reason Trojan relies on clinical psychologists, psychiatrists and cultural anthropologists to understand how men relate to condoms.[64]

Researchers approach consumer issues from different perspectives. You might remember a fable about blind men and an elephant. The gist of the story is that each man touched a different part of the animal, and, as a result, the descriptions each gave of the elephant were quite different. This analogy applies to consumer research as well. A similar consumer phenomenon can be studied in different ways and at different levels depending on the training and interests of the researchers studying it.

Figure 1.2 covers some of the disciplines in the field and the level at which each approaches research issues. These disciplines can be loosely characterized in terms of their focus on micro *vs* macro consumer behaviour topics. The fields closer to the top of the pyramid concentrate on the individual consumer (micro issues), while those towards the base are more interested in the aggregate activities that occur among larger groups of people, such as consumption patterns shared by members of a culture or subculture (macro issues).

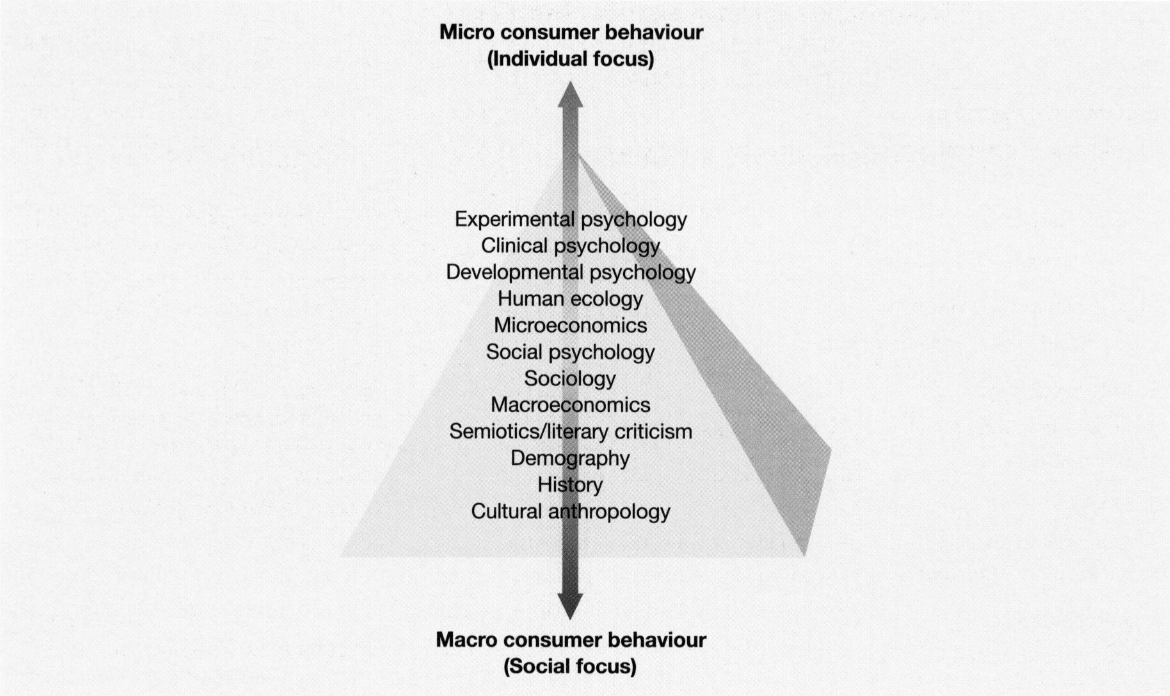

**Micro consumer behaviour
(Individual focus)**

Experimental psychology
Clinical psychology
Developmental psychology
Human ecology
Microeconomics
Social psychology
Sociology
Macroeconomics
Semiotics/literary criticism
Demography
History
Cultural anthropology

**Macro consumer behaviour
(Social focus)**

Figure 1.2 The pyramid of consumer behaviour

The issue of strategic focus

Many people regard the field of consumer behaviour as an applied social science. Accordingly, the value of the knowledge generated has traditionally been measured in terms of its ability to improve the effectiveness of marketing practice. Recently, though, some researchers have argued that consumer behaviour should not have a strategic focus at all; the field should not be a 'handmaiden to business'. It should instead focus on understanding consumption for its own sake, rather than because the knowledge can be applied by marketers.[65] This view is probably not held by most consumer researchers, but it has encouraged many to expand the scope of their work beyond the field's traditional focus on the purchase of consumer goods. And it has certainly led to some fierce debates among people working in the field! In fact, it can also be argued that business gets better research from non-strategic research projects because they are unbiased by strategic goals. Take a relatively simple and common consumer object like the women's magazine, found in every culture in a variety of versions. How much is there to say about the 'simple' act of buying such a magazine? Well, quite a lot. Table 1.3 lists some potential issues relevant for the marketing of or advertising in women's magazines which can be researched based on the variety of disciplines influencing consumer research.

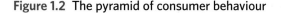

This more critical view of consumer research has led to the recognition that not all consumer behaviour and/or marketing activity is necessarily beneficial to individuals or to society. As a result, current consumer research is likely to include attention to the 'dark side' of consumer behaviour, such as addiction, prostitution, homelessness, shoplifting or environmental waste. This activity builds upon the earlier work of researchers who, as we have seen, have studied consumer issues related to public policy, ethics and consumerism.

The issue of two perspectives on consumer research

One general way to classify consumer research is in terms of the fundamental assumptions the researchers make about what they are studying and how to study it. This set of beliefs is

Table 1.3 Interdisciplinary research issues in consumer behaviour

Disciplinary focus	Magazine usage sample research issues
Experimental Psychology: product role in perception, learning and memory processes	How specific aspects of magazines, such as their design or layout, are recognized and interpreted; which parts of a magazine are most likely to be read
Clinical Psychology: product role in psychological adjustment	How magazines affect readers' body images (e.g. do thin models make the average woman feel overweight?)
Microeconomics/Human Ecology: product role in allocation of individual or family resources	Factors influencing the amount of money spent on magazines in a household
Social Psychology: product role in the behaviours of individuals as members of social groups	Ways that ads in a magazine affect readers' attitudes towards the products depicted; how peer pressure influences a person's readership decisions
Sociology: product role in social institutions and group through a social group relationships	Pattern by which magazine preferences spread
Macroeconomics: product role in consumers' relations with the marketplace	Effects of the price of fashion magazines and expense of items advertised during periods of high unemployment
Semiotics/Literary Criticism: product role in the verbal and visual communication of meaning	Ways in which underlying messages communicated by models and ads in a magazine are interpreted
Demography: product role in the measurable characteristics of a population	Effects of age, income and marital status of a magazine's readers
History: product role in societal changes over time	Ways in which our culture's depictions of 'femininity' in magazines have changed over time
Cultural Anthropology: product role in a society's beliefs and practices	Ways in which fashions and models in a magazine affect readers' definitions of masculine vs feminine behaviour (e.g. the role of working women, sexual taboos)

known as a **paradigm**. Like other fields of study, consumer behaviour is dominated by a paradigm, but some believe it is in the middle of a *paradigm shift*, which occurs when a competing paradigm challenges the dominant set of assumptions.

The basic set of assumptions underlying the current dominant paradigm is called **positivism**. This perspective has significantly influenced Western art and science since the late sixteenth century. It emphasizes that human reason is supreme and that there is a single, objective truth that can be discovered by science. Positivism encourages us to stress the function of objects, to celebrate technology and to regard the world as a rational, ordered place with a clearly defined past, present and future. Some feel that positivism puts too much emphasis on material well-being, and that its logical outlook is dominated by an ideology that stresses the homogeneous views of a predominantly Western and male culture.

The newer paradigm of **interpretivism** questions these assumptions. Proponents of this perspective argue that our society places too much emphasis on science and technology, and that this ordered, rational view of consumers denies the complexity of the social and cultural world in which we live. Interpretivists stress the importance of symbolic, subjective experience, and the idea that meaning is in the mind – that is, we each construct our own meanings based

Table 1.4 Positivist *vs* interpretivist approaches to consumer behaviour

Assumptions	Positivist approach	Interpretivist approach
Nature of reality	Objective, tangible	Socially constructed
	Single	Multiple
Goal	Prediction	Understanding
Knowledge generated	Time-free	Time-bound
	Context-independent	Context-dependent
View of causality	Existence of real causes	Multiple, simultaneous shaping events
Research relationship	Separation between researcher and subject	Interactive, co-operative, with researcher being part of phenomenon under study

Source: Adapted from Laurel A. Hudson and Julie L. Ozanne, 'Alternative ways of seeking knowledge in consumer research', *Journal of Consumer Research* 14 (March 1988): 508–21. Reprinted with the permission of The University of Chicago Press.

on our unique and shared cultural experiences, so that there are no single right or wrong references. To the value we place on products, because they help us to create order in our lives, is added an appreciation of consumption as a set of diverse experiences. The major differences between these two perspectives are summarized in Table 1.4.

In addition to the cross-cultural differences in consumer behaviour discussed earlier, it is also clear that research styles differ significantly between Europe and North America and also within European countries. For example, studies have shown that European researchers tend to consider the cultural dimension much more than their American counterparts.[66] A recent and more 'bridging' perspective on approaches to the study of consumer research argues that the study of particular consumption contexts are not an end in themselves, but rather that studying human behaviour in a consumption context is useful for generating new constructs and theoretical insights. This approach, consumer culture theory (CCT), embraces a variety of methodological approaches (used by both positivist and interpretivist), and recognizes that managers can make use of multiple methods to better understand trends in the marketplace, such as the complexities of lifestyle, multicultural marketing, and how consumers use media as part of their lives.[67]

Consumer research is still moving on. From its original emphasis on buying behaviour and the factors influencing the decision-making process, the field gradually widened to become a study of consumer behaviour in a more general sense, also taking into consideration what happened before and after the purchase. After the introduction of the interpretivist approach, a broader research perspective has included many new and non-psychological facets in the increasingly complex portraits of consumers. And it can be argued that the field increasingly looks beyond the single individual and their social background and environment to describe and analyse the complex relationships that have led us to start characterizing our present society as a **consumer society**.[68] The facts of living in a consumer society and being surrounded by consumer culture permeate this book but will be dealt with in more detail in Chapters 2 and 13.

TAKING IT FROM HERE: THE PLAN OF THE BOOK

This book covers many facets of consumer behaviour, and in the chapters to come we will highlight many of the research perspectives we briefly described in this one. The plan of the book is simple. It goes from micro to macro. Think of it as a sort of photograph album of consumer behaviour: each chapter provides a 'snapshot' of consumers, but the lens used to take each picture gets successively wider. The book begins with issues related to the individual consumer and expands its focus until it eventually considers the behaviours of large groups of people in their social settings.

PROFESSOR JULIE OZANNE
Virginia Tech

Consumer behaviour as I see it . . .

If you want to work to make the world a better place, then it is essential to understand consumers' behaviour. Consumption lies at the heart of the most important problems facing the global community. In economically developed countries, we are drowning in a sea of things that are depleting our limited global resources at an alarming rate. We are overconsuming food and raising a generation of overweight and unhealthy children. We are engaging in risky consumption behaviours such as smoking, drinking and gambling. Yet most of the people in the world face limited consumption opportunities and struggle to meet even basic nutritional needs.

Transformative Consumer Research is a new movement of consumer researchers who want to improve consumer well-being. Transformative consumer researchers engage in rigorous research to understand the nature of these pressing social problems. But then they seek to move outside the university to forge alliances with external stakeholders who can build programmes of social change to improve the quality of life. Consumer researchers stand in a unique position because they understand and respect the interests of both consumers and businesses. Thus, they have the potential to act as honest brokers working with consumer interest groups, public policy makers and business leaders to foster positive social transformation.

This is an exciting time in which to create new models of business and new forms of consumption that are more sustainable and can strengthen our communities. Nobel Peace Prize winner Muhammad Yunis envisioned offering microcredit loans to poor consumers who wanted to start their own businesses, which is a new model of consumer financing that has literally pulled millions of people out of poverty. New models of consumption are also being created. Paris encourages bike-sharing by distributing bikes throughout the city and does not charge for the first half-hour of rental so that short trips are free. Similarly, car-sharing, in which a fleet of cars is collectively owned and used, has grown to 600 cities worldwide.

In my recent research done in collaboration with my sister, Lucie Ozanne, we examine how the sharing of possessions and the exchange of services can build and strengthen the resiliency of local communities. For instance, toy-lending libraries operate similarly to book libraries by making toys available to children for a nominal fee. Networks of families form communities of sharing that become an important neighbourhood resource for advice and support. Children get to enjoy a wide range of toys while learning important lessons, such as the pleasures of sharing and a respect for collective goods. We are also studying timebanks that allow community members to exchange services in a system where each person's labour is valued equally. During the 2011 earthquakes in New Zealand, the local timebank leveraged this informal exchange network of neighbours who came to the aid of displaced families when civil services became overwhelmed.

Julie Ozanne

CHAPTER SUMMARY

Now that you have finished reading this chapter you should understand why:

→ We use products to help us define our identities in different settings. Products and services that we consume are all part of our 'lifelong identity project'.

→ Consumer behaviour is a process, and this process starts before a purchase even takes place, and continues through the purchase and post-purchase stages.

→ Marketers need to understand the wants and needs of different consumer segments. Whether within or across national boundaries, effective **market segmentation** delineates segments whose members are similar to one another in one or more characteristics and different from members of other segments. Depending on its goals and resources, a company may choose to focus on just one segment or several, or it may ignore differences among segments by pursuing a mass market strategy.

→ The web is changing consumer behaviour. The internet and its related technologies that gave birth to Web 2.0 make what we know today as social media possible and prevalent. Every day the influence of social media expands as more people join online communities. Facebook is a social utility that offers **synchronous interactions** (that occur in real-time like when you text back-and-forth with a friend) and **asynchronous interactions** (that don't require all participants to respond immediately, like when you email a friend and get an answer the next day). The web has made the marketplace much more transparent, and empowers consumers to be more participative in their consumption attitudes and behaviours.

→ Our beliefs and actions as consumers strongly connect to other issues in our lives. 'Buying, having, and being' are instrumental in weaving our social reality, and the nature of many of our relationships.

→ Many different types of specialists study consumer behaviour. Consumer researchers work for manufacturers, retailers, marketing research firms, governments and nonprofit organizations, and of course colleges and universities.

→ There are two major perspectives on consumer behaviour, the positivist approach, and the interpretivist approach. Each perspective has its strengths and limitations in terms of studying how we behave in the global/local marketplace.

KEY TERMS

Asynchronous interactions (p. 15)

B2C e-commerce (p. 14)

C2C e-commerce (p. 14)

Consumer behaviour (p. 3)

Consumer policy (p. 17)

Consumer society (p. 26)

Consumption communities (p. 4)

Culture of participation (p. 15)

Database marketing (p. 13)

Demographics (p. 9)

Digital native (p. 14)

Economics of information (p. 22)

Exchange (p. 6)

Global consumer culture (p. 13)

Horizontal revolution (p. 14)

Interpretivism (p. 25)

Market segmentation (p. 8)

Paradigm (p. 25)

Positivism (p. 25)

Psychographics (p. 9)

Relationship marketing (p. 12)

RFID tag (p. 14)

Role theory (p. 6)

Social marketing (p. 18)

Social media (p. 14)

Synchronous interactions (p. 15)

U-commerce (p. 13)

User-generated content (p. 15)

Web 2.0 (p. 15)

CONSUMER BEHAVIOUR CHALLENGE

1 This chapter states that people play different roles and that their consumption behaviours may differ depending on the particular role they are playing. State whether you agree or disagree with this perspective, giving examples from your own life.

2 Some researchers believe that the field of consumer behaviour should be a pure, rather than an applied, science. That is, research issues should be framed in terms of their scientific interest rather than their applicability to immediate marketing problems. Do you agree?

3 In recent years, there has been a large debate about the influence that internet shopping will have on our consumer lives. Try listing the changes that you personally have made in your buying and consumption patterns due to e-commerce. Compare these changes with changes experienced by other people from various social groups, e.g. somebody from your parents' generation, an IT freak, or somebody with a lower educational background.

4 Name some products or services that are widely used by your social group. State whether you agree or disagree with the notion that these products help to form bonds within the group, and support your argument with examples from your list of products used by the group.

5 Although demographic information on large numbers of consumers is used in many marketing contexts, some people believe that the sale of data on customers' incomes, buying habits and so on constitutes an invasion of privacy and should be banned. Comment on this issue from both a consumer's and a marketer's point of view.

6 List the three stages in the consumption process. Describe the issues that you considered in each of these stages when you made a recent important purchase.

7 State the differences between the positivist and interpretivist approaches to consumer research. For each type of inquiry, give examples of product dimensions that would be more usefully explored using that type of research over the other.

8 What aspects of consumer behaviour are likely to be of interest to a financial planner? To a university administrator? To a graphic arts designer? To a social worker in a government agency? To a nursing instructor?

9 Select a product and brand that you use frequently and list what you consider to be the brand's determinant attributes. Without revealing your list, ask a friend who is approximately the same age but of the opposite sex to make a similar list for the same product (the brand may be different). Compare and contrast the identified attributes and report your findings.

10 Collect ads for five different brands of the same product. Report on the segmentation variables, target markets and emphasized product attributes in each ad.

For additional material see the companion website at **www.pearsoned.co.uk/solomon**

NOTES

1. Full list of countries which are considered 'European countries': Austria, Azerbaijan, Albania, Andorra, Armenia, Belarus, Belgium, Bulgaria, Bosnia and Herzegovina, Vatican, Great Britain, Germany, Hungary, Cyprus, Denmark, Finland, Iceland, Ireland, Italy, Kazakhstan, Cyprus, Latvia, Lithuania, Liechtenstein, Luxembourg, Malta, Macedonia, Moldova, Monaco, Netherlands, Norway, Poland, Portugal, Romania, Russia, San Marino, Serbia, Slovakia, Slovenia, Turkey, Ukraine, Finland, France, Croatia, Montenegro, Czech Republic, Switzerland, Sweden, Estonia. To give the correct answer to the question: 'How many countries in Europe', keep in mind that an accurate count of the number of states located in Europe, depends on the definition of the borders of Europe and the criteria for the inclusion of unrecognized and partially recognized states, taking into account the dependent territories. It should be borne in mind that since traditional geographical boundaries of Europe and Asia are the Caucasus Mountains and the Black Sea straits, the inclusion of Armenia, Azerbaijan, Georgia, Hungary, Kazakhstan and Turkey to the list of European countries is based primarily on political, economic and cultural considerations and is not unique.

2. Andrea Davies, James Fitchett and Avi Shankar, 'An Ethno-consumerist Enquiry into International Consumer Behaviour', in Darach Turley and Stephen Brown (eds), *European Advances in Consumer Research: All Changed, Changed Utterly?* 6 (Valdosta, GA: Association for Consumer Research 2003):

102–7. See also: Jacobs, Frank, (2012) 'Where is Europe'? *New York Times*, accessed at: http://opinionator.blogs.nytimes.com/ 2012/01/09/where-is-europe/ and Buckley, Neil, (2011) 'West Meets East' *Financial Times*, accessed at: http://www. ft.com/cms/s/0/b7f7ee48-207a-11e1-8462-00144feabdc0. html#axzz1ij4vvqn4

3. Eurostat: Europe in Figures, Eurostat yearbook, 2010, available at: http://epp.eurostat.ec.europa.eu/cache/ITY_OFFPUB/ KS-CD-10-220/EN/KS-CD-10-220-EN.PDF; see also: http:// en.wikipedia.org/wiki/Demographics_of_the_European_ Union

4. 'Older Consumers in the Spotlight', April 2004, accessed at: http://www.cmdglobal.com/database/U/UFO/Understanding_ Fifties_and_Over

5. 'Recession: Shifting Consumer Responses', *Euromonitor International*, March 2012. Accessed at: http://blog.euromonitor.com/ survey-results/

6. Thompson, Christopher (2012) 'Valentine's Boost for Online Dating Sites' *Financial Times*, 10 February 2012, accessed at: http://www.ft.com/cms/s/2/874790d0-53df-11e1-9eac-00144feabdc0.html#axzz1rprOkgg8

7. Mike Featherstone (ed.), *Global Culture. Nationalism, Globalization, and Modernity* (London: Sage, 1990). For a critical review of the effects and reception of (American style) marketing, see Johansson, Johny K., *In Your Face: How American Marketing Excess Fuels Anti-Americanism* (Upper Saddle River, NJ: Financial Times Prentice Hall, 2004).

8. Daniel Miller, 'Consumption as the Vanguard of History', in D. Miller (ed.), *Acknowledging Consumption* (London: Routledge, 1995): 1–57.

9. Erving Goffman, *The Presentation of Self in Everyday Life* (Garden City, NY: Doubleday, 1959); George H. Mead, *Mind, Self, and Society* (Chicago: University of Chicago Press, 1934); Michael R. Solomon, 'The role of products as social stimuli: A symbolic interactionism perspective', *Journal of Consumer Research* 10 (December 1983): 319–29.

10. Yiannis Gabriel and Tim Lang, *The Unmanageable Consumer* (London: Sage, 1995).

11. Frank Bradley, *Marketing Management: Providing, Communicating and Delivering Value* (London: Prentice-Hall, 1995).

12. Evan Ramstad, 'Walkman's Plan for Reeling in the Ears of Wired Youths', *Wall Street Journal Interactive Edition* (18 May 2000).

13. http://www.meetic.com/

14. http://epp.eurostat.ec.europa.eu/portal/page/portal/eurostat/ home/

15. Päivi Munter and Norma Cohen, 'Ageing populations "will create crippling debt" ', *Financial Times* (31 March 2004).

16. Natalie Perkins, 'Zeroing in on consumer values', *Ad Age* (22 March 1993): 23. See also: 'Ageing, Children, and Gender Issues', *European Public Health Alliance*, 2008, http:// www.epha.org/r/37

17. Charles Goldsmith and Anne-Michelle Morice, 'Marie Claire wants to add some fun', *Wall Street Journal* (12 April 2004): B-1. See also: http://www.marieclaire.com/hair-beauty/ trends/world-hair-color-trends?click=main_sr#slide-1

18. Jennifer Lawrence, 'Gender-specific works for diapers – almost too well', *Ad Age* (8 February 1993): S-10 (2); see also: Dixon, John, 'On Discourse and Dirty Nappies', *Theory & Psychology*, vol. 14 no. 2, 167–189 (2004).

19. 'Wrangler ad ropes in men', *Marketing* (27 March 1997).

20. 'Gender Gap Alive and Well Online' BBC News, http:// news.bbc.co.uk/2/hi/technology/4555370.stm

21. Amy Barrett, 'Site blends frivolous, serious to draw French women online', *Wall Street Journal Interactive Edition* (11 April 2000).

22. http://www.meetic.com/

23. Charles M. Schaninger and William D. Danko, 'A conceptual and empirical comparison of alternative household life cycle models', *Journal of Consumer Research* 19 (March 1993): 580–94; Robert E. Wilkes, 'Household life-cycle stages, transitions, and product expenditures', *Journal of Consumer Research* 22(1) (June 1995): 27–42.

24. Richard P. Coleman, 'The continuing significance of social class to marketing', *Journal of Consumer Research* 10 (December 1983): 265–80.

25. Henry, Paul C. 'How Mainstream Consumers Think about Consumers Rights and Responsibilities' *Journal of Consumer Research*, 37, no. 4 (December 2010) 670–87. See also: Henry, Paul C. 'Social Class, Market Situation, and Consumers' Metaphors of (Dis)Empowerment' 31, no. 4 (March 2005), 766–778.

26. Janmohamed, Shelina (2012) 'The Muslim consumer: building your brand for a fast-growing segment', *Financial Times*, 5 January, accessed at: http://blogs.ft.com/beyondbrics/2012/01/05/the-muslim-consumer-building-your-brand-for-a-fast-growing-segment/; see also: Kerstin Hilt, 'Mail order firm ships a taste of home', *Deutsche Welle* (29 December 2004), http://www.dw-world.de/dw/article/ 0,1564,1441829,00.html. See also: *The Halal Journal*, http://www.halaljournal.com/artman/publish_php/cat_ index_66.php

27. Jean-Claude Usunier, *Marketing Across Cultures*, 4th edn (London: Prentice-Hall, 2005).

28. Søren Askegaard and Tage Koed Madsen, 'The local and the global: homogeneity and heterogeneity in food consumption in European regions', *International Business Review* 7(6) (1998): 549–68.

29. http://www.visitbritain.com/en/EN/ Vanessa Thorpe, 'London becomes Europe's pink capital', *The Observer* (9 January 2005), http://media.guardian.co.uk/site/story/0,14173, 1386236,00. html; see also: 'Hello Sailors: The United Queendom Wants You', *The Sunday Times* (5 February 2006).

30. *Markedsføring* 18 (7 September 2000): 16.

31. *Markedsføring* 17 (25 August 2000): 8.

32. Richard Vezina, Alain d'Astous and Sophie Deschamps, 'The Physically Disabled Consumer: Some Preliminary Findings and an Agenda for Future Research', in F. Hansen (ed.), *European Advances in Consumer Research* 2 (Provo, UT: Association for Consumer Research, 1995): 277–81.

33. *Samvirke* 3 (March 1997).

34. http://www.screenselect.co.uk/visitor/home.html and http://web.de/, 2005.

35. Barry Leventhal, 'An approach to fusing market research with database marketing', *Journal of the Market Research Society* 39(4) (1997): 545–58.

36. Brad Edmondson, 'The dawn of the megacity', *Marketing Tools* (March 1999): 64.

37. For a discussion of this trend, see Russell W. Belk, 'Hyperreality and globalization: Culture in the age of Ronald McDonald', *Journal of International Consumer Marketing* 8(3/4) (1995): 23–37.

38. For a fully fledged study of this process, see Tom O'Dell, *Culture Unbound. Americanization and Everyday Life in Sweden* (Lund: Nordic Academic Press, 1997).

39. Richard T. Watson, Leyland F. Pitt, Pierre Berthon and George M. Zinkhan, 'U-Commerce: Expanding the Universe of Marketing', *Journal of the Academy of Marketing Science* 30 (2002): 333–47.

40. Irina Slutsky, 'Get Hooked up With the Big Business of Online Dating', *Advertising Age* (14 February 2011), http://adage.com/article/ad-age-graphics/online-dating-a-a-1-3-billion-market/148845/, accessed 7 May 2011.

41. Prensky, Marc (2001) 'Digital Natives, Digital Immigrants', *On the Horizon* (MCB University Press, vol. 9 no. 5, October 2001).

42. Steve Spangler, 'Mentos Diet Coke Geyser', *SteveSpanglerScience.com*, http://www.stevespanglerscience.com/experiment/original-mentos-diet-coke-geyser, accessed 7 May 2011; Suzanne Vranica and Chad Terhune, 'Mixing Diet Coke and Mentos Makes a Gusher of Publicity', *Wall Street Journal* (12 June 2006): B1.

43. Facebook Statistics, available online: http://www.facebook.com/press/info.php?statistics, accessed 15 November 2010.

44. Chloe Albanesius, 'YouTube Users Uploading 35 Hours of Video Every Minute', *PCMag.com*, 11 November 2010, available online: http://www.pcmag.com/article2/0, 2817,2372511,00.asp, accessed 15 November 2010.

45. Parts of this section are adapted from Tracy Tuten and Michael R. Solomon, *Social Media Marketing* (2012), Upper Saddle River, NJ: Pearson Education, in press.

46. R. Pearce, 'Social responsibility in the marketplace: assymetric information in food labelling', *Business Ethics: A European Review* 8(1) (1999): 26–36.

47. 'Alcopop sales dry up for Diageo', 19 February 2004, BBC News, http://news.bbc.co.uk/2/hi/business/3503589.stm

48. Pasi Falk, 'The Advertising Genealogy', in P. Sulkunen, J. Holmwood, H. Radner and G. Schulze (eds), *Constructing the New Consumer Society* (London: Macmillan, 1997): 81–107.

49. Wayne, Teddy, 'The Mail-Order-Bride Trade is Flourishing', *Business Week*, 6 January 2011, accessed at: http://www.businessweek.com/magazine/content/11_03/b4211069050983.htm *Information* (2–3 September 2000): 11; Victor Malarek, *The Natashas: The New Global Sex Trade Book* (Viking Canada, 2003); see also: 'New crackdown on sex trafficking', 3 October 2007, *BBC News*, http://news.bbc.co.uk/2/hi/uk_news/7024646.stm

50. For scientific consumer research and discussions related to public policy issues, there is a special European journal, the *Journal of Consumer Policy* (available electronically via many university library journal databases).

51. Cookson, Clive, 'Biotech crops area increases 8%' *Financial Times*, 7 February 2012, accessed at: http://www.ft.com/cms/s/0/3562e8f8-4b44-11e1-a325-00144feabdc0.html#axzz1s2X3LL7l. See also: G.K. Hadfield and D. Thompson, 'An information-based approach to labeling bio-technology consumer products', *Journal of Consumer Policy* 21 (1998): 551–78; H. Sheehy, M. Legault and D. Ireland, 'Consumers and biotechnology: A synopsis of survey and focus group research', *Journal of Consumer Policy* 21 (1998): 359–86.

52. See Philip Kotler and Alan R. Andreasen, *Strategic Marketing for Nonprofit Organizations*, 7th edn (Englewood Cliffs, NJ: Prentice Hall, 2008); Jeff B. Murray and Julie L. Ozanne, 'The critical imagination: Emancipatory interests in consumer research', *Journal of Consumer Research* 18 (September 1991):

192–44; William D. Wells, 'Discovery-oriented consumer research', *Journal of Consumer Research* 19 (March 1993): 489–504.

53. See Chapter 9 and particularly the EU website which deals with these issues and publishes annual reports about 'Keeping consumers safe' http://ec.europa.eu/consumers/dyna/rapex/create_rapex.cfm?rx_id=423 (accessed 15 February 2012).

54. Bertil Swartz, '"Keep Control": The Swedish Brewers' Association Campaign to Foster Responsible Alcohol Consumption Among Adolescents', paper presented at the ACR Europe Conference, Stockholm, June 1997; Anna Oloffson, Ordpolen Informations AB, Sweden, personal communication, August 1997.

55. Roger Crisp, 'Persuasive advertising, autonomy, and the creation of desire', *Journal of Business Ethics* 6 (1987): 413–18.

56. Søren Askegaard and A. Fuat Firat, 'Towards a Critique of Material Culture, Consumption and Markets' in S. Pearce (ed.), *Experiencing Material Culture in the Western World* (London: Leicester University Press, 1997): 114–39.

57. William Leiss, Stephen Kline and Sut Jhally, *Social Communication in Advertising: Persons, Products & Images of Well-Being* (Toronto: Methuen, 1986); Jerry Mander, *Four Arguments for the Elimination of Television* (New York: William Morrow, 1977).

58. Packard (1957), quoted in Leiss *et al.*, *Social Communication*, 11.

59. Raymond Williams, *Problems in Materialism and Culture: Selected Essays* (London: Verso, 1980).

60. Leiss *et al.*, *Social Communication*, ibid.

61. George Stigler, 'The Economics of Information', *Journal of Political Economy* (1961): 69.

62. See Chapter 9 on neuromarketing and how your brain reacts to alternatives.

63. Suzanne Vranica, 'Ad Houses Will Need to Be More Nimble, Clients Are Demanding More and Better Use of Consumer Data, Web', *Wall Street Journal* (2 January 2008): B3.

64. Jack Neff, 'Mucus to Maxi Pads: Marketing's Dirtiest Jobs, Frank Talk About Diapers and Condoms Lifts Taboos and Helps Make a Difference in Consumers' Lives, Say Those in the Trenches', *Advertising Age* (17 February 2009), www.adage.com, accessed 17 February 2009.

65. Morris B. Holbrook, 'The Consumer Researcher Visits Radio City: Dancing in the Dark', in E.C. Hirschman and M.B. Holbrook (eds), *Advances in Consumer Research* 12 (Provo, UT: Association for Consumer Research, 1985): 28–31.

66. Jean-Claude Usunier, 'Integrating the Cultural Dimension into International Marketing', Proceedings of the Second Conference on the Cultural Dimension of International Marketing (Odense: Odense University, 1995): 1–23.

67. Eric J. Arnould and Craig J. Thompson, 'Consumer culture theory (CCT): Twenty years of research', *Journal of Consumer Research* 31 (March 2005): 868–82.

68. Per Østergaard and Christian Jantzen, 'Shifting Perspectives in Consumer Research: From Buyer Behaviour to Consumption Studies' in S.C. Beckmann and R. Elliott (eds), *Interpretive Consumer Research* (Copenhagen: Copenhagen Business School Press, 2000): 9–23.

2 A CONSUMER SOCIETY

CHAPTER OBJECTIVES

When you finish reading this chapter you will understand why:

→ The society we live in today can be described as a consumer society, and what we understand by a consumer culture.

→ Consumption within our society is more a matter of cultural meaning, than of utility.

→ We live in an experience economy.

→ Brands have become the most important symbolic vehicles in the marketplace.

→ Some consumers can be described as political consumers, who vote with their shopping baskets.

→ Standardized global marketing is more likely to work when the message appeals to basic values.

→ Consumers around the world adopt Western products and lifestyles but Westerners also adopt Eastern lifestyle elements.

→ Globalization is important when trying to understand the consumer society.

SIX WEEKS before St Valentine's Day, called Lovers' Day in Turkey, Ayşe starts planning for that special romantic evening. She remembers that last year she and her husband could not find a table in any restaurant in Ankara, all hotels and restaurants had been fully booked and florists had run out of red roses. So she acts early and makes a reservation for two at a good restaurant. She starts window shopping for a gift that she would like to receive. She sees a St Valentine's Day Swatch that she really likes. Two weeks before Lovers' Day, she starts asking her husband what he is thinking of getting her. She takes him to the shopping centre and shows him the St Valentine's Day Swatch and tells him that she'd like that *very* much. On Lovers' Day Ayşe's husband remembers that he has not yet bought anything, goes to get the St Valentine's Day Swatch – only to discover that the shop has run out of them. Instead he buys a much more expensive Swatch. When he comes home, he finds his wife, dressed up ready to go out for dinner. Excited, she closes her eyes and puts her arm forward, confident that he will put a watch around her wrist. And he does. But when she opens her eyes and sees that it is not the St Valentine's Day Swatch, she is upset – and furious. She bursts into tears; they have an argument; and Ayşe goes to the bedroom and takes off her nice clothes. They spend the evening at home, in separate rooms, not talking to each other. 'Some Lovers' Day!' she thinks.

Later, Ayşe tells the story to her friends, some of whom think it's very funny . . .

GÜLIZ GER, Bilkent University, Ankara

CONSUMER CULTURE

The opening vignette illustrates two of the processes related to changes in consumer societies that are discussed in this chapter, globalization and the importance of consumption in structuring our lives. Lovers' Day started to be celebrated in Turkey about a decade ago, first by exchanging cards among school friends. It has become more widespread in the last few years, mostly among the urban middle class who now exchange gifts and make a special evening of it. St Valentine's Day, appropriated as Lovers' Day, is taking root among married and unmarried couples in this Muslim country where traditional norms of respectability did not allow dating – dating is not what 'nice' girls were supposed to do, and many from conservative or lower-middle class families still frown on it. Beyond globalization, we can also see how important consumption is in the creation of a meaningful relationship and a meaningful cultural event such as St Valentine's Day. In fact, in contemporary modern society, it is hard to think of many kinds of social behaviour that do not involve consumption in one form or another. Consumption activities provide both meaning and structure to the way we live. A lot of our everyday imaginations are informed by consumer culture – our imaginations about health, perfect family life, the dream wedding, take shape using consumer culture as negative or positive frames of reference.[1] Brands are becoming ubiquitous signs of the importance of symbolic meanings in the marketplace. These are some of the processes we will deal with in this chapter.

Many people use the notion of the **consumer society** in order to describe the current type of social organization in the economically-developed world. This is not only because we live in a world full of things, which we obviously do, but also because the most decisive step in the construction of consumer society is the new role of consumption activities. We used to define ourselves primarily based on our role in the production process, i.e. our work. Increasingly, however, it is more decisive for our personal and social identities how we consume instead of what we do for a living. The plethora of goods and their varieties in range and styles allows consumption choices to become clear (or sometimes purposefully ambiguous) statements about our personality, our values, aspirations, sympathies and antipathies, and our way of handling social relations. Furthermore, in times of economic crisis such as the current period, consumers are time and again called upon for playing their crucial part in keeping the economies running. The standard economic logic is that if consumers stop buying, producers will have to stop producing. It is in many ways as simple as that – and one of the big challenges for a sustainable economy. Consumption is therefore a matter to be taken seriously – both on the personal, the social, and the economic level.[2]

Modern consumer society is thus characterized by consumption-based identities, but related features of a consumer society include many of the other topics discussed in this book: shopping as a leisure activity combined with the variety of shopping possibilities including shopping centres (the new 'temples of consumption'), easier access to credit, the growing attention to brand images and the communicative aspects of product and packaging as well as the pervasiveness of promotion, the increasing political organization of consumers in groups with a variety of purposes and the sheer impossibility of trying not to be a consumer and still participating in ordinary social life.[3] Things do matter.[4]

33

Popular culture

When it is said that contemporary culture is a **consumer culture**, we do not just refer to the central role of consumption in all of our daily activities.[5] We also underline the basic relationship between market forces, consumption processes and the basic characteristics of what we normally understand by 'a culture'. As we shall see, whether we talk about high culture (such as the fine arts etc.) or popular culture, our contemporary culture is basically something 'to be consumed'. Whether we talk about our way of travelling around, our styles of dressing, our music, our spectacles and sports events, tourism, fashion, popular music and sports are deeply commercialized consumer markets.[6] We consume 'spaces' and 'places' both in our cities when we are enjoying their commercial and/or cultural areas and offerings as well as on holidays; we are constantly consuming different styles and fashions, not only in clothing but also in food, home appliances, garden and interior design, music and so on and so forth. Marketing sometimes seems to exert a self-fulfilling prophecy on popular culture. As commercial influences on popular culture increase, marketer-created symbols make their way into our daily lives to a greater degree. Historical analyses of plays, best-selling novels and the lyrics of hit songs, for example, clearly show large increases in the use of brand names over time.[7]

Popular culture, the music, films, sports, books and other forms of entertainment consumed by the mass market, is both a product of and an inspiration for marketers. Our lives are also affected in more fundamental ways, ranging from how we acknowledge social events such as marriages, deaths or holidays to how we view societal issues such as air pollution, gambling and addiction. The football World Cup, Christmas shopping, tourism, newspaper recycling, cigarette smoking and Barbie dolls are all examples of products and activities that touch many of us in our lives.

Marketing's role in the creation and communication of popular culture is especially emphasized in this book. This cultural influence is hard to ignore, although many people fail to appreciate the extent to which their view of the world – their film and music icons, the latest fashions in clothing, food and interior design, and even the physical features that they find attractive or not in sexual partners – is influenced by the marketing system.

Consider the product characters that marketers use to create a personality for their products and brands. To speak of a brand personality is an example of the degree of anthropomorphism in marketing. From the Michelin Man to Ronald McDonald, popular culture is peopled with fictional heroes. A recent issue of an academic journal is consecrated to the study of such anthropomorphic figures and their impact on consumers and marketing.[8] In fact, it is likely that more consumers will recognize characters such as these than can identify former (or present!) prime ministers, captains of industry or artists. These characters may not exist, but many of us feel that we 'know' them, and they certainly are effective *spokes-characters* for the products and brands, they promote.

THE MEANING OF THINGS

For better or worse, we live in a world that is significantly influenced by marketers. We are surrounded by marketing stimuli in the form of advertisements, shops and products competing for our attention and our cash. Much of what we learn about the world is filtered by marketers, whether through conspicuous consumption depicted in glamorous magazine advertising or via the roles played by family figures in TV commercials. Ads show us how we ought to act with regard to recycling, alcohol consumption and even the types of house or car we aspire to. In many ways we are heavily influenced by and depend upon marketers, since we rely on them to sell us products that are safe and perform as promised, to tell us the truth about what they are selling, and to price and distribute these products fairly.

The meaning of consumption

One of the fundamental premises of consumer behaviour is that people often buy products not for what they do, but for what they *mean*.[9] This principle does not imply that a product's primary function is unimportant, but rather that the roles products play and the **meaning** that they have in our lives go well beyond the tasks they perform. The deeper meanings of a product may help it to stand out from other, similar goods and services – all things being equal, a person will choose the brand that has an image (or even a personality!) consistent with their underlying ideas. While this text takes multiple perspectives on how consumers view products in their lives, one of the recurring themes throughout is that consumer goods are an important medium in European (and other contemporary consumer) societies, that goods and services are loaded with both public and private meanings, and that we as consumers are constantly drawing meanings out of our possessions and using them to construct our domestic and public worlds.

Research has demonstrated that the cultural symbolism of product meanings influence physiological processes such as taste. When we think we adhere to the values represented by a product or a brand, we also think that it tastes better.[10] So such cultural symbols are very powerful and product meanings are to some extent self-fulfilling. Athletes swear by their favourite brand and may lose self-confidence and perform poorly if they cannot wear it, although objectively speaking they cannot run faster or jump higher if they are wearing Nikes rather than Reeboks. These arch rivals are marketed in terms of their image – meanings that have been carefully crafted with the help of legions of rock stars, athletes, slickly produced commercials – and many millions of dollars. So, when you buy a Nike 'Swoosh' you may be doing more than choosing footwear – you may also be making a lifestyle statement about the type of person you are, or want to be. For a relatively simple item made of leather and laces, that's quite a feat!

As Figure 2.1 shows, meaning transfer is largely accomplished by such marketing vehicles as the advertising and fashion industries, which associate products with symbolic qualities. These goods, in turn, impart their meanings to consumers through different forms of ritual and are used to create and sustain consumer identities. We will take a much closer look at how these rituals work in Chapter 13 and at the fashion system in Chapter 14. In this chapter, the model serves the more general purpose of underlining the importance of meaning for understanding contemporary consumption.

One can make the objection to the model in Figure 2.1, that there is a feedback arrow missing between the individual consumer and the cultural values and symbols. Cultural

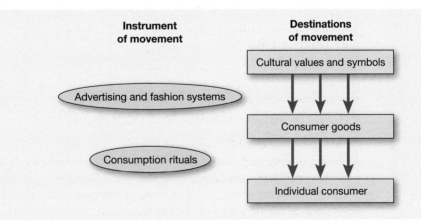

Figure 2.1 The movement of meaning

Source: Adapted from Grant McCracken, 'Culture and consumption: A theoretical account of the structure and movement of the cultural meaning of consumer goods', *Journal of Consumer Research* 13 (June 1986): 72. Reprinted with permission of The University of Chicago Press.

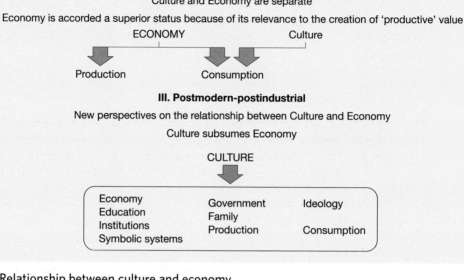

I. Pre-modern

No distinction between Culture and Economy. One implies the other

II. Modern

Culture and Economy are separate

Economy is accorded a superior status because of its relevance to the creation of 'productive' value

ECONOMY   Culture

Production   Consumption

III. Postmodern-postindustrial

New perspectives on the relationship between Culture and Economy

Culture subsumes Economy

CULTURE

Economy	Government	Ideology
Education	Family	
Institutions	Production	Consumption
Symbolic systems		

Figure 2.2 Relationship between culture and economy

Source: Alladi Venkatesh, 'Ethnoconsumerism: A New Paradigm to Study Cultural and Cross-Cultural Consumer Behavior', in J.A. Costa and G. Bamossy (eds), *Marketing in a Multicultural World* (Thousand Oaks, CA: Sage, 1995).

values and symbols obviously only exist in so far as people enact and use them. Therefore, it is also important to remind ourselves that the advertising and fashion industries, even though they are highly influential, are not dictatorial in establishing product meanings. We all give a helping hand. In a sense, in consumer society we are all 'lifestyle experts' to some degree, and many of us are trying to assert our uniqueness by mixing and matching styles and products that we can find in the marketplace. In a very existential sense, we can say that we are what we consume, an issue we will discuss in more detail in Chapter 5 on consumption and the self.

Consumer society, then, is a society where the social life is organized less around our identities as producers or workers in the production system, and more according to our roles as consumers in the consumption system. This expresses a relatively new idea. Until recently, many researchers treated culture as a sort of variable that would explain differences in what they saw as the central dimension in society: economic behaviour. However, in our post-industrial society it has become increasingly evident that the principles of economy are themselves expressions of a specific kind of culture. Figure 2.2 provides an overview of this evolving approach to the relationship between culture and economy, indicating the all-encompassing influence that culture has on consumers.

Cultural categories

Meanings that are imparted to products reflect underlying **cultural categories**, which correspond to the basic ways we characterize the world.[11] Our culture makes distinctions between different times of the day, such as between leisure and work hours, as well as other differences, such as between genders, occasions, groups of people, and so on. The fashion system provides us with products that signify these categories. For example, the clothing industry gives us clothing to denote certain times (evening wear, resort wear), it differentiates between leisure clothes and work clothes, and it promotes masculine, feminine or unisex styles.[12] Goods, then, are 'signs of the times' in which we live. The 'rocket designs' in the 1950s reflected the belief in the technological progress of that era. Political figures (and their relatives) and what they represent are also potential style icons. One of the first examples indicating the rise of consumer society was Jackie Kennedy. A more contemporary example is Kate Middleton, who seemingly takes the European economic crisis into consideration when shopping. It is not uncommon to see her wearing high-street fashions, which of course sell out as soon as the paparazzi images hit the internet.[13] What is important to retain, then, is that meanings of consumer goods and their designs are not universal but relative to given social and historical contexts or, to put it simply, are bound to particular times and particular places.

What do we do, when we consume? Product meanings in use

If consumption is not just about solving practical problems, but is also about the personal, and cultural meanings ascribed to the consumption practices, then it raises the important question about the cultural purposes of consumption. For example, we do not just eat because we are hungry, since most eating behaviours are linked to a myriad of cultural meanings and rituals. We will take a closer look at this in Chapter 13, but for now consider a more general explanation of consumption practices. In a fine proposal of a theory to answer this question, one consumer researcher has developed a classification scheme in an attempt to explore the different ways that products and experiences can provide meaning to people.[14] This consumption typology was derived from a two-year analysis of supporters of a baseball team in the US, but it is easily transferable to both the European context and to other types of consumption as well. But focusing on an event such as a baseball match – or to make it more familiar to Europeans a football match – is a useful reminder that when we refer to consumption, we are talking about intangible experiences, ideas and services (the thrill of a goal or the antics of a team mascot) in addition to tangible objects (like the food and drink consumed at the stadium). This analysis identified four distinct types of consumption activities:

1 *Consuming as experience* – when the consumption is a personal, emotional or aesthetic goal in itself. This would include activities like the pleasure derived from learning how to interpret the offside rule, or appreciating the athletic ability of a favourite player.

2 *Consuming as integration* – using and manipulating consumption objects to express aspects of the self. For example, some fans express their solidarity with the team by identifying with, say, the mascot and adopting some of its characteristic traits. Attending matches in person rather than watching them on TV allows the fan to integrate their experience more completely with their self – the feeling of 'having been there'.

3 *Consuming as classification* – the activities that consumers engage in to communicate their association with objects, both to self and to others. For example, spectators might dress up in the team's colours and buy souvenirs to demonstrate to others that they are diehard fans. Unfortunately, the more hard core express their contempt for opponents' supporters violently. There is a profound 'us' and 'them' dichotomy present here.

4 *Consuming as play* – consumers use objects to participate in a mutual experience and merge their identities with that of a group. For example, happy fans might scream in unison and engage in an orgy of jumping and hugging when their team scores a goal – this is a different dimension of shared experience compared with watching the game at home.

It is important to realize that these categories are not mutually exclusive, and that consumption activities may have traits of several or all of these aspects. On the other hand, one aspect may dominate in the understanding of one particular consumption situation.

Even though this typology takes its point of departure in the consumption of baseball, it is easy to see how it can be applied to other types of consumption as well. You can drive/consume your car for the experience of it, just you and your car and the feeling of the oneness of the driver and the machine, or you can drive it as an extended self, a confirmation of your personality (maybe it is a hybrid model that serves to underline your environmental consciousness). You can drive your car based on the playful togetherness and the freedom of movement it gives to you and your friends. And finally, it is hard to think of a car that does not in some sense classify its driver, be it a cheerfully painted Citroën 2CV, a sporty convertible Mini or a black Mercedes Benz 500 SE.[15]

A BRANDED WORLD

One of the most important ways in which meaning is created in consumer society is through the **brand**. Although defining exactly what a brand is, is a complex task,[16] the point of departure is that it refers to those strategic processes whereby managers try to create and sustain meanings attached to products, services, organizations, etc. The problem arises when we add that the brand is not limited by these strategically intended meanings but possibly first and foremost come to life in the minds of consumers. Hence, what the brand means in the marketplace is ultimately decided by the consumer, not by the brand manager. In the twenty-first century, there has been a tremendous growth in the interest in brands, whether product brands or corporate brands, and their increasing importance as vehicles of meaning for people/consumers. Few people will raise an eyebrow at the suggestion that a university, a school, a kindergarten, a politician, a sports club or even a type of sports can be thought of in terms of being a brand. In fact, today, it is not unheard of to think about oneself as a brand that must compete in the marketplace for friends, partners, jobs, success, etc.[17]

As we have already seen in Chapter 1, one of the hallmarks of marketing strategies at the beginning of the twenty-first century is an emphasis on building relationships with customers. The nature of these relationships can vary, and these bonds help us to understand some of the possible meanings products have for us. Here are some of the types of relationship a person may have with a brand:[18]

- *Self-concept attachment*: the product helps to establish the user's identity.
- *Nostalgic attachment*: the product serves as a link with a past self.
- *Interdependence*: the product is a part of the user's daily routine.
- *Love*: the product elicits bonds of warmth, passion or other strong emotion.

Brand identities are thus potentially very closely intertwined with consumer identities[19] and brands can elicit deep emotional engagement from consumers.[20] Even brands we do not like can be very important to us, because we often define ourselves in opposition to what we do not like.[21]

One of the 'discoveries' of consumer research in the twenty-first century is that consumers increasingly organize communities based on their consumption of and attachment to particular brands, so-called **brand communities**.[22] Such brand communities can range from core members of 'social clubs' or organizations to 'felt' memberships of some imagined community. For example, drivers of the classic British-produced MG cars in the US considered each other somehow linked through their MG ownership, and they engage in various types of communal commitment and sharing of help and information at the same time as they feel that they have a common cause in preserving this 'pristine brand'. Just the fact that they drive the same brand of cars makes the MG owners feel part of a special group of people set apart from the rest of society: a brand community.[23] Memberships of brand communities can also be very important in conveying a sense of authenticity and confirmation of one's identity as a member of some (youth) subculture oriented towards consumption of a particular style of fashion or type of music.[24] Brand communities do not have to be about expensive products such as computers or cars. A virtual brand community has formed around the hazelnut-based spread Nutella, where consumers online write or talk about and expose themselves in Nutella consumption situations and share their funniest or happiest 'Nutella moments'.[25] Some consumers form communities around brands, but some consumer communities form their own brands. Communities around websites such as **outdoorseiten.net** and **skibuilders.com** have engaged in developing equipment and branding based on what community members felt was lacking in the marketplace.[26]

What do people, as consumers, get out of participating in a brand community? Based on an overview of brand community studies, it has been concluded that, beyond the mere production of a social identity as an Apple user, a Star Trek fan or an MG driver, the following elements have been highlighted:[27]

- *Social networking.* Making sure that the community is inclusive and welcoming, keeping it together, making friends, etc.

- *Community engagement.* Making sure that the network is kept alive through active discussions, debates, differentiations, etc.

- *Impression management.* Promoting and justifying one's particular interest to others outside the community.

- *Brand use.* Becoming better at what one is already interested in through learning from the others inside the community.

Experience economy

Some marketers have suggested that the contemporary economy can be characterized as an **experience economy**.[28] They argue that the competition among different market offers has driven producers to distinguish otherwise almost identical product first through the services attached to acquiring the product but now increasingly through differentiating the experience that comes along with consuming the product. This historical shift, it is argued, can be exemplified through the consumption of a birthday cake. Historically, the standard way of creating a birthday party for one's child has gone from buying the ingredients for making a cake, buying a cake at the baker's/confectioner's shop, buying the cake as well as a number of other objects supposedly providing a thematized birthday (a Spiderman birthday, a ghost birthday, a Barbie birthday) to buying the whole birthday party at the local McDonald's, the local toy store, the local zoo or any other provider of a 'complete birthday experience'. Although it has been argued, that we should probably look for the origins of the experience economy somewhat earlier, for example in the rise of hedonic consumer culture in postwar Californian myths of 'fun in the sun',[29] it is obvious that contemporary corporations are doing their utmost to play the game. To the extent that consumers demand and companies provide more and more 'total experiences', we live in an experience economy.

Some of the most notable providers of consumable experiences are theme parks and amusement parks, such as the Disneylands, Legolands, Parc Asterix or other thematized spaces of leisurely consumption. But experience economy has also found its way to more mundane consumption activities. Even banks have tried different ways of turning the bank services into an experience. One Danish bank, in addition to the café corner, provided particular rooms with photos from around the world and an airplane-wing shaped table for talks about financing travels and provided about 30 different packages of brochures and information visualizing their product offers. If you were to talk about a loan for building or reconstructing a house, the information came in a box shaped and coloured like a brick. If discussing investments and savings, the box had the shape of a gold bar. If you were financing your first accommodation, moving out from your parents' home, the box came disguised as a moving box.[30]

Postmodernism

Many of the themes that we address in this book, such as the dominance of the brand (over whatever reality lies behind it), the possibility of engineering reality in the experience economy or the blurring of the fashion picture, are linked to major social changes. One proposed summary term for this change is **postmodernism** – one of the most widely discussed and disputed terms in consumer research in the past two decades.[31]

Postmodernists argue that we live in a period where the modern order, with its shared beliefs in certain central values of modernism and industrialism, is breaking up. Examples of these values include the fundamental belief in a progressing society, characterized by the benefits of economic growth and industrial production, and the infallibility of science. In opposition to currently held views, postmodernism questions the search for universal truths and values, and the existence of objective knowledge.[32] Thus a keyword is **pluralism**, indicating the co-existence of various truths, styles and fashions. Consumers (and producers) are relatively free to combine elements from different styles and domains to create their own personal expression. This pluralism, it is argued, has significant consequences for how we regard theories of marketing and consumer behaviour. Most importantly, pluralism does not mean that anything goes in terms of method or theory, but it does mean that no single theory or method can pretend to be universal in its accounting for consumer behaviour or marketing practices.[33]

There have been several attempts to sum up features of postmodernism and their implications for contemporary market conditions.[34] Together with pluralism, one European researcher has suggested that postmodernism can be described by six key features:[35]

1 *Fragmentation.* The splitting up of what used to be simpler and more mass oriented, exemplified by the ever-growing product ranges and brand extensions in more and more specialized variations. The advertising media have also become fragmented, with increasingly specialized TV channels, magazines, radio stations and websites for placing one's advertising.

2 *De-differentiation.* Postmodernists are interested in the blurring of distinctions between hierarchies such as 'high and low culture', 'advertising and programming' or 'politics and show business'. Examples would be the use of artistic works in advertising and the celebration of advertising as artistic works. Companies such as Coca-Cola, Nike and Guinness have their own museums. The blurring of gender categories also refers to this aspect of postmodernism.

MARKETING OPPORTUNITY

In London, the vodka brand absolut has opened a bar where the temperature is maintained artificially at minus five degrees. This cold environment evokes the imagery consumers have of Sweden, the vodka brand's country of origin, and the clear, crystalline feeling that drinking the vodka should convey. Equipped with a cape and gloves, consumers can sip their vodka from a glass made of ice, a truly glacial experience.[36] The company also rebuilds a hotel made of ice and snow every year in northern Sweden, complete with rooms, dining and meeting facilities, a sauna and, of course, another icebar for tasting the famous vodka.[37] The brand has thus recreated a hyperreal world in the image of its own 'crystal clear and icy' brand identity. In the contemporary experience economy, this promises to be one of a kind. Are you tempted?

3 **Hyperreality** refers to the spreading of simulations and the 'making real of what was just a fantasy'. Disneyland (and other theme parks) are quintessentially hyperreal. Marketers are among the prime creators of hyperreality.[38] But consumers contribute too! Film director

Quentin Tarantino lets some of his main characters in *Pulp Fiction* smoke a fictitious 'Red Apple' cigarette brand, which later appears on an advertising billboard in *Kill Bill*. Merchandise for this fictitious brand has subsequently been made real by certain consumers, presumably devoted Tarantino fans captured by the coolness of Red Apples smokers Butch Coolidge (Bruce Willis) and Mia Wallace (Uma Thurman), through the production of, e.g. tee shirts and ashtrays featuring the otherwise fictitious Red Apple brand![39]

MARKETING PITFALL

Sometimes companies may fall victim to their own hyperreality. It is the dream of many producers to create a strong brand with a solid position in cultural life. But as they do so, their brand images are incorporated into the general cultural sign system, and the company loses control over the signs attached to the brand name. For example, the name 'Barbie' today is much more than a brand name – it has almost become a name for a personality type. In 1997, when a Danish pop group, Aqua, enjoyed a global success with the song 'Barbie Girl', which contained lyrics alluding to the personal life of this hyperreal personality (e.g. 'you can dress my hair, undress me everywhere'), Mattel Inc. was not amused. It sued the pop group for abuse of the Barbie name and for destroying the pure and positive image of Barbie's world created through a long range of expensive campaigns. The case was dismissed by the US supreme court with reference to the lyrics being a parody. Ironically, in 2009 Mattel launched a series of campaigns where they made use of the song, albeit with altered 'no hanky-panky' lyrics.[40] But the important thing in this context is that it is yet another example of the blurring of marketing and popular culture, and the question is: can you patent culture?[41]

4 *Chronology.* This refers to the consumer's nostalgic search for the authentic and a preoccupation with the past.[42] A postmodern way of looking at the same phenomenon is *retro branding* conceptualized as 'the revival or re-launch of a brand from a prior historical period that differs from nostalgic brands by the element of updating'.[43] Retro brands are of relevance here as well because 'these revived brands invoke brand heritage which triggers personal and communal nostalgia'.[44]

5 **Pastiche.** A recent book on postmodern marketing is a pastiche of a novel. This novel's content is in itself a pastiche since it is a thinly veiled 'copy' of Dan Brown's bestseller, *The Da Vinci Code*, complete with murders, suspense and a sectarian society that acts as a keeper of the ultimate secret. The book, *The Marketing Code*, basically uses the format of the novel to discuss various marketing techniques, promoting the view that marketing is an art form rather than a science.[45] Such playful and ironic mixing of existing categories and styles is typical of pastiche.

6 *Anti-foundationalism.* This last feature of postmodern marketing efforts refers not to parody but to an outright 'anti-campaign campaign'. For example, some campaigns are encouraging the receiver of the message *not* to take notice of the message since somebody is trying to seduce and take advantage of them.

Postmodernism has also been attached to such themes as the ability of readers to see through the hype of advertising.[46] This may suggest that we are becoming more skilled consumers and readers/interpreters of advertising, recognizing ads as hyperreal persuasion or seduction attempts which do not intend to reflect our own daily experiences. Younger consumers especially may be prone to detect and enjoy the self-referencing or intertextuality of advertising.[47] Here, the self-consciousness of the brand as a brand and the ambivalence that follows from it is seen as the entertaining aspect of contemporary marketing.[48]

The seventeenth-century Danish landmark of the 'round tower' of Copenhagen has been recreated (in a slightly smaller version) in the simulated Danish environment of Solvang, California, founded as a 'little Denmark' by Danish immigrants in the nineteenth century, but gradually becoming more of a hyperreal theme park under the influence of marketing in the postwar period. The tower in Solvang houses a local pizza restaurant: Tower Pizza, of course!

Photo: Søren Askegaard.

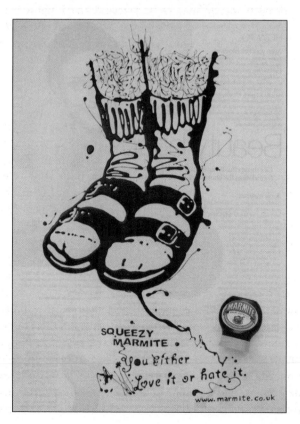

Self-parody is one postmodern approach to communication.

Unilever.

GLOBAL CONSUMER CULTURE

Consumer culture is becoming increasingly globalized, and brands have becomes signs of a global ideology of cultural (and commercial!) value and power.[49] In fact, the tempting imagery of contemporary consumer culture and marketing, the prime vehicles that bring this imagery about, may be considered some of the most important drivers of globalization. The process of **globalization** has attracted a tremendous amount of interest in the last couple of decades. But learning about the relationship between the global and the local in the practices of other cultures is more than just interesting – it is an essential task for any company that wishes to expand its horizons and become part of the international or global marketplace at the beginning of the new millennium.

This viewpoint represents an **etic perspective**, which focuses on commonalities across cultures. An etic approach assumes that there are common, general categories and measurements which are valid for all cultures under consideration. One such etic study identified four major clusters of consumer styles when they looked at data from the US, the UK, France, and Germany: *price-sensitive consumers, variety seekers, brand-loyal consumers* and *information seekers*.[50] On the other hand, many marketers choose to study and analyse a culture using an **emic perspective**, which attempts to explain a culture based on the cultural categories and experiences of the insiders. We will take a closer look at this perspective in the discussion of ethnoconsumerism in Chapter 13. For now, it will be sufficient to remember that in spite of the fact that technology, media and cultural exchange processes are bringing us closer to each other in many ways, cultural differences continue to prevail. For example, cultures vary sharply in the degree to which references to sex and nudity (and other controversial issues) are permitted. One study analysed responses to advertising for 'controversial products', including potentially offensive ads related to sexual behaviour such as ads for condoms, female contraceptives, underwear and (prevention of) sexually transmitted diseases. It was found that results for what was deemed controversial differed highly between the UK and New Zealand on the one hand and Turkey and Malaysia on the other. While negative reactions to sexual references differed, racist imagery was ranked among the most offensive in all samples. Good that we can agree on something like that![51]

A global consumer?

It is often asserted that global marketing works well with affluent people who are 'global citizens' and who are exposed to ideas from around the world through their travels, business contacts and media experiences, and as a result share common tastes.[52] One sector that comes across as inherently 'global' is the market for luxury goods, with its highly standardized and aesthetisized marketing campaigns and its cosmopolitan target market. Still, one study distinguished between a European type of luxury brands, based more on history, rarity and craftsmanship and an American type of luxury brands based on storytelling, marketing imagery and marketing finesse.[53] The differing business cultures, we can assume, also cover differences in the cultural meaning of luxury products across the Atlantic Ocean. Furthermore, differences in the perception and valorization of the concept of 'performance' (an important notion in many contemporary marketing campaigns) has led to different responses to the same advertisement in countries such as the US, Germany, France, Spain and Thailand.[54]

Another 'global segment' that is often referred to is young people whose tastes in music and fashion are strongly influenced by international pop culture broadcasting many of the same images and sounds to multiple countries.[55] On the other hand, one study of the global youth culture concluded that although similar existential conditions were found, including the search for an identity and the feeling of being a member of a global youth consumer culture, the way these similar existential conditions are lived out in reality varies a lot from context to context.[56]

This ad is targeting an allegedly global segment of cool, young (wealthy?) cosmopolitans.
SKYY Vodka.

A large-scale study with consumers in 41 countries identified the characteristics people associate with global brands, and it also measured the relative importance of those dimensions when consumers buy products.[57] The researchers grouped consumers who evaluate global brands in similar ways and they identified four major segments:

1 *Global citizens*. The largest segment (55 per cent of consumers) uses the global success of a company as a signal of quality and innovation. At the same time, they are concerned about whether companies behave responsibly on issues such as consumer health, the environment and worker rights.

2 *Global dreamers*. The second-largest segment, at 23 per cent, consists of consumers who see global brands as quality products and readily buy into the myths they author. They are not nearly as concerned with social responsibility as are the global citizens.

3 *Antiglobals*. Thirteen per cent of consumers are sceptical that transnational companies deliver higher-quality goods. They dislike brands that preach American values and do not trust global companies to behave responsibly. They try to avoid doing business with transnational firms.

4 *Global agnostics*. The remaining 9 per cent of consumers don't base purchase decisions on a brand's global attributes. Instead, they evaluate a global product by the same criteria they use to judge local brands and don't regard its global nature as meriting special consideration.

Coca-Colonization: exporting Western lifestyles

The West (and especially the US) is a *net exporter* of popular culture. Western symbols in the form of images, words and products have diffused throughout the world. This influence is eagerly sought by many consumers, who have learned to equate Western lifestyles in general and the English language in particular with modernization and sophistication. As a result, people around the world are being exposed to a blizzard of Western products that are attempting to become part of local lifestyles.

The allure of Western consumer culture has spread as people in other societies slowly but surely fall under the spell of far-reaching advertising campaigns, contact with tourists and the desire to form attachments with other parts of the world. This attraction sometimes results in bizarre permutations of products and services, as they are modified to be compatible with local customs. For example, in addition to traditional gifts of cloth, food and cosmetics, Nigerian Hausa brides receive cheap quartz watches although they cannot tell the time.[58] As indicated by this and many other examples, many formerly isolated cultures now incorporate Western objects into their traditional practices. In the process, the meanings of these objects are transformed and adapted to local tastes (at times in seemingly bizarre ways). Sometimes the process enriches local cultures; sometimes it produces painful stresses and strains on the local society.

However, the West is no longer the sole model for expanding consumer cultures. In the BRIC countries (Brazil, Russia, India, China), but also in many other places like, for example, Qatar, Turkey or Malaysia enormous new middle classes are producing consumer societies that both to some degree emulate what is known from the West but also establish their own particular variant of consumer culture. One of the most evident contemporary showcases for studying the impact of a rapid introduction of consumer culture is China. In the 1970s, the Chinese strove to attain what they called the 'three bigs': bikes, sewing machines and wristwatches. This wish list was later modified to become the 'new big six', adding refrigerators, washing machines and televisions. The list was then expanded with *colour* televisions, cameras and video recorders.[59] Today, although there are huge urban–rural variations, Chinese middle classes constitute a power consumer market – 'a new generation of brand-conscious individualists'[60] – and the Chinese economy is expected to become the world's biggest in the near future. The Chinese consumer culture of 2012 and the history behind it is described below.

PROFESSOR RUSSELL BELK
York University, Toronto

Consumer behaviour as I see it . . .

In a 1979 movie called *The China Syndrome*, a meltdown in an American nuclear reactor threatened to bore a hole through the earth to China. Today, there are much faster ways to reach China by e-mail, text messaging, satellite television, podcasts, websites, blogs and other such technologies. The year before *The China Syndrome* opened in theatres, China opened its doors to the world through a group of strategically positioned special economic zones. Deng Xiaoping had replaced Mao Zedong and 'market socialism' was beginning to replace the centralized planning of communism. Deng came to the special economic zone city of Shenzhen, across the border from Hong Kong, and pronounced a revolutionary new slogan. In sharp contrast to the old mottoes urging Chinese people to sacrifice and carry the revolution forward by hard work and austere consumption, the new slogan read: 'To Get Rich Is Glorious'.

This was the beginning of an outward-looking China that initiated a still-continuing period of remarkable economic growth toward becoming the world's largest economy (something it should achieve as soon as 2020 given its current rates of growth). It was also the start of an equally profound consumer revolution in China as the market-directed economy took hold. Especially in China's large cities, a prosperous new middle class arose along with a number of millionaires and more than a few billionaires. From drab stores, identical Sun Yat-Sen ('Mao') jackets, and advertising-free public spaces, Chinese consumer culture burst onto the scene in these cities in a spectacular way. China quickly became a natural laboratory in which we might observe the effects of consumerism, materialism and dramatic changes in material lifestyles. →

→ What sorts of effects are we seeing from these changes in Chinese consumption? One effect that seems apparent is that besides its nouveau riche consumers, China as a nation might be regarded as a nouveau riche country, with all the reckless and brash spending this implies. Shanghai now has more skyscrapers than New York City. Beijing totally revamped itself for the 2008 Olympics. And Shenzhen is now virtually indistinguishable from Hong Kong. Its several large amusement parks include Window on the World with a replica of the Eiffel Tower, an indoor ski mountain, and reconstructions of many famous world monuments and icons. It is said that the national bird of China is the construction crane. Whereas Japan remains the world's largest market for luxury brands such as Luis Vuitton, Prada and Chanel, Chinese consumption of such brands is not far behind and will soon eclipse Japan. And for those who can't yet afford such brands, there is an array of counterfeits that are graded 'A', 'B' and 'C' according to how perfectly they replicate the originals. There is also a category called 'clones' that are virtually indistinguishable from the real thing. In an eight-country study posing consumer 'ethical dilemmas' that included buying counterfeit goods, Giana Eckhardt, Tim Devinney and I found that Chinese consumers stood out by failing to see any ethical problem with such behaviour. They instead insisted that the famous brands were unethical because their prices were so outrageous. If the clever Chinese could find a way to right the balances with copies, then good for them, our Chinese interviewees said.

Something else that has changed in China is advertising. When advertising returned to China in the late 1970s, it was initially unemotional, informational and utilitarian in its appeals. But 35 years later, Nan Zhou and I found that Chinese advertising had become much more similar to Western advertising, including its use of many Caucasian models. This prompted a subsequent study examining portrayals of beauty and skin colour in several Asian countries. Results suggested that although lighter skin colour is held to be extremely important in these countries, this is not entirely because of a desire to look more Western or to attain a globalized standard of beauty. There are also distinctly Asian traditions of whiteness, such as those of Japanese geishas and Chinese opera. But the study also raises important questions about globalism, race and nationalism.

In studies I have done with Güliz Ger, we found that consumer materialism (believing that consumer goods are the major source of happiness in life) tends to increase during periods of sudden economic growth. Such growth appears to upset the status quo with regard to social prestige, and consumer goods increase in importance as a way to shore up or increase social status. The current China syndrome involving conspicuous consumption, luxury goods, counterfeit goods and volatile standards of beauty seems to be a key example of such a status scramble. At the same time, the formerly flat Chinese income distribution is becoming more polarized through extremes of wealth and poverty that differ between urban and rural areas, coastal and non-coastal areas, dominant Han and minority ethnic groups, and eastern and western China. Forty years is enough to see some of the effects of the consumer revolution in China, but the natural experiment is far from over. And we have only to contrast the consumer boom in pre-communist Shanghai of the 1930s versus the Chinese cultural revolution of the 1960s to realize that conditions can change dramatically in an equally short period of time. Today, as China joins the global consumer society, it is showing a fascinating amalgam of tastes. For example, Chinese rap music and Chinese opera both flourish. A secular version of Western Christmas is becoming popular (mostly as a couples holiday like Valentine's Day in the West), but it is not nearly as popular as the Chinese New Year, also known as the Spring Festival. And various regional Chinese cuisines continue to dominate even as the flood of Western fast foods continues to spread. One popular Chinese fast food chain, formerly called California Beef Noodle King, serves only Chinese foods and has no counterpart in the West. But the Chinese government thought the name was inappropriately Western and after a number of years of popularity it has now been renamed Lǐ Xiān Sheng. From a consumer behaviour perspective China may well be the most interesting place on earth.

Russell Belk

Consumption of global products and symbols: Japanese motorcyclists with 'chopped' bikes, jackets, jeans and that 'rebel' look.

Harley Davidson, Inc.

The Japanese often use Western words as shorthand for anything new and exciting, even if they do not understand their meaning. The resulting phenomenon is known as 'Japlish',[61] where new Western-sounding words are merged with Japanese. Cars are given names like Fairlady, Gloria and Bongo Wagon. Consumers buy *deodoranto* (deodorant) and *appuru pai* (apple pie). Ads urge shoppers to *stoppu rukku* (stop and look), and products are claimed to be *yuniku* (unique).[62] For an interesting and revealing website which features dozens of well-known Western celebrities doing commercials for Japanese media, spend some time at Japander![63]

The lure of Western consumption styles and the brands that carry this message have been some of the most effective tools in spreading Western-style consumer culture across the globe. But these tools are now used in order to maintain a particular cultural identity. Branding strategies are used by increasingly strong Asian managers in order to construct a universe of 'Asianness' that can be used to construct local brand value in the booming Asian markets. The Asia portrayed in these campaigns is not the traditional one of peasants working in rice fields but a modern, booming and busting self-confident transnational (not a priori tied to a specific country) Asian world. The result is a branding style that reinforces pride and self-confidence in the Asian region.[64] Consequently, for example, there is a growth in Chinese luxury brands. Do names like NE Tiger, Chow Tai Fook or Kweichow Mao Tai ring a bell? Well, in China they do – these are the top three on a recent list of the most prominent luxury brands in China, representing the fur and leather, jewellery and alcohol sectors respectively. Other products represented on the list are Mongolian cashmere, tea and silk.[65]

The lesson we have to draw is that the emerging economies are increasingly taking centre stage. This is not least true for Chinese corporations. The leading Chinese search engine Baidu (78.3 per cent market share as opposed to Google's 167 per cent) is trying to expand globally and is, for example, launching an attempt to gain foothold in the lucrative Brazilian market.[66]

Advertisement for Chow Tai Fook indicating the existence of a vibrant Chinese luxury brand scene. The ad combines signs of Chinese culture with classical Western signs of a luxury brand.

Bloomberg/Getty Images.

MULTICULTURAL DIMENSIONS

When Marvel comics launched 'Spiderman India', the first ethnic adaptation of the popular comic book series, the writers turned Peter Parker of New York City into Pavitr Prabhakar of Mumbai. Mary Jane became Meera Jain, and the villainous Norman Osbourne (aka the Green Goblin) is Nalin Oberoi. Spiderman changed from a semitragic figure representing the dangers of scientific experimentation into a hero trying to navigate a modern India still steeped in Hindu mysticism.[67]

Emerging consumer cultures in transitional economies

China and India are not the only emerging consumer societies. After the collapse of communism, eastern Europeans emerged from a long winter of deprivation of consumer goods into a springtime of abundance. The picture is not all rosy, however, since attaining consumer goods is not easy for many in **transitional economies**, where the economic system is still 'neither fish nor fowl', and governments ranging from Vietnam to Romania struggle with the difficult adaptation from a controlled, centralized economy to a free market system.[68] These problems stem from such factors as the unequal distribution of income among citizens, as well as striking rural–urban differences in expectations and values. The key aspect of a transitional economy is the rapid change required in social, political and economic dimensions as the populace is suddenly exposed to global communications and external market pressures. One study investigated how poor villagers migrating to a larger Turkish city coped with becoming acculturated to consumer society. The study basically concluded that these consumers-to-be would select one of three coping strategies. They would either shut out the whole modern consumer lifestyle altogether, trying to perpetuate village life in the poor shantytown outside the city, or collectively embrace the dreams proposed by consumer society by adopting ritualized consumption practices to the best of their humble means. A final strategy consists in giving up on both projects, which leads to shattered identities for the consumers involved, neither being able to maintain the traditional identity, nor to adopt a consumer identity.[69] Such a transitional process can have heartbreaking consequences. In Turkey one researcher met a rural consumer, a mother who deprived her child of nutritious milk from the family's cow and instead sold it in order to be able to buy sweets for her child because 'what is good for city kids is also good for my child'.[70]

Some of the consequences of the transition to capitalism thus include a loss of confidence and pride in the local culture, as well as alienation, frustration and an increase in stress as leisure time is sacrificed to work ever harder to buy consumer goods. The yearning for the trappings of Western material culture is perhaps most evident in parts of eastern Europe, where citizens who threw off the shackles of communism now have direct access to coveted consumer goods from the US and Europe – if they can afford them. One analyst observed, '. . . as former subjects of the Soviet empire dream it, the American dream has very little to do with liberty and justice for all and a great deal to do with soap operas and the Sears Catalogue'.[71] A recent huge analysis of the acceptance of brands and advertisements in social media among 57,000 consumers in 60 countries demonstrated a profound difference: whereas 57 per cent of consumers in the Western countries dislike commercial content in social media, this figure is much lower in emerging market economies such as China, India, Mexico or Vietnam.[72]

Glocalization

Based on these discussions, we are now able to reflect a little more on the character of the globalization process. The conclusion we can safely draw is that globalization is always inevitably a **glocalization** since all global phenomena exist and become meaningful in a local context. Even completely similar McDonald's restaurants, just to take one obvious example, have different meanings and play different roles for consumers when placed in Chicago, Bordeaux, Moscow or Middlesbrough. A recent introspective account of a Thai consumer researcher's experience of a paradoxical glocal consumer identity, reflecting both differences within the Thai culture's upper and lower classes as well as her experiences from being an expatriate during her studies in the UK witness the extent to which many of us, maybe in particular migrants, are today glocalized.[73] We will return to migrant populations in Chapter 15.

Globalization may even engender an increased focus on the local.[74] An anthropological study of developments in the British food culture revealed four different types of food consumption that are all consequences of globalization.[75] The first is the *global food* culture, represented mainly by the ubiquitous fast food of burgers and pizzas, convenience products like instant coffee, etc. that are found everywhere and belong nowhere in particular. Secondly, *expatriate food* refers to the search for authentic meals and products from other cultures – 'Indian', 'Mexican', Thai, etc. Thirdly, *nostalgia food* represents a search for local authenticity – in

Britain, for example, Stilton cheese, sticky toffee puddings – from the local cultural heritage that is under pressure from globalization. Finally, *creolization* of food involves blending various traditions into new ones, such as Chinese dishes omitting ingredients considered unappetizing in Western culture, spiced down Indonesian food in the Netherlands, or Indianized versions of sandwiches. Similar processes are found in all European cultures.

It is interesting to note that all four are related to globalization trends, but only global food leads to a tendency to standardize consumption patterns. We may consider these tendencies as relevant for all types of consumption, not just for consumption of food. So whether we look at retailing, interior decoration, tourism or musical tastes, we may find at least these four tendencies, taking the notion of globalization beyond the interpretation of it as homogenization. Glocalization also includes the increasing awareness of other styles and tastes, and the search for 'exotic authenticity', as well as the incorporation of this 'exoticism' into local habits and consumption styles. And finally, the exposure to all this 'otherness' often makes consumers more aware of their own cultural roots, and the tastes and consumption styles that they would define as 'our own'. All these offers of old and new, strange and familiar, authentic and creolized, tend to coexist in the marketplace.[76] Therefore, it is not so strange that some authors discuss globalization more in terms of fragmentation than in terms of homogenization.[77]

THE POLITICS OF CONSUMPTION

The issue of postmodernism and the suggestion that the focus on consumption in our current culture is basically a way of securing meaning and continuity through our private consumer lives in times where continuity is no longer provided by society[78] might suggest that consumption has become an independent sphere of playful self-realization without too much depth or seriousness attached to it. However, not all is well in consumer society and the globalization of consumer culture makes these problems even clearer because we can, so to speak, 'study the problems as they aggravate'. Many critics have attacked consumer society for a variety of reasons: that it erodes cultural differences, that it creates superficial and inauthentic forms of social interaction and that it inspires competition and individualism rather than solidarity and community. While many of these assertions may or may not bear close scrutiny,[79] consumer society in general does represent some serious challenges for our future development, not least in terms of the pressure on the environment, so it may not be so strange that these years are characterized by a hefty public and scientific debate about the ethics and moralities of consumption.[80]

The pressure of consumer society is not only felt on the environment but also on the individual consumer, sometimes with negative outcomes. **Compulsive buying** is a physiological and/or psychological dependency on products or services. While most people equate addiction with drugs, virtually any product or service can be seen as relieving some problem or satisfying some need to the point where reliance on it becomes extreme. Even the act of shopping itself is an addictive experience for some consumers.[81] Such compulsive consumption has been on the rise in Western societies throughout the last decades. But there is reason to believe that consumers in newly marketized economies are even more vulnerable. For example, evidence from Germany indicates that the rise of compulsive buying behaviour is bigger in the newly marketized parts of Central and Eastern Europe compared with the Western parts.[82] Finally, over-consumption should not be regarded strictly as an individual failure, but may also be viewed as a structural problem that has evolved in our affluent, consumer society.[83]

The central role of consumption in today's society has also led to an increasing interest in the social and political consequences of consumer society. The aggravating environmental crisis, the linkages between over-consumption and climate change, the unsustainability of many consumption practices, and a feeling that a consumer orientation has turned politics into marketing and branding – all these factors contribute to the feeling that consumer society is not a care- and risk-free lifestyle. There have been several investigations of various types of **anti-consumption** practices and movements.[84] Some critics have coined the term **affluenza**[85] to account for the negative sides of a society over-focused on its consumption. The animated successful movie from Pixar, *Wall-E*, is based on a grim projection of a future world as a victim of affluenza. On the other hand, as pointed out by a very influential consumer researcher, it might be wiser to analyse the pros and cons of consumer society in more detail concerning the variety of ways in which consumers can also make a positive difference, rather than making such sweeping 'consumption is bad' conclusions as indicated by the affluenza term.[86]

It has been suggested that we live in a **risk society**, where our ways of manufacturing goods are increasingly producing just as many and even more 'bads' or risks,[87] risks that the consumer will have to take into account in their decision making. Lots of these risks are linked to our consumption processes, whether they concern something we eat or drink, chemicals in the paint and surface coating of various construction materials, the content of phtalates (plasticizers) in toys and so on. The sense of risks is compounded by recurring food scandals such as the addition of melanine in Chinese milk products which has severely lowered consumer confidence in many foods 'made in China'[88] or the many scandals surrounding meat (for example the BSE scandal) or fake classifications of wine or olive oil.

One example of a product type where such risks have made consumers sceptical about the benefits suggested to them by the industry is that of genetically manipulated organisms (GMO). One fear expressed by consumers in a study of acceptance or rejection of GMO foods in Sweden and Denmark was of too great a concentration of power in a few giant corporations dominating both research and industry.[89] Similar results were found for several European countries in a cross-national study. Testing consumer attitudes and purchase intentions regarding GMO foods, it was concluded that an overall rejection of the technology as such was found in Denmark, Germany, the UK and Italy.[90] In connection with this study, various types of information material were also tested, some more informative, some more emotional, in order to estimate the potential of informational campaigns in changing negative attitudes. But whatever data was given to the consumers, it only made their attitude *more* negative, something which points to the deep-seated nature of this scepticism among European consumers. Instead, the demand for organic produce has increased tremendously in several European countries over the last few years. Although the current economic crisis may have led to a temporary setback in this demand in, for example, the UK,[91] other countries including the European leaders in organic food consumption continue to experience increased demand in spite of the crisis.[92]

The ethical consumer

The discussion above points to an increasing awareness of the political and moral consequences of consumption choices among many consumers. Consumers are not just individuals responsible solely for the private outcomes of their choices, they are also social citizens with social responsibilities.[93] How consumers feel these responsibilities and act upon them depends largely on how they perceive the robustness of nature in the face of so many consumers who intervene and use resources[94] but also on their beliefs regarding technology and its role for society.[95] This social and moral consciousness means that what started out predominantly as a green consumer is gradually being followed by, or perhaps is turning into, a political, or, as s/he is increasingly called, an **ethical consumer**.[96,97] The ethical consumers use their buying pattern as a weapon against companies they don't like and in support of the companies that reflect values similar to their own. This consumer type selects products

Table 2.1 Political consumption activities among food consumers in four European countries (percentage of population) (all results: $p = < 0.0001$)

	Norway N = 1002	Denmark N = 1005	Italy N = 2006	Portugal N = 1000
During last 12 months, I have been involved in the following activities:				
Refused to buy food types or brands to express opinion about a political or social issue	21%	35%	24%	25%
Bought particular food to support their sale	31%	38%	21%	14%
Participated in organized consumer boycott	3%	4%	13%	6%

Source: Adapted from Bente Halkier *et al.*, 'Trusting, complex, quality conscious or unprotected? Constructing the food consumer in different European national contexts', *Journal of Consumer Culture*, 7(3), 2007: 379–402.

according to the company's ethical behaviour, which includes respect for human rights, animal protection, environmental friendliness and support for various benevolent causes.

Although consumer boycott of, for example, South African produce during the apartheid regime has been known for some time, the term 'the political consumer' was first coined in Denmark in the 1990s following consumer protests against the dumping of a drilling platform in the North Sea and against France for its nuclear testing in the Pacific.[98] Today, political or ethical consumers are found in all countries, but significant differences are also found. One EU-based study concluded that Norwegian food consumers could generally be framed as trusting, Danish as complex, Italian as quality conscious and Portuguese as unprotected. Some results from that study are reproduced in Table 2.1.

The ethical consumer is supported by such agencies as the Vancouver-based Adbusters,[99] which engages in twisting campaigns from major companies that, for some reason, have come under their spotlight for immoral or harmful behaviour. For example, they made a spoof on the well-known Coca-Cola polar bear campaign by depicting a family of bears on a tiny ice floe, with the sign 'Enjoy Climate Change' written in that well-known type from the Coca-Cola logo, thereby protesting against the company's use of ozone-harming gases in its vending machines.[100] This kind of 'peaceful' rebelliousness against what is seen as control over our minds and imagination by major companies is called *culture jamming*.[101] Vigilante marketing is also emerging where new ads and ideas for campaigns appear without either client or agency involvement. These are often generated by freelancers, fans or agencies looking for work.[102]

The global brands are generally the target of such consumer activism. One study examined consumers' experiences of the global coffee shop chain Starbucks.[103] The authors concluded that although Starbucks has created a lot of followers in and outside the US who see Starbucks as the quintessential cool café environment, it has also produced significant consumer resistance among consumers who perceive Starbucks as inauthentic and no better in terms of the café culture than McDonald's is for the global food culture. As such, they must fight a negative shadow of their own brand image, a so-called *doppelgänger brand-image*.[104]

Not all companies are on the defensive, though. Companies such as The Body Shop are founded on the idea of natural and non-animal-tested products and a maximum of environmental concern. But their concerns are becoming directed towards a broader array of social values. They took up the debate over beauty ideals by introducing 'Ruby', a Barbie-lookalike doll but one with considerably rounder forms, in order to fight the tyranny of thinness and the impossible body ideal of the supermodels which are also endorsed by Barbie's shape. The reaction was predictable: Mattel Inc., the producers of Barbie, took out an injunction against The Body Shop because Ruby's face was too like Barbie's.

This Adbusters campaign against exploitation of cheap labour in Indonesia highlights the role of the major corporation, Nike, and uses its logo and line 'to be all you can be' to create individual awareness of the global impact of big corporations (and individual consumer choice of running shoe) on newly emerging economies and their labour forces.

www.adbusters.org

The Body Shop's Ruby, a Barbie-lookalike doll but with considerably rounder forms, introduced in order to fight the tyranny of thinness and impossible body ideal of the supermodels which are reinforced by Barbie's shape. The version you see here was not used, because Mattel claimed that Ruby had too much facial similarity with Barbie, hence another version was produced. See, for example, www.imforanimals.com/images/people/ruby_poster.jpg (accessed 9 January 2009).

With permission from The Body Shop (file supplied by The Advertising Archives).

Consumer boycotts

As we have seen, we live in a period when many consumers are becoming increasingly aware that their consumption pattern is part of a global political and economic system, to the extent that they become ethical consumers. Sometimes a negative experience can trigger an organized and devastating response, as when a consumer group organizes a *boycott* of a company's products. These efforts can include protests against everything from investing in a politically undesirable country (as when Carlsberg and Heineken both withdrew their investments from Myanmar following protests against this support for a repressive regime), to efforts to discourage consumption of products from certain companies or countries (as during the boycott of French wines and other products during the nuclear testing in the Pacific in 1996, an action which was especially strongly felt in The Netherlands and in the Scandinavian countries). Four factors are found to predict boycott participation:

1 The desire to make a difference.

2 The scope for self-enhancement.

3 Counterarguments that inhibit boycotting.

4 The cost to the boycotter of constrained consumption.[105]

Boycotts are not always effective – studies show that normally only a limited percentage of a country's consumers participate in them. However, those who do are disproportionately vocal and well educated, so they are a group companies especially do not want to alienate. One increasingly popular solution used by marketers is to set up a joint task force with the boycotting organization to try to iron out the problem. In the US, McDonald's used this approach with the Environmental Defense Fund, which was concerned about its use of such things as polystyrene containers, bleached paper and antibiotics in food. The company agreed to test a composting programme, to switch to plain brown bags and to eliminate the use of antibiotics in such products as poultry.[106]

Corporate social responsibility

Parallel to the changing consumer attitudes towards the political and environmental role of marketplace behaviour, consumption as well as production, changing attitudes among companies and businesses can be traced as they recognize the changing nature of their customer. **Corporate social responsibility (CSR)** has become increasingly prominent in companies' provision of and stakeholders' approaches to buying goods and services. CSR addresses two kinds of commercial responsibility: 'commercial responsibilities (that is running their businesses successfully) and social responsibilities (that is their role in society and the community)'.[107] CSR Europe is the leading European business network for corporate social responsibility with over 60 leading multinational corporations as members '. . . [committed to helping] companies integrate CSR into the way they do business every day'.[108] One large-scale EU sponsored survey concluded that the public's key priority for companies is a demonstration of corporate citizenship (e.g. quality and service; human health and safety; being open and honest) rather than just charitable or community giving.'[109] In turn the study also identified 'the active conscious consumer' or 'socially responsible activists' (SR activists) who were defined 'as those people who have participated in five or more socially responsible activities in the last twelve months'. Across Europe more than a quarter are activists. In Switzerland, Sweden and Belgium the proportion rises to two in five. In contrast, only around one in ten could be classified in this way in Germany, France, Portugal and Italy.

The growing attention to CSR has not prevented a series of business scandals in various countries emerging with the growing financial and economic crisis. This has also caused new reflections on the consumer society and the pitfalls and benefits that may emerge. It is too early to tell, but the fall in real estate value and risks of unemployment could contribute to a severe drop in consumer spending. This might also lead to a questioning of the consumer society as we know it. We can ask ourselves: 'Is it likely that some of the happy-go-lucky attitudes and expectations concerning ever-increasing consumption opportunities will be challenged by new consumer attitudes oriented towards values of modesty?'

MARKETING PITFALL

The Swedish-owned company Vattenfall which offers energy and heat in several European countries has tried to profile itself as a highly environmentally conscious corporation through large campaigns promoting imagery of unspoiled nature and through organizing a petition among consumers for imposing a global cost on CO_2 production. But at the same time, their own plans for expanding energy and heat production based on coal in countries such as Germany, and alleged behind-the-scenes activities for watering down upcoming agreements on climate change, have severely damaged this attempt.[110] Accusations of such so-called 'green-washing' of activities have recently also hit the fair trade organization Max Havelaar, when a TV documentary revealed that the working conditions in their tea plantations were hardly any better than in conventional commercially driven plantations.[111] The moral is: there are increasing demands of keeping one's path very clean, if a company is promoting itself through some form of corporate social responsibility.

CHAPTER SUMMARY

→ We live in a *consumer society*, where more and more of our personal identities and the relationships between people are mediated through consumption. Consumer society is thus characterized by a consumer culture.

→ The core of consumer culture is that consumption goes far beyond solving practical and utilitarian problems. Consumer society has become a reality when consumption becomes more a matter of *cultural meaning* and less a matter of utility. Consumption is first and foremost a way of creating meaningful lives in the context of personal identity and social relationships. Consumption, branding and marketing have become some of the prime reflectors of current cultural values, norms and social roles. Economy and cultures of consumption are thus closely intertwined.

→ We increasingly live in an *experience economy* that provides not only goods and services but complete staged events, or experiences, for the consumers.

→ Experience economy can be linked to *postmodernism*, which involves processes of social change in an era where the 'grand truths' of modernism, such as scientific knowledge or the progressiveness of economic growth, are no longer taken for granted. Postmodernism includes social processes such as fragmentation, de-differentiation, hyperreality, chronology, pastiche and anti-foundationalism.

→ The increasing political and moral significance of consumption has given birth to the *political* or *ethical consumer*, who 'votes with the shopping basket' in an attempt to influence companies to care for the natural as well as the human environment, adding issues such as human rights to the set of dimensions that influence purchases.

→ Followers of an *etic perspective* believe that the same universal messages will be appreciated by people in many cultures. Believers in an *emic perspective* argue that individual cultures are too unique to permit such standardization: marketers instead must adapt their approaches to be consistent with local values and practices. Attempts at global marketing have met with mixed success: in many cases this approach is more likely to work if the messages appeal to basic values and/or if the target markets consist of consumers who are more internationally rather than locally oriented.

→ The Western world is a net exporter of popular culture. Consumers around the world have eagerly adopted Western products, especially entertainment, vehicles and items that are linked symbolically to a uniquely Western lifestyle (e.g. Marlboro, Levi's, BMW, Nestlé). Despite or because of the continuing 'Americanization' or 'Westernization' of cultures in the world, some consumers are alarmed by this influence, and are instead emphasizing a return to local products and customs.

→ It is appropriate to consider the process of globalization as one of the most central in understanding the development of consumer society. But it is also important to bear in mind that globalization should almost always be considered as *glocalization*, due to the complex interactions between the global and the local that follows from it.

KEY TERMS

Affluenza (p. 51)

Anti-consumption (p. 51)

Brand (p. 38)

Brand communities (p. 38)

Compulsive buying (p. 50)

Consumer culture (p. 34)

Consumer society (p. 33)

Corporate social responsibility (CSR) (p. 54)

Cultural categories (p. 36)

Emic perspective (p. 43)

Ethical consumer (p. 51)

Etic perspective (p. 43)

Experience economy (p. 39)

Globalization (p. 43)

Glocalization (p. 49)

Hyperreality (p. 40)

Meaning (p. 35)

Pastiche (p. 41)

Pluralism (p. 40)

Popular culture (p. 34)

Postmodernism (p. 40)

Risk society (p. 51)

Transitional economies (p. 49)

CONSUMER BEHAVIOUR CHALLENGE

1 Try to consider some of your own patterns and behaviour in the light of the different types of consumption practices: experience, integration, play and classification. What do you conclude?

2 Reflect on your and your friends' consumption patterns in the same light. What do you see?

3 Try to consider your personal relationship to brands. Select one that you are absolutely positive about. How would you characterize your relationship to that brand? And then one you are absolutely negative about; what is your relationship to that? Which personal and cultural factors might explain your brand relationships?

4 Find three examples of how experience economy, i.e. the staging of complete consumer experiences, has altered some market offerings that you know about.

5 Try to collect advertisements that reflect the postmodern features of fragmentation, de-differentiation, hyperreality, chronology, pastiche and anti-foundationalism.

6 What role does the globalization process play in your personal consumption profile? After reflecting on that, take a walk in your nearest shopping area and look for signs of the global and the local. What is from 'somewhere else'? What is distinctively local? Are there mixtures, or are these two domains separate? Can you identify any *hegemonic brandscapes*?

7 Try to identify processes of glocalization in your own consumption patterns? And in your shopping neighbourhood?

8 Is the 'ethical consumer' a fad or a new and growing challenge and/or opportunity for marketers and producers? Discuss.

9 Go to your local supermarket to check the selection of politically correct products (organic produce, fair trade products, etc.). How are they presented in the store? What does that say about the way these products are regarded?

10 What do you think about boycotts as consumers' response to what is perceived as companies' unethical behaviour?

11 Identify and assess the importance of corporate social responsibility for companies, consumers and government policy.

For additional material see the companion website at **www.pearsoned.co.uk/solomon**

NOTES

1. Rebecca Jenkins, Elizabeth Nixon and Mike Molesworth, '"Just normal and homely": The presence, absence and othering of consumer culture in everyday imagining', *Journal of Consumer Culture*, vol. 11 no. 2 (2011): 261–281.

2. Don Slater, 'The Moral Seriousness of Consumption', *Journal of Consumer Culture*, vol. 10 no. 2 (2010): 280–84.

3. Celia Lury, *Consumer Culture* (New Brunswick, NJ: Rutgers University Press, 1996). Another excellent book on the rise of consumer culture is Don Slater, *Consumer Culture and Modernity* (Cambridge: Polity Press, 1997).

4. Daniel Miller, 'Why Some Things Matter', in D. Miller (ed.), *Material Cultures: Why Some Things Matter* (London: UCL Books, 1998): 3–21.

5. Eric J. Arnould and Craig J. Thompson, 'Consumer Culture Theory (CCT): Twenty Years of Research', *Journal of Consumer Research*, 31, 4 (March 2005): 868–882.

6. Steven Miles, *Consumerism – as a Way of Life* (London: Sage 1998).

7. T. Bettina Cornwell and Bruce Keillor, 'Contemporary Literature and the Embedded Consumer Culture: The Case of Updike's Rabbit', in Roger J. Kruez and Mary Sue MacNealy (eds), *Empirical Approaches to Literature and Aesthetics: Advances in Discourse Processes* 52 (Norwood, NJ: Ablex Publishing Corporation, 1996): 559–72; Monroe Friedman, 'The changing language of a consumer society: Brand name usage in popular American novels in the postwar era', *Journal of Consumer Research* 11 (March 1985): 927–37; Monroe Friedman, 'Commercial influences in the lyrics of popular American music of the postwar era', *Journal of Consumer Affairs* 20 (Winter 1986): 193.

8. *Journal of Marketing Management*, 29, 1 (2013), special issue on anthropomorphic marketing.

9. Sidney J. Levy, 'Symbols for sale', *Harvard Business Review* 37 (July–August 1959): 117–24.

10. Michael W. Allen, Richa Gupta and Arnaud Monnier, 'The interactive effect of cultural symbols and human values on taste evaluation', *Journal of Consumer Research*, vol. 35 (August 2008): 294–308.

11. Grant McCracken, 'Culture and consumption: A theoretical account of the structure and movement of the cultural meaning of consumer goods', *Journal of Consumer Research* 13 (June 1986): 71–84.

12. One example of such a cultural category is the definition of being 'a real woman'. For a cultural analysis of female identity and consumption of lingerie, see Christian Jantzen, Per Østergaard and Carla Sucena Vieira, 'Becoming a woman to the backbone. Lingerie consumption and the experience of female identity', *Journal of Consumer Culture*, vol. 6 no. 2 (2006): 177–202.

13. 'Kate Middleton's Zara dress sells out in an hour after Gary Barlow concert', *Metro*, 8 December 2011, http://www.metro.co.uk/lifestyle/884277-kate-middletons-zara-dress-sells-out-in-an-hour-after-gary-barlow-concert, accessed 3 May 2012.

14. Douglas B. Holt, 'How consumers consume: a typology of consumption practices', *Journal of Consumer Research* 22(1) (June 1995): 1–16.

15. See, e.g., Paul Hewer, Douglas Brownlie, Steven Treanor, Pauline Ferguson and Susan Hamilton, 'Peeps, Beemers and Scooby-doos; Exploring Community Value amongst Scottish Car Cruisers', in A.Y. Lee and D. Soman (eds), *Advances in Consumer Research*, vol. XXXV (Duluth, MN: Association for Consumer Research, 2008): 429–38.

16. Stephen Brown, 'Ambi-Brand Culture', in J. Schroeder and M. Salzer-Mörling (eds), *Brand Culture* (London: Routledge: 2006): 50–66.

17. Michael Solomon, Greg Marshall and Elnora Stuart, *Marketing. Real People, Real Choices* (Prentice Hall 2006).

18. Susan Fournier, 'Consumers and their brands. Developing relationship theory in consumer research', *Journal of Consumer Research* 24 (March 1998): 343–73.

19. Fabian F. Csaba and Anders Bengtsson, 'Rethinking Identity in Brand Management' in J. Schroeder and M. Salzer-Mörling (eds), *Brand Culture* (London: Routledge, 2006): 118–35.

20. Elisabeth A. Pichler and Andrea Hemetsberger, 'Driven by Devotion – How Consumers Interact with their Objects of Devotion', in A.Y. Lee and D. Soman (eds), *Advances in Consumer Research*, vol. XXXV (Duluth, MN: Association for Consumer Research, 2008): 439–43.

21. Margaret Hogg and Emma Banister, 'Dislikes, distastes and the undesired self: Conceptualising and exploring the role of the undesired end state in consumer experience', *Journal of Marketing Management*, vol. 17 no. 1–2 (2001): 73–104; Emma Banister and Margaret Hogg, 'Negative symbolic consumption and consumers' drive for self-esteem: The case of the fashion industry', *European Journal of Marketing*, vol. 38 no. 7 (2004): 850–68.

22. Albert Muñiz and Thomas O'Guinn, 'Brand communities', *Journal of Consumer Research*, vol. 27 no. 4 (2001): 412–32.

23. Thomas W. Leigh, Cara Peters and Jeremy Shelton, 'The Consumer Quest for Authenticity: The Multiplicity of Meanings Within the MG Subculture of Consumption', *Journal of the Academy of Marketing Science*, vol. 34 no. 4 (2006): 482–493.

24. Richard Elliott and Andrea Davies, 'Symbolic Brands and Authenticity of Identity Performance', in J. Schroeder and M. Salzer-Mörling (eds), *Brand Culture* (London: Routledge, 2006): 155–70.

25. Bernard Cova and Stefano Pace, 'Brand community of convenience products: New forms of customer empowerment – the case "my Nutella The Community"', *European Journal of Marketing*, vol. 40 no. 9/10 (2006): 1087–105. See also www.nutellaville.it

26. Johann Füller, Marius Luedicke and Gregor Jawecki, 'How Brands Enchant: Insights from Observing Community Driven Brand Creation', in A.Y. Lee and D. Soman (eds), *Advances in Consumer Research* (Duluth, MN: Association for Consumer Research, 2008): 359–66.

27. Hope Jensen Schau, Albert M. Muñiz and Eric J. Arnould, 'How Brand Community Practices Create Value', *Journal of Marketing*, vol. 73 (September 2009): 30–51.

28. B. Joseph Pine and James Gilmore, 'Welcome to the experience economy', *Harvard Business Review* (July/August 1998): 97–105.

29. Søren Askegaard, 'Experience Economy in the Making: Hedonism, Play and Coolhunting in Automotive Song Lyrics', *Consumption, Markets and Culture*, vol. 13 no. 4 (2010): 351–371.

30. www.brandbase.dk/arrangementer/reportager/oplev elsesokonomi-for-alle-pengene, accessed 8 January 2009.

31. Two special issues of *International Journal of Research in Marketing* 10(3) (1993) and 11(4) (1994), both edited by A. Fuat Firat, John F. Sherry Jr and Alladi Venkatesh, have been decisive for the introduction of themes of postmodernism in marketing and consumer research.

32. Craig J. Thompson, 'Modern truth and postmodern incredulity: A hermeneutic deconstruction of the metanarrative of "scientific truth" in marketing research', *International Journal of Research in Marketing* 10(3) (1993): 325–38.

33. Christina Goulding, 'Issues in representing the postmodern consumer', *Qualitative Market Research: An International Journal*, vol. 6 no. 3 (2003): 152–59.

34. See, for example, A. Fuat Firat and Alladi Venkatesh, 'Postmodernity: The age of marketing', *International Journal of Research in Marketing* 10(3) (1993): 227–49; James Ogilvy, 'This postmodern business', *Marketing and Research Today* (February 1990): 4–22; W. Fred van Raaij, 'Postmodern consumption', *Journal of Economic Psychology* 14 (1993): 541–63.

35. Stephen Brown, *Postmodern Marketing* (London: Routledge, 1995): 106 ff.

36. www.belowzerolondon.com/icebar/index.html, accessed 14 February 2008.

37. www.icehotel.com, accessed 14 February 2008.

38. Fuat Firat and Venkatesh, 'Postmodernity: The age of marketing', *op. cit.*

39. Laurent Muzellec, 'Ceci n'est pas une brand. Postmodernism and Brand Management', paper presented at the 36th EMAC Conference (Reykjavik 2007).

40. Stuart Elliott, 'Years later, Mattel embraces "Barbie Girl"', *New York Times*, 26 August 2009. http://mediadecoder.blogs.nytimes.com/2009/08/26/years-later-mattel-embraces-barbie-girl/?pagemode=print, accessed 3 May 2012.

41. Eric Arnould and Søren Askegaard, 'HyperCulture: The Next Stage in the Globalization of Consumption', paper presented at the 1997 Annual Association for Consumer Research Conference in Denver, Colorado, 16–19 October.

42. Aurélie Kessous and Elyette Roux, 'A semiotic analysis of nostalgia as as connection to the past', *Qualitative Market Research. An International Journal*, vol. 11 no. 2 (2008): 192–212.

43. Stephen Brown, Robert V. Kozinets and John F. Sherry Jr, 'Teaching old brands new tricks: Retro branding and the revival of brand meaning', *Journal of Marketing* 67 (July 2003): 19–33.

44. Brown, Kozinets and Sherry Jr, 'Teaching old brands new tricks', *ibid.*

45. Stephen Brown, *The Marketing Code* (London: Cyan Books, 2006).

46. Richard Elliott, Susan Eccles and Michelle Hodgson, 'Recoding gender representations: Women, cleaning products, and advertising's "New Man"', *International Journal of Research in Marketing* 10(3) (1993): 311–24.

47. Stephanie O'Donohoe, 'Raiding the postmodern pantry: Advertising intertextuality and the young adult audience', *European Journal of Marketing* 31(3/4) (1997): 234–53.

48. Stephanie O'Donohoe, 'Living with ambivalence: Attitudes towards advertising in postmodern times', *Marketing Theory*, vol. 1 no. 1 (2001): 91–108.

49. Søren Askegaard, 'Brands as a Global Ideoscape', in J. Schroeder and M. Salzer-Mörling (eds), *Brand Culture* (London: Routledge, 2006): 91–102.

50. Martin McCarty, Martin I. Horn, Mary Kate Szenasy and Jocelyn Feintuch, 'An exploratory study of consumer style: Country differences and international segments', *Journal of Consumer Behaviour* 6, no. 1 (2007): 48.

51. David Waller, Kim-Shyan Fam and B. Zafer Erdigan, 'Advertising of controversial products: A cross-cultural study', *Journal of Consumer Marketing*, vol. 22 no. 1 (2005): 6–13.

52. See, for example, Craig Thompson and Siok Kuan Tambyah, 'Trying to be cosmopolitan', *Journal of Consumer Research*, vol. 26 no. 3 (1999): 214–41.

53. Jean-Noël Kapferer, 'The Two Business Cultures of Luxury Brands', in J. Schroeder and M. Salzer-Mörling (eds), *Brand Culture* (London: Routledge, 2006): 67–76.

54. Sandra Diehl, Ralf Terlutter and Barbara Mueller, 'The Influence of Culture on Responses to the Globe Dimension of Performance Orientation in Advertising Messages – Results from the US, Germany, France, Spain, and Thailand', in A.Y. Lee and D. Soman (eds), *Advances in Consumer Research*, vol. XXXV (Duluth, MN: Association for Consumer Research, 2008): 269–75.

55. See also Ulf Hannerz, 'Cosmopolitans and Locals in World Culture', in Mike Featherstone (ed.), *Global Culture* (London: Sage, 1990): 237–52.

56. Dannie Kjeldgaard and Søren Askegaard, 'The glocalization of youth culture: The global youth segment as structures of common difference', *Journal of Consumer Research*, vol. 33 no. 2 (2006): 231–47.

57. Douglas B. Holt, John A. Quelch and Earl L. Taylor, 'How global brands compete', *Harvard Business Review* (September 2004): 68–75.

58. Eric J. Arnould and Richard R. Wilk, 'Why Do the Natives Wear Adidas? Anthropological Approaches to Consumer Research', in Elisabeth C. Hirschman and Morris B. Holbrook (eds), *Advances in Consumer Research* 12 (Provo, UT: Association for Consumer Research, 1985): 748–52.

59. David K. Tse, Russell W. Belk and Nan Zhou, 'Becoming a consumer society: A longitudinal and cross-cultural content analysis of print ads from Hong Kong, the People's Republic of China, and Taiwan', *Journal of Consumer Research* 15 (March 1989): 457–72; see also Annamma Joy, 'Marketing in modern China: An evolutionary perspective', *CJAS* (June 1990): 55–67, for a review of changes in Chinese marketing practices since the economic reforms of 1978.

60. Lilly Ye, Mousumi Bose and Lou Pelton, 'Dispelling the myth of Chinese consumers: A new generation of brand-conscious individualists', *Journal of Consumer Marketing*, 29 (3, 2012): 190–201.

61. See: http://www.tokyotales.com/japlish/ (accessed 30 July 2005).

62. John F. Sherry Jr and Eduardo G. Camargo, '"May your life be marvelous": English language labeling and the semiotics of Japanese promotion', *Journal of Consumer Research* 14 (September 1987): 174–88.

63. http://www.japander.com/japander/zz.htm (accessed 30 July 2005).

64. Julien Cayla and Giana Eckhardt, 'Asian brands and the shaping of a transnational imagined community', *Journal of Consumer Research*, vol. 35 no. 2 (2008): 216–30.

65. www.red-luxury.com/2010/08/10/Chinas-10-top-local-luxury-brands, accessed 16 February 2012.

66. 'Google konkurrent til Brasilien'; *Markedsføring*, 16 February 2012.

67. Jason Overdorf, 'Comics: Off to Save Mumbai', *Newsweek* (2 August 2004): 15.

68. Material in this section adapted from Güliz Ger and Russell W. Belk, 'I'd like to buy the world a Coke: Consumptionscapes of the "less affluent world"', *Journal of Consumer Policy* 19(3) (1996): 271–304; Russell W. Belk, 'Romanian Consumer Desires and Feelings of Deservingness', in Lavinia Stan (ed.), *Romania in Transition* (Hanover, NH: Dartmouth Press, 1997): 191–208; see also Güliz Ger, 'Human development and humane consumption: Well-being beyond the good life', *Journal of Public Policy and Marketing* 16(1) (1997): 110–25.

69. Tuba Üstüner and Douglas B. Holt, 'Dominated consumer acculturation: The social construction of poor migrant women's consumer identity projects in a Turkish squatter', *Journal of Consumer Research*, vol. 34 no. 1 (2007): 41–56.

70. Güliz Ger, 'The positive and negative effects of marketing on socioeconomic development: The Turkish case', *Journal of Consumer Policy* 15 (1992): 229–54.

71. Erazim Kohák, 'Ashes, ashes . . . Central Europe after forty years', *Daedalus* 121 (Spring 1992): 197–215, at 219, quoted in Belk, 'Romanian Consumer Desires and Feelings of Deservingness', *op. cit.*

72. Markedsføring, 10, November 2011.

73. Rungpaka Amy Tiwaskul and Chris Hackley, 'Postmodern Paradoxes in Thai–Asian Consumer Identity', *Journal of Business Research*, vol. 65 no. 4 (2012): 490–496.

74. Søren Askegaard and Dannie Kjeldgaard, 'Here, there and everwhere: Place branding and gastronomic glocalization in a macromarketing perspective', *Journal of Macromarketing*, vol. 27 no. 2 (2007): 138–47.

75. Allison James, 'Cooking the Books: Global or Local Identities in Contemporary British Food Cultures?' in David Howes (ed.), *Cross-Cultural Consumption* (London: Routledge, 1996): 77–92.

76. Søren Askegaard, Dannie Kjeldgaard and Eric Arnould, 'Reflexive Culture's Consequences', in C. Nakata (ed.), *Beyond Hofstede: Culture Frameworks for Global Marketing and Management* (Chicago: Palgrave Macmillan 2009): 101–122.

77. A. Fuat Firat, 'Globalization of fragmentation – a framework for understanding contemporary global markets', *Journal of International Marketing* 5(2) (1997): 77–86. See also T. Bettina Cornwell and Judy Drennan, 'Cross-cultural consumer/consumption research: Dealing with issues emerging from globalization and fragmentation', *Journal of Macromarketing*, vol. 24 no. 2 (2004): 108–21.

78. Zygmunt Bauman, 'Consuming Life', *Journal of Consumer Culture*, vol. 1 no. 1 (2001): 9–29.

79. Daniel Miller, 'Consumption as the Vanguard of History', in D. Miller (ed.), *Acknowledging Consumption* (London: Routledge, 1995): 1–57; see also Cornelia Dröge, Roger Calantone, Madhu Agrawal and Robert Mackay, 'The consumption culture and its critiques: A framework for analysis', *Journal of Macromarketing* (Fall 1993): 32–45.

80. Panel discussion: 'Critical and Moral Stances in Consumer Studies', *Journal of Consumer Culture*, vol. 10 no. 2 (2010): 274–291.

81. Richard Elliott, 'Addictive consumption: Function and fragmentation in postmodernity', *Journal of Consumer Policy* 17 (1994): 159–79; Thomas C. O'Guinn and Ronald J. Faber, 'Compulsive buying: A phenomenological exploration', *Journal of Consumer Research* 16 (1989): 147–57.

82. Michael Neuner, Gerhard Raab and Lucia A. Reisch, 'Compulsive Buying as a Consumer Policy Issue in East and West Germany', in K.G. Grunert and J. Thøgersen (eds), *Consumers, Policy and the Environment* (New York: Springer, 2005): 89–114.

83. Hans Kjellberg, 'Market practices and over-consumption', *Consumption, Markets and Culture*, vol. 11 no. 2 (2008): 151–67.

84. Cf, for example, *Consumption, Markets and Culture*, 13 (3, 2010), special issue on anti-consumption.

85. John de Graaf, David Wann, and Thomas H. Naylor, *Affluenza. The All-Consuming Epidemic* (San Francisco: Berrett-Koehler Publishers, 2001).

86. Craig Thompson, 'A Carnivalesque Approach to the Politics of Consumption (or) Grotesque Realism and the Analysis of the Excretory Economy', *ANNALS of the American Academy of Political and Social Science*, vol. 611 (2007): 112–125. See also the already cited panel discussion (op. cit.).

87. Ulrich Beck, *Risk Society* (London: Sage Publications, 1992).

88. http://blogs.wsj.com/chinajournal/2008/10/01/seeking-sources-of-information-on-melamine-tainted-food/ 20090118

89. Karin Ekström and Søren Askegaard, 'Daily Consumption in Risk Society: The Case of Genetically Modified Foods', in S. Hoch and R. Meyer (eds), *Advances in Consumer Research* 27 (Provo, UT: Association for Consumer Research, 2000): 237–43.

90. Lone Bredahl, 'Determinants of Consumer Attitudes and Purchase Intentions with Regard to Genetically Modified Foods – Results from a Cross-National Survey', MAPP Working Paper no. 69 (Aarhus: The Aarhus School of Business, 2000).

91. www.guardian.co.uk/environment/2011/apr/04/organic-food-sales-fail, accessed 16 February 2012.

92. Denmark's Radion Programme One News, 16 February 2012.

93. Liisa Uusitalo, 'Consumers as Citizens – Three Approaches to Collective Consumer Problems', in K.G. Grunert and J. Thøgersen (eds), *Consumers, Policy and the Environment*, (New York: Springer, 2005): 127–50. See also Yannis Gabriel and Tim Lang, *The Unmanageable Consumer*, 2nd edn (London: Sage, 2006).

94. Suzanne Beckmann, 'In the Eye of the Beholder: Danish Consumer-Citizens and Sustainability', in K.G. Grunert and J. Thøgersen (eds), *Consumers, Policy and the Environment, op. cit.*: 265–99.

95. On consumers and their ideologized narratives about technology, see Robert V. Kozinets, 'Technology/ideology: How ideological fields influence consumers' technology narratives', *Journal of Consumer Research*, vol. 34 no. 6 (2008): 865–81.

96. Bente Halkier, 'Consequences of the politicization of consumption: The example of environmentally friendly consumption practices', *Journal of Environmental Policy and Planning* 1 (1999): 25–41.

97. Oliver M. Freestone and Peter McGoldrick, 'Motivations of the ethical consumer', *Journal of Business Research*, 79 (2008), 445–467. See also *Journal of Marketing Management*, 28 (3–4, March 2012).

98. Richard Jones, 'Challenges to the notion of publics in public relations: Implications of the risk society for the discipline', *Public Relations Review*, vol. 28 no. 1 (2002): 49–62.

99. http://www.adbusters.org/home/ (accessed 30 July 2005).

100. www.cokespotlight.org; see also www.adbusters.org and www.corpspotlight.org (accessed 30 July 2005).

101. Kalle Lasn, 'Culture Jamming', in J.B. Schor and D.B. Holt (eds), *The Consumer Society Reader* (New York: The New Press, 2000): 414–32.

102. Nat Ives, 'Advertising: Unauthorized campaigns used by unauthorized creators become a trend', *New York Times* (23 December 2004); see www.gomotron.com and www.MadisonAveNew.com for posting suggestions for companies such as Coca-Cola, Mitsubishi Motors, North American and Alltel (accessed 30 July 2005).

103. Craig J. Thompson and Zeynep Arsel, 'The Starbucks brandscape and consumers' (anticorporate) experiences of glocalization', *Journal of Consumer Research* 31 (December 2004): 631–42.

104. Craig J. Thompson, Aric Rindfleisch and Zeynep Arsel, 'Emotional branding and the strategic value of the doppelgänger brand image', *Journal of Marketing*, vol. 70 no. 1 (2006): 50–64.

105. Jill Gabrielle Klein, N. Craig Smith and Andrew John, 'Why we boycott: Consumer motivation for boycott participation', *Journal of Marketing*, vol. 68 (July 2004): 92–109.

106. Marcus Mabry, 'Do Boycotts Work?' *Newsweek* 3 (6 July 1992): 35; 'McDonald's antibiotic project: No more playing chicken with antibiotics', retrieved 16 July 2005 at: http://www.environmentaldefense.org/partnership_project.cfm?subnav=project_fullstory&projectID=1

107. MORI, 'Stakeholder dialogue: consumer attitude' (November 2000), http://www.csreurope.org/whatwedo/consumerattitudes_page408.aspx

108. CSR Europe website, http://www.csreurope.org (accessed 15 March 2005).

109. http://mediadecoder.blogs.nytimes.com/2009/08/26/years-later-mattel-embraces-barbie-girl/?pagemode=print; Carlos J. Torelli, Alokparna Basu Monga, Andrew M. Kaikati, 'Doing Poorly by Doing Good: Corporate Social Responsibility and Brand Concepts', *Journal of Consumer Research*, 38, 5 (February 2012): 948–963.

110. 'Vattenfall vasker kulsort energi grøn', *Information*, 14 November 2008.

111. 'The Bitter Taste of Tea', TV documentary, Denmark's Radio TV, 26 November 2008, accessed 8 January 2009 on www.dr.dk/Dr1/dokumentar/2008/1120141500.htm

3 SHOPPING, BUYING AND EVALUATING

CHAPTER OBJECTIVES

When you finish reading this chapter you will understand why:

→ Many factors at the time of purchase dramatically influence the consumer's decision-making process.

→ The information a store or website provides strongly influences a purchase decision in addition to what a shopper already knows or believes about a product.

→ A salesperson often is the crucial connection to a purchase.

→ Marketers need to be concerned about a consumer's evaluations of a product after he or she buys it as well as before.

GRACE'S mobile phone was coming to the end of its life. She had two choices. Either she could buy a straightforward replacement for her mobile phone; or she could invest in a new smartphone, which sounded like an attractive but expensive option. As Grace currently has a 'pay as you go' phone she was keen to try and keep the costs of the purchase down, although most of the best phones seemed to come with expensive sounding 24-month contracts. She had a number of other concerns, in addition to the cost – most notably how to choose amongst all the different smartphones that are on the market? And how confident could she be, once she had bought a smartphone, that she would be able to operate it? Most especially, how easy would it be to set up the all important links to her existing e-mail account? What was meant by all the different mobile operating systems she had read about: Apple's iOS; Android with the Samsung or HTC phones [had she got that right?]; and RIM's BlackBerry OS? If she had a smartphone, she wanted to be able to check her e-mails and surf the net at the very least, and then she had to learn about downloading and using apps. She was nervous about making everything work – would everything be compatible? She'd heard that 'everything is simple', but she'd learnt that was not always true. What should she do? She did a little bit of web surfing for her homework, visiting a comparison site (e.g. **kelkoo.com**). Then she went along to some of her local high street stores (e.g. Orange; Vodafone; Apple) where she was rather overwhelmed by the array of choice. She decided to try and pick the brains of some of her friends who already had iPhones, BlackBerries and the latest Samsung and HTC models. In the end she decided, as she was most familiar with Samsung (as that was her current mobile phone), that she would upgrade to one of their smart phones – but which one? That would depend on the help and advice she got from the high street store, once she had done some more homework on the Samsung website and identified the models she really fancied. She could, of course, always purchase via the Orange or Vodafone website, but she thought it might be safer and better to make the purchase instore, so that she could go back and ask questions if she was having problems with understanding how to use all the various functions – all the stores offered lessons these days, so that helped alleviate some of her anxiety that she would make a purchase, and then be completely defeated by the complexity of the phone she had chosen.

INTRODUCTION

In this chapter we seek to understand the consumer within the marketplace. Grace's experience illustrates some of the concepts to be discussed in this chapter, as we examine issues related to the consumption cycle of search, choice, purchase and post-purchase evaluation (we deal with product disposal, the final stage in the consumption cycle, in Chapter 6). We begin the chapter by examining a number of important antecedent states that affect our consumer behaviour across all stages of the consumption cycle including situational factors (e.g. social and physical surroundings); temporal factors; mood and shopping motivations. Our previous consumer experiences influence firstly, our views about how best to collect information about the products we are interested in (note that Grace searched online and also in the high street); and secondly, our decisions about where to purchase (e.g. online sites; high street stores; or a combination of click and collect). The importance of the retail environment means that marketing managers invest a lot of effort in the experiences that their customers have either instore or online (e.g. store image; atmospherics; service levels; navigability of the website), so we spend some time in this chapter looking at servicescapes (retailing as theatre) where the consumer has many of his/her experiences of the marketplace. Towards the end of the chapter we discuss the important role played by expectations in affecting consumers' levels of satisfaction and dissatisfaction as the post-purchase experiences of the product or service are important for feeding through into the start of the next consumption cycle, whether for the same or a similar product or service. We finish the chapter firstly, by examining what happens when consumers decide to act on their dissatisfaction; and secondly, by discussing the EU systems in place for monitoring product quality and product failures.

CONSUMERS' CHOICES

Grace's story highlights the range of dilemmas many consumers face when making consumption choices (more on consumer decision-making in Chapter 9, with the difficulties faced by Daniel when choosing amongst different televisions), and how consumers try and manage the different types of perceived risk associated with their choices (e.g. the financial risk that Grace felt in choosing a smartphone). Grace's dilemma also highlights the importance of the purchase context (online versus offline) as well as her fears about the post-purchase experience.

Making a purchase is often not a simple, routine matter of going to a shop and choosing something. As illustrated in Figure 3.1, a consumer's choices are affected by many personal factors, such as mood, time pressure and the particular situation or context for which the product is needed. In some situations, like the purchase of a car or a home, the salesperson or the reference group (which we will discuss in Chapter 10) play a pivotal role in the final

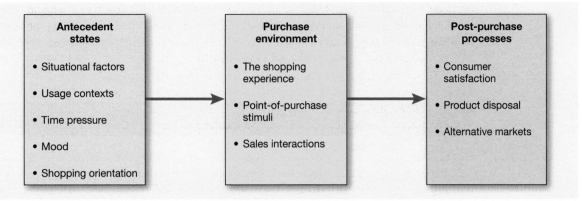

Antecedent states	Purchase environment	Post-purchase processes
• Situational factors • Usage contexts • Time pressure • Mood • Shopping orientation	• The shopping experience • Point-of-purchase stimuli • Sales interactions	• Consumer satisfaction • Product disposal • Alternative markets

Figure 3.1 Issues related to purchase and post-purchase activities

choice. And today people are using the web to arm themselves with product and price information before they even enter a store[1] (note Daniel's preliminary search for televisions via the internet in the opening vignette of Chapter 9), which puts added pressure on retailers to deliver the value customers expect.

The store environment also exerts a major influence: shopping is like a stage performance, with the customer involved either as a member of the audience or as an active participant. The quality of the performance is affected by the other *cast members* (salespeople or other shoppers), as well as by the *setting* of the play (the image of a particular store and the 'feeling' it imparts) and *props* (store fittings and promotional material which try to influence the shopper's decisions).

In addition, the consumer activity per se occurs *after* a product has been purchased and brought home. After using a product, the consumer must decide whether or not they are satisfied with it. The satisfaction process is especially important to marketers, who realize that the key to success is not selling a product once, but rather forging a relationship with the consumer so that they will continue to buy in the future. Finally, we must also consider how

Barbara Kruger, 'I shop therefore I am'.
Copyright Barbara Kruger, Courtesy: Mary Boone Gallery, New York.

consumers go about disposing of products and how secondary markets (e.g. eBay; second-hand car dealers) often play a pivotal role in product acquisition. This chapter considers many issues related to purchase and post-purchase phenomena (product disposal, recycling and second-hand goods are considered in Chapter 6).

ANTECEDENT STATES

A person's mood or physiological condition at the time of purchase can have a major impact on what is bought and can also affect how products are evaluated.[2] One reason for this is that behaviour is directed towards certain goal states, as will be discussed in Chapter 6. In addition, the person's particular social identity, or the role that is being played at a given time (and thus their *situational self-image*), will be influential.[3]

Situational effects: mood and consumption situations

A consumer's mood will have an impact on purchase decisions. For example, stress can reduce a consumer's information-processing and problem-solving abilities.[4] Two dimensions determine whether a shopper will react positively or negatively to a store environment: *pleasure* and *arousal*. A person can enjoy or not enjoy a situation, and they can feel stimulated or not. As Figure 3.2 indicates, different combinations of pleasure and arousal levels result in a variety of emotional states. For example, an arousing situation can be either distressing or exciting, depending on whether the context is positive or negative (e.g. a street riot *vs* a street festival). Maintaining an upbeat mood in a pleasant context is one factor behind the success of theme parks such as Disneyland, which try to provide consistent doses of carefully calculated stimulation to patrons.[5]

A specific mood is some combination of pleasure and arousal. For example, the state of happiness is high in pleasantness and moderate in arousal, while elation would be high in

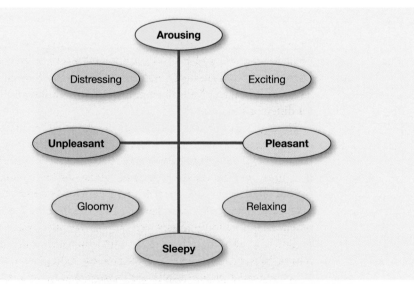

Figure 3.2 Dimensions of emotional states

Source: James Russell and Geraldine Pratt, 'A description of the affective quality attributed to environment', *Personality and Social Psychology* 38 (August 1980): 311–22.

both dimensions.[6] In general, a mood state (either positive or negative) biases judgements of products and services in that direction.[7] Put simply, consumers like things better when they are in a good mood (this may explain the popularity of the business lunch).

Moods can be affected by store design, the weather or other factors specific to the consumer. In addition, music and television programming can affect mood; this has important consequences for commercials.[8] When consumers hear happy music or watch happy programmes, they have more positive reactions to commercials and products, especially when the marketing appeals are aimed at arousing emotional reactions.[9] When we're in a good mood, we process ads with less elaboration. We pay less attention to the specifics of the message and we rely more on heuristics (see Chapter 9).[10]

Our emotional reactions to marketing cues are so powerful that some high-tech companies study mood in very small doses (in 1/30 of a second increments) as they analyse people's facial reactions when they see ads or new products. They measure happiness as they look for differences between, for example, a *true smile* (which includes a relaxation of the upper eyelid) and a *social smile* (which occurs only around the mouth). Whirlpool used this technique to test consumers' emotional reactions to a yet-to-be-launched generation of its Duet washers and dryers. The company's goal: to design an appliance that will actually make people happy. Researchers discovered that even though test subjects said they weren't thrilled with some out-of-the-box design options, such as unusual colour combinations, their facial expressions said otherwise.[11]

A *consumption situation* is defined by factors over and above the characteristics of the person and of the product. Situational effects can be behavioural (such as entertaining friends) or perceptual (being depressed, or feeling pressed for time).[12] Common sense tells us that people tailor their purchases to specific occasions or that the way we feel at a specific time affects what we feel like buying or doing.

One reason for this variability is that the role a person plays at any time is partly determined by their *situational self-image*: 'Who am I right now?' (see also Chapter 5).[13] Someone trying to impress his girlfriend by playing the role of 'man about town' may spend more lavishly, ordering champagne rather than beer and buying flowers – purchases he would never consider when he is with his male friends in a pub and playing the role of 'one of the boys'. As this example demonstrates, knowledge of what consumers are doing at the time a product is consumed may improve predictions of product and brand choice.[14]

Situational segmentation

By systematically identifying important usage situations, market segmentation strategies can be developed to position products that will meet the specific needs arising from these situations. Many product categories are amenable to this form of segmentation. The South African ad for Volkswagen, overleaf, emphasizes the versatility of the Volkswagen people carrier bus for different situations.[15]

Situations can be used to fine-tune a segmentation strategy. A study of 2,500 online customers[16] identified 'occasion-based segmentation'. Using variables such as length of session, time spent on each page of the website, and the user's familiarity with the site, seven different occasions were identified which could be classified into two groups. First, the group Loitering, Information Please and Surfing, spent between 33 and 70 minutes online, and was more likely to purchase. The second group, Quickies, Just the Facts, Single Mission and Do It Again, remained online for much shorter periods. 'It's only by decoding the type of occasion – such as gathering product information – that marketers can fully harness the web's interactive powers by aiming messages and offers at the right place at the right time.'[17]

Social media platforms also are looking at ways to adapt quickly to situational changes. Facebook is testing ads targeted in real time based on users' status updates ('What's on your mind?') and wall posts. Theoretically, a user who posts near the end of his workday could immediately be sent a promotion from a beer company.[18]

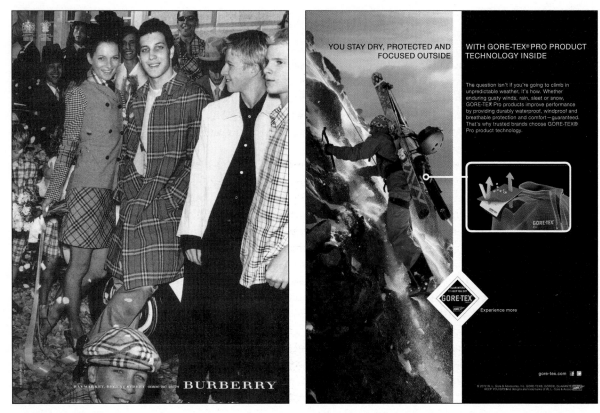

(*Left*) This Burberry ad shows the situational context for the consumption of their products, notably in social settings and by upper class, young adult consumers. The Advertising Archives.

(*Right*) Clothing choices often are heavily influenced by the situation in which they need to be worn. W.L. Gore & Associates, Inc. (Gore-Tex)

This South African ad for Volkswagen emphasizes that brand criteria can differ depending upon the situation in which the product will be used.

Courtesy of Volkswagen Group.

SOCIAL AND PHYSICAL SURROUNDINGS

A consumer's physical and social environment can make a big difference in affecting their motives for product purchase and also product evaluation. Important cues include the number and type of other consumers, as well as dimensions of the physical environment. Decor, smells (the use of scents in the retail environment can increase the pleasure and hedonic values derived from shopping)[19] and even temperature can significantly influence consumption.

In addition to physical cues, many of a consumer's purchase decisions are significantly affected by the groups or social settings in which these occur (as we shall see in Chapter 10). In some cases, the presence or absence of **co-consumers**, the other patrons in a setting, can be a determinant attribute (see the discussion in Chapter 9) and function as a product attribute, as when an exclusive resort or boutique promises to provide privacy to privileged customers. At other times, the presence of others can have positive value. A sparsely attended football match or an empty bar, in contrast, can be depressing sights.

The presence of large numbers of people in a consumer environment increases arousal levels, so a consumer's subjective experience of a setting tends to be more intense. This polarization can be both positive and negative. While the experience of other people creates a state of arousal, the consumer's actual experience depends on their *interpretation of* and *reaction to* this arousal. Crowding may result in avoidance (leaving the store earlier), aggressiveness (rushing others), opportunism (using the extra time to find bargains) or self-blame (for coming into the store at the wrong hour).[20] It is important, therefore, to distinguish between *density* and *crowding*. Density refers to the actual number of people occupying

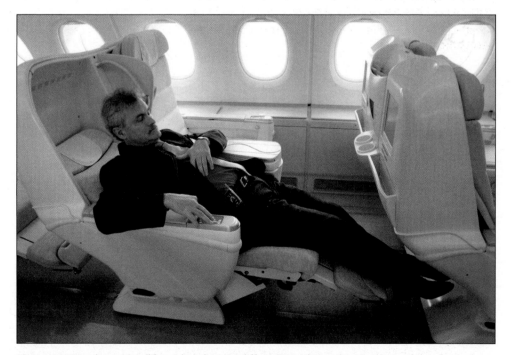

Many stores and services (like airlines) try to differentiate themselves in terms of the physical environments they offer, touting such amenities as comfort and space.

Photo of Qantas business class, courtesy of Press Association Images.

a space, while the psychological state of crowding exists only if a negative affective state occurs as a result of this density.[21] For example, 100 students packed into a classroom designed for 75 may result in an unpleasant situation for all concerned, but the same number of people jammed together at a party occupying a room of the same size might just make for a great party.

In addition, the *type* of consumers who patronize a store or service can serve as a store attribute; and the *type* of consumers who use a product can influence evaluations. We may infer something about a store by examining its customers. For this reason, some restaurants require men to wear a jacket for dinner, and bouncers at some 'hot' nightspots hand-pick patrons from the queue based on whether they have the right 'look' for the club. Royal Ascot has tightened up the dress code for its race meetings, banning the wearing of fascinators[22] from the Royal Enclosure, and announcing that all women's hats have to be four inches (10 cm) in diameter at the base, and banning strapless dresses; for men, waistcoats and ties will be compulsory and the wearing of cravats is banned. Charles Barnett (chief executive of Royal Ascot) said: 'We want to see modern and stylish dress at Royal Ascot, just within the parameters of formal wear, and the feedback we have received from our customers overwhelmingly supports that.'[23] However, policies can backfire, as in the case of Royal Ascot which 'was accused of demeaning spectators who had paid £28 to enter the Premier enclosure. Charles Barnett, Ascot's chief executive, admitted . . . that labelling the course's customers [with orange stickers] had been a mistake. "It is clear that we let down many of our Premier enclosure customers yesterday with a well-intentioned but misguided policy . . ." "No customer should be expected to pay for such an experience, and we have taken the view that all Premier enclosure visitors yesterday will receive a full refund."'[24] This cost the company £28,000.

Temporal factors

Time is one of consumers' most precious and limiting resources. Recent research indicates that there are significant time–money differences when consumers use heuristics ('rules-of-thumb for problem solving learnt by experiment or trial and error' (Merriam-Webster **http://www.merriam-webster.com/dictionary/heuristic**) for decision-making: i.e. 'decisions related to time rather than money foster an enhanced use of heuristics' which suggests that although time and money seem to be economically equivalent, they are, in fact, psychologically different[25] (see Chapter 9). Our perspectives on time can affect many stages of decision-making and consumption, such as needs that are stimulated, the amount of information search we undertake and so on. Common sense tells us that more careful information search and deliberation occurs when we have the luxury of taking our time. In online marketing **open rates** (the percentage of people who open an e-mail message from a marketer) vary throughout the day. The peak time for high open rates is mid-day on weekdays (presumably when all those people at work take a lunch break).[26]

Economic time

Time is an economic variable; it is a resource that must be divided among activities.[27] Consumers try to maximize satisfaction by allocating time to the appropriate combination of tasks. Of course, people's allocation decisions differ. An individual's priorities determine their **time style**.[28] Time style incorporates dimensions like economic time, past orientation, future orientation, time submissiveness and time anxiety.[29] Research identified four dimensions of time: social, temporal, planning and polychromic orientation. The social dimension refers to individuals' categorization of time as either 'time for me' or 'time with/for others'. The temporal orientation depicts the relative significance individuals attach to past, present or future. The planning orientation dimension alludes to different time management styles varying on a continuum from analytic to spontaneous. And lastly, polychromic orientation denotes doing-one-thing-at-a-time versus multitasking time styles. These multiple dimensions of time style push and pull individuals in different directions, which ultimately lead to psychological conflicts. From these dimensions, five emergent symbolic metaphors of time were proposed,[30] which reflected different perspectives on time and the process by which the perspective was created:

Time is a pressure cooker: Women who personify this metaphor are usually analytic in their planning, other oriented, and monochronic in their time styles. They treat shopping in a methodical manner and they often feel under pressure and in conflict.

Time is a map: Women who exemplify this metaphor are usually analytic planners, have a future temporal orientation and a polychronic time style. They often engage in extensive information search and in comparison shopping.

Time is a mirror: Women who come under this metaphor are also analytic planners and have a polychromic orientation. However, they have a past temporal orientation. Due to their risk averseness in time use, these women are usually loyal to products and services they know and trust.

Time is a river: Women whose time styles can be described through this metaphor are usually spontaneous in their planning orientation and have a present focus. They go on unplanned, short and frequent shopping trips undertaken on impulse.

Time is feast: These women are analytic planners who have a present temporal orientation. They view time as something to be consumed in the pursuit of sensory pleasure and gratification and, hence, they are motivated by hedonic and variety seeking desires in their consumption behaviour.[31]

Many consumers believe they are more pressed for time than ever before, a feeling called **time poverty**. This feeling may, however, be due more to perception than to fact. People may simply have more options for spending their time and feel pressured by the weight of it all. European research showed that women aged 15 to 24 spent more time on average on personal care, studying and unpaid work (e.g. cooking, cleaning, caring for children) than young men of the same age (15 to 24) who spent more time in paid work and leisure activities (e.g. sports, watching TV and playing computer games) (see Figure 3.3).[32] For some interesting (and revealing!) data on how we spend our time, see **http://ec.europa.eu/eurostat**[33] and Figures 3.4 and 3.5.

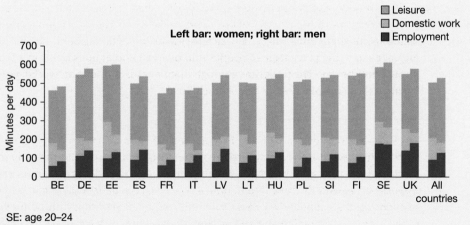

Figure 3.3 How young women and men aged 15–24 spend their time

Source: The life of women and men in Europe: A Statistical Portrait – 2008 edition, Figure 39, page 48, European Commission/Eurostat Luxembourg: Cat. No. KS-80-07-135-EN-N website http://ec.europa.eu/eurostat

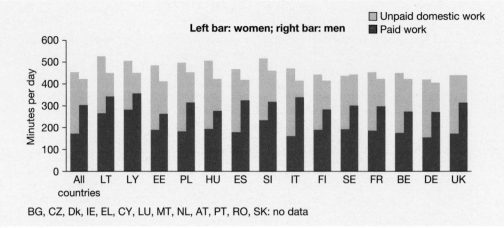

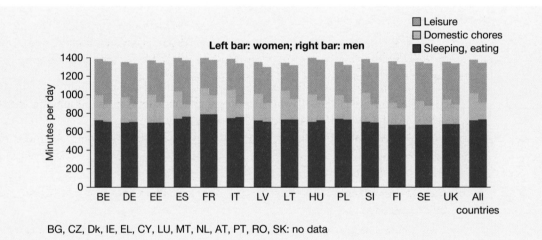

Figure 3.4 Time spent by women and men, aged 25–44, on paid work and unpaid domestic work

Source: The life of women and men in Europe: A Statistical Portrait – 2008 edition, Figure 121, page 111, European Commission/Eurostat Luxembourg: Cat. No. KS-80-07-135-EN-N website http://ec.europa.eu/eurostat

Figure 3.5 How women and men aged 65 and over spend their time

Source: The life of women and men in Europe: A Statistical Portrait – 2008 edition, Figure 158, page 147, European Commission/Eurostat Luxembourg: Cat. No. KS-80-07-135-EN-N website http://ec.europa.eu/eurostat

This sense of *time poverty* has made consumers very responsive to marketing innovations that allow them to save time. New online business concepts based on improved delivery are popping up all over the web. Delivery of videos, groceries, or dry cleaning to customers' doors are a few of the time-saving online possibilities.[34] In Hong Kong rush-hour commuters no longer need to stand and queue to buy Underground tickets. Instead, a scanner automatically reads an Octopus card and automatically deducts the fare from their account. The card doesn't even require contact to be read, so people can just pass their entire bag over the scanner and race to catch their trains.[35]

Convenience, variety and new packaging are themes in this Heinz soup ad, which is addressed to the time-pressed consumer (illustrating time poverty as a theme within food ads, as well as the application of new technology to product packaging and preparation, e.g. these microwaveable and portable soups for lunch at the office).

Courtesy of H.J. Heinz Company Limited.

Psychological time

The fluidity of time is important for marketers to understand, because we are more likely to be in a consuming mood at some times rather than others. We can identify time categories in terms of when people are likely to be receptive to marketing messages:[36]

- *Flow time*: In a flow state we become so absorbed in an activity we notice nothing else. Not a good time to be hitting people with ads.
- *Occasion time*: Special moments when something monumental occurs, such as a birth or an important job interview. Ads clearly relevant to the situation will be given our undivided attention.
- *Deadline time*: When we are working against the clock. This is the worst time to catch someone's attention.
- *Leisure time*: During down time, we are more likely to notice ads and perhaps try new things.
- *Time to kill*: Waiting for something to happen such as catching a plane or sitting in a waiting room. This is bonus time, where we feel we have the luxury to focus on extraneous things. As a result we are more receptive to commercial messages, even for products we do not normally use.

The psychological dimension of time – how we actually experience it – is an important factor in **queuing theory**, the mathematical study of waiting lines. As we all know, our experience when we wait has a big effect on our evaluations of what we get at the end of the wait. Although we assume that something must be pretty good if we have to wait for it, the negative feelings that long waits arouse can quickly turn people off.[37] In a survey, NCR Corp found queuing at retail outlets was one of the most frustrating consumer experiences, followed by registering at clinics or hospitals, checking in at airports, and ordering at fast-food restaurants. On average, consumers estimate that they spend more than two days per year waiting in line for service, and half believe they waste between 30 minutes and two hours each week in queues.[38]

Marketers use various devices to minimize psychological waiting time. These techniques range from altering customers' perceptions of the length of a queue to providing distractions that divert attention from waiting:[39]

● One hotel chain received excessive complaints about the waiting time for lifts, so it installed mirrors near the lifts. People's natural tendency to check their appearance reduced complaints, even though the actual waiting time was unchanged.

● Airline passengers often complain about the wait to claim their baggage. In one airport, they would walk one minute from the plane to the baggage carousel and then wait seven minutes for their luggage. When the airport changed the layout so that the walk to the carousel took six minutes and bags arrived two minutes after that, complaints disappeared.[40]

Queuing theory must take cultural differences into account, because these affect how we behave while we are waiting. A Disney executive claims that Europeans exhibit different behaviours depending on their nationality. He notes that at the Disneyland Resort Paris, British visitors are orderly but the French and Italians 'never saw a line they couldn't be in front of'.[41]

Social time

Social time has been proposed as an important but overlooked time dimension in consumer behaviour.[42] Social time refers to the time in relation to social processes and rhythms and schedules in society. It takes into account how determined our lives are by interrelated temporal phenomena, such as working hours, opening hours, eating hours and other institutionalized schedules.

To most Western consumers, time is something that is neatly compartmentalized: we wake up in the morning, go to school or work, come home, eat, go out, go to bed, then do it all

Multitasking has become a way of life for many of us.
Hewlett-Packard Development Company, L.P.

over again. This perspective is called linear separable time (or Christian time): events proceed in an orderly sequence and different times are well defined: 'There's a time and a place for everything.' In this worldwide 'modernized' conception of time, there is a clear sense of past, present and future, and the present is preferred to the past, whereas the future is generally rated better than the present.[43]

Some products and services are believed to be appropriate for certain times and not for others. Some products crossing cultural borders are also crossing over from consumption at one time of day to another time of day. In its home country of Italy, the cappuccino is known as a breakfast coffee. Now it has become popular all over Europe, and in these new markets it is drunk at all times of the day whenever a plain cup of coffee would traditionally have been appropriate. So the cappuccino has moved from a 'breakfast time' category to a more general 'coffee time' category.[44]

SHOPPING: MOTIVATIONS AND EXPERIENCES

People often shop even though they do not necessarily intend to buy anything at all, whereas others have to be dragged to the shopping centre. Shopping is a way to acquire needed products and services, but social motives for shopping are also important. Retailers need to understand the variety of shopping motivations because these all affect how consumers evaluate different aspects of their retail experience such as atmospherics, promotion and marketing communications.[45] One scholar has suggested that shopping activities have a lot to do with love and caring for significant others, to the extent that shopping can be seen as a person's (often the mother's) personal sacrifice of time and devotion for the well-being of the family.[46]

Other scholars distinguish between shopping as an activity performed for utilitarian (functional or tangible) or hedonic (pleasurable or intangible) reasons.[47] These different motives are illustrated by scale items used by researchers to assess people's underlying reasons for shopping. One item that measures hedonic value is: 'During the trip, I felt the excitement of the hunt.' When that type of sentiment is compared to a functionally related statement such as: 'I accomplished just what I wanted to on this shopping trip', the contrast between these two dimensions is clear.[48] European research identified the following hedonic shopping motives:[49]

- *Anticipated utility*: Desire for innovative products, expectations of benefits or hedonistic states which will be provided by the product to be acquired.

- *Role enactment*: Taking on the culturally prescribed roles regarding the conduct of shopping activity, such as careful product and price comparisons, possibly discussed with other shoppers.

- *Choice optimization*: Desire to find the absolutely best buy.

- *Negotiation*: To seek economic advantages and sports-like pleasure through bargaining interactions with sellers in a 'bazaar atmosphere'.

- *Affiliation*: Shopping centres are a natural place to affiliate. The shopping arcade has become a central meeting place for teenagers. It also represents a controlled, secure environment for other groups, such as the elderly.

- *Power and authority*: Entering a power game with the sales personnel and maybe feeling superior to the personnel. As every salesperson knows, some people love the experience of being waited on, even though they may not necessarily buy anything. One men's clothing salesman offered this advice: 'Remember their size, remember what you sold them last time. Make them feel important! If you can make people feel important, they are going to come back. Everybody likes to feel important!'[50]

● *Stimulation*: Searching for new and interesting things offered in the marketplace – shopping just for fun.

Consumers can also be segmented in terms of their **shopping orientation**, or general attitudes about shopping. These orientations may vary depending on the particular product categories and store types considered. Many people feel insecure about shopping for a car (many women, for instance, feel quite intimidated by car showrooms), but they may love to browse in bookshops. A shopper's motivation influences the type of shopping environment that will be attractive or annoying; for example, a person who wants to locate and buy something quickly may find loud music, bright colours or complex layouts distracting, whereas someone who is there to browse may enjoy the sensory stimulation.[51] Our feelings about shopping are also influenced by the culture in which we live. Several shopping types have been identified, although the following list does not cover the whole range of possibilities:[52]

● *The economic shopper*: a rational, goal-oriented shopper who is primarily interested in maximizing the value of their money.

● *The personalized shopper*: a shopper who tends to form strong attachments to store personnel ('I shop where they know my name').

● *The ethical shopper*: a shopper who likes to help out the underdog and will support local shops rather than chain stores.

● *The apathetic shopper*: one who does not like to shop and sees it as a necessary but unpleasant chore.

● *The recreational shopper*: a person who views shopping as a fun, social activity – a preferred way to spend leisure time.

Given what we said above, however, one type of shopper is missing from this list: *the hate-to-shop shopper*. They are emerging from research on a variety of examples of the aversive side of shopping, including the hassle of finding a parking space, shopping with a girl- or boyfriend with completely different shopping motivations, dealing with the fact that just when you've made a purchase you find something better or less expensive, or coping with intruding 'Can-I-help-you?' sales assistants.[53]

Trends in the purchase environment

We see bumper stickers and T-shirts everywhere: 'Shop 'til you drop', 'When the going gets tough, the tough go shopping', 'Born to shop'. Like it or not, shopping is a major activity for many consumers. The competition for shoppers among retailers is getting tougher, especially in the face of the economic downturn that has followed the credit crunch. In the UK alone such familiar retailing brands as Woolworths have closed down as they lost sales in a falling market, and as they lost touch with their consumers. Retailers must now offer something extra to lure shoppers, whether that something is excitement or, increasingly, just plain bargains.[54] 'Grocery shopping in Europe, North America and indeed around the world is changing in two main ways. Firstly, shoppers' attitudes towards the different elements of the retail offer are shifting. And secondly, these changing attitudes are encouraging the development of new forms of retail channel which shoppers are using in new and different ways.'[55]

Another European trend is the increase of trade from kiosks (for instance in Greece), and from smaller stores with extended opening hours carrying a small selection of daily goods as well as snack products, sweets, newspapers, etc., sometimes more or less like the 7–11 concept imported from the US. In many countries, such kiosks are well established and are often run by Middle Eastern or North African immigrants. But in countries such as Finland,

Table 3.1 Top 15 food retailers in Europe (turnover in Europe 2010 in billion €)

Rank	Retailer	Turnover	Headquarter
1	Carrefour	90.1	France
2	Metro	67.3	Germany
3	Schwarz	54 (2009)	Germany
4	Tesco	53	UK
5	Rewe	50 (2009)	Germany
6	Aldi	46	Germany
7	Edeka	44	Germany
8	Auchan	43	France
9	ITM	35	France
10	E.Leclerc	35	France
11	Casino	29	France
12	Sainsbury	28	UK
13	WalMart	21	USA
14	Morrison	19.3	UK
15	Systeme U	17.8	France

2010 data are the latest available data for comparisons
© 2011 Veraart Research[59]

where the introduction of kiosks is more recent, it has created a new feature in the retail channel system.[56]

In order to be able to compete in the European single market, many retail chains have undergone an internationalization process. The ten biggest companies controlled 30 per cent of the turnover in daily goods in Europe in the mid to late 1990s, and the concentration was growing fast at the end of the 1990s.[57] In 2010 (Table 3.1) the French-owned Carrefour remained the top food retailer in Europe (having held this position at least since 2007), and the second largest distribution company in the world operating globally; its main markets are in Europe, Latin America and Asia. With over 57 per cent of its business deriving from outside France, and a growing presence in international markets (e.g. China, Brazil, Indonesia, Poland and Turkey), it aims to support local suppliers by sourcing locally in so far as it can, with some 90–95 per cent of the products on its shelves sourced locally, depending on the country.[58]

German-owned Metro Group remained the second biggest food retailer in Europe.[60] Tesco, at fourth in the table, has an expanding international presence and now operates in fourteen markets across Europe, Asia and North America.[61]

Store loyalty

Faced with a turbulent retailing environment, including economic recession, retailers highly value store-loyal consumers. Consumers now have an abundance of choices regarding where to shop, including electronic alternatives, which have proved particularly attractive in the economic downturn. Sales online held up well in the traditional pre-Christmas trading period in 2008 for instance, compared with consumer expenditure in high street stores in the UK in the same period. People tend not to be as store-loyal as they once were.[62] Since the 1990s Tesco have gained a reputation for their very effective exploitation of the information gathered via their store loyalty Clubcards. Clubcard's quarterly mailings are so carefully customized

Internationalization of retail brands, illustrated by these outlets for the low-cost German grocery retailer Lidl, in Lodz, Poland (left), and France (above).

Photos from Charles Jean Marc/Sygma/Corbis (left), and Arnd Wiegmann/Reuters/Corbis (right).

that the company prints over four million variations for each mailing.[63] Research suggests that loyalty programmes, properly designed and targeted, can serve five goals: 'keep customers from defecting; win greater share of wallet; prompt customers to make additional purchases; yield insights into customer behaviour; and help turn a profit.'[64] 'Levers of loyalty' were identified as: first, the divisibility of rewards (i.e. redeemable points divided into attractive size clusters, e.g. two lots of 5,000 points rather than one set of 10,000 points); secondly, sense of momentum for the members; nature of rewards (more hedonic than utilitarian in emphasis); thirdly, expansion of relationship (by encouraging the customer to buy more *different* products rather than simply more of the same product); and fourthly, combined-currency flexibility (i.e. spending the alternative currencies represented by points such as air miles in smaller amounts in combination with cash purchase of an air ticket is more attractive than spending a lot of air miles in one go).[65] However, the same researchers warn of the dangers of designing schemes which reward the disloyal; reward volume over profit; give too much away in terms of profit margin; and promise more than can be delivered.[66] A recent study of customer relationships in the Swedish superstore Gekås Ullared[67] identified the importance for customer relationships of both product features (e.g. price, assortment, availability) and also service (e.g. attitude of staff) along with aspects of the physical environment.[68]

E-COMMERCE: CLICKS *VS* BRICKS

As more and more websites pop up to sell everything from fridge magnets to cars, marketers continue to debate how this **cyberspace** marketplace in the online world will affect how they conduct business.[69] Will e-commerce replace traditional retailing, or learn to work in concert with it? The European online buying population is well over 100 million,[70] with obvious differences between the older and younger segments (see Chapter 15 for a discussion of the changing patterns of internet access and online shopping across Europe). Between 2006 to 2011, online shopping in the EU increased from 27 per cent to 40 per cent (Eurostat, 2011a,

2011b).[71] A Swedish survey indicated that searching for product and service information were more important aspects of internet behaviour than actual purchases (note Daniel's behaviour in the opening vignette for Chapter 9). In 2000 only 9 per cent of consumers wanted to buy food online (and a mere 1 per cent had actually tried it), and even the highest scoring purchase product types like travel and ticket purchase did not exceed 30 per cent at that point.[72] However, the last decade has seen e-commerce take off globally so that the e-market is increasingly important. By 2008 'more than 85 per cent of the world's online population had used the internet to make a purchase, increasing the market for online shopping by 40 per cent in the past two years.'[73]

For marketers, the growth of online commerce is a sword that cuts both ways: on the one hand, they can reach customers around the world even if they are physically located 100 miles from nowhere. On the other hand, their competition now comes not only from the shop across the street, but from thousands of websites spanning the globe. A second problem is that offering products directly to consumers has the potential to cut out the middleman – the loyal store-based retailers who carry the firm's products and who sell them at a marked-up price.[74] The 'clicks *vs* bricks' dilemma is raging in the marketing world.

One marketing opportunity, increasingly employed by European retailers, is click and collect – a multi-channel strategy which allows companies to maximize the potential of both their online and offline retail offerings. Customers use the companies' websites to search for, order and pay for items (thus the click), and then go to the retail branch in the local shopping mall or high street to collect the item (this saves a lot of the hassle that consumers have experienced in waiting around for the delivery of goods).

> According to leading retail analysts, more of us – cash- and time-poor – will be turning to the internet. And major retailers are already adapting . . . the internet is now dictating strategies . . . The Interactive Media in Retail Group (IMRG) estimate a £68.2bn online spend in the UK in 2011 – a 16 per cent growth on 2010. 'Compared to offline, it is a massive thing', said the IMRG spokesman Andy Mulcahy. 'Click and collect, where customers can reserve items online and pick up in store, represented 10.4 per cent of all orders placed in the third quarter, up from 7.4 per cent the previous quarter. Mobile shopping is also increasing rapidly. Around 15 per cent of Google search queries now go through mobile devices – including iPads and internet-enabled Kindles', said Mulcahy.[75]

Many online shopping sites offer time-saving convenience. This French ad for a shopping/home delivery website says, 'stop the muscle training on Saturdays . . . yes, this is total laziness. But so what?'
Jean & Montmarin, Paris.

MARKETING OPPORTUNITY

Multi-channel retail strategy

'John Lewis is ramping up its online expansion programme by more than doubling its number of Click and Collect collection points around the country through the addition of a further 60 branches of its sister chain Waitrose.

This will bring the total of collection points around the UK to 119 by the end of October.

The initiative forms part of plans to increase the strength of the retailer's "multi-channel" operation – the overlap between its physical store presence and its online operation – and the fastest growing and potentially most profitable area of its business.

The first tranche of new Waitrose branches to offer the John Lewis Click and Collect service include Harrogate, Lincoln and Towcester.

Click and Collect accounts for 20 per cent of johnlewis.com orders and is the fastest growing purchasing method – growing at more than twice the rate of online sales.

Provided that orders are placed before 7pm, goods will be ready for customers to collect from 2pm the following day at the designated point.

Photograph by Darren Staples / Reuters.

Andy Street, managing director of John Lewis, said: "The collaboration with Waitrose has been hugely important in offering our customers the option to Click and Collect for their purchases. Looking to the future it will be a key element in developing our multi-channel strategy even further by extending collection points to many more parts of the country." [76]

So, what makes e-commerce sites successful?[77] According to a survey by NPD Online, 75 per cent of online shoppers surveyed said that good customer service would make them shop at the site again.[78] Fashion has proved to be an increasingly popular purchase with online consumers. New fashion sites, such as Net-a-Porter and Gilt Groupe, directly connect buyers and sellers so that designers can be more nimble and react quickly to changing consumer tastes. Others like Threadless, ModCloth, Lookk and Fabricly go a step farther: they crowd-source fashion to determine what styles they will actually produce based on what customers tell them they will buy. Indeed, the high-fashion site ModaOperandi bills itself as a **pretailer**; it provides exclusive styles by prodding manufacturers to produce catwalk pieces they wouldn't otherwise make because store buyers weren't sure anyone would pay the money for them.[79]

More generally, online shoppers value the following aspects of a website:

- The ability to click on an item to create a pop-up window with more details about the product, including price, size, colours, and inventory availability.
- The ability to click on an item and add it to your cart without leaving the page you're on.
- The ability to 'feel' merchandise through better imagery, more product descriptions and details.
- The ability to enter all data related to your purchase on one page, rather than going through several checkout pages.
- The ability to mix and match product images on one page to determine whether they look good together.[80]

Retailers and service providers are starting to integrate a range of technologies in their multi-channel strategies, combining offline and online facilities to provide extra value for customers and thus attracting and keeping customers. A variety of online banking services are becoming very popular.[81] And estate agents can provide much more information, floor plans and more appealing photographs of homes for sale as well as virtual guided tours, for example, than has been possible through the traditional print media. In a similar way companies such as Expedia have offered potential customers virtual tours of holiday destinations including pictures of hotel rooms and beaches.[82]

Figure 3.6 depicts the major domains in the development of consumer possibilities in cyberspace. Consumer experiences in cyberspace can be analysed according to two dimensions: *telepresence* and *bricolage*.[83] Telepresence expresses the degree to which the consumer feels immersed in the virtual environment, the time spent there and the positive feelings generated, whereas bricolage (a French word meaning 'getting by with whatever is at hand') is an indication of the interactive medium's possibilities for the consumer to be in control of the information gathered and used, presumably leading to a higher degree of involvement in and retention of the information.

However, all is not perfect in the virtual world. E-commerce does have its limitations. Security is one important concern. We hear horror stories of consumers whose credit cards and other identity information have been stolen. While an individual's financial liability in most theft cases is limited to approximately €60 or £55, the damage to one's credit rating can last for years.

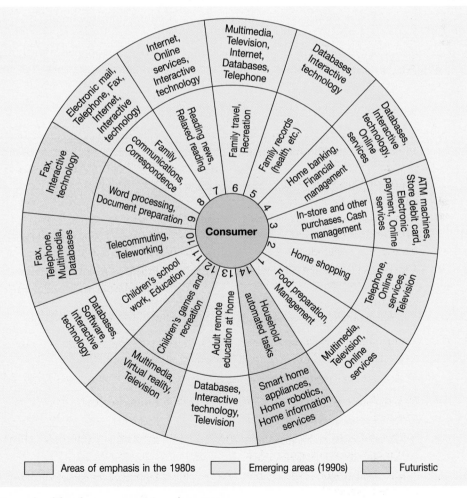

Figure 3.6 Everyday life of a consumer in cyberspace

Source: Alladi Venkatesh, 'Cybermarketscapes and consumer freedoms and identities', *European Journal of Marketing* 32(7/8) (1998): 664–76. Used with permission.

Other limitations of e-commerce relate to the actual shopping experience. While it may be satisfactory to buy a computer or a book on the internet, buying clothing and other items in which touching the item or trying it on is essential may be less attractive. Lack of tactile input (feeling material; smelling a bouquet) is one of the major factors which deters consumers from using the internet for buying goods. One study established that consumers with a higher need for tactile inputs tended not to use the internet so much for product purchase; and men tend to exhibit less need for tactile input than women when evaluating products.[84] Even though most companies have very liberal returns policies, consumers can still get stuck with large delivery and return postal charges for items where the material does not hang properly, or they don't fit, or they simply aren't the right colour. However, a potentially interesting counter-example to this is the purchase of wedding dresses online, where customers have the opportunity to co-design their dresses. This was a particularly attractive opportunity for customers who were already comfortable with technology and already owned personal technological devices; have already bought formal clothes online; and regularly spend time online.[85] Some of the pros and cons of e-commerce are summarized in Table 3.2. It is clear that traditional shopping isn't quite dead yet but bricks-and-mortar retailers are having to work harder to win and keep shoppers, and multi-channel strategies are one of their most successful recent innovations.

Many of the winners in the future retail scene will be those who can create a high degree of synergy between their online and offline outlets.[86] There is already evidence of the rewards for retailers who successfully link offline with online because the fastest-growing trend in consumer behaviour is combining patronage of offline company outlets (shops and/or mail order catalogues or car dealerships) with online company websites.[87]

Bricks-and-mortar retailers will need to work hard to give shoppers something they can not get (yet anyway) in the virtual world – a stimulating or pleasant environment in which to

Table 3.2 Pros and cons of e-commerce

Benefits of e-commerce	Limitations of e-commerce
For the consumer	**For the consumer**
Shop 24 hours a day	Lack of security
Less travelling	Fraud
Can receive relevant information in seconds from any location	Can't touch items
More choice of products	Exact colours may not reproduce on computer monitors
More products available to less-developed countries	Expensive to order and then return
Greater price information	Potential breakdown of human relationships
Lower prices so that less affluent can purchase	
Participate in virtual auctions	
Fast delivery	
Electronic communities	
For the marketer	**For the marketer**
The world is the marketplace	Lack of security
Decreases costs of doing business	Must maintain site to reap benefits
Very specialized businesses can be successful	Fierce price competition
Real-time pricing	Conflicts with conventional retailers
	Legal issues not resolved

Source: Adapted from Michael R. Solomon and Elnora W. Stuart, *Welcome to Marketing.Com: The Brave New World of E-Commerce* (Englewood Cliffs, NJ: Prentice Hall, 2001).

browse with sensory appeals not available online.[88] They will need to build emotional bonds with their customers through imaginative and entertaining retail design and merchandising strategies.[89] Now let's consider how they are doing that.

SERVICESCAPES: RETAILING AS THEATRE

Shopping can no longer be regarded as a simple act of purchasing.[90] A retail culture has arisen,[91] where the act of shopping has taken on new entertainment and/or experiential dimensions as retailers compete for customers' attention, not to mention their loyalty. The act of shopping ties into a number of central existential aspects of human life such as sexuality.[92] Furthermore, the customer may be regarded not as a passive recipient of the offerings of the purchase environment but rather as an active co-creator of this very environment and the meanings attached to it,[93] in a situation analogous to the focus among 'marketing mavens' (see Chapter 10) on flexibility in the area of product supply and tailormade marketing mixes for the individual consumer.[94] One of the most obvious trends in the retailing sector in Europe is the construction of shopping centres, often modelled on American prototypes. Once introduced into an area, shopping centres often bring with them a whole new combination of leisure activities, shopping and social encounters in safe environments.[95]

Shopping centres have tried to gain the loyalty of shoppers by appealing to their social motives as well as providing access to desired goods. It is now typical to find such features as children's rides and climbing walls in a suburban shopping centre. As one retailing executive put it, 'Malls are becoming the new mini-amusement parks.'[96] The importance of creating a positive, vibrant and interesting image has led innovative marketers to blur the line between shopping and the theatre. Shopping centres and individual stores have to create environments that stimulate people and allow them to shop and be entertained at the same time.[97]

Hard Rock Café: one of the oldest and most well-established themed consumer environments.
James Marshall/Corbis.

The Hard Rock Café, established in London over 25 years ago, now has over 45 restaurants around the world, and has become a sort of pilgrimage place in itself. The classic European counterpart to the American mall is the department store.[98] The first department stores can be seen as marking the introduction of a modern consumer culture, nourished by dreams of abundance.[99] The following are a few examples of 'performers' in the retailing theatre:

- The Powerscourt Townhouse Centre in Dublin succeeded in merging a variety of styles and features, including a grand piano on a stage in the central hall, to make a sort of new version of a Victorian marketplace atmosphere. Unlike the mall of America, it does not appear as a carefully planned environment but rather a happy blend of many consumption opportunities including an Italian restaurant, a modern hairstylist, an antique shop, etc. in a stylish classical setting.[100]

The quest to entertain means that many stores are going all-out to create imaginative environments that transport shoppers to fantasy worlds or provide other kinds of stimulation. This strategy is called **retail theming**. Innovative merchants today use four basic kinds of theming techniques:

- *Landscape themes* rely upon associations with images of nature, earth, animals and the physical body. Bass Pro Shops, for example, create a simulated outdoor environment including pools stocked with fish.
- *Marketscape themes* build upon associations with man-made places. An example is the Venetian Hotel in Las Vegas that lavishly recreates parts of the Italian city.
- *Cyberspace themes* are built around images of information and communications technology. eBay's retail interface instils a sense of community among its vendors and traders.
- *Mindscape themes* draw upon abstract ideas and concepts, introspection and fantasy, and often possess spiritual overtones. At the Seibu store in Tokyo, shoppers enter as neophytes at the first level. As they progress through the physical levels of the store each is themed to connote increasing levels of consciousness until they emerge at the summit as completed shoppers.[101]

Cutting-edge retailers are figuring out that they need to convert a store into a **being space** that resembles a commercial living room where we can go to relax, be entertained, hang out with friends, escape the everyday, or even learn. When you think of being spaces, Starbucks will probably come to your mind. The coffee chain's stated goal is to become our 'third place', where we spend the bulk of our time in addition to home and work. Starbucks led the way

A vintage pop-up market in Brick Lane, East London.

Photograph by Oli Scarff/ Getty Images.

when it fitted out its stores with comfy chairs and WiFi. But there are many other marketers who are meeting our needs for exciting commercial spaces – no matter what those needs are.

Pop-up stores are appearing in many forms around the world. Typically these are makeshift installations that do business only for a few days or weeks, and then disappear before they get old.

MARKETING OPPORTUNITY

Pop-up stores

Kira Cochrane writes:

'Temporary shops and restaurants were once a way for artists to subvert empty urban spaces. Now, they're just as likely to be part of a corporate marketing strategy . . . There have been pop-up shops, restaurants and gardens; pop-up galleries – one in an abandoned Woolworths in Leytonstone – and cinemas – Tilda Swinton even carted one around the Scottish Highlands. There have been pop-up gigs in launderettes; restaurants in front rooms; films projected in disused petrol stations or on to hay bales in fields.

Those are the more guerrilla projects, the grassroots events, often put together on a wing, a prayer and a stiflingly small bank loan. But alongside these are the corporate-backed pop-ups, the temporary shops and bars and restaurants that appear with increasing regularity, often hosted by well-known venues . . . A branch of Central Perk, the coffee shop from the TV series Friends, which opened in London's Soho for a fortnight last year (2009), was used to promote a limited-edition box set of the series . . . Gap has used a school bus, kitted out with merchandise instead of seats, as a travelling pop-up shop in the US . . . what unites these disparate projects is essentially a strong fascination with the temporary, with the here-today-and-gone-tomorrow, the idea of excitement, urgency and a dynamic interaction with urban (and it is usually urban) spaces. These are projects that stand in opposition to clone towns, to the idea of uniformity and unending drabness.

The debut of pop-up businesses is often traced back to 2004, when Rei Kawakubo of the cutting-edge fashion brand, Comme des Garçons, set up a temporary shop in a disused building in Berlin . . . While these businesses have counter-cultural roots, there's no doubt they've become a corporate concern. As Ali Madanipour, professor of urban design at Newcastle University says, there are two key readings of pop-ups, which aren't mutually exclusive. One is that they can be "a positive way of making more intensive use of urban space," he says, "bringing life to parts of the city that are under-used – they can provide space for local activity, civil society events, impromptu gatherings. But on the other hand, they can also be an aid to consumerism, in which brands create a stage setting, adding colour and texture to the general mall atmosphere that is the backdrop to many of our urban spaces. Pop-up businesses support shopping – they bring a festival atmosphere to shopping." . . . One of the attractions of pop-ups for businesses is that they can act as an informal, unacknowledged market research project. Last week [October 2010] the smoothie maker Innocent ran a pop-up event in London called the Five for Five café – offering a two-course meal designed to deliver five portions of fruit and veg for £5. Dan Germain, head of creative at Innocent, said that the event, held in a disused tramshed, was "a no-brainer. Put on a bit of a party for the people who buy the drinks, meet and hang out with them, and find out stuff you wouldn't discover in some weird research group . . . You get all these charts and graphs that say your customer is a certain age, that they live in a certain place, do a certain thing, and then you see the real people. We could just loiter in Sainsbury's by the fridges and watch the people who come and buy our drinks, but we'd probably get kicked out." . . . Any pop-up event this well thought out, prompting this much goodwill, is clearly an excellent piece of marketing. Germain says a pop-up event is better value for money than running an advertising campaign. Stephen Zatland, a partner at management consultancy Accenture, says that pop-up businesses give retailers other benefits which might not be immediately obvious to the consumer. It's a chance, he says, "to try out a new store location, to see if the kind of people they want to attract will start flocking there before they invest in a permanent site. Manufacturers can try out new products, new services, deliver them direct to the customer, promote a new brand, or try and re-invigorate an older brand" . . . The pop-up trend has been so big, for so long, that there have been whispers that it must be about to fizzle and die. But Zatland suggests this is unlikely. "There's another interesting trend for a more permanent kind of feature," he says, "where there's a site for maybe eight different pop-up stores, and the content of that site will rotate, change, every eight weeks, or every three weeks. That will be good, I think, because it encourages customers to keep coming back to see what the new feature is".'[102]

Spectacular consumption environments represent another example of servicescapes, where the emphasis is on *play*, and the co-creation of the experience by the producer and the consumer. Recent research within a themed retail environment, the ESPN Zone Chicago, examined the agency of the consumer in this type of environment and how the use of technology affected consumers' sense of reality. Consumers seemed to exercise creative control over the spectacular environment by using technology and their bodies to produce parts of the spectacle, and to create and alter space, suggesting a dialectical relationship between producers and consumers.[103] However an alternative view of retail spaces from recent research suggests that consumers also have bonds with what the researchers term 'ordinary places, i.e. small, informally branded or unthemed stores or restaurants' and these often constitute consumers' favourite commercial spaces.[104]

PROFESSOR PAULINE MACLARAN
Royal Holloway College, University of London

Consumer behaviour as I see it . . .

How do people make sense of the spaces and places around them, what is the difference between space and place, and how do spaces become places? To me these are fascinating questions that have been relatively overlooked in consumer research. Places, such as retail centres, restaurants, pubs and other consumption scapes, are much more than spatial co-ordinates or dots on a map. As places become intimately associated with life's events (whether routine or unique), they come to represent symbols of the experiences concerned. Places perform many socio-cultural functions that go unacknowledged in traditional marketing management texts where the 'P' of place is just another element of the marketing mix. Places can make us feel secure; they can evoke nostalgic memories; they can excite and stimulate; they can bind us to old friends or lead us to new ones. We form bonds with places that we know and they can often perform an important social role. Consider the pensioner who goes to her local supermarket everyday just to find a friendly face with whom to exchange a smile; or the young man who sits at the bar counter telling his woes to the patient bartender. A space thus becomes a place when it becomes invested with meanings by those who use it. Our relationships with places are dynamic, however, and the meaning that places hold for us changes and evolves as we move through the life-course.

My research often looks at how consumption intersects with spaces and places. For example, one of my studies, about a refurbishment of a festival marketplace, showed the deep emotional attachments that many people held for the centre, and how it was also tied in with their sense of self. They believed it held a special ambience that differentiated it strongly from normal high street shopping. As the refurbishment took place, and the centre moved towards mainstream retailing, consumers complained that it could now be anywhere and that it had lost its special ambience. Many consumers were very angry at the changes, believing that a unique place had been sacrificed to the encroaching forces of globalization and, indeed, that a part of their heritage had been taken away. They blamed the management of the centre and dissatisfaction with the new minimalist look only served to increase their nostalgia for the old centre which had once symbolized for them the antithesis of high street shopping.

This example also illustrates how marketers and consumers are involved in joint cultural production of spaces and how marketers need to be aware of the important social role they play in the organization of such spaces. Their relationships with consumers are enhanced by judicious use of marketing activities within the spaces concerned. When marketers overlook this social role their marketing activities may actually subvert, rather than support, consumers' interest in a particular space. In particular, it highlights the importance for management of understanding the meaning systems that consumers create around consumption scapes and how these may be very powerful and enduring.

Pauline Maclaran

Store image

With so many stores competing for customers, how do consumers select one rather than another? Like products, we can think of stores as having 'personalities'. Some stores have very clearly defined images (either good or bad). Others tend to blend into the crowd. They may not have anything distinctive about them and may be overlooked for this reason. This personality, or **store image**, is composed of many different factors. The design and general image of the store is central to the perception of the goods displayed there, whether we are talking about fashion,[105] food products[106] or any other type of good. Store features, coupled with such consumer characteristics as shopping orientation, help to predict which shopping outlets people will prefer.[107] Some of the important dimensions of a store's profile are location, merchandise suitability and the knowledge and congeniality of the sales staff.[108]

These features typically work together to create an overall impression. When shoppers think about stores, they may not say, 'Well, that place is fairly good in terms of convenience, the salespeople are acceptable, and services are good.' They are more likely to say, 'That place gives me the creeps', or 'I always enjoy shopping there.' Consumers evaluate stores in terms of both their specific attributes *and* a global evaluation, or the **store gestalt** (see Chapter 4).[109] This overall feeling may have more to do with such intangibles as interior design and the types of people one finds in the store than with aspects such as returns policies or credit availability. As a result, some stores are likely to be consistently in consumers' evoked sets (see Chapter 9), whereas others will never be considered.[110]

Atmospherics

Because a store's image is now recognized as a very important aspect of the retailing mix, store designers pay a lot of attention to **atmospherics**, or the 'conscious designing of space and its various dimensions to evoke certain effects in buyers'.[111] These dimensions include colours, scents and sounds. For any store or any shopping centre, one may think of this process as a careful *orchestration* of the various elements, each playing its part to form a whole.[112] A store's atmosphere in turn affects what we buy. In one study researchers who asked shoppers how much pleasure they were feeling five minutes after they entered a store predicted the amount of time and money they spent there.[113] To boost the entertainment value of shopping (and to lure online shoppers back to bricks-and-mortar stores), some retailers now offer **activity stores** that let consumers participate in the production of the products or services they buy there. At a chain of stores catering to preteen girls called Club Libby Lu, for instance, girls enter a fantasyland environment where they dress as princesses and mix their own fragrances.[114]

Many elements of store design can be cleverly controlled to attract customers and produce desired effects on consumers. Light colours impart a feeling of spaciousness and serenity, and signs in bright colours create excitement. One study found that brighter in-store lighting influenced people to examine and handle more merchandise.[115]

In addition to visual stimuli, all sorts of cues can influence behaviours.[116] For example, music can affect eating habits. A study found that diners who listened to loud, fast music ate more food. In contrast, those who listened to Mozart or Brahms ate less and more slowly. The researchers concluded that diners who choose soothing music at mealtimes can increase weight loss by at least five pounds a month![117] Classical music can have a positive effect on consumers' evaluation of store atmosphere.[118]

In-store decision-making

Despite all their efforts to 'pre-sell' consumers through advertising, marketers are increasingly recognizing the significant degree to which many purchases are strongly influenced by the store environment. Women tell researchers, for example, that store displays are one of the major information sources they use to decide what clothing to buy.[119] A Danish survey indicated that nine out of ten customers did not plan the purchase of at least one-third of the goods they acquired.[120] The proportion of unplanned purchases is even higher for other product categories such as food – it is estimated that about two out of every three supermarket purchases are decided in the aisles. And people with lists are just as likely to make spontaneous purchases as those without them.[121] Research evidence indicates that consumers have **mental budgets** for grocery trips that are typically composed of both an itemized portion and *in-store slack*. This means they typically decide beforehand on an amount they plan to spend, but then they have an additional amount in mind (slack) they are willing to spend on unplanned purchases – if they come across anything they really want to have. Thus stores should encourage consumers to spend all of their mental budgets by offering samples or posting reminder placards as they approach the checkout queues to remind them of things they may have forgotten.[122]

Mobile shopping apps on smartphones provide imaginative new ways for retailers to guide shoppers through the experience, as they do everything from locate merchandise, identify the nearest restroom in a mall, or scout out sales. Some help you remember where you parked your car; others actually provide reward points when you visit certain stores. The apps also promise to provide a solution to the major hassles that drive consumers away from bricks-and-mortar stores, especially long checkout times and incompetent sales assistants. One survey reported that nearly 3 in 10 store visits ended with an average of $132 (about £85 or just over 100 euros) unspent because shoppers gave up in frustration and abandoned their shopping trolleys. The study also found that more than 40 per cent of shoppers who received guidance from a retail assistant armed with a handheld mobile computer reported an improved shopping experience. To rub salt into the wound, more than half of store employees agreed that because use of online shopping tools is escalating, their customers were more knowledgeable about their products than the salespeople are.[123]

Marketers are scrambling to engineer purchasing environments in order to increase the likelihood that they will be in contact with consumers at the exact time they make a decision. This strategy even applies to drinking behaviour: Diageo, the world's largest liquor company, discovered that 60 per cent of bar customers do not know what they will drink until seconds before they place their orders. To make it more likely that the customer's order will include Smirnoff vodka, Johnnie Walker Scotch or one of its other brands, Diageo launched its Drinks Invigoration Team to increase what it calls its 'share of throat'. The Dublin-based team experimented with bar 'environments', bottle-display techniques and how to match drinks to customers' moods. For example, the company researchers discovered that bubbles stimulate the desire for spirits, so it developed bubble machines to put in the back of bars. Diageo has even categorized bars into types and is identifying the types of drinkers – and the drinks they prefer – who frequent each. These include 'style bars', where cutting-edge patrons like to sip fancy fresh-fruit martinis, and 'buzz bars', where the clientele is receptive to a drink made of Smirnoff and energy brew Red Bull.[124]

Spontaneous shopping

When a shopper is prompted to buy something in a shop, one of two different processes may be at work: **unplanned buying** may occur when a person is unfamiliar with a store's layout or perhaps when under some time pressure; or, a person may be reminded to buy something by seeing it on a store shelf. About one-third of unplanned buying has been attributed to the recognition of new needs while within the store.[125]

Impulse buying

In contrast, **impulse buying** occurs when the person experiences a sudden urge that they cannot resist. For this reason, so-called impulse items such as sweets and chewing gum are conveniently placed near the checkout. Similarly, many supermarkets have installed wider aisles to encourage browsing, and the widest tend to contain products with the highest margin. Low mark-up items that are purchased regularly tend to be stacked high in narrower aisles, to allow shopping trolleys to speed through.[126] A more recent high-tech tool has been added to encourage impulse buying: a device called 'The Portable Shopper', a personal scanning gun which allows customers to ring up their own purchases as they shop. The gun was initially developed for Albert Heijn, the Netherlands' largest grocery chain, to move customers through the store more quickly. It is now in use in over 150 supermarkets worldwide.[127]

One particular type of occasion where a lot of impulse buying goes on is in the seasonal sales, which appeal especially to younger and price-conscious shoppers according to one British study.[128] In general, shoppers can be categorized in terms of how much advance planning they do. *Planners* tend to know what products and specific brands they will buy beforehand, *partial planners* know they need certain products, but do not decide on specific brands until they are in the store, and *impulse purchasers* do no advance planning whatsoever.[129]

Point-of-purchase stimuli

Because so much decision-making apparently occurs while the shopper is in the purchasing environment, retailers are beginning to pay more attention to the amount of information in their stores, as well as to the way it is presented. It has been estimated that impulse purchases increase by 10 per cent when appropriate displays are used. Consumers' images of a good-value-for-money purchase are in many cases not induced by careful price examinations but by powerful and striking in-store information.[130] That explains why US companies spend about $19 billion each year on **point-of-purchase (POP) stimuli**.[131] A POP can be an elaborate product display or demonstration, a coupon-dispensing machine, or someone giving out free samples of a new perfume in the cosmetics aisles. Research indicated that European consumers responded more positively to spray samplers than to vials and plugs in the promotion campaign for a fragrance. 'Both fragrance marketers and retailers confirm[ed] that spray samplers successfully entice customers to try, experience and buy an upscale product. The sprays are able to effectively communicate the feel, gesture and essence of a brand' and are now being increasingly tried out in the US as an effective way of getting consumers to try a new fragrance.[132] Winning consumers in the store with packaging and displays is regarded as 'the first moment of truth'.[133]

Much of the growth in point-of-purchase activity has been in new electronic technologies.[134] Videotronic, a German hardware producer, has specialized in compact in-store video displays. The newest feature is a touch-screen selection with various pieces of information

Smart retailers recognize that many purchase decisions are made at the time the shopper is in the store. That's one reason why grocery carts sometimes resemble billboards on wheels.

Peter Byron/Photo Researchers, Inc.

which eventually provoke scent to be produced.[135] Some shopping trolleys have a small screen that displays advertising, which is keyed to the specific areas of the store through which the trolley is wheeled.[136] New interactive possibilities seem to enhance the effectiveness of POP information systems,[137] although the effect of in-store advertising and other POP continues to be difficult to assess. In-store *displays* are another commonly used device to attract attention in the store environment. While most displays consist of simple racks that dispense the product and/or related coupons, some highlight the value of regarding retailing as theatre by supplying the 'audience' with elaborate performances and scenery.

Place-based media

Advertisers are also being more aggressive about hitting consumers with their messages, wherever they may be. *Place-based media* is a specialized medium that has grown in popularity: it targets consumers based on the locations in which the message is delivered. Tesco followed Wal-Mart and installed TV in 300 stores where 'in between news clips, recipe tips and beauty advice, the screens will show ads for products in the aisles'.[138] In 2007 dunnhumby relaunched Tesco's in-store TV screens to provide a more tailored content proposition.[139] Twentieth Century Fox has negotiated a partnership deal with shopping centres owned by US General Growth Properties for the promotion of its films using methods which range from banners, posters and window stickers to tray liners and ad placements in eating areas.[140] Even MTV is in on the act: its Music Report, shown in record stores, is a two-hour 'video capsule' featuring video spots and ads for music retailers and corporate sponsors. An MTV executive observed, 'They're already out there at the retail environment. They're ready to spend money.'[141] A Dutch CD retailer, Free Record Shop, has installed a device that permits shoppers to compile and burn their own CD in-store. Consumers can select up to 74 minutes of music and are charged a per-song amount (up to €1.23). The teens are delighted about this legal way of making personalized compilations. The company planned to spread the system to their other stores in The Netherlands, Belgium, Norway and France.[142]

The salesperson

One of the most important in-store factors is the salesperson, who attempts to influence the buying behaviour of the customer.[143] This influence can be understood in terms of **exchange theory**, which stresses that every interaction involves an exchange of value. Each participant gives something to the other and hopes to receive something in return.[144]

What 'value' does the customer look for in a sales interaction? There are a variety of resources a salesperson might offer. For example, they might offer expertise about the product to make the shopper's choice easier. Alternatively, the customer may be reassured because the salesperson is an admired or likeable person whose tastes are similar and who is seen as someone who can be trusted.[145] A long stream of research attests to the impact of a salesperson's appearance on sales effectiveness. In sales, as in much of life, attractive people appear to hold the upper hand.[146] In addition, it's not unusual for service personnel and customers to form fairly warm personal relationships; these have been termed *commercial* friendships (think of all those patient bartenders who double as therapists for many people). Researchers have found that commercial friendships are similar to other friendships in that they can involve affection, intimacy, social support, loyalty and reciprocal gift giving. They also work to support marketing objectives such as satisfaction, loyalty and positive word-of-mouth.[147]

A buyer/seller situation is like many other dyadic encounters (two-person groups); it is a relationship where some agreement must be reached about the roles of each participant, when a process of *identity negotiation* occurs.[148] For example, if the salesperson immediately establishes themselves as an expert, they are likely to have more influence over the customer through the course of the relationship. Some of the factors that help to determine a salesperson's role (and relative effectiveness) are their age, appearance, educational level and motivation to sell.[149] Another variable is similarity between the seller and the buyer. In fact, even **incidental similarity**, such as a shared birthday or growing up in the same place, can be enough to boost the odds of a sale.[150]

In addition, more effective salespeople usually know their customers' traits and preferences better than do ineffective salespeople, since this knowledge allows them to adapt their approach to meet the needs of the specific customer.[151] The ability to be adaptable is especially vital when customers and salespeople differ in terms of their *interaction styles*.[152] Consumers, for example, vary in the degree of assertiveness they bring to interactions. At one extreme, non-assertive people believe that complaining is not socially acceptable and they may be intimidated in sales situations. Assertive people are more likely to stand up for themselves in a firm but non-threatening way. Aggressives may resort to rudeness and threats if they do not get their way.[153]

POST-PURCHASE SATISFACTION

In a survey of 480 chief marketing officers (CMOs), 58 per cent reported that their companies do not reward their employees if customer satisfaction improves. More than one-third said they have no way to track word of mouth among customers, and less than three in ten said their firms are good at resolving customers' complaints.[154] What's wrong with this picture? Companies that score high in customer satisfaction often have a big competitive advantage in building longer term relationships with their customers.

Our overall feelings about a product after we've bought it – what researchers call **consumer satisfaction/dissatisfaction (CS/D)** – obviously play a big role in our future behaviour. As consumers we engage in a constant process of evaluating the things we buy as we integrate these products into our daily consumption activities.[155] In a sense, each of us is a product reviewer, whether or not we bother to talk or blog about our experiences. Our post-purchase product experiences are an important part of our satisfaction (or dissatisfaction) with a product or service, and these experiences and post-purchase evaluations play a big role in our future purchasing choices. Despite evidence that customer satisfaction is steadily declining in many industries, good marketers are constantly on the lookout for sources of dissatisfaction so that they can improve.[156] Customer satisfaction has a real impact on profitability: a study conducted among a large sample of Swedish consumers found that product quality affects customer satisfaction, which in turn results in increased profitability among firms who provide quality products.[157] Quality is more than a marketing 'buzzword'.

Perceptions of product quality

Just what do consumers look for in products? The answer's easy: they want quality and value. Especially because of foreign competition, claims of product quality have become strategically crucial to maintaining a competitive advantage.[158] Consumers use a number of cues to infer quality, including brand name, price, and even their own estimates of how much money has been put into a new product's advertising campaign.[159] These cues, as well as others such as product warranties and follow-up letters from the company, are often used by consumers to relieve perceived risk and assure themselves that they have made smart purchase decisions.[160]

The importance of expectations

Satisfaction or dissatisfaction is more than a reaction to the actual performance quality of a product or service. First of all, satisfaction is not just a matter of functional but also of the hedonic performance of the product – something which may be more difficult for the producer to ensure beforehand. When we buy a book, we don't expect that the pages will come loose or fall out.[161]

This ad for Audi relies on a claim about quality based on technical excellence in engineering and design.
The Advertising Archives.

Satisfaction, then, is highly influenced by prior expectations regarding all aspects of quality. According to the **expectancy disconfirmation model**, consumers form beliefs about product performance based on prior experience with the product and/or communications about the product that imply a certain level of quality.[162] When something performs the way we thought it would, we may not think much about it. If, on the other hand, it fails to live up to expectations, negative affect may result. Furthermore, if performance happens to exceed our expectations, we are satisfied and pleased.

To understand this perspective, think about different types of restaurants. People expect to be provided with sparkling, clean glassware at high-class restaurants, and they might become upset if they discover a grimy glass. On the other hand, we may not be surprised to find fingerprints on our mug at a local 'greasy spoon'; we may even shrug it off because it contributes to the 'charm' of the place. An important lesson emerges for marketers from this perspective: don't over-promise if you can't deliver.[163]

This perspective underscores the importance of *managing expectations* – customer dissatisfaction is usually due to expectations exceeding the company's ability to deliver. Figure 3.7 illustrates the alternative strategies a firm can choose in these situations. When confronted with unrealistic expectations about what it can do, the firm can either accommodate these demands by improving the range or quality of the products it offers, alter the expectations, or perhaps even choose to abandon the customer if it is not feasible to meet their needs.[164] Expectations are altered, for example, when waiters tell patrons in advance that the portion size they have ordered will not be very big, or when new car buyers are warned of strange smells they will experience during the running-in period. A firm can also under-promise, as when Xerox inflates the time it will take for a service rep to visit. When the rep arrives a day earlier, the customer is impressed.

One approach to customer satisfaction, known as the *Kano-model*, operates with three kinds of expectation: basis, performance and enthusiasm expectations. The first includes the implicit and taken-for-granted qualities expected from a product. If these are not satisfied, the product will never be able to live up to the customer's requirements, but even if fulfilled, they do not profile the product because these qualities are taken for granted as a minimum. For the performance expectations satisfaction is proportional to how well the product lives up to the expectations. Such quality requirements are often specified and articulated by the customer. As for enthusiasm-related product features, it is wrong to call them expectations since their essential character is that they are *not* expected by the customer. Therefore, such positive surprises can lead to a very great feeling of satisfaction, since the product quality was even better than expected.[165] Furthermore, research evidence indicates that product experience is important for customer satisfaction. When people have no experience they are relatively easy to satisfy, but with growing experience they become harder to satisfy. Then, when they reach a certain level of experience, satisfaction again becomes easier to obtain,

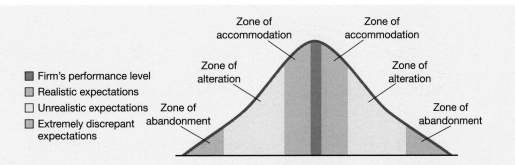

Figure 3.7 Customer expectation zones: managing quality expectations

since consumers are now 'experts' and this facilitates choice and generates more realistic expectations.[166]

Satisfaction levels are determined not only by the product purchased but also by the expectations about the quality of alternatives that were *not* purchased. In other words, the higher the expectations about unselected alternatives, the lower the level of satisfaction with the chosen good.[167] A general conclusion which one should draw from such a discussion is that consumer goals may be multiple and the product or service offer so complex to evaluate that any measurement of satisfaction must be used with caution.[168] A recent Italian study argued that consumers' schematic knowledge about a product, or the hopes associated with the subsequent consumption of the product, determined consumers' satisfaction judgements depending on their motivation and level of involvement.[169]

Quality and product failures

The power of quality claims is most evident when a company's product fails. Here, consumers' expectations are dashed and dissatisfaction results. In these situations, marketers must immediately take steps to reassure customers. When the company confronts the problem truthfully, consumers are often willing to forgive and forget, as was the case with Perrier when traces of benzene were found in the bottled water. When the company appears to be dragging its heels or covering up, on the other hand, consumer resentment will grow, as occurred during Union Carbide's chemical disaster in India, the massive Alaskan oil spill caused by the tanker *Exxon Valdez* or corporate scandals such as the collapse of Enron. The EC has seen a significant rise in national notifications of unsafe non-food products since 2003 (Figure 3.8). In 2010 Germany (10 per cent), Bulgaria (10 per cent), Hungary (10 per cent), Cyprus (9 per cent) and Greece (8 per cent) were the source of 47 per cent of the national notifications to the EC (Figures 3.9, 3.10 and 3.11).[170] Of national notifications to the EC in 2010, 32 per cent related to fashion, textiles and clothing items; 25 per cent to toys; 9 per cent to motor vehicles; 8 per cent to electrical appliances; and 4 per cent childcare items and children's equipment (Figures 3.12 and 3.13). 'More than one out of three products notified in 2007 was either a toy or a childcare article/children's equipment, thus confirming that child safety is a top-ranking priority for market surveillance authorities.'[171]

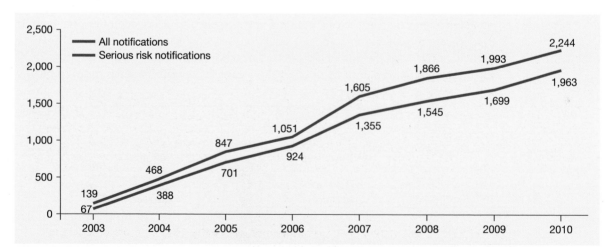

Figure 3.8 The total number of notifications to EC Health and Consumer Protectorate (2003–2010)

Source: 'Keeping European Consumers Safe', 2010 Annual Report on the operation of the Rapid Alert System for non-food consumer products, European Communities Health and Consumer Protection Directorate General, Luxembourg, 2011: 13.

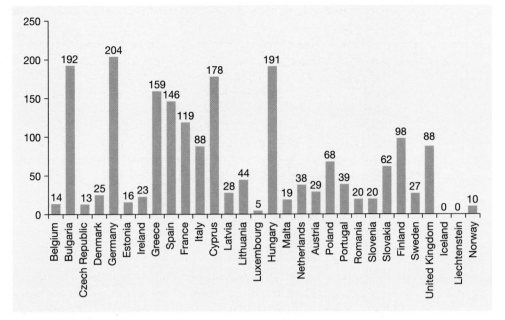

Figure 3.9 The total number of notifications by country (absolute values) of unsafe products to EC Health and Consumer Protectorate (2010)

Source: 'Keeping European Consumers Safe', 2010 Annual Report on the operation of the Rapid Alert System for non-food consumer products, European Communities Health and Consumer Protection Directorate General, Luxembourg, 2011: 15.

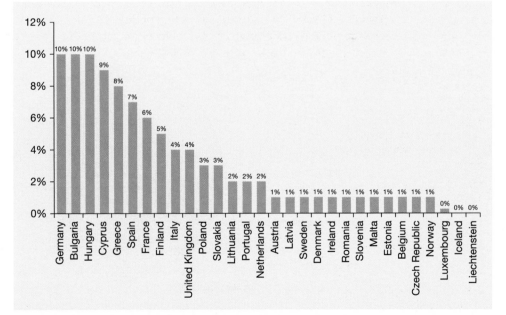

Figure 3.10 The total number of notifications by country (%) of unsafe products to EC Health and Consumer Protectorate (2010)

Source: 'Keeping European Consumers Safe', 2010 Annual Report on the operation of the Rapid Alert System for non-food consumer products, European Communities Health and Consumer Protection Directorate General, Luxembourg, 2011: 15.

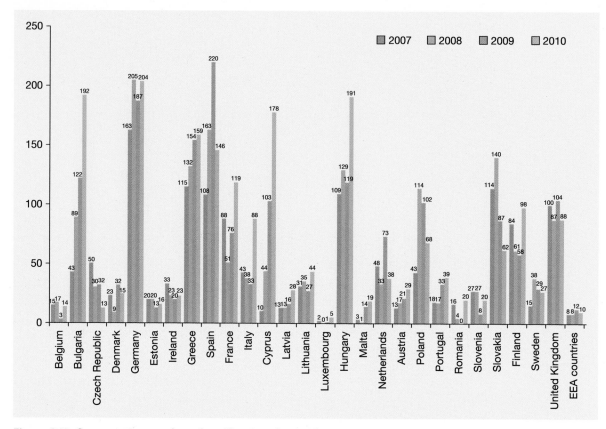

Figure 3.11 Comparative number of notifications by notifying country of unsafe products to EC Health and Consumer Protectorate (2007–2010)

Source: 'Keeping European Consumers Safe', 2010 Annual Report on the operation of the Rapid Alert System for non-food consumer products, European Communities Health and Consumer Protection Directorate General, Luxembourg, 2011: 16.

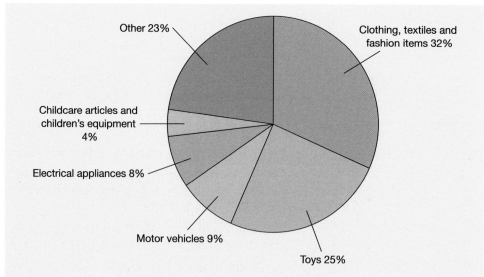

Figure 3.12 The five most frequently notified product categories of unsafe products to EC Health and Consumer Protectorate (2010)

Source: 'Keeping European Consumers Safe', 2010 Annual Report on the operation of the Rapid Alert System for non-food consumer products, European Communities Health and Consumer Protection Directorate General, Luxembourg, 2011: 19.

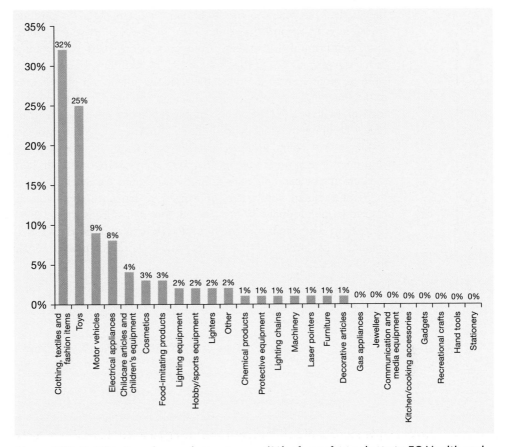

Figure 3.13 Notifications by product category (%) of unsafe products to EC Health and Consumer Protectorate (2010)

Source: 'Keeping European Consumers Safe', 2010 Annual Report on the operation of the Rapid Alert System for non-food consumer products, European Communities Health and Consumer Protection Directorate General, Luxembourg, 2011: 18.

Acting on dissatisfaction

If a person is not happy with a product or service, what can be done? Reasons for complaining include bad service, unsafe products, failure to respect consumer legislation, and lack of transparency or availability of information.[172] Essentially, a consumer can take one or more possible courses of action:[173]

1 *Voice response*: The consumer can appeal directly to the retailer for redress (e.g. a refund).

2 *Private response*: Express dissatisfaction about the store or product to friends and/or boycott the store. As will be discussed in Chapter 10, negative word-of-mouth (WOM) can be very damaging to a retailer's reputation.

3 *Third-party response*: The consumer can take legal action against the merchant, register a complaint with the Ombudsman, or perhaps write a letter to a newspaper.

A number of factors influence which route is taken. The consumer may in general be assertive or meek. Action is more likely to be taken for expensive products such as household durables, cars and clothing than for inexpensive products.[174] If the consumer does not believe that the store will respond positively to a complaint, the person will be more likely to switch brands than fight.[175] Ironically, marketers should *encourage* consumers to complain to them: people are more likely to spread the word about unresolved negative experiences to their friends than they are to boast about positive occurrences.[176] Consumers are more likely to spread negative information about a bad service than they are to spread information about a successful complaint handling. Complaint management is thus not as good an alternative as high-quality service in the first place.[177] In addition, consumers who are satisfied with a store are more likely to complain; they take the time to complain because they feel connected to the store. Older people are more likely to complain, and are much more likely to believe the store will actually resolve the problem. Shoppers who get their problems resolved feel even *better* about the store than if nothing went wrong.[178] A variety of factors affect consumers' willingness to complain including different national systems for consumer protection; consumers' perception of the likelihood of success; and consumers' different expectations of the outcome of a complaint. Within the EU, 'country-level analysis suggests that consumers living in northern Europe are more likely to launch a complaint than other Europeans. A socio-economic analysis of results indicates that citizens with higher education levels tend to be more assertive if they are not satisfied with their purchases and proceed to launch a complaint (21 per cent)'.[179] A sense of the scale of potential complainants can be grasped from Figures 3.14 and 3.15.[180]

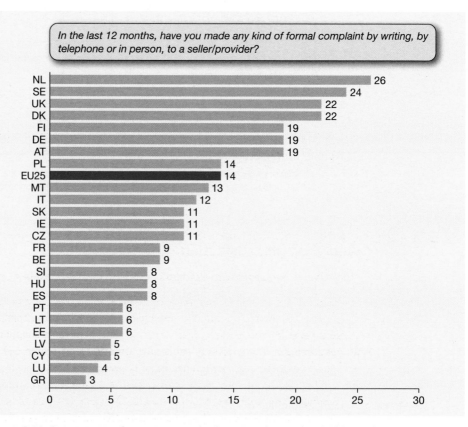

Figure 3.14 Percentage of consumers who have made any kind of formal complaint to a seller/provider – % of yes

Data source: Special Eurobarometer 252 – Consumer protection in the Internal Market, 2006.

Source: *The Consumer Markets Scoreboard Monitoring Consumer Outcomes in the Single Market*, COM (2008) 31, European Communities, Luxembourg, 2008, Figure 1: 18.

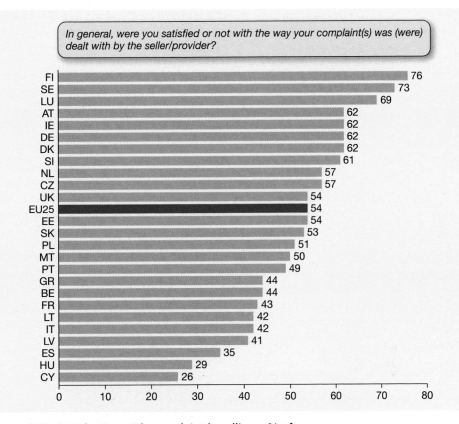

Figure 3.15 Satisfaction with complaint handling – % of yes

Data source: Special Eurobarometer 252 – Consumer protection in the Internal Market, 2006.

Source: *The Consumer Markets Scoreboard: Monitoring Consumer Outcomes in the Single Market*, COM (2008) 31, European Communities, Luxembourg, 2008, Figure 4: 20.

CHAPTER SUMMARY

Now that you have finished reading this chapter you should understand why:

→ **Factors at the time of purchase dramatically influence the consumer decision-making process.** Many factors affect a purchase. These include the consumer's antecedent state (e.g. his or her mood, time pressure, or disposition towards shopping). Time is an important resource that often determines how much effort and search will go into a decision. Our moods are influenced by the degree of pleasure and arousal a store environment creates.

The usage context of a product is a segmentation variable; consumers look for different product attributes depending on the use to which they intend to put their purchase. The presence or absence of other people (co-consumers) – and the types of people they are – can also affect a consumer's decisions.

The shopping experience is a pivotal part of the purchase decision. In many cases, retailing is like theatre: the consumer's evaluation of stores and products may depend on the type of 'performance' he witnesses. The actors (e.g. salespeople), the setting (the store environment), and the props (e.g. store displays) influence this evaluation. Like a brand personality, a number of factors, such as perceived convenience, sophistication, and expertise of salespeople, determine store image. With increasing competition from non-store alternatives, creating a positive shopping experience has never been more important.

Online shopping is growing in importance, and this new way to acquire products has both good (e.g. convenience) and bad (e.g. security) aspects.

→ **In addition to what a shopper already knows or believes about a product, information a store or website provides can strongly influence a purchase decision.** Because we don't make many purchase decisions until we're actually in the store, point-of-purchase (POP) stimuli are very important sales tools. These include product samples, elaborate package displays, place-based media, and in-store promotional materials such as 'shelf talkers'. POP stimuli are particularly useful in promoting impulse buying, which happens when a consumer yields to a sudden urge for a product. Increasingly, mobile shopping apps are also playing a key role.

→ **A salesperson can be the crucial link to a purchase.** The consumer's encounter with a salesperson is a complex and important process. The outcome can be affected by such factors as the salesperson's similarity to the customer and his or her perceived credibility.

→ **Marketers need to be concerned about a consumer's evaluations of a product after he buys it as well as before.** A person's overall feelings about the product after he buys it determine consumer satisfaction/dissatisfaction. Many factors influence our perceptions of product quality, including price, brand name and product performance. Our degree of satisfaction often depends on the extent to which a product's performance is consistent with our prior expectations of how well it will function.

KEY TERMS

Activity stores (p. 85)

Atmospherics (p. 85)

Being space (p. 82)

Co-consumers (p. 67)

Consumer satisfaction/dissatisfaction (CS/D) (p. 89)

Cyberspace (p. 76)

Exchange theory (p. 89)

Expectancy disconfirmation model (p. 91)

Impulse buying (p. 87)

Incidental similarity (p. 89)

Mental budgets (p. 86)

Mobile shopping apps (p. 86)

Open rates (p. 68)

Point-of-purchase stimuli (POP) (p. 87)

Pop-up stores (p. 83)

Pretailer (p. 78)

Queuing theory (p. 71)

Retail theming (p. 82)

Shopping orientation (p. 74)

Store gestalt (p. 85)

Store image (p. 85)

Time poverty (p. 69)

Time style (p. 68)

Unplanned buying (p. 87)

CONSUMER BEHAVIOUR CHALLENGE

1 Discuss some of the motivations for shopping described in the chapter. How might a retailer adjust their strategy to accommodate these motivations? What is the difference between unplanned buying and impulse buying?

2 Do you think shopping motives might be different between online and offline shopping?

If so, why? What are the pros and cons of e-commerce?

3 What factors help determine store image? What are the two dimensions that determine whether we will react positively or negatively to a purchase environment?

4 Describe the difference between density and crowding. Why is this difference relevant in purchase environments?

5 The store environment is heating up as more and more companies put their promotional resources into point-of-purchase efforts. Shoppers are now confronted by videos at the checkout, computer monitors attached to their shopping trolleys, and so on. Place-based media expose us to ads in non-shopping environments. Do you feel that these innovations are unacceptably intrusive? At what point might shoppers rebel and demand some peace while shopping? Do you see any market potential in the future for stores that 'counter-market' by promising a 'hands-off' shopping environment?

6 Find a spectacular consumption environment and examine how consumers' play is encouraged and constrained by producers. How is technology used by producers and consumers in this environment to create and alter the sense of reality and space in this spectacular environment? If you don't have a spectacular consumption environment near you, consider these questions (and the associated research findings) about the co-creation of meaning between producers and consumers within the context of the online world, e.g. computer games.

7 Is e-commerce going to replace the high street retailer?

8 Discuss the changing trends across online and high street shopping (e.g. click and collect), and identify the factors within consumer behaviour which have influenced the development of these trends (e.g. time scarcity). What new trends can you identify as online and offline consumer behaviour becomes increasingly integrated? Or will online and offline purchasing remain separate activities for different types of shoppers?

9 Are pop-up stores simply a fad, or a retailing concept that is here to stay?

10 Discuss the concept of 'time style'. Based on your own experiences, how might consumers be segmented in terms of their time styles?

11 What is time poverty, and how might it influence our purchase decisions?

12 Recent research (among American married and single women without children) has shown that there are major differences in individuals' attitudes and behaviours in relation to shopping across five metaphors of time: pressure cooker, map, mirror, river and feast. Consider how these temporal metaphors might vary across households (e.g. married with children); age (e.g. empty nest households); and culture.

13 Conduct naturalistic observation at a local mall or shopping centre. Sit in a central location and observe the activities of mall staff and customers. Keep a log of the non-retailing activity you observe (special performances, exhibits, socializing, etc.). Does this activity enhance or detract from business conducted at the mall or shopping centre? As malls become more like high-tech game rooms, how valid is the criticism that shopping areas are only encouraging more loitering by teenage boys, who do not spend a lot in stores and simply scare away other customers?

14 Select three competing clothing stores in your area and conduct a store image study for each one. Ask a group of consumers to rate each store on a set of attributes and plot these ratings on the same graph. Based on your findings, are there any areas of competitive advantage or disadvantage you could bring to the attention of store management? (This technique is described in Chapter 8.)

15 How do a consumer's prior expectations about product quality influence their satisfaction with the product after they buy it? List three actions a consumer can take if they are dissatisfied with a purchase.

16 Discuss and critique the view that 'shoppers who blend store, mail order catalogues and websites spend more.'[181]

17 New interactive tools are being introduced that allow surfers on sites such as landsend.com to view apparel product selections on virtual models in full, 360-degree rotational view. In some cases, the viewer can modify the bodies, face, skin colouring and hairstyles of these models. In others, the consumer can project their *own* likeness into the space by scanning a photo into a 'makeover' programme.[182] Visit landsend.com or another site that offers a personalized model. Surf around. Try on some clothes. How was your experience? How helpful was this model? When you shop for clothes online, would you rather see how they look on a body with dimensions the same as yours, or on a different body? What advice can you give website designers who are trying to personalize these shopping environments by creating lifelike models to guide you through the site?

18 Choy and Loker (2004)[183] explored and classified internet sites supporting the wedding industry and the purchase of a wedding gown in their study of mass customization. They identified four major categories: marketing, browsing, advice and customizing. Choose another industry (e.g. mother and baby; travel; leisure; pets; music) and classify the websites according to their characteristics and strategies. What categories can you identify?

19 The mall of the future will most likely be less about purchasing products than about exploring them in a physical setting. This means that retail environments will have to become places to build brand images, rather than just places to sell products. What are some strategies stores can use to enhance the emotional/sensory experiences they give to shoppers?

20 Identify three people who own the same technological product (e.g. electric coffeemaker; satnav; iPhone; iPad; Kindle). Then, observe them as they actually use the appliance. Based on these experiences, what recommendations might you make to the designer of a new appliance that would improve customers' experience with the product?

For additional material see the companion website at www.pearsoned.co.uk/solomon

NOTES

1. Brian T. Ratchford, Debabrata Talukdar and Myung-Soo Lee, 'The impact of the internet on consumers' use of information sources for automobiles: A re-inquiry', *Journal of Consumer Research* 34 (June 2007): 111–119.

2. Laurette Dube and Bernd H. Schmitt, 'The Processing of Emotional and Cognitive Aspects of Product Usage in Satisfaction Judgments', in Rebecca H. Holman and Michael R. Solomon (eds), *Advances in Consumer Research* 18 (Provo, UT: Association for Consumer Research, 1991): 52–6; Lalita A. Manrai and Meryl P. Gardner, 'The Influence of Affect on Attributions for Product Failure', in *ibid.*: 249–54.

3. Peter J. Burke and Stephen L. Franzoi, 'Studying situations and identities using experimental sampling methodology', *American Sociological Review* 53 (August 1988): 559–68.

4. Kevin G. Celuch and Linda S. Showers, 'It's Time To Stress *Stress*: the Stress-Purchase/Consumption Relationship', in Holman and Solomon (eds), *Advances in Consumer Research* 18: 284–9; Lawrence R. Lepisto, J. Kathleen Stuenkel and Linda K. Anglin, 'Stress: An Ignored Situational Influence', in *ibid.*: 296–302.

5. See Eben Shapiro, 'Need a little fantasy? A bevy of new companies can help', *New York Times* (10 March 1991): F4.

6. John D. Mayer and Yvonne N. Gaschke, 'The experience and meta-experience of mood', *Journal of Personality and Social Psychology* 55 (July 1988): 102–11. See also: Michael J. Barone, Paul Miniard and Jean B. Romeo, 'The influence of positive mood on brand extension evaluations', *Journal of Consumer Research* 26 (March 2000): 386–400; Eduardo B. Andrade, 'Behavioral Consequences of Affect: Combining Evaluative and Regulatory Mechanisms', *Journal of Consumer Research* 32 (December 2005): 355–362; Georgios A. Bakamitsos, 'A cue alone or a probe to think? The dual role of affect in product evaluations', *Journal of Consumer Research* 33 (December 2006): 403–412; Harper A. Roehm Jr and Michelle L. Roehm, 'Revisiting the effect of positive mood on variety seeking', *Journal of Consumer Research* 32 (September 2005): 330–336; Cheng Qiu and Catherine W.M. Yeung, 'Mood and comparative judgment: does mood influence everything and finally nothing?', *Journal of Consumer Research* 34 (February 2008): 657–669; Alexander Fedorikhin and Vanessa M. Patrick, 'Positive mood and resistance to temptation: the interfering influence of elevated arousal', *Journal of Consumer Research* 37 (December 2010): 698–711; Cassie Mogilner, Jennifer Aaker and Sepandar D. Kamvar, 'How happiness affects choice', *Journal of Consumer Research* 39 (August 2012) *published electronically*; Fabrizio Di Muro and Kyle B. Murray, 'An arousal regulation explanation of mood effects on consumer choice', *Journal of Consumer Research* 39 (October 2012) *published electronically*.

7. Meryl Paula Gardner, 'Mood states and consumer behavior: A critical review', *Journal of Consumer Research* 12 (December 1985): 281–300; Scott Dawson, Peter H. Bloch and Nancy M. Ridgway, 'Shopping motives, emotional states, and retail outcomes', *Journal of Retailing* 66 (Winter 1990): 408–27; Patricia A. Knowles, Stephen J. Grove and W. Jeffrey Burroughs, 'An experimental examination of mood states on retrieval and evaluation of advertisement and brand information', *Journal of the Academy of Marketing Science* 21 (April 1993): 135–43; Paul W. Miniard, Sunil Bhatla and Deepak Sirdeskmuhk, 'Mood as a determinant of postconsumption product evaluations: Mood effects and their dependency on the affective intensity of the consumption experience', *Journal of Consumer Psychology* 1 (1992) 2: 173–95; Mary T. Curren and Katrin R. Harich, 'Consumers' mood states: The mitigating influence of personal relevance on product evaluations', *Psychology and Marketing* 11(2) (March/April 1994): 91–107; Gerald J. Gorn, Marvin E. Goldberg and Kunal Basu, 'Mood, awareness,

and product evaluation', *Journal of Consumer Psychology* 2(3) (1993): 237–56.

8. Gordon C. Bruner, 'Music, mood, and marketing', *Journal of Marketing* 54 (October 1990): 94–104; Basil G. Englis, 'Music Television and its Influences on Consumers, Consumer Culture, and the Transmission of Consumption Messages', in Holman and Solomon (eds), *Advances in Consumer Research* 18: 111–14; see also Steve Oakes, 'Examining the Relationships Between Background Musical Tempo and Perceived Duration Using Different Versions of a Radio Ad', in B. Dubois, T. Lowrey, L.J. Shrum and M. Vanhuele (eds), *European Advances in Consumer Research* 4 (Provo, UT: Association of Consumer Research, 1999): 40–4.

9. Marvin E. Goldberg and Gerald J. Gorn, 'Happy and sad TV programs: How they affect reactions to commercials', *Journal of Consumer Research* 14 (December 1987): 387–403; Gorn, Goldberg and Basu, 'Mood, awareness, and product evaluation': *op. cit.*, 237–56; Curren and Harich, 'Consumers' mood states', *op. cit.*

10. Rajeev Batra and Douglas M. Stayman, 'The Role of Mood in Advertising Effectiveness', *Journal of Consumer Research* 17 (September 1990): 203; John P. Murry, Jr, and Peter A. Dacin, 'Cognitive Moderators of Negative-Emotion Effects: Implications for Understanding Media Context', *Journal of Consumer Research* 22 (March 1996): 439–47; see also Curren and Harich, 'Consumers' Mood States' *op. cit.*; Gorn, Goldberg, and Basu, 'Mood, Awareness, and Product Evaluation' *op. cit.*

11. Jeffrey Zaslow, 'Happiness Inc', *Wall Street Journal* (March 18, 2006): P1.

12. Pradeep Kakkar and Richard J. Lutz, 'Situational Influence on Consumer Behavior: A Review', in Harold H. Kassarjian and Thomas S. Robertson (eds), *Perspectives in Consumer Behavior*, 3rd edn (Glenview, IL: Scott, Foresman, 1981): 204–14.

13. Carolyn Turner Schenk and Rebecca H. Holman, 'A Sociological Approach to Brand Choice: The Concept of Situational Self-Image', in Jerry C. Olson (ed.), *Advances in Consumer Research* 7 (Ann Arbor, MI: Association for Consumer Research, 1980): 610–14.

14. Russell W. Belk, 'An exploratory assessment of situational effects in buyer behavior', *Journal of Marketing Research* 11 (May 1974): 156–63; U.N. Umesh and Joseph A. Cote, 'Influence of situational variables on brand-choice models', *Journal of Business Research* 16(2) (1988): 91–9; see also J. Wesley Hutchinson and Joseph W. Alba, 'Ignoring irrelevant information: Situational determinants of consumer learning', *Journal of Consumer Research* 18 (December 1991): 325–45.

15. Peter R. Dickson, 'Person–situation: segmentation's missing link', *Journal of Marketing* 46 (Fall 1982): 56–64.

16. Booz-Allen Hamilton's Digital Consumer Project and Nielsen/NetRatings reported in Laura Mazur, 'Web marketers must now adapt to the occasion', *Marketing* (29 May 2003): 16 (http://search.epnet.com/login.aspx?direct=true&db=buh&an=10029509).

17. Laura Mazur, 'Web marketers must now adapt to the occasion', *op. cit.*

18. Christopher Heine, 'Will Facebook Ads Soon Reflect "What's On Your Mind?",' *ClickZ* (23 March 2011), http://www.clickz.com/clickz/news/2036901/facebook-ads-soon-reflect-whats-mind, accessed 17 April 2011.

19. Anja Stöhr, 'Air-Design: Exploring the Role of Scents in Retail Environments', in B. Englis and A. Olofsson (eds), *European Advances in Consumer Research* 3 (Provo, UT: Association for Consumer Research, 1998): 126–32.

20. Delphine Dion, 'A Theoretical and Empirical Study of Retail Crowding', in Dubois, Lowrey, Shrum and Vanhuele (eds), *European Advances in Consumer Research* 4: 51–7.

21. Daniel Stokols, 'On the distinction between density and crowding: Some implications for future research', *Psychological Review* 79 (1972): 275–7.

22. Fascinators are worn on the head, but are smaller than hats and are seen as a way to wear some decoration on the head but without squashing the hair (as can happen with a hat). Fascinators are usually themed around feathers and netting, see http://www.prettycool.co.uk/fascinators--hats-79-c.asp (accessed 6 April 2012) for some illustrations.

23. http://www.guardian.co.uk/sport/2012/jan/18/royal-ascot-fascinators-hats-dresscode?INTCMP=SRCH; http://www.guardian.co.uk/lifeandstyle/gallery/2012/jan/18/royal-ascot-dress-rules?INTCMP=SRCH (accessed 23 January 2012), article and picture illustrations of updated dress code for Royal Ascot for summer 2012 (e.g. no fascinators to be worn as hats).

24. http://www.guardian.co.uk/sport/2012/jan/22/ascot-tieless-refund-orange-stickers?INTCMP=SRCH (accessed 23 January 2012).

25. Ritesh Saini and Ashwani Monga, 'How I decide depends on what I spend: Use of heuristics is greater for time than for money', *Journal of Consumer Research* 34 (April 2008): 921.

26. Tanya Irwin, 'ReachMail: Email Marketers Should Focus on Mid-Day', *Marketing Daily* (March 17, 2011), http://www.mediapost.com/publications/?fa=Articles.showArticle&art_aid=146883&nid=124807, accessed 18 April 2011.

27. Carol Felker Kaufman, Paul M. Lane and Jay D. Lindquist, 'Exploring more than 24 hours a day: A preliminary investigation of polychronic time use', *Journal of Consumer Research* 18 (December 1991): 392–401.

28. Laurence P. Feldman and Jacob Hornik, 'The use of time: An integrated conceptual model', *Journal of Consumer Research* 7 (March 1981): 407–19; see also Michelle M. Bergadaa, 'The role of time in the action of the consumer', *Journal of Consumer Research* 17 (December 1990): 289–302.

29. Jean-Claude Usunier and Pierre Valette-Florence, 'Individual time orientation: A psychometric scale', *Time and Society* 3(2) (1994): 219–41.

30. June Cotte, S. Ratneshwar and David Glen Mick, 'The times of their lives: Phenomenological and metaphorical characteristics of consumer timestyles', *Journal of Consumer Research* 31 (September 2004): 333–45.

31. June Cotte, S. Ratneshwar and David Glen Mick, *ibid*.

32. 'The life of women and men in Europe: A statistical portrait – 2008 edition': 47–49, European Commission/Eurostat Luxembourg: Cat. No. KS-80-07-135-EN-N, http://ec.europa.eu/eurostat

33. The life of women and men in Europe: A statistical portrait – 2008 edition: 111–113, European Commission/Eurostat Luxembourg: Cat. No. KS-80-07-135-EN-N, website: http://ec.europa.eu/eurostat

34. Jared Sandberg, 'NoChores.com', *Newsweek* (30 August 1999): 30(2).

35. 'Plugged in: Hong Kong embraces the Octopus Card', *The New York Times on the Web* (8 June 2002).

36. David Lewis and Darren Bridger, *The Soul of the New Consumer: Authenticity – What We Buy and Why in the New Economy* (London: Nicholas Brealey Publishing, 2000).

37. Dhruv Grewal, Julie Baker, Michael Levy and Glenn B. Voss, 'The Effects of Wait Expectations and Store Atmosphere Evaluations on Patronage Intentions in Service-Intensive Retail Store', *Journal of Retailing* 79 (2003): 259–68; cf. also Shirley Taylor, 'Waiting for Service: The Relationship Between Delays and Evaluations of Service', *Journal of Marketing* 58 (April 1994): 56–69.

38. 'We're Hating the Waiting; 43 per cent Prefer Self-Service', *Marketing Daily* (23 January 2007), www.mediapost.com, accessed 23 January 2007.

39. David H. Maister, 'The Psychology of Waiting Lines', in John A. Czepiel, Michael R. Solomon and Carol F. Surprenant (eds), *The Service Encounter: Managing Employee/ Customer Interaction in Service Businesses* (Lexington, MA: Lexington Books, 1985): 113–24.

40. David Leonhardt, 'Airlines Using Technology in a Push for Shorter Lines', *New York Times* (8 May 2000), www.nytimes.com, accessed 8 May 2000.

41. Henry Fountain, quoted in 'The Ultimate Body Language: How You Line Up for Mickey', *New York Times* (18 September 2005), www.nytimes.com, accessed 18 September 2005.

42. Sigmund Grønmo, 'Concepts of Time: Some Implications for Consumer Research', in Thomas K. Srull (ed.), *Advances in Consumer Research* 16 (Provo, UT: Association for Consumer Research 1989): 339–45.

43. Gabriele Morello and P. van der Reis, 'Attitudes towards time in different cultures: African time and European time', *Proceedings of the Third Symposium on Cross-Cultural Consumer and Business Studies* (Honolulu: University of Hawaii, 1990); Gabriele Morello, 'Our attitudes towards time', *Forum* 96/2 (European Forum for Management Development, 1996): 48–51.

44. Søren Askegaard and Tage Koed Madsen, 'The local and the global: Traits of homogeneity and heterogeneity in European food cultures', *International Business Review* 7(6) (1998): 549–68; for a thorough discussion of food culture, see Claude Fischler, *L'Homnivore* (Paris: Odile Jacob, 1990).

45. Mark J. Arnold and Kristy E. Reynolds, 'Hedonic shopping motivations', *Journal of Retailing* 79 (2003): 90–1.

46. Daniel Miller, *A Theory of Shopping* (Cambridge: Polity Press, 1998).

47. For a scale that was devised to assess these dimensions of the shopping experience, see Barry J. Babin, William R. Darden and Mitch Griffin, 'Work and/or fun: Measuring hedonic and utilitarian shopping value', *Journal of Consumer Research* 20 (March 1994): 644–56.

48. *Ibid.*

49. Adapted from Andrea Groeppel-Klein, Eva Thelen and Christoph Antretter, 'The Impact of Shopping Motives on Store Assessment', in Dubois, Lowrey, Shrum and Vanhuele (eds), *European Advances in Consumer Research* 4: 63–72.

50. Quoted in Robert C. Prus, *Making Sales: Influence as Inter-personal Accomplishment* (Newbury Park, CA: Sage Library of Social Research, Sage, 1989): 225.

51. V.D. Kaltcheva and B.A. Weitz (2006), 'When Should a Retailer Create an Exciting Store Environment?'

52. Gregory P. Stone, 'City shoppers and urban identification: Observations on the social psychology of city life', *American Journal of Sociology* 60 (1954): 36–45; Danny Bellenger and Pradeep K. Korgaonkar, 'Profiling the recreational shopper', *Journal of Retailing* 56(3) (1980): 77–92.

53. Stephen Brown and Rhona Reid, 'Shoppers on the Verge of a Nervous Breakdown', in S. Brown and D. Turley (eds), *Consumer Research: Postcards from the Edge* (London: Routledge, 1997): 79–149.

54. Nina Gruen, 'The retail battleground: Solutions for today's shifting marketplace', *Journal of Property Management* (July–August 1989): 14.

55. http://www.datamonitor.com/industries/research/?pid= DMCM4619&type=Report (accessed 25 April 2008).

56. Personal communication with a Finnish reviewer.

57. 'Slaget om Europa', *Jyllands Posten* (12 February 1997).

58. http://www.carrefour.com/cdc/group/our-group/ (accessed 16 February 2012).

59. http://www.retail-index.com/HOMESEARCH/ FoodRetailers/tabid/3496/Default.aspx (accessed 16 February 2012).

60. http://www.metrogroup.de/servlet/PB/menu/1179530_ l2/index.htm (accessed 20 August 2008); http://www. metrogroup.de/internet/site/metrogroup/node/9251/ Len/index.html (accessed 16 February 2012); http://www. metro-cc.com/dynasite.cfm?dsmid=103297&dspaid=844302 (accessed 16 February 2012) for an interactive map which shows the locations where this global company now operates.

61. http://www.tescocorporate.com/publiclibs/tesco/ International.pdf; for an interview with Sir Terry Leahy (former CEO of Tesco) discussing the Group's international strategy see http://w3.cantos.com/08/tesco-804-0lvon/ interviews.php?task=view&type=video&i=1&med=asx&cn t=bb&url=http://w3.cantos.com/08/tesco-804-0lvon/ video/tsco-d005-bb-v-5.asx accessed 20 August 2008; see also http://www.tescocorporate.com/publiclibs/tesco/ (accessed 16 February 2012).

62. Arieh Goldman, 'The shopping style explanation for store loyalty', *Journal of Retailing* 53 (Winter 1977–8): 33–46, 94; Robert B. Settle and Pamela L. Alreck, 'Hyperchoice shapes the marketplace', *Marketing Communications* (May 1988): 15.

63. Joseph C. Nunes and Xavier Dreze, 'Your loyalty program is betraying you', *Harvard Business Review* April 2006: 126.

64. Joseph C. Nunes and Xavier Dreze, 'Your loyalty program is betraying you', *Harvard Business Review* April 2006: 124–131, 125–128.

65. Joseph C. Nunes and Xavier Dreze, 'Your loyalty program is betraying you', *Harvard Business Review* April 2006: 128–9.

66. Joseph C. Nunes and Xavier Dreze, 'Your loyalty program is betraying you', *Harvard Business Review* April 2006: 129–131.

67. http://www.halland.se/en/forest-lakes/278397/

68. Daniel Hjelmgren, 'Creating positive experiences' in Alan Bradshaw, Chris Hackley and Pauline Maclaran (eds), *European Association for Consumer Research Conference* 2010, RHUL, page 7.

69. Some material in this section was adapted from Michael R. Solomon and Elnora W. Stuart, *Welcome to Marketing.com: The Brave New World of E-Commerce* (Upper Saddle River, NJ: Prentice Hall, 2001).

70. Seema Williams, David M. Cooperstein, David E. Weisman and Thalika Oum, 'Post-web retail', *The Forrester Report*, Forrester Research, Inc., September 1999; Catherine Arnold, 'Across the pond', *Marketing News* (28 October 2002): 3.

71. Eurostat 2011a Individuals having ordered/bought goods or services for private use over the Internet in the last three months. Retrieved 6 December 2011, http://epp.eurostat. ec.europa.eu/tgm/table.do?tab=table&init=1&language= en&pcode=tin00067; and Eurostat 2011b Information society statistics at regional level. Retrieved 6 December 2011, for Eurostat. Cited from Elfriede Penz and M.K. Hogg 'Consumer Decision Making in Online and Offline Environments' in *The Digital Consumer* (eds), R.W. Belk and Rosa Llamas (Routledge) 2013.

72. Mikael Lundström, 'E-handel inget för svensson', *Info* 8 (2000): 52–4.

73. The Nielsen Company Press Release 'Over 875 Million Consumers Have Shopped Online – the Number of Internet Shoppers Up 40 per cent in Two Years' http:// www.earthtimes.org/articles/show/over-875-million-consumers-have-shopped-online--the-number,263812. shtml accessed 20 August 2008.

74. Rebecca K. Ratner, Barbara E. Kahn and Daniel Kahneman, 'Choosing less-preferred experiences for the sake of variety', *Journal of Consumer Research* 26 (June 1999): 1–15.

75. Caroline Davies, 'Tesco sales slump part of consumer revolution changing the way we shop' *The Guardian*, 12 January 2012, http://www.guardian.co.uk/business/2012/ jan/12/tesco-consumer-revolution-internet-shopping? INTCMP=SRCH, accessed 24 January 2012.

76. Rebecca Smithers, 'John Lewis expands Collect and Click to Waitrose stores', *The Guardian*, 31 August 2011, http://www.guardian.co.uk/business/2011/aug/31/john-lewis-click-collect-waitrose?INTCMP=SRCH, accessed 24 January 2012.

77. A study of how online grocery shoppers negotiated three different store layouts, freeform, grid and racetrack, indicated that they found the freeform layout most useful for finding shopping list products within the store, and also by far the most entertaining to use. They also found the grid layout much easier to use than the other layouts. 'The grid layout is a rectangular arrangement of displays and long aisles that generally run parallel to one another. The freeform layout is a free-flowing and asymmetric arrangement of displays and aisles, employing a variety of different sizes, shapes and styles of display. In the racetrack/boutique layout, the sales floor is organized into individual, semi-separate areas, each built around a particular shopping theme', Adam P. Vrechopolous, Robert M. O'Keefe, Georgios I. Doukidis and George J. Siomkos, 'Virtual store layout: An experimental comparison in the context of grocery retail', *Journal of Retailing* 80 (2004): 13–22.

78. Jennifer Gilbert, 'Customer service crucial to online buyers', *Advertising Age* (13 September 1999): 52.

79. Alisa Gould-Simon, 'How Fashion Retailers Are Redefining E-Commerce with Social Media', *Mashable.com* (7 March 2011), http://mashable.com/2011/03/07/fashion-retailers-social-e-commerce/, accessed 17 April 2011.

80. www.allurent.com/newsDetail.php?newsid=20, accessed 29 January 2007. For questionnaire items for researching consumers' online experiences see also: Mary Wolfinbarger and Mary C. Gilly, 'eTailQ: Dimensionalizing, measuring and predicting etail quality', *Journal of Retailing* 79 (2003): Table 4.

81. Datamonitor predicted that by the end of 2003 almost 60 million European consumers would bank online; Laura Mazur, 'Web marketers must now adapt to the occasion', *Marketing* (29 May 2003): 16 (http://search.epnet.com/ login.aspx?direct=true&db=buh&an=10029509).

82. Bob Tedeschi, 'More e-commerce sites aim to add "sticky" content', *NYT Online* (9 August 2004).

83. Chuan-Fong Shih, 'Conceptualizing consumer experiences in cyberspace', *European Journal of Marketing* 32(7/8) (1998): 655–63.

84. Alka Varma Citrin, Donald E. Stern, Eric R. Spangenberg and Michael J. Clark, 'Consumer need for tactile input: An internet retailing challenge', *Journal of Business Research* 56 (2003): 915–22. See also Joann Peck and Terry L. Childers, 'Individual differences in haptic information processing: The need for touch scale', *Journal of Consumer Research* 30 (December 2003): 430–42, whose scale includes both instrumental and autotelic factors which differentiate between need for touch as part of the pre-purchase decision-making process, and the need for touch as an end in itself. The importance of touch (particularly as an end in itself) points to this as a potential barrier to the use of e-commerce by some consumers across all product groups.

85. Rita Choy and Suzanne Loker, 'Mass customization of wedding gowns: Design involvement on the internet', *Clothing and Textiles Research Journal* 22 (1 and 2) (2004): 79–87.

86. *Markedsføring* (17 February 2000): 20.

87. Kortney Stringer, 'Shoppers who blend store, catalog, web spend more', *The Wall Street Journal Online* (3 September 2004): A7.

88. Marc Gobé, *Emotional Branding: The New Paradigm for Connecting Brands to People* (New York: Allworth Press, 2001): xxv.

89. *Ibid*.

90. An excellent collection of articles on this topic is found in Pasi Falk and Colin Campbell (eds), *The Shopping Experience* (London: Sage, 1997).

91. C. Gardner and J. Sheppard, *Consuming Passion: The Rise of Retail Culture* (London: Unwin Hyman, 1989).

92. Stephen Brown, 'Sex "n" Shopping', Working Paper 9501 (University of Stirling: Institute for Retail Studies, 1995); see also Stephen Brown, 'Consumption Behaviour in the Sex "n" Shopping Novels of Judith Krantz: A Post-structuralist Perspective', in Kim P. Corfman and John G. Lynch, Jr (eds), *Advances in Consumer Research* 23 (Provo, UT: Association for Consumer Research, 1996): 43–8.

93. Véronique Aubert-Gamet, 'Twisting servicescapes: Diversion of the physical environment in a re-appropriation process', *International Journal of Service Industry Management* 8(1) (1997): 26–41.

94. Stephen Brown, *Postmodern Marketing* (London: Routledge, 1995), discussion on pp. 50 ff.; Lars Thøger Christensen

and Søren Askegaard, 'Flexibility in the marketing organization: The ultimate consumer orientation or Ford revisited?' *Marketing Today and for the 21st Century*, Proceedings of the XIV EMAC Conference (ed.), Michelle Bergadaà (Cergy-Pontoise: ESSEC, 1995): 1507–14.

95. Turo-Kimmo Lehtonen and Pasi Mäenpää, 'Shopping in the East Centre Mall', in Falk and Campbell (eds), *The Shopping Experience*: 136–65.

96. Quoted in Jacquelyn Bivins, 'Fun and mall games', *Stores* (August 1989): 35.

97. Sallie Hook, 'All the retail world's a stage: Consumers conditioned to entertainment in shopping environment', *Marketing News* 21 (31 July 1987): 16.

98. David Chaney, 'The department store as a cultural form', *Theory, Culture and Society* 1(3) (1983): 22–31.

99. Cecilia Fredriksson, 'The Making of a Swedish Department Store Culture', in Falk and Campbell (eds) *The Shopping Experience*: 111–35.

100. Pauline Maclaran and Lorna Stevens, 'Romancing the Utopian Marketplace', in S. Brown, A.M. Doherty and B. Clarke (eds), *Romancing the Market* (London: Routledge, 1998): 172–86.

101. Millie Creighton, 'The Seed of Creative Lifestyle Shopping: Wrapping Consumerism in Japanese Store Layouts', in John F. Sherry Jr (ed.), *Servicescapes: The Concept of Place in Contemporary Markets* (Lincolnwood, IL: NTC Business Books, 1998): 199–228.

102. Kira Cochrane, 'Why pop-ups pop up everywhere?', *Guardian*, 12 October 2010, http://www.guardian.co.uk/lifeandstyle/2010/oct/12/pop-up-temporary-shops-restaurants, accessed 24 January 2012.

103. Researchers identified two ludic (play related) elements that help us understand the role of *play* in consumption environments: firstly, '*Liminoid Real Estate*: This refers to the creation of new worlds through consumer play, which consumers interpret as different realities. This notion of transcendent surrender provides a link between play and religion, ritual, sacrifice and the sacred; and secondly *The Obverse Panapticon*: This refers to physical structures that are designed in a way that appeals to exhibitionistic desires of consumers by enabling them to be observed by others.' Robert V. Kozinets, John F. Sherry, Diana Storm, Adam Duhachek, Krittinee Nuttavuthisit and Benet DeBerry-Spence, 'Ludic agency and retail spectacle', *Journal of Consumer Research* 31 (December 2004): 658–72.

104. Stefania Borghini, John F. Sherry, Annamma Joy, 'Ordinary Spaces and Sense of Place' in Alan Bradshaw, Chris Hackley and Pauline Maclaran (eds), *European Association for Consumer Research Conference* 2010 RHUL, 33.

105. Patrick Hetzel and Veronique Aubert, 'Sales Area Design and Fashion Phenomena: A Semiotic Approach', in van Raaij and Bamossy (eds), *European Advances in Consumer Research* 1: 522–33.

106. Søren Askegaard and Güliz Ger, 'Product-Country Images as Stereotypes: A Comparative Analysis of the Image of Danish Food Products in Germany and Turkey', *MAPP Working Paper* 45 (Aarhus: The Aarhus School of Business, 1997).

107. Susan Spiggle and Murphy A. Sewall, 'A choice sets model of retail selection', *Journal of Marketing* 51 (April 1987): 97–111; William R. Darden and Barry J. Babin, 'The role of

emotions in expanding the concept of retail personality', *Stores* 76 (April 1994) 4: RR7–RR8.

108. Most measures of store image are quite similar to other attitude measures, as discussed in Chapter 5. For an excellent bibliography of store image studies, see Mary R. Zimmer and Linda L. Golden, 'Impressions of retail stores: A content analysis of consumer images,' *Journal of Retailing* 64 (Fall 1988): 65–93.

109. *Ibid.*

110. Spiggle and Sewall, 'A choice sets model of retail selection', *op. cit.*

111. Philip Kotler, 'Atmospherics as a marketing tool,' *Journal of Retailing* (Winter 1973–74): 10; Anna Mattila and Jochen Wirtz, 'Congruency of scent and music as a driver of in-store evaluations and behavior', *Journal of Retailing* 77 (Summer 2001): 273–89; J. Duncan Herrington, 'An Integrative Path Model of the Effects of Retail Environments on Shopper Behavior', in Robert L. King (ed.), *Marketing: Toward the Twenty-First Century* (Richmond, VA: Southern Marketing Association, 1991): 58–62; see also Ann E. Schlosser, 'Applying the functional theory of attitudes to understanding the influence of store atmosphere on store inferences', *Journal of Consumer Psychology* 7(4) (1998): 345–69.

112. Fabian Csaba and Søren Askegaard, 'Malls and the Orchestration of the Shopping Experience in a Historical Perspective', in Arnould and Scott (eds), *Advances in Consumer Research* 26: 34–40.

113. Robert J. Donovan, John R. Rossiter, Gilian Marcoolyn, and Andrew Nesdale, 'Store atmosphere and purchasing behavior', *Journal of Retailing* 70, no. 3 (1994): 283–94.

114. Alice Z. Cuneo, 'Malls seek boost with "activity" stores', *Advertising Age* (21 July 2003): 6.

115. Charles S. Areni and David Kim, 'The influence of in-store lighting on consumers' examination of merchandise in a wine store', *International Journal of Research in Marketing* 11(2) (March 1994): 117–25.

116. Jean-Charles Chebat, Claire Gelinas Chebat and Dominique Vaillant, 'Environmental background music and in-store selling', *Journal of Business Research* 54 (2001): 115–23; Judy I. Alpert and Mark I. Alpert, 'Music influences on mood and purchase intentions', *Psychology and Marketing* 7 (Summer 1990): 109–34.

117. Brad Edmondson, 'Pass the meat loaf', *American Demographics* (January 1989): 19.

118. Dhruv Grewal, Julie Baker, Michael Levy and Glenn B. Voss, 'The effects of wait expectations and store atmosphere evaluations on patronage intentions in service-intensive retail store', *Journal of Retailing* 79 (2003): 259–68.

119. 'Through the looking glass', *Lifestyle Monitor* 16 (Fall/Winter 2002).

120. 'Butikken er en slagmark', *Berlingske Tidende* (15 July 1996): 3.

121. Jennifer Lach, 'Meet you in aisle three', *American Demographics* (April 1999): 41.

122. Karen M. Stilley, J. Jeffrey Inman and Kirk L. Wakefield, 'Planning to Make Unplanned Purchases? The Role of In-Store Slack in Budget Deviation', *Journal of Consumer Research* 37, no. 2 (2010): 264–78.

123. 'Motorola Survey: Shoppers Better Connected to Information than Store Associates', *Chain Store Age* (17 January 2011),

http://www.chainstoreage.com/article/motorola-survey-shoppers-better-connected-information-store-associates, accessed 30 April 2011; Kris Hudson, 'Malls Test Apps to Aid Shoppers', *Wall Street Journal* (26 April 2011), http://online.wsj.com/article/SB1000142405274870433650457 6258740640080926.html?mod=dist_smartbrief, accessed 29 April 2011.

124. Ernest Beck, 'Diageo attempts to reinvent the bar in an effort to increase spirits sales', *The Wall Street Journal* (23 February 2001).

125. Easwar S. Iyer, 'Unplanned purchasing: Knowledge of shopping environment and time pressure', *Journal of Retailing* 65 (Spring 1989): 40–57; C. Whan Park, Easwar S. Iyer and Daniel C. Smith, 'The effects of situational factors on in-store grocery shopping', *Journal of Consumer Research* 15 (March 1989): 422–33.

126. Michael Wahl, 'Eye POPping persuasion', *Marketing Insights* (June 1989): 130.

127. 'Zipping down the aisles', *New York Times Magazine* (6 April 1997).

128. Peter McGoldrick, Erica J. Betts and Kathleen A. Keeling, 'Antecedents of Spontaneous Buying Behaviour During Temporary Markdowns', in Arnould and Scott (eds), *Advances in Consumer Research* 26: 26–33.

129. Cathy J. Cobb and Wayne D. Hoyer, 'Planned versus impulse purchase behavior', *Journal of Retailing* 62 (Winter 1986): 384–409; Easwar S. Iyer and Sucheta S. Ahlawat, 'Deviations from a Shopping Plan: When and Why Do Consumers Not Buy as Planned?' in Melanie Wallendorf and Paul Anderson (eds), *Advances in Consumer Research* 14 (Provo, UT: Association for Consumer Research, 1987): 246–9.

130. Andrea Groeppel-Klein, 'The Influence of the Dominance Perceived at the Point-of-Sale on the Price-Assessment', in Englis and Olofsson (eds), *European Advances in Consumer Research* 3: 304–11.

131. Emily Steel, 'Luring Shoppers to Stores', *Wall Street Journal* (26 August 2010), http://online.wsj.com/article/SB10001 42405274870454090457545184 1980063132.html, accessed April 18, 2011.

132. Dennis Desrochers, 'European consumers respond to spray samplers', *Global Cosmetic Industry* 171(16) (June 2003): 28.

133. Chairman-CEO A.G. Laffley, quoted in Jack Neff, 'P&G boosts design's role in marketing', *Advertising Age* (9 February 2004): 52.

134. William Keenan, Jr, 'Point-of-purchase: From clutter to technoclutter', *Sales and Marketing Management* 141 (April 1989): 96.

135. *Markedsføring* 13 (1999): 24.

136. Cyndee Miller, 'Videocart spruces up for new tests', *Marketing News* (19 February 1990): 19; William E. Sheeline, 'User-friendly shopping carts', *Fortune* (5 December 1988): 9.

137. Bernard Swoboda, 'Multimedia Customer Information Systems at the Point of Sale: Selected Results of an Impact Analysis', in Englis and Olofsson (eds), *European Advances in Consumer Research* 3: 239–46.

138. Erin White, 'Look up for new products in aisle 5: In-store TV advertising gains traction globally; Timely pitch at shoppers', *The Wall Street Journal Online* (23 March 2004): B11.

139. http://www.talkingretail.com/industry_announcements/6076/dunnhumby-relaunches-Tesco-in-.ehtml

140. Merissa Marr, 'Fox to pitch its movies at the mall as TV-ad costs escalate: Studio says new approach avoids broadcast clutter', *The Wall Street Journal Online* (15 July 2004): B6.

141. Cyndee Miller, 'MTV "Video Capsule" features sports for music retailers, corporate sponsors', *Marketing News* (3 February 1992): 5.

142. 'Dutch shop lets clients burn own CDs', *Wall Street Journal* (14 November 2000): B10.

143. See Robert B. Cialdini, *Influence: Science and Practice*, 2nd edn (Glenview, IL: Scott, Foresman, 1988).

144. Richard P. Bagozzi, 'Marketing as exchange', *Journal of Marketing* 39 (October 1975): 32–9; Peter M. Blau, *Exchange and Power in Social Life* (New York: Wiley, 1964); Marjorie Caballero and Alan J. Resnik, 'The attraction paradigm in dyadic exchange', *Psychology and Marketing* 3(1) (1986): 17–34; George C. Homans, 'Social behavior as exchange', *American Journal of Sociology* 63 (1958): 597–606; Paul H. Schurr and Julie L. Ozanne, 'Influences on exchange processes: Buyers' preconceptions of a seller's trustworthiness and bargaining toughness', *Journal of Consumer Research* 11 (March 1985): 939–53; Arch G. Woodside and J.W. Davenport, 'The effect of salesman similarity and expertise on consumer purchasing behavior', *Journal of Marketing Research* 8 (1974): 433–6.

145. Paul Busch and David T. Wilson, 'An experimental analysis of a salesman's expert and referent bases of social power in the buyer–seller dyad', *Journal of Marketing Research* 13 (February 1976): 3–11; John E. Swan, Fred Trawick Jr, David R. Rink and Jenny J. Roberts, 'Measuring dimensions of purchaser trust of industrial salespeople', *Journal of Personal Selling and Sales Management* 8 (May 1988): 1.

146. For a study in this area, see Peter H. Reingen and Jerome B. Kernan, 'Social perception and interpersonal influence: Some consequences of the physical attractiveness stereotype in a personal selling setting', *Journal of Consumer Psychology* 2 (1993): 25–38.

147. Linda L. Price and Eric J. Arnould, 'Commercial friendships: Service provider–client relationships in context', *Journal of Marketing* 63 (October 1999): 38–56.

148. Mary Jo Bitner, Bernard H. Booms and Mary Stansfield Tetreault, 'The service encounter: Diagnosing favorable and unfavorable incidents', *Journal of Marketing* 54 (January 1990): 7–84; Robert C. Prus, *Making Sales* (Newbury Park, CA: Sage, 1989); Arch G. Woodside and James L. Taylor, 'Identity Negotiations in Buyer–Seller Interactions', in Elizabeth C. Hirschman and Morris B. Holbrook (eds), *Advances in Consumer Research* 12 (Provo, UT: Association for Consumer Research, 1985): 443–9.

149. Barry J. Babin, James S. Boles and William R. Darden, 'Salesperson stereotypes, consumer emotions, and their impact on information processing', *Journal of the Academy of Marketing Science* 23(2) (1995): 94–105; Gilbert A. Churchill Jr, Neil M. Ford, Steven W. Hartley and Orville C. Walker Jr, 'The determinants of salesperson performance: A meta-analysis', *Journal of Marketing Research* 22 (May 1985): 103–18.

150. Jiang Lan, Joandrea Hoegg, Darren W. Dahl and Amitava Chattopadhyay, 'The Persuasive Role of Incidental Similarity on Attitudes and Purchase Intentions in a Sales

Context', *Journal of Consumer Research* 36, no. 5 (2010): 778–91.

151. Siew Meng Leong, Paul S. Busch and Deborah Roedder John, 'Knowledge bases and salesperson effectiveness: A script-theoretic analysis', *Journal of Marketing Research* 26 (May 1989): 164; Harish Sujan, Mita Sujan and James R. Bettman, 'Knowledge structure differences between more effective and less effective salespeople', *Journal of Marketing Research* 25 (February 1988): 81–6; Robert Saxe and Barton Weitz, 'The SOCCO scale: A measure of the customer orientation of salespeople', *Journal of Marketing Research* 19 (August 1982): 343–51; David M. Szymanski, 'Determinants of selling effectiveness: The importance of declarative knowledge to the personal selling concept', *Journal of Marketing* 52 (January 1988): 64–77; Barton A. Weitz, 'Effectiveness in sales interactions: A contingency framework', *Journal of Marketing* 45 (Winter 1981): 85–103.

152. Jagdish M. Sheth, 'Buyer–Seller Interaction: A Conceptual Framework,' in Beverlee B. Anderson (ed.), *Advances in Consumer Research* 3 (Cincinnati, OH: Association for Consumer Research, 1976): 382–6; Kaylene C. Williams and Rosann L. Spiro, 'Communication style in the salesperson–customer dyad', *Journal of Marketing Research* 22 (November 1985): 434–42.

153. Marsha L. Richins, 'An analysis of consumer interaction styles in the marketplace', *Journal of Consumer Research* 10 (June 1983): 73–82.

154. 'Voice of the Consumer Not Leveraged', Center for Media Research (3 February 2009), www.mediapost.com, accessed 3 February 2009.

155. Rama Jayanti and Anita Jackson, 'Service Satisfaction: Investigation of Three Models', in Holman and Solomon (eds), *Advances in Consumer Research* 18: 603–10; David K. Tse, Franco M. Nicosia and Peter C. Wilton, 'Consumer satisfaction as a process', *Psychology and Marketing* 7 (Fall 1990): 177–93. For a treatment of satisfaction issues from a more interpretive perspective, see Susan Fournier and David Mick, 'Rediscovering satisfaction,' *Journal of Marketing* 63 (October 1999): 5–23.

156. Constance L. Hayes, 'Service takes a holiday', *New York Times* (23 December 1998): C1.

157. Eugene W. Anderson, Claes Fornell and Donald R. Lehmann, 'Customer satisfaction, market share, and profitability: Findings from Sweden', *Journal of Marketing* 58(3) (July 1994): 53–66.

158. Robert Jacobson and David A. Aaker, 'The strategic role of product quality', *Journal of Marketing* 51 (October 1987): 31–44; for a review of issues regarding the measurement of service quality, see J. Joseph Cronin Jr and Steven A. Taylor, 'Measuring service quality: A reexamination and extension', *Journal of Marketing* 56 (July 1992): 55–68.

159. Anna Kirmani and Peter Wright, 'Money talks: Perceived advertising expense and expected product quality', *Journal of Consumer Research* 16 (December 1989): 344–53; Donald R. Lichtenstein and Scot Burton, 'The relationship between perceived and objective price-quality', *Journal of Marketing Research* 26 (November 1989): 429–43; Akshay R. Rao and Kent B. Monroe, 'The effect of price, brand name, and store name on buyers' perceptions of product quality: An integrative review', *Journal of Marketing Research* 26 (August 1989): 351–7.

160. Shelby Hunt, 'Post-transactional communication and dissonance reduction', *Journal of Marketing* 34 (January 1970): 46–51; Daniel E. Innis and H. Rao Unnava, 'The Usefulness of Product Warranties for Reputable and New Brands,' in Holman and Solomon (eds), *Advances in Consumer Research* 18: 317–22; Terence A. Shimp and William O. Bearden, 'Warranty and other extrinsic cue effects on consumers' risk perceptions', *Journal of Consumer Research* 9 (June 1982): 38–46.

161. Mia Stokmans, 'The Relation Between Postpurchase Evaluations and Consumption Experiences of Hedonic Products: A Case of Reading Fiction', in Englis and Olofsson (eds), *European Advances in Consumer Research* 3: 139–45.

162. Gilbert A. Churchill Jr and Carol F. Surprenant, 'An investigation into the determinants of customer satisfaction', *Journal of Marketing Research* 19 (November 1983): 491–504; John E. Swan and I. Frederick Trawick, 'Disconfirmation of expectations and satisfaction with a retail service', *Journal of Retailing* 57 (Fall 1981): 49–67; Peter C. Wilton and David K. Tse, 'Models of consumer satisfaction formation: An extension', *Journal of Marketing Research* 25 (May 1988): 204–12; for a discussion of what may occur when customers evaluate a new service for which comparison standards do not yet exist, see Ann L. McGill and Dawn Iacobucci, 'The Role of Post-Experience Comparison Standards in the Evaluation of Unfamiliar Services,' in John F. Sherry Jr and Brian Sternthal (eds) *Advances in Consumer Research* 19 (Provo, UT: Association for Consumer Research, 1992): 570–8; William Boulding, Ajay Kalra, Richard Staelin and Valarie A. Zeithaml, 'A dynamic process model of service quality: From expectations to behavioral intentions', *Journal of Marketing Research* 30 (February 1993): 7–27.

163. John W. Gamble, 'The expectations paradox: The more you offer customers, the closer you are to failure', *Marketing News* (14 March 1988): 38.

164. Jagdish N. Sheth and Banwari Mittal, 'A framework for managing customer expectations', *Journal of Market Focused Management* 1 (1996): 137–58.

165. Franz Bailom, Hans H. Hinterhuber, Kurt Matzler and Elmar Sauerwein, 'Das kano-modell der kundenzufriedenheit', *Marketing ZFP* 2 (2nd quarter 1996): 117–26.

166. Marit G. Engeset, Kjell Grønhaug and Morten Heide, 'The impact of experience on customer satisfaction as measured in direct surveys', in *Marketing for an Expanding Europe*, Proceedings of the 25th EMAC Conference, Berács, Bauer and Simon (eds): 403–17.

167. Andreas Herrmann, Frank Huber and Christine Braunstein, 'A Regret Theory Approach to Assessing Customer Satisfaction when Alternatives are Considered', in Dubois, Lowrey, Shrum and Vanhuele (eds), *European Advances in Consumer Research* 4: 82–8.

168. Kjell Grønhaug and Alladi Venkatesh, 'Products and services in the perspectives of consumer socialisation', *European Journal of Marketing* 21(10) (1987); Folke Ölander, 'Consumer Satisfaction – A Sceptic's View', in H.K. Hunt (ed.), *Conceptualization and Measurement of Consumer Satisfaction and Dissatisfaction* (Cambridge, MA: Marketing Science Institute, 1977): 453–88.

169. Alessandro M. Peluso and Gianluigi Guido, 'Testing antecedents and moderators in product evaluation:

towards a new model of consumer satisfaction' in Alan Bradshaw, Chris Hackley and Pauline Maclaran (eds), *European Association for Consumer Research Conference* 2010 RHUL, 15.

170. 'Keeping European Consumers Safe', *2010 Annual Report on the operation of the Rapid Alert System for non-food consumer products*, European Communities Health and Consumer Protection Directorate General, Luxembourg 2011: 14.

171. 'Keeping European Consumers Safe', *2010 Annual Report on the operation of the Rapid Alert System for non-food consumer products*, European Communities Health and Consumer Protection Directorate General, Luxembourg 2011: 36–7.

172. *The Consumer Markets Scoreboard: Monitoring Consumer Outcomes in the Single Market*, COM (2008) 31, European Communities, Luxembourg 2008: 17.

173. Mary C. Gilly and Betsy D. Gelb, 'Post-purchase consumer processes and the complaining consumer', *Journal of Consumer Research* 9 (December 1982): 323–8; Diane Halstead and Cornelia Droge, 'Consumer Attitudes Toward Complaining and the Prediction of Multiple Complaint Responses', in Holman and Solomon (eds), *Advances in Consumer Research* 18: 210–16; Jagdip Singh, 'Consumer complaint intentions and behavior: Definitional and taxonomical issues,' *Journal of Marketing* 52 (January 1988): 93–107.

174. Alan Andreasen and Arthur Best, 'Consumers complain – does business respond?', *Harvard Business Review* 55 (July/August 1977): 93–101.

175. Ingrid Martin, 'Expert–Novice Differences in Complaint Scripts', in Holman and Solomon (eds), *Advances in*

Consumer Research 18: 225–31; Marsha L. Richins, 'A multivariate analysis of responses to dissatisfaction', *Journal of the Academy of Marketing Science* 15 (Fall 1987): 24–31.

176. John A. Schibrowsky and Richard S. Lapidus, 'Gaining a competitive advantage by analysing aggregate complaints', *Journal of ConsumerMarketing* 11 (1994) 1: 15–26.

177. Veronica Liljander, 'Consumer Satisfaction with Complaint Handling Following a Dissatisfactory Experience with Car Repair', in Dubois, Lowrey, Shrum and Vanhuele (eds), *European Advances in Consumer Research* 4: 270–5.

178. Tibbett L. Speer, 'They complain because they care', *American Demographics* (May 1996): 13–14.

179. *The Consumer Markets Scoreboard: Monitoring Consumer Outcomes in the Single Market*, COM (2008) 31, European Communities, Luxembourg, 2008: 17.

180. Special Eurobarometer 252, Consumer Protection in the Internal Market 2006, Figure 1, *The Consumer Markets Score-board: Monitoring Consumer Outcomes in the Single Market*, COM (2008) 31, European Communities, Luxembourg.

181. See Kortnery Stringer, 'Shoppers who blend store, catalog, web spend more', *The Wall Street Journal Online* (3 September 2004): A7 for a detailed discussion of these issues.

182. William Echison, 'Designers climb onto the virtual catwalk', *Business Week* (11 October 1999): 164.

183. Rita Choy and Suzanne Loker, 'Mass customization of wedding gowns: Design involvement on the internet', *Clothing and Textiles Research Journal* 22(1&2) (2004): 79–87.

CASE STUDY 1

'Small is beautiful': the Mini brand community

PAULINE MACLARAN, Royal Holloway College, University of London, UK

KOK HOI BEH, De Montfort University, Leicester, UK

Associated with rebel culture in the swinging sixties, the Mini has been the most popular British car ever produced. Despite the fact that it ceased production in 2000, the Mini still has a huge following of loyal fans around the world. They maintain their Minis with extreme devotion, ensuring their cars remain in prime condition on our UK roads, where they serve as a continual reminder of the iconic status of this little car that we have all come to love. Significantly, BMW, who bought the Mini brand as part of their takeover of Rover, were able to trade on this nostalgia when they launched the new MINI (spelt with capitals to differentiate it from the classic Mini) in 2001. To understand the passion that these loyal fans hold for the original Mini, we need to understand the car's history and its evolution into a cultural icon.

The Mini was first launched by the British Motor Corporation (BMC) in 1959, in response to increasing competition from the German manufactured 'bubble cars', small three-wheelers that were highly economic to run at a time when fuel prices were soaring following the Suez Crisis. The Mini's designer, Sir Alex Issigonis, introduced several innovative features, and, in particular, the use of front wheel drive, to allow for more passenger and luggage space and to overcome the car's limitations of size.

The Mini quickly became the quintessential fashion item of the 60s. With its cheeky straplines, such as 'You don't need a big one to be happy. Happiness is Mini shaped,' it enabled a then young baby boom generation to rebel against parental values (Filby, 1981). It epitomised perfectly the hedonistic, fun-seeking youth culture that the 60s heralded (Broderick, Maclaran and Ma, 2003). Throughout this decade the Mini was continually associated with major celebrities of the time – Michael Caine, Peter Sellers, Ringo Starr, Britt Ekland, Lulu and a host of others – many of whom had specially customised models (**wikipedia.com**). Fashion designer, Mary Quant, whose famous mini skirt was another iconic symbol of the 60s, appeared in many photos alongside her Mini car. The Mini's subversive connotations were further enhanced when Marianne Faithful drove to Mick Jagger's drugs trial in her Mini, and George Harrison's psychedelic Mini appeared in the Beatles' *Magical Mystery Tour* film

(**wikipedia.com**). In 1969 the Mini's notoriety was ensured when it played a starring role in *The Italian Job*, a film about a gold bullion robbery that featured what has now become a classic car chase. The robbers used three Minis to make their dramatic and 'nippy' escape from the police which included racing down a flight of steps and many other daring stunts. This film was remade in 2003 using the new MINI.

The Mini's image was further enhanced by the launches of the Mini Cooper (in 1961) and the more powerful Mini Cooper S (in 1963). These high performance versions of the Mini attracted many international rally drivers and this gave the Mini a racy image, strongly reinforced when the Mini Cooper S won the Monte Carlo Rally in 1964, 1965 and 1967. In addition, well-known dare-devil racers such as Niki Lauda, Enzo Ferrari and Steve McQueen drove Mini Coopers.

At the height of its popularity the Mini was exported to markets around the world, including South Africa, Australia, New Zealand and Japan (where it still has a very loyal following). From the early 1980s onwards, however, sales of the Mini declined, as newer small car designs, such as the Ford Fiesta and Volkswagen Polo, captured the popular imagination. Although production volumes decreased significantly in response to this declining demand, special editions of the Mini were launched thereafter at regular intervals. This gave the car a niche market allure and exclusivity that enhanced its sense of style and appeal as a collector's item.

Through its wealth of associations with pop, style and sporting icons, the Mini has become a cultural icon that stands for fun, happiness and individuality. Its loyal fans take pride in the fact that no two Minis are the same and often creatively theme the car's interior, exterior and even their own attire. For example, one passionate devotee, who drives a pink-painted Mini, dresses all in pink and has pink accessories for both herself and her car when she attends regular Mini events. The Mini's faithful followers constitute a brand community in that they relate to each other through their ownership of a Mini, regardless of traditional community markers, such as geographic location, age, gender, class or ethnicity (Muniz and O'Guinn, 2001).

There are over 150 Mini clubs alone in the UK and many others around the world, particularly in Italy and Japan (Beh, 2008). These clubs were set up by groups of Mini enthusiasts in order to meet with each other, swop advice, exchange parts, tell stories and enjoy themselves. They also communicate online where many Mini cyber communities are now flourishing. The internet enables members to transcend their own locality and communicate about their passion with other like-minded aficionados of the Mini from around the globe. Wherever members of the Mini community go, nationally or internationally, they can be assured of a welcome from other Mini owners. The three markers of community identified by Muniz and O'Guinn (2001) – consciousness of kind, moral responsibility, rituals and tradition – are very evident in the way Mini owners behave towards each other.

1 Consciousness of kind

This refers to the essential connection that members feel towards one another, a sense of 'we-ness' that engenders deep bonds through their shared passion for the brand. Two interconnected mechanisms engender consciousness of kind, 'legitimacy' and 'oppositional brand loyalty'. Legitimacy is the process by which the community recognise their identity and distinguish between 'true' members, peripheral members, and those who are not members at all. Oppositional brand loyalty gives the community member a sense of distinctiveness from those who do not belong. Normally this would be against other competitive brands. However, the launch of the new BMW MINI has created additional grounds for an oppositional loyalty which is not so much inter-brand as it is *intra*-brand (Beh, 2008). Many Mini clubs do not permit new MINI owners to join. There are several reasons why many Mini brand community members feel that the BMW MINI is not a true Mini. First, many members feel that the design of the new MINI does not retain the authenticity of the orginal Mini, and they are indignant that the two designs should be associated. Second, the MINI is no longer British and there is a sense of betrayal. Frequent contributors to the Mini internet discussion boards refer to BMW as 'British Motor Wreckers', and a 'foreign imposter' (Beh, 2008). A third reason, according to certain members, is that the new MINI does not permit the same level of individual customisation and creative expression.

2 Moral responsibility

Mini community members feel a deep sense of responsibility not only to other members, but also to the community as a whole. They have two important communal missions. The first of these is the recruiting, integrating and retaining of members to ensure the continued existence of the club. Members spread the word about their passion for the Mini with a missionary zeal that has been noted in other brand communities such as the 'Cult of Macintosh' (Belk and Tumbat, 2003). The second communal mission is internal and is based on assisting members to care for their Minis in order to ensure a thriving community. For example, Mini drivers always stop to help each other if they see a Mini that has broken down (but they do not stop for a BMW MINI). They place great emphasis on a felt obligation to lend tools or exchange parts in order to help maintain each others' Minis.

3 Rituals and traditions

Holding regular events to celebrate the history of the brand reinforces the Mini community's sense of identity and allows certain rituals and traditions to evolve as members share stories about their experiences of the Mini. Mini events are colourful pageants where members parade and display their customized Minis to each other. Car accessories become ritual artefacts to assist these performances and the sales of Mini collectibles are an important part of this ritualized behaviour. Other unwritten traditions have evolved over the years, such as flashing headlights and waving when two Minis pass on the road. Interestingly, non-brand- and brand-related rituals sometimes become mutually reinforcing, as when a member receives Mini-related birthday and Christmas presents.

From the above analysis we can see how the relationships between Mini owners meet the essential criteria for being considered a community. The Mini brand community has been going through a certain amount of turmoil in recent years. Similar to the Apple Newton brand community (Muniz and Schau, 2005), some members felt abandoned when production of the original Mini ceased in 2000. Many others experienced a sense of betrayal when BMW commenced production of what they saw as a very different MINI. We suggest that much of the BMW MINI's success is due to the fact that the Mini brand community, acting independently from marketers, has kept the core values of the original Mini brand alive for nearly 50 years, values that once again resonate with a new generation of MINI owners.

QUESTIONS

1 What do you think are the key influences that enabled the Mini car to become a cultural icon?

2 In what ways has the launch of the new BMW MINI destabilised the Mini brand community?

3 How do you think the opposition between fans of the BMW MINI and the original Mini might be resolved in the future?

4 Identify a brand community; and assess it with respect to the three markers of community identified by Muniz and O'Guinn (2001), i.e. consciousness of kind; moral responsibility; and rituals and tradition.

Sources

Beh, K.H. (2008), 'Unity in Diversity? Identity, Relationship and Cultural Context in the Mini Brand Community', Unpublished doctoral dissertation, De Montfort University.

Belk, R.W. and Tumbat, G. (2003), 'The Cult of Macintosh (Video)', in D. Turley and S. Brown (eds), *European Advances in Consumer Research*, vol. 6, Provo, UT: Association for Consumer Research.

Broderick, A., Maclaran, P. and Ma, P. (2003), 'Brand meaning negotiation and the role of the online community: a Mini case study', *Journal of Customer Behaviour*, vol. 2(1), pp. 75–104.

Filby P. (1981), *Amazing Mini*, UK: Haynes Publishing.

Muniz, A.M. and Schau, H.J. (2005), 'Religiosity in the Abandoned Apple Newton Brand Community', *Journal of Consumer Research*, vol. 31 (March), pp. 737–747.

Muniz, A.M. and O'Guinn, T.C. (2001), 'Brand Community', *Journal of Consumer Research*, 27 (March), pp. 412–432.

Wikipedia.com, 'Mini', http://en.wikipedia.org/wiki/Mini, last accessed 10 May 8.

How different is different? IKEA's challenge to appeal to local tastes globally

SOFIA ULVER-SNEISTRUP AND PETER SVENSSON, Lund University, Sweden

Introduction

In an interview in 2005, an IKEA manager described the IKEA business in the following words:

> In a way our business is people's *tastes*, how things look. And that's a quite difficult thing for us here in America where the taste is quite traditional. [...] I *do* think IKEA should have an opinion about what we could call 'good taste' is. In the long run we want to attract more and more customers but we also want to educate our markets too, educate them to like IKEA and to share *our* points of view when it comes to home decoration.

The customers referred to above are not customers in general, but the lower income segments in the United States. Although IKEA continuously faces the problem of different taste preferences among consumers in different markets, as indeed do all global brands, in some markets this difference in taste preferences is a more serious threat to IKEA's global expansion than in others. Thus, in the United States IKEA has struggled for years with American low income consumers holding on to tastes for traditional and conventional styles, whereas the majority of IKEA's priority range is Scandinavian modern and mostly patronized by the more dynamic middle-class. This tension between IKEA's global range strategy on the one hand and local consumers' taste resistance on the other, highlights the following general theoretical and practical problems, representing three perspectives from which global marketing can be discussed:

1 *From a consumer perspective*. How do different consumer markets, and consumers within these markets, adapt to and/or resist global brands' taste instructions in different ways?
2 *From a management perspective*. How should these differences be managed across the marketing mix?
3 *From an ethical/political perspective*. How far should a company go in terms of trying to change local cultural tastes?

Needless to say, in marketing practice these questions are not separated from but are actualized in every marketing decision. In order to understand these issues better, in this case study we draw upon research carried out in three different countries (USA, Sweden, Turkey) both among IKEA management and among IKEA consumers (Ulver-Sneistrup, 2008).

Consumer perspective: the example of individualistic consumption

In 30 interviews with middle-class consumers from different age groups in their homes in Turkey, Sweden and the USA, styles were often seen to be materially different but the ways of talking about preferred versus despised tastes seemed to be quite similar. For instance, in general consumers celebrated the virtue of being individualistic in their consumption and having a unique style. However, among the Swedish and US consumers, 'being individualistic' meant something rather different from what was meant by the consumers from Turkey.

The Turkish respondents emphasized the value of having the courage to break with the strong traditions and conventions held by family, relatives and older generations. One man said that:

> [Regular] Turkish people prefer two couches, two or three. They also want to buy single armchairs. I don't know why they prefer that. Look, *we* don't have that! . . . And also, a typical piece of furniture is a *garderobe* something like this [drawing a *garderobe*]. A big piece with doors on it, some shelves and they put a lot of money into that. And they think that if there's not a piece of furniture like this in the living-room, the living-room will be empty [laughter]! This is a *must* for them [laughter]! I don't know why they prefer it. They put all the stuff in it. Cups, mugs, I don't know all the stuff they put in there [laughter]! So they buy something like this, it's a *must*, it's a *must*! This is Turkish culture, I can say that. . . . Most people are not rich in Turkey, and when they try to get married, oh, it's not easy to get married in Turkey! [laughter] Because you have to rent, rent a flat, buy furniture, and also you have to choose furniture that your parents like because they help their children to buy the furniture [laughter]! Also they will have some visitors because of their parents – because they have lots of relatives – for example, so you will have a lot of guests coming to see your house 'What's happening here?' [laughter]. So this is a very important point for Turkish people. We don't have an

isolated life. So lots of people, they prefer to choose furniture that everybody can like, you know. Half that they prefer and half that their relatives or other people prefer. They prefer to combine them, this feeling.   (Turkish male, 30)

Hence, going to IKEA to buy a set of furniture shown in the IKEA catalogue was seen as quite rebellious, as IKEA's room-sets were considered to be quite a contrast to the Turkish norms and conventions on how to furnish a home. For example, a Turkish sitting-room (a *salon*) should, according to traditional conventions, consist of a three-person couch, a two-person couch and at least two armchairs in the same elegant style. IKEA seldom offers a sofa with an accompanying large set. Neither do they offer the heavy, large and ornamented cupboards in dark wood with glass doors (*vitrines*) that are close to mandatory in the Turkish *salons*. In the interviews, the middle-class Turkish consumers emphasized that it was high status among the new generations within the pro-European Turkish elite, to have the courage to move away from the old conventions and to buy complete 'room solutions' such as those presented in advertisements and catalogues by modern retailers like IKEA.

In contrast, among the respondents from Sweden and USA, 'individuality' meant something completely different from the views expressed by the Turkish respondents. In Sweden and USA, imitating room-sets in catalogues from mass producers like IKEA was seen as the plain opposite to rebellion. An American woman explained that:

> When I say 'common' I would mean – I would say common or uninspired . . . regular people, regular people who, primarily blue-collar, working-class . . . young, very young professionals. Uhm, it's not high income bracket. Definitely. Uhm, except the high-income bracket people will come there and furnish an apartment for their child . . . or furnish a dorm-room there . . . things like that. So definitely not an intellectual crowd *at all* . . . The idea that that place [IKEA] gives – *allows* people to have . . . I don't know . . . style who would not normally have style, is a new concept. And now, somebody graduating from college can walk in there and just get a room, I mean their whole apartment can be set up relatively cheaply. Like *anybody* can do it. *Anybody* can do it!
> (American female, 35)

Buying pre-fabricated room sets, as presented by the marketing communications of large global brands like IKEA, was considered to show a lack of imagination and ultimately a lack of individuality and uniqueness. Instead, these consumers preferred anti-commercial 'eclectic', 'authentic' and 'historical' styles. That is, styles that the Turkish consumers thought were too close to the preferences held by their own grandparents, *or* – if the styles were too historical and rural in their expressions – too similar to the less educated and lower income groups' tastes.

Hence, in the American and Swedish homes, 'individuality' was expressed by mixing styles, such as old with new, cheap with expensive, dark with light, commercial with vintage and colonial with modern. In the fieldwork in Turkish homes, in contrast, 'individuality' was expressed through the entirely modern style solutions offered by companies such as IKEA. Still, what the respondents from the three countries *did* have in common was that they all perceived themselves to be 'individualistic' and anti-traditional consumers, different from the masses, and genuinely unique.

Management perspective: the example of social gatherings

At the time of writing, IKEA, the Swedish home furnishing retailer with the mission to 'create a better everyday life for the many people' has almost 300 stores in 35 countries globally (IKEA.com, 2008). The global marketing strategy in terms of global/local standardization or adaptation is continuously under evaluation and incessantly debated within the organization [IKEA manager interview, 2005]. Meanwhile, various standardization and adaptation strategies continue to be mixed and combined across the marketing mix. For example, the popular IKEA catalogue is standardized globally but does carry some local adaptations (e.g. front covers, products in focus on central pages etc.) based on global product range strategy in combination with the specific market's choice of range. Some products are globally mandatory to offer in the stores and some are not. Manuals by Inter IKEA Systems provide mandatory guidelines for its local managers about how to present the IKEA brand in external and internal communication; and yet advertisements, TV commercials, showrooms and websites are adapted for the local markets and stores.

The general idea behind IKEA's US strategy of targeting the lower income classes is founded on two arguments linked firstly, to the IKEA 'identity' (its range) and secondly, to the business idea (to offer function and design at a reasonable price to many people). The famous IKEA idea of 'democratic design' is based on targeting lower income groups, but it is also assumed to carry some additional economic advantages: (1) the lower income groups make lower demands on service than higher income groups; (2) the lower income groups welcome IKEA furniture into all rooms of their home whereas the higher income groups generally treat IKEA as more 'transitional' and for the lower-profile rooms of the home; and (3) the low income market is larger than the higher income market.

However, IKEA's strategy of *driving* the market in terms of tastes rather than being market-*driven* entails some problems. As mentioned earlier, the lower income markets are assumed to be less dynamic and open to change than the middle-class market. Consequently, the educative strategy needs to be long-term and focus persistently on lower income classes' exposure to Scandinavian and modern styles over time. According to the IKEA managers interviewed in the study, this can be accomplished by emphasizing, and even exaggerating, the range which internally within IKEA is called 'traditional' style and actually only constitutes 20 per cent of the total range – to make it look as if it constitutes 40 per cent of the range in order to give the impression that this style is more dominant in order to attract people to the store. Once inside the store shoppers are presented, early on, with traditional styles, but the rest of the items displayed tend to derive from the more 'modern' range which constitutes 80 per cent of IKEA's total range. This way, consumers visiting the IKEA store will immediately come across the traditional styles that they are already attracted to, but at the same time they are exposed to the attractive showrooms and settings of modern Scandinavian living. The idea is that this exposure will educate the consumers into a way of thinking (and tastes) that fits well with the IKEA product range. As one IKEA manager put it:

> The more inclusive we try to be, the more it is about giving people the *courage* and to . . . yes, that's perhaps where it turns into what we could call 'education'. We also know – another thing we know about our customers, and perhaps even more about our *potential* customers, is that once we expose them to IKEA, then many of them . . . because we have done a lot of focus groups etc, and some exercises where we have invited customers and non-customers to the stores on guided tours, and it is almost always the same result. If we only get them to the store, a large majority really likes the experience. So, that's one key. (IKEA manager)

Being 'inclusive' towards the lower income groups also means, as the IKEA manager makes clear, speaking to consumers with an IKEA voice but in a way that the target group wants to listen to. This has consequences for the global versus local marketing strategies, where ethnic groups and women are prioritized as target groups within the larger low income group. In terms of the ethnic groups for example, IKEA has hired advertising and media agencies who are experts on specific ethnic communities (e.g. on the Turkish community in Berlin, and on the Mexican community in Los Angeles) and know how and where to communicate with these groups (e.g. for the Mexican community via Hispanic soap operas on TV). Part of the strategy is to slightly adapt the room-settings in the ads and in the stores to the preferences expressed by these ethnic groups. For instance in the Mexican case, IKEA undertook ethnographic research within these communities and found that specific lifestyle aspects had a large impact on why IKEA furniture was seldom chosen by this group. One of these aspects was that IKEA's images of room-settings was seldom adapted to larger groups of people. The IKEA ethnograpers found that, in the Mexican communities, gatherings at home often included more than ten people, mixing families, friends and generations.

Moreover, the colours often portrayed in IKEA's images were perceived to be quite cold and unwelcoming.

Hence, to be more inclusive, the local IKEA store interior designers created room-settings that were vastly more Mexican in style, showing smart space solutions for large dinner parties with many chairs, and textiles and kitchen work space in hues of warm terracotta colours. At the same time IKEA launched local TV commercials in Spanish, broadcast only during the soap operas watched by the targeted Hispanic groups. The overall campaign was successful and set an example within IKEA globally for the local adaptation of marketing campaigns.

From an ethical/political perspective: home violators or taste teachers?

It is impossible to discuss global marketing enterprises such as that of IKEA without commenting on the ethical and political issues involved. The scope of this case study does not allow us to elaborate on the notions of ethics and politics at length. For the sake of the discussion we will just use ethics as an entry point into questions regarding the extent of IKEA's global responsibility that far transcends the usual financial and legal considerations. By politics is meant the exercise of power through IKEA's global marketing strategies.

Globalization is a key notion in this respect. The process by which we see a world society emerging is not just the result of an autonomous historical force, outside of and beyond the control of human activity and decision making. Corporations are not bystanders and passive observers of external globalization movements. On the contrary, globalization involves changes in the relationships between regions, nations and markets worldwide. Organizations – such as IKEA – have an active part in these globalization processes. In effect, IKEA is a paramount example of an organization that brings together the economic, political and cultural aspects of globalization in one business idea. The export of Swedish made furniture is not only about the global flow of goods; it is also, as discussed above, about the export of values, preferences and taste. The export of furniture and taste moreover carries with it political effects on the ideological power relations between regions, nations and perhaps even class. In that sense, the global marketing of IKEA furniture can be seen as a good example of what Pierre Bourdieu refers to as 'symbolic power' or 'symbolic violence' (Bourdieu, 1992; Bourdieu and Passeron, 1996), i.e. the ways in which symbols and representations are involved in the exercise of power. In the educative endeavour performed by IKEA strategists, to persuade potential customers about their room-sets, a certain representation of 'the home' is imposed upon and reproduced for the target market. The marketing of Scandinavian home style and fashion to Hispanic consumer segments in USA, for instance, goes to the heart of the fundamental question of what a home is and how the social space is to be organized in everyday, domestic life. In the example of Mexican consumers discussed above, the pivotal question asked and answered by the IKEA ethnographers was: How many people make up a social gathering? In other words, the marketing of IKEA here touched upon very fundamental cultural categories such as 'space', 'room' and 'group'.

The symbolic power (or violence), found in the tension between standardization and adaptation, creates difficult (and interesting) ethical challenges for the global marketer. These issues are quite familiar to us from the practice of colonialization. The relationship between coloniser and colonized appears to be of a similar kind to that between IKEA as educator and the consumer as student of taste. The enterprise of colonialization also involved the export, also violent but in a slightly different sense of the term, of values and tastes.

Ethical issues of this cultural-political kind are obviously devoid of simple solutions or decision models. What is important, however, is to acknowledge their existence. Their solutions can only be produced in concrete and practical marketing situations.

However, culture should not be seen as a static set of values and practices, and the relationship between global standardization and adaptation is hardly as simple as that between an authoritarian colonizer and an oppressed colonized. Culture exists in incessant change and transformation. Insofar as globalization has resulted in an increased volume of encounters between different cultures, values, styles and tastes, some researchers have argued that in these meetings, hybrids emerge, in-between, as it were, the colonizer and the colonized (see Bhabha, 1994). In these hybrid amalgams resides potential resistance against colonial power. This may also be the case for the business of global IKEA. In domestic practices, such as the above mentioned social gatherings, hybrid forms of using (consuming) the home and furnishing can appear. These hybridities are hard to predict and beyond the reach and control of IKEA's marketing management activities.

QUESTIONS

1 How would you describe IKEA's strategies to overcome the problem that the American market prefers the part of the range that IKEA does not actually want to emphasize?

2 How do *you* think IKEA should manage it? Should they change their own product range or should they change (educate) the consumers? Why?

3 How can consumers' tastes be seen as related to social class?

4 How can IKEA's market-driving strategy across markets be seen from this perspective on differing consumer tastes?

5 How can IKEA manage the paradox that consumers in different parts of the world may celebrate the same themes (e.g. in this case 'individuality') when they talk, but at the same time *mean* completely different things in practice?

6 Discuss IKEA's objective to 'educate' consumers globally into Northern European tastes from an ethical perspective. What are the political implications (i.e. power effects) of this conception of marketing as education?

7 Do you think some socio-historical settings are more prone to encourage resistance between older and younger generations than others? If you think so, then why?

8 Discuss how homes around the globe will look in the future, depending on whether or not IKEA succeeds with their objectives to educate 'the many people' on how to furnish a home tastefully.

Sources

Bhabha, H.K. (1994), *The Location of Culture*, London: Routledge.

Bordieu, P. (1992), *Language and Symbolic Power*, Cambridge: Polity Press.

Bourdieu, P. and Passeron, J. (1996), *Reproduction*, London: Sage.

Ulver-Sneistrup, S. (2008), *Status-Spotting – A Consumer Cultural Exploration into Ordinary Status Consumption of 'Home' and Home Aesthetics*. PhD Dissertation, Lund: Lund Business Press.

Dodge's last stand? Or who buys cars these days?

GRY HØNGSMARK KNUDSEN, University of Southern Denmark, Denmark

Super Bowl 2010 provided the American people with many new and creative commercials, as do all the Super Bowls. Most of them can be found on YouTube; both ordinary users and commercial users upload Super Bowl advertisements. The Super Bowl is a family event, where friends and families gather around the TV for a whole day. Super Bowl 2010 was no exception, in fact it was the most viewed programme of all times in the United States.[1] One of the most hotly debated ads shown during Super Bowl 2010 was Dodge's commercial, *Man's last stand*. As with other commercials it has been uploaded to YouTube by many users, as well as by Dodge, the company behind the original ad.

The commercial tells the story of how today's men suffer all kinds of injustices during their adult life. From walking the dog early in the morning to being bored in their work life to carrying around their girl friend's lip balm, these men endure all kinds of trivialities and as the commercial argues, they do so because the justification is to drive the car they want to drive – the Dodge Charger.

On YouTube the video has gained a life of its own; it has generated intense debate as well as numerous video responses. As of 22 August 2011, it had been viewed 1,483,312 times, a total of 3,463 viewers have voted on its 'likeability', and it had garnered 2,547 comments.[2] In relation to overall YouTube viewings and comments, these numbers are not particularly significant. The impact of *Man's last stand*, however, is apparent in the many unsolicited and unofficial uploads of *Man's last stand* on YouTube and in the numerous video remakes, responses and spoofs. The significance of the commercial is the interactional activity it has been generating on YouTube. The comments and video responses show how consumers engage in various reading strategies, and how they negotiate the meaning of the commercial in a collective space. Apparently, all the viewers agree that the commercial is about masculinity today, but they don't all interpret the validity of the message in the same way.

The social context that informs the reception of *Man's last stand* is the sociological debate about gender and especially the 'poor boys' debate (a debate not about poverty or economic status but about social position; 'poor' as in 'unfortunate'). The social sounding board for this individual struggle for a coherent masculinity is the Western 'poor boys' debate. The debate is about how boys and men become alienated from the educational system, how they lose the best job opportunities to the better educated women, and how in general they have little power over their everyday lives because of the empowerment of women and a general feminization of society.

Man's last stand

In the Dodge video, a montage is shown of four different males aged somewhere between the early thirties to the early forties. The first three men have motionless faces. The only move they make is to shrug their shoulders as if they were sighing. A voice-over supplements the impression of powerlessness and weakness by listing the things these men have to endure from their girlfriends, wives and bosses. The last man in the video is the exception. He is dressed in a business suit, whereas the other men are dressed more casually. The last man in the video does not sigh; instead as the camera zooms in on his face, he stares back without any movement. He is completely calm, yet vigilant – this is a man who has not given up! And the audience soon understands why. As the camera zooms in on his eyes, a roaring sound is heard, and the video cuts into a Dodge racing into the unknown. The last man's last stand is his Dodge Charger, which makes up for all the pressure, pain and frustration that life as an adult male living with women in a Western society entails.

http://www.youtube.com/watch?v=2RyPamyWotM
The commercial takes part in the debate about 'poor boys' and introduces the male viewer to a masculine construction process through the voice-over, as it emphasizes how far men go to please their girlfriends, wives and bosses. Also Dodge's own comment (attached to the video) highlights the breadwinner as self-sacrificing yet in need of a stronger feeling of masculinity: 'You've sacrificed a lot, but surely there is a limit to your chivalry. Drive the car you want to drive.'[3]

By speaking directly to the consumer through the use of 'you' in the text, the consumer is invited to put himself in the place of the men in the commercial and thereby to experience the emasculated tension of living the life of a breadwinner. The last man in the commercial introduces the solution on how to maintain a feeling of masculinity. Through his more upright posture and his business suit, he communicates a different and stronger masculinity than the three previous men. The business suit implies that the last man is someone who can successfully balance the responsibility of the breadwinner with masculinity in the modern world, without becoming a wimp. Thus, in the narrative of the commercial, the consumer is first confronted with his own lack of masculinity and next provided with a consumption solution to his problem.

The context of reception facilitates certain readings, and in the case of *Man's last stand*, the surrounding gender debate becomes part of the dialogue as consumers on YouTube respond to the commercial. Male and female consumers respond in many ways to the commercial, also a large number of video responses are connected to the commercial.

Woman's last stand

There are many variations in the video responses to *Man's last stand* on YouTube, and most of them are called *Woman's last stand*. Most of the videos paraphrase *Man's last stand* only with angry women as protagonists in the montage. The voice-over lists inequalities that many women experience during their adult lives, such as lower pay, sexual harassment, and mediated pressure to look thin and beautiful. However, contrary to the commercial, there is no car in sight to offer the women a well-earned reprieve from an unjust and unpleasant life. The videos' format is a paraphrased argument that is limited to the montage and the voice-over; it is not about selling cars, but about making a response to Dodge.

http://www.youtube.com/watch?v=ou5Ens-qNRc&feature=related

The discussion in comments and videos attached to Dodge's commercial implies that the discourse on gender equality is trenchant in the interpretive community that has been evoked by the commercial. The comments overflow with strong expressions, such as *feminazis* and *weiny* [sic] *bitches*, which suggests that the commentators have a strong emotional involvement in the discourse. At stake here is the political, social and cultural discourse on gender and the various interpretations of it. As a culturally embedded corporation, Dodge has entered into one of the omnipresent discourses in today's Western world. The viewers are caught in a discourse with very limited possibilities, which in turn polarizes the interpretations. In this case, the commercial becomes a battleground that allows consumers to negotiate and challenge the discourse, thereby entering the dialogue and co-creating meaning. In sum, the

usually implicit assumptions about other consumers and their knowledge and behaviour occurs in the discursive space of YouTube where the discourse is laid out openly.

Interestingly, it seems that Dodge has envisaged more perspectives on the discourse by making the commercial *Getaway car*, which places a woman as the strong, no nonsense, and independent character. The viewing ratings and comments attached to this second commercial were nowhere near as numerous as they were for *Man's last stand*, and since it has been removed from Dodge's official channel, the material related to *Getaway car* is limited.

Getaway car

Getaway car is about a woman who is leaving her boyfriend. She is seen standing on the lawn in front of a typical American suburban home at night. She seems resolute as she stands there watching her angry boyfriend throw stuff out of the upstairs window while he screams at her about whether she is also tired of this or that object that he sends flying to the grass below. Finally, he throws her jacket out. She bends down, but rather than take the jacket she reaches into the pocket and gets the car keys out. She turns around, walks to the car, gets in, and races off. The ending tagline is *Dodge – we make getaway cars.*

http://www.youtube.com/watch?v=Sro4p_f9HZE

Getaway car, however, did not resonate with the audience to the same extent that *Man's last stand* did. Part of the reason has to do with media convergence. Messages spread across media forms – and especially a commercial shown during Super Bowl – are amplified. But the gender discourse is also significantly reduced in *Getaway car*. Anyone can experience the need for a getaway car, but *Man's last stand* unmistakably echoes the poor boys debate and through that actualizes the interpretive community. Thus, the commercial *Man's last stand* dis-embeds a social, political, and cultural discourse from the ordinary public space and political world, and re-embeds it into popular culture in the commercial and onto YouTube, where the interpretive community emerges. The success of *Man's last stand* is directly related to the commercial's triumphant articulation of the poor boys debate.

It seems that the commercial address using a similar femininity negotiation has been seen as less to the point and thereby lacking authenticity for the potential audience and interpretive community. Where *Man's last stand* reaches directly into the hearts of American men by taking their masculinity seriously, *Getaway car* is not as precise when it comes to understanding the American women's existential dilemma. As she is portrayed in *Getaway car*, she is less than likable. She seems cold and unsympathetic to her ex-boyfriend as she races away in the car. And thus, the female target audience may simply not recognize themselves in the commercial and thereby not feel a need to interact with the message.

Further, the break-up story is a generic one, and even if it is supposed to be empowering to women, since the girl is the one walking away, the story does not pinpoint the feminine condition specifically. Consequently, one can speculate that *Getaway car* has been removed from the Dodge website in order to create an unambiguous message to the consumers. In this case, Dodge has foreseen the response from the interpretive community, but they haven't built it into the original commercial; rather, they have offered a different manifestation of the discourse. The text of *Getaway car* renders a woman as the strong independent person who lacks the interest or capacity to engage in a conversation about the break-up. In fact, this portrayal of women highlights the other side of the poor boys debate: women have become so independent and free that they no longer need or care about men; rather, women have become (ab) users of men.

QUESTIONS

1 Discuss the possibility that *Man's last stand* is Dodge's attempt to reach their brand community.

2 Consider who the audience on YouTube is. Do you think it is a good communication strategy to address the brand community via YouTube?

3 Could *Man's last stand* and *Getaway car* be ironic comments on the poor boys debate?

4 Who buys cars?

Sources

1. http://tvbythenumbers.com/2010/02/08/super-bowl-xliv-becomes-most-watched-program-of-all-time/41392, accessed 6 January 2010.

2. http://www.youtube.com/watch?v=2RyPamyWotM&list=FLmVrWHqn_5pjroB-fMIycoQ&index=26, accessed 22 August 2011.

3. http://www.youtube.com/watch?v=2RyPamyWotM&list=FLmVrWHqn_5pjroB-fMIycoQ&index=26, accessed 8/22/2011.

Part B

HOW CONSUMERS SEE THE WORLD AND THEMSELVES

The second part of this book deals with the questions of 'Who am I?' and 'How do I see the world?'. Building on the initial themes set out in the first part, these chapters examine how consumers' perceptions affect their understanding and interpretation of the marketplace, how they use consumption in constructing their sense of self, and how motivations, values and lifestyles affect their consumption.

4 PERCEPTION

CHAPTER OBJECTIVES

When you finish reading this chapter you will understand why:

→ Perception is a three-stage process that translates raw stimuli into meaning.

→ The design of a product today is a key driver of its success or failure.

→ Products and commercial messages often appeal to our senses, but because of the profusion of these messages most of them won't influence us.

→ The concept of a sensory threshold is important for marketing communication.

→ Subliminal advertising is a controversial – but largely ineffective – way to talk to consumers.

→ We interpret the stimuli to which we do pay attention according to learned patterns and expectations.

→ The field of semiotics helps us to understand how marketers use symbols to create meaning.

THE EUROPEAN VACATION has been wonderful, and this stop in Lisbon is no exception. Still, after two weeks of eating his way through some of the Continent's finest pastry shops and restaurants, Gary's getting a bit of a craving for his family's favourite snack – a good old American box of Oreos and an ice-cold carton of milk. Unbeknownst to his wife, Janeen, he had stashed away some cookies 'just in case' – this was the time to break them out.

Now, all he needs is the milk. On an impulse, Gary decides to surprise Janeen with a mid-afternoon treat. He sneaks out of the hotel room while she's napping and finds the nearest *grosa*. When he heads to the small refrigerated section, though, he's puzzled – no milk here. Undaunted, Gary asks the clerk, '*Leite, por favor*?' The clerk quickly smiles and points to a rack in the middle of the store piled with little white square boxes. No, that can't be right – Gary resolves to work on his Portuguese. He repeats the question, and again he gets the same answer.

Finally, he investigates and sure enough he sees the boxes with labels saying they contain something called ultra heat treated (UHT) milk. Nasty! Who in the world would drink milk out of a little box that's been sitting on a warm shelf for who knows how long? Gary dejectedly returns to the hotel, his snack time fantasies crumbling like so many stale cookies.

INTRODUCTION

We live in a world overflowing with sensations. Wherever we turn, we are bombarded by a symphony of colours, sounds and odours. Some of the 'notes' in this symphony occur naturally, such as the barking of a dog, the shadows of the evening sky or the heady smell of a rose bush. Others come from people; the person sitting next to you might have dyed blonde hair, bright pink jeans, and be wearing enough perfume to make your eyes water.

Marketers certainly contribute to this commotion. Consumers are never far from advertisements, product packages, radio and television commercials, and advertising hoardings that clamour for their attention. Whether it is the (culturally learned) bias of being suspicious of unrefrigerated UHT milk, the purchasing fresh fish from a vending machine in Spain,[1] or listening to a car blast out teeth-rattling 50 cent cuts from booming car speakers, each of us copes with the bombardment of sensations in the marketplace as we pay attention to some stimuli, and tune out others. When we do make a decision to purchase, we are responding not only to these influences but to our interpretations of them.

This chapter focuses on the process of perception, in which sensations are absorbed by the consumer and used to interpret the surrounding world. After discussing the stages of this process, the chapter examines how the five senses (sight, smell, sound, touch and taste) affect consumers. It also highlights some of the ways in which marketers develop products and communications that appeal to the senses.

The chapter emphasizes that the way in which a marketing stimulus is presented plays a role in determining whether the consumer will make sense of it or even notice it at all. The techniques and marketing practices that make messages more likely to be noticed are discussed. Finally, the chapter discusses the process of interpretation, in which the stimuli that are noticed by the consumer are organized and assigned meaning.

THE PERCEPTUAL PROCESS

As you sit in a lecture hall, you may find your attention shifting. One minute you are concentrating on the lecture, and in the next, you catch yourself daydreaming about the weekend ahead before you realize that you are missing some important points and tune back into the lecture.

People undergo stages of information processing in which stimuli are input and stored. However, we do not passively process whatever information happens to be present. Only a very small number of the stimuli in our environment are ever noticed. Of these, an even smaller number are attended to. And the stimuli that do enter our consciousness are not processed objectively. The meaning of a stimulus is interpreted by the individual, who is influenced by their unique biases, needs and experiences. These three stages of **exposure (or sensation)**, **attention** and **interpretation** make up the process of perception. The stages involved in selecting and interpreting stimuli are illustrated in Figure 4.1, which provides an overview of the perceptual process.

From sensation to perception

Sensation refers to the immediate response of our sensory receptors (e.g. eyes, ears, nose, mouth, fingers) to such basic stimuli as light, colour and sound. **Perception** is the process by which these stimuli are selected, organized and interpreted. We process raw data (sensation); however, the study of perception focuses on what we add to or take away from these sensations as we assign meaning to them.

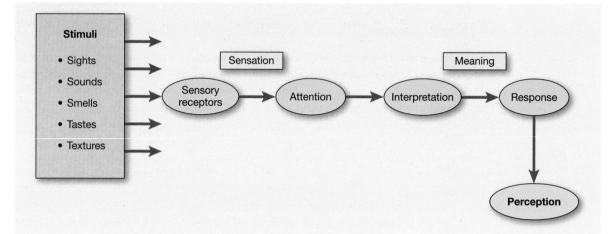

Figure 4.1 An overview of the perceptual process

The subjective nature of perception is demonstrated by this ad.

Courtesy of McCann Erickson.

The subjective nature of perception is demonstrated by this 'Ugly Truth/Your beauty Up in Smoke' ad. Whether from smoking, or from other 'long term' damaging behaviours to your appearance, such as going to tanning salons, young people tend to discount or outright reject messages of 'this could be you if you continue to do this' (smoke, ultra-tanning). Such interpretations or assumptions stem from **schemas**, or organized collections of beliefs and feelings. That is, we tend to group the objects we see as having similar characteristics, and the schema to which an object is assigned is a crucial determinant of how we choose to evaluate this object at a later time. I'm youthful, beautiful, cool looking now . . . these warnings don't apply to me, so I pay little or no attention to them.

The perceptual process can be illustrated by the purchase of a new aftershave. We have learned to equate aftershave with romantic appeal, so we search for cues that (we believe) will increase our attractiveness. We make our selection by considering such factors as the image associated with each alternative and the design of the bottle, as well as the actual scent. We thus access a small portion of the raw data available and process it to be consistent with our wants. These expectations are largely affected by our cultural background. For example, a male consumer self-conscious about his masculinity may react negatively to an overtly feminine brand name, even though other men may respond differently.[2]

A perceptual process can be broken down into the following stages:[3]

1 *Primitive categorization*, in which the basic characteristics of a stimulus are isolated: our male consumer feels he needs to bolster his image, so he chooses aftershave.

2 *Cue check*, in which the characteristics are analysed in preparation for the selection of a schema: everyone has his own unique, more or less developed schemas or categories for different types of aftershave, such as 'down-to-earth macho', 'mysterious' or 'fancy French'. We use certain cues, such as the colour of the bottle, to decide in which schema a particular cologne fits.

3 *Confirmation check*, in which the schema is selected: the consumer may decide that a brand falls into his 'mysterious' schema.

4 *Confirmation completion*, in which a decision is made as to what the stimulus is: the consumer decides he has made the right choice, and then reinforces this decision by considering the colour of the bottle and the interesting name of the aftershave.

Such experiences illustrate the importance of the perceptual process for product positioning. In many cases, consumers use a few basic dimensions to categorize competing products or services, and then evaluate each alternative in terms of its relative standing on these dimensions.

This tendency has led to the use of a very useful positioning tool – a **perceptual map**. By identifying the important dimensions and then asking consumers to place competitors within this space, marketers can answer some crucial strategic questions, such as which product alternatives are seen by consumers as similar or dissimilar, and what opportunities exist for new products that possess attributes not represented by current brands. Figure 4.2 offers a perceptual map of the iconic Burberry brand, showing its 'old' position from the 1980s and 1990s, and the shift in perceptions of the brand in more recent years.

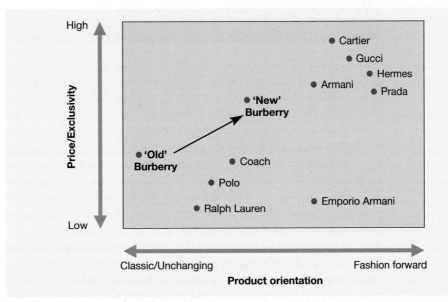

Figure 4.2 Perceptual map of the Burberry brand, relative to competitors

MARKETING OPPORTUNITY

While working in his olive grove in the rugged mountains near the Andalusian town of Jaén last fall, Juan Manuel Melero Aibar was approached by a man admiring one of his olive trees. After years of close pruning to optimize production, the tree resembled a very large bonsai. The stranger, Sr Aibar recalls, told him he could get €50,000 for it at auction. What piqued the potential buyer's interest in the tree wasn't the circumference of its trunk, which measured eight metres, or its yield of olives, roughly 600 kilograms every other year. It was the tree's age – estimated by a representative from the Agriculture Department at 1,200 to 1,500 years.

Sr Aibar decided not to sell his tree, and the stranger gave up trying to convince him to part with it. But a growing number of other farmers in the region have been less reluctant to cash in on theirs. Trees considered 'ancient' – more than 500 years old – can sell for several thousand euros apiece.

Olive trees, called olivos in Spanish and said originally to have been planted on the Iberian peninsula by the Romans, have stood witness to much of Spain's history. Today the country's vast groves make it the world's largest producer of olive oil. Many of these olive trees have a striking visual appeal: gnarled, thick trunks with cropped branches and silvery-green leaves. Landscape architects seek out old trees with aesthetic personality, or to suit a particular buyer's garden. During a 10-year building boom along Spain's southern coast in the early

2000s from Tarifa to Valencia, the trees – often uprooted by developers – found new homes in Spain and abroad as garden ornaments.

Buyers usually are not interested in the fruit the trees produce. They want works of landscape art. 'Olives are in their prime in terms of production capacity at 25 to 40 years old,' says Charles Butler Mackay, an olive grower in Jaén and publisher of the *Olive Oil Gazette*, an online journal of the olive business. 'That's centuries ago.' To farmers, this is reason enough to sell the trees; if they aren't adding to their annual yield – and are worth thousands of euros – why not offload them?

Most of the old trees are replanted in tourist areas, especially exclusive golf courses such as Monte Mayor and La Zagaleta courses in Malaga, to add a look of regional authenticity. Aaron Mount, owner of Ancient Olive Trees, a California-based transplant service that moves trees from Europe and Latin America to the US, says, 'When resorts and hotels open, they want to look established from day one. An old tree helps create that feel.'

A substantial number of trees are sold each year to individuals looking to adorn private gardens. Mr Mount says the appeal to buyers is the one-of-a-kind status they offer. 'Olive trees are like antiques,' he says. 'There is a story tied to each one, in this case stories that cover kingdoms rising and falling.'[4]

SENSORY SYSTEMS

When guests at Omni luxury hotels visit the hotel chain's website to reserve a room, they hear the sound of soft chimes playing. The signature scent of lemongrass and green tea hits them as they enter the lobby. In their rooms, they will find eucalyptus bath salts and Sensation Bars; minibars stocked with items such as mojito-flavoured jelly beans and miniature Zen gardens.

Welcome to the new era of **sensory marketing**, where companies pay extra attention to the impact of sensations on our product experiences. From hotels to carmakers to brewers, they recognize that our senses help us to decide which products appeal to us – and which ones stand out from a host of similar offerings in the marketplace. In this section, we'll take a closer look at how some smart marketers use our sensory systems to create a competitive advantage.

Sensory inputs evoke historical imagery, in which events that actually occurred are recalled. Fantasy imagery results when an entirely new, imaginary experience is the response to sensory data. These responses are an important part of **hedonic consumption**, or the multi-sensory, fantasy and emotional aspects of consumers' interactions with products.[5] The data that we receive from our sensory systems determine how we respond to products.

Although we usually trust our sensory receptors to give us an accurate account of the external environment, new technology is making the linkage between our senses and reality more

Virtual reality.
AFP/Getty Images.

questionable. Computer-simulated environments, or *virtual reality*, allow surgeons to 'cut into' a person without drawing blood or an architect to see a building design from different perspectives. This technology, which creates a three-dimensional perceptual environment which the viewer experiences as being virtually real, is already being adapted to everyday pursuits, such as virtual reality games.

Enterprising business people will no doubt continue to find new ways to adapt this technology for consumers' entertainment – the recent developments in 'virtual catalogues' now allow a person to browse through a shop without leaving their armchair (still no progress on delivering smells to your web browser, but it will come!). In this section, we will take a brief look at some of the processes involved in the business applications of sensory stimuli.

Vision

Sure, Apple's products usually work pretty well – but that's not why many people buy them. Sleek styling and simple, compact features telegraph an aura of modernity, sophistication and just plain 'cool'. Marketers rely heavily on visual elements in advertising, store design and packaging. They communicate meanings on the *visual channel* through a product's colour, size and styling.

Colour in the marketplace

Colours may even influence our emotions more directly. Evidence suggests that some colours (particularly red) create feelings of arousal and stimulate appetite, and others (such as blue) create more relaxing feelings – American Express launched its Blue card after its research found that people describe the colour as 'providing a sense of limitlessness and peace'.[6] Advertisements of products presented against a backdrop of blue are better liked than when shown against a red background, and cross-cultural research indicates a consistent preference for blue whether people live in Canada or Hong Kong.[7]

People who complete tasks when the words or images appear on red backgrounds perform better when they have to remember details, while they excel at tasks that require an imaginative response when these are displayed on blue backgrounds. Olympic athletes who wear red uniforms are more likely to defeat competitors in blue uniforms, and men rate women who wear red as more attractive than those who wear blue. In one study, interior designers created bars decorated primarily in red, yellow or blue and people were invited to choose one to hang out in. More people chose the yellow and red rooms, and these guests were more social and active – and ate more. But, partygoers in the blue room stayed longer.[8]

Some reactions to colour come from learned associations. In Western countries, black is the colour of mourning, whereas in some Eastern countries, notably Japan, white plays this role. In addition, we associate the colour black with power.

Other reactions are a result of biological and cultural differences. Women are drawn towards brighter tones and they are more sensitive to subtle shadings and patterns. Some scientists attribute this to biology; females see colour better than males do, and men are 16 times more likely to be colour blind. Age also influences our responsiveness to colour. As we get older, our eyes mature and our vision takes on a yellow cast. Colours look duller to older people, so they prefer white and other bright tones. This helps to explain why mature consumers are much more likely to choose a white car – Lexus, which sells heavily in this demographic, makes 60 per cent of its vehicles in white.

We now know that perceptions of a colour depend on both its physical wavelength and how the mind responds to that stimulus. Yellow is in the middle of wavelengths the human eye can detect so it is the brightest and attracts attention. The *Yellow Pages* originally were coloured yellow to heighten the attention level of bored telephone operators.[9] However, our culture and even our language affect the colours we see. For example, the Welsh language has no words that correspond to green, blue, grey or brown in English, but it uses other colours that English speakers don't (including one that covers part of green, part of grey, and the whole of our blue). Hungarian has two words for what we call red; Navajo Indians in North America have a single word for blue and green, but two words for black.[10]

Because colours elicit such strong emotional reactions, obviously the choice of a *colour palette* is a key issue in package design. These decisions help to 'colour' our expectations of what's inside the package. When it launched a white cheese as a 'sister product' to an existing blue 'Castello' cheese, a Danish company introduced it in a red package under the name of Castello Bianco. They chose this colour to provide maximum visibility on store shelves. Although taste tests were very positive, sales were disappointing. A subsequent analysis of consumer interpretations showed that the red packaging and the name gave the consumers wrong associations with the product type and its degree of sweetness. Danish consumers had trouble associating the colour red with the white cheese. Also, the name 'Bianco' connoted a sweetness that was incompatible with the actual taste of the product. The company relaunched it in a white package and named it 'White Castello'. Almost immediately, sales more than doubled.[11]

Some colour combinations come to be so strongly associated with a corporation that they become known as the company's **trade dress**, and the company may even be granted exclusive use of these colours. For example, Eastman Kodak has successfully protected its trade dress of yellow, black and red in court. As a rule, however, judges grant trade dress protection only when consumers might be confused about what they buy because of similar coloration of a competitor's packages.[12]

Of course, fashion trends strongly influence our colour preferences so it's no surprise that we tend to encounter a 'hot' colour on clothing and in home designs in one season that something else replaces the next season (as when the *fashionistas* proclaim: 'Brown is the new black!'). These styles do not happen by accident; most people don't know (but now *you* do) that a handful of firms produce *colour forecasts* that manufacturers and retailers buy so they can be sure they stock up on the next hot hue. For example, Pantone, Inc. (one of these colour arbiters), listed these colours as among its favourites for Fall 2011 women's fashions:[13]

- **Bamboo**: Like a filtered sunset on the waning days of fall, Bamboo is a standout yellow with a subtle green undertone.
- **Honeysuckle**: This playful, reddish pink works with any other colour in the palette, especially fall staples like Coffee Liqueur and Nougat.
- **Phlox**: A magical, deep purple with a hint of mystery.

The text in the ad reads 'Where would the bright orange be without Dreft?' Orange is the national colour of The Netherlands, so the ad simultaneously underlines the colour-protecting qualities of the product and, through the national colour code, refers to the strength of the Dutch nation.

Courtesy of Procter & Gamble.

In a given year, certain colours appear to be 'hot' and show up over and over again in clothing, home furnishings, cars and so on. But favourite colours disappear as fast as they come, to be replaced by another set of 'hot' colours the next year or season.

Smell

Odours can stir emotions or create a calming feeling. They can invoke memories or relieve stress. One study found that consumers who viewed ads for either flowers or chocolate and who also were exposed to flowery or chocolaty odours spent more time processing the product information and were more likely to try different alternatives within each product category.[14] Many consumers control the odours in their environments and this growing interest has spawned a lot of new products since Glade marketed the first air freshener to suburban families in 1956. Today, younger people are at the forefront of scented air as they take advantage of plug-ins, fragrance fans, diffusers and potpourri. Sensing a growing market, Procter & Gamble introduced Febreze air products in 2004 and appealed to twenty-somethings by making air freshener products seem cool – Scentstories is a Febreze dispenser P&G designed to look like a CD player, complete with 'stop' and 'play' buttons that radiate scents rather than music.[15] Almost anything is fair game to be scented today; even the country of Lithuania created a perfume (appropriately called Lithuania) it will use in hotels and embassies to convey the country's image.

Consumers' love of fragrances has contributed to a very large industry. Because this market is extremely competitive (30–40 new scents are introduced each year) and expensive (it costs an average of £30 million to introduce a new fragrance), manufacturers are scrambling to find new ways to expand the use of scents and odours in our daily lives. While traditional floral scents, such as rose and jasmine, are still widely used, newer fragrances feature such scents as melon peach (Elizabeth Arden's *Sunflowers*) and a blend of peach, mandarin orange, waterlily and white cloud rose (*Sun Moon Stars* by Karl Lagerfeld).[16] A later trend, supported by the marketing efforts of, among others, Calvin Klein, are perfumes positioned as unisex. In addition

127

This ad metaphorically illustrates the natural quality and taste sensation of a lemon as a substitute for salt.

Sunkist Growers, Inc.

to the perfume market, home fragrance products, consisting primarily of potpourri, room sprays and atomizers, drawer liners, sachets and scented candles, represent important markets. But the use of smell goes further than that. An association of employers in the wood industry used a scratch'n'sniff card to convince potential apprentices of the advantages of smell in the wood industry compared with other professions.[17]

Sound

Coca-Cola chose an obscure Somalian musician named N-Kaan and made his song *Wavin' Flag* the centerpiece of its $300 million global advertising campaign linked to the 2010 World Cup. The company rerecorded the song in over 20 regional versions that included duets with local musicians (the US version featured David Guetta and Will.i.am). The tune became embedded with the world games as people around the world found themselves singing it. As a music industry executive explained, 'Coke has used a technique we call audio watermarking. This is a popular and well-known trick that has been around for centuries and used by composers and producers to weave a sound/motif into a piece of music . . . watermarking acts like an "earworm", which gets inside our brains and becomes so compulsive that we go around humming it as we walk down the street and not understanding why. We effectively become living, walking, singing commercials for Coke.'[18]

Many aspects of sound affect people's feelings and behaviours. One British company stresses the importance of the sound a packaging gives when opened, after having watched consumers open, close and reopen it several times during a test, clearly also listening to the right sound of the opening procedure.[19] Two areas of research that have widespread applications in consumer contexts are the effects of background music on mood and the influence of speaking rate on attitude change and message comprehension.

Muzak is heard by millions of people every day. This so-called 'functional music' is played in stores, shopping centres and offices either to relax or stimulate consumers. There is general agreement that muzak contributes to the well-being and buying activities of customers, but no scientific proof exists. *Time compression* is a technique used by broadcasters to manipulate perceptions of sound. It is a way to pack more information into a limited time by speeding up an announcer's voice in commercials. The speaking rate is typically accelerated to about 120 to 130 per cent of normal. Most people fail to notice this effect.

The evidence for the effectiveness of time compression is mixed. It has been shown to increase persuasion in some situations but to reduce it in others. One explanation for a positive effect is that the listener uses a person's speaking rate to infer whether the speaker is confident; people seem to think that fast talkers must know what they are talking about.

Another explanation is that the listener is given less time to elaborate on the assertions made in the commercial. The acceleration disrupts normal responses to the ad and changes the cues used to form judgements about its content. This change can either hinder or facilitate attitude change, depending on other conditions.[20]

Touch

Hint to retailers: follow Apple's lead and encourage customers to handle your products in the store! One recent study demonstrated the potential power of touch; the researchers found that participants who simply touched an item (an inexpensive coffee mug) for 30 seconds or less created a greater level of attachment to the product; this connection in turn boosted what they were willing to pay for it.[21] Britain's Asda grocery chain removed the wrapping from several brands of toilet tissue in its stores so that shoppers could feel and compare textures. The result, the retailer says, was soaring sales for its own in-store brand, resulting in a 50 per cent increase in shelf space for the line.[22]

There are considerable cultural differences in the world as well as within Europe concerning the appropriate amount and kind of touching in interpersonal interactions. In general, northern Europeans touch less than their southern European counterparts. Many British think the French shake hands for too long.[23] Sensations that reach the skin, whether from a

We have a tendency to want to touch objects, although typing or using a mouse are skills we have to learn. The proliferation of touchscreens on computers, ATM machines, digital cameras, GPS devices and e-readers is an outgrowth of a philosophy of computer design known as *natural user interface*. This approach incorporates habitual human movements that we don't have to learn. Sony decided to offer touchscreens on its e-readers after its engineers repeatedly observed people in focus groups automatically swipe the screen of its older, nontouch models. Touchscreens also appear on exercise machines, in hospitals, at airport check-in terminals, and on Virgin America airplanes.

Shutterstock.com

Table 4.1 Tactile oppositions to fabrics

Perception	Male	Female	
High-class	Wool	Silk	Fine
Low-class	Denim	Cotton	↕
	Heavy	Light	Coarse

luxurious massage or the bite of a winter wind, stimulate or relax us. Researchers even have shown that touch can influence sales interactions. In one study, diners whom waiting staff touched gave bigger tips, and the same researchers reported that food demonstrators in a supermarket who lightly touched customers had better luck in getting shoppers to try a new snack product and to redeem coupons for the brand.[24]

Tactile cues have symbolic meaning. People associate the textures of fabrics and other products with underlying product qualities. The perceived richness or quality of the material in clothing, bedding or upholstery is linked to its 'feel', whether it is rough or smooth, soft or stiff. A smooth fabric such as silk is equated with luxury, while denim is considered practical and durable. The vibration of a mobile phone against the owner's body signals a personal telephone call coming in, as well as some degree of respect about not disturbing others in the area. Some of these tactile/quality associations are summarized in Table 4.1. Fabrics that are composed of rare materials or that require a high degree of processing to achieve their smoothness or fineness tend to be more expensive and thus are seen as being classier. Similarly, lighter, more delicate textures are assumed to be feminine. Roughness is often positively valued for men, while smoothness is sought by women.

Taste

Our taste receptors contribute to our experience of many products. Sensory analysis is used to account for the human perception of sensory product qualities. One study used sensory analysis to assess butter biscuits: the crispness, buttery-taste, rate of melt, density, 'molar packing' (the amount of biscuit that sticks to the teeth) and the 'notes' of the biscuit, such as sweetness, saltiness or bitterness.[25]

Food companies go to great lengths to ensure that their products taste as they should. Philips' highly successful Senseo coffee machine produces a creamy head of foam on the top of a cup of home-brewed coffee.[26] Companies may use a group of 'sensory panellists' as tasters. These consumers are recruited because they have superior sensory abilities, and are then given six months' training. Or they rely on lay people, i.e. ordinary consumers. In a blind taste test, panellists rate the products of a company and its competitors on a number of dimensions. The results of such studies are important to discover both different consumer preferences and, thus, different consumer segments, and the positioning of a company or a brand in terms of the most important sensory qualities of the product.[27]

Are blind taste tests worth their salt? While taste tests often provide valuable information, their results can be misleading when it is forgotten that objective taste is only one component of product evaluation. Sometimes taste test failures can be overcome by repositioning the product. For example, Vernor's ginger ale did poorly in a taste test against leading ginger ales. When the research team introduced it as a new type of soft drink with a tangier taste, it won easily. As an executive noted, 'People hated it because it didn't meet the preconceived expectations of what a ginger ale should be.'[28]

SENSORY THRESHOLDS

If you have ever blown a dog whistle and watched pets respond to a sound you cannot hear, you will know that there are some stimuli that people simply are not capable of perceiving. And, of course, some people are better able to pick up sensory information than are others. The science that focuses on how the physical environment is integrated into our personal, subjective world is known as **psychophysics**. By understanding some of the physical laws that govern what we are capable of responding to, this knowledge can be translated into marketing strategies.

The absolute threshold

When we define the lowest intensity of a stimulus that can be registered on a sensory channel, we speak of a threshold for that receptor. The **absolute threshold** refers to the minimum amount of stimulation that can be detected on a sensory channel. The sound emitted by a dog whistle is too high to be detected by human ears, so this stimulus is beyond our auditory absolute threshold. The absolute threshold is an important consideration in designing marketing stimuli. A billboard along the motorway might have the most entertaining story ever written, but this genius is wasted if the print is too small for passing motorists to read it.

The differential threshold

The **differential threshold** refers to the ability of a sensory system to detect changes or differences between two stimuli. A commercial that is intentionally produced in black and white might be noticed on a colour television because the intensity of colour differs from the programme that preceded it. The same commercial being watched on a black-and-white television would not be seen as different and might be ignored altogether.

The issue of when and if a change will be noticed is relevant to many marketing situations. Sometimes a marketer may want to ensure that a change is noticed, such as when merchandise is offered at a discount. In other situations, the fact that a change has been made is downplayed, as in the case of price increases or when the size of a product, such as a chocolate bar, is decreased.

A consumer's ability to detect a difference between two stimuli is relative. A whispered conversation that might be unintelligible on a noisy street can suddenly become public and embarrassing knowledge in a quiet library. It is the relative difference between the decibel level of the conversation and its surroundings, rather than the loudness of the conversation itself, that determines whether the stimulus will register.

The minimum change in a stimulus that can be detected is also known as the **JND**, which stands for 'just noticeable difference'. In the nineteenth century, Ernst Weber, a psychophysicist, found that the amount of change that is necessary to be noticed is related to the original intensity of the stimulus. The stronger the initial stimulus, the greater the change must be for it to be noticed. This relationship is known as **Weber's Law**. Many companies choose to update their packages periodically, making small changes that will not necessarily be noticed at the time. When a product icon is updated, the manufacturer does not want people to lose their identification with a familiar symbol.

Weber's Law, ironically, is a challenge to green marketers who try to reduce the sizes of packages when they produce concentrated (and more earth-friendly) versions of their products. Makers of laundry detergent brands have to convince their customers to pay the same price for about half the detergent. Also, because of pressure from powerful retailers such as Wal-Mart that want to fit more bottles on their shelves, the size of detergent bottles is shrinking significantly. Procter & Gamble, Unilever and Henkel all maintain that their new concentrated versions will allow people to wash the same number of loads with half the detergent. One perceptual trick they're using to try to convince consumers of this is the re-design of the bottle cap: both P&G and Church & Dwight use a cap with a broader base and shorter sides to persuade consumers that they need a smaller amount.[29]

PERCEPTUAL SELECTION

Augmented reality

Perceptual thresholds become even more interesting as we enter the new age of **augmented reality**. This term refers to media that combine a physical layer with a digital layer to create a combined experience. If you've ever watched a 3D movie with those clunky glasses, you've experienced one form of augmented reality. Or, if you've seen those ads changing to new and different ads on the walls surrounding the football pitch, you've also encountered AR in a simple form.

More likely, though, in the next few years you'll live AR through your smartphone. New apps like Google Goggles (for Android phones) and Layar (for Android and Apple devices) impose a layer of words and pictures on to whatever you see in your phone's viewer.

Augmented reality apps open new worlds of information (and marketing communica-tions). Do you want to know the bio-sketch of the singer you see on a CD cover? Who painted that cool mural in your local bar? How much did that house you were looking at sell for last month? Just point your smartphone at each and the information will be superimposed on your screen.[30]

Web-based AR

These techniques use your PC and webcam to offer an enhanced experience often via a marker, image or through motion capture. For example, the Fashionista dressing-room app you'll find in the online fashion boutique Tobi lets you 'virtually' try on clothing items using your webcam and a marker on a printed piece of paper.

Kiosk-based AR

This is similar to web-based AR, but you can often find more powerful applications that use 3D or facial tracking. At a toy store, shoppers can hold up a boxed Lego set to an in-store kiosk, and the kiosk will show an image of them holding the put-together Lego creation. At several shopping malls in the US, Chevrolet showcases its key brands in kiosks that let shop-pers use a virtual 'professional air sprayer' and their fingers to paint the car, then move on to choose the rims, tyres, decorative stripes, and other elements. When visitors finish building their cars, they are handed a 6 × 9-inch card with an augmented reality marker on the back. The person holds the card up to a camera mounted on a 65-inch TV screen that reads the marker and creates a computer-generated 3-D model of a Camaro. By moving the card, the person can 'drive' the car as they hear the engine roar.[31]

Mobile AR

These applications use the viewfinder on a mobile phone to access enhanced digital informa-tion. The iButterfly app the Dentsu advertising agency created in Japan lets you track and find digital butterflies using your iPhone GPS and camera. Hold your iPhone camera up at desig-nated spots and when you look at your surroundings through the camera, you'll see animated butterflies flapping by. Each iButterfly contains coupons for nearby businesses.[32] eBay's Fashion app 'See It On' allows the user to virtually try on sunglasses in real time. The app uses facial recognition to identify the user and apply virtual sunglasses to their video image. The user is able to adjust the fit, choose different styles, frames, lenses and colours to find their perfect look. Within the app they can then browse through eBay to find the perfect pair at the perfect price.[33]

Subliminal perception

Most marketers want to create messages *above* consumers' thresholds so people will notice them. Ironically, a good number of consumers instead believe marketers design many advertising messages so they will perceive them unconsciously, or *below* the threshold of recognition. Another word for threshold is *limen*, and we term stimuli that fall below the limen *subliminal*. **Subliminal perception** refers to a stimulus below the level of the consumer's awareness.

Subliminal perception is a topic that has captivated the public for more than 50 years, despite the fact that there is virtually no proof that this process has *any* effect on consumer behaviour. A survey of American consumers found that almost two-thirds believe in the existence of subliminal advertising, and more than one-half are convinced that this technique can get them to buy things they do not really want.[34] ABC rejected a Kentucky Fried Chicken (KFC) commercial that invited viewers to slowly replay the ad to find a secret message, citing the network's long-standing policy against subliminal advertising. KFC argued that the ad wasn't subliminal at all because the company told viewers about the message and how to find it. The network wasn't convinced.[35]

Like this KFC ad, most examples of subliminal advertising that people 'discover' are not subliminal at all – on the contrary, the images are quite apparent. Remember, if you can see it or hear it, it's not subliminal; the stimulus is above the level of conscious awareness. Nonetheless, the continuing controversy about subliminal persuasion has been important in shaping the public's beliefs about advertisers' and marketers' abilities to manipulate consumers against their will.

Subliminal messaging techniques

Marketers supposedly send *subliminal messages* on both visual and aural channels. Embeds are tiny figures they insert into magazine advertising via high-speed photography or airbrushing. These hidden figures, usually of a sexual nature, supposedly exert strong but unconscious influences on innocent readers. Some limited evidence hints at the possibility that embeds can alter the moods of men when they're exposed to sexually suggestive subliminal images, but the effect (if any) is very subtle – and may even work in the opposite direction if this creates negative feelings among viewers.[36] To date, the only real impact of this interest in hidden messages is to sell more copies of 'exposés' written by a few authors and to make some consumers (and students taking a consumer behaviour class) look a bit more closely at print ads – perhaps seeing whatever their imaginations lead them to see.

The possible effects of messages hidden on sound recordings also fascinate many consumers. We can see one attempt to capitalize on subliminal auditory perception techniques in the growing market for self-help audios. CDs and tapes, which typically feature the sounds of crashing waves or other natural sounds, supposedly contain subliminal messages to help listeners stop smoking, lose weight, gain confidence, and so on. Despite the rapid growth of this market, there is little evidence that subliminal stimuli transmitted on the auditory channel can bring about desired changes in behaviour.[37]

Does subliminal perception work?

Some research by clinical psychologists suggests that subliminal messages can influence people under very specific conditions, though it is doubtful that these techniques would be of much use in most marketing contexts. For this kind of message to have a prayer of working,

Nikon

The Nikon S60. Detects up to 12 faces.

This camera ad from Singapore reminds us that consumers tune out many stimuli that compete for their attention.

Source: Courtesy of Euro RSCG/ Singapore. Eurorscg.com

an advertiser has to tailor it specifically to an individual rather than the mass messages suitable for the general public.[38] The stimulus should also be as close to the liminal threshold as possible. Here are other discouraging factors:

- There are wide individual differences in threshold levels. In order for a message to avoid conscious detection by consumers who have low thresholds, it would have to be so weak that it would not reach those who have high thresholds.

- Advertisers lack control over consumers' distance and position from a screen. In a movie theatre, for example, only a small portion of the audience would be in exactly the right seats to be exposed to a subliminal message.

- The viewer must pay absolute attention to the stimulus. People who watch a television programme or a movie typically shift their attention periodically, and they might not even notice when the stimulus appears.

- Even if the advertiser induces the desired effect, it works only at a very general level. For example, a message might increase a person's thirst – but not necessarily for a specific drink. Because the stimulus just affects a basic drive, a marketer could find that after all the bother and expense of creating a subliminal message, demand for competitors' products increases as well!

    Clearly, there are better ways to get our attention – let's see how.

Attention

Attention is the degree to which consumers focus on stimuli within their range of exposure. Although we live in an 'information society', we can have too much of a good thing. Consumers often are in a state of **sensory overload**, where they are exposed to far more information than they can process. In our society, much of this bombardment comes from commercial sources, and the competition for our attention is steadily increasing. The average adult is exposed to about 3,500 pieces of advertising information every single day – up from about 560 per day 30 years ago. Because consumers are exposed to so many advertising stimuli, marketers are becoming increasingly creative in their attempts to gain attention for their products. Some successful advertisers such as Apple, Nike, Gap and Dyson have created a visual identity with their television ads, and then deliver more detailed product information in other places, such as websites and newspaper stories in which third party experts provide independent reviews.[39]

Multitasking and attention

Getting the attention of young people in particular is a challenge – as your professor probably knows! As of 2010, more than half of teens report that they engage in **multitasking**, where they process information from more than one medium at a time as they attend to their cell phones, TVs, instant messages, and so on – and that's just during the time when they are doing homework![40] One study observed 400 people for a day and found that 96 per cent of them were multitasking about a third of the time they used media.[41] Marketing researchers struggle to understand this new condition as they figure out how to reach people who do many things at once.

What impact does all this multitasking have on consumers' ability to absorb, retain and understand information? One possible consequence: these bursts of stimulation provoke the body to secrete dopamine, which is addicting. When we go without these squirts, we feel bored. Some scientists warn that our cravings for more stimulation distract us from more prolonged thought processes and reduce our ability to concentrate (don't text and drive!). Studies find that heavy multitaskers have more trouble focusing, and they experience more stress. One study found that people interrupted by e-mail reported significantly more stress than those who were allowed to focus on a task. The good news is that the brains of internet users become more efficient at finding information, while some videogame players develop better eyesight. One team of researchers found that players of fast-paced video games can track the movement of a third more objects on a screen than nonplayers. They say the games can improve reaction and the ability to pick out details amid clutter. For better or worse, technology seems to be rewiring our brains to try to pay attention to more stimuli. Today we consume three times as much information each day as people did in 1960. We constantly shift attention: computer users at work change windows or check e-mail or other programs nearly 37 times an hour. Computer users visit an average of 40 websites a day.[42]

How do marketers get our attention?

As we'll also see in later chapters, marketers constantly search for ways to break through the clutter and grab people's attention – at times with mixed results. Because the brain's capacity to process information is limited, consumers are very selective about what they pay attention to. The process of **perceptual selection** means that people attend to only a small portion of the stimuli to which they are exposed. Consumers practice a form of 'psychic economy', picking and choosing among stimuli to avoid being overwhelmed. How do they choose? Both personal and stimulus factors help to decide.

PERSONAL SELECTION FACTORS

Experience, which is the result of acquiring and processing stimulation over time, is one factor that determines how much exposure to a particular stimulus a person accepts. Remember Gary's reaction to UHT milk in Portugal? Gary's perceptual filters based on his past experiences and beliefs about milk influence what he decided to process . . . with some effort, he may have come to understand that UHT milk is perfectly good to drink!

Consumers are more likely to be aware of stimuli that relate to their current needs, a behaviour known as **perceptual vigilance**. A consumer who rarely notices car ads will become very much aware of them when she or he is in the market for a new car. A newspaper ad for a fast-food restaurant that would otherwise go unnoticed becomes significant when one sneaks a glance at the paper in the middle of a five o'clock class. And, individual variations in perceptual processing may account for some differences. Indeed, a recent study reported that women are better than men in terms of their ability to identify visually incongruent products that are promoted among competing products. Females discriminate relational information among competing advertisements and use this information to identify incongruent products that would otherwise go unidentified.[43]

The flip side of perceptual vigilance is **perceptual defence**. This means that people see what they want to see – and don't see what they don't want to see. If a stimulus is threatening to us in some way, we may not process it – or we may distort its meaning so that it's more acceptable. For example, a heavy smoker may block out images of cancer-scarred lungs because these vivid reminders hit a bit too close to home.

Still another factor is **adaptation**, the degree to which consumers continue to notice a stimulus over time. The process of adaptation occurs when consumers no longer pay attention to a stimulus because it is so familiar. A consumer can 'habituate' and require increasingly stronger 'doses' of a stimulus to notice it. A commuter *en route* to work might read a billboard message when it is first installed, but after a few days, it simply becomes part of the passing scenery. Several factors can lead to adaptation:

- **Intensity**. Less-intense stimuli (e.g. soft sounds or dim colours) habituate because they have less sensory impact.
- **Duration**. Stimuli that require relatively lengthy exposure in order to be processed habituate because they require a long attention span.
- **Discrimination**. Simple stimuli habituate because they do not require attention to detail.
- **Exposure**. Frequently encountered stimuli habituate as the rate of exposure increases.
- **Relevance**. Stimuli that are irrelevant or unimportant habituate because they fail to attract attention.

Stimulus selection factors

In addition to the receiver's mind-set, characteristics of the stimulus itself play an important role in determining what we notice and what we ignore. Marketers need to understand these factors so they can create messages and packages that will have a better chance to cut through the clutter. For example, when researchers measured what ads consumers look at using infrared eye-tracking equipment, they found that visually complex ads are more likely to capture attention.[44]

In general, we are more likely to notice stimuli that differ from others around them (remember Weber's Law). A message creates contrast in several ways:

- **Size**. The size of the stimulus itself in contrast to the competition helps to determine if it will command attention. Readership of a magazine ad increases in proportion to the size of the ad.[45]
- **Colour**. As we've seen, colour is a powerful way to draw attention to a product or to give it a distinct identity. When Black & Decker developed a line of tools it called DeWalt to target the residential construction industry, the company coloured the new line yellow instead of black; this made them stand out against other 'dull' tools.[46]
- **Position**. Not surprisingly, we stand a better chance of noticing stimuli that are in places we're more likely to look. That's why the competition is so heated among suppliers to have their products displayed in stores at eye level. In magazines, ads that are placed towards the front of the issue, preferably on the right-hand side, also win out in the race for readers' attention. (Hint: The next time you read a magazine, notice which pages you're more likely to spend time looking at.)[47] When you are doing your 'Google search', how far down the screen do you typically go in reviewing results? Do you often scroll to the second page of results?

● **Novelty**. Stimuli that appear in unexpected ways or places tend to grab our attention. One solution is to put ads in unconventional places, where there will be less competition for attention. These places include the backs of shopping carts, walls of tunnels, floors of sports stadiums, and yes, even public restrooms.[48] An outdoor advertising agency in London constructs huge ads in deserts and farm fields adjacent to airports so that passengers who look out the window can't help but pay attention. It prints the digital ads on pieces of PVC mesh that sit on frames a few inches above the ground.[49] Other entrepreneurs equip billboards with tiny cameras that use software to determine that a person is standing in front of an outdoor ad. Then the program analyses the viewer's facial features (like cheekbone height and the distance between the nose and the chin) to judge the person's gender and age. Once the software categorizes the passerby, it selects an advertisement tailored to this profile – a Spanish teenager, for example, sees a different message than the middle-aged Asian woman who walks behind him.[50]

INTERPRETATION: DECIDING WHAT THINGS MEAN

Interpretation refers to the meaning that people assign to sensory stimuli. Just as people differ in terms of the stimuli that they perceive, the eventual assignment of meanings to these stimuli varies as well. Two people can see or hear the same event, but their interpretation of it may be completely different.

Consumers assign meaning to stimuli based on the *schema*, or set of beliefs, to which the stimulus is assigned. During a process known as **priming**, certain properties of a stimulus are more likely to evoke a schema than others. As evidenced by the case of Castello cheese quoted earlier, a brand name can communicate expectations about product attributes and colour consumers' perceptions of product performance by activating a schema. One somewhat disturbing example of how this works comes from America. Children aged 3 to 5 who ate McDonald's French fries served in a McDonald's bag overwhelmingly thought they tasted better than those who ate the same fries out of a plain white bag. Even carrots tasted better when they came out of a McDonald's bag – more than half the children preferred them to the same carrots served in a plain package![51]

Stimulus organization

People do not perceive a single stimulus in isolation. Our brains tend to relate incoming sensations to imagery of other events or sensations already in our memory based on some fundamental organizational principles. A number of perceptual principles describe how stimuli are perceived and organized.

MARKETING OPPORTUNITY

Companies such as the Anglo-Dutch Unilever and France's Picard are attempting to change consumer perceptions of frozen foods. In supermarkets across the UK, it is the chiller cabinet rather than the freezer that increasing numbers of shoppers head for first. The chilled food section is where much of the innovation in convenience food is happening and where manufacturers compete most aggressively for space. Chilled food is perceived by the consumer as fresher and healthier. But, cry the champions of frozen food, it is food picked or prepared and immediately frozen that keeps its nutritional value, and does not rely on preservatives in the way that some chilled or ambient (tinned) food does. In the UK, frozen food already faces increasingly stiff competition from the chilled pretender, and suffers from stigma. 'In the UK, frozen food is seen as an inferior product, and consumer perception of freshness is warped. Frozen food is seen as the last resort, eaten when you can't get to the shops, or fed to the children.' This is less true in the other seven countries where the company operates. 'Perception of frozen food in southern Europe is that it is modern, so they have fewer hang-ups,' says Andrew Beattie, Unilever's Rotterdam-based marketing director for frozen foods.[52] Critical to the development of new perceptions regarding frozen foods is newly designed logo and packaging, with a warmer, more contemporary design, which implies that the food is the product of natural sunlight rather than factory freezing, and more pleasant lighting in the freezer area. In France, the main reasons for the surge in 'surgelé' (as frozen food is called) are two-career couples, children with overcommitted activities, and the desire to avoid spending whatever leisure time there is chopping, dredging and sautéing. In 1960, the French consumed only 2kg of frozen food products per year, while in 2001, this figure has gone up to over 30kg. Shopping for frozen packages in an antiseptic, ultra-white Picard store or in similar aisles at France's national supermarket chains may lack romance, but it is reliable.[53]

The gestalt

These principles are based on work in **gestalt psychology**, a school of thought maintaining that people derive meaning from the totality of a set of stimuli, rather than from any individual stimulus. The German word 'Gestalt' roughly means 'whole', 'pattern' or 'configuration', and this perspective is best summarized by the saying, 'the whole is greater than the sum of its parts'. A piecemeal perspective that analyses each component of the stimulus separately will be unable to capture the total effect. The gestalt perspective provides several principles relating to the way stimuli are organized. Three of these principles, or perceptual tendencies, are illustrated in Figure 4.3.

The gestalt **principle of closure** implies that consumers tend to perceive an incomplete picture as complete. That is, we tend to fill in the blanks based on our prior experience. This principle explains why most of us have no trouble reading a neon sign, even if one or two of its letters are burned out, or filling in the blanks in an incomplete message. The principle of closure is also at work when we hear only part of a jingle or theme. Utilization of the principle of closure in marketing strategies encourages audience participation, which increases the chance that people will attend to the message.

The **principle of similarity** tells us that consumers tend to group together objects that share similar physical characteristics. That is, they group like items into sets to form an integrated whole. This principle is used by companies who have extended product lines, but wish to keep certain features similar, such as the shape of a bottle, so that it is easy for the consumer to recognize that they are in fact buying a shampoo of brand X.

Another important gestalt concept is the **figure-ground principle** (see Wrangler ad), in which one part of a stimulus (the figure) will dominate while other parts recede into the background. This concept is easy to understand if one thinks of a photograph with a clear and

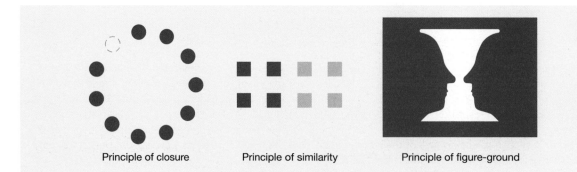

| Principle of closure | Principle of similarity | Principle of figure-ground |

Figure 4.3 Principles of stimulus organization derived from gestalt psychology

sharply focused object (the figure) in the centre. The figure is dominant, and the eye goes straight to it. The parts of the configuration that will be perceived as figure or ground can vary depending on the individual consumer as well as other factors. Similarly, in marketing messages that use the figure-ground principle, a stimulus can be made the focal point of the message or merely the context that surrounds the focus.

This billboard for Wrangler jeans makes creative use of the figure-ground principle.

BooneOakley Advertising.

The Australian postal service uses a unique application of the figure-ground principle.

M&C Saatchi Australia.

The role of symbolism in interpretation

When we try to make sense of a marketing stimulus, whether a distinctive package, an elaborately staged television commercial or perhaps a model on the cover of a magazine, we do so by **interpretation** of its meaning in the light of associations we have with these images. For this reason much of the meaning we take away is influenced by what we make of the symbolism we perceive. After all, on the surface many marketing images have virtually no literal connection to actual products. What does a cowboy have to do with a bit of tobacco rolled into a paper tube? How can a celebrity such as the football star Gary Lineker enhance the image of a potato crisp?[54]

For assistance in understanding how consumers interpret the meanings of symbols, some marketers are turning to a field of study known as **semiotics**, which examines the correspondence between signs and symbols and their role in the assignment of meaning.[55] Semiotics is important to the understanding of consumer behaviour, since consumers use products to express their social identities. Products have learned meanings, and we rely on advertising to work out what those meanings are. As one set of researchers put it, 'advertising serves as a kind of culture/consumption dictionary; its entries are products, and their definitions are cultural meanings'.[56]

According to the semiotician Charles Sanders Peirce, every message has three basic components: an object, a sign and an interpretant. A marketing message such as a Marlboro ad can be read on different levels. On the lowest level of reading, the **object** would be the product that is the focus of the message (Marlboro cigarettes). The **sign** is the sensory imagery that represents the intended meanings of the object (the contents of the ad, in this case, the cowboy). The **interpretant** is the meaning derived (this man smokes these cigarettes). But this man is not any man. He is a cowboy – and not just any cowboy. The interpretant 'man (cowboy) smoking these cigarettes' in itself becomes a sign, especially since we have already seen many examples of these ads from this company. So, on the second, connotative level, this sign refers to the fictive personality of 'the Marlboro Man', and its interpretant consists of all the connotations attached to the Marlboro Man, for example his being a 'rugged, individualistic American'. On the third level, called the ideological level, the interpretant of the 'rugged, individualistic American' becomes a sign for what is stereotypically American. So its object is 'America', and the interpretant all the ideas and characteristics that we might consider as typically and quintessentially American. This semiotic relationship is shown in Figure 4.4. By means of such a chain of meanings, the Marlboro ad both borrows from and contributes to reinforcing a fundamental 'myth of America'.

From the semiotic perspective of Peirce, signs are related to objects in one of three ways. They can resemble objects, be connected to them with some kind of causal or other relation, or be conventionally tied to them.[57]

An **icon** is a sign that resembles the product in some way (e.g. Apple Computers uses the image of an apple to represent itself). An **index** is a sign that is connected to a product because they share some property (e.g. the pine tree on certain cleaning products conveys the shared property of fresh, natural scent). A **symbol** is a sign that is related to a product through purely conventional associations (e.g. the Mercedes star which in addition to the Mercedes-Benz company provides associations with German industrial quality and ingenuity).

The use of symbols provides a powerful means for marketers to convey product attributes to consumers. For example, expensive cars, designer fashions and diamond jewellery – all widely recognized symbols of success – frequently appear in ads to associate products with affluence or sophistication. The rhetoric of advertising is an additional field of analysis which has been useful for the discussion of how advertising communicates its messages.[58] Semiotic analysis of ads has been connected to product and brand lifecycles in order to establish some guidelines about when to use the most complex advertising forms.[59]

One aspect of the semiotics of consumption, which used to be relatively neglected compared to the semiotics of advertising, is the semiotics of goods as such. In recent years, instead

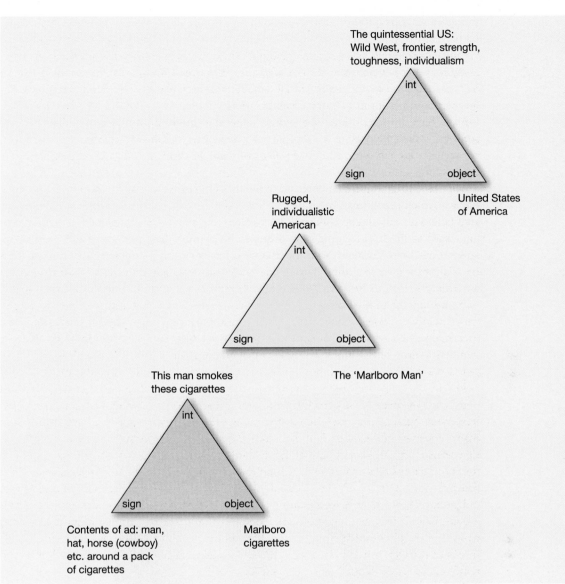

Figure 4.4 Relationship of components in semiotic analysis of meaning

of studying messages about commodities there has been an increased number of studies of commodities as messages.[60] Semiotics of consumer goods, then, focus on the ability of goods to communicate either by themselves or in connection with other goods. A related field of study is symbolic consumption,[61] which focuses not so much on the good as sign per se, but rather on the meanings attached to the act of consuming the good. Here, in many cases, the good becomes an indexical sign for some attributes that characterize the consumer, such as trendiness, wealth, femininity or others that place the consumer in some subcultural context.

Other uses of semiotics include industrial design[62] and design of distribution outlets. For example, in a semiotic study of the meanings and expectations consumers would attach to a new hypermarket, the researchers generated four different value profiles among potential customers. These profiles were linked to preferences for different designs of the hypermarket and its interior, thus helping the planners to conceive a type of hypermarket that was pleasing to most consumers.[63]

Semiotics plays a central role in much of the recent challenging consumer behaviour theory. The fact that consumers have become increasingly aware of how they communicate through their consumption as well as what they communicate has led to the designation of the present world as a 'semiotic world'.[64] Furthermore, it has been argued that we feel more confident in creating our own messages rather than just following what is proposed by marketing or fashion statements. This tendency to eclecticism means that we are increasingly likely to match things, such as articles of clothing, furniture or even lifestyles that traditionally have not been perceived as fitting together.

As we have already argued, one of the hallmarks of modern advertising is that it creates a condition where advertising is becoming self-referential. An increasing number of ads and commercials are referring, often ironically or tongue-in-cheek, to other advertisements, and thus creating a universe of their own, which in many ways is independent from the goods actually advertised. Advertising thus becomes an art in itself and is appreciated as such rather than as deceptive information about products.[65] **Hyperreality** refers to the becoming real of what is initially simulation or 'hype'.[66] Advertisers create new relationships between objects and interpretants by inventing new connections between products and benefits, such as equating Marlboro cigarettes with the American frontier spirit.[67] To a large extent, over time the relationship between the symbol and reality is increasingly difficult to discern, and the 'artificial' associations between advertisement symbols, product symbols and the real world may take on a life of their own.

For example, Tasters' Choice coffee perfected the concept of an ongoing series of 'soap opera' commercials where a romantic relationship is slowly cultivated between two actors, a commercial form later adopted by other coffee brands such as Nestlé's Gold Blend.

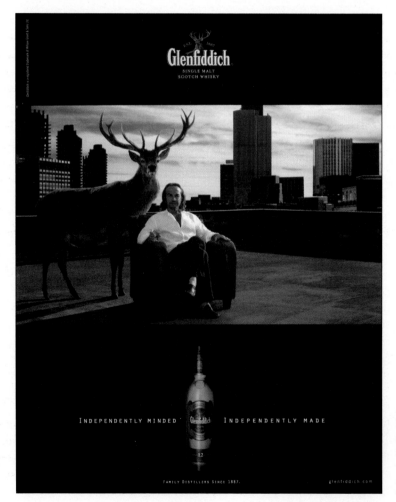

An illustration of how to read an advertisement semiotically.

The Advertising Archives.

Hyperreality will be discussed again in the final chapter of the book because it has been linked to the concept of postmodernism, the idea that we are living in a period of radical cultural change where certain hitherto dominant features and assumptions of modern societies are challenged.

PROFESSOR KENT GRAYSON
Northwestern University

Consumer behaviour as I see it . . .

How much would you be willing to pay for a dress? Perhaps £125,000? That's how much a bidder recently paid for a dress that Kate Middleton wore when she was in a fashion show at college. And – would someone really pay $350,000 for a single glove? That's what a Hong Kong businessman paid for the glove Michael Jackson was wearing when he performed his trademark *Moonwalk* dance in public for the first time.

Of course, no one would pay that much money for a glove that merely looks like the glove Michael Jackson wore, but which the singer never owned. Although there may be no *perceptual* difference between a glove worn by a celebrity and one sold in department store, why are people willing to pay thousands of times more for the glove worn by a star?

The answer comes from an American philosopher named Charles Peirce, who founded a school of thought called 'semiotics' in the late 1800s. As Peirce noted, when we perceive things, we don't just simply allow sights, sounds and smells to come directly into our senses from the outside world. Instead, we're always filtering and interpreting this information in relation to other things and experiences in our lives. For example, when someone asks us to buy a product, we think not only about whether the product is similar in appearance to other products (what Peirce called iconicity) but also how the product is physically connected to other things (indexicality) and what the product means to us and to other people (symbolism).

In other words, although two different dresses may be quite *iconic* (similar in appearance), they may nonetheless have very different marketplace values because their *indexicality* is different: one dress is connected to Kate Middleton and the other isn't. Because of this difference, the *symbolism* is also different – the dress worn by Kate Middleton means something different than an identical dress sold in a second-hand clothing store with no indexical connection to the Duchess of Cambridge. So if you're ever at a music concert and the singer throws you something that you sell for a mint on eBay . . . you can thank Charles Peirce's semiotics.

Kent Grayson

CHAPTER SUMMARY

Now that you have finished reading this chapter you should understand why:

→ **Perception is a three-stage process that translates raw stimuli into meaning.** Perception is the process by which physical sensations, such as sights, sounds, and smells, are selected, organized and interpreted. The eventual interpretation of a stimulus allows it to be assigned meaning. A perceptual map is a widely used marketing tool that evaluates the relative standing of competing brands along relevant dimensions.

→ **The design of a product today is a key driver of its success or failure.** In recent years the sensory experiences we receive from products and services have become a high priority when we choose among competing options. Consumers increasingly want to buy things that will give them hedonic value in addition to functional value. They often believe that most brands perform similarly, so they weigh a product's aesthetic qualities heavily when they select a brand.

→ **Products and commercial messages often appeal to our senses, but we won't be influenced by most of them.** Marketing stimuli have important sensory qualities. We rely on colours, odours, sounds, tastes, and even the 'feel' of products when we evaluate them. Not all sensations successfully make their way through the perceptual process. Many stimuli compete for our attention, and we don't notice or accurately interpret the majority of them. People have different thresholds of perception. A stimulus must be presented at a certain level of intensity before our sensory detectors can detect it. In addition, a consumer's ability to detect whether two stimuli are different (the differential threshold) is an important issue in many marketing contexts, such as package design, the size of a product, or its price.

→ **Subliminal advertising is a controversial – but largely ineffective – way to talk to consumers.** So-called subliminal persuasion and related techniques that expose people to visual and aural messages below the sensory threshold are controversial. Although evidence that subliminal persuasion is effective is virtually nonexistent, many consumers continue to believe that advertisers use this technique.

→ Some of the factors that determine which stimuli (above the threshold level) do get perceived include the amount of exposure to the stimulus, how much attention it generates, and how it is interpreted. In an increasingly crowded stimulus environment, advertising clutter occurs when too many marketing-related messages compete for attention.

→ **We interpret the stimuli to which we do pay attention according to learned patterns and expectations.** We don't attend to a stimulus in isolation. We classify and organize it according to principles of perceptual organization. A *gestalt*, or overall pattern, guides these principles. Specific grouping principles include closure, similarity and figure-ground relationships. The final step in the process of perception is interpretation. Symbols help us make sense of the world by providing us with an interpretation of a stimulus that others often share. The degree to which the symbolism is consistent with our previous experience affects the meaning we assign to related objects.

→ **The field of semiotics helps us to understand how marketers use symbols to create meaning.** Marketers try to communicate with consumers by creating relationships between their products or services and desired attributes. A semiotic analysis involves the correspondence between stimuli and the meaning of signs. The intended meaning may be literal (e.g. an icon such as a street sign with a picture of children playing). Or it may be indexical if it relies on shared characteristics (e.g. the red in a stop sign means danger). Meaning also can be conveyed by a symbol in which an image is given meaning by convention or by agreement of members of a society (e.g. stop signs are octagonal, whereas yield signs are triangular). Marketer-created associations often take on lives of their own as consumers begin to believe that hype is, in fact, real. We call this condition hyperreality.

KEY TERMS

Absolute threshold (p. 131)
Adaptation (p. 136)
Attention (pp. 121, 134)
Augmented reality (p. 132)
Differential threshold (p. 131)
Exposure (p. 121)
Figure-ground principle (p. 139)
Gestalt psychology (p. 138)
Hedonic consumption (p. 124)
Hyperreality (p. 142)
Icon (p. 140)
Index (p. 140)
Interpretant (p. 140)
Interpretation (p. 121)
JND (p. 131)
Multitasking (p. 135)
Object (p. 140)
Perception (p. 121)

Perceptual defence (p. 136)
Perceptual map (p. 123)
Perceptual selection (p. 135)
Perceptual vigilance (p. 135)
Priming (p. 137)
Principle of closure (p. 138)
Principle of similarity (p. 139)
Psychophysics (p. 131)
Schema (p. 122)
Semiotics (p. 140)
Sensation (p. 121)
Sensory marketing (p. 124)
Sensory overload (p. 134)
Sign (p. 140)
Subliminal perception (p. 133)
Symbol (p. 140)
Trade dress (p. 126)
Weber's Law (p. 131)

CONSUMER BEHAVIOUR CHALLENGE

1 Many studies have shown that our sensory detection abilities decline as we grow older. Discuss the implications of the absolute threshold for marketers attempting to appeal to the elderly.

2 Interview three to five male and three to five female friends regarding their perceptions of both men's and women's fragrances. Construct a perceptual map for each set of products. Based on your map of perfumes, do you see any areas that are not adequately served by current offerings? What (if any) gender differences did you obtain regarding both the relevant dimensions used by raters and the placement of specific brands along these dimensions?

3 Assume that you are a consultant for a marketer who wants to design a package for a new premium chocolate bar targeted to an affluent market. What recommendations would you provide in terms of such package elements as colour, symbolism and graphic design? Give the reasons for your suggestions.

4 Do you believe that marketers have the right to use any or all public spaces to deliver product messages? Where would you draw the line in terms of places and products that should be restricted?

5 Find one ad that is rich in symbolism and perform a semiotic analysis of it. Identify each type of sign used in the ad and the product qualities being communicated by each. Comment on the effectiveness of the signs that are used to communicate the intended message.

6 Using magazines archived in the library, track the packaging of a specific brand over time. Find an example of gradual changes in package design that may have been below the JND.

7 Collect a set of current ads for one type of product (e.g. personal computers, perfumes, laundry detergents or athletic shoes) from magazines, and analyse the colours employed. Describe the images conveyed by different colours, and try to identify any consistency across brands in terms of the colours used in product packaging or other aspects of the ads.

→

8 Look through a current magazine and select one ad that captures your attention over the others. Give the reasons why.

9 Find ads that utilize the techniques of contrast and novelty. Give your opinion of the effectiveness of each ad and whether the technique is likely to be appropriate for the consumers targeted by the ad.

For additional material see the companion website at **www.pearsoned.co.uk/solomon**

NOTES

1. 'Fish Vending Machine in Mungia, Spain' accessed 23 February 2012 at: http://guiagastronomika.diariovasco.com/noticias/maquina-dispensadora-pescado-201202231644.php

2. For an overview of Unilever's successful Axe/Lynx aftershave campaign, see: http://axeads.blogspot.com/2007/04/bomchickawahwah-france.html; also, as part of the masculine perceptions that Axe is trying to portray, the company has enlisted the help of Husky Injection Molding company, to rework the packaging of Axe. See: 'Unilever chooses Husky hot runners for redesigned Axe Lynx closure', at http://www.husky.ca/abouthusky/news/content-1085-106.html

3. Jerome S. Bruner, 'On perceptual readiness', *Psychological Review* 64 (March 1957): 123–52.

4. Synder, William R., *Wall Street Journal* (18 April 2008), http://online.wsj.com/article/SB120846638155724155.html

5. Elizabeth C. Hirschman and Morris B. Holbrook, 'Hedonic consumption: Emerging concepts, methods, and propositions', *Journal of Marketing* 46 (Summer 1982): 92–101.

6. Adam Bryant, 'Plastic Surgery at AmEx', *Newsweek* (4 October 1999): 55.

7. Amitava Chattopadhyay, Gerald J. Gorn and Peter R. Darke, 'Roses Are Red and Violets Are Blue – Everywhere? Cultural Universals and Differences in Color Preference Among Consumers and Marketing Managers' (unpublished manuscript, University of British Columbia, Fall 1999); Joseph Bellizzi and Robert E. Hite, 'Environmental Color, Consumer Feelings, and Purchase Likelihood', *Psychology & Marketing* 9 (1992): 347–63; Ayn E. Crowley, 'The Two-Dimensional Impact of Color on Shopping', *Marketing Letters* 4 (January 1993); Gerald J. Gorn, Amitava Chattopadhyay and Tracey Yi, 'Effects of Color as an Executional Cue in an Ad: It's in the Shade' (unpublished manuscript, University of British Columbia, 1994).

8. Pam Belluck, 'Reinvent Wheel? Blue Room. Defusing a Bomb? Red Room', *New York Times* (5 February 2009), www.nytimes.com, accessed 5 February 2009.

9. Marc Gobé, *Emotional Branding: The New Paradigm for Connecting Brands to People* (New York: Allworth Press, 2001).

10. Dirk Olin, 'Color Cognition', *New York Times* (30 November 2003), www.nytimes.com, accessed 30 November 2003.

11. 'Ny Emballage og New York Times Navn Fordoblede Salget', *Markedsføring* 12 (1992): 24. Adapted from Michael R. Solomon, Gary Bamossy and Soren Askegaard, *Consumer Behaviour: A European Perspective*, 2nd edn (London: Pearson Education, 2001).

12. Meg Rosen and Frank Alpert, 'Protecting Your Business Image: The Supreme Court Rules on Trade Dress', *Journal of Consumer Marketing* 11 (1994): 50–55.

13. Excerpted from http://www.pantone.com/pages/MYP_mypantone/mypInfo.aspx?ca=75&pg=20875, accessed 27 March 2011.

14. Deborah J. Mitchell, Barbara E. Kahn and Susan C. Knasko, 'There's something in the air: Effects of congruent or incongruent ambient odor on consumer decision-making', *Journal of Consumer Research* 22 (September 1995): 229–38; for a review of olfactory cues in store environments, see also Eric R. Spangenberg, Ayn E. Crowley and Pamela W. Henderson, 'Improving the store environment: Do olfactory cues affect evaluations and behaviors?', *Journal of Marketing* 60 (April 1996): 67–80.

15. Thom Forbes, 'P&G Noses Its Way into Youthful Air Freshener Market' (3 January 2007), available from mediapost.com, accessed 3 January 2007.

16. Suein L. Hwang, 'Seeking scents that no one has smelled', *The Wall Street Journal* (10 August 1994): B12.

17. 'En duft af træ', *Markedsføring* 13 (1996): 6.

18. Quoted in Sheila Shayon, 'World Cup Winner: Coca-Cola for Sonic Branding', *BrandChannel* (12 July 2010), http://www.brandchannel.com/home/post/2010/07/12/Coca-Cola-World-Cup-Wavin-Flag.aspx, accessed 28 March 2011.

19. *Marketing* (3 April 1997).

20. For research in time compression, see James MacLachlan and Michael H. Siegel, 'Reducing the costs of television commercials by use of time compression', *Journal of Marketing Research* 17 (February 1980): 52–7; James MacLachlan, 'Listener perception of time compressed spokespersons', *Journal of Advertising Research* 2 (April/May 1982): 47–51; Danny L. Moore, Douglas Hausknecht and Kanchana Thamodaran, 'Time compression, response opportunity, and persuasion', *Journal of Consumer Research* 13 (June 1986): 85–99.

21. 'You Can Look – But Don't Touch', *Science Daily* (20 January 2009), www.sciencedaily,com, accessed 30 January 2009; Joann Peck and Suzanne B. Shu (2009), 'The Effect of Mere

Touch on Perceived Ownership', *Journal of Consumer Research*, 36 (3), 434–447.

22. Sarah Ellison and Erin White, '"Sensory" Marketers Say the Way to Reach Shoppers Is the Nose', *Advertising Age* (24 November 2000): 1–3.

23. Jean-Claude Usunier, *Marketing Across Cultures* (Pearson, 2005).

24. Jacob Hornik, 'Tactile stimulation and consumer response', *Journal of Consumer Research* 19 (December 1992): 449–58.

25. Anne C. Bech, Erling Engelund, Hans Jørn Juhl, Kai Kristensen and Carsten Stig Poulsen, 'QFood. Optimal Design of Food Products', *MAPP Working Paper* no. 19 (Aarhus: The Aarhus School of Business, 1994); Hans Jørn Juhl, 'A Sensory Analysis of Butter Cookies – An Application of Generalized Procrustes Analysis', *MAPP Working Paper* no. 20 (Aarhus: The Aarhus School of Business, 1994).

26. Richard Tomkins, 'Products that aim for your heart', *Financial Times* (28 April 2005), http://news.ft.com/cms/s/d92c1660-b809-11d9-bc7c-00000e2511c8.html. Senseo has been so successful with this new product that they have a website for several European countries. See: http://www.senseo.com/content/default.html

27. Andreas Scharf, 'Positionierung neuer bzw. modifizierter Nahrungsund Genußmittel durch integrierte Marktund Sensorik-forschung', *Marketing ZFP* 1 (1st quarter 1995): 5–17.

28. Quoted in Davis, *ibid.*: 44.

29. Ellen Byron, 'Selling Detergent Bottles' Big Shrink Suds Makers' Challenge: Convince Consumers Less Isn't Really Less', *Wall Street Journal* (21 May 2007), www.Wall Street Journal.com, accessed 21 May 2007.

30. Bob Teheschi, 'Seeing the World Around You Through Your Phone', *New York Times*, (28 July 2010), http://www.New York Timesimes.com/2010/07/29/technology/personaltech/29smart.html?emc=tnt&tntemail0=y, accessed 28 March 2011.

31. Patricia Odell, 'Chevy Puts a New Spin on an Old Model', *PROMO* (10 January 2011), http://promomagazine.com/news/chevy-new-old-model-0110/, accessed 28 March 2011.

32. Matthew Szymczyk, 'Digital Marketing Guide: Augmented Reality', *Advertising Age*, (27 February 2011), http://adage.com/article/special-report-digital-marketing-guide/digital-marketing-guide-augmented-reality/149109/, accessed 28 March 2011.

33. 'Total Immersion and eBay Bring Virtual "See It On" Feature to eBay's Fashion App', *Business Wire* (1 February 2011), http://www.businesswire.com/news/home/20110201006053/en/Total-Immersion-eBay-Bring-Virtual-%E2%80%98See-On%E2%80%99, accessed 28 March 2011.

34. Michael Lev, 'No Hidden Meaning Here: Survey Sees Subliminal Ads', *New York Times* (3 May 1991): D7.

35. 'ABC Rejects KFC Commercial, Citing Subliminal Advertising', *Wall Street Journal* (2 March 2006), www.Wall Street Journal.com, accessed 2 March 2006.

36. Andrew B. Aylesworth, Ronald C. Goodstein and Ajay Kalra, 'Effect of Archetypal Embeds on Feelings: An Indirect Route to Affecting Attitudes?', *Journal of Advertising* 28, no. 3 (Fall 1999): 73–81.

37. Philip M. Merikle, 'Subliminal Auditory Messages: An Evaluation', *Psychology & Marketing* 5, no. 4 (1988): 355–72.

38. Joel Saegert, 'Why Marketing Should Quit Giving Subliminal Advertising the Benefit of the Doubt', *Psychology & Marketing* 4 (Summer 1987): 107–20; see also Dennis L. Rosen and Surendra N. Singh, 'An Investigation of Subliminal Embed Effect on Multiple Measures of Advertising Effectiveness', *Psychology & Marketing* 9 (March–April 1992): 157–73; for a more recent review, see Kathryn T. Theus, 'Subliminal Advertising and the Psychology of Processing Unconscious Stimuli: A Review of Research', *Psychology & Marketing* (May–June 1994): 271–90.

39. Gary Silverman, 'Image is everything in attention wars', *Financial Times* (17 January 2005), http://news.ft.com/cms/s/23a18ba4-68b3-11d9-9183-00000e2511c8,ft_acl=ftalert_ftarc_ftcol_ftfree_ftindsum_ftmywap_ftprem_ftspecial_ftsurvey_ftworldsub_ftym

40. Joseph Burris, 'Plugged-in Generation Multi-Tasking Big Time' (17 February 2010), *Baltimore Sun*, http://articles.baltimoresun.com/2010-02-17/features/bal-md.pa.kids 17feb17_1_cell-phones-multi-tasking-parental-controls, accessed 5 May 2011.

41. Sharon Waxman, 'At an Industry Media Lab, Close Views of Multitasking', *New York Times* (15 May 2006).

42. Matt Richtel, 'Attached to Technology and Paying a Price', *New York Times* (6 June 2010), http://www.New York Timesimes.com/2010/06/07/technology/07brain.html?pagewanted=1, accessed 17 April 2011.

43. Theodore J. Noseworthy, June Cotte and Seung Hwan (Mark) Lee, 'The Effects of Ad Context and Gender on the Identification of Visually Incongruent Products', *Journal of Consumer Research*, August 2011, in press, published online 24 January 2011.

44. Rik Pieters, Michel Wedel and Rajeev Batra (2010), 'The Stopping Power of Advertising: Measures and Effects of Visual Complexity', *Journal of Marketing*, 74 (September), 48–60.

45. Roger Barton, *Advertising Media* (New York: McGraw-Hill, 1964).

46. Suzanne Oliver, 'New Personality', *Forbes* (15 August 1994): 114.

47. Adam Finn, 'Print Ad Recognition Readership Scores: An Information Processing Perspective', *Journal of Marketing Research* 25 (May 1988): 168–77.

48. Michael R. Solomon and Basil G. Englis, 'Reality Engineering: Blurring the Boundaries Between Marketing and Popular Culture', *Journal of Current Issues and Research in Advertising* 16, no. 2 (Fall 1994): 1–18; Michael McCarthy, 'Ads Are Here, There, Everywhere: Agencies Seek Creative Ways to Expand Product Placement', *USA Today* (19 June 2001): 1B.

49. Linda Stern, 'Bigger Than at Times Square', 24 March 2008, www.newsweek.com.

50. Stephanie Clifford, 'Billboards That Look Back', *New York Times* (31 May 2008), www.nytimes.com, accessed 31 May 2008.

51. Bakalar Nicholas, 'If It Says McDonald's, Then It Must Be Good', *New York Times Online Edition*, accessed 14 August 2007.

52. Clare Dowdy, 'A fresh look inside the shop freezer', *Financial Times* (24 March 2004), http://news.ft.com/servlet/

ContentServer?pagename=FT.com/StoryFT/FullStory&c=StoryFT&cid=1079419893700&p=1059480266913.

53. Elaine Sciolino, 'Foie gras in the freezer? Just don't tell anyone!', *The New York Times* (19 December 2002), http://www.nytimes.com/2002/12/19/international/europe/19PARI.html?ex=1041353523&ei=1&en=4560794b5f85c27c

54. Apparently, many consumers think the answer is 'No!' See http://news.bbc.co.uk/2/hi/talking_point/3270473.stm for a discussion on whether celebrities should endorse 'junk food'. See also: (Spring 2008) 'Using celebrities to endorse products: What NOT to do', http://www.pannone-services.com/Subscription-Management/documents/celeritas/Spring-2008.htm

55. See David Mick, 'Consumer research and semiotics: Exploring the morphology of signs, symbols, and significance', *Journal of Consumer Research* 13 (September 1986): 196–213.

56. Teresa J. Domzal and Jerome B. Kernan, 'Reading advertising: The what and how of product meaning', *Journal of Consumer Marketing* 9 (Summer 1992): 48–64, at 49.

57. Winfried Nöth, *Handbook of Semiotics* (London: Sage, 1994); David Mick, 'Consumer research and semiotics', *op. cit.*; Charles Sanders Peirce, in Charles Hartshorne, Paul Weiss and Arthur W. Burks (eds), *Collected Papers* (Cambridge, MA: Harvard University Press, 1931–58).

58. Jacques Durand, 'Rhetorical Figures in the Advertising Image', in Jean Umiker-Sebeok (ed.), *Marketing and Semiotics. New Directions in the Study of Signs for Sale* (Berlin: Mouton de Gruyter, 1987): 295–318.

59. Alsted and Larsen, 'Toward a semiotic typology of advertising forms', *op. cit.*

60. Winfried Nöth, 'The language of commodities. Groundwork for a semiotics of consumer goods', *International Journal of Research in Marketing* 4 (1988): 173–86.

61. See the early introduction of the field: Elizabeth C. Hirschman and Morris B. Holbrook (eds), *Symbolic Consumer Behavior* (Ann Arbor, MI: Association for Consumer Research, 1981).

62. Odile Solomon, 'Semiotics and marketing. New directions in industrial design applications', *International Journal of Research in Marketing* 4 (1988): 201–15.

63. *Ibid.*

64. James Ogilvy, 'This postmodern business', *Marketing and Research Today* (February 1990): 4–22.

65. Chantal Cinquin, 'Homo Coca-Colens: From Marketing to Semiotics and Politics', in Umiker-Sebeok (ed.), *Marketing and Semiotics, op. cit.*: 485–95.

66. A. Fuat Firat and Alladi Venkatesh, 'Postmodernity: The age of marketing', *International Journal of Research in Marketing* 10(3) (1993): 227–49.

67. Jean Baudrillard, *Simulations* (New York: Semiotext(e), 1983).

5 THE SELF

CHAPTER OBJECTIVES

When you finish reading this chapter you will understand why:

→ The self-concept strongly influences consumer behaviour.

→ Products often play a key role in defining the self-concept.

→ Society's expectations of masculinity and femininity help to determine the products we buy to meet these expectations.

→ The way we think about our bodies (and the way our culture tells us we should think) is a key component of self-esteem.

→ Desire to live up to cultural expectations of appearance can be harmful.

→ Culture dictates certain types of body decoration or mutilation.

MATTHEW, a marketing director, is a happily married man, and his two children aged six and eight provide immense joy in his life. However, at 42 he feels younger than his years, and somewhat anxious about his totally family-oriented life – he has a nice house, a magnificent garden and takes regular family holidays in sunny Dubai. But he has begun to feel the loss of his previous, extravagant, carefree life, one in which he perceived himself to be a well-dressed, admired individual of good taste and discernment who always turned heads when he entered the room. He has a slight nagging worry that Matthew the family man is dominating his personality and has totally taken over his life's spirit. It's a life he very much loves and one which has his complete commitment, but one which he also views as very 'sensible and earnest'.

Some months into the development of these feelings, Matthew is contacted by his company's personnel department about replacing his company car. Three years earlier he had selected a sensible Audi 80 with the needs of the family in mind. In the meantime, he had bought his wife a BMW x5 which is always used for family travel. He has a widely envied budget allocated to car purchase, due to his long-term commitment and excellent contribution to company performance. As a result he can select almost any car he desires. He drives past a Bentley garage on the way home every day but thought the price tag of £185k on the one in the window was a little excessive, after extensive thought and research he decides on a Porsche Panamera.

The Porsche Panamera, a unique four seater, four door model is a well-designed and admired car for drivers of good taste and discernment, created for the sporty, confident, powerful individual. The current media campaign portrays a successful mid-forties man being admired at the traffic lights, in the office car park and occasionally the local school collecting his children. Whilst driving home Matthew plays his favourite music at full volume, exceeds the legal speed limit when he believes it is 'safe' to do so, and generally feels more like the much-revered Matthew who graduated over 20 years ago. Catching a glimpse of himself in the rear view mirror he decided he really doesn't look his age . . .

CAROLYN STRONG, University of Bath

PERSPECTIVES ON THE SELF

Matthew is not alone in feeling that his self-image and possessions affect his 'value' as a person. Consumers' insecurities about their appearance are rampant: it has been estimated that 72 per cent of men and 85 per cent of women are unhappy with at least one aspect of their appearance.[1] Even among married couples, the sense of presenting one's self is guarded. When it comes to being naked in front of one's partner, one-third of women are too shy to take their clothes off in front of their husband. In the same study, 80 per cent of women reported having real difficulty in showering or changing clothes in front of other women in the gym.[2] Reflecting this discontent, new cosmetics for men and new clinical 'beauty procedures' have grown rapidly in Europe in the past few years, and revenues for men's cosmetics are projected to approach €1 billion![3] Many products, from cars to aftershave, are bought because the person is trying to highlight or hide some aspect of the self. In this chapter, we will focus on how consumers' feelings about themselves shape their consumption habits, particularly as they strive to fulfil their society's expectations about how a male or female should look and act.

Does the self exist?

Most of us can't boast of coming close to Lady Gaga's ten million followers on Twitter, but many of us do have hundreds of followers in addition to legions of Facebook friends.[4] The explosion of these and other social networking services enables everyone to focus on him- or herself and share mundane or scintillating details about their lives with anyone who's interested (*why* they are interested is another story!).

Today it seems natural to think of ourselves as a potential celeb waiting for our 15 minutes of fame (as the pop icon Andy Warhol once predicted). However, the idea that each single human life is unique rather than a part of a group only developed in late medieval times (between the eleventh and fifteenth centuries). Furthermore, the emphasis on the unique nature of the self is much greater in Western societies.[5] Many Eastern cultures stress the importance of a *collective self*, where a person derives his or her identity in large measure from a social group. Both Eastern and Western cultures believe the self divides into an inner, private self and an outer, public self. But where they differ is in terms of which part they see as the 'real you' – the West tends to subscribe to an independent understanding of the self, which emphasizes the inherent separateness of each individual.

Non-Western cultures, in contrast, tend to focus on an interdependent self where we define our identities largely by our relationships with others.[6] For example, a Confucian perspective stresses the importance of 'face' – others' perceptions of the self and maintaining one's desired status in their eyes. One dimension of face is *mien-tzu* – the reputation one achieves through success and ostentation. Some Asian cultures developed explicit rules about the specific garments and even colours that certain social classes and occupations were allowed to display. These traditions live on today in Japanese style manuals that provide very detailed instructions for dressing and how to address people of differing status.[7]

That orientation is a bit at odds with such Western conventions as 'casual Friday', which encourages employees to express their unique selves (at least short of muscle shirts and flip-flops). To further illustrate these cross-cultural differences, a Roper Starch Worldwide survey compared consumers in 30 countries to see which were the most and least vain. Women who live in Venezuela were the chart toppers – 65 per cent said they thought about their appearance all the time.[8] Other high-scoring countries included Russia and Mexico. The lowest scorers lived in the Philippines and in Saudi Arabia, where only 28 per cent of consumers surveyed agreed with this statement. In the UK, a study of image consciousness showed that women in Liverpool check their appearance up to 71 times a day, while men check their appearance up to 66 times daily.

The self can be understood from many different theoretical vantage points. As you will read about in Chapter 6, a psychoanalytical or Freudian perspective regards the self as a system of competing forces riddled with conflict. Chapter 7 (Learning and memory) discusses the point that behaviourists tend to regard the self as a collection of conditioned responses. From a cognitive orientation, the self is an information-processing system, an organizing force that serves as a nucleus around which new information is processed.[9]

Self-concept

The **self-concept** refers to the beliefs a person holds about their attributes, and how they evaluate these qualities. While one's overall self-concept may be positive, there are certainly parts of the self that are evaluated more positively than others. For example, Matthew felt better about his professional identity than he did about his pending 'middle age' identity.

Components of the self-concept

The self-concept is a very complex structure. It is composed of many attributes, some of which are given greater emphasis when the overall self is being evaluated. Attributes of self-concept can be described along such dimensions as their content (for example, facial attractiveness *vs* mental aptitude), positivity or negativity (i.e. self-esteem), intensity, stability over time and accuracy (that is, the degree to which one's self-assessment corresponds to reality).[10] As we will see later in the chapter, consumers' self-assessments can be quite distorted, especially with regard to their physical appearance.

MARKETING OPPORTUNITY?

Time for your video-chat close up?

In 2012, Dr Sigal, a plastic surgeon in the US started a media frenzy when he publicized a new procedure that he said could help people look younger when they appear on Skype and other video chat services. He named the surgery the 'FaceTime Face-Lift', after the popular iPhone feature. 'People don't come in asking for a FaceTime Face-Lift per se', said the surgeon, in a YouTube video. 'What they'll say is that "I don't like the way I look when I'm video chatting."'

The blogosphere pounced on the news, often in moralizing tones that painted the plastic surgeon as predatory and his patients as vain. But it turns out that the FaceTime Face-Lift was more than just provocative branding. People usually gaze down into their video chat devices, which is just about the least flattering angle, foreshortening the face and accentuating any fat under the chin. Charging $10,000 for the procedure the surgeon reduces sagging necks but does not leave a scar under the chin – where the camera usually points – as traditional neck-lifts do.

The phenomenon is not surprising, given how pervasive video chats are becoming in everyday life, from job interviews to online dating. In a typical video conference or video chat, the screen shows not only the other party's face, but also the user's, in a corner inset.

As one recipient put it: 'When you're video calling someone, you can no longer ignore the fact that your face and neck are starting to droop . . . It's like a mirror on steroids.'[11]

Source: From The *New York Times*, 19 April © 2012 The New York Times. All rights reserved. Used by permission and protected by the Copyright Laws of the US. The printing, copying, redistribution, or retransmission of this Content without express written premission is prohibited.

Self-esteem

Self-esteem refers to the positivity of a person's self-concept. People with low self-esteem do not expect that they will perform very well, and they will try to avoid embarrassment, failure or rejection. In developing a new line of snack cakes, for example, Sara Lee found that consumers low in self-esteem preferred portion-controlled snack items because they felt they lacked self-control.[12] In contrast, people with high self-esteem expect to be successful, will take more risks and are more willing to be the centre of attention.[13] Self-esteem is often related to acceptance by others. As you probably remember, teenagers who are members of high-status groups have higher self-esteem than their excluded classmates.[14] Alberto-Culver uses a self-esteem appeal to promote a new product that reflects our changing society: Soft & Beautiful Just for Me Texture Softener, an alternative to hair pressing or relaxing. It is targeted to Caucasian mothers who don't know how to care for the hair of their multiracial children who have 'hair texture' issues. The self-esteem portion of the campaign, dubbed 'Love Yourself. Love Your Hair', includes a website, **texturesoftener.com**, that offers 'conversation starters' to help parents find ways to talk to their daughters about self-image.[15]

Marketing communications can influence a consumer's level of self-esteem. Exposure to ads can trigger a process of *social comparison*, where the person tries to evaluate their self by comparing it to the people depicted in these artificial images. This form of comparison appears to be a basic human motive, and many marketers have tapped into this need by supplying idealized images of happy, attractive people who just happen to be using their products. We even feel better about our self-image when we own and display products that are thought to be of high aesthetical value![16]

The social comparison process was illustrated in a study which showed that female college students do tend to compare their physical appearance with advertising models. Furthermore, study participants who were exposed to beautiful women in advertisements afterwards expressed lowered satisfaction with their own appearance, as compared to controls.[17] Another study demonstrated that young women's perceptions of their own body shapes and sizes can be altered after being exposed to as little as 30 minutes of television programming.[18] Finally, in what would seem to be a counter-intuitive finding, a recent study showed that while female subjects felt badly about themselves after viewing ads with thin female models, they also evaluated the brands being paired with the thin models more highly. Further, the subjects who saw ads depicting normal weight models did not feel bad about themselves, but they did rate the brands lower.[19]

Self-esteem advertising attempts to change product attitudes by stimulating positive feelings about the self.[20] One strategy is to challenge the consumer's self-esteem and then show a linkage to a product that will provide a remedy. Sometimes compliments are derived by comparing the person to others. One recent European advertising campaign even took to comparing different European nationalities, with the focus on self-esteem. British women face a stereotype: they are the plump ones on the beaches of Europe. Until now, that image has been fodder for jokes – not an advertising campaign. Slim-Fast, the diet brand, is running ads that rally British women to lose weight or lose face to sexier Continental counterparts in France, Spain and Sweden. One Slim-Fast ad is a photo of a French model and reads, 'I love British women. They make me look great.' Another spot shows a gorgeous Spanish woman: 'Face it, British women, it's not last year's bikini getting smaller.' One proposed ad read: 'You've got to be brave to share the beach with me.' After focus groups found it too insulting, the advertising agency softened the copy by making it more collective. It became: 'British women are so brave sharing the beach with us.' They also dropped the line, 'I bet your boyfriend thinks I look great in this.'[21]

Real and ideal selves

Self-esteem is influenced by a process where the consumer compares their actual standing on some attribute to some ideal. A consumer might ask, 'Am I as attractive as I would like to be?'

'Do I make as much money as I should?' and so on. The **ideal self** is a person's conception of how they would like to be, while the **actual self** refers to our more realistic appraisal of the qualities we have or lack.

We choose some products because we think they are consistent with our actual self, whereas we buy others to help us to reach more of an ideal standard. And we often engage in a process of **impression management** where we work hard to 'manage' what others think of us by strategically choosing clothing and other cues that will put us in a good light.[22] For example, an increasing number of Islamic men in Egypt have a *zebibah* (Arabic for 'raisin'); a dark circle of callused skin or a bump, between the hairline and the eyebrows. It marks the spot where the worshipper repeatedly presses his forehead into the ground during his daily prayers (observant Muslims pray five times a day). Some add prayers so that the bump will become even more pronounced; the owner of the mark thus broadcasts his degree of piousness on his head. As an Egyptian newspaper editor explains, '. . . there is a kind of statement in it. Sometimes as a personal statement to announce that he is a conservative Muslim and sometimes as a way of outbidding others by showing them that he is more religious or to say that they should be like him.'[23]

The ideal self is partly moulded by elements of the consumer's culture, such as heroes or people depicted in advertising who serve as models of achievement or appearance.[24] Products may be purchased because they are believed to be instrumental in helping us achieve these goals. Some products are chosen because they are perceived to be consistent with the consumer's actual self, while others are used to help reach the standard set by the ideal self. In a recent study looking at the willingness of young healthy adults to take (legal) drugs to enhance their social, emotional and cognitive traits, people were much more reluctant to take drugs which promised to enhance traits that they considered fundamental to their self identity (social comfort), and more likely to take drugs which were viewed as being less central to their self identity, such as performance enhancing drugs for memory. Advertising messages which promoted 'enabling' rather than 'enhancing' were more favourably received as well. Apparently, boosting one's ability to concentrate is more easily accepted than boosting one's mood![25]

Fantasy: bridging the gap between the selves

While most people experience a discrepancy between their real and ideal selves, for some consumers this gap is larger than for others. These people are especially good targets for marketing communications that employ *fantasy* appeals.[26] A fantasy or daydream is a self-induced shift in consciousness, which is sometimes a way of compensating for a lack of external stimulation or of escaping from problems in the real world.[27] Many products and services are successful because they appeal to consumers' tendency to fantasize. These marketing strategies allow us to extend our vision of ourselves by placing us in unfamiliar, exciting situations or by permitting us to try interesting or provocative roles. And with today's technology, like Dove's Real Beauty campaign[28] or the virtual digitized preview from the plastic surgeon's PC of how your new face-lift will probably look, consumers can experiment before taking the plunge in the real world.

Multiple selves

In a way, each of us is really a number of different people – your mother probably would not recognize the 'you' that emerges while you're on holiday with a group of friends! We have as many selves as we do different social roles. Depending on the situation, we act differently, use different products and services, and we even vary in terms of how much we like ourselves. A person may require a different set of products to play a desired role: she may choose a sedate, understated perfume when she is being her professional self, but splash on something more provocative on Saturday night as she becomes her *femme fatale* self. The dramaturgical perspective on consumer behaviour views people much like actors who play different roles. We each play many roles, and each has its own script, props and costumes.[29]

The self can be thought of as having different components, or *role identities*, and only some of these are active at any given time. Some identities (e.g. husband, boss, student) are more central to the self than others, but other identities (e.g. stamp collector, dancer or advocate for greater equality in the workplace) may be dominant in specific situations.[30] Indeed, some roles may conflict with one another – for example, one study of Iranian young people who live in the UK described what the authors termed the **torn self** where respondents struggle with retaining an authentic culture while still enjoying Western freedom (and dealing with assumptions of others who believe they might be terrorists).[31] Strategically, this means a marketer may want to ensure the appropriate role identity is active before she pitches products customers need to play a particular role. One obvious way to do that is to place advertising messages in contexts where people are likely to be well aware of that role identity – for example, when fortified drink and energy bar product companies hand out free product samples to runners at a marathon.

Virtual identity

In the influential cyberpunk novel *Snow Crash*, author Neal Stephenson envisioned a virtual world he called the *Metaverse* as a successor to the internet. In the Metaverse, everyday people take on glamorous identities in a 3-D immersive digital world. The book's main character delivers pizza in real life (RL), but in the Metaverse, he's a warrior prince and champion sword fighter.[32] The hugely popular *Matrix* movie trilogy paints a similar (though more sinister) picture of a world that blurs the lines between physical and digital reality, as did *Avatar* where the hero transforms from a disabled soldier to a ten foot tall blue warrior.

Today these fictional depictions come to life as we witness the tremendous growth of real-time, interactive virtual worlds that allow people to assume **virtual identities** in cyberspace. More than 11 million people worldwide belong to the virtual world of *Second Life*, more than 8 million play the online game *World of Warcraft*, and the majority of Korean adults belong to *CyWorld*. Add to that the millions more who play *The Sims Online* or who visit other **computer-mediated environments (CMEs)** such as *Webkinz, Habbo Hotel*, MTV's *Virtual Laguna Beach*, and more than 50,000 other virtual worlds and you're looking at a lot of serious role-playing.[33]

On these sites people assume visual identities, or **avatars**, that range from realistic versions of themselves to tricked-out versions with exaggerated physical characteristics or winged dragons or superheroes. Researchers are just starting to investigate how these online selves will influence

An author's personal correspondence with Xin Zhao, 2007.

Image courtesy of Xin Zhao.

consumer behaviour and how the identities we choose in CMEs relate to our RL (or 'meat-world') identities. Already we know that when people take on avatar forms, they tend to interact with other avatars much as their 'meat-world' selves interact with other RL people. For example, just as in the RL, males in *Second Life* leave more space between themselves when they talk to other males as opposed to females and they are less likely to maintain eye contact than females are. And when avatars get very close to one another, they tend to look away from each other – the norms of the RL steadily creep into the virtual world.[34] With new platforms like Microsoft's Kinect that eliminate the need for hand controllers, our online and offline selves will continue to fuse. Already, scientists have been able to transmit the minds of volunteers from their physical bodies to their avatars for the first time; in one project volunteers wore skullcaps that contained electrodes to monitor brain activity while they also wore a set of goggles that showed them a different body in a different world. Researchers found that the subjects started to react as if their avatar was their real body.[35]

KATHY KEELING
Manchester Business School, Manchester UK

Consumer behaviour as I see it . . .

Interactive technologies have had a profound influence on consumer behaviour. Many people have found the WWW, which is essentially a medium of text and 2D images, sufficiently compelling to form social networks via e-mail, instant messaging, chatrooms, etc. They browse, they shop, they exchange information, develop meaningful relationships and worldwide cyber communities. So imagine the possibilities as we look toward the 3D web, where websites become enriched 3D virtual spaces within which digital representations of users, also known as avatars, can interact with others.

As avatars, we can represent ourselves in almost any way we choose, changing gender, skin colour, shape and even species at will. We may question that avatars are 'ushers of a post-human era' (Meadows, 2008) but through them we can explore new identities, new worlds and play any number of possible (or even impossible) selves, mixing fantasy and reality. I am excited by the potential and questions posed for consumer research. The sense of presence invoked by the immersive avatar experience is capable of producing reactions in participants similar to the real world, so throwing into sharp relief the drivers of behaviour and self-representation.

If we actively use clothes, appearance and possessions to construct and symbolize self and identity in the offline world, we should not be surprised that digital goods are used in the same way. But we have a limited understanding of how they are used in virtual worlds, as the technology offers boundless behavioural possibilities. Moreover, what is rare is valuable; the value of digital goods may be based on the difficulty of creation (programing/scripting) and so differ markedly from actual goods. Research questions arise on three fronts. First, issues of personal representation and identity. Humans are nothing if not social beings; in these virtual yet social worlds, what shapes or constrains the choice of avatar appearance from the almost limitless possibilities? How is identity negotiated once we have chosen our display of avatar characteristics? Is avatar appearance accepted as a reliable and accurate symbolism of the user or partially or wholly discounted? What can the individual's choice of avatar and digital possessions tell us about emotional desires or cultural notions of the self? Do virtual experiences and identity exploration contribute to changes in the offline self? →

→ Second, we might imagine opportunities for modification or transformation of customer–business relationships in virtual worlds. The use of an avatar or the presence of other avatars will change the processes of customer interaction in contrast to most e-retailing, e.g. you can easily go shopping with a friend in virtual worlds. How best can business use avatars to connect with customers and consumers to augment purchase and consumption experiences? Does a trial virtual purchase lead to a real-world purchase, or will it depress offline consumption?

Third, we should choose carefully in applying existing theoretical models of consumer behaviour to the virtual world context where people have multiple representations of themselves (perhaps in different genders), can fly (with or without wings), change their body shape, eye colour, skin colour (try the purple) at will, and/or inhabit their (and others') fantasy worlds. How can theories of cognitive processing, motivation and social psychology inform our understanding? Virtual worlds promise unique opportunities for exploring and experimenting with consumer behaviour, as well as testing the boundaries of our present understanding and theories. It's going to be an interesting journey.

Kathy Keeling

Meadows, M.S. (2008). *I, Avatar: The Culture and Consequences of Having a Second Life*. Berkeley: New Riders.

Symbolic interactionism

If each person potentially has many social selves, how does each develop and how do we decide which self to 'activate' at any point in time? The sociological tradition of **symbolic interactionism** stresses that relationships with other people play a large part in forming the self.[36] This perspective maintains that people exist in a symbolic environment, and the meaning attached to any situation or object is determined by the interpretation of these symbols. As members of society, we learn to agree on shared meanings. Thus, we 'know' that a red light means stop, or that McDonald's 'golden arches' mean fast food.

Like other social objects, the meanings of consumers themselves are defined by social consensus. The consumer interprets their own identity, and this assessment is continually evolving as they encounter new situations and people. In symbolic interactionist terms, we *negotiate* these meanings over time. Essentially the consumer poses the question: 'Who am I in this situation?' The answer to this question is greatly influenced by those around us: 'Who do *other people* think I am?' We tend to pattern our behaviour on the perceived expectations of others in a form of *self-fulfilling prophecy*. By acting the way we assume others expect us to act, we may confirm these perceptions. This pattern of self-fulfilling behaviour is often expressed in our 'gendered roles', as we will see later in this chapter.

The looking-glass self

Some stores are testing a new interactive mirror that doubles as a high-resolution digital screen. When you choose an article of clothing, the mirror superimposes it on your reflection so that you can see how it would look on you. A camera relays live images of you modelling your virtual outfit to an internet site where your friends can log to instant message (IM) you to tell you what they think; their comments pop up on the side of the mirror for you to read. They can also select virtual items for you to try on that will be reflected in the 'magic' mirror.[37] This process of imagining the reactions of others towards us is known as 'taking the role of the other', or the **looking-glass self**.[38] According to this view, our desire to define ourselves operates as a sort of psychological sonar: we take readings of our own identity by 'bouncing' signals off others and trying to project what impression they have of us. The looking-glass image we receive will differ depending upon whose views we are considering.

THE STILETTO EFFECT

BIANCO.®
FOOTWEAR

While this Bianco Footwear ad is making a visually playful metaphor which likens the 'Stiletto Effect' of the model's legs to the stiletto heel of the shoes, an additional message to female consumers is also part of the ad – the message that thin is fashionable.
Bianco Footwear Danmark A/S.

Like the distorted mirrors in a funfair, our appraisal of who we are can vary, depending on whose perspective we are taking and how accurately we are able to predict their evaluations of us. A successful man like Matthew may have doubts about his role as a middle-aged 'family man' as it conflicts with his earlier self-image as dapper and carefree (whether these perceptions are true or not). A self-fulfilling prophecy may be at work here, since these 'signals' can influence Matthew's actual behaviour. If he does not believe he is dapper, he may choose clothing and behaviour that actually make him less dapper. On the other hand, his self-confidence in a professional setting may cause him to assume that others hold his 'executive self' in even higher regard than they actually do (we've all known people like that!).

Self-consciousness

If you have ever walked into a class in the middle of a lecture and you were convinced that all eyes were on you as you awkwardly searched for a seat, you can understand the feeling of *self-consciousness*. In contrast, sometimes we behave with shockingly little self-consciousness. For example, we may do things in a stadium, a riot or at a party we would never do if we were highly conscious of our behaviour (and add insult to injury when we post photos of these escapades to our Facebook page!).[39]

Some people seem in general to be more sensitive to the image they communicate to others (on the other hand, we all know people who act as if they are oblivious to the impression they are making). A heightened concern about the nature of one's public 'image' also results in more concern about the social appropriateness of products and consumption activities.

Several measures have been devised to measure this tendency. Consumers who score high on a scale of *public self-consciousness*, for example, are also more interested in clothing and are heavier users of cosmetics.[40] A similar measure is *self-monitoring*. High self-monitors are more attuned to how they present themselves in their social environments, and their product choices are influenced by their estimates of how these items will be perceived by others.[41] Self-monitoring is assessed by consumers' extent of agreement with such items as 'I suppose I put on a show to impress or entertain others', or 'I would probably make a good actor'.[42] High self-monitors are more likely than low self-monitors to evaluate products consumed in public in terms of the impressions they make on others.[43] Similarly, other research has looked at aspects of *vanity*, such as a fixation on physical appearance or on the achievement of personal goals. Perhaps not surprisingly, groups like body-builders and fashion models tend to score higher on this dimension.[44]

CONSUMPTION AND SELF-CONCEPT

By extending the dramaturgical perspective a bit further, it is easy to see how the consumption of products and services contributes to the definition of the self. For an actor to play a role convincingly, they need the correct props, stage setting and so on. Consumers learn that different roles are accompanied by *constellations* of products and activities which help to define these roles.[45] Some 'props' are so important to the roles we play that they can be viewed as a part of the *extended self*, a concept to be discussed shortly.

Products that shape the self: you are what you consume

Recall that the reflected self helps to shape self-concept, which implies that people see themselves as they imagine others see them. Since what others see includes a person's clothing, jewellery, furniture, car and so on, it stands to reason that these products also help to determine the perceived self. A consumer's products place them in a social role, which helps to answer the question, 'Who am I *now*?'

People use an individual's consumption behaviours to help them make judgements about that person's social identity. In addition to considering a person's clothes, grooming habits, and such like, we make inferences about personality based on a person's choice of leisure activities (squash *vs* soccer), food preferences (vegetarians *vs* 'steak and chips' people), cars or home decorating choices. People who are shown pictures of someone's sitting room, for example, are able to make surprisingly accurate guesses about their personality.[46] In the same way that a consumer's use of products influences others' perceptions, the same products can help to determine their *own* self-concept and social identity.[47]

A consumer exhibits *attachment* to an object to the extent that it is used by that person to maintain their self-concept.[48] Objects can act as a sort of security blanket by reinforcing our identities, especially in unfamiliar situations. For example, students who decorate their room or house with personal items are less likely to drop out. This coping process may protect the self from being diluted in an unfamiliar environment.[49]

The use of consumption information to define the self is especially important when an identity is yet to be adequately formed, something that occurs when a consumer plays a new or unfamiliar role. **Symbolic self-completion theory** predicts that people who have an incomplete self-definition tend to complete this identity by acquiring and displaying symbols associated with it.[50] Adolescent boys may use 'macho' products like cars and cigarettes to bolster their developing masculinity: these items act as a 'social crutch' to be leaned on during a period of uncertainty about identity.

Loss of self

The contribution of possessions to self-identity is perhaps most apparent when these treasured objects are lost or stolen. One of the first acts performed by institutions that want to repress individuality and encourage group identity, such as prisons or convents, is to confiscate personal possessions.[51] Victims of burglaries and natural disasters commonly report feelings of alienation, depression or of being 'violated'. One consumer's comment after being robbed is typical: 'It's the next worse thing to being bereaved; it's like being raped.'[52] Burglary victims exhibit a diminished sense of community, reduced sense of privacy and take less pride in their house's appearance than do their neighbours.[53]

The dramatic impact of product loss is highlighted by studying post-disaster conditions, when consumers may literally lose almost everything but the clothes on their backs following a fire, hurricane, flood or earthquake. Some people are reluctant to undergo the process of recreating their identity by acquiring all new possessions. Interviews with disaster victims reveal that some are reluctant to invest the self in new possessions and so become more detached about what they buy. This comment from a woman in her fifties is representative of this attitude: 'I had so much love tied up in my things. I can't go through that kind of loss again. What I'm buying now won't be as important to me.'[54]

MARKETING PITFALL ⊗

The automaker Renault avoided a big problem when a French judge ruled that the company can go forward with its plan to release a new electric car named Zoe in 2012 – even though the two plaintiffs in the case already have the name Zoe Renault. The lawyer who brought the unsuccessful suit argued that the girls would endure a lifetime of grief, as would the other 35,000 people in France who are also named Zoe. He claimed, 'Can you imagine what little Zoes would have to endure on the playground, and even worse, when they get a little bit older and someone comes up to them in a bar and says, "Can I see your air bags?" or "Can I shine your bumper?"'[55]

Self/product congruence

Because many consumption activities relate to self-definition, it is not surprising to learn that consumers demonstrate consistency between their values (see Chapter 4) and the things they buy.[56] **Self-image congruence models** suggest that we choose products when their attributes match some aspect of the self.[57] These models assume a process of *cognitive matching* between product attributes and the consumer's self-image.[58] Over time we tend to form relationships with products that resemble the bonds we create with other people – these include love, unrequited love (we yearn for it but can't have it), respect, and perhaps even fear or hate ('why is my computer out to get me?').[59] Researchers even report that after a 'breakup' with a brand, people tend to develop strong negative feelings and will go to great lengths to discredit it including bad-mouthing and even vandalism. As the saying (sort of) goes, 'Hell hath no fury like a (wo)man scorned.'[60]

While results are somewhat mixed, the ideal self appears to be more relevant as a comparison standard for highly expressive social products such as perfume. In contrast, the actual self is more relevant for everyday, functional products. These standards are also likely to vary by usage situation. For example, a consumer might want a functional, reliable car to commute to work everyday, but a flashier model with more 'zing' when going out on a date in the evening. Sadly, there are examples of people using products by which the goal of enhancing the ideal self ends up conflicting with and damaging the actual self. The body-building craze that swept through the US and the north-east of England resulted in an increasing number of young men using anabolic steroids for body-building. This steroid use may 'bulk up' the physique (and provide a faster attainment of the ideal self), but it also damages the actual self, since the steroids cause male infertility.[61]

An exploration of the conflicts Muslim women who choose to wear headscarves experience illustrates how even a simple piece of cloth reflects a person's aesthetic, political and moral dimensions.[62] The Turkish women in the study expressed the tension they felt in their ongoing struggle to reconcile ambiguous religious principles that simultaneously call for modesty and beauty. Society sends Muslim women contradictory messages in modern-day Turkey. Although the Koran denounces waste, many of the companies that produce religious headscarves introduce new designs each season and, as styles and tastes change, women are encouraged to purchase more scarves than necessary. Moreover, the authors point out that a wearer communicates her fashion sense by the fabrics she selects and by the way she drapes and ties her scarf. In addition, veiling sends contradictory images about the proper sex roles of men and women. On the one hand, women who cover their heads by choice feel a sense of empowerment. On the other, the notion that Islamic law exhorts women to cover themselves lest they threaten men's self-restraint and honour is a persistent sign that men exert control over women's bodies and restrict their freedom. As a compromise solution Nike designed a uniform for observant women in Somalia who want to play sports without abandoning the traditional *hijab* (a robe that wraps around the head and loosely drapes over the entire body). The company streamlined the garment so that volleyball players could move but still keep their bodies covered.[63]

While these findings make some intuitive sense, we cannot blithely assume that consumers will always buy products whose characteristics match their own. It is not clear that consumers really see aspects of themselves in down-to-earth, functional products that do not have very complex or human-like images. It is one thing to consider a brand personality for an expressive, image-oriented product like perfume and quite another to impute human characteristics to a toaster.

Another problem is the old 'chicken-and-egg' question: do people buy products because the products are seen as similar to the self, or do they *assume* that these products must be similar because they have bought them? The similarity between a person's self-image and the images of products purchased does tend to increase with ownership, so this explanation cannot be ruled out.

The extended self

As noted earlier, many of the props and settings consumers use to define their social roles in a sense become a part of their selves. Those external objects that we consider a part of us comprise the **extended self**. In some cultures, people literally incorporate objects into the self – they lick new possessions, take the names of conquered enemies (or in some cases ate them) or bury the dead with their possessions.[64] We don't usually go that far, but many people do cherish possessions as if they were a part of them. Many material objects, ranging from personal possessions and pets to national monuments or landmarks, help to form a consumer's identity. Just about everyone can name a valued possession that has a lot of the self 'wrapped up' in it, whether it is a treasured photograph, a trophy, an old shirt, a car or a cat. Indeed, it is often possible to construct a pretty accurate 'biography' of someone just by cataloguing the items on display in their bedroom or office.

In an important study on the self and possessions, four levels of the extended self were described. These range from very personal objects to places and things that allow people to feel like they are rooted in their larger social environments:[65]

- *Individual level.* Consumers include many of their personal possessions in self-definition. These products can include jewellery, cars, clothing and so on. The saying 'You are what you wear' reflects the belief that one's things are a part of what one is.
- *Family level.* This part of the extended self includes a consumer's residence and its furnishings. The house can be thought of as a symbolic body for the family and often is a central aspect of identity.

This Italian ad demonstrates that our favourite products are part of the extended self.

D'Adda, Lorenzini, Vigorelli, BBDO S.p.A. Photo: Ilan Rubin.

- *Community level.* It is common for consumers to describe themselves in terms of the neighbourhood or town from which they come. For farming families or residents with close ties to a community, this sense of belonging is particularly important.
- *Group level.* Our attachments to certain social groups can be considered a part of self. A consumer may feel that landmarks, monuments or sports teams are a part of the extended self.

GENDER ROLES

Sexual identity is a very important component of a consumer's self-concept. People often conform to their culture's expectations about how those of their gender should act, dress, speak and so on. Of course, these guidelines change over time, and they can differ radically across societies. Some societies are highly dichotomized, with little tolerance for deviation from gender norms. In other societies this is not the case, and greater freedom in behaviour, including behaviour stemming from sexual orientation, is allowed. In certain societies, lip-service is paid to gender equality, but inequalities are just under the surface; in others, there is greater sharing of power, of resources and of decision-making. To the extent that our culture is everything that we learn, then virtually all aspects of the consumption process must be affected by culture. It is not always clear to what extent sex differences are innate rather than culturally shaped – but they are certainly evident in many consumption decisions.[66]

Consider the gender differences market researchers have observed when comparing the food preferences of men and women. Women eat more fruit, men are more likely to eat meat. As one food writer put it, 'Boy food doesn't grow. It is hunted or killed.' Men are more likely to eat Frosted Flakes or Corn Flakes, while women prefer multigrain cereals. Men are more likely than women to consume soft drinks, while women account for the bulk of sales of bottled water. The sexes also differ sharply in the quantities of food they eat: when researchers at Hershey's discovered that women eat smaller amounts of sweets, the company created a white chocolate confection called Hugs, one of the most successful food launches of all time. However, a man in a Burger King Whopper ad ditches his date at a fancy restaurant, complaining that he is 'too hungry to settle for chick food'. Pumped up on Whoppers, a swelling mob of men shake their fists, punch one another, toss a van off a bridge, and sing, 'I will eat this meat until my innie turns into an outie', and 'I am hungry. I am incorrigible. I am man'.[67]

Gender differences in socialization

A society's assumptions about the proper roles of men and women are communicated in terms of the ideal behaviours that are stressed for each sex (in advertising, among other places). It is likely, for instance, that many women eat smaller quantities because they have been 'trained' to be more delicate and dainty.

Gender goals and expectations[68]

In many societies, males are controlled by **agentic goals**, which stress self-assertion and mastery. Females, on the other hand, are taught to value **communal goals**, such as affiliation and the fostering of harmonious relations.[69]

Every society creates a set of expectations regarding the behaviours appropriate for men and women, and finds ways to communicate these priorities. This training begins very young: even children's birthday stories reinforce sex roles. A recent analysis showed that while stereotypical depictions have decreased over time, female characters in children's books are still far more likely to take on nurturant roles such as baking and gift-giving. The adult who prepares the birthday celebration is almost always the mother – often no adult male is present at all. On the other hand, the male figure in these stories is often cast in the role of a miraculous provider of gifts.[70] Not surprisingly, we observe the same gender difference in social media: women are just more enthusiastic about connecting with others. Although there are more men online on the global internet, women spend about 8 per cent more time online, averaging 25 hours per month on the web. Women around the world over spend 20 per cent more time on retail sites overall than men. In a typical month, about 76 per cent of all women globally interact with a social networking site, as compared to only 70 per cent of men. And, women spend significantly more time on social networking sites than men, with women averaging 5.5 hours per month compared to 4 hours for men.[71]

Macho marketers?

Marketing has historically been defined largely by men, so it still tends to be dominated by male values. Competition rather than co-operation is stressed, and the language of warfare and domination is often used. Strategists often use distinctly masculine concepts: 'market penetration' or 'competitive thrusts', for example. Marketing articles in academic journals also emphasize agentic rather than communal goals. The most pervasive theme is power and control over others. Other themes include instrumentality (manipulating people for the good of an organization) and competition.[72] This bias may diminish in years to come, as more marketing researchers begin to stress such factors as emotions and aesthetics in purchase decisions, and as increasing numbers of women graduate in marketing. For the time being, it seems a slow process . . . A recent study indicates that our brains are 'wired' to react differently to males and females – and it may help to explain why men tend to objectify women. A study that used brain-scanning technology showed photos of women wearing bikinis to a group of heterosexual male students and tracked which areas of their brains lit up. The activated areas were the same as those that get aroused when males handle tools. In a follow-up study, men tended to associate bikini-clad women with first-person action verbs such as I 'push', 'handle' and 'grab' instead of the third-person forms such as she 'pushes', 'handles' and 'grabs'. On the other hand, when they saw photos of fully clothed women, they reverted to the third-person forms, which implied they perceived these women as being in control of their own actions. Female subjects who responded to both sets of pictures did not display this difference.[73]

Gender *vs* sexual identity

Sex role identity is a state of mind as well as body. A person's biological gender (i.e. male or female) does not totally determine whether they will exhibit **sex-typed traits**, or characteristics that are stereotypically associated with one sex or the other. A consumer's subjective feelings about their sexuality are crucial as well.[74]

Unlike maleness and femaleness, masculinity and femininity are *not* biological characteristics. A behaviour considered masculine in one culture may not be viewed as such in another. For example, the norm in northern Europe, and in Scandinavia in particular, is that men are stoic, while cultures in southern Europe and in Latin America allow men to show their emotions. Each society determines what 'real' men and women should and should not do.

Sex-typed products

Many products also are *sex-typed*: they take on masculine or feminine attributes, and consumers often associate them with one sex or another.[75] The sex-typing of products is often created or perpetuated by marketers (e.g. Princess telephones, boys' and girls' toys, and babies' colour-coded nappies). Even brand names appear to be sex-typed: those containing alphanumerics (e.g. Formula 409, 10W40, Clorox 2) are assumed to be technical and hence masculine.[76] Our gender also seems to influence the instrumentality of the products we buy. Studies have shown that men tend to buy instrumental and leisure items impulsively, projecting independence and activity, while women tend to buy symbolic and self-expressive goods concerned with appearance and emotional aspects of self. Other research has shown, for example, that men take a more self-oriented approach to buying clothing, stressing its use as expressive symbols of personality and functional benefits, whilst women have 'other-oriented' concerns, choosing to use clothes as symbols of their social and personal interrelatedness with others.[77]

This German ad evokes a masculine ideal of beauty to highlight the strength of a glue product.
Courtesy of DDB Tribal Hamburg.

Androgyny

Masculinity and femininity are not opposite ends of the same dimension. **Androgyny** refers to the possession of both masculine and feminine traits.[78] Researchers make a distinction between *sex-typed people*, who are stereotypically masculine or feminine, and *androgynous people*, whose mixture of characteristics allows them to function well in a variety of social situations.[79]

Differences in sex-role orientation can influence responses to marketing stimuli, at least under some circumstances.[80] For example, research evidence indicates that females are more likely to undergo elaborate processing of message content, so they tend to be more sensitive to specific pieces of information when forming a judgement, while males are more influenced by overall themes.[81] In addition, women with a relatively strong masculine component in their sex-role identity prefer ad portrayals that include non-traditional women.[82] Some research indicates that sex-typed people are more sensitive to the sex-role depictions of characters in advertising, although women appear to be more sensitive to gender role relationships than are men. A study demonstrated that sex-role assumptions travel into cyberspace as well. The researchers asked each volunteer to interact with another respondent via a chat room. They showed subjects an avatar to represent the other person, with images ranging from 'an obviously female' blonde to one with no clear gender to a strong-jawed male. The subjects rated their partners as less 'credible' when they saw an androgynous avatar than when they saw one with sex-typed facial characteristics.[83]

Sex-typed people in general are more concerned with ensuring that their behaviour is consistent with their culture's definition of gender appropriateness.

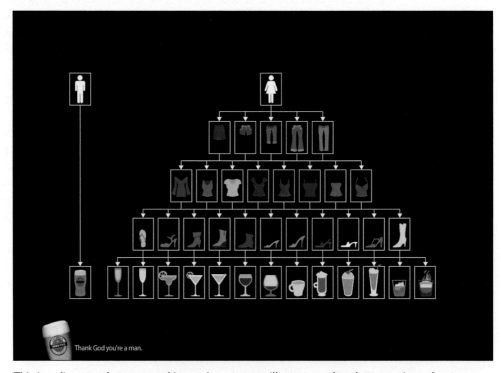

This Israeli poster that appeared in men's restrooms illustrates cultural assumptions about sex role differences.

Courtesy of McCann Erickson (Photograph by Goldstar).

Female gender roles

Gender roles for women are changing rapidly. Social changes, such as the dramatic increase in the proportion of women in waged work, have led to an upheaval in the way women are regarded by men, the way they regard themselves and in the products they choose to buy. Modern women now play a greater role in decisions regarding traditionally male purchases. For example, more than 60 per cent of new car buyers under the age of 50 are female, and women even buy almost half of all condoms sold.[84]

Segmenting women

In the 1949 movie *Adam's Rib*, Katherine Hepburn played a stylish and competent lawyer. This film was one of the first to show that a woman can have a successful career and still be happily married. Today, the evolution of a new managerial class of women has forced marketers to change their traditional assumptions about women as they target this growing market. For example, Suzuki is going out of its way to appeal to the growing number of women in India who are achieving financial independence and buying their own cars. Its Zen Estilo (*Estilo* means 'style' in Spanish) model comes in eight colours, including 'purple fusion', 'virgin blue' and 'sparkling olive'.[85] Ironically, it seems that in some cases marketers have overcompensated for their former emphasis on women as housewives. Many attempts to target the vast market of females employed outside the home tend to depict all these women in glamorous, executive positions. This portrayal ignores the fact that the majority of women do not hold such jobs, and that many work because they have to, rather than for self-fulfilment. This diversity means that not all women should be expected to respond to marketing campaigns that stress professional achievement or the glamour of the working life.

Whether or not they work outside the home, many women have come to value greater independence and respond positively to marketing campaigns that stress the freedom to make their own lifestyle decisions. American Express has been targeting women for a long time, but the company found that its 'Do you know me?' campaign did not appeal to women as much as to men. A campaign aimed specifically at women featured confident women using their American Express cards. By depicting women in active situations, the company greatly increased its share of the women's credit card market.[86]

Although women continue to be depicted in traditional roles, this situation is changing as advertisers scramble to catch up with reality. For example, the highly successful Dove Real Beauty campaign has significantly changed women's perceptions of what is 'beautiful', particularly with respect to the notion of beauty and natural ageing. The campaign shows women in various roles, and at varying ages, and the notion of 'beauty' is central to the discussions.[87] Women are now as likely as men to be central characters in television commercials. But while males are increasingly depicted as spouses and parents, women are still more likely than men to be seen in domestic settings. Also, about 90 per cent of all narrators in commercials are male. The deeper male voice is apparently perceived as more authoritative and credible.[88]

Some ads now feature *role reversal*, where women occupy traditional men's roles. In other cases, women are portrayed in romantic situations, but they tend to be more sexually dominant. Ironically, current advertising is more free to emphasize traditional female traits now that sexual equality is becoming more of an accepted fact. This freedom is demonstrated in a German poster for a women's magazine. The caption reads, 'Today's women can sometimes show weakness, because they are strong'.

Male sex roles

While the traditional conception of the ideal male as a tough, aggressive, muscular man who enjoys 'manly' sports and activities is not dead, society's definition of the male role is evolving.

As with female roles, this evolution is a slow process. When global entrepreneur and CEO of Virgin Airlines Richard Branson lost a racing bet to the owner of AirAsia, his 'sentence' was to dress as a female flight attendant for the winner's airline. The winner gloated, '. . . I'm looking forward to him sucking up to me as a stewardess!'[89] Starting in the late 1990s, men were allowed to be more compassionate and to have close friendships with other men. In contrast to the depiction of macho men who do not show feelings, some marketers were promoting men's 'sensitive' side. An emphasis on male bonding was the centrepiece of many ad campaigns, especially for beers.[90] Just as for women, however, the true story is more complicated than that. Indeed, scholars of **masculinism** study the male image and the complex cultural meanings of masculinity.[91] Like women, men receive mixed messages about how they are supposed to behave and feel. No doubt one of the biggest marketing buzzwords over the past few years is the **metrosexual**, a straight, urban male who is keenly interested in fashion, home design, gourmet cooking, and personal care. For another take on the presentation and fashion of males, and the evolution to the 'retrosexual', see the case 'Being a Real Man About Town' at the end of this Part. A gay writer named Mark Simpson actually coined the term way back in a 1994 article when he 'outed' British soccer star and pop icon David Beckham as a metrosexual. Simpson noted that Beckham is 'almost as famous for wearing sarongs and pink nail polish and panties belonging to his wife, Victoria (aka Posh from the Spice Girls), as he is for his impressive ball skills. In the second decade of the 2000s, you can insert your more contemporary favourite: Zac Efron? Ryan Seacreast? Hugh Jackman?'[92]

Some analysts argue that men are threatened because they do not necessarily recognize themselves in the powerful male stereotypes against which feminists protest.[93] One study examined how American men pursue masculine identities through their everyday consumption. The researchers suggest that men are trying to make sense out of three different models of masculinity that they call *breadwinner*, *rebel* and *man-of-action hero*, as they figure out just who they are supposed to be. On the one hand, the breadwinner model draws from the American myth of success and celebrates respectability, civic virtues, pursuit of material success and organized achievement. The rebel model, on the other hand, emphasizes rebellion, independence, adventure and potency. The man-of-action hero is a synthesis that draws from the better of the other two models.[94]

One consequence of the continual evolution of sex roles is that men are concerned as never before with their appearance. Men spend $7.7 billion on grooming products globally each year. A wave of male cleansers, moisturizers, sunscreens, depilatories and body sprays is washing up on US shores, largely from European marketers. L'Oréal Paris reports that men's skincare product is now its fastest-growing sector. In Europe, 24 per cent of men younger than age 30 use skincare products – and 80 per cent of young Korean men do. Men are a bit more store-loyal than women when shopping for beauty cosmetics (for brick and mortar stores), and a bit more likely to make use of the internet once they have found a brand that works for them.[95]

Beefcake: the depiction of men in advertising

Men as well as women are often depicted in a negative fashion in advertising. They frequently come across as helpless or bumbling. As one advertising executive put it, 'The woman's movement raised consciousness in the ad business as to how women can be depicted. The thought now is, if we can't have women in these old-fashioned traditional roles, at least we can have men being dummies.'[96]

Just as advertisers are criticized for depicting women as sex objects, so the same accusations can be made about how males are portrayed – a practice correspondingly known as 'beefcake'.[97] An advertising campaign for Sansabelt trousers featured the theme, 'What women look for in men's pants.' Ads featured a woman who confides, 'I always lower my eyes when a man passes [pause] to see if he's worth following.' One female executive commented, 'Turnabout is fair play . . . If we can't put a stop to sexism in advertising . . . at least we can have some fun with it and do a little leering of our own.'[98]

Gay, lesbian, bisexual and transgender (LGBT) consumers

Gay and lesbian consumers are still largely ignored by marketers. This situation is starting to change, however, as some marketers are acknowledging the upmarket demographic profile of these consumers.[99] IKEA, the Swedish furniture retailer with outlets throughout Europe and in several major US cities, broke new ground by running a TV spot featuring a gay male couple purchasing a dining-room table at the shop.[100] Other major companies making an effort to market to homosexuals include AT&T, Anheuser-Busch, Apple Computers, Benetton, Philip Morris, Seagram and Sony.[101] Gay consumers can even get their own credit card – a Rainbow Visa card issued by Travelers Bank USA. Using tennis star Martina Navratilova as spokeswoman, such groups as the National Center for Lesbian Rights are benefited by users of the card. The card allows people who don't qualify based on income to apply with a same-sex partner.[102] Kurt, the gay character on the hit show *Glee* (played by actor Chris Colfer) is but the latest celebrity to publicize the issues GLBT consumers face. To promote better understanding of these problems, Google Chrome created a supportive video for LGBT teens as part of the 'It Gets Better' campaign that aired during a 2011 episode; actors included Adam Lambert, Lady Gaga, Kathy Griffin and even Woody from *Toy Story*. Among other celebrities who are participating in this effort, the US President, Barach Obama uploaded a video on the campaign's YouTube channel to let LGBT teens know that 'there are people out there who love you and care about you just the way you are'.[103] Slowly but surely, the gay market is going mainstream.

The percentage of the population that is gay and lesbian is difficult to determine, and efforts to measure this group have been controversial.[104] However, the respected research company Yankelovich Partners Inc., which has tracked consumer values and attitudes since 1971 in its annual Monitor survey, now includes a question about sexual identity in its survey. This study was virtually the first to use a sample that reflects the population as a whole instead of polling only smaller or biased groups (such as readers of gay publications) whose responses may not be representative of all consumers. About 6 per cent of respondents identified themselves as gay/homosexual/lesbian. As of 2012, there has been tremendous growth in marketing and public relations firms which specialize in consulting with and for companies of all sizes regarding the LGBT market, globally.

As civil rights gains are made by gay activists, the social climate is becoming more favourable for firms targeting this market segment.[105] In one of the first academic studies in this field, the conclusion was that gays and lesbians did not qualify as a market segment because they did not satisfy the traditional criteria of being identifiable, accessible and of sufficient size.[106] Subsequent studies have argued that the segmentation criteria rely on outdated assumptions regarding the nature of consumers, marketing activities and the ways in which media are used in the contemporary marketplace. Here, the argument is that identifiability is an unreliable construct for socially subordinated groups, and really is not the issue anyway. How marketers segment (by race, ethnicity, gender or, in this case, sexuality) is not as important as whether the group itself expresses consumption patterns in identifiable ways. Similarly, the accessibility criterion continues with the assumption of active marketers who contact passive consumers. This criterion also needs to take into account the dramatic changes in media over the past two decades, in particular the use of speciality media by marketers to access special-interest segments. Gay consumers are also active web surfers: the website **Gay.com** attracts 1 million consumers a month. As many as 65 per cent of gay and lesbian internet users go online more than once a day and over 70 per cent make purchases online.[107] Finally, sufficient size assumes separate campaigns are necessary to reach each segment, an assumption that ignores consumers' ability and willingness to explore multiple media.[108]

At least in some parts of the US and Europe, homosexuality appears to be becoming more mainstream and accepted.[109] Mattel even sells an Earring Magic Ken doll, complete with *faux*-leather vest, lavender mesh shirt and two-tone hair (though the product has become a favourite of gay men, the company denied it was targeted at that group). More importantly, the LGBT community is becoming better organized, particularly in terms of having their 'consumer voice' heard. Global companies are all now aware of and working for high ratings from the LGBT segment.[110]

MARKETING OPPORTUNITY

Lesbian consumers have recently been in the cultural spotlight, perhaps due in part to the actions of such high-profile cultural figures as Martina Navratilova, singers k.d. lang and Melissa Etheridge, and actress Ellen DeGeneres. Whatever the reason, American Express, Stolichnaya vodka, Atlantic Records and Naya bottled water are among those corporations now running ads in lesbian publications (an ad for American Express Travellers Cheques for Two shows two women's signatures on a cheque). Acting on research that showed that lesbians are four times as likely to own one of their cars, Subaru of America recently began to target this market as well.[111]

BODY IMAGE

For many women, trying on jeans is a painful exercise. Levi Strauss' recently launched an online fitting service called the Curve ID system to make the process a little more comfortable. The digital offering is available in 20 languages and 50 countries; it is based on 60,000 women's figures worldwide and its goal is to provide a more customized experience to ease

University student Galia Slayen created a 'life-size' Barbie (39 inch bust, 18 inch waist and 33 inch hips) for an eating disorders awareness event at her school. When she was interviewed about the impact the doll had on her as she was growing up, she commented, 'I'm not blaming Barbie [for her own eating disorder] . . . I'm blond and blue-eyed and I figured that was what I was supposed to look like. She was my idol. It impacted the way I looked at myself.'
Courtesy of Galia Slayen.

the frustration many women feel as they search for the perfect pair of jeans.[112] A person's physical appearance is a large part of their self-concept. **Body image** refers to a consumer's subjective evaluation of their physical self. As was the case with the overall self-concept, this image is not necessarily accurate. A man may think of himself as being more muscular than he really is, or a woman may think she is fatter than is the case. In fact, it is not uncommon to find marketing strategies that exploit consumers' tendencies to distort their body images by preying upon insecurities about appearance, thereby creating a gap between the real and the ideal physical self and, consequently, the desire to purchase products and services to narrow that gap.

Body cathexis

A person's feelings about their body can be described in terms of **body cathexis**. Cathexis refers to the emotional significance of some object or idea to a person, and some parts of the body are more central to self-concept than others. One study of young adults' feelings about their bodies found that these respondents were most satisfied with their hair and eyes and had least positive feelings about their waists. These feelings were related to consumption of grooming products. Consumers who were more satisfied with their bodies were more frequent users of such 'preening' products as hair conditioner, hairdryers, aftershave, artificial tanning products, toothpaste and pumice soap.[113] In a large-scale study of older women in six European countries, the results showed that women would like to 'grow old beautifully', and that they were prepared to follow diets, exercise and use cosmetics to reach this goal. Wrinkles were the biggest concern, and Greek and Italian women were by far the most concerned about how to combat ageing, with northern European women expressing more agreement with the statement that ageing was natural and inevitable.[114]

As suggested by this Emporio Armani ad, a global perspective on ideals of beauty is resulting in more ways to be considered attractive.

Getty Images.

Ideals of beauty

A person's satisfaction with the physical image they present to others is affected by how closely that image corresponds to the image valued by their culture. In fact, infants as young as two months show a preference for attractive faces.[115] An ideal of beauty is a particular model, or exemplar, of appearance. Ideals of beauty for both men and women may include physical features (big breasts or small, bulging muscles or not) as well as clothing styles, cosmetics, hairstyles, skin tone (pale *vs* tan) and body type (petite, athletic, voluptuous, etc.).

Is beauty universal?

It's no secret that despite the popular saying 'You can't judge a book by its cover', people can and do. Fairly or not, we assume that more attractive people are smarter, more interesting, and more competent – researchers call this the *'what is beautiful is good'* stereotype.[116] Indeed, recent research evidence indicates there is some truth to this assumption – beautiful people are generally happier than average or below average looking people and economists calculate that about half of that boost stems from the fact that they make more money![117] By the way, this bias affects both men and women – men with above-average looks earn about five per cent more than those of average appearance, and those who are below average in appearance make an average of nine per cent less than the norm.

Recent research indicates that preferences for some physical features over others are 'wired in' genetically, and that these reactions tend to be the same among people around the world. Specifically, people appear to favour features associated with good health and youth, attributes linked to reproductive ability and strength. Men are also more likely to use a woman's body shape as a sexual cue, and it has been theorized that this is because feminine curves provide evidence of reproductive potential. During puberty a typical female gains almost 15kg of 'reproductive fat' around hips and thighs which supplies the approximately 80,000 extra calories needed for pregnancy. Most fertile women have waist:hip ratios of 0.6:0.8, an hour-glass shape that happens to be the one men rank highest. Even though preferences for total weight change, waist:hip ratios tend to stay in this range – even the super-thin model Twiggy (who pioneered the 'waif' look decades before Kate Moss) had a ratio of 0.73.[118] Other positively valued female characteristics include a higher forehead than average, fuller lips, a shorter jaw and a smaller chin and nose. Women, on the other hand, favour men with a heavy lower face, those who are slightly above average height and those with a prominent brow.

Of course, the way these faces are 'packaged' still varies enormously, and that is where marketers come in. Advertising and other forms of mass media play a significant role in determining which forms of beauty are considered desirable at any point in time. An ideal of beauty functions as a sort of cultural yardstick. Consumers compare themselves to some standard (often advocated by the fashion media) and are dissatisfied with their appearance to the extent that it does not match up to it. These mass media portrayals have been criticized not only on social grounds, but on issues of health as well. In a study of New Zealand print advertisements over the period 1958–88, the findings confirmed that advertising models became thinner and less curvaceous over the 30-year period, resulting in contemporary models being approximately 8.5kg lighter than they would be if they had the same body shape as models of the late 1950s. To achieve the currently fashionable body shape, a young woman of average height would have to weigh approximately 42kg, which is far below the recommended level for good health.[119] Clearly, what constitutes 'beauty' for women involves a number of complex relationships – a recent study in The Netherlands found that Dutch women consider friendliness, self-confidence, happiness and humour are the most important pillars of female beauty, while only two per cent found 'pretty' a description for female beauty. A majority of the over 3,200 women in the study felt that the media's depiction of the 'ideal' female beauty was unrealistic. Most of the women in the study complained slightly of their weight and the shape of their body.[120]

Ideals of beauty over time

While beauty may be only skin deep, throughout history and across cultures women in particular have worked very hard to attain it. They have starved themselves, painfully bound their feet, inserted plates into their lips, spent countless hours under hairdryers, in front of mirrors and beneath ultraviolet lights, and have undergone breast reduction or enlargement operations to alter their appearance and meet their society's expectations of what a beautiful woman should look like.

Periods of history tend to be characterized by a specific 'look' or ideal of beauty. American history can be described in terms of a succession of dominant ideals. For example, in sharp contrast to today's emphasis on health and vigour, in the early 1800s it was fashionable to appear delicate to the point of looking ill. The poet John Keats described the ideal woman of that time as 'a milk white lamb that bleats for man's protection'. Other looks have included the voluptuous, lusty woman as epitomized by Lillian Russell, the athletic Gibson Girl of the 1890s, and the small, boyish flapper of the 1920s as exemplified by Clara Bow.[121]

Throughout much of the nineteenth century, the desirable waistline for American women was 18 inches, a circumference that required the use of corsets pulled so tight that they routinely caused headaches, fainting fits, and possibly even the uterine and spinal disorders common among women of the time. While modern women are not quite as 'strait-laced', many still endure such indignities as high heels, body waxing, eye-lifts and liposuction. In addition to the millions spent on cosmetics, clothing, health clubs and fashion magazines, these practices remind us that – rightly or wrongly – the desire to conform to current standards of beauty is alive and well.

The ideal body type of Western women has changed radically over time, and these changes have resulted in a realignment of *sexual dimorphic markers* – those aspects of the body that distinguish between the sexes. For example, analyses of the measurements of *Playboy* centrefolds over a 20-year period from 1958 to 1978 show that these ideals became thinner and more muscular. The average hip measurement went from 36 inches in 1958 to just over 34 inches in 1978. Average bust size shrank from almost 37 inches in 1958 to about 35 inches in 1978.[122]

The Dove campaign emphasizes that our ideals about beauty, and what is beautiful, vary over time, place and age.
Unilever.

171

Is the ideal getting real?

Fed up because you don't get mistaken for a svelte supermodel on the street? Dove's well-known Campaign for Real Beauty that features women with imperfect bodies in their underwear may help. One ad reads, 'Let's face it, firming the thighs of a size 8 supermodel wouldn't have been much of a challenge.' Unilever initiated the campaign after its research showed that many women didn't believe its products worked because the women shown using them were so unrealistic.[123] When the company asked 3,200 women around the world to describe their looks, most summed themselves up as 'average' or 'natural'. Only two per cent called themselves 'beautiful'.

Marketers of its Dove brand sensed an opportunity, and they set out to reassure women about their insecurities by showing them as they are – wrinkles, freckles, pregnant bellies and all. Taglines ask 'Oversized or Outstanding?' or 'Wrinkled or Wonderful?' The brand also sponsored a survey of 1,800 American women to assess how they felt about their looks. Overall, they found that women were satisfied with who they are, and these positive feelings were even stronger in sub-groups such as African American and Hispanic women, younger women, and wealthier women. Fifty-two per cent of women between the ages of 18 and 39 said that 'looking beautiful' describes them very well, whereas 37 per cent of women aged 40 and older feel the same. And 75 per cent of the women agree that beauty does not come from a woman's looks but from her spirit and love of life. Only 26 per cent feel that our society uses reasonable standards to evaluate women's beauty.[124]

However, Unilever's experience with Chinese women reminds us again that appearance norms are strongly rooted in culture. Dove's Campaign for Real Beauty flopped in China – after the fact Unilever's research showed that many Chinese women *do* believe they can attain the kind of airbrushed beauty they see in advertising. As a result the company scrapped the campaign there and instead launched a Chinese version of *Ugly Betty* – a successful American sitcom, which was in turn adapted from a Colombian telenovela. The show, *Ugly Wudi*, focuses on fictional ad agency employee Lin Wudi, who strives to unveil her own beauty – aided by the numerous Dove products that appear in the show. As you might expect, it helps that the actress who played Wudi has perfect skin and actually is quite attractive once you strip away the oversized glasses and the fake braces.[125]

We can also distinguish among ideals of beauty for men in terms of facial features, musculature and facial hair – who could confuse Johnny Depp with Mr Bean? In fact, one national survey which asked both men and women to comment on male aspects of appearance found that the dominant standard of beauty for men is a strongly masculine, muscled body – though women tend to prefer men with less muscle mass than men themselves strive to attain.[126] Advertisers appear to have the males' ideal in mind – a study of men appearing in advertisements found that most sport the strong and muscular physique of the male stereotype.[127]

Working on the body

Because many consumers are motivated to match up to an ideal appearance, they often go to great lengths to change aspects of their physical selves. From cosmetics to plastic surgery, tanning salons to diet drinks, a multitude of products and services are directed towards altering or maintaining aspects of the physical self in order to present a desirable appearance. It is difficult to overstate the importance of the physical self-concept (and the desire by consumers to improve their appearance) to many marketing activities.

Sizeism

As reflected in the expression 'you can never be too thin or too rich', many Western societies have an obsession with weight. Even primary school children perceive obesity as worse than being disabled.[128] The pressure to be slim is continually reinforced both by advertising and by

There are 3 billion women who don't look like supermodels and only 8 who do.

THE BODY SHOP
KNOW YOUR MIND LOVE YOUR BODY

The Body Shop taps into the growing sentiment against unrealistic ideals of beauty.
Reproduced with the kind permission of The Body Shop.

peers. Americans in particular are preoccupied by what they weigh. They are continually bombarded by images of thin, happy people.

How realistic are these appearance standards? In Europe, the public discourse on appearance and body weight is becoming more active and visible, particularly with respect to the weight of European children. Of the 77 million children in the EU, 14 million are overweight. The EU has launched a 'platform' on diet, physical activity and health as a public policy approach to the issue of weight. Obesity is especially acute in Mediterranean countries, underscoring concerns that people in the southern region are turning away from the traditional diet of fish, fruits and vegetables to fast food, high in fat and refined carbohydrates.[129] Still, many consumers focus on attaining an unrealistic ideal weight, sometimes by relying on height and weight charts which show what one should weigh. These expectations are communicated in subtle ways. Even fashion dolls, such as the ubiquitous Barbie, reinforce the ideal of thinness. The dimensions of these dolls, when extrapolated to average female body sizes, are unnaturally long and thin.[130] In spite of Americans' obsession about weight, as a country they continue to have a greater percentage of obesity in the general population relative to all European countries, as shown in Figure 5.1. Within Europe, female and male consumers aged 15 to 24 from Malta, Germany and England lead the EU in measures of obesity.[131]

Want to calculate your own body mass index? Go to **http://www.consumer.gov/weightloss/bmi.htm#BMI** and fill in your personal data.

Body image distortions

While many people perceive a strong link between self-esteem and appearance, some consumers unfortunately exaggerate this connection even more, and sacrifice greatly to attain what they consider to be a desirable body image. Women tend to be taught to a greater degree than men that the quality of their bodies reflects their self-worth, so it is not surprising that most major distortions of body image occur among females.

Men do not tend to differ in ratings of their current figure, their ideal figure and the figure they think is most attractive to women. In contrast, women rate both the figure they think is

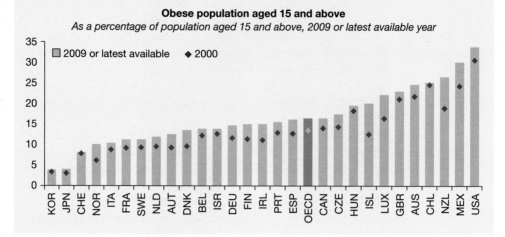

Figure 5.1 Obese population comparison

Source: OECD (2011), *OECD Health Statistics*, OECD Publishing.

most attractive to men and their ideal figure as much thinner than their actual figure.[132] In one survey, two-thirds of college women admitted resorting to unhealthy behaviour to control weight. Advertising messages that convey an image of slimness help to reinforce these activities by arousing insecurities about weight.[133]

A distorted body image has been linked to the rise in eating disorders, which are particularly prevalent among young women. People with anorexia regard themselves as fat, and starve themselves in the quest for thinness. This condition may be accompanied by bulimia, which involves two stages: first, binge eating occurs (usually in private), where more than 5,000 calories may be consumed at one time. The binge is then followed by induced vomiting, abuse of laxatives, fasting and/or overly strenuous exercise – a 'purging' process that reasserts the woman's sense of control.

Most eating disorders are found in white, teenaged girls and students. Victims often have brothers or fathers who are hypercritical of their weight. In addition, binge eating may be encouraged by one's peers. Groups such as athletic teams and social clubs at school may develop positive norms regarding binge eating. In one study of a female social club, members' popularity within the group increased the more they binged.[134]

Eating disorders do affect some men as well. They are common among male athletes who must also conform to various weight requirements, such as jockeys, boxers and male models.[135] In general, though, most men who have distorted body images consider themselves to be too light rather than too heavy: society has taught them that they must be muscular to be masculine. Men are more likely than women to express their insecurities about their bodies by becoming addicted to exercise. In fact, striking similarities have been found between male compulsive runners and female anorexics. These include a commitment to diet and exercise as a central part of one's identity and susceptibility to body image distortions.[136]

Cosmetic surgery

The Cosmetic Surgery Europe website (**http://www.cosmetic-surgery-europe.com/**) lists hundreds of clinics, and several websites also point out to Western Europeans that the options for highly skilled, safe and very affordable cosmetic surgery can be found in Eastern European countries such as Poland and the Czech Republic. There is no longer much (if any) psychological stigma associated with having this type of operation: it is commonplace and accepted among many segments of consumers.[137] In fact, men now account for as many as

20 per cent of plastic surgery patients. Popular operations include the implantation of silicon pectoral muscles (for the chest) and even calf implants to fill out 'chicken legs'.[138]

Many women turn to surgery either to reduce weight or to increase sexual desirability. The use of liposuction, where fat is removed from the thighs with a vacuum-like device, has almost doubled since it was introduced in the US in 1982.[139] Some women believe that larger breasts will increase their allure and undergo breast augmentation procedures. Although some of these procedures have generated controversy due to possible negative side effects, it is unclear whether potential medical problems will deter large numbers of women from choosing surgical options to enhance their (perceived) femininity. The importance of breast size to self-concept resulted in an interesting and successful marketing strategy undertaken by an underwear company. While conducting focus groups on bras, an analyst noted that small-chested women typically reacted with hostility when discussing the subject. They would unconsciously cover their chests with their arms as they spoke and felt that their needs were ignored by the fashion industry. To meet this overlooked need, the company introduced a line of A-cup bras called 'A-OK' and depicted wearers in a positive light. A new market segment was born. Other companies are going in the opposite direction by promoting bras that create the illusion of a larger cleavage. In Europe and the US, both Gossard and Playtex are aggressively marketing specially designed bras offering 'cleavage enhancement' which use a combination of wires and internal pads to create the desired effect. Recently, the market for women's bras has had to contend with at least one natural development: unaugmented breasts (no surgery) are getting bigger by themselves, as a result of using the pill and changes in diet. The average cup size in Britain has grown from 34B to 36C over the past 30 years, and bra designers such as Bioform and Airotic, and retailers such as Knickerbox and Victoria's Secret, have all responded with new product offerings to meet what they consider to be a long-term market trend.[140]

Body decoration and mutilation

The body is adorned or altered in some way in every culture. Decorating the self serves a number of purposes.[141]

- *To separate group members from non-members.* The Chinook Indians of North America used to press the head of a newborn baby between two boards for a year, permanently altering its shape. In our society, teenagers go out of their way to adopt distinctive hair and clothing styles that will distinguish them from adults.

- *To place the individual in the social organization.* Many cultures engage in rites of passage at puberty when a boy symbolically becomes a man. Young men in Ghana paint their bodies with white stripes to resemble skeletons to symbolize the death of their child status. In Western culture, this rite may involve some form of mild self-mutilation or engaging in dangerous activities.

- *To place the person in a gender category.* The Tchikrin Indians of South America insert a string of beads in a boy's lip to enlarge it. Western women wear lipstick to enhance femininity. At the turn of the century, small lips were fashionable because they represented women's submissive role at that time.[142] Today, big, red lips are provocative and indicate an aggressive sexuality. Some women, including a number of famous actresses and models, have collagen injections or lip inserts to create large, pouting lips (known in the modelling industry as 'liver lips').[143]

- *To enhance sex-role identification.* Wearing high heels, which podiatrists agree are a prime cause of knee and hip problems, backaches and fatigue, can be compared with the traditional Oriental practice of foot-binding to enhance femininity. As one doctor observed, 'When they [women] get home, they can't get their high-heeled shoes off fast enough. But every doctor in the world could yell from now until Doomsday, and women would still wear them.'[144]

● *To indicate desired social conduct.* The Suya of South America wear ear ornaments to emphasize the importance placed in their culture on listening and obedience. In Western society gay men may wear an earring to signal how they expect to be identified.

● *To indicate high status or rank.* The Hidates Indians of North America wear feather ornaments that indicate how many people they have killed. In our society, some people wear glasses with clear lenses, even though they do not have eye problems, to increase their perceived intellectual or fashion status.

● *To provide a sense of security.* Consumers often wear lucky charms, amulets, rabbits' feet and so on to protect them from the 'evil eye'. Some modern women wear a 'mugger whistle' around their necks for a similar reason.

Tattoos

Tattoos – both temporary and permanent – are a popular form of body adornment.[145] This body art can be used to communicate aspects of the self to onlookers and may serve some of the same functions that other kinds of body painting do in primitive cultures. In fact, much of the recent literature and discourse on tattoos centres on the theme of users as 'Modern Primitives'.[146] Tattoos (from the Tahitian *ta-tu*) have deep roots in folk art. Until recently, the images were crude and were primarily either death symbols (e.g. a skull), animals (especially panthers, eagles and snakes), pin-up women or military designs. More current influences include science fiction themes, Japanese symbolism and tribal designs.

A tattoo may be viewed as a fairly risk-free (?) way of expressing an adventurous side of the self. Tattoos have a long history of association with people who are social outcasts. For example, the faces and arms of criminals in sixth-century Japan were tattooed as a way of identifying them, as were Massachusetts prison inmates in the nineteenth century. These emblems are often used by marginal groups, such as bikers or Japanese *yakuze* (gang members), to express group identity and solidarity. In Europe today, the growth of tattoos on individuals of all ages

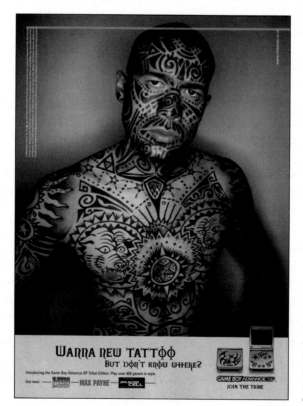

Body decoration can be permanent, or temporary, in order to distinguish oneself, shock others, signify group membership, or express a particular mood or message.

Leo Burnett Worldwide Ad Agency.

and social classes can be seen both as a form of communication, and a growth in commodification. European consumers are more and more often using their own skin as part of their expression of consumer culture.[147]

Body piercing

Decorating the body with various kinds of metallic inserts has evolved from a practice associated with some fringe groups to become a popular fashion statement. Piercings can range from a hoop protruding from a navel to scalp implants, where metal posts are inserted in the skull (do not try this at home!). Publications such as *Piercing Fans International Quarterly* are seeing their circulations soar and websites featuring piercings and piercing products are attracting numerous followers. This popularity is not pleasing to hard-core piercing fans, who view the practice as a sensual consciousness-raising ritual and are concerned that now people just do it because it is trendy. As one customer waiting for a piercing remarked, 'If your piercing doesn't mean anything, then it's just like buying a pair of platform shoes.'[148]

CHAPTER SUMMARY

Now that you have finished reading this chapter you should understand why:

→ **The self-concept strongly influences consumer behaviour.** Consumers' self-concepts are reflections of their attitudes towards themselves. Whether these attitudes are positive or negative, they will help to guide many purchase decisions; we can use products to bolster self-esteem or to 'reward' the self.

→ **Products often play a pivotal role in defining the self-concept.** We choose many products because we think that they are similar to our personalities. The symbolic interactionist perspective of the self implies that each of us actually has many selves, and we require a different set of products as props to play each role. We view many things other than the body as part of who we are. People use valued objects, cars, homes, and even attachments to sports teams or national monuments to define the self, when they incorporate these into the extended self.

→ **Society's expectations of masculinity and femininity help to determine the products we buy to be consistent with these expectations.** A person's sex-role identity is a major component of self-definition. Conceptions about masculinity and femininity, largely shaped by society, guide the acquisition of 'sex-typed' products and services.

The media play a key role in teaching us how to behave as 'proper' males and females. Advertising and other media play an important role because they socialize consumers to be male and female. Although traditional women's roles have often been perpetuated in advertising depictions, this situation is changing somewhat. The media do not always portray men accurately either.

→ **The way we think about our bodies (and the way our culture tells us we should think) is a key component of self-esteem.** A person's conception of his or her body also provides feedback to self-image. A culture communicates specific ideals of beauty, and consumers go to great lengths to attain these. Many consumer activities involve manipulating the body, whether through dieting, cosmetic surgery, piercing, or tattooing.

→ **Our desire to live up to cultural expectations of appearance can be harmful.** Sometimes these activities are carried to an extreme, as people try too hard to live up to cultural ideals. One common manifestation is eating disorders, diseases in which women in particular become obsessed with thinness.

→ **Every culture dictates certain types of body decoration or mutilation.** Body decoration or mutilation may serve such functions as separating group members from nonmembers, marking the individual's status or rank within a social organization or within a gender category (e.g. homosexual), or even providing a sense of security or good luck.

KEY TERMS

Actual self (p. 153)
Agentic goals (p. 162)
Androgyny (p. 164)
Avatars (p. 154)
Body cathexis (p. 169)
Body image (p. 169)
Communal goals (p. 162)
Computer-mediated environments (CMEs) (p. 154)
Extended self (p. 160)
Ideal self (p. 153)

Impression management (p. 153)
Looking-glass self (p. 156)
Masculinism (p. 166)
Metrosexual (p. 166)
Self-concept (p. 151)
Self-image congruence models (p. 159)
Sex-typed traits (p. 163)
Symbolic interactionism (p. 156)
Symbolic self-completion theory (p. 158)
Torn self (p. 154)
Virtual identities (p. 154)

CONSUMER BEHAVIOUR CHALLENGE

1 How might the creation of a self-conscious state be related to consumers who are trying on clothing in changing rooms? Does the act of preening in front of a mirror change the dynamics by which people evaluate their product choices? Why?

2 Is it ethical for marketers to encourage infatuation with the self?

3 List three dimensions by which the self-concept can be described.

4 Compare and contrast the real *vs* the ideal self. List three products for which each type of self is likely to be used as a reference point when a purchase is considered.

5 Watch a series of ads featuring men and women on television. Try to imagine the characters with reversed roles (the male parts played by women, and vice versa). Can you see any differences in assumptions about sex-typed behaviour?

6 To date, the bulk of advertising targeted at gay consumers has been placed in exclusively gay media. If it was your decision, would you consider using mainstream media to reach gays, who constitute a significant proportion of the general population? Or, bearing in mind that members of some targeted segments have serious objections to this practice, especially when the product (e.g. alcohol, cigarettes) may be viewed as harmful in some way, do you think gays should be singled out at all by marketers?

7 Do you agree that marketing strategies tend to have a male-oriented bias? If so, what are some possible consequences for specific marketing activities?

8 Construct a 'consumption biography' of a friend or family member. Make a list of and/or photograph their favourite possessions, and see if you or others can describe this person's personality just from the information provided by this catalogue.

9 Some consumer advocates have protested at the use of super-thin models in advertising, claiming that these women encourage others to starve themselves in order to attain the 'waif' look. Other critics respond that the media's power to shape behaviour has been overestimated, and that it is insulting to people to assume that they are unable to separate fantasy from reality. What do you think?

For additional material see the companion website at **www.pearsoned.co.uk/solomon**

NOTES

1. Daniel Goleman, 'When ugliness is only in patient's eye, body image can reflect mental disorder', *New York Times* (2 October 1991): C13. See also: Duncan Robertson (2007), 'Too Shy to Strip in Front of a Man' www.dailymail.co.uk/news/article-445068/Too-shy-strip-man.html

2. Duncan Robertson, 'Too Shy to Strip in Front of a Man', *Daily Mail*, 28 March 2007, based on a survey of 3,500 women for SHUC, a bathroom equipment company www.dailymail.co.uk/news/article-445068/Too-shy-strip-man.html

3. Sims, Josh, 'Anti-aging Cosmetics for Men' *Financial Times*, 3 September 2010; see also: Tatiana Boncompagni, 'Newest wrinkle in the anti-ageing war', *Financial Times* (12 March 2004), http://news.ft.com/servlet/ContentServer?pagename=FT.com/StoryFT/FullStory&c=StoryFT&cid=1078381734673&p=1016625900932; Rhymer Rigby, 'Grooming the male market', *Financial Times* (3 February 2004), http://news.ft.com/servlet/ContentServer?pagename=FT.com/StoryFT/FullStory&c=StoryFT&cid=1073281521382&p=1059480266913

4. http://wiki.answers.com/Q/Who_has_the_most_Twitter_followers, accessed 28 May 2011.

5. Harry C. Triandis, 'The Self and Social Behavior in Differing Cultural Contexts', *Psychological Review* 96, no. 3 (1989): 506–20; H. Markus and S. Kitayama, 'Culture and the Self: Implications for Cognition, Emotion, and Motivation', *Psychological Review* 98 (1991): 224–53.

6. Wong, P. and M.K. Hogg, 'Exploring cultural differences in the extended self' in *Identity and Consumption*, A. Ruvio and R. Belk, Routledge (eds), (2013, forthcoming); Wong, P., M.K. Hogg and M. Vanharanta, 'Consumption Narratives of Extended Possessions and the Extended Self', *Journal of Marketing Management* (2013, forthcoming); Markus and Kitayama, 'Culture and the Self', *op. cit.*

7. Nancy Wong and Aaron Ahuvia, 'A Cross-Cultural Approach to Materialism and the Self', in Dominique Bouchet (ed.), *Cultural Dimensions of International Marketing* (Denmark: Odense University, 1995): 68–89.

8. Lisa M. Keefe, 'You're so Vain', *Marketing News* (28 February 2000): 8.

9. Anthony G. Greenwald and Mahzarin R. Banaji, 'The self as a memory system: Powerful, but ordinary', *Journal of Personality and Social Psychology* 57 (1989) 1: 41–54; Hazel Markus, 'Self Schemata and Processing Information About the Self', *Journal of Personality and Social Psychology* 35 (1977): 63–78.

10. Morris Rosenberg, *Conceiving the Self* (New York: Basic Books, 1979); M. Joseph Sirgy, 'Self-concept in consumer behavior: A critical review', *Journal of Consumer Research* 9 (December 1982): 287–300.

11. Considine, Austin, 'Ready for my video chat close up' *New York Times*, 19 April 2012, accessed at: http://www.nytimes.com/2012/04/19/fashion/ready-for-my-video-chat-close-up.html?_r=1

12. Emily Yoffe, 'You are what you buy', *Newsweek* (4 June 1990): 59. See also: (2008) 'Therapy hope for eating disorders', http://news.bbc.co.uk/2/hi/health/7779468.stm. See also: http://www.eatingdisorderexpert.co.uk/

13. Roy F. Baumeister, Dianne M. Tice and Debra G. Hutton, 'Self-presentational motivations and personality differences in self-esteem', *Journal of Personality* 57 (September 1989): 547–75; Ronald J. Faber, 'Are Self-Esteem Appeals Appealing?' *Proceedings of the 1992 Conference of the American Academy of Advertising* (ed.), Leonard N. Reid (1992): 230–5.

14. B. Bradford Brown and Mary Jane Lohr, 'Peer-group affiliation and adolescent self-esteem: An integration of ego identity and symbolic-interaction theories', *Journal of Personality and Social Psychology* 52 (1987) 1: 47–55.

15. Christine Bittar, 'Alberto-Culver Ties Hair Relaxer to Self-Esteem', available from www.mediapost.com, accessed 15 February 2007. See also: http://texturesoftener.com/

16. Townsend, Claudia and Sanjay Sood, 'Self-Affirmation Through the Choice of Highly Aesthetic Products', *Journal of Consumer Research* 39 (2012) 3: 415–28.

17. Marsha L. Richins, 'Social comparison and the idealized images of advertising', *Journal of Consumer Research* 18 (June 1991): 71–83; Mary C. Martin and Patricia F. Kennedy, 'Advertising and social comparison: Consequences for female preadolescents and adolescents', *Psychology and Marketing* 10 (November/December 1993) 6: 513–30.

18. Philip N. Myers Jr and Frank A. Biocca, 'The elastic body image: The effect of television advertising and programming on body image distortions in young women', *Journal of Communication* 42 (Summer 1992): 108–33.

19. Jeremy Kees, Karen Becker-Olsen and Milos Mitric (2008) 'The Use of Thin Models in Advertising: The Moderating Effect of Self-Monitoring on Females' Body Esteem and Food Choices', in John Kozup, Charles R. Taylor and Ronald Paul Hill (eds), *Marketing and Public Policy Proceedings* (Philadelphia, PA).

20. Jeffrey F. Durgee, 'Self-esteem advertising', *Journal of Advertising* 14 (1986) 4: 21.

21. Erin White and Deborah Ball, 'Slim-Fast pounds home tough talk ads aimed at U.K. women offer steady diet of barbs to encourage weight loss', *The Wall Street Journal* (28 May 2004): B3.

22. For the seminal treatment of this process, *cf.* Erving Goffman, *The Presentation of Self in Everyday Life* (New York: Doubleday, 1959).

23. Quoted in Michael Slackman, 'Fashion and Faith Meet, on Foreheads of the Pious', *New York Times* (18 December 2007), www.nytimes.com, accessed 18 December 2007.

24. Sigmund Freud, *New Introductory Lectures in Psycho-analysis* (New York: Norton, 1965).

25. Jason Riis, Josepht P. Simmons and Geoffrey P. Goodwin (2008) 'Preferences for enhancement pharmaceuticals: The reluctance to enhance fundamental traits', *Journal of Consumer Research* 35 (October 2008): 495–508.

26. Harrison G. Gough, Mario Fioravanti and Renato Lazzari, 'Some implications of self versus ideal-self congruence on the revised adjective check list', *Journal of Personality and Social Psychology* 44 (1983) 6: 1214–20.

27. Steven Jay Lynn and Judith W. Rhue, 'Daydream believers', *Psychology Today* (September 1985): 14.

28. http://campaignforrealbeauty.co.uk (accessed 5 August 2005).

29. Erving Goffman, *The Presentation of Self in Everyday Life* (Garden City, NY: Doubleday, 1959); Michael R. Solomon, 'The role of products as social stimuli: A symbolic interactionism perspective', *Journal of Consumer Research* 10 (December 1983): 319–29.

30. Yinlong Zhang and L.J. Shrum (2009) 'The influence of self construal on impulsive consumption', *Journal of Consumer Research*, 35, 5 (February 2009): 838–50.

31. Aliakbar Jafari and Christina Goulding (2008) '"We are Not Terrorists!" UK-Based Iranians, Consumption Practices and the "Torn Self",' *Consumption Markets and Culture*, 11 (June), 73–91.

32. Neal Stephenson, *Snow Crash* (New York: Bantam Books, 1992).

33. Virtual World Web Reaches 50,000 Virtual Worlds, *San Francisco Chronicle* (31 March 2011), http://www.sfgate.com/cgi-bin/article.cgi?f=/g/a/2011/03/31/prweb8256005.DTL, accessed 28 May 2011.

34. Natalie Wood and Michael R. Solomon (2010) (eds), *Virtual Social Identity* (Newport Beach, CA: Sage); Peter Svensson, 'Study: Virtual Men Are Standoffish Too' *MyFox 21* (February 2007), http://matei.org/ithink/2007/02/22/study-virtual-men-are-standoffish-too-yahoo-news/, accessed 22 February 2007.

35. 'Virtual reality avatars created', *The Drum* (17 February 2011), http://www.thedrum.co.uk/news/2011/02/17/18810-virtual-reality-avatars-created/, accessed 10 April 2011.

36. George H. Mead, *Mind, Self and Society* (Chicago: University of Chicago Press, 1934).

37. Natasha Singer, 'If the Mirror Could Talk (It Can)', *New York Times Online* (18 March 2007), accessed 18 March 2007.

38. Charles H. Cooley, *Human Nature and the Social Order* (New York: Scribner's, 1902).

39. J. G. Hull and A. S. Levy, 'The Organizational Functions of the Self: An Alternative to the Duval and Wicklund Model of Self-Awareness', *Journal of Personality and Social Psychology* 37 (1979): 756–68; Jay G. Hull, Ronald R. Van Treuren, Susan J. Ashford, Pamela Propsom and Bruce W. Andrus, 'Self-Consciousness and the Processing of Self-Relevant Information', *Journal of Personality and Social Psychology* 54, no. 3 (1988): 452–65.

40. Arnold W. Buss, *Self-Consciousness and Social Anxiety* (San Francisco: W.H. Freeman, 1980); Lynn Carol Miller and Cathryn Leigh Cox, 'Public self-consciousness and makeup use', *Personality and Social Psychology Bulletin* 8 (1982) 4: 748–51; Michael R. Solomon and John Schopler, 'Self-consciousness and clothing', *Personality and Social Psychology Bulletin* 8 (1982) 3: 508–14.

41. Morris B. Holbrook, Michael R. Solomon and Stephen Bell, 'A re-examination of self-monitoring and judgments of furniture designs', *Home Economics Research Journal* 19 (September 1990): 6–16; Mark Snyder and Steve Gangestad, 'On the nature of self-monitoring: matters of assessment, matters of validity', *Journal of Personality and Social Psychology* 51 (1986): 125–39.

42. Snyder and Gangestad, 'On the nature of self-monitoring', *ibid.*

43. Timothy R. Graeff, 'Image congruence effects on product evaluations: The role of self-monitoring and public/private consumption', *Psychology and Marketing* 13(5) (August 1996): 481–99.

44. Richard G. Netemeyer, Scot Burton and Donald R. Lichtenstein, 'Trait aspects of vanity: Measurement and relevance to consumer behavior', *Journal of Consumer Research* 21 (March 1995): 612–26.

45. Michael R. Solomon and Henry Assael, 'The forest or the trees? A gestalt approach to symbolic consumption', in Jean Umiker-Sebeok (ed.), *Marketing and Semiotics: New Directions in the Study of Signs for Sale* (Berlin: Mouton de Gruyter, 1987): 189–218.

46. Jack L. Nasar, 'Symbolic meanings of house styles', *Environment and Behavior* 21 (May 1989): 235–57; E.K. Sadalla, B. Verschure and J. Burroughs, 'Identity symbolism in housing', *Environment and Behavior* 19 (1987): 599–687.

47. Douglas B. Holt and Craig J. Thompson, 'Man-of-action heroes: The pursuit of heroic masculinity in everyday consumption', *Journal of Consumer Research* 31 (September 2004): 425–40; Michael R. Solomon, 'The role of products as social stimuli: A symbolic interactionism perspective', *Journal of Consumer Research* 10 (December 1983): 319–28; Robert E. Kleine III, Susan Schultz-Kleine and Jerome B. Kernan, 'Mundane consumption and the self: A social-identity perspective', *Journal of Consumer Psychology* 2 (1993) 3: 209–35; Newell D. Wright, C.B. Claiborne and M. Joseph Sirgy, 'The Effects of Product Symbolism on Consumer Self-Concept', in John F. Sherry Jr and Brian Sternthal (eds), *Advances in Consumer Research* 19 (Provo, UT: Association for Consumer Research, 1992): 311–18; Susan Fournier, 'A Person Based Relationship Framework for Strategic Brand Management', PhD dissertation, University of Florida, 1994.

48. A. Dwayne Ball and Lori H. Tasaki, 'The role and measurement of attachment in consumer behavior', *Journal of Consumer Psychology* 1 (1992) 2: 155–72.

49. William B. Hansen and Irwin Altman, 'Decorating personal places: A descriptive analysis', *Environment and Behavior* 8 (December 1976): 491–504.

50. R.A. Wicklund and P.M. Gollwitzer, *Symbolic Self-Completion* (Hillsdale, NJ: Lawrence Erlbaum, 1982).

51. Erving Goffman, *Asylums* (New York: Doubleday, 1961).

52. Quoted in Floyd Rudmin, 'Property crime victimization impact on self, on attachment, and on territorial dominance', *CPA Highlights, Victims of Crime Supplement* 9 (1987) 2: 4–7.

53. Barbara B. Brown, 'House and Block as Territory', paper presented at the Conference of the Association for Consumer Research, San Francisco, 1982.

54. Quoted in Shay Sayre and David Horne, 'I Shop, Therefore I Am: The Role of Possessions for Self Definition', in Shay Sayre and David Horne (eds), *Earth, Wind, and Fire and Water: Perspectives on Natural Disaster* (Pasadena, CA: Open Door Publishers, 1996): 353–70. Recently in Germany, the 'loss of self' was taken to the ultimate extreme when a 43-year-old German from Berlin advertised on the internet that he would like to be eaten. His ad was answered and, with his consent, he was cut into pieces, frozen and placed in the freezer next to the takeaway pizza. See: 'Cannibal to face murder charge at retrial', *The Guardian* (23 April 2005), http://www.guardian.co.uk/international/story/0,,1468373,00.html

55. Quoted in Fred Meier, 'Girls Named Zoe Lose Suit against Renault for Naming Electric Car Zoe', *DriveOn* (10 November 2010), http://content.usatoday.com/communities/driveon/

post/2010/11/girls-lose-renault-zoe-electric-car-lawsuit-over-name/1, accessed 10 April 2011.

56. Deborah A. Prentice, 'Psychological Correspondence of Possessions, Attitudes, and Values', *Journal of Personality and Social Psychology* 53, no. 6 (1987): 993–1002.

57. Jennifer L. Aaker, 'The Malleable Self: The Role of Self-Expression in Persuasion', *Journal of Marketing Research* 36 (February 1999): 45–57; Sak Onkvisit and John Shaw, 'Self-Concept and Image Congruence: Some Research and Managerial Implications', *Journal of Consumer Marketing* 4 (Winter 1987): 13–24. For a related treatment of congruence between advertising appeals and self-concept, see George M. Zinkhan and Jae W. Hong, 'Self-Concept and Advertising Effectiveness: A Conceptual Model of Congruency, Conspicuousness, and Response Mode', in Rebecca H. Holman and Michael R. Solomon (eds), *Advances in Consumer Research* 18 (Provo, UT: Association for Consumer Research, 1991): 348–54.

58. C.B. Claiborne and M. Joseph Sirgy, 'Self-Image Congruence as a Model of Consumer Attitude Formation and Behavior: A Conceptual Review and Guide for Further Research', paper presented at the Academy of Marketing Science Conference, New Orleans, 1990.

59. Susan Fournier and Julie L. Yao, 'Reviving Brand Loyalty: A Reconceptualization Within the Framework of Consumer-Brand Relationships', *International Journal of Research in Marketing*, Volume 14, Issue 5, December 1997: 451–472; Caryl E. Rusbult, 'A Longitudinal Test of the Investment Model: The Development (and Deterioration) of Satisfaction and Commitment in Heterosexual Involvements', *Journal of Personality and Social Psychology*, 1983, vol. 45, no. 1, 101–117.

60. Allison R. Johnson, Maggie Matear and Matthew Thomson, 'A Coal in the Heart: Self-Relevance as a Post-Exit Predictor of Consumer Anti-Brand Actions', *Journal of Consumer Research*, Volume 38, Number 1, June 2011, 108–125.

61. Liz Hunt, 'Rise in infertility linked to craze for body building', *The Independent* (12 July 1995): 12; Paul Kelso, Duncan Mackay and Matthew Taylor, 'From gym to club to school: the shock spread of steroid abuse', *The Guardian* (14 November 2003), http://www.guardian.co.uk/uk_news/story/0,,1084792,00.html. See also: 'Anabolic Steroids, Use and Abuse', (July 2006) http://menshealth.about.com/cs/fitness/a/anab_steroids.htm

62. Özlem Sandikci and Güliz Ger, 'Aesthetics, Ethics and Politics of the Turkish Headscarf', in Susanne Küchler and Daniel Miller (eds), *Clothing as Material Culture* (Oxford: Berg, 2005): Chapter 4.

63. Marc Lacey, 'Where Showing Skin Doesn't Sell, a New Style is a Hit', *New York Times* (20 March 2006).

64. Ernest Beaglehole, *Property: A Study in Social Psychology* (New York: Macmillan, 1932).

65. Russell W. Belk, 'Possessions and the extended self', *Journal of Consumer Research* 15 (September 1988): 139–68.

66. Janeen Arnold Costa, 'Introduction', in J.A. Costa (ed.), *Gender Issues and Consumer Behavior* (Thousand Oaks, CA: Sage, 1994).

67. Rozin, Paul, Julia M. Hormes, Myles S. Faith and Brian Wansink, 'Is Meat Male? A Quantitative Multimethod Framework to Establish Metaphoric Relationships', *Journal of Consumer Research*, vol. 39 (3), October 2012, 629–43.

See also: Nina M. Lentini, 'McDonald's Tests "Angus Third Pounder" in California', *Marketing Daily* (27 March 2007), www.mediapost.com, accessed 27 March 2007.

68. For an up-to-date overview of Gender and Consumer Behaviour research which has a strong global perspective, see: Cele C. Otnes and Linda Tuncay Zayer (eds), *Gender, Culture and Consumer Behavior*, New York/London: Routledge.

69. Joan Meyers-Levy, 'The influence of sex roles on judgment', *Journal of Consumer Research* 14 (March 1988): 522–30.

70. Kimberly J. Dodson and Russell W. Belk, 'Gender in Children's Birthday Stories' in Janeen Costa (ed.), *Gender, Marketing, and Consumer Behavior* (Salt Lake City, UT: Association for Consumer Research, 1996): 96–108.

71. Gavin O'Malley, 'Study: Men Are from Hulu, Women Are from Facebook', *Online Media Daily* (28 July 2010), http://www.mediapost.com/publications/?fa=Articles.showArticle&art_aid=132841&nid=117095, accessed 10 April 2011.

72. Elizabeth C. Hirschman, 'A Feminist Critique of Marketing Theory: Toward Agentic-Communal Balance', working paper, School of Business, Rutgers University, New Brunswick, NJ, 1990.

73. Elizabeth Landau, 'Men See Bikini-Clad Women as Objects, Psychologists Say', *CNN* (19 February 2009), www.cnnhealth.com, accessed 19 February 2009.

74. Eileen Fischer and Stephen J. Arnold, 'Sex, gender identity, gender role attitudes, and consumer behavior', *Psychology and Marketing* 11 (March/April 1994) 2: 163–82.

75. Kathleen Debevec and Easwar Iyer, 'Sex Roles and Consumer Perceptions of Promotions, Products, and Self: What Do We Know and Where Should We Be Headed', in Richard J. Lutz (ed.), *Advances in Consumer Research* 13 (Provo, UT: Association for Consumer Research, 1986): 210–14; Joseph A. Bellizzi and Laura Milner, 'Gender positioning of a traditionally male-dominant product', *Journal of Advertising Research* (June/July 1991): 72–9.

76. Janeen Arnold Costa and Teresa M. Pavia, 'Alpha-numeric brand names and gender stereotypes', *Research in Consumer Behavior* 6 (1993): 85–112.

77. Helga Dittmar, Jane Beattie and Susanne Friese, 'Gender identity and material symbols: Objects and decision considerations in impulse purchases', *Journal of Economic Psychology* 16 (1995): 491–511; Jason Cox and Helga Dittmar, 'The functions of clothes and clothing (dis)satisfaction: A gender analysis among British students', *Journal of Consumer Policy* 18 (1995): 237–65.

78. Sandra L. Bem, 'The measurement of psychological androgyny', *Journal of Consulting and Clinical Psychology* 42 (1974): 155–62; Deborah E.S. Frable, 'Sex typing and gender ideology: Two facets of the individual's gender psychology that go together', *Journal of Personality and Social Psychology* 56 (1989) 1: 95–108.

79. Who is your favorite androgynous celebrity? Go to: http://www.rankopedia.com/Most-Androgynous-Looking-Celebrity/Step1/25834/.htm and place your vote!

80. See D. Bruce Carter and Gary D. Levy, 'Cognitive aspects of early sex-role development: The influence of gender schemas on preschoolers' memories and preferences for sex-typed toys and activities', *Child Development* 59 (1988): 782–92; Bernd H. Schmitt, France Le Clerc and Laurette Dube-Rioux, 'Sex typing and consumer behavior: A test of

gender schema theory', *Journal of Consumer Research* 15 (June 1988): 122–7.

81. Carol Gilligan, *In a Different Voice: Psychological Theory and Women's Development* (Cambridge, MA: Harvard University Press, 1982); Joan Meyers-Levy and Durairaj Maheswaran, 'Exploring differences in males' and females' processing strategies', *Journal of Consumer Research* 18 (June 1991): 63–70.

82. Lynn J. Jaffe and Paul D. Berger, 'Impact on purchase intent of sex-role identity and product positioning', *Psychology and Marketing* (Fall 1988): 259–71; Lynn J. Jaffe, 'The unique predictive ability of sex-role identity in explaining women's response to advertising', *Psychology and Marketing* 11 (September/October 1994) 5: 467–82.

83. 'Gender-Bending Avatars Suffer Lack of Trust', *SAWF News* (11 July 2007), http://news.sawf.org/Lifestyle/39848.aspx, accessed 11 July 2007.

84. Sexual Health, U.K., *Mintel*, July 2011; see also: Julie Candler, 'Woman car buyer – don't call her a niche anymore', *Advertising Age* (21 January 1991): S-8; see also Robin Widgery and Jack McGaugh, 'Vehicle message appeals and the new generation woman', *Journal of Advertising Research* (September/October 1993): 36–42; Blayne Cutler, 'Condom mania', *American Demographics* (June 1989): 17.

85. Eric Bellman, 'Suzuki's Stylish Compacts Captivate India's Women', *Wall Street Journal* (11 May 2007): B1.

86. B. Abrams, 'American Express is gearing new ad campaign to women', *Wall Street Journal* (4 August 1983): 23.

87. http://campaignforrealbeauty.co.uk (accessed 5 August 2005).

88. Daniel J. Brett and Joanne Cantor, 'The portrayal of men and women in U.S. television commercials: A recent content analysis and trends over 15 years', *Sex Roles* 18 (1988): 595–609.

89. Quoted in Barry Silverstein, 'Ever the Publicity Hound, Branson Readies to be an Airline Hostess', *BrandChannel* (18 November 2010), http://www.brandchannel.com/home/post/2010/11/18/Richard-Branson-Loses-Bet.aspx, accessed 10 April 2011.

90. Gordon Sumner, 'Tribal rites of the American male', *Marketing Insights* (Summer 1989): 13.

91. Barbara B. Stern, 'Masculinism(s) and the Male Image: What Does It Mean to Be a Man?' in Tom Reichert and Jacqueline Lambiase (eds), *Sex in Advertising: Multidisciplinary Perspectives on the Erotic Appeal* (Mahwah, NJ: Erlbaum, 2003).

92. 'Defining Metro sexuality', *Metrosource* (September/October/November 2003).

93. Rinallo, Diego, 'Metro/Fashion/Tribes of men: Negotiating the boundaries of men's legitimate consumption', in B. Cova, R. Kozinets and A. Shankar (eds), *Consumer Tribes: Theory, Practice, and Prospects* (Elsevier/Butterworth-Heinemann, 2007).

94. Douglas B. Holt and Craig J. Thompson, 'Man-of-action heroes: The pursuit of heroic masculinity in everyday consumption', *Journal of Consumer Research* 31 (September): 425–40.

95. 'Beauty Retailing: U.K.', *Mintel*, January 2012. See also: Vivian Manning-Schaffel, 'Metrosexuals: A Well-Groomed Market?' www.brandchannel.com, accessed 22 May 2006.

96. Quoted in Jennifer Foote, 'The ad world's new bimbos', *Newsweek* (25 January 1988): 44.

97. Maples, 'Beefcake marketing', *op. cit.*

98. Quoted in Lynn G. Coleman, 'What do people really lust after in ads?', *Marketing News* (6 November 1989): 12.

99. For an up-to-date census on gay European consumers, see: http://www.glcensus.org/ Riccardo A. Davis, 'Marketers game for gay events', *Advertising Age* (30 May 1994): S-1 (2); Cyndee Miller, 'Top marketers take bolder approach in targeting gays', *Marketing News* (4 July 1994): 1 (2); see also Douglas L. Fugate, 'Evaluating the US male homosexual and lesbian population as a viable target market segment', *Journal of Consumer Marketing* 10(4) (1993) 4: 46–57; Laura M. Milner, 'Marketing to Gays and Lesbians: A Review', unpublished manuscript, the University of Alaska, 1990.

100. Kate Fitzgerald, 'IKEA dares to reveal gays buy tables, too', *Advertising Age* (28 March 1994): 3(2); Miller, 'Top marketers take bolder approach in targeting gays': 1(2); Paula Span, 'ISO the gay consumer', *Washington Post* (19 May 1994): D1 (2).

101. Kate Fitzgerald, 'AT&T addresses gay market', *Advertising Age* (16 May 1994): 8.

102. James S. Hirsch, 'New credit cards base appeals on sexual orientation and race', *Wall Street Journal* (6 November 1995): B1 (2).

103. Ben Parr, 'Google Chrome Commercial Lets Gay Teens Know "It Gets Better",' Mashable.com, http://mashable.com/2011/05/04/google-chrome-it-gets-better/, accessed 28 May 2011.

104. Projections of the incidence of homosexuality in the general population are often influenced by assumptions of the researchers, as well as the methodology they employ (e.g. self-report, behavioural measures, fantasy measures). For a discussion of these factors, see Edward O. Laumann, John H. Gagnon, Robert T. Michael and Stuart Michaels, *The Social Organization of Homosexuality* (Chicago: University of Chicago Press, 1994).

105. Lisa Peñaloza, 'We're here, we're queer, and we're going shopping! A critical perspective on the accommodation of gays and lesbians in the U.S. marketplace', *Journal of Homosexuality* 31(1/2) (1966): 9–41.

106. Fugate, 'Evaluating the U.S. male homosexual and lesbian population as a viable target market segment'. See also Laumann, Gagnon, Michael and Michaels, *The Social Organization of Homosexuality*.

107. Laura Koss-Feder, 'Out and about', *Marketing News* (25 May 1998): 1(2); Rachel X. Weissman, 'Gay market power', *American Demographics* 21 (June 1999) 6: 32–3.

108. Peñaloza, 'We're here, we're queer, and we're going shopping!' *op. cit.*

109. For an up-to-date overview of gay consumption, lifestyle and markets, see: http://www.gayeuro.com/

110. 'Buying for Workplace Equality 2012: A Guide to Companies, Products and Services that support Lesbian, Gay, Bisexual and Transgender workplace inclusion' accessed at: http://www.hrc.org/files/assets/resources/2012_BuyersGuide.pdf

111. Michael Wilke, 'Subaru adds lesbians to niche marketing drive', *Advertising Age* (4 March 1996): 8. See also: http://lesbianlife.about.com/od/otherfunstuff/tp/LesbianCars.htm for the top ten brands of cars purchased by gay women.

112. Sheila Shayon, 'Levi's for Women: Shape, Not Size, Matters', *BrandChannel* (17 September 2010), http://www.brandchannel.com/home/post/2010/09/17/Levis-Women-Curve-ID-Digital.aspx, accessed 10 April 2011; http://us.levi.com/shop/index.jsp?categoryId=3146849&AB=CMS_Home_CurveID_081010, accessed 28 May 2011.

113. Dennis W. Rook, 'Body Cathexis and Market Segmentation', in Michael R. Solomon (ed.), *The Psychology of Fashion* (Lexington, MA: Lexington Books, 1985): 233–41.

114. 'Nederlandse vrouw krijt lachend rimpels', *De Telegraaf* (26 April 1997): TA5.

115. Jane E. Brody, 'Notions of beauty transcend culture, new study suggests', *New York Times* (21 March 1994): A14.

116. Karen K. Dion, 'What Is Beautiful Is Good', *Journal of Personality and Social Psychology* 24 (December 1972): 285–90.

117. Sharon Jayson, 'Study: Beautiful People Cash in on Their Looks', *USA Today* (31 March 2011), http://www.usatoday.com/money/perfi/basics/2011-03-30-beauty30_ST_N.htm, accessed April 10, 2011.

118. Geoffrey Cowley, 'The biology of beauty', *Newsweek* (3 June 1996): 61–6.

119. Michael Fay and Christopher Price, 'Female body-shape in print advertisements and the increase in anorexia nervosa', *European Journal of Marketing* 28 (1994): 12.

120. 'Vrouwen hebben complexe relatie met schoonheid' ('Women have a complex relationship with beauty') *De Telegraaf* (31 January 2005), http://www2.telegraaf.nl/binnenland/17688091/_Vrouwen_hebben_complexe_relatie_met_schoonheid_.html

121. Lois W. Banner, *American Beauty* (Chicago: The University of Chicago Press, 1980); for a philosophical perspective, see Barry Vacker and Wayne R. Key, 'Beauty *and* the beholder: The pursuit of beauty through commodities', *Psychology and Marketing* 10 (November/December 1993) 6: 471–94.

122. David M. Garner, Paul E. Garfinkel, Donald Schwartz and Michael Thompson, 'Cultural expectations of thinness in women', *Psychological Reports* 47 (1980): 483–91.

123. Erin White, 'Dove "Firms" with Zaftig Models: Unilever Brand Launches European Ads Employing Non-Supermodel Bodies', *Wall Street Journal* (21 April 2004): B3.

124. 'The Dove Report: Challenging Beauty', *Unilever 2004*, www.dove.com/real_beauty/article.asp?id=430, accessed 15 June 2005.

125. Geoffrey A. Fowler, 'Unilever Gives "Ugly Betty" A Product-Plug Makeover in China', *Wall Street Journal* (29 December 2008), www.wallstreetjournal.com, accessed 29 December 2008.

126. Jill Neimark, 'The beefcaking of America', *Psychology Today* (November/December 1994): 32 (11).

127. Richard H. Kolbe and Paul J. Albanese, 'Man to man: A content analysis of sole-male images in male-audience magazines', *Journal of Advertising* 25(4) (Winter 1996): 1–20.

128. 'Girls at 7 think thin, study finds', *New York Times* (11 February 1988): B9.

129. Smeesters, Dirk, Thomas Mussweiler and Naomi Mandel, 'The Effects of Thin and Heavy Media Images on Overweight and Underweight Consumers: Social Comparison Processes and Behavioral Implications', *Journal of Consumer Research*, vol. 36, April 2010, 930–49; McFerran, Brent, Darren W. Dahl, Gavan J. Fitzsimons and Andrea C. Morales, 'I'll have What She's Having: Effects of Social Influence and Body Type on the Food Choices of Others', *Journal of Consumer Research*, vol. 36, April 2010, 915–29; Dubois, David, Derek D. Rucker and Adam D. Galinsky, 'Super Size Me: Product Size as a Signal of Status', *Journal of Consumer Research*, vol. 38, April 2012, 1047–62; see also: Beth Carney, 'In Europe, the fat is in the fire', *Business Week* (8 February 2005), http://www.businessweek.com/bwdaily/dnflash/feb2005/nf2005028_5771_db016.htm?chan=gb. For a comprehensive report on obesity in the EU, go to http://www.iotf.org

130. Elaine L. Pedersen and Nancy L. Markee, 'Fashion dolls: Communicators of ideals of beauty and fashion', paper presented at the International Conference on Marketing Meaning, Indianapolis, 1989; Dalma Heyn, 'Body hate', *Ms.* (August 1989): 34; Mary C. Martin and James W. Gentry, 'Assessing the internalization of physical attractiveness norms', *Proceedings of the American Marketing Association Summer Educators' Conference* (Summer 1994): 59–65.

131. 'So Germans can be gourmets too', *The Economist* (9 December 2000): 57. See also The European Commission, Eurostat, and 'International survey: Teens fattest in the U.S.', CNN (6 January 2004), http://www.cnn.com/2004/HEALTH/parenting/01/05/obese.teens.ap/index.html

132. Debra A. Zellner, Debra F. Harner and Robbie I. Adler, 'Effects of eating abnormalities and gender on perceptions of desirable body shape', *Journal of Abnormal Psychology* 98 (February 1989): 93–6.

133. Robin T. Peterson, 'Bulimia and anorexia in an advertising context', *Journal of Business Ethics* 6 (1987): 495–504.

134. Christian S. Crandall, 'Social contagion of binge eating', *Journal of Personality and Social Psychology* 55 (1988): 588–98.

135. Judy Folkenberg, 'Bulimia: Not for women only', *Psychology Today* (March 1984): 10.

136. Eleanor Grant, 'The exercise fix: What happens when fitness fanatics just can't say no?' *Psychology Today* 22 (February 1988): 24.

137. Annette C. Hamburger and Holly Hall, 'Beauty quest', *Psychology Today* (May 1988): 28.

138. Emily Yoffe, 'Valley of the silicon dolls', *Newsweek* (26 November 1990): 72.

139. Keith Greenberg, 'What's hot: Cosmetic surgery', *Public Relations Journal* (June 1988): 23.

140. 'Bra wars', *The Economist* (2 December 2000): 64.

141. Ruth P. Rubinstein, 'Color, Circumcision, Tattoos, and Scars', in Solomon (ed.), *The Psychology of Fashion*: 243–54; Peter H. Bloch and Marsha L. Richins, 'You look "mahvelous": The pursuit of beauty and marketing concept', *Psychology and Marketing* 9 (January 1992): 3–16.

142. Sondra Farganis, 'Lip service: The evolution of pouting, pursing, and painting lips red', *Health* (November 1988): 48–51.

143. Michael Gross, 'Those lips, those eyebrows: New face of 1989 (new look of fashion models)', *New York Times Magazine* (13 February 1989): 24.

144. Quoted in 'High heels: Ecstasy's worth the agony', *New York Post* (31 December 1981).

145. Dannie Kjeldgaard and Anders Bengtsson (2005), 'Consuming the Fashion Tattoo', *Advances in Consumer Research* 32, Geeta Menon and Akshay R. Rao (eds), (Duluth, MN: Association for Consumer Research): 172–7.

146. Mike Featherstone (ed.), *Body Modification* (Thousand Oaks, CA: Sage, 2000); Anne M. Velliquette and Jeff B. Murray, 'The New Tattoo Subculture', in *Mapping the Social Landscape: Readings in Sociology* (ed.), Susan Ferguson (Mountain View, CA: Mayfield, 1999): 56–68; Anne M. Velliquette, Jeff B. Murray and Elizabeth H. Creyer, 'The Tattoo Renaissance: An Ethnographic Account of Symbolic Consumer Behavior', in Joseph W. Alba and J. Wesley Hutchinson (eds), *Advances in Consumer Research* 25 (Provo, UT: Association for Consumer Research, 1998): 461–7; Anne M. Velliquette, 'Modern Primitives: The Role of Product Symbolism in Lifestyle Cultures and Identity', dissertation, University of Arkansas Press, 2000; Margo DeMello, *Bodies of Inscription: A Cultural History of the Modern Tattoo Community* (Durham, NC: Duke University Press, 2000); Anne Veliquette and Gary Bamossy, 'Modern Primitives: The Role of the Body and Product Symbolism in Lifestyle Cultures and Identity', in Andrea Groppel-Klein and Franz-Rudolf Esch (eds), *European Advances in Consumer Research* 5 (Valdosta, GA: Association for Consumer Research, 2001): 21–2.

147. Jonathan Schroeder, 'Branding the Body: Skin and Consumer Communication', in Darach Turley and Stephen Brown (eds), *European Advances in Consumer Research: All Changed, Changed Utterly?* 6 (Valdosta, GA: Association for Consumer Research 2003): 23; Maurice Patterson and Richard Elliott, 'Harsh Beauty: The Alternative Aesthetic of Tattooed Women', in Turley and Brown (eds), *European Advances in Consumer Research* 6: 23; Dannie Kjeldgaard and Anders Bengtsson, 'Acts, Images, and Meaning of Tattooing', in Turley and Brown (eds), *European Advances in Consumer Research* 6: 24; Jonathan Schroeder and Janet Borgerson, 'Skin Signs: The Epidermal Schema in Contemporary Marketing Communications', in Turley and Brown (eds), *European Advances in Consumer Research* 6: 26; Roy Langer, 'SKINTWO: (Un)covering the Skin in Fetish Carnivals', in Turley and Brown (eds), *European Advances in Consumer Research* 6: 27.

148. Quoted in Wendy Bounds, 'Body-piercing gets under America's skin', *Wall Street Journal* (4 April 1994): B1 (2), B4.

6 MOTIVATION, VALUES AND LIFESTYLES

CHAPTER OBJECTIVES

When you finish reading this chapter you will understand why:

→ It is important for marketers to recognize that products can satisfy a range of consumer needs.

→ A consumer's **personality** influences the way he responds to marketing stimuli, but efforts to use this information in marketing contexts meet with mixed results.

→ The way we evaluate and choose a product depends on our degree of involvement with the product, the marketing message, and/or the purchase situation.

→ Our deeply held cultural values dictate the types of products and services we seek out or avoid.

→ Consumers vary in the importance they attach to worldly possessions, and this orientation in turn influences their priorities and behaviours.

→ Products that succeed in one culture may fail in another if marketers fail to understand the differences among consumers in each place.

→ Psychographics go beyond simple demographics to help marketers understand and reach different consumer segments.

→ Getting rid of products when consumers no longer need or want them is a major concern both to marketers and to public policymakers.

RUFUS and his Italian girlfriend, Adrienne, have just found a table for lunch at a restaurant in Kolonaki that Rufus found recommended on TripAdvisor.[1] It had been Rufus's turn to choose where to eat as Adrienne had suggested the Cretan restaurant where they had had dinner the previous night. Rufus studies the menu hard. Rufus is reflecting on what a man will do for love. Adrienne is keen that they both eat healthily. She's not yet managed to persuade him to follow her conversion to vegetarianism. However, she's slowly but surely persuading him to give up burgers and pizzas for healthier, preferably organic, fare; and swop his beer drinking for wine. At least while they are on holiday he can hide from tofu and the other vegan delights which confront him as the menu choices at their favourite local café when he visits her in Bergamo. The café has just started offering 'veggie' alternatives to its usual rich Bergamasque cuisine of casconcelli (pasta stuffed with sausagemeat), all types of charcuterie, game and rabbit.

Adrienne is still prepared to eat dairy products, so she is not a vegan. She argues that eating this way not only cuts out unwanted fat, but is also good for the environment. Just Rufus's luck to fall head-over-heels for a green, organic-food-eating environmentalist who is into issues of sustainability. As Rufus gamely tries to decide between the stuffed artichokes with red pepper vinaigrette and the grilled, marinated zucchini, he wonders if he might be able to choose the soutzoukakia smyrneika (meatballs cooked with cumin, cinnamon and garlic in a tomato sauce) – after all, they are on holiday and in Greece?

INTRODUCTION

As a lacto-ovo-vegetarian (rather than a lacto-vegetarian or a vegan),[2] Adrienne certainly is not alone in believing that eating organic foods are good for the body, the soul and the planet.[3] 'About one quarter of the 6.5 billion people who live on our planet enjoy a mostly vegetarian diet.'[4] In 2006 between 2 per cent and 4 per cent of the population in Western Europe were vegetarians (the exception was the United Kingdom where 6 per cent were vegetarian); and in Eastern Europe the number of vegetarians varied between 0.3 per cent and 1.9 per cent of the population.[5] There has been a lively debate in Europe about genetically modified foods compared with the US, although genetic modification for medical purposes has not met with such widespread hostility in Europe. Consumers see 'functional foods as placed midway on the combined "naturalness–healthiness continuum" from organically processed to genetically modified'[6] but tend to remain unconvinced that genetically modified foods can offer any significant health benefits.[7] However, concerns about adult, and more especially childhood, obesity means that diet has become a burning issue for many European governments.[8] It is obvious our menu choices have deep-seated consequences.

The forces that drive people to buy and use products are generally straightforward, as when a person chooses what to have for lunch. As hard-core vegans demonstrate, however, even the consumption of basic food products may also be related to wide-ranging beliefs regarding what is appropriate or desirable. Among the more general population there are strong beliefs about genetically modified foods, which have proved difficult to alter via information campaigns.[9] In some cases, these emotional responses create a deep commitment to the product. Sometimes people are not even fully aware of the forces that drive them towards some products and away from others. Often a person's *values* – their priorities and beliefs about the world – influence these choices. Choices are not always straightforward. Often there are tradeoffs to be made.

THE MOTIVATION PROCESS: WHY ASK WHY?

To understand motivation is to understand *why* consumers do what they do. Why do some people choose to bungee jump off a bridge (which is close to being an important rite of passage for young Europeans on their gap year visiting New Zealand) while others choose to do gardening for their relaxation;[10] whilst still others spend their leisure time online playing games or visiting the virtual world of **secondlife.com**? Whether to quell the pangs of hunger like Rufus and Adrienne, kill boredom, or to attain some deep spiritual experience, we do everything for a reason, even if we can't always articulate what that reason is. Marketing students are taught from Day One that the goal of marketing is to satisfy consumers' needs.

However, this insight is useless unless we can discover *what* those needs are and *why* they exist. A beer commercial once asked, 'Why ask why?' In this chapter, we'll find out.

Motivation refers to the processes that cause people to behave as they do. From a *psychological perspective* motivation occurs when a **need** is aroused that the consumer wishes to satisfy. Once a need has been activated, a state of tension exists that drives the consumer to attempt to reduce or eliminate the need. This need may be *utilitarian* (a desire to achieve some functional or practical benefit, as when Adrienne eats green vegetables for nutritional reasons) or it may be *hedonic* (an experiential need, involving emotional responses or fantasies, as when Rufus thinks longingly about the rich Bergamasquan cuisine of charcuterie and game). The distinction between the two is, however, a matter of degree. The desired end-state is the consumer's **goal**. Marketers try to create products and services that will provide the desired benefits and permit the consumer to reduce this tension.

Whether the need is utilitarian or hedonic, a discrepancy exists between the consumer's present state and some ideal state. This gulf creates a state of tension. The magnitude of this tension determines the urgency the consumer feels to reduce the tension. This degree of arousal is called a **drive**. A basic need can be satisfied in any number of ways, and the specific path a person chooses is influenced both by their unique set of experiences and by the values instilled by cultural, religious, ethnic or national background (also discussed in Chapter 15). In Adrienne's case, her Italian upbringing means that breakfast is not a particularly important meal. Lunch, with her mother's home-cooked food, is normally her main meal of the day, and for supper she will usually prepare something lighter for herself.[11]

These personal and cultural factors combine to create a **want**, which is one manifestation of a need. For example, hunger is a basic need that must be satisfied by all; the lack of food creates a tension state that can be reduced by the intake of such products as paella, bouillabaisse, pasta, cheeses, smoked herring, chocolate biscuits or bean sprouts. The specific route to drive reduction is culturally and individually determined. Once the goal is attained, tension is reduced and the motivation recedes (for the time being). Motivation can be described in terms of its *strength*, or the pull it exerts on the consumer, and its *direction*, or the particular way the consumer attempts to reduce motivational tension.

MOTIVATIONAL STRENGTH

The degree to which a person is willing to expend energy to reach one goal as opposed to another reflects their underlying motivation to attain that goal. Many theories have been advanced to explain why people behave the way they do. Most share the basic idea that people have some finite amount of energy that must be directed towards certain goals. A conceptual distinction has been made between goal setting and goal striving.[12] Recent research has extended Bagozzi and Dhokalia's modelling of goals by examining consumers' willingness to *persistently* strive to achieve goals. In a study of assisted reproductive technologies, the researchers identify the important interplay between culture and cognition in affecting consumers' persistence in achieving goals, in this case the highly emotional goal of parenthood.[13]

Biological *vs* learned needs

Early work on motivation ascribed behaviour to *instinct*, the innate patterns of behaviour that are universal in a species. This view is now largely discredited. The existence of an instinct is difficult to prove or disprove. The instinct is inferred from the behaviour it is supposed to explain (this type of circular explanation is called a *tautology*).[14] It is like saying that a consumer buys products that are status symbols because they are motivated to attain status, which is hardly a satisfactory explanation.

Pirelli uses the sport metaphor of world-class competition to emphasize motivation and top performance.

With permission from Pirelli (file from The Advertising Archives).

This ad for health clubs and exercise regimes shows men an undesired state (lack of muscle tone and fitness, as dictated by contemporary Western culture), and suggests a solution to the problem of spare inches around the waist (purchase of health club membership in order to attain a fit and healthy body).

The Advertising Archives.

Drive theory

Drive theory focuses on biological needs that produce unpleasant states of arousal (e.g. your stomach grumbles during the first lecture of the day – you missed breakfast). We are motivated to reduce the tension caused by this arousal. Tension reduction has been proposed as a basic mechanism governing human behaviour.

In a marketing context, tension refers to the unpleasant state that exists if a person's consumption needs are not fulfilled. A person may be grumpy or unable to concentrate very well if they haven't eaten. Someone may be dejected or angry if they cannot afford that new car they want. This state activates goal-oriented behaviour, which attempts to reduce or eliminate this unpleasant state and return to a balanced one called **homeostasis**.

Those behaviours that are successful in reducing the drive by satisfying the underlying need are strengthened and tend to be repeated. (This *reinforcement* aspect of the learning process will be discussed in Chapter 7.) Your motivation to leave your lecture early to buy a snack would be greater if you hadn't eaten in the previous 24 hours than if you had eaten breakfast only two hours earlier. If you did sneak out and experienced indigestion after, say, wolfing down a packet of crisps, you would be less likely to repeat this behaviour the next time you wanted a snack. One's degree of motivation, then, depends on the distance between one's present state and the goal.

Drive theory, however, runs into difficulties when it tries to explain some facets of human behaviour that run counter to its predictions. People often do things that *increase* a drive state rather than decrease it. For example, people may delay gratification. If you know you are going out for a five-course dinner, you might decide to forgo a snack earlier in the day even though you are hungry at that time. And the most rewarding thing may often be the tension of the drive state itself rather than its satisfaction. It's not the kill, it's the thrill of the chase.

Expectancy theory

Most explanations of motivation currently focus on cognitive rather than biological factors in order to understand what drives behaviour. **Expectancy theory** suggests that behaviour is largely pulled by expectations of achieving desirable outcomes – *positive incentives* – rather than being pushed from within. We choose one product over another because we expect this choice to have more positive consequences for us. Thus the term *drive* is used here more loosely to refer to both physical and cognitive, i.e. learned, processes.

MOTIVATIONAL DIRECTION

Motives have direction as well as strength. They are goal oriented in that they drive us to satisfy a specific need. Most goals can be reached by a number of routes, and the objective of a company is to convince consumers that the alternative it offers provides the best chance to attain the goal. For example, a consumer who decides that they need a pair of jeans to help them reach their goal of being accepted by others can choose among Levi's, Wranglers, Diesel, Calvin Klein, Pepe, Gap, Hugo Boss, Stone Island and many other alternatives, each of which promises to deliver certain functional as well as symbolic benefits.

Needs *vs* wants

The specific way a need is satisfied depends on the individual's unique history, learning experiences and their cultural environment. The particular form of consumption used to satisfy a need is termed a want. For example, two classmates may feel their stomachs rumbling during a lunchtime lecture. If neither person has eaten since the night before, the strength of their respective needs (hunger) would be about the same. However, the way each person goes about satisfying this need might be quite different. The first person may be a vegetarian like Adrienne who fantasizes about large bowls of salad, whereas the second person like Rufus might be equally aroused by the prospect of a large plateful of Greek meatballs in tomato sauce.

What do we need?

A start to the discussion of needs and wants can best be illustrated by considering two basic types of need. People are born with a need for certain elements necessary to maintain life, such as food, water, air and shelter. These are called *biogenic needs*. People have many other needs, however, that are not innate. We acquire *psychogenic needs* as we become members of a specific culture. These include the need for status, power, affiliation, and so on. Psychogenic needs reflect the priorities of a culture, and their effect on behaviour will vary in different environments. For example, an Italian consumer may be driven to devote a good portion of their income to products that permit them to display their individuality, whereas their Scandinavian counterpart may work equally hard to ensure that they do not stand out from their group.

This distinction is revealing because it shows how difficult it is to distinguish needs from wants. How can we tell what part of the motivation is a psychogenic need and what part is a want? Both are profoundly formed by culture, so the distinction is problematic at best. As for the biogenic needs, we know from anthropology that satisfaction of these needs leads to some of the most symbolically rich and culturally based activities of humankind. The ways we want to eat, dress, drink and provide shelter are far more interesting to marketers than our need to do so. Hence, the idea of satisfaction of biogenic needs is more or less a given thing for marketing and consumer research because it is on the most basic level nothing more than a simple prerequisite for us to be here. Beyond that level, and of much greater interest (and challenge) to marketers, is a concept embedded in culture such as wants.[15]

We can also be motivated to satisfy either utilitarian or hedonic needs. When we focus on a *utilitarian need*, we emphasize the objective, tangible attributes of products, such as miles per gallon in a car; the amount of fat, calories and protein in a cheeseburger; or the durability of a pair of blue jeans. *Hedonic needs* are subjective and experiential; here we might look to a product to meet our needs for excitement, self-confidence or fantasy – perhaps to escape the mundane or routine aspects of life.[16] Many items satisfy our hedonic needs. Luxury brands in particular thrive when they offer the promise of pleasure to the user. Of course, consumers can be motivated to purchase a product because it provides *both* types of benefits. For example, a mink coat might be bought because it feels soft against the skin, because it keeps one warm through the long cold winters of northern Europe, and because it has a luxurious image. But again the distinction tends to hide more than it reveals, because functionality can bring great pleasure to people and is an important value in the modern world.[17] Indeed, recent research on novel consumption experiences indicates that even when we choose to do unusual things (like eating bacon ice cream or staying in a freezing ice hotel), we may do so because we have what the authors term a **productivity orientation**. This refers to a continual striving to use time constructively: trying new things is a way to check them off our checklist of experiences we want to achieve before moving on to others.

We expect today's technical products to satisfy our needs – instantly.

With permission from Apple Inc. (file supplied by The Advertising Archives).

Motivation and emotion

Motivation is largely driven by raw emotions, or what social scientists call **affect**. At the most basic level, we are driven to heighten positive emotion, or mood, and to reduce negative feelings. Thinking about the learning processes which we discuss in Chapter 7, our emotional reactions in turn influence the likelihood that we will engage in an activity next time – they positively or negatively reinforce us. That explains why so many marketing activities and messages focus on altering mood and linking products or services to affect.[18] This appeal to emotions also explains the popularity of soap operas, as well as reality TV shows. They encourage viewers to engage emotionally with the participants and to develop a 'relationship' with them. So, in a sense marketers/producers harness consumers' emotions and convert them into capital, as this affect is what they use to build loyalty to the product.[19]

How social media tap into our emotions

Social media platforms also strongly relate to our moods. We may share particularly good or bad feelings on Facebook or Twitter, or even resort to corny emoticons like ☺ in texts or emails to convey how we feel. It's so common for people to express their moods and also their emotional reactions to products that these posts can be a treasure trove for marketers who want to learn more about how their offerings make people feel. A technique called **sentiment analysis** does this; this refers to a process (sometimes also called *opinion mining*) that scours the social media universe to collect and analyse the words people use when they describe a specific product or company. When people feel a particular way, they are likely to choose certain words that tend to relate to the emotion. From these words, the researcher creates a **word-phrase dictionary** (sometimes called a *library*) to code the data. The programme scans the text to identify whether the words in the dictionary appear.[20]

MOTIVATIONAL CONFLICTS

A goal has *valence*, which means that it can be positive or negative. A positively valued goal is one towards which consumers direct their behaviour; they are motivated to *approach* the goal and will seek out products that will help them to reach it. However, not all behaviour is motivated by the desire to approach a goal. As we will see in the discussion of negative reinforcement (Chapter 7), consumers may instead be motivated to *avoid* a negative outcome.[21] They will structure their purchases or consumption activities to reduce the chances of attaining this end result. For example, many consumers work hard to avoid rejection, a negative goal. They will stay away from products that they associate with social disapproval. Products such as deodorants and mouthwash frequently rely on consumers' negative motivation by depicting the onerous social consequences of underarm odour or bad breath.

Because a purchase decision can involve more than one source of motivation, consumers often find themselves in situations where different motives, both positive and negative, conflict with one another.[22] Because marketers are attempting to satisfy consumers' needs, they can also be helpful by providing possible solutions to these dilemmas. As shown in Figure 6.1, three general types of conflicts can occur: approach–approach; approach–avoidance and avoidance–avoidance.

Approach–approach conflict

In an **approach–approach conflict**, a person must choose between two desirable alternatives. As a student, Adrienne might be torn between going home for the holidays or going on a skiing trip with friends. Or, she might have to choose between two CDs.

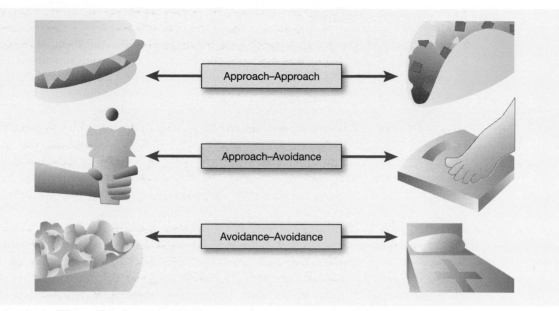

Figure 6.1 Three types of motivational conflict

The **theory of cognitive dissonance** is based on the premise that people have a need for order and consistency in their lives and that a state of tension is created when beliefs or behaviours conflict with one another. The conflict that arises when choosing between two alternatives may be resolved through a process of *cognitive dissonance reduction*, where people are motivated to reduce this inconsistency (or dissonance) and thus eliminate unpleasant tension.[23]

A state of dissonance occurs when there is a psychological inconsistency between two or more beliefs or behaviours. It often occurs when a consumer must make a choice between two products, where both alternatives usually possess both good and bad qualities. By choosing one product and not the other, the person gets the bad qualities of the chosen product and loses out on the good qualities of the one not chosen.

This loss creates an unpleasant, dissonant state that the person is motivated to reduce. People tend to convince themselves, after the fact, that the choice they made was the right one by finding additional reasons to support the alternative they chose, or perhaps by 'discovering' flaws with the option they did not choose (sometimes we call this 'rationalization'). A marketer can resolve an approach–approach conflict by bundling several benefits together. For example, many low calorie products claim that they have 'all the taste' *and* 'half the calories', e.g. Müller Light Yoghurts,[24] 'deliciously thick and creamy tasting and still fat free', allowing the consumer to avoid having to choose between better taste and fewer calories.

Approach-avoidance conflict

Many of the products and services we desire have negative consequences attached to them as well. We may feel guilty or ostentatious when buying a status-laden product such as a fur coat, or we might feel like a glutton when contemplating a box of chocolates. When we desire a goal but wish to avoid it at the same time, an **approach-avoidance conflict** exists. Some solutions to these conflicts include the proliferation of fake furs, which eliminate guilt about harming animals to make a fashion statement; and the success of low calorie and diet foods,

This ad from the National Drugs Helpline points out the negative consequences of drug addiction for those who are tempted to start.

The Advertising Archives.

such as those produced by WeightWatchers, that promise good food without the calories (**weight-watchers.com**). Some marketers counter consumer resistance to overconsumption and spending by promising more (benefits) from less, whereas other marketers try to overcome guilt by convincing consumers that they deserve luxuries (such as when the model for L'Oréal cosmetics states, 'Because I'm worth it!'). Sometimes consumers go outside the conventional marketplace to satisfy their needs, wants and desires, for instance drag-racing in Moscow where young Russian car fanatics fulfil their drive for thrill-seeking outside the law.[25]

Avoidance–avoidance conflict

Sometimes consumers find themselves 'caught between a rock and a hard place'. They may face a choice between two undesirable alternatives, for instance the option of either investing more money into an old car with more repairs or buying a new one. Marketers frequently address an **avoidance–avoidance conflict** with messages that stress the unforeseen benefits of choosing one option (e.g. by emphasizing special credit plans to ease the pain of new car payments).

HOW CAN WE CLASSIFY CONSUMER NEEDS?

Much research has been done on classifying human needs. On the one hand, some psychologists have tried to define a universal inventory of needs that could be traced systematically to explain virtually all behaviour. One such effort, developed by Henry Murray, delineates a set of 20 psychogenic needs that (sometimes in combination) result in specific behaviours. These needs include such dimensions as *autonomy* (being independent), *defendance* (defending the self against criticism), and even *play* (engaging in pleasurable activities).[26]

Murray's needs structure serves as the basis for a number of widely used personality tests such as the Thematic Apperception Technique (TAT) and the Edwards' Personal Preference Schedule (EPPS). In the TAT, test subjects are shown four to six ambiguous pictures and are asked to write answers to four questions about the pictures. These questions are: (1) What is happening? (2) What has led up to this situation? (3) What is being thought? (4) What will happen? Each answer is then analysed for references to certain needs and scored whenever that need is mentioned. The theory behind the test is that people will freely project their own subconscious needs onto the stimulus. By getting their responses to the picture, you are really getting at the person's true needs for achievement or affiliation or whatever other need may be dominant. Murray believed that everyone has the same basic set of needs, but that individuals differ in their priority ranking of these needs.[27]

Other motivational approaches have focused on specific needs and their ramifications for behaviour. For example, individuals with a high *need for achievement* strongly value personal accomplishment.[28] They place a premium on products and services that signify success because these consumption items provide feedback about the realization of their goals. These consumers are good prospects for products that provide evidence of their achievement. One study of working women found that those who were high in achievement motivation were more likely to choose clothing they considered businesslike, and less likely to be interested in apparel that accentuated their femininity.[29] Some other important needs that are relevant to consumer behaviour include the following:

● *Need for affiliation* (to be in the company of other people):[30] this need is relevant to products and services that are 'consumed' in groups and alleviate loneliness, such as team sports, bars and shopping centres.

● *Need for power* (to control one's environment):[31] many products and services allow consumers to feel that they have mastery over their surroundings, ranging from cars with 'souped up' engines and loud sound systems that impose the driver's musical tastes on others, to luxury resorts that promise to respond to every whim of their pampered guests.

● *Need for uniqueness* (to assert one's individual identity):[32] products can satisfy this need by pledging to accentuate a consumer's distinctive qualities. For example, Cachet perfume claims to be 'as individual as you are'.

Maslow's hierarchy of needs

Psychologist Abraham Maslow originally developed his influential **hierarchy of needs** to understand personal growth and how people attain spiritual 'peak experiences'. Marketers later adapted his work to understand consumer motivations.[33] Maslow proposed a hierarchy of biogenic and psychogenic needs that specifies certain levels of motives. This *hierarchical* structure implies that the order of development is fixed – that is, we must attain a certain level before we activate a need for the next, higher one. Marketers embraced this perspective because it (indirectly) specifies certain types of product benefits people might look for, depending on their stage of mental or spiritual development or on their economic situation.[34] However, as we shall see it, contains many problems, and we shall devote space to it here

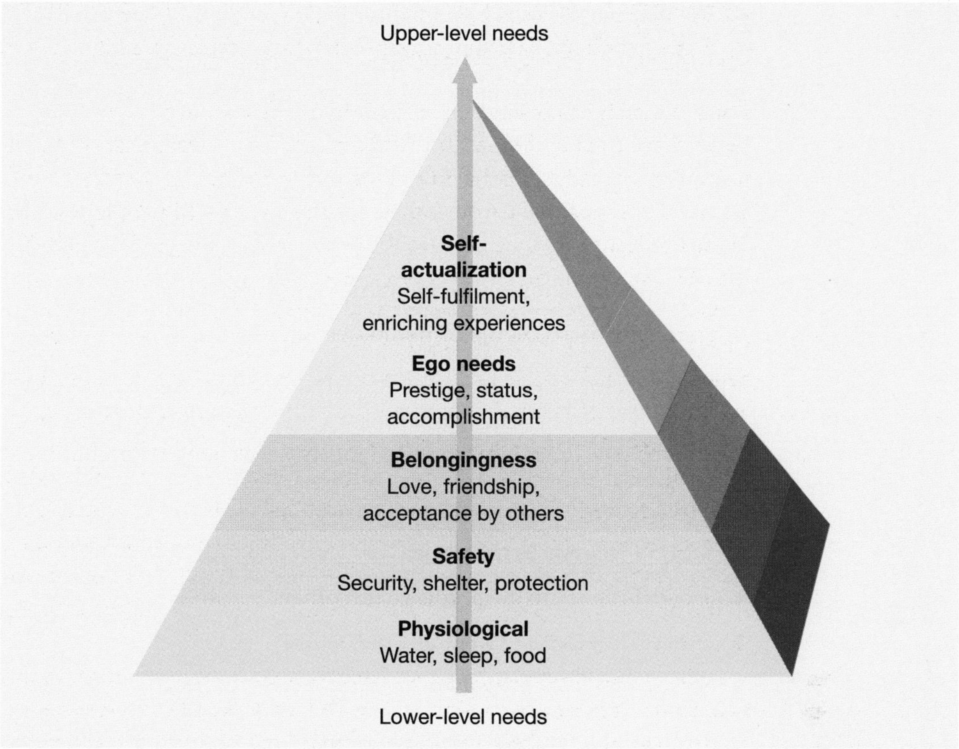

Upper-level needs

Self-actualization
Self-fulfilment,
enriching experiences

Ego needs
Prestige, status,
accomplishment

Belongingness
Love, friendship,
acceptance by others

Safety
Security, shelter, protection

Physiological
Water, sleep, food

Lower-level needs

Figure 6.2 Levels of need in the Maslow hierarchy

because it is a 'standard' in marketing knowledge rather than because we believe in its theoretical and practical value.

Maslow's levels are summarized in Figure 6.2. At each level, different priorities exist in terms of the product benefits a consumer is looking for. Ideally, an individual progresses up the hierarchy until their dominant motivation is a focus on 'ultimate' goals, such as justice and beauty. Unfortunately, this state is difficult to achieve (at least on a regular basis); most of us have to be satisfied with occasional glimpses, or *peak experiences*. One study of men aged 49 to 60 found respondents engaged in three types of activities to attain self-fulfilment:

1 Sport and physical activity.

2 Community and charity.

3 Building and renovating.

Regardless of whether these activities related to their professional work, these so-called *magnetic points* gradually took the place of those that were not as fulfilling.[35]

The implication of Maslow's hierarchy is that one must first satisfy basic needs before progressing up the ladder (i.e. a starving man is not interested in status symbols, friendship or self-fulfilment).[36] This suggests that consumers value different product attributes depending upon what is currently available to them.

Satisfying needs via social media

Our online behaviours can also satisfy needs at different levels of Maslow's hierarchy, especially when we participate in social networks like Facebook. **Web**-based companies can build loyalty if they keep these needs in mind when they design their offerings:

● We satisfy physiological needs when we use the web to research topics such as nutrition or medical questions.

- The web enables users to pool information and satisfy safety needs when they call attention to bad practices, flawed products, or even dangerous predators.
- Profile pages on Facebook and MySpace let users define themselves as individuals.
- Online communities, blogs and social networks provide recognition and achievement to those who cultivate a reputation for being especially helpful or expert in some subject.
- Users can seek help from others and connect with people who have similar tastes and interests.
- Access to invitation-only communities provides status.
- Spiritually based online communities can provide guidance to troubled people.[37]

The application of this hierarchy by marketers has been somewhat simplistic, especially as the same product or activity can satisfy a number of different needs. One example would be gardening, which has been found to satisfy needs at every level of the hierarchy:[38]

- *Physiological*: 'I like to work in the soil'.
- *Safety*: 'I feel safe in the garden'.
- *Social*: 'I can share my produce with others'.
- *Esteem*: 'I can create something of beauty.'
- *Self-actualization*: 'My garden gives me a sense of peace'.

Another problem with taking Maslow's hierarchy too literally is that it is culture-bound. The assumptions of the hierarchy may be restricted to a highly rational, materialistic and individualistic Western culture. People in other cultures may question the order of the levels as specified. A religious person who has taken a vow of celibacy would not necessarily agree that physiological needs must be satisfied before self-fulfilment can occur. Neither do all people in Western cultures seem to live according to Maslow's hierarchy. In fact, spiritual survival can be seen as a stronger motivator than physical survival, as can be seen from patriots or freedom fighters giving their life for the idea of nation, political or religious fanatics for their beliefs.[39]

Similarly, many Asian cultures value the welfare of the group (belongingness needs) more highly than needs of the individual (esteem needs). The point is that Maslow's hierarchy, while widely applied in marketing, is only helpful to marketers in so far as it reminds us that consumers may have different need priorities in different consumption situations and at different stages in their lives – not because it exactly specifies a consumer's progression up the ladder of needs. It also does not take account of the cultural formation of needs.

How and why do consumers use social media?

In search of a deeper understanding of consumers' use of social media, and particularly of how social media can best satisfy consumers' basic needs and lead to the most positive outcomes, Hoffman and Novak argued that 'the fundamental interactivity of social media allows for four higher-order goals: connect, create, consume, and control. These "4Cs" capabilities of social media undoubtedly explain in part why so many people spend so much of their time using social media and why social media are so popular.' In earlier research they had found that 'individuals who experience flow during their online navigational experiences are more likely to achieve positive outcomes compared to individuals who cannot attain these compelling online experiences.' Using this as a starting point, they studied how the 4Cs of connecting, creating, consuming and controlling social media experiences are used to organize consumers' social media goals '. . . Results suggested that connect goals ("social" goals) are associated with relatedness needs, an external locus of control, intrinsic motivation to connect with others, and positive evaluations of the social media groups to which consumers belong (private collective self-esteem). Consumers' pursuit of create goals is associated with autonomy, competence, and relatedness needs; an external locus of control; higher social media involvement; and contribution to sense of self (identity self-esteem). Consume goals ("non-social" goals) appear to be intrinsically motivated and negatively associated with autonomy and competence. Control goals satisfy autonomy and competence needs, and are associated with an external locus of causality and social media knowledge . . .' Hoffman and Novak concluded that 'different social media goals are supported by different needs and motivations'.[40]

HIDDEN MOTIVES: THE PSYCHOANALYTICAL PERSPECTIVE ON PERSONALITY

A motive is an underlying reason for behaviour and not something researchers can see or easily measure. The same behaviour can be caused by a configuration of different motives. To compound the problem of identifying motives, the consumer may be unaware of the actual need/want they are attempting to satisfy, or alternatively they may not be willing to admit that this need exists. Because of these difficulties, motives must often be *inferred* by the analyst. Although some consumer needs undoubtedly are utilitarian and fairly straightforward, some researchers feel that a great many purchase decisions are not the result of deliberate, logical decisions. On the contrary, people may do things to satisfy motives of which they are not even aware.

Sigmund Freud had a profound, if controversial, impact on many basic assumptions about human behaviour. His work changed the way we view such topics as adult sexuality, dreams and psychological adjustment. **Freudian theory** developed the idea that much of human behaviour stems from a fundamental conflict between a person's desire to gratify their physical needs and the necessity to function as a responsible member of society. This struggle is carried out in the mind among three systems. (Note that these systems do not refer to physical parts of the brain.)

The *id* is entirely oriented towards immediate gratification – it is the 'party animal' of the mind. It operates according to the pleasure principle: behaviour is guided by the primary desire to maximize pleasure and avoid pain. The *id* is selfish and illogical. It directs a person's psychic energy towards pleasurable acts without regard for the consequences.

The **superego** is the counterweight to the *id*. This system is essentially the person's conscience. It internalizes society's rules (especially as communicated by parents) and works to prevent the *id* from seeking selfish gratification.

Finally, the **ego** is the system that mediates between the *id* and the *superego*. It is in a way a referee in the fight between temptation and virtue. The *ego* tries to balance these two opposing forces according to the reality principle. It finds ways to gratify the *id* that will be acceptable to the outside world. These conflicts occur on an unconscious level, so the person is not necessarily aware of the underlying reasons for their behaviour.

Some of Freud's ideas have also been adapted by consumer researchers. In particular, his work highlights the potential importance of unconscious motives underlying purchases. The implication is that consumers cannot necessarily tell us their true motivation for choosing a product, even if we can devise a sensitive way to ask them directly. The Freudian perspective also hints at the possibility that the *ego* relies on the symbolism in products to compromise between the demands of the *id* and the prohibitions of the *superego*. The person channels their unacceptable desires into acceptable outlets by using products that signify these underlying desires. This is the connection between product symbolism and motivation: the product stands for, or represents, a consumer's true goal, which is socially unacceptable or unattainable. By acquiring the product, the person is able to vicariously experience the forbidden fruit.

Motivational research

The first attempts to apply Freudian ideas to understand the deeper meanings of products and advertisements were made in the 1950s as a perspective known as **motivational research** was developed. This approach was largely based on psycho-analytic (Freudian) interpretations, with a heavy emphasis on unconscious motives. A basic assumption is that socially unacceptable needs are channelled into acceptable outlets. Product use or avoidance is motivated by unconscious forces which are often determined in childhood.

This form of research relies on *depth interviews* probing deeply into each person's purchase motivations. These can be derived only after questioning and interpretation on the part of a carefully trained interviewer. This work was pioneered by Ernest Dichter, a psychoanalyst who was trained in Vienna in the early part of the twentieth century (see Table 6.1). Dichter conducted in-depth interview studies on over 230 different products, and many of his findings have been incorporated into marketing campaigns.[41] For example, Esso (or Exxon) for many

Table 6.1 Major motives for consumption as identified by Ernest Dichter

Motive	
Power – masculinity virility	Power: sugary products and large breakfasts (to charge oneself up), bowling, electric trains, hot rods, power tools
	Masculinity virility: coffee, red meat, heavy shoes, toy guns, buying fur coats for women, shaving with a razor
Security	Ice cream (to feel like a loved child again), full drawer of neatly ironed shirts, real plaster walls (to feel sheltered), home baking, hospital care
Eroticism	Sweets (to lick), gloves (to be removed by woman as a form of undressing), a man lighting a woman's cigarette (to create a tension-filled moment culminating in pressure, then relaxation)
Moral purity – cleanliness	White bread, cotton fabrics (to connote chastity), harsh household cleaning chemicals (to make housewives feel moral after using), bathing (to be equated with Pontius Pilate, who washed blood from his hands), oatmeal (sacrifice, virtue)
Social acceptance	Companionship: ice cream (to share fun), coffee
	Love and affection: toys (to express love for children), sugar and honey (to express terms of affection)
	Acceptance: soap, beauty products
Individuality	Gourmet foods, foreign cars, cigarette holders, vodka, perfume, fountain pens
Status	Scotch, ulcers, heart attacks, indigestion (to show one has a high-stress, important job!); carpets (to show one does not live on bare earth like peasants)
Femininity	Cakes and biscuits, dolls, silk, tea, household curios
Reward	Cigarettes, sweets, alcohol, ice cream, biscuits
Mastery over environment	Kitchen appliances, boats, sporting goods, cigarette lighters
Disalienation (a desire to feel connectedness to things)	Home decorating, skiing, morning radio broadcasts (to feel 'in touch' with the world)
Magic – mystery	Soups (having healing powers), paints (change the mood of a room), carbonated drinks (magical effervescent property), vodka (romantic history), unwrapping of gifts

Source: Adapted from Jeffrey F. Durgee, 'Interpreting Dichter's Interpretations: An Analysis of Consumption Symbolism in *The Handbook of Consumer Motivation*', *Marketing and Semiotics: Selected Papers from the Copenhagen Symposium*, Hanne Hartvig-Larsen, David Glen Mick and Christian Alsted (eds) (Copenhagen: Handelshøjskolens forlag, 1991).

years reminded consumers to 'Put a Tiger in Your Tank', after Dichter found that people responded well to powerful animal symbolism containing vaguely suggestive overtones.

Criticisms of motivational research

Motivational research has been attacked for two quite different reasons. Some feel it does not work, while others feel it works *too* well. On the one hand, social critics attacked this school of thought for giving advertisers the power to manipulate consumers.[42] On the other hand, many consumer researchers felt the research lacked sufficient rigour and validity, since interpretations were subjective and indirect.[43] Because conclusions are based on the analyst's own judgement and are derived from discussions with a small number of people, some researchers are doubtful about the degree to which these results can be generalized to a large market. In addition, because the original motivational researchers were heavily influenced by orthodox Freudian theory, their interpretations usually carried strong sexual overtones. This emphasis tends to overlook other plausible causes for behaviour.

The positive side of motivational research

Motivational research had great appeal at least to some marketers for several reasons, some of which are detailed here.

● Motivational research tends to be less expensive than large-scale, quantitative survey data because interviewing and data processing costs are relatively small.

● The knowledge derived from motivational research may help in the development of marketing communications that appeal to deep-seated needs and thus provide a more powerful hook to relate a product to consumers. Even if they are not necessarily valid for all consumers in a target market, these insights can be valuable when used in an exploratory way. For example, the rich imagery that may be associated with a product can be used creatively when developing advertising copy.

● Some of the findings seem intuitively plausible after the fact. For example, motivational studies concluded that coffee is associated with companionship, that people avoid prunes because they remind them of old age, and that men fondly equate the first car they owned as a young man with the onset of their sexual freedom.

Despite its drawbacks, motivational research continues to be employed as a useful diagnostic tool. Its validity is enhanced, however, when it is used in conjunction with other research techniques available to the consumer researcher.

Neo-Freudian theories

Freud's work had a huge influence on subsequent theories of **personality**. Although he opened the door to the realization that explanations for behaviour may lurk beneath the surface, many of his colleagues and students felt that an individual's personality is more influenced by how he handles relationships with others than by how he resolves sexual conflicts. We call these theorists *neo-Freudian* (meaning following from or being influenced by Freud). One of the most prominent neo-Freudians was Karen Horney who described people as moving towards others (*compliant*), away from others (*detached*), or against others (*aggressive*).[44] Other well-known neo-Freudians include Alfred Adler, who proposed that a prime motivation is to overcome feelings of inferiority relative to others; and Harry Stack Sullivan, who focused on how personality evolves to reduce anxiety in social relationships.[45]

Carl Jung was also a disciple of Freud. However, Jung was unable to accept Freud's emphasis on sexual aspects of personality and he developed his own method of psychotherapy, which he called *analytical psychology*. Jung believed that the cumulative experiences of past generations shape who we are today. He proposed that we each share a *collective unconscious*, a storehouse of memories we inherit from our ancestors. These shared memories create **archetypes**, or universally recognized ideas and behaviour patterns. Archetypes involve themes, such as birth, death or the devil, that appear frequently in myths, stories and dreams. Advertising messages often include archetypes (e.g. 'old wise man'; the 'earth mother').[46]

Trait theory

Popular online matchmaking services such as **match.com** and **eharmony.com** offer to create your 'personality profile' and then hook you up with other members whose profiles are similar. This approach to personality focuses on the quantitative measurement of **personality traits**, defined as the identifiable characteristics that define a person. What are some crucial personality traits? One is that we tend to describe people in terms of whether they are socially outgoing (the trait of *extroversion*) or not (the trait of *introversion*).[47] Some research evidence suggests that ad messages that match how a person thinks about himself are more persuasive.[48]

According to research firm Mindset Media, personality traits are better predictors of the type of media consumers choose than are demographic variables such as age, gender and income. The company also claims that the TV shows you watch offer marketers insights into your personality and the types of brands you're likely to prefer, based upon your dominant personality traits and the (perceived) matchup with a brand's image. To find out which personalities are attracted to which TV shows, it recently analysed self-reported data from about 25,000 TV viewers across more than 70 TV shows. These are some of the media/trait/brand linkages the company generated in its analysis:[49]

- Viewers of *Mad Men* are emotionally sensitive and intellectually curious types who often tend to be dreamers rather than realists. Good brand matches are Apple and the Audi A6.

- Viewers of *Family Guy* are rebels who don't like authority, rules or structure they deem unfair, and usually won't hesitate to make their feelings known with anger or sarcasm. Good brand matches are DiGiorno and the Ford F150.

- Viewers of *Glee* are open people who believe that imagination and intellectual pursuits contribute to a good life, and go out in search of unique and varied experiences. They are in touch with their own feelings and may even feel happiness or sadness more intensely than others. Good brand matches are Evian and the Volkswagen Jetta.

- Viewers of *The Office* consider themselves superior to others and like to brag about their accomplishments. They also like to be in charge. Good brand matches are Starbucks and the BMW Series 3.

Some specific traits relevant to consumer behaviour include *innovativeness* (the degree to which a person likes to try new things), *materialism* (the amount of emphasis a person places on acquiring and owning products as discussed in later in this chapter), *self-consciousness* (the degree to which a person deliberately monitors and controls the image of the self that he or she projects to others, as discussed in Chapter 5), and *need for cognition* (the degree to which a person likes to think about things and, by extension, expends the necessary effort to process brand information).[50]

Frugality

Another trait relevant to consumer behaviour is *frugality*. Frugal people deny short-term purchasing whims; they choose instead to resourcefully use what they already own. For example, this personality type tends to favour cost-saving measures such as timing showers and bringing leftovers from home to have for lunch at work.[51] Obviously, during tough economic times many consumers search for ways to save money. In 2008, as the recession started, Google searches for the term *frugality* increased by roughly 2,500 per cent.

Problems with trait theory in consumer research

Because consumer researchers categorize large numbers of consumers according to whether they exhibit various traits, we can apply this approach to segment markets. If a car manufacturer, for example, determines that drivers who fit a given trait profile prefer a car with certain features, it can use this information to great advantage. The notion that consumers buy products that are extensions of their personalities makes intuitive sense. As we'll see shortly, many marketing managers endorse this idea as they try to create *brand personalities* to appeal to different types of consumers.

Unfortunately, the use of standard personality trait measurements to predict product choices has met with mixed success at best. In general, marketing researchers simply have not been able to predict consumers' behaviours on the basis of measured personality traits. The following are some logical explanations for these less-than-stellar results:[52]

- Many of the scales are not sufficiently valid or reliable; they do not adequately measure what they are supposed to measure, and their results may not be stable over time.

- Psychologists typically develop personality tests for specific populations (e.g. people who are mentally ill); marketers then 'borrow' them to apply to a more general population where they have questionable relevance.

- Often marketers don't administer the tests under the appropriate conditions; people who are not properly trained may give them in a classroom or at a kitchen table.

- The researchers often make changes in the instruments to adapt them to their own situations and needs; in the process they may add or delete items and rename variables. These *ad hoc* changes dilute the validity of the measures and also reduce researchers' ability to compare results across consumer samples.

- Many trait scales measure gross, overall tendencies (e.g. emotional stability or introversion); marketers then use these results to make predictions about purchases of specific brands.

- In many cases, marketers ask consumers to respond to a large number of scales with no advance thought about how they will relate these measures to consumer behaviour. The researchers then use a 'shotgun approach', as they follow up on anything that happens to look interesting. As any statistician will tell you, this approach capitalizes on chance and can produce distorted results that may not be reproducible (or surface at all) in other studies.

Although marketing researchers largely abandoned the use of personality measures after many studies failed to yield meaningful results, some researchers have not given up on the early promise of this line of work. More recent efforts (mainly in Europe) try to learn from past mistakes. Researchers use more specific measures of personality traits that they have reason to believe are relevant to economic behaviour. They try to increase the validity of these measures, primarily by including multiple measures of behaviour rather than just a single personality scale. In addition, these researchers tone down their expectations of what personality traits can tell them about consumers. They now recognize that traits are only part of the solution; they have to incorporate personality data with information about people's social and economic conditions for it to be useful.[53] As a result, some more recent research has had better success at relating personality traits to such consumer behaviours as alcohol consumption among young men or shoppers' willingness to try new, healthier food products.[54]

BRAND PERSONALITY

Do products have personalities, or influence their owners' traits? Are Apple users better than the rest of us? Many of us know an 'Apple-holic' who likes to turn up his or her nose at the uneducated masses that have to get by with their primitive PCs or Android phones. A survey of 20,000 people claims that iPad users are unkind and have little empathy; it labels them a 'selfish elite'. It also described them as 'six times more likely to be wealthy, well-educated, power-hungry, over-achieving, sophisticated, unkind and non-altruistic 30- to 50-year-olds. They are self-centered workaholics with an overwhelming interest in business and finance who cherish "power and achievement" and will not cross the street to help others.'[55]

Today thousands of brands borrow personality traits of individuals or groups to convey an image they want customers to form of them. A **brand personality** is the set of traits people attribute to a product as if it were a person. An advertising agency wrote the following memo to help it figure out how to portray one of its clients. Based on this description of the 'client', can you guess who he is? 'He is creative . . . unpredictable . . . an imp. . . . He not only walks and talks, but has the ability to sing, blush, wink, and work with little devices like pointers. . . . He can also play musical instruments. . . . His walking motion is characterized as a "swagger". . . . He is made of dough and has mass.'[56] Of course, we all know today that packaging and other physical cues create a 'personality' for a product (in this case, the Pillsbury Doughboy).

Many of the most recognizable figures in popular culture are spokes-characters for long-standing brands, such as the Jolly Green Giant.[57] These personalities periodically get a make-over to keep their meanings current. Like people, brand personalities do change over time – whether marketers like Alka-Seltzer want them to or not. To give you an idea of how much things change, Americans ranked these brands as the most stylish in 1993: Levis; Nike; Bugle Boy; and Guess and L.A. Gear. By 2008, the top five were: Victoria's Secret; Ralph Lauren; Nine West; Calvin Klein; and Coach.[58]

Forging a successful brand personality often is key to building brand loyalty, but it's not as easy to accomplish as it might appear. One reason is that many consumers (particularly younger ones) are very alert to when a brand doesn't live up to its claims or is somehow inauthentic. When this happens, the strategy may backfire as consumers rebel. They may create websites to attack the brand or post parodies that make fun of it on YouTube. One set of researchers terms this phenomenon a **Doppelgänger brand image** (one that looks like the original but is in fact a critique of it).

Our feelings about a brand's personality are part of *brand equity*, which refers to the extent to which a consumer holds strong, favourable and unique associations with a brand in memory – and the extent to which she or he is willing to pay more for the branded version of a product than for a nonbranded (generic) version.[59] Building strong brands is good business. In a study of 760 *Fortune* 1,000 companies after the stock market took a nosedive in October 1997, for example, the 20 strongest corporate brands (e.g. Microsoft, GE) actually gained in market value, whereas the 20 weakest lost an average of $1 billion each.[60]

So, how do people think about brands? Advertisers are keenly interested in this question, and ad agencies often conduct extensive consumer research to help them understand how consumers will relate to a brand before they roll out campaigns. DDB Worldwide does a global study called 'Brand Capital' of 14,000 consumers; Leo Burnett's 'Brand Stock' project involves 28,000 interviews. WPP Group has 'BrandZ' and Young & Rubicam uses its BrandAsset Valuator®. DDB's worldwide brand planning director observes, 'We're not marketing just to isolated individuals. We're marketing to society. How I feel about a brand is directly related to and affected by how others feel about that brand.'[61] Some researchers argue that, just as they use the two basic dimensions of warmth and competence to judge people, consumers employ the same labels when they form perceptions of firms; one study found that people perceive nonprofits as being warmer than for-profits but also as being less competent.[62]

We use some personality dimensions to compare and contrast the perceived characteristics of brands in various product categories, including these:[63]

- Old-fashioned, wholesome, traditional.
- Surprising, lively, 'with it'.
- Serious, intelligent, efficient.
- Glamorous, romantic, sexy.
- Rugged, outdoorsy, tough, athletic.

Consumers appear to have little trouble assigning personality qualities to all sorts of inanimate products, from personal care products to more mundane, functional ones – including kitchen appliances. A product that creates and communicates a distinctive brand personality stands out from its competition and inspires years of loyalty. However, personality analysis helps marketers identify a brand's weaknesses that have little to do with its functional qualities: Adidas asked kids in focus groups to imagine that the brand came to life and was at a party, and to tell what they would expect the brand to be doing there. The kids responded that Adidas would be hanging around the bar with its pals, talking about girls. Unfortunately, they also said Nike would *be with* the girls![64] The results reminded Adidas' brand managers that they had some work to do. We compare this process to **animism**, the common cultural practice whereby people attribute to inanimate objects qualities that make them somehow alive.[65]

We tend to *anthropomorphize* objects, which happens when we attribute human characteristics to them. We may think about a cartoon character or mythical creation as if it were a person and even assume that it has human feelings. Again, think about familiar spokes-characters such as the Michelin Man or the Jolly Green Giant.

In a sense, a brand personality is a statement about the brand's market position. Understanding this is crucial to marketing strategy, especially if consumers don't see the brand the way its makers intend them to and they must attempt to *reposition* the product (i.e., give it a personality makeover). That's the problem Volvo now faces: its cars are renowned for safety, but drivers don't exactly see them as exciting or sexy. A safe and solid brand personality makes it hard to sell a racy convertible like the C70 model, so a British ad tried to change that perception with the tagline, 'Lust, envy, jealousy. The dangers of a Volvo.' Just as with people, however, you can only go so far to convince others that your personality has changed. Volvo has been trying to jazz up its image for years, but for the most part consumers aren't buying it. In an earlier attempt in the United Kingdom, the company paired action images like a Volvo pulling a helicopter off a cliff with the headline 'Safe Sex' – but market research showed that people didn't believe the new image. As one brand consultant observed, 'You get the sort of feeling you get when you see your grandparents trying to dance the latest dance. Slightly amused and embarrassed.'[66] Still, Volvo keeps trying to morph into a sexy brand. It calls its new S60 model the Naughty S60, and to launch the car in Europe the company hosted underground parties in London, Paris, Milan, Berlin and Madrid (check out the videos on Volvo's Subject360YouTube channel).[67]

CONSUMER INVOLVEMENT

Do consumers form strong relationships with products and services? People can become pretty attached to products. As we have seen, a consumer's motivation to attain a goal increases their desire to expend the effort necessary to acquire the products or services they believe will be instrumental in satisfying that goal. However, not everyone is motivated to the same extent – one person might be convinced they can't live without the latest Apple iPhone, while another is perfectly happy with their three year-old LG.

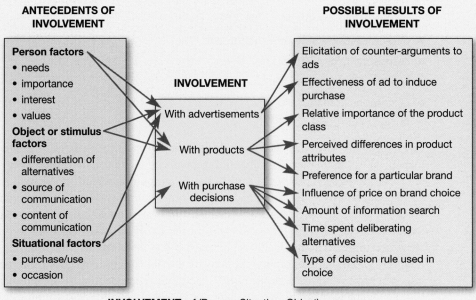

ANTECEDENTS OF INVOLVEMENT

Person factors
- needs
- importance
- interest
- values

Object or stimulus factors
- differentiation of alternatives
- source of communication
- content of communication

Situational factors
- purchase/use
- occasion

INVOLVEMENT

With advertisements

With products

With purchase decisions

POSSIBLE RESULTS OF INVOLVEMENT

Elicitation of counter-arguments to ads

Effectiveness of ad to induce purchase

Relative importance of the product class

Perceived differences in product attributes

Preference for a particular brand

Influence of price on brand choice

Amount of information search

Time spent deliberating alternatives

Type of decision rule used in choice

INVOLVEMENT = f (Person, Situation, Object)

The level of involvement may be influenced by one or more of these factors.
Interactions among persons, situation, and object factors are likely to occur.

Figure 6.3 Conceptualizing components of involvement

Involvement is defined as 'a person's perceived relevance of the object based on their inherent needs, values, and interests'.[68] The word *object* is used in the generic sense and refers to a product (or a brand), an advertisement, or a purchase situation. Consumers can find involvement in all these *objects*. Figure 6.3 shows that because involvement is a motivational construct, different antecedents can trigger it. These factors can be something about the person, something about the object, or something about the situation, which can combine to determine the consumer's motivation to process product-related information at a given point in time. When consumers are intent on doing what they can to satisfy a need, they will be motivated to pay attention and process any information felt to be relevant to achieving their goals. On the other hand, a person may not bother to pay any attention to the same information if it is not seen as relevant to satisfying some need. Adrienne, for instance, who prides herself on her knowledge of the environment and green issues, may read everything she can find about the subject, while another person may skip over this information without giving it a second thought.

Involvement can be viewed as the motivation to process information.[69] To the degree that there is a perceived linkage between a consumer's needs, goals or values and product knowledge, the consumer will be motivated to pay attention to product information. When relevant knowledge is activated in memory, a motivational state is created that drives behaviour (e.g. shopping). As felt involvement with a product increases, the consumer devotes more attention to ads related to the product, exerts more cognitive effort to understand these ads, and focuses more attention on the product-related information in them.[70] However, this kind of 'rational' involvement may be the exception rather than the rule.[71]

Levels of involvement: from inertia to passion

The type of information processing that will occur thus depends on the consumer's level of involvement. It can range from *simple processing*, where only the basic features of a message

An example of a collage which illustrates higher levels of involvement, particularly passionate intensity.

are considered, all the way to *elaboration*, where the incoming information is linked to one's pre-existing knowledge system.[72]

Inertia

We can think of a person's degree of involvement as a continuum, ranging from absolute lack of interest in a marketing stimulus at one end to obsession at the other. Consumption at the low end of involvement is characterized by **inertia**, where decisions are made out of habit because the consumer lacks the motivation to consider alternatives. At the high end of involvement, we can expect to find the type of passionate intensity reserved for people and objects that carry great meaning for the individual. For the most part a consumer's involvement level with products falls somewhere in the middle, and the marketing strategist must determine the relative level of importance to understand how much elaboration of product information will occur.

When consumers are truly involved with a product, an ad or a website, they enter what has been called a **flow state**. This state is the Holy Grail of **web** designers who want to create sites that are so entrancing that the surfer loses all track of time as they become engrossed in the site's contents (and hopefully buys things in the process!). The web is 'a part of the internet accessed through a graphical user interface and containing documents often connected by hyperlinks' (**www.merriam-webster.com/dictionary/worldwideweb**). Flow is an optimal experience characterized by:

- a sense of playfulness;
- a feeling of being in control;
- concentration and highly focused attention;
- mental enjoyment of the activity for its own sake;
- a distorted sense of time;
- a match between the challenge at hand and one's skills.[73]

The many faces of involvement

As previously defined, involvement can take many forms. It can be cognitive, as when a 'web-head' is motivated to learn all they can about the latest spec of a new multimedia PC, or emotional, as when the thought of a new Armani suit gives a clothes horse goose pimples.[74] Further, the very act of buying the Armani suit may be very involving for people who are passionately devoted to shopping. To complicate matters further, advertisements, such as those produced for Nike or Adidas, may themselves be involving for some reason (for example, because they make us laugh, cry, or inspire us to work harder). It seems that involvement is a fuzzy concept, because it overlaps with other things and means different things to different people. Indeed, the consensus is that there are actually several broad types of involvement related to the product, the message, or the perceiver.[75]

Product involvement is related to a consumer's level of interest in a particular product. Many sales promotions are designed to increase this type of involvement. Perhaps the most powerful way to enhance product involvement is to invite consumers to play a role in designing or personalizing what they buy. **Mass customization** is the personalization of products and services for individual customers at a mass-production price.[76] Improved manufacturing techniques in many industries are allowing companies to produce made-to-order products for many customers at a time. Dell is now offering customized paint jobs on its notebooks, as part of the design revolution in personal computers aimed at giving a unique look and feel to Dell IT products. This design revolution recognizes the changing role of digitial technologies in consumers' lives, where the emphasis is as much on the form as on the function of these IT products.[77]

Message-response involvement (also known as *advertising involvement*), refers to the consumer's interest in processing marketing communications.[78] Television is considered a low-involvement medium because it requires a passive viewer who exerts relatively little control (remote control 'zapping' notwithstanding) over content. In contrast, print is often seen as a high-involvement medium. The reader is actively involved in processing the information and is able to pause and reflect on what they have read before moving on.[79] In fact, some messages (including really well-made advertisements) are so involving that they trigger a stage of **narrative transportation**, where people become immersed in the storyline (much like the flow state we described earlier).[80] We'll discuss the role of message characteristics in changing attitudes in Chapter 8.

Strategies to increase involvement

Although consumers differ in their levels of involvement with respect to a product message, marketers do not have to simply sit back and hope for the best. By being aware of some basic factors that increase or decrease attention, they can take steps to increase the likelihood that product information will get through. A marketer can boost a person's motivation to process relevant information via one or more of the following techniques:[81]

- *Appeal to the consumers' hedonic needs.* Ads that use sensory appeals generate higher levels of attention.[82]
- *Use novel stimuli, such as unusual cinematography, sudden silences, or unexpected movements, in commercials.* When a British firm called Egg Banking introduced a credit card to the French

market, its ad agency created unusual commercials to make people question their assumptions. One ad stated, 'Cats always land on their paws', and then two researchers in white lab coats dropped a kitten off a rooftop – never to see it again (animal rights activists were not amused).[83]

- *Use prominent stimuli, such as loud music and fast action, to capture attention in commercials.* In print formats, larger ads increase attention. Also, viewers look longer at coloured pictures than at black-and-white ones.

- *Include celebrity endorsers to generate higher interest in commercials.* As we'll see in Chapter 8, people process more information when it comes from someone they admire.

- *Provide value that customers appreciate.* Charmin bathroom tissue set up public toilets in Times Square that hordes of grateful visitors used. Thousands more people visited the brand's website to view the display.[84]

- *Let customers make the messages.* **Consumer-generated content**, where freelancers and fans film their own commercials for favourite products, is one of the hottest trends in marketing right now. 'The explosion in Consumer Generated Media over the last few years means that this reliance on word of mouth, over other forms of referral, looks set to increase.'[85] Advertisers will probably spend about $2.6 billion (over 1.7 billion euros) 'to place ads on social networking sites by 2012.'[86] This important trend helps to define the so-called era of Web 2.0; the rebirth of the internet as a social, interactive medium from its original roots as a form of one-way transmission from producers to consumers. This practice creates a high degree of *message–response involvement* (also called *advertising involvement*), which refers to the consumer's interest in processing marketing communications.[87]

At the least, give customers a say if you're contemplating a change: Gap found this out the hard way when it rolled out an updated version of its logo on its website without warning fans first. Almost instantly, more than 2,000 customers posted complaints on Facebook. The company first tried to stand by its decision, but eventually it gave in and returned to the tried-and-tested logo. The president of Gap Brand North America admitted that the company 'did not go about this in the right way' and missed the 'opportunity to engage with the online community'.[88]

What are some other tactics to increase message involvement? One is to invent new media platforms to grab our attention. Procter & Gamble printed trivia questions and answers on its Pringles snack chips with ink made of blue or red food colouring.[89] Another tactic is to create **spectacles** or *performances*, where the message is itself a form of entertainment. In the early days of radio and television, ads literally were performances – show hosts integrated marketing messages into the episodes. Today live advertising is making a comeback as marketers try harder and harder to captivate jaded consumers:[90]

- A British show broadcast a group of skydivers who performed a dangerous jump to create a human formation in the air that spelled out the letters *H*, *O*, *N*, *D* and *A*.

- To promote the 25th anniversary of the Michael Jackson album *Thriller*, which featured zombies dancing in a music video, Sony BMG staged such a performance on the London Underground. A group of 'passengers' suddenly burst into a zombie-like dance before they disappeared into the crowd – and this videotaped scene was posted online. The video inspired similar performances in other countries, and within a week more than a million people had downloaded these films.

- In a similar stunt for T-Mobile, several hundred commuters at a Liverpool railway station broke into a dance; more than 15 million people watched the performance on YouTube in the following weeks. These (not so) spontaneous **flashmobs** have become increasingly common – which probably means they will wane in popularity as the spectacle of hundreds of people suddenly exploding into dance or song becomes almost an ordinary experience.

Television is considered a low-involvement medium because it requires a passive viewer who exerts relatively little control.

Source: Simon Marcus/Corbis/ photolibrary.com.

The quest to heighten message involvement is fuelling the rapid growth of **interactive mobile marketing** where consumers participate in real-time promotional campaigns via their trusty mobile phones, usually by text-messaging entries to on-air TV contests. These strategies are very popular in the UK, for example, where revenue from phone and text-messaging services for TV programmes bring in almost half a billion dollars (over 680 million euros) a year. Viewers sent over 500,000 text-message votes within two days during the reality show *Big Brother*.[91]

Purchase situation involvement refers to differences that may occur when buying the same object for different contexts. Here the person may perceive a great deal of social risk or none at all. For example, when you want to impress someone you may try to buy a brand or a product with a certain image that you think reflects good taste. When you have to buy a gift for someone in an obligatory situation, like a wedding gift for a cousin you do not really like, you may not care what image the gift portrays. Or you may actually pick something cheap that reflects your desire to distance yourself from that cousin. Again, some smart retailers are waking up to the value of increasing purchase situation involvement by appealing to hedonic shoppers who are looking to be entertained or otherwise engaged in addition to just 'buying stuff'.[92] We saw how they are doing this via the creation of themed retailing venues and other strategies in Chapter 3.

Many of us experience heightened purchase situation involvement when we log in to our favourite social media sites. Some of the most successful new applications involve some form of **social game**: a multiplayer, competitive, goal-oriented activity with defined rules of engagement and online connectivity among a community of players. Most social games include a few key elements:

- *Leaderboards* a listing of the leaders in the game competition.
- *Achievement badges* symbols awarded to show game levels achieved, shared with the community.
- *Friend (buddy) lists* with a chat list of contacts with whom one plays and the ability to communicate within the game.

Brands can utilize social games for marketing in several ways. When the Microsoft search engine Bing ran an ad that offered players the chance to earn *FarmVille* cash for becoming a fan of Bing on Facebook, the brand won 425,000 new fans in the first day.[93] One specific tactic we will see more of in the booming world of social games is **transactional advertising** which rewards players if they respond to a request.[94] The offers can be for *virtual goods* (which

A study about clubbing (or 'raves') illustrates how a social activity is co-created by producers and consumers. These experiences started in the UK as spontaneous gatherings in empty warehouses. Although these events are banned in many places, the consumer researchers showed how the promoters and the clubbers cooperate with local authorities to make possible this 'contained illegality': for example, by regulating the drugs (particularly Ecstasy) that are consumed and instituting safeguards to prevent violence.

Source: dwphotos/istockphoto.

players can use in the game or offer as gifts to friends), *currency* (used to advance in the game), or *codes* (used to unlock prizes and limited-access player experiences). Players are rewarded with the virtual goods, currencies, or codes if they make a purchase, 'friend' the brand, watch a commercial, or perhaps answer a survey. The hugely popular *FarmVille* social game teamed up with the also hugely popular Lady Gaga in 2011 to launch a special version of the game called *GagaVille*; an entire area inside the game with Gaga-themed items like unicorns. Fans who bought a $25 game card from Best Buy also received her album *Born This Way* as a free download.[95]

VALUES

Generally speaking, a **value** can be defined as a belief about some desirable end-state that transcends specific situations and guides selection of behaviour.[96] Thus, values are general and different from attitudes in that they do not apply to specific situations only. A person's set of values plays a very important role in their consumption activities, since many products and services are purchased because (it is believed) they will help us to attain a value-related goal. Two people can believe in and exhibit the same behaviours (for example, vegetarianism) but their underlying belief systems may be quite different (animal activism *vs* health concerns). The extent to which people share a belief system is a function of individual, social and cultural forces. Advocates of a belief system often seek out others with similar beliefs, so that social networks overlap and as a result believers tend to be exposed to information that supports their beliefs (e.g. environmentalists rarely socialize with factory farmers).[97]

Core values

Every culture has a set of **core values** that it imparts to its members.[98] For example, people in one culture might feel that being a unique individual is preferable to subordinating one's identity to the group, while another group may emphasize the virtues of group membership. In many cases, values are universal. Who does not desire health, wisdom or world peace? But on the other hand, values can vary across cultures and do change over time. In Japan young people are working hard to adopt Western values and behaviours – which explains why the current fashion for young people is bleached, blond hair, chalky make-up and a deep tan. Government policies have encouraged this type of consumer spending. However, changing patterns of consumption have increased feelings of personal liberation among the younger generation. They are now challenging many of the values of the past as shown, for instance, by the increasing school drop-out rate, which has grown by 20 per cent since 1997.[99] Similar concerns about the consequences of what is often called a value crisis are also discussed in European societies. Likewise, one may wonder what happened to the traditional Scandinavian modesty – in both Denmark and Sweden people are now showing more willingness to share their private lives with thousands of others in either talk shows or docu-soaps of the *Big Brother* variety.

Or, take the core value of cleanliness: everyone wants to be clean, but some societies are more fastidious than others and won't accept products and services that they think cut corners. Italian women on average spend 21 hours a week on household chores other than cooking – compared with only four hours for Americans, according to Procter & Gamble's research. The Italian women wash kitchen and bathroom floors at least four times a week, Americans only once. Italian women typically iron nearly all their wash, even socks and sheets, and they buy more cleaning supplies than women elsewhere do.

So they should be ideal customers for cleaning products, right? That's what Unilever thought when it launched its all-purpose Cif spray cleaner there, but it flopped. Similarly, P&G's best-selling Swiffer wet mop bombed big time. Both companies underestimated this market's desire for products that are tough cleaners, not timesavers. Only about 30 per cent of Italian households have dishwashers, because many women don't trust machines to get dishes as clean as they can get them by hand, manufacturers say. Many of those who do use

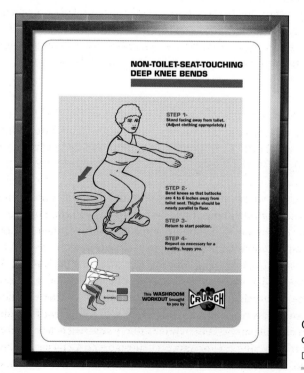

Cleanliness is a core value in many cultures.

DiMassimo, Inc.

Many advertisements appeal to people's values to persuade them to change or modify their behaviours, such as this Dogs Trust ad.

The Advertising Archives.

machines tend to thoroughly rinse the dishes before they load them into the dishwasher. The explanation for this value: after the Second World War, Italy remained a poor country until well into the 1960s, so labour-saving devices, such as washing machines, which had become popular in wealthy countries, arrived late. Italian women joined the workforce later than many other European women and in smaller numbers. Young Italian women increasingly work outside the home, but they still spend nearly as much time as their mothers did on housework.

When Unilever did research to determine why Italians didn't take to Cif, they found that these women weren't convinced that a mere spray would do the job on tough kitchen grease or that one product would adequately clean different surfaces (it turns out that 72 per cent of Italians own more than eight different cleaning products). The company reformulated the product and reintroduced it with different varieties instead of as an all-in-one. It also made the bottles 50 per cent bigger, because Italians clean so frequently, and changed its advertising to emphasize the products' cleaning strength rather than convenience. P&G also reintroduced its Swiffer, this time adding beeswax and a Swiffer duster that is now a bestseller. It sold five million boxes in the first eight months, twice the company's forecasts.[100]

Value systems

Every culture is characterized by its members' endorsement of a **value system**. These end-states may not be equally endorsed by everyone, and in some cases values may even seem to contradict one another (e.g. Westerners in general appear to value both conformity and individuality, and seek to find some accommodation between the two). Nonetheless, it is usually possible to identify a general set of *core values* which uniquely define a culture.

How do we find out what a culture values? We term the process of learning the beliefs and behaviours endorsed by one's own culture **enculturation**. In contrast, we call the process of learning the value system and behaviours of another culture (often a priority for those who wish to understand consumers and markets in foreign countries) **acculturation**.[101] *Socialization agents* including parents, friends and teachers impart these beliefs to us. Another important type of agent is the media; we learn a lot about a culture's priorities by looking at the values communicated by advertising. Sales strategies, for example, differ significantly between the US and China. American commercials are more likely to present facts about products and suggestions from credible authorities, while Chinese advertisers tend to focus more on emotional appeals without bothering too much to substantiate their claims. American ads tend to be youth-oriented, while Chinese ads are more likely to stress the wisdom of older people.[102]

Italians don't like online publicity because online ads represent obstacles as they try to navigate a website. Nearly 70 per cent of Italians interviewed complained that the publicity was a violation of their privacy, and about 40 per cent found online advertising invasive.[103]

In many cases, values are universal. What sets cultures apart is the *relative importance*, or ranking, of these universal values. This set of rankings constitutes a culture's **value system**.[104] Core values must be understood in the local context – that is, the meaning of the values changes when the cultural context shifts. This is a serious challenge to the idea that it is possible to compare value systems by studying the rankings of universal sets of values across countries. For example, one study found that North Americans have more favourable attitudes towards advertising messages that focus on self-reliance, self-improvement, and the achievement of personal goals as opposed to themes stressing family integrity, collective goals, and the feeling of harmony with others. Korean consumers exhibited the reverse pattern.[105]

Core values such as freedom, youthfulness, achievement, materialism and activity characterize American culture. In contrast, most Japanese are happy to trade off a bit of independence for security and a feeling of safety – especially when it comes to their children. It's common for communities to post guards along school routes and for parents to place global positioning system (GPS) devices and safety buzzers in their kids' backpacks. Numerous indoor parks in Japan are highly secure environments designed to ease parents' minds.[106] Despite living under enormous stress and deprivation after the 2011 earthquake and tsunami, thousands of Japanese who were marooned in public shelters still found ways to maintain order and hygiene to the greatest extent possible.[107]

DR DIEGO RINALLO
Bocconi University, Milan

Consumer behaviour as I see it . . .

One of my ongoing research interests is fashion, which I consider an interesting setting in which to explore how consumer values and lifestyles are evolving. Being Italian and living in Milan, my foreign colleagues regularly say that I'm definitely in the right place. One recent development is that fashion increasingly speaks to men. In the past, women were the only targets of companies in the fashion and beauty businesses. After the French Revolution men renounced fashion – on the basis of the cultural principle that judgement of a man's worth should be based on accomplishments rather than on simple appearance. In the 1980s, however, fashion designers like Armani, Versace, Dolce & Gabbana, Calvin Klein – to name just a few prominent examples – started employing muscular and handsome male models in their ads who were far from the average-looking guy next door. Such beauty ideals, which are shaped by gay aesthetics, are difficult (not to say impossible) to achieve for most men. In some cases, these images were rejected by male consumers for being unrealistic or even exploitative of psychological fragilities. However, many male consumers are seduced by these beautiful representations of masculinity, which stimulate consumer narcissism and lead men to look at themselves and other men as objects of beauty. People who are now in their twenties and early thirties have grown up immersed in a media environment full of these hyper-real images of masculinity, which have influenced male consumer aesthetics. Young straight men, increasingly, look like gay men, particularly when living in metropolitan areas. Accordingly, fashion involvement is no longer a predominantly female trait.

However, the fashion-conscious guy may face stigma – particularly outside big cities. Sure, men have to abide by minimum requirements to be socially accepted. However, there are boundaries that cannot be crossed without risks. Men who spend too much time and money on looking beautiful or adopt extreme fashions to attract attention to their physical appearance may be considered unmanly: vain, superficial, effeminate, and even gay. In contexts characterized by homophobia, such evaluations engender negative social consequences. Even those fashion innovators who would like to experiment with new products and styles are constrained by the fear of being misjudged or made fun of by family, friends, and acquaintances. These facts show that important aspects of consumer behaviour – such as consumer involvement and the acquisition of expertise regarding certain product categories – may be shaped by cultural norms about what is gender appropriate for men and women. Such norms are internalized by consumers and, in cases of transgressions, actively sanctioned through the judgemental gaze of relevant others.

As early fashion theorists have often reminded us, fashion is based on ambivalence between two opposing needs: expressing individuality on the one hand, and being socially accepted on the other. In Italy, people are often said to be obsessed with bella figura (literally, a good figure, which can be roughly translated as making a good impression). Bella figura in fashion requires standing out in the crowd, but without going to the extreme. Virtue resides in the middle, according to an old Latin proverb. However, the 'middle' is socially constructed and marketers, through their mass production of visual images of beauty, constantly try to redefine it. Outside of Italy, national cultural differences may play important roles in configuring what constitutes excess in men's fashion and physical appearance. I leave male readers to ponder the limits of an acceptable involvement with fashion and beauty in their own country and social milieu.

How can marketers target fashion-involved men in an effective way? In my view, all marketing mix elements can be deployed for this purpose. Male models in advertising should be beautiful, but not impossibly so, in order to avoid consumer rejection. Celebrity endorsers should be selected on the basis of what they have achieved, rather than just on their looks. In addition, promotion, product design, distribution channels and price should in general help male consumers avoid social criticism while indulging in narcissism. For example, a cheap moisturizing cream bought in a supermarket may be much more socially acceptable than an expensive, top brand purchased at a cosmetics counter in an up-market department store; an anti-wrinkle cream may be redefined as 'regenerating' and its use linked to special circumstances ('I wouldn't buy it, but my skin needs to be fresh for tomorrow's meeting with my boss').

Diego Rinallo

How do values link to consumer behaviour?

Despite their importance, values have not been as widely applied to direct examinations of consumer behaviour as might be expected. One reason is that broad-based concepts such as freedom, security or inner harmony are more likely to affect general purchasing patterns rather than to differentiate between brands within a product category. For this reason, some researchers have found it convenient to make distinctions among broad-based *cultural values* such as security or happiness; *consumption-specific values* such as convenient shopping or prompt service; and *product-specific values* such as ease of use or durability, that affect the relative importance people in different cultures place on possessions.[108] One way we can clearly see the impact of shifting cultural values on consumption is to look at the increasing emphasis placed on the importance of health and wellness.

A recent study of product-specific values looked in depth at Australians who engage in extreme sports like surfing, snowboarding and skateboarding. The researchers identified four dominant values that drove brand choice: freedom, belongingness, excellence and connection. For example, one female surfer they studied embraced the value of belongingness. She expressed this value by wearing popular brands of surfing apparel even when these major brands had lost their local roots by going mainstream. In contrast, another surfer in the study

Research identified four dominant values that drove brand choice amongst extreme sports' enthusiasts: freedom, belongingness, excellence and connection.

Source: DavidPu'u/Corbis/photolibrary.com

valued connection; he expressed this by selecting only locally-made brands and going out of his way to support local surfing events.[109]

While some aspects of brand image such as sophistication tend to be common across cultures, others are more likely to be relevant in specific places. The characteristic of peacefulness is valued to a larger extent in Japan, while the same holds true for passion in Spain and ruggedness in the US.[110] Because values drive much of consumer behaviour (at least in a very general sense), we might say that virtually all consumer research ultimately is related to the identification and measurement of values. This process can take many forms, ranging from qualitative research techniques such as ethnography to quantitative techniques such as laboratory experiments and large-scale surveys. This section will describe some specific attempts by researchers to measure cultural values and apply this knowledge to marketing strategy.

A number of companies track changes in values through large-scale surveys. For instance, one Young and Rubicam study tracked the new segment of single, professional career women without any ambitions of having a family. They are among the highest consuming segments and are characterized by central values such as freedom and independence.[111] Many companies use value inventories in order to adapt their strategies. SAS, the airline, which for a long time addressed 'hard values' of their key segment, business travellers, realized that this segment had started to express more informal and 'softer' values, and they changed their communication profile accordingly.[112]

Such ideas are reflected in a relatively recent theory of consumer value. According to this theory, value for a consumer is the consumer's evaluation of a consumer object in terms of which general benefit the consumer might get from consuming it.[113] As such, the value at stake in consumption is tied much more to the consumption experience than to general existential values of the person. Thus, it is suggested that the consumer experience may generate eight distinct types of consumer value:

1 *Efficiency*: referring to all products aimed at providing various kinds of convenience for the consumer.

2 *Excellence*: addressing situations where the experience of quality is the prime motivation.

3 *Status*: when the consumer pursues success and engages in impression management and conspicuous consumption.

4 *(Self-)esteem*: situations where the satisfaction of possessing is in focus, as is the case with materialism.

5 *Play*: the value of having fun in consuming.

6 *Aesthetics*: searching for beauty in one's consumption, e.g. designer products, fashion or art.

7 *Ethics*: referring to motivations behind consumption, e.g. morally or politically correct consumption choices.

8 *Spirituality*: experiencing magical transformations or sacredness in the consumption, as felt by devoted collectors.[114]

The Rokeach Value Survey

The psychologist Milton Rokeach identified a set of **terminal values**,[115] or desired end-states, that apply (to various degrees) to many different cultures. The *Rokeach Value Survey*, a scale used to measure these values, also includes a set of **instrumental values**,[116] which are composed of actions needed to achieve these terminal values (Table 6.2).[117] These sets of values have been used in many studies, for example to investigate the changes in the value system of post-Soviet Russia.[118]

Some evidence indicates that differences on these global values do translate into product-specific preferences and differences in media usage. Nonetheless, marketing researchers have not widely used the Rokeach Value Survey.[119] One reason is that our society is evolving into smaller and smaller sets of *consumption micro-cultures* within a larger culture, each with its own set of core values.

Table 6.2 Terminal and instrumental values

Instrumental values	Terminal values
Ambitious	A comfortable life
Broadminded	An exciting life
Capable	A sense of accomplishment
Cheerful	A world of peace
Clean	A world of beauty
Courageous	Equality
Forgiving	Family security
Helpful	Freedom
Honest	Happiness
Imaginative	Inner harmony
Independent	Mature love
Intellectual	National security
Logical	Pleasure
Loving	Salvation
Obedient	Self-respect
Polite	Social recognition
Responsible	True friendship
Self-controlled	Wisdom

Source: Richard W. Pollay, 'Measuring the Cultural Values Manifest in Advertising', *Current Issues and Research in Advertising* (1983): 71–92. Reprinted by permission, CtC Press. All rights reserved.

The List of Values (LOV)

The **List of Values** identifies nine consumer values which can be related to differences in consumption behaviours, and thus has more direct marketing applications. It includes the following values: sense of belonging, fun and enjoyment in life, excitement, warm relationships with others, self-fulfilment, being well respected, a sense of accomplishment, self-respect and security. The nine consumer segments identified by LOV include consumers who place priorities on such values as a sense of belonging, excitement, warm relationships with others, and security. For example, people who endorse the sense-of-belonging value are older, are more likely to read *Reader's Digest* and *TV Guide*, drink and entertain more, and prefer group activities more than people who do not endorse this value as highly. In contrast, those who endorse the value of excitement are younger and prefer *Rolling Stone* magazine.[120] A comparative study of French and German consumers which used this instrument found that the values of sense of belonging and self-respect were much more popular in Germany, whereas the values of fun and enjoyment in life, self-fulfilment and self-accomplishment were chosen as the most important values in France significantly more often.[121]

However, it should be noted that the cross-cultural validity of such value instruments is, at best, difficult to obtain since, as we have already said, the meaning of values may differ significantly in different cultural contexts.[122] For example, the LOV did not do very well in a test of its cross-cultural validity.[123]

Schwartz value survey

This very elaborate set of values, containing 56 different values organized in ten so-called motivational domains, has been demonstrated to be among the more cross-culturally valid set of instruments.[124] The structuring of values in interrelated motivational domains provides a theoretical framework for this approach to values which many researchers find more satisfactory compared to other value inventories. More specifically, it has been demonstrated to distinguish between cultures[125] and types of media consumption behaviour[126] better than the traditional dichotomy of **individualism** and collectivism. The values are located in a space demarcated by the poles 'openness to change' *vs* 'conservation' and 'self-transcendence' *vs* 'self-enhancement'. These dimensions seem relatively universal for a lot of syndicated lifestyle and value surveys. A mapping of the motivational domains can be seen in Figure 6.4. The

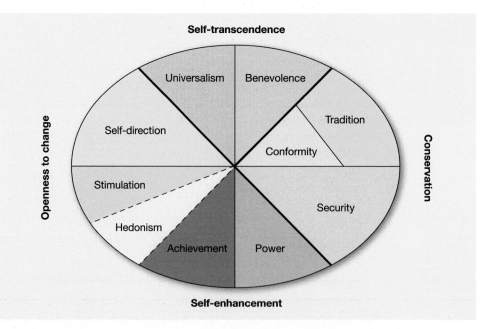

Figure 6.4 The motivational domains of the Schwartz value survey

Schwartz value survey was used to profile Danish consumers with environmentally friendly attitudes and behaviour, where it turned out that such values as 'protecting the environment' and 'unity with nature' but also 'mature love', 'broadminded' and 'social justice' characterized the 'green' segment, whereas values such as 'authority', 'social power', 'national security' and 'politeness' were the values most characteristic of the non-green segment.[127]

THE MEANS-END CHAIN MODEL

Another research approach that incorporates values is termed a **means-end chain model**. This approach assumes that people link very specific product attributes (indirectly) to terminal values: we choose among alternative means to attain some end state that we value (such as freedom or safety). Thus, we value products to the extent that they provide the means to some end we desire. Through a technique called **laddering**, researchers can uncover consumers' associations between specific attributes and these general consequences. Using this approach, consumers are helped to climb up the 'ladder' of abstraction that connects functional product attributes with desired end-states.[128] Based upon consumer feedback, researchers create *hierarchical value maps* that show how specific product attributes get linked to end-states (see Figure 6.5).

To understand how laddering works, consider somebody who expresses a liking for a light beer. Probing might reveal that this attribute is linked to the consequence of not getting drunk. A consequence of not getting drunk is that they will be able to enjoy more interesting conversations, which in turn means that they will be more sociable. Finally, better sociability results in better friendship, a terminal value for this person.[129]

Laddering is not without problems, however, since the laddering technique might generate invalid answers if the respondent is pushed up the ladder by too strong an emphasis on the sequence in the means–end chain. Consumers should be allowed to jump back and forth, to make loops and forks and take blind alleys, which requires more skill on the part of the interviewer but is also a more accurate representation of the respondent's thought processes.[130] Furthermore, it has been argued that in researching the demand for status goods, using laddering techniques can be problematic since motivations for conspicuous consumption are difficult for consumers to express or reveal.[131]

MECCAs

The notion that products are consumed because they are instrumental in attaining more abstract values is central to one application of this technique, called the Means–End Conceptualization of the Components of Advertising Strategy (**MECCAs**). In this approach, researchers first generate a map depicting relationships between functional product or service attributes and terminal values. This information is then used to develop advertising strategy by identifying elements such as the following:[132]

- *Message elements*: the specific attributes or product features to be depicted.
- *Consumer benefit*: the positive consequences of using the product or service.
- *Executional framework*: the overall style and tone of the advertisement.
- *Leverage point*: the way the message will activate the terminal value by linking it with specific product features.
- *Driving force*: the end value on which the advertising will focus.

Figure 6.5 shows three different hierarchical value maps, or sets of ladders, from a study of consumers' perceptions and motivations with regard to cooking oils. The three ladders demonstrate some important differences between the three markets. Health is the central

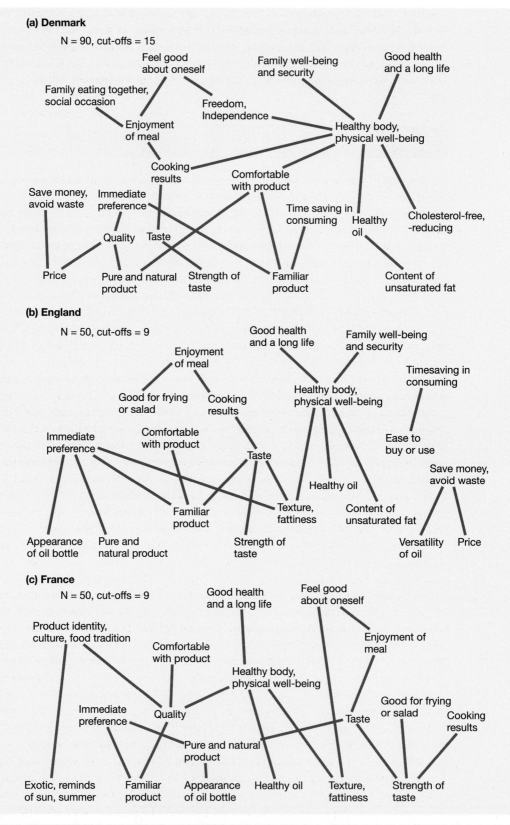

Figure 6.5 Hierarchical value maps for vegetable oil in three countries

Source: N.A. Nielsen, T. Bech-Larsen and K.G. Grunert, 'Consumer purchase motives and product perceptions: a laddering study on vegetable oil in three countries', *Food Quality and Preference* 9(6) (1998): 455–66.

concept most often referred to for the Danes and is linked to several personal values. The British also focus on health but the links to personal values are fewer and less differentiated, indicating a lower product involvement. Saving money and avoiding waste is more important to the British than to the other samples. The French focus a lot on previous knowledge of the product, indicating more routine with buying oils. Theirs is also the only culture that links oil (especially olive oil) with cultural identity and fundamental food culture.[133] These ladders illustrate the central importance of cultural and contextual differences for consumers' motivation structures.

Syndicated surveys

A number of companies who track changes in values through large-scale surveys sell the results of these studies to marketers, who often also pay a fee to receive regular updates on changes and trends. This approach originated in the mid-1960s. It is often useful to go beyond simple demographics like a person's age to understand the values and preferences a group of people might have in common. We discuss these surveys (e.g. RISC and CCA) in more detail later in this chapter.

MATERIALISM: ANOTHER PERSPECTIVE ON THE 'WHY' OF CONSUMPTION?

Materialism may be considered a more general value underlying other consumer values, thus reassuring us that an obvious way of realizing one's values is through consumption. Materialism refers to the importance people attach to worldly possessions. Westerners in general (and Americans in particular) are often stereotyped as being members of a highly materialistic society where people often gauge their worth and that of others in terms of how much they own.

Materialists are more likely to value possessions for their status and appearance-related meanings, whereas those who do not emphasize this value tend to prize products that connect them to other people or that provide them with pleasure in using them.[134] As a result, products valued by high materialists are more likely to be publicly consumed and to be more expensive.[135] The priorities of materialism tend to emphasize the well-being of the individual versus the group, which may conflict with family or religious values. That conflict may help to explain why people with highly material values tend to be less happy.[136] A recent study has identified the important role that self-esteem plays in potentially explaining the variation in levels of materialism among children and adolescents. Results indicated that materialism increased from middle childhood to early adolescence (between 8 and 13 years old) and decreased from early adolescence onwards (between 13 and 18). Increasing levels of materialism amongst 8- to 13-year-olds was linked to declining levels of self-esteem in this age group. The researchers argue that 'a drop in self-esteem experienced by many children as they enter adolescence triggers a focus on material goods, primarily as a means of self-enhancement. As self-esteem rebounds in late adolescence, the need for self-enhancement of any sort, including the use of material goods, declines along with a decrease in materialistic orientation.'[137] A study that compared specific items that low versus high materialists value found that people low on the materialism value cherished items such as a mother's wedding gown, picture albums, a rocking chair from childhood or a garden, whereas those who scored high preferred things such as jewelry, china or a vacation home.[138] Materialistic people appear to link more of their self-identity to products (see also Chapter 5). One study found that when people who score high on this value fear the prospect of dying, they form even stronger connections to brands.[139] Another study reported that consumers who are 'love-smitten' with their possessions tend to use these relationships to compensate for loneliness and a lack of affiliation with social networks.[140]

In Europe, we often take the existence of an abundance of products and services for granted, until we remember how recent many of these developments are; and how subject these developments are to economic conditions, e.g. the market downturn towards the end of 2008. The widespread ownership of cars, freezers, telephones and televisions is all a post-1950s phenomenon. Nowadays many young people could not imagine a life without mobile phones, iPods and other creature comforts. In fact, one way to think about marketing is as a system that provides a certain standard of living to consumers. To some extent, then, our lifestyles are influenced by the standard of living we have come to expect and desire. However, there is evidence that how much money we have does not relate directly to happiness: 'as long as people are not battling poverty, they tend to rate their happiness in the range of 6 or 7, or higher, on a 10-point scale'.[141] The World Values survey rated Denmark as the happiest country in the world, followed by other European countries: Iceland (4), Northern Ireland (5), Ireland (6) Switzerland (7), the Netherlands (8) and Austria (10).[142]

Of course, not everyone stresses the value of materialism to the same degree. Individual differences have been found among consumers in terms of this emphasis. One approach partitions the value of materialism into three categories: success, centrality and happiness.[143] Cross-cultural differences in materialism have also been analysed. One study of 12 countries resulted in the following ranking in degree of materialism from highest to lowest: Romania, US, New Zealand, Ukraine, Germany, Turkey, Israel, Thailand, India, UK, France and Sweden.[144] From these results, several conclusions can be drawn. First of all, materialism is not directly linked to affluence, as has often been proposed. On the contrary, some of the most materialistic cultures are the ones where most consumers (feel that they) lack a lot of things. But this obviously is not the only explanation, since the US, New Zealand and Germany score relatively high as well, and India scores low. Since neither wealth, 'Western-ness', nor any other single variable can explain these differences, it must be concluded that materialism is a consequence of several factors, including such things as social stability, access to information, reference models, as well as historical developments and cultural values.

This study was followed up by another based on qualitative depth interviews, adding more insight into consumers' different ways of coping with their own materialism, which was generally perceived as something negative. Basically, two ways of dealing with materialism were found, justifying versus excusing oneself: either you condemn materialism and provide an explanation why your personal materialism is a particularly good one, or you admit to being a 'bad' materialist but provide an excuse for being so.[145]

Large numbers of consumers are trying to reduce their reliance on possessions by **downshifting**. This means learning to get by with less, avoiding the use of credit cards, and in extreme cases living totally 'off the grid' without using commercial services. Other evidence of the disenchantment among some people with a culture dominated by materialist values and big corporations shows up in events that promote uniqueness and anti-corporate statements. Probably the most prominent movement in the US is the annual Burning Man project. This is a week-long annual anti-market event, where thousands of people gather at Black Rock Desert in Nevada to express themselves and proclaim their emancipation from Corporate America. The highlight of the festival involves the burning of a huge figure of a man made out of wood that symbolizes the freedom from market domination. Ironically, some critics point out that even this high-profile anti-market event is being commercialized as it becomes more popular each year.[146]

Research on the relationship between consumption and happiness tends to show that people are happier when they spend money on experiences instead of material objects, when they relish what they plan to buy long before they buy it, and when they stop trying to outdo their neighbours. One study reported that the only consumption category that was positively related to happiness involved leisure: vacations, entertainment, sports and equipment like golf clubs and fishing poles. This finding is consistent with changes in buying patterns, which show that consumers have tended to choose experiences over objects during the last couple of years.

Participants at the anti-corporate Burning Man Festival find novel ways to express their individuality.
Courtesy of Professor Robert Kozinets.

Another factor is just how much of a 'buzz' we get from the stuff we buy. The research evidence points to the idea that consumers get more 'bang for their buck' when they buy a bunch of smaller things over time, rather than blowing it all on one big purchase. This is due to what psychologists call **hedonic adaptation**; it basically means that to maintain a fairly stable level of happiness, we tend to become used to changes, big or small, wonderful or terrible. That means that over time the rush from a major purchase will dissipate and we're back to where we started (emotionally speaking). So, the next time you get a bonus or find an envelope stuffed with cash on the street, take a series of long weekends instead of splurging on that three-week trip to Maui.[147]

A value that's related to materialism is **cosmopolitanism**. Researchers define a *cosmopolitan* as someone who tries to be open to the world and who strives for diverse experiences. This is a quality that used to be linked to the wealthy, but now with improved access to media and of course the internet, it's no longer necessary to be rich to express an interest in a range of culturally diverse products. Cosmopolitans respond well to brands that have a 'worldly' (i.e. international or global) image. They think it's important to own consumer electronics products and are more likely to engage in electronic media activities such as email, web surfing and buying DVDs.[148]

SUSTAINABILITY: A NEW CORE VALUE?

Are European consumers finally going green – for real?[149] In a US 2007 survey, fully 8 in 10 US consumers said they believe it is important to buy green brands and products from green companies, and that they will pay more to do so. The US consumer's focus on personal health is merging with a growing interest in global health. Some analysts call this new value **conscientious consumerism**.[150] A recent study has suggested that 'the translation of concern over sustainability to sustainable consumption practices is based on the promotion of self-efficacy, through the reduction of ambivalent feelings by enforcing knowledge-based trust between institutions and individuals'.[151]

Who is driving this change? In the US marketers point to a segment of consumers who practice **LOHAS** – an acronym for 'lifestyles of health and sustainability'. This label refers to people who worry about the environment, want products to be produced in a sustainable way, and who spend money to advance what they see as their personal development and potential. These so-called 'Lohasians' (others refer to this segment as *Cultural Creatives*) repre-sent a great market for products such as organic foods, energy-efficient appliances and hybrid cars as well as alternative medicine, yoga tapes and eco-tourism. One organization that tracks this group estimates they make up about 16 per cent of the adults in the US, or 35 million people; it values the market for socially conscious products at over $200 billion.[152]

Marketers and retailers are responding with thousands of new eco-friendly products and programmes. L'Oréal acquired The Body Shop. Kellogg introduced organic versions of some of its best-selling cereals like Rice Krispies. We are seeing a significant increase in products with better-for-you positioning, but new products that take an ethical stance are also driving this trend, whether the claim links to fair trade, sustainability or ecological friendliness. Whereas in the past it was sufficient for companies to offer recyclable products, this new movement is creating a whole new vocabulary as consumers begin to 'vote with their forks' by demanding food, fragrances and other items that are made with no *GMOs* (genetically modified ingredients); hormone-free; no animal clones; no animal testing; locally grown; and cage-free, to name a few.[153]

Not content to wait for companies to change their practices, ordinary consumers are taking action. Many are joining numerous organizations like Slow Food to agitate for lifestyle changes. One such movement called 'Local First' stresses the value of buying locally made products. This group (some members call themselves 'locavores') values small community businesses, but it is also reacting to the waste it sees occurring as people import things they need from long distances.[154]

Still other consumers are rebelling against the huge market for bottled water. They object to the fact that some brands come from as far away as Fiji. These imports create pollution because of the tanker ships that have to cart them halfway around the world and the waste from millions of discarded plastic bottles.[155] The environmental effect of an object seemingly as innocent as a plastic water bottle points to the concern that many now have about the size of their **carbon footprint**.[156] This measures in units of carbon dioxide the impact that human activities have on the environment in terms of the amount of greenhouse gases they produce.[157]

Another emerging environmental issue for the developed world is the **virtual water footprint** which represents how much water is required to produce a product: 'when virtual water is taken into account, consumers in developed nations are leaving a large water foot-print not just in their own countries but across the globe too'.[158] In the case of the UK, for instance, under 40 per cent of the country's total footprint is met from its own resources; more than 60 per cent is met by the rest of the world. 'A can of fizzy drink might contain 0.35 litres of water, for instance, yet it also requires about 200 litres to grow and process the sugar that goes into it.'[159] This means that the average Briton consumes about 4,645 litres of water a day once these hidden factors are included. World Water Forum experts are 'increasingly talking of fresh water as "the new oil"'.[160]

Greenwashing

Consumers sometimes just don't believe the green claims that companies make about their brands. According to one report, more than 95 per cent of consumer products marketed as 'green', including all toys surveyed, make misleading or inaccurate claims. Another survey found that the number of products claiming to be green has increased by 73 per cent since 2009 – but of the products investigated, almost a third had fake labels, and 70 made green claims without offering any proof to back them up.[161]

All of this hype results in so-called **greenwashing**,[162] and causes consumers not to believe the claims marketers make and in some cases consumers actually avoid brands that promise they are green. One survey reported that 71 per cent of respondents say they will stop buying a product if they feel they've been misled about its environmental impact, and 37 per cent are so angry about greenwashing that they believe this justifies a complete boycott of everything the company makes.[163]

LIFESTYLES AND CONSUMPTION CHOICES

Consumers choose products, services and activities that help them define a unique *lifestyle*. This section first explores how marketers approach the issue of lifestyle and how they use information about these consumption choices to tailor products and communications to individual lifestyle segments, and secondly how marketers use **psychographics** to obtain a more nuanced picture of consumer behaviour.

Lifestyle: who we are, what we do

In traditional societies, class, caste, village or family largely dictate a person's consumption options. In a modern consumer society, however, people are freer to select the products, services and activities that define themselves and, in turn, create a social identity they communicate to others. One's choice of goods and services makes a statement about who one is and about the types of people with whom one wishes to identify – and even some whom we wish to avoid. **Lifestyle** refers to a pattern of consumption that reflects a person's choices about how they spend time and money, but in many cases it also refers to the attitudes and values attached to these behavioural patterns. Many of the factors discussed in this book, such as a person's self-concept, reference group and social class, are used as 'raw ingredients' to fashion a unique lifestyle. In an economic sense, your lifestyle represents the way you elect to allocate income, both in terms of relative allocations to different products and services, and to specific alternatives within these categories.[164] Other somewhat similar distinctions describe consumers in terms of their broad patterns of consumption, such as those differentiating people by those who devote a high proportion of their total expenditure to food, or advanced technology, or to such information-intensive goods as entertainment and education. Often, these allocations create a new kind of status system based less on income than on accessibility to information about goods and how these goods function as social markers.[165]

Lifestyles may be considered as group identities. Marketers use demographic and economic approaches in tracking changes in broad societal priorities, but these approaches do not begin to embrace the symbolic nuances that separate lifestyle groups. Lifestyle is more than the allocation of discretionary income. It is a statement about who one is in society and who one is not. Group identities, whether of hobbyists, athletes, footballers (e.g. Bobby's friends in Chapter 10) or drug users, take their form based on acts of expressive symbolism. The self-definitions of group members are derived from the common symbol system to which the group is dedicated. Such self-definitions have been described by a number of terms, including *lifestyle, public taste, consumer group, symbolic community* and *status culture*.[166]

Many people in similar social and economic circumstances may follow the same general consumption pattern. Still, each person provides a unique 'twist' to this pattern which allows them to inject some individuality into a chosen lifestyle. For example, a 'typical' student (if

This ad states 'YOUR bedroom' in the headline. However, the ad illustrates how a product offering can be highly complementary to the lifestyle of the decision-maker, in this case the wife and mother in the family who seems to have decorated the room in terms of her own tastes rather than necessarily those of the intended occupant (who presumably would like the clean, simple and unfussy lines of Scandinavian taste in decor as offered by IKEA).
S.C.P.F., Patricia Luján, Carlitos. Photo: Biel Capllonch

there is such a thing) may dress much like their friends, go to the same places and like the same foods, yet still indulge a passion for running marathons, stamp collecting or community service, activities which make them unique.

Lifestyles don't last forever, and are not set in stone. Unlike deep-seated values people's tastes and preferences evolve over time, so that consumption patterns that were viewed favourably at one point in time may be laughed at or sneered at a few years later. If you don't believe that, simply think back to what you, your friends and your family were wearing, doing and eating five or ten years ago: where *did* you find those clothes? Because people's attitudes regarding physical fitness, social activism, sex roles for men and women, the importance of home life and family, and many other things, do change, it is vital for marketers to monitor the social landscape continually to try to anticipate where these changes will lead.

PSYCHOGRAPHICS

Marketers often find it useful to develop products that appeal to different lifestyle groups – simply knowing a person's income does not necessarily predict which type of car he or she might drive. Consumers can share the same demographic characteristics and still be very different people. For this reason, marketers need a way to 'breathe life' into demographic data to identify, understand and target consumer segments that will share a set of preferences for their products and services. In Chapter 5 we discussed some of the important differences in consumers' self-concepts and personalities that play a big role in determining product choices. When marketers combine personality variables with knowledge of lifestyle preferences, they have a powerful lens that they can focus on consumer segments. This tool is known as **psychographics**, which involves the 'use of psychological, sociological and anthropological factors . . . to determine how the market is segmented by the propensity of groups within the market – and their reasons – to make a particular decision about a product, person, ideology, or otherwise hold an attitude or use a medium.'[167]

Psychographic research was first developed in the 1960s and 1970s to address the short-comings of two other types of consumer research: motivational research and quantitative survey research. *Motivational research*, which involves intensive personal interviews and projective tests, yields a lot of information about individual consumers. The information gathered, however, was often idiosyncratic and deemed to be not very useful or reliable.[168] At the other extreme, *quantitative survey research*, or large-scale demographic surveys, yields only a little information about a lot of people. As some researchers observed, 'The marketing manager who wanted to know why people ate the competitor's cornflakes was told "32 per cent of the respondents said *taste*, 21 per cent said *flavour*, 15 per cent said *texture*, 10 per cent said *price*, and 22 per cent said *don't know* or *no answer*".'[169]

In many applications, the term 'psychographics' is used interchangeably with 'lifestyle' to denote the separation of consumers into categories based on differences in choices of consumption activities and product usage. While there are many psychographic variables that can be used to segment consumers, they all share the underlying principle of going beyond surface charac-teristics to understand consumers' motivations for purchasing and using products. Demo-graphics allow us to describe *who* buys, but psychographics helps us understand *why* they buy.

How do we perform a psychographic analysis?

Some early attempts at lifestyle segmentation 'borrowed' standard psychological scales (often used to measure pathology or personality disturbances) and tried to relate scores on these tests to product usage. As might be expected, such efforts were largely disappointing. These tests were never intended to be related to everyday consumption activities and yielded little in the way of explanation for purchase behaviours. The technique is more effective when the variables included are more closely related to actual consumer behaviours. If you want to understand purchases of household cleaning products, you are better off asking people about their attitudes towards household cleanliness than testing for personality disorders.

Psychographic studies can take several different forms:

- A *lifestyle profile* looks for items that differentiate between users and non-users of a product.

- A *product-specific profile* identifies a target group and then profiles these consumers on product-relevant dimensions.

- A *general lifestyle segmentation* places a large sample of respondents into homogeneous groups based on similarities of their overall preferences.

- A *product-specific segmentation* tailors questions to a product category. For example, if a researcher wants to conduct research for a stomach medicine, they might rephrase the item, 'I worry too much' as, 'I get stomach problems if I worry too much'. This allows them to more finely discriminate among users of competing brands.[170]

Most contemporary psychographic research attempts to group consumers according to some combination of three categories of variables – **a**ctivities, **i**nterests and **o**pinions – which are known as **AIOs**. Using data from large samples, marketers create profiles of customers who resemble each other in terms of their activities and patterns of product usage.[171] The dimensions used to assess lifestyle are **Activities** (Work, Hobbies, Social events, Holiday, Entertainment, Club membership, Community, Shopping, Sports), **Interests** (Family, Home, Job, Community, Recreation, Fashion, Food, Media, Achievements), **Opinions** (Themselves, Social issues, Politics, Business, Economics, Education, Products, Future, Culture), **Demographics** (Age, Education, Income, Occupation, Family size, Dwelling, Geography, City size, Stage in life cycle). (These lifestyle dimensions are based on William D. Wells and Douglas J. Tigert, 'Activities, interests and opinions', *Journal of Advertising Research* 11 (August 1971): 27–35.)

To group consumers into common AIO categories, researchers give respondents a long list of statements, and respondents are asked to indicate how much they agree with each one. Lifestyle is thus teased out by discovering how people spend their time, what they find interesting and important, and how they view themselves and the world around them, as well as demographic information.

Typically, the first step in conducting a psychographic analysis is to determine which lifestyle segments are producing the bulk of customers for a particular product. According to a very general rule of thumb that marketers call the **80/20 rule** – only 20 per cent of a product's users account for 80 per cent of the volume of product a company sells. Researchers attempt to determine who uses the brand and try to isolate heavy, moderate and light users. They also look for patterns of usage and attitudes towards the product. In some cases, just a few lifestyle segments account for the majority of brand users.[172] Marketers primarily target these heavy users, even though they may constitute a relatively small number of total users.

After marketers identify and understand their heavy users, they consider more specifically how these customers relate to the brand. Heavy users may have quite different reasons for using the product; they can be further subdivided in terms of the *benefits* they derive from using the product or service. For instance, marketers at the beginning of the walking shoe craze assumed that purchasers were basically burned-out joggers. Subsequent psychographic research showed that there were actually several different groups of 'walkers', ranging from those who walk to get to work to those who walk for fun. This realization resulted in shoes aimed at different segments.

How do we use psychographic data?

Marketers use the data from psychographic surveys in a variety of ways.

- *To define the target market.* This information allows the marketer to go beyond simple demographic or product usage descriptions (such as middle-aged men or frequent users).

- *To create a new view of the market.* Sometimes marketers create their strategies with a 'typical' customer in mind. This stereotype may not be correct because the actual customer may not match these assumptions. For example, marketers of a facial cream for women were surprised to find their key market was composed of older, widowed women who turned out to be their heavy users, rather than the younger, more sociable women to whom they were pitching their appeals.

- *To position the product.* Psychographic information can allow the marketer to emphasize features of the product that fit in with a person's lifestyle. A company that wants to target people whose lifestyle profiles show a high need to be around other people might focus on its product's ability to help meet this social need.

- *To better communicate product attributes.* Psychographic information can offer very useful input to advertising creatives who must communicate something about the product. The artist or writer obtains a much richer mental image of the target consumer than they can obtain through simply looking at dry statistics, and this insight improves their ability to 'talk' to that consumer.

- *To develop product strategy.* Understanding how a product fits, or does not fit, into consumers' lifestyles allows the marketer to identify new product opportunities, chart media strategies and create environments most consistent and harmonious with these consumption patterns. For example, inexpensive airline tickets have become very popular in Germany, with intra-country fares often lower than the price of a train ticket. The increase in flights has sparked concern of environmental worries among 'the greens', even though the greens are one of the market segments most likely to book the low fare airline tickets. Research has shown that conflicting values (in this case, low fares vs. air pollution and the carbon footprint) can be addressed in promotions by better understanding the motives that cause the tensions.[173]

● *To market social and political issues.* Psychographic segmentation can be an important tool in political campaigns and policymakers can also employ the technique to find similarities among types of consumers who engage in destructive behaviours, such as drug use, excessive gambling or binge drinking. A psychographic study of men aged 18 to 24 who drink and drive highlighted the potential for this perspective to help in the eradication of harmful behaviours. Researchers divided this segment into four groups: 'good timers', 'well adjusted', 'nerds' and 'problem kids'. They found that one group in particular – 'good timers' – is more likely to believe that it is fun to be drunk, that the chances of having an accident while driving drunk are low, and that drinking increases one's appeal to the opposite sex. Because the study showed that this group is also the most likely to drink at rock concerts and parties, is most likely to watch MTV and tends to listen to album-oriented rock radio stations, reaching 'good timers' with a prevention campaign was made easier because messages targeted to this segment could be placed where these drinkers were most likely to see and hear them.[174]

LIFESTYLE MARKETING

The lifestyle concept is one of the most widely used in modern marketing activities. It provides a way to understand consumers' everyday needs and wants, and a mechanism to allow a product or service to be positioned in terms of how it will allow a person to pursue a desired lifestyle. A **lifestyle marketing perspective** recognizes that people sort themselves into groups on the basis of the things they like to do, how they like to spend their leisure time and how they choose to spend their disposable income.[175] These choices in turn create opportunities for market segmentation strategies that recognize the potency of a consumer's chosen lifestyle in determining both the types of products purchased and the specific brands more likely to appeal to a designated lifestyle segment.

Psychographic segmentation typologies

Marketers are constantly on the lookout for new insights that will allow them to identify and reach groups of consumers that are united by a common lifestyle. To meet this need, many research companies and advertising agencies have developed their own *segmentation typologies* which divide people into segments. Respondents answer a battery of questions that allow the researchers to cluster them into a set of distinct lifestyle groups. The questions usually include a mixture of AIOs, plus other items relating to their perceptions of specific brands, favourite celebrities, media preferences and so on. These systems are usually sold to companies wanting to learn more about their customers and potential customers.

At least at a superficial level, many of these typologies are fairly similar to one another, in that a typical typology breaks up the population into roughly five to ten segments. Each cluster is given a descriptive name, and a profile of the 'typical' member is provided to the client. Categories in this system include such segments as 'avant-gardians' (interested in change), 'pontificators' (traditionalists, very British), 'chameleons' (follow the crowd) and 'sleepwalkers' (contented underachievers). Unfortunately, it is often difficult to compare or evaluate different typologies, since the methods and data used to devise these systems are frequently *proprietary* – this means that the information is developed and owned by the company, and the company feels that it would not be desirable to release this information to outsiders.

Such psychographic segmentation typologies and their associated lifestyle analyses have been widely used in Europe and the USA.[176] Below we discuss two European examples (RISC and CCA) of such international lifestyle segmentation efforts.

RISC

Since 1978, the Paris-based Research Institute on Social Change (RISC) has conducted international measurements of lifestyles and socio-cultural change in more than 40 countries, including most European countries.[177] RISC asks a battery of questions to identify people's values and attitudes about a wide range of issues. It combines the answers to measure 40 'trends' such as 'spirituality' or 'blurring of the sexes'. Based on statistical analysis of the respondents' scores on each trend, each individual is located in a virtual space described by three axes, representing the three most discriminating dimensions in the data material. RISC then divides the population into ten segments referring to their position in this virtual space. The three axes are:

1 *Exploration/stability*: the vertical axis separates people motivated by change, creativity, volatility and openness from people motivated by stability, familiarity, tradition and structure.

2 *Social/individual*: the horizontal axis distinguishes people oriented towards collective needs from people oriented more towards satisfaction of individual needs.

3 *Global/local*: the third axis indicates a distance between people who are comfortable with broad and unfamiliar environments, multiple loose connections and large-scale networking from people preferring close-knit relationships and a desire for the elements of life to be connected in a predictable manner. Figure 6.6 illustrates the ten segments (G for global, L for Local (behind)) and their main life aspirations.

The use of RISC typically involves identifying users of a brand and understanding those users better; it is also used to monitor changes in the profiles of users over time. Furthermore, potential target groups, the product benefits and the kind of communication that would attract and reach them can be indicated by systems such as RISC. In the example in Figure 6.7 we see the lifestyle profiling of German car brand B (approximately 21 per cent of the population)

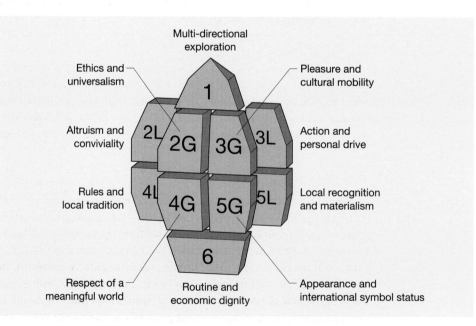

Figure 6.6 The ten RISC segments

Source: RISC Methodology (Paris: RISC International, 1997): 14.

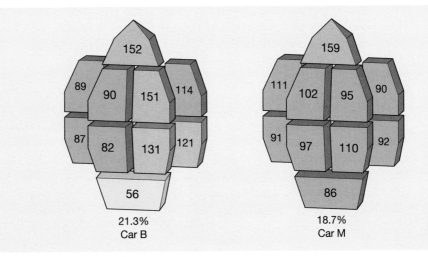

Figure 6.7 Choice of brand for the next new car, Germany, brand B/brand M 1995

Source: RISC Methodology (Paris: RISC International, 1997): 14.

and car brand M (approximately 19 per cent) as their first, second or third choice if they were going to buy a new car. Car brand B has a strong profile, individual and experimental, with both global and local orientations. Car brand M, in contrast, has a more uniform profile, with evidence of popularity across all segments of the population. However, there is a very strong presence in cell 1, the group that is most interested in new designs, technologies and functions.

CCA socio-styles

A Paris-based agency, the CCA (Centre de Communication Avancé), introduced a European lifestyle typology in the early 1990s. Although the mapping principle of this lifestyle typology is similar to that of most other typologies, they use a somewhat different methodological approach since their questionnaires are not attitude-based, but use a variety of question formats and also projective techniques, such as various scenario descriptions of future social forms or consumption types that the respondent must relate to, or suggestive drawings and vignettes.[178] The CCA study divided the European population into 16 lifestyles, regrouped into six so-called 'mentalities'. The resulting lifestyle map, presented in the usual suggestive vignette format, is seen in Figure 6.8. One of the advantages of this system was that the 16 individual lifestyles could be gathered into other larger groups rather than just the mentalities to form marketing segments specifically adapted to a specific product sector. So some lifestyles would be grouped to form food segments, others to form car segments.[179]

The value of lifestyle typologies

Generally, lifestyle analyses of consumers are exciting because they seek to provide a sort of complete sociological view of the market and its segments and trends, but their general character is their biggest weakness, since the underlying assumption – that these general segments have relatively homogeneous patterns of consumer behaviour – is far from proven.[180] One needs only to consider the index numbers in Figure 6.7 to realize that the predictive power of this typology is not extraordinary. Add to this the generally weak theoretical foundation and the problems of reliability and validity linked to the large-scale questionnaires and to the operationalization of complex social processes in simple variables, and it is understandable why some marketers see lifestyles more as a way of 'thinking the market' and as an input to creative strategies than as descriptions of segments defined by their consumer behaviour.[181]

229

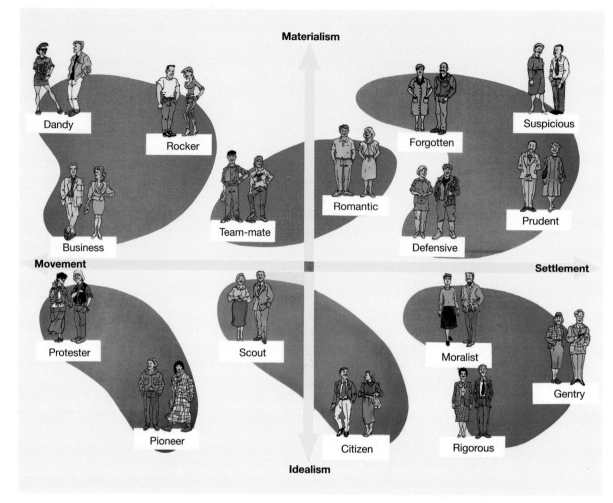

Figure 6.8 CCA Eurostyles: 16 lifestyles in 6 mentalities

Source: CCA, Paris, 1990.

One attempt to overcome the problem of generally defined segments was the introduction of sectorial lifestyles, proposed by the CCA in the 1980s. The principle behind sectorial lifestyles is that only variables (attitudes, behaviour, etc.) that are considered relevant to a specific domain of consumption are included in the survey. The lifestyles defined on the basis of such an approach thus pertain to this specific sector of consumption only. Recent work on internet users has suggested that online emotions might provide a way to 'construct typologies of internet users [as] . . . "nervous", "invisible", "confident but reserved", and "confident and carefree". These clusters [were found to] discriminate on the basis of age, working status and perceptions towards online brands'.[182]

Behavioural targeting

The latest and hottest extension of lifestyle marketing is **behavioural targeting**, which refers to presenting people with advertisements based on their internet use. In other words, with today's technology it has become fairly easy for marketers to tailor the ads you see to websites you have visited. Some critics feel this is a mixed blessing because it implies that big companies are tracking where we go and keeping this information.

Indeed, there are important privacy issues still to be resolved, but interestingly many consumers seem more than happy to trade off some of their personal information in exchange for information they consider more useful to them. A 2006 survey on this issue reported that 57 per cent of the consumers it polled say they are willing to provide demographic information in exchange for a personalized online experience. And three-quarters of those involved in an online social network felt that this process would improve their experience because it would serve to introduce them to others who share their tastes and interests. However, a majority still express concern about the security of their personal data online.[183] Pro or con, it is clear that behavioural targeting is starting to take off in a big way.

Microsoft combines personal data from the 263 million users of its free Hotmail e-mail service – the biggest in the world – with information it gains from monitoring their searches. When you sign up for Hotmail, the service asks you for personal information including your age, occupation and address (though you are not required to answer). If you use Microsoft's search engine it calls Live Search, the company keeps a record of the words you search for and the results you clicked on. Microsoft's behavioural targeting system will allow its advertising clients to send different ads to each person surfing the web. For instance, if a 25-year-old financial analyst living in a big city is comparing prices of cars online, BMW could send them an ad for a Mini Cooper. But it could send a 45-year-old suburban businessperson with children who is doing the same search an ad for the X5 SUV.[184]

Claria released its PersonalWeb service that allows people to download a piece of tracking software and receive a home page filled with news stories and other information tailored to their interests. If a man, for example, downloaded the software for and surfed through stories about the UEFA cup and car reviews, his PersonalWeb home page would reflect those interests the next time he clicked on it. It might also include ads from car companies and from stores selling merchandise for his favourite football team.

MySpace uses personal details users put on their profile pages and blogs to sell highly targeted advertising in ten broad categories such as finance, autos, fashion and music. Facebook is hard at work on a similar system, and it hopes to use sophisticated software to decide how receptive a user will be to an ad based not only on their personal information but that of their friends – even if they haven't explicitly expressed interest in that topic.[185]

However, behavioural lifestyle marketing brings threats was well as opportunities for consumers, as represented by **cybercrime**, i.e. criminal behaviour online (e.g. theft of money; identity).

PRODUCT DISPOSAL

How do our changing consumer values around sustainability and environmentalism affect our consumer behaviour when disposing of products? Because we form strong attachments to some products, it can be painful to dispose of things. Our possessions anchor our identities; our past lives on in our things.[186] Some Japanese ritually 'retire' worn-out sewing needles, chopsticks, and even computer chips when they burn them in a ceremony to thank them for years of good service.[187] Still, although some of us have more problems than others in discarding things, we all have to get rid of our 'stuff' at some point, either because it has served its purpose or perhaps because it no longer fits with our view of ourselves. In many cases we acquire a new product even though the old one still functions (e.g. our cars or our mobile phones). Reasons to replace an item include a desire for new features, a change in the individual's environment (e.g. moving to a house with a smaller kitchen so we need to change the large fridge for a more compact one); or a change in the person's role or self-image.[188]

Disposal options

When a consumer decides that a product is no longer of use, several choices are available. The person can either (1) keep the item, (2) temporarily dispose of it, or (3) permanently dispose

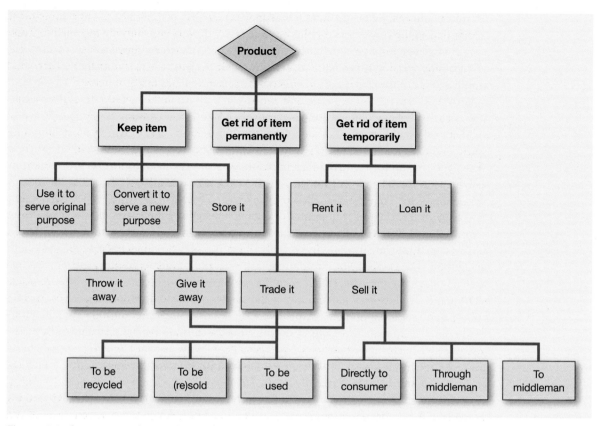

Figure 6.9 Consumers' disposal options

Source: Adapted from Jacob Jacoby, Carol K. Berning and Thomas F. Dietvorst, 'What about disposition?' *Journal of Marketing*, 41 (April 1977): 23.

of it. Figure 6.9 provides an overview of consumers' disposal options. Compared with the original scheme, we have added the opportunity of 'to be recycled' in the lower left corner. This is interesting because it bears witness to the fact that thinking about recycling as a 'natural' thing to do is a rather recent occurrence. The issue of product disposal is doubly vital because of its enormous public policy implications.

We live in a throwaway society, which creates problems for the environment and also results in a great deal of unfortunate waste. One study reported that we never use as much as 12 per cent of the grocery products we buy; consumers buy nearly two-thirds of these **abandoned products** for a specific purpose such as a particular recipe and then change their plans. Because we don't use these items immediately, they slowly get pushed to the back of the cupboard and forgotten.[189] The consumers most likely to save things are older people and those who live alone.[190] A recent study examined whether messages framed around loss were more or less effective than messages framed around gain in influencing consumer behaviour towards recycling. The researchers found that 'loss frames were more efficacious paired with lower-level, concrete mindsets, whereas gain frames were more effective paired with higher-level, abstract mindsets . . . [so that] a pairing of messages that activate more concrete (abstract) mindsets leads to enhancing processing efficiency, increased efficacy, and, as a result, more positive recycling outcomes'.[191]

However, rather than assuming that disposal represents the terminal point for goods, rather disposal might 'be regarded as a new point in the valuing of objects and, by implication, also a new point in the relationship of people to goods'.[192] Training consumers to recycle has become a priority in many countries. Japan recycles about 40 per cent of its rubbish, and this relatively high rate of compliance is partly due to the social value the Japanese place on recycling: citizens are encouraged by dustbin lorries that periodically rumble through the streets playing classical music or children's songs.[193] Companies continue to search for ways to use resources more efficiently, often at the prompting of activist consumer groups. For example, McDonald's restaurants bowed to pressure by eliminating the use of styrofoam packages, and its outlets in Europe experimented with edible breakfast plates made of maize.[194]

A study examined the relevant goals consumers have when they recycle. It used a means–end chain analysis of the type described above to identify how consumers link specific instrumental goals to more abstract terminal values. Researchers identified the most important lower-order goals to be 'avoid filling up landfills', 'reduce waste', 'reuse materials,' and 'save the environment'. They linked these to the terminal values of 'promote health/avoid sickness', 'achieve life-sustaining ends' and 'provide for future generations'.

Another study reported that the perceived effort involved in recycling was the best predictor of whether people would go to the trouble. This pragmatic dimension outweighed general attitudes towards recycling and the environment in predicting intention to recycle.[195] When researchers apply these techniques to study recycling and other product disposal behaviours, it will be easier for social marketers to design advertising copy and other messages that tap into the underlying values that will motivate people to increase environmentally responsible behaviour.[196] Of course, one way to ease the pain is to reward consumers for recycling. Gap tried this when it teamed up with Cotton Incorporated to collect old denim, which will be turned into insulation and donated to communities to help them build new houses. The sweetener in the deal: those who donated got a 30 per cent discount on new jeans purchases and a 40 per cent discount to those who buy the pants on Gap's Facebook page.[197] In the UK the major retailer M&S undertook a similar campaign in conjunction with the charity Oxfam in spring 2011, offering £5 store vouchers to customers who brought in their old M&S clothing and donated it to Oxfam.[198] Recent research examined the relationship between disposal and identity, using a study of mothers' disposal of their children's products to show how consumer behaviour 'is used to build, maintain and signal both individual and social identity' and to illustrate 'how complexities, conflicts and coping strategies are an inherent part of disposal as an identity marker.'[199]

Get a £5 M&S voucher when you donate to Oxfam.

Source: With kind permission from Marks and Spencer plc.

Xmas tree recycling.

Corbis/Image Source.

This Dutch ad says: 'And when you've had enough of it, we'll clear it away nicely.'

Courtesy of Volkswagen Group.

Lateral cycling: junk *vs* 'junque'

Interesting consumer processes occur during **lateral cycling**, where already-purchased objects are sold to others or exchanged for yet other things. Many purchases are made second-hand, rather than new. The reuse of other people's things is especially important in our throwaway society because, as one researcher put it, 'there is no longer an "away" to throw things to'.[200]

Flea markets, garage sales, classified advertisements, bartering for services, hand-me-downs, car-boot sales, charity shops and the black market all represent important alternative marketing systems that operate alongside the formal marketplace. In the United States alone, there are more than 3,500 flea markets. Economic estimates of this **underground economy** range from 3 to 30 per cent of the gross national product of the United States and up to 70 per cent of the gross domestic product of other countries. Trade publications offer reams of practical advice to consumers who want to bypass formal retailers and swap merchandise. Interest in antiques, period accessories and specialized magazines catering for this niche is increasing, e.g. Lassco (London Architectural Salvage and Supply Company) is a reclamation business. '**Reclaimers** are not, strictly speaking, antique dealers, and very definitely not junk merchants . . . they are not in the business of plundering the past, they are in the business of rescuing large lumps of history from the wrecking ball . . . reclaiming is . . . part of the current craze for 'collectables' (architectural salvage is big on eBay).'[201] Other growth areas include student markets for used computers and textbooks, as well as ski swaps, at which consumers exchange millions of dollars worth of used ski equipment. A new generation of secondhand store owners is developing markets for everything from used office equipment to cast-off kitchen sinks. Many are nonprofit ventures started with government funding. A trade association called the Reuse Development Organization (**redo.org**) encourages them.[202]

The internet has revolutionized the lateral cycling process, as millions of people flock to eBay to buy and sell their 'treasures'. This phenomenally successful online auction site started as a trading post for Beanie Babies and other collectibles. Now two-thirds of the site's sales are for practical goods. eBay expects to sell $2 billion worth of used cars and $1 billion worth of computers a year. Coming next are event tickets, food, industrial equipment and property.[203] However, eBay has recently hit a slight hiccup with the award by a French court against the company of €38.6 million in damages to 'LVMH, the luxury giant behind Louis Vuitton and Christian Dior for negligence in allowing the sale of fake bags and clothes, and of perfume that it was not licensed to sell. The ruling comes hot on the heels of a judgement by another French court that ordered eBay to pay 20,000 euros to Hermès for allowing the sale of fake bags. L'Oréal has lawsuits pending against eBay in five European countries, including the UK, and there is another filed by Tiffany in the US. As part of its case, LVMH presented evidence to the court that of the 300,000 products purporting to be Louis Vuitton or Christian Dior sold on the site in the second quarter of 2006, 90 per cent were fakes.'[204]

Again, social media platforms offer new ways to recycle. Numerous **sharing sites** like **SnapGoods**, **NeighborGoods.com** and ShareSomeSugar base their business models around allowing people to share, exchange and rent goods in a local setting. In fact, some research indicates that people who participate in these sites also benefit because they feel they are part of a community. One study found that when people post messages on Twitter (also part of a community), this releases oxytocin, a neurotransmitter that evokes feelings of contentment and is thought to help induce a sense of positive social bonding. The researcher observed that this interaction 'reduces stress hormones, even through the web. You're feeling a real physiological relationship to that person, even if they are online'.[205]

An economic slowdown is good news for auction sites like eBay, because it is the kind of business that prospers when other businesses aren't doing well. As one analyst explained, 'The interesting thing about eBay is that it may benefit because some people may choose not to buy something new, like a computer or consumer electronics.' Hobbies and crafts also are selling strongly, which may be due to the number of people staying at home rather than travelling.

Luxury items are often found for sale on eBay.
Getty Images.

Despite its success, there's sometimes a bittersweet quality to eBay. Some of the sellers are listing computers, fancy cars, jewellery and other luxury items because they desperately need the money. As one vendor explained when he described the classic convertible he wanted to sell, 'I am out of money and need to pay my rent, so my toys have to be sold'. The site witnessed a particularly strong surge in these kinds of messages following 9/11 when many people were laid off in the wake of a sluggish economy. In the words of an accountant who lost his job, 'Things were bad before, and then they got really bad after the bombings. Everything completely dried up.' Noting that he used to sell merchandise on eBay as a hobby but is now forced to sell some of his own possessions, including his BMW and his wife's jewellery, he commented, 'If it weren't for eBay, I'm not sure what I'd be doing. We definitely would not be able to pay the bills.'[206]

Lateral cycling is literally a lifestyle for some people with an anticonsumerist bent who call themselves **freegans** (this label is a takeoff on *vegans*, who shun all animal products). Freegans are modern-day scavengers who live off discards as a political statement against corporations and consumerism. They forage through supermarket waste bins and eat the slightly bruised produce or just-expired canned goods that we routinely throw out, and negotiate gifts of surplus food from sympathetic stores and restaurants. Freegans dress in castoff clothes and furnish their homes with items they find on the street. They get the word on locations where people throw out a lot of stuff (end-of-semester dorm cleanouts are a prime target) as they check out postings at **freecycle.org**, where users post unwanted items and at so-called *freemeets* (flea markets where no one exchanges money).[207] **Freecycling** is the practice of giving away useful but unwanted goods to keep them out of landfills and maybe to help someone less fortunate in the process. Free recycling – which already existed in a number of forms offline, for example, jumble sales and donations to charity shops and church institutions (such as the Salvation Army) – has

Flea markets are an important form of lateral cycling.
Alamy/Stockfolio.

emerged online with the establishment of **www.freecycle.org** by a consumer in Tucson, Arizona, keen to give away a queen-size bed and some packaged peanuts. What started as an e-mail circular to friends turned into a website for the exchange of unwanted items. 'Free, legal and appropriate for all ages': these are the only constraints on what is offered via the site. At **freecycle.org**, roughly three million people from more than 70 countries exchange unwanted items.[208] A recent study has examined how participation in Freecycling served 'to increase community cohesion and personal and social sustainability goals'.[209]

If our possessions do indeed come to be a part of us, how do we bring ourselves to part with these precious items? Some researchers recently examined the ways consumers practise **divestment rituals**, where they take steps to gradually distance themselves from things they treasure so that they can sell them or give them away (more on rituals in Chapter 13). As they observed people getting items ready to be sold at garage sales, the researchers identified these rituals:

- *Iconic transfer ritual*: taking pictures and videos of objects before selling them.
- *Transition-place ritual*: putting items in an out-of-the way location such as a garage or attic before disposing of them.
- *Ritual cleansing*: washing, ironing, and/or meticulously wrapping the item.[210]

The 'why' of consumption

As we have seen in this chapter, there are many reasons why we want to engage in consumption activities. One of the main lessons to retain is probably that the 'why?' question cannot stand alone, but must be asked with reference to a number of other questions such as 'who?' indicating personal, group and cultural differences; 'when?' and 'where?' indicating situational and contextual differences; 'how?' pointing to the reflexive and emotional processes involved; and finally 'what' kind of consumption items and consumer behaviour are we talking about? These dimensions, which are all to some extent addressed throughout this book, are illustrated in Figure 6.10.

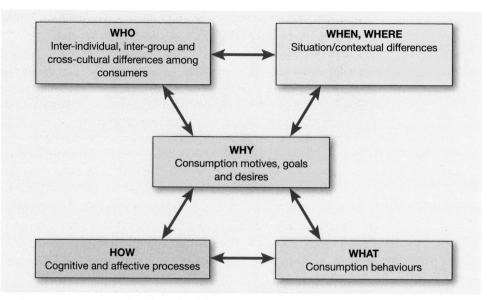

Figure 6.10 Contextualizing the 'why' of consumption

Source: Adapted from S. Ratneshaw, D.G. Mick and C. Huffman, 'Introduction', in S. Ratneshaw, D.G. Mick and C. Huffman (eds), *The Why of Consumption* (London: Routledge, 2000): 1–8.

CHAPTER SUMMARY

Now that you have finished reading this chapter you should understand why:

→ **It's important for marketers to recognize that products can satisfy a range of consumer needs.** Marketers try to satisfy consumer needs, but the reasons people purchase any product can vary widely. The identification of consumer motives is an important step to ensure that a product will satisfy appropriate needs. Traditional approaches to consumer behaviour focus on the abilities of products to satisfy rational needs (utilitarian motives), but hedonic motives (e.g. the need for exploration or for fun) also play a key role in many purchase decisions.

As Maslow's hierarchy of needs demonstrates, the same product can satisfy different needs, depending on the consumer's state at the time. In addition to this objective situation (e.g. have basic physiological needs already been satisfied?), we must also consider the consumer's degree of involvement with the product.

→ **A consumer's personality influences the way he responds to marketing stimuli, but efforts to use this information in marketing contexts meet with mixed results.** The concept of *personality* refers to a person's unique psychological makeup and how it consistently influences the way that person responds to his or her environment. Marketing strategies based on personality differences have met with mixed success, partly because of the way researchers have measured and applied these differences in *personality traits* to consumption contexts. Some analysts try to understand underlying differences in small samples of consumers by employing techniques based on Freudian psychology and variations of this perspective, whereas others have tried to assess these dimensions more objectively in large samples using sophisticated, quantitative techniques.

→ **The way we evaluate and choose a product depends on our degree of involvement with the product, the marketing message, and/or the purchase situation.** Product involvement can range from very low, where purchase decisions are made via inertia, to very high, where consumers form very strong bonds with what they buy. In addition to considering the degree to which consumers are involved with a product, marketing strategists also need to assess consumers' extent of involvement with marketing messages and with the purchase situation.

→ **Our deeply held cultural values dictate the types of products and services we seek out or avoid.** Values are basic, general principles used to judge the desirability of end-states. Underlying values often drive consumer motivations. Products thus take on meaning because a person thinks they will help him or her to achieve some goal that is linked to a value, such as individuality or freedom. All cultures form a value system which sets them apart from other cultures. Each culture is characterized by a set of core values to which many of its members adhere. Some researchers have developed lists to account for such value systems and used them in cross-cultural comparisons. One approach to the study of values is the means–end chain, which tries to link product attributes to consumer values via the consequences that usage of the product will have for the consumer.

→ **Consumers vary in the importance they attach to worldly possessions, and this orientation in turn has an impact on their priorities and behaviours.** *Materialism* refers to the importance people attach to worldly possessions. Although we describe many consumers as materialists, there are indications of a value shift across Europe – and this accompanies much greater interest in environmentally sustainable products and services.

→ **Products that succeed in one culture may fail in another if marketers fail to understand the differences among consumers in each place.** Because a consumer's culture exerts such a big influence on his or her lifestyle choices, marketers take account of such differences in cultural norms and preferences when they are marketing. One important issue is the extent to which we need to tailor our marketing strategies to each culture.

→ **Psychographics goes beyond simple demographics to help marketers understand and reach different consumer segments.** *Psychographic* techniques classify consumers in terms of psychological, subjective variables in addition to observable characteristics (demographics). Marketers have developed systems to identify consumer 'types' and to differentiate them in terms of their brand or product preferences, media usage, leisure time activities, and attitudes towards broad issues such as politics and religion.

→ **Getting rid of products when consumers no longer need or want them is a major concern to both marketers and public policymakers.** Product disposal is an increasingly important problem. Recycling is one option that will become more crucial as consumers' environmental awareness grows. Lateral cycling occurs when we buy, sell or barter secondhand objects.

KEY TERMS

80/20 rule (p. 226)
Abandoned products (p. 232)
Acculturation (p. 211)
Affect (p. 191)
AIOs (p. 225)
Animism (p. 203)
Approach–approach conflict (p. 191)
Approach–avoidance conflict (p. 192)
Archetypes (p. 200)
Avoidance–avoidance conflict (p. 193)
Behavioural targeting (p. 230)
Brand personality (p. 202)
Carbon footprint (p. 222)
Conscientious consumerism (p. 222)

Consumer-generated content (CGC) (p. 207)
Core values (p. 210)
Cosmopolitanism (p. 221)
Cybercrime (p. 231)
Divestment rituals (p. 237)
Doppelgänger brand image (p. 202)
Downshifting (p. 220)
Drive (p. 187)
Drive theory (p. 188)
Ego (p. 197)
Enculturation (p. 211)
Expectancy theory (p. 189)
Flashmobs (p. 207)
Flow state (p. 205)

→

→ **Freecycling** (p. 236)
Freegans (p. 236)
Freudian theory (p. 197)
Goal (p. 187)
Greenwashing (p. 223)
Hedonic adaptation (p. 221)
Hierarchy of needs (p. 194)
Homeostasis (p. 188)
Id (p. 197)
Individualism (p. 216)
Inertia (p. 205)
Instrumental values (p. 215)
Interactive mobile marketing (p. 208)
Involvement (p. 204)
Laddering (p. 217)
Lateral cycling (p. 235)
Lifestyle (p. 223)
Lifestyle marketing perspective (p. 227)
List of Values (LOV) (p. 216)
LOHAS (p. 222)
Mass customization (p. 206)
Materialism (p. 219)
Means-end chain model (p. 217)
MECCAs (p. 217)

Motivation (p. 187)
Motivational research (p. 198)
Narrative transportation (p. 206)
Need (p. 187)
Personality (pp. 185, 199)
Personality traits (p. 200)
Productivity orientation (p. 190)
Psychographics (pp. 223, 224)
Reclaimers (p. 235)
Sentiment analysis (p. 191)
Sharing sites (p. 235)
Social game (p. 208)
Spectacles (p. 207)
Superego (p. 197)
Terminal values (p. 215)
Theory of cognitive dissonance (p. 192)
Transactional advertising (p. 208)
Underground economy (p. 235)
Values (p. 209)
Value system (p. 211)
Virtual water footprint (p. 222)
Want (p. 187)
Web (p. 195)
Word-phrase dictionary (p. 191)

CONSUMER BEHAVIOUR CHALLENGE

1 What is motivation, and how is motivation relevant to consumer behaviour? What is the difference between a need and a want?

2 Describe three types of motivational conflicts, citing an example of each from current marketing campaigns.

3 Consumer researchers have the right to probe into the consumer's unconscious. Is this a violation of privacy, or just another way to gather deep knowledge of purchase motivations?

4 What is cognitive dissonance? Why is it important for marketers to understand how this works?

5 Devise separate promotional strategies for an article of clothing, each of which stresses one of the levels of Maslow's hierarchy of needs.

6 Describe the id, ego and superego and discuss how they work together according to Freudian theory.

7 Describe three personality traits relevant to marketers. What problems arise when we try to apply trait theory to marketing contexts?

8 Define a brand personality and give two examples.

9 What is consumer involvement? Give examples of the three types of consumer involvement. How do these types of involvement relate to motivation?

10 'High involvement is just a fancy term for expensive.' Do you agree?

11 Describe how a man's level of involvement with his car would affect how he is influenced by different marketing stimuli. How might you design a strategy for a line of car batteries for a segment of low-involvement consumers, and how would this strategy differ from your attempts to reach a segment of men who are very involved in working on their cars?

12 Collect a sample of ads that appeals to consumers' values. What value is being communicated in each ad, and how is this done? Is this an effective approach to designing a marketing communication?

13 'University students' concerns about ethics, sustainability, the environment, carbon footprints, genetically modified foods and vegetarianism are just passing fads; a way to look "cool".' Do you agree?

14 Assess the role of materialism in consumer behaviour. Think about some of the excuses or explanations you have used towards yourself or towards others for materialistic wants. How do they correspond to the explanations and excuses accounted for here?

15 If you were segmenting European consumers in terms of their relative level of materialism, how might your advertising and promotional strategy take this difference into account? Construct two versions of an ad for a suntan lotion, one to appeal to a high materialism country and one to appeal to a low materialism country (under the untenable assumption of all other things being equal).

16 Describe at least two alternative techniques marketing researchers have used to measure values. What might be the cultural issues to be considered when applying these techniques?

17 Core values evolve over time. What do you think are the three to five core values that best describe your country today? Can you see differences between present day core values and those of your parents' and grandparents' generations? What might be the implications for marketing managers?

18 Visit the *Business Week* website, **http://images. businessweek.com/ss/08/08/0819_happiest_ countries/index.htm**. Read the latest report by the World Value Survey of the happiest countries. Identify and discuss the key features used to assess happiness in the descriptions of these European countries. How would you describe and evaluate your own society using these criteria?

19 Construct a hypothetical means–end chain model for the purchase of a bouquet of roses. How might a florist use this approach to construct a promotional strategy?

20 Define psychographics, and describe three ways that marketers might use it.

21 Compare and contrast the concepts of lifestyle and social class. How does lifestyle differ from income?

22 In what situations is demographic information likely to be more useful than psychographic data, and vice versa?

23 What are three specific kinds of AIOs?

24 What are RISC and CCA, and how do marketers use them?

25 Behavioural targeting techniques give marketers access to a wide range of information about a consumer by telling them what websites they visit. Do you believe this 'knowledge power' presents any ethical problems with regard to consumers' privacy? Should the government regulate access to such information? Should consumers have the right to limit access to these data?

26 What is the basic philosophy behind a lifestyle marketing strategy?

27 Discuss some concrete situations in which international similarities in lifestyles may be more relevant than national cultural differences for market segmentation and for the understanding of consumer behaviour.

28 Compile a set of recent ads that attempt to link consumption of a product with a specific lifestyle. How is this goal usually accomplished?

29 Construct separate advertising executions for a cosmetics product targeted to three of the RISC segments: ethics and universalism; appearance and international symbol status; and action and personal drive. How would the basic appeal differ for each group?

30 There are, of course, people of most lifestyle types in all European countries, but their numbers vary. Try to determine which lifestyles are the most common in some European countries that you know.

31 Extreme sports. Chat rooms. Vegetarianism. Can you predict what will be 'hot' in the near future? Identify a lifestyle trend that is just surfacing in your universe. Describe this trend in detail, and justify your prediction. What specific styles and/or products are part of this trend?

32 The movement away from a 'disposable consumer society' towards one that emphasizes creative recycling creates many opportunities for marketers. Can you identify some?

33 What is the underground economy and why is it important to marketers?

34 Interview people who are selling items at a flea market or garage sale. Ask them to identify some items to which they had a strong attachment. Then, see if you can prompt them to describe one or more divestment rituals they went through as they prepared to offer these items for sale.

For additional material see the companion website at www.pearsoned.co.uk/solomon

NOTES

1. http://www.tripadvisor.com/ShowUserReviews-g189400-d695900-r118454869-Filippou-Athens_Attica.html, accessed 6 April 2012.

2. For detailed definitions of different types of vegetarianism see http://www.vegsoc.org/info/definitions.html

3. See Susan Baker, Keith E. Thompson and Julia Engelken, 'Mapping the values driving organic food choice: Germany *vs* the UK', *European Journal of Marketing* 38 (2004): 995 ff. Their study showed that although there were similarities between German and UK consumers of organic products in terms of values related to health, well-being and enjoyment, there were differences in terms of product attributes linked to achieving these values. A major difference was that UK consumers did not necessarily link organic food with the environment.

4. Vegetarian Society quickfacts1: http://www.youngveggie.org/Information/quick%20facts1.pdf, accessed 22 August 2008.

5. Mintel report 2006 cited in Russell Eaton, 'Vegetarian populations around the world', published February 2010: http://articles.submityourarticle.com/Russell-Eaton-6911/types-of-vegetarians-79577.php, accessed 6 April 2012; see also Jess Halliday, 'The market for vegetarian supplements' Nutra Ingredients.com, free newsletter, 20 January 2006, http://www.nutraingredients.com/news/ng.asp?n=65255-vegetarian-supplements

6. Tino Bech-Larsen and Klaus G. Grunert, 'The Influence of Tasting Experience and Health Benefits on Nordic Consumers' Rejection of Genetically Modified Foods', in Andrea Groppel-Klein and Franz-Rudolf Esch (eds), *European Advances in Consumer Research* 5 (Valdosta, GA: Association for Consumer Research, 2001): 11–14.

7. *Ibid.*

8. Laura Smith, 'Childhood obesity fuelled by cartoons', *The Guardian* (24 February 2005): 5.

9. Bech-Larsen and Grunert, 'The Influence of Tasting Experience and Health Benefits', *op. cit.*: 11–14.

10. Paul Hewer, 'Consuming Gardens: Representations of Paradise, Nostalgia and Postmodernism', in Darach Turley and Stephen Brown (eds), *European Advances in Consumer Research* 6 (Valdosta, GA: Association for Consumer Research, 2003): 327–31.

11. http://www.study-in-italy.it/about/eating.html

12. Richard Bagozzi and Utpal Dholakia, 'Goal setting and goal striving in consumer behavior', *Journal of Marketing* 63 (October 1999): 19–23.

13. Eileen Fischer, Cele C. Otnes and Linda Tuncay, 'Pursuing parenthood: Integrating cultural and cognitive perspectives on persistent goal striving', *Journal of Consumer Research* 34 (December 2007): 425–40.

14. Robert A. Baron, *Psychology: The Essential Science* (Needham, MA: Allyn & Bacon, 1989).

15. Jean Baudrillard, 'La genèse idéologique des besoins', *Cahiers internationaux de sociologie* 47 (1969): 45–68.

16. Russell W. Belk, Guliz Ger and Søren Askegaard, 'The Fire of Desire: A Multisited Inquiry into Consumer Passion', *Journal of Consumer Research*, 30 (2003): 326–51; cf. also Yu Chen, 'Possession and Access: Consumer Desires and Value Perceptions Regarding Contemporary Art Collection and Exhibit Visits', *Journal of Consumer Research* 35 (April 2009): 925–40.

17. Søren Askegaard and A. Fuat Firat, 'Towards a Critique of Material Culture, Consumption, and Markets', in S. Pearce (ed.), *Experiencing Material Culture in the Western World* (London: Leicester University Press, 1997): 114–39.

18. For a study that looks at cross-cultural differences in expression of emotion, cf. Ana Valenzuela, Barbara Mellers and Judi Strebel (2010), 'Pleasurable Surprises: A Cross-Cultural Study of Consumer Responses to Unexpected Incentives', *Journal of Consumer Research* 36, no. 5 (2010): 792–805.

19. Samuel K. Bonsu, Aron Darmody and Marie-Agnes Parmentier (2010), 'Arrested Emotions in Reality Television', *Consumption Markets & Culture* 13, no. 1 (2010): 91–107.

20. For more on this, see Tracy Tuten and Michael R. Solomon, *Social Media Marketing* (Upper Saddle River, NJ: Pearson Education, 2012); Jennifer Van Grove, 'How a Sentiment Analysis Startup Profits by Checking Emotion in E-mail, *Mashable* (20 January 2011), http://mashable.com/2011/01/20/lymbix/?utm_source=feedburner&utm_medium=email&utm_campaign=Feed%3A+Mashable+%28Mashable%29, accessed 29 April 2011.

21. See for instance the discussion in Emma N. Banister and Margaret K. Hogg, 'Negative symbolic consumption and consumers' drive for self-esteem: the case of the fashion industry', *European Journal of Marketing* 38(7) (2004): 850–68.

22. Thomas Kramer and Song-Oh yoon, 'Approach–Avoidance Motivation and the Use of affect as Information', *Journal of Consumer Psychology* 17, no. 2 (2007): 128–38.

23. Leon Festinger, *A Theory of Cognitive Dissonance* (Stanford, CA: Stanford University Press, 1957).

24. http://www.visit4info.com/advert/Muller-Light-Yoghurt-Muller-Yoghurt-Fromage-Frais-Range/55309#

25. Jeannie Whalen, 'Meet the leader of the pack: Moscow's drag-racing queen Katya Karenina organizes illicit matches under the nose of the city police force', *The Wall Street Journal* (9 December 2002) jeanne.whalen@wsj.com

26. See Paul T. Costa and Robert R. McCrae, 'From catalog to classification: Murray's needs and the five-factor model', *Journal of Personality and Social Psychology* 55 (1988): 258–65; Calvin S. Hall and Gardner Lindzey, *Theories of Personality*, 2nd edn (New York: Wiley, 1970); James U. McNeal and Stephen W. McDaniel, 'An analysis of need-appeals in television advertising', *Journal of the Academy of Marketing Science* 12 (Spring 1984): 176–90.

27. Michael R. Solomon, Judith L. Zaichkowsky and Rosemary Polegato, *Consumer Behaviour: Buying, Having, and Being – Canadian Edition* (Scarborough, Ontario: Prentice Hall Canada, 1999).

28. See David C. McClelland, *Studies in Motivation* (New York: Appleton-Century-Crofts, 1955).

29. Mary Kay Ericksen and M. Joseph Sirgy, 'Achievement Motivation and Clothing Preferences of White-Collar Working Women', in Michael R. Solomon (ed.), *The*

Psychology of Fashion (Lexington, MA: Lexington Books, 1985): 357–69.

30. See Stanley Schachter, *The Psychology of Affiliation* (Stanford, CA: Stanford University Press, 1959).

31. Eugene M. Fodor and Terry Smith, 'The power motive as an influence on group decision making', *Journal of Personality and Social Psychology* 42 (1982): 178–85.

32. C.R. Snyder and Howard L. Fromkin, *Uniqueness: The Human Pursuit of Difference* (New York: Plenum, 1980).

33. Abraham H. Maslow, *Motivation and Personality*, 2nd edn (New York: Harper & Row, 1970).

34. An integrative view of consumer goal structures and goal-determination processes proposes six discrete levels of goals wherein higher-level (versus lower-level) goals are more abstract, more inclusive, and less mutable. In descending order of abstraction, these goal levels are life themes and values, life projects, current concerns, consumption intentions, benefits sought and feature preferences. See Cynthia Huffman, S. Ratneshwar and David Glen Mick, 'Consumer Goal Structures and Goal-Determination Processes: An Integrative Framework', in S. Ratneshwar, David Glen Mick and Cynthia Huffman (eds), *The Why of Consumption* (London: Routledge, 2000): 9–35.

35. Henry, Paul (2006), 'Magnetic points for lifestyle shaping: The contribution of self-fulfillment, aspirations and capabilities', *Qualitative Market Research* 9(2): 170.

36. See, however, Primo Levi, *If This Is A Man* (London: Abacus by Sphere Books, 1987); his discussion of the importance of friendship for surviving extreme conditions of deprivation; and his description of the loss of his concentration camp friend and companion Alberto: 161.

37. Adapted in part from Jack Loechner, 'Emotional Business Bonding on Social Networks', *Research Brief*, Center for Media Research (27 December 2007), http://blogs.mediapost.com/research_brief/?p=1603, accessed 27 December 2007.

38. Study conducted in the Horticulture Department at Kansas State University, cited in 'Survey tells why gardening's good', *Vancouver Sun* (12 April 1997): B12; see also Paul Hewer and Douglas Brownlie (2006), 'Constructing "Hortiporn": On the Aesthetics of Stylized Exteriors', *Advances in Consumer Research* 33(1).

39. Richard Maddock, 'A Theoretical and Empirical Substructure of Consumer Motivation and Behaviour', in Flemming Hansen (ed.), *European Advances in Consumer Research* 2 (Provo, UT: Association for Consumer Research, 1995): 29–37.

40. Donna Hoffman, 'Consumer Behavior as I See IT', *Consumer Behavior*, 10th edn, Michael R. Solomon (2012) Pearson.

41. Ernest Dichter, *A Strategy of Desire* (Garden City, NY: Doubleday, 1960); Ernest Dichter, *The Handbook of Consumer Motivations* (New York: McGraw-Hill, 1964); Jeffrey J. Durgee, 'Interpreting Dichter's Interpretations: An Analysis of Consumption Symbolism in *The Handbook of Consumer Motivations*', *Marketing and Semiotics. Selected Papers from the Copenhagen Symposium*, Hanne Hartvig Larsen, David G. Mick and Christian Alsted (eds), (Copenhagen: Handelshøjskolens Forlag 1991): 52–74; Pierre Martineau, *Motivation in Advertising* (New York: McGraw-Hill, 1957).

42. Vance Packard, *The Hidden Persuaders* (New York: D. McKay, 1957).

43. Harold Kassarjian, 'Personality and consumer behavior: A review', *Journal of Marketing Research* 8 (November 1971): 409–18.

44. Karen Horney, *Neurosis and Human Growth* (New York: Norton, 1950). See also: Joel B. Cohen, 'An Interpersonal Orientation to the Study of Consumer Behavior', *Journal of Marketing Research* 6 (August 1967): 270–78; Pradeep K. Tyagi, 'Validation of the CAD Instrument: A Replication', in Richard P. Bagozzi and Alice M. Tybout (eds), *Advances in Consumer Research 10* (Ann Arbor, MI: Association for Consumer Research, 1983): 112–14.

45. For a comprehensive review of classic perspectives on personality theory, see Calvin S. Hall and Gardner Lindzey, *Theories of Personality*, 2nd edn (New York: Wiley, 1970).

46. See Carl G. Jung, 'The Archetypes and the Collective Unconscious', in H. Read, M. Fordham and G. Adler (eds), *Collected Works*, vol. 9, part 1 (Princeton, NJ: Princeton University Press, 1959).

47. For an application of trait theory, cf. Adam Duhachek and Dawn Iacobucci, 'Consumer Personality and Coping: Testing Rival Theories of Process', *Journal of Consumer Psychology* 15, no. 1 (2005): 52–63.

48. S. Christian Wheeler, Richard E. Petty and George Y. Bizer, 'Self-Schema Matching and Attitude Change: Situational and Dispositional Determinants of Message Elaboration,' *Journal of Consumer Research* 31 (March, 2005): 787–97.

49. Adapted from information presented in Beth Snyder Bulik, 'You Are What You Watch: Market Data Suggest Research Links Personality Traits to Consumers' Viewing Habits, Helps Marketers Match Brands with Audiences', *Advertising Age* (1 November 2010), http://adage.com/article/news/research-links-personality-traits-tv-viewing-habits/146779/, accessed 13 April 2011.

50. Linda L. Price and Nancy Ridgway, 'Development of a Scale to Measure Innovativeness', in Richard P. Bagozzi and Alice M. Tybout (eds), *Advances in Consumer Research 10* (Ann Arbor, MI: Association for Consumer Research, 1983): 679–84; Russell W. Belk, 'Three Scales to Measure Constructs Related to Materialism: Reliability, Validity, and Relationships to Measures of Happiness', in Thomas C. Kinnear (ed.), *Advances in Consumer Research 11* (Ann Arbor, MI: Association for Consumer Research, 1984): 291; Mark Snyder, 'Self-Monitoring Processes', in Leonard Berkowitz (ed.), *Advances in Experimental Social Psychology* (New York: Academic Press, 1979), 85–128; Gordon R. Foxall and Ronald E. Goldsmith, 'Personality and Consumer Research: Another Look', *Journal of the Market Research Society* 30, no. 2 (1988): 111–25; Ronald E. Goldsmith and Charles F. Hofacker, 'Measuring Consumer Innovativeness', *Journal of the Academy of Marketing Science* 19, no. 3 (1991): 209–21; Curtis P. Haugtvedt, Richard E. Petty and John T. Cacioppo, 'Need for Cognition and Advertising: Understanding the Role of Personality Variables in Consumer Behavior', *Journal of Consumer Psychology* 1, no. 3 (1992): 239–60.

51. John L. Lastovicka, Lance A. Bettencourt, Renee Shaw Hughner and Ronald J. Kuntze, 'Lifestyle of the Tight and Frugal: Theory and Measurement', *Journal of Consumer Research* 26 (June 1999): 85–98; The Hartman Group, 'The

Continuing Economic Maelstrom & the US Consumer: Implications for CPG, Restaurant and Retail January 2009', 9, http://www.hartman-group.com/publications/white-papers/the-continuing-economic-maelstrom-the-us-consumer, accessed 3 September 2011; Joseph Lazzaro, 'US Savings Rate Soars to 14-Year High', *Daily Finance* (1 June 2009), www.dailyfinance.com/2009/06/01/us-savings-rate-soars-to-14-year-high, accessed 1 June 2009; Andrea K. Walker, 'Economy Breeds a Frugal Consumer', *Baltimore Sun* (20 April 2009), www.baltimoresun.com/business/bal-te.bz.shoppinghabits19apr20,0,1577826.story, accessed 1 June 2009.

52. Jacob Jacoby, 'Personality and Consumer Behavior: How Not to Find Relationships', in *Purdue Papers in Consumer Psychology*, no. 102 (Lafayette, IN: Purdue University, 1969); Harold H. Kassarjian and Mary Jane Sheffet, 'Personality and Consumer Behavior: An Update', in Harold H. Kassarjian and Thomas S. Robertson (eds), *Perspectives in Consumer Behavior*, 4th edn (Glenview, IL: Scott Foresman, 1991): 291–353; John Lastovicka and Erich Joachimsthaler, 'Improving the Detection of Personality Behavior Relationships in Consumer Research', *Journal of Consumer Research* 14 (March 1988): 583–87. For an approach that ties the notion of personality more directly to marketing issues, see Jennifer L. Aaker, 'Dimensions of Brand Personality', *Journal of Marketing Research* 34 (August 1997): 347–57.

53. See Girish N. Punj and David W. Stewart, 'An Interaction Framework of Consumer Decision-Making', *Journal of Consumer Research* 10 (September 1983): 181–96.

54. J.F. Allsopp, 'The Distribution of On-Licence Beer and Cider Consumption and Its Personality Determinants Among Young Men', *European Journal of Marketing* 20, no. 3 (1986): 44–62; Gordon R. Foxall and Ronald E. Goldsmith, 'Personality and Consumer Research: Another Look', *Journal of the Market Research Society* 30, no. 2 (April 1988): 111–25.

55. Quoted in Stuart O'Brien, 'iPad Owners are "Self-Centered Workaholics"', *Mobile Entertainment* (30 July 2010), http://www.mobile-ent.biz/news/read/ipad-owners-are-self-centered-workaholics, accessed 13 April 2011.

56. Bradley Johnson, 'They All Have Half-Baked Ideas', *Advertising Age* (12 May 1997): 8.

57. Yongjun Sung and Spencer F. Tinkham, 'Brand Personality Structures in the United States and Korea: Common and Culture-Specific Factors', *Journal of Consumer Psychology* 15, no. 4 (2005): 334–50; Beverly T. Venable, Gregory M. Rose, Victoria D. Bush and Faye W. Gilbert, 'The Role of Brand Personality in Charitable Giving: An Assessment and Validation', *Journal of the Academy of Marketing Science* 33 (July 2005): 295–312.

58. Susan Nelson, 'Our Changing View of Style', *Marketing Daily* (17 February 2009), www.mediapost.com, accessed 17 February 2009.

59. Kevin L. Keller, 'Conceptualization, Measuring, and Managing Customer-Based Brand Equity', *Journal of Marketing* 57 (January 1993): 1–22.

60. Linda Keslar, 'What's in a Name?', *Individual Investor* (April 1999): 101–2.

61. Kathryn Kranhold, 'Agencies Beef up Brand Research to Identify Consumer Preferences', *Wall Street Journal*

Interactive Edition (9 March 2000), accessed 9 March 2000.

62. Jennifer Aaker, Kathleen D. Vohs and Cassie Mogilner (2010), 'Nonprofits Are Seen as Warm and For-Profits as Competent: Firm Stereotypes Matter', *Journal of Consumer Research* 37, no. 2 (2010): 224–37.

63. Jennifer L. Aaker, 'Dimensions of Brand Personality', *Journal of Marketing Research* 34 (August 1997): 347–57.

64. Seth Stevenson, 'How to Beat Nike', *New York Times* (5 January 2003), www.nytimes.com, accessed 5 January 2003.

65. Susan Fournier, 'Consumers and Their Brands: Developing Relationship Theory in Consumer Research', *Journal of Consumer Research* 24, no. 4 (March 1998): 343–73.

66. Quoted in Erin White, 'Volvo Sheds Safe Image for New, Dangerous Ads', *Wall Street Journal* (June 14, 2002), www.wsj.com, accessed 14 June 2002; Viknesh Vijayenthiran, 'Volvo's Upmarket Plans Hindered by Brand Image, Poor CO2 Emissions', *Motor Authority* (24 November 2008), www.motorauthority.com/volvo-continuing-with-plans-to-move-upmarket.html, accessed 1 June 2009.

67. Shirley Brady, 'Volvo's Naughty S60 Experiment', *BrandChannel* (28 July 2010), http://www.brandchannel.com/home/post/2010/07/28/Volvo-Naughty-S60-Experiment.aspx, accessed 13 April 2011.

68. Judith Lynne Zaichkowsky, 'Measuring the involvement construct in marketing', *Journal of Consumer Research* 12 (December 1985): 341–52.

69. Andrew Mitchell, 'Involvement: A Potentially Important Mediator of Consumer Behaviour', in William L. Wilkie (ed.), *Advances in Consumer Research* 6 (Provo, UT: Association for Consumer Research, 1979): 191–6.

70. Richard L. Celsi and Jerry C. Olson, 'The role of involvement in attention and comprehension processes', *Journal of Consumer Research* 15 (September 1988): 210–24.

71. Ton Otker, 'The highly involved consumer: A marketing myth?' *Marketing and Research Today* (February 1990): 30–6.

72. Anthony G. Greenwald and Clark Leavitt, 'Audience involvement in advertising: Four levels', *Journal of Consumer Research* 11 (June 1984): 581–92.

73. Mihaly Csikszentmihalyi, *Flow: The Psychology of Optimal Experience* (New York: HarperCollins, 1991); Donna L. Hoffman and Thomas P. Novak, 'Marketing in hypermedia computer-mediated environments: Conceptual foundations', *Journal of Marketing* (July 1996), 60, 50–68.

74. Judith Lynne Zaichkowsky, 'The Emotional Side of Product Involvement', in Paul Anderson and Melanie Wallendorf (eds), *Advances in Consumer Research* 14 (Provo, UT: Association for Consumer Research): 32–5.

75. For a discussion of interrelationship between situational and enduring involvement, see Marsha L. Richins, Peter H. Bloch and Edward F. McQuarrie, 'How enduring and situational involvement combine to create involvement responses', *Journal of Consumer Psychology* 1(2) (1992): 143–53. For more information on the involvement construct see 'Special issue on involvement' *Psychology and Marketing* 10(4) (July/August 1993).

76. Joseph B. Pine II and James H. Gilmore, *Markets of One – Creating Customer-Unique Value through Mass Customization* (Boston: Harvard Business School Press, 2000); www.managingchange.com/masscust/overview.htm, accessed 30 May 2005.

77. http://search.ft.com/ftArticle?queryText=personalization &y=4 &aje=false&x=16&id=070913000705&ct=0, accessed 26 April 2008; http://adfarm.mediaplex.com/ad/fm/ 54649?mpt=5640053&mpvc=, accessed 27 April 2008.

78. Rajeev Batra and Michael L. Ray, 'Operationalizing Involvement as Depth and Quality of Cognitive Responses', in Alice Tybout and Richard Bagozzi (eds), *Advances in Consumer Research* 10 (Ann Arbor, MI: Association for Consumer Research, 1983): 309–13.

79. Herbert E. Krugman, 'The impact of television advertising: Learning without involvement', *Public Opinion Quarterly* 29 (Fall 1965): 349–56.

80. Brent McFerran, Darren W. Dahl, Gerald J. Gorn and Heather Honea, 'Motivational Determinants of Transportation into Marketing Narratives', *Journal of Consumer Psychology* 20, no. 3 (2010): 306–16.

81. David W. Stewart and David H. Furse, 'Analysis of the Impact of Executional Factors in Advertising Performance', *Journal of Advertising Research* 24 (1984): 23–26; Deborah J. MacInnis, Christine Moorman and Bernard J. Jaworski, 'Enhancing and Measuring Consumers' Motivation, Opportunity, and Ability to Process Brand Information from Ads', *Journal of Marketing* 55 (October 1991): 332–53.

82. Morris B. Holbrook and Elizabeth C. Hirschman, 'The Experiential Aspects of Consumption: Consumer Fantasies, Feelings, and Fun', *Journal of Consumer Research* 9 (September 1982): 132–40.

83. Elaine Sciolino, 'Disproving Notions, Raising a Fury', *New York Times* (21 January 2003), www.nytimes.com, accessed 21 January 2003.

84. Louise Story, 'Times Sq. Ads Spread via Tourists' Cameras', *New York Times* (11 December 2006), www.nytimes.com, accessed 11 December 2006.

85. The Nielsen Company Press Release 'Over 875 Million Consumers Have Shopped Online – the Number of Internet Shoppers Up 40 per cent in Two Years', http://www. earthtimes.org/articles/show/over-875-million-consumers-have-shopped-online--the-number,263812.shtml, accessed 20 August 2008.

86. Knowledge@Wharton, 'Fast Forward: Tech Giants Scramble for Bigger Piece of Growing Online Ad Market', 23 July 2008, http://knowledge.wharton.upenn.edu/

87. Rajeev Batra and Michael L. Ray, 'Operationalizing Involvement as Depth and Quality of Cognitive Responses', in Alice Tybout and Richard Bagozzi (eds), *Advances in Consumer Research 10* (Ann Arbor, MI: Association for Consumer Research, 1983): 309–13.

88. Quoted in 'Gap Scraps New Logo after Online Outcry', *Reuters* (12 October 2010), http://www.reuters.com/article/ 2010/10/12/us-gap-idUSTRE69B05Z20101012?utm_ source=feedburner&utm_medium=feed&utm_campaign= Feed%3A+Reuters%2FInternetNews+%28News+%2F+US +%2F+Internet+News%29, accessed 30 April 2011.

89. 'Ads That Stay with You', *Newsweek* (19 November 2007), www.newsweek.com/Id/68904, accessed 19 November 2007.

90. Stephanie Clifford, 'Axe Body Products Puts Its Brand on the Hamptons Club Scene', *New York Times* (22 May 2009): B6; Alana Semuels, 'Honda Finds a Groovy New Way to Pitch Products: The Musical Road', *Los Angeles Times* (13 October 2008), www.latimes.com/Business/ La-Fi-Roads13-2008oct13,0,4147014.Story, accessed 13 October 2008; Eric Pfanner, 'A Live Promotion, At 14,000 Feet', *New York Times* (6 June 2008), www.nytimes.com, accessed 6 June 2008; Les Luchter, 'Jameson Whiskey Texts Targets on N.Y. Streets', *Marketing Daily* (8 August 2008), www.mediapost.com, accessed 8 August 2008; Doreen Carvajal, 'Dancers in the Crowd Bring Back "Thriller"', *New York Times* (10 March 2008), www.nytimes.com, accessed 10 March 2008; Eric Pfanner, 'When Consumers Help, Ads Are Free', *New York Times* (21 June 2009), www.nytimes.com, accessed 22 June 2009.

91. Li Yuan, 'Television's New Joy of Text Shows With Vote by Messaging Are on the Rise as Programmers Try To Make Live TV Matter', *Wall Street Journal* (20 July 2006): B1.

92. Mark J. Arnold and Kristy E. Reynolds, 'Hedonic shopping motivations', *Journal of Retailing* 79 (2003): 77–95.

93. Drew Elliott, 'Opportunities for Brands in Social Games', *Ogilvy PR Blog* (May 2010), http://blog.ogilvypr.com/ 2010/05/opportunities-for-brands-in-social-games/, accessed 12 July 2010.

94. Andiara Petterle, 'Reaching Latinos through Virtual Goods', *Media Post* (10 June 2010), http://www.mediapost.com/ publications/?fa=Articles.showArticle&art_aid=129857, accessed 13 July 2010.

95. 'Gagaville', http://gagaville.org/, accessed 12 May 2011.

96. Shalom H. Schwartz and Warren Bilsky, 'Toward a universal psychological structure of human values', *Journal of Personality and Social Psychology* 53 (1987): 550–62.

97. Ajay K. Sirsi, James C. Ward and Peter H. Reingen, 'Microcultural analysis of variation in sharing of causal reasoning about behavior', *Journal of Consumer Research* 22 (March 1996): 345–72.

98. Richard W. Pollay, 'Measuring the cultural values manifest in advertising', *Current Issues and Research in Advertising* (1983): 71–92.

99. Howard W. French, 'Vocation for dropouts is painting Tokyo red', *New York Times on the Web* (5 March 2000).

100. Deborah Ball, 'Women in Italy Like to Clean but Shun the Quick and Easy: Convenience Doesn't Sell When Bathrooms Average Four Scrubbings a Week', *Wall Street Journal* (25 April 2006): A1.

101. See, for instance, the discussion of acculturation issues and British South East Asian women in A.M. Lindridge, M.K. Hogg and M. Shah, 'Imagined multiple worlds: How South Asian women in Britain use family and friends to navigate the "border crossings" between household and societal contexts', *Consumption, Markets and Culture* 7(3) (September 2004): 211–38.

102. Carolyn A. Lin, 'Cultural values reflected in Chinese and American television advertising', *Journal of Advertising* 30 (Winter 2001): 83–94.

103. Sante J. Achille, 'Italians dislike online publicity', http:// www.multilingual-search.com/italians-dislike-online-publicity/22/07/2008, accessed 20 August 2008.

104. Milton Rokeach, *The Nature of Human Values* (New York: Free Press, 1973).

105. Sang-Pil Han and Sharon Shavitt, 'Persuasion and Culture: Advertising Appeals in Individualistic and Collectivistic Societies', *Journal of Experimental Social Psychology* 30 (1994): 326–50.

106. Chisaki Watanabe, 'Japanese Parents Embrace Ultra-Secure Children's Park', *Philadelphia Inquirer* (4 September 2006): A2.

107. Jay Alabaster and Ryan Nakashima, 'Japanese Comforted or Cramped in Evacuee Shelters', *MSNBC.com* (19 April 2011), http://www.msnbc.msn.com/id/42672467/ns/world_news-asia-pacific/t/japanese-comforted-or-cramped-evacuee-shelters/, accessed 10 May 2011.

108. Donald E. Vinson, Jerome E. Scott and Lawrence R. Lamont, 'The role of personal values in marketing and consumer behaviour', *Journal of Marketing* 41 (April 1977): 44–50; John Watson, Steven Lysonski, Tamara Gillan and Leslie Raymore, 'Cultural values and important possessions: A cross-cultural analysis', *Journal of Business Research* 55 (2002): 923–31.

109. Quester, Pascale, Michael Beverland and Francis Farrelly (2006), 'Brand-personal values fit and brand meanings: Exploring the role individual values play in ongoing brand loyalty in extreme sports subcultures', *Advances in Consumer Research* 33(1).

110. Jennifer Aaker, Veronica Benet-Martinez and Jordi Garolera, 'Consumption symbols as carriers of culture: A study of Japanese and Spanish brand personality constructs', *Journal of Personality and Social Psychology* (2001).

111. *Markedsføring* (25 August 2000): 8. See also Amelia Hill and Anushka Asthana, 'She's young, gifted and ahead of you at the till', *Observer* (2 January 2005): 7, http://observer.guardian.co.uk/uk_news/story/0,6903,1382042,00.html which describes 10 million twenty-to-thirty somethings in UK 'who are the new darlings of the retailers and politicians want their vote'. They are key decision makers and spenders in homeware stores.

112. *Markedsføring* (12 November 1999): 2.

113. Morris B. Holbrook, *Consumer Value* (London: Routledge, 1999).

114. *Ibid.* This book contains a chapter by various consumer researchers on each of the value types.

115. A comfortable life; an exciting life; a sense of accomplishment; a world at peace; a world of beauty; equality; family security; freedom; happiness; inner harmony; mature love; national security; pleasure; salvation; self-respect; social recognition; true friendship; and wisdom.

116. Ambitious; broad-minded; capable; cheerful; clean; courageous; forgiving; helpful; honest; imaginative; independent; intellectual; logical; loving; obedient; polite; responsible; and self-controlled.

117. Milton Rokeach, *Understanding Human Values* (New York: The Free Press, 1979); see also J. Michael Munson and Edward McQuarrie, 'Shortening the Rokeach Value Survey for Use in Consumer Research', in Michael J. Houston (ed.), *Advances in Consumer Research* 15 (Provo, UT: Association for Consumer Research, 1988): 381–86.

118. Jacques-Marie Aurifeille, 'Value Changes and Their Marketing Implications: A Russian Survey', in W.F. van Raaij and G. Bamossy (eds), *European Advances in Consumer Research* 1 (Provo, UT: Association for Consumer Research, 1993): 249–61.

119. B.W. Becker and P.E. Conner, 'Personal values of the heavy user of mass media', *Journal of Advertising Research* 21 (1981): 37–43; Scott Vinson and Lamont Vinson, 'The role of personal values in marketing and consumer behavior': 44–50.

120. Sharon E. Beatty, Lynn R. Kahle, Pamela Homer and Shekhar Misra, 'Alternative Measurement Approaches to Consumer Values: The List of Values and the Rokeach Value Survey', *Psychology & Marketing* 2 (1985): 181–200; Lynn R. Kahle and Patricia Kennedy, 'Using the List of Values (LOV) to Understand Consumers', *Journal of Consumer Marketing* 2 (Fall 1988): 49–56; Lynn Kahle, Basil Poulos and Ajay Sukhdial, 'Changes in Social Values in the United States During the Past Decade', *Journal of Advertising Research* 28 (February–March 1988): 35–41; see also Wagner A. Kamakura and Jose Alfonso Mazzon, 'Value Segmentation: A Model for the Measurement of Values and Value Systems', *Journal of Consumer Research* 18 (September 1991): 28; Jagdish N. Sheth, Bruce I. Newman and Barbara L. Gross, *Consumption Values and Market Choices: Theory and Applications* (Cincinnati, OH: South-Western, 1991).

121. Pierre Valette-Florence, Suzanne C. Grunert, Klaus G. Grunert and Sharon Beatty, 'Une comparaison franco-allemande de l'adhésion aux valeurs personnelles', *Recherche et Applications en Marketing* 6(3) (1991): 5–20.

122. Klaus G. Grunert, Suzanne C. Grunert and Sharon Beatty, 'Cross-cultural research on consumer values', *Marketing and Research Today* 17 (1989): 30–9.

123. Suzanne C. Grunert, Klaus G. Grunert and Kai Kristensen, 'Une méthode d'estimation de la validité interculturelle des instruments de mesure: Le cas de la mesure des valeurs des consommateurs par la liste des valeurs LOV', *Recherche et Applications en Marketing* 8(4) (1993): 5–28. Beatty, Kahle, Homer and Misra, 'Alternative measurement approaches to consumer values': 181–200; Lynn R. Kahle and Patricia Kennedy, 'Using the List of Values (LOV) to understand consumers', *Journal of Consumer Marketing* 2 (Fall 1988): 49–56; Lynn Kahle, Basil Poulos and Ajay Sukhdial, 'Changes in social values in the United States during the past decade', *Journal of Advertising Research* 28 (February/March 1988): 35–41; see also Wagner A. Kamakura and Jose Alfonso Mazzon, 'Value segmentation: A model for the measurement of values and value systems', *Journal of Consumer Research* 18 (September 1991): 28; Jagdish N. Sheth, Bruce I. Newman and Barbara L. Gross, *Consumption Values and Market Choices: Theory and Applications* (Cincinnati: South-Western Publishing Co., 1991).

124. Shalom H. Schwartz and Warren Bilsky, 'Toward a theory of universal content and structure of values: Extensions and cross-cultural replications', *Journal of Personality and Social Psychology* 58 (1990): 878–91; Shalom H. Schwartz, 'Universals in the Content and Structure of Values: Theoretical Advance and Empirical Test in 20 Countries', in M. Zanna (ed.), *Advances in Experimental Social Psychology* 25 (San Diego, CA: Academic Press, 1992): 1–65.

125. Shalom H. Schwartz, 'Beyond Individualism/Collectivism: New Cultural Dimensions of Values' in U. Kim *et al.* (eds), *Individualism and Collectivism* (Thousand Oaks, CA: Sage, 1994): 85–119.

126. Sarah Todd, Rob Lawson and Haydn Northover, 'Value Orientation and Media Consumption Behavior', in B. Englis and A. Olofsson (eds), *European Advances in Consumer Behaviour* 3 (Provo, UT: Association for Consumer Research): 328–32.

127. Suzanne C. Grunert and Hans Jørn Juhl, 'Values, environmental attitudes, and buying of organic foods', *Journal of Economic Psychology* 16 (1995): 39–62.

128. Thomas J. Reynolds and Jonathan Gutman, 'Laddering theory, method, analysis, and interpretation', *Journal of Advertising Research* (February/March 1988): 11–34; Beth Walker, Richard Celsi and Jerry Olson, 'Exploring the Structural Characteristics of Consumers' Knowledge', in Melanie Wallendorf and Paul Anderson (eds), *Advances in Consumer Research* 14 (Provo, UT: Association for Consumer Research, 1986): 17–21.

129. Andreas Hermann, 'Wertorientierte produktund werbegestaltung', *Marketing ZFP* 3 (3rd quarter 1996): 153–63.

130. Klaus G. Grunert and Suzanne C. Grunert, 'Measuring subjective meaning structures by the laddering method: Theoretical considerations and methodological problems', *International Journal of Research in Marketing* 12(3) (1995): 209–25. This volume of *IJRM* is a special issue on means–end chains and the laddering technique.

131. Roger Mason, 'Measuring the Demand for Status Goods: An Evaluation of Means–End Chains and Laddering', in Hansen (ed.), *European Advances in Consumer Research* 2: 78–82.

132. Thomas J. Reynolds and Alyce Byrd Craddock, 'The application of the MECCAS model to the development and assessment of advertising strategy: A case study', *Journal of Advertising Research* (April/May 1988): 43–54.

133. N.A. Nielsen, T. Bech-Larsen and K.G. Grunert, 'Consumer purchase motives and product perceptions: A laddering study on vegetable oil in three countries', *Food Quality and Preference* 9(6) (1998): 455–66.

134. Marsha L. Richins, 'Special possessions and the expression of material values', *Journal of Consumer Research* 21 (December, 1994): 522–33.

135. *Ibid.*

136. James E. Burroughs and Aric Rindfleisch, 'Materialism and well-being: A conflicting values perspective', *Journal of Consumer Research* 29 (December 2002): 348ff.

137. Lan Nguyen Chaplin and Deborah Roedder John, 'Growing Up in a Material World: Age Differences in Materialism in Children and Adolescents', *Journal of Consumer Research* 34 (December 2007): 490.

138. Marsha L. Richins, 'Special Possessions and the Expression of Material Values', *Journal of Consumer Research* 21 (December 1994): 522–33.

139. Aric Rindfleisch, James E. Burroughs and Nancy Wong, 'The Safety of Objects: Materialism, Existential Insecurity and Brand Connection', *Journal of Consumer Research* 36 (June 2009): 1–16.

140. John L. Lastovicka and Nancy J. Sirianni, 'Truly, Madly, Deeply: Consumers in the Throes of Material Possession Love', *Journal of Consumer Research* 38 (August 2011): 323–342.

141. Daniel Kahneman cited in Benedict Carey, 'TV time, unlike child care, ranks high in mood study', *NYTimes.com* (3 December 2004); see also Richard Tomkins, 'Materialism damages well-being,' *Financial Times* (27 November 2003), http://news.ft.com/servlet/ContentServer?pagename=FT.com/StoryFT/FullStory&c=StoryFT&cid=1069493548137&p=1012571727088

142. Matt Mabe 'Got Warm Feelings?' Business Week report on World Values Survey on the happiest countries, 20 August 2008, http://images.businessweek.com/ss/08/08/0819_happiest_countries/index.htm accessed 22 August 2008. Note that the World Value Survey will undertake a new wave of surveys 2010–2012, http://www.worldvaluessurvey.org/, accessed 23 February 2012.

143. Marsha L. Richins and Scott Dawson, 'A consumer values orientation for materialism and its measurement: Scale development and validation', *Journal of Consumer Research* 20 (December 1992).

144. Güliz Ger and Russell Belk, 'Cross-cultural differences in materialism', *Journal of Economic Psychology* 17 (1996): 55–77.

145. Güliz Ger and Russell Belk, 'Accounting for materialism in four cultures', *Journal of Material Culture* 4(2) (1999): 183–204.

146. Robert V. Kozinets, 'Can consumers escape the market? Emancipatory illuminations from burning man', *Journal of Consumer Research* 29 (June 2002): 20–38; see also Douglas B. Holt, 'Why do brands cause trouble? A dialectical theory of consumer culture and branding', *Journal of Consumer Research* 29 (June 2002): 70–90.

147. Stephanie Rosenbloom, 'But Will It Make You Happy?', *New York Times* (7 August 2010), http://www.nytimes.com/2010/08/08/business/08consume.html?pagewanted=1&_r=2&ref=business, accessed 10 April 2011.

148. Mark Cleveland, Michel Laroche and Nicolas Papadopoulos, 'Cosmopolitanism, Consumer Ethnocentrism, and Materialism: An Eight-Country Study of Antecedents and Outcomes', *Journal of International Marketing* 17, no. 1 (2009): 116–46.

149. See http://www.hltlaw.it/public/files/2009-05-green-marketing-in-europe-pp_211.pdf, for summary of debate about how 'real' the concern is amongst consumers in the face of marketing campaigns which employ the theme of 'green'.

150. Emily Burg, 'Whole Foods Is Consumers' Favorite Green Brand', *Marketing Daily*, mediapost.com (10 May 2007).

151. Cristina Cardigo and Paulo Rita, 'Fostering sustainable consumption practices through consumer empowerment' in Alan Bradshaw, Chris Hackley and Pauline Maclaran (eds), *European Association for Consumer Research Conference*, 2010, RHUL, page 55.

152. www.lohas.com/about.htm, accessed 30 June 2007.

153. Adrienne W. Fawcett, 'Conscientious Consumerism Drives Record New Product Launches in 2006', *New York Timesimes.com/magazine* (24 January 2007).

154. Mya Frazier, Farmstands vs. Big Brands: With Consumers Interested in Locally Produced Goods, Marketers Scramble to Get in on a Movement Going Mainstream, advertisingage.com (5 June 2007).

155. Cecilia M. Vega, 'Mayor to cut off flow of city money for bottled water', http://sfgate.com/cgi-bin/article.cgi?f=/c/a/2007/06/22/BAGE8QJVIL1.DTL, accessed 22 June 2007.

156. http://www.carbonfootprint.com/carbon_footprint.html, accessed 30 June 2007.

157. Note that a carbon footprint comprises two parts, the direct/primary footprint and the indirect/secondary footprint: firstly, the primary footprint is a measure of our direct emissions of CO_2 from the burning of fossil fuels including domestic energy consumption and transportation

(e.g. car and plane); and secondly the secondary footprint is a measure of the indirect CO_2 emissions from the whole lifecycle of products we use – those associated with their manufacture and eventual breakdown.

158. Editorial, 'Water: Go Against the Flow', *The Guardian*, 20 August 2008: 30, http://www.guardian.co.uk/commentisfree/2008/aug/20/water.food, accessed 20 August 2008.

159. *Ibid.*

160. Felicity Lawrence, 'Revealed: the massive scale of UK's water consumption', *The Guardian*, 20 August 2008: 1, http://www.guardian.co.uk/environment/2008/aug/20/water.food1, accessed 20 August 2008.

161. Wendy Koch, '"Green" Product Claims Are Often Misleading', *USA Today* (26 October 2010), http://content.usatoday.com/communities/greenhouse/post/2010/10/green-product-claims/1?csp=34money&utm_source=feedburner&utm_medium=feed&utm_campaign=Feed%3A+UsatodaycomMoney-TopStories+%28Money+-+Top+Stories%29, accessed 10 April 2011.

162. See Gary Bamossy and Basil Englis video: 'In Green', http://vimeo.com/10409261 which gets into the 'burnout' of Green.

163. Mark Dolliver, 'Thumbs Down on Corporate Green Efforts', *Adweek* (31 August 2010), http://www.adweek.com/aw/content_display/news/client/e3i84260d4301c885f91b2cd8a712f323cf, accessed 10 April 2011; Sarah Mahoney, 'Americans Hate Faux Green Marketers', *Marketing Daily* (25 March 2011), http://www.mediapost.com/publications/?fa=Articles.showArticle&art_aid=147415&nid=125122, accessed 10 April 2011.

164. Pierre Valette-Florence, *Les styles de vie* (Paris: Nathan, 1994); Benjamin Zablocki and Rosabeth Moss Kanter, 'The differentiation of life-styles', *Annual Review of Sociology* (1976): 269–97.

165. Mary T. Douglas and Baron C. Isherwood, *The World of Goods* (New York: Basic Books, 1979).

166. Richard A. Peterson, 'Revitalizing the culture concept', *Annual Review of Sociology* 5 (1979): 137–66.

167. See Lewis Alpert and Ronald Gatty, 'Product Positioning by Behavioral Life Styles', *Journal of Marketing* 33 (April 1969): 65–69; Emanuel H. Demby, 'Psychographics Revisited: The Birth of a Technique', *Marketing News* (2 January 1989): 21; William D. Wells, 'Backward Segmentation', in Johan Arndt (ed.), *Insights into Consumer Behavior* (Boston: Allyn & Bacon, 1968): 85–100.

168. Bill Schlackman, 'An Historical Perspective', in S. Robson and A. Foster (eds), *Qualitative Research in Action* (London: Edward Arnold, 1989): 15–23.

169. William D. Wells and Douglas J. Tigert, 'Activities, interests, and opinions', *Journal of Advertising Research* 11 (August 1971): 27.

170. Piirto Heath, 'Psychographics: "Q'est-ce que c'est"?', *American Demographics* (November 1995).

171. Alfred S. Boote, 'Psychographics: Mind over matter', *American Demographics* (April 1980): 26–9; William D. Wells, 'Psychographics: A critical review', *Journal of Marketing Research* 12 (May 1975): 196–213.

172. Joseph T. Plummer, 'The concept and application of life style segmentation', *Journal of Marketing* 38 (January 1974): 33–7.

173. J.E. Burroughs and A. Rindfleisch, 'Materialism and well-being: a conflicting values perspective', *Journal of Consumer Research* 29(3): 348–70; Hugh Williamson, 'All the rage in Germany: Cheap flights', *Financial Times* (26 March 2004), http://news.ft.com/servlet/ContentServer?pagename=FT.com/StoryFT/FullStory&c=StoryFT&cid=1079419851116&p=1079419860606

174. John L. Lastovicka, John P. Murry, Erich A. Joachimsthaler, Gurav Bhalla and Jim Scheurich, 'A lifestyle typology to model young male drinking and driving', *Journal of Consumer Research* 14 (September 1987): 257–63.

175. Søren Askegaard, 'Livsstilsundersøgelser: henimod et teoretisk fundament', doctoral dissertation, School of Business and Economics: Odense University, 1993.

176. For information about international lifestyle segmentation approaches in the US, e.g. the psychographic segmentation typology VALS2™ and its associated lifestyle analyses go to http://www.strategicbusinessinsights.com/vals/ and www.strategicbusinessinsights.com/vals/presurvey.shtml, accessed 6 April 2012.

177. Internal document, RISC.

178. Bernard Cathelat, *Socio-Styles-Système* (Paris: Editions D'Organisation, 1990).

179. Askegaard, 'Livsstilsundersøgelser: henimod et teoretisk fundament', *op. cit.*: 67–77.

180. Valette-Florence, *Les styles de vie*, *op. cit.*

181. Askegaard, 'Livsstilsundersøgelser: henimod et teoretisk fundament', *op. cit.*

182. George Christodoulides, Nina Michaelidou and Nikoletta-Theofania Siamagka 'Segmenting Internet Users Using Emotions' in Alan Bradshaw, Chris Hackley and Pauline Maclaran (eds), *European Association for Consumer Research Conference* 2010 RHUL page p. 9.

183. 'Consumers Willing to Trade Off Privacy for Electronic Personalization', available from www.mediapost.com, accessed 23 January 2007.

184. Aaron O. Patrick, 'Microsoft Ad Push Is All about You: "Behavioral Targeting" Aims to Use Customer Preferences to Hone Marketing Pitches', *Wall Street Journal* (26 December 2006): B3; Brian Steinberg, 'Next Up on Fox: Ads That Can Change Pitch', *Wall Street Journal* (21 April 2005): B1; Bob Tedeschi, 'Every Click You Make, They'll Be Watching You', *New York Times Online* (3 April 2006); David Kesmodel, 'Marketers Push Online Ads Based on Your Surfing Habits', *Wall Street Journal on the Web* (5 April 2005).

185. Associated Press, 'MySpace Launches Targeted Ad Program', *New York Times Online* (18 September 2007), accessed 18 September 2007; Vauhini Vara, 'Facebook Gets Personal with Ad Targeting Plan', *Wall Street Journal* (23 August 2007): B1.

186. Russell W. Belk, 'The Role of Possessions in Constructing and Maintaining a Sense of Past', in Marvin E. Goldberg, Gerald Gorn and Richard W. Pollay (eds), *Advances in Consumer Research 17* (Provo, UT: Association for Consumer Research, 1989): 669–76.

187. David E. Sanger, 'For a Job Well Done, Japanese Enshrine the Chip', *New York Times* (11 December 1990): A4.

188. Jacob Jacoby, Carol K. Berning and Thomas F. Dietvorst, 'What about Disposition?' *Journal of Marketing* 41 (April 1977): 22–28.

189. Brian Wansink, S. Adam Brasel and Steven Amjad, 'The Mystery of the Cabinet Castaway: Why We Buy Products We Never Use', *Journal of Family & Consumer Sciences* 92, no. 1 (2000): 104–7.

190. Jennifer Lach, 'Welcome to the Hoard Fest', *American Demographics* (April 2000): 8–9.

191. Katherine White, Rhiannon MacDonnell and Darren Dahl, 'It's the Mindset that Matters: The Role of Construal Level and Message Framing in Influencing Consumer Conservation Behaviors' in Alan Bradshaw, Chris Hackley and Pauline Maclaran (eds), *European Association for Consumer Research Conference* 2010 RHUL p. 15.

192. Jan Brace-Govan and Elizabeth Parsons, 'Reduce, Re-use, Recycle Practice Theory' in Alan Bradshaw, Chris Hackley and Pauline Maclaran (eds), *European Association for Consumer Research Conference* 2010 RHUL page p. 7.

193. Mike Tharp, 'Tchaikovsky and toilet paper', *U.S. News and World Report* (December 1987): 62; B. Van Voorst, 'The recycling bottleneck', *Time* (14 September 1992): 52–4; Richard P. Bagozzi and Pratibha A. Dabholkar, 'Consumer recycling goals and their effect on decisions to recycle: A means–end chain analysis,' *Psychology and Marketing* 11 (July/August 1994): 313–40.

194. 'Finally, something at McDonald's you can actually eat', *UTNE Reader* (May/June 1997): 12.

195. Debra J. Dahab, James W. Gentry and Wanru Su, 'New Ways to Reach Non-Recyclers: An Extension of the Model of Reasoned Action to Recycling Behaviors', in *Advances in Consumer Research* Volume 22, Frank R. Kardes and Mita Sujan (eds), Provo, UT: Association for Consumer Research, 251–256.

196. Richard P. Bagozzi and Pratibha A. Dabholkar, 'Consumer Recycling Goals and Their Effect on Decisions to Recycle', *Psychology & Marketing* 11, no. 4 (1994): 313–40; see also L.J. Shrum, Tina M. Lowrey and John A. McCarty, 'Recycling as a Marketing Problem: A Framework for Strategy Development', *Psychology & Marketing* 11 (July–August 1994): 393–416; Dahab, Gentry and Su, 'New Ways to Reach Non-Recyclers'.

197. 'Gap Asks Consumers to Recycle Their Jeans', *RetailingToday.com* (5 October 2010), http://www.retailingtoday.com/ article/gap-asks-consumers-recycle-their-jeans, accessed 18 April 2011.

198. http://www.look.co.uk/fashion/get-a-%C2%A35-ms-voucher-when-you-donate-to-oxfam, accessed 13 February 2012.

199. Barbara Phillips and Trina Sego 'The Role of Identity in Disposal: Lessons from Mothers' Disposal of Children's Products' in Alan Bradshaw, Chris Hackley and Pauline Maclaran (eds), *European Association for Consumer Research Conference* 2010 RHUL, 67.

200. John F. Sherry Jr, 'A socio-cultural analysis of a Midwestern American flea market', *Journal of Consumer Research* 17 (June 1990): 13–30.

201. John Sutherland, 'The price of nostalgia', *Guardian G2*, 28 March 2005: 5 (http://www.guardian.co.uk/g2/story/ 0,,1446610,00.html).

202. www.redo.org, accessed 4 June 2011.

203. Saul Hansell, 'Meg Whitman and eBay, net survivors', *The New York Times on the Web*, 5 May 2002.

204. Jess Cartner-Morley, 'In search of the real deal', *The Guardian*, 2 July 2008, http://www.guardian.co.uk/technology/ 2008/jul/02/ebay.consumeraffairs, accessed 20 August 2008.

205. Quoted in Jenna Wortham, 'Neighborly Borrowing, Over the Online Fence', *New York Times* (28 August 2010), http://www.nytimes.com/2010/08/29/business/29ping. html?_r=1&scp=1&sq=collaborative%20consumption&st =cse, accessed 18 April 2011; www.snapgoods.com, accessed 4 June 2011; www.neighborgoods.com, accessed 4 June 2011; www.sharesomesugar.com, accessed 4 June 2011.

206. Quoted in Stephanie Stoughton, 'Unemployed Americans turn to e-Bay to make money', *The Boston Globe*, 16 October 2001.

207. http://freegan.info/?page_id=2, accessed 9 June 2009; Steven Kurutz, 'Not Buying It', *New York Times* (21 June 2007), www.nytimes.com, accessed 21 June 2007.

208. Rob Walker, 'Unconsumption', *New York Times Magazine* (7 January 2007): 19; Tina Kelley, 'Socks? With Holes? I'll Take It', *New York Times on the Web*, 16 March 2004.

209. Zeynep Arsel and Susan Dobscha, 'Local Acts, Global Impacts? Examining the Pro-Social, Non-Reciprocal Nature of Freecyclers' in Alan Bradshaw, Chris Hackley and Pauline Maclaran (eds), *European Association for Consumer Research Conference* 2010 RHUL, 11–12.

210. John L. Lastovicka and Karen V. Fernandez, 'Three paths to disposition: The movement of meaningful possessions to strangers', *Journal of Consumer Research* 31 (March 2005): 813–23.

Fertility in Europe: what's next?

INGEBORG ASTRID KLEPPE, Norwegian School of Economics, Bergen, Norway

Arguably one of the most important decisions in life is the decision about whether or not to have children; and if so, the number and the timing. Fertility decisions are of great interest to manufacturers, marketers, and politicians as it is key information in making predictions about future needs for goods and services in a population. You – the students of today on the threshold of adulthood (and of one of the key markers of adulthood, i.e. family life) – are the next generation who will make these decisions. The big question is: What choices will you make about family lifestyle?

The ability of individuals to 'decide freely and responsibly the number and spacing of one's children' has become a global consumer and citizen rights issue (World WGNRR – Women's Network for Reproductive Rights). These rights were made possible primarily by common access to effective contraceptives from the 1960s onwards – particularly in Europe and the USA (Frejka and Sobotka, 2008). As a consequence of the ability to choose whether or not to have children, fertility has become a strategic consumption and lifestyle decision, which has long-term implications for the individual consumer, for the household, and for society in general (Bagozzi and Van Loo, 1978).

Evidence from fertility research suggests that firstly, the long-term commitment, and secondly, the irreversibility of becoming a parent, are strong incentives to postpone or opt out of parenthood (Kohler, Billari and Ortega, 2002). There are two current trends in the patterns of fertility in Europe that reflect this: (1) a trend towards delayed fertility that is universal across Europe and (2) a trend towards a north–south gap in the level of fertility (Frejka and Sobotka, 2008). Women in Europe now enter motherhood at an average age of around 29 years old, compared to the age of 25 years old in the early 1970s. In Italy and Spain women over 30 years old represent almost 60 per cent of the overall total national fertility pattern (Frejka and Sobotka, 2008). The rationale behind the postponement of the decision to have children can be linked to the desire to reduce the uncertainties associated with the costs of bringing up children, household economy, and relationships in early adulthood (Kohler, Billari and Ortega 2002, p. 652). Moreover, improved fertility health technology has also given consumers greater flexibility in the timing of

parenthood, and this has probably also been reinforced by an emerging popular cultural narrative that includes representations of first-time mothers in their forties. A Google search on 'pregnancy after 40' produces millions of hits.

Since the 1970s all European countries have had fertility rates below the average number of children each woman would be required to have for a population to replace itself in the long term, without migration. The fertility replacement rate is 2.1. However, there are some interesting differences between countries that are worth mentioning. Since the 1970s we have seen the development of a geographical map of 'higher' and 'lower' fertility regions in Europe. Countries in the 'higher' fertility regions of Western and Northern Europe (such as Belgium, France, Ireland, Luxemburg, the Netherlands, UK, Denmark, Finland, Iceland, Norway and Sweden) have maintained a stable fertility rate of about 1.8 since the 1970s. Some countries in this 'higher' region even have rates at or above population replacement – e.g. Ireland 2.22; Norway, 2.07; France 2.02 (Frejka and Sobotka, 2008). In contrast, all the other countries of Europe (including the German-speaking countries: Austria, Germany and Switzerland; Central Eastern countries and Southern European countries) have had low fertility rates, ranging between 1.2 and 1.5. Italy and Spain are two cases in point. In the mid-1970s both countries had the highest fertility rates (around 2.8) in Europe. Twenty years later in 1996 the fertility rates in both Italy and Spain had fallen to the lowest in Europe – well below the replacement rate at a level of around 1.2. In spite of a small recovery in these fertility rates, Southern European countries are still in the lowest-to-low fertility category (Frejka and Sobotka, 2008).

Low fertility rates reflect two types of fertility decisions: firstly, women or couples who opt out of parenthood altogether; and secondly, those who choose to have only one child. The latter option is also associated with late parenthood. Spanish and Swiss women are the oldest first-time mothers in Europe with a mean age of around 30 years (Frejka and Sobotka, 2008, p. 20).

There are various explanations for these new regional differences in fertility such as: differences in the character of the family and gender equality; differences in welfare state regimes; differences in family policies; and cultural differences (Ahn and Mira, 2002; Kohler *et al.* 2002; Zuanna, 2001). The falling rates of fertility in the 1970s are often attributed to the women's liberation movement and women's entry into the labour force. However, this explanation is not supported by the fact that the countries with the highest female labour force participation also have the highest fertility rates (Rønsen, 2004). Another explanation is that the lack of family orientation and values reduces interest in having children. If we take Italy, for example, research suggests that strong family values interact with socio-political conditions to reduce fertility. Italian 'familism' means families prefer to have their children stay at home longer since they do not want their children to experience low incomes and expensive housing on their own. Needless to say, staying at home has a negative impact on the desire and capacity to start a family of procreation (Zuanna, 2001). In Spain research suggests that several socio-political and historical circumstances work in concert (opposition to the Church, high unemployment, inflation, high public depth, and women's liberation) to explain low fertility rates. These examples demonstrate that there is probably no one single factor or simple explanation for people's fertility choices.

There is also a qualitative perspective on the behaviour of specific age cohorts. Ryder (1965) suggests that each age cohort constitute their own brand as they have been exposed to the same socio-historic events at the same time in their lives. Hence they will be formed and influenced in certain ways that are unique to their age. This is evidenced by certain behaviours as they make their way through social institutions such as the family; working life; politics; cultural institutions; and society at large. Some cohorts are named after time époques that brand their values, attitudes and behaviour. The beatnik generation and the hippie generation of the 1950s and 60s, for example, associate these age cohorts with opposition towards and actions against established authority and their parents' norms for relationships and sexuality. At the same time the hippies were part of the huge growth in higher and university education. Both their attitudinal opposition to their parents and to social institutions (like the family) and their educational levels set them apart from their parents and may explain the low fertility rates from the 1970s and onwards.

Young people of today have been assigned their own brand label based on the massive social changes enabled by technologies such as the www, smartphones, YouTube, Facebook and social media in general (Jenkins, 2006). Labels such as the Internet generation, the Social media generation circulate in popular culture. The question is whether and how the new communication technology and the global participatory culture in social media will change people's outlook on life and influence lifestyle choices,

including decisions about whether or not to have children, and if so: how many and when. It is interesting to speculate about what individual choices lie behind these aggregate measures of fertility discussed above because in the end fertility decisions come down to the individual consumer, family and household; and to consider the implications for consumption and the marketplace.

EXERCISES

1 Form groups (4–6) of students from countries representing regions with higher and lower rates of fertility. As preparation each student should prepare:
  (a) a list of factors that she/he thinks were important for her/his parents' fertility choices,
  (b) a list of issues that she/he thinks will be important to her/him in thinking about whether or not to start a family and have children,
  (c) a list of reflections on how their parents' and also their own choices impact on consumer behaviour and marketing practices.

2 When the group meets the students should share the points on their lists, and then the group should:
  (a) discuss the differences and similarities which can be identified by various countries of origin and for each generation (their parents' and their own),
  (b) how these differences and similarities across countries and across generations impact on consumer behaviour, consumer markets and marketing practices.

3 If you were a market researcher commissioned to study fertility rates across Europe in order to identify markets for new products in such categories as maternity wear; baby clothing and products; technology products for the family – how and where would you start? And which markets would you recommend as having growth potential; and which markets would you suggest being more cautious about? (hint: for fertility figures try the OECD website: http://www.oecd.org/home/0,2987,en_2649_201185_1_1_1_1_1,00.html; OECD Society at a Glance publications: http://www.oecd.org/document/24/0,3746,en_2649_37419_2671576_1_1_1_37419,00.html; and Eurostat portal: http://epp.eurostat.ec.europa.eu/portal/page/portal/eurostat/home/; and Eurostat statistics: http://epp.eurostat.ec.europa.eu/portal/page/portal/statistics/themes

Sources

Ahn, Namkee and Pedro Mira (2001), 'Job bust, baby bust?: Evidence from Spain', *Journal of Population Economics*, vol. 14, 505–21.

Bagozzi, Richard P. and M. Frances Van Loo (1978), 'Fertility as Consumption: Theories from the Behavioral Sciences', *Journal of Consumer Research*, vol. 4 (March), 199–228.

Frejka, Tomas and Tomás Sobotka (2008), 'Fertility in Europe: Diverse, delayed and below replacement', *Demographic Research*, vol. 19, Article 3, 15–46.

Jenkins, Henry (2006), *Convergence Culture: Where Old and New Media Collide*, New York University Press, New York: USA.

Kohler, Hans-Peter, Fransesco C. Billari and José Antonio Ortega (2002), 'The Emergence of Lowest-Low Fertility in Europe During the 1990s', *Population and Development Review*, vol. 28 (4), December, 641–80.

Ryder, Norman B. (1965), 'The Cohort as a Concept in the Study of Social Change', *American Sociological Review*, vol. 30 (6), December, 843–61.

Rønsen, Marit (2004), 'Fertility and family policy in Norway – A reflection on trends and possible connections', *Demographic Research*, vol. 10, Article 10, 265–86.

Van De Kaa (1996), 'Anchored Narratives: The Story and Findings of Half a Century of Research into the Determinants of Fertility', *Population Studies*, vol. 50, 389–432.

WGNRR – Women's Network for Reproductive Rights – http://www.wgnrr.org/access-contraceptives

Zuanna, Gianpiero Dalla (2001), 'The banquet of Aeolus: A familistic interpretation of Italy's lowest low fertility', *Demographic Research*, vol. 4, Article 5, 133–162.

Being a real man about town: the challenge of the 'new masculinity'

JACOB ÖSTBERG, Stockholm University School of Fashion, Sweden

Stockholm, like most other reasonably large cities, has a rich nightlife. Also, like most other reasonably large cities, the people at the centre of the Stockholm nightlife circuit are convinced that the particular nightlife in the city is spectacular; more akin to Paris, London, New York or LA than other similarly sized cities such as, heaven forbid, Copenhagen. Especially, they are convinced that Stockholm has a unique sense of fashion and style that is surmounted by only the hippest of the hip. Be that as it may. What is given, however, is that the activities in and around the nightclubs in Stockholm are gaining a fair share of attention in both mainstream and specialized media. Not least various internet sites, with as many as 340,000 unique visitors per month (**www.stureplan.se**), are chronicling everyone's whereabouts on the nightclub circuit. Most notably they are publishing thousands of pictures every week where the lucky ones whose photo gets published are given a chance to show the world what an exquisite sense of style they have got. The chance to get your image displayed to thousands of viewers is, however, a double-edged sword. On the one hand you have a fantastic opportunity to make an impact, but on the other hand you only have a flash of a moment to make that impression. The challenge is to communicate *who you are* clearly and distinctly without overdoing it and becoming a parody. Needless to say, fervent image management activities are taking place in these places.

One group who finds this especially challenging is those people aspiring to be connected to the old elite in Sweden. Whether they are indeed old aristocrats is beside the point, the interesting issue is that there is a rather large group on the Stockholm nightclub scene that affiliate themselves with some sort of faux-aristocracy, claiming lineage to the old aristocratic families or, at least, being on a first name basis with the princesses or the prince of Sweden. The members of this group have traditionally been expressing their masculine identities through knowledge and practice of refined consumption, and have thus set themselves apart from the masses by being more stylish.

The last couple of years, however, it has been proposed that we see a *'new hegemonic masculinity'* (Patterson and Elliott, 2002), which includes a feminization of masculinity, and invites men from all social positions to partake in the carnival of consumption in ways previously reserved predominantly for female consumers (Schroeder and Zwick, 2004). Due to this change in mainstream masculinity, the traditional elite – who have long been concerned with appearances and are expressing their masculine identities through a knowledge and practice of refined consumption – is challenged in their roles as tastemakers *par excellence* (Osgerby, 2001). The advent of popular-culture outlets for new gender ideologies – such as the TV-show *Queer Eye for the Straight Guy*, self-help books such as *The Metrosexual Guide to Style*, not to mention the abundant availability of men's lifestyle magazines and, increasingly, blogs – make the cultural capital previously reserved for the higher social classes available to the masses. Consequently, the legacy of the traditional elite is challenged. The question is how young men from social groups that have historically paid particular attention to appearance respond to the popularization – and perhaps vulgarization – of their traditional consumption codes? What strategies are utilized by the traditional elite to strengthen their sense of masculinity in light of this new, allegedly feminized, consumption ethos?

Defenders of timeless stability: the retrosexuals

The first characteristic of the traditional elite's consumption is that they do not regard themselves as representing something new, or as following contemporary trends. Instead, they see themselves as defenders of stability and providing a timeless, classic (and classy) masculinity as an alternative to all the currently available fast-moving consumer fads. They are characterized more by conservatism and a willingness to uphold – what they perceive to be – traditional values, than the more rebellious traits usually upheld by similar youth constellations (cf. Hodkinson, 2002). Instead of manifesting their identity by rebelling against the parent generation, they act in a rebellious fashion by trying to resurrect conservative values of an imagined past. They are thus escaping the temporality of contemporary, faddish consumption, of which they would regard the new feminized masculine consumption as a prime example, by attaching themselves to a timeless ethos of style. In the online communities, references are made many times to how they – the traditional elite – do things with style, whereas others – particularly the new elite – lack the ability, both economically and culturally, to be stylish. One principal way for them to distinguish their consumption from that of the new elite is to frame the latter's consumption behaviours as overly conscious or even girlish; if one *really* has style, one rarely has to show it in the explicit way utilized by the new elite. One of the official tastemakers of the Stockholm nightclub scene, Roland-Philippe Krezschmar, fashion editor of the webpage '*Stureplan: La publication glamoreuse, superfashion et tres exclusif*' strongly suggests that when it comes to style, just buying a fancy outfit won't cut it, you need some depth and history in your closet, you need to be a 'retrosexual':

> It is not until you have 7 suits, 7 pairs of shoes and 21 shirts [. . .], that you can start experimenting with jeans, t-shirts, slacks, sneakers and jackets. You are smart, so you never go for fashion-fashion, but for the timeless classics. Call it preppy, call it carefree, call it retrosexual . . .

The oh-so-stylish Mr Krezschmar continues by drawing lines between those who have understood what style is and the others that are just anxiously following the lead of whoever is portrayed as the fashion guru of the day:

> . . . The retrosexual man, when it comes to appearance, is a man who is strategic, long-term, and smart. It's all about investing in one's lifelong success, not about day trading with one's appearance. It's about being confidently relaxed in oneself and not about being a fashion-poof who dances to Tom Ford's pipe. It's about Ralph Lauren but not Karl Lagerfeld, Adrian Brody but not Kevin Federline, Bernard Arnault but not Donald Trump. It's about men with class, finesse, and natural panache.

In this way, the traditional elite express that they do not *need* brands and fashion to show that they are stylish. Instead, this quality seems to be almost inherent in who they are. The crux of the matter is that the traditional elite wants to at least imagine that this comes naturally to them, while it might be hard for onlookers to know who is just posing and who was born that way. Despite their calls to stay true to the eternal codes of style rather than follow the whims of fashion, what is stylish at any given point of time is constantly changing. Distinguishing the exclusive classic style from the marketized version available to the masses is becoming increasingly hard. A few years ago, the Spanish company *Zara* introduced a new line of suits that catered to the stylish gentleman. One of the features was that the cuffs could be unbuttoned, traditionally a sign

that the jacket was made by a tailor. The elite used to wear one button unbuttoned to subtly signal to the likeminded that they were wearing an expensive jacket. On the *Zara* suits there was a little tag explaining this behaviour to the prospective buyers and thus giving away the secret code. When these codes are spread to the masses the elite has to adapt. The following quote, taken from a webpage catering to the ones more interested in classic style than fashion (**asuitablewardrobe.dynend.com**), illustrates how the elite has to vulgarize their old behaviours in order to stay one step ahead of the crowd:

> When struck by the urge to undo a jacket sleeve button, walk quickly to a large public men's room. Unbutton and roll up your sleeves and wash your hands. Then dry your hands and button the sleeves again. You'll demonstrate that your sleeve buttons work to many men without embarrassing yourself and after a few repetitions the urges will cease.

Connecting to a global elite

Another common denominator for what is deemed stylish, and thus a suitable blueprint for the construction of masculinity, is that it should be connected to what other, imagined, groups of similar consumers around the world are engaging in. In this way, the traditional elite tries to escape the spatial restrictions of their present consumption by attaching themselves to an imagined community of global cosmopolitans. By viewing these global soul mates as their points of reference rather than the upward-striving new elitists, or at least the ones posing as such, they manage to downplay the similarities between their respective consumption behaviours. Again, they have to walk a thin line to be able to show off in a manner that can easily be de-coded from a snapshot posted on a webpage, while not coming across as overtly conscious about appearing in a particular way. The trick is to frame others' behaviours as vulgar and one's own as sophisticated. One behaviour that has been used in such a manner lately is the spraying of champagne, an activity that perhaps could come across as always unsophisticated. But no, apparently it all depends on *how* you do it. If you spray it for effect, to get as much attention as possible, you are not getting it right, you have to adopt the right blasé attitude to make it look like it is just something that needs to be done. Again, the fashionable webpage *Stureplan* shows how it should be done by alluding to the really stylish people in faraway places with this description followed by a dozen pictures of people pouring champagne into the pool at the nightclub *Le Cave de Roy* in St Tropez: 'What do the real players look like in St Tropez, New York or Shanghai? Yes, you guessed it – like real men, not like overgrown teenagers.' How vulgar it is to ostentatiously *spray* champagne. You then come across as an attention-seeking teenager dying for the world to pay attention to you. To be stylish, in the right cosmopolitan manner, you should just turn the bottle upside-down and casually let the liquid glide from the (100 dollar-) bottle at its own pace.

QUESTIONS

1 Discuss the groups of consumers described in this case from the perspective of lifestyles?

2 What (if any) is the difference between style, as defined by the traditional elite, and fashion?

3 What challenges are there for companies trying to market to groups of consumers who strive to be elitists?

EXERCISE

The group of consumers described in this case is symbolically fighting over the right to define what should be deemed masculine and stylish. Try to come up with other examples of consumption domains where groups of consumers are fighting over the right to define what's hot and what's not.

Sources

Hodkinson, Paul (2002), *Goth: Identity, Style and Subculture*, Oxford and New York: Berg.

Osgerby, Bill (2001), *Playboys in Paradise: Masculinity, Youth and Leisure-style in Modern America*, Oxford and New York: Berg.

Patterson, Maurice and Elliott, Richard (2002), 'Negotiating Masculinities: Advertising and the Inversion of the Male Gaze', *Consumption, Markets and Culture*, 5 (3), 231–246.

Schroeder, Jonathan E. and Zwick, Detlev (2004), 'Mirrors of Masculinity: Representation and Identity in Advertising Images', *Consumption, Markets and Culture*, 7 (1), 21–52.

Greek women's desired and undesired selves, identity conflicts and consumption

KATERINA KARANIKA, University of Exeter, UK

Context

This case is a discussion vehicle for a number of issues around real, ideal and multiple selves and role identities, symbolic self-completion theory and the extended self. The case helps us to identify the motivational conflicts, dilemmas and challenges faced by consumers in their everyday lives, and it potentially provides a forum for discussing self-relevant consumption.

Introduction

Desired and undesired selves have been described as imagined selves (Markus and Nurius, 1986) and they can be either positive or negative. Consumers' different views of themselves can play a significant role in consumption. Products and services play an important role for consumers firstly, in helping them to *portray* a desired self-concept, e.g. fashionable, popular self (Belk, 1988; Levy, 1959; Solomon, 1983; Wright, Claiborne and Sirgy, 1992); and secondly, in helping them to avoid portraying undesired possible selves (Schouten, 1991; Patrick and MacInnis, 2002; Ahuvia, 2005) e.g. unpopular and unfashionable self. In addition, consumers can also decide to avoid products and services in order firstly, to *approach* a desired self (e.g. avoiding untrendy clothes with implicitly negative fashion messages in order to ensure that they come closer to approaching a desired fashionable self); and secondly, to *avoid* an undesired self-concept (e.g. avoiding untrendy clothes in order not to be associated with what they see as an undesired unfashionable self (Banister and Hogg, 2001; Wilk, 1997).

At the same time, consumers often experience identity conflicts (e.g. Thompson *et al.*, 1990; Thompson, 1996; Fournier, 1998; Ahuvia, 2005). Several dilemmas can colour consumers' consumption experiences such as 'looking feminine or feeling comfortable', 'being healthy or indulging myself'. Consumers who experience an identity conflict are faced with the dilemma of choosing between possible identities, which can involve both a desired and an undesired self (Karanika and Hogg, 2010). This case examines two Greek female consumers' stories regarding their experiences with their important possessions, products and consumption activities in relation to their desired and undesired selves; and the associated identity conflicts that these women were faced with.

Maria's story

Maria is 46 years old and lives with her husband, their daughter (aged 18) and son (aged 10). Maria works in a clerical position in a service company, but is considering taking early retirement. Her mothering identity is central for her and she says that she has no personal goals for herself as all her goals are entirely centred on her children; particularly in helping them with their studies. Maria particularly values two of her possessions (a necklace and her house) because she associates these with strong interpersonal ties and affiliation. The importance of affiliation and also of being a mother comes through clearly in Maria's discussion of her necklace. In line with the notion of the extended self (Belk, 1988), this necklace is a reflection of Maria's mothering identity. She says:

> If I lost this necklace I would die from a broken heart . . . I bought it when I gave birth to my daughter. I promised always to wear it. I've not taken it off for over eighteen years . . . not even on the beach, in the shower or when I sleep. I always wear it. I associate it with my daughter's birth; the happiest moment in my life. Although I hadn't realized before what it means to be a parent . . . I feel my daughter is like this necklace; she is part of me . . . it is this connection [. . .] Until I gave birth to my son, my entire world revolved around my daughter . . . I neglected myself. I was doing everything for her and if any time, energy and money were left over then I would do something for me . . . When she was born I was 28 years old. I had changed. I had got fatter, I stopped taking care of myself, wearing makeup and dressing up . . . I used to stay in, doing household tasks. I did not go out with friends for entertainment in order to take care of my daughter . . . Until my son was born I felt that my life was over. I was telling myself to only focus on and take care of my daughter, not to enjoy myself anymore . . . sometimes we have incorrect thoughts but we convince ourselves that that's how it should be done and we pressure ourselves; I escaped

from these feelings with the birth of my son. I was 36 years old when my son was born . . . I felt old. My behaviour and appearance were those of a woman of 46 not of a 36 year old woman . . . I had to stop being like I had been before and renew myself as if I didn't, people would think I was my son's grandmother and not his mother. I neglected myself for my daughter and I found myself for my son. The change is obvious. Everybody says I've changed; my dress style is more modern and my behaviour more energetic. I have a young son and I have to be young too and enjoy myself. The opposite shouldn't happen.

Maria feels that by cleaning and tidying the house, which is one of her major possessions, she takes care of her family; living up to her desired caring self. But by doing so she feels she neglects herself, putting up with her undesired self of 'not enjoying herself'. At times she enjoys self-grooming activities and going out with friends, but then feels that she is somehow neglecting her children. Other times she takes care of her children, and does various household tasks but then she feels she is not enjoying herself. Therefore, she experiences the need to compromise and has a love-and-hate relationship with her important possession, her house which she associates both with her desired self (caring mother; by doing household tasks) and with her undesired self (not enjoying herself; by doing household tasks). She says:

> I wanted to take care of my children. Thus, I neglected myself. If a friend asks me now to go out, I won't stop to think to stay in and do household tasks as in the past. Before I wasn't able to go out and enjoy myself if I didn't have the house perfectly clean and tidy [. . .] When I am retired then I will do things for me (going out with friends, shopping, reading), that is I will enjoy myself but not at the expense of others, without neglecting the others . . . I will be calmer and more satisfied. Sometimes now when I enjoy myself I feel I neglect the others. I feel I do something for myself but at the expense of the others.

Nancy's story

Nancy is 31 years old. She works in a museum and lives with her parents. She has been in a long distance relationship for over two years. She describes a lonely present because her friends and boyfriend live far away. Therefore, her undesired 'alone-lonely' self means that her mobile phone is a very important possession for her. She says:

> I don't want to be alone. This idea is what really scares me, stresses me out and panics me . . . I cannot think of myself without my mobile phone as it enables me to communicate with my friends and my partner. Unluckily they are far away and I love and miss them so much. My mobile phone is communication for me.

Nancy's desire to stand out from the crowd positively and her desired self to be 'more knowledgeable than others' drove her desire for travelling because with travelling she felt she would 'learn and see more things than most people'. Following this desired self, Nancy feels satisfied with the kind and number of trips she has undertaken this year and the ones she has already planned because, as she said, 'lots of people aren't able to do these'. Nancy's concern to stand out from other people is also reflected in her relationship with her clothes and clothing accessories that she identified as important to her. She carefully chooses and buys her clothing items, being driven by two completely different undesired selves of hers: 'being and standing out as very different from others' and 'being and standing out as too similar to others'. She values her clothes and accessories for feeling they disable and represent separation from these two opposite undesired selves of hers, and for feeling they enable and represent her desired self of 'being and standing out as somewhat different from the mass'.

Nancy is pleased she has some economic independence and thus is sometimes able to allocate her time as she wishes and to go on trips 'without taking money from anyone' to quote her words. At the same time, she is dissatisfied with not being completely financially independent and with having to live with her parents for financial reasons. However, she saves money in order to be able to rent a house of her own and buy her own furniture in a few months' time. Her 'independent' desired self and her 'dependent' undesired self also make her car as one of her most important possessions. She says:

> I adore my car . . . it enables me to go anywhere I want; to annihilate the distances . . . I don't want to depend on others for transportation. I can choose the time of departure and place to go to. I can do everything. It gives me independence . . . Getting it fulfilled a fervent desire.

Security also emerges as significant for Nancy in her discussion of her car. One desired self for Nancy is being 'safe-secure-protected' and she values her car also because of the sense of security that her car offers her, reflecting that possessions are often valued due to the sense of security that derives from them (Wallendorf and Arnould, 1988). She says:

> I adore my car. I gave it a name. It is a boy to protect me. It suits it to be a boy. It is a car I can depend on, for a trip. I went on a trip with a friend who has the same model of car and it performed really well. Yaris is a very credible car. My father trusts Japanese cars and he has passed this view on to me. I wanted a car that would make me feel safe and this one does.

Nancy anthropomorphized her car (i.e. she projected human traits onto an inanimate object) feeling that her car enables her desired self ('*safe-secure-protected*'). Note also the role of important others (in Nancy's case, her father) in influencing values, purchasing decisions and consumption experiences.

257

QUESTIONS

1 Choose a product, an object or a consumption activity that is important to you and about which you feel a special fondness.

   (a) Write a brief description of that product or object or consumption activity.

   (b) Compose a short story explaining why or how you came to feel special affection for the product or object or consumption activity.

   (c) Provide a brief self-description in terms of your age, gender, ethnic group, family form, socio-economic status (as you perceive yourself or family), country of origin, and any other information that you consider relevant to your liking for the product or object or activity of interest.

   (d) In small groups, share your personal stories. Try and identify the key themes that occurred in your statements.

   (e) From your comparison of everyone's stories, develop a set of themes (with evidence) that your group thinks characterise the phenomenon of self-relevant consumption.

   (f) Share your analysis of the themes from your story with the whole class, in order to try and generate a collective view on self-relevant consumption.

2 Identify the themes that characterised Maria's, Nancy's and your classmates' desired and undesired selves (based on the case study that you have just read and your fellow students' stories of their meaningful possessions, products and consumption activities) (Tutors might want to give a hint about how best to get started with this task; e.g. what a matrix that maps themes to different aspects of the self (desired and undesired) might look like.)

3 Compare and contrast Maria's and Nancy's stories. What similarities are there? What differences? Who (if any) of the two women experience an identity conflict, Maria or Nancy? And how has she dealt with her identity conflict i.e. identify different strategies employed to deal with an identity conflict.

4 Can you think of a time when you have had an identity conflict? What did you do - i.e. how did you work through this conflict?
- Strategies employed?
- Purposeful or not?
- Why different strategies have been followed?

Sources

Ahuvia, A.C. (2005), 'Beyond the Extended Self: Loved Objects and Consumers' Identity Narratives', *Journal of Consumer Research*, 32, 171–184.

Banister, E.N. and Hogg, M.K. (2001), 'Mapping the Negative Self: From "So Not Me" . . . to "Just Not Me"', *Advances in Consumer Research*, vol. 28, 242–248.

Belk, R.W. (1988), 'Possessions and the Extended Self', *Journal of Consumer Research*, 15 (2), 139–68.

Fournier Susan (1998), 'Consumers and their brands: Developing relationship theory in consumer research', *Journal of Consumer Research*; 24, 4; p. 343.

Karanika, K. and Hogg, M.K. (2010), 'The interrelationship between desired and undesired selves and consumption: The case of Greek female consumers' experiences', special issue on multicultural perspectives in customer behaviour, *Journal of Marketing Management*, vol. 26, issue 11–12, 1091–1111.

Levy, S.J. (1959), 'Symbols for Sale', *Harvard Business Review*, no. 37, 4, 117.

Markus, H. and Nurius, P. (1986), 'Possible Selves', *American Psychologist*, 41, 9, 954.

Patrick, V.M. and MacInnis, D.J. (2002), 'Approaching What We Hope For and Avoiding What We Fear: The Role of Possible Selves in Consumer Behaviour', *Advances in Consumer Research*, vol. 29, 270–276.

Schouten, J. (1991), 'Selves in Transition: Symbolic Consumption in Personal Rites of Passage and Identity Reconstruction', *Journal of Consumer Research*, 17: 412.

Solomon, M.R. (1983), 'The Role of Products as Social Stimuli: A Symbolic Interactionism Perspective', *Journal of Consumer Research*, vol. 10, 319–329.

Thompson, C., Locander W. and Pollio, H. (1990), 'The Lived Meaning of Free Choice: An Existential-Phenomenological Description of Everyday Consumer Experiences of Contemporary Married Women', *Journal of Consumer Research*, 17: 346.

Thompson, C.J. (1996), 'Caring Consumers: Gendered Consumption Meanings and the Juggling Lifestyle', *Journal of Consumer Research*, vol. 22, 4, 388–407.

Wallendorf, M. and Arnould, E. (1988), 'My Favorite Things: A Cross-Cultural Inquiry into Object Attachment, Possessiveness and Social Linkage', *Journal of Consumer Research*, 14 (March), 531–547.

Wilk, R.R. (1997), 'A Critique of Desire: Distaste and Dislike in Consumer Behavior' *Consumption, Markets and Culture*, 1, 2, 175–196.

Wright, N.D., Claiborne, C.B. and Sirgy, M.J. (1992), 'The Effects of Product Symbolism on Consumer Self-Concept', *Advances in Consumer Research*, 19, 311.

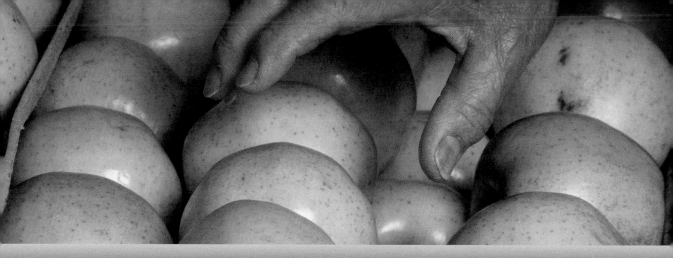

Part C

CONSUMERS AS DECISION-MAKERS

This part explores how individuals make choices and discusses many of the internal influences involved in the process of consumer decision-making. Chapter 7 considers how decisions are affected by what we have learnt and what we have remembered. Chapter 8 provides an overview of how attitudes are formed and changed; and also discusses how influences such as advertising affect our consumer choices and our predisposition to make certain consumption decisions. Chapter 9 focuses on the basic sequence of steps we undergo when making a decision.

7 LEARNING AND MEMORY

CHAPTER OBJECTIVES

When you finish reading this chapter you will understand why:

→ It is important to understand how consumers learn about products and services.

→ Conditioning results in learning.

→ Learned associations with brands generalize to other products, and why is this important to marketers.

→ There is a difference between classical and instrumental conditioning, and both processes help consumers to learn about products.

→ We learn about products by observing others' behaviour.

→ Our brains process information about brands to retain them in memory.

→ The other products we associate with an individual product influence how we will remember it.

→ Products help us to retrieve memories from our past.

MARIO ROSSI is a 60-year-old Italian insurance man, and still very active in his field. He is a pleasant, sociable and easy going fellow, and has made a very good career for himself. Together with his wife and four children, he lives in a comfortable flat in the suburbs of Rome. Although Rome is full of historical sites to visit, Mario is a staunch nature lover, and he prefers to 'get back to nature' in his free time.

Mario's dog, Raphael, recognizes the sound of his master's old Fiat drawing up outside as he arrives home late after work, and Raphael begins to get excited at the prospect of having his master back home. Mario's 'first love' was a Fiat 126, and in spite of his good income he keeps the old car running. Relaxing and sipping a glass of Chianti is just what he needs after a hard day's work. The pieces of furniture in his sitting room, and even his television set, are not the latest models, but he likes it that way – the old objects give him a sense of security. Slowly unwinding, he looks forward to spending the weekend with his family and friends at his house in the countryside. He grew up there, and is very attached to the old villa and everything in it.

He often imagines what it will be like when he retires, when he will be able to live there permanently, surrounded by his family. It will be like the good old days, when he was a boy and life was uncomplicated, less chaotic. He pictures them all sitting around the table enjoying a leisurely meal (with pasta, of course!) made from home-grown produce, and afterwards sitting together.

This peaceful fantasy is in stark contrast to the reality of last weekend. His two eldest sons had gone off to a football match. The youngest ones restlessly complained about the fact that there was still such a slow internet connection in the house, and then went into another room to settle down in front of the television for what they called an afternoon's entertainment!

GABRIELE MORELLO, GMA-Gabriele Morello and Associates, Palermo, Italy

INTRODUCTION

Learning refers to a relatively permanent change in behaviour which comes with experience. This experience does not have to affect the learner directly: we can learn vicariously by observing events that affect others.[1] We also learn even when we are not trying to do so. Consumers, for example, recognize many brand names and can hum many product jingles, even for those product categories they themselves do not use. This casual, unintentional acquisition of knowledge is known as *incidental learning*. Like the concept of perception discussed in an earlier chapter, learning is an ongoing process. Our knowledge about the world is constantly being revised as we are exposed to new stimuli and receive feedback that allows us to modify behaviour in other, similar situations. The concept of learning covers a lot of ground, ranging from a consumer's simple association between a stimulus such as a product logo (such as Coca-Cola) and a response (e.g. 'refreshing soft drink') to a complex series of cognitive activities (like writing an essay on learning for a consumer behaviour exam). Psychologists who study learning have advanced several theories to explain the learning process. These range from those focusing on simple stimulus–response associations to perspectives that regard consumers as complex problem-solvers who learn abstract rules and concepts by observing others. Understanding these theories is important to marketers as well, because basic learning principles are at the heart of many consumer purchase decisions. In this chapter we will explore how learned associations among feelings, events and products – and the memories they evoke – are an important aspect of consumer behaviour.

BEHAVIOURAL LEARNING THEORIES

Behavioural learning theories assume that learning takes place as the result of responses to external events. Psychologists who subscribe to this viewpoint do not focus on internal thought processes. Instead, they approach the mind as a 'black box' and emphasize the observable aspects of behaviour, as depicted in Figure 7.1. The observable aspects consist of

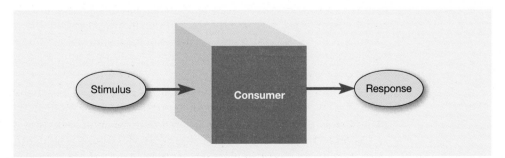

Figure 7.1 The consumer as a 'black box': a behaviourist perspective on learning

things that go into the box (the stimuli, or events perceived from the outside world) and things that come out of the box (the responses, or reactions to these stimuli).

This view is represented by two major approaches to learning: classical conditioning and instrumental conditioning. People's experiences are shaped by the feedback they receive as they go through life. Similarly, consumers respond to brand names, scents, jingles and other marketing stimuli based on the learned connections they have formed over time. People also learn that actions they take result in rewards and punishments, and this feedback influences the way they respond in similar situations in the future. Consumers who are complimented on a product choice will be more likely to buy that brand again, while those who get food poisoning at a new restaurant will not be likely to patronize it in the future.

MARKETING OPPORTUNITY

Popcorn, and perhaps body odour, are the scents usually associated with a trip to the movies. But in a European cinema, you might just smell bread, chocolate or whatever else an advertiser wants you to.

A company called Cinescent is giving marketers the chance to pump out the scent of their brands in German theatres, where it first tested the technology for Beiersdorf's Nivea. For the test, a specially made 60-second spot showed a typical sunny beach scene, with people lying around on deck chairs or sunbathing on towels while waves crashed and seagulls cried in the background. As people wondered what the ad was for, the scent of Nivea sun cream permeated the cinema, and a Nivea logo appeared on screen along with the words, 'Nivea. The scent of summer'. The results were significant: cinema exit polls showed a 515 per cent rise in recall for the Nivea ad compared with moviegoers who saw the spot without the scent. The same ad, when combined with only a subliminal whiff of scent, scored a 25 per cent lift. Cinescent works by pumping smells through the cinema's air-conditioning system to distribute a scent that covers other odours without being overpowering. Using this method, much finer fragrance molecules reach the audience, minimizing the allergy and irritation problems encountered by previous attempts, when smells were dispensed via boxes located among the audience.

Mike Hope-Milne, enterprise director at Pearl & Dean, which sells cinema advertising, is so impressed by the German results that he is bringing the technology to the UK. 'We are talking to a handful of clients, including sun cream, bread, coffee, perfume, air fresheners and chocolate manufacturers. It is most cost-effective when working with scent-based products that have the scent oils already to hand,' he said.

One of the advertisers lined up is a car manufacturer that wants to promote its Cabriolet version by evoking the smell of fresh country air and newly cut grass. The argument is that scents provide a dynamic psychological and emotional trigger that can be invaluable to brands.

Mr Hope-Milne is also hoping to drum up new business with the technology, noting that three of the companies he's talking to have never advertised in cinemas before. 'It's encouraging people to reappraise the medium,' he said. The Cinescent idea works best, he said, when advertising a product that appeals to a broad audience. 'Perfume is probably a bit of a risk and is better off using sampling.'[2]

Classical conditioning

Classical conditioning occurs when a stimulus that elicits a response is paired with another stimulus that initially does not elicit a response on its own. Over time, this second stimulus causes a similar response because it is associated with the first stimulus. This phenomenon was first demonstrated in dogs by Ivan Pavlov, a Russian physiologist doing research on digestion in animals.

Pavlov induced classically conditioned learning by pairing a neutral stimulus (a bell) with a stimulus known to cause a salivation response in dogs (he squirted dried meat powder into their mouths). The powder was an unconditioned stimulus (UCS) because it was naturally capable of causing the response. Over time, the bell became a conditioned stimulus (CS): it did not initially cause salivation, but the dogs learned to associate the bell with the meat powder and began to salivate at the sound of the bell only. The drooling of these canine consumers over a sound, now linked to feeding time, was a conditioned response (CR), just as Mario's dog Raphael begins to get excited hearing his master's Fiat 126 coming close to home.

This basic form of classical conditioning primarily applies to responses controlled by the autonomic (e.g. salivation) and nervous (e.g. eye blink) systems. That is, it focuses on visual and olfactory cues that induce hunger, thirst or sexual arousal. When these cues are consistently paired with conditioned stimuli, such as brand names, consumers may learn to feel hungry, thirsty or aroused when later exposed to the brand cues.

Classical conditioning can have similar effects for more complex reactions, too. Even a credit card becomes a conditioned cue that triggers greater spending, especially since it is a stimulus that is present only in situations where consumers are spending money. People learn that they can make larger purchases when using credit cards, and they also have been found to leave larger tips than they do when using cash.[3] Small wonder that American Express reminds us, 'Don't leave home without it.' Conditioning effects are more likely to occur after the conditioned and unconditioned stimuli have been paired a number of times.[4] Repeated exposures increase the strength of stimulus–response associations and prevent the decay of these associations in memory.

Conditioning will not occur or will take longer if the CS is only occasionally presented with the UCS. One result of this lack of association may be **extinction**, which occurs when the effects of prior conditioning are reduced and finally disappear. This can occur, for example, when a product is overexposed in the marketplace so that its original allure is lost. Some research indicates that the intervals between exposures may influence the effectiveness of this strategy as well as the type of medium the marketer uses; the most effective repetition strategy is a combination of spaced exposures that alternate in terms of media that are more and less involving, such as television advertising complemented by print media.[5]

Stimulus generalization refers to the tendency of stimuli similar to a CS to evoke similar, conditioned responses.[6] Pavlov noticed in subsequent studies that his dogs would sometimes salivate when they heard noises that only resembled a bell (e.g. keys jangling). People react to other, similar stimuli in much the same way that they responded to an original stimulus.

Positive reinforcement occurs after consumers try a new product and like it.
Frito-Lay North America, Inc.

A chemist shop's bottle of own-brand mouthwash deliberately packaged to resemble Listerine mouthwash may evoke a similar response among consumers who assume that this 'me-too' product shares other characteristics of the original. These 'lookalikes' tactics work, and companies have targeted well-known brands ranging from Unilever's Blue Band margarine, and Calvé peanut butter, to Hermès scarves. Similar colours, shapes and designs are all stimuli which consumers organize and interpret, and up to a point, these tactics are perfectly legal.[7]

Stimulus discrimination occurs when a stimulus similar to a CS is not followed by a UCS. In these situations, reactions are weakened and will soon disappear. Part of the learning process involves making a response to some stimuli but not to other, similar stimuli. Manufacturers of well-established brands commonly urge consumers not to buy 'cheap imitations' because the results will not be what they expect.

Operant conditioning

Operant conditioning, also known as instrumental conditioning, occurs as the individual learns to perform behaviours that produce positive outcomes and to avoid those that yield negative outcomes. This learning process is most closely associated with the psychologist B.F. Skinner, who demonstrated the effects of instrumental conditioning by teaching animals to dance, pigeons to play ping-pong, and so on, by systematically rewarding them for desired behaviours.[8]

While responses in classical conditioning are involuntary and fairly simple, those in instrumental conditioning are made deliberately to obtain a goal and may be more complex. The desired behaviour may be learned over a period of time, as intermediate actions are rewarded in a process called *shaping*. For example, the owner of a new shop may award prizes to shoppers just for coming in, hoping that over time they will continue to drop in and eventually buy something.

Also, classical conditioning involves the close pairing of two stimuli. Instrumental learning occurs as a result of a reward received following the desired behaviour and takes place over a period in which a variety of other behaviours are attempted and abandoned because they are not reinforced. A good way to remember the difference is to keep in mind that in instrumental learning the response is performed because it is instrumental to gaining a reward or avoiding a punishment. Consumers over time come to associate with people who reward them and to choose products that make them feel good or satisfy some need.

Operant conditioning (instrumental learning) occurs in one of three ways. When the environment provides **positive reinforcement** in the form of a reward, the response is strengthened, and appropriate behaviour is learned. For example, a woman who is complimented after wearing Obsession perfume will learn that using this product has the desired effect, and she will be more likely to keep buying the product. **Negative reinforcement** also strengthens responses so that appropriate behaviour is learned. A perfume company, for example, might run an ad showing a woman sitting alone on a Saturday night because she did not use its fragrance. The message to be conveyed is that she could have avoided this negative outcome if only she had used the perfume. In contrast to situations where we learn to do certain things in order to avoid unpleasantness, **punishment** occurs when a response is followed by unpleasant events (such as being ridiculed by friends for wearing an offensive-smelling perfume). We learn not to repeat these behaviours.

When trying to understand the differences between these mechanisms, keep in mind that reactions from a person's environment to behaviour can be either positive or negative and that these outcomes or anticipated outcomes can be applied or removed. That is, under conditions of both positive reinforcement and punishment, the person receives a reaction after doing something. In contrast, negative reinforcement occurs when a negative outcome is avoided: the removal of something negative is pleasurable and hence is rewarding. Finally, when a positive outcome is no longer received, extinction is likely to occur, and the learned

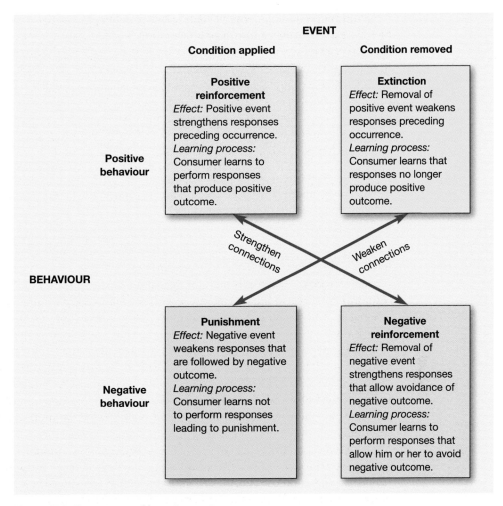

Figure 7.2 Four types of learning outcome

stimulus–response connection will not be maintained (as when a woman no longer receives compliments on her perfume). Thus, positive and negative reinforcement strengthen the future linkage between a response and an outcome because of the pleasant experience. This tie is weakened under conditions of both punishment and extinction because of the unpleasant experience. The relationships among these four conditions are easier to understand by referring to Figure 7.2.

An important factor in operant conditioning is the set of rules by which appropriate reinforcements are given for a behaviour. The issue of what is the most effective reinforcement schedule to use is important to marketers, because it relates to the amount of effort and resources they must devote to rewarding consumers in order to condition desired behaviours.

- *Fixed-interval reinforcement.* After a specified period has passed, the first response that is made brings the reward. Under such conditions, people tend to respond slowly immediately after being reinforced, but their responses speed up as the time for the next reinforcement approaches. For example, consumers may crowd into a store for the last day of its seasonal sale and not reappear again until the next one.

- *Variable-interval reinforcement.* The time that must pass before reinforcement is delivered varies around some average. Since the person does not know exactly when to expect the reinforcement, responses must be performed at a consistent rate. This logic is behind retailers' use of so-called secret shoppers – people who periodically test for service quality by posing as customers at unannounced times. Since store employees never know exactly when to expect a visit, high quality must be constantly maintained.

● *Fixed-ratio reinforcement.* Reinforcement occurs only after a fixed number of responses. This schedule motivates people to continue performing the same behaviour over and over again. For example, a consumer might keep buying groceries at the same store in order to earn a gift after collecting 50 books of trading stamps.

● *Variable-ratio reinforcement.* The person is reinforced after a certain number of responses, but they do not know how many responses are required. People in such situations tend to respond at very high and steady rates, and this type of behaviour is very difficult to extinguish. This reinforcement schedule is responsible for consumers' attraction to slot machines. They learn that if they keep feeding money into the machine, they will eventually win something (if they don't go broke first).

Cognitive learning theory

Cognitive learning occurs as a result of mental processes. In contrast to behavioural theories of learning, cognitive learning theory stresses the importance of internal mental processes. This perspective views people as problem-solvers who actively use information from the world around them to master their environment. Supporters of this viewpoint also stress the role of creativity and insight during the learning process.

The issue of consciousness

A lot of controversy surrounds the issue of whether or when people are aware of their learning processes. While behavioural learning theorists emphasize the routine, automatic nature of conditioning, proponents of cognitive learning argue that even these simple effects are based on cognitive factors: that is, expectations are created that a stimulus will be followed by a response (the formation of expectations requires mental activity). According to this school of thought, conditioning occurs because subjects develop conscious hypotheses and then act on them.

There is some evidence for the existence of non-conscious procedural knowledge. People apparently do process at least some information in an automatic, passive way, which is a condition that has been termed mindlessness.[9] When we meet someone new or encounter a new product, for example, we have a tendency to respond to the stimulus in terms of existing categories, rather than taking the trouble to formulate different ones. Our reactions are activated by a trigger feature, some stimulus that cues us towards a particular pattern. For example, men in one study rated a car in an ad as superior on a variety of characteristics if a seductive woman (the trigger feature) was present in the ad, despite the fact that the men did not believe the woman's presence actually had an influence.[10] A recent study which reviewed the literature on knowledge (a meta-analysis) took the approach of looking at what consumers' know, versus what they think they know. Results suggest that we are better at having objective knowledge about products (as opposed to services), and that we have a stronger sense of subjective knowledge (what we think we know) when the information comes to us from an expert in the product category.[11] Ultimately, our ability to retrieve information comes from our actual knowledge, as well as from what we think we know. A recent study also suggests that our subjective knowledge about the 'fairness' of how the product was manufactured (ethical, humane working conditions) influences how we evaluate brands.[12]

Nonetheless, many modern theorists are beginning to regard some instances of conditioning as cognitive processes, especially where expectations are formed about the linkages between stimuli and responses. Indeed, studies using masking effects, in which it is difficult for subjects to learn CS/UCS associations, show substantial reductions in conditioning.[13] For example,

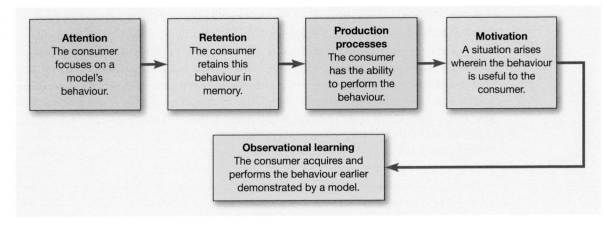

Figure 7.3 Components of observational learning

an adolescent girl may observe that women on television and in real life seem to be rewarded with compliments and attention when they smell nice and wear alluring clothing. She works out that the probability of these rewards occurring is greater when she wears perfume and deliberately wears a popular scent to obtain the pay-off of social acceptance.

Observational learning

Observational learning occurs when people watch the actions of others and note the reinforcements they receive for their behaviours. This type of learning is a complex process: people store these observations in memory as they accumulate knowledge, perhaps using this information at a later point to guide their own behaviours. This process of imitating the behaviour of others is called modelling. For example, a woman shopping for a new kind of perfume may remember the reactions a friend received when wearing a certain brand several months earlier, and she will base her behaviour on her friend's actions. In order for observational learning in the form of modelling to occur, four conditions must be met (see Figure 7.3).[14]

1 The consumer's attention must be directed to the appropriate model who, for reasons of attractiveness, competence, status or similarity, it is desirable to emulate.

2 The consumer must remember what is said or done by the model.

3 The consumer must convert this information into actions.

4 The consumer must be motivated to perform these actions.

MARKETING APPLICATIONS OF LEARNING PRINCIPLES

Understanding how consumers learn is very important to marketers. After all, many strategic decisions are based on the assumption that consumers are continually accumulating information about products and that people can be 'taught' to prefer some alternatives over others.

Behavioural learning applications

Many marketing strategies focus on the establishment of associations between stimuli and responses. Behavioural learning principles apply to many consumer phenomena, ranging from the creation of a distinctive brand image to the perceived linkage between a product and an underlying need.

How marketers take advantage of classical conditioning principles

The transfer of meaning from an unconditioned stimulus to a conditioned stimulus explains why 'made-up' brand names like Marlboro, Coca-Cola or IBM can exert such powerful effects on consumers. The association between the Marlboro Man and the cigarette is so strong that in some cases the company no longer even includes the brand name in its ad. When nonsense syllables (meaningless sets of letters) are paired with such evaluative words as beauty or success, the meaning is transferred to the nonsense syllables. This change in the symbolic significance of initially meaningless words shows that complex meanings can be conditioned. Recent studies have shown that attitudes formed through classical conditioning are enduring.[15]

These conditioned associations are crucial to many marketing strategies that rely on the creation and perpetuation of positive **brand equity**, in which a brand has strong positive associations in a consumer's memory and commands a lot of loyalty as a result.[16] As we will see in the next chapter, a product with brand equity holds a tremendous advantage in the marketplace.

Repetition One advertising researcher argues that more than three exposures are wasted. The first creates awareness of the product, the second demonstrates its relevance to the consumer, and the third serves as a reminder of the product's benefits.[17] However, even this bare-bones approach implies that repetition is needed to ensure that the consumer is actually exposed to (and processes) the ad at least three times. Marketers attempting to condition an association must ensure that the consumers they have targeted will be exposed to the stimulus a sufficient number of times.

On the other hand, it is possible to have too much of a good thing. Consumers can become so used to hearing or seeing a marketing stimulus that they cease to pay attention to it (see Chapter 4). This problem, known as advertising wear-out, can be reduced by varying the way in which the basic message is presented.

Conditioning product associations Advertisements often pair a product with a positive stimulus to create a desirable association. Various aspects of a marketing message, such as music, humour or imagery, can affect conditioning. In one study, subjects who viewed a photograph of pens paired with either pleasant or unpleasant music were more likely later to select the pen that appeared with pleasant music.[18]

Advertising often pairs a product with a positive stimulus (the attractive male model), or to a positive outcome (kind to his skin).
The Advertising Archives.

The order in which the conditioned stimulus and the unconditioned stimulus is presented can affect the likelihood that learning will occur. Generally speaking, the unconditioned stimulus should be presented prior to the conditioned stimulus. The technique of backward conditioning, such as showing a soft drink (the CS) and then playing a jingle (the UCS), is generally not effective.[19] Because sequential presentation is desirable for conditioning to occur, classical conditioning is not very effective in static situations, such as in magazine ads, where (in contrast to TV or radio) the marketer cannot control the order in which the CS and the UCS are perceived.

Just as product associations can be formed, so they can be extinguished. Because of the danger of extinction, a classical conditioning strategy may not be as effective for products that are frequently encountered, since there is no guarantee they will be accompanied by the CS. A bottle of Pepsi paired with the refreshing sound of a carbonated beverage being poured over ice may seem like a good example of conditioning. Unfortunately, the product would also be seen in many other contexts where this sound was absent, reducing the effectiveness of the conditioning.

By the same reasoning, a novel tune should be chosen over a popular one to pair with a product, since the popular song might also be heard in many situations in which the product is not present.[20] Music videos in particular may serve as effective UCSs because they often have an emotional impact on viewers and this effect may transfer to ads accompanying the video.[21]

Applications of stimulus generalization The process of stimulus generalization is often central to branding and packaging decisions that attempt to capitalize on consumers' positive associations with an existing brand or company name, as exemplified by a hairdressing establishment called United Hairlines.[22] In one 20-month period, Procter & Gamble introduced almost 90 new products. Not a single product carried a new brand name. In fact, roughly 80 per cent of all new products are actually extensions of existing brands or product lines.[23] Strategies based on stimulus generalization include the following:

- *Family branding*, in which a variety of products capitalize on the reputation of a company name. Companies such as Campbell's, Heinz, Philips and Sony rely on their positive corporate images to sell different product lines.

- *Product line extensions*, in which related products are added to an established brand. Dole, which is associated with fruit, was able to introduce refrigerated juices and juice bars, while Sun Maid went from raisins to raisin bread. Other recent extensions include Woolite rug cleaner, and the various models of Nike Air shoes.[24]

- *Licensing*, in which well-known names are 'rented' by others. This strategy is increasing in popularity as marketers try to link their products and services with well established figures. Companies as diverse as McDonald's, Disney, Vogue and Harley-Davidson have authorized the use of their names on products.

- Marketers are increasingly capitalizing on the public's enthusiasm for films[25] and popular TV programmes by developing numerous *product tie-ins*.

- *Lookalike packaging*, in which distinctive packaging designs create strong associations with a particular brand. This linkage is often exploited by makers of generic or private-label brands who wish to communicate a quality image by putting their products in very similar packages. As one chemist chain store executive commented, 'You want to tell the consumer that it's close to the national brand. You've got to make it look like, within the law, close to the national brand. They're at least attracted to the package.'[26]

Applications of stimulus discrimination An emphasis on communicating a product's distinctive attributes vis-à-vis its competitors is an important aspect of positioning, in which consumers learn to differentiate a brand from its competitors (see Chapter 4). This is not

Many marketing strategies focus on the establishment of associations between stimuli and responses. Associating products with the imagery of riding in a Toyota with one's comfortable, modern living room is one example of this stimulus–response application.

Toyota Singapore and Saatchi & Saatchi Ltd.

always an easy task, especially in product categories where the brand names of many of the alternatives look and sound alike. For example, one survey showed that many consumers have a great deal of trouble distinguishing between products sold by the top computer manufacturers. With a blur of names like OmniPlex, OptiPlex, Premmia, Premium, ProLinea, ProLiant, etc., this confusion is not surprising.[27]

Companies with a well-established brand image try to encourage stimulus discrimination by promoting the unique attributes of their brands: the constant reminders for American Express Travellers Cheques: 'Ask for them by name . . .' On the other hand, a brand name that is used so widely that it is no longer distinctive becomes part of the public domain and can be used by competitors, as has been the case for such products as aspirin, cellophane, yo-yos and escalators.

How marketers take advantage of instrumental conditioning principles

Principles of instrumental conditioning are at work when a consumer is rewarded or punished for a purchase decision. Business people shape behaviour by gradually reinforcing consumers for taking appropriate actions. For example, a car dealer might encourage a reluctant buyer to try sitting in a showroom model, then suggest a test drive, and so on.

Marketers have many ways of reinforcing consumers, ranging from a simple thank you after a purchase to substantial rebates and follow-up phone calls. For example, a life insurance company obtained a much higher rate of policy renewal among a group of new customers who received a thank you letter after each payment compared to a control group that did not receive any reinforcement.[28]

A popular technique known as **frequency marketing** reinforces regular purchasers by giving them prizes with values that increase along with the amount purchased. This operant learning strategy was pioneered by the airline industry, which introduced 'frequent-flyer' programmes in the early 1980s to reward loyal customers. Well over 20 per cent of food stores now offer trading stamps or some other frequent-buyer promotion. Manufacturers in the fast-moving consumer goods (FMCG) category also make use of this technique in food stores. For example, Douwe Egberts, the coffee manufacturer owned by Sara Lee, offers stamps which can be saved and redeemed for a whole range of coffee-related products such as espresso makers, service sets and coffee grinders, including their classic (and nostalgic) hand coffee grinder.

In some industries, these reinforcers take the form of clubs, including a Hilton Hotel Club. Club members usually earn bonus points to set against future purchases, and some get privileges such as magazines and free telephone numbers and sometimes even invitations to exclusive outings.

How marketers take advantage of cognitive learning principles

Consumers' ability to learn vicariously by observing how the behaviour of others is reinforced makes the lives of marketers much easier. Because people do not have to be directly reinforced for their actions, marketers do not necessarily have to reward or punish them for purchase behaviours. Instead, they can show what happens to desirable models who use or do not use their products and know that consumers will often be motivated to imitate these actions at a later time. For example, a perfume commercial may depict a woman surrounded by a throng of admirers who are providing her with positive reinforcement for using the product. Needless to say, this learning process is more practical than providing the same personal attention to each woman who actually buys the perfume!

Consumers' evaluations of models go beyond simple stimulus–response connections. For example, a celebrity's image is often more than a simple reflexive response of good or bad: it is a complex combination of many attributes.[29] In general, the degree to which a model will be emulated depends upon their social attractiveness. Attractiveness can be based upon several components, including physical appearance, expertise or similarity to the evaluator.

These factors will be addressed further in Chapter 8, which discusses personal characteristics that make a communication's source more or less effective in changing consumers' attitudes. In addition, many applications of consumer problem-solving are related to ways in which information is represented in memory and recalled at a later date. This aspect of cognitive learning is the focus of Part C.

PROFESSOR STIJN VAN OSSELAER
Rotterdam School of Management,
Erasmus University

Consumer behaviour as I see it . . .

Tie it to the brand

When consumers decide to buy products, they often base their decisions on what they have learned about those products. Thus, it is important to understand how people learn about products. My research has shown that a lot of the learning consumers do is based on relatively simple processes not unlike the ones we see in rats and pigeons. Luckily, more and more research suggests that rats and pigeons are not nearly as stupid as people sometimes think they are. It turns out that even very simple learning rules can lead to quite sophisticated behaviour. When they learn, it's almost as if rats and pigeons are performing regression analyses, for example.

With my co-authors Chris Janiszewski and Joseph Alba, I have documented how many of these rat-like learning processes play out when consumers learn about brands.* For example, when rats repeatedly encounter a light and a tone presented together followed by the appearance of food, they learn to anticipate the appearance of food as soon as the light and tone are presented (together). However, when after those *learning trials* the light →

→ or the tone is presented separately, there is only a weak anticipatory response. This is quite smart. It is almost as if the rats are doing some sophisticated reasoning about the cause of the food's appearance. Was it the light that caused the food to appear or the tone? Because light and tone were always presented together, you can't really know.

In our lab, we found that people do something similar with brands. If a marketer always presents the brand name together with information about a product characteristic such as an ingredient, the presence of the ingredient decreases learning of the connection between the brand and its benefits. For example, if you say that Calvé brand peanut butter tastes great because it has 97 per cent peanuts, people don't learn the relationship between the brand name (*Calvé*) and the benefit (*tastes great*) very well. Basically, the brand name (*Calvé*) is like the light, the ingredient (*97 per cent peanuts*) is like the tone, and the benefit (*tastes great*) is like the appearance of the food in the rat example. What happens is that instead of having all your brand equity in the brand name, your *locus of equity* shifts, in part, to the ingredient. That is, the brand equity is no longer mostly in the brand name itself, but in an ingredient. This is a problem if competitors can also claim the ingredient (e.g. if Aldi peanut butter also has 97 per cent peanuts) or if you want to introduce a new product (e.g. Calvé chocolate spread) that doesn't contain the ingredient. The bottom line is clear: you need to make sure people learn that the brand name (and not its ingredients) is the main predictor of the product's benefits. This can be done by focusing your advertising on the *brand* and what it does for consumers (e.g. provide a great taste) instead of focusing on ingredients.**

Stijn van Osselaer

*van Osselaer, Stijn M.J. (2008), 'Associative Learning and Consumer Decisions', in *Handbook of Consumer Psychology*, Curtis P. Haugtvedt, Paul M. Herr and Frank R. Kardes (eds), New York, Erlbaum: 699–729.
**See also: van Osselaer, Stijn M.J. and Chris Janiszewski, 'A Goal Based Model of Product Evaluation and Choice', *Journal of Consumer Research*, Vol. 39, (August 2012).

THE ROLE OF LEARNING IN MEMORY

Memory involves a process of acquiring information and storing it over time so that it will be available when needed. Contemporary approaches to the study of memory employ an information-processing approach. They assume that the mind is in some ways like a computer: data are input, processed and output for later use in revised form. In the **encoding** stage, information is entered in a way the system will recognize. In the **storage** stage, this knowledge is integrated with what is already in memory and 'warehoused' until needed. During **retrieval**, the person accesses the desired information.[30] The memory process is summarized in Figure 7.4.

As suggested by Mario's memories and musings at the beginning of the chapter, many of our experiences are locked inside our heads, and we maintain those memories and recall those experiences if prompted by the right cues. Marketers rely on consumers to retain information they have learned about products and services, trusting that it will later be applied in

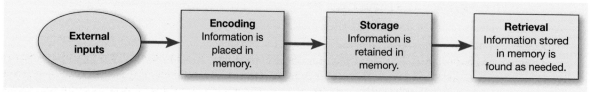

Figure 7.4 The memory process

situations where purchase decisions must be made. During the consumer decision-making process, this internal memory is combined with external memory – which includes all the product details on packages in shopping lists, and through other marketing stimuli – to permit brand alternatives to be identified and evaluated.[31] Research supports the idea that marketers can distort a consumer's recall of a product experience. What we think we 'know' about products can be influenced by advertising messages to which we are exposed after using them. This *post-experience advertising* is more likely to alter actual memories when it is very similar or activates memories about the actual experience. For example, advertising can make a remembered product experience more favourable than it actually was.[32]

Encoding of information for later retrieval

The way information is encoded or mentally programmed helps to determine how it will be represented in memory. In general, incoming data that are associated with other information already in memory stand a better chance of being retained. For example, brand names that are linked to physical characteristics of a product category (such as Coffee-mate creamer or Sani-flush toilet bowl cleaner) or that are easy to visualize (e.g. Tide or Omo detergent) tend to be more easily retained in memory than more abstract brand names.[33] Today, one of the biggest memory problems relates to our need to retain the numerous passwords we have to remember to function in our high-tech society. In fact, one in nine consumers keeps their passwords written down in electronic form – making the whole system so insecure that government regulators require online banks to add more layers of authentication. Both Google/Firefox and the Mac OS systems offer add-ons to manage your many passwords, and take the strain off your memory!

Types of memory

A consumer may process a stimulus simply in terms of its sensory meaning, such as its colour or shape. When this occurs, the meaning may be activated when the person sees a picture of the stimulus. We may experience a sense of familiarity on seeing an ad for a new snack food we recently tasted, for example.

In many cases, though, meanings are encoded at a more abstract level. *Semantic meaning* refers to symbolic associations, such as the idea that rich people drink champagne or that fashionable men wear an earring.

Episodic memories are those that relate to events that are personally relevant, such as Mario's.[34] As a result, a person's motivation to retain these memories will be strong. Couples often have 'their song' that reminds them of their first date or wedding. The memories that might be triggered upon hearing this song would be quite different and unique for them.

Commercials sometimes attempt to activate episodic memories by focusing on experiences shared by many people. Recall of the past may have an effect on future behaviour. A university fund-raising campaign can get higher donations by evoking pleasant memories. Some especially vivid associations are called *flashbulb* memories. These are usually related to some highly significant event. One method of conveying product information is through a *narrative* or a story. Much of the social information that an individual acquires is represented in memory this way. Therefore, utilizing this method in product advertising can be an effective marketing technique. Narratives persuade people to construct a mental representation of the information they are viewing. Pictures aid in this construction and allow for a more developed and detailed mental representation.[35]

Memory systems

According to the information-processing perspective, there are three distinct memory systems: sensory memory, short-term memory (STM) and long-term memory (LTM). Each plays a role in processing brand-related information. The interrelationships of these memory systems are summarized in Figure 7.5.

This French ad for Pictionary requires the viewer to invest a fair amount of effort to understand it.

Ogilvy & Mather, Paris.

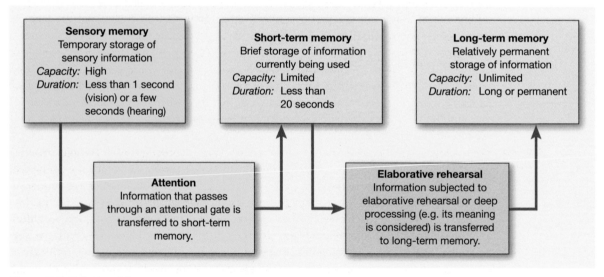

Figure 7.5 Relationships among memory systems

Sensory memory permits storage of the information we receive from our senses. This storage is very temporary: it lasts a couple of seconds at most. For example, a person might be walking past a bakery and get a brief, but enticing, whiff of bread baking inside. While this sensation would only last for a few seconds, it would be sufficient to allow the person to determine if they should investigate further. If the information is retained for further processing, it passes through an attentional gate and is transferred to short-term memory.

Short-term memory also stores information for a limited period of time, and its capacity is limited. Similar to a computer, this system can be regarded as working memory: it holds the information we are currently processing. Verbal input may be stored acoustically (in terms of how it sounds) or semantically (in terms of its meaning).

The information is stored by combining small pieces into larger ones in a process known as 'chunking'. A chunk is a configuration that is familiar to the person and can be manipulated as a unit. For example, a brand name can be a chunk that summarizes a great deal of detailed information about the brand.

Initially, it was believed that STM was capable of processing five to nine chunks of information at a time, and for this reason phone numbers were designed to have seven digits.[36] It now appears that three to four chunks is the optimum size for efficient retrieval (seven-digit phone numbers can be remembered because the individual digits are chunked, so we may remember a three-digit exchange as one piece of information).[37]

Long-term memory is the system that allows us to retain information for a long period of time. In order for information to enter into long-term memory from short-term memory, elaborative rehearsal is required. This process involves thinking about the meaning of a stimulus and relating it to other information already in memory. Marketers sometimes assist in the process by devising catchy slogans or jingles that consumers repeat on their own.

Storing of information in memory

Relationships among the types of memory are a source of some controversy. The traditional perspective, known as multiple-store, assumes that STM and LTM are separate systems. More recent research has moved away from the distinction between the two types of memory, instead emphasizing the interdependence of the systems. This work argues that, depending upon the nature of the processing task, different levels of processing occur that activate some aspects of memory rather than others. These approaches are called **activation models of memory**.[38] The more effort it takes to process information (so-called deep processing), the more likely it is that information will be placed in long-term memory.

Activation models propose that an incoming piece of information is stored in an associative network containing many bits of related information organized according to some set of relationships. The consumer has organized systems of concepts relating to brands, stores, and so on.

Knowledge structures

These storage units, known as **knowledge structures**, can be thought of as complex spiders' webs filled with pieces of data. This information is placed into nodes, which are connected by associative links within these structures. Pieces of information that are seen as similar in some way are chunked together under some more abstract category. New, incoming information is interpreted to be consistent with the structure already in place.[39] According to the hierarchical processing model, a message is processed in a bottom-up fashion: processing begins at a very basic level and is subject to increasingly complex processing operations that require greater cognitive capacity. If processing at one level fails to evoke the next level, processing of the ad is terminated, and capacity is allocated to other tasks.[40]

Links form between nodes as an associative network is developed. For example, a consumer might have a network for 'perfumes'. Each node represents a concept related to the category. This node can be an attribute, a specific brand, a celebrity identified with a perfume, or even a related product. A network for perfumes might include concepts like the names Chanel, Obsession and Charlie, as well as attributes like sexy and elegant.

When asked to list perfumes, the consumer would recall only those brands contained in the appropriate category. This group constitutes that person's **evoked set**. The task of a new entrant that wants to position itself as a category member (e.g. a new luxury perfume) is to provide cues that facilitate its placement in the appropriate category. A sample network for perfumes is shown in Figure 7.6.

Spreading activation

A meaning can be activated indirectly: energy spreads across nodes at varying levels of abstraction. As one node is activated, other nodes associated with it also begin to be triggered. Meaning

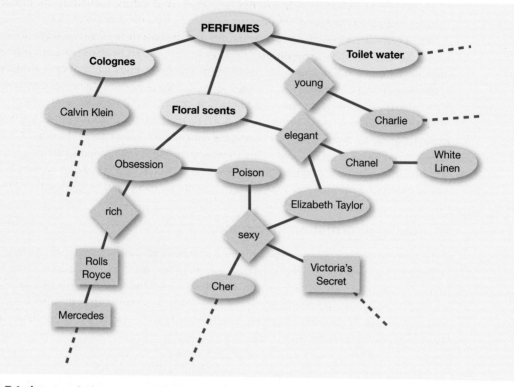

Figure 7.6 An associative network for perfumes

thus spreads across the network, bringing up concepts including competing brands and relevant attributes that are used to form attitudes towards the brand.

This process of spreading activation allows consumers to shift back and forth between levels of meaning. The way a piece of information is stored in memory depends upon the type of meaning assigned to it. This meaning type will, in turn, determine how and when the meaning is activated. For example, the memory trace for an ad could be stored in one or more of the following ways:

- *Brand-specific*: in terms of claims made for the brand.
- *Ad-specific*: in terms of the medium or content of the ad itself.
- *Brand identification*: in terms of the brand name.
- *Product category*: in terms of how the product works, where it should be used, or experiences with the product.
- *Evaluative reactions*: in terms of whether 'that looks like fun'.[41]

Levels of knowledge

Knowledge is coded at different levels of abstraction and complexity. Meaning concepts are individual nodes (e.g. elegant). These may be combined into a larger unit, called a *proposition* (also known as a *belief*). A proposition links two nodes together to form a more complex meaning, which can serve as a single chunk of information. For example, a proposition might be that 'Chanel is a perfume for elegant women'.

Propositions are, in turn, integrated to produce a complex unit known as a **schema**. A schema is a cognitive framework that is developed through experience. Information that is consistent with an existing schema is encoded more readily.[42] The ability to move up and down between levels of abstraction greatly increases processing flexibility and efficiency. For this reason, young children, who do not yet have well-developed schemas, are not able to make efficient use of purchase information compared with older children.[43]

One type of schema that is relevant to consumer behaviour is a script, a sequence of procedures that is expected by an individual. For example, consumers learn service scripts that guide expectations and purchasing behaviour in business settings. Consumers learn to expect a certain sequence of events, and they may become uncomfortable if the service departs from the script. A service script for your visit to the dentist might include such events as (1) driving to the dentist, (2) reading old magazines in the waiting room, (3) hearing your name called and sitting in the dentist's chair, (4) having the dentist probe your teeth, (5) having the dentist scale and polish your teeth, and so on. This desire to follow a script helps to explain why such service innovations as automatic bank machines and self-service petrol stations have met with resistance by some consumers, who have trouble adapting to a new sequence of events.[44]

Retrieving of information for purchase decisions

Retrieval is the process whereby information is accessed from long-term memory. As evidenced by the popularity of the board game *Trivial Pursuit*, or the television programmes *Who Wants to Be a Millionaire?* or *Eggheads* people have a vast quantity of information stored in their heads that is not necessarily available on demand. Although most of the information entered in long-term memory does not go away, it may be difficult or impossible to retrieve unless the appropriate cues are present.

Factors influencing retrieval

Individual cognitive or physiological factors are responsible for some of the differences we see in retrieval ability among people.[45] Some older adults consistently display inferior recall ability for current items, such as prescription drug instructions, although they may recall events that happened to them when they were younger with great clarity.[46] The recent popularity of puzzles, such as Sudoku, and centres that offer 'mental gymnastics' attest to emerging evidence that we can keep our retrieval abilities sharp by exercising our minds just as we keep our other muscles toned by working out on a regular basis.

Other factors that influence retrieval are situational; they relate to the environment in which the message is delivered. Not surprisingly, recall is enhanced when we pay more attention to the message in the first place. Some evidence indicates that we can retrieve information about a *pioneering brand* (the first brand to enter a market) more easily from memory than we can for *follower brands* because the first product's introduction is likely to be distinctive and, for the time being, no competitors divert our attention.[47] In addition, we are more likely to recall descriptive brand names than those that do not provide adequate cues as to what the product is.[48]

Not surprisingly, the way a marketer presents their message influences the likelihood we will be able to recall it later. The **spacing effect** describes the tendency for us to recall printed material more effectively when the advertiser repeats the target item periodically rather than presenting it repeatedly in a short time period.[49] The viewing environment of a marketing message also affects recall. For example, General Electric found that its commercials fared better in television shows with continuous activity, such as stories or dramas, compared to variety shows or talk shows that are punctuated by a series of acts.[50] Finally, a large-scale analysis of TV commercials found that viewers recall commercials shown first in a series of ads better than those they see last.[51]

State-dependent retrieval In a process termed state-dependent retrieval, people are better able to access information if their internal state is the same at the time of recall as it was when the information was learned.

This phenomenon, called the *mood congruence effect*, underscores the desirability of matching a consumer's mood at the time of purchase when planning exposure to marketing communications. A consumer is more likely to recall an ad, for example, if their mood or level of arousal at the time of exposure is similar to that in the purchase environment. By recreating the cues that were present when the information was first presented, recall can be enhanced.[52]

Familiarity and recall As a general rule, prior familiarity with an item enhances its recall. Indeed, this is one of the basic goals of marketers who are trying to create and maintain awareness of their products. The more experience a consumer has with a product, the better use that person is able to make of product information.[53] Finally, research suggests a **highlighting effect**, where the order in which consumers learn about brands determines the strength of association between these brands and their attributes. Consumers more strongly associate common attributes with early learned brands and unique attributes with late-learned brands. More generally, we are more likely to recognize words, objects and faces we learn early in life than similar items we learn later. This applies to brands as well; managers who introduce new entries into a market with well-established brand names need to work harder to create learning and memory linkages by exposing consumers to information about them more frequently.[54]

However, there is a possible fly in the ointment: as noted earlier in the chapter, some evidence indicates that overfamiliarity can result in inferior learning and/or recall. When consumers are highly familiar with a brand or an advertisement, they may attend to fewer attributes because they do not believe that any additional effort will yield a gain in knowledge.[55] For example, when consumers are exposed to the technique of radio replay, where the audio track from a television ad is replayed on the radio, they do very little critical, evaluative processing and instead mentally replay the video portion of the ad.[56]

Salience and recall The salience of a brand refers to its prominence or level of activation in memory. As noted in Chapter 4, stimuli that stand out in contrast to their environment are more likely to command attention, which, in turn, increases the likelihood that they will be recalled. Almost any technique that increases the novelty of a stimulus also improves recall (a result known as the von Restorff effect).[57] This effect explains why unusual advertising or distinctive packaging tends to facilitate brand recall.[58]

As we saw in Chapter 4, introducing a surprise element in an ad can be particularly effective. This strategy aids recall even if the stimulus is not relevant to the factual information being presented.[59] In addition, so-called mystery ads, where the brand is not identified until the end, are more effective at building associations in memory between the product category and that brand – especially in the case of novel brands.[60]

Pictorial *vs* verbal cues There is some evidence for the superiority of visual memory over verbal memory, but this advantage is unclear because it is more difficult to measure recall of pictures.[61] However, the available data indicate that information presented in pictorial form is more likely to be recognized later.[62] Certainly, visual aspects of an ad are more likely to grab a consumer's attention. In fact, eye-movement studies indicate that about 90 per cent of viewers look at the dominant picture in an ad before they bother to view the copy.[63]

While pictorial ads may enhance recall, however, they do not necessarily improve comprehension. One study found that television news items presented with illustrations (still pictures) as a backdrop result in improved recall for details of the news story, even though understanding of the story's content does not improve.[64] Visual imagery can be especially effective when it includes verbal cues that relate to the consumer's existing knowledge.

Factors influencing forgetting

Marketers obviously hope that consumers will not forget their products. However, in a poll of more than 13,000 adults, over half were unable to remember any specific ad they had seen, heard or read in the previous 30 days.[65] Forgetting is obviously a problem for marketers.

Early memory theorists assumed that memories fade due to the simple passage of time. In a process of decay, the structural changes in the brain produced by learning simply go away. Forgetting also occurs due to **interference**: as additional information is learned, it displaces the earlier information.

Stimulus–response associations will be forgotten if the consumers subsequently learn new responses to the same or similar stimuli in a process known as *retroactive interference*. Or prior learning can interfere with new learning, a process termed *proactive interference*. Since pieces of information are stored in memory as nodes that are connected to one another by links, a meaning concept that is connected by a larger number of links is more likely to be retrieved. But, as new responses are learned, a stimulus loses its effectiveness in retrieving the old response.[66]

These interference effects help to explain problems in remembering brand information. Consumers tend to organize attribute information by brand.[67] Additional attribute information regarding a brand or similar brands may limit the person's ability to recall old brand information. Recall may also be inhibited if the brand name is composed of frequently used words. These words cue competing associations and result in less retention of brand information.[68]

In one study, brand evaluations deteriorated more rapidly when ads for the brand appeared with messages for 12 other brands in the same category than when the ad was shown with ads for 12 dissimilar products.[69] By increasing the salience of a brand, the recall of other brands can be impaired.[70] On the other hand, calling a competitor by name can result in poorer recall for one's own brand.[71]

Finally, a phenomenon known as the *part-list cueing effect* allows marketers to utilize the interference process strategically. When only a portion of the items in a category are presented to consumers, the omitted items are not as easily recalled. For example, comparative advertising that mentions only a subset of competitors (preferably those that the marketer is not very worried about) may inhibit recall of the unmentioned brands with which the product does not compare favourably.[72]

Products as memory markers

Products and ads can themselves serve as powerful retrieval cues. Indeed, the three types of possessions most valued by consumers are furniture, visual art and photos. The most common explanation for this attachment is the ability of these things to summon memories of the past.[73] Products are particularly important as markers when our sense of past is threatened, as when a consumer's current identity is challenged due to some change in role caused by divorce, moving, graduation, and so on.[74] Products have mnemonic qualities that serve as a form of external memory by prompting consumers to retrieve episodic memories. For example, family photography allows consumers to create their own retrieval cues, with the 11 billion amateur photos taken annually forming a kind of external memory bank for our culture.

Researchers are just beginning to probe the effects of autobiographical memories on buying behaviour. These memories appear to be one way that advertisements create emotional responses: ads that succeed in getting us to think about our own past also appear to get us to like these ads more – especially if the linkage between the nostalgia experience and the brand is strong.[75] Recent research even argues that movies we've seen a second (or third) time, and books that we've re-read, even after years since the first reading add to a deeper sense of understanding and appreciation for the film or book.[76]

The marketing power of nostalgia

Marketers often resurrect popular characters and stories from days gone by; they hope that consumers' fond memories will motivate them to revisit the past. We had a 1950s revival in the 1970s, and consumers in the 1980s got a heavy dose of memories from the 1960s. Today, it seems that popular characters only need to be gone for a few years before someone tries to bring them back. **Nostalgia** describes a bittersweet emotion where we view the past with both sadness and longing.[77] References to 'the good old days' are increasingly common, as advertisers call up memories of youth – and hope these feelings will translate to what they are selling today. Researchers find that valued possessions can evoke thoughts about prior events on several dimensions, including sensory experiences, friends and loved ones, and breaking away from parents or former partners.[78] That helps to explain the popularity of photo-sharing sites like *Flickr* – this platform alone hosts over five billion pictures and offers 'Share This' tools for use on *Facebook* and *Twitter*.[79] A new app called Memolane goes a step farther: it lets you create a visual timeline from the posts on your social media accounts. You can compile these into a searchable, scrollable image that lets you remember the sequence of events from that memorable vacation or even (but let's hope not) that awesome first date.[80]

Many European companies are making use of nostalgic appeals, some of which are based on the not-too-distant past. Berlin's Humboldt University and City Museum have staged a fashion show of the 1960s, displaying clothes, appliances and posters from the communist era. The show, entitled *Ostalgie*, which is a play on words for 'East Nostalgia' in the German language, gave a nostalgic view of a time when goods might have been shoddy but when there was no unemployment or homelessness. There is growing interest in the Trabant (the joke used to be that you could double the value of a Trabant by filling it with sand) which has resulted in the Son of Trabant, built in the same factory where they used to build the original. Likewise, Western European multinationals are relaunching local brands of East European origin in response to a backlash against the incursion of foreign products. From cigarettes to yoghurt, multinationals are trying to lure consumers by combining yesteryear's product names with today's quality. Local brands like Nestlé's Chokito or Unilever's Flora margarine brands are now among the companies' best-selling products in Eastern European markets.

Considerable care goes into the production values of campaigns which are intended to evoke nostalgia. Mulino Bianco, the Italian producer of cakes, biscuits and cereals, carefully developed a campaign depicting the quiet aspects of rural life to increase sales of cakes, which are typically served only on special occasions. The campaign showed a white farmhouse on a green hill, next to a watermill. Parents, children and friends are shown in a slow, relaxed, informal atmosphere, far from the hectic urban commitments of work. The object was to evoke a relationship between 'the good old days' and cakes, and to present cakes as genuine food to be eaten every day during normal meals. In Italy, where the tension to escape from the hectic urban life is high, the campaign was quite successful. In France, where eating habits are different, and the appeal to rural life is weaker, the same campaign was not successful.[81] As you notice from the examples above, food can be a particularly nostalgic product category! A recent study looked at how favourite recipes stimulate memories of the past. When the researchers asked informants to list three of their favourite recipes and to talk about these choices, they found that people tended to link them with memories of past events such as childhood memories, family holidays, milestone events (such as dishes they only make on special holidays like corned beef and cabbage on St Patrick's Day), heirlooms (recipes handed down across generations), and the passing of time (e.g. only eating blueberry cobbler in the summer).[82] Indeed, one of the most famous literary references is from the classic (3,000 page!) novel *Remembrance of Things Past* by the French novelist Marcel Proust. The narrator dips a pastry (a 'madeleine') into his tea, and this action unleashes a flood of memories that drive the rest of the book.

MARKETING OPPORTUNITY

Oiled herring and vodka shot

The bartenders in white shirts and black bow ties served endless shots of vodka followed by platefuls of herring in oil, and the occasional kielbasa, on small white plates as the crowds eagerly downed their drinks with an enthusiastic toast: 'Na zdrowie!' Polish for 'Cheers'.

If not for the designer handbags and ubiquitous iPhones, this could have been a time capsule from when Poland was behind the Iron Curtain and small bars like this one were common. Back then, Poles jealously guarded their culture, their heritage, their gastronomic delights against the smothering grip of Communism. But when Communism fell in 1989 the novelty of the West overran the capital, with rum cocktails, fast food and Asian fusion restaurants.

After the fall of the Iron Curtain, capitalism brought Poles their fairy-tale visions of life in the West, particularly fast-food restaurants and cocktail bars. But as the years passed, so did their appetite for the things they were denied under Communism, and a bit of nostalgia for the old ways began to creep in. This sentiment has been at least partly caused by the sizable emigration from Poland that followed Polish accession to the European Union in 2004. In a search for jobs, at least two million Poles left for Great Britain, Ireland, The Netherlands and elsewhere.

Today, Poles have come full circle and are feeling a lot more confident, embracing their traditions rather than rushing to welcome the latest foreign trends. These new establishments, standing-room-only bars, known as zakaskas bars, try to recreate the Soviet-era ambience, with intentionally shabby décor, little or no furniture and cheap offerings. These simple gathering spots try to build a sense of community by combining several Polish traditions. 'Zakaska' is Polish for any of several appetizers that accompany a drink, usually vodka. The most popular zakaskas besides herring in oil are steak tartare, kielbasa or pâté.

'Everything associated with Polish tradition was identified as being trashy and crude, an indicator of Poles' alleged low socioeconomic background', said Tomasz Szlendak, a sociologist. 'So people tried to recreate the world from "Dynasty",' the former prime-time American soap opera, he said. Poles began consuming sushi at the highest rate outside of Japan, he added, thinking that was a sign they had arrived and were no longer a Communist-era backwater, a punchline for jokes.

As they began to feel better about themselves, Poles began to explore their past in a variety of ways, from historical documentaries to retro crime novels. Zakaskas bistros fit right into that trend. More than a dozen opened up in the capital alone, and the rest of Poland followed suit. 'I didn't want a fussy place', said one owner, who owns three zakaskas bistros in Warsaw. 'I wanted something even a bit ugly, where one wouldn't feel the need to show off'. 'I wanted to create a place where elegant ladies could come and not feel embarrassed about having a couple of shots of vodka', she said with determination.[83]

Memory and aesthetic preferences

In addition to liking ads and products that remind us of our past, our prior experiences also help to determine what we like now. Some recent research indicates that people's tastes in such products as films and clothing are influenced by what was popular during certain critical periods of their youth. For example, liking for specific songs appears to be related to how old a person was when those songs were popular: on average, songs that were popular when an individual was 23 to 24 years old are the most likely to be favoured.[84] In addition, it seems that men form preferences for women's clothing styles that were in vogue when these men were in their early twenties.[85]

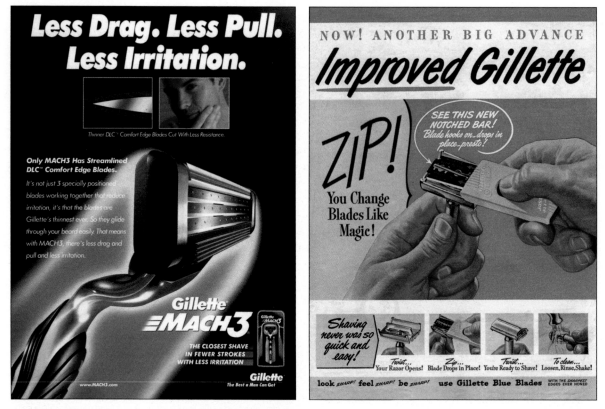

The Gillette brand has always positioned itself as innovative. This 'innovative' brand association is learned, and reinforced, over their customers' lifetime.

The Advertising Archives.

More generally, many marketers understand that life-long brand loyalties are formed at a fairly early age: they view the battle for the hearts (and wallets) of students and young adults as a long-term investment. These age-related preferences will be further addressed in Chapter 11.

Measuring memory for advertising

Because advertisers pay so much money to place their messages in front of consumers, they are naturally concerned that people will actually remember these messages at a later point. It seems that they have good reason to be concerned. In one study, less than 40 per cent of television viewers made positive links between commercial messages and the corresponding products; only 65 per cent noticed the brand name in a commercial; and only 38 per cent recognized a connection to an important point.[86]

More worryingly, only 7 per cent of television viewers can recall the product or company featured in the most recent television commercial they watched. This figure represents less than half the recall rate recorded in 1965 and may be attributed to such factors as the increase of 30- and 15-second commercials, the highly fragmented media consumption of consumers in the twenty-first century, and the practice of airing television commercials in clusters rather than in connection with single-sponsor programmes.[87] Small wonder that noticing a brand is becoming more difficult, especially among young consumers. A recent study of 'digital natives' (consumers in their 20s, who grew up with computers, smart phone and tablets) shows that during non-working hours, they switch media venues up to 27 times an hour![88]

Recognition *vs* recall

One indicator of good advertising is, of course, the impression it makes on consumers. But how can this impact be defined and measured? Two basic measures of impact are recognition and recall. In the typical recognition test, subjects are shown ads one at a time and asked if they have seen them before. In contrast, free recall tests ask consumers to produce independently previously acquired information and then perform a recognition test on it.

Under some conditions, these two memory measures tend to yield the same results, especially when the researchers try to keep the viewers' interest in the ads constant.[89] Generally, though, recognition scores tend to be more reliable and do not decay over time in the way recall scores do.[90] Recognition scores are almost always better than recall scores because recognition is a simpler process and more retrieval cues are available to the consumer.

Both types of retrieval play important roles in purchase decisions. Recall tends to be more important in situations where consumers do not have product data at their disposal, and so they must rely upon memory to generate this information.[91] On the other hand, recognition is more likely to be an important factor in a store, where consumers are confronted with thousands of product options and information (i.e. where external memory is abundantly available) and where the task may simply be to recognize a familiar package. Unfortunately, package recognition and familiarity can have a negative consequence in that warning labels may be ignored, since their existence is taken for granted and not really noticed.[92]

The Starch Test

A widely used commercial measure of advertising recall for magazines is called the Starch Test, a syndicated service founded in 1932. This service provides scores on a number of aspects of consumers' familiarity with an ad, including such categories as 'noted', 'associated' and 'read most'. It also scores the impact of the component parts of an overall ad, giving such information as 'seen' for major illustrations and 'read some' for a major block of copy.[93] Such factors as the size of the ad, whether it appears towards the front or the back of the magazine, if it is on the right or left page, and the size of illustrations play an important role in affecting the amount of attention given to an ad as determined by Starch scores.

Problems with memory measures

While the measurement of an ad's memorability is important, the ability of existing measures to assess these dimensions accurately has been criticized for several reasons.

Visual aspects of an ad grab a consumer's attention, especially when they are novel. That is certainly the case for this 'pile of trash' that is actually an outdoor ad on a Dutch street for the Mini Cooper.
UbachsWisbrun/JWT Amsterdam.

Response biases Results obtained from a measuring instrument are not necessarily due to what is being measured, but rather to something else about the instrument or the respondent. This form of contamination is called a **response bias**. For example, people tend to give 'yes' responses to questions regardless of what is asked. In addition, consumers are often eager to be 'good subjects' by pleasing the experimenter. They will try to give the responses they think they are looking for. In some studies, the claimed recognition of bogus ads (ads that have not been seen before) is almost as high as the recognition rate of real ads.[94]

Memory lapses People are also prone to forgetting information unintentionally. Typical problems include omitting (the leaving out of facts), averaging (the tendency to 'normalize' things and not report extreme cases), and telescoping (the inaccurate recall of time).[95] These distortions call into question the accuracy of various product usage databases that rely upon consumers to recall their purchase and consumption of food and household items. In one study, for example, people were asked to describe what portion of various foods – small, medium or large – they ate in a normal meal; however, different definitions of 'medium' were used (e.g. 185ml *vs* 375ml). Regardless of the measurement specified, about the same number of people claimed they normally ate medium portions.[96]

Memory for facts *vs* feelings Although techniques are being developed to increase the accuracy of memory scores, these improvements do not address the more fundamental issue of whether recall is necessary for advertising to have an effect. In particular, some critics argue that these measures do not adequately tap the impact of 'feeling' ads where the objective is to arouse strong emotions rather than to convey concrete product benefits. Many ad campaigns, including those for Hallmark cards, Chevrolet and Pepsi, use this approach.[97] An effective strategy relies on a long-term build-up of feeling rather than on a one-shot attempt to convince consumers to buy the product.

Also, it is not clear that recall translates into preference. We may recall the benefits touted in an ad but not believe them. Or the ad may be memorable because it is so obnoxious, and the product becomes one we 'love to hate'. The bottom line is that while recall is important, especially for creating brand awareness, it is not necessarily sufficient to alter consumer preferences. To accomplish this, marketers need more sophisticated attitude-change strategies. These issues will be discussed in Chapter 8.

CHAPTER SUMMARY

Now that you have finished reading this chapter you should understand why:

→ **It's important to understand how consumers learn about products and services.** Learning is a change in behaviour that is caused by experience. Learning can occur through simple associations between a stimulus and a response or via a complex series of cognitive activities.

→ **Conditioning results in learning.** Behavioural learning theories assume that learning occurs as a result of responses to external events. Classical conditioning occurs when a stimulus that naturally elicits a response (an unconditioned stimulus) is paired with another stimulus that does not initially elicit this response. Over time, the second stimulus (the conditioned stimulus) elicits the response even in the absence of the first.

→ **Learned associations can generalize to other things and this is important to marketers.** This response can also extend to other, similar stimuli in a process we call stimulus generalization. This process is the basis for such marketing strategies as licensing and family branding, where a consumer's positive associations with a product transfer to other contexts.

→ **There is a difference between classical and instrumental conditioning.** Operant, or instrumental, conditioning occurs as the person learns to perform behaviours that produce positive outcomes and avoid those that result in negative outcomes. Whereas classical conditioning involves the pairing of two stimuli, instrumental learning occurs when reinforcement occurs following a response to a stimulus. Reinforcement is positive if a reward follows a response. It is negative if the person avoids a negative outcome by not performing a response. Punishment occurs when an unpleasant event follows a response. Extinction of the behaviour will occur if reinforcement no longer occurs.

→ **We learn by observing others' behaviour.** Cognitive learning occurs as the result of mental processes. For example, observational learning occurs when the consumer performs a behaviour as a result of seeing someone else performing it and being rewarded for it.

→ **Our brains process information about brands to retain them in memory.** Memory is the storage of learned information. The way we encode information when we perceive it determines how we will store it in memory. The memory systems we call sensory memory, short-term memory and long-term memory each play a role in retaining and processing information from the outside world.

→ **The other products we associate with an individual product influence how we will remember it.** We don't store information in isolation; we incorporate it into knowledge structure where our brains associate it with other related data. The location of product information in associative networks, and the level of abstraction at which it is coded, help to determine when and how we will activate this information at a later time. Some factors that influence the likelihood of retrieval include the level of familiarity with an item, its salience (or prominence) in memory, and whether the information was presented in pictorial or written form.

→ **Products help us to retrieve memories from our past.** Products also play a role as memory markers; consumers use them to retrieve memories about past experiences (autobiographical memories), and we often value them because they are able to do this. This function also encourages the use of nostalgia in marketing strategies.

→ **Marketers measure our memories about products and ads.** We can use either recognition or recall techniques to measure memory for product information. Consumers are more likely to recognize an advertisement if it is presented to them than they are to recall one without being given any cues. However, neither recognition nor recall automatically or reliably translates into product preferences or purchases.

KEY TERMS

Activation models of memory (p. 275)

Behavioural learning theories (p. 261)

Brand equity (p. 268)

Classical conditioning (p. 262)

Cognitive learning (p. 266)

Encoding (p. 272)

Evoked set (p. 275)

Extinction (p. 263)

Frequency marketing (p. 270)

Highlighting effect (p. 278)

Interference (p. 279)

Knowledge structures (p. 275)

Learning (p. 261)

Long-term memory (p. 275)

Memory (p. 272)

Negative reinforcement (p. 264)

Nostalgia (p. 280)

Observational learning (p. 267)

Operant conditioning (p. 264)

Positive reinforcement (p. 264)

Punishment (p. 264)

Response bias (p. 284)

CONSUMER BEHAVIOUR CHALLENGE

1 Identify three patterns of reinforcement and provide an example of how each is used in a marketing context.

2 Describe the functions of short-term and long-term memory. What is the apparent relationship between the two?

3 Devise a 'product jingle memory test'. Compile a list of brands that are or have been associated with memorable jingles, such as Opal Fruits or Heinz Baked Beans. Read this list to friends, and see how many jingles are remembered. You may be surprised at the level of recall.

4 Identify some important characteristics for a product with a well-known brand name. Based on these attributes, generate a list of possible brand extension or licensing opportunities, as well as some others that would be unlikely to be accepted by consumers.

5 Collect some pictures of 'classic' products that have high nostalgia value. Show these pictures to consumers and allow them to make free associations. Analyse the types of memories that are evoked, and think about how these associations might be employed in a product's promotional strategy.

For additional material see the companion website at www.pearsoned.co.uk/solomon

NOTES

1. Robert A. Baron, *Psychology: The Essential Science* (Boston: Allyn & Bacon, 1989).

2. Dowdey, Sarah (2012) 'Does What you Smell Determine What you Buy?' *How Stuff Works*, The Discovery Channel, http://money.howstuffworks.com/scent-marketing.htm, accessed 20 April 2012; see also: Emma Hall (2008), 'What's that Smell in the Movie Theatre? It's an Ad', *Adage*, 24 July 2008, http://adage.com/article?article_id=129864

3. Richard A. Feinberg, 'Credit cards as spending facilitating stimuli: A conditioning interpretation', *Journal of Consumer Research* 13 (December 1986): 348–56.

4. R.A. Rescorla, 'Pavlovian conditioning: It's not what you think it is', *American Psychologist* 43 (1988): 151–60; Elnora W. Stuart, Terence A. Shimp and Randall W. Engle, 'Classical conditioning of consumer attitudes: Four experiments in an advertising context', *Journal of Consumer Research* 14 (December 1987): 334–9; Terence A. Shimp, Elnora W. Stuart and Randall W. Engle, 'A program of classical conditioning experiments testing variations in the conditioned stimulus and context', *Journal of Consumer Research* 18(1) (June 1991): 1–12.

5. C. Janiszewski, H. Noel and A.G. Sawyer, 'A Meta-analysis of the Spacing Effect in Verbal Learning: Implications for Research on Advertising Repetition and Consumer Memory', *Journal of Consumer Research* 30, no. 1 (2003): 138–49.

6. Baron, *Psychology, op. cit.*

7. Caitlin Ingrassia, 'Counterfeiter, imitators: fine line, *The Wall Street Journal* (16 January 2004), http://online.wsj.com/article/0,,SB107421653820930400,00.html?mod=article-outset-box; see also: 'AH moet twee verpakkingen aanpassingen' (video), *RTL Nieuws* (28 April 2005), http://www.rtl.nl/actueel/rtlnieuws/video/; see also: Elder, Ryan S. and Aradhna Krishna, 'The "Visual Depiction Effect" in Advertising: Facilitating Embodied Mental Simulation through Product Orientation', *Journal of Consumer Research*, vol. 38, no. 6, (April 2012): 988–1003.

8. For a comprehensive approach to consumer behaviour based on operant conditioning principles, see Gordon R. Foxall, 'Behavior analysis and consumer psychology', *Journal of Economic Psychology* 15 (March 1994): 5–91. Foxall also sets out some consumer behaviour based on a neo-behaviourist perspective. By identifying environmental determinants, he develops four classes of consumer behaviour: *accomplishment*, *pleasure*, *accumulation* and *maintenance*. For an extensive discussion on this approach, see the entire special issue of Gordon R. Foxall, 'Science and interpretation in consumer behavior: A radical behaviourist perspective', *European Journal of Marketing* 29(9) (1995): 3–99.

9. Ellen J. Langer, *The Psychology of Control* (Beverly Hills, CA: Sage, 1983); Klaus G. Grunert, 'Automatic and strategic

processes in advertising effects', *Journal of Marketing* 60 (1996): 88–91.

10. Robert B. Cialdini, *Influence: Science and Practice*, 2nd edn (New York: William Morrow, 1984).

11. Jay P. Carlson, Leslie H. Vincent, David M. Hardesty and William O. Bearden (2009) 'Objective and subjective knowledge relationships: A quantitative analysis of consumer research findings', *Journal of Consumer Research* 35 (February 2009): 864–76.

12. Gershoff, Andrew D., Ran Kivetz and Anat Keinan, 'Consumer Response to Versioning: How Brands' Production Methods Affect Perceptions of Unfairness', *Journal of Consumer Research*, vol. 39, (August, 2012) in press. See also: Nuttall Chris and Richard Waters, 'Apple responds to critical report on Foxconn', *Financial Times*, 29 March 2012, http://www.ftsyndication.com/preview.php?id=201203290001FT_____FT_COM__ff2a84c4-79df-11e1-9900-00144fe_6670.2

13. Chris T. Allen and Thomas J. Madden, 'A closer look at classical conditioning', *Journal of Consumer Research* 12 (December 1985): 301–15.

14. Albert Bandura, *Social Foundations of Thought and Action: A Social Cognitive View* (Englewood Cliffs, NJ: Prentice Hall, 1986); Baron, *Psychology, op. cit.*

15. Allen and Madden, 'A closer look at classical conditioning', *op. cit.*; Chester A. Insko and William F. Oakes, 'Awareness and the conditioning of attitudes', *Journal of Personality and Social Psychology* 4 (November 1966): 487–96; Carolyn K. Staats and Arthur W. Staats, 'Meaning established by classical conditioning', *Journal of Experimental Psychology* 54 (July 1957): 74–80; Randi Priluck Grossman and Brian D. Till, 'The persistence of classically conditioned brand attitudes', *Journal of Advertising* 21(1) (Spring 1998): 23–31.

16. Stijn M.J. van Osselaer and Joseph W. Alba, 'Consumer learning and brand equity', *Journal of Consumer Research* 27(1) (June 2000): 1–16; Kevin Lane Keller, 'Conceptualizing, measuring, and managing customer-based brand equity', *Journal of Marketing* 57 (January 1993): 1–22; Patrick Bawise, 'Brand equity: Snark or boojum?' *International Journal of Research in Marketing* 10 (1993): 93–104; W. Fred van Raaij and Wim Schoonderbeer, 'Meaning Structure of Brand Names and Extensions', in W. Fred van Raaij and Gary J. Bamossy (eds), *European Advances in Consumer Research* 1 (Provo, UT: Association for Consumer Research, 1993): 479–84; Gil McWilliam, 'The Effect of Brand Typology on Brand Extension Fit: Commercial and Academic Research Findings', in van Raaij and Bamossy (eds), *European Advances in Association for Consumer Research* 1: 485–91; Elyette Roux and Frederic Lorange, 'Brand Extension Research: A Review', in van Raaij and Bamossy (eds), *European Advances in Consumer Research* 1: 492–500; 'The art of perception', *Marketing* (28 November 1996): 25–9.

17. Herbert Krugman, 'Low recall and high recognition of advertising', *Journal of Advertising Research* (February/March 1986): 79–86.

18. Gerald J. Gorn, 'The effects of music in advertising on choice behavior: A classical conditioning approach', *Journal of Marketing* 46 (Winter 1982): 94–101.

19. Calvin Bierley, Frances K. McSweeney and Renee Vannieuwkerk, 'Classical conditioning of preferences for stimuli', *Journal of Consumer Research* 12 (December 1985): 316–23; James J. Kellaris and Anthony D. Cox, 'The effects of background music in advertising: A reassessment', *Journal of Consumer Research* 16 (June 1989): 113–18.

20. Frances K. McSweeney and Calvin Bierley, 'Recent developments in classical conditioning', *Journal of Consumer Research* 11 (September 1984): 619–31.

21. Basil G. Englis, 'The Reinforcement Properties of Music Videos: "I Want My . . . I Want My . . . I Want My . . . MTV"' (paper presented at the meetings of the Association for Consumer Research, New Orleans, 1989).

22. 'Giving bad puns the business', *Newsweek* (11 December 1989): 71.

23. Bernice Kanner, 'Growing pains – and gains: Brand names branch out', *New York* (13 March 1989): 22.

24. Peter H. Farquhar, 'Brand equity', *Marketing Insights* (Summer 1989): 59.

25. Product placements in film and TV programmes is also a very common marketing approach to building learning and awareness, and to associate a product or service with a particular actor, or popular cultural event. Go to: http://www.brandchannel.com/brandcameo_films.asp?movie_year=2012#movie_list to see just how prevalent this practice is for films.

26. Quoted in 'Look-alikes mimic familiar packages', *New York Times* (9 August 1986): D1; 'Action fails to match spirit of lookalike law', *Marketing* (27 March 1997): 19.

27. Laurie Hays, 'Too many computer names confuse too many buyers', *Wall Street Journal* (29 June 1994): B1 (2 pp.).

28. Blaise J. Bergiel and Christine Trosclair, 'Instrumental learning: Its application to customer satisfaction', *Journal of Consumer Marketing* 2 (Fall 1985): 23–8.

29. Terence A. Shimp, 'Neo-Pavlovian Conditioning and Its Implications for Consumer Theory and Research', in Thomas S. Robertson and Harold H. Kassarjian (eds), *Handbook of Consumer Behavior* (Englewood Cliffs, NJ: Prentice Hall, 1991).

30. K.K. Desai and Wayne Hoyer, 'Descriptive characteristics of memory-based consideration sets: Influence of usage occasion frequency and usage location familiarity', *Journal of Consumer Research* 27(3) (December 2000): 309–23; R.C. Atkinson and R.M. Shiffrin, 'Human Memory: A Proposed System and Its Control Processes', in K.W. Spence and J.T. Spence (eds), *The Psychology of Learning and Motivation: Advances in Research and Theory* (New York: Academic Press, 1968): 89–195.

31. James R. Bettman, 'Memory factors in consumer choice: a review', *Journal of Marketing* (Spring 1979): 37–53. For a study that explored the relative impact of internal versus external memory on brand choice, see Joseph W. Alba, Howard Marmorstein and Amitava Chattopadhyay, 'Transitions in preference over time: The effects of memory on message persuasiveness', *Journal of Marketing Research* 29 (November 1992): 406–17. For other research on memory and advertising, see H. Shanker Krishnan and Dipankar Chakravarti, 'Varieties of Brand Memory Induced by Advertising: Determinants, Measures, and Relationships', in David A. Aaker and Alexander L. Biel (eds), *Brand Equity and Advertising: Advertising's Role in Building Strong Brands* (Hillsdale, NJ: Lawrence Erlbaum Associates, 1993): 213–31; Bernd H. Schmitt, Nader T. Tavassoli and Robert T. Millard, 'Memory for print ads: Understanding relations among brand name, copy, and picture', *Journal of Consumer*

Psychology 2(1) (1993): 55–81; Marian Friestad and Esther Thorson, 'Remembering ads: The effects of encoding strategies, retrieval cues, and emotional response', *Journal of Consumer Psychology* 2(1) (1993): 1–23; Surendra N. Singh, Sanjay Mishra, Neeli Bendapudi and Denise Linville, 'Enhancing memory of television commercials through message spacing', *Journal of Marketing Research* 31 (August 1994): 384–92.

32. Kathryn R. Braun, 'Postexperience advertising effects on consumer memory', *Journal of Consumer Research* 25 (March 1999): 319–34. See also: Gal Zauberman, Rebecca K. Ratner and B. Kyu Kim (2008), 'Memories as assets: Strategic memory protection in choice over time', *Journal of Consumer Research* 35 (February 2009): 715–28.

33. Kim Robertson, 'Recall and recognition effects of brand name imagery', *Psychology and Marketing* 4 (Spring 1987): 3–15.

34. Endel Tulving, 'Remembering and knowing the past', *American Scientist* 77 (July/August 1989): 361.

35. Perkins, Andrew W. and Mark R. Forehand, 'Implicit Self Referencing: The Effect of Non-volitional Self-Association on Brand and Product Attitude', *Journal of Consumer Research*, vol. 39 (June, 2012), in press. See also: Rashmi Adaval and Robert S. Wyer Jr, 'The role of narratives in consumer information processing', *Journal of Consumer Psychology* 7(3) (1998): 207–46.

36. George A. Miller, 'The magical number seven, plus or minus two: Some limits on our capacity for processing information', *Psychological Review* 63 (1956): 81–97.

37. James N. MacGregor, 'Short-term memory capacity: Limitation or optimization?' *Psychological Review* 94 (1987): 107–8.

38. See Catherine A. Cole and Michael J. Houston, 'Encoding and media effects on consumer learning deficiencies in the elderly', *Journal of Marketing Research* 24 (February 1987): 55–64; A.M. Collins and E.F. Loftus, 'A spreading activation theory of semantic processing', *Psychological Review* 82 (1975): 407–28; Fergus I.M. Craik and Robert S. Lockhart, 'Levels of processing: A framework for memory research', *Journal of Verbal Learning and Verbal Behavior* 11 (1972): 671–84.

39. Walter A. Henry, 'The effect of information-processing ability on processing accuracy', *Journal of Consumer Research* 7 (June 1980): 42–8.

40. Anthony G. Greenwald and Clark Leavitt, 'Audience involvement in advertising: Four levels', *Journal of Consumer Research* 11 (June 1984): 581–92. See also: Anirban Mukhopadhyay, Jaideep Sengupta, and Suresh Ramanathan (2008), 'Recalling past temptations: An information processing perspective on the dynamics of self control', *Journal of Consumer Research* 35 (December 2008): 586–99.

41. Kevin Lane Keller, 'Memory factors in advertising: The effect of advertising retrieval cues on brand evaluations', *Journal of Consumer Research* 14 (December 1987): 316–33. For a discussion of processing operations that occur during brand choice, see Gabriel Biehal and Dipankar Chakravarti, 'Consumers' use of memory and external information in choice: Macro and micro perspectives', *Journal of Consumer Research* 12 (March 1986): 382–405.

42. Susan T. Fiske and Shelley E. Taylor, *Social Cognition* (Reading, MA: Addison-Wesley, 1984).

43. Deborah Roedder John and John C. Whitney Jr, 'The development of consumer knowledge in children: A cognitive structure approach', *Journal of Consumer Research* 12 (March 1986): 406–17.

44. Michael R. Solomon, Carol Surprenant, John A. Czepiel and Evelyn G. Gutman, 'A role theory perspective on dyadic interactions: The service encounter', *Journal of Marketing* 49 (Winter 1985): 99–111.

45. S. Danziger, S. Moran and V. Rafaely, 'The influence of ease of retrieval on judgment as a function of attention to subjective experience', *Journal of Consumer Psychology* 16(2) (2006): 191–95.

46. Roger W. Morrell, Denise C. Park and Leonard W. Poon, 'Quality of instructions on prescription drug labels: Effects on memory and comprehension in young and old adults', *The Gerontologist* 29 (1989): 345–54.

47. Frank R. Kardes, Gurumurthy Kalyanaram, Murali Chandrashekaran and Ronald J. Dornoff, 'Brand retrieval, consideration set composition, consumer choice, and the pioneering advantage' (unpublished manuscript, University of Cincinnati: Ohio, 1992).

48. Judith Lynne Zaichkowsky and Padma Vipat, 'Inferences from Brand Names', paper presented at the European meeting of the Association for Consumer Research, Amsterdam, June 1992.

49. H. Noel, 'The spacing effect: Enhancing memory for repeated marketing stimuli', *Journal of Consumer Psychology* 16(3) (2006): 306–20; for an alternative explanation, see S.L. Appleton-Knapp, R.A. Bjork and T.D. Wickens, 'Examining the spacing effect in advertising: Encoding variability, retrieval processes, and their interaction', *Journal of Consumer Research* 32(2) (2005): 266–76.

50. Herbert E. Krugman, 'Low recall and high recognition of advertising', *Journal of Advertising Research* (February–March 1986): 79–86.

51. Rik G.M. Pieters and Tammo H.A. Bijmolt, 'Consumer memory for television advertising: A field study of duration, serial position, and competition effects', *Journal of Consumer Research* 23 (March 1997): 362–72.

52. Margaret G. Meloy, 'Mood-driven distortion of product information', *Journal of Consumer Research* 27(3) (December 2000): 345–59.

53. Eric J. Johnson and J. Edward Russo, 'Product familiarity and learning new information', *Journal of Consumer Research* 11 (June 1984): 542–50.

54. Marcus Cunha Jr and Juliano Laran (2009), 'Asymmetries in the Sequential Learning of Brand Associations: Implications for the Early Entrant Advantage', *Journal of Consumer Research*, 35(5), 788–799; Andrew W. Ellis, Selina J. Holmes and Richard L. Wright (2010), 'Age of acquisition and the recognition of brand names: On the importance of being early', *Journal of Consumer Psychology*, 20(1), 43–52.

55. Eric J. Johnson and J. Edward Russo, 'Product Familiarity and Learning New Information', in Kent Monroe (ed.), *Advances in Consumer Research* 8 (Ann Arbor, MI: Association for Consumer Research, 1981): 151–5; John G. Lynch and Thomas K. Srull, 'Memory and attentional factors in consumer choice: Concepts and research methods', *Journal of Consumer Research* 9 (June 1982): 18–37.

56. Julie A. Edell and Kevin Lane Keller, 'The information processing of coordinated media campaigns', *Journal of Marketing Research* 26 (May 1989): 149–64.

57. Lynch and Srull, 'Memory and attentional factors in consumer choice', *op. cit.*

58. Joseph W. Alba and Amitava Chattopadhyay, 'Salience effects in brand recall', *Journal of Marketing Research* 23

(November 1986): 363–70; Elizabeth C. Hirschman and Michael R. Solomon, 'Utilitarian, Aesthetic, and Familiarity Responses to Verbal Versus Visual Advertisements', in Thomas C. Kinnear (ed.), *Advances in Consumer Research* 11 (Provo, UT: Association for Consumer Research, 1984): 426–31.

59. Susan E. Heckler and Terry L. Childers, 'The role of expectancy and relevancy in memory for verbal and visual information: What is incongruency?' *Journal of Consumer Research* 18 (March 1992): 475–92.

60. Russell H. Fazio, Paul M. Herr and Martha C. Powell, 'On the development and strength of category–brand associations in memory: The case of mystery ads', *Journal of Consumer Psychology* 1(1) (1992): 1–13.

61. Hirschman and Solomon, 'Utilitarian, aesthetic, and familiarity responses to verbal versus visual advertisements', *op. cit.*

62. Terry Childers and Michael Houston, 'Conditions for a picture-superiority effect on consumer memory', *Journal of Consumer Research* 11 (September 1984): 643–54; Terry Childers, Susan Heckler and Michael Houston, 'Memory for the visual and verbal components of print advertisements', *Psychology and Marketing* 3 (Fall 1986): 147–50.

63. Werner Krober-Riel, 'Effects of Emotional Pictorial Elements in Ads Analyzed by Means of Eye Movement Monitoring', in Kinnear (ed.), *Advances in Consumer Research* 11: 591–6.

64. Hans-Bernd Brosius, 'Influence of presentation features and news context on learning from television news', *Journal of Broadcasting and Electronic Media* 33 (Winter 1989): 1–14.

65. Raymond R. Burke and Thomas K. Srull, 'Competitive interference and consumer memory for advertising', *Journal of Consumer Research* 15 (June 1988): 55–68.

66. *Ibid.*

67. Johnson and Russo, 'Product Familiarity and Learning New Information', *op. cit.*

68. Joan Meyers-Levy, 'The influence of brand names association set size and word frequency on brand memory', *Journal of Consumer Research* 16 (September 1989): 197–208.

69. Michael H. Baumgardner, Michael R. Leippe, David L. Ronis and Anthony G. Greenwald, 'In search of reliable persuasion effects: II. Associative interference and persistence of persuasion in a message-dense environment', *Journal of Personality and Social Psychology* 45 (September 1983): 524–37.

70. Alba and Chattopadhyay, 'Salience effects in brand recall', *op. cit.*

71. Margaret Henderson Blair, Allan R. Kuse, David H. Furse and David W. Stewart, 'Advertising in a new and competitive environment: persuading consumers to buy', *Business Horizons* 30 (November/December 1987): 20.

72. Lynch and Srull, 'Memory and attentional factors in consumer choice', *op. cit.*

73. Russell W. Belk, 'Possessions and the extended self', *Journal of Consumer Research* 15 (September 1988): 139–68.

74. Russell W. Belk, 'The Role of Possessions in Constructing and Maintaining a Sense of Past', in Marvin E. Goldberg, Gerald Gorn and Richard W. Pollay (eds), *Advances in Consumer Research* 16 (Provo, UT: Association for Consumer Research, 1990): 669–78.

75. Hans Baumgartner, Mita Sujan and James R. Bettman, 'Autobiographical memories, affect and consumer information processing', *Journal of Consumer Psychology* 1 (January 1992): 53–82; Mita Sujan, James R. Bettman and Hans Baumgartner, 'Influencing consumer judgments using autobiographical memories: A self-referencing perspective', *Journal of Marketing Research* 30 (November 1993): 422–36.

76. Russell, Christel Antonia and Sidney J. Levy, 'The Temporal and Focal Dynamics of Volitional Reconsumption: A Phenomenological Investigation of Repeated Hedonic Experiences', *Journal of Consumer Research*, vol. 39 (August, 2012) in press.

77. Loveland, Katherine E., Dirk Smeesters and Naomi Mandel, 'Still Preoccupied with 1995: The Need to Belong and Preferences for Nostalgic Products', *Journal of Consumer Research*, vol. 37 (October 2010) 393–408; Zhou, Xinyue, Tim Wildschut, Constatine Sekikides Kan Shi and Cong Feng, 'Nostalgia: The Gift that Keeps on Giving' *Journal of Consumer Research*, vol. 39 (June, 2012) in press; Bardhi, Fleura, Giana M. Eckhardt and Eric J. Arnould, 'Liquid Relationship to Possessions', *Journal of Consumer Research*, vol. 39 (October 2012) in press. See also: Susan L. Holak and William J. Havlena, 'Feelings, fantasies, and memories: An examination of the emotional components of nostalgia', *Journal of Business Research* 42 (1998): 217–26.

78. Morris B. Holbrook and Robert M. Schindler, 'Nostalgic Bonding: Exploring the Role of Nostalgia in the Consumption Experience', *Journal of Consumer Behavior* 3, no. 2 (December 2003): 107–27.

79. Alexia Tsotsis, 'Flickr Dips Its Toes Into Social with Twitter and Facebook "Share This" Features', (30 March 2011), *TechCrunch*, http://techcrunch.com/2011/03/30/flickr-dips-its-toes-into-social-with-twitter-and-facebook-share-this-features/, accessed 6 April 2011.

80. Sarah Kessler, 'Memolane Creates an Automatic Scrapbook of Your Social Media Activity', (11 March 2011), *Mashable*, http://mashable.com/2011/03/11/memolane/, accessed 4 April 2011.

81. Gabriella Stern, 'VW hopes nostalgia will spur sales of retooled Beetle, fuel US comeback', *Wall Street Journal, Europe* (7 May 1997): 4; 'Ostalgie for the day when they'd never had it so good', *The Independent* (10 February 1997); Almar Latour, 'Shelf wars', *Central European Economic Review* 4 (Dow Jones, May 1997); G. Morello, *The Hidden Dimensions of Marketing* (Amsterdam: Vrije Universiteit, 1993): 13.

82. Stacy Menzel Baker, Holli C. Karrer and Ann Veeck, 'My Favorite Recipes: Recreating Emotions and Memories Through Cooking', *Advances in Consumer Research* 32, no. 1 (2005): 304–305.

83. Berendt, Joanna, 'Flavor of Nostalgia Grows More Appealing to Poles Brimming With Pride', *New York Times*, 18 April 2012, accessed at: http://www.nytimes.com/2012/04/19/world/europe/flavor-of-nostalgia-grows-more-appealing-to-puffed-up-poles.html?_r=1

84. Morris B. Holbrook and Robert M. Schindler, 'Some exploratory findings on the development of musical tastes', *Journal of Consumer Research* 16 (June 1989): 119–24.

85. See Morris B. Holbrook, 'Nostalgia and consumption preferences: Some emerging patterns of consumer tastes', *Journal of Consumer Research* 20 (September 1993): 245–56; Robert M. Schindler and Morris B. Holbrook, 'Critical periods in the development of men's and women's tastes in personal appearance', *Psychology and Marketing* 10(6) (November/December 1993): 549–64; Morris B. Holbrook and Robert M.

Schindler, 'Age, sex, and attitude toward the past as predictors of consumers' aesthetic tastes for cultural products', *Journal of Marketing Research* 31 (August 1994): 412–22.

86. 'Only 38 per cent of T.V. audience links brands with ads', *Marketing News* (6 January 1984): 10.

87. 'Terminal television', *American Demographics* (January 1987): 15.

88. Steinberg, Brian, 'Young Consumers Switch Media 27 Times an Hour', *Advertising Age*, 9 April 2012, accessed at: http://adage.com/article/news/study-young-consumers-switch-media-27-times-hour/234008/?utm_source=digital_email&utm_medium=newsletter&utm_campaign=adage

89. Richard P. Bagozzi and Alvin J. Silk, 'Recall, recognition, and the measurement of memory for print advertisements', *Marketing Science* (1983): 95–134.

90. Adam Finn, 'Print ad recognition readership scores: An information processing perspective', *Journal of Marketing Research* 25 (May 1988): 168–77.

91. Bettman, 'Memory factors in consumer choice', *op. cit.*

92. Mark A. deTurck and Gerald M. Goldhaber, 'Effectiveness of product warning labels: effects of consumers' information processing objectives', *Journal of Consumer Affairs* 23(1) (1989): 111–25.

93. Finn, 'Print ad recognition readership scores', *op. cit.*

94. Hung, Iris W. and Anirban Mukhopadhyay, 'Lenses of the Heart: How Actors' and Observers' Perspectives Influence Emotional Experiences', *Journal of Consumer Research*, vol. 38 (April, 2012), 1103–15; see also: Surendra N. Singh and Gilbert A. Churchill Jr, 'Response-bias-free recognition tests to measure advertising effects', *Journal of Advertising Research* 29 (June/July 1987): 23–36.

95. William A. Cook, 'Telescoping and memory's other tricks', *Journal of Advertising Research* 27 (February/March 1987): 5–8.

96. 'On a diet? Don't trust your memory', *Psychology Today* (October 1989): 12.

97. Hubert A. Zielske and Walter A. Henry, 'Remembering and forgetting television ads', *Journal of Advertising Research* 20 (April 1980): 7–13.

8 ATTITUDES

CHAPTER OBJECTIVES

When you finish reading this chapter you will understand why:

→ Understanding attitudes is important to consumer researchers.

→ Attitudes are more complex than they appear.

→ Attitudes are formed in several ways.

→ Consistency is important in attitude formation.

→ Attitude models are used to identify specific components of an attitude towards a brand, a product or an advertisement.

→ Persuasion can change attitudes.

→ Likelihood of persuasion depends on the source's credibility and attractiveness.

→ A buzz can be a very effective marketing tool.

→ The appeal of a message often depends on fear, sex and humour.

IT'S SATURDAY EVENING, and Leah, Lynn and Nicki are hanging out at Nicki's flat in Manchester. While waiting to go out on the town, they are doing some channel-surfing. Leah clicks to the sports channel and the three friends see there's a football game on, being tele-vised from Ukraine. Portugal is playing against Germany. Leah has been a fan for as long as she can remember – perhaps as a result of having three older brothers and growing up in a house which had Manchester United souvenirs in every room. She loves the subtle intensity of the game, of any game – the traps, the moves, the way players make it look easy to move a ball around a huge field as if it were a small patch of grass. Further, she's proud of Manchester United's rich history as a club, and its success as a business operation. But don't ask her opin-ion of having her beloved team's ownership taken over by some American businessman who doesn't even understand the game![1] Nicki's a glutton for thrills and chills – at least when it comes to the national team: she converted to football 10 years ago after seeing the England team beat Germany 5–1 in a qualifying game for the 2002 World Cup. But this game does not include the English team, and so she is somewhat less interested. Lynn, on the other hand, doesn't know a corner kick from a penalty kick. For her, the most interesting part of the match was the footage being shown of the Portuguese player Christiano Ronaldo's spectacular play-ing skills. She thinks he is the cutest thing – and even considered asking her boyfriend to get a haircut like Ronaldo's. Still, soccer doesn't really ring her chimes – but as long as she gets to hang out with her girlfriends she doesn't really care if they watch non-contact sports like football or contact sports like *Celebrity Big Brother!*

THE POWER OF ATTITUDES

All over Europe, football has a long and rich tradition, but as a sport it has been dominated by male patronage at the stadiums and male viewership on the television. A long running campaign for the Danish national betting corporation plays on the widespread attitude that women are not into football. With the pay-off line 'There's so much that women do not understand', the humourous TV spots illustrate female misunderstandings of a variety of expressions in football jargon, thereby maintaining an image of football as a male domain (or refuge?). Not so in the US, where attitudes towards the game are much more positive towards women's football.

On the other hand, football clubs, sports gear producers and other market agents generally welcome female consumers among their ranks. For example, Leah is just the kind of fan sponsoring companies like Nike, Gatorade and Adidas hope will turn more women into an ongoing source of football fanaticism. It is obvious that a variety of hero myths are necessary in order to mobilize such new fan groups. However, following Beckham's, Ronaldo's and others' stardom as male sex symbols rather than as footballers, certain people believe that too much focus is moving away from the sport and onto something which should be secondary. According to this attitude, it is one (acceptable) thing to use the hero myth to sell something related to the sport,[2] it is another to sell something completely unrelated to the sport (see for example David Beckham's promotion of Armani, Chapter 10).

Any which way, football is big business, but how it operates in the life of the single consumer is very much a question of attitude, as we have seen with Leah, Nicki and Lynn. As you'll see throughout this chapter and this book, attitudes can vary significantly along gender lines, and from one culture to another. Attitudes obviously also vary over time. Since most of us are also consuming banking services and other financial products, we may be able to relate to the attitudinal statement, 'I have confidence in the financial sector'. How would that rate in an attitude measurement in the spring of 2008 versus the spring of 2012 (i.e. before or after the financial crisis)? Effectively, part of the problem is exactly that the shift in attitudes vis-à-vis the financial sector is provoking much lower degrees of confidence which in itself aggravates the crisis.

The term **attitude** is widely used in popular culture. You might be asked, 'What is your attitude towards abortion?' A parent might scold, 'Young man, I don't like your attitude.' Some bars even euphemistically refer to Happy Hour as 'an attitude adjustment period'. For our purposes, though, an attitude is a lasting, general evaluation of people (including oneself), objects, advertisements or issues.[3] Anything towards which one has an attitude is called an **attitude object (A$_o$)**.

This chapter will consider the contents of an attitude, how attitudes are formed, how they can be measured, and review some of the surprisingly complex relationships between attitudes and behaviour. Both as a theoretical concept, and as a tool to be used in the marketplace, the notion and dynamics of attitudes remain one of the most studied and applied of all behavioural constructs.[4] In the final part of the chapter, we will take a closer look at how attitudes can be changed – as this is certainly an issue of prime importance to marketers.

THE FUNCTION OF ATTITUDES

The **functional theory of attitudes** was initially developed by the psychologist Daniel Katz to explain how attitudes facilitate social behaviour.[5] According to this pragmatic approach, attitudes exist because they serve a function for the person. That is, they are determined by a person's motives. Consumers who expect that they will need to deal with similar information at a future time will be more likely to start forming attitudes in anticipation of an event.[6]

Two people can each have the same attitude towards an object for very different reasons. As a result, it can be helpful for a marketer to know why an attitude is held before attempting to change it. The following are attitude functions as identified by Katz:

- *Utilitarian function.* The utilitarian function is related to the basic principles of reward and punishment. We develop some of our attitudes towards products simply on the basis of whether these products provide pleasure or pain. If a person likes the taste of a cheeseburger, that person will develop a positive attitude towards cheeseburgers. Ads that stress straightforward product benefits (e.g. you should drink Diet Coke 'just for the taste of it') appeal to the utilitarian function.

- *Value-expressive function.* Attitudes that perform a value-expressive function express the consumer's central values or self-concept. A person forms a product attitude not because of its objective benefits, but because of what the product says about them as a person (e.g. 'What sort of woman reads *Elle*?'). Value-expressive attitudes are highly relevant to lifestyle analyses, where consumers cultivate a cluster of activities, interests and opinions to express a particular social identity.

- *Ego-defensive function.* Attitudes that are formed to protect the person, from either external threats or internal feelings, perform an ego-defensive function. An early marketing study indicated that housewives in the 1950s resisted the use of instant coffee because it threatened their conception of themselves as capable homemakers.[7] Notice how this attitude has certainly changed! Products that promise to help a man project a 'macho' image (e.g. Marlboro cigarettes) may be appealing to his insecurities about his masculinity. Another example of this function is deodorant campaigns that stress the dire, embarrassing consequences of underarm odour.

- *Knowledge function.* Some attitudes are formed as the result of a need for order, structure or meaning. This need is often present when a person is in an ambiguous situation or is confronted with a new product (e.g. 'Bayer wants you to know about pain relievers').

An attitude can serve more than one function, but in many cases a particular one will be dominant. By identifying the dominant function a product serves for consumers (i.e. what benefits it provides), marketers can emphasize these benefits in their communications and packaging. Ads relevant to the function prompt more favourable thoughts about what is being marketed and can result in a heightened preference for both the ad and the product.

One American study determined that for most people coffee serves more of a utilitarian function than a value-expressive function. As a consequence, subjects responded more positively to copy for a fictitious brand of coffee that read, 'The delicious, hearty flavour and aroma of Sterling Blend coffee comes from a blend of the freshest coffee beans' (i.e. a utilitarian appeal) than they did to copy that read, 'The coffee you drink says something about the type of person you are. It can reveal your rare, discriminating taste' (i.e. the value-expressive function). In European countries with a strong 'coffee culture', such as Germany, the Benelux and Scandinavian countries, ads are more likely to stress the value-expressive function, in which the more social and ritualistic aspects of coffee consumption are expressed.[8] Attitudes, then, obviously vary with cultural context. A large-scale comparative study of attitudes towards sustainability principles in pig meat production resulted in a typology of consumers

Table 8.1 Comparison among types of citizens in terms of sustainability related characteristics

	Indifferent ambivalent	Environmentally conscious	Animal well-being conscious	Small farming supporters	Food safety conscious	Industrial production oriented
EU	59.1%	17.1%	12.3%	11.5%	–	–
Brazil	71.6%	16.0%	–	12.4%	–	–
China	44.1%	–	–	–	31.5%	23.0%

Source: Adapted from Athanasios Krystalis, Klaus G. Grunert, Marcia D. de Barcellos, Toula Perrea and Wim Verbeke, 'Consumer Attitudes towards Sustainability Aspects of Food Production: Insights from Three Continents', *Journal of Marketing Management*, 28 (3–4 March 2012), 334–372.

that showed some clear differences between EU, Brazil and China (see Table 8.1). While the results for EU and Brazil were fairly similar (although the level of ambivalence or indifference towards the sustainability issue is higher in Brazil than in Europe), the issue of animal welfare came out as significant in the EU sample unlike Brazil, where it did not appear. In China, the segment of the indifferent showed a higher degree of indifference, but perhaps surprisingly, this segment was smaller than on the other two continents. China, having been plagued by a number of food production scandals, was shown to have segments much more concerned about food safety and industrial farming (as opposed to small scale farming in EU and Brazil).[9] The same food safety issue might also explain the fact that personal (rather than social) motives seems to dominate the small but emerging demand for organic produce in China.[10]

As we saw in the experiences of the three Manchester women watching a football game, the importance of an attitude object may differ quite a bit for different people. Understanding the centrality of an attitude to an individual and to others who share similar characteristics can be useful to marketers who are trying to devise strategies that will appeal to different customer segments. A study of football game attendance illustrates that varying levels of commitment result in different fan 'profiles'.[11] The study identified three distinct clusters of fans:[12]

- One cluster consisted of the real diehard fans like Leah who were highly committed to their team and who displayed an enduring love of the game. To reach these fans, the researchers recommended that sports marketers should focus on providing them with greater sports knowledge and relate their attendance to their personal goals and values.

- A second cluster was like Nicki – their attitudes were based on the unique, self-expressive experience provided by the game. They enjoyed the stimulation of cheering for a team and the drama of the competition itself. These people are more likely to be 'brand switchers', fair-weather fans who shift allegiances when the home team no longer provides the thrills they need. This segment can be appealed to by publicizing aspects of the visiting teams, such as advertising the appearance of stars who are likely to give the fans a game they will remember.

- A third cluster was like Lynn – they were looking for camaraderie above all. These consumers attend games primarily to take part in small-group activities such as a pre- or post-game party which may accompany the event. Marketers could appeal to this cluster by providing improved peripheral benefits, such as making it easier for groups to meet at the stadium, improving parking, and offering multiple-unit pricing.

The ABC model of attitudes and hierarchies of effects

Most researchers agree that an attitude has three components: affect, behaviour and cognition. **Affect** refers to the way a consumer feels about an attitude object. Behaviour involves the person's intentions to do something with regard to an attitude object (but, as will be discussed later, an intention does not always result in an actual behaviour). **Cognition** refers to the beliefs a consumer has about an attitude object. These three components of an attitude can be remembered as the **ABC model of attitudes**.

This model emphasizes the interrelationships between knowing, feeling and doing. Consumers' attitudes towards a product cannot be determined simply by identifying their beliefs about it. For example, a researcher may find that shoppers 'know' a particular digital camera has a 10X optical zoom lens, auto-focus and can also shoot *QuickTime Movies*, but such findings do not indicate whether they feel these attributes are good, bad or irrelevant, or whether they would actually buy the camera.

While all three components of an attitude are important, their relative importance will vary depending upon a consumer's level of motivation with regard to the attitude object. Attitude researchers have developed the concept of a **hierarchy of effects** to explain the relative impact of the three components. Each hierarchy specifies that a fixed sequence of steps occurs en route to an attitude. Three different hierarchies are summarized in Figure 8.1.

The standard learning hierarchy

Think→Feel→Do: Leah's positive attitude towards football closely resembles the process by which most attitudes have been assumed to be constructed. A consumer approaches a product decision as a problem-solving process. First, they form beliefs about a product by accumulating knowledge (beliefs) regarding relevant attributes. Next, the consumer evaluates these beliefs and forms a feeling about the product (affect).[13] Over time, Leah assembled information about the sport, began to recognize the players, and learned which teams were superior to others. Fnally, based on this evaluation, the consumer engages in a relevant behaviour, such as buying the product or supporting a particular team by wearing its shirt. This careful choice process often results in the type of loyalty displayed by Leah: the consumer 'bonds' with the product over time and is not easily persuaded to experiment with other brands. The standard learning hierarchy assumes that a consumer is highly involved in making a purchase decision.[14] The person is motivated to seek out a lot of information, carefully weighs alternatives, and comes to a thoughtful decision. As we saw in Chapter 6, this process is likely to occur if the decision is important to the consumer or in some way central to the consumer's

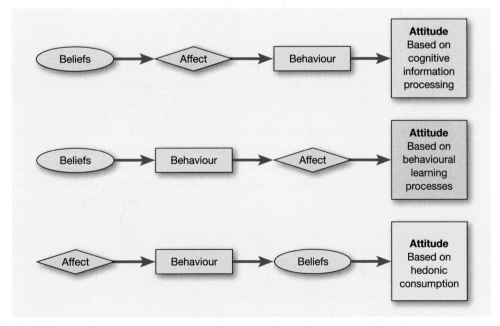

Figure 8.1 Three hierarchies of effects

self-concept. If you understand the level of fan support for Manchester United, then you will appreciate just how central Leah's attitudes about football (or, in this case, Manchester United) are for her.

While the attitudes that Leah holds towards Manchester United may be well understood to be positive, it is not always an easy and straightforward task to assume that any related product purchases she makes will be consistent with her positive attitudes towards the team. Imagine that Leah is considering the purchase of some Nike football shoes for herself, and as part of gathering information about the shoes, she comes across an article on globalization, and Nike's use of outsourcing the labour for making football shoes to factories in low labour cost countries such as Vietnam. Leah's attitudes towards globalization, coupled with her own cognitive beliefs about the labour conditions in these factories may in fact lead her to have a negative affect towards the Nike shoes. At the same time, Leah's attitude towards buying a well-made football shoe at a very competitive price might be quite positive! So possibly she is likely to still buy the shoes. In a different context, it has been shown that satisfaction with the brand's performance is more directly related to brand loyalty than corporate image.[15]

The low-involvement hierarchy

Do→Feel→Think: In contrast to Leah, Nicki's interest in the attitude object (football) is at best lukewarm. She is not particularly knowledgeable about the sport, and she may have an emotional response to an exciting game but not to a specific team (excluding the English national team). Nicki is typical of a consumer who forms an attitude via the *low-involvement hierarchy of effects*. In this sequence, the consumer does not initially have a strong preference for one brand over another, but instead acts on the basis of limited knowledge and then forms an evaluation only after the product has been purchased or used.[16] The attitude is likely to come about through behavioural learning, in which the consumer's choice is reinforced by good or bad experiences with the product after purchase. Nicki will probably be more likely to tune in to future games if they continue to have the same level of drama and excitement as the classic Germany–England match.

The possibility that consumers simply do not care enough about many decisions to assemble a set of product beliefs carefully and then evaluate them is important, because it implies that all of the concern about influencing beliefs and carefully communicating information about product attributes may be largely wasted. Consumers are not necessarily going to pay attention anyway; they are more likely to respond to simple stimulus–response connections when making purchase decisions. For example, a consumer choosing between paper towels might remember that 'Brand X absorbs more quickly than Brand Y', rather than bothering to compare systematically all of the brands on the shelf. Such automatically evoked attitudes are also called implicit attitudes and may have significant influences on purchase decisions.[17]

The notion of low involvement on the part of consumers is a bitter pill for some marketers to swallow. Who wants to admit that what they market is not very important or involving? A brand manager for, say, a brand of chewing gum or cat food may find it hard to believe that consumers do not put that much thought into purchasing their product because they themselves spend many of their waking (and perhaps sleeping) hours thinking about it.

For marketers, the ironic silver lining to this low-involvement cloud is that, under these conditions, consumers are not motivated to process a lot of complex brand-related information. Instead, they will be swayed by principles of behavioural learning, such as the simple responses caused by conditioned brand names, point-of-purchase displays, and so on. This results in what we might call the *involvement paradox*: the less important the product is to consumers, the more important are many of the marketing stimuli (e.g. packages, jingles) that must be devised to sell it.

The experiential hierarchy

Feel→Think→Do: In recent years researchers have begun to stress the significance of emotional response as a central aspect of an attitude. According to the experiential hierarchy of

While Leah may have very positive attitudes towards soccer, and for the soccer boot made by one of her favourite brands, Nike, she still needs to sort out her conflicting attitudes towards globalization, and labour practices, which Nike and other shoe manufacturers use.

Photo: Gary Bamossy.

effects, consumers act on the basis of their emotional reactions (just as Lynn enjoys watching TV with her friends, regardless of what is on). Although the factors of beliefs and behaviour are recognized as playing a part, a consumer's overall evaluation of an attitude object is considered by many to be the core of an attitude.

This perspective highlights the idea that attitudes can be strongly influenced by intangible product attributes such as package design, and by consumers' reactions to accompanying stimuli such as advertising and even the brand name. As an example, consider one Swedish study which underlined the importance of the book covers with sexually charged images in the forming of the attitude towards the book.[18] Such emotional involvement and feelings of connectedness also play a role in relation to sales people. Another study concluded that an incidental similarity between a customer and a salesperson, like a shared birthday or originating from the same town, can lead to a more positive attitude and a higher likelihood of purchase.[19] Numerous studies indicate that the mood a person is in when exposed to a marketing message influences how the ad is processed, the likelihood that the information presented will be remembered, and how the person will feel about the advertised item and related products in the future.[20] Furthermore, feelings may not be uniform, as we saw with Leah: Manchester United and Nike shoes. They can be mixed positive and negative. There are indications that people with Eastern cultural backgrounds are better at accepting mixed emotions in the formation of an attitude than Westerners, since they have a less dichotomizing way of looking at life, and instead understand the balancing of contradictory principles, as seen in the principle of yin and yang.[21]

One important debate about the experiential hierarchy concerns the independence of cognition and affect. On the one hand, the *cognitive–affective model* argues that an affective judgement is the last step in a series of cognitive processes. Earlier steps include the sensory registration of stimuli and the retrieval of meaningful information from memory to categorize these stimuli.[22]

On the other hand, the *independence hypothesis* takes the position that affect and cognition involve two separate, partially independent systems; affective responses do not always require

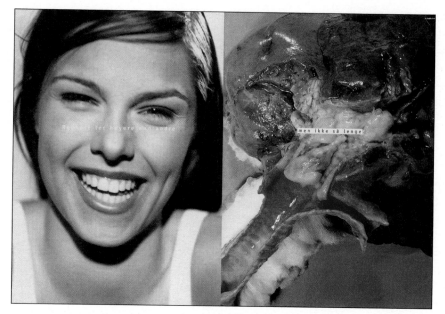

'Smokers are more sociable than others . . . while it lasts.' This Norwegian ad represents the many anti-smoking campaigns running in European markets.

John Hopkins Bloomberg School of Public Health.

prior cognitions.[23] The number one song in the 'Top Ten' hit parade may possess the same attributes as many other songs (dominant bass guitar, raspy vocals, persistent downbeat), but beliefs about these attributes cannot explain why one song becomes a classic while another sharing the same characteristics ends up in the bargain bin on iTunes! The independence hypothesis does not eliminate the role of cognition in experience. It simply balances this traditional, rational emphasis on calculated decision-making by paying more attention to the impact of aesthetic, subjective experience. This type of holistic processing is more likely to occur when the product is perceived as primarily expressive or delivers sensory pleasure rather than utilitarian benefits.[24]

There is more to marketing than product attitudes

Marketers who are concerned with understanding consumers' attitudes have to contend with an even more complex issue: in decision-making situations, people form attitudes towards objects other than the product itself that can influence their ultimate selections. One additional factor to consider is attitudes towards the act of buying in general or attitudes towards a particular shop.[25] As we will see later in the chapter, sometimes people are reluctant, embarrassed or just too lazy to expend the effort to obtain a desired product or service. In addition, consumers' reactions to a product, over and above their feelings about the product itself, are influenced by their evaluations of its advertising. Our evaluation of a product can be determined solely by our appraisal of how it is depicted in marketing communications – that is, we do not hesitate to form attitudes about products we have never even seen personally, much less used.

The **attitude towards the advertisement (A_{ad})** is defined as a predisposition to respond in a favourable or unfavourable manner to a particular advertising stimulus during a particular exposure occasion. The feelings generated by advertising can have a direct impact on brand attitudes. Commercials can evoke a wide range of emotional responses, from disgust to happiness. Further, there is evidence that emotional responses will vary from one group of consumers to another. In an empirical study of students and housewives in Belgium and Holland, the results showed that the Belgians were more positive towards the hedonic and sociocultural aspects of advertising than their Dutch counterparts. In the UK, Ford's ad campaign research on the Ford Ka, which is targeting an image-oriented market, showed it annoyed

41 per cent of 55- to 64-year-olds, compared with only 18 per cent of 25- to 34-year-olds. These feelings can be influenced both by the way the ad is done (i.e. the specific advertising execution) and by the consumer's reactions to the advertiser's motives. For example, many advertisers who are trying to craft messages for adolescents and young adults are encountering problems because this age group, having grown up in a 'marketing society', tends to be quite literate about attempts to persuade them to buy things.[26]

MARKETING PITFALL

Is there a European attitude towards humour in advertising?

One of the reasons the use of humour is so widespread is that it is such a versatile tool. 'It has a surprisingly broad range of applications. It can act as a razor-sharp discriminator, allowing advertisers to address very tightly defined demographic and attitudinal segments, but because humour is universal it can also act as a catch-all, a way of appealing to everyone,' says advertising psychologist David Lewis.

Humour may be universal, but few nations use it to the extent it is used in the UK. Research carried out by the University of Luton into the devices used in beer advertising found that 88 per cent of British beer ads used humour, compared with a third of Dutch beer ads and only 10 per cent of German beer commercials. The British reliance on humour reflects historic and cultural factors peculiar to this country, say commentators. A major ingredient is our antipathy to 'the sell', argues writer and communications consultant Paul Twivy, who has written comedy scripts for television and run a major advertising agency. 'It's a feature of the British malaise. We are embarrassed about the hard sell. Germany for instance has a tradition of revering engineering, so they are quite happy to talk unironically about product quality. We on the other hand still look down on commerce and value amateurism and effortless success in a way that can be traced back to the nineteenth century. So humour which entertains is a way of selling, while not being seen to sell.' Others say that it reflects a narrow range of emotional responses and attitudes within the national culture. 'Other countries are much more open about expressing a wide range of attitudes. We tend to be repressed and self-deprecating and consider it rude to wear our emotions on our sleeve. So we use humour as a way of not expressing what we really feel,' says Andy Nairn, joint planning director at advertising agency Miles Calcraft Briginshaw Duffy. 'The upshot is that American advertising, for instance, has a much wider emotional repertoire than British, using joy, love, ambition and desire in a way that would simply make British audiences gag.'[27] How do you respond to humorous ads from different countries in Europe? Do they all strike you as 'funny', and does the approach improve your attitude towards the advertiser'?

HOW DO WE FORM ATTITUDES?

We all have lots of attitudes, and we do not usually question how we got them. No one is born with the conviction that, say, Pepsi is better than Coke or that heavy metal music liberates the soul. Where do these attitudes come from?

An attitude can form in several different ways, depending on the particular hierarchy of effects in operation. It can occur because of classical conditioning, in which an attitude object, such as the name Pepsi, is repeatedly paired with a catchy jingle ('You're in the Pepsi Generation . . .'). Or it can be formed through instrumental conditioning, in which consumption of the attitude object is reinforced (Pepsi quenches the thirst). Alternatively, the learning of an attitude can be the outcome of a very complex cognitive process. For example, a teenager may come to model the behaviour of friends and media endorsers, such as Beyoncé, who drink Pepsi because they believe that this will allow them to fit in with the desirable lifestyle Pepsi commercials portray.

Is it possible to build positive attitudes to and even recall of experiences of something that does not exist? Indeed! Experiments have shown that advertisements, especially those with more vivid imagery, can even lead consumers to believe that they have had experiences with a product that does not, in fact, exist, a belief that in turn is likely to reinforce the attitude towards the product, a phenomenon known as the 'false experience effect'.[28] Such research demonstrates a certain unreliability of attitudes as expressed by consumers.

It is thus important to distinguish between types of attitudes, since not all are formed the same way.[29] A highly brand-loyal consumer like Leah, the Manchester United fan, has an enduring, deeply-held positive attitude towards an attitude object, and this involvement will be difficult to weaken. On the other hand, another consumer like Nicki, who likes the drama and excitement more than the subtle aspects of soccer, may have a mildly positive attitude towards a product but be quite willing to abandon it when something better comes along. This section will consider the differences between strongly and weakly held attitudes and briefly review some of the major theoretical perspectives that have been developed to explain how attitudes form and relate to one another in the minds of consumers.

Levels of commitment to an attitude

Consumers vary in their commitment to an attitude, and the degree of commitment is related to their level of involvement with the attitude object.[30] Consumers are more likely to consider brands that engender strong positive attitudes.[31] Let's look at three (increasing) levels of commitment:

- *Compliance*. At the lowest level of involvement, compliance, an attitude is formed because it helps in gaining rewards or avoiding punishments from others. This attitude is very superficial: it is likely to change when the person's behaviour is no longer monitored by others or when another option becomes available. A person may drink Pepsi because that is the brand the café sells and it is too much trouble to go elsewhere for a Coca-Cola.

- *Identification*. A process of identification occurs when attitudes are formed in order for the consumer to be similar to another person or group. Advertising that depicts the social consequences of choosing some products over others is relying on the tendency of consumers to imitate the behaviour of desirable models, cf. Chapter 10 on group influences.

- *Internalization*. At a high level of involvement, deep-seated attitudes are internalized and become part of the person's value system. These attitudes are very difficult to change because they are so important to the individual. For example, many consumers had strong attitudes towards Coca-Cola and reacted very negatively when the company attempted to switch to the New Coke formula. This allegiance to Coke was obviously more than a minor preference for these people: the brand had become intertwined with their social identities, taking on patriotic and nostalgic properties.

The consistency principle

Have you ever heard someone say, 'Pepsi is my favourite soft drink. It tastes terrible', or 'I love my husband. He's the biggest idiot I've ever met'? If we disregard the use of irony, perhaps not very often for the simple reason that these beliefs or evaluations are not consistent with one another. According to the **principle of cognitive consistency**, consumers value harmony among their thoughts, feelings and behaviours, and they are motivated to maintain uniformity among these elements. This desire means that, if necessary, consumers will change their thoughts, feelings or behaviours to make them consistent with their other experiences. The consistency principle is an important reminder that attitudes are not formed in a vacuum. A significant determinant of the way an attitude object will be evaluated is how it fits with other related attitudes we already hold.

MARKETING PITFALL

Attitudes to countries: Who do we love?

The top 10 most valuable global brands as measured by Interbrand are still American. For more than half a century, the US and its products have stood for progress, glamour and freedom in the minds of consumers around the world. Yet there seems to be a growing challenge for US companies in the attitudes of people. The critique of Wall Street and its role in the financial crisis, scandals such as Enron and reckless crooks such as Bernard Madoff have headlined news from the American business world. A qualitative study of brand reputations in the UK and Germany confirmed that due to imagery of a rather rough form of capitalism, consumers associate American corporations with a relatively high likelihood of unethical behaviour compared to companies in, for example, Scandinavia.[32] On the other hand, trying to position oneself as 'the good guys' can also backfire. Karen, a young blonde with a baby boy in her arms,

appeared on YouTube in 2009, addressing 'everyone' out there in the search for the boy's father. Not resentful in any way she just wanted to see if she could find this tourist of no name and no origin, to let him know that the boy existed. The touching story made more than a million people watch the video on Karen's YouTube profile and generated a lot of sympathy for the single mother. At least until it was revealed that 'Karen' was actually an actress and that the video had been planted by the Danish national tourist board VisitDenmark as a viral campaign to influence people's attitudes towards Denmark as a free-spirited and easygoing country. A lot of people turned their sympathy to anger, feeling betrayed and emotionally exploited. VisitDenmark withdrew the video[33] – but of course, it has not been off the internet since . . .

Cognitive dissonance theory revisited

In Chapter 6, we discussed the role played by cognitive dissonance when consumers are trying to choose between two desired products. Cognitive dissonance theory has other important ramifications for attitudes, since people are often confronted with situations in which there is some conflict between their attitudes and behaviours.[34]

The theory proposes that, much like hunger or thirst, people are motivated to reduce this negative state by making things fit with one another. The theory focuses on situations where two cognitive elements are inconsistent with one another.

A cognitive element can be something a person believes about themselves, a behaviour they perform or an observation about their surroundings. For example, the two cognitive elements 'I know smoking cigarettes causes cancer' and 'I smoke cigarettes' are dissonant. This psychological inconsistency creates a feeling of discomfort that the smoker is motivated to reduce. The magnitude of dissonance depends upon both the importance and the number of dissonant elements.[35] In other words, the pressure to reduce dissonance is more likely to be observed in high-involvement situations in which the elements are more important to the individual.

Dissonance reduction can occur by either eliminating, adding or changing elements. For example, the person could stop smoking (eliminating) or remember Great Aunt Sophia, who smoked until the day she died at age 90 (adding). Alternatively, they might question the research that links cancer and smoking (changing), perhaps by believing industry-sponsored studies that try to refute this connection.

Dissonance theory can help to explain why evaluations of a product tend to increase after it has been purchased, i.e. post-purchase dissonance. The cognitive element 'I made a stupid decision' is dissonant with the element 'I am not a stupid person', so people tend to find even more reasons to like something after buying it. Gamblers have been shown to evaluate their chosen horses more highly and were more confident of their success after they had placed a bet than before. Since the gambler is financially committed to the choice, they reduce dissonance by increasing the attractiveness of the chosen alternative relative to the unchosen ones.[36] Similar effects have been found for technological products, but it was also found that such increased positivity was fragile.[37] One implication of this phenomenon is that consumers actively seek support for their purchase decisions, so marketers should supply them with additional reinforcement to build positive brand attitudes.

While the consistency principle works well in explaining our desire for harmony among thoughts, feelings and behaviours, and subsequently in helping marketers understand their target markets, it is not a perfect predictor of the way in which we hold seemingly *related* attitudes, as we saw in the case of Leah's attitudes towards soccer, Nike and labour practices in our globalized economy.

Self-perception theory

Do attitudes necessarily change following behaviour because people are motivated to feel good about their decisions? **Self-perception theory** provides an alternative explanation of dissonance effects.[38] It assumes that people use observations of their own behaviour to determine what their attitudes are, just as we assume that we know the attitudes of others by watching what they do. The theory states that we maintain consistency by inferring that we must have a positive attitude towards an object if we have bought or consumed it (assuming that we freely made this choice).

Self-perception theory is relevant to the low-involvement hierarchy, since it involves situations in which behaviours are initially performed based on implicit attitudes. After the fact, the cognitive and affective components of attitude fall into line. Thus, buying a product out of habit may result in a positive attitude towards it after the fact – namely, why would I buy it if I didn't like it?

Self-perception theory helps to explain the effectiveness of a sales strategy called the **foot-in-the-door technique**, which is based on the observation that a consumer is more likely to comply with a request if they have first agreed to comply with a smaller request.[39] The name of this technique comes from the practice of door-to-door selling, when the salesperson was taught to plant their foot in a door so the prospect could not slam it shut. A good salesperson knows that they are more likely to get an order if the customer can be persuaded to open the door and talk. By agreeing to do so, the customer has established that they are willing to listen. Placing an order is consistent with this self-perception. This technique is especially useful for inducing consumers to answer surveys or to donate money to charity. Recent research also points to the possibility that when salespeople ask consumers to make a series of choices, these decisions are cognitively demanding and deplete the resources the person has available to monitor his behaviour. As a result, the target will opt for easier decisions down the road; in some cases it may be easier just to comply with the request than to search for reasons why you shouldn't.[40]

Social judgement theory

Social judgement theory assumes that people assimilate new information about attitude objects in the light of what they already know or feel.[41] The initial attitude acts as a frame of reference, and new information is categorized in terms of this existing standard. Just as our decision that a box is heavy depends in part on other boxes we have lifted, so we develop a subjective standard when making judgements about attitude objects.

One important aspect of the theory is the notion that people differ in terms of the information they will find acceptable or unacceptable. They form **latitudes of acceptance and rejection** around an attitude standard. Ideas that fall within a latitude will be favourably received, while those falling outside this zone will not. There are plenty of examples of how latitudes of acceptance and rejection are influencing marketing practices and consumers' behaviour in Europe: childhood obesity has become an alarming European issue, prompting the Belgian parliament's ban of Coca-Cola machines in Belgium's elementary schools.[42] Similar steps have been taken in other countries as well. Likewise, European attitudes towards smoking have clearly evolved towards a latitude of rejection – providing GlaxoSmithKline with the opportunity to launch new anti-smoking products such as nicotine replacement gums and patches.[43] Furthermore, a positive attitude towards consumption of nicotine replacement therapy has been shown to be the single most influential factor in establishing a behavioural desire to quit smoking.[44] Nowadays, in more and more European countries, pubs, bars, restaurants and other public facilities have faced new legislation banning smoking in public rooms. The widespread acceptance of this legislation, also among smokers, reflects these changing attitudes towards smoking.

Messages that fall within the latitude of acceptance tend to be seen as more consistent with one's position than they actually are. This process is called an *assimilation effect*. On the other hand, messages falling in the latitude of rejection tend to be seen as even further from one's position than they actually are, resulting in a *contrast effect*.[45]

Balance theory

Balance theory considers relations among elements a person might perceive as belonging together.[46] This perspective involves relations (always from the perceiver's subjective point of view) among three elements, so the resulting attitude structures are called *triads*. Each triad contains (1) a person and their perceptions of (2) an attitude object and (3) some other person or object. These perceptions can be positive or negative. More importantly, people *alter* these perceptions in order to make relations among them consistent. The theory specifies that people desire relations among elements in a triad to be harmonious, or balanced. If they are not, a state of tension will result until perceptions are changed and balance is restored.

Elements can be perceived as going together in one of two ways. They can have a *unit relation*, where one element is seen as belonging to or being a part of the other (something like a belief), or a *sentiment relation*, where the two elements are linked because one has expressed a preference (or dislike) for the other. A couple might be seen as having a positive sentiment relation. If they marry, they will have a positive unit relation. The process of divorce is an attempt to sever a unit relation.

To see how balance theory might work, consider the following scenario:

- Monica would like to go out with Anthony, who is in her consumer behaviour class. In balance theory terms, Monica has a positive sentiment relation with Anthony.
- One day, Anthony attends class wearing clothing that allows his fellow students to see his tattoo. Anthony has a positive unit relation with the tattoo. It belongs to him and is literally a part of him.
- Monica does not like tattooed men. She has a negative sentiment relation with tattoos.

According to balance theory, Monica faces an unbalanced triad, and she will experience pressure to restore balance by altering some aspect of the triad, as shown in Figure 8.2. She could, for example, decide that she does not like Anthony after all. Or her liking for Anthony could prompt a change in her attitude towards tattoos. Finally, she could choose to 'leave the field' by thinking no more about Anthony and his controversial tattoo. Note that while the theory does not specify which of these routes will be taken, it does predict that one or more of Monica's perceptions will have to change in order to achieve balance. While this distortion is an oversimplified representation of most attitude processes, it helps to explain a number of consumer behaviour phenomena. Consider, for example, how consumers tend to perceive the same dish – say, a pasta salad – as more healthy when it is classified as salad than when it is classified as a pasta dish. Since consumers, and especially dieters, have established negative associations with the pasta category and positive with the salad category, these negative and positive associations rub off on a dish classified under one and the other, even if the dish is the same.[47]

Balance theory reminds us that when perceptions are balanced, attitudes are likely to be stable. On the other hand, when inconsistencies are observed we are more likely to observe

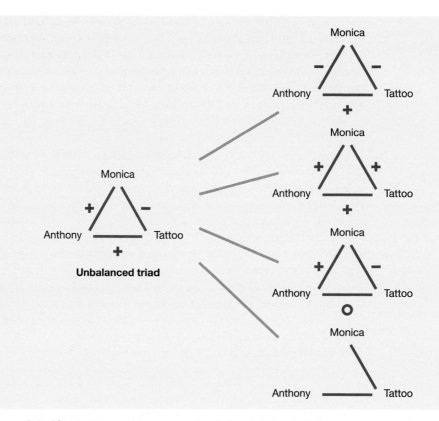

Figure 8.2 Alternative routes to restoring balance in a triad

changes in attitudes. Balance theory also helps to explain why consumers like to be associated with positively valued objects. Forming a unit relation with a popular product (buying and wearing fashionable clothing or driving a high-performance car) may improve one's chances of being included as a positive sentiment relation in other people's triads.

This 'balancing act' is at the heart of celebrity endorsements, in which marketers hope that the star's popularity will transfer to the product or when a nonprofit organization gets a celebrity to discourage harmful behaviours.[48] We will consider this strategy in more detail towards the end of the chapter. For now, it pays to remember that creating a unit relation between a product and a star can backfire if the public's opinion of the celebrity endorser shifts from positive to negative. This happened when Pepsi pulled an ad featuring Madonna after she released a controversial music video involving religion and sex and when celebrity bad girl Paris Hilton got busted (see also page 315). The strategy can also cause trouble if people question the star–product unit relation: this happened when the late singer Michael Jackson, who also did promotions for Pepsi, subsequently confessed that he did not drink soda at all.

ATTITUDE MODELS

A consumer's overall evaluation of a product sometimes accounts for the bulk of their *attitude* towards it. When market researchers want to assess attitudes, it can often be sufficient for them simply to ask the consumer, 'How do you feel about Heineken?' or 'How do you feel about the proposals for solving the crisis of the Greek national debt?'

However, as we saw earlier, attitudes can be a lot more complex than that. One problem is that a product or service may be composed of many attributes or qualities – some of which may be more important than others to particular people. Another problem is that a person's decision to act on their attitude is affected by other factors, such as whether it is felt that buying a product will meet with approval of friends or family (if Leah's closest friends are strongly opposed to using cheap labour for the making of Nike soccer boots, this may be a key reason for her not to buy Nike). For these reasons, attitude models have been developed that try to specify the different elements that might work together to influence people's evaluations of attitude objects.

Multi-attribute attitude models

A simple response does not always tell us everything we need to know about why the consumer has certain feelings towards a product or about what marketers can do to change the consumer's attitude. For this reason, **multi-attribute attitude models** have been extremely popular among marketing researchers. This type of model assumes that a consumer's attitude (evaluation) of an attitude object (A_o) will depend on the beliefs they have about several or many attributes of the object. The use of a multi-attribute model implies that an attitude towards a product or brand can be predicted by identifying these specific beliefs and combining them to derive a measure of the consumer's overall attitude. We will describe how these work, using the example of a consumer evaluating a complex attitude object that should be very familiar: a university.

Basic multi-attribute models specify three elements:[49]

- *Attributes* are characteristics of the A_o. Most models assume that the relevant characteristics can be identified. That is, the researcher can include those attributes that consumers take into consideration when evaluating the A_o. For example, scholarly reputation is an attribute of a university.

- *Beliefs* are cognitions about the specific A_o (usually relative to others like it). A belief measure assesses the extent to which the consumer perceives that a brand possesses a particular attribute. For example, a student might have a belief that the University of Southern Denmark has a strong academic standing in consumer research.

- *Importance weights* reflect the relative priority of an attribute to the consumer. Although an A_o can be considered on a number of attributes, some will be more important than others (i.e. they will be given greater weight), and these weights are likely to differ across consumers. In the case of universities, for example, one student might stress the school's reputation for project based learning, while another might assign greater weight to the social environment in which the university is located, for example in terms of access to internships.

Measuring attitude elements

Suppose a supermarket chain wanted to measure shoppers' attitudes towards its retail outlets. The firm might administer one of the following types of attitude scales to consumers by mail, phone or in person.[50]

Single-item scales One simple way to assess consumers' attitudes towards a store or product is to ask them for their general feelings about it. Such a global assessment does not provide much information about specific attributes, but it does give managers some sense of consumers' overall attitudes. This single-item approach often uses a Likert scale, which measures respondents' overall level of agreement with or feelings about an attitude statement.

How satisfied are you with your grocery store?
☐ Very satisfied   ☐ Somewhat satisfied   ☐ Satisfied   ☐ Not at all satisfied

Multiple-item batteries Attitude models go beyond such a simple measure, since they acknowledge that an overall attitude may often be composed of consumers' perceptions about multiple elements. For this reason, many attitude measures assess a set of beliefs about an issue and combine these reactions into an overall score. For example, the supermarket might ask customers to respond to a set of Likert scales and combine their responses into an overall measure of store satisfaction:

1   My supermarket has a good selection of produce.
2   My supermarket maintains sanitary conditions.
3   I never have trouble finding exotic foods at my supermarket.

☐ Agree   ☐ Agree   ☐ Neither agree   ☐ Disagree   ☐ Disagree
  strongly   somewhat   nor disagree   somewhat   strongly

The *semantic-differential scale* is useful for describing a person's set of beliefs about a company or brand, and it is also used to compare the images of competing brands. Respondents rate each attribute on a series of rating scales, where each end is anchored by adjectives or phrases, such as this one:

My supermarket is

Dirty 1—2—3—4—5—6—7 Clean

Semantic-differential scales can be used to construct a profile analysis of the competition, where the images of several stores or products can be compared visually by plotting the mean ratings for each object on several attributes of interest. This simple technique can help to pinpoint areas where the product or store diverges sharply from the competitors (in either a positive or a negative way).

The Fishbein model

The most influential multi-attribute model is the Fishbein model, named after its primary developer.[51] The model measures three components of attitude.

1 *Salient beliefs* people have about an A_o (those beliefs about the object that are considered during evaluation).

2 *Object-attribute linkages*, or the probability that a particular object has an important attribute.

3 *Evaluation* of each of the important attributes.

Note, however, that the model makes some assumptions that may not always be warranted. It assumes that we have been able to specify adequately all the relevant attributes that, for example, a student will use in evaluating their choice about which college to attend. The model also assumes that they will go through the process (formally or informally) of identifying a set of relevant attributes, weighing them and summing them. Although this particular decision is likely to be highly involving, it is still possible that their attitude will be formed by an overall affective response (a process known as *affect-referral*).

By combining these three elements, a consumer's overall attitude towards an object can be computed. (We will see later how this basic equation has been modified to increase its accuracy.) The basic formula is

$$A_{ijk} = \Sigma B_{ijk} I_{ik}$$

where i = attribute; j = brand; k = consumer; I = the importance weight given attribute i by consumer k; B = consumer k's belief regarding the extent to which brand j possesses attribute i; and A = a particular consumer k's attitude score for brand j.

Table 8.2 The basic multi-attribute model: Sandra's camera decision

		Beliefs (b)		
		Canon	Minolta	Nikon
Attribute (i)	Importance (I)	Digital Ixus	Dimage F100	Coolpix
Price	6	5	3	7
Brand reputation	5	5	5	7
Size	4	5	4	6
No. of pixels	3	5	3	6
Type of screen	2	2	2	3
Zoom	1	3	4	1
Attitude score		97	76	126

Note: These hypothetical ratings are scored from 1 to 10, and higher numbers indicate 'better' standing on an attribute. For a negative attribute (e.g. price), higher scores indicate that the camera is believed to have 'less' of that attribute (i.e. to be cheaper).

The overall attitude score (A) is obtained by multiplying a consumer's rating of each attribute for all the brands considered by the importance rating for that attribute.

To see how this basic multi-attribute model might work, let's suppose we want to predict which digital camera a young girl is likely to buy. Sandra has now reduced her choice to three alternatives. Since she must now decide between these, we would first like to know which attributes Sandra will consider in forming an attitude towards each camera. We can then ask Sandra to assign a rating regarding how well each camera performs on each attribute and also determine the relative importance of the attributes to her. An overall attitude score for each camera can then be computed by summing scores on each attribute (after weighing each by its relative importance). These hypothetical ratings are shown in Table 8.2. Based on this analysis, it seems that Sandra has the most favourable attitude towards Nikon Coolpix.

Strategic applications of the multi-attribute model

Imagine you are the director of marketing for Minolta, another brand that Sandra is considering. How might you use the data from this analysis to improve your image?

Capitalize on relative advantage If one's brand is viewed as being superior on a particular attribute, consumers like Sandra need to be convinced that this particular attribute is an important one. For example, while Sandra rates Minolta's zoom highly, she does not believe this attribute is a very important one for a camera. As Minolta's marketing director, you might emphasize the importance of good zoom in terms of the increased possibilities and pleasures that the camera offers.

Strengthen perceived product/attribute linkages A marketer may discover that consumers do not equate their brand with a certain attribute. This problem is commonly addressed by campaigns that stress the product's qualities to consumers (e.g. 'new and improved'). Sandra apparently does not think much of Minolta's screen, nor its pixel resolution quality. You might develop an informational campaign to improve these perceptions (e.g. 'Little-known facts about Minolta cameras').

Add a new attribute Product marketers frequently try to create a distinctive position from their competitors by adding a product feature. Minolta might try to emphasize some unique aspect, such as an improved technique for linking the camera with a cell phone's MMS function.

307

DO ATTITUDES PREDICT BEHAVIOUR?

Although multi-attribute models have been used by consumer researchers for many years, they have been plagued by a major problem: in many cases, knowledge of a person's attitude is not a very good predictor of behaviour. In a classic demonstration of 'do as I say, not as I do', many studies have obtained a very low correlation between a person's reported attitude towards something and their actual behaviour towards it. Some researchers have been so discouraged that they have questioned whether attitudes are of any use at all in understanding behaviour.[52] This questionable linkage can be a big headache for advertisers when consumers love a commercial yet fail to buy the product. During the 2012 superbowl, the ads for Bud Light and Dorito's chips were the most popular and generated the most buzz (see later this chapter), but according to market research did not make people want to buy the product.[53]

MARKETING PITFALL

The gulf between what consumers say and what they do is apparent when we look at sales of environmentally friendly products. Especially since the recession hit, the demand for green products has declined in USA[54] and other countries, while no such decline can be detected in terms of people's environmental attitudes. One study revealed such a gap between widespread positive attitudes towards ethical fashion but no actual consumption. Consumers blamed the price and the lack of accessibility for this discrepancy.[55]

Extended Fishbein models

The original Fishbein model, which focused on measuring a consumer's attitude towards a product, has been extended in a number of ways to improve its predictive ability. The revised version is called the **theory of reasoned action**.[56] An even more elaborate model, including also the degree to which one thinks that one is able to actually carry what is intended is called **theory of planned behaviour**.[57] The model is still not perfect, but its ability to predict relevant behaviour has been improved.[58] Some of the modifications to this model are considered here.

Intentions *vs* behaviour

As the old saying goes, 'the road to hell is paved with good intentions'. Many factors might interfere with actual behaviour, even if the consumer's intentions are sincere. You might save up with the intention of buying an iPod. In the interim, though, any number of things – having to spend your savings on unexpected expenses or finding that the desired model has been replaced by a new (and more expensive) one – could happen. It is not surprising, then, that in some instances past purchase behaviour has been found to be a better predictor of future behaviour than is a consumer's behavioural intention.[59] The theory of reasoned action aims to measure behavioural intentions, recognizing that certain uncontrollable factors inhibit prediction of actual behaviour.

Social pressure

The theory acknowledges the power of other people in influencing behaviour. Most of our behaviour is not determined in isolation. Much as we sometimes may hate to admit it, what we think others would like us to do may be more relevant than our own individual preferences. In the case of Sandra's camera choice, note that she is very positive about purchasing a

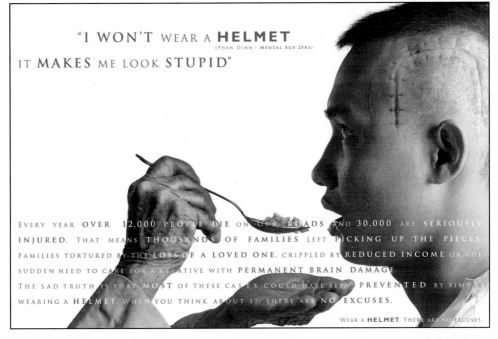

This Vietnamese ad employs social pressure (the subjective norm) to address people's attitudes to wearing helmets.

Ogilvy & Mather/Asia Injury Prevention Foundation; Photo by Pro-I Studio.

less expensive model. However, if she feels that this choice would be unpopular (perhaps her friends will think she is mad), she might ignore or downgrade this preference when making her final decision. A new element, the subjective norm (SN), was thus added to include the effects of what we believe other people think we should do. The value of SN is arrived at by including two other factors: (1) the intensity of a normative belief (NB) that others believe an action should be taken or not taken, and (2) the motivation to comply (MC) with that belief (i.e. the degree to which the consumer takes others' anticipated reactions into account when evaluating a course of action or a purchase). One study demonstrated how hotel guests were more likely to reuse towels if told that 'most guests in this hotels choose to reuse towels' than if told that doing so is 'good for the environment'. If told that most guests 'in this room' have chosen to reuse towels, the effect was even stronger. Social pressure also works even if you are never confronted with those exercising it.[60]

Attitude towards buying

Some models measure **attitude towards the act of buying (A_{act})**, rather than only the attitude towards the product itself. In other words, the focus is on the perceived consequences of a purchase. Knowing how someone feels about buying or using an object proves to be more valid than merely knowing the consumer's evaluation of the object itself.[61]

To understand this distinction, consider a problem that might arise when measuring attitudes towards condoms. Although a group of college students might have a positive attitude towards condom use, does this necessarily predict that they will buy and use them? A better prediction would be obtained by asking the students how likely they are to buy condoms. While a person might have a positive A_o towards condoms, A_{act} might be negative due to the embarrassment or the trouble involved. Different shopping contexts, such as seasonal sales, are also met with different attitudes, since consumers weigh the benefits and costs of such sales differently. One factor to consider is whether such sales are actually sales or just a marketing trick. In order to improve the trustworthiness and therefore the positive attitude, it has been suggested that shops produce a 'seasonal sales charter', promising good ethical conduct in their sales policies.[62]

Finally, in these days when more and more shopping takes place online, it is also useful to consider yet another attitude type: attitude towards the site (A_{site}). One study concluded, however, that affect (mood state based mainly on interactivity and aesthetics of the website) was more influential in producing purchase intentions than the attitude towards the website.[63]

Obstacles to predicting behaviour

Despite improvements to the Fishbein model, problems arise when it is misapplied. In many cases the model is used in ways for which it was not intended or where certain assumptions about human behaviour may not be warranted.[64] One study added an emotional dimension to a theory of planned behaviour approach to predicting the usage of electric cars, and concluded that the emotional component, together with the attitudes towards the car, actually were the strongest determinants of usage intentions.[65] We will look at emotions in terms of their persuasive function later in the chapter. Other obstacles to predicting behaviour are as follows:

1 The model was developed to deal with actual behaviour (e.g. taking a slimming pill), not with the outcomes of behaviour (e.g. losing weight) which are assessed in some studies.

2 Some outcomes are beyond the consumer's control, such as when the purchase requires the co-operation of other people. For instance, someone might seek a mortgage, but this intention will be worthless if they cannot find a banker to give them one.

3 The basic assumption that behaviour is intentional may be invalid in a variety of cases, including those involving impulsive acts, sudden changes in one's situation, novelty-seeking or even simple repeat-buying. One study found that such unexpected events as having guests, changes in the weather or reading articles about the health qualities of certain foods exerted a significant effect on actual behaviours.[66]

4 Measures of attitude often do not really correspond to the behaviour they are supposed to predict, either in terms of the A_o or when the act will occur. One common problem is a difference in the level of abstraction employed. For example, knowing a person's attitude towards sports cars may not predict whether they will purchase a Porsche 911. It is very important to match the level of specificity between the attitude and the behavioural intention.

5 A similar problem relates to the time-frame of the attitude measure. In general, the longer the time between the attitude measurement and the behaviour it is supposed to assess, the weaker the relationship will be. For example, predictability would improve markedly by asking consumers the likelihood that they would buy a house in the next week as opposed to within the next five years.

6 Attitudes formed by direct, personal experience with an A_o are stronger and more predictive of behaviour than those formed indirectly, such as through advertising.[67] According to the attitude accessibility perspective, behaviour is a function of the person's immediate perceptions of the A_o in the context of the situation in which it is encountered. An attitude will guide the evaluation of the object, but only if it is activated from memory when the object is observed. These findings underscore the importance of strategies that induce trial (e.g. by widespread product sampling to encourage the consumer to try the product at home, by taste tests, test drives, etc.) as well as those that maximize exposure to marketing communications.

MARKETING PITFALL

Animal welfare is an increasingly salient social issue for farmers, and animal rights activists have targeted a variety of production types all over Europe. Fur farming, for example, has been prohibited for more than a decade in countries such as Austria and the UK following massive consumer protests and activities. In order to try to avoid a similar fate, the fur industry in Denmark has openly admitted to the problems of the business, for example, the issue that mink bite each other in captivity. And the farmers raise the question: is there a place for us in this country? By showing photos of mink with gaping wounds,

the message from these ads is that while such problems exist, they are smaller in Denmark than elsewhere due to the high standards in the industry. Through the campaign, the industry invites consumers to have a continuous and open dialogue about how to improve animal welfare in fur farming. The Danish minister for food and agriculture has welcomed the campaign and its invitation to join the debates on these issues.[68] Ongoing research will investigate the role of animal welfare imagery on the world market for the Danish fur industry.[69]

MULTICULTURAL DIMENSIONS

The theory of reasoned action has primarily been applied in the West. Certain assumptions inherent in the model may not necessarily apply to consumers from other cultures. Several of the following diminish the universality of the theory of reasoned action:

- The model was developed to predict the performance of any voluntary act. Across cultures, however, many consumer activities, ranging from taking exams and entering military service to receiving an inoculation or even choosing a marriage partner, are not necessarily voluntary.
- The relative impact of subjective norms may vary across cultures. For example, Asian cultures tend to value conformity and face-saving, so it is possible that subjective norms involving the anticipated reactions of others to the choice will have an even greater

impact on behaviour for many Asian consumers.
- The model measures behavioural intentions and thus presupposes that consumers are actively anticipating and planning future behaviours. The intention concept assumes that consumers have a linear time sense, i.e. they think in terms of past, present and future. As will be discussed in a later chapter, this time perspective is not held by all cultures.
- A consumer who forms an intention is (implicitly) claiming that they are in control of their actions. Some cultures tend to be fatalistic and do not necessarily believe in the concept of free will. Indeed, one study comparing students from the US, Jordan and Thailand found evidence for cultural differences in assumptions about fatalism and control over the future.[70]

Trying to consume

Other theorists have proposed different perspectives on the attitude–behaviour connection. One perspective focuses on consumers' goals and what they believe they have to do to attain them. The **theory of trying** states that the criterion of behaviour in the reasoned action model should be replaced with *trying* to reach a goal.[71] This perspective recognizes that additional factors might intervene between intent and performance – both personal and environmental barriers might prevent the individual from attaining the goal. For example, a person who intends to lose weight may have to deal with numerous issues: they may not believe they are capable of slimming down, they may have a roommate who loves to cook and who leaves tempting goodies lying around the apartment, their friends may be jealous of their attempts to diet and encourage them to pig out, or they may be genetically predisposed to obesity and cutting down on calories simply will not produce the desired results.

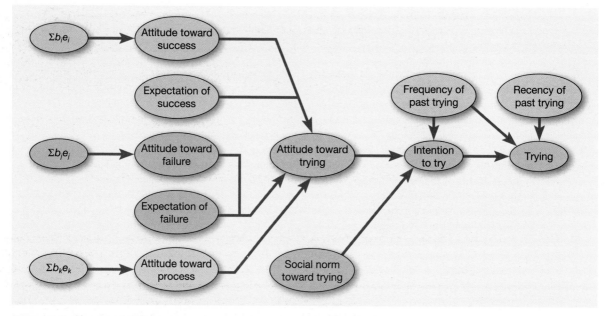

Figure 8.3 Theory of trying

The theory of trying includes several new components that attempt to account for the complex situations in which many factors either help or hurt our chances of turning intentions into actions, as Figure 8.3 shows. To predict whether someone would try to lose weight, here are a few sample issues that a researcher might address:

- *Past frequency*: how many times in the past year did the person try to lose weight?
- *Recency*: did they try to lose weight in the past week?
- *Beliefs*: did they believe they would be healthier if they lost weight?
- *Evaluations of consequences*: did they believe their girlfriend/boyfriend would be happier if they succeeded in losing weight? Did they believe their friends would make fun of them if they tried but failed to lose weight?
- *The process*: would the diet make them uncomfortable or depressed?
- *Expectations of success and failure*: did they believe it likely that they would be able to lose weight if they tried?
- *Subjective norms towards trying*: would the people who are important to them approve of their efforts to lose weight?

Tracking attitudes over time

An attitude survey is like a snapshot taken at a single point in time. It may tell us a lot about the position of a person, issue or object at that moment, but it does not permit many inferences about progress made over time or any predictions about possible future changes in consumer attitudes. To accomplish these tasks, it is necessary to develop an attitude-tracking programme. This activity helps to increase the predictability of behaviour by allowing researchers to analyse attitude trends over an extended period of time. It is more like a film than a snapshot. Attitude tracking involves the administration of an attitude survey at regular intervals. Preferably, the same methodology will be used each time so that results can be reliably compared. Several services, such as Gallup, the Henley Centre or the Yankelovich Monitor, track consumer attitudes over time.

Table 8.3 Recycling rate of container glass (per cent)

Country	1990	1995	1996	1997	1998	1999	2000	2001	2002	2003	2004	2010
Austria	60	n.a.	n.a.	88	86	84	84	83	87	86	88	n.a.
Belgium	59	67	66	75	n.a.	n.a.	87	88	95	88	90	90+
Denmark	40	63	66	70	63	63	65	65	76	71	75	88
Finland	46	50	63	62	69	78	89	91	92	73	72	n.a.
France	41	70	50	52	55	55	55	55	55	58	58	68
Germany	54	75	79	79	81	81	83	87	90	88	91	81
Greece	16	35	29	26	27	25	26	27	27	30	24	n.a.
Ireland	19	39	46	38	37	35	35	40	49	67	69	75
Italy	49	53	53	34	37	41	40	55	58	59	61	74
Netherlands	66	80	81	82	85	91	78	78	78	81	76	n.a.
Norway	34	75	75	76	81	83	85	88	88	86	90	89
Portugal	23	42	42	44	42	42	40	34	35	38	39	n.a.
Spain	27	32	35	37	41	40	31	33	36	38	41	n.a.
Sweden	35	61	72	76	84	84	86	84	87	92	96	90+
Switzerland	61	85	89	91	91	93	91	92	94	96	96	90+
Turkey	30	12	13	20	31	25	24	24	23	22	24	n.a.
United Kingdom	21	27	22	23	24	26	29	34	34	36	44	61

n.a. = Not available

Source: FEVE (European Container Glass Federation); *Consumers in Europe: Facts and Figures*, Eurostat, Theme 3: Population and Social Statistics (Luxembourg, 2001). http://www.euwid-recycling.com/news/business/single/Artikel/container-glass-recycling-rate-remains-high.html

For example, a longitudinal survey conducted by Eurostat of Europeans' attitudes regarding recycling behaviour shows how attitudes can shift over a decade of time, and across countries. Table 8.3 shows the results of a large-scale study carried out in 17 countries. The percentage of respondents reporting that they recycle container glass (and thus exposuing a positive attitude) has grown over the past decade, but at uneven rates, and at very different starting points for each country in the EU. By 2010, Belgium, Switzerland, Luxemburg and Sweden were reported to have reached recycling rates above 90 per cent followed by Norway 89 per cent, Denmark 88 per cent and Germany 81 per cent. By comparison, Ireland was at 75 per cent, France and Italy were at 68 per cent and 74 per cent respectively, and the UK trailing (at least by western European standards) at 61 per cent.[72]

These results would suggest that even as Europe moves towards a more integrated union with a common currency, consumers from individual countries vary in their recycling attitudes.[73]

HOW DO MARKETERS CHANGE ATTITUDES?

As consumers we are constantly bombarded by messages inducing us to change our attitudes. These persuasion attempts can range from logical arguments to graphic pictures, and from intimidation by peers to exhortations by celebrity spokespeople. And, communications flow both ways – the consumer may seek out information sources in order to learn more about these options, for instance by surfing the net. The increasing choice of ways to access marketing messages is changing the way we think about persuasion attempts. Our focus will be on some basic aspects of communication that specifically help to determine how and if attitudes will be created or modified. This objective relates to **persuasion**, which refers to an active attempt to change attitudes. Persuasion is, of course, the central goal of many marketing communications.

CONNIE PECHMANN
University of California, Irvine

Consumer behaviour as I see it . . .

Television networks increasingly try to include educational content in the plots of their television shows, particularly in shows for young people. The networks view this as a public service and call it 'entertainment education'. Previously the networks aired public service announcements at the commercial breaks, typically late at night to minimize the loss in paid advertising revenue. Now the networks prefer entertainment education because it reaches prime-time viewers, and they believe that messages in television shows are more credible and persuasive. If your favourite television actors tell you something within their show, you listen, or so they believe.

I study the effects of different types of educational messages on young people. I go into high schools and arrange for students to be released from a class, watch one type of educational show, and then complete a survey. I test television shows that try to discourage youths from smoking. In a typical show, attractive youths smoke but their friends disapprove and tell them to quit. I found this works; it makes viewers less likely to want to smoke. However, in other educational shows, the characters' reactions to the smoking are more mixed; some approve while others disapprove. Mixed messages are more realistic but they don't discourage viewers from smoking. Also many shows include a short epilogue before the closing credits in which the characters reappear and restate their antismoking message. This boomerangs or actually encourages smokers to light up because they don't want television characters telling them what to do.

Connie Pechmann

Consumers: ad readers or ad users?

In a traditional communications model, advertising is essentially viewed as the process of transferring information to the buyer before a sale. As such, there is a 'real' meaning of the ad based on the intentions of the sender of the message. This meaning can then be transferred to the consumer, if the message is clear enough and the medium is easy to get access to. In other words, if there is not too much 'noise' (as it was called!) on the line, the message should pass undistorted to the consumer. In this perspective, the power of creating the content of the message lies exclusively with the sender.[74]

Is this an accurate picture of the way we relate to marketing communications? In **reader-response theory**,[75] it is argued that it is better to conceive of the communication process as consisting of two communicators, both actively engaged in a process of making sense in and of some message. Instead of the 'machine-like' transmission of information, advertising must be understood as a particular type of communication, a particular genre, and it is understood and interpreted by consumers using particular strategies. Persuading consumers through advertising is not a technical but a cultural process.[76] In other words, when there is uncertainty about how consumers understand and interpret ads, this cannot be explained by 'noise' disturbing the 'real message', but must instead be understood based on consumers' own personal and cultural backgrounds.[77]

Proponents of **uses and gratification theory** add to this argument that consumers are an active, goal-directed audience who draw on mass media as a resource to satisfy needs. Instead of asking what media do *for* or *to* people, they ask what people do *with* the media.[78] Research with young people in the UK finds that they rely on advertising for many gratifications, including entertainment (some report that the 'adverts' are better than the programmes), escapism, play (some report singing along with jingles, others make posters out of magazine ads), and self-affirmation (ads can reinforce their own values or provide role models).[79]

Credibility and attractiveness

Regardless of whether a message is received by passive or, as it seems, more active consumers, common sense tells us that the same words uttered or written by different people can have very different effects. Research on *source effects* has been carried out for more than 50 years. By attributing the same message to different sources and measuring the degree of attitude change that occurs after listeners hear it, it is possible to determine which aspects of a communicator will induce attitude change.[80] Two particularly important source characteristics are *credibility* and *attractiveness*.[81]

Source credibility refers to a source's perceived expertise, objectivity or trustworthiness. This characteristic relates to consumers' beliefs that a communicator is competent, and is willing to provide the necessary information to evaluate competing products adequately. A credible source can be particularly persuasive when the consumer has not yet learned much about a product or formed an opinion of it.[82] The decision to pay an expert or a celebrity to promote a product can be a very costly one, but researchers have concluded that on average the investment is worth it simply because the announcement of an endorsement contract is often used by market analysts to evaluate a firm's potential profitability, thereby affecting its expected return. On average, then, the impact of endorsements appears to be so positive that it offsets the cost of hiring the spokesperson.[83] The credibility is reinforced if the consumer/advertisement reader thinks that the source's qualifications are relevant to the product he or she endorses. On the other hand, teen idol Justin Bieber has promoted almost anything, including . . . nail polish.[84]

What's more, the early evidence indicates that celebrities exert the same impact on messages we receive from social media platforms. One study found that brand endorsements streamed by celebrities directly to friends and followers on platforms such as Facebook and Twitter are significantly more effective (in fact, greater than 50 per cent more) than conventional display ads placed on social media pages. The celebrities in the study included Drew Brees, Snoop Dogg, Matt Hasselbeck, Enrique Iglesias, Khloe Kardashian, Nick Swisher and Kendra Wilkinson.[85]

Celebrity endorsement in advertising. Note that in 2011 TAG Heuer dropped the collaboration with Tiger Woods following the scandals concerning his private life; see the discussion on balance theory.

Getty Images.

These celebrities are not only credible due to their status. A good number of them are also credible, simply because they are good looking. **Source attractiveness** refers to the source's perceived social value. This quality can emanate from the person's physical appearance, personality, social status, or their similarity to the receiver (we like to listen to people who are like us). A compelling source has great value and endorsement deals are constantly in the works. Even dead sources can be attractive: the great-grandson of the artist Renoir is putting his famous ancestor's name on bottled water, and the Picasso family licensed their name to the French car maker Citroën.[86] The use of celebrity endorsers is an expensive but commonly used strategy. While a celebrity endorsement strategy is expensive, it can pay off handsomely.[87] Celebrities increase awareness of a firm's advertising and enhance both company image and brand attitudes.[88] More generally, star power works because celebrities represent *cultural meanings* – they symbolize important categories such as status and social class (a 'business icon' such as Richard Branson), gender (a 'manly man' like Mel Gibson, or a strong feminine character, such as Kate Winslet), age (the boyish Brad Pitt or the mature and serene Sean Connery) and even personality types (the noble humanitarian George Clooney). Ideally, the advertiser decides what meanings the product should convey (that is, how it should be positioned in the marketplace), and then chooses a celebrity who has come to evoke that meaning. The product's meaning thus moves from the manufacturer to the consumer, using the star as a vehicle.[89]

MULTICULTURAL DIMENSIONS

Does this work for you?

Park Jin Sung combs through a rack of button-down shirts at a clothes shop in Seoul. After close examination, he picks out one in light blue that has a stiff, narrow collar and buttons spaced just right, so that the top two can be left open without exposing too much chest. 'Bill would wear this. The collar on this other one is too floppy. Definitely not Bill's style,' Mr Park says. William H. Gates, Chairman of Microsoft Corp., may not be considered the epitome of chic in Europe, but in Seoul, Korea, he is a serious style icon. Young South Koreans believe that 'dressing for success' means copying Mr Gates's wardrobe, down to his round, tortoise-shell glasses, unpolished shoes and wrinkle-free trousers.[90] While Bill Gates doesn't even try to be an endorser of style in Korea, or elsewhere, some celebrities choose to maintain their credibility by endorsing products only in other countries. Many celebrities who do not do many American advertisements appear frequently in Japan. Mel Gibson endorses Asahi beer, Sly Stallone appears for Kirin beer, Sean Connery plugs Ito hams and the singer Sheena was featured in ads for Shochu liquor – dressed in a kimono and wig. Even the normally reclusive comedian and film director Woody Allen featured in a campaign for a large Tokyo department store.[91] **Japander.com** is a website where consumers can see Hollywood stars in Japanese commercials, for example Nathalie Portman for Lux soap or Nicholas Cage promoting a videogame (both 2006).[92]

Hype *vs* buzz: the corporate paradox

Obviously many marketers spend lavishly to create marketing messages that they hope will convince hordes of customers that they are the best. There's the rub – in many cases they may be trying too hard! We can think of this as the **corporate paradox** – the more involved a company appears to be in the dissemination of news about its products, the less credible it becomes.[93] As we will see in Chapter 10, consumer word-of-mouth is typically the most convincing kind of message. As Table 8.4 shows, **buzz** is word-of-mouth that is viewed as authentic and generated by customers. In contrast, **hype** is dismissed as inauthentic – corporate propaganda planted by a company with an axe to grind. So, the challenge to marketers is to get the word out and about without it looking like they are trying too hard.

The now-famous *Blair Witch Project* that led many viewers to believe the fictional treatment was in fact a real documentary demonstrated the power of a brand that seems as if it is not

Table 8.4 Hype versus buzz

Hype	Buzz
Advertising	Word-of-mouth
Overt	Covert
Corporate	Grassroots
Fake	Authentic
Scepticism	Credibility

one. In 2010, actor Joaquin Phoenix created a lot of buzz when rumours had it that he was altering his life path profoundly, changing his personality and pursuing a new career as a rapper. What looked like a documentation of this transformation, the film *I'm Still Here*, was, in fact, a *mockumentary*, a story looking as if it was real (through the making of the film, Joaquin Phoenix never stepped out of his character even in numerous public appearances) but was in fact a comment on our obsession with reality TV shows and personality change.[94] Some marketers are trying to borrow the veneer of buzz by mounting 'stealth' campaigns that seem as if they are untouched by the corporate world. *Buzz building* has become the new mantra for many companies that recognize the power of underground word-of-mouth.[95] Indeed, a small cottage industry has sprung up as some firms begin to specialize in the corporate promotion business by planting comments on websites which are made to look as if they originated from actual consumers. One of the first really successful examples was when Honda launched its Honda HRV in Europe – this was prior to YouTube, so films had to be made so they could be e-mailed. Starting with only e-mails to 500 employees, Honda ended up with more than 4.5 million visitors to their promoted website.[96] A contemporary example from the car industry includes Volkswagen's campaign for the new Beetle in 2011, where a mixture of impressive billboards in urban environments and the opportunity for downloading apps that permitted playing with the billboard scenery in an augmented reality format created a lot of . . . buzz.[97]

As powerful as these tactics are, they have the potential to poison the well in a big way. Web surfers, already sceptical about what they see and hear, may get to the point where they assume every 'authentic' site they find is really a corporate front. Until then, however, buzz building online is growing strongly. Still, there is no beating the impact of a marketing message that really does originate with product users.

Types of message appeals

The *way* something is said can be as significant as *who* says it. A persuasive message can tug at the heartstrings or scare you, make you laugh, make you cry or leave you yearning to learn more, depending on the **appeal** used. In this section, we will briefly review the major alternatives available to communicators who wish to appeal to a message recipient.

The first alternative often considered is whether to use rational or emotional appeals; or, in other words, appeal to the head or to the heart? As with the other types of appeals, there is no single given 'right' or 'wrong' answer to this question. The answer always depends upon the nature of the product, the type of relationship consumers have with it, and the current competitive situation in the market. Although they are hard to gauge, it has not prevented researchers from trying to predict the precise effects of rational *vs* emotional appeals. Even if recall of ad contents tends to be better for 'thinking' ads than for 'feeling' ads, conventional measures of advertising effectiveness (e.g. day-after recall) may not be adequate to assess cumulative effects of emotional ads. These open-ended measures are oriented towards cognitive responses, and feeling ads may be penalized because the reactions are not as easy to articulate.[98]

This ad from Dubai clearly uses an emotional appeal.

Courtesy of Y&R Dubai.

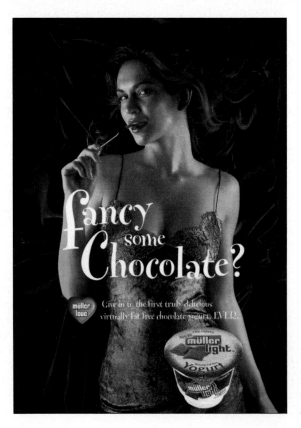

Chocolate is always seductive – also in a fat free form. An ad employing a sexual appeal.

The Advertising Archives.

Echoing the widely held belief that 'sex sells', many marketing communications – for everything from perfumes to cars – feature heavy doses of erotic suggestions that range from subtle hints to blatant displays of flesh. Of course, the prevalence of sex appeals varies from country to country. American firms run ads abroad that would not go down well in the US. For example, a recent 'cheeky' ad campaign designed to boost the appeal of American-made Lee Jeans among Europeans features a series of bare buttocks. The messages are based on the concept that if bottoms could choose jeans, they would opt for Lee: 'Bottoms feel better in Lee Jeans'.[99]

Does sex work? Although the use of sex does appear to draw attention to an ad, it may actually be counter-productive to the marketer. Ironically, a provocative picture can be *too* effective; it attracts so much attention that it hinders processing and recall of the ad's other contents, such as the brand. Some researchers also suggest that strong use of sexual appeals are generally received negatively.[100] In one survey, an overwhelming 61 per cent of the respondents said that sexual imagery in a product's ad made them less likely to buy it.[101] However, as in all attitude measurements, it is important to remember that such statements are highly influenced by the moral picture that consumers like to present, not only to the researcher, but also to themselves.

MULTICULTURAL DIMENSIONS

Sexy ads . . . now also in India

The Indian advertising scene has traditionally been very prudent with showing too much skin and making too many allusions towards sexyness. No longer so – as one advertising executive remarks, the Indian advertising industry seemingly had run out of ideas and therefore recently turned to the (in the West) good old-fashioned formula of sexy ads, voluptuous women and flirtatious behaviour. Apparently it works – one brand experienced a 40 per cent growth following a campaign featuring a sexy air hostess coming into the cockpit and tempting the pilot to put the aircraft on autopilot, thereby freeing his hands for . . . and here the rest is left to the viewers' imaginations. Little wonder that sex in advertising is on the rise in India, remember over half the population is below 25 years of age. Not exactly a hormone-free zone . . .[102]

Perhaps not surprisingly, female nudity in print ads generates negative feelings and tension among female consumers, whereas men's reactions are more positive – although women with more liberal attitudes towards sex are more likely to be receptive.[103] Women also respond more positively to sexual themes when they occur in the context of a committed relationship rather than just gratuitous lust.[104]

MARKETING OPPORTUNITY

Sex, fame and humour – a combination only for the big and powerful?

Is the use of sexy and famous endorsers only for the big corporations? Cocio, a Danish producer of chocolate milk and ice-coffee thinks not, and has aligned itself with actress Eva Mendes in an attempt to further enhance their market shares nationally but especially internationally. A first execution using Eva Mendes was launched a couple of years ago, and now a new TV commercial should hopefully follow up on the success. Two young boys are hitchhiking on a rainy night, when Eva Mendes arrives in a classic Volkswagen Cocio van. She stops and invites them to either 'squeeze up with her' or 'sit in the back'. One boy is obviously thrilled by the possibility of rubbing thighs with Eva Mendes, but his friend, discovering the chocolate milk cargo in the back, pulls him back there, exclaiming: 'How lucky can you be!' Eva Mendes, through her skin colour, also metaphorically expresses the Cocio product (cf. the section on metaphors below).[105]

And what about humour? Does humour work? Overall, humorous advertisements do get attention. One study found that recognition scores for humorous alcohol ads were better than average. However, the verdict is mixed as to whether humour affects recall or product attitudes in a significant way.[106] One function it may play is to provide a source of *distraction*. A funny ad inhibits the consumer from *counter-arguing* (thinking of reasons why they don't agree with the message), thereby increasing the likelihood of message acceptance.[107]

Humour is more likely to be effective when the brand is clearly identified and the funny material does not 'swamp' the message. This danger is similar to that of beautiful models diverting attention from copy points. Furthermore, subtle humour is usually better, as it presents the product or brand as 'clever'. Finally, the humour can make fun of the brand (and its producers), something which makes them appear as 'more cool', but generally not of the potential consumer.

MARKETING OPPORTUNITY

Marketing with double entendres – football and music: Messi or messy?

Pepsi is well-known for its long-term usage of celebrity endorsers. The corporation has summoned football stars such as Lionel Messi, Dider Drogba and Frank Lampard for their 2012 campaign 'Kick in the mix'. Together with DJ Calvin Harris, they are supposed to create a particular universe which is neither football field nor a dance clubbing party, but a beach festival kind of environment, where the joy and passion for music and football is supposedly united for players and fans alike. The tempo of football and the beats of the music are supposed to be aligned in a total experience of bodily rhythm and leisurely enthusiasm. The question is obviously whether this combination is a credible one – what do you think?[108]

Fear appeals highlight the negative consequences that can occur unless the consumer changes a behaviour or an attitude. The arousal of fear is a common tactic for social policy issues, such as encouraging consumers to change to a healthier lifestyle by stopping smoking, using contraception, taking more exercise, eating a more balanced diet, drinking without driving (by relying on a designated driver in order to reduce physical risk to themselves or others). It can also be applied to social risk issues by threatening one's success with the opposite sex, career and so on. One French study made a direct comparison of fear appeals, guilt appeals and shame appeals in terms of persuading consumers to refrain from excessive alcohol consumption; fear and shame were found to have the biggest persuasive impact.[109] (See also the case by Effi Raftopoulou at the end of Part C in this book.)

Does fear work? Fear appeals, it has been argued, are usually most effective when only a moderate amount of fear is induced and when a solution to the problem is presented.[110] If the threat is too great, the audience tends to deny that it exists as a way to rationalize the danger. Consumers will tune out of the ad because they can do nothing to solve the problem.[111] This approach also works better when source credibility is high.[112]

Some of the research on fear appeals may be confusing a threat (the literal content of a message, such as saying 'engage in safe sex or die') with fear (an emotional response to the message). According to this argument, greater fear does result in greater persuasion – but not all threats are equally effective because different people will respond differently to the same threat. Therefore, the strongest threats are not always the most persuasive because they may not have the desired impact on the perceiver. For example, raising the spectre of AIDS is about the strongest threat that can be delivered to sexually active young people – but this tactic is only effective if they believe they will get the disease. Because many young people (especially those who live in fairly affluent areas) do not believe that 'people like them' will be exposed to the AIDS virus, this strong threat may not actually result in a high level of fear.[113] The bottom line is that more precise measures of actual fear responses are needed before definitive conclusions can be drawn about the impact of fear appeals on consumption decisions.

Humourous ads like this one from Budapest grab our attention.

McCann-Erickson, New York.

Fear, humour, or any other communicative strategy – most of them remind us that marketers today are storytellers, who supply visions of reality similar to those provided by authors, poets and artists. These communications take the form of stories often because the product benefits they describe are intangible and must be given tangible meaning by expressing them in a form that is concrete and visible. Advertisers (consciously or not) rely on various literary

Fairy uses a bomb metaphor in its sales pitch for Lemon Fairy with its antibacterial agents that will 'elemonate' the germs.

The Advertising Archives.

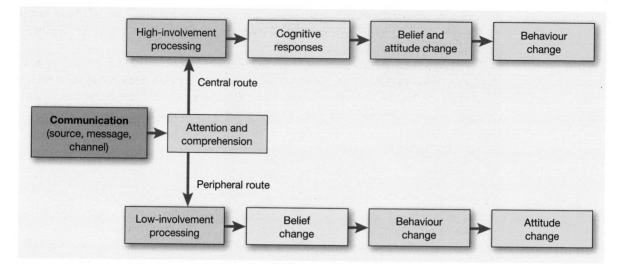

Figure 8.4 The elaboration likelihood model of persuasion

Source: From *Consumer Behavior,* 2nd edn, by John C. Mowen, Macmillan Publishing Company.

devices to communicate these meanings. To do this, they often use metaphors, which involves placing two dissimilar things in a close relationship by expressing one thing in terms of another. 'Love is a battlefield' is one example of metaphor. 'Argument is war' is another.[114] Such usage of metaphors is both an expression of and a development of some of those cultural values and symbols used by the advertising industry in connection with providing meaning to a product or brand, as we saw in Figure 2.1. (See also the case by Lampros Gkiouzepas at the end of Part C in this book.)

The elaboration likelihood model

Some major features of the persuasion process, like the qualities of the source and the appeals have been discussed. Which aspect has more impact in persuading consumers to change their attitudes? Should marketers worry more about *what* is said, or *how* it is said and *who* says it?

The answer is, it depends. Variations in a consumer's level of involvement, as discussed in Chapter 6, result in the activation of very different cognitive processes when a message is received. Research indicates that this level of involvement will determine which aspects of a communication are processed. The situation appears to resemble a traveller who comes to a fork in the road: one or the other path is chosen, and this choice has a big impact on the factors that will make a difference in persuasion attempts.

The **elaboration likelihood model (ELM)** assumes that once a consumer receives a message they begin to process it.[115] Depending on the personal relevance of this information, one of two routes to persuasion will be followed. Under conditions of high involvement, the consumer takes the *central route* to persuasion. Under conditions of low involvement, a *peripheral route* is taken instead. This model is shown in Figure 8.4.

The central route to persuasion

When the consumer finds the information in a persuasive message to be relevant or somehow interesting, they will carefully attend to the message content. The person is likely actively to think about the arguments presented and generate *cognitive responses* to these arguments. On hearing a radio message warning about drinking alcohol while pregnant, an expectant mother might say to herself, 'She's right. I really should stop drinking alcohol now that I'm pregnant.' Or, she might offer counter-arguments, such as, 'That's a load of nonsense. My mother had a cocktail every night when she was pregnant with me, and I turned out OK.' If a person generates counter-arguments in response to a message, it is less likely that they will yield to the message, whereas the generation of further supporting arguments by the consumer increases the probability of compliance.[116]

The central route to persuasion is likely to involve the traditional hierarchy of effects, as discussed earlier in the chapter. Beliefs are carefully formed and evaluated, and the resulting strong attitudes will be likely to guide behaviour. The implication is that message factors, such as the quality of arguments presented, will be important in determining attitude change. Prior knowledge about a topic results in more thoughts about the message and also increases the number of counter-arguments.[117]

The peripheral route to persuasion

In contrast, the peripheral route is taken when the person is not motivated to think deeply about the arguments presented. Instead, the consumer is likely to use other cues in deciding on the suitability of the message. These cues might include the product's package, the attractiveness of the source, or the context in which the message is presented. Sources of information extraneous to the actual message content are called *peripheral cues* because they surround the actual message.

The peripheral route to persuasion highlights the paradox of low involvement discussed in Chapter 6: when consumers do not care about a product, the stimuli associated with it increase in importance. The implication here is that low-involvement products may be purchased chiefly because the marketer has done a good job in designing a 'sexy' package, choosing a popular spokesperson, or perhaps just creating a pleasant shopping environment.

Support for the ELM model

The ELM model has received a lot of research support.[118] In one study, undergraduates were exposed to one of several mock advertisements for Break, a new brand of low-alcohol beer. Using the technique of *thought listing*,[119] they were asked to provide their thoughts about the ads, which were later analysed.[120] Three independent variables crucial to the ELM model were manipulated.

1 *Message-processing involvement*. Some subjects were motivated to be highly involved with the ads. They were promised a gift of low-alcohol beer for participating in the study and were told that the brand would soon be available in their area. Low-involvement subjects were not promised a gift and were told that the brand would be introduced in a distant area.

2 *Argument strength*. One version of the ad used strong, compelling arguments to drink Break (e.g. 'Break contains one-half of the amount of alcohol of regular beers and, therefore, has fewer calories than regular beer'), whereas the other listed only weak arguments (e.g. 'Break is just as good as any other regular beer').

3 *Source characteristics*. Ads contained a photo of a couple drinking the beer, but their relative social attractiveness was varied by their dress, their posture and nonverbal expressions, and the background information given about their educational achievements and occupations.

Consistent with the ELM model, high-involvement subjects had more thoughts related to the ad messages than did low-involvement subjects, who devoted more cognitive activity to the sources used in the ad. The attitudes of high-involvement subjects were more likely to be swayed by powerful arguments, whereas the attitudes of low-involvement subjects were more likely to be influenced by the ad version using attractive sources. The results of this study, paired with numerous others, indicate that the relative effectiveness of a strong message and a favourable source depends on consumers' level of involvement with the product being advertised.

It is important to remember, however, that the same communications variable can be both a central and a peripheral cue, depending on its relation to the attitude object. The physical attractiveness of a model might serve as a peripheral cue in a car commercial, but her beauty might be a central cue for a product such as shampoo, where the product's benefits are directly tied to enhancing attractiveness.[121]

CHAPTER SUMMARY

→ An attitude is a predisposition to evaluate an object or product positively or negatively.

→ Social marketing refers to attempts to change consumers' attitudes and behaviours in ways that are beneficial to society as a whole.

→ Attitudes are made up of three components: beliefs, affect and behavioural intentions.

→ Attitude researchers traditionally assumed that attitudes were learned in a predetermined sequence, consisting first of the formation of beliefs (cognitions) regarding an attitude object, followed by an evaluation of that object (affect) and then some action (behaviour). Depending on the consumer's level of involvement and the circumstances, though, attitudes can result from other hierarchies of effects.

→ A key to attitude formation is the function the attitude plays for the consumer (e.g. is it utilitarian or ego-defensive?).

→ One organizing principle of attitude formation is the importance of consistency among attitudinal components – that is, some parts of an attitude may be altered to conform with others. Such theoretical approaches to attitudes as cognitive dissonance theory, balance theory and congruity theory stress the vital role of consistency.

→ The complexity of attitudes is underscored by multi-attribute attitude models, in which sets of beliefs and evaluations are identified and combined to predict an overall attitude. Factors such as subjective norms and the specificity of attitude scales have been integrated into attitude measures to improve predictability.

→ *Persuasion* refers to an attempt to change consumers' attitudes.

→ Two important characteristics that characterize a message source are its *attractiveness* and *credibility*. Although celebrities are often used with the purpose of enhancing these characteristics, their credibility is not always as strong as marketers hope. Marketing messages that consumers perceive as buzz (that are authentic and consumer-generated) tend to be more effective than those they categorize as hype (that are inauthentic, biased and company-generated).

→ Some elements of a message that help to determine its effectiveness in terms of attitude change are whether an emotional or a rational appeal is employed and whether the message includes fear, humour or sexual references.

→ The relative influence of the source versus the message depends on the receiver's level of involvement with the communication. The *elaboration likelihood model* specifies that a less involved consumer will more likely be swayed by source effects, whereas a more involved consumer will be more likely to attend to and process components of the actual message.

KEY TERMS

ABC model of attitudes (p. 295)

Affect (p. 294)

Appeal (p. 317)

Attitude (p. 292)

Attitude object (A$_o$) (p. 292)

Attitude towards the act of buying (A$_{act}$) (p. 309)

Attitude towards the advertisement (A$_{ad}$) (p. 298)

Balance theory (p. 303)

Buzz (p. 316)

Cognition (p. 295)

Corporate paradox (p. 316)

Elaboration likelihood model (ELM) (p. 322)

Foot-in-the-door technique (p. 302)

Functional theory of attitudes (p. 293)

Hierarchy of effects (p. 295)

CONSUMER BEHAVIOUR CHALLENGE

1 Contrast the hierarchies of effects outlined in the chapter. How will strategic decisions related to the marketing mix be influenced by which hierarchy is operative among target consumers?

2 List three functions played by attitudes, giving an example of how each function is employed in a marketing situation. To examine European countries' attitudes towards a wide variety of issues, go to the website: **http://europa.eu.int/en/comm/dg10/ infcom/epo/eo.html**. Which sorts of attitudes expressed in different countries seem utilitarian, value-expressive or ego-defensive? Why?

3 Think of a behaviour exhibited by an individual that is inconsistent with their attitudes (e.g. attitudes towards cholesterol, drug use or even buying things to attain status or be noticed). Ask the person to elaborate on why they do the behaviour, and try to identify the way the person has resolved dissonant elements.

4 Using a series of semantic-differential scales, devise an attitude survey for a set of competing cars. Identify areas of competitive advantage or disadvantage for each model you incorporate.

5 Construct a multi-attribute model for a set of local restaurants. Based on your findings, suggest how restaurant managers can improve their establishments' image using the strategies described in the chapter.

6 A government agency wants to encourage the use of designated drivers by people who have been drinking. What advice could you give the organization about constructing persuasive communications? Discuss some factors that might be important, including the structure of the communications, where they should appear, and who should deliver them. Should fear appeals be used, and if so, how?

7 The Coca-Cola company pulled a UK internet promotion campaign after parents accused it of targeting children by using references to a notorious pornographic movie. As part of its efforts to reach young social media users for its Dr Pepper brand, the company took over consenting users' Facebook status boxes. Then, the company would post mildly embarrassing questions such as 'Lost my special blankie. How will I go sleepies?,' and 'What's wrong with peeing in the shower?' But, when a parent discovered that her 14-year-old daughter's profile had been updated with a message that directly referred to a hardcore porn film, the plan backfired and Coke had to pull the promotion.[122] What does it take to get the attention of jaded young people, who get exposed to all kinds of messages in cyberspace? What guidelines (if any) should marketers follow when they try to talk to young people on social media platforms?

8 Why would a marketer consider saying negative things about their product? When is this strategy feasible? Can you find examples of it?

9 Create a list of celebrities who match up with products in your country. What are the elements of the celebrities and products that make for a 'good match'? Why? Which celebrities have a global or European-wide appeal, and why?

10 A marketer must decide whether to incorporate rational or emotional appeals in a communication strategy. Describe conditions that are more favorable to one or the other in terms of changing attitudes.

For additional material see the companion website at **www.pearsoned.co.uk/solomon**

NOTES

1. 'It's a funny old game', *The Economist* (10 February 2001): 57–8.

2. See, for example, Sven Bergvall and Mikolaj Dymek, 'Uncovering Sport Game Covers – The Consumption of Video Game Packages', in K. Ekström and H. Brembeck (eds), *European Advances in Consumer Research*, vol. 7 (Valdosta, GA: Association for Consumer Research, 2007): 310–16.

3. Robert A. Baron and Donn Byrne, *Social Psychology: Understanding Human Interaction*, 5th edn (Boston: Allyn & Bacon, 1987).

4. D. Albarracín, B.T. Johnson and M.P. Zanna (eds), *The Handbook of Attitudes* (Mahwah, NJ: Erlbaum, 2005); see also: J.R. Priester, D. Nayakankuppan, M.A. Fleming and J. Godek, 'The A(2)SC(2) model: The influence of attitudes and attitude strength on consideration set choice', *Journal of Consumer Research* 30(4) (2004): 574–87 for a study on how the strength of attitudes influences and guides a consumer's consideration of brands.

5. Daniel Katz, 'The functional approach to the study of attitudes', *Public Opinion Quarterly* 24 (Summer 1960): 163–204; Richard J. Lutz, 'Changing brand attitudes through modification of cognitive structure', *Journal of Consumer Research* 1 (March 1975): 49–59.

6. Russell H. Fazio, T.M. Lenn and E.A. Effrein, 'Spontaneous attitude formation', *Social Cognition* 2 (1984): 214–34.

7. Mason Haire, 'Projective techniques in marketing research', *Journal of Marketing* 14 (April 1950): 649–56.

8. Sharon Shavitt, 'The role of attitude objects in attitude functions', *Journal of Experimental Social Psychology* 26 (1990): 124–48; see also J.S. Johar and M. Joseph Sirgy, 'Value-expressive versus utilitarian advertising appeals: When and why to use which appeal', *Journal of Advertising* 20 (September 1991): 23–34.

9. Athanasios Krystalis, Klaus G. Grunert, Marcia D. de Barcellos, Toula Perrea and Wim Verbeke, 'Consumer Attitudes towards Sustainability Aspects of Food Production: Insights from Three Continents', *Journal of Marketing Management*, 28 (3–4 March 2012): 334–372.

10. John Thøgersen and Yanfeng Zhou, 'Chinese consumers' adoption of a "green" innovation – The case of organic food', *Journal of Marketing Management*, 28 (3–4 March 2012): 313–333.

11. For the original work that focused on the issue of levels of attitudinal commitment, see H.C. Kelman, 'Compliance, identification, and internalization: Three processes of attitude change', *Journal of Conflict Resolution* 2 (1958): 51–60.

12. Lynn R. Kahle, Kenneth M. Kambara and Gregory M. Rose, 'A functional model of fan attendance motivations for college football', *Sports Marketing Quarterly* 5(4) (1996): 51–60.

13. For a study that found evidence of simultaneous causation of beliefs and attitudes, see Gary M. Erickson, Johny K. Johansson and Paul Chao, 'Image variables in multi-attribute product evaluations: Country-of-origin effects', *Journal of Consumer Research* 11 (September 1984): 694–9.

14. Michael Ray, 'Marketing Communications and the Hierarchy-of-Effects', in P. Clarke (ed.), *New Models for Mass Communications* (Beverly Hills, CA: Sage, 1973): 147–76.

15. Jung Chae Suh and Youjae Yi, 'When brand attitudes affect the customer satisfaction–loyalty relation: The moderating role of product involvement', *Journal of Consumer Psychology* 16(2): 145–55.

16. Herbert Krugman, 'The impact of television advertising: Learning without involvement', *Public Opinion Quarterly* 29 (Fall 1965): 349–56; Robert Lavidge and Gary Steiner, 'A model for predictive measurements of advertising effectiveness', *Journal of Marketing* 25 (October 1961): 59–62.

17. Melanie A. Dempsey and Andrew A. Mitchell, 'The Influence of Implicit Attitudes on Choice When Consumers Are Confronted with Conflicting Attribute Information', *Journal of Consumer Research*, 37 (December 2010): 614–625.

18. Magnus Söderlund, 'Judging Fiction Books by the Cover: An Examination of the Effects of Sexually Charged Cover Images', in S. Borghini, M.A. McGrath and C.C. Otnes (eds), *European Advances in Consumer Research* 8 (Duluth, MN: Association for Consumer Research, 2008): 500–4.

19. Lan Jiang, Joandrea Hoegg, Darren W. Dahl and Amitava Chattopadhyay, 'The Persuasive Role of Incidental Similarity on Attitutdes and Purchase Intentions in a Sales Context', *Journal of Consumer Research*, 36 (February 2010): 778–791.

20. For some studies on this topic see Andrew B. Aylesworth and Scott B. MacKenzie, 'Context is key: The effect of program-induced mood on thoughts about the ad', *Journal of Advertising*, 27(2) (Summer 1998): 15–17 (at 15); Angela Y. Lee and Brian Sternthal, 'The effects of positive mood on memory', *Journal of Consumer Research* 26 (September 1999): 115–28; Michael J. Barone, Paul W. Miniard and Jean B. Romeo, 'The influence of positive mood on brand extension evaluations', *Journal of Consumer Research* 26 (March 2000): 386–401. For a study that compared the effectiveness of emotional appeals across cultures, see Jennifer L. Aaker and Patti Williams, 'Empathy versus pride: The influence of emotional appeals across cultures', *Journal of Consumer Research* 25 (December 1998): 241–61.

21. See, for example, Özlem H. Sanaktekin, 'Moderating Role of Valence Sequence in the Mixed Affective Approach', in S. Borghini, M.A. McGrath and C.C. Otnes (eds), *European Advances in Consumer Research* 8 (Duluth, MN: Association for Consumer Research, 2008): 150–54.

22. Punam Anand, Morris B. Holbrook and Debra Stephens, 'The formation of affective judgments: The cognitive – affective model versus the independence hypothesis', *Journal of Consumer Research* 15 (December 1988): 386–91; Richard S. Lazarus, 'Thoughts on the relations between emotion and cognition', *American Psychologist* 37(9) (1982): 1019–24.

23. Robert B. Zajonc, 'Feeling and thinking: Preferences need no inferences', *American Psychologist* 35(2) (1980): 151–75.

24. Banwari Mittal, 'The role of affective choice mode in the consumer purchase of expressive products', *Journal of Economic Psychology* 4(9) (1988): 499–524.

25. Dirk Morschett, Bernhard Swoboda and Hanna Schramm-Klein, 'Shopping Orientations as Determinants of Attitude Towards Food Retailers and Perception of Store Attributes', in K. Ekström and H. Brembeck (eds), *European Advances in Consumer Research* 7 (Duluth, MN: Association for Consumer Research, 2006): 160–67.

26. For a study examining the impact of scepticism on advertising issues, see David M. Boush, Marian Friestad and Gregory M. Rose, 'Adolescent skepticism toward TV advertising and knowledge of advertiser tactics', *Journal of Consumer Research* 21 (June 1994): 165–75; see also Lawrence Feick and Heribert Gierl, 'Skepticism about advertising: A comparison of East and West German consumers', *International Journal of Research in Marketing* 13 (1996): 227–35; Rik Pieters and Hans Baumgartner, 'The Attitude Toward Advertising of Advertising Practitioners, Homemakers and Students in The Netherlands and Belgium', in W. Fred van Raaij and Gary J. Bamossy (eds), *European Advances in Consumer Research* 1 (Provo, UT: Association for Consumer Research, 1993): 39–45.

27. Alex Benady, 'Advertisers' funny business', *Financial Times* (17 February 2004), http://news.ft.com/servlet/ContentServer?pagename=FT.com/StoryFT/FullStory&c=StoryFT&cid=1075982574327&p=1012571727085

28. Priyali Rajagopal and Nicole Votolato Montgomery, 'I Imagine, I Experience, I Like: The False Experience Effect' *Journal of Consumer Research*, 38 (October 2011): 578–594.

29. Kelman, 'Compliance, identification, and internalization', *op. cit.*: 51–60.

30. See Sharon E. Beatty and Lynn R. Kahle, 'Alternative hierarchies of the attitude–behaviour relationship: The impact of brand commitment and habit', *Journal of the Academy of Marketing Science* 16 (Summer 1988): 1–10.

31. J.R. Priester, D. Nayakankuppan, M.A. Fleming and J. Godek, 'The A(2)SC(2) model: The influence of attitudes and attitude strength on consideration set choice', *Journal of Consumer Research* 30(4) (2004): 574–87.

32. Katja Brunk, 'Reputation Building: Beyond Our Control? Inferences in Consumers' Ethical Perception Formation', *Journal of Consumer Behaviour*, 9 (2010): 275–292.

33. http://adland.tv/commercials/karen26-karen-denmark seeking-augusts-father-2009-denmark, accessed 6 May 2012.

34. Leon Festinger, *A Theory of Cognitive Dissonance* (Stanford, CA: Stanford University Press, 1957).

35. Chester A. Insko and John Schopler, *Experimental Social Psychology* (New York: Academic Press, 1972).

36. Robert E. Knox and James A. Inkster, 'Postdecision dissonance at post time', *Journal of Personality and Social Psychology* 8(4) (1968): 319–23.

37. Ab Litt and Zakary L. Tormala, 'Fragile Enhancement of Attitudes and intentions Following Difficult Decisions', *Journal of Consumer Research*, 37 (December 2010): 584–598.

38. Daryl J. Bem, 'Self-Perception Theory', in Leonard Berkowitz (ed.), *Advances in Experimental Social Psychology* (New York: Academic Press, 1972): 1–62.

39. Jonathan L. Freedman and Scott C. Fraser, 'Compliance without pressure: the foot-in-the-door technique', *Journal of Personality and Social Psychology* 4 (August 1966): 195–202; for further consideration of possible explanations for this effect, see William DeJong, 'An examination of self-perception mediation of the foot-in-the-door effect', *Journal of Personality and Social Psychology* 37 (December 1979): 221–31; Alice M. Tybout, Brian Sternthal and Bobby J. Calder, 'Information availability as a determinant of multiple-request effectiveness', *Journal of Marketing Research* 20 (August 1988): 280–90.

40. Bob Fennis, Loes Janssen and Kathleen D. Vohs, 'Acts of Benevolence: A Limited-Resource Account of Compliance with Charitable Requests,' *Journal of Consumer Research* (December 2009): 906–25.

41. Muzafer Sherif and Carl I. Hovland, *Social Judgment: Assimilation and Contrast Effects in Communication and Attitude Change* (New Haven, CT: Yale University Press, 1961); for a recent treatment see Yong-Soon Kang and Paul M. Herr, 'Beauty and the beholder: Toward an integrative model of communication source effects', *Journal of Consumer Research*, 33 (June 2006): 123–130.

42. 'Cola geweerd uit Belgische basisscholen', *De Telegraaf* (4 January 2005), http://www2.telegraaf.nl/buitenland/16939271/Cola_geweerd_uit_Belgische_basisscholen.html

43. Andrew Jack, 'GSK launches a 5m NiQuitin marketing drive', *Financial Times* (10 January 2005), http://news.ft.com/cms/s/042bcb56-62ad-11d9-8e5d-00000e2511c8.html; Peter John, 'Wetherspoon to stub out smoking in its 650 pubs', *Financial Times* (25 January 2005), http://news.ft.com/cms/s/2b37e7d8-6e75-11d9-a60a-00000e2511c8.html

44. Edward Shiu, Louise M. Hassan, Jennifer A. Thomson and Deirdre Shaw, 'An Empirical Examination of the Extended Model of Goal-Directed Behaviour: Assessing the Role of Behavioural Desire', in S. Borghini, M.A. McGrath and C.C. Otnes (eds), *European Advances in Consumer Research* 8 (Duluth, MN: Association for Consumer Research, 2008): 66–79.

45. Joan Meyers-Levy and Brian Sternthal, 'A two-factor explanation of assimilation and contrast effects', *Journal of Marketing Research* 30 (August 1993): 359–68.

46. Fritz Heider, *The Psychology of Interpersonal Relations* (New York: Wiley, 1958).

47. Caglar Irmak, Beth Vallen and Stephanie Rosen Robinson, 'The Impact of Product Name on Dieters' and Nondieters' Food Evaluations and Consumption' *Journal of Consumer Research*, 38 (August 2011): 390–405.

48. Debra Z. Basil and Paul M. Herr, 'Attitudinal balance and cause-related marketing: An empirical application of balance theory', *Journal of Consumer Psychology* 16(4) (2006): 391–403.

49. William L. Wilkie, *Consumer Behavior* (New York: Wiley, 1986).

50. A number of criteria beyond the scope of this book are important in evaluating methods of attitude measurement, including such issues as reliability, validity and sensitivity. For an excellent treatment of attitude-scaling techniques, see David S. Aaker and George S. Day, *Marketing Research*, 4th edn (New York: Wiley, 1990).

51. Martin Fishbein, 'An investigation of the relationships between beliefs about an object and the attitude toward that object', *Human Relations* 16 (1983): 233–40.

52. Allan Wicker, 'Attitudes versus actions: The relationship of verbal and overt behavioral responses to attitude objects', *Journal of Social Issues* 25 (Autumn 1969): 65.

53. Chris Smith, 'Doritos is most popular but Chevrolet is Superbowl's runaway winner', *Forbes*, 6.2. 2012, http://www.forbes.com/sites/chrissmith/2012/02/06/doritos-is-most-popular-but-chevrolet-is-super-bowls-runaway-winner/, accessed 6 May 2012.

54. 'As consumers cut spending, "green" products lose allure', *New York Times*, 21 April 2011, http://www.nytimes.com/2011/04/22/business/energy-environment/22green.html?_r=2&hp

55. Lynn Sudbury and Sebastian Böltner, 'Fashion Marketing and the Ethical Movement versus Individualist Consumption: Analysing the Attitude-Behaviour Gap', paper presented at the European Conference for the Association for Consumer Research, London, 30 June–3 July 2010.

56. Icek Ajzen and Martin Fishbein, 'Attitude–behavior relations: A theoretical analysis and review of empirical research', *Psychological Bulletin* 84 (September 1977): 888–918.

57. Icek Ajzen, 'The theory of planned behavior', *Organizational Behavior and Human Decision Processes*, 50 (2, 1991): 179–211.

58. Morris B. Holbrook and William J. Havlena, 'Assessing the real-to-artificial generalizability of multi-attribute attitude models in tests of new product designs', *Journal of Marketing Research* 25 (February 1988): 25–35; Terence A. Shimp and Alican Kavas, 'The theory of reasoned action applied to coupon usage', *Journal of Consumer Research* 11 (December 1984): 795–809.

59. Richard P. Bagozzi, Hans Baumgartner and Youjae Yi, 'Coupon Usage and the Theory of Reasoned Action', in Holman and Solomon (eds), *Advances in Consumer Research* 18: 24–7; Edward F. McQuarrie, 'An alternative to purchase intentions: The role of prior behavior in consumer expenditure on computers', *Journal of the Market Research Society* 30 (October 1988): 407–37; Arch G. Woodside and William O. Bearden, 'Longitudinal Analysis of Consumer Attitude, Intention, and Behavior Toward Beer Brand Choice', in William D. Perrault Jr (ed.), *Advances in Consumer Research* 4 (Ann Arbor, MI: Association for Consumer Research, 1977): 349–56.

60. Noah J. Goldstein, Robert B. Cialdini and Vladas Griskevicius, 'A room with a viewpoint: Using social norms to motivate environmental conservation in hotels', *Journal of Consumer Research*, 35 (October 2008): 472–482.

61. Michael J. Ryan and Edward H. Bonfield, 'The Fishbein Extended Model and consumer behavior', *Journal of Consumer Research* 2 (1975): 118–36.

62. Christine Gonzalez and Michaël Korchia, 'Attitudes Toward Seasonal Sales: An Exploratory Analysis of the Concept and its Antecedents', in K. Ekström and H. Brembeck (eds), *European Advances in Consumer Research* 7 (Duluth, MN: Association for Consumer Research, 2006): 485–94.

63. Anis Allagui and Jean-Francois Lemoine, 'Web Interface and Consumers' Buying Intention in e-Tailing: Results from and Online Experiment', in S. Borghini, M.A. McGrath and C.C. Otnes (eds), *European Advances in Consumer Research* 8 (Duluth, MN: Association for Consumer Research 2008): 24–30.

64. Blair H. Sheppard, Jon Hartwick and Paul R. Warshaw, 'The theory of reasoned action: A meta-analysis of past research with recommendations for modifications and future research', *Journal of Consumer Research* 15 (December 1988): 325–43.

65. Ingrid Moons and Patrick de Pelsmacker, 'Emotions as determinants of electric car usage intention', *Journal of Marketing Management*, 28 (2–3, March 2012): 195–237.

66. Joseph A. Cote, James McCullough and Michael Reilly, 'Effects of unexpected situations on behavior–intention differences: A garbology analysis', *Journal of Consumer Research* 12 (September 1985): 188–94.

67. Russell H. Fazio, Martha C. Powell and Carol J. Williams, 'The role of attitude accessibility in the attitude-to-behavior process', *Journal of Consumer Research* 16 (December 1989): 280–8; Robert E. Smith and William R. Swinyard, 'Attitude–behavior consistency: The impact of product trial versus advertising', *Journal of Marketing Research* 20 (August 1983): 257–67.

68. http://epn.dk/landbrug/article2752561.ece, accessed 18 April 18 2012.

69. Søren Askegaard, 'The Fur Industry and its Doppelgänger Brand Image', research project proposal, Danish National Council for Strategic Research.

70. Joseph A. Cote and Patriya S. Tansuhaj, 'Culture Bound Assumptions in Behavior Intention Models', in Thom Srull (ed.), *Advances in Consumer Research* 16 (Provo, UT: Association for Consumer Research, 1989): 105–9.

71. Richard P. Bagozzi and Paul R. Warshaw, 'Trying to consume', *Journal of Consumer Research* 17 (September 1990): 127–40.

72. http://www.euwid-recycling.com/news/business/single/Artikel/container-glass-recycling-rate-remains-high.html, accessed 18 April 2012.

73. In terms of the relative importance of structural conditions (equipment) and attitudes in determining recycling behaviour, see also Folke Ölander and John Thøgersen, 'The A-B-C of Recycling', in K. Ekström and H. Brembeck (eds), *European Advances in Consumer Research* 7 (Duluth, MN: Association for Consumer Research, 2006): 297–307.

74. For a good introduction to various classical perspectives on human communication, see R. Aubrey Fischer, *Perspectives on Human Communication* (New York: Macmillan, 1978).

75. See, for example, Umberto Eco, *The Role of the Reader*, (Bloomington: Indiana University Press, 1979).

76. See, for example, Linda M. Scott, 'The Bridge from Text to Mind: Adapting Reader-Response Theory to Consumer Research', *Journal of Consumer Research* 21 (December 1994): 461–80.

77. David G. Mick and Claus Buhl, 'A meaning-based model of advertisement experiences', *Journal of Consumer Research* 19 (December 1992): 317–38.

78. First proposed by Elihu Katz, 'Mass communication research and the study of popular culture: An editorial note on a possible future for this journal', *Studies in Public Communication* 2 (1959): 1–6. For a more recent discussion of this approach, see Stephanie O'Donohoe, 'Advertising uses and gratifications', *European Journal of Marketing* 28(8/9) (1994): 52–75.

79. Mark Ritson and Richard Elliott, 'The social uses of advertising: an ethnographic study of adolescent advertising audiences', *Journal of Consumer Research* 25(3) (December 1999): 260–78.

80. Carl I. Hovland and W. Weiss, 'The influence of source credibility on communication effectiveness', *Public Opinion Quarterly* 15 (1952): 635–50.

81. Herbert Kelman, 'Processes of opinion change', *Public Opinion Quarterly* 25 (Spring 1961): 57–78; Susan M. Petroshuis and Kenneth E. Crocker, 'An empirical analysis of spokesperson characteristics on advertisement and product evaluations', *Journal of the Academy of Marketing Science* 17 (Summer 1989): 217–26.

82. S. Ratneshwar and Shelly Chaiken, 'Comprehension's role in persuasion: The case of its moderating effect on the persuasive impact of source cues', *Journal of Consumer Research* 18 (June 1991): 52–62.

83. Jagdish Agrawal and Wagner A. Kamakura, 'The economic worth of celebrity endorsers: An event study analysis', *Journal of Marketing* 59 (July 1995): 56–62.

84. Robert Klara, 'Brands by Bieber', *Brandweek* (1 January 2011), http://www.adweek.com/news/advertising-branding/brands-bieber-126241, accessed 23 February 2011.

85. Joe Mandese, 'Tweet This: Social Endorsements Beat Social Media Ad Buys', *Online Media Daily* (10 March 2011), http://www.mediapost.com/publications/?fa_Articles.showArticle&art_aid_146459&nid_124651, accessed 30 April 2011.

86. Kruti Trivedi, 'Great-grandson of artist Renoir uses his name for marketing blitz', *The Wall Street Journal Interactive Edition* (2 September 1999).

87. Judith Graham, 'Sponsors line up for rockin' role', *Advertising Age* (11 December 1989): 50.

88. Michael A. Kamins, 'Celebrity and noncelebrity advertising in a two-sided context', *Journal of Advertising Research* 29 (June–July 1989): 34; Joseph M. Kamen, A.C. Azhari and J.R. Kragh, 'What a spokesman does for a sponsor', *Journal of Advertising Research* 15(2) (1975): 17–24; Lynn Langmeyer and Mary Walker, 'A First Step to Identify the Meaning in Celebrity Endorsers', in Rebecca H. Holman and Michael R. Solomon (eds), *Advances in Consumer Research* 18 (Provo, UT: Association for Consumer Research, 1991): 364–71.

89. Grant McCracken, 'Who is the celebrity endorser? Cultural foundations of the endorsement process', *Journal of Consumer Research* 16(3) (December 1989): 310–21.

90. Choi Hae Won, 'Bill Gates, style icon? Oh yes – in Korea, where geek is chic', *Wall Street Journal* (4 January 2001): A1.

91. Marie Okabe, 'Fading yen for foreign stars in ads', *Singapore Straits Times* (1986).

92. www.japander.com, accessed 6 May 2012.

93. This section is based upon a discussion in Michael R. Solomon, *Conquering Consumerspace: Marketing Strategies for a Branded World* (New York: AMACOM, 2003); see also David Lewis and Darren Bridger, *The Soul of the New Consumer: Authenticity – What We Buy and Why in the New Economy* (London: Nicholas Brealey Publishing, 2000).

94. See for example the puzzled reception of the movie by *The Guardian*'s critic: http://www.guardian.co.uk/film/2010/sep/06/still-here-film-review, accessed 6 May 2012.

95. Jeff Neff, 'Pressure points at IPG', *Advertising Age* (December 2001): 4.

96. Greg Metz Thomas Jr, 'Building the buzz in the hive mind', *Journal of Consumer Behaviour*, 4 (1, 2004): 64–72.

97. http://bengnyexperience.blogspot.com/2011/10/volkswagen-launches-new-beetle-with-ar.html, accessed 19 April 2012.

98. H. Zielske, 'Does day-after recall penalize "feeling" ads?' *Journal of Advertising Research* 22 (1982): 19–22.

99. Allessandra Galloni, 'Lee's cheeky ads are central to new European campaign', *Wall Street Journal Online* (15 March 2002).

100. Michael S. LaTour and Tony L. Henthorne, 'Ethical judgments of sexual appeals in print advertising', *Journal of Advertising* 23(3) (September 1994): 81–90.

101. Rebecca Gardyn, 'Where's the lovin'?', *American Demographics* (February 2001): 10.

102. Asheesh Sharma, 'It's raining sexy ads', *Hindustan Times*, 28 April 2012, http://www.hindustantimes.com/Brunch/Brunch-Stories/It-s-raining-sexy-ads/Article1-847528.aspx, accessed 6 May 2012.

103. Jaideep Sengupta and Darren W. Dahl, 'Gender-related reactions to gratuitous sex appeals', *Journal of Consumer Psychology*, 18 (2008): 62–78.

104. Darren W. Dahl, Jaideep Sengupta and Kathleen Vohs, 'Sex in advertising: Gender differences and the role of relationship commitment', *Journal of Consumer Research*, 36 (August 2009): 215–231.

105. Lars Winther, 'Cocio skal ud I verden', *Food & Culture*, no. 2, 2011, p. 30.

106. Thomas J. Madden, 'Humor in Advertising: An Experimental Analysis' (working paper, no. 83–27, University of Massachusetts, 1984); Thomas J. Madden and Marc G. Weinberger, 'The effects of humor on attention in magazine advertising', *Journal of Advertising* 11(3) (1982): 8–14; Weinberger and Spotts, 'Humor in U.S. versus U.K. TV commercials'; see also Ashesh Mukherjee and Laurette Dubé, 'The Use of Humor in Threat-Related Advertising', unpublished manuscript, McGill University, June 2002.

107. David Gardner, 'The distraction hypothesis in marketing', *Journal of Advertising Research* 10 (1970): 25–30.

108. 'Messi sparker Pepsi-kampagne i gang', *Markedsføring*, 27 February 2012.

109. Imene Becheur, Hayan Dib, Dwight Merunka and Pierre Valette-Florence, 'Emotions of Fear, Guilt or Shame in Anti-Alcohol Messages: Measuring Direct Effects on Persuasion and the Moderating Role of Sensation Seeking', in S. Borghini, M.A. McGrath and C.C. Otnes (eds), *European Advances in Consumer Research* 8 (Duluth, MN: Association for Consumer Research, 2008): 99–108.

110. Michael L. Ray and William L. Wilkie, 'Fear: The potential of an appeal neglected by marketing', *Journal of Marketing* 34 (1970) 1: 54–62.

111. *Ibid.*

112. Brian Sternthal and C. Samuel Craig, 'Fear appeals: Revisited and revised', *Journal of Consumer Research* 1 (December 1974): 22–34.

113. Prof. Herbert J. Rotfeld, Auburn University, personal communication, 9 December 1997; Herbert J. Rotfeld, 'Fear appeals and persuasion: assumptions and errors in advertising research', *Current Issues and Research in Advertising* 11(1) (1988): 21–40; Michael S. LaTour and Herbert J. Rotfeld, 'There are threats and (maybe) fear-caused arousal: Theory and confusions of appeals to fear and fear arousal itself', *Journal of Advertising* 26(3) (Fall 1997): 45–59.

114. For a classical discussion of the importance of metaphors in our culture, see George Lakoff and Mark Johnson, *Metaphors We Live By* (University of Chicago Press, 1980).

115. Richard E. Petty, John T. Cacioppo and David Schumann, 'Central and peripheral routes to advertising effectiveness: The moderating role of involvement', *Journal of Consumer Research* 10(2) (1983): 135–46.

116. Jerry C. Olson, Daniel R. Toy and Philip A. Dover, 'Do cognitive responses mediate the effects of advertising content on cognitive structure?' *Journal of Consumer Research* 9(3) (1982): 245–62.

117. Julie A. Edell and Andrew A. Mitchell, 'An Information Processing Approach to Cognitive Responses,' in S.C. Jain (ed.), *Research Frontiers in Marketing: Dialogues and Directions* (Chicago: American Marketing Association, 1978).

118. See Mary Jo Bitner and Carl Obermiller, 'The Elaboration Likelihood Model: Limitations and Extensions in Marketing', in Elizabeth C. Hirschman and Morris B. Holbrook (eds), *Advances in Consumer Research* 12 (Provo, UT: Association for Consumer Research, 1985): 420–5; Meryl P. Gardner, 'Does attitude toward the ad affect brand attitude under a brand evaluation set?', *Journal of Marketing Research* 22 (1985): 192–98; C.W. Park and S.M. Young, 'Consumer response to television commercials: The impact of involvement and background music on brand attitude formation', *Journal of Marketing Research* 23 (1986): 11–24; Petty, Cacioppo and Schumann, 'Central and peripheral routes to advertising effectiveness'; for a discussion of how different kinds of involvement interact with the ELM, see Robin A. Higie, Lawrence F. Feick and Linda L. Price, 'The Importance of Peripheral Cues in Attitude Formation for Enduring and Task-Involved Individuals', in Holman and Solomon (eds), *Advances in Consumer Research* 18: 187–93.

119. For a recent extension of this technique, see Yanliu Huang and J. Wesley Hutchinson, 'Counting every thought: Implicit measures of cognitive responses to advertising', *Journal of Consumer Research* 35 (June 2008): 98–118.

120. J. Craig Andrews and Terence A. Shimp, 'Effects of involvement, argument strength, and source characteristics on central and peripheral processing in advertising', *Psychology and Marketing* 7 (Fall 1990): 195–214.

121. Richard E. Petty, John T. Cacioppo, Constantine Sedikides and Alan J. Strathman, 'Affect and persuasion: a contemporary perspective', *American Behavioral Scientist* 31(3) (1988): 355–71.

122. Vikram Dodd, 'Coca-Cola Forced to Pull Facebook Promotion after Porn References', *Guardian.co.uk* (18 July 2010), http://www.guardian.co.uk/ business/2010/jul/18/ coca-cola-facebook-promotion-porn, accessed 15 April 2011.

9 INDIVIDUAL DECISION-MAKING

CHAPTER OBJECTIVES

When you finish reading this chapter you will understand why:

→ Consumer decision-making is a central part of consumer behaviour, but the way we evaluate and choose products (and the amount of thought we put into these choices) varies widely, depending on such dimensions as the degree of novelty or risk in the decision.

→ A purchase decision actually is composed of a series of stages that results in the selection of one product over competing options.

→ Decision-making is not always rational.

→ Our access to online sources changes the way we decide what to buy.

→ We often fall back on well-learned 'rules-of-thumb' to make decisions.

→ Consumers rely on different decision rules when they evaluate competing options.

DANIEL is really frustrated with his small portable TV. The final straw was when he could barely tell the runners apart in the Men's Olympics 100m final.[1] When he finally went next door – in total exasperation – to watch the rest of that day's Olympics Men's athletics finals on Lily's new HDTV, he realized what he had been missing out on. Budget or not, it was time to act: a man has to get his priorities right, especially as he felt he was miles behind all his friends in getting the latest digital television technology.

Where to start looking? The web, naturally. Daniel does a quick search on YouTube (www.youtube.com) for HDTVs, and then checks out an independent online consumer guide (www.hdtvorg.co.uk) – there's no point in slogging around the high street shops at this early stage. After narrowing down his options, he ventures out to look at the possible HDTVs which he has identified. He knows he will get some good advice at the small specialist high street retailer about the merits of particular brands so he decides to start there; and then he can hunt around for the best buy by visiting a couple of comparison-shopping websites such as Kelkoo and PriceRunner (www.pricerunner.co.uk). He reckons he'll probably find the most affordable models at one of the out-of-town 'big shed' retailers. At the local specialist retailer, Daniel goes straight to the television section, where he can browse quietly. Eventually, one of the sales assistants asks him if he wants any help. Daniel asks some questions, and gets some useful advice and tips about what features to think about when making his purchase; and one or two recommendations about current good buys. Before leaving the shop, Daniel asks the salesperson to write down the model names and numbers (and prices) for him. At this point Daniel does some more searching online, this time visiting the manufacturers' and brand websites in order to compare the respective features of the different models more carefully. Daniel then visits one of the out-of-town 'big shed' retailers. When he gets there he heads for the Video Zone at the back – barely noticing the rows of toasters, microwave ovens and stereos on his way. Within minutes, a smiling salesperson in a cheap suit accosts him. Daniel reckons that these guys don't know what they're talking about, and they're just out to make a sale, no matter what. Anyway, he has already collected all the information he needs for making his decision.

Daniel starts to look at the new HDTVs. He knew his friend Christopher had a set by Prime Wave that he really liked, and his fellow hockey player, Hannah, had warned him to stay away from the Kamashita. Although Daniel finds a Prime Wave model loaded with features such as a sleep timer, on-screen programming menu, cable compatible tuner, and picture-in-picture, he chooses the less-expensive Precision 2000X because it has one feature that really catches his fancy: stereo broadcast reception; and it had been highly recommended by the high street specialist retailer.

Later that day, Daniel is a happy man as he sits in his armchair watching Formula 1 racing. If he's going to be a couch potato, he's going to do it in style . . .

CONSUMERS AS PROBLEM-SOLVERS

A consumer purchase is a response to a problem, which in Daniel's case is the perceived need for a new TV, partly because the screen on his existing TV is too small; and partly because he feels he has fallen behind with the trends.

> 'The number of digital TV homes will double between 2010 and 2016 to 1,189 million, according to a report covering 73 countries published by Digital TV Research. The Digital TV World Household Forecasts Report estimated that digital penetration will climb from 42.5 per cent at end-2010 to 80.0 per cent by 2016. By 2016, 33 countries will be completely digital, compared with only one (Finland) at end-2010 . . . Of the 613 million digital TV households to be added between 2010 and 2016, 388 million will be in the Asia Pacific region, bringing its total to 607 million. China became the largest digital TV household nation in 2010, and will boast 352 million digital homes by end-2016.'[2]

Daniel is probably right to feel that he has not kept up with the Joneses (see Figure 9.1).

Daniel's situation is similar to that encountered by consumers virtually every day of their lives (even deciding not to make any decision is still a decision). Daniel realizes that he wants to make a purchase, and he goes through a series of steps in order to make it. These steps can be described as: (1) problem recognition, (2) **information search**, (3) evaluation of alternatives, and (4) product choice. After the decision is made, the quality of that decision affects the final step in the process, when learning occurs based on how well the choice worked out. This learning process influences the likelihood that the same choice will be made the next time the need for a similar decision occurs. There is also evidence that suggests that 'more optimistic expectations of future goal pursuit . . . have a greater impact on immediate choices'.[3]

Figure 9.2 provides an overview of this decision-making process (and Professor Suzanne C. Beckmann offers a critique of this five-stage model below). This chapter begins by considering various approaches consumers use when faced with a purchase decision. We then focus on three of the steps in the decision process: how we recognize the problem, or need for a product; how we search for information about product choices; and the ways in which we

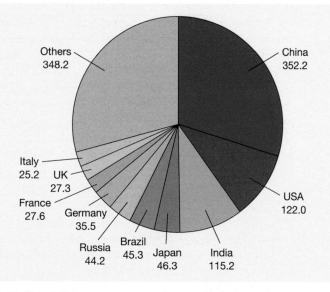

Figure 9.1 Top 10 digital TV countries at end-2016 (million)

Source: Digital TV World Household Forecasts report by Simon Marsh, cited by Clarke in 'Digital TV homes to double within five years' *Broadband TV News Correspondent inShare* 17 June 2011 http://www.broadbandtvnews.com/2011/06/17/digital-tv-homes-to-double-within-five-years/ accessed 17 February 2012.

evaluate alternatives to arrive at a decision. Chapter 3 considered influences in the actual purchase situation, as well as the person's satisfaction with the decision.

Since some purchase decisions are more important than others, the amount of effort we put into each one differs. Sometimes the decision-making process is done almost automatically; we seem to make snap judgements based on very little information. At other times, reaching a purchase decision begins to resemble a full-time job. A person may literally spend days or weeks thinking about an important purchase such as a new home, even to the point of obsession. This intensive decision-making process becomes even more complicated in today's environment where we have so many options from which to choose. Ironically, for many modern consumers one of the biggest problems they face is not having *too few* choices but having *too many*. We describe this profusion of options as **consumer hyperchoice**, a condition where the large number of available options forces us to make repeated choices that may drain psychological energy while decreasing our abilities to make smart decisions.[4] A recent German study has argued that in the face of choice under conditions of high product variety, consumers might disengage and evade the choice process by choosing an avoidant option, in effect the consumers become paralyzed when faced with too much choice.[5]

Two of the most powerful global brands.

Songquan Deng/ Shutterstock.com Bikeworldtravel/ Shutterstock.com

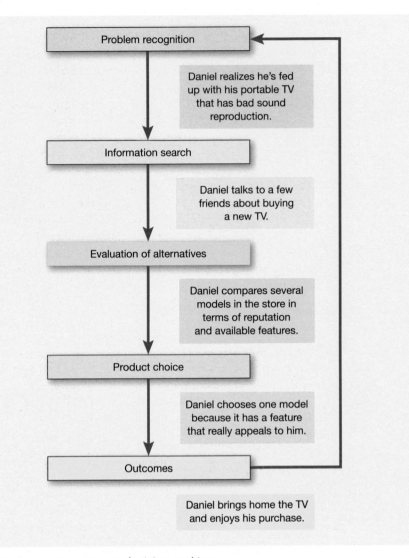

Figure 9.2 Stages in consumer decision-making

Although we tend to assume that more choice is always better, in fact this preference varies across the world. In some cultures people prefer to have hard choices made for them. For example, one study compared American and French consumers who live in different medical cultures: the US norm is to emphasize patient autonomy, whereas in France it's more typical for a doctor to make important decisions on behalf of the patient. The researchers studied families that had to decide whether to take their gravely ill infants off life support. Although the American parents claimed the right to make this difficult choice, they also had greater trouble with their grief and coping processes than the French parents who left this decision to their physicians.[6]

Perspectives on decision-making

Traditionally, consumer researchers have approached decision-making from a **rational perspective**. In this view, people calmly and carefully integrate as much information as possible with what they already know about a product, painstakingly weighing the pluses and minuses of each alternative, and arriving at a satisfactory decision. This traditional decision-making perspective incorporates the *economics of information* approach to the search process; it assumes that consumers will gather as much data as they need in order to make an informed decision. Consumers form expectations of the value of additional information and continue to search to the extent that the rewards of doing so (what economists call the *utility*) exceed the costs. This utilitarian assumption also implies that the person will collect the most valuable units of information first. They will absorb additional pieces only to the extent that they think they will add to what they already know.[7] In other words, people will put themselves out to collect as much information as possible, as long as the process of gathering it is not too onerous or time-consuming.[8]

This process implies that steps in decision-making should be carefully studied by marketing managers in order to understand how consumers obtain information, how consumers form beliefs, and what criteria consumers use to make product or service choices. Companies can then develop products or services that emphasize the appropriate attributes, and marketers can tailor promotional strategies to deliver the types of information consumers are most likely to desire, via the best channels, and in the most effective formats.[9]

How valid is this perspective? Professor Beckmann acknowledges the value and limitations of this perspective, and illustrates some of the complexities involved in consumer decision-making in her commentary (see below).[10] While consumers do follow these decision-making steps when making some purchases, such a rational process does not accurately portray many of our purchase decisions.[11] Consumers simply do not go through this elaborate sequence every time they buy something. If they did, their entire lives would be spent making such decisions, leaving them with very little time to enjoy the things they eventually decide to buy. Some of our consumption behaviours simply don't seem 'rational' because they don't always seem to serve a logical purpose (e.g. people who break the law to collect the eggs of the osprey (a rare bird) in Scotland even though the eggs have no (legal) monetary value).[12] Other purchase behaviours are undertaken with virtually no advance planning at all (e.g. impulsively grabbing that tempting bar of chocolate at the checkout till while waiting to pay for groceries in the supermarket). Still other actions are actually contrary to those predicted by rational models. For example, **purchase momentum** occurs when these initial impulses actually increase the likelihood that we will buy even more (instead of less as our needs are satisfied), almost as if we get caught up in a spending spree.[13] Research also hints that people differ in terms of their **cognitive processing style**. Some of us tend to have a *rational system of cognition* that processes information analytically and sequentially using rules of logic, whereas others rely on an *experiential system of cognition* that processes information more holistically and in parallel.[14]

Researchers are now beginning to realize that decision-makers actually possess a repertoire of strategies. A consumer evaluates the effort required to make a particular choice, and then they choose a strategy best suited to the level of effort required. This sequence of events is known as *constructive processing*. Rather than using a big stick to kill an ant, consumers tailor their degree of cognitive 'effort' to the task at hand.[15] When the task requires a well-thought-out, rational approach, we'll invest the brainpower required for the decision. Otherwise, we look for short cuts or fall back upon learned responses that 'automate' these choices. Researchers are also beginning to understand the role that controlling the information flow can have on consumers' decisions, as increased control leads to increased performance. These new insights promise to be particularly important in the new online environments where 'marketers have the potential to integrate interactive communication systems back into mass communication'[16] where controlling the information flow can particularly influence the quality of consumers' decisions, memory, knowledge and confidence.[17] Research on information structure (the amount of information in a choice set) is also relevant in the new electronic marketplaces, where consumers are regularly faced with information overload when making decisions.[18] One study suggests that: 'consumers adapt their acquisition of information in response to changes in information structure. When a choice set contains more information per element, fewer acquisitions are made, more time is spent per acquisition, and customers are more selective in their information acquisition.'[19] Other recent research has identified how consumers integrate the internet into other product information sources such as retailers and media during their search for information. Car buyers, for instance, often use the manufacturer and dealer internet

This ad for the US Postal Service presents a problem, illustrates the decision-making process and offers a solution.

sources to substitute for more traditional information search via visits to car dealerships.[20] Daniel also used the internet for informal information gathering, and then for price searching when looking for his new HDTV, thus integrating the net into his search activities.

Some decisions are made under conditions of low involvement, as discussed in Chapter 3. In many of these situations, our decision is a learned response to environmental cues (see Chapter 7), as when we decide to buy something on impulse that is being promoted as a special offer in a shop. A concentration on these types of decisions can be described as the **behavioural influence perspective**. Under these circumstances, managers must concentrate on assessing the characteristics of the environment that influence members of a target market,[21] such as the design of a retail outlet or whether a package is enticing.

In other cases, consumers are highly involved in a decision, but still we cannot explain their selections entirely rationally. For example, the traditional approach is hard pressed to explain a person's choice of art, music or even a partner. In these cases, no single quality may be the determining factor. Instead, the **experiential perspective** stresses the *Gestalt*, or totality (see Chapter 4), of the product or service.[22] Marketers in these areas focus on measuring consumers' affective responses to products or services and developing offerings that elicit appropriate subjective reactions.

PROFESSOR SUZANNE C. BECKMANN, CBS
Copenhagen Business School, Denmark

Consumer behaviour as I see it . . .

Individual decision-making

The five-stage model of decision-making (Figure 9.2) is the core of the classic view in consumer behaviour about how consumers make decisions, based on the idea that a consumer is an information processing 'machine'. Although certainly helpful in structuring this sequence by putting the various events in boxes connected by arrows, the model is not always useful in understanding real life consumer decisions. For one simple reason: neither problem recognition nor information search nor evaluation of alternatives nor product choice take place in isolation from each other and without the impact of any external influences. Human beings are social beings, and the number of 'problems' that are truly individual are quite few and far between, and are mostly related to biological needs. It is obvious that consumers' interaction with others – family, friends, peers – will to a large extent determine where to search for information, which features to look for when evaluating alternatives, and what ultimately to buy. Hence, much of the consumer research in our department uses the classical model as a backcloth, but not as a driver for study designs.

There is, for instance, the complexity issue. How do consumers decide between products in a world full of brands, when confronted with so much information? Lots of information does not necessarily mean that choices are easier or quicker to make for the individual consumer. Take the case of grocery shopping – how do consumers incorporate other aspects such as health, pleasure or status into their decision-making process? One group in our department works with 'supra-complex' decision-making in the food market, suggesting that the construct of perceived complexity will help us in better understanding how consumers actually make use of informational cues. And why is health and nutrition information more often than not overlooked? We distinguish between four levels of perceived complexity, with price being the least complex of all the indicators. The Danish label 'Varefakta' is an example of the next level of complexity, because it contains core objective information on product content, but it is not a quality label. The third situation relates to product labels provided by producers such as 'light' or 'natural' that are used by consumers as a surrogate when they are evaluating products. And the highest level of complexity is reached when all these other informational cues are supplemented by labels concerning fair trade, ecology or energy saving. Admittedly, it is the individual consumer who perceives complexity in decision-making but it is the environment, the interaction with others and societal requirements that increase this complexity.

Consumers are not only consumers but have many different roles in daily life vis-à-vis other people. And these roles are played out in different situations. How they are played out depends to a large degree on personality, values and beliefs. Therefore, another group in our department has developed 'CUBEicle thinking' = customer universe based execution for designing marketing strategies. The core idea is to know the customer type combined with a certain role and a certain situation or context and to plot this into a Necker 3-D cube-type graphic. Consider air transportation as an example: a woman arriving at the airport with her briefcase on the way to a business meeting has different needs and expectations about what the airport should offer her whilst waiting for the departure of her flight compared with the same woman arriving a few days later with her two small children and on her way on holiday with her young family. The challenge of this approach is to determine exactly the content of the three sides of the cube that takes account of all the individual and social determinants of decision-making.

→

→ A third example from our research are our studies on brand relevance. We assume that there are situations where brands are less relevant than in others. One important dimension here is product category, i.e. not all categories necessarily have the same brand relevance for all consumers. One of our findings is that brand loyalty competes with store loyalty in out-of-stock situations: certain consumers will switch supermarket when their preferred brand in a category is not available, while others will be prepared to substitute with another brand. Yet, this behaviour is dependent on category, since the propensity for store switching is greater, for instance, in the case of shampoo than it is for marinated herring. While the decision to switch or not to switch is made individually at the point of purchase, the drivers for this decision could very well be other people within the decision-making unit: 'I know that my husband doesn't care which brand of marinated herring I buy' versus 'My daughter will be furious if I take home the wrong shampoo.'

Finally, the most recent example of our endeavours relates to multisensory branding, more specifically consumers' responses to sound as an integral part of conveying a brand's identity. As an emerging field in both academic research and practitioner applications we are confronted with a number of fascinating methodological challenges, yet findings show so far that sound is an important brand equity driver – and in this particular case, it is a very individual and idiosyncratic response.

Suzanne C. Beckmann

Types of consumer decisions

One helpful way to characterize the decision-making process is to consider the amount of effort that goes into the decision each time we must make it. Consumer researchers have found it convenient to think in terms of a continuum, which is anchored at one end by habitual decision-making and at the other extreme by extended problem-solving. Many decisions fall somewhere in the middle and so we characterize these as limited problem solving. This continuum is presented in Figure 9.3.

Extended problem-solving

Decisions involving **extended problem-solving** correspond most closely to the traditional decision-making perspective. As indicated in Table 9.1, we usually initiate this careful process when the decision we have to make relates to our self-concept (see Chapter 5), and we feel that the outcome may be risky in some way. In that case we try to collect as much information

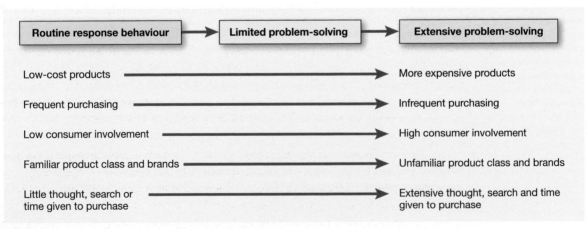

Figure 9.3 A continuum of buying decision behaviour

Table 9.1 Characteristics of limited *vs* extended problem-solving

	Limited problem-solving	Extended problem-solving
Motivation	Low risk and involvement	High risk and involvement
Information search	Little search	Extensive search
	Information processed passively	Information processed actively
	In-store decision likely	Multiple sources consulted prior to store visits
Alternative evaluation	Weakly held beliefs	Strongly held beliefs
	Only most prominent criteria used	Many criteria used
	Alternatives perceived as basically similar	Significant differences perceived among alternatives
	Non-compensatory strategy used	Compensatory strategy used
Purchase	Limited shopping time; may prefer self-service	Many outlets visited if necessary
	Choice often influenced by store displays	Communication with store personnel often desirable

as possible, both from our memory (internal search) and from outside sources such as Google or YouTube (as Daniel did when looking for information about HDTVs) (external search). Based on the importance of the decision, we carefully evaluate each product alternative, often considering the attributes of one brand at a time and seeing how each brand's attributes shape up to some set of desired characteristics or outcomes that we hope to achieve through our choice.

In the past few years we've witnessed huge growth in extended problem solving in the online space, mostly due to the tremendous popularity of complex and engrossing games that people play on social media platforms. A **social game** is a multiplayer, competitive, goal-oriented activity with defined rules of engagement and online connectivity among a community of players. Because the phenomenal growth of social games is attributed largely to Facebook's game platform and the blockbuster game *FarmVille*, social games are sometimes thought of as games that people play within a social network. However, other game formats, such as Xbox Live with Kinect, also adopt social elements, including the ability to play online with other geographically dispersed players and to share game achievements on social profiles.[23]

These games, especially the so-called *core games* like *Call of Duty: Black OPS* that extend over time and involve hundreds or thousands of players, tend to morph from extended decision-making to produce the kind of flow state discussed in Chapter 6.

Social games are built upon several layers, including platform, mode, milieu and genre.[24] Let's briefly review the basic dimensions of social games:

- A **game platform** refers to the hardware systems on which the game is played. Platforms include *game consoles* (consoles are interactive, electronic devices used to display video games, such as Sony's PlayStation3, Microsoft's Xbox 360, and Nintendo's Wii), computers (including both online games and those that require software installation on the player's computer hard drive), and portable devices that may include smartphones or devices specifically for game play such as the Sony PSP or Nintendo DS.[25]

- **Mode** refers to the way players experience the game world. It includes aspects such as whether a player's activities are highly structured, whether the game is single-player or multiplayer, whether the game is played in close physical proximity to other players (or by virtual proximity), and whether the game is real-time or turn-based.

- **Milieu** describes the visual nature of the game, such as science fiction, fantasy, horror and retro.

- The **genre** of a game refers to the method of play. Popular genres include simulation, action and role-playing. *Simulation games* attempt to depict real-world situations as accurately as possible. There are several subgenres, including racing simulators, flight simulators and 'Sim' games that enable players to simulate the development of an environment. Among social games, simulations include the highly popular *FarmVille*, *Pet Resort* and *FishVille*. *Action games* consist of two major subgenres: *first-person shooters (FPS)*, where you 'see' the game as your avatar sees it, and third-person games. Examples of social action games are *Epic Goal*, a live-action soccer game; *Paradise Paintball*, a first-person shooter social game; and *Texas Hold 'Em*, a social gambling game. In *role-playing games* (RPGs), the players play a character role with the goal of completing some mission. Perhaps the best-known RPG started its life as a tabletop game: *Dungeons and Dragons*. Players adopt the identity of a character in the game story and go about completing tasks and collecting points and items as they strive to accomplish the intended goal. **MMORPGs** – *massively multiplayer online role-playing games* – are a type of RPG that truly encompass the social aspects of gaming. *World of Warcraft* is the largest of these. with more than 11 million subscribers. Social RPGs on Facebook include *Haven*, *Mafia Wars*, *Battle Stations*, and *Tennis Mania*.[26]

It's important for us to understand these new platforms for extended decision-making, because many analysts feel that these will be a very important place to talk to consumers in the next few years as **game-based marketing** tactics accelerate. Brands can utilize social games for marketing in several ways. Games offer a targeted audience, a large and wide reach, a high level of engagement, low-intrusion methods of promotion, and a way to interact with brand fans. Numerous companies are already experimenting with different formats for embedding their messages into game play:

- *Display ads* are integrated in a game's environment as billboards, movie posters and store-fronts. The display advertising may be static or dynamic and may include text, images or rich media. Rich-media advertising can run pre-roll (before the game begins), interlevel (between stages of the game), or post-roll (at the game's conclusion), though interlevel is the most common placement.

- *Static ads* are hard-coded into the game and ensure that all players view the advertising. Bing's display ad in FarmVille is an example of an in-game, static display ad. The ad offered players the chance to earn FarmVille cash by becoming a fan of Bing on Facebook. In the first day the ad ran, Bing earned 425,000 new fans.[27]

- *Dynamic ads* are variable; they change based on specified criteria. This technique is managed by networks like Google AdWords, which offers insertion technology to place ads across multiple games. The networks contract with game publishers to place advertising in their games. By combining games from several publishers, networks create a large portfolio of in-game media opportunities for advertisers. The network works with publishers to strategically embed advertising, sell the placement to advertisers, serve the ads into the games in the network, and manage the billing and accounting for the process. Advertisers can choose specific game placement or allow Google AdWords to place the ads dynamically within games in the Google Display Advertising Network. Playfish's game portfolio includes *Word Challenge*, *Hotel City*, *Who Has The Biggest Brain?* and others. Players of these games will be exposed to commercials that run between levels of the game.

Limited problem-solving

Limited problem-solving is usually more straightforward and simple. In this case we are not nearly as motivated to search for information or to evaluate each alternative rigorously. Instead, we are likely to use simple *decision rules* to choose among alternatives. These cognitive short cuts (more about these later) enable consumers to fall back on general guidelines, instead of having to start from scratch every time we need to make a decision.

Habitual decision-making

Both extended and limited problem-solving modes involve some degree of information search and deliberation, though they vary in the degree to which we engage in these activities. At the other end of the choice continuum, however, lies **habitual decision-making**; choices that we make with little or no conscious effort. Many purchase decisions are so routinized that we may not realize we have made them until we look in our shopping trolleys. We make these choices with minimal effort and without conscious control; researchers call this process *automaticity*.[28]

While this kind of thoughtless activity may seem dangerous at worst or stupid at best, it is actually quite efficient in many cases. The development of habitual, repetitive behaviour allows consumers to minimize the time and energy spent on mundane purchase decisions. On the other hand, habitual decision-making poses a problem when a marketer tries to introduce a new way of doing an old task. In this case consumers must be convinced to 'unfreeze' their former habit and replace it with a new one – perhaps by using digital banking rather than the local branch of the bank; or using an ATM machine instead of a live bank teller; or switching to self-service petrol pumps instead of being served by an attendant.

Steps in the decision-making process

Daniel did not suddenly wake up and crave a new HDTV. He went through several steps between feeling the need for a better quality television picture for watching sporting fixtures, and actually purchasing a new television. Let's review the basic steps in this process.

PROBLEM RECOGNITION

Ford's plan to promote its Fusion hybrid model focused on people who aren't thinking about buying a new car – at least not right now. Its TV commercials targeted what the car industry terms the 'upper funnel', or potential buyers down the road. Ford's research found that a large number of US drivers are still unaware of the Fusion. The company is confident that it can achieve sales if and when customers decide to buy a new car. But, its weak spot is to get people into the frame of mind where they want to do that. To create desire where none exists yet, visitors to a special website entered a competition to win a trip and a new Fusion. Ford publicized the sweepstakes on Twitter and Facebook; during the first two weeks of the promotion, almost 70,000 people requested more information about the car.[29]

Problem recognition occurs at what Ford terms 'the upper funnel' when we experience a significant difference between our current state of affairs and some desired or ideal state. We realize that to get from here to there we need to solve a problem, which may be large or small, simple or complex. A person who unexpectedly runs out of petrol on the motorway or autobahn has a problem, as does the person who becomes dissatisfied with the image of their car, even though there may be nothing mechanically wrong with it. Although the quality of Daniel's TV had not changed, for example, his *standard of comparison* had altered, and he was confronted with a desire he did not have prior to watching his friend Lily's HDTV.

Problem creation

Figure 9.4 shows that a problem can arise in one of two ways. As in the case of the person who runs out of petrol, the quality of the consumer's *actual state* can sometimes move downwards or decrease (*need recognition*). On the other hand, as in the case of the person who craves a high performance car, the consumer's *ideal state* can move upward (*opportunity recognition*). Either way, a gulf occurs between the actual state and the ideal state.[30] In Daniel's case, a

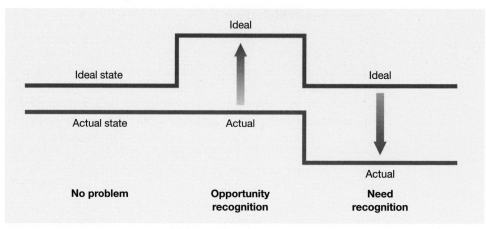

Figure 9.4 Problem recognition: shifts in actual or ideal states

problem was perceived as a result of opportunity recognition; his ideal state in terms of the television reception and viewing quality that he wanted.

Need recognition can occur in several ways. A person's actual state can decrease if they run out of a product, or if they buy a product that doesn't adequately satisfy their needs, or if they realize that they have a new need or desire (e.g. buying a house can set off an avalanche of other choices, because many new things will be needed to furnish the house – assuming that there's any money left over). In contrast, opportunity recognition often occurs when we're exposed to different or better-quality products. This happens because our circumstances have somehow changed, as when an individual goes to university or gets a new job. As our frame of reference shifts, we make purchases to adapt to the new environment.

Marketers' role in problem creation

While problem recognition can and does occur naturally, this process is often spurred by marketing efforts. In some cases, marketers attempt to create *primary demand*, where consumers are encouraged to use a product or service regardless of the brand they choose. Such needs are often encouraged in the early stages of a product's lifecycle, as, for example, when microwave ovens were first introduced. *Secondary demand*, where consumers are prompted to prefer a specific brand instead of others, can occur only if primary demand already exists. At this point, marketers must convince consumers that a problem can be best solved by choosing their brand over others in the same category.

INFORMATION SEARCH

Once a problem has been recognized, consumers need adequate information to resolve it. **Information search** is the process by which the consumer surveys their environment for appropriate data to make a reasonable decision. In this section we will review some of the factors this search involves.[31]

Types of information search

A consumer may recognize a need and then search the marketplace for specific information (a process called *pre-purchase search*). On the other hand, many consumers, especially veteran shoppers, enjoy browsing just for the fun of it, or because they like to stay up-to-date on what's happening in the marketplace. Those shopaholics are engaging in *ongoing search*.[32] Some differences between these two search modes are described in Table 9.2.

Table 9.2 A framework for consumer information search

	Pre-purchase search	Ongoing search
Determinants	Involvement in the purchase Market environment Situational factors	Involvement with the product Market environment Situational factors
Motives	Making better purchase decisions	Building a bank of information for future use Experiencing fun and pleasure
Outcomes	Increased product and market knowledge Better purchase decisions Increased satisfaction with the purchase outcome	Increased product and market knowledge, leading to – future buying efficiencies – personal influences Increased impulse buying Increased satisfaction from search and other outcomes

Source: Peter H. Bloch, Daniel L. Sherrell and Nancy M. Ridgway, 'Consumer search: An extended framework', *Journal of Consumer Research* 13 (June 1986): 120. Reprinted with permission by The University of Chicago Press.

Internal *vs* external search

Information sources can be roughly broken down into two kinds: internal and external. As a result of prior experience and simply living in a consumer culture, each of us often has some degree of knowledge about many products already in our memory. When confronted with a purchase decision, we may engage in *internal search* by scanning our own memory bank to assemble information about different product alternatives (see Chapter 7). Usually, though, even the most market-aware of us needs to supplement this knowledge with external search, by which we obtain the information from advertisements, friends, or just plain people-watching. A study in Finland recently demonstrated how what our neighbours buy impacts our own decision making. The researchers discovered that when one of a person's ten nearest neighbours bought a car, the odds that they would buy a car of the same make during the next week and a half jumped 86 per cent. The effect was even stronger for used car purchases – low-income families and those who lived in rural areas were more likely to be influenced by their neighbours than were wealthy Helsinki residents. They explained this finding in terms of the information value of these choices – because used cars are less reliable, a neighbour's endorsement of one kind over others might carry more weight.[33]

Deliberate *vs* 'accidental' search

Our existing knowledge of a product may be the result of *directed learning*: on a previous occasion we might already have searched for relevant information or experienced some of the alternatives. A parent who bought a birthday cake for one child last month, for example, probably has a good idea of the best kind to buy for another child this month.

Alternatively, we may acquire information in a more passive manner. Even though a product may not be of direct interest to us right now, exposure to advertising, packaging, sales promotion and viral marketing activities may result in *incidental learning*. Mere exposure over time to conditioned stimuli and observations of others results in the learning of much material that may not be needed for some time, if ever. For marketers, this is one of the benefits of steady, 'low-dose' advertising, as they establish and maintain product associations until the time we need them.[34]

In some cases, we may be so expert about a product category (or at least believe we are) that no additional search is undertaken. Frequently, however, our own existing state of knowledge is not sufficient to make an adequate decision, and we must look elsewhere for

This ad for Arm & Hammer demonstrates the strategy of identifying new problems an existing product can solve.

Church & Dwight Co., Inc.

more information. The sources we consult for advice vary. They may be impersonal and marketer-dominated sources, such as retailers, retailers' websites and catalogues; they may be friends and family members; or they may be unbiased third parties such as *Which?* magazine or other consumer reports which are published in a number of European countries.[35]

MARKETING OPPORTUNITY

Tangled web

Internet search engines (especially Google) are huge players now when it comes to searching. Yahoo found that consumers spend 10 per cent more for televisions and digital cameras they buy in stores when they research these purchases online first using a search engine, and people who use these engines consult twice as many information sources as those who don't.[36]

When we search online for product information, we're a perfect target for advertisers because we're declaring our desire to make a purchase. Recognizing this, many companies pay search engines to show ads to users who have searched for their brand names. However, when DoubleClick (an online marketing company) looked closely at what people search for, it found that searches including brand names account for a small share of our queries. Instead, most pre-purchase searches use only generic terms, like 'hard drive'. Consumers tend to make these searches early on, and then conduct a small flurry of brand-name queries right

before buying.[37] The internet is increasingly integrated into overall search strategies.[38] Hence Daniel's iteration between online and offline sources of information as he assessed the variety of choices available to him before purchasing his new HDTV. There is also evidence of migration from printed sources of objective information to online sources of objective information.[39] 'However, possibly because friends/relatives convey different types of information, the internet does not appear to have a significant effect on the use of friends/relatives as a source [of information].'[40] However, Nielsen's latest research suggests where friends and relatives are important is in suggesting websites to try 'recommendations from fellow consumers – whether they are people they know or fellow online shoppers – play an enormous role in the decision-making process. The explosion in Consumer Generated Media over the last year means that this reliance on word of mouth, over other forms of referral, looks set to increase.'[41]

Not surprisingly, social media platforms now play a major role in the search process. Although about 60 per cent of consumers now start their online process by typing queries into a search engine such as Google or Bing; 40 per cent now continue their quest for more information on other social media platforms such as blogs, YouTube, Twitter and Facebook. The goal here is not to collect more technical or performance information, but to get other people's opinions about options in the product category – and to eliminate some brands from consideration when others criticise them. What's more, after they buy a brand, about three-quarters of shoppers who use social media in the process choose to follow it on the company's Facebook page so they can continue to engage with it in the future.[42]

Do consumers always search rationally?

This assumption of rational search is not always supported. As we've seen, consumers don't necessarily engage in a rational search process where they carefully identify every alternative before choosing one they prefer. The amount of external search that we do for most products is surprisingly small, even when we would benefit by having more information. For example, lower-income shoppers, who have more to lose by making a bad purchase, actually search *less* prior to buying than more affluent people do.[43]

One widely used distinction is between a decision strategy that seeks to deliver the best possible result (**maximizing**) and one that simply tries to yield an adequate solution, often as a way to reduce the costs of the decision-making process. This is called a **satisficing** solution (economist Herbert Simon won a Nobel Prize for this idea in 1978). Because we rarely have the resources (especially the time) to weigh every possible factor into a decision, we will often happily settle for a solution that is just good enough. This perspective on decision making is called **bounded rationality**. These two extremes have huge implications for marketing and retailing strategy, because they imply very different approaches to customers. Indeed, the maximizer strongly resembles the high-involvement consumer we discussed in Chapter 6; she is going to go all out to explore as much information as she can before she decides. In contrast, the satisficer resembles the low-involvement consumer who will probably use some simple shortcuts (that we'll discuss shortly) to just pick something decent and get on with her life. Indeed, some recent research suggests that maximizers may be so thorough they don't even rely on their past experiences to guide their current choice. Instead, they start almost from scratch to research options for each unique decision situation. The researchers term this the **Sisyphus effect**.[44] Sisyphus was a famous figure in Greek mythology; he was sentenced for all eternity to push a huge boulder up a hill, only to watch it roll back down just before it reached the top so that he had to begin again.

Like Daniel, some consumers typically visit only one or two stores and often don't seek out unbiased information sources prior to making a purchase decision, especially when there is little time to do so.[45] This pattern is especially prevalent for decisions regarding durable goods such as appliances or cars, even when these products represent significant investments. There is also some evidence that even having information available on the package does not necessarily mean that consumers make use of it. Environmentally friendly products in Finland are beginning to carry the Nordic Environmental Label to assist consumers in their choice of environmentally safe products. In a study which asked Finnish consumers to evaluate detergent and batteries choices, little use was made of and little trust was placed in the 'green label' on the packages, in spite of the positive attitudes that Finnish citizens have towards the environment. The results suggest that marketers have a long way to go in order to provide clear, easily comprehensible and unbiased information regarding 'green' products.[46]

This tendency to avoid external search is less prevalent when consumers consider the purchase of symbolic items, such as clothing. In those cases, not surprisingly, people tend to do a fair amount of external search, although most of it involves seeking the opinions of peers.[47] Although the stakes may be lower financially, people may see these self-expressive decisions as having dire social consequences if they make the wrong choice. The level of perceived risk, a concept to be discussed shortly, is high.

In addition, consumers are often observed to engage in *brand switching*, even if their current brand satisfies their needs.[48] Sometimes, it seems that people simply like to try new things – we crave variety as a form of stimulation or to reduce boredom. **Variety seeking**, the desire to choose new alternatives over more familiar ones, even influences us to switch from our favourite products to ones we like less. This can occur even before we become *satiated*, or tired of our favourite product. Research supports the idea that we are willing to trade enjoyment for variety because the unpredictability itself is rewarding. One study suggests that although consumers frequently consume items to the point where they no longer enjoy them, the marketer can counteract this **variety amnesia** simply by prompting them to recall the variety of alternative items they have consumed in the past.[49]

Variety seeking is a choice strategy that occurs as a result of pleasurable memories of ringing the changes.[50] Variety seeking is especially likely to occur when we are in a good mood, or when there is relatively little stimulation elsewhere in our environment.[51] In the case of foods and beverages, variety seeking can occur due to a phenomenon known as *sensory-specific satiety*. Put simply, this means the pleasantness of a recently consumed food item drops, while the pleasantness of uneaten foods remains unchanged.[52] So even though we have favourites, we still like to sample other possibilities. Ironically, consumers may actually switch to less-preferred options for variety's sake even though they enjoy the more familiar option more. On the other hand, when the decision situation is ambiguous or when there is little information about competing brands, we tend to opt for the safe choice by selecting familiar brands and maintaining the status quo. Figure 9.5 shows the brand attributes consumers consider most important when choosing among alternatives, according to a survey *Advertising Age* conducted.

Brand familiarity influences confidence about a brand, which in turn affects purchase intention.[53] Still, the tendency of consumers to shift brand choices over time means that marketers can never relax in the belief that once they have won a customer, they are necessarily theirs forever.[54]

Biases in the decision-making process

Consider the following scenario: you've been given a free ticket to an important football match. At the last minute, though, a sudden snowstorm makes getting to the football ground somewhat dangerous. Would you still go? Now, assume the same game and snowstorm, except this time you paid a lot of money for the ticket. Would you go?

Analyses of people's responses to this situation and to other similar puzzles illustrates principles of **mental accounting**. This process demonstrates that the way we pose a problem (we call this **framing**) and whether it's phrased in terms of gains or losses, influences our decisions.[55] In this case, researchers found that people are more likely to risk their personal safety in the storm if they paid for the football ticket than if it was a freebie. Only the most diehard fan would fail to recognize that this is an irrational choice, because the risk is the same regardless of whether or not you got a great bargain on the ticket. This decision-making bias is called the *sunk-cost fallacy* – having paid for something makes us reluctant to waste it.

Behavioural economics

In recent years, the recognition that many decisions are not based on a maximization strategy has contributed to the huge resurgence of the field of **behavioural economics**, a blend of psychology and economics that studies how consumers make economic decisions. Unlike more traditional economic approaches, this hybrid perspective recognizes that our decisions are not always based on 'logical' factors such as price or quality. Rather, they are coloured by our emotions and even by very subtle cues in the environment that steer us towards some products and away from others. Numerous books and blogs, including the huge bestsellers *Freakonomics* and *Predictably Irrational*, come from and promote this view of the less-than-logical consumer.[56]

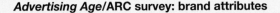

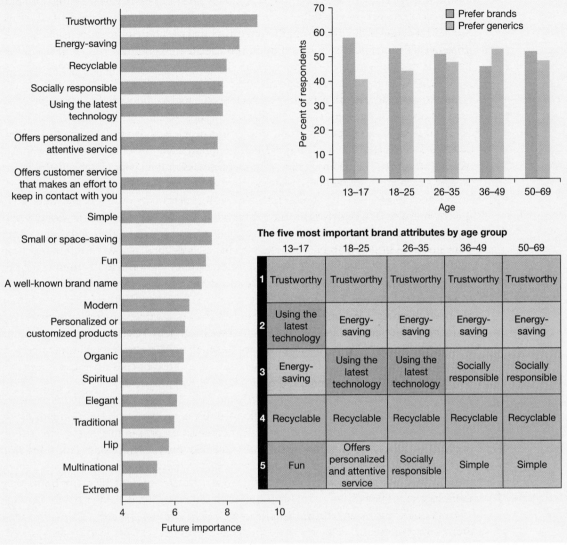

Figure 9.5 *Advertising Age* poll: importance of brand attitudes

As we'll see shortly, many of the principles in behavioural economics deal with the way a choice is put into context (earlier we referred to this as *framing*), along with the bias and experience that each consumer brings to that purchase. Daniel Kahneman, the 'father' of behavioural economics (he won a Nobel Prize in Economics in 2002 for his seminal work) gave an example of one type of framing called **anchoring**, which refers to the fact that when people are given a number, they tend to use that number as the standard for future judgements. He noted that when he asked people if the tallest tree in the world is more or less than 900 feet, most people would correctly guess that is way too tall. Now, however, he's made you think of very tall trees, so perhaps a 500-foot-tall tree would seem small to you. The opposite would have been true if he had used 100 feet as an 'anchor' number.[57]

Whether we focus on the present or the future is another example of how the way we frame an issue influences the options we choose and how we feel about them. The condition of hyperopia (the medical term for people who have far sighted vision) describes people who are so obsessed with preparing for the future that they can't enjoy the present. College students who participated in a study on this phenomenon reported that they regretted not working, studying, or saving money during their winter breaks. But, when researchers asked them to imagine how they will feel about this break a year from now, their biggest regrets were that they didn't have enough fun or travel enough. In another study, female subjects received a ticket for a lottery that would be held three months later. They had to choose in advance from one of two prizes if they won: either $85 in cash or an $80 voucher for a massage or facial at a spa. Even though they were reminded that they could use the $85 in cash to get a spa treatment and pocket the $5 difference, more than a third of the women chose the voucher. Researchers found similar results in other situations: when people had to choose between cash and prizes such as bottles of wine or dinners out, many of them chose the luxuries even though the cash was a better deal. One participant observed, 'If I took the cash it would end up going into the rent.'[58]

Loss aversion is another bias. This means we emphasize our losses more than our gains. For example, for most people losing money is more *unpleasant* than gaining money is *pleasant*. A recent study has distinguished between two types of loss aversion (or, as the authors suggest thinking about aversion in this context, as either loss sensitivity or loss exaggeration). First, one type of loss aversion focuses on losses and gains defined in terms of desirability or valence. In this case a desirable change is defined as a valence gain (e.g. passing an examination; surviving surgery), and an undesirable change is defined as a valence loss (catching a cold; being in a car crash; having one's house destroyed by a tornado). Secondly, the other type of loss aversion concentrates on changes in possessions and ownership. Giving up a possession becomes a 'possession loss' (e.g. the removal of a bad debt; removal of a tumour; although this possession loss can also involve the loss of a valued possession such as house or money). Receiving an item represents a 'possession gain' (e.g. winning a scholarship). From here, it is argued that this distinction between types of loss aversion allows for a clearer understanding of possession loss aversion within the context of consumer decision-making. The **Psychology of Loss Aversion (PLA)** particularly helps to predict 'opposite patterns of staying and switching between choices involving goods and bads. Consequently, PLA can simultaneously explain both the traditional endowment effect (i.e. the tendency to value more highly an item that is already in one's possession) and also the fact that people may sometimes strongly desire to switch from a current negative state to an alternative negative state' (see Table 9.3).[59]

Prospect theory, which describes how people make choices, finds that utility is a function of gains and losses. Our sense of risk differs when we face options involving gains versus those involving losses.[60]

To illustrate this bias, consider the following choices. For each, would you take the safe bet or choose to gamble?

● *Option 1*. You're given €100 and then offered a chance to flip a coin: heads you win €30; tails you lose €30.

Table 9.3 Example of valence gains/losses and possession gains/losses

	Possession gain (receiving an item)	Possession loss (giving up an item)
Valence gain (positive changes)	Receiving an attractive item (e.g. winning $100)	Giving up an unattractive item (e.g. giving up the speeding ticket)
Valence loss (negative changes)	Receiving an unattractive item (e.g. receiving a speeding ticket)	Giving up an attractive item (e.g. losing $100)

Source: Lyle Brenner, Yuval Rottenstreich, Sanjay Sood and Baler Bilgin, 'On the psychology of loss aversion: Possession, valence, and reversals of the endowment effect', *Journal of Consumer Research* 34 (October 2007): Table 1: 370. *The Journal of Consumer Research* by AMERICAN ASSOC. FOR PUBLIC OPINION RESEARCH. Reproduced with permission of UNIVERSITY OF CHICAGO PRESS.

- *Option 2*. You're given a choice of getting €100 outright, or accepting a coin flip that will win you either €115 or €85.

In one study, 70 per cent of those given Option 1 chose to gamble, compared to just 43 per cent of those offered Option 2. Yet, the odds are the same for both options! The difference is that people prefer 'playing with the house money'; they are more willing to take risks when they perceive they're using someone else's resources. So, contrary to a rational decision-making perspective, we value money differently depending on its source. This explains why someone might choose to spend a big bonus on some frivolous purchase, but they would never consider taking that same amount out of their savings account for this purpose.

Finally, research in mental accounting demonstrates that extraneous characteristics of the choice situation can influence our selections, even though they wouldn't *if* we were totally rational decision-makers. As one example, participants in a survey were provided with one of two versions of this scenario:

> You are lying on the beach on a hot day. All you have to drink is iced water. For the last hour you have been thinking about how much you would enjoy a nice cold bottle of your favourite brand of beer. A companion gets up to go and make a phone call and offers to bring back a beer from the only nearby place where beer is sold (either a fancy resort hotel or a small, run-down grocery store, depending on the version you're given). They say that the beer might be expensive and so asks how much you are willing to pay for it . . . What price do you tell them?

In this survey, the median price given by participants who were in the fancy resort version was $2.65 (about €2), but those given the grocery store version were only willing to pay $1.50 (just over €1)! In both versions the consumption act is the same, the beer is the same, and no 'atmosphere' is consumed because the beer is being brought back to the beach.[61] So much for rational decision-making!

Researchers continue to identify other factors that bias our decisions. Recent work has examined the role of emotions in decision-making. One study looked at 'the pain of paying'; and argued that immediate emotions experienced at the point of choice could affect consumer behaviour. These researchers examined the emotion of 'pain of paying' and identified that the 'anticipatory pain of paying drives "tightwads" to spend less than they would ideally spend. "Spendthrifts", by contrast, experience too little pain of paying and typically spend more than they would ideally like to spend.'[62]

Many other factors operate beneath the level of conscious awareness. For example, during the 2010 New York Republican gubernatorial primary, one candidate (Carl Paladino) posted thousands of campaign ads impregnated with the smell of rotting garbage. The tagline was 'Something Stinks in Albany' and the mail shots included photos of scandal-tainted New York Democrats (the message had its intended effect, but the candidate lost for other reasons).

Many researchers believe that the primitive emotion of disgust evolved to protect us from contamination; we learned over the years to avoid putrid meat and other foul substances linked to pathogens. As a result, even the slight odour of something nasty elicits a universal reaction – the wrinkling of the nose, curling of the upper lips, and protrusion of the tongue. Wrinkling the nose has been shown to prevent pathogens from entering through the nasal cavity, and sticking out the tongue aids in the expulsion of tainted food and is a common precursor to vomiting. What does disgust have to with marketing and persuasion? Well, disgust also exerts a powerful effect on our judgements. People who experience this emotion become harsher in their judgements of moral offenses and offenders. In one experiment, people who sat in a foul-smelling room or at a desk cluttered with dirty food containers judged acts like lying on a résumé or keeping a wallet found on the street as more immoral than individuals who were asked to make the same judgements in a clean environment. In another study, survey respondents who were randomly asked to complete the items while they stood in front of a hand sanitizer gave more conservative responses than those who stood in another part of the hallway.[63] Scientists continue to identify other, similar effects of subtle environmental cues that carry over onto our judgements of people and products; for instance, people who hold a cold cup of water before they are asked to make ratings judge other people and objects as 'colder' than do those who were given a hot cup of coffee.

Non-conscious processes in consumer decision-making

Professor Gavan Fitzsimmons (Duke University) argues that researchers are placing increasing emphasis on understanding the processes of which consumers are less consciously aware when they make decisions:

> consumers are influenced by stimuli they don't realize they have been exposed to, processes occur in the consumers' minds they are unaware of, and consumers even engage in behaviour that they are not conscious of (e.g. consider many habitual behaviours). These non-conscious processes are often adaptive and helpful for the consumer, but can also at times be detrimental. One example from our own lab involved subliminally exposing consumers to brand logos – in several studies, either an Apple or an IBM logo. Incidental brand exposures occur every day (recent estimates range between 3,000 and 10,000 times in a single day for the typical American consumer) and thus we were curious if they could influence consumer behaviour in meaningful ways. Apple or IBM logos were flashed on a screen for very brief intervals – from 10 to 50 milliseconds – to mimic this real-world incidental brand exposure. Participants had no conscious experience of seeing a brand, and believed they were only seeing a box on the left or right of the screen. Our results showed that non-conscious exposure to the Apple logo led consumers to be significantly more creative than consumers similarly exposed to an IBM logo. This **incidental brand exposure** activated a goal in consumers that they actively pursued until they could satisfy it. Similar studies have shown dramatic increases in choices of one brand versus another as a result of incidental brand exposure. Some of the most interesting questions deal with exactly how nonconscious processes work, and when they may be adaptive versus harmful. If helpful, how can consumers, firms and public policymakers embrace and encourage them?[64]

How much do we search?

As a general rule, search activity is greater when the purchase is important, when we have more of a need to learn more about the purchase, and/or when the relevant information is easily obtained and utilized.[65] Consumers differ in the amount of search they tend to undertake, regardless of the product category in question. All things being equal, younger, better-educated people who enjoy the shopping/fact-finding process tend to conduct more information search. Women are more inclined to search than men are, as are those who place greater value on style and the image they present.[66] A recent study of information search in high technology markets suggested that use of information channels can be segmented by age and education, with older consumers accessing information channels with less complex information compared with more highly educated consumers who tend to search all information channels. In addition, 'during each segment of the search consumers tend to use multiple sources of information'.[67]

The consumer's prior expertise

Should prior product knowledge make it more or less likely that consumers will engage in search? The answer to this question is not as obvious as it first appears. Product experts and novices use very different procedures during decision-making. Novices who know little about a product should be the most motivated to find out more about it. However, experts are more familiar with the product category, so they should be able to better understand the meaning of any new product information they might acquire.

So, who searches more? The answer is neither: search tends to be greatest among those consumers who are *moderately knowledgeable* about the product. There is an inverted-U relationship between knowledge and external search effort, as shown in Figure 9.6. People with very limited expertise may not feel they are capable of searching extensively. In fact, they may

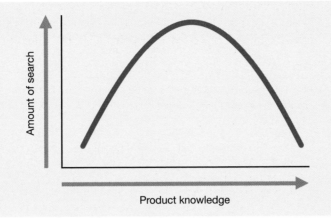

Figure 9.6 The relationship between amount of information search and product knowledge

not even know where to start. Daniel, who did spend a lot of time researching his purchase, is only partly representative of this situation. He used the web to do some research at the beginning, and again after he'd visited a specialist store for advice. At that point, he'd largely made up his mind and so went to the second store to make his final purchase where the prices were very competitive. In other respects Daniel resembled other shoppers with very limited expertise who typically limit their search by looking at only a few brands with which they are already familiar; and focus on only a small number of product features. They usually also tend to limit their visits to stores.[68]

The *type* of search undertaken by people with varying levels of expertise differs as well. Because experts have a better sense of what information is relevant to the decision, they tend to engage in *selective search*, which means their efforts are more focused and efficient. In contrast, novices are more likely to rely on the opinions of others and to rely on 'non-functional' attributes, such as brand name and price, to distinguish among alternatives. They may also process information in a 'top-down' rather than a 'bottom-up' manner, focusing less on details than on the big picture. For instance, they may be more impressed by the sheer amount of technical information presented in an ad than by the actual significance of the claims made.[69]

Consumers who have details about a product before they buy it do *not* expect to be as happy with it as do those who got only ambiguous information. The so-called **blissful ignorance effect** apparently occurs because we want to feel like we've bought the right thing – and if we know precisely how the product performs, it's not as easy to rationalize away any shortcomings. In one experiment, some subjects were told of a manufacturer's claims about a hand lotion and informed that separate research had shown that 50 per cent of people in fact obtained these benefits. Another set of subjects also heard about the manufacturers' claims, but they were told that the results from independent research were not yet available. Those who were provided with less information (the latter group) actually expected the product to perform better. In other words, the less we know about something, the easier it is to persuade ourselves that we like it.[70]

Perceived risk

As a rule, purchase decisions that involve extensive search also entail some kind of **perceived risk**, or the belief that the product has potentially negative consequences from using or not using the product or service. Perceived risk may be present if the product is expensive or is complex and difficult to understand, or if the brand is unfamiliar. Mood effects on consumers' attitudes and perceptions about risk are stronger when brands are unfamiliar.[71] Perceived risk can also be a factor when a product choice is visible to others and we run the risk of embarrassment if we make the wrong choice.[72]

MARKETING PITFALL

In recent years, some researchers have started to focus on the plight of consumers who really have trouble searching – because they have difficulty reading. When we do consumer research, we typically assume that our respondents are fully literate so they are able to find information, identify products, and conduct transactions with few problems. However, it's worth noting that, in fact, more than half of the US population reads at or below the equivalent of sixth-grade school level (i.e. 11 or 12 years of age) – and that roughly half are unable to master specific aspects of shopping. In the UK this would represent national curriculum levels 3 and 4 (entry level 3 of the core curriculum for literacy) and constitutes about 3.5 million people aged between 16 and 65 in the UK.[73] This fact reminds us to think more about the **low-literate consumer** who is at a big disadvantage in the marketplace. Some of these people (whom researchers term *social isolates*) cope with the stigma of illiteracy by avoiding situations where they will have to reveal this problem. They may avoid eating at a restaurant with an unfamiliar menu, for example. Low-literate consumers rely heavily on visual cues, including brand logos and store layouts, to navigate in retail settings, but they often make mistakes when they select similarly packaged products (for example, brand line extensions). They also encounter problems with *innumeracy* (understanding numbers); many low-literate people have difficulty knowing, for example, whether they have enough money to purchase the items in their cart and are vulnerable to being cheated out of the correct amount of change due. Not surprisingly, these challenges create an emotional burden for low-literate consumers, who experience stress, anxiety, fear, shame and other negative emotions before, during, and after they shop.[74] Some groups of European consumers are equally vulnerable in the marketplace (see Table 9.4).[75]

Table 9.4 Low achievers

Benchmark 2010/2020: By 2010 the share of low achievers in reading should decrease by 20 per cent (to 17 per cent). By 2020 the share of low achievers in reading, maths and science should be less than 15 per cent.

Trends: In the EU (comparable data available for 18 countries) performance improved from 21.3 per cent low performers in reading in 2000 to 20.0 per cent (girls: 13.3 per cent, boys: 26.6 per cent) in 2009.

Best EU performers: Finland, Estonia and Netherlands.

	Reading	Reading	Maths	Science
	2000	2009	2009	2009
EU (18/25)	21.3	20.0	22.2	17.7
Belgium	19.0	17.7	19.1	18.0
Bulgaria	40.3	41.0	47.1	38.8
Czech Rep.	17.5	23.1	22.3	17.3
Denmark	17.9	15.2	17.1	16.6
Germany	22.6	18.5	18.6	14.8
Estonia	:	13.3	12.7	8.3
Ireland	11.0	17.2	20.8	15.2
Greece	24.4	21.3	30.3	25.3
Spain	16.3	19.6	23.7	18.2
France	15.2	19.8	22.5	19.3
Italy	18.9	21.0	24.9	20.6
Cyprus	:	:	:	:
Latvia	30.1	17.6	22.6	14.7
Lithuania	:	24.3	26.2	17.0
Luxembourg	(35.1)	26.0	23.9	23.7
Hungary	22.7	17.6	22.3	14.1
Malta	:	:	:	:
Netherlands	(9.5)	14.3	13.4	13.2
Austria	19.3	27.5	23.2	:
Poland	23.2	15.0	20.5	13.1
Portugal	26.3	17.6	23.7	16.5
Romania	41.3	40.4	47.0	41.4
Slovenia	:	21.2	20.3	14.8
Slovakia	:	22.3	21.0	19.3
Finland	7.0	8.1	7.8	6.0
Sweden	12.6	17.4	21.1	19.1
UK	(12.8)	18.4	20.2	15.0
Croatia	:	22.5	33.2	18.5
Iceland	14.5	16.8	17.0	17.9
Turkey	:	24.5	42.1	30.0
Liechtenstein	22.1	15.6	9.5	11.3
Norway	17.5	14.9	18.2	15.8

() = not comparable
Cyprus has not yet participated in the survey, results for Malta not yet available
Reading: EU result for 18 countries with comparable data
Maths and science: EU result for 25 countries with comparable data
(:) not available
Source: OECD (PISA).

Figure 9.7 lists five kinds of risk – including objective (e.g. physical danger) and subjective factors (e.g. social embarrassment) – as well as the products that tend to be affected by each type. As this figure notes, perceived risk is less of a problem for consumers who have greater 'risk capital' because they have less to lose from a poor choice. For example, a highly self-confident person might worry less about the social risk inherent in a product, whereas a more vulnerable, insecure consumer might be reluctant to take a chance with a product or brand that might not be seen as cool and thus not be accepted by peers. Within the EU complaints about the physical risks associated with consumer products are particularly related to the categories of toys, motor vehicles, electrical appliances, lighting equipment, cosmetics, children's equipment, clothing and household appliances (Figures 9.8 and 9.9).[76] A recent study of Italian consumers suggested that issues of food safety was the major determining influence in the motivation of regular consumers of organic foods, whereas occasional organic food consumers were influenced by ethical issues.[77]

	Buyers most sensitive to risk	**Purchases most subject to risk**
Monetary risk	Risk capital consists of money and property. Those with relatively little income and wealth are most vulnerable.	High-price items that require substantial expenditures are most subject to this form of risk.
Functional risk	Risk capital consists of alternate means of performing the function or meeting the need. Practical consumers are most sensitive.	Products or services whose purchase and use requires the buyer's exclusive commitment and precludes redundancy are most sensitive.
Physical risk	Risk capital consists of physical vigour, health and vitality. Those who are elderly, frail, or in ill health are most vulnerable.	Mechanical or electrical goods (such as vehicles or flammables), drugs and medical treatment, and food and beverages are most sensitive.
Social risk	Risk capital consists of self-esteem and self-confidence. Those who are insecure and uncertain are most sensitive.	Socially visible or symbolic goods, such as clothes, jewellery, cars, homes, or sports equipment are most subject to it.
Psycho-logical risk	Risk capital consists of affiliations and status. Those lacking self-respect or attractiveness to peers are most sensitive.	Expensive personal luxuries that may engender guilt; durables; and services whose use demands self-discipline or sacrifice are most sensitive.

Figure 9.7 Five types of perceived risk

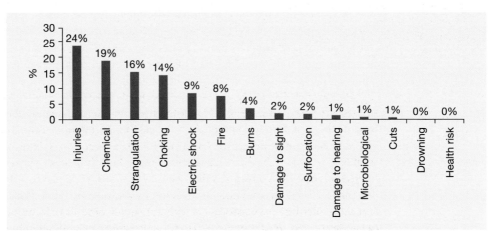

Figure 9.8 Notifications by type of risk of unsafe non-food products to EC Health and Consumer Protectorate (2010)

Source: *Keeping European Consumers Safe*, 2010 Annual Report on the operation of the Rapid Alert System for non-food consumer products, European Communities Health and Consumer Protection Directorate General, Luxembourg, 2011: 24.

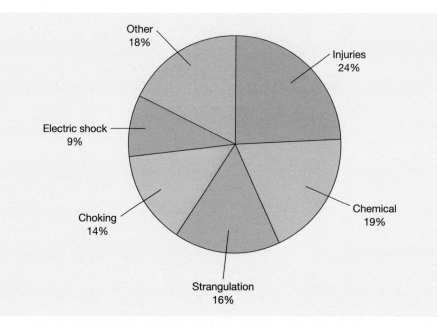

Figure 9.9 Five most frequently notified types of risk of unsafe non-food products to EC Health and Consumer Protectorate (2010)

Source: Keeping European Consumers Safe, 2010 Annual Report on the operation of the Rapid Alert System for non-food consumer products, European Communities Health and Consumer Protection Directorate General, Luxembourg, 2011: 25.

EVALUATION OF ALTERNATIVES

Much of the effort we put into a purchase decision occurs at the stage in which a choice must be made from the available alternatives. This may not be easy; modern consumer society abounds with choices. In some cases, there may be literally hundreds of different brands (as in cigarettes) or different variations of the same brand (as in shades of lipstick), each clamouring for our attention.

Ask a friend to name all the brands of perfume she can think of. The odds are she will reel off three to five names rather quickly, then stop and think awhile before she comes up with a few more. She's probably very familiar with the first set of brands, and in fact she probably wears one or more of these. Her list may also contain one or two brands that she doesn't like; to the contrary, they come to mind because she thinks she doesn't like the way they smell or she might think that they are unsophisticated. Note also that there are many, many more brands on the market that she did not name at all.

If your friend goes to the store to buy perfume, it is likely that she will consider buying some or most of the brands she listed initially. She might also entertain a few more possibilities if these come to her attention while she's at the fragrance counter (for example, if an employee approaches her with a scent sample as she walks down the aisle).

Identifying alternatives

How do we decide which criteria are important, and how do we narrow down product alternatives to an acceptable number and eventually choose one instead of the others? The answer varies depending upon the decision-making process we are using. A consumer engaged in extended problem-solving may carefully evaluate several brands, whereas someone making a habitual decision may not consider any alternatives to their normal brand. Furthermore, some evidence indicates that we do more extended processing in situations that arouse

This BT Cellnet ad appeals to the need for social recognition and approbation from peer groups.

Courtesy of BT Image Library (File supplied by The Advertising Archives).

negative emotions due to conflicts among the available choices. This is most likely to occur when there are difficult trade-offs, for example, when a person must choose between the risks involved in undergoing a heart bypass operation versus the potential improvement in their life if the operation is successful.[78]

We call the alternatives a consumer knows about their **evoked set**; and the ones they actually consider their **consideration set** (because often we do not seriously consider every single brand in a category because of issues such as price, a prior negative experience, and so on).[79] The evoked set comprises those products already in memory (the retrieval set), plus those prominent in the retail environment. For example, recall that Daniel did not know much about the technical aspects of HDTVs, and he had only a few major brands in memory. Of these, two were acceptable possibilities and one was not. The alternatives that the consumer is aware of but would not consider buying are their *inept set*, while those not under consideration at all comprise the *inert set*. You can easily guess in which set a marketer wants its brand to appear! These categories are depicted in Figure 9.10.

Consumers often include a surprisingly small number of alternatives in their evoked set. One study combined results from several large-scale investigations of consumers' evoked sets. It found that people overall include a small number of products in these sets, although this amount varies by product category and across countries.[80]

For obvious reasons, a marketer who finds that their brand is not in their target market's evoked set has cause to worry. You don't often get a second chance to make a good first impression. A consumer is not likely to place a product in his evoked set after they have already considered it and rejected it. Indeed, we are more likely to add a new brand to the evoked set than one that we had previously considered but passed over, even after a marketer has provided additional positive information about the brand.[81] For marketers, consumers'

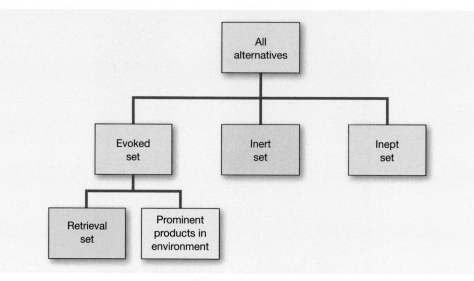

Figure 9.10 Identifying alternatives: getting in the game

unwillingness to give a rejected product a second chance underlines the importance of ensuring that it performs well from the time it is introduced.

Product categorization

Remember that when consumers process product information, they do not do so in a vacuum. Instead, they evaluate a product stimulus in terms of what they already know about a product or other similar ones. A person evaluating a particular digital camera will most likely compare it with other digital cameras rather than to a 35mm camera, and would be unlikely to compare it with a DVD player or iPod. Since the category in which a product is placed determines the other products it will be compared with, *categorization* is a crucial determinant of how a product is evaluated. These classifications derive from different product attributes, including appearance (e.g. we assume that chocolates in silver or gold wrappings are more upscale), price (we view items with price endings in .99 as cheaper than those that end in .00), or previously learned connections (if it has the name Porsche on it, it must be expensive).[82]

The products in a consumer's evoked set are likely to share some similar features. This process can either help or hurt a product, depending on what people compare it with. For example, in one survey about 25 per cent of consumers said they would be less likely to buy a product made of hemp if they know it is derived from the same plant from which marijuana comes (but without the latter's effects). When faced with a new product, consumers refer to their already existing knowledge in familiar product categories to form new knowledge.[83] We tend to place the new product into an existing category rather than create a new category.[84] Of course, that's one of the big hurdles a new form of technology has to clear: before people will buy a smartphone, tablet, MP3 player, or GPS, they need to make sense out of the category to which it belongs.

It is important to understand how consumers cognitively represent this information in a **knowledge structure**, a set of beliefs and the way we organize these beliefs in our minds.[85] We discussed these knowledge structures in Chapter 7.[86] Their makeup matters to marketers because they want to ensure that customers correctly group their products.

Levels of categorization

Not only do people group things into categories, but these groupings occur at different levels of specificity. Typically, we represent a product in a cognitive structure at one of three levels. To understand this idea, consider how someone might respond to these questions about an

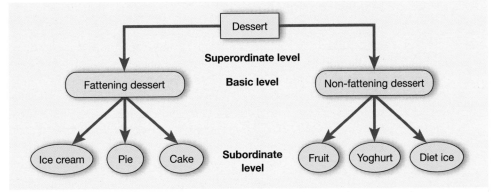

Figure 9.11 Levels of abstraction in categories of dessert

ice-cream: what other products share similar characteristics, and which would be considered as alternatives to eating an ice-cream?

These questions may be more complex than they first appear. At one level, an ice-cream is similar to an apple, because both could be eaten as a dessert. At another level, an ice-cream is similar to a slice of pie, because both are eaten for dessert and both are fattening. At still another level, an ice-cream is similar to an ice-cream sundae – both are eaten for dessert, are made of ice cream and are fattening.

It is easy to see that the items a person associates with, say, the category 'fattening dessert' influence the choices they will make for what to eat after dinner. The middle level, known as the *basic level category*, is typically the most useful in classifying products, because at this level the items we group together tend to have a lot in common with each other, but still permit us to consider a broad enough range of alternatives. The broader *superordinate category* is more abstract, whereas the more specific *subordinate category* often includes individual brands.[87] These three levels are depicted in Figure 9.11.

Of course, not all items fit equally well into a category. Apple pie is a better example of the subordinate category 'pie' than is rhubarb pie, even though both are types of pie. Apple pie is thus more *prototypical*, and would tend to be considered first, especially by category novices. In contrast, pie experts will tend to have knowledge about both typical and atypical category examples.[88]

Strategic implications of product categorization

The way we categorize products has many strategic implications. This process affects which products consumers will compare with our product and also the criteria they will use to decide if they like us or our competitors.

Product positioning

The success of a *positioning strategy* often hinges on the marketer's ability to convince the consumer that their product should be considered within a given category. For example, the orange juice industry tried to reposition orange juice as a drink that could be enjoyed all day long ('It's not just for breakfast anymore'). On the other hand, soft drinks companies are now attempting the opposite by portraying carbonated drinks as suitable for breakfast consumption. They are trying to make their way into consumers' 'breakfast drink' category, along with orange juice, grapefruit juice and coffee. Of course, this strategy can backfire, as PepsiCo discovered when it introduced Pepsi A.M. and positioned it as a coffee substitute. The company did such a good job of categorizing the drink as a morning beverage that customers wouldn't drink it at any other time, and the product failed.[89]

Identifying competitors

At the abstract, superordinate level, many different product forms compete for membership. The category 'entertainment' might comprise both bowling and the ballet, but not many people would consider the substitution of one of these activities for the other. Products and services that on the surface are quite different, however, actually compete with each other at a broad level for consumers' discretionary cash. While bowling or ballet may not be a likely trade-off for many people, it is feasible, for example, that a symphony orchestra might try to lure away season ticket-holders to the ballet by positioning itself as an equivalent member of the category 'cultural event'.[90]

We are often faced with choices between non-comparable categories, where we cannot directly relate the attributes of one category to those in another category (the old problem of comparing apples and oranges). When we can create an overlapping category that encompasses both items (for instance, entertainment, value, usefulness) and then rate each alternative in terms of that superordinate category comparison, the process is easier.[91]

Exemplar products

As we saw with the case of apple pie versus rhubarb, if a product is a really good example of a category, it is more familiar to consumers and they more easily recognize and recall it.[92] The characteristics of **category exemplars** tend to exert disproportionate influence on how people think of the category in general.[93] In a sense, brands that are strongly associated with a category 'call the shots' by defining the evaluative criteria that should be used to evaluate all category members.

Being a bit less than prototypical is not necessarily a bad thing, however. Products that are moderately unusual within their product category may stimulate more information processing and positive evaluations, because they are neither so familiar that we will take them for granted nor so different that we will not consider them at all.[94] A brand that is strongly discrepant may occupy a unique niche position, whereas those that are moderately discrepant remain in a distinct position within the general category.[95]

Locating products

Product categorization also can affect consumers' expectations regarding the places where they can locate a desired product. If products do not clearly fit into categories (is a carpet furniture?), this may diminish our ability to find them or work out what they are meant to do, once we have found them. For instance, a frozen dog food that had to be thawed and cooked failed in the market, partly because people could not adapt to the idea of buying dog food in the 'frozen foods for people' section of their supermarkets.

PRODUCT CHOICE: SELECTING AMONG ALTERNATIVES

Once we assemble and evaluate the relevant options in a category, we have to choose one.[96] Recall that the decision rules guiding choice can range from very simple and quick strategies to complicated processes requiring much attention and cognitive processing.[97] The choice can be influenced by integrating information from sources such as prior experience with the product or a similar one, information present at the time of purchase, and beliefs about the brands that have been created by advertising.[98]

Our job isn't getting any easier as we often find that there are more and more features to evaluate. We deal with 50-button remote controls, digital cameras with hundreds of mysterious features and book-length manuals, and cars with dashboard systems worthy of the space shuttle. Experts call this spiral of complexity **feature creep**, also known as **feature fatigue** or **feature bloat**.[99] As evidence that the proliferation of gizmos is counter-productive, Philips

Electronics found that at least half of returned products have nothing wrong with them – consumers simply couldn't figure out how to use them! What's worse, on average the person spent only 20 minutes trying to figure out how to use the product before giving up.

Why don't companies avoid this problem? One reason is that when we look at a new product in a store we tend to think that the more features there are, the better. It is only once we get the product home and try to use it that we realize the virtues of simplicity. We tend to rely on indirect experience when choosing products, so that before using a product our preference tends to be for many features and capabilities. It is only after we have had direct experience of a product that we tend to prefer simpler products that we find easier to use.[100] In one study,[101] consumers chose among three models of a digital device that varied in terms of how complex each was. More than 60 per cent chose the one with the most features. Then, the participants got the chance to choose from up to 25 features to customize their product – the average person chose 20 of these add-ons. But when they actually used the devices, it turns out that the large number of options only frustrated them – they ended up being much happier with the simpler product. As the saying goes, 'Be careful what you wish for . . .'[102]

Evaluative criteria

When Daniel was looking at different HDTVs, he focused on one or two product features and completely ignored several others. He narrowed down his choices by only considering two specific brand names, and from the Prime Wave and Precision models, he chose one that featured stereo capability. A survey carried out by different European manufacturers showed that they had identified a range of criteria used by consumers in Germany, Netherlands and Czech Republic when choosing televisions. Purchase price, design and technology emerged as key considerations for consumer decision-making in this product category (Figure 9.12).[103]

Evaluative criteria are the dimensions we use to judge the merits of competing options. In comparing alternative products, Daniel could have chosen from among any number of criteria, ranging from very functional attributes ('does this TV have a remote control?') to experiential ones ('does this TV's sound reproduction make me imagine I'm in a concert hall?').

Another important point is that criteria on which products *differ* from one another carry more weight in the decision process than do those where the alternatives are *similar*. If all

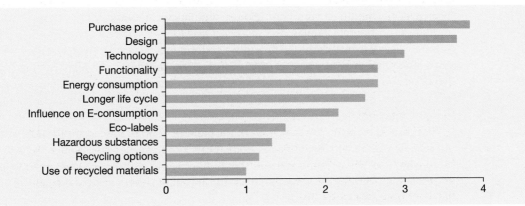

Figure 9.12 Importance of aspects in the buying decision for TVs (weighting by seven TV producers)

Data source: Manufacturers' questionnaires from Germany, Netherlands and Czech Republic.

Source: Lutz Stobbe, EuP Preparatory Studies 'Televisions' (Lot 5) Final Report on Task 3 'Consumer Behaviour and Local Infrastructure' (TREN/ D1/40 lot 5-2005), compiled by Deutsche Umwelthilfe and Fraunhofer IZM, contractor: Fraunhofer Institute for Reliability and Microintegration, IZM, Berlin, 2 August 2007: 5.

brands being considered rate equally well on one attribute (e.g. if all TVs come with remote control), consumers will have to find other reasons to choose one over another. **Determinant attributes** are the features we actually use to differentiate among our choices.

Reflecting consumers' renewed interest in ethical and sustainable marketing (see Chapter 6) it makes sense that a company's reputation for social responsibility is emerging as one of the most important determinant attributes when people choose among brands. Each year Harris Interactive and *The Wall Street Journal* conduct a survey and rank corporate reputations on 20 attributes in six categories: financial performance, social responsibility, workplace environment, quality of products and services, vision and leadership and emotional appeal.[104] Although Microsoft has its share of critics, in 2007 it achieved the number one ranking – helped to a large extent by founder Bill Gates' philanthropy. The company beat Johnson & Johnson into number two place, although their emotionally appealing baby products business had kept Johnson & Johnson in first place for seven consecutive years. However, the corporate world's overall reputation remains dismal as new scandals continue to emerge, e.g. Parmalat, Madoff and Satyam.[105] About 69 per cent of respondents graded corporate America's reputation as either 'not good' or 'terrible'.

Marketers can play a role in educating consumers about which criteria should be used as determinant attributes. For example, research indicated that many consumers view the use of natural ingredients as a determinant attribute. The result was promotion of toothpaste made from baking soda, which the company, Church & Dwight, already manufactured for its Arm & Hammer brand.[106] The decision about which attributes to use is the result of *procedural learning*, in which a person undergoes a series of cognitive steps before making a choice. These steps include identifying important attributes, remembering whether competing brands differ on those attributes, and so on. In order for a marketer to recommend a new decision criterion effectively, their communication should convey three pieces of information:[107]

1 It should point out that there are significant differences among brands on the attribute.

2 It should supply the consumer with a decision-making rule, such as *if* (deciding among competing brands), *then* . . . (use the attribute as a criterion).

3 It should convey a rule that can be easily integrated with how the person has made this decision in the past. Otherwise, the recommendation is likely to be ignored because it requires too much mental work.

Neuromarketing: how your brain reacts to alternatives

Is there a 'buy button' in your brain? Some corporations are teaming up with neuroscientists to find out.[108] **Neuromarketing** uses *functional magnetic resonance imaging* (or *MRI*), a brain-scanning device that tracks blood flow as we perform mental tasks. In recent years, researchers have discovered that regions in the brain, such as the amygdala, the hippocampus, and the hypothalamus, are dynamic switchboards that blend memory, emotions and biochemical triggers. These interconnected neurons shape the ways that fear, panic, exhilaration and social pressure influence our choices.

Scientists know that specific regions of the brain light up in these scans to show increased blood flow when a person recognizes a face, hears a song, makes a decision, or senses deception. Now they are trying to harness this technology to measure consumers' reactions to movie trailers, choices about automobiles, the appeal of a pretty face, and loyalty to specific brands. British researchers recorded brain activity as shoppers toured a virtual store. They claim to have identified the neural region that becomes active when a shopper decides which product to pluck from a supermarket shelf. DaimlerChrysler took brain scans of men as they looked at photos of cars and confirmed that sports cars activated their reward centres. The company's scientists found that the most popular vehicles – the Porsche- and Ferrari-style sports cars – triggered activity in a section of the brain they call the *fusiform face area*, which governs facial recognition. A psychiatrist who ran the study commented, 'They were reminded of faces when they looked at the cars. The lights of the cars look a little like eyes.'

One study of brain scans reported that pictures of celebrities triggered many of the same brain circuits as images of shoes, cars, chairs, wristwatches, sunglasses, handbags and water bottles. All of these objects set off a rush of activity in a part of the cortex that neuroscientists know links to a sense of identity and social image. The scientists also identified types of consumers based on their responses. At one extreme were people whose brains responded intensely to 'cool' products and celebrities with bursts of activity but who didn't respond at all to 'uncool' images. They dubbed these participants 'cool fools', likely to be impulsive or compulsive shoppers. At the other extreme were people whose brains reacted only to the unstylish items, a pattern that fits well with people who tend to be anxious, apprehensive or neurotic. Many researchers remain sceptical about how helpful this technology will be for consumer research. If indeed researchers can reliably track consumers' brand preferences by seeing how their brains react, there may be many interesting potential opportunities for new research techniques that rely on what we (or at least our brains) do rather than what we say.

MARKETING OPPORTUNITY

Neuro-marketing and neuroscience

'The world's biggest companies have got a new way of convincing you to buy their products – by getting inside your head. Brands, including Google, Facebook and ITV, are turning to mind-reading technology to help them develop products and create adverts that people like . . . Faced with the prospect of consumers hiding their emotions . . . a new breed of "neuromarketer" has emerged, armed with medical technology to probe consumers' brains for genuine responses.

"We put a cap on your head that measures your brain impulses," said A.K. Pradeep, a pioneer of neuromarketing science and chief executive of NeuroFocus, one of the biggest players in a booming industry. "We measure all parts of your brain continuously. Second by second, we measure how much attention you're paying. We get [to learn] what emotions you're experiencing and what memories you're memorising."

Pradeep says watching people's brains via caps covered in electrodes or magnetic scanners that are normally used by hospitals to detect cancer is better than direct questioning because, "when you ask people to tell you how they feel, the very act of thinking about a feeling changes the feeling" . . . A spokesman for NeuroFocus, which was bought last year by the $5bn global measurement and analytics firm Nielsen, said the company has worked with Google, Microsoft, Intel, Facebook, PayPal, Hewlett-Packard and Citigroup, but refused to provide details of adverts or products involved. "It's not just one company and one advertiser; it is all sorts of companies and brands around the world," Pradeep said. Gemma Calvert, a former Oxford University neurologist who founded rival company Neurosense, said neuromarketing

The Mynd wireless EEG headset developed by NeuroFocus to read the brain's emotional responses to products.

Photograph: NeuroFocus.

. . . is now so advanced that she is "able to predict how customers will behave" . . . "Neuroscience has completely changed our understanding of the brain. This information is not a flash-in-the-pan," Calvert said. "We are trying to find out what aspects of the images [in adverts] are having effect on the reward system – and making them [the brand] more likeable." Her company's website lists clients including McDonald's, Unilever, Procter & Gamble and GlaxoSmithKline . . . She said the research has led to brands changing their logos, packaging and even theme tunes: "We are changing the way brands understand themselves so they can better understand their audiences." The techniques are also used in the development of new products: "There are lots of products that have been developed with knowledge about the brain and psychology that's been derived from this stuff," she said.'[109]

Cybermediaries

As anyone who's ever typed a phrase such as 'home theatres' into Google or another search engine, the web delivers enormous amounts of product and retailer information in seconds. In fact (recall our earlier discussion of the problem of *hyperchoice*), the biggest problem web surfers face these days is to narrow down their choices, not to increase them. In cyberspace, simplification is key.

With the tremendous number of websites available and the huge number of people surfing the web each day, how can people organize information and decide where to click? A **cybermediary** often is the answer. This is an intermediary that helps to filter and organize online market information so that customers can identify and evaluate alternatives more efficiently.[110] Many consumers regularly link to comparison-shopping sites, such as **Bizrate.co.uk** or **Pricegrabber.co.uk**, for example, that list many online retailers that sell a given item along with the price each charges.[111]

Cybermediaries take different forms:[112]

- *Directories* and *portals*, such as Yahoo! are general services that tie together a large variety of different sites.

- *Forums*, *fan clubs*, and *user groups* offer product-related discussions to help customers sift through options (more on these in Chapter 10). It's clear that customer product reviews are a key driver of satisfaction and loyalty. In one large survey, about half of the respondents who bought an item from a major website remembered seeing customer product reviews. This group's satisfaction with the online shopping experience was 5 per cent higher than for shoppers who didn't recall customer reviews.[113] Another advantage is that consumers get to experience a much wider array of options – and at the same time products such as movies, books and CDs that aren't 'blockbusters' are more likely to sell. At Netflix, the online DVD rental company, for example, fellow subscribers recommend about two-thirds of the films that people order. In fact, between 70 and 80 per cent of Netflix rentals come from the company's back catalogue of 38,000 films rather than recent releases.[114]

This aspect of online customer review is one important factor that's fueling a new way of thinking, which one writer calls the **long tail**.[115] The basic idea is that we no longer need to rely solely on big hits (such as blockbuster movies or best-selling books) to find profits. Companies can also make money if they sell small amounts of items that only a few people want – *if* they sell enough different items. For example, **Amazon.com** maintains an inventory of 3.7 million books, compared to the 100,000 or so you'll find in a large high street book retail outlet. Most of these will sell only a few thousand copies (if that), but the 3.6 million books that are not carried by the mainstream book retailers make up a quarter of Amazon's revenues. Other examples of the long tail include successful microbreweries and TV networks that make money on reruns of old shows on channels such as BBC Gold in the UK.

Intelligent agents are sophisticated software programs that use *collaborative filtering* technologies to learn from past user behaviour in order to recommend new purchases.[116] When you let **Amazon.com** suggest a new book, the site uses an intelligent agent to propose novels based on what you and others like you have bought in the past. Collaborative filtering is still in its infancy. In the next few years, expect to see many new web-based methods to simplify the consumer decision-making process.

Researchers work hard to understand how consumers find information online, and in particular how they react to and integrate recommendations received from different kinds of online agents into their own product choices. An **electronic recommendation agent** is a software tool that tries to understand a human decision maker's multiattribute preferences for a product category as it asks the user to communicate his preferences. Based on that data, the software then recommends a list of alternatives sorted by the degree to which they fit these criteria. These agents do appear to influence consumers' decision making, though some evidence indicates that they're more effective when they recommend a product based on utilitarian attributes (functionality such as nutritional value) rather than hedonic attributes (such as design or taste).[117]

Although engineers continually improve the ability of electronic recommendation agents to suggest new things we might like, we still rely on other people to guide our search. About 80 per cent of online shoppers rely on customer reviews before they buy. We call the people who supply these reviews **brand advocates**. Yahoo! estimates that 40 per cent of people who spend time online are advocates and that they influence purchases two to one over nonadvocates. Marketers who adjust their strategies to acknowledge this impact find it's worth their while.[118]

The huge growth in demand for user reviews in turn fuels new opinion-based sites, such as TripAdvisor for travel, and Urbanspoon for restaurants. People who take the time to post to these sites don't do it for money, but they do generate an income in the form of props for good recommendations. Analysts refer to this reward system as the **reputation economy**: many thousands of consumers devote significant time to editing Wikipedia entries, serving as brand advocates, or uploading clips to YouTube simply because they enjoy the process and want to boost their reputation as knowledgeable advisors.[119]

Heuristics: mental short cuts

Do we actually perform complex mental calculations every time we make a purchase decision? Of course not! When we are not relying on a website to steer us to the right place, we often use other decision rules to simplify our choices. For example, Daniel relied on certain assumptions as substitutes for a prolonged information search. In particular, he assumed the selection at the out-of-town big shed retailer would be more than sufficient, so he did not bother to investigate any of its competitors. This assumption served as a short cut to more extended information processing.[120] Daniel could have chosen a heuristic approach based either on compromise or anchoring. A compromise strategy might have involved following one of the options used by his friends in choosing a new HDTV, e.g. Hannah might have done an exhaustive web-based search; Lily might have visited every high street and out-of-town stockist; and Christopher might have read all the independent consumer reports. Daniel's compromise would have been to have done some web-searching, visited one high street retailer, and then made a purchase after visiting just one large out-of-town stockist.[121] Alternatively, Daniel could have pursued anchoring (Tversky and Kahneman, 1974),[122] i.e. 'the tendency to rely heavily, or anchor, on one piece of information in order to arrive at a decision'.[123]

Ask Jeeves, one of the popular search engines/shopping 'bots' available on the web to simplify the consumer decision-making process via online searches.

Especially when limited problem-solving occurs prior to making a choice, we often fall back on **heuristics**, or mental rules-of-thumb that lead to a speedy decision. These rules range from the very general ('Higher-priced products are higher-quality products' or 'Buy the same brand I bought last time') to the very specific ('Buy Silver Spoon, the brand of sugar my mother always bought').[124] Recent research has 'demonstrated that decision making is more heuristic in situations that involve spending time rather than money'.[125]

Sometimes these short cuts may not be in our best interests. A consumer who personally knows one or two people who have had problems with a particular make of car, for example, might assume they would have similar trouble with it rather than taking the time to find out that it has an excellent repair record.[126] The influence of such assumptions may be enhanced if the product has an unusual name, which makes it *and* the experiences with it more distinctive.[127]

Relying on a product signal

One short cut we often use is to infer hidden dimensions of products from attributes we can observe. In these cases the visible element acts as a **product signal** that communicates some underlying quality. This explains why someone trying to sell a used car takes great pains to be

i want everything at my party to be yellow. i want yellow balloons, yellow cups, and yellow icing on my cake because yellow is the prettiest color ever. except for pink. i want everything at my party to be pink.

www.iparty.com > birthdays > basics > **pink** > cups/plates/napkins/favors > order

i want. i click. iparty.com

aol keyword: iparty

Consumers often simplify choices by using heuristics such as automatically choosing a favourite colour or brand.
iParty Corp.

sure the car's exterior is clean and shiny. Potential buyers often judge the vehicle's mechanical condition by its appearance, even though this means they may drive away in a shiny, clean death trap.[128]

When we only have incomplete product information, we often base our judgements on our beliefs about *co-variation*; the associations we have among events that may or may not actually influence one another.[129] For example, a consumer may judge product quality by the length of time a manufacturer has been in business. Other signals or attributes consumers tend to believe co-exist with good or bad products include well-known brand names, country of origin, price and the retail outlets that carry the product. The perceptions of UK consumers of Italian luxury design, fashion, food and beverage products, for instance, were found to be influenced by a combination of the Italianate elements of the brands (i.e. country of origin effect) as well as brand trust and brand experience.[130]

Market beliefs: is it better if I have to pay more for it?

We are constantly forming assumptions about companies, products and stores. These market beliefs then become the short cuts that guide our decisions – regardless of whether or not these beliefs are accurate.[131] Recall, for instance, that Daniel chose to shop at a large 'electronics supermarket' because he *assumed* the prices would be more competitive there than at a specialized shop. A large number of **market beliefs** have been identified. Some of these are listed in Table 9.5. How many do you share?

Do higher prices mean higher quality? The assumption of a *price–quality relationship* is one of the most pervasive market beliefs.[132] Novice consumers may in fact consider price as the *only* relevant product attribute. Experts also consider this information, although they tend to use price for its informational value, especially for products (e.g. virgin wool) they know vary widely in quality. When this quality level is more standard or strictly regulated (e.g. Harris Tweed sports jackets), experts do not weigh price in their decisions. For the most part, this belief is justified; you do tend to get what you pay for. However, let the buyer beware: the price–quality relationship is not always justified.[133]

Country of origin as a product signal

Modern consumers choose among products made in many countries. European consumers may buy Portuguese, Italian or Brazilian shoes, Japanese cars, clothing imported from Taiwan or microwave ovens built in South Korea. A product's 'address' matters. Consumers' reactions to these imports are mixed. In some cases, people have come to assume that a product made overseas is of better quality (cameras, cars), whereas in other cases the knowledge that a product has been imported tends to lower perceptions of product quality (apparel).[134] In general, people tend to rate their own country's products more favourably than do foreigners, and products from industrialized countries are rated better than are those from developing countries. **Ethnocentrism** is the tendency to prefer products or people of one's own culture to those of other countries. Ethnocentric consumers are likely to feel it is wrong to buy products made elsewhere, particularly because this may have a negative effect on the domestic economy. Marketing campaigns that stress the desirability of buying locally appeal to ethnocentric consumers. The Consumer Ethnocentric Scale (CETSCALE) for measuring this trait was originally developed in the US[135] and its applicability in other cultural contexts such as Spain has been examined.[136]

As briefly discussed in Chapter 8 when we were talking about persuasive communication, a product's **country of origin** in some cases is an important piece of information in the decision-making process.[137] A product's origin, then, is often used as a signal of quality. Certain items are strongly associated with specific countries, and products from those countries often attempt to benefit from these linkages. Sometimes, however, the country of origin can act as a negative signal. Recent reports of poor experiences with goods has undermined some national manufacturing reputations. In an EC report China (including Hong Kong) accounted

Table 9.5 Common market beliefs

Brand	All brands are basically the same.
	Generic products are just name brands sold under a different label at a lower price.
	The best brands are the ones that are purchased the most.
	When in doubt, a national brand is always a safe bet.
Store	Specialized shops are good places to familiarize yourself with the best brands; but once you know what you want, it's cheaper to buy it at a discount outlet.
	A store's character is reflected in its window displays.
	Salespeople in specialized shops are more knowledgeable than other sales personnel.
	Larger stores offer better prices than small stores.
	Locally-owned stores give the best service.
	A store that offers a good value on one of its products probably offers good value on all of its items.
	Credit and return policies are most lenient at large department stores.
	Stores that have just opened usually charge attractive prices.
Prices/discounts/sales	Sales are typically run to get rid of slow-moving merchandise.
	Stores that are constantly having sales don't really save you money.
	Within a given store, higher prices generally indicate higher quality.
Advertising and sales promotion	'Hard-sell' advertising is associated with low-quality products.
	Items tied to 'giveaways' are not good value (even with the freebie).
	Coupons represent real savings for customers because they are not offered by the store.
	When you buy heavily advertised products, you are paying for the label, not for higher quality.
Product/packaging	Largest-sized containers are almost always cheaper per unit than smaller sizes.
	New products are more expensive when they're first introduced; prices tend to settle down as time goes by.
	When you are not sure what you need in a product, it's a good idea to invest in the extra features, because you'll probably wish you had them later.
	In general, synthetic goods are lower in quality than goods made of natural materials.
	It's advisable to stay away from products when they are new to the market; it usually takes the manufacturer a little time to sort out the bugs.

Source: Adapted from Calvin P. Duncan, 'Consumer Market Beliefs: A Review of the Literature and an Agenda for Future Research', in Marvin E. Goldberg, Gerald Gorn and Richard W. Pollay (eds), *Advances in Consumer Research* 17 (Provo, UT: Association for Consumer Research, 1990): 729–35.

for over half of the notifications in 2010 (58 per cent compared with 60 per cent in 2009) of substandard non-food products (Figure 9.13).[138]

Countries, in their turn, can be very protective of product names which potentially provide them with an important competitive advantage in winning customers. The EU has been trying to achieve a global trade agreement to protect some of its product names such as champagne and wines like Beaujolais, chianti and Madeira; cheeses such as Roquefort, Feta and Gorgonzola; as well as meat products like Parma ham and Mortadella sausages. This has been opposed in some non-EU countries where these names are seen as generic.[139] Country of origin can function as a **stereotype** – a knowledge structure based on inferences across products. These stereotypes may be biased or inaccurate, but they do play a constructive role in simplifying complex choice situations.[140] A recent study of UK consumers' brand perceptions of Italian goods across a range of categories (e.g. luxury design, fashion, food and beverages) showed that 'brand image, brand trust and brand experience . . . [were all] highly important in influencing the relationship between consumers and Italian luxury brands'.[141]

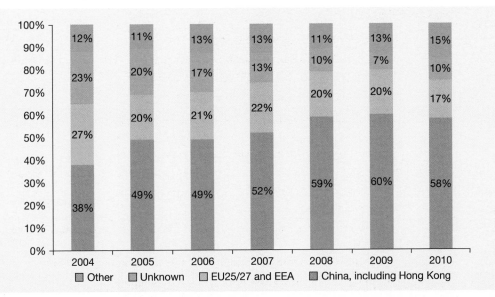

Figure 9.13 Notifications by country of origin of unsafe non-food products to EC Health and Consumer Protectorate (comparison 2004–2010)

Source: Keeping European Consumers Safe, 2010 Annual Report on the operation of the Rapid Alert System for non-food consumer products, European Communities Health and Consumer Protection Directorate General, Luxembourg, 2011: 23.

Recent evidence indicates that learning of a product's country of origin is not necessarily good or bad. Instead, it has the effect of stimulating the consumer's interest in the product to a greater degree. The purchaser thinks more extensively about the product and evaluates it more carefully.[142] The origin of the product can thus act as a product attribute that combines with other attributes to influence evaluations.[143] In addition, the consumer's own expertise with the product category moderates the effects of this attribute. When other information is

cafédirect, a pioneer company in ethical business, is associated with three major coffee-producing countries: Peru, Costa Rica and Mexico.

The Advertising Archives.

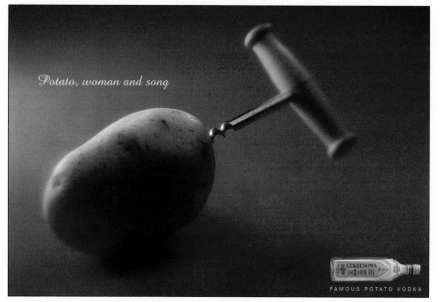

Potato, woman and song

LUKSUSOWA

FAMOUS POTATO VODKA

Some countries are strongly associated with certain types of alcoholic products. This Polish ad plays on these stereotypes.

Grey Worldwide Warszawa. Photo: Jacek Wolowski.

available, experts tend to ignore country-of-origin information, whereas novices continue to rely on it. However, when other information is unavailable or ambiguous, both experts and novices will rely on this attribute to make a decision.[144]

Do we choose familiar brand names because of loyalty or habit?

Branding is a marketing strategy that often functions as a heuristic. When you fall in love with a brand, it may be your favourite for a lifetime. People form preferences for a favourite brand, and then they literally may never change their minds in the course of a lifetime. In a study of the market leaders in 30 product categories by the Boston Consulting Group, it was found that 27 of the brands that were number one in 1930 in the US remain at the top today. These include such perennial American favourites as Ivory Soap, Campbell's Soup and Gold Medal Flour.[145] As this study demonstrates, some brands in a sense are well known because they are well known; we assume that if so many people choose a product, it must be good. Clearly, choosing a well-known brand name is a powerful heuristic. A recent study has applied cultural theory to understanding how brands become icons over time.[146]

Indeed, our tendency to prefer a number-one brand to the competition is so strong that it seems to mimic a pattern scientists find in other domains ranging from earthquakes to linguistics. **Zipf's Law** describes this pattern. In the 1930s, a linguist named George Kingsley Zipf found that *the* – the most-used English word – occurs about twice as often as *of* (second place), about three times as often as *and* (third), and so on. Since then, scientists have found similar relationships between the size and frequency of earthquakes and a variety of other natural and artificial phenomena.

A marketing researcher decided to apply Zipf's Law to consumer behaviour. His firm asked Australian consumers to identify the brands of toilet paper and instant coffee they use and to rank them in order of preference. As the model predicted, people spend roughly twice as much of their toilet paper budget on the top choice than on the second-ranked brand, about twice as much on the number-two brand as on the third-ranked brand, and about twice as much on the number-three brand as on the number-four brand. One ramification is that a brand that moves from number two to number one in a category will see a much greater jump in sales than will, say, a brand that moves from number four to number three. Brands that dominate their markets are as much as 50 per cent more profitable than their nearest competitors (see Table 9.6 for Brandz listing of top brands for 2011).[147]

Table 9.6 The Brandz top 100 most powerful brands in 2011 compiled by Millward Brown

No.	Brand	Brand value 2011 ($M)	% Brand value change 2011 vs 2010	No.	Brand	Brand value 2011 ($M)	% Brand value change 2011 vs 2010	No.	Brand	Brand value 2011 ($M)	% Brand value change 2011 vs 2010	No.	Brand	Brand value 2011 ($M)	% Brand value change 2011 vs 2010
1	Apple	153,285	84%	26	Louis Vuitton	24,312	23%	50	Mercedes	15,344	12%	76	Telcel	11,558	7%
2	Google	111,498	−2%	27	Toyota	24,198	11%	51	Shell	15,168	0%	77	Santander	11,363	−37%
3	IBM	100,849	17%	28	HSBC	22,587	−4%	52	Tencent	15,131	N/A	78	PetroChina	11,291	−19%
4	Macdonalds	81,016	23%	29	Baidu	22,555	141%	53	ICICI Bank	14,900	3%	79	Nintendo(⁵)	11,147	−37%
5	Microsoft	78,243	2%	30	BMW	22,425	3%	54	SUBWAY	14,306	19%	80	MTC	10,883	12%
6	Coca-Cola(¹)	73,752	8%	31	Tesco	21,834	−15%	55	Colgate	14,258	0%	81	Nokia	10,735	−28%
7	at&t	69,916	N/A	32	Gillette	19,782	−4%	56	Honda	14,182	−1%	82	eBay	10,731	15%
8	Marlboro	67,522	18%	33	China Life Insurance	19,542	N/A	57	Nike	13,917	10%	83	Ping An	10,540	N/A
9	China Mobile	57,326	9%	34	Pampers	19,350	11%	58	Intel	13,904	−2%	84	US Bank	10,525	26%
10	GE	50,318	12%	35	Facebook	19,102	246%	59	Carrefour	13,754	−8%	85	Sony(⁶)	10,443	19%
11	ICBC	44,440	1%	36	Orange	17,597	N/A	60	Mastercard	13,543	16%	86	Zara	10,335	15%
12	Vodafone	43,647	−2%	37	Bank of China	17,530	−20%	61	Petrobras	13,421	39%	87	Scotiabank	10,076	N/A
13	Verizon	42,828	N/A	38	Disney	17,290	15%	62	H&M	13,006	7%	88	Nissan	10,072	17%
14	Amazon	37,628	37%	39	RBC	17,182	3%	63	Pepsi(⁴)	12,931	1%	89	Home Depot	9,877	10%
15	Walmart	37,277	−5%	40	American Express	17,115	23%	64	BP	12,542	−27%	90	Itaú	9,600	29%
16	Wells Fargo	36,876	97%	41	Exxon Mobil	16,973	10%	65	Target	12,471	3%	91	China Telecom	9,587	N/A
17	UPS	35,737	35%	42	TD	16,931	19%	66	Porsche	12,413	3%	92	Bank of America	9,358	−43%
18	Hewlett-Packard	35,404	−11%	43	Agricultural Bank of China	16,909	N/A	67	Samsung	12,160	7%	93	RedBull(⁷)	9,263	4%
19	T Mobile(²)	29,774	N/A	44	Cisco	16,314	−2%	68	Chase	12,083	−3%	94	ALDI	9,251	6%
20	Visa	28,553	15%	45	Budweiser(³)	15,952	0%	69	Standard Chartered Bank	12,033	45%	95	TIM	8,838	21%
21	Movistar	27,249	N/A	46	L'Oréal	15,719	11%	70	Siemens	11,998	29%	96	Barclays	8,760	4%
22	Oracle	26,948	9%	47	Citigroup	15,674	17%	71	Hermès	11,917	41%	97	China Merchants Bank	8,668	5%
23	SAP	26,078	7%	48	Docomo	15,449	19%	72	Starbucks	11,901	40%				
24	China Construction Bank	25,524	22%	49	Accenture	15,427	5%	73	FedEx	11,759	25%	98	Bradesco	8,600	15%
25	BlackBerry	24,623	−20%	50	Mercedes	15,344	12%	74	O2	11,694	N/A	99	Sberbank	8,535	N/A
								75	Telecom Italia	11,609	N/A	100	Goldman Sachs	8,439	−9%

(¹) The brand value of Coca-Cola includes Lites, Diets and Zero
(²) Deutsche Telekom is in the process of re-branding its business to 'T', which incorporates T-Mobile, T-Home and T-Systems
(³) The brand value of Budweiser includes Bud Light
(⁴) The brand value of Pepsi includes Lites, Diets and Zero
(⁵) The brand value of Nintendo includes Wii and Nintendo DS
(⁶) The brand value of Sony includes Playstation 2 and 3, as well as PSP
(⁷) The brand value of Red Bull includes sugar-free and Cola
Source: Millward Brown Optimor (including data from Brand Z, Kantar Worldpanel and Bloomberg).

Inertia

Many people tend to buy the same brand just about every time they go shopping. This consistent pattern is often due to **inertia** – we buy a brand out of habit merely because it requires less effort. If another product is introduced that is for some reason easier to buy (for instance, it is cheaper or the original product is out of stock), we will not hesitate to change our minds. A competitor who is trying to change a buying pattern based on inertia often can do so rather easily, because the shopper won't hesitate to jump to the new brand if it offers the right incentive. When we have little to no underlying commitment to a particular brand, marketers find it easy to 'unfreeze' our habit when they use promotional tools such as point-of-purchase displays, extensive couponing or noticeable price reductions. Some analysts predict that we are going to observe this kind of fickle behaviour more and more as consumers flit from one brand to the next. Indeed, one industry observer labels this variety-seeking consumer a *brand slut*; she points out that from 2004 to 2007 the number of women who say a manufacturer's brand name is very influential in their decision to buy a beauty product decreased by 21 percentage points to stand at 19 per cent.[148]

Brand loyalty: a 'friend', tried and true

This kind of fickleness or promiscuity will not occur if true **brand loyalty** exists. In contrast to inertia, brand loyalty describes repeat purchasing behaviour that reflects a *conscious* decision to continue buying the same brand.[149] For brand loyalty to exist, a pattern of repeat purchase must be accompanied by an underlying positive attitude towards the brand, rather than simply buying the same brand out of habit. Brand loyalty may be initiated by customer preference based on objective reasons, but after the brand has existed for a long time and is heavily advertised it can also create an emotional attachment, either by being incorporated into the consumer's self-image or because it is associated with prior experiences.[150] Purchase decisions based on brand loyalty also become habitual over time, though in these cases the underlying commitment to the product is much firmer.

Compared to inertia, a situation in which the consumer passively accepts a brand, a brand-loyal consumer is actively (sometimes passionately) involved with their favourite. Because of the emotional bonds that can come about between brand-loyal consumers and products, 'true-blue' users react more vehemently when these products are altered, redesigned or withdrawn.[151] Recall, for example, when Coca-Cola replaced its tried-and-true formula with New Coke in the 1980s.

A decade ago, marketers struggled with the problem of *brand parity*, which refers to consumers' beliefs that there are no significant differences among brands. For example, one survey at that time found that more than 70 per cent of consumers worldwide believed that all paper towels, all soaps and all crisps are alike.[152] Some analysts even proclaimed the death of brand names, predicting that private label or generic products that offered the same value for less money would kill off the tried-and-true products.

However, the reports of this death appear to be premature – major brands are making a dramatic comeback. Brand sluts aside, today branding is king. Some attribute this renaissance to information overload (as mentioned by Suzanne C. Beckmann above) – with too many alternatives (many of them unfamiliar names) to choose from, people seem to be looking for a few clear signals of quality. Following a period in the late 1980s and early 1990s when people had strong doubts about the ability of large companies to produce quality products, more recent surveys indicate consumers are slowly beginning to trust major manufacturers again.[153] Brand names are very much alive.

Decision rules we use when we care

We have seen that we use different rules to choose among competing products depending on the decision's complexity and how important the choice is to us. Sometimes we use a simple

Table 9.7 Hypothetical alternatives for an HDTV

Attribute	Importance ranking	Brand ratings		
		Kamashita	Prime Wave	Precision
Size of screen	1	Excellent	Excellent	Excellent
Stereo broadcast capability	2	Good	Poor	Excellent
Brand reputation	3	Poor	Excellent	Excellent
On-screen programming	4	Poor	Excellent	Poor
Cable-ready capability	5	Good	Good	Good
Sleep timer	6	Good	Excellent	Poor

heuristic, but at other times we carefully weigh alternatives. We can describe the processes we use when we are giving more thought to these decisions by dividing the types of rules we use into two categories: *compensatory* and *non-compensatory*. To aid the discussion of some of these rules, Table 9.7 summarizes the attributes of the HDTV sets Daniel considered. It is now possible to see how some of these rules result in different brand choices.

Non-compensatory decision rules

We use **non-compensatory decision rules** when we feel that a product with a low standing on one attribute cannot compensate for this flaw by doing better on another attribute. Simple non-compensatory decision rules are therefore short cuts to making choices. In other words we simply eliminate all options that do not meet some basic standards. A consumer like Daniel who uses the decision rule, 'Only buy well-known brand names', would not consider a new brand, even if it were equal or superior to existing ones. When people are less familiar with a product category or are not very motivated to process complex information, they tend to use simple, non-compensatory rules, which are summarized below:[154]

The lexicographic rule When a person uses *the lexicographic rule*, they select the brand that is the best on the most important attribute selected. If they feel two or more brands are equally good on that attribute, the consumer then compares them on the second most important attribute. This selection process goes on until the tie is broken. In Daniel's case, because both the Prime Wave and Precision models were tied on his most important attribute (screen size), he chose the Precision because of its rating on this second most important attribute – its stereo capability.

The elimination-by-aspects rule Using the elimination-by-aspects rule, the buyer also evaluates brands on the most important attribute. In this case, though, they impose specific cut-offs. For example, if Daniel had been more interested in having a sleep timer on his HDTV (if that had had a higher importance ranking), he might have stipulated that his choice 'must have a sleep timer'. Because the Prime Wave model had one and the Precision did not, he would have chosen the Prime Wave.

The conjunctive rule Whereas the two former rules involve processing by attribute, the *conjunctive rule* entails processing by brand. As with the elimination-by-aspects procedure, the decision-maker establishes cut-offs for each attribute. They choose a brand if it meets all of the cut-offs, while failure to meet any one cut-off means they will reject it. If none of the brands meet all of the cut-offs, they may delay the choice, change the decision rule, or modify the cut-offs they choose to apply.

If Daniel had stipulated that all attributes had to be rated 'good' or better, he would not have been able to choose any of the options. He might then have modified his decision rule, conceding that it was not possible to attain these high standards in the price range he was considering. In this case, Daniel might decide that he could live without on-screen programming, so he would again consider the Precision model.

Compensatory decision rules

Unlike non-compensatory decision rules, **compensatory decision rules** give a product a chance to make up for its shortcomings. Consumers who employ these rules tend to be more involved in the purchase and so they are willing to exert the effort to consider the entire picture in a more exacting way. The willingness to let good and bad product qualities balance out can result in quite different choices. For example, if Daniel had not been concerned about having stereo reception, he might have chosen the Prime Wave model. But because this brand doesn't feature this highly ranked attribute, it doesn't stand a chance when he uses a non-compensatory rule.

Two basic types of compensatory rules have been identified. When they use the *simple additive rule*, the consumer merely chooses the alternative that has the largest number of positive attributes. This choice is most likely to occur when their ability or motivation to process information is limited. One drawback to this approach for the consumer is that some of these attributes may not be very meaningful or important. An ad containing a long list of product benefits may be persuasive, despite the fact that many of the benefits included are actually standard within the product class and are not determinant attributes at all.

The *weighted additive rule* is a more complex version.[155] When using this rule, the consumer also takes into account the relative importance of positively rated attributes, essentially multiplying brand ratings by importance weights. If this process sounds familiar, it should. The calculation process strongly resembles the multi-attribute attitude model described in Chapter 8.

Recent research argues that the difficulties faced by consumers in making decisions derives not just from the evaluation and trading off of different attributes (as described by the different decision rules above), but also derives from some degree of incompatibility between the *task* of choosing itself, and the valence of the alternatives within the decision set. When the consumer experiences conflict between the task of choosing and the valence of the alternatives then they face greater difficulties in making decisions; and take longer to make the decision. In the case of Daniel, for instance, if he had been faced with choices between HDTVs that he had not liked, then this would have compounded the difficulty involved in the task itself, i.e. making a decision. When all of the alternatives are unattractive, then decision-making increases in difficulty. The conflict Daniel would have faced in making a decision, when confronted by alternatives that he did not like, would have been heightened because he was faced with making a choice that he did not wish to make; and he would have taken longer to make a decision.[156]

CHAPTER SUMMARY

Now that you have finished reading this chapter you should understand why:

→ **Consumer decision making is a central part of consumer behaviour, but the way we evaluate and choose products (and the amount of thought we put into these choices) varies widely, depending on such dimensions as the degree of novelty or risk related to the decision.** We almost constantly need to make decisions about products. Some of these decisions are very important and entail great effort, whereas we make others on a virtually automatic basis. The decision-making task is further complicated because of the sheer number of decisions we need to make in a marketplace environment characterized by consumer hyperchoice.

Perspectives on decision making range from a focus on habits that people develop over time to novel situations involving a great deal of risk in which consumers must carefully collect and analyse information before making a choice. Many of our decisions are highly automated; we make them largely by habit. This trend is accelerating as marketers begin to introduce smart products that enable silent commerce, where the products literally make their own purchase decisions (e.g. a malfunctioning appliance that contacts the repair person directly).

→ **A decision is actually composed of a series of stages that results in the selection of one product over competing options.** A typical decision process involves several steps. The first is problem recognition, when we realize we must take some action. This recognition may occur because a current possession malfunctions or perhaps because we have a desire for something new.

Once the consumer recognizes a problem and sees it as sufficiently important to warrant some action, he begins the process of information search. This search may range from doing a simple scan of his memory to determine what he's done before to resolve the same problem to extensive fieldwork during which he consults a variety of sources to amass as much information as possible. In many cases, people engage in surprisingly little search. Instead, they rely on various mental shortcuts, such as brand names or price, or they may simply imitate others' choices.

In the evaluation-of-alternatives stage, the product alternatives a person considers constitute his evoked set. Members of the evoked set usually share some characteristics; we categorize them similarly. The way the person mentally groups products influences which alternatives she will consider, and usually we associate some brands more strongly with these categories (i.e. they are more prototypical).

→ **Decision making is not always rational.** Research in the field of behavioural economics illustrates that decision making is not always strictly rational. Principles of mental accounting demonstrate that the way a problem is posed (called *framing*) and whether it is put in terms of gains or losses influences what we decide.

→ **Our access to online sources is changing the way we decide what to buy.** The world wide web has changed the way many of us search for information. Today, our problem is more likely to be about weeding out excess detail rather than searching for more information. Comparative search sites and intelligent agents help to filter and guide the search process. We may rely on cybermediaries, such as web portals, to sort through massive amounts of information as a way to simplify the decision-making process.

→ **We often fall back on well-learned 'rules-of-thumb' to make decisions.** Very often, we use heuristics, or mental rules-of-thumb, to simplify decision making. In particular, we develop many market beliefs over time. One of the most common beliefs is that we can determine quality by looking at the price. Other heuristics rely on well-known brand names or a product's country of origin as signals of product quality. When we consistently purchase a brand over time, this pattern may be the result of true brand loyalty or simply inertia because it's the easiest thing to do.

→ **Consumers rely on different decision rules when evaluating competing options.** When the consumer eventually must make a product choice from among alternatives, he uses one of several decision rules. Non-compensatory rules eliminate alternatives that are deficient on any of the criteria we've chosen. Compensatory rules, which we are more likely to apply in high-involvement situations, allow us to consider each alternative's good and bad points more carefully in order to arrive at the overall best choice.

KEY TERMS

Anchoring (p. 347)

Behavioural economics (p. 346)

Behavioural influence perspective (p. 336)

Blissful ignorance effect (p. 351)

Bounded rationality (p. 345)

Brand advocates (p. 363)

Brand loyalty (p. 370)

Category exemplars (p. 358)

Cognitive processing style (p. 335)

Compensatory decision rules (p. 372)

Consideration set (p. 355)

Consumer hyperchoice (p. 333)

Country of origin (p. 365)

Cybermediary (p. 362)

Determinant attributes (p. 360)

Electronic recommendation agent (p. 362)

Ethnocentrism (p. 365)

Evaluative criteria (p. 359)

Evoked set (p. 355)

Experiential perspective (p. 336)

Extended problem-solving (p. 338)

Feature bloat (p. 358)

Feature creep (p. 358)

Feature fatigue (p. 358)

Framing (p. 346)

Game-based marketing (p. 340)

Game platform (p. 339)

Genre (p. 340)

Habitual decision-making (p. 341)

Heuristics (p. 364)

Hyperopia (p. 348)

Incidental brand exposure (p. 350)

Inertia (p. 370)

Information search (p. 332)

Intelligent agents (p. 362)

Knowledge structure (p. 356)

Limited problem-solving (p. 340)

Long tail (p. 362)

Low-literate consumer (p. 352)

Market beliefs (p. 365)

Maximising (p. 345)

Mental accounting (p. 346)

Milieu (p. 339)

MMORPGs (massively multiplayer online role-playing games) (p. 340)

Mode (p. 339)

Neuromarketing (p. 360)

Neuroscience (p. 361)

Non-compensatory decision rules (p. 371)

Perceived risk (p. 351)

Problem recognition (p. 341)

Product signal (p. 364)

Prospect theory (p. 348)

Psychology of Loss Aversion (PLA) (p. 348)

Purchase momentum (p. 335)

Rational perspective (p. 334)

Reputation economy (p. 363)

Satisficing (p. 345)

Search engines (p. 344)

Sisyphus effect (p. 345)

Social game (p. 339)

Stereotype (p. 366)

Variety amnesia (p. 346)

Variety seeking (p. 346)

Zipf's Law (p. 368)

CONSUMER BEHAVIOUR CHALLENGE

1 What is the difference between the behavioural influence and experiential perspectives on decision making? Give an example of the type of purchase that each perspective would help to explain.

2 If people are not always rational decision-makers, is it worth the effort to study how purchasing decisions are made? What techniques might be employed to understand experiential consumption and to translate this knowledge into marketing strategy?

3 What is prospect theory? Does it support the argument that we are rational decision makers?

4 Give an example of the sunk-cost fallacy.

5 Describe the difference between a superordinate category, a basic level category, and a subordinate category. What is an example of an exemplar product?

6 Describe the relationship between a consumer's level of expertise and how much they are likely to search for information about a product.

7 List three types of perceived risk, and give an example of each.

8 List three product attributes that can be used as quality signals and provide an example of each.

9 Explain the 'evoked set'. Why is it difficult to place a product in a consumer's evoked set after it has already been rejected? What strategies might a marketer use in an attempt to accomplish this goal?

10 Define the three levels of product categorization described in the chapter. Diagram these levels for a health club.

11 How does a brand function as a heuristic?

12 Describe the difference between inertia and brand loyalty.

13 Discuss two different non-compensatory decision rules and highlight the difference(s) between them. How might the use of one rule versus another result in a different product choice?

14 Choose a friend or parent who shops for groceries on a regular basis and keep a log of their purchases of common consumer products during the term. Can you detect any evidence of brand loyalty in any categories based on consistency of purchases? If so, talk to the person about these purchases. Try to determine if their choices are based on true brand loyalty or on inertia. What techniques might you use to differentiate between the two?

15 Form a group of three. Pick a product and develop a marketing plan based on each of the three approaches to consumer decision-making: rational, experiential and behavioural influence. What are the major differences in emphasis among the three perspectives? Which is the most likely type of problem-solving activity for the product you have selected? What characteristics of the product make this so?

16 Find a person who is about to make a major purchase. Ask that person to make a chronological list of all the information sources consulted prior to making a decision. How would you characterize the types of sources used (i.e., internal versus external, media versus personal, etc.)? Which sources appeared to have the most impact on the person's decision?

17 Perform a survey of country-of-origin stereotypes. Compile a list of five countries and ask people what products they associate with each. What are their evaluations of the products and likely attributes of these different products? The power of a country stereotype can also be demonstrated in another way. Prepare a brief description of a product, including a list of features, and ask people to rate it in terms of quality, likelihood of purchase, and so on. Make several versions of the description, varying only the country from which it comes. Do ratings change as a function of the country of origin?

18 In the past few years, several products made in China have been recalled because they are dangerous or even fatal to use (see **http://ec.europa.eu/consumers/dyna/rapex/create_rapex.cfm?rx_id=423** (accessed 15 February 2012) for an up-to-date list). If the Chinese government hired you as a consultant to help it repair some of the damage to the reputation of products made there, what actions would you recommend?

19 What is neuromarketing, and is it dangerous? Identify the advantages and disadvantages of neuromarketing from the perspective firstly of the consumer, secondly of the market researcher, and thirdly of the marketing brand manager.

Ask a friend to 'talk through' the process they used to choose one brand rather than others during a recent purchase. Based on this description, can you identify the decision rule that was most likely employed?

20 Technology has the potential to make our lives easier by reducing the amount of clutter we need to work through in order to access the information on the internet that really interests us. On the other hand, perhaps intelligent agents that make recommendations based only on what we and others like us have chosen in the past limit us – they reduce the chance that we will stumble upon something (e.g. a book on a topic we've never heard of, or a music group that's different from the style we usually listen to). Will the proliferation of shopping bots make our lives too predictable by only giving us more of the same? If so, is this a problem?

21 What is the future of social gaming? How do you evaluate the potential of these activities for marketing?

22 Read Rust, Thompson and Hamilton's article in *Harvard Business Review* (February 2006: 98ff) on 'Defeating feature fatigue'. Summarize their main arguments and examples into a paragraph. Working in groups of three, write a brief for a marketing manager, first, explaining why consumers prefer capability to usability; secondly, identifying the disadvantages for both consumers and managers of consumers' tendency to prefer capability to usability; and thirdly, suggesting strategies that managers might adopt to counter feature fatigue amongst consumers.

23 'Too many features can make a product overwhelming for consumers and difficult to use' (Thompson, Rust and Hamilton, 2005: 431, Debora V. Thompson, Rebecca W. Hamilton and Roland T. Rust, 'Feature fatigue: when product capabilities become too much of a good thing', *Journal of Marketing Research* 42 (November 2005): 431–442). Debate this in class, using the material on adoption and diffusion from Chapter 14. How might marketing managers overcome barriers to adoption of their technically sophisticated products?

24 Give one of the scenarios described in the section on biases in decision-making to between 10 and 20 people. How do the results you obtain compare with those reported in the chapter?

25 Think of a product you recently shopped for online. Describe your search process. How did you become aware you wanted/needed the product? How did you evaluate alternatives? Did you end up buying online? Why, or why not? What factors would make it more or less likely that you would buy something online rather than in a traditional store?

26 Consider the five types of perceived risk in Figure 9.7 within the context of making a decision to purchase a new diamond. Review the following websites, and discuss the kinds of risk you would consider in buying a diamond on the web: **www.diamond.com**, **www.mondera.com**, **www.bluenile.com**.

27 Find examples of electronic recommendation agents on the web. Evaluate these – are they helpful? What characteristics of the sites you locate are likely to make you buy products you wouldn't have bought on your own?

28 It is increasingly clear that many postings on blogs and product reviews on websites are fake or are posted there to manipulate consumers' opinions. For example, a mini-scandal erupted in 2007 when the press learned that the CEO of Whole Foods had regularly been blasting competitor Wild Oats on blogs under a pseudonym.[157] How big a problem is this if consumers are increasingly looking to consumer-generated product reviews to guide their purchase decisions? What steps, if any, can marketers take to nip this problem in the bud?

29 Visit the EC website with video briefings about systems of consumer protection in the EC: **http://ec.europa.eu/dgs/health_consumer/press/index_en.htm#consumers** (accessed 15 February 2012). Debate in class the reasons why there is increasing concern about 'keeping consumers safe'; and how far is it the role of national governments or international institutions (like the EC) to undertake this? What about the traditional view of the consumer's responsibility, i.e. buyer beware or *caveat emptor*?

For additional material see the companion website at www.pearsoned.co.uk/solomon

NOTES

1. http://www.london2012.com/athletics

2. Simon Marsh, Digital TV World Household Forecasts Report, http://www.ekmpowershop4.com/ekmps/shops/broadbandtv/digital-tv-world-household-forecasts-1-5-users-104-p.asp, accessed 17 February 2012 cited by Clarke in 'Digital TV homes to double within five years' Broadband TV News Correspondent in Share, 17 June 2011, http://www.broadbandtvnews.com/2011/06/17/digital-tv-homes-to-double-within-five-years/, accessed 17 February 2012.

3. Ying Zhang, Ayelet Fishback and Ravi Dhar, 'When thinking beats doing: The role of optimistic expectations in goal-based choice', *Journal of Consumer Research* 34 (December 2007): 567.

4. David Glen Mick, Susan M. Broniarczyk and Jonathan Haidt, 'Choose, choose, choose, choose, choose, choose, choose: Emerging and prospective research on the deleterious effects of living in consumer hyperchoice', *Journal of Business Ethics* 52 (2004): 207–11; see also Barry Schwartz, *The Paradox of Choice: Why More Is Less* (New York: Ecco, 2005).

5. Frank Huber, Sören Köcher, Frederik Meyer and Johannes Vogel, 'The Paralyzed Customer: An Empirical Investigation of Antecedents and Consequences of Decision Paralysis' in Alan Bradshaw, Chris Hackley and Pauline Maclaran (eds), *European Association for Consumer Research Conference* 2010 RHUL, page 82.

6. Simona Botti, Kristina Orfali and Sheena S. Iyengar, 'Tragic Choices: Autonomy and Emotional Responses to Medical Decisions', *Journal of Consumer Research* 36 (October 2009): 337–52; cf. also Hazel Rose Markus and Barry Schwartz, 'Does Choice Mean Freedom and Well Being?' *Journal of Consumer Research* 37, no. 2 (2010): 344–55.

7. Itamar Simonson, Joel Huber and John Payne, 'The relationship between prior brand knowledge and information acquisition order', *Journal of Consumer Research* 14 (March 1988): 566–78.

8. John R. Hauser, Glenn L. Urban and Bruce D. Weinberg, 'How consumers allocate their time when searching for information', *Journal of Marketing Research* 30 (November 1993): 452–66; George J. Stigler, 'The economics of information', *Journal of Political Economy* 69 (June 1961): 213–25. For a set of studies focusing on online search costs, see John G. Lynch, Jr and Dan Ariely, 'Wine online: Search costs and competition on price, quality, and distribution', *Marketing Science* 19(1) (2000): 83–103.

9. John C. Mowen, 'Beyond consumer decision making', *Journal of Consumer Marketing* 5(1) (1988): 15–25.

10. See Deborah. J. MacInnis and Valerie S. Folkes, 'The Disciplinary Status of Consumer Behavior: A Sociology of Science Perspective on Key Controversies', *Journal of Consumer Research* 36 (April 2010): 899–914 for an up-to-date discussion of the variety of debates about researching topics in the field of consumer behaviour.

11. Richard W. Olshavsky and Donald H. Granbois, 'Consumer decision making – fact or fiction', *Journal of Consumer Research* 6 (September 1989): 93–100.

12. Chris Marks, 'As two osprey nests are raided, fears that thieves see Scotland as a soft option', *Daily Mail* (14 May 2002).

13. Ravi Dhar, Joel Huber and Uzma Khan, 'The Shopping Momentum Effect', paper presented at the Association for Consumer Research, Atlanta, Georgia, October 2002.

14. Thomas P. Novak and Donna L. Hoffman, 'The Fit of Thinking Style and Situation: New Measures of Situation-Specific Experiential and Rational Cognition', *Journal of Consumer Research* 36 (December 2009): 56–72.

15. James R. Bettman, 'The Decision Maker Who Came in from the Cold' (presidential address), in Leigh McAllister and Michael Rothschild (eds), *Advances in Consumer Research* 20 (Provo, U.T.: Association for Consumer Research, 1993): 7–11; John W. Payne, James R. Bettman and Eric J. Johnson, 'Behavioral decision research: A constructive processing perspective', *Annual Review of Psychology* 4 (1992): 87–131; J.R. Bettman, M.F. Luce and J.W. Payne 'Constructive consumer choice processes', *Journal of Consumer Research* 25(3) (December 1998): 187–217; for an overview of recent developments in individual choice models, see Robert J. Meyer and Barbara E. Kahn, 'Probabilistic Models of Consumer Choice Behavior', in Thomas S. Robertson and Harold H. Kassarjian (eds), *Handbook of Consumer Behavior* (Upper Saddle River, N.J.: Prentice Hall, 1991): 85–123.

16. Dan Ariely, 'Controlling the information flow: Effects on consumers' decision making and preferences', *Journal of Consumer Research*, 27 (September 2000): 245; John Deighton, 'The future of interactive marketing', *Harvard Business Review* 74(6) (1996): 151–62.

17. Ariely, 'Controlling the information flow' *ibid.*: 233–48.

18. Nicholas H. Lurie, 'Decision making in information-rich environments: The role of information structure', *Journal of Consumer Research* 30 (March 2004): 473–86.

19. *Ibid.*, 484–5.

20. Brian T. Ratchford, Debabrata Talukdar and Myung-Soo Lee, 'The impact of the internet on consumers' use of information sources for automobiles: A re-inquiry', *Journal of Consumer Research* 34 (June 2007): 111–9.

21. Mowen, 'Beyond consumer decision making', *op. cit.*

22. The Fits-Like-a-Glove (FLAG) framework is a new decision-making perspective that views consumer decisions as a holistic process shaped by the person's unique context: see Douglas E. Allen, 'Toward a theory of consumer choice as sociohistorically shaped practical experience: The fits-like-a-glove (FLAG) framework', *Journal of Consumer Research* 28 (March 2002): 515–32.

23. Material in this section is adapted and abridged from Tracy Tuten and Michael R. Solomon, *Social Media Marketing* (Upper Saddle River, NJ: Pearson Education, 2012).

24. Thomas Apperley, 'Genre and Game Studies: Toward a Critical Approach to Video Game Genres', *Simulation & Gaming* 37, no. 1 (2006): 6–23.

25. Interactive Advertising Bureau, *IAB Game Advertising Platform Status Report*, http://www.iab.net/media/file/games-reportv4.pdf, accessed 31 May 2011.

26. Apperley, 'Genre and Game Studies: Toward a Critical Approach to Video Game Genres'.

27. Drew Elliott, 'Opportunities for Brands in Social Games', *Ogilvy PR Blog* (May 2010), http://blog.ogilvypr.com/2010/05/opportunities-for-brands-in-social-games/, accessed 12 July 2010.

28. Joseph W. Alba and J. Wesley Hutchinson, 'Dimensions of consumer expertise', *Journal of Consumer Research* 13 (March 1988): 411–54.

29. Jean Halliday, 'With Fusion Campaign, Ford Targets "Upper Funnel" Car Buyers: $60M to $80M Ad Blitz Aimed at Consumers Not Yet Ready to Buy New Vehicle', *Advertising Age* (2 March 2009), www.advertisingage.com, accessed 2 March 2009.

30. Gordon C. Bruner III and Richard J. Pomazal, 'Problem recognition: The crucial first stage of the consumer decision process', *Journal of Consumer Marketing* 5(1) (1988): 53–63.

31. For a study that examined tradeoffs in search behaviour among different channels, cf. Judi Strebel, Tulin Erdem and Joffre Swait, 'Consumer Search in High Technology Markets: Exploring the Use of Traditional Information Channels', *Journal of Consumer Psychology* 14, nos 1 and 2 (2004): 96–104.

32. Peter H. Bloch, Daniel L. Sherrell and Nancy M. Ridgway, 'Consumer search: An extended framework', *Journal of Consumer Research* 13 (June 1986): 119–26.

33. *Ibid.*

34. Girish Punj, 'Presearch decision making in consumer durable purchases', *Journal of Consumer Marketing* 4 (Winter 1987): 71–82.

35. H. Beales, M.B. Jagis, S.C. Salop and R. Staelin, 'Consumer search and public policy', *Journal of Consumer Research* 8 (June 1981): 11–22.

36. Laurie Petersen, 'Study Places Value On Marketing At Consumer Research Stage', *Marketing Daily* (27 June 2007): www.medipost.com

37. Alex Mindlin, 'Buyers Search Online, but Not by Brand', *New York Times* (13 March 2006); see also Jessica Twentyman, 'New customers: retailers experiment on ways to win loyalty' 24 January 2012, ft.com: http://www.ft.com/cms/s/0/41628e10-41c6-11e1-a586-00144feab49a.html#axzz1sPj2BhoK, accessed 19 April 2012.

38. Brian T. Ratchford, Debabrata Talukdar and Myung-Soo Lee, 'The impact of the internet on consumers' use of information sources for automobiles: A re-inquiry', *op. cit.*

39. Brian T. Ratchford, Debabrata Talukdar and Myung-Soo Lee, 'The Impact of the Internet on Consumers' Use of Information Sources for Automobiles: A Re-Inquiry', *op. cit.*: 112.

40. *Ibid.*

41. The Nielsen Company Press Release, 'Over 875 Million Consumers Have Shopped Online – the Number of Internet Shoppers Up 40 per cent in Two Years', http://www.earthtimes.org/articles/show/over-875-million-consumers-have-shopped-online--the-number,263812.shtml, accessed 20 August 2008.

42. Greg Sterling, 'Search + Social Media Increases CTR by 94 Percent: Report', *Search Engine Land* (28 February 2011), http://searchengineland.com/search-social-media-increases-ctr-by-94-percent-report-66231?utm_source=feedburner&utm_medium=feed&utm_campaign=Feed%3A+searchengineland+%28Search+Engine+Land%3A+Main+Feed%29, accessed 30 April 2011.

43. Cathy J. Cobb and Wayne D. Hoyer, 'Direct observation of search behavior', *Psychology and Marketing* 2 (Fall 1985): 161–79.

44. Francois A. Carrillat, Daniel M. Ladik and Renaud Legoux, 'When the Decision Ball Keeps Rolling: An Investigation of the Sisyphus Effect among Maximizing Consumers', *Marketing Letters* (September 2010): 1–14.

45. Sharon E. Beatty and Scott M. Smith, 'External search effort: An investigation across several product categories', *Journal of Consumer Research* 14 (June 1987): 83–95; William L. Moore and Donald R. Lehmann, 'Individual differences in search behavior for a nondurable', *Journal of Consumer Research* 7 (December 1980): 296–307.

46. See the Terrachoice website: Sins of greenwashing (home and family edition) http://sinsofgreenwashing.org/, accessed 19 April 2012; also Kiel and Layton, 'Dimensions of consumer information seeking behavior'; Srinivasan and Ratchford, 'An empirical test of a model of external search for automobiles'; Mari Niva, Eva Heiskanen and Päivi Timonen, 'Environmental information in consumer decision making', *National Consumer Research Centre* (Helsinki, July 1996).

47. David F. Midgley, 'Patterns of interpersonal information seeking for the purchase of a symbolic product', *Journal of Marketing Research* 20 (February 1983): 74–83.

48. Cyndee Miller, 'Scotland to U.S.: "This Tennent's for you"', *Marketing News* (29 August 1994): 26.

49. Jeff Galak, Joseph P. Redden and Justin Kruger (2009), 'Variety Amnesia: Recalling Past Variety Can Accelerate Recovery from Satiation', *Journal of Consumer Research* 36, no. 4 (2009): 575–84.

50. Rebecca K. Ratner, Barbara E. Kahn and Daniel Kahneman, 'Choosing less-preferred experiences for the sake of variety', *Journal of Consumer Research* 26 (June 1999): 1–15.

51. Satya Menon and Barbara E. Kahn, 'The impact of context on variety seeking in product choices', *Journal of Consumer Research* 22 (December 1995): 285–95; Barbara E. Kahn and Alice M. Isen, 'The influence of positive affect on variety seeking among safe, enjoyable products', *Journal of Consumer Research* 20 (September 1993): 257–70.

52. J. Jeffrey Inman, 'The Role of Sensory-Specific Satiety in Consumer Variety Seeking Among Flavors' (unpublished manuscript, A.C. Nielsen Center for Marketing Research, University of Wisconsin-Madison, July 1999).

53. Michael Laroche, Chankon Kim and Lianxi Zhou, 'Brand familiarity and confidence as determinants of purchase intention: An empirical test in a multiple brand context', *Journal of Business Research* 37 (1996): 115–20.

54. Barbara E. Kahn, 'Understanding Variety-Seeking Behavior From a Marketing Perspective', unpublished manuscript, University of Pennsylvania, University Park, 1991; Leigh McAlister and Edgar A. Pessemier, 'Variety-seeking behavior: An interdisciplinary review', *Journal of Consumer Research* 9 (December 1982): 311–22; Fred M. Feinberg, Barbara E. Kahn and Leigh McAlister, 'Market share response when consumers seek variety', *Journal of Marketing Research* 29 (May 1992): 228–37; Kahn and Isen, 'The influence of positive affect on variety seeking among safe, enjoyable products', *op. cit.*

55. Gary Belsky, 'Why smart people make major money mistakes', *Money* (July 1995): 76; Richard Thaler and Eric J.

Johnson, 'Gambling with the house money or trying to break even: The effects of prior outcomes on risky choice', *Management Science* 36 (June 1990): 643–60; Richard Thaler, 'Mental accounting and consumer choice', *Marketing Science* 4 (Summer 1985): 199–214.

56. Steven J. Levitt and Stephen G. Dubner, *Freakonomics: A Rogue Economist Explores the Hidden Side of Everything* (New York, NY: Harper Perennial, 2009); Dan Ariely, *Predictably Irrational: The Hidden Forces That Shape Our Decisions* (New York, NY: HarperCollins, 2008).

57. Beth Snyder Bulik, 'Behavioral Economics Helping Marketers Better Understand Consumers Practice Gives Advertisers Insight into Shoppers' Brand Selection', *Ad Age CMO Strategy* (26 July 2010), http://adage.com/article/cmo-strategy/behavioral-economics-helping-marketers-understand-consumers/145091/, accessed 17 April 2011; cf. also Robin L. Soster, Ashwani Monga and William O. Bearden, 'Tracking Costs of Time and Money: How Accounting Periods Affect Mental Accounting', *Journal of Consumer Research* 37, no. 4 (2010): 712–21.

58. Quoted in John Tierney, 'Oversaving, a Burden for Our Times', *New York Times* (23 March 2009), www.nytimes.com/2009/03/24/science/24tier.html?_r=1, accessed 23 March 2009.

59. Lyle Brenner, Yuval Rottenstreich, Sanjay Sood and Baler Bilgin, 'On the Psychology of Loss Aversion Aversion: Possession, Valence, and Reversals of the Endowment Effect', *Journal of Consumer Research* 34 (October 2007): 376.

60. Daniel Kahneman and Amos Tversky, 'Prospect theory: An analysis of decision under risk,' *Econometrica* 47 (March 1979): 263–91; Timothy B. Heath, Subimal Chatterjee and Karen Russo France, 'Mental accounting and changes in price: The frame dependence of reference dependence', *Journal of Consumer Research* 22(1) (June 1995): 90–7.

61. Quoted in Thaler, 'Mental accounting and consumer choice', *op. cit.*: 206.

62. Scott I. Rick, Cynthia E. Cryder and George Loewenstein, 'Tightwads and Spendthrifts', *Journal of Consumer Research* 34 (April 2008): 767.

63. Peter Lieberman and David Pizarro, 'All Politics Is Olfactory', *New York Times* (23 October 2010), http://www.nytimes.com/2010/10/24/opinion/24pizarro.html?_r=1&ref=todayspaper, accessed 29 April 2011.

64. Gavan Fitzsimons, 'CB As I See It' in M. Solomon, *Consumer Behavior*, 10th edn (Pearson 2012).

65. Girish N. Punj and Richard Staelin, 'A model of consumer search behavior for new automobiles', *Journal of Consumer Research* 9 (March 1983): 366–80.

66. Cobb and Hoyer, 'Direct observation of search behavior', *op. cit.*; Moore and Lehmann, 'Individual differences in search behavior for a nondurable', *op. cit.*; Punj and Staelin, 'A model of consumer search behavior for new auto-mobiles', *op. cit.*

67. Judi Strebel, Tulin Erdem and Joffre Swait, 'Consumer search in high technology markets: Exploring the use of traditional information channels', *Journal of Consumer Psychology* 14 (1 and 2) (2004): 96–104.

68. James R. Bettman and C. Whan Park, 'Effects of prior knowledge and experience and phase of the choice process on consumer decision processes: A protocol analysis', *Journal of Consumer Research* 7 (December 1980): 234–48.

69. Alba and Hutchinson, 'Dimensions of consumer expertise'; Bettman and Park, 'Effects of prior knowledge and experience and phase of the choice process on consumer decision processes', *op. cit.*; Merrie Brucks, 'The effects of product class knowledge on information search behavior', *Journal of Consumer Research* 12 (June 1985): 1–16; Joel E. Urbany, Peter R. Dickson and William L. Wilkie, 'Buyer uncertainty and information search', *Journal of Consumer Research* 16 (September 1989): 208–15.

70. Alina Tugend, 'Some Blissful Ignorance Can Cure Chronic Buyer's Remorse', *New York Times* (15 March 2008), www.nytimes.com/2008/03/15/Business/15shortcuts.Html?Scp=1&Sq=Tugend&St=Nyt, accessed 15 March 2008.

71. Alexander Fedorikhin and Catherine A. Cole, 'Mood effects on attitudes, perceived risk and choice: Moderators and mediators', *Journal of Consumer Psychology*, 14(1 and 2) (2004): 2–12.

72. For a discussion of 'collective risk', where consumers experience a reduction in perceived risk by sharing their exposure with others who are also using the product or service, see an analysis of Hotline, an online file-sharing community in Markus Geisler, 'Collective Risk', working paper, Northwestern University, March 2003.

73. DfES Skills for Life national needs and impact survey 2003, http://www.literacytrust.org.uk/database/stats/adultstats.html, and http://www.literacytrust.org.uk/Policy/adultlevels.html, accessed 23 August 2008.

74. Natalie Ross Adkins and Julie L. Ozanne, 'The low literate consumer', *Journal of Consumer Research* 32(1) (2005): 93; Madhubalan Viswanathan, Jose Antonio Rosa and James Edwin Harris, 'Decision making and coping of functionally illiterate consumers and some implications for marketing management', *Journal of Marketing* 69(1) (2005): 15.

75. Leaflet: *Education benchmarks for Europe* [with country-specific data], http://ec.europa.eu/education/lifelong-learning-policy/doc/benchmarks10_en.pdf, accessed 17 February 2012 via 'Progress and performance in education and training in EU countries – report, 19 April 2011' http://www.eubusiness.com/topics/education/progress-11/accessed, 17 February 2012.

76. 'Keeping European Consumers Safe', 2007 Annual Report on the operation of the Rapid Alert System for non-food consumer products, European Communities Health and Consumer Protection Directorate General, Luxembourg, 2008, page 10; see also weekly updates: http://ec.europa.eu/consumers/dyna/rapex/create_rapex.cfm?rx_id=196

77. Gianluigi Guido, M. Irene Prete and Giovanni Pino, 'Purchasing motivations of regular and occasional organic food consumers: The incidence of food safety and ethical concern' in Alan Bradshaw, Chris Hackley and Pauline Maclaran (eds), *European Association for Consumer Research Conference* 2010 RHUL, page 17.

78. Mary Frances Luce, James R. Bettman and John W. Payne, 'Choice processing in emotionally difficult decisions', *Journal of Experimental Psychology: Learning, Memory, and Cognition* 23 (March 1997): 384–405; example provided by Prof. James Bettman, personal communication, 17 December 1997.

79. Some research suggests that structural elements of the information available, such as the number and distribution

of attribute levels, will influence how items in a consideration set are processed; *cf.* Nicholas H. Lurie, 'Decision making in information-rich environments: The role of information structure', *Journal of Consumer Research* 30 (March 2004): 473–86.

80. John R. Hauser and Birger Wernerfelt, 'An evaluation cost model of consideration sets', *Journal of Consumer Research* 16 (March 1990): 393–408.

81. Robert J. Sutton, 'Using empirical data to investigate the likelihood of brands being admitted or readmitted into an established evoked set', *Journal of the Academy of Marketing Science* 15 (Fall 1987): 82.

82. Cf., for example, Kenneth C. Manning and David E. Sprott, 'Price Endings, Left-Digit Effects, and Choice', *Journal of Consumer Research* 36, no. 2 (2009): 328–35; Sandra J. Milberg, Francisca Sinn and Ronald C. Goodstein, 'Consumer Reactions to Brand Extensions in a Competitive Context: Does Fit Still Matter?' *Journal of Consumer Research* 37, no. 3 (2010): 543–53; David Sleeth-Keppler and Christian S. Wheeler, 'A Multidimensional Association Approach to Sequential Consumer Judgments,' *Journal of Consumer Psychology* 21, no. 1 (2011): 14–23; Aner Sela, Jonah Berger and Wendy Liu, 'Variety, Vice, and Virtue: How Assortment Size Influences Option Choice', *Journal of Consumer Research* 35, no. 6 (2009): 941–51.

83. Cyndee Miller, 'Hemp is latest buzzword', *Marketing News* (17 March 1997): 1.

84. Stuart Elliott, 'A Brand Tries to Invite Thought', *New York Times* (7 September 2007), www.nytimes.com, accessed 7 September 2007.

85. Alba and Hutchinson, 'Dimensions of consumer expertise'; Joel B. Cohen and Kunal Basu, 'Alternative models of categorization: Toward a contingent processing framework', *Journal of Consumer Research* 13 (March 1987): 455–72.

86. Robert M. McMath, 'The perils of typecasting', *American Demographics* (February 1997): 60.

87. Eleanor Rosch, 'Principles of Categorization', in E. Rosch and B.B. Lloyd (eds), *Recognition and Categorization* (Hillsdale, N.J.: Erlbaum, 1978).

88. Michael R. Solomon, 'Mapping product constellations: A social categorization approach to symbolic consumption', *Psychology and Marketing* 5(3) (1988): 233–58.

89. McMath, 'The perils of typecasting', *op. cit.*

90. Elizabeth C. Hirschman and Michael R. Solomon, 'Competition and Cooperation Among Culture Production Systems', in Ronald F. Bush and Shelby D. Hunt (eds), *Marketing Theory: Philosophy of Science Perspectives* (Chicago: American Marketing Association, 1982): 269–72.

91. Michael D. Johnson, 'The differential processing of product category and noncomparable choice alternatives', *Journal of Consumer Research* 16 (December 1989): 300–9.

92. Mita Sujan, 'Consumer knowledge: Effects on evaluation strategies mediating consumer judgments', *Journal of Consumer Research* 12 (June 1985): 31–46.

93. Rosch, 'Principles of categorization', *op. cit.*

94. Joan Meyers-Levy and Alice M. Tybout, 'Schema congruity as a basis for product evaluation', *Journal of Consumer Research* 16 (June 1989): 39–55.

95. Mita Sujan and James R. Bettman, 'The effects of brand positioning strategies on consumers' brand and category

perceptions: Some insights from schema research', *Journal of Marketing Research* 26 (November 1989): 454–67.

96. See William P. Putsis Jr and Narasimhan Srinivasan, 'Buying or just browsing? The duration of purchase deliberation', *Journal of Marketing Research* 31 (August 1994): 393–402.

97. Robert E. Smith, 'Integrating information from advertising and trial: Processes and effects on consumer response to product information', *Journal of Marketing Research* 30 (May 1993): 204–19.

98. *Ibid.*

99. Roland T. Rust, Debora V. Thompson and Rebecca W. Hamilton, 'Defeating feature fatigue', *Harvard Business Review* 84 (February 2006): 100.

100. Rebecca W. Hamilton and Debora Viana Thompson, 'Is there a substitute for direct experience? Comparing consumers' preferences after direct and indirect product experiences', *Journal of Consumer Research* 34 (December 2007): 546–55.

101. Debora V. Thompson, Rebecca W. Hamilton and Roland T. Rust, 'Feature fatigue: when product capabilities become too much of a good thing', *Journal of Marketing Research* 42 (November 2005): 431–42; Roland T. Rust, Debora V. Thompson and Rebecca W. Hamilton, 'Defeating feature fatigue', *op. cit.*: 98–107.

102. Robert E. Smith, 'Integrating information from advertising and trial: Processes and effects on consumer response to product information', *op. cit.*

103. Lutz Stobbe, EuP Preparatory Studies, 'Televisions' (Lot 5) Final Report on Task 3 'Consumer Behaviour and Local Infrastructure' (TREN/D1/40 lot 5-2005), compiled by Deutsche Umwelthilfe and Fraunhofer IZM (contractor: Fraunhofer Institute for Reliability and Microintegration, IZM: Berlin) (2 August 2007): 5.

104. James Surowiecki, 'Feature Presentation', *The New Yorker* (28 May 2007), accessed 23 May 2007, www.NewYorker.com

105. Sikka, Prem, 'Sleeping watchdogs', http://www.guardian.co.uk/commentisfree/2009/jan/14/corporatefraud, accessed 14 January 2009.

106. Jack Trout, 'Marketing in tough times', *Boardroom Reports* 2 (October 1992): 8.

107. Amna Kirmani and Peter Wright, 'Procedural learning, consumer decision making and marketing communication', *Marketing Letters* 4(1) (1993): 39–48.

108. *Ibid.*

109. Rupert Neate, 'Ad men use brain scanners to probe our emotional response', *The Guardian* (14 January 2012) http://www.guardian.co.uk/media/2012/jan/14/neuroscience-advertising-scanners?INTCMP=SRCH, accessed 27 January 2012.

110. www.neurosciencemarketing.com/blog, accessed 7 June 2009; Hotz, 'Searching for the Why of Buy'; Blakeslee, 'If You Have a "Buy Button" in Your Brain, What Pushes It?'; Thompson, 'There's a Sucker Born in Every Medial Prefrontal Cortex.'

111. Michael Porter, *Competitive Advantage* (New York: Free Press, 1985).

112. Linda Stern, 'Wanna Deal? Click Here', *Newsweek* (22 March 2004): 65.

113. Material in this section was adapted from Michael R. Solomon and Elnora W. Stuart, *Welcome to Marketing.com:*

The Brave New World of E-Commerce (Upper Saddle River, NJ: Prentice Hall, 2001).

114. 'Customer Product Reviews Drive Online Satisfaction and Conversion', *Marketing Daily* (24 January 2007), www.mediapost.com, accessed 24 January 2007.

115. Chris Anderson, *The Long Tail: Why the Future of Business Is Selling Less of More* (New York: Hyperion, 2006).

116. Jeffrey M. O'Brien, 'You're Sooooooo Predictable', *Fortune* (27 November 2006): 230.

117. Joseph Lajos, Amitava Chattopadhyay and Kishore Sengupta, 'When Electronic Recommendation Agents Backfire: Negative Effects on Choice Satisfaction, Attitudes, and Purchase Intentions', *INSEAD Working Paper Series* (2009).

118. Emily Burg, 'Leverage User-Generated Content to Boost Brands', *Marketing Daily* (13 March 2007), www.mediapost.com, accessed 13 March 2007.

119. Sangkil Moon, Paul K. Bergey and Dawn Iacobucci, 'Dynamic Effects among Movie Ratings, Movie Revenues, and Viewer Satisfaction', *Journal of Marketing* 74 (January 2010): 108–21; http://www.yelp.com/search?find_desc=restaurants&find_loc=Philadelphia%2C+PA&action_search=Search, accessed 31 May 2011; Anya Kamenetz, 'The Perils and Promise of the Reputation Economy', *Fast Company* (3 December 2008), www.fastcompany.com/magazine/131/on-the-internet-everyone-knows-youre-a-dog.html, accessed 3 December 2008.

120. Robert A. Baron, *Psychology: The Essential Science* (Boston: Allyn & Bacon, 1989); Valerie S. Folkes, 'The availability heuristic and perceived risk', *Journal of Consumer Research* 15 (June 1989): 13–23; Daniel Kahneman and Amos Tversky, 'Prospect theory: An analysis of decision under risk', *Econometrica* 47 (1979): 263–91.

121. Example developed from Ritesh Saini and Ashwani Monga, 'How I decide depends on what I spend: Use of heuristics is greater for time than for money', *Journal of Consumer Research* 34 (April 2008): 914–22.

122. Amos Tversky and Daniel Kahneman, 'Judgment under uncertainty: Heuristics and biases', *Science* 27, 185 (September 1974): 1124–131.

123. Ritesh Saini and Ashwani Monga, 'How I decide depends on what I spend', *op. cit.*: 915.

124. Wayne D. Hoyer, 'An examination of consumer decision making for a common repeat purchase product', *Journal of Consumer Research* 11 (December 1984): 822–9; Calvin P. Duncan, 'Consumer Market Beliefs: A Review of the Literature and an Agenda for Future Research', in Marvin E. Goldberg, Gerald Gorn and Richard W. Pollay (eds), *Advances in Consumer Research* 17 (Provo, U.T.: Association for Consumer Research, 1990): 729–35; Frank Alpert, 'Consumer market beliefs and their managerial implications: An empirical examination', *Journal of Consumer Marketing* 10(2) (1993): 56–70.

125. Ritesh Saini and Ashwani Monga, 'How I Decide Depends on What I Spend', *op. cit.*: 920.

126. Michael R. Solomon, Sarah Drenan and Chester A. Insko, 'Popular induction: When is consensus information informative?' *Journal of Personality* 49(2) (1981): 212–24.

127. Folkes, 'The availability heuristic and perceived risk', *op. cit.*

128. Beales *et al.*, 'Consumer search and public policy', *op. cit.*

129. Gary T. Ford and Ruth Ann Smith, 'Inferential beliefs in consumer evaluations: An assessment of alternative processing strategies', *Journal of Consumer Research* 14 (December 1987): 363–71; Deborah Roedder John, Carol A. Scott and James R. Bettman, 'Sampling data for covariation assessment: The effects of prior beliefs on search patterns', *Journal of Consumer Research* 13 (June 1986): 38–47; Gary L. Sullivan and Kenneth J. Berger, 'An investigation of the determinants of cue utilization', *Psychology and Marketing* 4 (Spring 1987): 63–74.

130. Raffaella Pacioloa and Li-Wei Mai, 'The Impact of Italianate on Consumers' Brand Perceptions of Luxury Brands', *European Association for Consumer Research Conference* (2010): 61.

131. Duncan, 'Consumer market beliefs', *op. cit.*

132. Chr. Hjorth-Andersen, 'Price as a risk indicator', *Journal of Consumer Policy* 10 (1987): 267–81.

133. David M. Gardner, 'Is there a generalized price–quality relationship?' *Journal of Marketing Research* 8 (May 1971): 241–3; Kent B. Monroe, 'Buyers' subjective perceptions of price', *Journal of Marketing Research* 10 (1973): 70–80.

134. Durairaj Maheswaran, 'Country of origin as a stereotype: Effects of consumer expertise and attribute strength on product evaluations', *Journal of Consumer Research* 21 (September 1994): 354–65; Ingrid M. Martin and Sevgin Eroglu, 'Measuring a multi-dimensional construct: Country image', *Journal of Business Research* 28 (1993): 191–210; Richard Ettenson, Janet Wagner and Gary Gaeth, 'Evaluating the effect of country of origin and the "Made in the U.S.A." campaign: A conjoint approach', *Journal of Retailing* 64 (Spring 1988): 85–100; C. Min Han and Vern Terpstra, 'Country-of-origin effects for uni-national and bi-national products', *Journal of International Business* 19 (Summer 1988): 235–55; Michelle A. Morganosky and Michelle M. Lazarde, 'Foreign-made apparel: Influences on consumers' perceptions of brand and store quality', *International Journal of Advertising* 6 (Fall 1987): 339–48.

135. See Sung-Tai Hong and Dong Kyoon Kang, 'Country-of-Origin Influences on Product Evaluations: The Impact of Animosity and Perceptions of Industriousness Brutality on Judgments of Typical and Atypical Products', *Journal of Consumer Psychology* 16, no. 3 (2006): 232–39; Richard Jackson Harris, Bettina Garner-Earl, Sara J. Sprick and Collette Carroll, 'Effects of Foreign Product Names and Country-of-Origin Attributions on Advertisement Evaluations', *Psychology & Marketing* 11 (March–April 1994): 129–45; Terence A. Shimp, Saeed Samiee and Thomas J. Madden, 'Countries and Their Products: A Cognitive Structure Perspective', *Journal of the Academy of Marketing Science* 21 (Fall 1993): 323–30; Durairaj Maheswaran, 'Country of Origin as a Stereotype: Effects of Consumer Expertise and Attribute Strength on Product Evaluations', *Journal of Consumer Research* 21 (September 1994): 354–65; Ingrid M. Martin and Sevgin Eroglu, 'Measuring a Multi-Dimensional Construct: Country Image', *Journal of Business Research* 28 (1993): 191–210; Richard Ettenson, Janet Wagner, and Gary Gaeth, 'Evaluating the Effect of Country of Origin and the "Made in the U.S.A." Campaign: A Conjoint Approach', *Journal of Retailing* 64 (Spring 1988): 85–100; C. Min Han and Vern Terpstra, 'Country-of-Origin Effects for Uni-National

and Bi-National Products', *Journal of International Business* 19 (Summer 1988): 235–55; Michelle A. Morganosky and Michelle M. Lazarde, 'Foreign-Made Apparel: Influences on Consumers' Perceptions of Brand and Store Quality', *International Journal of Advertising* 6 (Fall 1987): 339–48.

136. Teodoro Luque-Martinez, Jose-Angel Ibanez-Zapata and Salvador del Barrio-Garcia, 'Consumer ethnocentrism measurement – an assessment of the reliability and validity of the CETSCALE in Spain', *European Journal of Marketing* 34(11/12) (2000): 1353ff.

137. See Richard Jackson Harris, Bettina Garner-Earl, Sara J. Sprick and Collette Carroll, 'Effects of foreign product names and country-of-origin attributions on advertisement evaluations', *Psychology and Marketing* 11 (March/April 1994): 129–45; Terence A. Shimp, Saeed Samiee and Thomas J. Madden, 'Countries and their products: A cognitive structure perspective', *Journal of the Academy of Marketing Science* 21 (Fall 1993): 323–30.

138. 'Keeping European Consumers Safe', 2010 Annual Report on the operation of the Rapid Alert System for non-food consumer products, European Communities Health and Consumer Protection Directorate General, Luxembourg, 2011: 23.

139. 'EU steps up global battle over Parma ham, Roquefort cheese', *NYT online* (28 August 2003).

140. Durairaj Maheswaran, 'Country of origin as a stereotype: Effects of consumer expertise and attribute strength on product evaluations', *Journal of Consumer Research* 21 (September 1994): 354–65.

141. Raffaella Paciolla and Li-Wei Mai, 'The Impact of Italianate on Consumers' Brand Perceptions of Luxury Brands', in Alan Bradshaw, Chris Hackley and Pauline Maclaran (eds), *European Association for Consumer Research Conference 2010 RHUL*, page 61.

142. Sung-Tai Hong and Robert S. Wyer Jr, 'Effects of country-of-origin and product-attribute information on product evaluation: An information processing perspective', *Journal of Consumer Research* 16 (September 1989): 175–87; Marjorie Wall, John Liefeld and Louise A. Heslop, 'Impact of country-of-origin cues on consumer judgments in multi-cue situations: A covariance analysis', *Journal of the Academy of Marketing Science* 19(2) (1991): 105–13.

143. Wai-Kwan Li and Robert S. Wyer Jr, 'The role of country of origin in product evaluations: Informational and standard-of-comparison effects', *Journal of Consumer Psychology* 3(2) (1994): 187–212.

144. Maheswaran, 'Country of origin as a stereotype', *op. cit.*

145. Richard W. Stevenson, 'The brands with billion-dollar names', *New York Times* (28 October 1988): A1.

146. Douglas B. Holt, *How Brands Become Icons: The Principles of Cultural Branding* (Boston: Harvard Business School Press, 2004).

147. Richard W. Stevenson, 'The Brands with Billion-Dollar Names', *New York Times* (28 October 1988): A1; Eric Pfanner, 'Zipf's Law, or the Considerable Value of Being Top Dog, as Applied to Branding', *New York Times* (21 May 2007); Ronald Alsop, 'Enduring Brands Hold Their Allure by Sticking Close to Their Roots', *Wall Street Journal*, centennial edn (1989): B4.

148. Greg Morago, 'Envy: The Brand Sluts – Many Who Covet Their Retailers' Garb No Longer Look at the Logo', *Hartford Courant on the Web* (1 January 2007).

149. Jacob Jacoby and Robert Chestnut, *Brand Loyalty: Measurement and Management* (New York: Wiley, 1978).

150. Anne B. Fisher, 'Coke's brand loyalty lesson', *Fortune* (5 August 1985): 44.

151. Jacoby and Chestnut, *Brand Loyalty, op. cit.*

152. Ronald Alsop, 'Brand loyalty is rarely blind loyalty', *The Wall Street Journal* (19 October 1989): B1.

153. Betsy Morris, 'The brand's the thing', *Fortune* (4 March 1996): 72(8).

154. C. Whan Park, 'The effect of individual and situation-related factors on consumer selection of judgmental models', *Journal of Marketing Research* 13 (May 1976): 144–51.

155. Joseph W. Alba and Howard Marmorstein, 'The effects of frequency knowledge on consumer decision making', *Journal of Consumer Research* 14 (June 1987): 14–25.

156. Anish Nagpal and Parthasarathy Krishnamurthy, 'Attribute conflict in consumer decision making: The role of task compatibility', *Journal of Consumer Research* 34 (February 2008): 696–705.

157. David Kesmodel and John R. Wilke, 'Whole Foods Is Hot, Wild Oats a Dud – So Said "Rahodeb" Then Again, Yahoo Poster Was a Whole Foods Staffer, the CEO to Be Precise', *Wall Street Journal* (12 July 2007): A1.

How research into consumer attitudes led to the creation of the O₂ brand

JIM FREUND, Lancaster University Management School, UK

'. . . this case is emblematic of how brand engineering can transform not just the metrics of a business, but the morale of its staff, the esteem of its public, its ability to sustain competitive advantage and its potential to deliver future earnings.'

From 'It only works if it all works: how troubled BT Cellnet transformed into thriving O₂', written by VCCP, O₂'s advertising agency in *Advertising Works 13* published by the UK Institute of Practitioners in Advertising (IPA)

Background

In 2000 BT (the trading name of British Telecommunications plc) was keeping a careful eye on the rapidly changing global mobile market. There were several strong international mobile network operators, but two brands in particular looked as though they were on course to become truly global: Vodafone and Orange.

Vodafone was known for its great size and had a strong brand and reputation among business users. Orange, on the other hand, was particularly strong among consumers, and had since its creation in 1984 been known as a mould-breaking brand, with its daring abstract name, and its brilliant strapline – 'The future's bright, the future's Orange' – which summarised the essence of the Orange brand: optimism.

BT owned shares in many mobile companies around the world, and had a controlling share in mobile network operators in four European countries; but each of these four controlled businesses traded under a different brand:

- **BT Cellnet** in the UK
- **Esat Digifone** in the Republic of Ireland
- **Viag Interkom** in Germany
- **Telfort** in the Netherlands

Logos used by permission of BT.

In July 2000 BT formed a global mobile division called BT Wireless to manage all these diverse wireless interests. It was clear that considerable integration benefits could be realised by creating a single international mobile brand that could compete with the likes of Vodafone and Orange.

Research

A global research programme was commissioned by BT's Group Brand Team to understand what users felt about the current mobile brands, and understand what characteristics this new brand should have to appeal to those customers. The research examined the existing quantitative brand tracking in each country, and then qualitative research, consisting of focus groups with consumers and depth interviews with business customers, was carried out. The research was conducted in the UK, Germany, Ireland, the Netherlands, Spain, Japan and USA.

Japan was included in the research because it was ahead of Europe in terms of both the development of mobile technology and services, and consumer adoption of these new applications. And the USA was included because of its potential as a marketplace and because it had a very different perspective from Europe and Asia and a much more fragmented set of competing brands.

If the re-branding was going to go ahead, BT Cellnet in the UK was going to be the most important country at launch, not only because the brand owner was based there, but because it was financially the biggest of the companies that would be rebranded, therefore the risk of getting it wrong was the greatest.

The main research findings were:

1 Mobiles had become an essential tool and were highly integrated into people's lives. People could no longer imagine life without their mobile and 'would feel naked without it' (see slide from research debrief).

2 The physical handset brands, especially Nokia, were more emotionally involving than the network brands. Handsets encapsulate the benefit, whereas networks were generally seen as being associated with the monthly bill, the price you pay.

383

3 Desirable characteristics for a new mobile brand were found to be 'Liberating', 'Cool' and 'Tomorrow'.

4 Overall, there was little loyalty among customers to the four owned brands. Each of the four brands had quite a different image from the others, and only one of them – Digifone – was seen as being positive on both functional and emotional characteristics. BT was not well known by consumers outside the UK, and so should probably not be used as an element in the new brand. BT Cellnet in the UK was seen as an older brand and as being more for business customers than for consumers. The name Cellnet was seen as functional and pretty boring (Cellular-Network).

The fact that none of the existing brands were particularly strong opened the door to taking the big risk of rebranding them all. The fear was that the rebranding could be expensive and disrupting, might not be accepted by the customers and the media, and could damage the business of some or all of the companies. But the upside was that the new brand could revitalise all of the businesses, and create an integrated new European business that could soon become much greater than the sum of its parts.

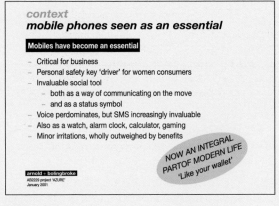

Figure 1

By permission of BT.

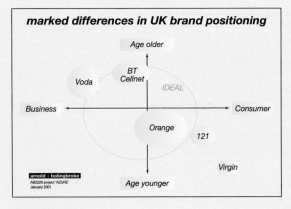

Figure 2

By permission of BT.

384

strong emotional and functional differences between brands

Figure 3

By permission of BT.

New brand

Once the evidence of this major research programme had been accepted, there was the exciting prospect (and anxiety) of creating a major new European communications brand. A pitch was arranged between four design agencies. The brief was written to inspire different thinking and create a truly original but relevant new brand name and visual identity. The agencies were told about the research findings and the new brand was described as follows:

It's serious. It's simple. It's global. It's cool.

It gets things done.

It makes you feel you can always get around things. Unless you leave it behind – then you're stuffed.

It's a very powerful thing to have – socially, at work, and just for the fun of it.

It's essential equipment for the modern world.

As regards the name, the requirement in the brief was:

Short is beautiful.

Real words are best.

Works globally.

Reflects the simplicity and power of the brand.

This brief led first to the name idea 'Oxygen', which was evolved into O_2 and the core idea: Essential for life. The winning agency Lambie-Nairn initially presented ideas in the pitch which included the bubbles in water as a way of visualising the invisible element O_2.

In that pitch presentation the O_2 logo was written using a font that was metallic silver in colour and looked solid, as though it was made of mercury. This prototype O_2 logo was designed to contrast with the fluidity of the water and oxygen imagery, and to represent graphically the solidity of the handset that had been found to be so popular with consumers in contrast to the intangible qualities of the network. This metallic logo was at first intended for use with various background colours including red, green and blue.

The pitch was unanimously awarded to Lambie-Nairn for transforming the strategic thinking and customer insights into a brilliant creative solution. Over the following weeks the early ideas were debated, researched and developed. The metallic logo was changed to plain white and was set in the Frutiger font – this was done so as not to distract from the impact of the main idea – the freshness and vitality of O_2 as depicted by the images of bubbles in blue water. For the same reason, the other background colours were also dropped.

What remained was a short, intriguing, original name, and a compelling and single-minded visual idea, based on a well researched customer insight. Like the new mobile services, it felt liberating and refreshing; it was everywhere; it was essential for life. The new name, visuals and brand ideas were tested among the various audiences and countries of interest. Some groups of customers in certain markets found the new name and branding too cold or abstract, and felt that people wouldn't get the link between oxygen and mobility; but other groups were very enthusiastic about the new name and graphics, especially younger consumers. The branding team felt it was an acceptable risk to push ahead with the O_2 brand, as it was considered more important to appeal strongly to some demographic groups, rather than to avoid offending any group.

Various factors have since made O_2 into a multi-billion pound brand: their extremely consistent application of the name and visual identity across their entire range of marketing communications, products and shops; their inspired use of sponsorship as a brand-building medium; their focus on keeping their existing customers happy rather than chasing new ones; their bold targeting of younger customers without alienating older ones; and their high standards of treatment of their employees – and all of this latter activity was set off on the right footing with the creation of a brand and identity that was original, relevant and based on customer insight.

This case study contains some important lessons in branding:

1 Take great care and adequate time to make the right naming and branding decisions at the outset of a venture.
2 Base your new brand on a strong idea.
3 The creative process occurs in a haphazard series of steps or leaps forward, e.g. new research insights or name ideas or visuals or core brand ideas can each spark off new ways of improving the other elements to build a coherent and integrated solution.

4 Sometimes elements of a solution that seem important and relevant need to be eliminated in order not to dilute and distract from the main idea. Less is often more.
5 Test your ideas on the audience at each stage – but don't be afraid occasionally to ignore parts of their feedback if you have a good reason to do so.
6 Once you have a great idea, be single-minded and ruthless in applying it and nothing else. O_2's rallying cry for marketing communications is 'It only works if it all works'.

'They have done a superb job. They have done a superb job on branding.'

Hans Snook, the founder of Orange, *The Times*, February 2004

QUESTIONS

1 What mobile brands operate in your country? Which ones are global and which ones are local? What are their strengths and weaknesses from a customer's point of view? Can you draw a positioning map which will draw out the main differences between the competing brands?

2 Can you think of any major brands that have rebranded and entirely changed their name and identity? Was the rebranding successful, or not? Did they just change the surface of the brand (how it looks, what it's called, the campaigns), or did the entire philosophy of the brand change (the services and products, pricing, distribution, the way they treat customers, brand personality, tone of voice).

3 Do you believe that qualitative or quantitative stakeholder research is most important to inform the process of creative development?

4 Set yourself a branding and naming challenge: select a product or service category that you are interested in (e.g. perfumes, mobile networks, beer) in your country. Imagine that you're rebranding one of the biggest brands in that category. Try to come up with the new brand including the name, the logo, the design look and feel, a strapline, and a definition of what the new brand should mean to its customers. What customer insight is your new brand based on? Will it use any elements from the existing brand, or do you believe you need to take the risk to kill off the old brand and launch a completely new brand? How is the new or revised brand positioned differently from the other brands?

Fear, guilt and shame: the use of emotions in advertising to change public behaviour

EFFI RAFTOPOULOU, Keele University, UK

Advertisers have always used a range of techniques to attract attention, increase the memorability of advertisements, create particular brand associations and ultimately sell their products or services to consumers. The use of emotion appeals in adverts has been quite popular as advertisers have always believed that the stimulation of emotions can exert a strong influence on audiences. The strength of the emotion generated by an ad is thought to be directly linked to consumers' reactions to adverts. Advertisements are frequently quite entertaining, funny, sexy or moving. However advertising is not only just about creating positive emotions. Advertisements also employ negative emotions, such as fear, shock, embarrassment, guilt or shame.

Despite the prominence of emotions in adverts, their effectiveness has been questioned by researchers, e.g. whether or not consumers actually feel the emotions intended by advertising (Campbell, 1995; Englis, 1990). In addition, advertisers have also been accused of manipulation by playing on people's emotions. This has been particularly the case with advertisements that draw upon negative emotions.

Negative emotions in advertisements

Negative emotion appeals have been used by commercial organisations. The (in)famous Benetton advertising campaigns in the 1990s is a particularly prominent example. The Benetton campaign drew on such hot topics as religion, homosexuality and AIDS in order to shock viewers. Negative emotional appeals are also frequently employed in charity and public sector advertising. Recent examples from the UK include an advertisement aimed at convincing people to stop smoking. The ad showed a hook going through a woman's mouth to represent the addiction to smoking. Another advertisement against child abuse depicts a scared little girl sitting in her room, listening out for the sound of approaching footsteps (presumably of a potential abuser).

Such advertising campaigns are often notorious for attracting a significant number of complaints from viewers disturbed by the images. The Advertising Standards Authority (ASA, UK) is typical of the organizations that seek to regulate advertisements as well as other promotional activities. The ASA are often faced with decisions about whether or not certain appeals are acceptable. The aforementioned anti-smoking advert, for example, has received the highest number of complaints in 2007 from viewers disturbed by the graphic imagery (Advertising Standards Authority and Committee of Advertising Practice, 2007). Similarly, an advert that showed a woman slapping her husband in a furniture shop also drew complaints from the public.

The Code of Advertising Practice states clearly that fear, violent images or distress should not be used without good reason or disproportionately; and that advertisers should avoid causing distress or offence to members of the public. However, this can be often a rather subjective call, particularly in cases where guilt, shame or embarrassment appeals are used. In view of the mounting criticism of advertising's manipulative tactics (e.g. Campbell, 1995; Cotte, Coulter and Moore, 2005), the question arises about whether or not such types of appeals should be used at all by advertisers in order to promote a product, service or a particular behaviour.

In this case study we examine a campaign against benefit fraud, which plays on emotions in a more subtle and indirect way. We begin by outlining the historical background of the campaign; and then we describe some of the ads used in the campaign which employed negative emotions such as fear and guilt.

The background

The campaign against benefit fraud was commissioned by the Department for Work and Pensions (hereafter DWP) in the UK. The issue of benefit fraud was particularly important for the Labour government from when it came to power in 1997. Benefit fraud was seen as an important problem for the DWP as it was estimated that around £2 billion pounds are lost every year through fraud and error in the system, 60 per cent of which relate to claims for Income Support, Jobseeker's Allowance and Housing Benefit (House of Commons Committee of Public Accounts, 2003). Benefit fraud remains an ongoing problem. The latest report from the Audit commission (May

2008) revealed a record £140 million of fraud and over-payments by local councils in England, up by 26 per cent on the previous year. This included £24 million in housing benefit fraud in this period (**http://www.guardian.co.uk/money/2008/may/20/scamsandfraud.localgovernment**).

On coming to power the Labour government tried to establish a strategy for the consistent evaluation and pre-vention of fraud. An influential report prepared by Lord Grabiner (2000) on the 'informal economy', argued that publicity and in particular advertising, should be used in order to change the culture of tolerance that sustains fraud. More specifically, it was suggested that advertising could be used in order, firstly to further publicise the benefit fraud hotline that had been in operation since 1997; and sec-ondly to change attitudes towards benefit fraud and show its consequences to the general public.

May 2000 saw the launch of the pilot campaign for Benefit Fraud. This campaign ran in the North West until November 2000 (National Audit Office, 2003). During July 2000, the first independent Benefit Fraud website was also launched. The same advertising campaign was launched nationally (February 2001), following evalu-ation of the pilot. The campaign has had several phases since then, with some changes in its advertising material and website.

In 2005, a strategy document 'Reducing Fraud in the Benefit System' (DWP, 2005) argued that the benefit fraud campaign (characterised as a campaign of deterrence) had achieved its goals of influencing public attitudes towards fraud and of raising awareness. The DWP proclaimed that the Targeting Fraud campaign would continue, with the aim of warning fraudsters and deterring potential cheats. The Benefit Fraud Hotline would remain as a medium for the deterrence of fraudsters.

So far, there are conflicting opinions about the cam-paign's effectiveness. Whereas an independent report suggests some viewers of the pilot perceived benefit fraud as easier to commit (DSS, Targeting Fraud Campaign Evaluation, 2001), the Minister of DSS claimed that evaluation results were encouraging (Rooker, J., Hansard, 26 April 2001).

The 'Reducing Fraud in the Benefit System' report (DWP, 2005) suggests that campaign evaluation (on the 5th wave of the campaign) shows that the belief that the Government takes benefit fraud seriously has strengthened, and attitudes against those who deliberately cheat the system have hardened. In addition it suggests that each phase of the campaign has led to a significant increase in the number of calls from the public about suspected fraud to the National Benefit Fraud Hotline. The DWP claims that the reduction in benefit fraud and error from 1998 until 2005 was 41 per cent (DWP, 2005), although the referrals from the website and the telephone hotline slowed down by 25 per cent in 2001–2 (the year when the campaign was most heavily promoted) as did the rate in the reduction of fraud (House of Commons Committee of Public Accounts, 2003).

The campaign has attracted a lot of attention in the media with several articles in the newspapers and a TV programme (*Panorama* programme on government advert-ising on BBC, May 26th 2002). The campaign also gener-ated discussion in Parliament (e.g. 25th April 2001, 26th October 2001). What made this campaign so significant for the media and politicians was that it demonstrated the increasing reliance of the UK government on advertising rather than on any other form of publicity (National Audit Office, 2003). In addition, the government was reportedly, during that time period, the biggest spender on advertising in the UK. This DWP campaign on benefit fraud received the highest funding from the Government in 2000–1 (£3.442 million) (Cozens, 2001).

Description of the campaign

The campaign makes use of a number of different media including the internet, television, radio, press and outdoor advertisements. The main aims of this campaign are firstly, to create a climate of intolerance towards benefit fraud and to undermine its social acceptability; and secondly to warn fraudsters or people that may be thinking about committing fraud that they will be caught and punished (DWP, 2005, p. 14). The target audiences are, therefore, not only benefit fraudsters or potential fraudsters but also the public, who may not perceive fraud as a real crime or may potentially assist fraudsters (National Audit Office, 2003).

A large number of the benefit fraud adverts depict a similar scene: a person, who is presumably a benefit fraud-ster, is pictured in a work setting. Usually this involves some type of seasonal or temporary work, e.g. decorating a house, working as a waitress at a seaside café, or working at a fairground. The viewer observes the situation through the camera lenses and the person in the advert seems to be unaware of the fact that they are being observed. A white spotlight is beamed at the central person in the ad. The cheat is captured in the spotlight, and the potential fraud-ster is shown at the centre of what appears to be a target (rather like a darts board). A caption underneath the adverts establishes the context for the situation by stating that it is benefit fraud not to declare employment; and that the DWP monitors and investigates benefit fraud. The advert then gives people who want to report fraud details of the confidential hotline and website.

This particular campaign therefore works on a rather subtle emotional level. It creates a sense of surveillance by suggesting the monitoring and targeting of benefit fraud-sters or of people that are thinking of committing fraud. The aim is to prevent the benefit cheats. The white spotlight-target signifies that the fraudster has been caught in the act, creating a sense that fraudsters cannot escape the vigilance of the authorities. The ad also seeks to deter potential fraudsters. Furthermore, the most recent adverts used the logo: 'no ifs, no buts', signalling a firmness and strictness towards benefit fraudsters.

Concluding thoughts

This campaign is one of the many advertising campaigns used by the government in order to try and solve social problems. It seems that the use of advertising for these purposes is an increasingly common practice in a number of countries. Since these campaigns concern important social issues and deep-seated attitudes, it is particularly important to ensure that appropriate and ethical advertising practices are adopted, particularly in the use of emotional appeals in the campaign messages.

QUESTIONS

1 Make a list of campaigns that are aimed at solving (or ameliorating) social problems. Which elements make these campaigns effective (or not)?

2 Is the use of emotional appeals in advertisements that help in the solution of social problems justified and if so, why (or if not, why not)?

3 What are the merits of using emotion campaigns in this context? What may be the potential adverse consequences?

4 The campaign on benefit fraud uses emotions (such as fear and guilt) in a rather subtle way. Discuss the ethical issues that may arise from this use of emotions; and assess the need for regulation of the use of emotions in marketing campaigns.

Sources

Advertising Standards Authority and Committee of Advertising Practice (2007), 'Advertising Standards Authority Annual Report 2007–8', available at http://www.asa.org.uk/NR/rdonlyres/F1CB4D0C-74BB-4B6E-8F48-01BA2465957D/0/Annual_Statement_20072008.pdf

Campbell, M.C. (1995), 'When Attention-Getting Advertising Tactics Elicit Consumer Inferences of Manipulative Intent', *Journal of Consumer Psychology*, 4, 3, 225–254.

Cotte, J., Coulter, R.A. and Moore, M. (2005), 'Enhancing or disrupting guilt: the role of ad credibility and perceived manipulative intent', *Journal of Business Research*, vol. 58, i. 3, pp. 361–368.

Cozens, C. (2001), 'Labour's 172 Advertising Campaigns', *The Guardian*, 26 April.

Department for Work and Pensions (October 2005), 'Reducing Fraud in the Benefit System: Achievements and Ambitions', in Fraud and Error Strategy Division, London.

Englis, B.G. (1990), 'Consumer emotional reactions to television advertising and their effects on message recall', in Agres, S.J., Edell, J.A. and Dubitsky, T.M. (eds), *Emotion in advertising: theoretical and practical explorations*, New York, Quorum Books.

House of Commons Committee of Public Accounts (2003), 'Tackling Benefit Fraud: Thirty First Report of Session 2002–3', The Stationery Office, London.

Lord Grabiner Q.C. (2000), 'The Informal Economy', The Public Enquiry Unit, HM Treasury, London.

National Audit Office (2003), 'Government Advertising', The Stationery Office, London.

Rooker, J., Hansard (26 April 2001), Column: 317W.

What do consumers do with advertising? 'This lemon is a bomb': how consumers read rhetorical visual imagery in advertising

LAMPROS GKIOUZEPAS, Technological Educational Institute of Thessaloniki, Greece

Context

This case study explores some of the issues faced by advertisers in creating visual metaphors in ads, and by consumers in interpreting visual metaphors in ads. Advertisers seem to use visual metaphors – like verbal metaphors – to make indirect claims about their brands. They have to make a number of decisions, e.g. about metaphorical terms; visual syntax; representation techniques; and the accompanying text. Consumers in their turn, as readers, have to recognize the relevance of the ad; to choose among alternative readings; and decide whether or not they should disregard counter-intuitive meanings.

Daphne's reading of the visual metaphor in the elemonate ad

Relevance

While Daphne was initially baffled by the ad visual of the lemon as an exploding bomb it did not strike her that the ad was merely a tragic advertising gaffe. Daphne felt sure that there was a reason for such a bizarre image and it was up to her to figure it out. Her *presumption* was that the ad visual was *relevant* in some way. Actually, she believes that every ad carries such a *promise of relevance*.

Interpreting the visual imagery

To start with, Daphne was rather puzzled about the significance of merging a real lemon with the top of a salt cellar (Sunkist, p. 128, Chapter 4). Then, she noticed that another lemon was about to explode (Fairy, p. 321, Chapter 8). A fuse was burning on the top of this second lemon. The headline for that ad 'explained' that this was because *Fairy* detergent can *elemonate* when it is used for washing-up. This was the first clue, and from here it did not take Daphne long to start working out the meaning of what – at first sight – seemed to be a rather strange image of an exploding lemon.

Visual syntax*

Fusing a lemon with a bomb might be one way to link these two objects together. Simply placing a lemon next to a bomb on a single page might be another way to point to a relationship between them (Figure 1). It seems, however, that the visual syntax (i.e. the way the objects within the ad are organized visually in relation to each other) differs in each case. In the first case, the advertiser is physically

---

*Visual syntax relates to the rules for ordering and combining visual elements in an advertisement so that the ads are comprehensible to consumers who read and interpret the adverts.

Figure 1 Lemon and bomb placed side by side

Procter & Gamble

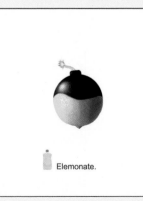

Figure 2 Lemon and bomb merged

Figure 3 Lemon resembling bomb

merging the two objects (see also Figure 2). This might be the equivalent of having the advertising say that the lemon *is* a bomb. In the second case, the advertiser seems to adopt a more subtle syntax. The objects are depicted in their entirety, separated from each other. It might be that the advertiser now says that the lemon *is like* a bomb. Still another way to present this metaphor visually might be to place lemons in such a way as to resemble the shape of a bomb. In this third case, the bomb is not physically present. Our fictitious reader, Daphne, would only have understood this point from the shape of the lemons (as they resembled the roundness of bombs in their physical appearance, rather than the more usual conical shapes of lemons). In this case it would be as if the advertiser had implicitly described lemons in terms of a bomb, but by exercising a certain amount of discretion never mentioned the word *bomb* explicitly by name. Similarly, the lemon's dried stalk could also be made to function like a fuse. The advertiser just had to make it burn (Figure 3). Alternatively, the lemon might prominently replace a bomb inside a wooden box stacked with explosive devices, fuses, and other bombs. Here, the advertiser does not describe the bomb or mention its name but gives away all its 'friends and acquaintances'. Volkswagen seems to adopt this latter visual syntax in its ad for the Passat Highline (Figure 4).

Recognition and visual representation

If the choices involved in the figurative use of the image of a lemon seem obscure, the skills required to understand such ads are probably even more complex. Daphne needs to be familiar with the objects to understand that what is visually depicted refers to a lemon, a bomb, a salt cellar or a pair of shoes. This might seem a case of elementary perception and recognition ability for Daphne, but this cannot be safely assumed for every reader. In addition, it is not even certain that Daphne has understood these objects in the same way as the advertiser does. The reading process becomes particularly demanding when some of the objects

Figure 4 Cars replacing a pair of shoes
Image courtesy of Volkswagen Group.

are only partially depicted or merely suggested by the rest of the visual. In the Passat ad, for example, the pair of shoes is not physically present in the picture. Daphne has to be familiar not only with the missing object (the shoes) but with an extended array of associated items and combinations, such as shoe boxes and labels, as well as the neat alignment of a new pair of shoes in their box, carefully wrapped up in tissue paper.

In addition, the viewer has to be accustomed to the representation technique used by the advertiser. Photographic records of the world might seem to be the easiest pictures for Daphne to read. And yet, even in the case of photography, slight variations in the camera angle used to depict objects might make their recognition more or less difficult. This implies that some angles of vision might be easier to understand than others. For instance, a picture of a lemon (standing upright) might come closer to an accepted norm than another picture of a lemon (where only the top of the lemon is visible). The importance of such prototypical views, in helping us understand the visual syntax of ads, is illustrated by the picture of the lemon in the *Fairy* ad. The lemon standing upright (Figure 5) or

Figure 5 A straight on view of a lemon
Procter & Gamble

Figure 6 A top view of a lemon

lying on its side is usually easier to identify as a lemon, compared with when only the top of the lemon is visible (Figure 6). In this respect, the Passat ad seems to be at a disadvantage because the pair of shoes never appear in the ad, they are 'absent' and can only be construed from hints and careful interpretation of the visual syntax. Furthermore, the car is shown in a rather unusual position. Importantly for the Passat, its sales are not as entirely dependent upon recognition of the product (drawing on the ad) at the point of purchase, compared with fast moving consumer products. For a product like *Fairy*, recognition is important as consumers walk along the aisles of the supermarket choosing their preferred product for cleaning dishes.

Interpretation

Daphne almost instantly inferred that what the advertiser implied was that the lemon had some of the (fatal) properties of a bomb. However, it seemed to Daphne that if it were not for her knowing that *Fairy* apparently does not sell bombs, the visual metaphor alone could be understood the other way around. That is, she could have understood the bomb in terms of the lemon; even if this just meant that the bomb was to be seen as a fresh one. Daphne, knowing the detergent product category and the brand, *Fairy*, decided against this rather bizarre interpretation. Nonetheless, she had to suppress some of the other properties that could be 'transferred' from the bomb and the lemon to the advertised product. For example, it crossed her mind that the detergent could be harsh for the skin. Both the explosive power of a bomb and the acidity of a lemon can bear testimony to this effect after all. Although nothing prevented her from drawing such inferences, Daphne thought that this was not what the advertiser wanted to convey to the reader. This interpretation did not seem legitimate to her.

Daphne also inferred that the detergent must be suitable for heavy professional use. The comparison with the bomb also suggested to her that *Fairy* could tackle tough stains. Furthermore, Daphne expected that this product would help her to do the washing-up faster. However, an additional interpretation could be that the dishes needed to soak in the detergent for a while in order to be completely clean, just as one has to wait a while before a bomb with a slow-burning fuse explodes. For some reason, Daphne also thought that the detergent should produce rich foam. Daphne had already drawn quite a few inferences about the ad's meaning but she was not quite sure which one to believe or what was actually its main message.

Anchored in text

The 'elemonate' title in the *Fairy* ad had already provided a very clear hint about the meaning of the ad visual. The combination of a noun (*lemon*) and a verb (*eliminate*) produced a new word, which was clearly anomalous and yet still comprehensible. Daphne could work out from the word elemonate that the detergent had some eliminating properties, and that also, somehow, lemon was responsible for these eliminating properties. Lemon had been a cleaning agent in many societies before the invention of detergents. However, Daphne still sensed that she had not fully uncovered the ad's main message. At this point, the verbal part of the ad came to her rescue. Daphne read, at the bottom of the ad, that *Fairy* can stop bacteria breeding on the sponge. The ad's main message was much clearer now. It might even be that the ad was so clear now that too much information had been given away, which might threaten the satisfaction that readers might derive from working out the solution implicitly posed by the ad (i.e. the role of lemon in eliminating dirt, odours and germs) without too much help. The solution was contained in fine print so that Daphne did not notice these extra clues to the puzzle in the ad at the beginning. Daphne regarded this as the final solution to the visual puzzle but she was unsure whether or not she was entitled to retain her other inferences or even draw yet more meanings from the ad.

Substantiation

The connections and the links that Daphne had to comprehend did not seem to stop either with understanding the combination of words or with interpreting what the synthesis of objects meant. The ad clearly implied a relationship between the lemon and the dish-washing detergent. Specifically, the ad seemed to propose that the lemon, somehow, stands for the advertised brand. This type of metonymical association is yet another instance of figurative 'language', where the whole is represented by the use of an associated element. Such a link might seem evident, but, in fact, Daphne remained clueless as to its real nature. For example, Daphne wondered whether the liquid detergent contains either a real lemon; or an artificial added lemon aroma; or just some of the ingredients of lemon. Or maybe the lemon and the liquid detergent bear no real relationship to each other? Although the advertiser could visually link the advertised product directly to the bomb, the advertiser preferred that the relationship between the bomb-like destructive powers of the detergent (towards dirt and germs) should be mediated by a lemon. Daphne, sceptical as she was, wandered whether it might be just as plausible for the consumer to believe in the detergent's power to stop bacteria when this is presented through the lemon, regardless of the nature of such an association between a lemon and the brand.

More visual connotations

The decisions which advertisers make when choosing visual objects for ads do not seem to depend solely on the product attributes that need to be communicated. Put another way, the message in this ad might not just be all about communicating the antibacterial power of a detergent. A highly prominent metaphorical object might also affect the mood of the ad as a whole. For example, the tone of an ad using a bomb might look aggressive. The choice did look threatening to Daphne. She would have preferred *Fairy* to use the magic power of a fairy as a gentler way to communicate its antibacterial action. However, on second thoughts, she wandered whether using the magic power of a fairy would have made the ad less realistic and thus less persuasive. Although she did not fully understand the link between the lemon and the detergent product, she thought that the link between a fairy and *Fairy* brand would have been even more irrational. She also thought, on the spur of the moment, that a plain white background would make the ad look more classy, rather like the Passat ad. She had always liked minimalist art.

QUESTIONS

1 Do you believe that all the product inferences drawn by Daphne are justified? Why did negative product attributes not prevail in her interpretation of the ad? Which communication model better supports your answer?

2 Text that explains a rhetorical visual might direct the interpretation of a visual. What might be the consequences of explaining either too much or too little to consumers in terms of ad liking, persuasion and comprehension?

3 Collect examples of advertisements that use visuals metaphors and try to identify the different ways used to visually link two objects. Can you classify them into meaningful categories? (*Hint*: think of the three ways suggested for combining pictures of lemons and bombs in the discussion of visual syntax above.) Consider how each category could affect important consumer responses such as attention, comprehension, ad liking and elaboration.

4 What is meant by syntax? (*Hint*: look up a definition in **http://dictionary.reference.com/browse/syntax**.) What is meant by visual syntax? What rules do you think advertising has to obey in order for consumers to be able to read the advertisements and understand them?

5 Choose one ad from the examples you collected of ads which use visual metaphor; and analyse the meaning as Daphne did for the elemonate ad, e.g. relevance; visual syntax; visual representation; interpretation; verbal syntax (anchored in the text); substantiation; more visual connotations. Does the ad you've found meet the key criteria of marketing managers, i.e. does it communicate the brand message effectively? If so, why? If not, why not?

Sources

Forceville, Charles (1996), *Pictorial Metaphor in Advertising*, London: Routledge.

Larsen, Val, David Luna and Laura A. Peracchio (2004), 'Points of View and Pieces of Time: A Taxonomy of Image Attributes', *Journal of Consumer Research*, 31(1): 102–11.

McQuarrie, Edward F. and David Glen Mick (1999), 'Visual Rhetoric in Advertising: Text-Interpretive, Experimental, and Reader-Response Analyses', *Journal of Consumer Research*, 26(1): 37–54.

McQuarrie, Edward F. and Barbara J. Phillips (2005), 'Indirect Persuasion in Advertising', *Journal of Advertising* 34(2): 7–20.

Phillips, Barbara J. (2000), 'The Impact of Verbal Anchoring on Consumer Response to Image Ads', *Journal of Advertising* 29(1): 15–24.

Pracejus, John W., Douglas G. Olsen and Thomas C. O'Guinn (2006), 'How Nothing Became Something: White Space, Rhetoric, History, and Meaning', *Journal of Consumer Research* 33(1): 82–90.

Scott, Linda M. (1994), 'Images in Advertising: The Need for a Theory of Visual Rhetoric', *Journal of Consumer Research* 21(2): 252–73.

Sperber, Dan and Deirdre Wilson (1986), *Relevance: Communication and Cognition*, Oxford: Blackwell.

Part D

EUROPEAN CONSUMERS AND THEIR SOCIAL GROUPS

The chapters in this part consider some of the range of social influences that help to determine who we are as well as our consumer behaviour. Chapter 10 looks at the influences that groups and social media have on consumer behaviour, and the particular influences that opinion leaders exert on our consumption deliberations. Chapter 11 provides a discussion of family structures in Europe, and identifies the many instances in which our purchase decisions are made in conjunction with the family. The chapter also points out the strong influence that age has on our behaviours as consumers, with an emphasis on the bonds we share with others who were born at roughly the same time. Chapter 12 focuses on factors that define our social classes, and how membership of a social class exerts a strong influence on what we buy with the money we make.

10 GROUPS AND SOCIAL MEDIA

CHAPTER OBJECTIVES

When you finish reading this chapter you will understand why:

→ Other people and groups, especially those who possess some kind of social power, often influence our decisions about what to buy.

→ We seek out others who share our interests in products or services.

→ We are motivated to buy or use products in order to be consistent with what other people do.
  - Certain people are especially likely to influence others' product choices.
  - The things other consumers tell us about products (good and bad) often are more influential than the advertising we see.
  - Online technologies accelerate the impact of word-of-mouth communication.
  - Social media are changing the way companies and consumers interact.

BOBBY tries to play sport just about every day. The obsession that started with football has expanded to include cricket, tennis and squash (depending on the season). He will happily leave work early to play for his company team, especially the 11-a-side league on a Monday evening. The original work team that Bobby played for now includes some of his closest friends, and they try to celebrate an important victory with a few drinks, with the importance of turning up for work the next day feeling fresh relegated to a poor second against the joys of forging a great team spirit.

Recently Bobby decided he needed new football boots, since the grip of his old trusty Puma boots had worn away, meaning rain, ice and whatever else happened to be on the football pitch was causing him to lose his footing. He has also got a bit sick of his mates ribbing him for his flashy shoes, which are the leftovers of uni days when the fashion was for garishly white boots. Amongst his workmates there is a certain amount of prestige to be upheld and since he has had his boots for so long, he feels he deserves some new ones anyway.

Bobby's mates had rather mixed things to say about Nike football boots. Bobby was tempted by the Nike Tiempo Legend IV Elite boot, which also offered customization by NIKEid. But Bobby really wondered if he could justify spending quite that much money on football boots. His friend Pete had also pointed out that the Nike Mercurial Vapors came in very strong colours, so Bobby decided those probably would not suit him. He would have liked to have stayed with Puma boots but there wasn't really the choice that he was looking for in their current offering. So that left Adidas (possibly Copa Mundial or the Kaisers), Umbro or maybe the T90s from the Nike range. Adidas represented his final choice, helped by the fact that many of his team mates wore them and said good things about the quality of the boot. The next decision was whether to get screw-in studs or moulded studs. Screw-ins invariably fell out in Bobby's experience, however much you tightened them, whereas moulded studs stayed in and could be used not just on grass but on good quality artificial pitches as well. However, Bobby had seen fellow team mates with moulded studs struggling to keep their balance on wet, muddy pitches, and since English pitches were frequently muddy Bobby decided he had to go for screw-ins, despite the fact he would have to buy a set of replacement studs. The only thing Bobby had to do now was to buy the most classic looking pair he could find. After all, some people want to stand out in the crowd, to be individual and different, but football is a team game . . .

R.J.W. HOGG, London

INTRODUCTION

Football is central to Bobby's identity: he was a sports-loving student, and remains an enthusiastic football player now that he is in the world of work; and his team mates influence many of his buying decisions for sports kit. We all belong to many different types of groups, some formal and some informal, some from our personal worlds (e.g. fellow football players) and some from our professional worlds (e.g. work colleagues). Our behaviour is often heavily influenced by the groups to which we belong, and we often seek affirmation from our fellow group members via our consumption choices.

This chapter focuses on how other people, whether fellow footballers and team mates, coworkers, friends and family or just casual acquaintances, influence our purchase decisions. It considers how our preferences are shaped by our positive group memberships, as well as by our dissociative reference groups, by our desire to please or be accepted by others, even by the actions of famous people whom we've never met. Finally, it explores why some people are more influential than others in affecting consumers' product preferences, and how marketers go about finding those people and enlisting their support in the persuasion process.

REFERENCE GROUPS

Humans are social animals. We belong to groups, try to please others, and look to others' behaviour for clues about what we should do in public settings. In fact, our desire to 'fit in' or to identify with desirable individuals or groups is the primary motivation for many of our consumption behaviours. We may go to great lengths to please the members of a group whose acceptance we covet,[1] and to avoid the group with which we do not wish to be associated.[2]

Bobby's football team is an important part of his identity, and this membership influences many of his buying decisions. Bobby doesn't model himself on just *any* footballer – only the people with whom he really identifies can exert that kind of influence. For example, Bobby primarily identifies with other sport enthusiasts, especially football players. The English Football League represents one of Bobby's most important *reference groups* whilst the English Rugby Union represents one of his dissociative groups.

A **reference group** is 'an actual or imaginary individual or group conceived of having significant relevance upon an individual's evaluations, aspirations, or behaviour'.[3] Reference

Table 10.1 Three forms of reference group influence

Informational influence	The individual seeks information about various brands from an association of professionals or independent group of experts.
	The individual seeks information from those who work with the product as a profession.
	The individual seeks brand-related knowledge and experience (such as how Brand A's performance compares to Brand B's) from those friends, neighbours, relatives or work associates who have reliable information about the brands.
	The brand the individual selects is influenced by observing a seal of approval of an independent testing agency (such as Good Housekeeping).
	The individual's observation of what experts do (such as observing the type of car that police drive or the brand of television that repairers buy) influences their choice of a brand.
Utilitarian influence	So that they satisfy the expectation of fellow work associates, the individual's decision to purchase a particular brand is influenced by their preferences.
	The individual's decision to purchase a particular brand is influenced by the preferences of people with whom they have social interaction.
	The individual's decision to purchase a particular brand is influenced by the preferences of family members.
	The desire to satisfy the expectations that others have of them has an impact on the individual's brand choice.
Value-expressive influence	The individual feels that the purchase or use of a particular brand will enhance the image others have of them.
	The individual feels that those who purchase or use a particular brand possess the characteristics that they would like to have.
	The individual sometimes feels that it would be nice to be like the type of person that advertisements show using a particular brand.
	The individual feels that the people who purchase a particular brand are admired or respected by others.
	The individual feels that the purchase of a particular brand would help show others what they are or would like to be (such as an athlete, successful business person, good parent, etc.).

Source: Adapted from C. Whan Park and V. Parker Lessig, 'Students and housewives: Differences in susceptibility to reference group influence', *Journal of Consumer Research*, 4 (September 1977): 102. Reprinted with permission of The University of Chicago Press.

groups influence consumers in three ways. These influences, *informational, utilitarian* and *value-expressive*, are described in Table 10.1. In this chapter we'll focus on how other people, whether fellow bikers, coworkers, friends, family or simply casual acquaintances, influence our purchase decisions. We'll consider how our group memberships shape our preferences because we want others to accept us or even because we mimic the actions of famous people we've never met. We'll also explore why some people in particular affect our product preferences and how marketers find those people and enlist their support to persuade consumers to jump on the bandwagon.

When are reference groups important?

Recent research on smoking cessation programmes powerfully illustrates the impact of reference groups. The study found that smokers tend to quit in groups: when one person quits, this creates a ripple effect that motivates others in his social network to give up cigarettes as well. The researchers followed thousands of smokers and nonsmokers for more than 30 years, and they also tracked their networks of relatives, coworkers, and friends. They discovered that over the years, the smokers tended to cluster together (on average in groups of three). As the overall US smoking rate declined dramatically during this period, the number of clusters in the sample decreased, but the remaining clusters stayed the same size; this indicated that people quit in groups rather than as individuals. Not surprisingly, some social connections were more powerful than others. A spouse who quit had a bigger impact than did a friend, whereas friends had more influence than siblings. Coworkers had an influence only in small firms where everyone knew one another.[4]

Reference group influences don't work the same way for all types of products and consumption activities. For example, we're not as likely to take others' preferences into account when we choose products that are not very complex, that are low in perceived risk (see Chapter 9), or that we can try before we buy.[5] In addition, knowing what others prefer may influence us at a general level (e.g. owning or not owning a computer, eating junk food versus health food), whereas at other times this knowledge guides the specific brands we desire within a product category (e.g. if we wear Levi's jeans versus Diesel jeans, or smoke Marlboro cigarettes rather than a national brand).

Two dimensions that influence the degree to which reference groups are important are whether we will consume the item publicly or privately and whether it is a luxury or a necessity. As a rule, reference group effects are more robust for purchases that are (1) luxuries rather than necessities (e.g. yachts), because products that we buy using discretionary income are subject to individual tastes and preferences, whereas necessities do not offer this range of choices; and (2) socially conspicuous or visible to others (e.g. living room furniture or clothing), because we do not tend to be swayed as much by the opinions of others if no one but ourselves will ever see what we buy.[6] The relative effects of reference group influences on some specific product classes are shown in Figure 10.1. This obviously does not mean that a reference group cannot exert influence on the consumption of private necessities.

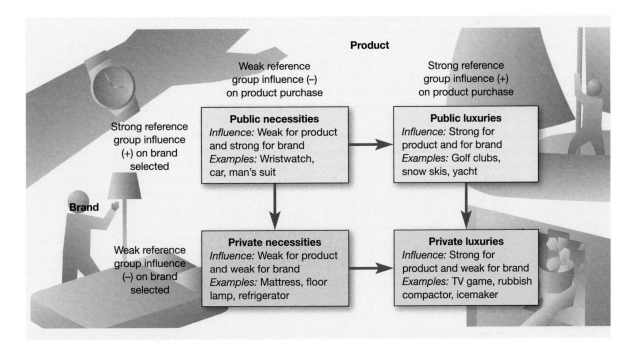

Figure 10.1 Relative effects of reference groups

Source: Adapted from William O. Bearden and Michael J. Etzel, 'Reference group influence on product and brand purchase decisions', *Journal of Consumer Research*, 9 (September 1982): 185. Reprinted with permission of The University of Chicago Press.

The power of reference groups

Why are reference groups so persuasive? The answer lies in the potential power they wield over us. **Social power** is 'the capacity to alter the actions of others.'[7] To the degree to which you are able to make someone else do something, regardless of whether they do it willingly, you have power over that person. The following classification of power bases helps us to distinguish among the reasons a person exerts power over another, the degree to which the influence is voluntary, and whether this influence will continue to have an effect even when the source of the power isn't around.[8]

Referent power

If a person admires the qualities of a person or a group, he tries to copy the referent's behaviours (e.g. choice of clothing, cars, leisure activities), just as Bobby's team mates affected his preferences. Prominent people in all walks of life affect our consumption behaviours by virtue of product endorsements (e.g. Lady Gaga for Polaroid), distinctive fashion statements (e.g. Kim Kardashian's displays of high-end designer clothing), or championing causes (e.g. Brad Pitt for UNICEF). **Referent power** is important to many marketing strategies because consumers voluntarily modify what they do and buy in order to identify with a referent.

Information power

A person possesses **information power** simply because she knows something others would like to know. Editors of trade publications such as *Women's Wear Daily* often possess tremendous power because of their ability to compile and disseminate information that can make or break individual designers or companies. People with information power are able to influence consumer opinion by virtue of their (assumed) access to the 'truth'.

Legitimate power

Sometimes we grant power by virtue of social agreements, such as the authority we give to police officers, border security officers at airports and ports and the armed forces. The **legitimate power** a uniform confers wields authority in consumer contexts, including teaching hospitals where medical students don white coats to enhance their standing with patients.[9] Marketers may borrow this form of power to influence consumers. For example, an ad that shows a model who wears a white doctor's coat adds an aura of legitimacy or authority to the presentation of the product.

Expert power

To attract the casual internet user, US Robotics signed up British physicist Stephen Hawking to endorse its modems. A company executive commented, 'We wanted to generate trust. So we found visionaries who use US Robotics technology, and we let them tell the consumer how it makes their lives more productive.' Hawking, who has Lou Gehrig's (motor neurone) disease and speaks via a synthesizer, said in one TV spot, 'My body may be stuck in this chair, but with the internet my mind can go to the end of the universe.'[10] Hawking's **expert power** derives from the knowledge he possesses about a content area. This helps to explain the weight many of us assign to professional critics' reviews of restaurants, books, movies and cars – even though, with the advent of blogs and open-source references such as Wikipedia, it's getting a lot harder to tell just who is really an expert![11]

Reward power

A person or group with the means to provide positive reinforcement (see Chapter 7) has **reward power**. The reward may be the tangible kind, as when an employee is given a pay rise. Or it can be more intangible, such as the approval the judges on *Strictly Come Dancing* deliver to contestants.

FUTURE GEOMETRIC AW 2012   FOR EVERY WOMAN YOU ARE *Only at* M&S

LEFT TO RIGHT: per una Dress £39.50 \ M&S Woman Top £19.50, Skirt £25 \ Limited Collection Dress £39.50 \   M&S Woman Coat £89 \ Limited Collection Jumper £29.50, Trousers £35 \ Limited Collection Jacket £55, Jeans £35

This Marks and Spencer advertising campaign used non-celebrities to endorse its message, 'For every woman you are'.
With kind permission from Marks and Spencer plc.

Coercive power

We exert coercive power when we influence someone because of social or physical intimidation. A threat is often effective in the short term, but it doesn't tend to produce permanent attitudinal or behavioural change because we revert fairly quickly to our original behaviour. Fortunately, marketers rarely try to use this type of power. However, we can see elements of this power base in the fear appeals we talked about in Chapter 8, as well as in intimidating salespeople who try to succeed with a 'hard sell'.

MULTICULTURAL DIMENSIONS

Norms change slowly over time, but there is general agreement within a society about which ones should be obeyed, and we adjust our way of thinking to conform to these norms. A powerful example is the change in attitudes towards smoking since the 1960s, when this practice was first linked with health concerns such as cancer and emphysema. By the mid-1990s, some communities in the US had outlawed smoking in public places. New York City did this in 2002. The Netherlands banned smoking from many public places in January 2004; Eire banned smoking in all public places in March 2004; Norway banned smoking in restaurants and bars in June 2004; Italy banned smoking in public places in January 2005; and Scotland introduced a ban in June 2006, followed by England in July 2007. In October 2003 the French government raised the price of cigarettes by 20 per cent in an attempt to cut levels of smoking; banned smoking in public places such as hospitals and government buildings in July 2007; and then extended the ban on smoking to include bars, cafés,

399

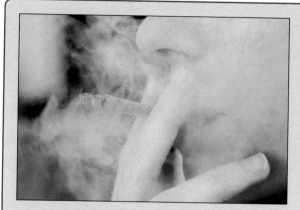

Around 10 million adults in the UK are smokers: 22 per cent of men and 21 per cent of women, compared with 51 per cent of men and 41 per cent of women in 1974.

Source: The Guardian, http://www.guardian.co.uk/society/2011/ jan/24/smoking-message-hits-home-cancer-rates
Photograph: Shutterstock.com

restaurants, hotels and night clubs with effect from January 2008. In Germany the ban on smoking in public places was introduced in January 2008, but met with some resistance.[12] Siggi Ermer (chairman of Germany's largest anti-tobacco lobby) argued that 'The smoking ban is a failure, it hasn't worked in the same way that it has in Italy, France and Britain. The difference is that there in each case you have a clear law that has put in place an absolute ban. Here we have a host of laws and major interpretation problems.'[13] However lung cancer remains a major cause of death amongst EU consumers (Figures 10.2 and 10.3 and Table 10.2).

There seems to be some evidence of downward trends in cigarette smoking, and a Citigroup report in 2011 suggested that 'Taking the very long view, it's hard to ignore 50 years of data. Smoking rates appear to be falling in a series of straight lines. If this continues, and it has for 50 years, then it means that the percentage declines in volumes will gradually accelerate . . . No-one

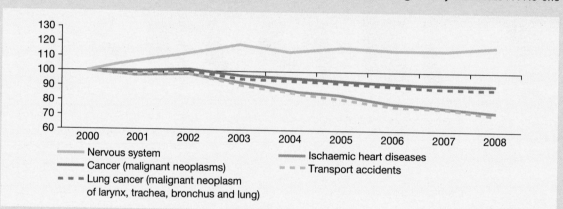

Figure 10.2 Causes of death: EU males 2000–2008

Source: Europe in figures – Eurostat yearbook 2011 p. 167, http://epp.eurostat.ec.europa.eu/cache/ITY_OFFPUB/KS-CD-11-001/EN/ KS-CD-11-001-EN.PDF, accessed 20 February 2012.

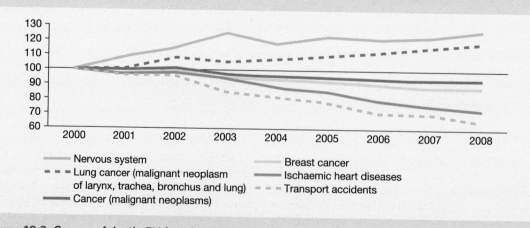

Figure 10.3 Causes of death: EU females 2000–2008

Source: Europe in figures – Eurostat yearbook 2011 p. 169, http://epp.eurostat.ec.europa.eu/cache/ITY_OFFPUB/KS-CD-11-001/EN/ KS-CD-11-001-EN.PDF, accessed 20 February 2012.

Table 10.2 Causes of death – standardized death rate, 2008 ([1]) (per 100,000 inhabitants)

	Total							Females	
	Cancer ([2])	Lung cancer ([3])	Colorectal cancer	Circulatory disease	Heart disease ([4])	Respiratory diseases	Transport accidents	Breast cancer	Uterus cancer
EU-27	**173.0**	**39.6**	**19.3**	**227.2**	**84.1**	**44.7**	**8.3**	**23.7**	**7.4**
Belgium	174.5	46.3	18.4	198.2	67.5	68.9	10.6	29.4	6.2
Bulgaria	171.6	38.9	22.7	611.3	126.0	41.7	13.3	23.3	13.1
Czech Republic	201.0	42.0	27.9	355.8	176.2	40.2	10.3	21.2	9.7
Denmark	208.0	53.9	26.2	193.7	71.6	60.6	5.8	31.1	7.0
Germany	162.6	35.0	18.8	223.2	86.4	37.7	5.4	24.6	5.6
Estonia	190.3	40.4	19.7	451.4	224.4	26.5	11.4	22.6	13.4
Ireland	176.7	37.7	20.6	190.7	102.3	64.8	6.2	31.1	7.8
Greece	157.2	40.8	12.4	258.9	67.3	53.5	14.1	21.7	4.9
Spain	154.6	36.5	19.8	151.4	47.4	52.8	7.2	18.2	5.7
France	166.0	36.6	16.7	124.7	33.8	27.3	6.9	24.1	6.4
Italy	163.7	35.9	17.6	179.1	62.0	29.6	9.2	23.6	5.4
Cyprus	121.6	22.0	9.4	208.6	73.9	36.3	11.6	22.8	7.1
Latvia	191.9	38.0	20.0	505.9	263.5	25.0	15.9	24.7	13.7
Lithuania	195.0	37.0	21.2	520.1	321.3	39.5	16.8	25.1	15.4
Luxembourg	167.7	44.4	20.5	210.8	63.8	43.4	8.7	20.5	7.3
Hungary	241.7	70.0	33.7	428.6	216.9	43.4	11.7	26.6	10.5
Malta	155.0	25.7	21.4	231.5	119.9	52.2	3.6	27.9	10.2
Netherlands	184.4	47.2	21.2	159.3	46.8	53.4	4.1	29.0	5.5
Austria	161.6	33.2	17.2	212.7	97.4	28.6	7.4	21.8	6.2
Poland	204.6	54.5	22.1	356.4	102.2	40.0	14.6	21.2	12.1
Portugal	155.6	25.5	22.4	184.9	44.4	62.0	9.1	19.8	7.7
Romania	179.7	41.5	18.8	557.9	194.1	49.5	16.6	21.6	17.8
Slovenia	201.9	43.2	26.2	234.9	67.4	36.4	11.5	27.4	8.8
Slovakia	201.7	38.6	30.3	465.0	280.5	49.9	13.3	22.1	13.3
Finland	137.0	26.0	13.3	224.0	128.8	22.3	6.9	19.8	5.0
Sweden	149.1	25.9	17.5	200.9	93.0	30.8	5.0	20.0	6.3
United Kingdom	178.1	41.1	17.8	188.7	93.0	73.7	5.3	26.8	5.9
Iceland	159.2	39.3	11.4	173.7	93.7	43.4	4.9	27.3	5.2
Norway	160.5	35.0	22.5	167.2	69.6	49.9	6.0	18.7	6.7
Switzerland	146.1	30.4	15.1	161.2	66.1	27.2	5.0	22.1	5.1
Croatia	212.6	49.4	28.6	402.7	157.1	33.7	15.0	25.8	9.8
FYR of Macedonia	170.0	41.7	18.1	573.9	92.2	37.8	6.0	23.9	13.4

([1]) Italy, Luxembourg, Malta, Sweden, the United Kingdom and Switzerland, 2007; Denmark, 2006; Belgium, 2005.
([2]) Malignant neoplasms.
([3]) Malignant neoplasm of larynx, trachea, bronchus and lung.
([4]) Ischaemic heart diseases.
Source: Eurostat (hlth_cd_asdr), http://appsso.eurostat.ec.europa.eu/nui/show.do?dataset=hlth_cd_asdr&lang=en

can be certain how smoking rates will play out in the distant future. [There are] three broad possibilities: Scenario A just extends the existing trend line until it hits zero. In Scenario B gradually fewer people quit, as we approach some sort of hard core of smokers, but in Scenario C smoking gets to a tipping point, as it becomes increasingly unacceptable and hence easier to regulate against. . . . We think that each scenario is quite plausible.

[But] it is quite possible that there will be no smokers left in Britain or many other developed countries in about 30–50 years. It is interesting to note that Finland passed an anti-tobacco law in September [2010] that declared its aim is 'to end the use of tobacco' in Finland. As far as we know this is the first example of a country putting such an aim in law. No target date was given, but the ASH Finland says 2040 should be the target. For us,

2060–80 seems a more realistic target to us, judging by the trends in the last 20 years in Finland.[14]

Much of the motivation to begin smoking at an early age is due to peer pressure; the alluring advertising images of smokers as cool, sexy or mature help to convince many young people that beginning the habit is a path to social acceptance. Because the power of advertising to influence attitudes is widely recognized, some groups have tried to fight fire with fire by creating anti-smoking ads that depict smoking as an ugly habit that turns people off.

Are these ads effective? One study of nonsmoking seventh graders examined their perceptions of smokers after being exposed to both cigarette ads and anti-smoking ads. Results were promising: the researchers found that those who saw the anti-smoking ads were more likely to rate smokers lower in terms of both personal appeal and common sense. These findings imply that it is possible to use advertising to debunk myths about the glamour of smoking, especially if used in tandem with other health education efforts.[15]

Types of reference groups

Although two or more people are normally required to form a group, the term *reference group* is often used a bit more loosely to describe *any* external influence that provides social cues.[16] The referent may be a cultural figure and have an impact on many people (e.g. Nelson Mandela or Michelle Obama); or a sportsman (e.g. the success of the World Road Champion cyclist, Mark Cavendish, in winning the coveted BBC Sportsman of the Year trophy in 2011, alongside Bradley Wiggins' success in the Tour de France, London Olympics and the same trophy in 2012 is forecast to stimulate cycling as a hobby, and thus the market for bicycles, in the UK[17]); or a person or group whose influence only operates in the consumer's immediate

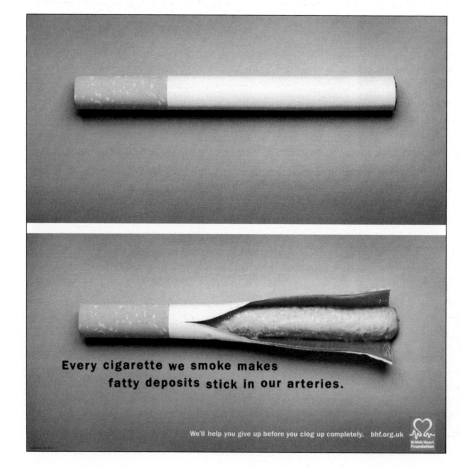

Every cigarette we smoke makes fatty deposits stick in our arteries.

We'll help you give up before you clog up completely. bhf.org.uk

This anti-tobacco advertisement draws on the legitimate and expert power represented by The British Heart Foundation, and combines it with stark images of the effects which smoking has on arteries – and thus on our health – to create a strong anti-smoking message.
Courtesy of British Heart Foundation.

'Family cycling in the Cotswolds. Cycling has soared in popularity in recent years.'
Photograph: Nick Turner/Alamy Images.
Source: The Observer, http://www.guardian.co.uk/lifeandstyle/2012/jan/29/cycling-boom-olympics?INTCMP=SRCH, accessed 31 January 2012.

environment (e.g. Bobby's various football teams, 5-a-side and 11-a-side). Reference groups that affect consumption can include parents, fellow football enthusiasts and team members, classmates, other leisure activity enthusiasts, a political party or even sports clubs such as Manchester United and bands such as U2 and Coldplay.

Some people influence us simply because we feel similar to them. Have you ever experienced a warm feeling when you pull up at a light next to someone who drives the exact same car as yours? One reason that we feel a bond with fellow brand users may be that many of us are a bit narcissistic; we feel an attraction to people and products that remind us of ourselves. That may explain why we feel a connection to others who happen to share our name. Research on the **name-letter effect** finds that, other things being equal, we like others who share our names or even initials better than those who don't. When researchers look at large databases like internet phone directories or Social Security records, they find that Johnsons are more likely to wed Johnsons, and people whose surname is Lane tend to have addresses that include the word *lane*, not *street*.[18]

Some groups and individuals exert a greater influence than others and affect a broader range of consumption decisions. For example, our parents may play a pivotal role in forming our values towards many important issues, such as attitudes about marriage and the family or where to go to university. We call this **normative influence** – that is, the reference group helps to set and enforce fundamental standards of conduct. In contrast, a Harley-Davidson club or Manchester United fan club exerts **comparative influence**, whereby decisions about specific brands or activities are affected.[19]

Formal *vs* informal groups

A reference group can take the form of a large, formal organization that has a recognized structure, regular meeting times and officers. Or it can be small and informal, such as a group of friends or students living in a university hall of residence. Marketers tend to have more control over their influencing of formal groups because they are more easily identifiable and accessible.

In general, small, informal groups exert a more powerful influence on individual consumers. These groups tend to be more involved in our day-to-day lives and to be more important to us, because they are high in normative influence. Larger, formal groups tend to be more product or activity-specific and thus are high in comparative influence.

Membership *vs* aspirational reference groups

Some reference groups consist of people we actually know; whereas others are composed of people we can either *identify with* or admire. These people are likely to be successful business

403

This ad of David Beckham promoting Emporio Armani underwear illustrates the use of celebrity endorsement in advertising campaigns; and also the importance of David Beckham as a cultural referent within the context of aspirational reference group influences.

Photograph: Getty Images.

people, athletes, performers, or whosoever appeals to us. Not surprisingly, many marketing efforts that specifically adopt a reference group appeal concentrate on highly visible, widely admired figures (such as well-known athletes or performers) and link these people to brands so that the products they use or endorse also take on this aspirational quality.[20] For instance David Beckham endorses a number of different products including Armani, and a large poster from the June 2009 campaign was reputed to have stopped the traffic when it was unveiled outside Selfridges.[21] One study of business students who aspired to the 'executive' role found a strong relationship between products they associated with their *ideal selves* (see Chapter 5) and those they assumed that real executives own.[22] Of course, it's worth noting that as social media usage increases, the line between those we 'know' and those we 'friend' gets blurrier. Still, whether offline or online, we tend to seek out others who are similar. Indeed, one study even found that people on Twitter tend to follow others who share their mood: people who are happy tend to re-tweet or reply to others who are happy, while those who are sad or lonely tend to do the same with others who also post negative sentiments.[23]

Identificational reference groups

Because we tend to compare ourselves with those who are similar to us, many promotional strategies include 'ordinary' people whose consumption activities provide informational social influence. How can we predict which people you know will become part of your **identificational membership reference group**? Several factors make it more likely:

- *Propinquity*. As physical distance between people decreases and opportunities for inter-action increase, relationships are more likely to form. We call this physical nearness **propinquity**. An early study on friendship patterns in a housing complex showed this factor's strong effects: residents were much more likely to be friends with the people next door than with those who lived only two doors away. Furthermore, people who lived next to a staircase had more friends than those at the ends of a corridor (presumably, they were more likely to 'bump into' people using the stairs).[24] Physical structure has a lot to do with who we get to know and how popular we are.

- *Mere exposure*. We come to like persons or things simply as a result of seeing them more often, which social scientists call the **mere exposure phenomenon**.[25] Greater frequency of contact, even if unintentional, may help to determine one's set of local referents. The same effect holds when evaluating works of art or even political candidates.[26] One study pre-dicted 83 per cent of the winners of political primaries solely by the amount of media exposure given to candidates.[27]

- *Group cohesiveness*. **Cohesiveness** refers to the degree to which members of a group are attracted to each other and how much each values their group membership. As the value of the group to the individual increases, so too does the likelihood that the group will influence their consumption decisions. Smaller groups tend to be more cohesive because in larger groups the contributions of each member are usually less important or noticeable. By the same token, groups often try to restrict membership to a select few, which increases the value of membership to those who are admitted. Exclusivity of membership is a benefit often promoted by credit card companies, book clubs and so on, even though the actual membership base might be fairly large.

Positive *vs* negative reference groups

Reference groups may exert either a positive or a negative influence on consumption behav-iours. In most cases, we model our behaviour to be consistent with what we think the group expects us to do. Sometimes, however, we also deliberately do the opposite if we want to distance ourselves from other people or groups who function as **avoidance** or **dissociative groups**. We may carefully study the dress or mannerisms of a disliked group and scrupulously avoid buying anything that might identify us with that group. Many consumers find it diffi-cult to express what they want whereas they can quite clearly express what they do not want. In fact, some researchers suggest that the phenomenon of distaste is much more decisive for our consumption choices but harder to study than tastes, since our choices are quite obvious compared to all the non-selected alternatives.[28] For example, rebellious adolescents often resent parental influence and may deliberately do the opposite of what their parents would like as a way of making a statement about their independence. In one study, college students reported consuming less alcohol and restaurant patrons selected less fattening food when drinking alcohol and eating junk food linked to members of avoidance groups.[29]

The motivation to distance oneself from a negative reference group can be as or more powerful than the desire to please a positive group.[30] That is why advertisements occasionally show an undesirable person using a competitor's product to subtly make the point that you can avoid winding up like *that* kind of person by staying away from the products they buy. As a once-popular book reminded us, 'Real men *don't* eat quiche!'[31] Today, others have adapted this avoidance group appeal to point out the ways we define ourselves by not consuming some products or services. For example, a T-shirt for sale on a computer-oriented website proudly proclaims, 'Real Men Don't Click Help'. Recent research suggests that 'dissociative reference groups have a greater impact on consumers' self-brand connections, product evalu-ations, and choices than do products associated with out-groups more generally'.[32] The web has encouraged the rise of a new kind of group – **anti-brand communities** (more on brand communities below). These groups coalesce around a celebrity, store or brand – but in this case they're united by their disdain for it. One team of researchers that studies these communities observes that they tend to attract social idealists who advocate non-materialistic lifestyles. After they interviewed members of online communities who oppose Walmart, Starbucks and McDonald's, they concluded that these anti-brand communities provide a meeting place for those who share a moral stance; a support network to achieve common goals; a way to cope with workplace frustrations (many members actually work for the companies they bash!); and a hub for information, activities and related resources.[33] Another study chronicles the level of opposition the Hummer inspires. For example, whereas brand enthusiasts celebrate the Hummer's road safety because of its size and weight, anti-branders who drive smaller cars criticise the vehicle's bulk. One driver posted this message: 'The H2 is a death machine. You'd better hope that you don't collide with an H2 in your economy car. You can kiss your ass goodbye thanks to the H2's massive weight and raised bumpers. Too bad you couldn't afford an urban assault vehicle of your own.'[34]

Before it released the popular Xbox game *Halo 2*, Bungie Studios put up a website to explain the story line. However, there was a catch: the story was written from the point of view of the Covenant (the aliens who are preparing to attack Earth in the game) – and in *their* language. Within 48 hours, avid gamers around the world shared information in gaming chat rooms to crack the code and translate the text. More than 1.5 million people preordered the game before its release.[35] This cooperative effort illustrates a major trend in consumer behaviour.

Brand communities and tribes

Some marketing researchers are embracing a new perspective on reference groups as they identify groups built around a shared allegiance to a product or activity. A **brand community** is a set of consumers who share a set of social relationships based upon usage of or interest in a product. Unlike other kinds of communities, these members typically do not live near each other – and they often meet only for brief periods at organized events called **brand-fests**, such as those sponsored by Jeep, Saturn or Harley-Davidson. These brand-fests help owners to 'bond' with fellow enthusiasts and strengthen their identification with the product as well as with others they meet who share their passion. In virtually any category, you'll find passionate brand communities (in some cases devoted to brands that don't even exist anymore); examples include the Apple Newton (discontinued personal digital assistant), and the BMW MINI (car) (see the case study by Maclaran and Beh at the end of Part A).

Researchers find that people who participate in these events feel more positive about the products as a result and this enhances brand loyalty. They are more forgiving than others of product failures or lapses in service quality, and less likely to switch brands even if they learn that competing products are as good or better. Furthermore, these community members become emotionally involved in the company's welfare, and they often serve as brand missionaries by carrying its marketing message to others.[36]

There is also evidence that brand community members do more than help the product build buzz; their inputs actually create added value for themselves and other members as they develop better ways to use and customize products. For example, it's common for experienced users to coach 'newbies' in ways to maximize their enjoyment of the product so that more and more people benefit from a network of satisfied participants. In other cases members benefit because their communities empower them to learn; for example, a study that looked at people who suffered from thyroid problems and who indicated they were uninformed and ill prepared to make decisions about their treatment later exhibited more active involvement and informed decision making after they participated in an online community with others who shared their health issues.[37] Figure 10.4 demonstrates this process of **collective value creation**.[38]

The notion of a **consumer tribe** is similar to a brand community; it is a group of people who share a lifestyle and who can identify with each other through a shared allegiance to an

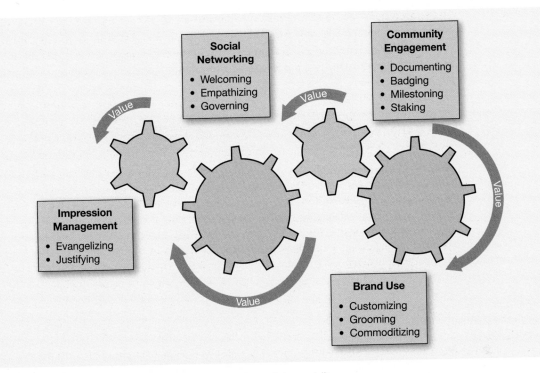

Figure 10.4 Collective value creation (Shau, Muniz and Arnould)

Source: Reprinted with permission from *Journal of Marketing*, published by the American Marketing Association, Schau, Hope Jensen, Albert M. Muñiz, and Eric J. Arnould, September 2009, 73, 30–51.

activity or a product. Although these tribes are often unstable and short-lived, at least for a time members identify with others through shared emotions, moral beliefs, styles of life, and of course the products they jointly consume as part of their tribal affiliation. Some companies, especially those that are more youth oriented, are using **tribal marketing** to link their product to the needs of a group as a whole. Many tribes devoted to activities like skateboarding or football are youth oriented, and we will talk more about these in Chapter 11. However, there are also plenty of tribes with older members, such as car enthusiasts who gather to celebrate such cult products (see Chapter 6) as the Citroën and Mini Cooper in Europe and the Ford Mustang in the US.[39]

Other research has identified **communities of practice** as a potentially valuable way of understanding and interpreting group behaviour. Communities of practice are 'an aggregate of people who come together around mutual engagement in an endeavour'.[40] Developed from work in socio-linguistics, communities of practice are usually defined by three characteristics: 'mutual engagement; a joint enterprise; and a shared repertoire'.[41] A study of Bolton schoolgirls showed how consumption symbols (e.g. Rockport shoes) could be combined with other social symbols (e.g. language) in order to create meanings related to group identity:[42] 'we are surrounded by stylistic material, and as long as we can position ourselves in relation to the sources of that material, and attribute meaning to it, we can use it'.[43]

When reference groups are important

Reference group influences are not equally powerful for all types of products and consumption activities, as we have seen above. However, we know that we can get away with more when we are in a group, for instance in the purchase of services. With more people in a group, it becomes less likely that any one member will be singled out for attention. People in larger groups, or those in situations where they are unlikely to be identified, tend to focus less attention on themselves, so normal restraints on behaviour are reduced. You may have observed that people sometimes behave more wildly at fancy dress parties, at hen or stag parties or partying on, for example, charter holidays, than they would normally do. This phenomenon is known as **de-individuation**. This is a process in which individual identities get submerged within a group.

MULTICULTURAL DIMENSIONS

University parties sometimes illustrate the dark side of de-individuation when students are encouraged by their peers to consume almost superhuman volumes of alcohol in group settings. About 4.5 million young people in the US are estimated to be alcohol-dependent or problem drinkers. Binge drinking among university students is reaching epidemic proportions. In a two-week period, 42 per cent of all college students engage in binge drinking (more than five drinks at a time) versus 33 per cent of their non-university counterparts. One in three students drinks primarily to get drunk, including 35 per cent of university women. For most, social pressure to abandon all inhibitions is the culprit.[44] Binge drinking is also increasingly recognized as a problem in the UK,[45] and not only among university students.[46] A recent UK study identified how students seek to 'neutralise potential feelings of guilt and stigmatisation regarding their alcohol consumption . . . Analysis highlights the importance of alcohol consumption in students' lifestyles, but also the potential identity conflicts experienced by all drinkers, regardless of the amount consumed. Heavy drinkers primarily employ neutralisation techniques as a means to rationalise the negative impacts of their actions, whereas abstainers and near-abstainers mainly use counter-neutralisation techniques as a means to reinforce their commitment to lifestyles which run counter to mainstream student life expectations. However, regardless of the amount of alcohol consumed, all participants employed neutralizing and counter-neutralizing arguments in some social situations.[47]

Social loafing is a similar effect. It happens when we do not devote as much effort to a task because our contribution is part of a larger group effort.[48] Waiting staff are painfully aware of social loafing: people who eat in groups tend to tip less per person than when they are eating alone.[49] For this reason, many restaurants automatically add on a fixed gratuity for groups of six or more.

Furthermore, the decisions we make as part of a group tend to differ from those that each of us might choose if we were on our own. The **risky shift effect** refers to the observation that in many cases, group members show a greater willingness to consider riskier alternatives following group discussion than they would if each group member made his or her decision without talking about it with others.[50] Psychologists propose several explanations for this increased riskiness. One possibility is that something similar to social loafing occurs. As more people are involved in a decision, each individual is less accountable for the outcome, resulting in *diffusion of responsibility*.[51] The practice of placing blanks in at least one of the rifles used by a firing squad is one way of diffusing each soldier's responsibility for the death of a prisoner because it is never certain who actually shot him. Another explanation is termed the *value hypothesis* which states that our culture values risky behaviour, so when people make decisions in groups they conform to this expectation.[52]

Research evidence for the risky shift is mixed. A more general finding is that group discussion tends to increase **decision polarization**. Therefore, whichever direction the group members were leaning towards before discussion began – whether towards a risky choice or towards a more conservative choice – becomes even more extreme in that direction after discussion. Group discussions regarding product purchases tend to create a risky shift for low-risk items, but they yield more conservative group decisions for high-risk products.[53]

Shopping patterns

Even shopping behaviour changes when people do it in groups. For example, people who shop with at least one other person tend to make more unplanned purchases, buy more and

Costumes hide our true identities and encourage de-individuation.
Martin Dalton/Alamy Images.

cover more areas of a store than those who go alone.[54] These effects are due to both normative and informational social influence. Group members may buy something to gain the approval of the others, or the group may simply be exposed to more products and stores by pooling information with the group. For these reasons, retailers are well advised to encourage group shopping activities.

The famous Tupperware party is a successful example of a **home shopping party** that capitalizes on group pressure to boost sales.[55] A company representative makes a sales presentation to a group of people who have gathered in the home of a friend or acquaintance. The shopping party works because of **informational social influence**. Participants model the behaviour of others who provide them with information about how to use certain products, especially since the home party is likely to be attended by a relatively homogeneous group (e.g. neighbourhood housewives). Normative social influence also operates because others can easily observe our actions. Pressures to conform may be particularly intense and may escalate as more and more group members begin to 'cave in' (this process is sometimes termed the *bandwagon effect*). In addition, these parties may activate de-individuation and/or the risky shift. As consumers get caught up in the group, they may find themselves willing to try new products they would not normally consider. These same dynamics underlie the latest wrinkle on the Tupperware home-selling technique: the Botox party. The craze for Botox injections that paralyze facial nerves to reduce wrinkles (for up to 6 months) is fuelled by gatherings where dermatologists or plastic surgeons redefine the definition of house calls. For patients, mixing cocktail hour with cosmetic injections takes some of the anxiety out of the procedure. Egged on by the others at the party, a doctor can dewrinkle as many as 10 patients in an hour. An advertising executive who worked on the Botox marketing strategy explained that the **membership reference group** appeal is more effective than the traditional route that uses a celebrity spokesperson to tout the injections in advertising: 'We think it's more persuasive to think of your next-door neighbour using it.'[56]

CONFORMITY

In every age there are those who 'march to the beat of their own drum'. However, most people tend to follow society's expectations regarding how they should act and look (with a little improvisation here and there, of course). **Conformity** refers to a change in beliefs or actions as a reaction to real or imagined group pressure. In order for a society to function, its members develop **norms**, or informal rules that govern behaviour. If such a system of agreements and rules did not evolve, chaos would result. Imagine the confusion if a simple norm such as sitting down to attend class did not exist.

We conform in many small ways every day – even though we don't always realize it. Unspoken rules govern many aspects of consumption. In addition to norms regarding appropriate use of clothing and other personal items, we conform to rules that include gift-giving (we expect birthday presents from loved ones and get upset if they do not materialize), sex roles (men were often expected to pick up the bill on a first date, though this convention is changing) and personal hygiene (we are expected to shower or bathe regularly to avoid offending others). We also observe conformity in the online world; research supports the idea that consumers are more likely to show interest in a product if they see that it is already very popular. One study analysed how millions of Facebook users adopted apps to personalize their pages. Researchers tracked, on an hourly basis, the rate at which 2,700 apps were installed by 50 million Facebook users. They discovered that once an app had reached a rate of about 55 installations a day, its popularity started to soar. Facebook friends were notified when one of their online buddies adopted a new app, and they could also see a list of the most popular ones. Apparently this popularity feedback was the key driver that determined whether still more users would download the software.[57]

Types of social influence

Just as the bases for social power can vary, so the process of social influence operates in several ways.[58] Sometimes a person is motivated to model the behaviour of others because this mimicry is believed to yield rewards such as social approval or money. At other times, the social influence process occurs simply because the person honestly does not *know* the correct way to respond and is using the behaviour of the other person or group as a cue to ensure that they are responding correctly.[59] **Normative social influence** occurs when a person conforms to meet the expectations of a person or group.

In contrast, **informational social influence** refers to conformity that occurs because the group's behaviour is taken as evidence of reality: if other people respond in a certain way in an ambiguous situation, we may mimic their behaviour because this appears to be the correct thing to do.[60]

Reasons for conformity

Conformity is not an automatic process, and many factors contribute to the likelihood that consumers will pattern their behaviour after others.[61] Among the factors that affect the likelihood of conformity are the following:

- *Cultural pressures*. Different cultures encourage conformity to a greater or lesser degree. The American slogan 'Do your own thing' in the 1960s reflected a movement away from conformity and towards individualism. In contrast, Japanese society is characterized by the dominance of collective well-being and group loyalty over individuals' needs. Most European societies are situated somewhere between these two, in this respect, 'extreme' cultures. In an analysis of the reading of a soft drinks TV commercial, Danish consumers stressed the group solidarity that they saw in the ad, an aspect not mentioned at all by the American sample.[62]

- *Fear of deviance*. The individual may have reason to believe that the group will apply *sanctions* to punish nonconforming behaviours. It is not unusual to observe adolescents shunning a peer who is 'different' or a corporation or university passing over a person for promotion because they are not a 'team player'.

- *Commitment.* The more people are dedicated to a group and value their membership in it, the more motivated they are to do what the group wants. Rock groupies and followers of religious sects may do anything that is asked of them, and terrorists (or martyrs and freedom fighters, depending on the perspective) may be willing to die for the good of their cause. According to the **principle of least interest**, the person that is least committed to staying in a relationship has the most power, because that party doesn't care as much if the other person rejects them.[63]

- *Group unanimity, size and expertise.* As groups gain in power, compliance increases. It is often harder to resist the demands of a large number of people than just a few, and this difficulty is compounded when the group members are perceived to know what they are talking about.

- *Susceptibility to interpersonal influence.* This trait refers to an individual's need to have others think highly of them. This enhancement process is often accompanied by the acquisition of products the person believes will impress their audience and by the tendency to learn about products by observing how others use them.[64] Consumers who are low on this trait have been called *role-relaxed*; they tend to be older, affluent and to have high self-confidence. Based on research identifying role-relaxed consumers, Subaru created a communications strategy to reach these people. In one commercial, a man is heard saying, 'I want a car . . . Don't tell me about wood panelling, about winning the respect of my neighbours. They're my neighbours. They're not my heroes.'

Social comparison: 'How am I doing?'

Informational social influence implies that sometimes we look to the behaviour of others to provide a yardstick about reality. **Social comparison theory** asserts that this process occurs as a way of increasing the stability of one's self-evaluation, especially when physical evidence is unavailable.[65] Social comparison even applies to choices for which there are no objectively correct answers. Such stylistic decisions as tastes in music and art are assumed to be a matter of individual choice, yet people often assume that some choices are 'better' or more 'correct' than others.[66] If you have ever been responsible for choosing the music to play at a party, you can probably appreciate the social pressure involved in choosing the right 'mix'.

Although people often like to compare their judgements and actions with those of others, they tend to be selective about precisely who they will use as benchmarks. Similarity between the consumer and others used for social comparison boosts confidence that the information is accurate and relevant (though we may find it more threatening to be outperformed by someone similar to ourselves).[67] We tend to value the views of obviously dissimilar others only when we are reasonably certain of our own.[68]

Social comparison theory has been used to explore the effects of advertising images on women's self-perceptions of their physical attractiveness and their levels of self-esteem.[69] Many early studies showed that social comparison, when studied in terms of only self-evaluation, is likely to have a negative effect on self-esteem. However, the incorporation of the specific goal (self-evaluation; self-improvement; or self-enhancement)[70] suggests that social comparison can have either positive or negative effects on self-feelings depending on the goal for social comparison.[71] One study suggests that the direction of spontaneous social comparison and social evaluation processes may be determined by fairly subtle cues. Whereas most advertising research suggests that comparisons with idealized models lead to contrast, this study found evidence that comparisons can also lead to assimilation of standards into the self-evaluation.[72]

In general people tend to choose a *co-oriented peer*, or a person of equivalent standing, when performing social comparison. For example, a study of adult cosmetics users found that women were more likely to seek information about product choices from similar friends to

Dove deodorant 7 day test

This advert for deodorant illustrates a message appeal based on conforming to the unspoken rule about personal hygiene in many societies.

With kind permission from Unilever (file supplied by The Advertising Archives).

reduce uncertainty and to trust the judgements of similar others.[73] The same effects have been found for evaluations of products as diverse as men's suits and coffee.[74]

Resistance to influence

Many people pride themselves on their independence, unique style or ability to resist the best efforts of salespeople and advertisers to buy products.[75] Indeed, individuality should be encouraged by the marketing system: innovation creates change and demand for new products and styles.

Anti-conformity *vs* independence

It is important to distinguish between *independence* and *anti-conformity*; in anti-conformity, defiance of the group is the actual object of behaviour.[76] Some people will go out of their way *not* to buy whatever happens to be in fashion. Indeed, they may spend a lot of time and effort to ensure that they will not be caught 'in style'. This behaviour is a bit of a paradox, because in order to be vigilant about not doing what is expected, one must always be aware of what is expected. In contrast, truly independent people are oblivious to what is expected; they 'march to the beat of own drum'.

Reactance and the need for uniqueness

People have a deep-seated need to preserve freedom of choice. When they are threatened with a loss of this freedom, they try to overcome this loss. This negative emotional state is termed **reactance**, and results when we are deprived of our freedom to choose.[77] This feeling can drive us to value forbidden things even if they wouldn't be that interesting to us otherwise. For example, efforts to censor books, television shows or rock music because some people find the content objectionable may result in an *increased* desire for these products by the public.[78] Similarly, extremely overbearing promotions that tell consumers they must or should use a product may lose customers in the long run, even those who were already loyal to the advertised brand. Reactance is more likely to occur when the perceived threat to one's freedom increases and as the threatened behaviour's importance to the consumer also increases.

If you have ever arrived at a party wearing the same outfit as someone else, you know how upsetting it can be, a reaction resulting from a search for uniqueness.[79] Consumers who have been led to believe they are not unique are more likely to try to compensate by increasing their creativity, or even to engage in unusual experiences. In fact, this is one explanation for the purchase of relatively obscure brands. People may try to establish a unique identity by deliberately *not* buying market leaders.

This desire to carve out a unique identity was the rationale behind Saab's shift from stressing engineering and safety in its marketing messages to appealing to people to 'find your own road'. According to a Saab executive, 'Research companies tell us we are moving into a period where people feel good about their choices because it fits their own self-concept rather than social conventions.'[80]

OPINION LEADERSHIP

Although consumers get information from personal sources, they tend not to ask just *anyone* for advice about purchases. If you decide to buy a new stereo, you will most likely seek advice from a friend who knows a lot about sound systems. This friend may own a sophisticated system, or she may subscribe to specialized magazines such as *Stereo Review* and spend free time browsing through electronics stores. On the other hand, you may have another friend who has a reputation for being stylish and who spends his free time reading fashion and lifestyle magazines and shopping at trendy boutiques. While you might not bring up your stereo problem with them, you may take them with you to shop for a new wardrobe.

The nature of opinion leadership

Everyone knows people who are knowledgeable about products and whose advice others take seriously. This individual is an **opinion leader**, a person who is frequently able to influence others' attitudes or behaviours.[81] Clearly, some people's recommendations carry more weight than others. Opinion leaders are extremely valuable information sources because they possess the social power we discussed earlier in the chapter:

- They are technically competent, so they possess expert power.[82]
- They prescreen, evaluate and synthesize product information in an unbiased way, so they possess knowledge power.[83]
- They are socially active and highly interconnected in their communities.[84]
- They are likely to hold offices in community groups and clubs and to be active outside of the home. As a result, opinion leaders often wield legitimate power by virtue of their social standing.
- They tend to be similar to the consumer in terms of their values and beliefs, so they possess referent power. Note that although opinion leaders are set apart by their interest or expertise in a product category, they are more convincing to the extent that they are *homophilous* rather than *heterophilous*. **Homophily** refers to the degree to which a pair of individuals is similar in terms of education, social status and beliefs.[85] Effective opinion leaders tend to be slightly higher in terms of status and educational attainment than those they influence, but not so high as to be in a different social class.
- Opinion leaders are often among the first to buy new products, so they absorb much of the risk. This experience reduces uncertainty for the rest of us who are not as courageous. Furthermore, whereas company-sponsored communications tend to focus exclusively on the positive aspects of a product, the hands-on experience of opinion leaders makes them more likely to impart *both* positive and negative information about product performance. Thus, they are more credible because they have no 'axe to grind'.

Opinion leadership is a big factor in the marketing of athletic shoes. Many styles first become popular in the inner city and then spread by word-of-mouth.

Carl Schneider/Getty Images.

Whereas individual behavioural and psychological traits are the most important in identifying opinion leaders, there are some indications that opinion leadership does not function the same way in different cultures. For example, there are cultural differences in how much people rely on impersonal *vs* personal information. In a study of opinion leadership in 14 European countries plus the US and Canada, the countries most characterized by the use of impersonal information-seeking (from consumer magazines, etc.) were Denmark, Norway, Sweden and Finland, whereas the countries least characterized by impersonal information-seeking were Italy, Portugal and Spain.[86]

How influential is an opinion leader? The extent of an opinion leader's influence

When marketers and social scientists initially developed the concept of the opinion leader, they assumed that certain influential people in a community would exert an overall impact on group members' attitudes. Later work, however, began to question the assumption that there is such a thing as a *generalized opinion leader*, somebody whose recommendations we seek for all types of purchases. Very few people are capable of being expert in a number of fields. Sociologists distinguish between those who are *monomorphic*, or expert in a limited field, and those who are *polymorphic*, or expert in several fields.[87] Even opinion leaders who are polymorphic, however, tend to concentrate on one broad domain, such as electronics or fashion.

Research on opinion leadership generally indicates that although opinion leaders do exist for multiple product categories, expertise tends to overlap across similar categories. It is rare to find a generalized opinion leader. An opinion leader for home appliances is likely to serve a similar function for home cleaners but not for cosmetics. In contrast, a *fashion opinion leader* whose primary influence is on clothing choices, may also be consulted for recommendations on cosmetics purchases, but not necessarily on microwave ovens.[88] A reexamination of the traditional perspective on opinion leadership reveals that the process isn't as clear-cut as some researchers thought.[89] The original framework is called the **two-step flow model of influence**. It proposes that a small group of *influencers* disseminate information because they can modify the opinions of a large number of other people. When the authors ran extensive computer simulations of this process, they found that the influence is driven less by **influentials** and more by the interaction among those who are easily influenced; they communicate the information vigorously to one another and they also participate in a two-way dialogue with the opinion leader as part of an **influence network**. These conversations create **information cascades**, which occur when a piece of information triggers a sequence of interactions (much like an avalanche). They concluded that 'influentials are only modestly more important than average individuals'[90] and thus influentials are less central to the process of diffusion of innovations or early adoption than hitherto assumed.[91]

It's worth noting that consumer researchers and other social scientists continue to debate the dynamics of these networks. For example, the jury is still out about just how influential it is when different people tweet about a product. On the one hand, an online service called 'Klout' claims to measure precisely just how influential each of us is. It awards pop sensation Justin Bieber, with his 6.4 million Twitter followers, a perfect score of 100; go there and see how influential you are.[92] Although many marketers today focus on identifying key influencers and motivating them to spread the word about a brand, another camp believes that it's more productive simply to get your message out to as many people as possible. They argue that it's very difficult to predict what will trigger a cascade, so it's better to hedge your bets by simply getting the word out as widely as possible.[93] The science of understanding online influence is racing to keep up with the mushrooming usage of these new platforms.

Types of opinion leaders *vs* other consumer types

Early conceptions of the opinion leader role assumed a static, one-way process: the opinion leader absorbs information from the mass media and in turn transmits data to opinion receivers. This view has turned out to be overly simplified; it confuses the functions of several different types of consumers. Furthermore, research has shown some evidence that the flow of influence is not one-way but two-way, so that opinion leaders are influenced by the responses of their followers.[94] This would reflect a more complex communication situation as discussed in Chapter 8.

Opinion leaders may or may not be purchasers of the products they recommend. Early purchasers are known as *innovators* and like to take risks and try new things (see Chapter 14). Researchers call opinion leaders who are also early purchasers **innovative communicators**. One study identified a number of characteristics of male university students who were innovative communicators for fashion products. These men were among the first to buy new fashions, and their fashion opinions were incorporated by other students into their own clothing purchases. Other characteristics of these men included:[95]

- They were socially active.
- They were appearance-conscious and narcissistic (i.e. they were quite fond of themselves and self-centered).
- They were involved in rock culture.
- They were heavy magazine readers.
- They were likely to own more clothing, and a broader range of styles, than other students.

Opinion leaders also are likely to be **opinion seekers**. They are generally more involved in a product category and actively search for information. As a result, they are more likely to talk about products with others and to solicit others' opinions as well.[96] Contrary to the static view of opinion leadership, most product-related conversation does not take place in a

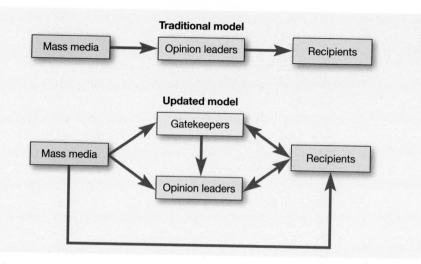

Figure 10.5 Updated opinion leadership model

'lecture' format in which one person does all of the talking. A lot of product-related conversation is prompted by the situation and occurs in the context of a casual interaction rather than as formal instruction.[97] One study, which found that opinion seeking is especially high for food products, revealed that two-thirds of opinion seekers also view themselves as opinion leaders.[98] This updated view of interpersonal product communication is contrasted with the traditional view in Figure 10.5.

The market maven

A **market maven** is a person who likes to transmit marketplace information of all types. Market mavens are not necessarily interested in certain products and may not necessarily be early purchasers of products; they are just interested in staying on top of what is happening in the marketplace. They come closer to the function of a generalized opinion leader because they tend to have a solid overall knowledge of how and where to procure products. They are also more confident in their ability to make smart purchase decisions. Researchers use scale items to identify market mavens (Figure 10.6). Respondents are asked to indicate how much they agree or disagree with the statements.[99]

1. I like introducing new brands and products to my friends.

2. I like helping people by providing them with information about many kinds of products.

3. People ask me for information about products, places to shop, or sales.

4. If someone asked me where to get the best buy on several types of products, I could tell him or her where to shop.

5. My friends think of me as a good source of information when it comes to new products or sales.

6. Think about a person who has information about a variety of products and likes to share this information with others. This person knows about new products, sales, stores, and so on, but does not necessarily feel he or she is an expert on one particular product. How well would you say this description fits you?

Figure 10.6 Scale items used to identify market mavens

Source: Adapted from Lawrence Feick and Linda Price, 'The market maven: A diffuser of marketplace information', *Journal of Marketing* 51 (January 1987): 83–7.

The surrogate consumer

In addition to everyday consumers who are instrumental in influencing others' purchase decisions, a class of marketing intermediary called the **surrogate consumer** often influences what we buy. A surrogate consumer is a person whom we hire to provide input into our purchase decisions. Unlike the opinion leader or market maven, the surrogate is usually compensated for their advice (e.g. personal shoppers in major department flagship stores).

Interior designers, stockbrokers or professional shoppers can all be thought of as surrogate consumers. Whether or not they actually make the purchase on behalf of the consumer, surrogates' recommendations can be enormously influential. The consumer, in essence, relinquishes control over several or all decision-making functions, such as information search, the evaluation of alternatives, or the actual purchase. For example, a client may commission an interior designer to update their house, and a broker may be entrusted to make crucial buy/sell decisions on behalf of investors. The involvement of surrogates in a wide range of purchase decisions tends to be overlooked by many marketers, who may be mistargeting their communications to end-consumers instead of to the surrogates who are actually sifting through product information and deciding among product alternatives on behalf of their clients, and making the final recommendations about purchase.[100]

How do we find opinion leaders?

Because most opinion leaders are everyday consumers rather than celebrities, they are hard to find. A celebrity or an influential industry executive is by definition easy to locate. That person has national or at least regional visibility or is listed in published directories. In contrast, opinion leaders tend to operate at the local level and may influence only a small group of consumers rather than an entire market segment. And yet because opinion leaders are so central to consumer decision-making, marketers are very interested in identifying influential people for a product category. In fact, many ads are intended to reach these influentials rather than the average consumer, especially if the ads contain a lot of technical information.

Professional opinion leaders

Perhaps the easiest way to find opinion leaders is to target people who are paid to give expert opinions. *Professional opinion leaders* are people such as doctors or scientists who obtain specialized information from technical journals and other practitioners.

Marketers who are trying to gain consumer acceptance for their products sometimes find it easier to try to win over professional opinion leaders, who (they hope) will, in turn, recommend their products to customers. A case in point is the effort by Roc SA, maker of Europe's leading brand of hypoallergenic lotions, to break into the lucrative American market for skincare products. Instead of competing head-to-head with the lavish consumer advertising of Revlon or Estée Lauder, the French company decided first to gain medical acceptance by winning over pharmacists and dermatologists. In 1994 the company began advertising in medical journals, and the product was distributed to dermatologists and to pharmacies patronized by patients of dermatologists. A free telephone number was established to provide interested consumers with the names of pharmacies carrying the range.[101]

Of course, this approach may backfire if it is carried to an extreme and compromises the credibility of professional opinion leaders. In several countries, the medical industry has a dubious reputation of 'bribing' doctors with invitations to product presentations disguised as conferences, often held in glamorous places. A recent examination of registers of gifts and donations to doctors in the UK showed the scale of sponsorship by pharmaceutical companies of all-expenses-paid conference trips around the world ran into millions of pounds.[102]

Consumer opinion leaders

Consumer opinion leaders tend to operate at the local level and may influence five to ten consumers rather than an entire market segment. In some cases, companies have tried to identify influentials and involve them directly in their marketing efforts, hoping to create a 'ripple effect' as these consumers sing the company's praises to their friends. Many department stores, for instance, sponsor fashion panels, usually composed of adolescent girls, who provide input into fashion trends, participate in fashion shows and so on.

Because of the difficulties involved in identifying specific opinion leaders in a large market, most attempts to do so instead focus on *exploratory studies*. Researchers aim to identify the profile of a representative opinion leader and then generalize these insights to the larger market. This knowledge helps marketers target their product-related information to appropriate settings and media. For example, one attempt to identify financial opinion leaders found that these consumers were more likely to be involved in managing their own finances and tended to use a computer to do so. They were also more likely to follow their investments on a daily basis and to read books and watch television shows devoted to financial issues.[103]

The self-designating method

The most commonly used technique to identify opinion leaders is simply to ask individual consumers whether they consider themselves to be opinion leaders. However, there are obvious problems with self-designation. Although respondents who report a greater degree of interest in a product category are more likely to be opinion leaders, the results of surveys intended to identify *self-designated opinion leaders* must be viewed with some scepticism. Some people have a tendency to inflate their own importance and influence, whereas others who really are influential might not admit to this quality or be conscious of it.[104] Just because we transmit advice about products does not mean other people *take* that advice. For someone to be considered a bona fide opinion leader, opinion seekers must actually heed their advice. An alternative is to select certain group members (*key informants*) who in turn are asked to identify opinion leaders. The success of this approach hinges on locating those who have accurate knowledge of the group and on minimizing their response biases (the tendency to inflate one's own influence on the choices of others).

The self-designating method is not as reliable as a more systematic analysis (in which we can verify individual claims of influence by asking others if they agree), but it does have the advantage of being easy to apply to a large group of potential opinion leaders. In some cases not all members of a community are surveyed. Figure 10.7 shows one of the measurement scales researchers use for this kind of self-designation.

Sociometry

A web-based service has been created that is based on the popular play *Six Degrees of Separation*. The basic premise of the plot is that everyone on the planet is separated by only six other people. The website (**www.sixdegrees.com**) allows a person to register and provide names and email addresses of other people, so that when the user needs to network a connection is made with others in the database. Indeed, social scientists estimate that the average person has 1,500 acquaintances and that five to six intermediaries could connect any two people in the United States.[105]

This site is a digital version of more conventional **sociometric methods**, which trace communication patterns among group members and allow researchers systematically to map out the interactions that take place among group members. By interviewing participants and asking them to whom they go for product information, researchers can identify those who tend to be sources of product-related information. In many cases one or a few people emerge as the 'nodes' in a map – and *voila*, we have found our opinion leaders. This method is the most

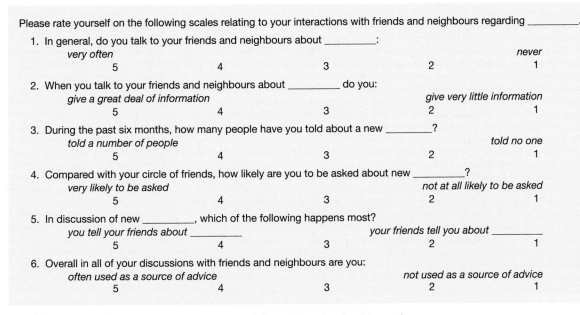

Please rate yourself on the following scales relating to your interactions with friends and neighbours regarding _____.

1. In general, do you talk to your friends and neighbours about _____:
   very often   never
   5   4   3   2   1

2. When you talk to your friends and neighbours about _____ do you:
   give a great deal of information   give very little information
   5   4   3   2   1

3. During the past six months, how many people have you told about a new _____?
   told a number of people   told no one
   5   4   3   2   1

4. Compared with your circle of friends, how likely are you to be asked about new _____?
   very likely to be asked   not at all likely to be asked
   5   4   3   2   1

5. In discussion of new _____, which of the following happens most?
   you tell your friends about _____   your friends tell you about _____
   5   4   3   2   1

6. Overall in all of your discussions with friends and neighbours are you:
   often used as a source of advice   not used as a source of advice
   5   4   3   2   1

Figure 10.7 A revised and updated version of the opinion leadership scale

Source: Adapted from Terry L. Childers, 'Assessment of the psychometric properties of an opinion leadership scale', *Journal of Marketing Research* 23 (May 1986): 184–8; and Leisa Reinecke Flynn, Ronald E. Goldsmith and Jacqueline K. Eastman, 'The King and Summers opinion leadership scale: revision and refinement', *Journal of Business Research* 31 (1994): 55–64.

precise, but it is very hard and expensive to implement because it involves very close study of interaction patterns in small groups. For this reason, sociometric techniques are best applied in a closed, self-contained social setting, such as in hospitals, prisons, and army bases, where members are largely isolated from other social networks.

A sociometric study on obesity provides a striking example of how our social networks influence our consumption behaviours. The researchers analysed a sample of more than 12,000 people who participated in the Framingham Heart Study, which closely documented their health from 1971 to 2003. They discovered that obesity can spread from person to person, much like a virus (we'll talk more about how consumer trends spread in this way in Chapter 14). The investigators knew who was friends with whom as well as who was a spouse or sibling or neighbour, and they knew how much each person weighed at various times over three decades so they could reconstruct what happened over the years if study participants became obese. Guess what? When one person gains weight, close friends tend to gain weight, too – a person's chances of being obese if a close friend put on the pounds increased by 57 per cent. The friend's influence remained even if they lived hundreds of miles away. The researchers speculated that the reason for this 'social contagion' effect is that when our best friends get fat, this alters our perception of normal body weight so we are not as concerned when we put on a few pounds as well. The moral of the story: Hang out with thin people.[106]

Many professionals (e.g. accountants, lawyers) and services marketers (e.g. cleaning services) depend primarily on word-of-mouth to generate business. In many cases consumers recommend a service provider to a friend or fellow worker, and in other cases business people will make recommendations to their customers. For example, only 0.2 per cent of respondents in one study reported choosing a physician based on advertising. Advice from family and friends was the most widely used criterion.[107]

We use sociometric analyses to better understand *referral behaviour* and to locate strengths and weaknesses in terms of how one's reputation flows through a community.[108] *Network analysis* focuses on communication in social systems, considers the relations among people in a *referral network*, and measures the *tie strength* among them. To understand how a network guides what we buy, consider a study researchers conducted among women who lived together in a sorority house. They found evidence that sub-groups, or *cliques*, within the sorority were likely to share preferences for various products. In some cases, the sisters even shared their choices of 'private' (i.e. socially inconspicuous) products (probably because of shared bathrooms in the sorority house).[109]

Tie strength refers to the nature of the bond between people. It can range from *strong primary* (e.g. one's partner) to *weak secondary* (e.g. an acquaintance whom one rarely sees). A strong tie relationship may be thought of as a primary reference group; interactions are frequent and important to the individual.

While strong ties are important, weak ties can perform a *bridging function*. This type of connection allows a consumer access between sub-groups. For example, you might have a regular group of friends who serve as a primary reference group (strong ties). If you have an interest in tennis, say, one of these friends might introduce you to a group of people who play on the tennis team at the local club. As a result, you gain access to their valuable expertise through this bridging function. This referral process demonstrates the strength of weak ties.[110]

MARKETING OPPORTUNITY

The tangled web

The 'Whopper Sacrifice' was a US advertising campaign Burger King launched to promote its new Angry Whopper sandwich. You could earn a free burger, but to get it you had to sacrifice 10 of your Facebook friends. After you delete these names, you get a coupon in the mail. Your ex-friends get a note informing them that they were dumped for a freebie sandwich. The burger costs $3.69 (£2.33 or 2.78 euros), so when you do the sums, each former friend is worth about 37 cents (23 pence or 28 [European] cents). Although it sounds cruel to give up a friend for this amount, many Facebookers jumped at the chance to purge their friend lists. As one student with several hundred friends commented, 'It's a good excuse to get rid of old girlfriends and their families on my account and get a Whopper out of it.'[111]

PROFESSOR DARACH TURLEY
Dublin City University, Ireland

Consumer behaviour as I see it . . .

We're told that people nowadays are becoming less similar to each other and that, as a result, markets are becoming more fragmented. In such a world it becomes harder to make general statements about consumers. However, despite this trend, one such statement still holds: some day each of us is going to die – and we know it. But why mention death in this chapter on groups? Well, much of my own research has sought to explore possible interfaces between consumer behaviour and mortality, death and mourning, and much of this consumer behaviour inevitably takes place in a social context.

I think that three topics in this area hold particular promise for consumer researchers in the years ahead. First is the impact of impending death on people's consumption. Pavia and Mason's study is an insightful example.[112] Faced with a terminal diagnosis, do consumers, for example, renew or cancel their gym subscription, purchase a new car or hold on to their existing model, take that dream holiday or stay at home? The answer would appear to be that consumer behaviour can both influence and be influenced by such medical conditions. The second area concerns those left behind after the recent loss of a loved one. Working with my research colleague, Dr Stephanie O'Donohoe, I've come to see how the journey through grief can involve a number of demanding and often poignant consumer decisions: whether to hold a burial or cremation, whether to sell the family home and downsize, when and how to dispose of the dead person's possessions. The third area takes a broader time horizon to examine memorializing consumer behaviour. Survivors invest more money, time and emotion in deciding on headstones and anniversary celebrations, for example, than they do in many of their more routine purchases. Very often consumers who can least afford it spend the most. Is this form of consumer behaviour simply repaying the dead person or might it have more to do with keeping their memory alive? Might it even be a means of working on relationships with those who are no longer with us physically? The growth in online memorial sites offers intriguing insights into how this relationship-work may develop in the years ahead.[113]

So to return to my original question, why discuss bereaved consumers in a chapter on groups? People seem unhappy talking about death and uncomfortable meeting those touched by it. In turn, those who have lost a loved one recently often sense this unease in others and experience a certain social isolation, a feeling of being out of step with mainstream society through no fault of their own. In this sense they can be seen as an involuntary aversion group. This chapter also looks at opinion leadership. Typically the opinion leader is seen as a living person; however, our encounters with bereaved persons suggest that some people can continue to exercise leadership on consumer choices, especially on family decisions, from beyond the grave.

Darach Turley

Online opinion leaders

The internet makes opinion leaders even more powerful – it's like giving a football player steroids (only legal). Instead of reaching only those within earshot, now an influential person can sway the opinions of thousands or even millions of people around the world. In online groups, opinion leaders sometimes are called **power users**. They have a strong communication network that gives them the ability to affect purchase decisions for a number of other consumers, directly and indirectly.[114]

Much like their offline counterparts, power users are active participants at work and in their communities. Their social networks are large and well developed. Others trust them and find them to be credible sources of information about one or more specific topics. They tend to have a natural sense of intellectual curiosity, which may lead them to new sources of information. And they post an awful lot of brand-related content: Forrester Research has dubbed these brand-specific mentions **influence impressions**. In advertising terms, an *impression* refers to a view or an exposure to an advertising message. Forrester estimates that each year, American consumers generate 256 billion influence impressions as people talk about their lives with each other, telling stories and experiences that invariably include brands.[115] These influence impressions are primarily delivered by power users: only 6.2 per cent of social media users are responsible for about 80 per cent of these brand mentions. Forrester calls these influencers **mass connectors**.

As mass connectors spread influence impressions, the impact of the message grows due to the **momentum effect**.[116] Influencers publish the message on blogs, share widgets, place a brand logo on their Facebook pages, and so on. Friends share with friends who share with friends. If a brand is well-liked, relevant and buzz-worthy, the media value originating from nonpaid, word-of-mouth referrals for brand can be enormous.

WORD-OF-MOUTH COMMUNICATION

Despite the abundance of formal means of communication (such as newspapers, magazines and television), much information about the world is conveyed by individuals on an informal basis.[117] **Word-of-mouth (WOM)** is product information that individuals transmit to other individuals. If you think carefully about the content of your own conversations in the course of a normal day, you will probably agree that much of what you discuss with friends, family members or coworkers is product-related: whether you compliment someone on her dress and ask her where she bought it, recommend a new restaurant to a friend, or complain to your neighbour about the shoddy treatment you got at the bank, you are engaging in word-of-mouth communication (WOM). Recall, for example, that Bobby's choice of football boots was directly initiated by comments and suggestions from his friends and team mates. This kind of communication can be an efficient marketing tool. When the film *The Blair Witch Project* became a big success, it was almost assured beforehand because of the pre-premiere WOM sparked by a good website and heavy exploitation of the blurring of reality and fiction.

Information obtained from those we know or talk to directly tends to be more reliable and trustworthy than that received through more formal channels and, unlike advertising, it is often backed up by social pressure to conform to these recommendations.[118] Another factor in the importance of WOM is the decline in people's faith in institutions. As traditional endorsers are becoming increasingly problematical to use, celebrities because they can be unreliable and classical authority figures because of the withering of their authority, and, indeed, as people are becoming more cynical about all sorts of commercial communications, they turn to sources which they feel are above commercial exploitation: friends and family.[119] The importance of personal, informal product communication to marketers is further underscored by one advertising executive, who stated, 'Today, 80 per cent of all buying decisions are influenced by someone's direct recommendations.'[120] In one survey, 69 per cent of interviewees said they relied on a personal referral at least once over the course of a year to help them choose a restaurant, 36 per cent reported they used referrals to decide on computer hardware and software, and 22 per cent got help from friends and associates to decide where to travel.[121] Marketers have been aware of the power of WOM for many years, but recently they've been more aggressive about trying to promote and control it instead of sitting back and hoping people will like their products enough to talk them up. Companies like BzzAgent enlist thousands of 'agents' who try new products and spread the word about those they like.[122] Many sophisticated marketers today also precisely track WOM. For example, the ongoing TalkTrack study reports which brands consumers mention the most in different categories. Based on online surveys of 14,000 women, it reports that middle-aged (baby boomer) women talk about Kraft more than any other packaged-goods food brand, and they discuss Olay the most among beauty products.[123]

However, research has challenged the traditional assumption that consumers weigh **negative word-of-mouth** more heavily than positive word-of-mouth where judgement and choice are concerned. These researchers suggest that negative word-of-mouth will be outweighed in cases where consumers positively evaluate the agent (the agent could be *inter alia* a friend, family member, online poster, or professional critic) who is the source of the word of mouth. This means that if the consumer judges the agent as having similar tastes to their own or as being a suitable source of information, then the consumer will potentially weigh that agent's positive evaluation more heavily than negative word of mouth from other sources.[124]

In the 1950s communications theorists began to challenge the assumption that advertising primarily determines what we buy. As a rule, advertising is more effective when it reinforces our existing product preferences than when it tries to create new ones.[125] Studies in both industrial and consumer purchase settings underline the idea that, although information from impersonal sources is important for creating brand awareness, consumers rely on word-of-mouth in the later stages of evaluation and adoption.[126] Quite simply, the more positive information consumers get about a product from peers, the more likely they will be to adopt the product.[127]

The influence of others' opinions is at times even more powerful than one's own perceptions. In one study of furniture choices, consumers' estimates of how much their friends would like the furniture was a better predictor of purchase than their *own* evaluations.[128]

WOM is especially powerful when the consumer is relatively unfamiliar with the product category. We would expect such a situation in the case of new products (e.g. medications to prevent hair loss) or those that are technologically complex (e.g. smartphones). One way to reduce uncertainty about the wisdom of a purchase is to talk about it. Talking gives the consumer an opportunity to generate supporting arguments for the purchase and to garner support for this decision from others. For example, the strongest predictor of a person's intention to buy a residential solar water-heating system is the number of solar-heat users the person knows.[129]

You talk about products for several reasons:[130]

- A person might be highly involved with a type of product or activity and get pleasure in talking about it. Computer hackers, avid birdwatchers, football fans and 'fashion plates' seem to share the ability to steer a conversation towards their particular interests.

- A person might be knowledgeable about a product and use conversations as a way to let others know it. Thus, word-of-mouth communication sometimes enhances the ego of the individual who wants to impress others with their expertise.

- A person might initiate such a discussion out of genuine concern for someone else. We are often motivated to ensure that people we care about buy what is good for them, do not waste their money, and so on.

Most WOM campaigns happen spontaneously, as a product begins to develop a regional or a sub-cultural following, but occasionally a 'buzz' is created intentionally. For example, when launching a new brand of beer, called Black Sheep, bottles were distributed and maximum exposure to opinion leaders in the trade ensured in order to pave the way for a massive word-of-mouth effect, intended as the vehicle for carrying the new brand towards success.[131] A similar *word-of-mouth advertising* technique was used when a group of opinion leaders, or 'influencers', was used to market services in the insurance market.[132]

Efficiency of WOM

Interpersonal transmissions can be quite rapid. The producers of *Batman* showed a trailer to 300 Batman fans months before its release to counteract widespread anger about the casting of Michael Keaton as the hero. The film-makers attribute the film's eventual huge success to the positive word-of-mouth that quickly spread following the screening.[133]

Negative WOM

Word-of-mouth is a two-edged sword that can cut both ways for marketers. Informal discussions among consumers can make or break a product or store. Furthermore, consumers weigh **negative word-of-mouth** more heavily than they do positive comments. According to one study, 90 per cent of unhappy customers will not do business with a company again. Each of these people is likely to share their grievance with at least nine other people, and 13 per cent of these disgruntled customers will go on to tell *more than 30* people of their negative experience.[134]

Especially when we're considering a new product or service, we're likely to pay more attention to negative information than positive information and tell others of our nasty experience.[135] Some consumers may even use negative WOM in order to restore their own positive self-image, for example in cases where a product offering is judged not to have corresponded to the person's self-image. Instead of blaming oneself for a misjudgment which would harm self-images of rationality and being in control, negative WOM may be the outcome.[136] Research shows that negative WOM reduces the credibility of a firm's advertising and influences consumers' attitudes toward a product as well as their intention to buy it.[137] And negative WOM is even easier to spread online. Dell found this out the hard way when bloggers denounced the computer maker's quality and service levels; then the popular media picked up this discontent and magnified it.[138] Many dissatisfied customers and disgruntled former employees have been 'inspired' to create websites just to share their tales of woe with others. For example, a website for people to complain about the Dunkin' Donuts chain became so popular the company bought it in order to control the bad press it was getting. It grew out of a complaint by the original owner because he could not get skimmed milk for his coffee.[139]

In an in-depth study of 40 complaint websites such as **walmartsucks.com**, the authors use *protest-framing theory* that sociologists developed to understand how people define a social situation to others in order to influence their behaviour.[140] They identify three basic subframes, or themes:

1 *Injustice*: consumer protestors frequently talk about their repeated attempts to contact the company, only to be ignored.

2 *Identity*: posters characterize the violator (often top management) as evil, rather than simply wrong.

3 *Agency*: individual website creators try to create a collective identity for those who share their anger with a company. They evoke themes of crusades and heroism to rally others to believe that they have the power to change the *status quo* in which companies can wrong consumers without retribution.

Rumours

A **rumour** can be very dangerous, especially when it is false. In the 1930s, 'professional rumourmongers' were hired to organize word-of-mouth campaigns to promote clients' products and criticize those of competitors.[141] More recently, Bio Business International, a small Canadian company that markets 100 per cent cotton nonchlorine-bleached tampons under the name Terra Femme, encouraged women to spread a message that the tampons its American competitors make contain dioxin. There is very little evidence to support the claim that these products are dangerous, but as a result of this rumour, Procter & Gamble received thousands of complaints about its feminine hygiene products.[142]

As information is transmitted among consumers, it tends to change. The resulting message usually does not resemble the original at all. Social scientists who study rumours have examined the process by which information gets distorted. The British psychologist Frederic Bartlett used the method of *serial reproduction* to examine how content mutates. A subject is asked to reproduce a stimulus, such as a drawing or a story. Another subject is given this reproduction and asked to copy that, and so on. This technique is shown in Figure 10.8. The figure illustrates how the message changes as it is reproduced. Bartlett found that distortions almost inevitably follow a pattern: they tend to change from ambiguous forms to more

Original drawing

Figure 10.8 The transmission of misinformation. These drawings provide a classic example of the distortions that can occur as information is transmitted from person to person. As each person reproduces the figure, it gradually changes from an owl to a cat

Source: Kenneth J. Gergen and Mary Gergen, *Social Psychology* (New York: Harcourt Brace Jovanovich, 1981): p. 365. Adapted from F.C. Bartlett, *Remembering* (Cambridge: Cambridge University Press, 1932).

conventional ones as subjects try to make them consistent with pre-existing schemas. He called this process *assimilation*, and he noted that it often occurs as people engage in *levelling*, when they omit details to simplify the structure, or *sharpening*, when they exaggerate prominent details.

In general, people have been shown to prefer transmitting good news rather than bad, perhaps because they like to avoid unpleasantness or dislike arousing hostility. However, this reluctance does not appear to occur when companies are the topic of conversation. Corporations such as Procter & Gamble and McDonald's have been the subjects of rumours about their products, sometimes with marked effects on sales.

Rumours are thought to reveal the underlying fears of a society. While rumours sometimes die out by themselves, in other instances a company may take direct action to counteract them. A French margarine was rumoured to contain contaminants, and the company addressed this in its advertising by referring to the story as 'The rumour that costs you dearly'.[143]

The web is a perfect medium for spreading rumours and hoaxes. Modern-day hoaxes abound; many of these are in the form of email chain letters promising instant riches if you pass the message on to 10 friends. Some hoaxes involve major corporations. A popular one promised that if you tried Microsoft products, you would win a free trip to Disneyland. Nike received several hundred pairs of old trainers a day after the rumour spread that you would

425

get a free pair of new shoes in exchange for your old, smelly ones (pity the delivery people who had to cart these packages to the company). Procter & Gamble received more than 10,000 irate calls after a rumour began to spread on newsgroups that its Febreze fabric deodorant kills dogs. In a preemptive strike, the company registered numerous website names such as **febrezekillspet.com**, **febrezesucks.com** and **ihateprocterandgamble.com** to be sure angry consumers didn't use them.

A new form of malicious rumour is **cyberbullying**, which occurs when one or more people post malicious comments online about someone else in a coordinated effort to harass the targeted individual. In South Korea, a famous actress named Choi Jinsil hung herself after online rumours claimed she had driven another actor to take his life. A Korean singer killed herself because rumours claimed she had had plastic surgery. In the United States, the most high-profile case involved the suicide of a 13-year-old girl after classmates created a fake boy online who first flirted with the girl and then taunted her with the claim that the world would be better off without her. The hoax allegedly began because the mother of one of the classmates wanted to find out what the victim was saying about her daughter online. One of the most recent cases was in Germany where it was alleged that Claudia Boerner's suicide was sparked by a series of attacks by internet haters and bloggers on her appearance after she had taken part in a TV cookery show, *Perfect Dinner*.[144]

Buzz building

A few years ago, here's how a toy company would launch a new product:

> Unveil a hot holiday toy during a spring trade fair, run a November–December saturation television ad campaign during cartoon prime time to sell the toy to children, sit back and watch as desperate parents scrambled through the aisles at Toys 'R' Us, and then wait for the resulting media coverage to drive still more sales.

Fast-forward to a recent toy story: a Hong Kong company called Silverlit Toys makes the $30 Picoo Z helicopter. At one point a Google search for the term Picoo produced more than 109,000 URLs, with many of those links pointing to major online global gift retailers like Hammacher–Schlemmer and Toys 'R' Us. Do you think this huge exposure was the result of a meticulously planned promotional strategy? Think again. By most accounts, a 28-year-old tech worker in Chicago started the Picoo Z buzz; he bought his helicopter after he read about it on a hobbyist message board. A few months later he uploaded his homemade video of the toy on YouTube. Within two weeks, 15 of his friends had also bought the toy, and they in turn posted their own videos and pointed viewers to the original video. Internet retailers who troll online conversations for fresh and exciting buzz identified the toy and started to add their own links to the clips. Within a few short months, there were hundreds of Picoo Z videos and more than a million people had viewed them (find one at **youtube.com/watch?v=y6t1R3yB-cs**).[145]

Guerrilla marketing

To promote their hip hop albums, Def Jam and other labels started building a buzz months before a release, leaking advance copies to DJs who put together 'mix tapes' to sell on the street. If the kids seemed to like a song, *street teams* then pushed it to club DJs. As the official release date neared, these groups of fans started slapping up posters around the inner city. They plastered telephone poles, sides of buildings and car windscreens with promotions announcing the release of new albums by artists such as Public Enemy, Jay-Z, DMX or L.L. Cool J.[146]

These streetwise strategies started in the mid-1970s, when pioneering DJs promoted their parties through graffiti-style flyers. This type of grass-roots effort epitomizes **guerrilla marketing**, promotional strategies that use unconventional locations and intensive word-of-mouth campaigns to push products. The term implies that the marketer 'ambushes' the unsuspecting recipient. As Ice Cube observed, 'Even though I'm an established artist, I still like to leak my music to a kid on the street and let him duplicate it for his homies before it hits radio.'[147]

These campaigns often recruit legions of real consumers who agree to engage in some kind of street theatre or other activity to convince others to use the product or service. Scion, for example, often reaches out to its young buyers with street teams that distribute merchandise and hang wild posters wherever they can to encourage twenty-somethings to check out the carmaker's videos and multiplayer games on its website.[148]

Today, big companies are buying into guerrilla marketing strategies in a big way. Coca-Cola did it for a Sprite promotion, Nike did it to build interest in a new shoe model.[149] Upmarket fashion companies are adopting this strategy, in order to offer shoppers a different retailing experience compared with conventional retail outlets. Comme des Garçons Guerrilla Store opened in New York in February 2004: '[I]n the first example of provisional retailing by an established fashion house, the store plans to close in a year even if it is making money. All 20 stores that the Tokyo-based company plans to open by next year, including one in Brooklyn in September [2004], will adopt the same guerrilla strategy, disappearing after a year.'[150]

When RCA Records wanted to create a buzz around teen pop singer Christina Aguilera, they hired a team of young people to swarm the web and chat about her on popular teen sites. They posted information casually, sometimes sounding like fans. Just before one of her albums debuted, RCA also hired a direct marketing company to e-mail electronic postcards filled with song snippets and biographical information to 50,000 web addresses.[151] Guerrilla marketing delivers: the album quickly went to No. 1 in the charts.

Adele's singing career was launched when a friend posted Adele's recordings of three songs on Myspace which attracted the attention of the music label XL Recordings.

Paul Mccarten/Landov/Press Association Images (PA Photos).

Viral marketing refers to the strategy of getting visitors to a website to forward information on the site to their friends in order to make still more consumers aware of the product. It usually takes off when an organization creates online content that is entertaining or just plain weird.

The Google search engine finds many matches for key word searches. For instance, the elaborate viral marketing campaign for the film *A.I.* (Artificial Intelligence) was based around key word searches on Google for 'Jeanine Salla'.

Used with permission from Google, Inc.

Role-playing computer games involve thousands of players worldwide in interactive, online communities.

© Susan Goldman/The Image Works/ Topfoto.

THE SOCIAL MEDIA REVOLUTION

The odds are that you've interacted with social media today. If you checked into your Facebook page, fired off a tweet, read a restaurant review on Yelp!, or maybe even killed off some nasty orcs on *World of Warcraft,* you're part of the social media revolution that is changing how consumers interact with the marketplace and with one another. Sometimes people define social media in terms of hardware (like Android smartphones) or software (like Wikipedia), but really it's first and foremost about *community*: the collective participation of members who together build and maintain a site.[152]

Social media and community

The Skittles sweet brand changed its website into a social media hub and in the process significantly boosted consumers' awareness of the product. Instead of seeing corporate-produced content, a visitor to the site finds links to Twitter to read tweets about Skittles (good and bad). Another link guides her to Skittles videos and photos on YouTube and Flickr, and if she clicks 'Friends', she'll go directly to the brand's Facebook area.[153]

Marketers like Skittles are stumbling over one another to adapt their strategies to a Web 2.0 environment. These new communications platforms can be as varied as a social networking site like Facebook, a social shopping site like Groupon, or a virtual world like MTV's Virtual Laguna Beach. Nonetheless, they share some basic characteristics:

- They improve as the number of users increase. For example, Amazon's ability to recommend books to you based on what other people with similar interests buy gets better as it tracks more and more people who enter search queries.
- Their currency is eyeballs. Google makes money as it charges advertisers according to the number of people who see their ads after they type in a search term.
- They are free and in perpetual change. Wikipedia, the online encyclopedia, gets updated constantly by volunteer editors who 'correct' others' errors.
- They categorize entries according to a **folksonomy** rather than a *taxonomy* (a pre-established labelling hierarchy). Instead, sites rely on users to sort contents. Listeners at **Pandora.com** create their own 'radio stations' that play songs by artists they choose, as well as other similar artists.[154] People who upload their photos to Flickr tag them with the labels *they* think best describe the pictures.

In some ways, online communities are not much different from those we find in our physical environment. The *Merriam-Webster Dictionary* (online version, of course) defines **community** as 'a unified body of individuals, unified by interests, location, occupation, common history, or political and economic concerns'. In fact, one social scientist refers to an online community as a **cyberplace** where 'people connect online with kindred spirits, engage in supportive and sociable relationships with them, and imbue their activity online with meaning, belonging, and identity'.[155]

Social networks

Let's take a closer look at the social fabric of social media. Each application consists of a **social network**, a set of socially relevant nodes connected by one or more relations.[156] **Nodes** are members of the network (e.g. the 600-million-plus Facebook users). Members (whom we also refer to as **network units**) are connected by their relationships with (or **ties** to) each other. Relationships are based on various affiliations, such as kinship, friendship and affective ties, shared experiences, and shared hobbies and interests. When we think of community, we tend to think of people, but in principle members of a network can be organizations, articles, countries, departments, or any other definable unit. A good example is your university alumni association. The association is a community of networked individuals and organizations. Social networks are sometimes called **social graphs**, though this term may also refer to a diagram of the interconnections of units in a network.

Nodes in a network experience **interactions**; these are behaviour-based ties like talking with each other, attending an event together, or working together. If you chat online with a prospective dating partner on **Match.com**, you are a node engaging in an interaction with another node. And, if that actually works out and you participate in an online forum that shares experiences about wedding photographers in your area, you engage in interactions with other nodes who are also getting hitched. Interactions are participative in nature; they are shared activities among members in the network.

Flows occur between nodes. Flows are exchanges of resources, information, or influence among members of the network. On Facebook you share news, updates about your life, opinions on favourite books and films, photos, videos and notes. As you share content, you create flows from among those in your network. In social media, these flows of communication go in many directions at any point in time and often on multiple platforms – a condition we term **media multiplexity**. Flows are not simply two-way or three-way; they may go through an entire community, a list or group within a network, or several individuals independently. Flows of communication also occur outside the community platform. Whereas the online community may exist entirely within a web space, the flows of communication may extend to other domains as well, like e-mails, text messages, virtual worlds and even face-to-face **meetups** in which members of an online network arrange to meet in a physical location.

For marketers, flows are especially important because they are the actionable components of any social network system in terms of the sharing of information, delivery of promotional materials and sources of social influence. The extent of this social influence (where one person's attitudes or behaviour change as a result of others' attempts) varies depending upon the power or attractiveness of other nodes.

Social object theory suggests that social networks will be more powerful communities if there is a way to activate relationships among people and objects. In this perspective, an *object* is something of common interest and its primary function is to mediate the interactions between people. All relationships have social objects embedded in the relationship. In the online world, a site like Facebook provides venues for several object formats to ensure that relationships can thrive within the site's framework. One factor that drives Facebook's stunning success is that it offers so many objects for users to share; these include events, family and friends, quizzes, and so on. Other **social networking** sites (SNSs) provide a more specialized or focused set of objects. For example, consider how each of these SNSs incorporates objects as part of its mission. On Flickr, users participate because they want to share photos. These images are the objects that give meaning to the platform and motivate people to visit. Video is the social object around which YouTube centres. On Diigo, the objects are URLs (uniform resource locator). On foursquare, the objects are places. On Dogster, the objects are our canine companions.

Object sociality, the extent to which an object can be shared in social media, is clearly related to an audience's unique interests, by virtue of tying the site relationships to a specific object such as photos of people's dogs or bookmarked websites that provide details about the history of alternative music. The audience becomes specialized at least to a degree. Importantly, though, SNSs oriented around object sociality are likely to be **passion-centric**. That is, the people who join those communities not only share an interest in the object in question, but chances are also high that they are obsessed with it. We all know people who devote countless hours to a hobby or who (to an outsider) seem insanely obsessed about the finer details of *Star Wars* characters, vintage wines, or warring guilds in *World of Warcraft*.

Characteristics of online communities

All communities, whether they are online or in the physical world, share important characteristics: participants experience a feeling of membership, a sense of proximity to one another (even though in online groups other members' physical selves may be thousands of miles away), and in most cases some interest in the community's activities. Members may identify with one another due to a common mission (e.g. a Twitter campaign to donate money for oil spill relief) or simply because they come from the same neighbourhood or belong to the same sorority (e.g. **classmates.com** connects people who attended the same high school).

Communities help members meet their needs for affiliation, resource acquisition, entertainment and information. Above all else, communities are social! Whether online or offline, they thrive when the members participate, discuss, share and interact with others as well as recruit new members to the community. Members do vary in their degree of participation, but the more active the membership, the healthier the community.

Social media provide the fuel that fans the fires of online communities. In the Web 1.0 era, people visited a lot of websites to get content that interested them. But these really weren't communities, because the flow of information was all one way. In today's Web 2.0 environment, all that has changed as interactive platforms enable online communities to exhibit the following basic characteristics:[157]

- **Conversations**. Communities thrive on communication among members. These conversations are not based on talking or writing but on a hybrid of the two. If you communicate with a friend via AIM or Facebook chat, you may feel that you actually 'talked' to her.

- **Presence**. Though online communities exist virtually rather than at a physical location, the better ones supply tangible characteristics that create the sensation of actually being in a place. This is particularly true for virtual-world communities that include three-dimensional depictions of physical spaces, but it also applies to visually simplistic online communities like message board groups. **Presence** is defined as the effect that people experience when they interact with a computer-mediated or computer-generated environment.[158] Social media sites can enhance a sense of presence by enabling interactions among visitors and making the environment look and feel real.[159]

- **Collective interest**. Just as your offline communities are based on family, religious beliefs, social activities, hobbies, goals, place of residence and so on, your online communities also need commonalities to create bonds among the members. These groups come together to allow people to share their passions, whether these are for indie bands, white wines, or open-source apps.

- **Democracy**. The political model of most online communities is democratic; leaders emerge due to the reputation they earn among the general membership. In this context, **democracy** is a descriptive term that refers to rule by the people. The leaders are appointed or elected by the community based on their demonstrated ability to add value to the group. For instance, in the online community 4chan, an online bulletin board devoted to the sharing of images related to and discussion of Japanese *anime*, members widely acknowledge that the person who posts under the name of 'moot' is a leader. His leadership comes from his role in the creation of the community as well as from his ongoing participation and the quality of his contributions.

Because of the horizontal structure of social media, we typically find that control over what appears on the platform shifts from a small elite to the larger mass. **Media democratization** means that the members of social communities, not traditional media publishers like magazines or newspaper companies, control the creation, delivery and popularity of content.

- **Standards of behaviour**. Virtual communities need rules that govern behaviour in order to operate. Some of these rules are spelled out explicitly (e.g. if you buy an item on eBay, you agree that you have entered into a legal contract to pay for it), but many of them are unspoken. A simple example is discouragement of the practice of **flaming**, when a POST CONTAINS ALL CAPITAL LETTERS TO EXPRESS ANGER.

- **Level of participation**. For an online community to thrive, a significant proportion of its members must participate. Otherwise the site will fail to offer fresh material and ultimately traffic will slow. Participation can be a challenge, though. Most users are **lurkers**: they absorb content that others post, but they don't usually contribute their own. Researchers estimate that only 1 per cent of a typical community's users regularly participate, and another 9 per cent do so only intermittently. The remaining 90 per cent just observe what's on the site, so they don't add a lot of value – other than adding to the number of 'eyeballs' the site can claim when it tries to convince advertisers to buy space. How can a site convert lurkers into active users? The easier it is to participate, the more likely it is that the community can generate activity among a larger proportion of visitors. In part this means ensuring that there are several ways to participate that vary in ease of use. Facebook is an example of an online community that has figured out how to offer several forms of participation. Members can post status updates (very easy), make comments, upload pictures, share notes and links, play social games, answer quizzes, decorate their profiles, upload videos and create events (a bit harder), among other forms of participation.

- **Crowd power**. Social media change the fundamental relationship between marketers and consumers: companies no longer market *to* customers, they market *with* them. Although many organizations resist this change, others build new business models on the **wisdom of crowds** perspective (from a book of that name). This argues that under the right circumstances, groups are smarter than the smartest people in them. If this is true, it implies that large numbers of consumers can predict successful products.[160] For example, at Threadless, customers rank T-shirt designs ahead of time, and the company prints the winning ideas. Every week, contestants upload T-shirt designs to the site, where about 700 compete to be among the six that are printed during that time. Threadless visitors score designs on a scale of 0 to 5, and the staff members select winners from the most popular entrants. The six lucky artists each get $2,000 in cash and merchandise. *Threadless sells out of every shirt it offers.* This business model has made a small fortune for a few designers 'the crowd' particularly likes. One pair of Chicago-based artists sold $16 million worth of T-shirts. To keep the judges and buyers coming back, the owners offer rewards: upload a photo of yourself wearing a Threadless T-shirt and you get a store credit of $1.50. Refer a friend who buys a T-shirt and you get $3. The site sells more than 1,500 T-shirts in a typical day.[161]

Here are some more crowd-based sites to watch:

- At Quirky, people submit ideas for innovative products like a Boil Buoy that floats in a pot and rings when it's hot, or Cordies that organize your power cords. Quirky's users choose the products they like; if the company gets a sufficient number of purchase commitments, the items are manufactured and sent.[162]

- Sermo is a social network for physicians. It has no advertising, job listings or membership fees. It makes its money (about $500,000 a year so far) by charging institutional investors for the opportunity to listen in as approximately 15,000 doctors chat among themselves. Say, for example, a young patient breaks out in hives after he takes a new prescription. A doctor might post whether she thinks this is a rare symptom or a drug side effect. If other doctors feel it's the latter, this negative news could affect the drug manufacturer's stock, so their opinions have value to analysts. Doctors who ask or answer a question that paying observers deem especially valuable receive bonuses of $5 to $25 per post.[163]

At **threadless.com**, users vote on which T-shirt designs the company will print and sell.

© Threadless.com, 2009.

- How about social networking sites that 'create' a concert as they persuade an artist to perform in a certain city or country? At **Eventful.com**, fans demand events and performances in their town and spread the word to make them happen. Or how about actually buying a piece of the bands you like? Go to **SellaBand**, where fans ('believers') buy 'parts' in a band for $10 per share. Once the band sells 5,000 parts, SellaBand arranges a professional recording, including top studios, A&R (Artists & Repertoire) managers (industry talent scouts), and producers. Believers receive a limited-edition CD of the recording. Believers get a piece of the profits, so they're likely to promote the band wherever they can.[164]

- The St Louis Cardinals invited fans to send the team scouting reports on promising college players. The idea is to collect intelligence on talent at small colleges that scouts don't routinely visit. One of the team's executives explained, 'We don't have a monopoly on baseball knowledge. Just looking at the fan sites and posting boards, you see an amazing amount of energy. Why not harness it?'[165]

433

NET PROFIT

As we saw in Chapter 3, consumption in online spaces such as websites, virtual worlds and video games is growing rapidly. Indeed, **digital virtual consumption (DVC)** may well be the next frontier of marketing. In 2011, Americans spent about $1.6 billion to buy **virtual goods** for their avatars in **virtual worlds** like *Second Life* and **MMOGs (massively multiplayer online games)** like *World of Warcraft*.[166] The majority of virtual worlds are 3-D and employ sophisticated computer graphics to produce photorealistic images. Furthermore, unlike most of today's relatively static networking sites, individuals who enter these worlds (or at least their avatars) can walk, fly, teleport, try on clothes, try out products, attend in-world events (educational classes, concerts, political speeches, etc.), and interact in real time (via textchat, IM and VoIP) with other avatars around the world. This unprecedented level of interactivity facilitates consumers' engagement and often creates the *flow state* we discussed in Chapter 6. Thousands of in-world residents design, create and purchase clothing, furniture, houses, vehicles and other products their avatars need – and many do it in style as they acquire the kind of 'bling' they can only dream about in real life. Some forward-thinking marketers understand that these platforms are the next stage they can use to introduce their products into people's lives, whether real or virtual. Today, for example, people who play *The Sims* can import actual pieces of furniture from IKEA into their virtual homes; the use of this sort of platform to accelerate purchases for real homes is unexplored territory. With more than 150 of these immersive 3-D environments now live or in development, we may well see other social networks like Facebook migrate to these platforms in the near future. Whether via your computer or even your mobile phone, you and your 'friends' will hang out together (or at least your avatars will), and you'll shop and compare your choices wherever you are. This is *not* a fad: as of 2011, more than 1 billion people worldwide were registered in at least one virtual world.

CHAPTER SUMMARY

Now that you have finished reading this chapter you should understand why:

→ **Other people and groups, especially those who possess some kind of social power, often influence us.** We belong to or admire many different groups, and a desire for them to accept us often drives our purchase decisions. Individuals or groups whose opinions or behaviour are particularly important to consumers are reference groups. Both formal and informal groups influence the individual's purchase decisions, although such factors as the conspicuousness of the product and the relevance of the reference group for a particular purchase determine how influential the reference group is.

   Individuals have influence in a group to the extent that they possess social power. Types of social power include information power, referent power, legitimate power, expert power, reward power and coercive power.

→ **We seek out others who share our interests in products or services.** Brand communities unite consumers who share a common passion for a product. **Brand-fests**, which companies organize to encourage this kind of community, can build brand loyalty and reinforce group membership.

→ **We are motivated to buy or use products in order to be consistent with what other people do.** We conform to the desires of others for two basic reasons: (1) People who model their behaviour on others because they take others' behaviour as evidence of the correct way to act are conforming because of informational social influence; and (2) those who conform to satisfy the expectations of others or to be accepted by the group are affected by normative social influence. Group members often do things they would not do as individuals because their identities become merged with the group; they become deindividuated.

→ **Certain people are particularly likely to influence others' product choices.** Opinion leaders who are knowledgeable about a product and whose opinions are highly regarded tend to influence others' choices. Specific opinion leaders are somewhat hard to identify, but marketers who know their general characteristics can try to target them in their media and promotional strategies. Other influencers include market mavens, who have a general interest in marketplace activities; and surrogate consumers, who are compensated for their advice about purchases.

→ **The things that other consumers tell us about products (good and bad) are often more influential than the advertising we see.** Much of what we know about products we learn through word-of-mouth (WOM) communication rather than formal advertising. We tend to exchange product-related information in casual conversations. Guerrilla marketing strategies try to accelerate the WOM process when they enlist consumers to help spread the word. Although WOM often is helpful to make consumers aware of products, it can also hurt companies when damaging product rumours or negative WOM occur.

→ **Online technologies accelerate the impact of word-of-mouth communication.** The web greatly amplifies our exposure to numerous reference groups. Virtual consumption communities unite those who share a common bond – usually enthusiasm about, or knowledge of, a specific product or service. Emerging marketing strategies try to leverage the potential of the web to spread information from consumer to consumer extremely quickly. Viral marketing techniques enlist individuals to tout products, services, websites and so on to others on behalf of companies. Blogging allows consumers to easily post their thoughts about products for others to see.

→ **Social networking is changing the way companies and consumers interact.** Social networking, where members post information and make contact with others who share similar interests and opinions, changes the way we think about marketing. As Web 2.0 continues to develop, companies and consumers increasingly interact directly. The wisdom-of-crowds perspective argues that under the right circumstances, groups are smarter than the smartest people in them. If this is true, it implies that large numbers of consumers can predict successful products.[167] In a sense, a lot of social networking sites let their members dictate purchase decisions.

KEY TERMS

Anti-brand communities (p. 406)

Aspirational reference groups (p. 403)

Avoidance reference groups (p. 405)

Brand community (p. 406)

Brand-fests (pp. 406, 434)

Coercive power (p. 399)

Cohesiveness (p. 405)

Collective value creation (p. 406)

Communities of practice (p. 407)

Community (p. 429)

Comparative influence (p. 403)

Conformity (p. 410)

Consumer tribe (p. 406)

Cyberbullying (p. 426)

Cyberplace (p. 429)

Decision polarization (p. 408)

De-individuation (p. 408)

Democracy (p. 431)

Digital virtual consumption (p. 434)

Dissociative reference groups (p. 405)

Expert power (p. 398)

Flaming (p. 432)

Flows (p. 430)

Folksonomy (p. 429)

Guerrilla marketing (p. 426)

Home shopping parties (p. 409)

Homophily (p. 413)

Identificational membership reference group (p. 405)

Influence impressions (p. 421)

Influence network (p. 415)

Influentials (p. 415)

Information cascades (p. 415)

Information power (p. 398)

Informational social influence (p. 409)

Innovative communicators (p. 415)

Interactions (p. 430)

Legitimate power (p. 398)

Lurkers (p. 432)

Market maven (p. 416)

Mass connectors (p. 421)

Media democratization (p. 431)

Media multiplexity (p. 430)

Meetups (p. 430)

Membership reference group (p. 409)

Mere exposure phenomenon (p. 405)

MMOGS (massively multiplayer online games) (p. 434)

Momentum effect (p. 422)

Name-letter effect (p. 403)

Negative word-of-mouth (pp. 422, 424)

Network units (p. 429)

Nodes (p. 429)

Normative influence (p. 403)

Normative social influence (p. 410)

Norms (p. 410)

Object sociality (p. 430)

Opinion leaders (p. 413)

Opinion seekers (p. 415)

Passion-centric (p. 430)

Power users (p. 421)

Presence (p. 431)

Principle of least interest (p. 411)

Propinquity (p. 405)

Reactance (p. 412)

Reference group (p. 395)

Referent power (p. 398)

Reward power (p. 398)

Risky shift effect (p. 408)

Rumour (p. 424)

Social comparison theory (p. 411)

Social graphs (p. 430)

Social loafing (p. 408)

Social network (p. 429)

Social networking (p. 430)

Social object theory (p. 430)

Social power (p. 398)

Sociometric methods (p. 419)

Surrogate consumer (p. 417)

Tie strength (p. 420)

Ties (p. 429)

Tribal marketing strategy (p. 407)

Two-step flow model of influence (p. 415)

Viral marketing (p. 428)

Virtual goods (p. 434)

Virtual worlds (p. 434)

Wisdom of crowds (p. 432)

Word-of-mouth (WOM) (p. 422)

CONSUMER BEHAVIOUR CHALLENGE

1 Compare and contrast the five bases of power described in the text. Which are most likely to be relevant for marketing efforts?

2 Why is referent power an especially potent force for marketing appeals? What factors help to predict whether or not reference groups will be a powerful influence on a person's purchase decisions?

3 Identify the differences between a membership and an aspirational reference group. Give an example of each.

4 What is a brand community, and why is it of interest to marketers? Describe the four types of virtual community members identified in this chapter; and assess their relevance to marketers.

5 Evaluate the strategic soundness of the concept of guerrilla marketing. For what types of product categories is this strategy most likely to be a success?

6 Discuss some factors that determine the amount of conformity likely to be observed among consumers.

7 Define de-individuation. Does de-individuation cause binge drinking? What can or should be done to discourage this type of behaviour?

8 What is the risky shift? How does this affect going shopping with friends? See if you can demonstrate risky shift. Get a group of friends together and ask each privately to rate the likelihood, on a scale from 1 to 7, that they would try a controversial new product (e.g. a credit card that works with a chip implanted in a person's wrist). Then ask the group to discuss the product and rate the idea again. If the average rating changes from the first rating, you have just observed a risky shift.

9 Under what conditions are we more likely to engage in social comparison with dissimilar others versus similar others? How might this dimension be used in the design of marketing appeals?

10 Discuss some reasons for the effectiveness of home shopping parties as a selling tool. What other products might be sold this way? Are home shopping parties, which put pressure on friends and neighbour to buy, ethical?

11 Discuss some factors that influence whether membership groups will have a significant influence on a person's behaviour.

12 Why is word-of-mouth communication often more persuasive than advertising? Which is more powerful, positive or negative word-of-mouth? Describe some ways in which marketers use the internet to encourage positive WOM.

13 What is viral marketing? Guerrilla marketing? Give an example of each.

14 Is there such a thing as a generalized opinion leader? What is likely to determine if an opinion leader will be influential with regard to a specific product category? How can marketers use opinion leaders to help them promote their products or services?

15 The adoption of a certain brand of shoe or apparel by athletes can be a powerful influence on students and other fans. Should secondary school and university coaches be paid to determine what brand of athletic equipment their players will wear?

16 The power of unspoken social norms often becomes obvious only when these norms are violated. To witness this result first hand, try one of the following: stand facing the back wall in a lift; serve dessert before the main course; offer to pay cash for dinner at a friend's home; wear pyjamas to class; or tell someone not to have a nice day.

17 Identify a set of avoidance groups for your peers. Can you identify any consumption decisions that are made with these groups in mind?

18 Identify fashion opinion leaders at your university or business school. Do they fit the profile discussed in the chapter?

19 Although social networking is red-hot, could its days be numbered? Many people have concerns about privacy issues. Others feel that platforms like Facebook are too overwhelming. What are your views? Will people start to tune out all of these networks?[168]

20 What are sociometric techniques? Conduct a sociometric analysis within your hall of residence or neighbourhood. For a product category such as music or cars, ask each individual to identify other individuals with whom they share information. Systematically trace all of these avenues of communication, and identify opinion leaders by locating individuals who are repeatedly named as providing helpful information.

21 The strategy of *viral marketing* gets customers to sell a product to other customers on behalf of the company. That often means convincing your friends to climb on the bandwagon, and sometimes you get a small percentage return (or other reward) if they end up buying something.[169] Some might argue that means you are selling out your friends (or at least selling to your friends) in exchange for a marketing reward. Others might say you are just sharing the wealth with those you care about. Have you been involved in viral marketing by passing along names of your friends or sending them to a website such as **hotmail.com**? If so, what happened? How do you feel about this practice? Discuss the pros and cons of viral marketing.

22 Mobile social networking is the next frontier in technology, as companies race to adapt platforms like Facebook to our mobile phones. Marketers are not far behind, especially because there are 3.3 billion mobile phone subscribers worldwide; that number is far greater than the number of internet users. One report says that about 2 per cent of all mobile users already use their mobile phones for social networking, such as chat and multimedia sharing; it forecasts that this proportion will zoom to at least 12.5 per cent in a few years. Mobile social networks are appealing in part because companies can identify precisely where users are in the physical world. For example, the SpaceMe service from GyPSii displays a map that identifies your friends' locations as well as photos, videos, and other information about them. A Dutch network called Bliin lets users update their location every 15 seconds.[170] This enhanced capability creates some fascinating marketing possibilities – but perhaps it also raises some ethical red flags. What do you see as the opportunities and the threats as we inevitably move to a world where our whereabouts are known to others?

23 Trace a referral pattern for a service provider such as a hair stylist by tracking how clients came to choose them. See if you can identify opinion leaders who are responsible for referring several clients to the businessperson. How might the service provider take advantage of this process to grow their business?

For additional material see the companion website at **www.pearsoned.co.uk/solomon**

NOTES

1. Joel B. Cohen and Ellen Golden, 'Informational social influence and product evaluation', *Journal of Applied Psychology* 56 (February 1972): 54–59; Robert E. Burnkrant and Alain Cousineau, 'Informational and normative social influence in buyer behavior', *Journal of Consumer Research* 2 (December 1975): 206–15; Peter H. Reingen, 'Test of a list procedure for inducing compliance with a request to donate money', *Journal of Applied Psychology* 67 (1982): 110–18.
2. Katherine White and Darren, W. Dahl, 'To be or not to be? The influence of dissociative reference groups on consumer preferences', *Journal of Consumer Psychology* 16 (2006:4): 404–414; Katherine White and Darren W. Dahl, 'Are all out-groups created equal? Consumer identity and dissociative influence', *Journal of Consumer Research* 34 (December 2007): 525–36.
3. C. Whan Park and V. Parker Lessig, 'Students and house-wives: Differences in susceptibility to reference group influence', *Journal of Consumer Research* 4 (September 1977): 102–10.
4. Gina Kolata, 'Study Finds Big Social Factor in Quitting Smoking', *New York Times* (22 May 2008), www.nytimes.com/2008/05/22/science/22smoke.html?ex=1369195200&en=0a10910fcde1a1ac&ei=5124&partner=permalink&exprod=permalink, accessed 22 May 2008. Do you know which European country has the highest percentage of smokers? Go to: http://tobaccocontrol.bmj.com/content/20/1/e4.full for an overview (Tobacco Control, 21 October 2010).
5. Jeffrey D. Ford and Elwood A. Ellis, 'A Re-examination of Group Influence on Member Brand Preference', *Journal of Marketing Research* 17 (February 1980): 125–32; Thomas S. Robertson, *Innovative Behavior and Communication* (New York: Holt, Rinehart & Winston, 1980), ch. 8.
6. William O. Bearden and Michael J. Etzel, 'Reference group influence on product and brand purchase decisions', *Journal of Consumer Research* 9 (1982): 183–94.
7. Kenneth J. Gergen and Mary Gergen, *Social Psychology* (New York: Harcourt Brace Jovanovich, 1981): 312.
8. J.R.P. French Jr and B. Raven, 'The Bases of Social Power', in D. Cartwright (ed.), *Studies in Social Power* (Ann Arbor, MI: Institute for Social Research, 1959): 150–67.
9. Michael R. Solomon, 'Packaging the Service Provider', *The Service Industries Journal* 5 (March 1985): 64–72.
10. Tamar Charry, 'Unconventional Spokesmen Talk up U.S. Robotics' Fast Modems in a New TV Campaign', *New York Times* (6 February 1997), http://www.nytimes.com/1997/02/06/business/unconventional-spokesmen-talk-

up-us-robotics-fast-modems-in-a-new-tv-campaign.html? scp=44&sq=Tamar+Charry&st=nyt, accessed 13 September 2011.

11. Patricia M. West and Susan M. Broniarczyk, 'Integrating Multiple Opinions: The Role of Aspiration Level on Consumer Response to Critic Consensus', *Journal of Consumer Research* 25 (June 1998): 38–51.

12. BBC News, 'Smoking curbs: the global picture': http://news.bbc.co.uk/1/hi/world/4016477.stm (accessed 1 March 2005); Claire Fowlder, 'Where there's smoke there's Germans', Guardian online, 8 July 2008, http://www.guardian.co.uk/commentisfree/2008/jul/08/smoking, accessed 15 July 2008.

13. Claire Fowlder 'Where there's smoke there's Germans', *ibid.*

14. Citigroup report cited in Nick Fletcher's MarketForcesLiveBlog (Guardian online) 'Imperial Tobacco and BAT fall as Citi says smoking could disappear by 2050', http://www.guardian.co.uk/business/marketforceslive/2011/jan/07/imperial-bat-smoking-disappear accessed 20 February 2012.

15. Cornelia Pechmann and S. Ratneshwar, 'The effects of anti-smoking and cigarette advertising on young adolescents' perceptions of peers who smoke', *Journal of Consumer Research* 21 (September 1994): 236–51.

16. Kenneth J. Gergen and Mary Gergen, *Social Psychology* (New York: Harcourt Brace Jovanovich, 1981).

17. Zoe Wood, 'Olympics fever will help to make 2012 the year of the bike', *The Observer* 29 January 2012, http://www.guardian.co.uk/lifeandstyle/2012/jan/29/cycling-boom-olympics?INTCMP=SRCH, accessed 31 January 2012.

18. Stephanie Rosenbloom, 'Names That Match Forge a Bond on the Internet', *New York Times* (10 April 2008), www.nytimes.com/2008/04/10/us/10names.html?ref=us, accessed 10 April 2008.

19. Harold H. Kelley, 'Two Functions of Reference Groups', in Harold Proshansky and Bernard Siedenberg (eds), *Basic Studies in Social Psychology* (New York: Holt, Rinehart & Winston, 1965): 210–14.

20. A. Benton Cocanougher and Grady D. Bruce, 'Socially distant reference groups and consumer aspirations', *Journal of Marketing Research* 8 (August 1971): 79–81.

21. Jason Gregory, 'David Beckham Bares His Body in the latest Armani Campaign', 11 June 2009, http://www.entertainmentwise.com/news/48836/david-beckham-bares-his-body-in-latest-armani-campaign–pictures, accessed 1 February 2012.

22. A. Benton Cocanougher and Grady D. Bruce, 'Socially Distant Reference Groups and Consumer Aspirations', *Journal of Marketing Research* 8 (August 1971): 79–81.

23. Nick Bilton, 'Twitter Users Congregate Based on Mood, Study Says', *New York Times* (16 March 2011), http://bits.blogs.nytimes.com/2011/03/16/twitter-users-congregate-based-on-mood-study-says/, accessed 29 April 2011.

24. L. Festinger, S. Schachter and K. Back, *Social Pressures in Informal Groups: A Study of Human Factors in Housing* (New York: Harper, 1950).

25. R.B. Zajonc, H.M. Markus and W. Wilson, 'Exposure effects and associative learning', *Journal of Experimental Social Psychology* 10 (1974): 248–63.

26. D.J. Stang, 'Methodological factors in mere exposure research', *Psychological Bulletin* 81 (1974): 1014–25; R.B. Zajonc, P. Shaver, C. Tavris and D. Van Kreveid, 'Exposure, satiation and stimulus discriminability', *Journal of Personality and Social Psychology* 21 (1972): 270–80.

27. J.E. Grush, K.L. McKeogh and R.F. Ahlering, 'Extrapolating laboratory exposure research to actual political elections', *Journal of Personality and Social Psychology* 36 (1978): 257–70.

28. Richard Wilk, 'A critique of desire: Distaste and dislike in consumer behavior', *Consumption, Culture and Markets* 1(2) (1997): 175–96; see also Pierre Bourdieu, *Distinction: A Social Critique of the Judgement of Taste* (London: Routledge, 1984); E.N. Banister and M.K. Hogg, 'Negative symbolic consumption and consumers' drive for self-esteem: The case of the fashion industry', *European Journal of Marketing* 7 (2004): 850–68; B.S. Turner and J. Edmunds, 'The distaste of taste: Bordieu, cultural capital and the Australian postwar elite', *Journal of Consumer Culture* 2(2) (2002): 219–40.

29. Jonah Berger and Lindsay Rand, 'Shifting Signals to Help Health: Using Identity Signaling to Reduce Risky Health Behaviors', *Journal of Consumer Research* 35, no. 3 (2008): 509–18.

30. Basil G. Englis and Michael R. Solomon, 'To be and not to be: Reference group stereotyping and *The Clustering of America*', *Journal of Advertising* 24 (Spring 1995): 13–28; Michael R. Solomon and Basil G. Englis, 'I Am Not, Therefore I Am: The Role of Anti-Consumption in the Process of Self-Definition', Special Session at the Association for Consumer Research meetings, October 1996, Tucson, Arizona.

31. Bruce Feirstein, *Real Men Don't Eat Quiche* (New York: Pocket Books, 1982); www.auntiefashions.com, accessed 31 December 2002.

32. Katherine White and Darren W. Dahl, 'Are all out-groups created equal? Consumer identity and dissociative influence', *Journal of Consumer Research* 34 (December 2007): 525.

33. Candice R. Hollenbeck and George M. Zinkhan, 'Consumer Activism on the Internet: The Role of Anti-Brand Communities', *Advances in Consumer Research* 33, no. 1 (2006): 479–85.

34. Marius K. Luedicke, 'Brand Community under Fire: The Role of Social Environments for the Hummer Brand Community', *Advances in Consumer Research* 33, no. 1 (2006): 486–93.

35. http://halo.xbox.com/en-us/intel/titles/halo2, accessed 15 June 2011; Kris Oser, 'Microsoft's Halo 2 Soars on Viral Push', *Advertising Age* (25 October 2004): 46.

36. James H. McAlexander, John W. Schouten and Harold F. Koenig, 'Building brand community', *Journal of Marketing* 66 (January 2002): 38–54; Albert Muniz and Thomas O'Guinn, 'Brand community', *Journal of Consumer Research* (March 2001): 412–32.

37. Rama K. Jayanti and Jagdip Singh, 'Framework for Distributed Consumer Learning in Online Communities', *Journal of Consumer Research* 36, no. 6 (2010): 1058–81.

38. Schau, Muñiz and Arnould, 'How Brand Community Practices Create Value'.

39. Veronique Cova and Bernard Cova, 'Tribal aspects of postmodern consumption research: The case of French in-line roller skaters', *Journal of Consumer Behavior* 1 (June 2001): 67–76.

40. Penelope Eckert and Sally McConnell-Ginet, 'Think practically and look locally: Language and gender as community-based practice', *Annual Review of Anthropology* (1992): 461–90, at 464, cited in Emma Moore, 'Approaches to Identity: Lesson from Sociolinguistics', Seminar paper, Customer Research Academy, Manchester School of Management, UMIST, UK (22 April 2004): 2.

41. Etienne Wenger, *Communities of Practice: Learning, Meaning and Identity* (Cambridge: Cambridge University Press, 1998), cited in Moore, 'Approaches to Identity', *op. cit.*

42. Emma Moore, 'Learning Style and Identity: A Socio-linguistic Analysis of a Bolton High School', unpublished Ph.D. dissertation, University of Manchester (2003).

43. Penelope Eckert, 'Constructing Meaning in Socio-linguistic Variation', paper presented at the Annual Meeting of the American Anthropological Association, New Orleans, USA (November 2002) (accessible at www.stanford.edu/~eckert/AAA02.pdf), cited in Moore 'Approaches to Identity', *op. cit.*: 3.

44. J. Craig Andrews and Richard G. Netemeyer, 'Alcohol Warning Label Effects: Socialization, Addiction, and Public Policy Issues', in Ronald P. Hill (ed.), *Marketing and Consumer Research in the Public Interest* (Thousand Oaks, CA: Sage, 1996): 153–75; 'National study finds increase in college binge drinking', *Alcoholism and Drug Abuse Weekly* (27 March 2000): 12–13; Emma Banister and Maria Piacentini, '"Binge Drinking: Do They Mean Us?" Living Life to the Full in Students' Own Words', in C. Pechmann and L. Price (eds), *Advances in Consumer Research* 33 (forthcoming).

45. Maria Piacentini and Emma N. Banister, 'Getting hammered? . . . Students coping with alcohol', *Journal of Consumer Behaviour* 5(2) (Spring 2006).

46. BBC Online, http://www.bbc.co.uk/insideout/southeast/series2/nhs_binge_drinking_alcohol_abuse_drunk_alcoholism.shtml (17 February 2003); *Guardian*, http://society.guardian.co.uk/drugsandalcohol/story/0,8150,874700,00.html (14 January 2003).

47. Maria G. Piacentini, Andreas Chatzidakis and Emma N. Banister (2012), 'Making Sense of Drinking: The Role of Techniques of Neutralisation and Counter-Neutralisation in Negotiating Alcohol Consumption', *Sociology of Health and Illness*, vol. 34, no. 6 *forthcoming*.

48. B. Latane, K. Williams and S. Harkins, 'Many hands make light the work: The causes and consequences of social loafing', *Journal of Personality and Social Psychology* 37 (1979): 822–32.

49. S. Freeman, M. Walker, R. Borden and B. Latane, 'Diffusion of responsibility and restaurant tipping: Cheaper by the bunch', *Personality and Social Psychology Bulletin* 1 (1978): 584–7.

50. Nathan Kogan and Michael A. Wallach, *Risk Taking* (New York: Holt, Rinehart & Winston, 1964).

51. Nathan Kogan and Michael A. Wallach, 'Risky shift phenomenon in small decision-making groups: A test of the information exchange hypothesis', *Journal of Experimental Social Psychology* 3 (January 1967): 75–84; Kogan and Wallach, *Risk Taking*; Arch G. Woodside and M. Wayne DeLozier, 'Effects of word-of-mouth advertising on consumer risk taking', *Journal of Advertising* (Fall 1976): 12–19.

52. Roger Brown, *Social Psychology* (New York: The Free Press, 1965).

53. David L. Johnson and I.R. Andrews, 'Risky shift phenomenon tested with consumer product stimuli', *Journal of Personality and Social Psychology* 20 (1971): 382–5; see also Vithala R. Rao and Joel H. Steckel, 'A polarization model for describing group preferences,' *Journal of Consumer Research* 18 (June 1991): 108–18.

54. Donald H. Granbois, 'Improving the study of customer in-store behavior', *Journal of Marketing* 32 (October 1968): 28–32.

55. Len Strazewski, 'Tupperware locks in new strategy', *Advertising Age* (8 February 1988): 30.

56. Melanie Wells, 'Smooth Operator', *Forbes* (13 May 2002): 167–68.

57. Tanya Irwin, 'Study: Facebook Users Show "Herding Instinct"', *Marketing Daily* (12 October 2010), http://www.mediapost.com/publications/?fa=Articles.showArticle&art_aid=137340&nid=119587, accessed 29 April 2011.

58. See Robert B. Cialdini, *Influence: Science and Practice*, 2nd edn (New York: Scott, Foresman, 1988) for an excellent and entertaining treatment of this process.

59. For the seminal work on conformity and social influence, see Solomon E. Asch, 'Effects of Group Pressure Upon the Modification and Distortion of Judgments', in D. Cartwright and A. Zander (eds), *Group Dynamics* (New York: Harper & Row, 1953); Richard S. Crutchfield, 'Conformity and character', *American Psychologist* 10 (1955): 191–8; Muzafer Sherif, 'A study of some social factors in perception', *Archives of Psychology* 27 (1935): 187.

60. Robert E. Burnkrant and Alain Cousineau, 'Informational and normative social influence in buyer behavior', *Journal of Consumer Research* 2 (December 1975): 206–15.

61. For a study attempting to measure individual differences in proclivity to conformity, see William O. Bearden, Richard G. Netemeyer and Jesse E. Teel, 'Measurement of consumer susceptibility to interpersonal influence', *Journal of Consumer Research* 15 (March 1989): 473–81.

62. Douglas B. Holt, Søren Askegaard and Torsten Ringberg, '7 ups and Downs', unpublished manuscript, Penn State University.

63. John W. Thibaut and Harold H. Kelley, *The Social Psychology of Groups* (New York: Wiley, 1959); W.W. Waller and R. Hill, *The Family, a Dynamic Interpretation* (New York: Dryden, 1951).

64. Bearden, Netemeyer and Teel, 'Measurement of consumer susceptibility to interpersonal influence'; Lynn R. Kahle, 'Observations: Role-relaxed consumers: A trend of the nineties', *Journal of Advertising Research* (March/April 1995): 66–71; Lynn R. Kahle and Aviv Shoham, 'Observations: Role-relaxed consumers: Empirical evidence', *Journal of Advertising Research* (May/June 1995): 59–62.

65. Leon Festinger, 'A theory of social comparison processes', *Human Relations* 7 (May 1954): 117–40.

66. Chester A. Insko, Sarah Drenan, Michael R. Solomon, Richard Smith and Terry J. Wade, 'Conformity as a function of the consistency of positive self-evaluation with being liked and being right', *Journal of Experimental Social Psychology* 19 (1983): 341–58.

67. Abraham Tesser, Murray Millar and Janet Moore, 'Some affective consequences of social comparison and reflection processes: The pain and pleasure of being close', *Journal of Personality and Social Psychology* 54(1) (1988): 49–61.

68. L. Wheeler, K.G. Shaver, R.A. Jones, G.R. Goethals, J. Cooper, J.E. Robinson, C.L. Gruder and K.W. Butzine, 'Factors determining the choice of a comparison other', *Journal of Experimental Social Psychology* 5 (1969): 219–32.

69. M.L. Richins, 'Social comparison and the idealized images of advertising', *Journal of Consumer Research* 18 (June 1991): 71–83; M.C. Martin and P.F. Kennedy, 'Advertising and social comparison: Consequences for female preadolescents and adolescents', *Psychology and Marketing* 10(6) (1993): 513–29; M.C. Martin and P.F. Kennedy, 'Social Comparison and the Beauty of Advertising Models: The Role of Motives in Comparison', in Chris T. Allen and Deborah Roedder John (eds), *Advances in Consumer Research* 21 (Provo, UT: Association for Consumer Research, 1994): 365–71; M.C. Martin and N.J. Gentry, 'Stuck in the model trap: The effects of beautiful models in ads on female pre-adolescents and adolescents', *Journal of Advertising* 26(2) (Summer 1997): 19–33.

70. See J.V. Wood, 'Theory and research concerning social comparisons of personal attributes', *Psychological Bulletin* 106 (September 1989): 231–48 for a detailed exposition of the evolving debates around the theory of social comparison.

71. Martin and Kennedy, 'Advertising and social comparison'; Martin and Kennedy, 'Social Comparison and the Beauty of Advertising Models'; Martin and Gentry, 'Stuck in the model trap'; Margaret K. Hogg, Margaret Bruce and Kerry Hough, 'Female images in advertising: The implications of social comparison for marketing', *International Journal of Advertising* 18(4) (1999): 445–73; Margaret K. Hogg and Aikaterini Fragou, 'Social comparison goals and the consumption of advertising: towards a more contingent view of young women's consumption of advertising', *Journal of Marketing Management* 19(7–8) (September 2003): 749–80.

72. Michael Hafner, 'How dissimilar others may still resemble the self: Assimilation and contrast after social comparison', *Journal of Consumer Psychology* 14(1 and 2) (2004): 187–96.

73. George P. Moschis, 'Social comparison and informal group influence', *Journal of Marketing Research* 13 (August 1976): 237–44.

74. Burnkrant and Cousineau, 'Informational and normative social influence in buyer behavior'; M. Venkatesan, 'Experimental study of consumer behavior conformity and independence', *Journal of Marketing Research* 3 (November 1966): 384–7.

75. Kenneth J. Gergen and Mary Gergen, *Social Psychology* (New York: Harcourt Brace Jovanovich, 1981).

76. L.J. Strickland, S. Messick and D.N. Jackson, 'Conformity, anticonformity and independence: Their dimensionality and generality', *Journal of Personality and Social Psychology* 16 (1970): 494–507.

77. Jack W. Brehm, *A Theory of Psychological Reactance* (New York: Academic Press, 1966).

78. R.D. Ashmore, V. Ramchandra and R. Jones, 'Censorship as an Attitude Change Induction', paper presented at meeting of Eastern Psychological Association, New York, 1971; R.A. Wicklund and J. Brehm, *Perspectives on Cognitive Dissonance* (Hillsdale, NJ: Erlbaum, 1976).

79. C.R. Snyder and H.L. Fromkin, *Uniqueness: The Human Pursuit of Difference* (New York: Plenum Press, 1980).

80. Quoted in Raymond Serafin, 'Non-conformity sparks Saab', *Advertising Age* (3 April 1995): 27.

81. Everett M. Rogers, *Diffusion of Innovations*, 3rd edn (New York: Free Press, 1983); cf. also Duncan J. Watts and Peter Sheridan Dodds, 'Influentials, Networks, and Public Opinion Formation', *Journal of Consumer Research* 34 (December 2007): 441–58; Morris B. Holbrook and Michela Addis, 'Taste versus the Market: An Extension of Research on the Consumption of Popular Culture', *Journal of Consumer Research* 34 (October 2007): 415–24.

82. Dorothy Leonard-Barton, 'Experts as Negative Opinion Leaders in the Diffusion of a Technological Innovation', *Journal of Consumer Research* 11 (March 1985): 914–26; Rogers, *Diffusion of Innovations*; cf. also Jan Kratzer and Christopher Lettl, 'Distinctive Roles of Lead Users and Opinion Leaders in the Social Networks of Schoolchildren', *Journal of Consumer Research* 36 December (2009): 646–59.

83. Herbert Menzel, 'Interpersonal and Unplanned Communications: Indispensable or Obsolete?', in Edward B. Roberts (ed.), *Biomedical Innovation* (Cambridge, MA: MIT Press, 1981), 155–63.

84. Meera P. Venkatraman, 'Opinion Leaders, Adopters, and Communicative Adopters: A Role Analysis', *Psychology & Marketing* 6 (Spring 1989): 51–68.

85. Everett M. Rogers, *Diffusion of Innovations*, 3rd edn (New York: Free Press, 1983).

86. Niraj Dawar, Philip M. Parker and Lydia J. Price, 'A cross-cultural study of interpersonal information exchange', *Journal of International Business Studies* (3rd quarter 1996): 497–516.

87. Robert Merton, *Social Theory and Social Structure* (Glencoe, IL: Free Press, 1957).

88. King and Summers, 'Overlap of opinion leadership across consumer product categories', *op. cit*; see also Ronald E. Goldsmith, Jeanne R. Heitmeyer and Jon B. Freiden, 'Social values and fashion leadership', *Clothing and Textiles Research Journal* 10 (Fall 1991): 37–45; J.O. Summers, 'Identity of women's clothing fashion opinion leaders', *Journal of Marketing Research* 7 (1970): 178–85.

89. Duncan J. Watts and Peter Sheridan Dodds, 'Influentials, Networks, and Public Opinion Formation', *Journal of Consumer Research* 34 (December 2007): 441–58.

90. *Ibid.*, 442.

91. *Ibid.*, 441–58.

92. http://klout.com/home, accessed 15 June 2011.

93. Matthew Creamer, 'Your Followers Are No Measure of Your Influence', *Advertising Age* (3 January 2011), http://adage.com/article/special-report-influencers-2010/facebook-followers-measure-influence/147957/, accessed 30 April 2011.

94. Gerrit Antonides and Gulden Asugman, 'The communication structure of consumer opinions', in Flemming Hansen (ed.), *European Advances in Consumer Research* 2 (Provo, UT: Association for Consumer Research, 1995): 132–7.

95. Steven A. Baumgarten, 'The innovative communicator in the diffusion process', *Journal of Marketing Research* 12 (February 1975): 12–18.

96. Laura J. Yale and Mary C. Gilly, 'Dyadic perceptions in personal source information search', *Journal of Business Research* 32 (1995): 225–37.

97. Russell W. Belk, 'Occurrence of Word-of-Mouth Buyer Behavior as a Function of Situation and Advertising Stimuli', in Fred C. Allvine (ed.), *Combined Proceedings of*

the American Marketing Association series, no. 33 (Chicago: American Marketing Association, 1971): 419–22.

98. Lawrence F. Feick, Linda L. Price and Robin A. Higie, 'People Who Use People: The Other Side of Opinion Leadership', in Richard J. Lutz (ed.), *Advances in Consumer Research* 13 (Provo, UT: Association for Consumer Research, 1986): 301–5.

99. For discussion of the market maven construct, see Lawrence F. Feick and Linda L. Price, 'The market maven', *Managing* (July 1985): 10; scale items adapted from Lawrence F. Feick and Linda L. Price, 'The market maven: A diffuser of marketplace information', *Journal of Marketing* 51 (January 1987): 83–7.

100. Michael R. Solomon, 'The missing link: Surrogate consumers in the marketing chain', *Journal of Marketing* 50 (October 1986): 208–18.

101. Andra Adelson, 'A French skin-care line seeks to take America by first winning over pharmacists', *New York Times* (14 February 1994): D7.

102. Sarah Boseley and Rob Evans, 'Drug giants accused over doctors' perks', *The Guardian*, 23 August 2008: 1–2.

103. Stern and Gould, 'The consumer as financial opinion leader', *op. cit.*

104. William R. Darden and Fred D. Reynolds, 'Predicting opinion leadership for men's apparel fashions', *Journal of Marketing Research* 1 (August 1972): 324–8. A modified version of the opinion leadership scale with improved reliability and validity can be found in Terry L. Childers, 'Assessment of the psychometric properties of an opinion leadership scale', *Journal of Marketing Research* 23 (May 1986): 184–8.

105. Dan Seligman, 'Me and Monica', *Forbes* (23 March 1998): 76.

106. Gina Kolata, 'Find Yourself Packing It On? Blame Friends', *New York Times Online Edition* (26 July 2007).

107. 'Referrals top ads as influence on patients' doctor selections', *Marketing News* (30 January 1987): 22.

108. Peter H. Reingen and Jerome B. Kernan, 'Analysis of referral networks in marketing: Methods and illustration', *Journal of Marketing Research* 23 (November 1986): 370–8.

109. Peter H. Reingen, Brian L. Foster, Jacqueline Johnson Brown and Stephen B. Seidman, 'Brand congruence in interpersonal relations: a social network analysis', *Journal of Consumer Research* 11 (December 1984): 771–83; see also James C. Ward and Peter H. Reingen, 'Sociocognitive Analysis of Group Decision-Making among Consumers', *Journal of Consumer Research* 17 (December 1990): 245–62.

110. Peter H. Reingen, Brian L. Foster, Jacqueline Johnson Brown and Stephen B. Seidman, 'Brand congruence in interpersonal relations: A social network analysis', *Journal of Consumer Research* 11 (December 1984): 771–83; see also James C. Ward and Peter H. Reingen, 'Sociocognitive analysis of group decision-making among consumers', *Journal of Consumer Research* 17 (December 1990): 245–62.

111. Jenna Wortham, 'What's the Value of a Facebook Friend? About 37 Cents', *New York Times* (9 January 2009), www.nytimes.com, accessed 9 January 2009.

112. T.M. Pavia and M.J. Mason (2004), 'The reflexive relationship between consumer behavior and adaptive coping', *Journal of Consumer Research* 31(2): 441–54.

113. See also some of their recent work: Darach Turley and Stephanie O'Donohoe 'Grief goods: material possessions and meaning construction in bereavement' in Alan Bradshaw, Chris Hackley and Pauline Maclaran (eds), *European Association for Consumer Research Conference* 2010 RHUL page p. 29. This uses 'a close reading of Didion's narrative [The Year of Magical Thinking] . . . [to] explore the symbiotic relationship between goods and grieving and how material possessions are marshalled in the service of meaning construction'.

114. Ed Keller and Jon Berry, *The Influentials* (New York: Simon & Schuster, 2003).

115. 'Introducing Peer Influence Analysis: 500 Billion Peer Impressions Each Year', *Empowered* (20 April 2010), http://forrester.typepad.com/groundswell/2010/04/introducing-peer-influence-analysis.html, accessed 31 December 2010.

116. 'MySpace, Isobar & Carat, Never Ending Friending: A Journey into Social Networking', http://creative.myspace.com/groups/_ms/nef/images/40161_nef_onlinebook.pdf, accessed 31 December 2010; cf. also Malcolm Gladwell, *The Tipping Point* (New York: Little, Brown, 2000).

117. See for instance the *Daily Princetonian*'s editorial about Thefacebook.com as 'possibly the biggest word-of-mouth trend to hit campus since St Ives Medicated Apricot Scrub found its ways into the women's bathroom', cited by Peter Applebome, 'On campus, hanging out by logging on', *NYT Online* (1 December 2004); see also note 99.

118. Johan Arndt, 'Role of product-related conversations in the diffusion of a new product', *Journal of Marketing Research* 4 (August 1967): 291–5.

119. '"Word-of-mouth" to become true measure of ads', *Marketing* (9 February 1995): 7.

120. Quoted in Barbara B. Stern and Stephen J. Gould, 'The consumer as financial opinion leader', *Journal of Retail Banking* 10 (Summer 1988): 43–52.

121. Douglas R. Pruden and Terry G. Vavra, 'Controlling the grapevine', *MM* (July–August 2004): 23–30.

122. www.bzzagent.com, accessed 15 June 2011.

123. Les Luchter, 'Kraft, Folgers, Olay Top Baby Boomer Gals' WOM', *Marketing Daily*, (18 November 2008), www.mediapost.com/publications/?fa=Articles.showArticle&art_aid=95000, accessed 18 November 2008.

124. Andrew D. Gershoff, Ashesh Mukherjee and Anirban Mukhopadjyay, 'Few ways to love, but many ways to hate: Attribute ambiguity and the positivity effect in agent evaluation', *Journal of Consumer Research* 33 (March 2007): 499–505.

125. Elihu Katz and Paul F. Lazarsfeld, *Personal Influence* (Glencoe, IL: Free Press, 1955).

126. John A. Martilla, 'Word-of-mouth communication in the industrial adoption process', *Journal of Marketing Research* 8 (March 1971): 173–8; see also Marsha L. Richins, 'Negative word-of-mouth by dissatisfied consumers: A pilot study', *Journal of Marketing* 47 (Winter 1983): 68–78.

127. Arndt, 'Role of product-related conversations in the diffusion of a new product', *op. cit.*

128. James H. Myers and Thomas S. Robertson, 'Dimensions of opinion leadership', *Journal of Marketing Research* 9 (February 1972): 41–6.

129. Dorothy Leonard-Barton, 'Experts as Negative Opinion Leaders in the Diffusion of a Technological Innovation', *Journal of Consumer Research* 11 (March 1985): 914–26.

130. James F. Engel, Robert J. Kegerreis, and Roger D. Blackwell, 'Word-of-Mouth Communication by the Innovator', *Journal of Marketing* 33 (July 1969): 15–19; cf. also Rajdeep Growl, Thomas W. Cline and Anthony Davies, 'Early-Entrant Advantage, Word-of-Mouth Communication, Brand Similarity, and the Consumer Decision Making Process', *Journal of Consumer Psychology* 13, no. 3 (2003): 187–97.

131. 'Black sheep of the Theakston family', *Marketing* (3 December 1992): 24.

132. Kimberley Paterson, 'Giving a boost to word-of-mouth advertising', *Rough Notes Co. Inc.* (April 1999).

133. Bill Barol, 'Batmania', *Newsweek* (26 June 1989): 70.

134. Chip Walker, 'Word-of-mouth', *American Demographics* (July 1995): 38–44.

135. Richard J. Lutz, 'Changing brand attitudes through modification of cognitive structure', *Journal of Consumer Research* 1 (March 1975): 49–59; for some suggested remedies to bad publicity, see Mitch Griffin, Barry J. Babin and Jill S. Attaway, 'An Empirical Investigation of the Impact of Negative Public Publicity on Consumer Attitudes and Intentions', in Rebecca H. Holman and Michael R. Solomon (eds), *Advances in Consumer Research* 18 (Provo, UT: Association for Consumer Research, 1991): 334–41; Alice M. Tybout, Bobby J. Calder and Brian Sternthal, 'Using information processing theory to design marketing strategies', *Journal of Marketing Research* 18 (1981): 73–9; see also Russell N. Laczniak, Thomas E. DeCarlo and Sridhar N. Ramaswami, 'Consumers' responses to negative word-of-mouth communication: An attribution theory perspective', *Journal of Consumer Psychology* 11(1) (2001): 57–74.

136. Gulden Asugman, 'An Evaluation of Negative Word-of-Mouth Research for New Extensions', in B. Englis and A. Olofsson (eds), *European Advances in Consumer Research* 3 (Provo, UT: Association for Consumer Research, 1998): 70–5.

137. Robert E. Smith and Christine A. Vogt, 'The effects of integrating advertising and negative word-of-mouth communications on message processing and response', *Journal of Consumer Psychology* 4(2) (1995): 133–51; Paula Fitzgerald Bone, 'Word-of-mouth effects on short-term and long-term product judgments', *Journal of Business Research* 32 (1995): 213–23.

138. Keith Schneider, 'Brands for the Chattering Masses', *New York Times* (17 December 2006), www.nytimes.com, accessed 3 October 2007.

139. 'Dunkin' donuts buys out critical web site', *The New York Times on the Web* (27 August 1999); for a discussion of ways to assess negative WOM online, see David M. Boush and Lynn R. Kahle, 'Evaluating negative information in online consumer discussions: From qualitative analysis to signal detection', *Journal of Euro Marketing* 11(2) (2001): 89–105.

140. James C. Ward and Amy L. Ostrom, 'Complaining to the masses: The role of protest framing in customer-created complaint web sites', *Journal of Consumer Research* 33(2) (2006): 220.

141. Charles W. King and John O. Summers, 'Overlap of opinion leadership across consumer product categories', *Journal of Marketing Research* 7 (February 1970): 43–50.

142. Michael Fumento, 'Tampon Terrorism', *Forbes* (17 May 1999): 170.

143. John Leo, 'Psst! Wait 'till you hear this: A scholar says rumors reveal our fears and desires', *Time* (16 March 1987): 76.

144. Mary Papenfuss, 'Internet haters tied to model's suicide: Claudia Boerner 32 found dead after TV show appearance sparks attacks', Newser, 10 April 2012, http://www.newser.com/story/143714/internet-haters-linked-to-cooking-model-suicide.html, accessed 16 April 2012.

145. youtube.com/watch?v=y6t1R3yB-cs, accessed 15 June 2011.

146. Sonia Murray, 'Street marketing does the trick', *Advertising Age* (20 March 2000): S12.

147. Quoted in 'Taking to the streets', *Newsweek* (2 November 1998): 70–3, at 71.

148. Karl Greenberg, 'Scion's Web-Based Pre-Launch Scorns Tradition', *Marketing Daily* (6 March 2007), www.mediapost.com, accessed 6 March 2007.

149. Constance L. Hays, 'Guerrilla marketing is going mainstream', *New York Times on the Web* (7 October 1999).

150. Cathy Horyn, 'A store made for right now: You shop until it's dropped', *NYTOnline* (17 February 2004).

151. Wayne Friedman, 'Street marketing hits the internet', *Advertising Age* (1 May 2000): 32; Erin White, 'Online buzz helps album skyrocket to top of charts', *Wall Street Journal Interactive Edition* (5 October 1999).

152. The material in this section is adapted from Tracy Tuten and Michael R. Solomon, *Social Media Marketing* (Englewood Cliffs, NJ: Pearson, 2012).

153. Karlene Lukovitz, 'Marketers Praise Skittles' Gutsy Site Move', *Marketing Daily* (March 3, 2009), www.mediapost.com, accessed 3 March 2009.

154. www.pandora.com, accessed 15 June 2011.

155. Barry Wellman, 'Physical Place and Cyberplace: The Rise of Personalized Networking', *International Journal of Urban & Regional Research* 24, no. 2 (2001): 227–52.

156. Alexandra Marin and Barry Wellman, 'Social Network Analysis: An Introduction', in *Handbook of Social Network Analysis* (London: Sage, 2010).

157. John Coate, 'Cyberspace Innkeeping: Building Online Community' (1998), http://www.cervisa.com/innkeeping, accessed 31 December 2010.

158. T.B. Sheridan, 'Further Musings on the Psychophysics of Presence', *Presence: Teleoperators and Virtual Environments* 5 (1994): 241–46.

159. Matthew Lombard and Theresa Ditton, 'At the Heart of It All: The Concept of Presence', *Journal of Computer Mediated Communication* 3, no. 2 (1973), http://jcmc.indiana.edu/vol3/issue2/lombard.html, accessed 31 December 2010.

160. James Surowiecki, *The Wisdom of Crowds* (New York: Anchor, 2005); Jeff Howe, 'The Rise of Crowdsourcing', *Wired* (June 2006), www.wired.com/wired/archive/14.06/crowds.html, accessed 3 October 2007.

161. Mark Weingarten, 'Designed to Grow', *Business2.0* (June 2007): 35–37. For a contrarian view, cf. Joseph P. Simmons, Leif D. Nelson, Jeff Galak and Shane Frederick,

'Intuitive Biases in Choice versus Estimation: Implications for the Wisdom of Crowds', *Journal of Consumer Research* 38, no. 1 (June 2011): 1–15.

162. www.quirky.com, accessed 15 June 2011.

163. www.sermo.com, accessed 15 June 2011; Susanna Hamner, 'Cashing in on Doctors' Thinking', *Business 2.0* (June 2006): 40.

164. www.eventful.com, accessed 15 June 2011; www.sellaband. com, accessed 15 June 2011.

165. Quoted in Darren Everson, 'Baseball Taps Wisdom of Fans', *Wall Street Journal* (7 March 2008): W4.

166. Janice Denegri-Knot and Mike Molesworth, 'Concepts and Practices of Digital Virtual Consumption', *Consumption Markets & Culture* 13, no. 2 (2010): 109–32; Natalie T. Wood and Michael R. Solomon, 'Adonis or Atrocious: Spokesavatars and Source Effects in Immersive Digital Environments', in Matthew S. Eastin, Terry Daugherty and Neal M. Burns (eds), *Handbook of Research on Digital Media*

and Advertising: User Generated Content Consumption (Hershey, PA: IGI Global, 2011): 521–34.

167. James Surowiecki, *The Wisdom of Crowds* (New York: Anchor, 2005); Jeff Howe, 'The Rise of Crowdsourcing', *Wired* (June 2006), www.wired.com/wired/archive/14.06/ crowds.html, accessed 3 October 2007.

168. Quoted in Suzanne Vranica, 'Ad Houses Will Need to Be More Nimble, Clients Are Demanding More and Better Use of Consumer Data, Web', *Wall Street Journal* (2 January 2008): B3.

169. Thomas E. Weber, 'Viral marketing: Web's newest ploy may make you an unpopular friend', *The Wall Street Journal Interactive Edition* (13 September 1999).

170. Victoria Shannon, 'Social Networking Moves to the Cellphone', *New York Times* (6 March 2008), www. nytimes.com/2008/03/06/technology/06wireless.html?ex= 1362459600&en=571b090085db559d&ei=5088&partner =rssnyt&emc=rss, accessed 6 March 2008.

11 EUROPEAN FAMILY STRUCTURES, HOUSEHOLD DECISION-MAKING AND AGE COHORTS

CHAPTER OBJECTIVES

When you finish reading this chapter you will understand why:

→ Marketers often need to understand consumers' behaviour, rather than a consumer's behaviour.

→ Our traditional notions about families are outdated.

→ Many important demographic dimensions of a population relate to family and household structure.

→ Members of a family unit play different roles and have different amounts of influence when the family makes purchase decisions.

→ Children learn over time what and how to consume.

→ We have many things in common with others because they are about the same age (age cohorts).

→ Teens are a critically important age segment for marketers.

→ Baby Boomers continue to be the most powerful age segment economically in the EU.

→ Seniors continue to increase in size and spending power as a market segment, and marketers are making more and better efforts to understand this segment.

ALTHOUGH it was still three days before Christmas, Liane was intent on making a large cauldron of Dutch pea soup, while her partner Joost was in the process of chopping ingredients for several Indonesian dishes. They agreed that all these dishes taste best if they are cooked a few days before actually eating them.

Although pea soup isn't always a part of Christmas dinner in Holland, it definitely has its place in the Dutch 'winter menu'. The best pea soup is thick in texture with peas, potatoes, celery root, onions, leek, carrots and generous chunks of

ham. Hot pea soup and dark bread topped with thinly sliced bacon (*Snert met roggebrood en spek*) leaves everyone feeling warm and content. The only concession to 'store bought' ingredients that Liane will make is to add a sliced Unox rookworst (sausage) on the day the soup is served. Joost, on the other hand, turns his nose up at the very idea of using anything from a package. While many Dutch rely on prepared Indonesian seasoning from Conimex, Joost considers himself a serious cook, and uses only traditional, freshly prepared dishes, which means lots of chopping, blending, mixing and marinating for days!

As in many other European countries, Christmas is a busy family time in Holland. Everyone has social events to attend, some of which are personal and joyful, while others seem more 'obligatory'. For Joost and Liane, the Dutch tradition of celebrating two Christmas days (December 25 and 26) is particularly helpful as they try to find time to visit everyone. Joost's parents divorced 18 years ago, and his mother lives in the east of Holland, while his father is two hours away in Amsterdam. In addition to Joost's parents, there is also Liane's family. Family, food, and lots of train travel . . . all part of the Christmas season for Joost and Liane.

INTRODUCTION

Joost and Liane's efforts to celebrate Christmas with their families is fairly typical of the joint nature of many consumer decisions. The individual decision-making process we described in detail in Chapter 9 is, in many cases, overly simplistic. This is because more than one person often participates in the problem-solving sequence, from initial problem recognition and information search to evaluation of alternatives and product choice. To further complicate matters, these decisions often include two or more people, or families, all with differing expectations, who may not have the same level of investment in the outcome, the same tastes and preferences, or the same consumption priorities.

Whether they are choosing a can of tuna or buying a new multimedia entertainment system for the home, consumers commonly work together. This section of the chapter examines issues related to *collective decision-making*, where more than one person is involved in the purchasing process for products or services that may be used by multiple consumers. We focus specifically on one of the most important organizations to which we all claim membership – the family unit. We will consider how members of a family negotiate among themselves, and how important changes in the modern family structure are affecting this process. The chapter concludes by discussing how we use age in consumer research as a predictor of behaviour, and the appeals that marketers make to diverse age subcultures.

THE FAMILY

Constructing and deconstructing the family in Europe

While it might still be too early to draw definite conclusions, it is reasonable to speculate that historians will regard the period from the 1990s to 2015 as one of the most politically, socially and economically turbulent timeframes in modern history. Radical political and market changes throughout Western and Eastern Europe are reflections and outcomes of intense social change in European societies that have been under way since the 1950s. While the extent and pace of changes and the national perceptions of social change have differed from one country to another, it is clear that many of our social institutions have been altered over the past four decades, not least of which is the notion of 'family'. In 2012 the population of the EU27 was just over a half-billion, projected to grow to 521 million by 2035, and to decline to 506 million by 2060.[1] While the newest EU member countries have more similarities than differences with the 'former 15' EU members in terms of family structure, there are some important trends in age distributions, marriage patterns, employment, salary rates between men and women and ageing of the populations of our individual member states which will have a major impact on consumer consumption patterns of European families in the decades to come.

Before moving on to a discussion of the forces that have changed our notions of family, and what these changes mean in terms of consumer behaviour, we need to spend a moment tackling the thorny question, 'What is the family, and how do we gather data about it?' There is a great deal of family diversity throughout Europe, and the conceptualization of *family* is based on ideology, popular mythology and conventions that are firmly rooted in each country's historical, political, religious, economic and cultural traditions. Certainly, European governments have had a strong history of requiring regular and up-to-date socio-demographic information on the behaviour of families (birth rates, fertility rates, divorce rates), and about family forms (size, structure and organization). This sort of information is an essential component in governments' policy-making processes.

Yet, despite a long history of international collaboration and the growing need for reliable information about demographic trends in Europe, data on households and families in the EU are still far from comparable, particularly from a historical perspective.[2] Attempts to standardize data collection methods across countries have had to deal with issues such as national political priorities and ideologies, the centralization and autonomy of the organizations responsible for data collection, and the reluctance of some governments to accept decisions taken at the supranational level. As an example of the problems of comparing families across Europe, consider the problem of dealing with the *age of children living at home*. In most EU member states, no age limit was applied during the 1991 census. However, in Denmark, Finland and Sweden, children were considered as part of the family up to the age of 18, and in Luxembourg to 25. France applied a limit of 25 years until 1982, but this was abolished for the 1991 census, which increased the proportion of lone-parent families by 35 per cent! In today's Europe, increasing migration rates, falling fertility rates, and delaying marriage until later in life (or cohabitation instead of marriage) all influence the reporting and analyses of statistics used to paint a portrait of the European family. As Europe moves further into the new millennium, more standardized and comparable forms of data about the family will be collected (see Figure 11.1).

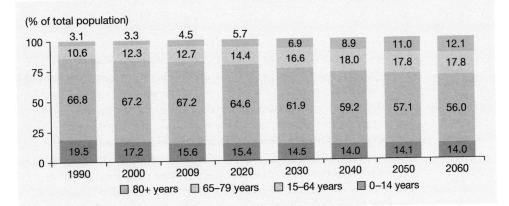

Figure 11.1 Population structure by major age groups, EU27 (¹)[3]

(¹) Excluding French overseas departments; 2020 to 2060 data are EUROPOP2008 convergence scenario.

Source: Eurostat (demo_pjandind and proj_08c2150p).

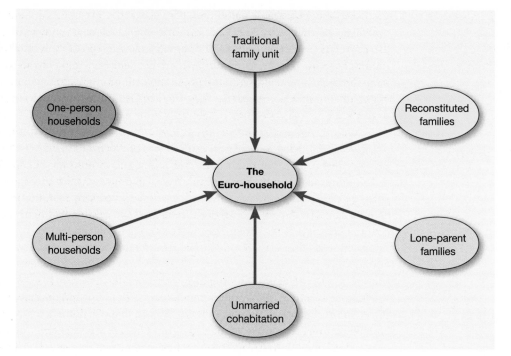

Figure 11.2 Components of the 'modern family'

From both a statistical as well as a sociological perspective, 'family' is hard to nail down. However, one thing is certain – the concept of family will continue to exist and will manifest itself in varying forms over time and across countries throughout Europe. Figure 11.2 provides an overview of the many components which make up our notion of a European household.

Defining the modern family

Some experts have argued that as traditional family living arrangements have declined, people are placing even greater emphasis on the role of siblings, close friends and other relatives to provide companionship and social support.[4] Many marketers have focused on the renewed interest in family life brought about by the more flexible definitions of what constitutes a family. Recent research on the family has shown this social unit to be of key importance in providing insights for marketers in understanding the strength of relationships in family structure, and how this understanding leads to better development of the key value propositions that need to be offered in the marketing of goods and services to the family such as vacations and mobile phones.[5] While families were indeed out of fashion in the 1960s and 1970s, being seen by some as an infringement of personal freedom, 90 per cent of the respondents in one recent survey confirmed that family life was one of the most important things to them.[6] The **extended family** was once the most common family unit. It consisted of three generations living together and often included not only the grandparents, but aunts, uncles and cousins. The **nuclear family**, a mother and a father and one or more children (perhaps with a dog thrown in for good measure), became the model family unit over time.

Just what is a household?

For statistical purposes, Eurostat has implemented the United Nation's definition of the family unit based on the 'conjugal family concept'. *The family* is defined in the narrow sense of a family nucleus as follows: 'The persons within a private or institutional household who are related as husband and wife or as parent and never-married child by blood or adoption.' Thus, a family nucleus comprises a married couple without children or a married couple with one or more never-married children of any age, or one parent with one or more never-married children of any age. The definition tries to take into account whenever possible, couples who report that they are living in consensual unions, regardless of whether they are legally married. Under the more recent European Community Household Panel, a **family household** is more broadly defined, as a 'shared residence and common housekeeping arrangement'. Marketers are interested in both of these units, not only for their similarities, but as a way of understanding differences. Changes in consumers' family structures, such as cohabitation, delayed marriage and delayed childbirth, the return of mothers to the work-force and the upheaval caused by divorce, often represent opportunities for marketers as normal purchasing patterns become unfrozen and people make new choices about products and brands.[7]

Age of the family

Since 1960 the EU has seen a trend of falling numbers of marriages and an increase in the number of divorces. Moreover, people are remarrying more often than they did before the 1960s, and men are more likely to form a new family than women. Couples marry youngest in Portugal and oldest in Denmark, and the greatest age difference between husbands and wives is to be found in Greece. Overall, consumers aged between 35 and 44 were responsible for the largest increase in the number of households, growing by almost 40 per cent since 1980. The 'crude marriage rate' (number of marriages per thousand of a country's population) has fallen from 7.9 in 1970, to 4.9 in 2007, a reduction in marriage rates by 38 per cent.[8] A key segment to change in the coming 20 years will be the significant increase in adults living alone – a segment which will increase to over 62 million households by 2025.[9]

Family size

Worldwide, surveys show that almost all women want smaller families than they did a decade ago. In 1980, the average European household contained 2.8 people, but today that number has slipped to 2.6 people. Furthermore, the current average number of children per woman is below the generational replacement threshold level, with a fertility rate for Europe of 1.44 children per woman in 1993 (compared to almost double this in 1964). A UK study predicts that one in five women born in the 1960s to 1980s will remain childless – a halving of the birth rate of their mother's generation.[10] The **fertility rate** is determined by the number of births per year per 1,000 women of childbearing age. For several decades now fertility rates in the EU have remained clearly below population replacement levels of 2.1, a trend which is reinforced by the enlargement of the EU to the EU27. Among the new member states only Cyprus (1.57 children per woman) and Malta (1.51) are a little above the average for EU15 (1.47).[11] A variety of European studies on the dynamics that underlie family size show that size is dependent on such factors as educational level, the availability of birth control and religion. Not only is the EU's fertility rate below replacement rate, the median age of women giving birth for the first time is rising to just under 30 years of age (see Ingeborg Kleppe's case on 'Fertility in Europe' at the end of Part B).

Recent research has also shown that the division of labour within the household between partners (husband and wife, or however the relationship is defined) also matters in Europe. Consider the situation of women in Italy and The Netherlands. While there is a greater percentage of Dutch women than Italian women in the workforce, the fertility rate in the Netherlands is significantly higher (1.73 in The Netherlands, compared to 1.33 in Italy). In both countries, people tend to have traditional views about gender roles, but Italian society is considerably more conservative in this regard, and this seems to be a decisive difference.

How realistic are these role models for your country and your generation?

Luc Ubaghs/Shutterstock.

Women who do more than 75 per cent of the housework and child care are less likely to want to have another child than women whose husbands or partners share the load. Put differently, Dutch fathers change more nappies, pick up more kids after soccer practice and clean up the living room more often than Italian fathers; therefore, relative to the population, there are more Dutch babies than Italian babies being born. In Europe, many countries with greater gender equality have a greater social commitment to day care and other institutional support for working women, which gives those women the possibility of having second or third children.[12]

Marketers keep a close eye on the population's birth rate to gauge how the pattern of births will affect demand for products in the future. Even when a married couple does live with children, the structure of family size is declining – the number of European households comprising one or two people is increasing, and the number of households with four or more people is falling.[13] The number of unmarried adults and one-person households is steadily rising (they now account for 26 per cent of European households, and are projected to be the fastest growing segment through to the year 2025). Some marketers are beginning to address the fact that this group is under-represented in advertising.[14] Gold Blend coffee built a very popular TV ad campaign around a romance between two single neighbours, while Procter & Gamble introduced Folger's Singles 'single-serve' coffee bags for people who live alone and don't need a full pot.[15] On the other hand, many singles report that they avoid buying single-size food portions or eating alone in restaurants since both remind them of their unattached status – they prefer takeaway food.[16]

Single men and women constitute quite different markets. More than half of single men are under the age of 35, while among people over the age of 65 women account for 80 per cent of one-person households. Despite single males' greater incomes, single women dominate many markets because of their spending patterns. Single women are more likely than single men to own a home, and they spend more on housing-related items and furniture. Single men, in contrast, spend more overall in restaurants and on cars. However, these spending patterns are also significantly affected by age: middle-aged single women, for example, spend *more* than their male counterparts on cars.[17]

LINDA L. PRICE
University of Arizona

Family matters

Marketers have long been interested in how to drive brand loyalty. Brands compete for 'share of market', 'share of mind', 'share of wallet', and more recently 'share of heart'. When marketers refer to 'share of heart', they are asking, 'Compared to my competitors, where is my brand in consumers' hearts?' In an effort to better capture consumers' hearts much recent consumer research has stressed the significance of affective, identity-affirming bonds between consumers and their brands. This research encourages marketers to ask, 'How can I make my brand central to the identity of my consumers?' Brand communities that emerge around brands such as Harley-Davidson, Jones Soda, Threadless and Apple underscore the powerful loyalty potential and customer lifetime value of brands that capture the hearts and support the identities of consumers. Certainly, firms should pay attention to developing and nurturing these affective bonds!

But ask a room full of consumers, even young global consumers, how many of them are active participants in even one brand community and you'll find that only a few hands go up. Now ask a room full of consumers what they are loyal to and care about, and there's a good chance not even one consumer will mention a brand or commercial service. You may capture more share of heart than your competitor but often it is still a pretty miniscule share – brands are not nearly as important to consumers as the family dog or cat. If you ask consumers what they do care about, family and family relationships are far and away most important. For companies, there's a simple metric, 'Where is your brand in what matters most to consumers?' This is an entirely different way of thinking about 'share of heart'. To answer this question, marketers need to examine how their brands and services help consumers: 'be a family' – to reconcile individual work ambitions and family goals; 'be a couple' – with young children underfoot and competing individual pursuits. Simply stated, families are trying to manage individual, relational and family goals and identities and they give their hearts to the brands and services that help them juggle their complicated, bundled lives. In mundane oversimplified terms, families are trying to fit in some exercise time for Mom, get John home from soccer practice, make sure the family eats dinner together, homework gets done and parents save a little couple time to keep the marriage alive. Marketers have to think about how they are a resource in the family ties that truly do bind consumers' everyday lives. It may not matter if you own Mom's favourite restaurant if no one else in the family will eat there. From a network perspective, what matters is how central and unique your brand or service is as a relational resource. If you are the 'go to' resource for the relationships that matter to consumers you may come out on top of individually preferred alternatives again and again. If your brand helps families navigate their individual, relational and collective goals you can truly earn a meaningful share of heart.

Much of my research over the past 15 years has dealt with family consumption and the important roles that families play in what consumers buy, integrate into family practices, come to love and pass forward to the next generation. If you've ever watched *The Antiques Road Show*, you've met consumers who discover Great Grandma's hope chest is worth a lot of money, but they would never sell it because it is 'priceless' – it has come to represent the history, values and future of the family, and perhaps most especially the women in the family. It's quite likely that you are already the recipient or the intended recipient of a family treasure – an object that simply must 'remain in the family'. Maybe you recall preparing or eating family recipes that replicate traditions, rituals and practices passed down through generations to preserve and define your

→ family. But now turn your attention to more mundane and everyday consumption choices. How do you use cell phones, Face Book, e-mail and even television to manage family relationships? What sort of cell phone plan would work best for your family? For example, if we define a cell phone as a close relationship management device, how would we design and market it? When your family takes a vacation, how important is 'being a family' in choosing where to go and what to do? How does your family balance individual, relational and collective interests and goals in vacation travel? If we define 'being a family' as a primary vacation goal, how do we design our offerings? Many business opportunities are lurking hidden in the goals and practices of family networks.

It's ironic that even though family is extremely important to most consumers relatively little consumer research and marketing effort focuses on studying family identity as a source of insight into consumer loyalty. Most research has instead focused on individual identity or how a group (such as a brand community) is important to an individual's identity. Perhaps the relative neglect of family research is in part because families are more fluid, elective and difficult to define than they were in the past. Increasingly common blended, single-parent, bi-cultural and gay family forms may depart from dominant discourses about family. However, despite varied and elective types most people believe they belong to a family uniquely defined by structure, character and generations over time and this collective dramatically shapes the brands, objects, activities and services they consume (Epp and Price 2008). The time is ripe for consumer researchers to reconsider family consumption with new methods and perspectives. To do this we need to move beyond our conventional understandings of family, family lifecycle and family decision making and question our stereotypes about what strengthens and weakens family communications.

Linda L. Price

*Not so coincidentally, my research on family consumption began about the same time I became a parent. My research was also vitally inspired by and co-created with many wonderful co-authors especially Carolyn Folkman Curasi, Amber M. Epp and Eric J. Arnould. For more information see Amber M. Epp and Linda L. Price (2008), 'Family Identity: A framework of identity interplay in consumption practices', *Journal of Consumer Research*, June: 50–70.

Non-traditional family structures

The European Community Household Panel regards any occupied housing unit as a household, regardless of the relationships among people living there. Thus, one person living alone, three room-mates or two lovers all constitute households. Less traditional households will rapidly increase these if trends persist. One-parent households are increasing steadily throughout Europe (most common in the UK, Denmark and Belgium, least common in Greece). Although these households are in the majority of cases headed by women, there is also an increasing trend for fathers to take on this role.[18]

Effects of family structure on consumption

A family's needs and expenditures are affected by such factors as the number of people (children and adults) in the family, their ages, and whether one, two or more adults are employed outside of the home.

Two important factors determining how a couple spend time and money are whether they have children and whether the woman works. Couples with children generally have higher expenses, and not just for the 'basics' such as food and utilities bills. Studies in the UK estimate that the costs of keeping a teenager 'in the style to which they aspire' run close to £66,000, and that a 2010 study estimates that the costs of getting a child from birth to the age of 21 is approaching a staggering £200,000.[19] In addition, a recently married couple make very different expenditures compared with people with young children, who in turn are quite different from a couple with children in college, and so on. Families with working mothers must often make allowances for such expenses as nursery care and a working wardrobe for the woman.

MULTICULTURAL DIMENSIONS

The Euro-housewife: considerable differences between EU member states

- The percentage of women aged between 25 and 59 who describe themselves as housewives varies considerably between member states. While the EU average is 33 per cent, it ranges from a high of 60 per cent in Ireland (Spain, Greece, Italy and Luxembourg are also high), to a mere 4 per cent in Denmark.

- Barely 6 per cent of women between 25 and 39 without children stay at home, compared with 36 per cent with one child under 5 and 52 per cent with at least two children under 5.

- EU-wide, only 7 per cent of today's housewives stopped working because of marriage – but this number peaked

at 15 per cent in Greece and 14 per cent in Spain. However, 42 per cent stop because of children.

- Family obligations, such as housework, caring for children or others are the main reason why 84 per cent of housewives are not looking for work.

- Being a housewife is strongly related to the level of education. Housewives represent 45 per cent of EU women aged from 25 to 59 with lower secondary education, 26 per cent with upper secondary education, and only 13 per cent of women with higher educational levels.[20]

The family lifecycle

Recognizing that family needs and expenditures change over time, the concept of the **family lifecycle (FLC)** has been widely used by marketers. The FLC combines trends in income and family composition with the changes in demands placed upon this income. As we grow older, our preferences for products and activities tend to change. In many cases, our income levels tend to rise (at least until retirement), so that we can afford more as well. In addition, many purchases that must be made at an early age do not have to be repeated very often. For example, we tend to accumulate durable goods, such as furniture, and only replace them as necessary.

A lifecycle approach to the study of the family assumes that pivotal events alter role relationships and trigger new stages of life which modify our priorities. These events include the birth of a first child, the departure of the last child from the house, the death of a spouse, retirement of the principal wage earner and divorce.[21] Movement through these life stages is accompanied by significant changes in expenditures on leisure, food, durables and services, even after the figures have been adjusted to reflect changes in income.[22]

This focus on longitudinal changes in priorities is particularly valuable in predicting demand for specific product categories over time. For example, the money spent by a couple with no children on eating out and holidays will probably be diverted for quite different purchases after the birth of a child. While a number of models have been proposed to describe family lifecycle stages, their usefulness has been limited because in many cases they have failed to take into account such important social trends as the changing role of women, the acceleration of alternative lifestyles, childless and delayed-child marriages and single-parent households.

Four variables are necessary to describe these changes: age, marital status, the presence or absence of children in the home, and their ages. In addition, our definition of marital status (at least for analysis purposes) must be relaxed to include any couple living together who are in a long-term relationship. Thus, while room mates might not be considered 'married', a man and a woman who have established a household would be, as would two homosexual men or women who have a similar understanding.

Lifecycle effects on buying

As might be expected, consumers classified into different stages of a family lifecycle show marked differences in consumption patterns. Young bachelors and newlyweds have the most 'modern' sex-role attitudes, are the most likely to exercise regularly, to go to pubs, concerts, the cinema and restaurants, and to go dancing; and they consume more alcohol. Families with young children are more likely to consume health foods such as fruit, juice and yogurt, while those made up of single parents and older children buy more junk foods. The monetary value of homes, cars and other durables is lowest for bachelors and single parents, but increases as people go through the full nest and childless couple stages. Perhaps reflecting the bounty of wedding gifts, newlyweds are the most likely to own appliances such as toasters, ovens and electric coffee grinders. Babysitter and day care usage is, of course, highest among single-parent and full nest households, while home maintenance services (e.g. lawn mowing) are most likely to be employed by older couples and bachelors. Recent studies have shown that families also place a significant emotional and financial attachment to possessions that they own when those possessions are part of the family's bonding and history. This goes well beyond our earlier notion of the importance of 'inheritance', and considers our sense of family well-being, continuity, history, and the important role as 'caretaker' of the family's identity over generations.[23]

The growth of these additional categories creates many opportunities for enterprising marketers. For example, divorced people undergo a process of transition to a new social role. This change is often accompanied by the disposal of possessions linked to the former role and the need to acquire a set of possessions that help to express the person's new identity as they experiment with new lifestyles.[24]

THE INTIMATE CORPORATION: FAMILY DECISION-MAKING

The decision process within a household unit in some ways resembles a business conference. Certain matters are put up for discussion, different members may have different priorities and agendas, and there may be power struggles to rival any tale of corporate intrigue. In just about every living situation, whether a conventional family, students sharing a house or apartment, or some other non-traditional arrangement, group members seem to take on different roles just as purchasing agents, engineers, account executives and others do within a company.

Household decisions

Two basic types of decisions are made by families.[25] In a **consensual purchase decision**, the group agrees on the desired purchase, differing only in terms of how it will be achieved. In these circumstances, the family will probably engage in problem-solving and consider alternatives until the means for satisfying the group's goal is found. For example, a household considering adding a dog to the family but concerned about who will take care of it might draw up a chart assigning individuals to specific duties.

Unfortunately, life is not always that easy. In an **accommodative purchase decision**, group members have different preferences or priorities and cannot agree on a purchase that will satisfy the minimum expectations of all involved. It is here that bargaining, coercion, compromise and the wielding of power are all likely to be used to achieve agreement on what to buy or who gets to use it. Family decisions are often characterized by an accommodative rather than a consensual decision. Conflict occurs when there is incomplete correspondence in family members' needs and preferences. While money is the most common source of conflict between marriage partners, television choices come a close second![26] Some specific factors determining the degree of family decision conflict include the following:[27]

- *Interpersonal need* (a person's level of investment in the group). A child in a family situation may care more about what their family buys for the house than a college student who is living in student accommodation.

- *Product involvement and utility* (the degree to which the product in question will be used or will satisfy a need). A family member who is an avid coffee drinker will obviously be more interested in the purchase of a new coffeemaker to replace a malfunctioning one than a similar expenditure for some other item.

- *Responsibility* (for procurement, maintenance, payment, and so on). People are more likely to have disagreements about a decision if it entails long-term consequences and commitments. For example, a family decision about getting a dog may involve conflict regarding who will be responsible for walking and feeding it.

- *Power* (or the degree to which one family member exerts influence over the others in making decisions). In traditional families, the husband tends to have more power than the wife, who in turn has more than the oldest child, and so on. In family decisions, conflict can arise when one person continually uses the power they have within the group to satisfy their priorities.

In general, decisions will involve conflict among family members to the extent that they are important or novel and/or if individuals have strong opinions about good and bad alternatives. The degree to which these factors generate conflict determines the type of decision the family will make.[28]

Sex roles and decision-making responsibilities

Traditionally, some buying decisions, termed **autocratic decisions**, were made by one spouse. Men, for instance, often had sole responsibility for selecting a car, while most decorating choices fell to women. Other decisions, such as holiday destinations, were made jointly; these are known as **syncratic decisions**. According to a study conducted by Roper Starch Worldwide, wives tend to have the most say when buying groceries, children's toys, clothes and medicines. Syncratic decisions are common for cars, holidays, homes, appliances, furniture, home electronics, interior design and long-distance phone services. As the couple's education increases, more decisions are likely to be made together.[29]

Identifying the decision-maker

The nature of consumer decision-making within a particular product category is an important issue for marketers, so that they know who to target and whether or not they need to reach both spouses to influence a decision. Researchers have paid special attention to which spouse plays the role of what has been called the **family financial officer (FFO)**, who keeps track of the family's bills and decides how any surplus funds will be spent. Among newlyweds, this role tends to be played jointly, and then over time one spouse or the other tends to take over these responsibilities.[30] Spouses usually exert significant influence on decision-making, even after one of them has died. An Irish study found that many widows claim to sense the continued presence of their dead husband, and to conduct 'conversations' with them about household matters.[31]

In traditional families (and especially those with low educational levels), women are primarily responsible for family financial management. While the man is usually the wage earner, the woman in these traditional family structures typically decides how the money is spent.[32] Each spouse 'specializes' in certain activities.[33] The pattern is different among families where spouses adhere to more modern sex-role norms. These couples believe that there should be more shared participation in family maintenance activities. In these cases, husbands assume more responsibility for laundering, house cleaning, day-to-day shopping, and so on, in addition to such traditionally 'male' tasks as home maintenance and waste removal.[34]

Of course, cultural background is an important determinant of the dominance of the husband or wife. Husbands tend to be more dominant in decision-making among couples with a strong Mediterranean ethnic identification.[35] Even in northern Europe, the pattern of traditional 'male' and 'female' roles is still fairly strong.

Four factors appear to determine the degree to which decisions will be made jointly or by one or the other spouse:[36]

1 *Sex-role stereotypes.* Couples who believe in traditional sex-role stereotypes tend to make individual decisions for sex-typed products (i.e. those considered to be 'masculine' or 'feminine').

2 *Spousal resources.* The spouse who contributes more resources to the family has the greater influence.

3 *Experience.* Individual decisions are made more frequently when the couple has gained experience as a decision-making unit.

4 *Socio-economic status.* More joint decisions are made by middle-class families than in either higher- or lower-class families.

Despite recent changes in decision-making responsibilities, women are still primarily responsible for the continuation of the family's **kin network system**: they perform the rituals intended to maintain ties among family members, both immediate and extended. This function includes such activities as coordinating visits among relatives, phoning and writing to family members, sending greetings cards, making social engagements, and so on.[37] This organizing role means that women often make important decisions about the family's leisure activities, and are more likely to decide with whom the family will socialize.

Heuristics in joint decision-making

The *synoptic ideal* calls for the husband and wife to take a common view and act as joint decision-makers. According to this ideal, they would very thoughtfully weigh alternatives, assign to one another well-defined roles, and calmly make mutually beneficial consumer decisions. The couple would act rationally, analytically and use as much information as possible to maximize joint utility. In reality, however, spousal decision-making is often characterized by the use of influence or methods that are likely to reduce conflict. A couple 'reaches' rather than 'makes' a decision. This process has been described as 'muddling through'.[38]

One common technique for simplifying the decision-making process is the use of *heuristics* (see Chapter 9). Some decision-making patterns frequently observed when a couple makes decisions in buying a new house illustrate the use of heuristics:

● The couple's areas of common preference are based upon salient, objective dimensions rather than more subtle, hard-to-define cues. For example, a couple may easily agree on the number of bedrooms they need in the new home, but will have more difficulty achieving a common view of how the home should look.

● The couple agrees on a system of *task specialization*, where each is responsible for certain duties or decision areas and does not interfere in the other's. For many couples, these assignments are likely to be influenced by their perceived sex roles. For example, the wife may seek out houses in advance that meet their requirements, while the husband determines whether the couple can obtain a mortgage.

● Concessions are based on the intensity of each spouse's preferences. One spouse will yield to the influence of the other in many cases simply because their level of preference for a certain attribute is not particularly intense, where in other situations they will be willing to exert effort to obtain a favourable decision.[39] In cases where intense preferences for different attributes exist, rather than attempt to influence each other, spouses will 'trade off' a less-intense preference for a more strongly felt one. For example, a husband who is indifferent to kitchen design may yield to his wife, but expect that in turn he will be allowed to design his own garage workshop. It is interesting to note that many men apparently want to be very involved in making some decorating decisions and setting budgets – more than women want them to be. According to one survey, 70 per cent of male respondents felt the husband should be involved in decorating the family room, while only 51 per cent of wives wanted them to be.[40]

CHILDREN AS DECISION-MAKERS: CONSUMERS-IN-TRAINING

Anyone who has had the 'delightful' experience of supermarket shopping with one or more children knows that children often have a say in what their parents buy, especially for products like breakfast cereal.[41] In addition, children increasingly are being recognized as a potential market for traditionally adult products. For example, Kodak is putting a lot of promotional effort into encouraging children to become photographers. Most children nowadays own or have access to a digital camera, and taking photos is seen as a cool pursuit. Websites which will post photos and mail printed photos to children are flourishing, as children take more control of their own photo collections.

Parental yielding occurs when a parental decision maker is influenced by a child's request and 'surrenders'. The likelihood of this occurring is partly dependent on the dynamics within a particular family – as we all know, parental styles range from permissive to strict, and they also vary in terms of the amount of responsibility children are given to make decisions.[42] The strategies children use to request purchases were documented in one study. While most children simply asked for things, other common tactics included saying they had seen it on television, saying that a sibling or friend had it, or bargaining by offering to do chores. Other actions were less innocuous; they included directly placing the object in the trolley and continuous whining – often a 'persuasive' behaviour![43]

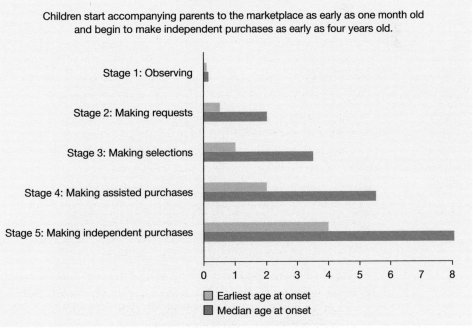

Figure 11.3 Five stages of consumer development by earliest age at onset and median age at onset.

Consumer socialization

Children do not spring from the womb with consumer skills already in memory. **Consumer socialization** has been defined as the process 'by which young people acquire skills, knowledge, and attitudes relevant to their functioning in the marketplace'.[44] Where does this knowledge come from? Friends and teachers certainly participate in this process. For instance, children talk to one another about consumer products, and this tendency increases with age.[45] Especially for young children, though, the two primary socialization sources are the family and the media. Some recent research has highlighted children's very varied experiences within the family, such that the family represents not a homogeneous but rather a heterogeneous consumption environment in which children grow up.[46] (See also Ben Kerrane's case 'Good child, bad child: observing experiences of consumer socialization in the 21st century family' at the end of Part C.)

Influence of parents

Parents' influences in consumer socialization are both direct and indirect. They deliberately try to instil their own values about consumption in their children ('you're going to learn the value of the pound/euro'). Parents also determine the degree to which their children will be exposed to other information sources, such as television, salespeople and peers.[47] Grown-ups serve as significant models for observational learning (see Chapter 7). Children learn about consumption by watching their parents' behaviour and imitating it. This modelling is facilitated by marketers who package adult products in child versions.

The process of consumer socialization begins with infants, who accompany their parents to shops where they are initially exposed to marketing stimuli. Within the first two years of life, children begin to make requests for desired objects. As children learn to walk, they also begin to make their own selections when they are in shops. By the age of five, most children are making purchases with the help of parents and grandparents, and by eight most are making independent purchases and have become fully-fledged consumers.[48]

Children begin making selections and purchases of products at an early age. By the time they reach their teens, the process of socialization and peer influence is well underway.

Photo: Gary Bamossy.

European and global brands are part of the social expression of young children, as well as their parents!

The Advertising Archives.

MARKETING PITFALL

Three dimensions combine to produce different 'segments' of parental styles. Parents characterized by certain styles have been found to socialize their children differently.[49] 'Authoritarian parents', who are hostile, restrictive and emotionally uninvolved, do not have warm relationships with their children, are active in filtering the types of media to which their children are exposed, and tend to have negative views about advertising. 'Neglecting parents' also do not have warm relationships, but they are more detached from their children and exercise little control over what their children do. In contrast, 'indulgent parents' communicate more with their children about consumption-related matters and are less restrictive. They believe that children should be allowed to learn about the marketplace without much interference.

Influence of television: 'the electric babysitter'

It is no secret that children watch a lot of television. As a result, they are constantly bombarded with messages about consumption, both contained in commercials and in the programmes themselves. The medium teaches people about a culture's values and myths. The more a child is exposed to television, whether the programme is a local 'soap' or *Baywatch*, the more they will accept the images depicted there as real.[50] In Britain, *Teletubbies* went a step further – it was made for viewers from three months to two years old. It is unclear if this show would succeed in the US, since babies are not seen as a lucrative market for advertising messages (yet). In the meantime, you can always entertain your infants by letting them dance virtually with *Teletubbies* characters on the show's website![51]

In addition to the large volume of programming targeted directly at children, children also are exposed to idealized images of what it is like to be an adult. Since children over the age of 6 spend about a quarter of their television viewing during prime-time, they are affected by programmes and commercials targeted at adults. For example, young girls exposed to adult lipstick commercials learn to associate lipstick with beauty.[52]

Sex-role socialization

Children pick up on the concept of gender identity at an earlier age than was previously believed – perhaps as young as the age of one or two. By the age of three, most children categorize driving a truck as masculine and cooking and cleaning as feminine.[53] Even cartoon characters who are portrayed as helpless are more likely to wear frilly or ruffled dresses.[54] Toy companies perpetuate these stereotypes by promoting gender-linked toys with commercials that reinforce sex-role expectations through their casting, emotional tone and copy.[55]

One function of child's play is to rehearse for adulthood. Children 'act out' different roles they might assume later in life and learn about the expectations others have of them. The toy industry provides the props children use to perform these roles.[56] Depending on which side of the debate you are on, these toys either reflect or teach children about what society expects of males versus females. While pre-school boys and girls do not exhibit many differences in toy preferences, after the age of five they part company: girls tend to stick with dolls, while boys gravitate towards 'action figures' and high-tech diversions. Industry critics charge that this is because the toy industry is dominated by males, while toy company executives counter that they are simply responding to children's natural preferences.[57]

Cognitive development

The ability of children to make mature, 'adult' consumer decisions obviously increases with age (not that grown-ups always make mature decisions). Children can be segmented by age in terms of their **stage of cognitive development**, or ability to comprehend concepts of increasing complexity. Some recent evidence indicates that young children are able to learn consumption-related information surprisingly well, depending on the format in which the information is presented (for instance, learning is enhanced if a videotaped vignette is presented to small children repeatedly).[58]

The foremost proponent of the idea that children pass through distinct stages of **cognitive development** was the Swiss psychologist Jean Piaget, who believed that each stage is characterized by a certain cognitive structure the child uses to handle information.[59] In one classic demonstration of cognitive development, Piaget poured the contents of a short, squat glass of lemonade into a taller, thinner glass. Five-year-olds, who still believed that the shape of the glass determined its contents, thought this glass held more liquid than the first glass. They are in what Piaget termed a *preoperational stage of development*. In contrast, six-year-olds tended to be unsure, but seven-year-olds knew the amount of lemonade had not changed.

Many developmental specialists no longer believe that children necessarily pass through these fixed stages at the same time. An alternative approach regards children as differing in information-processing capability, or the ability to store and retrieve information from memory (see Chapter 7). The following three segments have been identified by this approach:[60]

1 *Limited.* Below the age of six, children do not employ storage and retrieval strategies.

2 *Cued.* Children between the ages of six and twelve employ these strategies, but only when prompted.

3 *Strategic.* Children aged twelve and older spontaneously employ storage and retrieval strategies.

This sequence of development underscores the notion that children do not think like adults, and they cannot be expected to use information in the same way. It also reminds us that they do not necessarily form the same conclusions as adults do when presented with product information. For example, children are not as likely to realize that something they

see on television is not 'real', and as a result they are more vulnerable to persuasive me.
The remaining section of this chapter also considers the role that age plays in our consump
but from the perspective of how age groups (cohorts) influence our behaviours, and
consumers from different generations truly differ in their approaches to consumption.

AGE AND CONSUMER IDENTITY

The era in which a consumer grows up creates for that person a cultural bond with the millions of others born during the same time period. As we grow older, our needs and preferences change, often in unison with others who are close to our own age. For this reason, a consumer's age exerts a significant influence on their identity. All things being equal, we are more likely than not to have things in common with others of our own age. In the remaining section of this chapter, we explore some of the important characteristics of some key age groups, and consider how marketing strategies must be modified to appeal to diverse age subcultures.

Age cohorts: 'my generation'

An **age cohort** consists of people of similar ages who have undergone similar experiences. They share many common memories about cultural heroes (e.g. Clint Eastwood *vs* Brad Pitt, or Frank Sinatra *vs* Kurt Cobain *vs* Justin Bieber), important historical events (e.g. the 1968 student demonstrations in Paris *vs* the fall of the Berlin Wall in 1989), and so on. Although there is no universally accepted way to divide people into age cohorts, each of us seems to have a pretty good idea of what we mean when we refer to 'my generation'.

Marketers often target products and services to one or more specific age cohorts. They recognize that the same offering will probably not appeal to people of different ages, nor will the language and images they use to reach them. In some cases separate campaigns are developed to attract consumers of different ages. For example, travel agencies throughout Europe target youth markets during the months of May and June for low-cost summer holidays to Mallorca, and then target middle-aged, more affluent consumers for the same destination during September and October. What differs in the two campaigns are the media used, the images portrayed and the prices offered.

The appeal of nostalgia

Because consumers within an age group confront crucial life changes at roughly the same time, the values and symbolism used to appeal to them can evoke powerful feelings of nostalgia. Adults aged 30+ are particularly susceptible to this phenomenon.[61] However, young people as well as old are influenced by references to their past. In fact, research indicates that some people are more disposed to be nostalgic than others, regardless of age.

Product sales can be dramatically affected by linking a brand to vivid memories and experiences, especially for items that are associated with childhood or adolescence. Vespa scooters, Hornby electric trains and the coupon 'saving points' from Douwe Egberts coffee are all examples of products that have managed to span two or more generations of loyal consumers, giving the brand a strong equity position in competitive and crowded markets.

Many advertising campaigns have played on the collective memories of consumers by using older celebrities to endorse their products such as campaigns by Hendricks Gin, Bailey's Original Irish Crème.[62] To assess just how pervasive nostalgia is, pay attention to television commercials, and notice how often they are produced against a background of 'classic songs'. *Memories* magazine, which was founded to exploit the nostalgia boom, even offers advertisers a discount if they run old ads next to their current ones.

MULTICULTURAL DIMENSIONS

Warsaw

The taste of home is here, behind a cold steel counter dominated by a serving lady with an impassive, lined face and a white apron. Tangy pickled cabbage, steaming potatoes, and the watery red slosh of beet soup . . . a timeless combination that has warmed the hearts of generations of Poles, through centuries of hardship and four grim decades of Soviet rule.

To the untrained eye, Warsaw, Poland's gleaming capital, appears to be caught up in a mad race to out-Westernize the West. Here, capitalism is king – skyscrapers plastered in garish billboards dominate the city centre, while European chains like H&M and Zara have taken over brand-new shopping malls, where 20-somethings strut, sipping blended coffees. For a country so recently freed from the clutches of communism, the transformation is astounding. But behind the glittering façade beats the heart of a very different Poland. Milk bars (*bar mleczny*), bare-bones cafés set up by the communist authorities in the 1950s to ensure that everyone had at least one hot meal a day, have somehow managed to survive the onslaught of capitalism. In fact, they are thriving, even in Warsaw's most fashionable districts, and to many Poles they represent a part of Polish culture that all the wonders of the free market can never replace.

Eating in a milk bar is a far cry from fine dining, but for many Poles the experience is priceless. It's a scene that harks back to the days when shiny shopping malls and designer brands were nothing more than vague rumours from the other side of the Iron Curtain. But despite the changes sweeping through Poland, milk bars still attract a fiercely loyal following. At mealtimes the lines can stretch out the door.

Most milk bars seem to have been frozen in time. The interiors, while clean, range from basic to downright drab. Some offer little décor aside from a handful of sturdy potted plants, whitewashed walls, and a menu of classic Polish dishes posted beside the cash register. The staff are apathetic, sometimes even rude. Customers order, are given a ticket to present at the kitchen window, then wait beside the steel-topped counter for their meals to appear.

Incomes have been rising rapidly, and with an abundance of new restaurants cropping up across the country, the Polish government has begun to question the need for milk bars. But Poles refuse to let them go.

Alicja Samarcew, a psychologist who still frequents milk bars about once a week, always makes a point of taking foreign visitors there because, she says, 'It's something really Polish'. Ms Samarcew has her own theories on why these sparse cafés are still relevant in Poland, and how an institution imposed by a repressive regime could remain so firmly rooted in the country's collective self-image. 'For one thing, it's a place to socialize,' she says. 'I still meet people there that I've seen for years. They tell the same stories, and everybody knows them. It provides a sense of continuity in people's lives.'

But, she points out, milk bars play an even more important social role. 'I wouldn't say it's real because there are poor people, it's not about that. But you are exposed to different categories of people in a milk bar, and I think this is really important. Old people come, often alone and lonely, and it can be hard to see. When we go to a restaurant, it's easy for us in the middle class to think we're the only people in the city. But when you go to a milk bar, that illusion is gone. Maybe it's something really Polish that we don't isolate these people in ghettos.'[63]

THE TEEN MARKET: IT TOTALLY RULES

With a spending capacity of more than 61 billion euros per year, the European youth market of teens is a powerful demographic and an important culture to understand intimately for businesses looking to grow and maintain relevancy in the future. In 1956, the label 'teenage' first entered the (American) vocabulary, as Frankie Lymon and the Teenagers became the first pop group to identify themselves with this new subculture. The concept of teenager is a fairly new cultural construction; throughout most of history a person simply made the transition from child to adult (often accompanied by some sort of ritual or ceremony, as we will see in a later chapter). As anyone who has been there knows, puberty and adolescence can be both the best of times and the worst of times. Many exciting changes happen as individuals leave the role of child and prepare to assume the role of adult. These changes create a lot of uncertainty about the self, and the need to belong and to find one's unique identity as a person becomes extremely important. At this age, choices of activities, friends and 'looks' are crucial to social acceptance. Teenagers actively search for cues from their peers and from advertising for the 'right' way to look and behave. Advertising geared to teenagers is typically action-oriented and depicts a group of 'in' teenagers using the product. Teenagers use products to express their identities, to explore the world and their new-found freedom in it, and also to rebel against the authority of their parents and other socializing agents. Marketers often do their best to assist in this process. The range of consumer products targeted at teenagers (and particularly young ones) is greater than ever. Then again, so is teenagers' disposable income from part-time jobs and weekly pocket money.[64]

Teenagers in every culture grapple with fundamental developmental issues as they make the transition from childhood to adult. According to research by Saatchi & Saatchi, there are four themes of conflict common to all teens:

1 *Autonomy vs belonging.* Teenagers need to acquire independence so they try to break away from their families. On the other hand, they need to attach themselves to a support structure, such as peers, to avoid being alone. A thriving internet subculture has developed to serve this purpose, as has text messaging via mobile phones.[65] The internet (world wide web) has become the preferred method of communication for many young people, since its anonymity makes it easier to talk to people of the opposite sex, or of different ethnic and racial groups.[66]

2 *Rebellion vs conformity.* Teenagers need to rebel against social standards of appearance and behaviour, yet they still need to fit in and be accepted by others. Cult products that cultivate a rebellious image are prized for this reason.

3 *Idealism vs pragmatism.* Teenagers tend to view adults as hypocrites, while they see themselves as being sincere. They have to struggle to reconcile their view of how the world should be with the realities they perceive around them.

4 *Narcissism vs intimacy.* Teenagers can be obsessed with their appearance and needs. On the other hand, they also feel the desire to connect with others on a meaningful level.[67]

Teenagers throughout history have had to cope with insecurity, parental authority and peer pressure. At the start of the new millennium, however, these issues are compounded by concerns about the environment, racism, AIDS and other pressing social problems. Today's teenagers often have to cope with additional family pressures as well, especially if they live in non-traditional families where they must take significant responsibility for shopping, cooking and housework. Marketers have a difficult time 'defining' the values of today's European teens, perhaps because they are living in such socially dynamic and demanding times. A study among 500 young opinion leaders aged 14–20 across 16 European countries suggests that this age group's credo should be: 'Don't define us – we'll define ourselves.' Respondents were asked their opinions on a wide range of subjects, from new technology to family relationships, divorce, drugs, alcohol, politics, fashion, entertainment, sex and advertising. Some of the highlights of this study[68] are:

● Living life to the 'fullest' is mandatory; ambition drives them, as does the fear of failure. Young eastern Europeans strongly believe that hard work will give them a high standard of living and education is their passport to this better life.

● They perceive the 'digitized' future as one that lacks warmth – something Europe's teenagers, a divorce-experienced generation, is actively seeking.

● Immersive and engaging technology which allows for '24-hour commerce' will lead to further stress for this generation, and a blurring of home/office means they will work longer and harder than any previous generation.

Marketers often influence public policy by creating messages to influence behaviours like smoking and drug use. This mosaic was used to promote Lorillard Tobacco's Youth Smoking Prevention Program.

Lorillard Inc. c/o Lowe Worldwide.

- This is a very visually literate generation, with clear understanding of a commercial's aims. Clichés will not be tolerated, and will lead to immediate rejection, particularly in the Nordic countries. Only eastern European teens have yet to achieve this level of 'advertising cynicism'.

- This generation is both brand-aware and brand-dismissive. It represents an opportunity, but not a homogeneous market. The successful marketer will be aware that for these consumers, an aspirational quality is essential, that heritage is an advantage, and that nothing is forever.

BABY BUSTERS: 'GENERATION X'

The cohort of consumers between the ages of 18 and 29 consists of over 30 million Europeans who will be a powerful force in years to come. This group, which has been labelled '**Generation X**', 'slackers' or 'busters' was profoundly affected by the economic downturn in the first part of the 1990s, and then again in the new/ongoing recession of 2012. So-called baby busters include many people, both in and out of higher education, whose tastes and priorities are beginning to be felt in fashion, popular culture, politics and marketing. While the percentage of Europeans aged 25–29 is high in terms of completing upper secondary education (71 per cent, compared with 50 per cent of persons aged 50–59), this group also has a large drop-out rate, with one in five Europeans between the ages of 18 and 24 leaving the education system without completing a qualification beyond lower secondary schooling. Given recent harsh economic conditions, children from this age cohort are more likely to live at home after college rather than taking their own place. Demographers call these returnees **boomerang kids** (you throw them out . . . they keep coming back). In today's shrinking job market many young people are forced to redefine the assumption that college graduation automatically means living on their own.[69]

Edinburgh from £9.50 one way.

national express

Many boomerang kids today return home to live with their parents – voluntarily or not.
McGarry Bowen.

Marketing to busters or marketing bust?

Although the income of this age cohort is below expectations, they still constitute a formidable market segment – partly because so many still live at home and have more discretionary income. Busters in their twenties are estimated to have an annual spending power of $125 billion, and their purchases are essential to the fortunes of such product categories as beer, fast food and cosmetics.

Because many busters have been doing the family shopping for a long time, marketers are finding that they are much more sophisticated about evaluating advertising and products. They are turned off by advertising that either contains a lot of hype or takes itself too seriously. They see advertising as a form of entertainment but are turned off by over commercialization.[70]

Perhaps one reason why marketers' efforts to appeal to X-ers with messages of alienation, cynicism and despair have not succeeded is that many people in their twenties are not depressed after all! Generation X-ers are quite a diverse group – they don't all wear reversed baseball caps and work in temporary, low-paid, mindless jobs. Despite the birth of dozens of magazines catering to 'riot grrrls' and other angry X-ers with names like *Axcess*, *Project X* and *KGB*, the most popular magazine for 20-something women is *Cosmopolitan*. What seems to make this age cohort the angriest is constantly being labelled as angry by the media![71]

BABY BOOMERS

The baby boomers cohort (born between 1946 and 1964) are the source of many fundamental cultural and economic changes. The reason: power in numbers. As the Second World War ended, Boomer's parents turned to new lives, and began to establish families and careers at a record pace. Imagine a large python that has swallowed a mouse: the mouse moves down the length of the python, creating a moving bulge as it goes. So it is with baby boomers. In 2003 there were 76 million elderly people aged 65 and over in the EU27 countries, compared with only 38 million in 1960. The baby boomers, ageing, coupled with extended longevity, and the overall lower fertility levels in the EU means that the population will continue to grow older for the coming decades.[72]

The market impact of boomers

Figure 11.4 shows a series of age pyramids of the European population for all ages for the period, from 2019 to 2060.[73] Note how the top of the pyramid continues to get wider in each

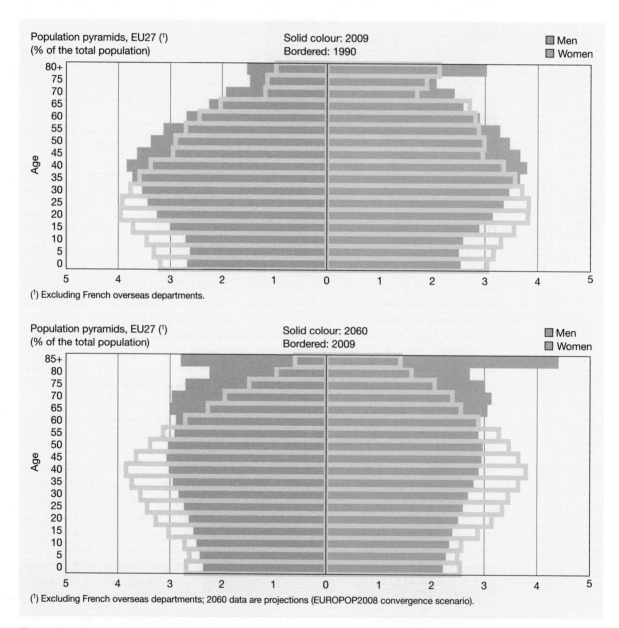

Population pyramids, EU27 (¹)
(% of the total population)

Solid colour: 2009
Bordered: 1990

■ Men
■ Women

(¹) Excluding French overseas departments.

Population pyramids, EU27 (¹)
(% of the total population)

Solid colour: 2060
Bordered: 2009

■ Men
■ Women

(¹) Excluding French overseas departments; 2060 data are projections (EUROPOP2008 convergence scenario).

Figure 11.4 European age pyramids

Source: Eurostat (demo_pjangroup and proj_08c2150p)

successive projection. This increase in the proportion of older citizens and decrease in the proportion of youth is often referred to as the 'greying and de-greening' of the European population, a structural trend which has major implications for the marketing of goods and services.

As teenagers in the 1960s and 1970s, this generation created a revolution in style, politics and consumer attitudes. As they have aged, their collective will has been behind cultural events as diverse as the Paris student demonstrations and hippies in the 1960s and Thatcherism and yuppies in the 1980s. Now that they are older, they continue to influence popular culture in important ways, redefining 'chronological age', and what 'retirement' means.

This 'mouse in the python' has moved into its mid-forties to early sixties, and is the age group that exerts the most impact on consumption patterns. Most of the growth in the market will be accounted for by people who are moving into their peak earning years. As one commercial for VH1, the music-video network that caters to those who are a bit too old for MTV, pointed out, 'The generation that dropped acid to escape reality . . . is the generation that drops antacid to cope with it'. Boomers tend to have different emotional and psychological needs from those who came before them, and this is being played out again throughout European markets. In the first decade of the twenty-first century, Boomers are busy rethinking their role in 'retirement' (which is to say, new identities and new consumption activities). Boomers see themselves not so much in chronological age, but as simply entering into a new life stage which is full of new opportunities.[74]

THE GREY MARKET

The old widowed woman sits alone in her clean but sparsely furnished apartment, while the television blares out a soap opera. Each day, she slowly and painfully makes her way out of the apartment and goes to the corner shop to buy essentials, bread, milk and vegetables, always being careful to pick the least expensive offering. Most of the time she sits in her rocking chair, thinking sadly of her dead husband and the good times she used to have.

Is this the image you have of a typical elderly consumer? Until recently, many marketers did. As a result, they largely neglected the elderly in their feverish pursuit of the baby boomer market. But as our population ages and people are living longer and healthier lives, the game is rapidly changing. A lot of businesses are beginning to replace the old stereotype of the poor recluse. The newer, more accurate image is of an elderly person who is active, interested in what life has to offer, and is an enthusiastic consumer with the means and willingness to buy many goods and services.

Grey power: shattering stereotypes

As of 2010, 20 per cent of Europeans are aged 62 or older. This fastest-growing age segment can be explained by the ageing of 'boomers', an increase in awareness of healthy lifestyles and nutrition, coupled with improved medical diagnoses and treatment. Over the past 50 years, life expectancy of men and women has risen steadily: by around 10 years for each sex. Throughout the EU, women live longer than men. Estimates are that the life expectancy of women and men may reach 84 and 78 years respectively by the year 2020.[75] Not only is this segment growing and living longer, but older adults have large amounts of discretionary income, since, typically, they have paid off their mortgage, and no longer have the expense of raising and educating children.

Most elderly people lead more active, multidimensional lives than we assume. Many engage in voluntary work, continue to work and/or are involved in daily care of a grandchild. Still, outdated images of mature consumers persist.

Seniors' economic clout

There is abundant evidence that the economic health of elderly consumers is good and getting better. Some of the important areas that stand to benefit from the surging **grey market** include holidays, cars, home improvements, cruises and tourism, cosmetic surgery and skin treatments, health, finance and legal matters, and 'how-to' books for learning to cope with retirement.

It is crucial to remember that income alone does not capture the spending power of this group. As mentioned above, elderly consumers are no longer burdened with the financial obligations that drain the income of younger consumers. Elderly consumers are much more likely to own their home, have no mortgage or have a (low-cost or subsidized) rented house or apartment. Across Europe, approximately 50 per cent of pensioners' income still comes from state pensions, yet it is clear that older consumers are time-rich, and have a significant amount of discretionary income to spend.[76] The relatively high living standards of future retirees (the baby boomers) and the stability of public finances (until the current economic forecast) in different European states has led to an active discussion of pension reform plans throughout the EU. Nonetheless, pensions will continue to play an important role in the discretionary incomes of Europe's retired population. As a final note on the two major demographic trends in Europe, let's link together the 'greying' and the 'de-greening' populations. Figure 11.5 shows the dependency ratio of the number of people in the EU27 countries over the age of 65, relative to the number of people aged 15–64 (those who are theoretically still employed).[77] While Japan (JP) faces the most critical scenario, the EU is also looking at a future with a greater percentage of the elderly, relative to a smaller percentage of younger people. This will have significant implications for social security payments, and the offerings of goods and services.

Researchers have identified a set of key values that are relevant to older consumers. For marketing strategies to succeed, they should be related to one or more of these factors:[78]

● *Autonomy*. Mature consumers want to lead active lives and to be self-sufficient. Financial services and financial planning are increasing markets for the elderly segment, who have a

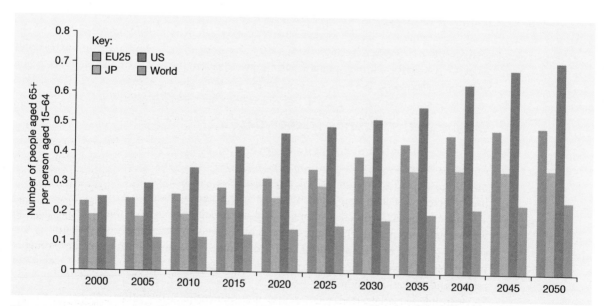

Figure 11.5 Old age dependency ratio

strong need to remain independent. While companies are the largest purchasers of cars in the UK, the majority of private buyers are 'greys' – a further sign of their financial muscle and desire for autonomy.[79]

- *Connectedness*. Mature consumers value the bonds they have with friends and family. While the 'grey' do not relate well to their own age group (most elderly report feeling on average ten years younger than they are, and feel that 'other' elderly behave 'older' than they do), they do value information which communicates clear benefits to cohorts in their age group. Advertisements which avoid patronizing stereotypes are well received.

- *Altruism*. Mature consumers want to give something back to the world. Thrifty Car Rental found in a survey that over 40 per cent of older consumers would select a rental car company if it sponsored a programme that gives discounts to senior citizens' centres. Based on this research, the company launched its highly successful 'Give a Friend a Lift' programme.

- *Personal growth*. Mature consumers are very interested in trying new experiences and developing their potential. By installing user-friendly interactive touch-screen computer stations in European stores, GNC has found that older consumers have become better educated about health issues, and are loyal to the brand.[80]

Europe's fastest-growing age segment continues to re-define the meaning of 'ageing' by remaining active, and having multidimensional lifestyles and activities.

Courtesy of Saga Publishing Ltd.

Perceived age: you're only as old as you feel

The 'grey' market does not consist of a uniform segment of vigorous, happy, ready-to-spend consumers – nor is it a group of senile, economically marginalized, immobile people. In fact, research confirms the popular wisdom that age is more a state of mind than of body. A person's mental outlook and activity level has a lot more to do with their longevity and quality of life than does *chronological age*, or the actual number of years lived. In addition to these psychological dimensions of age, there are also cultural influences on what constitutes ageing, and perceptions of what is 'elderly' across different European markets.[81]

A better yardstick to categorize the elderly is **perceived age**, or how old a person feels. Perceived age can be measured on several dimensions, including 'feel-age' (how old a person feels) and 'look-age' (how old a person looks).[82] The older consumers get, the younger they feel relative to actual age. For this reason, many marketers emphasize product benefits rather than age appropriateness in marketing campaigns, since many consumers will not relate to products targeted to their chronological age.[83]

MARKETING PITFALL ⊗

Some marketing efforts targeted at the elderly have backfired because they reminded people of their age or presented their age group in an unflattering way. One of the more infamous blunders was committed by Heinz. A company analyst found that many elderly people were buying baby food because of the small portions and easy chewing consistency, so Heinz introduced a line of 'Senior Foods' made especially for denture wearers. Needless to say, the product failed. Consumers did not want to admit that they required strained foods (even to the supermarket cashier). They preferred to purchase baby foods, which they could pretend they were buying for a grandchild.

In Holland, a country where bicycles are an important mode of personal transportation, a specially designed 'elderly bicycle' was a resounding failure in spite of its competitive product benefits. While conventional marketing wisdom would suggest that a firm communicate its unique functional benefits to a target market, this wisdom backfired for the Dutch 'greys'. Positioning the bicycle as an easy-to-pedal 'senior bicycle' was met with a negative response, as the Dutch elderly who still ride a bicycle (a common sight in Holland) feel too young to be riding a 'senior' bike.[84]

Finally, there is growing evidence throughout the UK and Europe that National Health Care Programmes in these countries need to start paying more attention to the elderly with respect to informative messages regarding the risk and spread of Sexually Transmitted Infections (!). As an age cohort, Seniors are increasingly likely to be single or undergoing relationship changes and put themselves at risk by not using condoms (contraception no longer being an issue), and not knowing the sexual history of their partners. Increased international travel, internet dating, the growing use of drugs such as Viagra to counter erectile dysfunction and overlapping sexual networks have been identified to be factors.[85]

Segmenting seniors

The senior subculture represents an extremely large market: the number of Europeans aged 62 and over exceeds the entire population of Canada.[86] Because this group is so large, it is helpful to think of the mature market as consisting of four subsegments: an 'older' group (aged 55–64), an 'elderly' group (aged 65–74), an 'aged' group (aged 75–84) and finally a 'very old' group (85+).[87]

The elderly market is well suited for segmentation. Older consumers are easy to identify by age and stage in the family lifecycle. Most receive social security benefits so they can be located without much effort, and many subscribe to one of the magazines targeted to the elderly. *Saga Magazine* in the UK has the largest circulation of any European magazine, with over 750,000 monthly readers. Selling holidays and insurance to the over-50s, the parent company also makes use of a database with over 4 million over-50s.

Several segmentation approaches begin with the premise that a major determinant of elderly marketplace behaviour is the way a person deals with being old.[88] *Social ageing theories* try to understand how society assigns people to different roles across the lifespan. For example, when someone retires they may reflect society's expectations for someone at this life stage – this is a major transition point when people exit from many relationships.[89] Some people become depressed, withdrawn and apathetic as they age, some are angry and resist the thought of ageing, and some appear to accept the new challenges and opportunities this period of life has to offer.

In general, the elderly have been shown to respond positively to ads that provide an abundance of information. Unlike other age groups, these consumers are not usually amused, or persuaded, by imagery-oriented advertising. A more successful strategy involves the construction of advertising that depicts the aged as well-integrated, contributing members of society, with emphasis on them expanding their horizons rather than clinging precariously to life.

Some basic guidelines have been suggested for effective advertising to the elderly. These include the following:[90]

- Keep language simple.
- Use clear, bright pictures.
- Use action to attract attention.
- Speak clearly, and keep the word count low.
- Use a single sales message, and emphasize brand extensions to tap consumers' familiarity.
- Avoid extraneous stimuli (excessive pictures and graphics can detract from the message).

CHAPTER SUMMARY

→ Many purchasing decisions are made by more than one person. Collective decision-making occurs whenever two or more people are involved in evaluating, selecting or using a product or service.

→ Demographics are statistics that measure a population's characteristics. Some of the most important of these relate to family structure, e.g. the birth rate, the marriage rate and the divorce rate. In Europe, collecting reliable and comparable data regarding the family unit has not always been a straightforward process.

→ A household is an occupied housing unit. The number and type of European households is changing in many ways, for example through delays in getting married and having children, and in the composition of family households, which increasingly are headed by a single parent. New perspectives on the family lifecycle, which focuses on how people's needs change as they move through different stages in their lives, are forcing marketers to consider more seriously such consumer segments as homosexuals, divorcees and childless couples when they develop targeting strategies.

→ Families must be understood in terms of their decision-making dynamics. Spouses in particular have different priorities and exert varying amounts of influence in terms of effort and power. Children are also increasingly influential during a widening range of purchase decisions.

→ Children undergo a process of socialization, whereby they learn how to be consumers. Some of this knowledge is instilled by parents and friends, but a lot of it comes from exposure to mass media and advertising. Since children are in some cases so easily persuaded, the ethical aspects of marketing to them are hotly debated among consumers, academics and marketing practitioners.

→ Europeans have many things in common with others merely because they are about the same age or live in the same country, or same part of the country. Consumers who grew up at the same time share many cultural memories, so they may respond to marketers' *nostalgia* appeals that remind them of these experiences.

→ Important age cohorts include teenagers, 18- to 29-year-olds, baby boomers and the elderly. *Teenagers* are making a transition from childhood to adulthood, and their self-concepts tend to be unstable. They are receptive to products that help them to be accepted and enable them to assert their independence. Because many teenagers receive allowances, and/or earn pocket money but have few financial obligations, they are a particularly important segment for many non-essential or expressive products, ranging from chewing gum to hair gel, to clothing fashions and music. Because of changes in family structure, many teenagers are taking more responsibility for their families, day-to-day shopping and routine purchase decisions.

→ *'Generation X-ers'*, consumers aged 18–29, are a difficult group for marketers to 'get a clear picture of'. They will be a powerful force in the years to come, whose tastes and priorities will be felt in fashion, popular culture, politics and marketing.

→ *Baby boomers* are the most powerful age segment because of their size and economic clout. As this group has aged, its interests have changed and marketing priorities have changed as well. The needs and desires of baby boomers have a strong influence on demands for housing, childcare, cars, clothing and so on. Only a small proportion of boomers fit into an affluent, materialistic category.

→ As the population ages, the needs of *elderly* consumers will also become increasingly influential. Many marketers traditionally ignored the elderly because of the stereotype that they are inactive and spend too little. This stereotype is no longer accurate. Most of the elderly are healthy, vigorous and interested in new products and experiences – and they have the income to purchase them. Marketing appeals to this age subculture should focus on consumers, self-concepts and perceived ages, which tend to be more youthful than their chronological ages. Marketers should emphasize the concrete benefits of products, since this group tends to be skeptical of vague, image-related promotions. Personalized service is of particular importance to this segment.

KEY TERMS

Accommodative purchase decision (p. 454)

Age cohort (p. 461)

Autocratic decisions (p. 455)

Boomerang kids (p. 464)

Cognitive development (p. 460)

Consensual purchase decision (p. 454)

Consumer socialization (p. 458)

Extended family (p. 448)

Family financial officer (FFO) (p. 455)

Family household (p. 449)

Family lifecycle (FLC) (p. 453)

Fertility rate (p. 449)

Generation X (p. 464)

Grey market (p. 468)

Kin network system (p. 456)

Nuclear family (p. 448)

Parental yielding (p. 457)

Perceived age (p. 470)

Stage of cognitive development (p. 460)

Syncratic decisions (p. 455)

CONSUMER BEHAVIOUR CHALLENGE

1 Review a number of popular media which are published in countries in southern Europe as well as media targeted for northern European countries. How do the ads' depictions of *family* seem to differ by region? In what sorts of consumption situations do they seem highly similar? Why?

2 For each of the following five product categories – groceries, cars, holidays, furniture and appliances – describe the ways in which you believe a married couple's choices would be affected if they had children.

3 In identifying and targeting newly divorced couples, do you think marketers are exploiting these couples' situations? Are there instances where you think marketers may actually be helpful to them? Support your answers with examples.

4 Arrange to interview two married couples, one younger and one older. Prepare a response form listing five product categories – groceries, furniture, appliances, holidays and cars – and ask each spouse to indicate, without consulting the other, whether purchases in each category are made by joint or unilateral decisions and to indicate whether the unilateral decisions are made by the husband or the wife. Compare each couples' responses for agreement between husbands and wives relative to who makes the decisions and compare both couples' overall responses for differences relative to the number of joint versus unilateral decisions. Report your findings and conclusions.

5 Collect ads for three different product categories in which the family is targeted. Find another set of ads for different brands of the same items in which the family is not featured. Prepare a report on the effectiveness of the approaches.

6 Observe the interactions between parents and children in the cereal section of a local supermarket. Prepare a report on the number of children who expressed preferences, how they expressed their preferences and how parents responded, including the number who purchased the child's choice.

7 Select a product category and, using the lifecycle stages given in the chapter, list the variables that will affect a purchase decision for the product by consumers in each stage of the cycle.

8 Consider three important changes in modern European family structure. For each, find an example of a marketer who has attempted to be conscious of this change as reflected in product communications, retailing innovations, or other aspects of the marketing mix. If possible, also try to find examples of marketers who have failed to keep up with these developments.

9 Why did baby boomers have such an important impact on consumer culture in the second half of the twentieth century?

10 How has the baby boomlet changed attitudes towards child-rearing practices and created demand for different products and services?

11 Is it practical to assume that people aged 55 and older constitute one large consumer market? What are some approaches to further segmenting this age subculture?

12 What are some important variables to keep in mind when tailoring marketing strategies to the elderly?

13 Find good and bad examples of advertising targeted at elderly consumers. To what degree does advertising stereotype the elderly? What elements of ads or other promotions appear to determine their effectiveness in reaching and persuading this group?

For additional material see the companion website at **www.pearsoned.co.uk/solomon**

NOTES

1. *Eurostat Yearbook 2011*; see also: http://europa.eu/rapid/pressReleasesAction.do?reference=STAT/08/119

2. T. Eggerickx and F. Bégeot, 'Les recensements en Europe dans les années 1990. De la diversité des pratiques nationales à la comparabilité internationales des résulats', *Population* 41(2) (1993): 327–48. Standardization efforts continue. See *The Social Situation in the European Union*, an annual report commissioned by the European Council, and published by Eurostat.

3. Europe in Figures: *Eurostat Yearbook 2011*, p. 122.

4. Robert Boutilier, 'Diversity in family structures', *American Demographics Marketing Tools* (1993): 4–6; W. Bradford Fay, 'Families in the 1990s: Universal values, uncommon experiences', *Marketing Research* 5 (Winter 1993) 1: 47.

5. Amber M. Epp and Linda L. Price (2008), 'Family identity: A framework of identity interplay in consumption practices', *Journal of Consumer Research*, June: 50–70; see also David Cheal, 'The ritualization of family ties', *American Behavioral Scientist* 31 (July/August 1988): 632.

6. 'Women and men in the European Union: a statistical portrait' (Luxembourg: Office for Official Publications of the European Communities, 1996); 'Families come first', *Psychology Today* (September 1988): 11.

7. Alan R. Andreasen, 'Life status changes and changes in consumer preferences and satisfaction', *Journal of Consumer Research* 11 (December 1984): 784–94; James H. McAlexander, John W. Schouten and Scott D. Roberts, 'Consumer behavior and divorce', *Research in Consumer Behavior* 6 (1993): 153–84.

8. Europe in Figures: *Eurostat Yearbook 2011*, p. 129. See also: 'Men and women in the European Union: a statistical portrait' (Luxembourg: Office for Official Publications of the European Communities, 1995); 'The big picture', *American Demographics* (March 1989): 22–7; Thomas G. Exter, 'Middle-aging households', *American Demographics* (July 1992): 63.

9. 'Trends in households in the European Union: 1995–2025', *Eurostat, Statistics in Focus*, Theme 3-24/2003 (Luxembourg: Office for Official Publications of the European Communities, 2004).

10. 'The population of the EU on 1 January, 1995', *Statistics in Focus. Population and Social Conditions*, no. 8 (Luxembourg: Office for Official Publications of the European Communities, 1995); Nicholas Timmins, 'One in five women to remain childless', *The Independent* (4 October 1995).

11. 'Trends in households in the European Union: 1995–2025', *op. cit.*: 14.

12. Edward del Rosario (2008), 'No Babies?' *New York Times*, 26 June 2008, http://www.nytimes.com/2008/06/29/magazine/29Birth-t.html?_r=2&oref=slogin&oref=slogin

13. 'Men and women in the European Union: a statistical portrait', *op. cit.*: 72.

14. Peg Masterson, 'Agency notes rise of singles market', *Advertising Age* (9 August 1993): 17.

15. Christy Fisher, 'Census data may make ads more single minded', *Advertising Age* (20 July 1992): 2.

16. Calmetta Y. Coleman, 'The unseemly secrets of eating alone', *The Wall Street Journal* (6 July 1995): B1 (2).

17. Stephanie Shipp, 'How singles spend', *American Demographics* (April 1988): 22–7; Patricia Braus, 'Sex and the single spender', *American Demographics* (November 1993): 28–34.

18. 'Men and women in the European Union: a statistical portrait', *op. cit.*: 76.

19. O'Neill, Moira, 'Why Finding a Good Nanny can be Taxing', *Financial Times*, 17 December 2010; see also: Gary Younge, 'Parents face a £66,000 bill', *The Guardian* (27 May 1996); Liz Hunt, 'The cost of growing: School-children need huge sums', *The Independent* (19 August 1996).

20. 'Trends in households in the European Union: 1995–2025', *op. cit.*

21. Mary C. Gilly and Ben M. Enis, 'Recycling the Family Life Cycle: A Proposal for Redefinition', in Andrew A. Mitchell (ed.), *Advances in Consumer Research* 9 (Ann Arbor, MI: Association for Consumer Research, 1982): 271–6.

22. Charles M. Schaninger and William D. Danko, 'A conceptual and empirical comparison of alternative household life cycle models', *Journal of Consumer Research* 19 (March 1993): 580–94; Robert E. Wilkes, 'Household life-cycle stages, transitions, and product expenditures', *Journal of Consumer Research* 22(1) (June 1995): 27–42.

23. Carolyn F. Curasi, Linda L. Price and Eric J. Arnould (2004), 'How individuals' cherished possessions become families' inalienable wealth', *Journal of Consumer Research* 31 (December): 609–22; Tonya Williams Bradford (2009), 'Intergenerationally gifted asset disposition', *Journal of Consumer Research* 36, in press.

24. James H. McAlexander, John W. Schouten and Scott D. Roberts, 'Consumer Behavior and Divorce', in *Research in Consumer Behavior* (Greenwich, CT: JAI Press, 1992); Michael R. Solomon, 'The role of products as social stimuli: A symbolic interactionism perspective', *Journal of Consumer Research* 10 (December 1983): 319–29; Melissa Martin Young, 'Disposition of Possession During Role Transitions', in Rebecca H. Holman and Michael R. Solomon (eds), *Advances in Consumer Research* 18 (Provo, UT: Association for Consumer Research, 1991): 33–9.

25. Harry L. Davis, 'Decision making within the household', *Journal of Consumer Research* 2 (March 1972): 241–60; Michael B. Menasco and David J. Curry, 'Utility and choice: An empirical study of wife/husband decision making', *Journal of Consumer Research* 16 (June 1989): 87–97; for a recent review, see Conway Lackman and John M. Lanasa, 'Family decision-making theory: An overview and assessment', *Psychology and Marketing* 10 (March/April 1993) 2: 81–94.

26. Shannon Dortch, 'Money and marital discord', *American Demographics* (October 1994): 11(3).

27. Daniel Seymour and Greg Lessne, 'Spousal conflict arousal: Scale development', *Journal of Consumer Research* 11 (December 1984): 810–21.

28. For recent research on factors influencing how much influence adolescents exert in family decision-making, see Ellen Foxman, Patriya Tansuhaj and Karin M. Ekstrom, 'Family members' perceptions of adolescents' influence in family decision making', *Journal of Consumer Research* 15 (March 1989) 4: 482–91; Sharon E. Beatty and Salil Talpade, 'Adolescent influence in family decision making: A replication with

extension', *Journal of Consumer Research* 21 (September 1994) 2: 332–41.

29. Diane Crispell, 'Dual-earner diversity', *American Demographics* (July 1995): 32–7.

30. Robert Boutilier, *Targeting Families: Marketing To and Through the New Family* (Ithaca, NY: American Demographics Books, 1993).

31. Darach Turley, 'Dialogue with the departed', in F. Hansen (ed.), *European Advances in Consumer Research* 2 (Provo, UT: Association for Consumer Research, 1995): 10–13.

32. Dennis L. Rosen and Donald H. Granbois, 'Determinants of role structure in family financial management', *Journal of Consumer Research* 10 (September 1983): 253–8.

33. Robert F. Bales, *Interaction Process Analysis: A Method for the Study of Small Groups* (Reading, MA: Addison-Wesley, 1950); for a cross-gender comparison of food shopping strategies, see Rosemary Polegato and Judith L. Zaichkowsky, 'Family food shopping: Strategies used by husbands and wives', *The Journal of Consumer Affairs* 28 (1994): 2.

34. Alma S. Baron, 'Working parents: Shifting traditional roles', *Business* 37 (January/March 1987): 36; William J. Qualls, 'Household decision behavior: The impact of husbands' and wives' sex role orientation', *Journal of Consumer Research* 14 (September 1987): 264–79; Charles M. Schaninger and W. Christian Buss, 'The relationship of sex role norms to household task allocation', *Psychology and Marketing* 2 (Summer 1985): 93–104.

35. Cynthia Webster, 'Effects of Hispanic ethnic identification on marital roles in the purchase decision process', *Journal of Consumer Research* 21 (September 1994) 2: 319–31; for a recent study that examined the effects of family depictions in advertising among Hispanic consumers, see Gary D. Gregory and James M. Munch, 'Cultural values in international advertising: an examination of familial norms and roles in Mexico', *Psychology and Marketing* 14(2) (March 1997): 99–120.

36. Gary L. Sullivan and P.J. O'Connor, 'The family purchase decision process: A cross-cultural review and framework for research', *Southwest Journal of Business and Economics* (Fall 1988): 43; Marilyn Lavin, 'Husband-dominant, wife-dominant, joint', *Journal of Consumer Marketing* 10 (1993) 3: 33–42; Nicholas Timmins, 'New man fails to survive into the nineties', *The Independent* (25 January 1996). See also Roger J. Baran, 'Patterns of Decision Making Influence for Selected Products and Services Among Husbands and Wives Living in the Czech Republic', in Hansen (ed.), *European Advances in Consumer Research* 2; Jan Pahl, 'His money, her money: Recent research on financial organization in marriage', *Journal of Economic Psychology* 16 (1995): 361–76; Carole B. Burgoyne, 'Financial organization and decision-making within Western "households"', *Journal of Economic Psychology* 16 (1995): 421–30; Erich Kirchler, 'Spouses' joint purchase decisions: Determinants of influence tactics for muddling through the process', *Journal of Economic Psychology* 14 (1993): 405–38.

37. Micaela DiLeonardo, 'The female world of cards and holidays: Women, families, and the work of kinship', *Signs* 12 (Spring 1942): 440–53.

38. C. Whan Park, 'Joint decisions in home purchasing: A muddling through process', *Journal of Consumer Research* 9 (September 1982): 151–62; see also William J. Qualls and Françoise Jaffe, 'Measuring Conflict in Household Decision Behavior:

Read My Lips and Read My Mind', in John F. Sherry Jr and Brian Sternthal (eds), *Advances in Consumer Research* 19 (Provo, UT: Association for Consumer Research, 1992).

39. Kim P. Corfman and Donald R. Lehmann, 'Models of co-operative group decision-making and relative influence: An experimental investigation of family purchase decisions', *Journal of Consumer Research* 14 (June 1987).

40. Alison M. Torrillo, 'Dens are men's territory', *American Demographics* (January 1995): 11(2).

41. Charles Atkin, 'Observation of parent–child interaction in supermarket decision-making', *Journal of Marketing* 42 (October 1978).

42. Les Carlson, Ann Walsh, Russell N. Laczniak and Sanford Grossbart, 'Family communication patterns and market-place motivations, attitudes, and behaviors of children and mothers', *Journal of Consumer Affairs* 28(1) (Summer 1994): 25–53; see also Roy L. Moore and George P. Moschis, 'The role of family communication in consumer learning', *Journal of Communication* 31 (Autumn 1981): 42–51.

43. Kerrane, Ben, M.K. Hogg and Shona Bettany, 'Children's strategies in practice: Exploring the co-constructed nature of children's influence strategies in family consumption', *Journal of Marketing Management*, 2013 (accepted February 2012, publication date tbc); *see also*: Leslie Isler, Edward T. Popper and Scott Ward, 'Children's purchase requests and parental responses: Results from a diary study', *Journal of Advertising Research* 27 (October/November 1987).

44. Scott Ward, 'Consumer Socialization', in Harold H. Kassarjian and Thomas S. Robertson (eds), *Perspectives in Consumer Behavior* (Glenville, IL: Scott, Foresman, 1980): 380.

45. Thomas Lipscomb, 'Indicators of materialism in children's free speech: Age and gender comparisons', *Journal of Consumer Marketing* (Fall 1988): 41–6.

46. Kerrane, B. and M.K. Hogg, 'Shared or Non-Shared: Children's Different Consumer Socialization Experiences within the Family Environment', *European Journal of Marketing*, 2013 (accepted June 2011 publication date tbc).

47. George P. Moschis, 'The role of family communication in consumer socialization of children and adolescents', *Journal of Consumer Research* 11 (March 1985): 898–913.

48. James U. McNeal and Chyon-Hwa Yeh, 'Born to shop', *American Demographics* (June 1993): 34–9.

49. See Les Carlson, Sanford Grossbart and J. Kathleen Stuenkel, 'The role of parental socialization types on differential family communication patterns regarding consumption', *Journal of Consumer Psychology* 1 (1992) 1: 31–52.

50. See Patricia M. Greenfield, Emily Yut, Mabel Chung, Deborah Land, Holly Kreider, Maurice Pantoja and Kris Horsley, 'The program-length commercial: A study of the effects of television/toy tie-ins on imaginative play', *Psychology and Marketing* 7 (Winter 1990): 237–56 for a study on the effects of commercial programming on creative play.

51. http://www.teletubbies.com/en/default.asp, accessed 27 April 2012; see also: Jill Goldsmith, 'Ga, ga, goo, goo, where's the remote? TV show targets tots', *Dow Jones Business News* (5 February 1997), accessed via *The Wall Street Journal Interactive Edition* (6 February 1997).

52. Gerald J. Gorn and Renee Florsheim, 'The effects of commercials for adult products on children', *Journal of Consumer Research* 11 (March 1985): 9, 62–7; for a study that assessed the impact of violent commercials on children, see V. Kanti

Prasad and Lois J. Smith, 'Television commercials in violent programming: an experimental evaluation of their effects on children', *Journal of the Academy of Marketing Science* 22 (1994) 4: 340–51.

53. Glenn Collins, 'New studies on "girl toys" and "boy toys"', *New York Times* (13 February 1984): D1.

54. Susan B. Kaiser, 'Clothing and the social organization of gender perception: A developmental approach', *Clothing and Textiles Research Journal* 7 (Winter 1989): 46–56.

55. D.W. Rajecki, Jill Ann Dame, Kelly Jo Creek, P.J. Barrickman, Catherine A. Reid and Drew C. Appleby, 'Gender casting in television toy advertisements: Distributions, message content analysis, and evaluations', *Journal of Consumer Psychology* 2 (1993) 3: 307–27.

56. Lori Schwartz and William Markham, 'Sex stereotyping in children's toy advertisements', *Sex Roles* 12 (January 1985): 157–70.

57. Joseph Pereira, 'Oh boy! In toyland, you get more if you're male', *The Wall Street Journal* (23 September 1994): B1 (2); Joseph Pereira, 'Girls' favorite playthings: dolls, dolls, and dolls', *The Wall Street Journal* (23 September 1994): B1 (2).

58. Laura A. Peracchio, 'How do young children learn to be consumers? A script-processing approach', *Journal of Consumer Research* 18 (March 1992): 4, 25–40; Laura A. Peracchio, 'Young children's processing of a televised narrative: Is a picture really worth a thousand words?' *Journal of Consumer Research* 20 (September 1993) 2: 281–93; see also M. Carole Macklin, 'The effects of an advertising retrieval cue on young children's memory and brand evaluations', *Psychology and Marketing* 11 (May/June 1994) 3: 291–311.

59. Jean Piaget, 'The child and modern physics', *Scientific American* 196 (1957) 3: 46–51; see also Kenneth D. Bahn, 'How and when do brand perceptions and preferences first form? A cognitive developmental investigation', *Journal of Consumer Research* 13 (December 1986): 382–93.

60. Deborah L. Roedder, 'Age differences in children's responses to television advertising: An information processing approach', *Journal of Consumer Research* 8 (September 1981): 1, 44–53; see also Deborah Roedder John and Ramnath Lakshmi-Ratan, 'Age differences in children's choice behavior: The impact of available alternatives', *Journal of Marketing Research* (29 May 1992): 216–26; Jennifer Gregan-Paxton and Deborah Roedder John, 'Are young children adaptive decision makers? A study of age differences in information search behavior', *Journal of Consumer Research* (1995).

61. Bickley Townsend, 'Où sont les neiges d'antan?' ('Where are the snows of yesteryear?'), *American Demographics* (October 1988): 2.

62. Lindstrom, Martin, 'Bottling the Past: Using Nostalgia to Connect with Consumers', *Fast Company*, 23 August 2011.

63. Adapted from: Hilary Heuler (2009), 'Poles Find Solidarity in Milk Bars', *Christian Science Monitor*, 26 January 2009, http://features.csmonitor.com/backstory/2009/01/26/poles-find-solidarity-in-milk-bars/; see also: Esche, Christine, Katarina Timm and Sandra Topalska, 'Lost and Found: Communism Nostalgia and Communism Chic Among Poland's Old and Young Generations' *Humanity in Action*, http://www.humanityinaction.org/knowledgebase/62-lost-and-found-communism-nostalgia-and-communist-chic-among-polands-old-and-young-generations, accessed 27 April 2012.

64. 'Same kids, more money', *Marketing* (29 June 1995): 37; see also the following websites for some overviews of allowances: http://www.kiplinger.com/drt.drthome.html and http://pages.prodigy.com/kidsmoney/.

65. Birgitte Tufte and Jeanetter Rasmussen, 'Children on the Net: State of the Art and Future Perspectives Regarding Danish Children's Use of the Internet', in Darach Turley and Stephen Brown (eds), *European Advances in Consumer Research: All Changed, Changed Utterly?* 6 (Valdosta, GA: Association for Consumer Research, 2003: 142–6; Anthony Patterson, Kim Cassidy and Steve Baron, 'Communication and Marketing in a Mobilized World: Diary Research on "Generation Txt"', in Turley and Brown (eds), *European Advances in Consumer Research*: 147–52; Hanman, Natalie, 'The kids are all writing', *The Guardian* (9 June 2005), http://www.guardian.co.uk/online/story/0,,1501803,00.html.

66. 'Same kids, more money', *op. cit.*; Scott McCartney, 'Society's subcultures meet by modem', *Wall Street Journal* (8 December 1994): B1 (2).

67. Junu Bryan Kim, 'For savvy teens: Real life, real solutions', *Advertising Age* (23 August 1993): Special Report 1.

68. 'Hopes and fears: Young European opinion leaders', GfK, adapted from *Marketing Week* (25 June 1998) (study of 500 opinion leaders aged 14–20 from 16 western and eastern European countries).

69. Gordon, Barry, 'The Boomerang Generation: Why more grown up kids are returning home to lodge with their parents', *Daily Record*, 21 December 2010; see also: 'Living Conditions in Europe: Statistical handbook', *Eurostat* (Luxembourg: Office for Official Publications of the European Communities, 2000): 29.

70. 'Generation next', *Marketing* (16 January 1997): 25.

71. Scott Donaton, 'The media wakes up to Generation X', *Advertising Age* (1 February 1993): 16(2); Laura E. Keeton, 'New magazines aim to reach (and rechristen) Generation X', *Wall Street Journal* (17 October 1994): B1.

72. 'Trends in households in the European Union: 1995–2025', *op. cit.*: 38.

73. Europe in Figures, *Eurostat Yearbook*, 2011, p. 121. See also: 'Europe in Figures', *Eurostat Yearbook*, 2008, Figure SP.9: 29.

74. Hope Schau, Mary C. Gilly and Mary Wolfinbarger (2009), 'Consumer identity renaissance: The resurgence of identity-inspired consumption in retirement', *Journal of Consumer Research* 36, August, in press.

75. 'Living conditions in Europe: Statistical handbook', *op. cit.*: 101.

76. 'Shades of grey', *op. cit.*

77. 'Trends in households in the European Union: 1995–2025', *op. cit.*: 93.

78. David B. Wolfe, 'Targeting the mature mind', *American Demographics* (March 1994): 32–6.

79. 'Shades of grey', *op. cit.*

80. Allyson Steward-Allen, 'Marketing in Europe to the consumer over age fifty', *Marketing News* 31(16) (4 August 1997): 18.

81. Gabriele Morello, 'Old is Gold, But What is Old?', ESOMAR seminar on 'The Untapped Gold Mine: The Growing Importance of the Over-50s' (Amsterdam: ESOMAR, 1989); Gabriele Morello, 'Sicilian time', in *Time and Society* (London: Sage, 1997): 6(1): 55–69. See also 'Living conditions in Europe: Statistical handbook', *op. cit.*: 9–21.

82. Benny Barak and Leon G. Schiffman, 'Cognitive Age: A Nonchronological Age Variable', in Kent B. Monroe (ed.),

Advances in Consumer Research 8 (Provo, UT: Association for Consumer Research, 1981): 602–6.

83. David B. Wolfe, 'An ageless market', *American Demographics* (July 1987): 27–55.

84. 'Baby boom generatie moet oud-zijn modieus maken', *op. cit.*

85. Lisa Power and Terrence Higgins Trust (2008), 'Sex is not the preserve of the young, and gonorrhoea and syphilis are no respecters of age', BBC News, 29 June 2008, http://news.bbc.co.uk/go/pr/fr/-/2/hi/health/7477739.stm

86. 'Demographic statistics 1997', *Eurostat* (Luxembourg: Office for Official Publications of the European Communities, 1997); see also http://europa.eu.int (accessed 5 August 2005); Lenore Skenazy, 'These days, it's hip to be old', *Advertising Age* (15 February 1988).

87. This segmentation approach is based on the US population and follows William Lazer and Eric H. Shaw, 'How older Americans spend their money', *American Demographics* (September 1987): 36. See also 'Shades of grey', *op. cit.*, for a two-segment approach to the UK elderly market, and 'Living conditions in Europe: Statistical handbook', *op. cit.*: 9–21.

88. Ellen Day, Brian Davis, Rhonda Dove and Warren A. French, 'Reaching the senior citizen market(s)', *Journal of Advertising Research* (December/January 1987/88): 23–30; Warren A. French and Richard Fox, 'Segmenting the senior citizen market', *Journal of Consumer Marketing* 2 (1985): 61–74; Jeffrey G. Towle and Claude R. Martin Jr, 'The Elderly Consumer: One Segment or Many?' in Beverlee B. Anderson (ed.), *Advances in Consumer Research* 3 (Provo, UT: Association for Consumer Research, 1976): 463.

89. Catherine A. Cole and Nadine N. Castellano, 'Consumer behavior', *Encyclopedia of Gerontology* 1 (1996): 329–39.

90. J. Ward, 'Marketers slow to catch age wave', *Advertising Age* (22 May 1989): S-1.

12 INCOME AND SOCIAL CLASS

CHAPTER OBJECTIVES

When you finish reading this chapter you will understand why:

→ Both personal and social conditions influence how we spend our money.

→ Economic recession is highly significant for consumption patterns.

→ We group consumers into social classes based on factors like income, occupation and education.

→ Social stratification creates a status hierarchy, where some goods come to signify the social class of their owners.

→ Social class is not only determined by income, but is also determined by factors such as place of residence, cultural interests and worldview.

→ Conspicuous consumption is a way of displaying ones status, especially common among the nouveaux riches.

→ Products can be used to communicate real as well as desired social class.

→ Not only economic capital, but also social and cultural capitals are relevant when distinguishing social classes from one another.

→ Socially adopted practices are important for understanding how we consume in daily life.

FINALLY, the big day has come! David is going home with Julia to meet her parents. David had been doing some contracting work at the publishing company where Julia works, and it was love at first sight. Even though David had attended the 'School of Hard Knocks' on the streets of Liverpool, while Julia studied Classics at Trinity College, Oxford, somehow they knew they could work things out despite their vastly different social backgrounds. Julia's been hinting that the Caldwells have money from *several* generations back, but David doesn't feel intimidated. After all, he knows plenty of guys from both Liverpool and London who have wheeled-and-dealed their way into six figures; he thinks he can handle one more big shot in a silk suit, flashing a roll of bills and showing off his expensive modern furniture with mirrors and gadgets everywhere you look.

When they arrive at the family estate 90 minutes outside London, David looks for a Rolls-Royce parked at the end of the long, tree-lined driveway, but he sees only a Jeep Cherokee – which, he decides, must belong to one of the servants. Once inside, David is surprised by how simply the house is decorated and by how understated everything seems. The hall floor is covered with a faded Oriental rug, and all the furniture looks really old – in fact, there doesn't seem to be a stick of new furniture anywhere, just a lot of antiques.

David is even more surprised when he meets Mr Caldwell. He had half-expected Julia's father to be wearing a tuxedo and holding a large glass of cognac like the people he saw in the movie *Gosford Park*. In fact, David had put on his best Italian silk suit in anticipation and was wearing his large cubic zirconium ring so Mr Caldwell would know that he had money too. When Julia's father emerges from his study wearing an old rumpled cardigan and plimsolls, David realizes he's definitely not in the same world . . .

CONSUMER SPENDING AND ECONOMIC BEHAVIOUR

As David's eye-opening experience at the Caldwells' suggests, there are many ways to spend money, and a wide gulf exists between those who have it and those who don't. Perhaps an equally wide one exists between those who have had it for a long time and those who made it more recently. This chapter begins by considering briefly how general economic conditions affect the way consumers allocate their money. Then, reflecting the adage, 'The rich are different', it will explore how people who occupy different positions in society consume in very different ways. Whether a person is a skilled worker like David or a child of privilege like Julia, their social class has a profound impact on what they do with their money and on how consumption choices reflect the person's 'place' in society.

As this chapter illustrates, these choices play another purpose as well. The specific products and services we buy are often intended to make sure *other* people know what our social standing is – or what we would like it to be. Products are frequently bought and displayed as markers of social class: they are valued as **status symbols**. Indeed, it is quite common for a product to be positioned on the basis of its (presumed) place in the **social hierarchy**. The chapter continues with an assessment of the evolving nature of such status symbols, and it considers some reasons why status-driven products are not always accurate indicators of a consumer's true social standing.

The way income and social class influences consumer behaviour can be approached from an individual or a more social perspective. The field of **behavioural economics**, or economic psychology, is concerned with the 'individual' and 'psychological' side of economic decisions. Beginning with the pioneering work of the psychologist George Katona, this discipline studies how consumers' motives and their expectations about the future affect their current spending, and how these individual decisions add up to affect a society's economic welfare.[1]

The chapter concludes with a section reflecting on the relation between social class and lifestyle based on the work of French sociologist Pierre Bourdieu.[2] Bourdieu also has been very influential in formulating a theory of practices, describing how culture is learned not so much by personal choices, nor by subjecting ourselves to explicit values and norms, but by adopting routinized types of behaviour that, for us, represent the 'ways things are done'. This approach is decisive in arguing why social inequalities have a tendency to reproduce themselves in society.

Income patterns

In Europe, we have been used to many years of relatively steady growth in income, so the average European's standard of living continued to improve. Gross Domestic Product more than doubled and in some EU countries quadrupled between 1980 and 1995. Although there were a few conjuncture-based fluctuations and although this boom was by no means shared equally among all consumer groups,[3] optimism generally endured until 2008. Individual income shifts were linked to two key factors: a shift in women's roles and increases in educational attainment.[4] But with the financial crisis turning into an economic crisis and into a crisis of public debt, these last years have witnessed a growing pessimism and the economic recession has had a serious impact on people's income and livelihoods. For instance, in the UK women have been particularly hard hit in terms of employment as they are more often found in the public sector (which has experienced extensive cuts) and in part-time work. Unemployment rates are soaring in several countries, mainly Spain and Greece, but what may be equally bad is the unemployment rates of young people hitting around 45 per cent (Spain, Greece) or around 30 per cent and over (several countries including Ireland, Italy and Lithuania).[5] It is obvious that such unemployment rates severely influences income and consumption patterns. For example, a lot more young people stay with their parents for a longer period, and money for leisure and fun may be lacking (or plentiful, if all the money saved from rent etc. can go into having fun – i.e. mum and dad do not ask for rent or contribution).[6]

Furthermore, Europe may be experiencing a new phenomenon, the 'working poor' – people with employment but making less than necessary to make ends meet. This struggling population, known from American society, is increasingly found not just in Spain and Greece but also in France and Germany. Usual welfare systems are ill-suited to cater for such people, who are employed and therefore technically self-sustained.[7]

Woman's work

One reason for the increase in income in European households up until the recent recession is that there has also been a larger proportion of people of working age participating in the labour force. While men are more likely to have paid employment than women are, the greatest increases in paid employment in EU countries over the past decades have been among women. This steady increase in the numbers of working women is a primary cause of the pre-recession steady increase in household incomes. Still, throughout the Union, women's average full-time earnings are less than men's, and 30 per cent of women in employment are working part-time, against only 6.5 per cent of men. Female part-time work is particularly prevalent in The Netherlands, where it accounts for almost 75 per cent of female employment, and the UK (44 per cent).[8] As can be seen in Figure 12.1, in 2009, the average gross

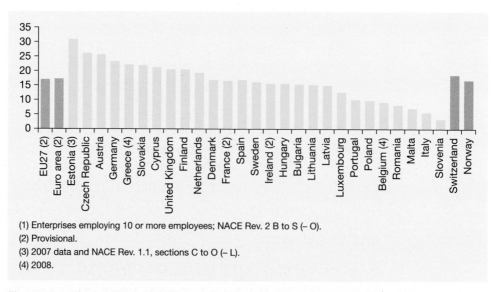

(1) Enterprises employing 10 or more employees; NACE Rev. 2 B to S (– O).
(2) Provisional.
(3) 2007 data and NACE Rev. 1.1, sections C to O (– L).
(4) 2008.

Figure 12.1 The unadjusted difference between men's and women's hourly average earnings as a percentage of men's hourly average earnings, 2009

Source: Eurostat, http://epp.eurostat.ec.europa.eu/tgm/table.do?tab=table&plugin=1&language=en&pcode=tsiem040.

hourly wage of women working on a full-time basis was 17 per cent lower than the earnings of a man. The explanations for this are related to the kinds of jobs typically held by women, the consequences of breaks in careers for child-bearing and a number of other factors. The differences in pay are particularly high among older workers, the highly educated and those employed with supervisory job status. Men are not only more concentrated in higher paid sectors and occupations, but within these sectors and occupations they are also more likely than women to hold supervisory responsibilities and if they do so their earnings tend to be relatively higher.[9] Women are also more likely to be in part-time work, a situation which reflects the more traditional activities of caring for the household and children living at home – activities that are still seen as primarily their responsibility. As discussed in the previous chapter, family situation, the number and age of children living at home and the educational level of women heavily influence their employment activities.

Yes, it pays to go to school!

Another factor that determines who gets a bigger slice of the pie is education. Although the expense of going to college often entails great sacrifice, it still pays in the long run. University and higher professional study graduates earn about 50 per cent more than those who have gone through secondary school only during the course of their lives. Close to half of the increase in consumer spending power during the past decade came from these more highly educated groups. Full-time employees with a tertiary education qualification earn on average considerably more than those who have completed upper secondary school (A-levels, *Baccalauréat*, Abitur, HBO or equivalent). In general, the trend is that the younger generation of Europeans is better qualified than the older generations. In 2008, 78.5 per cent of the younger generation aged 20–24 had completed at least upper secondary education (*Baccalauréat*, Abitur, HBO, apprenticeship).[10] This figure has been rising steadily over the years, a development driven by the increase in outsourcing of jobs requiring lower skills and thus the smaller number of job opportunities for the less skilled.

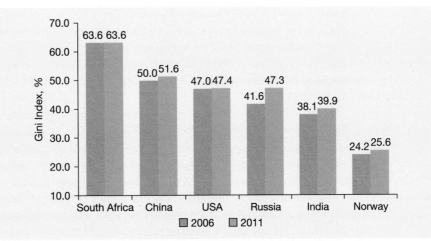

Figure 12.2 Gini index of selected countries, 2006–2011

Note: A society that scores 0 per cent on the Gini index has perfect equality, where every inhabitant has the same income. The higher the number over 0 per cent, the higher the inequality, and a score of 100 per cent indicates total inequality, where only one person receives all the income.

Source: *Euromonitor International* from national statistics.

To spend or not to spend, that is the question

A basic assumption of economic psychology is that consumer demand for goods and services depends on both our ability *and* willingness to buy. While demand for necessities tends to be stable over time, other expenditures can be postponed or eliminated if people do not feel that now is a good time to spend.[11] For example, a person may decide to 'make do' with their current car for another year rather than buy a new car now.

Discretionary spending

Discretionary income is the money available to a household over and above that required for a comfortable standard of living. European consumers are estimated to have discretionary spending power in billions of euros per year, and it is consumers aged 35–55 whose incomes are at a peak who account for the greatest amounts. As might be expected, discretionary income increases as overall income goes up – and it goes down for many people during recessionary times such as the current one.

While some populations are struggling, the crisis obviously did not hit everyone equally hard. All countries have felt a degree of recession, but the burdens are far from equally distributed. Income inequality is on the rise and is a potential source for unrest in much of the Western world.[12] In some parts of the world, like Indonesia and Russia, the rise in income inequality is due to the growth of an upper and upper middle class (and in Russia also a class of super rich), whereas in the developed economies the rise may well be due to the fact that not all parts of the population carry the same burden of economic recession. And even if there are large differences among the developed countries (ranging from USA with the highest income inequality to Norway with the lowest), the inequality is growing pretty much everywhere.[13] This is seen in Firgure 2.2, which shows the *Gini index*, a measure of social inequality, for selected countries between 2006 and 2011.

Within Europe, the top (richest) 20 per cent of the population received five times as much of the total income as the bottom (poorest) 20 per cent received. This gap between the most and least well-off persons (known as the *share ratio S80/S20*) is smallest in Slovenia (3.4) and Norway (3.4). It is generally widest in Spain (6.9) and Portugal (6.0) but also in the Baltic states, for example, Latvia has a wide gap (6.4).[14] While discretionary income is a powerful tool for predicting certain types of consumer behaviour, it is not always a measure from which straightforward comparisons between countries can be easily made. Factors such as different levels of sales tax (VAT) or varying levels of direct family benefits for children under 19 years of age living at home in various EU countries account for differences in what constitutes true discretionary income. Price levels also vary in spite of the homogenizing effect of the European free market. Buying power is therefore often a better measurement of wealth, at least in relation to the daily costs of living. Figure 12.3 gives a graphic overview of regional buying power for Europe 2012–13.

Individual attitudes towards money

Many consumers are entertaining doubts about their individual and collective futures, and are anxious about holding on to what they have. A consumer's anxieties about money are not necessarily related to how much they actually have: acquiring and managing money is sometimes more a state of mind than of wallet. Times of crisis, like the current one, impact a lot of people directly on their income, as we have seen. But even those that are not directly touched by the recession tend to be more prudent with their money and their spending, both out of precaution for an uncertain future but also because crisis can be 'talked up'. This psychological mechanism has been demonstrated for financial markets[15] but it also works for ordinary people, for example when they are experiencing talk of crisis in all media. Based on this particular 'crisis mood', they may alter their spending patterns without it really being a measure of caution or some other rational decision. The change may, however, go in two

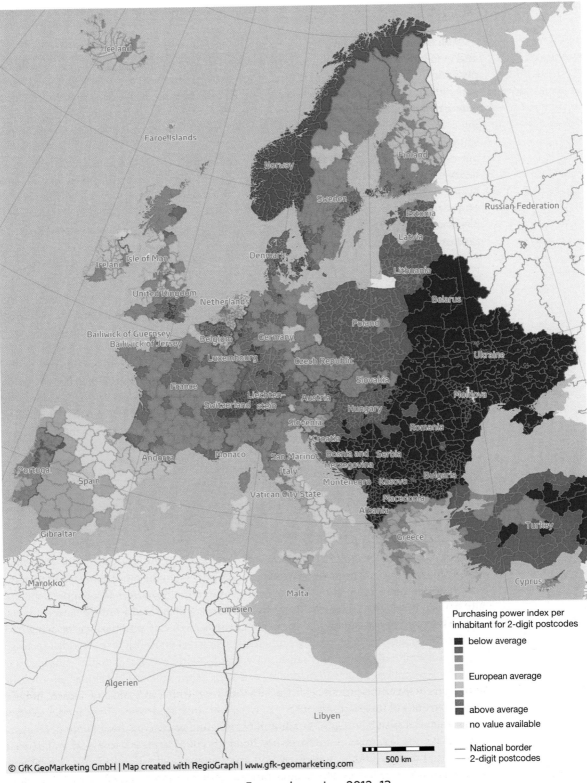

Figure 12.3 Buying power per capita across Europe, by region, 2012–13

Source: www.gfk-geomarketing.de/fileadmin/newsletter/pressrelease/purchasing-power-europe.html, © GfK GeoMarketing, study 'GfK Purchasing Power Europe 2012/2013'.

directions since instead of being more cautious, especially young people might also decide that since the future is not to be relied upon, we might as well have the fun we can right away.[16]

Money can have a variety of complex psychological meanings: it can be equated with success or failure, social acceptability, security, love, freedom and . . . sex appeal.[17] Some clinical psychologists even specialize in treating money-related disorders, and report that people feel guilty about their success and deliberately make bad investments to ease this feeling! Other clinical conditions include atephobia (fear of being ruined), harpaxophobia (fear of becoming a victim of robbers), peniaphobia (fear of poverty) and aurophobia (fear of gold).[18] A study that approached money as a social resource explored some interesting links between our need for acceptance and feelings about cash. In one case participants were either led to believe that a group had rejected them or that it had accepted them. They then completed a number of measures that reflected their desire for money. Those whom the group rejected expressed a greater desire for money. At another stage, subjects counted either real money or pieces of paper and then experienced physical pain. Those who counted money reported they felt less pain than did those who just counted paper![19]

Consumer confidence

A consumer's beliefs about what the future holds is an indicator of **consumer confidence**, which reflects the extent to which people are optimistic or pessimistic about the future health of the economy and how they will fare in the future. These beliefs influence how much money a consumer will pump into the economy when making discretionary purchases.

Hence, it is no surprise that many businesses take forecasts about anticipated spending very seriously, and periodic surveys attempt to 'take the pulse' of the European consumer. The Henley Centre conducts a survey of consumer confidence, as does Eurostat and the *EuroMonitor*. The following are the types of attitudinal statements presented to consumers in these surveys:[20]

'My standard of living will change for the better over the next year.'

'My quality of life will improve over the next year.'

'I will have a lack of money when I retire.'

'I spend too much of my income, and intend to spend less next year.'

'I am concerned about the amount of free time I have.'

When people are pessimistic about their prospects and about the state of the economy, they tend to cut back their spending and take on less debt. On the other hand, when they are optimistic about the future, they tend to reduce the amount they save, take on more debt and buy discretionary items. The overall **savings rate** thus is influenced by individual consumers' pessimism or optimism about their personal circumstances (for example, fear of being laid off vs. a steady increase in personal wealth due to rising real estate prices or a sudden increase in personal wealth due to an inheritance), as well as by world events (for example the election of a new government or an international crisis such as the collapse of Lehman Brothers in September 2008; or the current EU financial sector crisis (think of Spain and Greece, and the current tensions of the Euro).)[21]

The financial crisis starting in the autumn of 2008 and marked by the collapse of Lehman Brothers is a good example of how mass psychology is linked to the economy. When financial markets go up, the rise is basically based on expectations (and a lot of what is bought and sold in the financial markets are expectations, and even expectations of expectations). Likewise, when the market goes down. When everybody expects greater risks of losses (rather than gains) due to bankruptcies, failing demand, unemployment, etc., investors, buyers *and* consumers become more prudent, which slows down the turnover in the marketplace and aggravates the symptoms of crisis. This is why indexes of consumer confidence are received and read with great interest and sometimes anxiety these days.

Seeking value *vs* quality

In an era of diminished resources, Europeans are redefining traditional relationships among price, value and quality. In the past (most notably in the 1980s), people seemed to be willing to pay almost anything for products and services. Consumers still claim to want quality – but at the right price. In surveys, most people report that they regret the conspicuous consumption of the 1980s and feel the need to live with less. The attitude of the 1990s was more practical and reflected a 'back to basics' orientation. People today want more hard news instead of 'hype' from advertising, and they appreciate ads that feature problem-solving tips or that save money or time – or both. Online and app-based services offering consumer-to-consumer buying and selling opportunities are proliferating, car sharing programs are popping up in many places[22] and sharing in general is becoming a new buzzword in marketing and consumer research.[23]

Nonetheless, the general quality of life, and life satisfaction of European consumers is high, with some important distinctions: there are big differences between the EU15 countries and the new member states with respect to perceived quality of life and life satisfaction. A higher degree of materialism is often found in relatively poorer countries that have a direct way of comparing themselves to richer 'relatives', such as the Central and East European countries still undergoing a marketizing process.[24] Also, levels of satisfaction are more heterogeneous among citizens of the new member states and in the EU15.

MARKETING OPPORTUNITY

Second-hand stores – the new in-place for consumers?

With the financial crisis turning into an economic crisis, new market opportunities replace the ones that went away with the carefree years that opened the twenty-first century. Second-hand shops are experiencing a boom in many European countries, not only for reasons of frugality, but also because many consumers consider this type of recycling a more ethical approach to consumption than the use-and-throw-away logic of former days. In the UK, Oxfam has experienced a boom in demand as soon as the economic crisis began[25] and has continued to grow. A sure sign of crisis is that in the same period, donations have gone down: 'Recession bites'.[26] In Denmark, second-hand shopping has also soared, and growth rates in some online second-hand services have exceeded 40 per cent over the last couple of years. This can hardly be explained by the crisis alone

– it probably also reflects a changed attitude towards second-hand consumption. Old stuff both makes it easier to feel unique through one's finds, there may be more stories attached to the old things, and finally – in contemporary consumer society of relative affluence, it might no longer be seen as socially downgrading to shop for recycled things, since it might be a sign of smartness and ability to locate 'good stuff' rather than lack of means.[27] Finally, second-hand is not just in order to get a cheap bargain. So called commission stores have sprung up, where consumers ready to make a bit of a change in their wardrobe put their designer clothes and accessories up for sale. A price is agreed between store owner and seller, and once the Louis Vuitton bag is sold, they split the amount often fifty-fifty.[28]

SOCIAL CLASS

All societies can be roughly divided into the haves and the have-nots (though sometimes 'having' is a question of degree). While social equality is a widely held value throughout Europe, the fact remains that some people seem to be more equal than others. As David's encounter with the Caldwells suggests, a consumer's standing in society, or **social class**, is determined by a complex set of variables, including income, family background and occupation.

The place one occupies in the social structure is not just an important determinant of *how much* money is spent. It also influences *how* it is spent. David was surprised that the Caldwells, who clearly had a lot of money, did not seem to flaunt it. This understated way of living is a hallmark of so-called 'old money'. People who have had it for a long time do not need to prove they have it. In contrast, consumers who are relative newcomers to affluence might allocate the same amount of money very differently.

Striving for access to resources

In many animal species, a social organization develops whereby the most assertive or aggressive animals exert control over the others and have the first pick of food, living space and even mating partners. Chickens, for example, develop a clearly defined dominance–submission hierarchy. Within this hierarchy, each hen has a position in which she is submissive to all of the hens above her and dominates all of the ones below her (hence the origin of the term *pecking order*).[29]

People are not much different. We also develop a pecking order that ranks us in terms of our relative standing in society. This ranking to a large degree determines our access to such resources as education, housing and consumer goods. And people try to improve their ranking by moving up the social order whenever possible. This desire to improve one's lot, and often to let others know that one has done so, is at the core of many marketing strategies.

Just as marketers try to carve society into groups for segmentation purposes, sociologists have developed ways to describe meaningful divisions of society in terms of people's relative social and economic resources. Some of these divisions involve political power, while others revolve around purely economic distinctions. Karl Marx argued that position in a society was determined by one's relationship to the *means of production*. Some people (the haves) control resources, and they use the labour of others to preserve their privileged positions. The have-nots lack control and depend on their own labour for survival, so these people have the most to gain by changing the system. Distinctions among people that entitle some to more than others are perpetuated by those who will benefit by doing so.[30] The sociologist Max Weber showed that the rankings people develop are not one-dimensional. Some involve prestige or 'social honour' (he called these *status groups*), some rankings focus on power (or *party*), and some revolve around wealth and property (*class*).[31]

The term 'social class' is now used more generally to describe the overall rank of people in a society. People who are grouped within the same social class are approximately equal in terms of their social standing in the community. They work in roughly similar occupations, and they tend to have similar lifestyles by virtue of their income levels and common tastes. These people tend to socialize with one another and share many ideas and values regarding the way life should be lived.[32] Indeed, 'birds of a feather do flock together'. We tend to marry people in a similar social class to ours, a tendency sociologists call **homogamy**, or 'assortative mating'.

Social class is as much a state of being as it is of having: as David saw, class is also a question of what one *does* with one's money and how one defines one's role in society. Although people may not like the idea that some members of society are better off or 'different' from others, most consumers do acknowledge the existence of different classes and the effect of class membership on consumption. In Figure 12.4 you can see the class distribution for selected countries. Note that only in Germany, social class B is larger than social class A. What does that indicate?

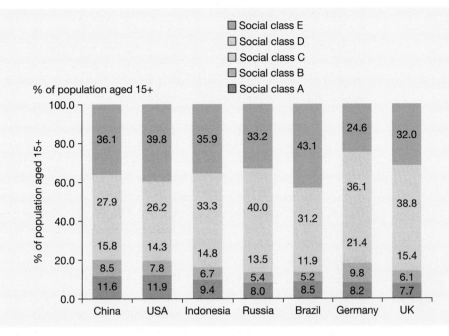

Figure 12.4 Distribution of social class in selected countries, 2011

Note: Social class data refer to the number of individuals whose incomes fall within a specified range of the average gross income of all individuals aged 15+ in that country or region. Social class A: +200 per cent; Social class B: between 150 per cent and 200 per cent; Social class C: between 100 per cent and 150 per cent; Social class D: between 50 per cent and 100 per cent and Social class E: less than 50 per cent of the average gross income.

Source: Euromonitor International from national statistics.

MARKETING PITFALL

Steinar gazes over the expansive new verandah of his summer cottage on a tranquil island off Norway's south-eastern coast, chatting on his cell phone. The 50-year-old Oslo accountant recently added a host of amenities such as hot running water to his *hytte*, as Norwegians call their rustic summer cabins. Now he plans to put in a paved road to his front door and a swimming pool in the garden. 'There's nothing wrong with a little comfort', says Steinar. Well, maybe not in other summer playgrounds such as France's Côte d'Azur, but here in austere Norway, the words 'comfort' and 'vacation' are not synonymous. Thanks to the recent oil boom, many Norwegians are spending their new-found wealth upgrading spartan summer chalets with tennis courts, jacuzzis and even helipads. But in a country where simplicity and frugality are cherished virtues, and egalitarianism is strong, the display of wealth and money is suspect. Some politicians have suggested bulldozing the houses of the wealthy if they block access to the sea, and trade union leaders have blasted a new breed of Norwegians who favour showy yachts and life in the fast lane, and who build fences around private property.

'The rich can be quite vulgar', grumbles Steinar's neighbour Brit, who demanded that he trim a metre or so off his verandah because she and her husband, Gustav, could see it from their cabin lower down the hill. Both teachers, Brit and Gustav are nearing retirement, and have a more traditional Norwegian view of how to spend their summer, and how to spend their money. At stake, many say, are Norwegian ideals of equality and social democracy. These dictate that all Norwegians should have the same quality of life and share the national wealth equally. Norwegians champion austerity because they haven't always been prosperous. Before oil was discovered about 35 years ago, only a few families were considered wealthy. This frugality is obvious even in the capital, Oslo. For all the new oil money, plus low inflation, the city isn't a brash 'Kuwait of the North'.

Summer chalets should reflect the spartan mood, die-hards say, and vacation activities must be limited. Scraping down paint is popular, as is hammering down loose floorboards. So is swimming in lakes, fishing for supper and chopping wood. But not much else. As another neighbour, Aase, puts it: 'We like to, uh, sit here. I'd like the rich to stay away from here. They would ruin the neighbourhood.'[33]

Social stratification

In virtually every context, some people seem to be ranked higher than others. Patterns of social arrangements evolve whereby some members get more resources than others by virtue of their relative standing, power and/or control in the group.[34] The phenomenon of **social stratification** refers to this creation of such culturally instituted divisions in a society: 'those processes in a social system by which scarce and valuable resources are distributed unequally to status positions that become more or less permanently ranked in terms of the share of valuable resources each receives.'[35] We see these distinctions both offline and online as the reputation economy takes shape; recall that this term refers to the 'currency' people earn when they post online and others recommend their comments.[36] Retailers may 'sort' clientele in terms of their ability to afford the retailers' products or services (e.g. some investment firms only accept clients with a certain net worth). Or, consider ASmallWorld.net, a social networking site that gives the wealthy access to one another in cyberspace – while keeping the rest of us out. It's an invitation-only site that's grown to about 150,000 registered users. The site's founders promote it as a Facebook for the social elite. A few recent postings help us to understand why. One person wrote, 'I need to rent 20 very luxury sports cars for an event in Switzerland. . . . The cars should be: Maserati–Ferrari–Lamborghini–Aston Martin ONLY!' Another announced: 'If anyone is looking for a private island, I now have one available for purchase in Fiji.' The rich *are* different.[37]

Achieved *vs* ascribed status

If you recall groups you've belonged to, both large and small, you will probably agree that in many instances some members seemed to get more than their fair share while others were not so lucky. Some of these resources may have gone to people who earned them through hard work or diligence. This allocation is due to **achieved status**. Other rewards may have been obtained because the person was lucky enough to be born into wealthy circles. Such good fortune reflects **ascribed status**. The most obvious contemporary example of ascribed status is the existence of royal families in a number of European countries. But, possibly in particular in the UK, the imagery of the aristocratic 'landed class' continues to be an important reference of ascribed social status. The dominance of inherited wealth appears to be fading in Britain's traditionally aristocratic society. According to a survey, 86 of the 200 wealthiest people in England made their money the old-fashioned way: they earned it. Even the sanctity of the Royal Family, which

The UK came to a virtual standstill during the royal wedding between Prince William and Kate Middleton on 29 April 2011.

Wayne Howes/Shutterstock.com.

epitomizes the aristocracy, has been diluted because of tabloid exposure and the antics of younger family members who have been transformed into celebrities more like rock stars than royalty.[38]

Although we tend to believe that in modern democratic societies there should be few inherited privileges, experience shows that ascribed status is more difficult to overcome than we would (like to) think. We will return to this issue in our discussion about social mobility below, but one reason might be how we raise our children. A research report looked at the way different social classes spend their money on activities and products oriented towards children's learning and development. In the early 1970s, the gap between the top fifth of the population in the US and the bottom fifth, meant that the former spent about four times as much on their children's learning and development as the bottom fifth. By 2006 the gap had widened to approximately seven times as much.[39]

Whether rewards go to the 'best and the brightest' or to someone who happens to be related to the boss, allocations are rarely equal within a social group. Most groups exhibit a structure, or status hierarchy, in which some members are somehow better off than others. They may have more authority or power, or they are simply more liked or respected. It is important to note, that in contemporary societies, status hierarchies may be of different types and they are not necessarily congruent. In other words, it is possible to have high status in some hierarchies but lower in others (cf. discussion of status crystallization below).

Components of social class

When we think about a person's social class, there are a number of pieces of information we can consider. Two major ones are occupation and income. A third important factor is educational attainment, which is strongly related to income and occupation.

Inherited or earned wealth, there are professionals who would help you spend the money 'the right way'.
Phoenix Wealth Management.

Occupational prestige

In a system where (like it or not) a consumer is defined to a great extent by what they do for a living, *occupational prestige* is one way to evaluate the 'worth' of people. Hierarchies of occupational prestige tend to be quite stable over time, and they also tend to be similar in different societies. Similarities in occupational prestige have been found in countries as diverse as Brazil, Ghana, Guam, Japan and Turkey.[40]

A typical ranking includes a variety of professional and business occupations at the top (e.g. director of a large corporation, doctor or college lecturer), while those jobs hovering near the bottom include shoeshiner, unskilled labourer and dustman. Because a person's occupation tends to be strongly linked to their use of leisure time, allocation of family resources, political orientation and so on, this variable is often considered to be the single best indicator of social class.

Income

The distribution of wealth is of great interest to social scientists and to marketers, since it determines which groups have the greatest buying power and market potential. Wealth is by no means distributed evenly across the classes. While there is a more equitable distribution of wealth across European countries relative to Latin America, Asia and America (the top fifth of the population in the US controls about 75 per cent of all assets),[41] there is still a disportionate share of wealth controlled by a small segment of the European population. As we have seen, income per se is often not a very good indicator of social class, since the way money is spent is more telling. Still, people need money to allow them to obtain the goods and services that they require in order to express their tastes, so obviously income is still very important.

The relationship between income and social class

Although consumers tend to equate money with class, the precise relationship between other aspects of social class and income is not clear and has been the subject of debate among social scientists.[42] The two are by no means synonymous, which is why many people with a lot of money try to use it to improve their social class.

The UK in many ways still seems very much a class-conscious country, and, at least until recently, consumption patterns were pre-ordained in terms of one's inherited position and family background. Members of the upper class were educated at public schools such as Eton and Harrow, and had a distinctive accent. Remnants of this rigid class structure can still be found. 'Hooray Henrys' (wealthy young men) play polo at Windsor and at the moment hereditary peers can still take their seat in the House of Lords.[43] The UK, together with Poland and the Baltic states, is the country in northern Europe with the highest inequality in income distribution.[44]

That said, a straightforward relationship between income and social class is not so easily established. One problem is that even if a family increases its household income by adding wage earners, each additional job is likely to be of lower status. For example, a housewife who gets a part-time job is not as likely to get one that is of equal or greater status than the primary wage earner's. In addition, the extra money earned may not be pooled for the common good of the family. Instead it may be used by the individual for their own personal spending. More money does not then result in increased status or changes in consumption patterns, since it tends to be devoted to buying more of the same rather than upgrading to higher-status products.[45]

The following general conclusions can be made regarding the relative value of social class (i.e. place of residence, occupation, cultural interests, etc.) *vs* income in predicting consumer behaviour:

- Social class appears to be a better predictor of purchases that have symbolic aspects, but low-to-moderate prices (e.g. cosmetics, alcohol).

- Income is a better predictor of major expenditures that do not have status or symbolic aspects (e.g. major appliances).
- Social class and income data together are better predictors of purchases of expensive, symbolic products (e.g. cars, homes, luxury goods).[46]

Social mobility

To what degree do people tend to change their social class? In some traditional societies social class is very difficult to change, but in Europe, any man or woman can become prime minister. **Social mobility** refers to the 'passage of individuals from one social class to another'.[47] Internationally speaking, social mobility is lower in countries like the USA and the UK compared with, for example, France, while mobility is highest in Scandinavian countries, for example, Denmark.[48]

- This mobility can be upward, downward or even horizontal. *Horizontal mobility* refers to movement from one position to another roughly equivalent in social status, such as becoming a nurse instead of a junior school teacher. *Downward mobility* is, of course, not very desirable, but this pattern is unfortunately quite evident in recent years as redundant workers have been forced to join the dole queue or have joined the ranks of the homeless. Even temporary downward mobility may be experienced as an embarrassment that requires various coping strategies, such as, for example, being downgraded in airplane seating.[49]
- Despite the discouraging trends generated by the crisis, hitting harder in countries such as Spain and Greece but nevertheless felt all over Europe, demographics decree that there must be *upward mobility* in European society. The middle and upper classes reproduce less than the lower classes (an effect known as *differential fertility*), and they tend to restrict family size below replacement level. Therefore, so the reasoning goes, positions of higher status over time must be filled by those of lower status.[50] Overall, though, the offspring of blue-collar consumers tend also to be blue-collar while the offspring of white-collar consumers tend also to be white-collar.[51] People tend to improve their positions over time, but these increases are not usually dramatic enough to catapult them from one social class to another.

Measurement of social class

Because social class is a complex concept which depends on a number of factors, not surprisingly it has proved difficult to measure. Early measures included the Index of Status Characteristics developed in the 1940s and the Index of Social Position developed by Hollingshead in the 1950s.[52] These indices used various combinations of individual characteristics (such as income, type of housing) to arrive at a label of class standing. The accuracy of these composites is still a subject of debate among researchers; one recent study claimed that for segmentation purposes, raw education and income measures work as well as composite status measures.[53]

Blue-collar workers with relatively high-income jobs still tend to view themselves as working class, even though their income levels may be equivalent to those of many white-collar workers.[54] This fact reinforces the idea that the labels 'working class' or 'middle class' are very subjective. Their meanings say at least as much about self-identity as they do about economic well-being.

Problems with measures of social class

Market researchers were among the first to propose that people from different social classes can be distinguished from each other in important ways. While some of these dimensions still exist, others have changed.[55] Unfortunately, many of these measures are badly dated and are not as valid today for a variety of reasons, some of which are discussed here.[56]

Most measures of social class were designed to accommodate the traditional nuclear family, with a male wage earner in the middle of his career and a female full-time homemaker. Such measures have trouble accounting for two-income families, young singles living alone, or households headed by women which are so much more prevalent in today's society (see Chapter 11).

Another problem with assigning people to a social class is that they may not be equal in their standing on all of the relevant dimensions. A person might come from a low-status ethnic group but have a high-status job, while another may live in a fashionable part of town but did not complete secondary school. The concept of **status crystallization** was developed to assess the impact of inconsistency on the self and social behaviour.[57] It was thought that since the rewards from each part of such an 'unbalanced' person's life would be variable and unpredictable, stress would result. People who exhibit such inconsistencies tend to be more receptive to social change than are those whose identities are more firmly rooted.

A related problem occurs when a person's social class standing creates expectations that are not met. Some people find themselves in the not unhappy position of making more money than is expected of those in their social class. This situation is known as an *overprivileged condition* and is usually defined as an income that is at least 25–30 per cent over the median for one's class.[58] In contrast, *underprivileged* consumers, who earn at least 15 per cent less than the median, must often devote their consumption priorities to sacrificing in order to maintain the appearance of living up to class expectations.

Lottery winners are examples of consumers who become overprivileged overnight. As attractive as winning is to many people, it has its problems. Consumers with a certain standard of living and level of expectations may have trouble adapting to sudden affluence and engage in flamboyant and irresponsible displays of wealth. Ironically, it is not unusual for lottery winners to report feelings of depression in the months after the win. They may have trouble adjusting to an unfamiliar world, and they frequently experience pressure from friends, relatives and business people to 'share the wealth'.

The traditional assumption is that husbands define a family's social class, while wives must live it. Women borrow their social status from their husbands.[59] Indeed, the evidence indicates that physically attractive women tend to 'marry up' to a greater extent than attractive men. Women trade the resource of sexual appeal, which historically has been one of the few assets they were allowed to possess, for the economic resources of men.[60] The accuracy of this assumption in today's world must be questioned. Many women now contribute equally to the family's well-being and work in positions of comparable or even greater status than their spouses. *Cosmopolitan* magazine offered this revelation: 'Women who've become liberated enough to marry any man they please, regardless of his social position, report how much more fun and spontaneous their relationships with men have become now that they no longer view men only in terms of their power symbols.'[61]

Employed women tend to average both their own and their husband's respective positions when estimating their own subjective status.[62] Nevertheless, a prospective spouse's social class is often an important 'product attribute' when evaluating alternatives in the interpersonal marketplace (as David and Julia were to find out). *Cosmopolitan* also discussed this dilemma, implying that social class differences are still an issue in the mating game: 'You've met the (almost) perfect man. You both adore Dashiell Hammett thrillers, Mozart and tennis. He taught you to jet ski; you taught him the virtues of tofu . . . The problem? You're an executive earning ninety-thousand dollars a year. He's a taxi driver . . .'[63]

Problems with social class segmentation: a summary

Social class remains an important way to categorize consumers. Many marketing strategies do target different social classes. However, marketers have failed to use social class information as effectively as they could for the following reasons:

- They have ignored status inconsistency.
- They have ignored intergenerational mobility.
- They have ignored subjective social class (i.e. the class a consumer identifies with rather than the one they objectively belong to).
- They have ignored consumers' aspirations to change their class standing.
- They have ignored the social status of working wives.

MULTICULTURAL DIMENSIONS

Anyone mingling with the crowd when India plays cricket at the Oval or shopping in areas with a large Asian population, such as Harrow or Slough or Wolverhampton, would find ample evidence of the material aspirations of young British Asians.

Asians as a group seem an attractive target for businesses. They are increasing in numbers (growing from 2.3m, according to the 2001 census); younger than the white population overall; more likely to be found in big cities; and making important economic advances. Indeed, most of the Asian population is British-born and one, two or even three, generations removed from their countries of ancestral origin. While the first generation had to save money and establish themselves, their children and grandchildren have British roots and are subject to tensions between their cultural upbringing and their degree of Britishness (remember *Bend it like Beckham*?). One study concluded that 'the resulting bi-cultural self is one of both joy and frustration but above all it is one of continual negotiation and compromise'.[64]

Yet, communications professionals have tended to put them in a niche or ignore them. In January 2003, just 2 per cent of advertising campaigns featured actors from ethnic minorities – despite blacks and Asians making up 8 per cent of the population. In an effort to correct this imbalance, marketing consultant Anjna Raheja coined the term 'brown pound'. 'It was intended', she says, 'to draw attention to the growing economic power of Asian – and black – consumers.'[65] In 2009, the first TV channel oriented specifically towards young Asians in the UK, Brit Asia TV, opened with a focus on the British Asian music scene and youth culture, yet another example of the proliferation of specialized media in the digital age.[66]

Class structure around the world

Every society has some type of hierarchical class structure, where people's access to products and services is determined by their resources and social standing. Of course, the specific 'markers' of success depend on what is valued in each culture. We may consider these class structures 'exotic', since we are used to considering that consumer societies are located in Western or 'Westernized' contexts. But consider the prediction of OECD for 2050 (see Figure 12.5) in terms of the size of the consuming middle classes – Westerners will increasingly be the 'oddity' while the majority of the consuming middle classes will be Asian.

Profound changes in global income distribution drive this shift. Traditionally, it was common to find a huge gulf between the rich and the poor countries: you were either one or the other. Today, rising incomes in many economically developing countries, such as South Korea and China, coupled with decreasing prices for quality consumer goods and services, level the playing field. The current recession aside, more and more consumers around the globe participate in the global economy. The biggest emerging markets go by the acronym BRIC nations: Brazil, Russia, India and China. These four countries today account for 15 per cent of the $60 trillion global economy, but analysts project they will overtake the European and American economies within by 2030.[67] (As an aside, sometimes they are referred to as BRICS, throwing South Africa in there for good measure.)

This change fuels demand for mass-consumed products that still offer some degree of panache. Companies such as H&M, Zara, EasyJet and L'Oréal provide creature comforts to a consumer

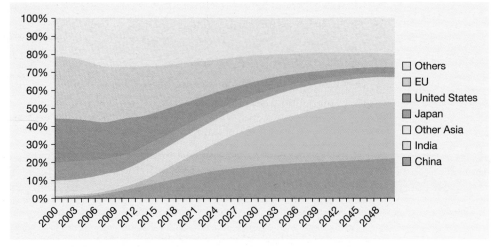

Figure 12.5 Shares of global middle class consumption 2000–2050

Source: Homi Kharas, 'The Emerging Middle Class in Developing Countries', OECD Development Centre, Working Paper no. 285 (OECD 2010).

segment that analysts label mass class. This refers to the hundreds of millions of global consumers who now enjoy a level of purchasing power that's sufficient to let them afford high-quality products – except for big-ticket items such as college educations, housing or luxury cars.

China

In China, an economic boom is rapidly creating a middle class of more than 130 million people that analysts project to grow to more than 400 million by 2020. During the cultural revolution, Mao's Red Guards seized on even the smallest possessions – a pocket watch or silk scarf – as evidence of 'bourgeois consciousness'. Change came rapidly in the early 1990s, after Mao's successor Deng Xiaoping uttered the phrase that quickly became the credo of the new China: 'To get rich is glorious.' Because costs are low, a family with an annual income €10–12,000 can enjoy middle-class comforts, including stylish clothes, Chinese-made colour televisions, DVD players and mobile phones. Wealthier Chinese entrepreneurs can indulge in Cuban Cohiba cigars that sell for €20 each, a quarter of the average Chinese labourer's monthly wage. In bustling Shanghai, newly minted 'yuppies' drop their kids off for golf lessons; visit Maserati and Ferrari showrooms; buy some luxury items from Louis Vuitton, Hugo Boss or Prada; then pick up some Häagen-Dazs ice cream before heading to an Evian spa to unwind. One cultural difference that may help to account for this love of branded goods is that Asians tend to be highly sensitive to cues that communicate social standing, and well-known brand names help to manage this impression. Indeed, even in the United States researchers report that Asian immigrants and Asian Americans prefer branded goods to generic products compared to other Americans.[68]

Nike, which consumers in a recent survey named China's coolest brand, profits mightily from the rise of the Chinese middle class. Nike shoes are a symbol of success, and the company opens an average of 1.5 new stores a day there. The company worked for a long time to attain this status; it started by outfitting top Chinese athletes and sponsoring all the teams in China's pro basketball league. Still, becoming a fashion icon (and persuading consumers to spend twice the average monthly salary ona pair of shoes) is no mean feat in a country that is not exactly sports-crazy. So Nike affiliated with the NBA (which had begun televising games in China), bringing over players such as Michael Jordan for visits. Slowly but surely, in-the-know Chinese came to call sneakers 'Nai-ke'.[69]

The class differences in China are very much a question about rural and urban populations, as demonstrated in Figure 12.6. The figure indicates the tremendous changes in terms of

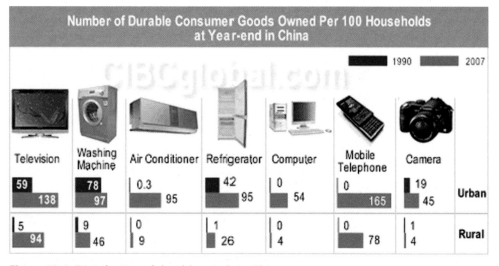

Figure 12.6 Distribution of durable goods in China

Source: China International Business Consulting, http://cibcglobal.com/s/marketing1.html, accessed 23 April 2012.

material wealth that has taken place in China since 1990. Also note the television and the telephone are common even in rural households, the washing machine less so, while the home computer is still very much a status marker.

India

Like China, India's economy has undergone a big booming period and many higher-end global brands are catching on. India's economy is among the fastest growing in the world, and brands like Gucci, Hermès and others are scrambling to open stores. One of Bollywood's biggest stars, Shahrukh Khan, is 'brand ambassador' for Tag Heuer watches, which cost thousands of dollars. He gives them away on the Indian version of *Who Wants to Be a Millionaire?* India's ascendancy is fairly recent; for decades after the country became independent from Britain, its economy was a relatively closed one. Today, a lot of young consumers watch satellite TV, surf the internet, read international fashion magazines, and are embracing the power of plastic; credit-card spending in India has risen by 30 per cent a year from 2002 to 2007 and is still rising.[70] Indian consumers have even (re-)discovered yoga! As a recent study points out, Indians are increasingly consuming yoga in a variety of fitness and wellness centres, both as a modern relaxation and wellness technique but also as a sign of traditional cultural identity. As such, it has become a new middle class marker in India.[71]

Not everybody is invited to the party, though. Inequality in China as well as India is out of proportion compared to what we know in the Western world, and economic development often happens at the expense of the poor population of so-called subaltern consumers, typically farmers, fishermen, unskilled workers and people of other traditional occupations.[72]

MARKETING PITFALL ⊗

A recent flap illustrates the cleavage in Indian society. Vogue India ran a 16-page spread of poor people surrounded by luxury goods: a toothless old woman holds a child who wears a Fendi bib, a woman and two other people ride on a motorbike as she sports a Hermès bag that sells for more than $10,000, a street beggar grips a Burberry umbrella. A columnist denounced the spread as 'not just tacky but downright distasteful'. The magazine's editor commented that the shoot's message is simply that 'fashion is no longer a rich man's privilege. Anyone can carry it off and make it look beautiful.'[73]

Japan

Japan is a highly status-conscious society, where upmarket, designer labels are popular and new forms of status are always being sought. In spite of this modernization of the Japanese consumer society, spiritual dimensions remain very important for the meanings Japanese attach to a variety of consumption rituals.[74]

Although the devastation wrought by the 2011 tsunami reduced demand for luxury goods among many Japanese, their love affair with top brands started in the 1970s when the local economy was booming and many Japanese could buy Western luxury accessories for the first time. Some analysts say Japan's long slump since that time may have fostered a psychological need to splurge on small luxuries to give people the illusion of wealth and to forget their anxieties about the future. Single, working women are largely responsible for fueling Japan's luxury-goods spending; about three-quarters of Japanese women aged 25 to 29 work outside the home. As we saw in Chapter 11, these 'office ladies' save money by living with their parents, so this leaves them with cash on hand to spend on clothes, accessories and vacations.

Middle East

In contrast to the Japanese, few Arab women work, so searching for the latest in Western luxury brands is a major leisure activity. Dressing rooms are large, with antechambers to accommodate friends and family members who often come along on shopping sprees. A major expansion of Western luxury brands is under way across the Middle East, home to some of the fashion industry's best customers. High-end retailers such as Saks Fifth Avenue and Giorgio Armani operate opulent stores to cater to this growing market. However, fashion retailers must take cultural and religious considerations into account. Missoni makes sure that collections include longer pants and skirts, and evening gowns with light shawls to cover heads or bare shoulders. And advertising and display options are more limited: erotic images don't work. In the strict religious culture of Saudi Arabia, mannequins can not reveal a gender or human shape. At Saks' Riyadh store, models are headless and do not have fingers. Half of the two-level store is off-limits to men.[75] This division of gendered spaces for consumption is not only established in public but also in private homes.[76]

Among the extremely wealthy locals in the Gulf states of Qatar and the United Arab Emirates, balancing modesty and vanity has led to a particular status game, where the local dresses, the *abaya*, supposedly covering the body and preventing desire, have become another status and fashion item, both separating the (often extremely wealthy) locals from the (often poorer) expatriate workers and providing tailors and fashion designers and brands with a new playground for innovativeness.[77]

HOW SOCIAL CLASS AFFECTS PURCHASE DECISIONS

Different products and stores are often, and possibly rightly so, perceived by consumers to be appropriate for certain social classes.[78] And income inequalities are growing in many societies in the West, notably in the United States but also elsewhere – a fact that contributed to the 'Occupy Wall Street' and 'We are the 99 per cent' protest movements. However, due to other changes in market society, it has become tougher for the casual observer to accurately place a consumer in a certain class by looking at the products he buys. That's because a lot of 'affordable luxuries' now are within reach of many consumers who could not have acquired them in the past. This being said, social differences persist in forming different consumer cultures in different layers of the population.

Class differences in worldview

A major social class difference involves the *worldview* of consumers. The world of the working class (including the lower-middle class) is more intimate and constricted. For example, working-class men are more likely to name local sports figures as heroes and are less likely to take long holidays in out-of-the-way places.[79] Immediate needs, such as a new refrigerator or TV, tend to dictate buying behaviour for these consumers, while the higher classes tend to focus on more long-term goals, such as saving for college fees or retirement.[80]

Working-class consumers depend heavily on relatives for emotional support and tend to orient themselves in terms of the community rather than the world at large. They are more likely to be conservative and family oriented. Maintaining the appearance of one's home and property is a priority, regardless of the size of the house. One recent study that looked at social class and how it relates to consumers' feelings of *empowerment* reported that lower-class men are not as likely to feel they have the power to affect their outcomes. Respondents varied from those who were what the researcher calls *potent actors* (those who believe they have the ability to take actions that affect their world) to *impotent reactors* (those who feel they are at the mercy of their economic situations). This orientation influenced consumption behaviours; for example, the professionals in the study who were likely to be potent actors set themselves up for financial opportunity and growth. They took very broad perspectives on investing and planned their budgets strategically.[81]

While good things appear to go hand in hand with higher status and wealth, the picture is not that clear. The social scientist Emile Durkheim observed that suicide rates are much higher among the wealthy. He wrote in 1897, 'the possessors of most comfort suffer most'.[82] The quest for riches has the potential to result in depression, deviant behaviour and ruin. In fact, a survey of affluent American consumers (they made an average of $176,000 a year) supports this notion. Although these people are in the top 2.5 per cent income bracket in America, only 14 per cent said they are very well off.[83]

The concept of a **taste culture**, which differentiates people in terms of their aesthetic and intellectual preferences, is helpful in understanding the important yet subtle distinctions in consumption choices among the social classes. Taste cultures largely reflect education (and are also income-related).[84] A distinction is often made between low-culture and high-culture groups (this is discussed in more detail towards the end of this chapter).

While such perspectives have met with criticism due to the implicit value judgements involved, they are valuable because they recognize the existence of groupings based on shared tastes in literature, art, home decoration and so on. In one of the classic studies of social differences in taste, researchers catalogued homeowners' possessions while asking more typical questions about income and occupation. Clusters of furnishings and decorative items which seemed to appear together with some regularity were identified, and different clusters were found depending on the consumer's social status. For example, religious objects, artificial flowers and still-life portraits tended to be found together in relatively lower-status living rooms, while a cluster containing abstract paintings, sculptures and modern furniture was more likely to appear in a higher-status home (see Figure 12.7).[85] We all carry stereotypical imagery of taste cultures in our heads. If you are told about one person that they like to visit museums and attend live theatre and about another that they like camping and fishing and like to attend a boxing match, which one would you place in the highest social class segment? You were probably right.[86]

Another approach to social class focuses on differences in the types of *codes* (the ways meanings are expressed and interpreted by consumers) used within different social strata. Discovery of these codes is valuable to marketers, since this knowledge allows them to communicate to markets using concepts and terms most likely to be understood and appreciated by specific consumers.

The nature of these codes varies among social classes. **Restricted codes** are dominant among the working class, while elaborated codes tend to be used by the middle and upper classes. Restricted codes focus on the content of objects, not on relationships among objects.

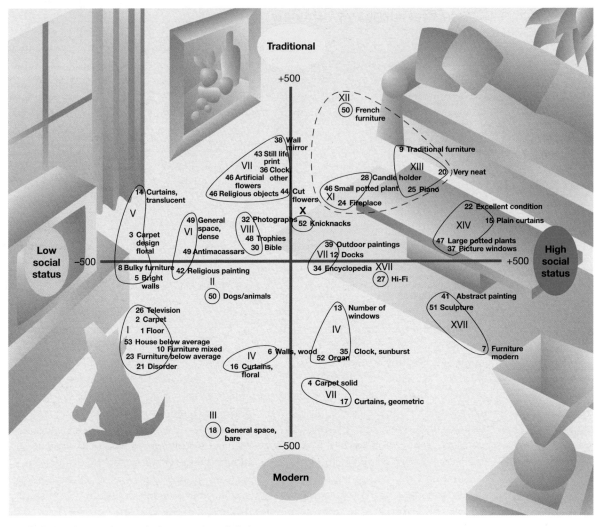

Figure 12.7 Living room clusters and social class

Source: Edward O. Laumann and James S. House, 'Living room styles and social attributes: The patterning of material artifacts in a modern urban community', *Sociology and Social Research 54* (April 1970): 321–42.

Elaborated codes, in contrast, are more complex and depend upon a more sophisticated world-view. Some differences between these two general types of codes are provided in Table 12.1. As this table indicates, these code differences extend to the way consumers approach such basic concepts as time, social relationships and objects. The brand as a code in itself constitutes an interesting issue: a study of the importance of brands in a choice among lunch boxes among British school children confirmed the importance of the brand code among those children, recruited from the lower class.[87] A study of high-end consumers in Scandinavia reached the exact opposite conclusion, that brands were something to be highly skeptical about.[88] We might conclude that according to an elaborated code, brands are not as trustworthy.

Marketing appeals that are constructed with these differences in mind will result in quite different messages. For example, a life insurance ad targeted at a lower-class person might depict in simple, straightforward terms a hard-working family man who feels good immediately after purchasing a policy. An upmarket appeal might depict a more affluent older couple surrounded by photos of their children and grandchildren and contain extensive copy emphasizing the satisfaction that comes from planning for the future and highlighting the benefits of a whole-life insurance policy.

Table 12.1 Effects of restricted versus elaborated codes

	Restricted codes	Elaborated codes
General characteristics	Emphasize description and contents of objects	Emphasize analysis and interrelationships between objects, i.e., hierarchical organization and instrumental connections
	Have implicit meanings (context dependent)	Have explicit meanings
Language	Use few qualifiers, i.e., few adjectives or adverbs	Have language rich in personal, individual qualifiers
	Use concrete, descriptive, tangible symbolism	Use large vocabulary, complex conceptual hierarchy
Social relationships	Stress attributes of individuals over formal roles	Stress formal role structure, instrumental relationships
Time	Focus on present; have only general notion of future	Focus on instrumental relationship between present activities and future rewards
Physical space	Locate rooms, spaces in context of other rooms and places: e.g. 'front room', 'corner shop'	Identify rooms, spaces in terms of usage; formal ordering of spaces: e.g. 'dining room', 'financial district'
Implications for marketers	Stress inherent product quality, contents (or trustworthiness, goodness of 'real-type'), spokesperson	Stress differences, advantages vis-à-vis other products in terms of some autonomous evaluation criteria
	Stress implicit fit of product with total lifestyle	Stress product's instrumental ties to distant benefits
	Use simple adjectives, descriptors	Use complex adjectives, descriptors

Source: Adapted from Jeffrey F. Durgee, 'How Consumer Sub-Cultures Code Reality: A Look at Some Code Types', in Richard J. Lutz (ed.), *Advances in Consumer Research* 13 (Provo, UT: Association for Consumer Research, 1986): 332.

Targeting the poor

While poor people obviously have less to spend than rich ones, they have the same basic needs as everyone else. Low-income families purchase such staples as milk, bread and tea at the same rates as average-income families. And minimum-wage level households spend a greater than average share on over-the-counter medicine, rent and food consumed at home. Equality among the poor raises overall satisfaction levels, but paradoxically also generates a tendency to destroy this equality since it increases the propensity to spend a little extra since it can improve one's relative position.[89] In 2010 the percentage of people at risk for poverty in EU was 23 per cent, up from 17 per cent in 2008.[90] A sure sign of crisis which, it must be added, has struck very differently in the different EU countries. Certain household types are typically more likely to be at risk of poverty: single parents with dependent children (these single parents are overwhelmingly female parents), old people living alone, single females and two-adult households with three or more dependent children.

The unemployed do feel alienated in a consumer society, since they are unable to obtain many of the items that our culture tells us we 'need' to be successful. However, idealized advertising portrayals do not seem to appeal to low-end consumers who have been interviewed by researchers. Apparently, one way to preserve self-esteem is by placing oneself outside the culture of consumption and emphasizing the value of a simple way of life with less emphasis on materialism. If you remain in the consumer culture, however, your relative feeling of powerlessness might induce you to choose larger portion sizes, as one American study concluded, adding worse to bad in terms of the health and obesity problems often associated with lower social classes.[91]

In some cases, the poor enjoy the advertising as entertainment without actually yearning for the products; a comment by one 32-year-old British woman is typical: 'They're not aimed at me, definitely not. It's fine to look at them, but they're not aimed at me so in the main I just pass over them.'[92] A more recent study identified other coping strategies among poor people when confronted with the consumption consequences of their own poverty. Such coping strategies could be rooted in the fulfilling of role expectations, for example, through the feeling of being a good mother in spite of not being able to give the children a lot in material terms, in the feeling of independence coming from not being dependent on others in spite of a low income, or in the consolation that others are worse off.[93] Furthermore, a variety of strategies for avoiding conflict are applied in order to avoid poverty-generated conflict in the family, for example, by being open about the economic troubles of the household.[94]

Some marketers are developing products and services for low-income consumers. These strategies may be obvious in some cases (or even bordering on the insulting), as when S.C. Johnson & Son, manufacturers of Raid insect spray, regularly hosts 'cockroach evictions' at inner-city housing developments. Other strategies raise important ethical issues, especially when marketers of so-called 'sin products' such as alcohol and tobacco single out what many feel is a vulnerable audience.

Still, a lot of companies are taking a second look at marketing to the poor because of their large numbers. The economist C.K. Prahalad added fuel to this fire with his book *The Fortune at the Bottom of the Pyramid*, which argued big companies could profit and help the world's four billion poor or low-income people by finding innovative ways to sell them soap and refrigerators.[95] And maybe he was not all wrong in pointing out this potential. A recent report by the market research agency Nielsen concluded that much of the impressive Brazilian retail growth of 5.5 per cent in value in 2010 was driven by low income groups.[96]

Some companies are getting into these vast markets by revamping their distribution systems or making their products simpler and less expensive. When Nestlé Brazil shrank the package size of its Bono cookies (no relation to the U2 singer) from 200 grams to 140 grams and dropped the price, sales jumped 40 per cent. Unilever called a new soap brand Ala so that illiterate people in Latin America could easily recognize it. In Mexico, cement company Cemex improved housing in poor areas after it introduced a pay-as-you-go system for buying building supplies.[97]

Muhammad Yunus, a Bangladeshi economist, won the 2006 Nobel Prize in Economics for pioneering the concept of **microloans**. His Grameen Bank loans small sums – typically less than $100 – to entrepreneurs in developing countries. Many of these go to 'cell-phone women', who rent time on the phones to others in their remote villages. The bank has issued about 6 million loans to date, and almost 99 per cent of recipients repay them (compared to a 50 per cent repayment rate for a typical bank in a developing country).[98] Today, there are a number of such microloan institutions.

Targeting the rich

We live in an age where elite department stores sell Donna Karan and Calvin Klein Barbies, and Mattel's Pink Splendor Barbie comes complete with crystal jewellery and a bouffant gown sewn with 24-carat threads.[99] To dress that 'living doll', Victoria's Secret offers its Million Dollar Miracle Bra, with over 100 carats of real diamonds.[100] *Somebody* must be buying this stuff . . .

Many marketers try to target affluent markets. This practice often makes sense, since these consumers obviously have the resources to expend on costly products (often with higher profit margins). *The Robb Report*, a magazine targeted at the very affluent has traditionally focused on the American market, but today publishes reports also on countries such as China, Russia, Brazil and Turkey. In these times of crisis, they have had to defend themselves against attacks from journalists and citizens who are bringing these super rich lifestyles into discredit.[101]

However, it is a mistake to assume that everyone with a high income should be placed in the same market segment. As noted earlier, social class involves more than absolute income: it is also a way of life, and affluent consumers' interests and spending priorities are significantly affected by such factors as where they got their money, how they got it, and how long they have had it.[102] For example, the marginally rich tend to prefer sporting events to cultural activities, and are only half as likely as the super rich to frequent art galleries or the opera.[103]

MULTICULTURAL DIMENSIONS

In a land where one-child families are the rule, Chinese parents spare few expenses when bringing up baby. They want to show off their pampered child and are eager to surround their 'little emperors' with status goods. To meet this need, foreign companies are rushing in, hawking the staples of Western baby care from disposable nappies to Disney cot sheets. These items are expensive luxuries in China, and plenty of families are splurging. Chinese families spend one-third to one-half of their disposable income on their children, according to industry estimates. The Disney Babies line of T-shirts, rattles and cot linens – all emblazoned with likenesses of baby Mickey Mouse and other familiar characters – are available in department stores in a dozen or so Chinese cities. These products are true extravagances: a Disney cotton T-shirt, for example, sells for the local equivalent of about $7.25–$8.45, compared to $1.20 for a Chinese-made shirt. But as a Disney spokesman observed, 'New parents are willing to pay the extra. Mickey is portrayed as fun and intelligent in China – characteristics parents want for their children.'[104]

Old money

When people have enough money for all intents and purposes to buy just about anything they want, ironically social distinctions no longer revolve around the amount of money they have. Instead, it appears to be important to consider *where* the money came from and *how* it is spent. The 'top out-of-sight class' (such as Julia's parents) live primarily on inherited money. People who have made vast amounts of money from their own labour do not tend to be included in this select group, though their flamboyant consumption patterns may represent an attempt to prove their wealth.[105] The mere presence of wealth is thus not sufficient to achieve social prominence. It must be accompanied by a family history of public service and philanthropy, which is often manifested in tangible markers that enable these donors to achieve a kind of immortality (e.g. Rockefeller University or the Whitney Museum).[106] 'Old money' consumers tend to make distinctions among themselves in terms of ancestry and lineage rather than wealth.[107] Old money people (like the Caldwells) are secure in their status. In a sense, they have been trained their whole lives to be rich and hence feel less the urgency to demonstrate their wealth at any given opportunity. As the saying goes, discretion is a matter of honour.

The nouveaux riches

Other wealthy people do not know how to be rich. The Horatio Alger myth, the dream of going from 'rags to riches' through hard work and a bit of luck, is still a powerful force in Western society and, more recently, in Asian societies as well. Although many people do in fact become 'self-made millionaires', they often encounter a problem (although not the worst problem one could think of!) after they have become wealthy and have changed their social status: consumers who have achieved extreme wealth and have relatively recently become members of upper social classes are known as the *nouveaux riches*, a term that is sometimes used in a derogatory manner to describe newcomers to the world of wealth.

The *nouveau riche* phenomenon is also widespread in Russia and other eastern European countries, where the transition to capitalism has paved the way for a new class of wealthy consumers who are spending lavishly on luxury items. One study of wealthy Russians identified a group of 'super-spenders', who spend as much on discretionary items as they do on rent. They would like to spend more money, but are frustrated by the lack of quality products and services available to them.[108]

An uncommon blend of rare woods, exotic metal, supple leather and discriminating owners.

This ad demonstrates the power of the 'old money imagery' of the British upper class.

The Advertising Archives.

Alas, many *nouveaux riches* are plagued by *status anxiety*. They monitor the cultural environment to ensure that they are doing the 'right' thing, wearing the 'right clothes', being seen in the 'right places', using the 'right' caterer, and so on.[109] Flamboyant consumption can thus be viewed as a form of symbolic self-completion, where the excessive display of symbols thought to denote 'class' is used to make up for an internal lack of assurance about the 'correct' way to behave.[110]

STATUS SYMBOLS

People have a deep-seated tendency to evaluate themselves, their professional accomplishments, their material well-being and so on, in relation to others. The popular phrase 'keeping up with the Joneses' (in Japan, 'keeping up with the Satos') refers to the comparison between one's standard of living and that of one's neighbours. This is true even in the details of life. One study demonstrated how we assign value to loyalty programmes (e.g. when airlines award you special status based on the number of miles you fly) at least in part based on our level in the hierarchy relative to other members. Subjects were assigned to 'gold status' in a programme where they were in the only tier, or a programme where there was also a silver tier. Although both groups were 'gold', those in the programme that also offered a lower level felt better about it.[111]

Satisfaction is a relative concept, however. We hold ourselves to a standard defined by others that is constantly changing. Unfortunately, a major motivation for the purchase and display of products is not to enjoy them, but rather to let others know that we can afford them. In other words, these products function as status symbols. The desire to accumulate these 'badges of achievement' is summarized by the slogan 'He who dies with the most toys, wins'. Status-seeking is a significant source of motivation to procure appropriate products and services that the user hopes will let others know that they have 'made it'. The popular movie *The Joneses* from 2009 illustrate the consequences of this logic – but also that the chase of 'the most toys' may end up taking your life.

Conspicuous consumption

The motivation to consume for the sake of consuming was first discussed by the social analyst Thorstein Veblen at the turn of the last century. Veblen felt that a major role of products was for invidious distinction – they are used to inspire envy in others through display of wealth or power. Veblen coined the term **conspicuous consumption** to refer to people's desire to provide prominent visible evidence of their ability to afford luxury goods. Veblen's work was motivated by the excesses of his time. He wrote in the era of the robber barons, where the likes of J.P. Morgan, Henry Clay Frick, William Vanderbilt and others were building massive financial empires and flaunting their wealth by throwing lavish parties. Some of these events of excess became legendary, as described in this account:

> there were tales, repeated in the newspapers, of dinners on horseback; of banquets for pet dogs; of hundred-dollar bills folded into guests' dinner napkins; of a hostess who attracted attention by seating a chimpanzee at her table; of centerpieces in which lightly clad living maidens swam in glass tanks, or emerged from huge pies; of parties at which cigars were ceremoniously lighted with flaming banknotes of large denominations.[112]

MARKETING OPPORTUNITY ✔

In this age of fitness and active lifestyle, cycling has been taken up by many as a new way of getting exercise, getting around in the cities without getting stuck in the traffic and even getting out into nature and the countryside (provided you don't live in the centre of a metropolitan area!). As a reference to some of the world's 'bicycling capitals', terms like Copenhagenizing or Amsterdamizing are now being used to describe other cities' attempts to make life easier for cyclists through bike paths, separate traffic etc.

With the increased focus on bicycling comes also an increased consciousness of its status value, and the inconspicuous bicycle is rapidly becoming a new way of showing off for some. Even in China, where consumers have rushed from bicycle to car transportation, a few up-market consumers are following the biking trend.[113]

For the really wealthy among you, what about a Damien Hirst designed Butterfly Trek Madone Bike auctioned at 500,000 USD. But that is of course one of a kind – in terms of (small) serial products, what about a 24 carat gold-coated Montante bike with python leather finish and 11,000 Swarovski crystals for adornment; only 46,000 USD. No? Well then check out some of the other possibilities for really showing off on your bike on bornrich.com.[114]

The modern potlatch

Veblen was inspired by anthropological studies of the Kwakiutl Indians, who lived in the American Pacific Northwest. These Indians had a ceremony called a **potlatch**, a feast where the host showed off his wealth and gave extravagant presents to the guests. The more one gave away, the better one looked to the others. Sometimes, the host would use an even more radical strategy to flaunt his wealth. He would publicly destroy some of his property to demonstrate how much he had.

This ritual was also used as a social weapon: since guests were expected to reciprocate, a poorer rival could be humiliated by being invited to a lavish potlatch. The need to give away as much as the host, even though he could not afford it, would essentially force the hapless guest into bankruptcy. If this practice sounds 'primitive', think for a moment about many modern weddings. Parents commonly invest huge sums of money to throw a lavish party and compete with others for the distinction of giving their daughter the 'best' or most extravagant wedding, even if they have to save for 20 years to do so.

The leisure class

This process of conspicuous consumption was, for Veblen, most evident among what he termed the *leisure class*, people for whom productive work is taboo. In Marxist terms, this reflects a desire to link oneself to ownership or control of the means of production, rather than to the production itself. Any evidence that one actually has to work for a living is to be shunned, as suggested by the term the 'idle rich'.

Like the potlatch ritual, the desire to convince others that one has a surplus of resources creates the need for evidence of this abundance. Accordingly, priority is given to consumption activities that use up as many resources as possible in non-constructive pursuits. This *conspicuous waste* in turn shows others that one has the assets to spare. Veblen noted that 'we are told of certain Polynesian chiefs, who, under the stress of good form, preferred to starve rather than carry their food to their mouths with their own hands'.[115]

MARKETING OPPORTUNITY

Consolidating for luxury

The luxury goods sector in Europe has undergone an important consolidation, as smaller groups find it increasingly difficult to compete with bigger rivals in terms of advertising spending, retail networks and production capacity. As a result, groups such as French luxury goods giant LVMH and Gucci have been buying up smaller names over the past years. Perhaps the biggest 'fashion family' is LVMH, with its stable of fashion brands including Louis Vuitton, Moët Hennessy, Christian Dior, Givenchy, Christian Lacroix, Celine, Loewe, Kenzo, Fendi and Emilio Pucci.

LVMH is not suffering too much from the current crisis - the Chinese (and other newly rich populations in, e.g. the Middle East, Russia, South Asia, Latin America, . . .) are flocking to buy luxury goods. LVMH has gone into mall construction in Shanghai, since the important thing is not to have a store with your brand - it is to have several stores with several brands enough to attract consumers to come and check out the selection.[116] But LVMH are also building up their internet presence, launching a Chinese version of their 'Nowness' website. This website, while also featuring some of the LVMH brands, is much more than a virtual advertising site; it is a magazine discussing the cutting edge events and trends in art and culture in China as well as abroad.[117]

The death – and rebirth – of status symbols

While ostentatious products fell out of favour in the 1970s, as a result of the rebellious previous decade, the 1990s and the early part of the twenty-first century (at least until the crisis set in in 2008) has seen a resurgence of interest in luxury goods. European companies such as Hermès International, LVMH, Moët Hennessy, Louis Vuitton and Baccarat enjoyed sales gains of between 13 and 16 per cent, as affluent consumers once again indulged their desires for the finer things in life. One market researcher termed this trend 'the pleasure revenge' – people were tired of buying moderately, eating low-fat foods and so on, and as a result sales boomed for self-indulgent products from fur coats to premium ice creams and caviar. As the Chairman of LVMH put it: 'The appetite for luxury is as strong as ever. The only difference is that in the 1980s, people would put a luxury trademark on anything. Today only the best sells.'[118] Think of the earlier quote concerning the conspicuous consumption around the shift from the nineteenth to the twentieth century – which examples of similarly spectacular (and excessive?) conspicuous consumption can you find dating from the recent turn of the century?

MULTICULTURAL DIMENSIONS

Although to most Americans the now-defunct Hummer vehicle is a symbol of excess, Iraqis still regard the huge gas-guzzlers as an alluring symbol of power. An Iraqi Hummer dealer observed, 'In Iraq, people judge you by your car, and you're not a man without one.' People there use an Arabic phrase to explain the need to have the biggest car: *hasad thukuri*, which roughly translates as 'penis envy'.[119]

Largely because of an oil boom, there are at least 25 billionaires and 88,000 millionaires in Russia (though the recession has also taken a big bite out of the Russian economy). Muscovites crave luxury goods to show off their newfound wealth. Some buy the GoldVish cell phone that glitters with 120 carats of diamonds encrusting a case of white gold. The desire to spend as much as possible on indulgences fuels a popular joke in Moscow: A wealthy businessman tells a friend he bought a tie for $100. The friend responds, 'You fool! You can get the same tie for $200 just across the street.'[120] In Indonesia, as in many countries, a cell phone is a status symbol – but instead of a sleek iPhone, a decade-old Nokia model users call 'the Brick' is the one to have. This 'smart phone' never took off in the West; its bulky design makes it look dated. But in Jakarta, its heft is what people like about it. At a whopping half-pound, it doesn't fit into a pocket, so it's very visible when models, politicians, and other celebrities cart it around with them. Nokia even sells a gold-plated version for $2,500. In the world of status symbols, anything goes as long as others don't have it.[121]

'The real power doesn't show': As this French ad for a Visa card with infinite credit underlines, there may be truth in that really high class tends to be discreet.
Visa USA.

Parody display

As the competition to accumulate status symbols escalates, sometimes the best tactic is to switch gears and go into reverse. One way to do this is to deliberately *avoid* status symbols – that is, to seek status by mocking it. This sophisticated form of conspicuous consumption has been termed **parody display**.[122] A good example of parody display is the home-furnishing style known as High Tech, which was in vogue in America a few years ago. This motif incorporated the use of industrial equipment (e.g. floors were covered with plates used on the decks of destroyers), and pipes and support beams were deliberately exposed.[123] This decorating strategy was intended to show that one is so witty and 'in the know' that status symbols are not necessary. Hence, the popularity of old, torn blue jeans and 'utility' vehicles such as jeeps among the upper classes. 'True' status is thus shown by the adoption of product symbolism that is deliberately not fashionable.

CAPITAL AND PRACTICES: CLASS-BASED LIFESTYLES

We can now try to summarize the relationship between social class and consumption, by integrating a lot of what we have described in the preceding pages into one conceptual framework. The French sociologist Pierre Bourdieu described society in terms of a competition for different types of **capital**.[124] Capital, for Bourdieu, is resources that are acknowledged and can be used as assets in various contexts. He distinguished primarily between economic (money, as well as access to money, i.e. financing possibilities), cultural (education, cultural knowledge) and social (networks, social connections) capital. Cultural capital, however, is not exclusively a matter of formal education but also, more generally speaking, a matter of 'manners'. Take the example of dining out. This is one domain (or field as Bourdieu would call it), where there can be a lot at stake. Remember that scene from *Pretty Woman*, where Julia Roberts is trying to learn which fork is used for what in a highly formal dinner setting? This is an example of trying to pick up cultural capital. But it does not have to be as high-brow as that. Just knowing a little about what to expect from an Indian versus a Thai or a Chinese restaurant, how to compose a meal from a menu, what to drink with which course – all these little 'knowledges' also constitute cultural capital. And that capital must be mobilized whenever we are eating out, whereby we reveal something about how much of it we have and which kinds of class and other distinctions are brought into play, when we sit down at the table.[125]

For Bourdieu, social life can be seen as a number of games, which people constantly win or lose to varying degrees. Social domination, then, is an outcome of how these resources or types of capital are distributed and brought to use strategically in the social games. Business, of course, is such a game. But family (how to make a good one) is also considered a game. As such, the games are played in different fields, such as the already mentioned business and family, but also politics, sports, news, education, entertainment, science, art and so on. Hence, it is obvious that the same types of capital do not apply in all fields – it is difficult to qualify as a sports hero based on a doctoral dissertation. But not all great sports people become sports heroes – certain of them seem have this extra 'star quality', which may be rooted in their abilities to play the games well and exploit their capital to the maximum. And speaking of sports: the notion of cultural capital was used to analyse the distinction between the inner circle of hard core football fans and the larger circle of the wider fan community in the football clubs Liverpool FC (England) and Cork City (Ireland). It was found that part of the build-up of cultural capital for the die-hard fans was through the sacrifices made for the club and for attending the matches. Thus having sacrificed a lot of time, money, effort and even family events for the club provided a particular status for the football consumers.[126]

The position of each individual in these status games and their resources constitute the basis for a person's **habitus**, a structuring set of classifications and tastes that permeates our lives

CAPITAL AND PRACTICES: CLASS-BASED LIFESTYLES

and determine our ways of behaviour as well as our judgement of different social phenomena, in short, our lifestyles. These systems of judgement permeate our lives and are also what permits the lower class people to not necessarily be envious of the rich, since apart from the lack of economic worries (which, as we have seen, the lower class people also attribute to the higher class people), there is not much to be envious about. Much of the high cultural and economic capital leisurely activities appear to be outright boring to the lower class, just as there is a tendency to consider high class social gatherings as less warm and heartfelt compared to lower class social gatherings. Hence the driver of this whole system, according to Bourdieu, is the process of **distinction**. This process works in terms of the social differences that exist in society, the aspirations to overcome them through social mobility or the aspirations to keep them (from above as well as from below) in order to reconfirm one's own social universe.

Figure 12.8 presents a simplified lifestyle mapping based on Bourdieu's work. Bourdieu distinguishes between the general level of capital (since there is a high correlation between cultural

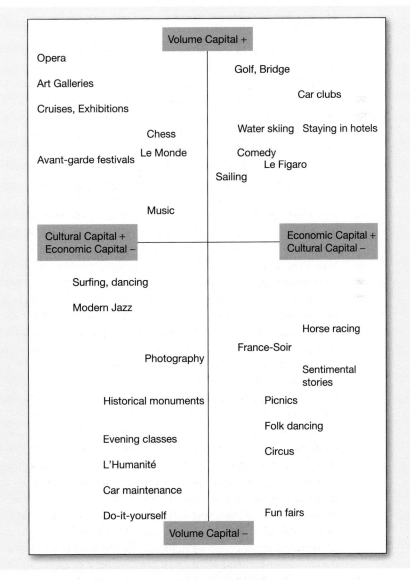

Figure 12.8 Bourdieu's lifestyle map with examples of leisure consumption

Source: Adapted from B. Moingeon, 'La sociologie de P. Bourdieu et son apport au marketing', *Recherches et Applications en Marketing*, vol. VIII no. 2 (1993) p. 123.

and economic capital in society. Remember: going to school pays off) and the relative weight of cultural versus economic capital on the other. We can see the clear positioning and correlation between reading *Le Monde* (an intellectual daily newspaper), going to the opera and being a university professor, being a manager in the private sector, playing golf and reading the more conservative and business-friendly *Le Figaro*, being a worker, reading *L'Humanité* (traditionalist communist newspaper) and engaging in car repair and finally being a craftsman, reading the popular newspaper *France-Soir* and engaging in betting on horses in one's spare time.

This approach has been applied within American consumer research to distinguish between consumer tastes among various social groupings.[127] Furthermore, an attempt has been made to translate Bourdieu's terms into a relatively simple lifestyle categorization scheme. Based on Bourdieu's notions of economic capital (income and wealth) and cultural capital (education plus the ability to distinguish between cultural styles and categories) combined with Mary Douglas's grid-group theory,[128] four different but fundamental consumer types are proposed (see Figure 12.9). Notice that this model is basically the same as in Figure 12.8 except that Bourdieu's hypothesized high correlation between cultural and economic capital has been replaced by a straightforward 2×2 matrix and the model has been turned 180 degrees around its vertical axis.

The distinction between grid and group refers to an individual's relation to their own social group and to the general social system (or grid). So the model distinguishes between people with high and low group identification and a more or less affirmative (high and low) relation to the organization of society (the grid). The model ends up with the following segments:

- *1st quadrant*. Professional, career-oriented people, with higher education and income, and with a rather individualistic attitude and an unproblematic relation to the social organization (they are responsible for much of it anyway). Their search for meaning is characterized by ambition for power and wealth.

- *2nd quadrant*. Well-educated intellectuals with less well-paid career opportunities (many university professors here), with a high degree of identification with their professional group, but with a critical attitude towards society. Their search for meaning lies in the realization of their own intellectual ideals.

- *3rd quadrant*. Relatively wealthy people, with low education and/or not so culturally interested (the stereotypical self-made (wo)man). Being preoccupied first and foremost with their own private lives, they do not show any particular interest in society, neither on a group level nor on a social level, and they may even tend to consider the rest of society (and everything strange) as relatively hostile. Often looked down upon by people from the second quadrant because of their alleged poor cultural tastes and their lack of social engagement.

High cultural capital High economic capital Low group High grid	High cultural capital Low economic capital High group Low grid
Low cultural capital High economic capital Low group Low grid	Low cultural capital Low economic capital High group High grid

Figure 12.9 A lifestyle model based on grid-group theory and capital

Source: Adapted from Henrik Dahl, *Hvis din nabo var en bil* (Copenhagen: Akademisk Forlag, 1997, 2nd edn 2006).

- *4th quadrant.* Low on both types of capital, money and education, but with strong group affiliation and a relatively affirmative attitude towards society, these people tend to be locally oriented. The search for meaning is rooted in their daily activities and daily lives.[129]

Practice theory and consumer behaviour

When Bourdieu was doing fieldwork in Algeria, he noticed the following things about the relation between what people actually did and what they said they did (remember the attitude–behaviour gap from Chapter 8?). First of all, as we have already discussed, there was not a very good correspondence between people's actions and their own accounts of these actions. In other words, people are not very accurate in accounting for their own behaviour. But what was more revealing was that the way people acted was not really in accordance with their own explicit values and norms either.[130] In other words, it was as if people often behaved in ways that was difficult to explain based on their own individual accounts. In order to find a word that would take into consideration this distance between our reflections and our behaviour, Bourdieu came up with a theory of practice.

Remember Bourdieu's fondness for considering social life as constituted of competitive games? **Practice theory** is normally described in terms of the sportsperson's 'feel' for the game.[131] It is very difficult for, say, a footballer to explain how to play football. It is also impossible for the same footballer to go through a lot of conscious decision processes when deciding how to move on the field, what to do with the ball, etc. There is simply no time for evaluating alternatives. Instead they act spontaneously based on experiences with how the game may unfold. That is not to say that their behaviour is determined, but it does follow certain logics or templates that the footballer can master to a greater or lesser degree.

A practice then, is, a routinised type of behaviour which involves both bodily and mental activities (the footballer moves and 'thinks' even if they do not engage in rational decision making as we have described it earlier), it involves things and their use (a football field of a certain size and design), a ball (rather important) and possibly appropriate clothes (in specific colours, goals with posts, net, etc.) and some background knowledge (knowing what all this is used for, what the different lines mean, etc.).[132]

Now, the trick is to consider not just playing a football match but all our daily activities along those lines. How do we know how to go to the movies? Go to a party? To bike? To shop in the supermarket? And so on and so forth. According to practice theory, all these things are embedded in certain routines (that is we do not make decisions in the classical sense while doing them). The fact that practices are routinized explain why they are discussed in this chapter on social class – quite simply because, as we have already seen, there is strong sociological evidence that our routines, as well as our ways of combining our own personal sources and the marketplace resources at our disposal,[133] are highly dependent on our upbringing and the capitals we have acquired. The routines are also embedded in the things and their design. We grab a cup by its handle, because it is there – and we are made aware of this when for instance offered tea in glasses as in Turkey or elsewhere in the Middle East. This is why practice theory is especially interested in how the presence and design of the things around us influence the way we use them.[134] In fact, not even digital consumption is without materiality – there are iPods, hard drives, and other devices that are crucial to digital consumption. Certain types of materiality may lose importance, but others seem to replace them.[135]

Just as practice theory considers whether the design of things determine their use (rather than the other way round), so it also suggests that activities generate wants (remember the discussion of effect hierarchies). In other words, it is because we engage in certain activities that we generate personal wants and desires, not our wants and desires that make us participate in certain activities. This might not sound very revolutionary, but a lot of consumer research actually assumes that wants (motivations, that is) come first and lead us to engage in certain types of consumption. Practice theorists say that practices in many cases are more likely to come first, and then generate wants.[136] For example, if we have established certain types of cooking routines (or cooking practices) in our family (for example, cooking from scratch and not relying on ready-to-eat meals), these practices generate the wants for fresh produce, etc.

Practice theory does not turn us into robots of our own social background, because the schemes of social practice are hardly ever very precise about what exactly to do. Consider how to eat 'properly'. How do we know when that practice is 'obeyed'? Not because of a very precise manual; in fact our children can point out our practices, when they act as if there is a very careful prescription of how to perform it, cutting the meat with excessively pointing little fingers, lifting the fork with great care to the mouth and slowly and without smearing anything on the side of the mouth, putting the bite in, then chewing it carefully with an exaggerated expression of satisfaction and happiness on their faces. In other words, if practices are performed consciously, they often stop being 'normal social practices' and become overdramatized performances instead. A good actor is someone who knows about this and can perform the practices of a persona in such a way that the audience cannot see that the actor is just performing a newly learned script.

Why is practice theory important to consumer research? Well, for one thing it reminds us how much of our consumption is carried out without us being really conscious about it since it is neither part of a calculation of benefits, nor is it part of our explicit identity projects and we do not consider it a symbolic expression of anything in particular (others might still interpret it but that is a different story!).[137] Secondly, it might contribute to our understanding of why it is so difficult to alter people's consumption behaviour to more sustainable types and possibly help to solve that problem (see Alan Warde's reflections in his 'CB as I see it' column), since a lot of our daily unsustainable consumption seems to be embedded in practices rather than deliberate choices. We all know we ought to recycle, right? Why don't we then just do it (as the Nike slogan goes)? Well, maybe it is because changing practices is not so easy. One study looked at the effects of a behaviour change initiative in a corporate setting – so-called 'Environment Champions' – and how the material environment and employee practices created obstacles or opportunities and in particular obstacles for implementing a recycling policy.[138]

Sustainability, then, seems largely practice-driven.[139] Likewise, other things we do often without even thinking about it may be absolutely crucial to the degree to which we live sustainable lives. Mundane activities such as energy consumption in the household (switching lights on and off, putting electronic equipment on stand-by) have attracted the attention of practice theorists.[140] Or consider the consumption of water! How many of you shower more or less 'on autopilot' in the morning, or maybe several times during the day? Do you 'choose' to shower? Well, not really, right? You just do it (here was that Nike logic again). Not so many decades ago, showering was not a daily routine for most people, the most critical places were washed in front of the washbowl, and the weekly or so bath took care of the thorough cleaning. How did showering become such a 'normal routine' in a few decades that we hardly think about it anymore?[141] Well, this is a good example of how practices work.

Since practices are embedded in our social background with its resources of capital, it can also profoundly alter the way we look at decision making and the way our social class background influences it. You would believe that the choice of where to study is an extremely rational one, since it basically influences your career opportunities and thereby to a large extent determines a lot of your social and economic possibilities for the rest of your life. One study examined the choice of college from a practice perspective and concluded that, especially for people of a working-class background, the fit of the school with previous life experiences was the deciding factor for choice. So students from this background tended to choose based on how much they felt 'at home' during the college visit rather than based on 'abstract information' like academic reputation, the academic quality of the curricula, etc.[142] Hence, it was the practical experience of the school 'fitting like a glove' to oneself that proved decisive. Again, this helps explain why social inequalities and class backgrounds tend to reproduce themselves from generation to generation.

ALAN WARDE
University of Manchester, UK

Consumer behaviour as I see it . . .

Consumption and practice

Much of my research has been directed towards developing sociological explanations which go beyond models which put at their core a portrait of the consumer as an individual decision maker. In both contemporary sociological and psychological ways of studying the consumer the point of departure is the individual, either as someone acting according to a set of norms and values, or someone acting according to theories of rational decision-making. My quest is to find and explore much needed alternative theoretical and conceptual approaches to consumption, ones which neither turn the consumer into a dupe of the commercial and industrial system nor into a utility-maximizer. A theory of practice is one candidate.

The appeal of theories of practice is that they start from a look at the consumer as neither an individual decision maker, as with rational action theory, nor as someone who just obeys the norms and rules of a society or an organization. Instead, from this perspective, analysis begins from understanding the history and development of practices, for example eating or driving. The term practice implies types of behaviour collectively shared (we all do it, to some degree), historically established (we have learned it from copying others), normatively regulated (there are certain 'rights' and 'wrongs') and routinely reproduced (we don't have to think about 'how' we do it in daily life). Practices are not very precisely prescribed, even if we all have some idea about 'how it should be done'. Practices thus tend to change gradually through improvisation as people go about their everyday lives.

Participants in a practice exhibit common understanding, know-how, and belief in the value of the practice. They act in accordance with a set of conventions which seem appropriate given their resources, dispositions and previous experience. Hence everyone does not perform the practice in an identical manner; there are class, gender and generational differences, and also differentiation of roles and positions based on expertise and experience within, for instance, a particular class setting.

The relevance to consumption comes from the insight that items 'consumed' are put to use in the course of engaging in particular practices and that being a competent practitioner requires appropriate consumption of goods and services. The practice, so to speak, requires that competent practitioners will avail themselves of the requisite services, possess the appropriate tools, and devote a suitable level of attention to the conduct of the practice. In this sense, practices precede individuals; practices determine the basic parameters of behaviour, including the purchase and use of commodities.

What is the use of practice theory? Well, today, malign consequences of ordinary and routine consumption associated with everyday practices have escalated into a public issue – most notably regarding environmental sustainability. Collective bad habits, from wasting food and water, to the polluting effects of transport and energy generation, seem globally unsustainable. The principal current solutions focus on changing the behaviour of individuals. Yet changing popular expectations about the right to consume freely looks close to impossible: giving people information is not very effective in altering their behaviour; changing their values so that they wish to act better has proven extremely difficult; and they tend to resist state regulation and protest against taxation designed to reform their consumption patterns. →

→ This is where practice theory may be of use. The principal implication of a theory of practice is that the sources of changed behaviour lie in the processes whereby practices themselves are repeated or transformed. Perhaps we can devise more effective ways of modifying or eliminating damaging behaviour by pursuing the insight that consumption exists for the sake of practices and work at that level rather than on individuals. Hence my current research objective is to understand how practices change.

Alan Warde

CHAPTER SUMMARY

Now that you have finished reading this chapter you should understand why:

→ The field of behavioural economics considers how consumers decide what to do with their money. In particular, *discretionary expenditures* are made only when people are able and willing to spend money on items above and beyond their basic needs. *Consumer confidence* – the state of mind consumers have about their own personal situation, as well as their feelings about their overall economic prospects – helps to determine whether they will purchase goods and services, take on debt or save their money.

→ In the past ten years, consumers overall have been relatively pessimistic about their future prospects. A lower level of resources has caused a shift towards an emphasis on quality products that are reasonably priced. Consumers are less tolerant of exaggerated or vague product claims, and they are more sceptical about marketing activities. Consumers in their twenties are particularly sceptical about the economy and marketing targeted at their age group.

→ A consumer's *social class* refers to their standing in society. It is determined by a number of factors, including education, occupation and income.

→ Virtually all groups make distinctions among members in terms of relative superiority, power and access to valued resources. This *social stratification* creates a status hierarchy, where some goods are preferred over others and are used to categorize their owners' social class.

→ While income is an important indicator of social class, the relationship is far from perfect since social class is also determined by such factors as place of residence, cultural interests and worldview.

→ Purchase decisions are sometimes influenced by the desire to 'buy up' to a higher social class or to engage in the process of *conspicuous consumption*, where one's status is flaunted by the deliberate and non-constructive use of valuable resources. This spending pattern is a characteristic of the *nouveaux riches*, whose relatively recent acquisition of income, rather than ancestry or breeding, is responsible for their increased *social mobility*.

→ Products are used as status symbols to communicate real or desired social class. *Parody display* occurs when consumers seek status by deliberately avoiding fashionable products.

→ Theories of capital explains how resources come in different types and for different uses in various social settings. Most important are cultural capital (education, knowledge, manners) and economic capital (wealth or access to financing), but social capital (the networks you can draw from) is also important. Different types of capital distinguish different social classes.

→ Theories of practice explain our behaviour, rooted in routinised patterns that we have learned, most significantly from our class background. Practice thus offers a different perspective on consumer behaviour that is less dependent on conscious decision making.

KEY TERMS

Achieved status (p. 488)

Ascribed status (p. 488)

Behavioural economics (p. 479)

Capital (p. 506)

Conspicuous consumption (p. 503)

Consumer confidence (p. 484)

Discretionary income (p. 482)

Distinction (p. 507)

Elaborated codes (p. 498)

Habitus (p. 506)

Homogamy (p. 486)

Microloans (p. 500)

Parody display (p. 506)

Potlatch (p. 503)

Practice theory (p. 509)

Restricted codes (p. 497)

Savings rate (p. 484)

Social class (p. 485)

Social hierarchy (p. 479)

Social mobility (p. 491)

Social stratification (p. 488)

Status crystallization (p. 492)

Status symbols (p. 479)

Taste culture (p. 497)

CONSUMER BEHAVIOUR CHALLENGE

1 The concepts *income* and *wealth* are measured in different ways throughout Europe, in spite of the standardization of currency that took place in 1999. Look through several recent issues of *Review of Income and Wealth* to get an idea of how these concepts differ across countries. For marketers, do you have any suggestions as to how to segment income groups for a Europe-wide strategy?

2 What are some of the obstacles to measuring social class in European society? Discuss some ways to get around these obstacles.

3 What consumption differences might you expect to observe between a family characterized as underprivileged *vs* one whose income is average for its social class?

4 When is social class likely to be a better predictor of consumer behaviour than mere knowledge of a person's income?

5 How do you assign people to social classes, or do you at all? What consumption cues do you use (e.g. clothing, speech, cars, etc.) to determine social standing?

6 Thorstein Veblen argued that women were often used as a vehicle to display their husbands' wealth. Is this argument still valid today?

7 Given present environmental conditions and dwindling resources, what is the future of 'conspicuous waste'? Can the desire to impress others with affluence ever be eliminated? If not, can it take on a less dangerous form?

8 Some people argue that status symbols are dead. Do you agree?

9 Compile ads that depict consumers of different social classes. What generalizations can you make about the reality of these ads and about the media in which they appear?

10 Identify a current set of fraudulent status symbols, and construct profiles of consumers who are wearing or using these products. Are these profiles consistent with the images portrayed in each product's promotional messages?

11 The chapter observes that some marketers are finding 'greener pastures' by targeting low-income people. How ethical is it to single out consumers who cannot afford to waste their precious resources on discretionary items? Under what circumstances should this segmentation strategy be encouraged or discouraged?

12 The model in Figure 12.9 has so far only been applied in Denmark. However, its theoretical foundations are rather general, so it might also apply in other countries. Discuss whether it is or not – and which alterations might be necessary?

For additional material see the companion website at **www.pearsoned.co.uk/solomon**

NOTES

1. Fred van Raaij, 'Economic psychology', *Journal of Economic Psychology* 1 (1981): 1–24.

2. Pierre Bourdieu, *Distinction: A Social Critique of the Judgment of Taste* (Cambridge, MA: Harvard University Press, 1984).

3. Peter S.H. Leeflang and W. Fred van Raaij, 'The changing consumer in the European Union: A meta-analysis', *International Journal of Research in Marketing* 12 (1995): 373–87.

4. Data in this section are adapted from Fabian Linden, *Consumer Affluence: The Next Wave* (New York: The Conference Board, Inc., 1994); 'Trends in households in the European Union: 1995–2025', *Eurostat, Statistics in Focus*, Theme 3–24/2003 (Luxembourg: Office for Official Publications of the European Communities, 2004).

5. http://epp.eurostat.ec.europa.eu/statistics_explained/index.php/Unemployment_statistics, accessed 2 May 2012.

6. *Euromonitor*, 'Q&A: How is the global economic downturn affecting young people and their lifestyles, http://0-www.portal.euromonitor.com.library.lausys.georgetown.edu/Portal/Pages/Search/SearchResultsList.aspx, accessed 2 May 2012.

7. Liz Aldermen, 'Ranks of working poor grow in Europe', *New York Times*, 2 April 2012, http://www.nytimes.com/2012/04/02/world/europe/in-rich-europe-growing-ranks-of-working-poor, accessed 2 May 2012.

8. 'Trends in households in the European Union: 1995–2025', *ibid.*: 51.

9. 'Trends in households in the European Union: 1995–2025', *op. cit.*, 'Earnings of men and women', *op. cit.*: 80; see also Hugh Muir, 'Women in less than 10 per cent of top jobs', *The Guardian* (5 January 2004), http://www.guardian.co.uk/gender/story/0,11812,1116127,00.html; Melissa Benn, 'Jobs for the Boys', *The Guardian* (5 January 2004).

10. European Centre for the Development of Vocational Training, http://www.cedefop.europa.eu/EN/articles/4407.aspx, accessed 23 April 2012.

11. Christopher D. Carroll, 'How does future income affect current consumption?', *Quarterly Journal of Economics* 109 (February 1994) 1: 111–47.

12. *Information*, 1 May 2012.

13. http://blog.euromonitor.com/2012/03/special-report-income-inequality-rising-across-the-globe.html, accessed 2 May 2012.

14. http://appsso.eurostat.ec.europa.eu/nui/show.do?dataset=ilc_di11&lang=en

15. Oliver Fischer and Lorenz Fischer, 'The financial crisis: An economic psychological analysis', *Wirtschaftspsychologie*, 13 (2011): 5–23.

16. *Euromonitor*, 'Q&A: How is the global economic downturn...', *op. cit.*

17. Jose J.F. Medina, Joel Saegert and Alicia Gresham, 'Comparison of Mexican-American and Anglo-American attitudes toward money', *Journal of Consumer Affairs* 30(1) (1996): 124–45.

18. Kirk Johnson, 'Sit down. Breathe deeply. This is *really* scary stuff', *New York Times* (16 April 1995): F5. For a scale that measures consumer frugality, see John L. Lastovicka, Lance A. Bettencourt, Renee Shaw Hughner and Ronald

J. Kuntze, 'Lifestyle of the tight and frugal: Theory and measurement', *Journal of Consumer Research* 26 (June 1999): 85–98.

19. Xinyue Zhou, Kathleen D. Vohs and Roy F. Baumeister, 'The Symbolic Power of Money: Reminders of Money Alter Social Distress and Physical Pain', *Psychological Science* 20, no. 6 (2009): 700–6.

20. 'Frontiers: Planning or consumer change in Europe 96/97', 2 (London: The Henley Centre, 1996).

21. George Katona, 'Consumer saving patterns', *Journal of Consumer Research* 1 (June 1974): 1–12.

22. Fleura Bardhi and Giana Eckhardt, 'Access-based consumption', *Journal of Consumer Research*, forthcoming.

23. Russell W. Belk, 'Sharing', *Journal of Consumer Research*, 36 (February 2010), 715–734; Russell W. Belk and Rosa Llamas, 'The nature and effect of sharing in consumer behavior', D.G. Mick, S. Pettigrew, C. Pechmann and J.L. Ozanne (eds), *Transformative Consumer Research for Personal and Collective Well-being*, (London: Routledge 2011), 625–646.

24. Güliz Ger and Russell Belk, 'Cross-Cultural Differences in Materialism', *Journal of Economic Psychology*, 17(1) (1996): 55–77; Güliz Ger and Russell Belk, 'Accounting for materialism in four cultures', *Journal of Material Culture* 4(2) (1999): 183–204.

25. http://www.journallive.co.uk/lifestyle-news/fashion-news-tips/2009/01/20/second-hand-rose-61634-22732469/, accessed 23 April 2012.

26. BBC News, 'Oxfam sales rise but donations fall as recession bites', 20 September 2010, http://www.bbc.co.uk/news/business-11371687, accessed 1 May 2012.

27. Henrik Jensen, 'Nyt er yt – genbrug har bidt sig fast', http://www.fri.dk/personlig-udvikling/nyt-er-yt-genbrug-har-bidt-sig-fast, accessed 23 April 2012.

28. Source: berlingske mediehus, http://www.b.dk/tv/20417, accessed 23 April 2012.

29. Floyd L. Ruch and Philip G. Zimbardo, *Psychology and Life*, 8th edn (Glenview, IL: Scott, Foresman, 1971).

30. Jonathan H. Turner, *Sociology: Studying the Human System*, 2nd edn (Santa Monica, CA: Goodyear, 1981).

31. *Ibid.*

32. Richard P. Coleman, 'The continuing significance of social class to marketing', *Journal of Consumer Research* 10 (December 1983): 265–80; Turner, *Sociology*, *op. cit.*

33. Ernest Beck, 'Cabin fever swirls around posh cottages on Norwegian coast', *Wall Street Journal Europe* (6 August 1997): 1.

34. Turner, *Sociology*, *op. cit.*

35. *Ibid.*

36. Anya Kamenetz, 'The Perils and Promise of the Reputation Economy', *Fast Company* (25 November 2008), www.fastcompany.com/magazine/131/on-the-internet-everyone-knows-youre-a-dog.html, accessed 17 June 2009.

37. Ruth LaFerla, 'A Facebook for the Few', *New York Times* (6 September 2007), www.nytimes.com, accessed 6 September 2007; www.asmallworld.net, accessed 16 June 2011.

38. Robin Knight, 'Just you move over,' Enry 'Iggins: A new regard for profits and talent cracks Britain's old class system', *U.S. News & World Report* 106 (24 April 1989): 40.

39. Greg Duncan and Richard Murnane (eds), *Whither Opportunity? Rising Inequality, Schools and Children's Life Chances*, New York: Russell Sage Foundation, 2011.

40. Richard Coleman, Lee Rainwater and Kent McLelland, *Social Standing in America: New Dimensions of Class* (New York: Basic Books 1978), p. 220.

41. Turner, *Sociology, op. cit.*

42. See Coleman, 'The continuing significance of social class to marketing', *op. cit.*; Charles M. Schaninger, 'Social class versus income revisited: An empirical investigation', *Journal of Marketing Research* 18 (May 1981): 192–208.

43. This may be just about to change as a series of alterations to the membership of the House of Lords to turn it into a largely elected chamber are currently being debated.

44. http://epp.eurostat.ec.europa.eu/tgm/table.do?tab=table&init=1&plugin=1&language=en&pcode=tsdsc260, accessed 2 December 2008.

45. Coleman, 'The continuing significance of social class to marketing', *op. cit.*

46. Bernard Dubois and Gilles Laurent, 'Is There a Euroconsumer for Luxury Goods?' in W. Fred van Raaij and Gary J. Bamossy (eds), *European Advances in Consumer Research* 1 (Provo, UT: Association for Consumer Research, 1993): 59–69; Bernard Dubois and Gilles Laurent, 'Luxury Possessions and Practices: An Empirical Scale', in F. Hansen (ed.), *European Advances in Consumer Research* 2 (Provo, UT: Association for Consumer Research, 1995): 69–77; Bernard Dubois and Patrick Duquesne, 'The market for luxury goods: Income versus culture', *European Journal of Marketing* 27(1) (1993): 35–44.

47. Turner, *Sociology, op. cit.*: 260.

48. *New York Times*, special section, class matter, www.nytimes.com/packages/html/national/20050515_class_graphic/index_03, accessed 24 April 2012.

49. Iain R. Black, 'Sorry not today: Self and temporary consumption denial', *Journal of Consumer Behaviour*, 10 (2011): 267–278.

50. Joseph Kahl, *The American Class Structure* (New York: Holt, Rinehart & Winston, 1961).

51. Leonard Beeghley, *The Structure of Social Stratification in The United States*, 3rd edn (Allyn and Bacon, 2000).

52. August B. Hollingshead and Fredrick C. Redlich, *Social Class and Mental Illness: A Community Study* (New York: John Wiley, 1958).

53. John Mager and Lynn R. Kahle, 'Is the whole more than the sum of the parts? Re-evaluating social status in marketing', *Journal of Business Psychology* 10(1) (1995): 3–18.

54. R. Vanneman and F.C. Pampel, 'The American perception of class and status', *American Sociological Review* 42 (June 1977): 422–37.

55. Donald W. Hendon, Emelda L. Williams and Douglas E. Huffman, 'Social class system revisited', *Journal of Business Research* 17 (November 1988): 259.

56. Coleman, 'The continuing significance of social class to marketing', *op. cit.*

57. Gerhard E. Lenski, 'Status crystallization: A non-vertical dimension of social status', *American Sociological Review* 19 (August 1954): 405–12.

58. Richard P. Coleman, 'The Significance of Social Stratification in Selling', in *Marketing: A Maturing Discipline, Proceedings of the American Marketing Association* 43rd National Conference, Martin L. Bell (ed.), (Chicago: American Marketing Association, 1960): 171–84.

59. E. Barth and W. Watson, 'Questionable assumptions in the theory of social stratification', *Pacific Sociological Review* 7 (Spring 1964): 10–16.

60. Zick Rubin, 'Do American women marry up?' *American Sociological Review* 33 (1968): 750–60.

61. Sue Browder, 'Don't be afraid to marry down', *Cosmopolitan* (June 1987): 236.

62. K.U. Ritter and L.L. Hargens, 'Occupational positions and class identifications of married working women: A test of the asymmetry hypothesis', *American Journal of Sociology* 80 (January 1975): 934–48.

63. Browder, 'Don't be afraid to marry down', *op. cit.*: 236.

64. Yasmin K. Sekhon and Isabelle Szmigin, 'Acculturation and identity: Insights from second-generation Indian Punjabis', *Consumption, Markets and Culture*, 14 (March 2011): 79–98.

65. Aditya Chakrabortty, 'Out with curry and Bollywood', *The Financial Times* (24 November 2004), http://news.ft.com/cms/s/54595ae4-3e4a-11d9-a9d7-00000e2511c8.html

66. www.britasia.tv, accessed 24 April 2012.

67. Gleb Bryanski and Guy Faulconbridge, 'BRIC Demands More Clout, Steers Clear of Dollar Talk', Reuters (16 June 2009), www.reuters.com/article/ousiv/idUSTRE55F47D20090616, accessed 17 June 2009; Guy Faulconbridge, 'BRIC Seeks Global Voice at First Summit', Reuters (14 June 2009), http://www.reuters.com/article/2009/06/14/us-russia-bricidUSLE11928120090614, accessed 17 June 2009.

68. Heejung S. Kim and Aimee Drolet, 'Cultural differences in preferences for brand name versus generic products', *Personality & Social Psychology*, 35 (12, December 2009), 1555–66.

69. Howard W. French, 'Chinese Children Learn Class, Minus the Struggle', *New York Times Online* (22 September 2006), accessed 22 September 2006; Bay Fang, 'The Shanghai High Life', *U.S. News & World Report* (20 June 2005), www.usnews.com/usnews/biztech/articles/050620/20china.b2.htm, accessed 20 June 2005, http://travel.guardian.co.uk/cities/story/0,7450,489488,00.html, accessed 20 June 2005; Russell Flannery, 'Long Live the $25 Cigar', *Forbes* (27 December 2004): 51; Clay Chandler, 'China Deluxe', *Fortune* (26 July 2004): 149–56; Matthew Forney, 'How Nike Figured Out China', *Time* (November 2004): A10–A14; J. David Lynch, 'Emerging Middle Class Reshaping China', *USA Today* (November 12, 2002): 13A.

70. Eric Bellman, 'Name Game: As Economy Grows, India Goes for Designer Goods', *Wall Street Journal* (27 March 2007): A1.

71. Søren Askegaard and Giana Echardt, 'Glocal yoga: Re-appropriation in the Indian consumptionscape, *Marketing Theory*, 12 (1, 2012), 45–60.

72. Rohit Varman and Ram Manohar Vikas, 'Freedom and consumption: Towards conceptualizing systemic constraints for sualtern consumers in a capitalist society', *Consumption, Markets and Culture* 10(2) (2007): 117–31.

73. Heather Timmons, 'Vogue's Fashion Photos Spark Debate in India', *New York Times* (31 August 2008), www.nytimes.com/2008/09/01/business/worldbusiness/01vogue.html?_r1&refbusi, accessed 1 September 2008.

74. Yukon Minowa, 'Practicing *Qi* and consuming *Ki*: Folk epistemology and consumption rituals in Japan', *Marketing Theory*, 12 (1, 2012), 27–44.

75. Cecilie Rohwedder, 'Design Houses Build Stores, Pamper Demanding Shoppers in Fashion-Industry Hot Spot', *Wall Street Journal on the Web* (23 January 2004).

76. Rana Sobh and Russell W. Belk, 'Privacy and gendered spaces in Arab Gulf homes', *Home Cultures*, 8 (3, November 2011), 317–340.

77. Rana Sobh, Russell Belk and Justin Gressel, 'The scented winds of change: Conflicting notions of modesty and vanity among young Qatari and Emirati women', *Advances in Consumer Research*, vol. XXXVIII, (2008) 342–343.

78. J. Michael Munson and W. Austin Spivey, 'Product and brand-user stereotypes among social classes: Implications for advertising strategy', *Journal of Advertising Research* 21 (August 1981): 37–45.

79. Coleman, 'The continuing significance of social class to marketing', *op. cit.*

80. Jeffrey F. Durgee, 'How Consumer Sub-Cultures Code Reality: A Look at Some Code Types', in Richard J. Lutz (ed.), *Advances in Consumer Research* 13 (Provo, UT: Association for Consumer Research, 1986): 332–7.

81. Paul C. Henry, 'Social class, market situation, and consumers' metaphors of (dis)empowerment', *Journal of Consumer Research* 31 (March 2005): 766–78.

82. Durkheim (1958), quoted in Roger Brown, *Social Psychology* (New York: The Free Press, 1965).

83. Lenore Skenazy, 'Affluent, like masses, are flush with worries', *Advertising Age* (10 July 1989): 55.

84. Herbert J. Gans, 'Popular Culture in America: Social Problem in a Mass Society or Social Asset in a Pluralist Society?' in Howard S. Becker (ed.), *Social Problems: A Modern Approach* (New York: Wiley, 1966); Helga Dittmar, 'Material possessions as stereotypes: Material images of different socio-economic groups', *Journal of Economic Psychology* 15 (1994): 561–85; Helga Dittmar and Lucy Pepper, 'To have is to be: Materialism and person perception in working class and middle class British adolescents', *Journal of Economic Psychology* 15 (1994): 233–5.

85. Edward O. Laumann and James S. House, 'Living room styles and social attributes: The patterning of material artifacts in a modern urban community', *Sociology and Social Research* 54 (April 1970): 321–42; see also Stephen S. Bell, Morris B. Holbrook and Michael R. Solomon, 'Combining esthetic and social value to explain preferences for product styles with the incorporation of personality and ensemble effects', *Journal of Social Behavior and Personality* (1991) 6: 243–74.

86. Eugene Sivadas, George Mathew and David J. Curry, 'A preliminary examination of the continuing significance of social class to marketing: A geodemographic replication', *Journal of Consumer Marketing* 41(6) (1997): 463–79. See also Morris B. Holbrook, Michael J. Weiss and John Habich, 'Class-related distinctions in American cultural tastes', *Empirical Studies of the Arts* 22(1) (2004): 91–115.

87. Stuart Roper and Caroline La Niece, 'The importance of brands in the lunch-box choices of low income British school children', *Journal of Consumer Behaviour*, 8 (2009), 84–99.

88. Sofia Ulver-Sneistrup, Søren Askegaard and Dorthe Brogård Kristensen, 'The new work ethics of consumption and the paradox of mundane brand resistance', *Journal of Consumer Culture*, 11 (2, 2011), 215–238.

89. Nadaliya Ordabayeva and Pierre Chandon, 'Getting ahead of the Joneses: When equality increases conospicuous consumption among bottom-tier consumers', *Journal of Consumer Research*, 38 (June 2011), 27–41.

90. http://epp.eurostat.ec.europa.eu/cache/ITY_PUBLIC/3-08022012-AP/EN/3-08022012-AP-EN.PDF and http://epp.eurostat.ec.europa.eu/cache/ITY_PUBLIC/3-18012010-AP/EN/3-18012010-AP-EN.PDF, both accessed 1 May 2012.

91. David Dubois, Derek Rucker and Adam Galisnky, 'Super size me: Product size as signal of status', *Journal of Consumer Research* 38 (April 2012), 1047–1062.

92. Quoted in Richard Elliott, 'How do the unemployed maintain their identity in a culture of consumption?' in Hansen (ed.), *European Advances in Consumer Research* 2: 1–4, at 3.

93. Kathy Hamilton and Miriam Catterell, 'I Can Do It! Consumer Coping and Poverty', in A.Y. Lee and D. Soman (eds), *Advances in Consumer Research* XXXV (2008): 551–6.

94. Kathy Hamilton, 'Consumer decision making in low-income families: The case of conflict avoidance', *Journal of Consumer Behavior*, 8 (2009), 252–267.

95. C.K. Pralahad, *The Fortune at the Bottom of the Pyramid: Eradicating Poverty Through Profits* (Philadelphia: Wharton School Publishing, 2004).

96. http://blog.nielsen.com/nielsenwire/consumer/lower-income-groups-drive-brazilian-retail-growth-in-2010/, accessed 24 April 2012.

97. Antonio Regalado, 'Marketers Pursue the Shallow-Pocketed', *Wall Street Journal* (26 January 2007): B3.

98. www.radicalcongruency.com/20061014-microfinance-wins-the-nobel-prize (22 July 2007), accessed 24 July 2007.

99. Cyndee Miller, 'New Line of Barbie dolls targets big, rich kids', *Marketing News* (17 June 1996): 6.

100. Cyndee Miller, 'Baubles are back', *Marketing News* (14 April 1997): 1(2).

101. The Robb Report, 'Putting luxury into perspective', editorial, 1 June 2009.

102. 'Reading the Buyer's Mind', *U.S. News & World Report* (16 March 1987): 59.

103. Rebecca Piirto Heath, 'Life on easy street', *American Demographics* (April 1997): 33–8.

104. Quoted in 'Western companies compete to win business of Chinese babies', *Wall Street Journal Interactive Edition* (15 May 1998).

105. Paul Fussell, *Class: A Guide Through the American Status System* (New York: Summit Books, 1983): 29.

106. Elizabeth C. Hirschman, 'Secular immortality and the American ideology of affluence', *Journal of Consumer Research* 17 (June 1990): 31–42.

107. Coleman Rainwater and McLelland, *Social Standing in America, op. cit.*: 150.

108. M.H. Moore, 'Homing in on Russian "Super Spenders"', *Adweek* (28 February 1994): 14–16. See also: Carol Vogel, 'Fabergé collection bought by Russian for a return home', *The New York Times* (5 February 2004), http://www.nytimes.com/2004/02/05/arts/design/05FABE.html?th=&pagewanted=print&position.

109. Jason DeParle, 'Spy anxiety: The smart magazine that makes smart people nervous about their standing', *Washingtonian Monthly* (February 1989): 10.

110. For an examination of retailing issues related to the need for status, see Jacqueline Kilsheimer Eastman, Leisa Reinecke Flynn and Ronald E. Goldsmith, 'Shopping for status: The retail managerial implications', *Association of Marketing Theory and Practice* (Spring 1994): 125–30.

111. Xavier Drèze and Joseph C. Nunes, 'Feeling superior: the impact of loyalty program structure on consumers perceptions of status', *Journal of Consumer Research*, 35 (April 2009): 890–905.

112. John Brooks, *Showing off in America* (Boston: Little, Brown, 1981): 13.

113. http://www.theurbancountry.com/2011/09/bicycle-as-status-symbol.html, accessed 2 May 2012.

114. http://www.bornrich.com/entry/world-s-most-expensive-bicycles-for-eco-luxurious-ride/, accessed 31 March 2012. Thanks to Richard Wilk for drawing our attention to this site – under the header 'more nonsense for rich people'!

115. Thorstein Veblen, *The Theory of the Leisure Class* (1899; reprint, New York: New American Library, 1953): 45.

116. Timothy Coglan, 'LVMH create luxury shopping paradise in Shanghai', 8 May 2011, http://maosuit.com/real-estate/lvmh-create-luxury-shopping-paradise-in-shanghai/

117. Barry Silverstein, 'Digital watch: LVMH engages Chinese with Nowness', 25 April 2012, http://www.brandchannel.com/home/post/2012/04/25/LVMH-Nowness-China-042512.aspx

118. Quoted in Miller, 'Baubles are back', *op. cit.*; Elaine Underwood, 'Luxury's tide turns', *Brandweek* (7 March 1994): 18–22. See also Ball, 'Italy's Finpart to acquire Cerruti', *op. cit.*

119. Rod Nordland, 'Iraqis Snap Up Hummers as Icons of Power', *New York Times* (29 March 2009), http://www.nytimes.com/2009/03/30/world/Middleeast/30hummer.html?scp_1&sq_Iraqis%20Snap%20Up%20Hummers%20as%20Icons%20of%20Power&st_cse, accessed 29 March 2009.

120. Andrew E. Kramer, 'New Czars of Conspicuous Consumption', *New York Times* (1 November 2006), www.nytimes.com, accessed 1 November 2006.

121. Tom Wright, 'Ringing Up Sales in Indonesia: Nokia's Bulky Smart Phones Find Niche Following There as Business Status Symbol', *Wall Street Journal* (22 May 2007): B1.

122. Brooks, *Showing off in America, op. cit.*

123. *Ibid.*: 31–2.

124. Pierre Bourdieu, *La Distinction: Critique Social du Jugement* (Paris: Editions de Minuit, 1979; Eng. trans. 1984).

125. Alan Warde, Lydia Martens and Wendy Olsen, 'Consumption and the problem of variety: Cultural omnivorousness, social distinction, and dining out', *Sociology* 33(1) (1999): 105–27.

126. Brendan Richardson and Darach Turley, 'It's Far More Important Than That: Football Fandom and Cultural Capital', in S. Borghini, M.A. McGrath and C. Otnes (eds), *European Advances in Consumer Research* (Duluth, MN: Association for Consumer Research, 2008): 33–8.

127. Douglas B. Holt, 'Does cultural capital structure American consumption?' *Journal of Consumer Research* 25 (June 1998): 1–25.

128. Mary Douglas, *Natural Symbols* (New York: Random House, 1973).

129. Henrik Dahl, *Hvis din nabo var en bil* (Copenhagen: Akademisk forlag 1997), 55–81.

130. Cf. Giana Eckhardt, Russell W. Belk and Timothy M. Devinney, 'Why don't consumers consume ethically?', *Journal of Consumer Behavior*, 9 (2010), 426–436.

131. Pierre Bourdieu, *The Logic of Practice* (Stanford, CA: Stanford University Press, 1990).

132. Andreas Reckwitz, 'Toward a theory of social practices: A development in culturalist theorizing', *European Journal of Social Theory* 5(2) (2002): 243–63.

133. Richard Elliott, 'Making Up People: Consumption as a Symbolic Vocabulary for the Construction of Identity', in K. Ekström and H. Brembeck (eds) *Elusive Consumption*, (Oxford: Berg 2004): 129–143.

134. Elizabeth Shove, Matthew Watson, Martin Hand and Jack Ingram, *The Design of Everyday Life* (Oxford: Berg, 2007).

135. Paolo Magaudda, 'When materiality "bites back": Digital music consumption practices in the age of dematerialization', *Journal of Consumer Culture*, 11(1) (2011): 15–36.

136. Alan Warde, 'Consumption and theories of practice', *Journal of Consumer Culture* 5(2) (2005): 131–53.

137. Søren Askegaard and Jeppe Trolle Linnet, 'Towards an epistemology of consumer culture theory: Phenomenology and the context of context', *Marketing Theory*, 11 (4, 2011), 381–404.

138. Tom Hargreaves, 'Practice-ing behavior change: Applying social practice theory to pro-environmental behavior change', *Journal of Consumer Culture*, 11 (1, 2011), 77–99.

139. Iain Black and Helene Cherrier, 'Anti-consumption as part of daily living a sustainable lifestyle: Daily practices, contextual motivations and subjective values', *Journal of Consumer Behaviour*, 9 (2010): 437–453.

140. Kirsten Gram-Hanssen, 'Understanding change and continuity in residential energy consumption', *Journal of Consumer Culture* 11 (1, 2011): 61–78.

141. Elisabeth Shove, 'Users, technologies and experiences of comfort, cleanliness and convenience', *Innovation. The European Journal of Social Science Research* 16(2) (2003): 193–206.

142. Douglas E. Allen, 'Toward a theory of consumer choice as sociohistorically shaped practical experience: The fits-like-a-glove (FLAG) framework', *Journal of Consumer Research* 28 (March 2002): 515–32.

Good child, bad child: observing experiences of consumer socialization in a twenty-first century family

BEN KERRANE, Manchester Business School, University of Manchester, UK

Context

Families play a large part in our lives. Indeed many decisions and purchases which we make in our adult lives are likely to be shaped and informed by our childhood experiences, and by the influence of family members. Within the family we learn to walk and talk, and how to interact with other people. We also learn about consumption in families: as children we may have been taken with our parents on many shopping trips; taught to save our pocket money and to carefully research our consumption choices; and we may have learnt how to influence the decisions of our parents and siblings. These experiences are part of the process of consumer socialization, from which we learn about consumption and acquire consumer skills. The family has therefore been described as *the* socialization unit, because it has such a tremendous influence on our consumption.

However, much of our current academic knowledge about families originates from research which was conducted in the 1960s and 1970s. These studies tended to concentrate on the experiences of husband and wives, when collecting data. These studies also focused on nuclear families, comprising heterosexual couples who live in the same home with one or more children (biological or adopted). At the start of the twenty-first century many consumer researchers have called for family research to move beyond nuclear families.

Similarly much of what we know about consumer socialization derives from research which was conducted some decades ago. This research characterized the family as being homogenous, i.e. all the children in a family were believed to be treated in the same way by their parents. Earlier marketing research suggested that parents adopt a uniform socialization style and communication pattern when dealing with all their children.

The family story below paints a rather different picture of how children experience their family environments; and hints at some of the changes in our understanding of life in family settings.*

*The name of this family and of the individual family members are fictional.

The Baldwin family story

Carole and Ray Baldwin got married two years ago. Before this they had spent several years cohabiting. They met following the death of Carole's first husband and the breakdown of Ray's first marriage. Carole and Ray both have children from their first marriages. Ray has two non-resident children, Jamie and Andrew, who live with their mother. Carole has four children from her first marriage; three are now fully grown adults (George, Kathy and Marie) and live away from the family home. Carole's fourth child, Jessica (aged fourteen), lives with Carole and Ray in the new family home alongside Carole and Ray's biological child, Nina (aged five).

Carole and Ray have very different opinions of Jessica and Nina. While Nina is clearly the apple of her parents' eyes, Jessica is often ostracised by her mother and stepfather, and she is frequently excluded from many family activities. As Carole comments, the couple believe that they have 'a good child [Nina] and a bad child [Jessica]', with Ray going even further, claiming that 'it's not a bad child; it's a pain in the arse child'. The roles of step parents can be very unclear, and this seems to be the case for the Baldwin family with Ray adopting a disengaged parenting style towards his stepdaughter, Jessica. Ray chooses instead to spend much of his time with Nina, his biological daughter. For example, Ray and Nina are beginning to learn Spanish together after school.

Jessica is very aware of her mother's and her stepfather's favourable opinions of Nina. Jessica reckons that Nina 'doesn't have to ask for things off Mum, she just gets them'. The ways in which Jessica and Nina attempt to ask for things, and influence their parents' behaviour, therefore differs dramatically. Jessica adopts a range of influence strategies in attempts to get her own way. These include the use of deal making, crying, and refusing to eat until she gets what she wants. Nina, in contrast, does not need to go to such great lengths.

In view of her parents' opinions, Jessica faces considerable parental resistance to her influence strategies. As a result Jessica often uses violence and issues threats to try and get what she wants. She has realised that she stands little chance of success in influencing her parents when she acts alone. Jessica realizes she needs to have Nina as an ally in her attempts to influence Carole and Ray. Nina, on the other hand, does not need to deploy such influence strategies. Her requests are regularly granted with minimal parental resistance. Ray, in particular, often buys Nina expensive products much to her half sister's annoyance. Indeed Nina's parents often anticipate Nina's desire for products, and purchase items for her without Nina having to instigate the process. For instance, Carole and Ray recently purchased a new mobile phone for Nina even though Jessica had been constantly asking for one for weeks before. Nina did not even ask to be bought a mobile phone. As Ray commented: 'No, Nina didn't ask for it, it was our treat. Jessica had been on at me for ages to get her one, but she goes about asking for things the wrong way. Nina just doesn't ask for things, but Jessica's like a dripping tap, and she goes on and on at you'.

Carole and Ray act as the gatekeepers of Nina and Jessica's consumption, having the ability to pay for what the children want. Carole and Ray are also therefore the recipients of their daughters' respective influence strategies, because they have the power (and money) to grant or reject their daughters' influence attempts. The relationship that the parents have with Nina and Jessica largely determines the success of the influence strategies the girls use. Realising that alone she stands little chance of influencing her parents' decisions, Jessica recruits Nina to help her get what she wants, forming a coalition with Nina. The family recalled one occasion when Jessica wanted to purchase a toy that connected to Jessica's SONY PlayStation. Individually Jessica could not afford the toy. Jessica recognized that she would not be able to persuade her parents by herself to buy it for her. Jessica subsequently persuaded Nina to contribute towards the cost (even though Nina initially showed no interest in the product) to ensure that Jessica got the toy that she wanted. Realising that Carole and Ray would not reject the wishes of their younger favourite daughter, and with Nina working as an intermediary for Jessica's influence strategy, Jessica got the toy that she wanted with minimal parental resistance.

Jessica, aware that her mother and stepfather spend a larger proportion of their time with her half sister than with her, spends a great deal of time with her own friends. Consequently Jessica is often away from the family home. When Jessica is at home she spends a great deal of her time on the family computer, logged in to online chat rooms where she talks to her friends and surfs the internet. For Jessica her friends act as an important reference group, and they are often the source of lots of consumer information and advice. Whereas Nina is taken on shopping trips and on family days out, is involved and has an input in decisions relating to her family's consumption (particularly in terms of where they go on holiday), Jessica does not. The family, therefore, appears to be very important in Nina's consumer socialization, but plays a much less dominant role in Jessica's consumer socialization. This is perhaps not entirely surprising given Jessica's age, with adolescents often seeking consumption advice from their peers instead of from their parents as it is rather un-cool to be too closely associated with one's family's opinions and views as a teenager.

QUESTIONS

1 Jessica and Nina experience different environments within the family home. How and why? Identify and evaluate the features which distinguish the two environments experienced by Jessica and Nina.

2 How did the different treatment of Jessica and Nina affect their success in deploying influence strategies? How might their different experiences affect their consumer socialization?

3 Reflecting on your own family experiences, did your parents treat you and your siblings in a similar way? What influence strategies did you use to influence your parents/guardians? Do you think that these were effective, and if so, why?

4 How far can families be characterized as offering a homogeneous environment to children?

5 How far can the family be described as *the* socialization unit? Using evidence from the case, and elsewhere, justify your answer.

6 Why should marketers be interested in understanding family decision making, and in particular child consumers?

7 Traditional family decision-making models assume that families have a nuclear family form.

   (a) What impact might 'alternative' families have on such models?

   (b) What role may other family members play in shaping family decision making, and the socialization of children?

Further reading

Carlson, L. and Grossbart, S. (1988), 'Parent Style and Consumer Socialisation of Children', *Journal of Consumer Research*, vol. 15, pp. 77–94.

Carlson, L., Walsh, A., Laczniak, R.N. and Grossbart, S. (1994), 'Family Communication Patterns and Marketplace Motivations, Attitudes, and Behaviours of Children and Mothers', *Journal of Consumer Affairs*, vol. 28(1) pp. 25–53.

Geuens, M., Mast, G. and Pelsmacker, P. (2002), 'Children's influence on family purchase behaviour: The role of family structure', *Asia Pacific Advances in Consumer Research*, vol. 5, pp. 130–135.

John, D.R. (1999), 'Consumer Socialization of Children: A Retrospective Look at Twenty-Five Years of Research', *Journal of Consumer Research*, vol. 26, pp. 183–213.

McNeal, J. (1998) 'Tapping the Three Kids' Markets', *American Demographics*, vol. 20 (April), pp. 37–41.

Palan, K.M., and Wilkes, R.E. (1997), 'Adolescent–Parent Interaction in Family Decision Making', *Journal of Consumer Research*, vol. 24, pp. 159–169.

Ward, S. (1974) 'Consumer Socialization', *Journal of Consumer Research*, vol. 2, pp. 1–16.

CASE STUDY 11

What is mothering really all about? And how does consumption fit into the picture?

SUSANNA MOLANDER, Stockholm University School of Business, Sweden

Consumption can be seen as a way to construct, express and negotiate identity (Arnould and Thompson, 2005), including that of being a mother. Encoded in advertisements, brands, retail settings and material goods, the marketplace provides the consumer with a broad range of symbolic meanings which she may tap into in the course of her identity construction as a mother (e.g. Hogg *et al.*, 2011; Scott, 2006). Furthermore, this identity construction does not only concern what she buys, but also what she does with what she buys and can include how things are used or changed (cf. Lury, 1996). There are numerous activities that may be involved in mothering but several studies and theorists confirm that those related to food are of major importance (cf. Charles and Kerr, 1988; DeVault, 1991; Lupton, 1996). In the following we will spend an afternoon with each of the single mothers, Marie and Linda, and take a look at their approach to mothering and meal consumption.

Dinner on the table – no matter what

Marie, a single mother in her 40s, was already late from work when she came to pick up her eighteen-month-old daughter Melina from the daycare centre around four o'clock one Thursday afternoon in March. Marie worked part time as a communications manager for a middle-sized firm outside town, and part time as a consultant from home, which was an apartment in central Stockholm. She liked the arrangement since it allowed her to spend as much time as possible with Melina of whom she had full custody. After picking Melina up, the plan was to go and buy dinner in a grocery store nearby and, as always, she had already planned what to have. Some weeks she went for more ambitious dinners 'made from scratch' and other weeks, due to a lack of time and energy, she thought it was okay to 'retreat' and fix something easier like pasta, soup or pancakes.

This Thursday Marie was not feeling great as she was suffering one of her migraine attacks but despite her dreadful headache there was no question of skipping dinner. It had to be made, regardless of how she felt and whether or not she was eating herself. Fortunately, this was an easy week and she had already decided to go for something simple. She bought a ready-made tomato soup, a grilled chicken and risoni, a rice-like kind of pasta. But while the soup was really good, she noted that it probably wasn't that healthy as it contained additives like glutamate and 'things like that'. When she had finished shopping, Marie took the receipt to go through it later. She laughed and said she did it to at least 'appear' as if she was an orderly person. She stored the food in the space underneath the pram and headed home. Once home, she had to rush with the cooking because Melina was hungry and Marie did not want her daughter to get full from snacking before dinner. Marie started cleaning the chicken thoroughly and cut it into neat pieces while heating the soup and the risoni. The risoni, she argued, was not only filling but also spot on size-wise for Melina. After her careful preparations, she laid the table, lit a candle and served her daughter the soup with bread and butter. Because of the pain she felt throbbing in her temples, Marie could not make herself eat anything at all but she managed to concentrate on Melina's eating. Melina did not eat much of the soup either. She focused on the butter on her sandwich. Most of the food fell on the floor and on the table. Marie, however, was okay with that and underlined the importance of letting Melina experiment under her supervision.

Dinners are important to Marie. She sees it as her mission to educate Melina into structures and routines and the everyday dinner was an indispensable tool in this. According to Marie, lack of routines risked leading to frustration and misery for both mothers and children and she had various cautionary examples of children who never ate full meals and constantly snacked instead. Marie herself had grown up in a working class home together with her mother, father and brother and was used to her mother serving dinners every evening; dinners which mostly consisted of meat, potatoes and gravy. They were usually pretty quick affairs and nobody really spoke. Marie, however, wanted Melina to experience other kinds of dinners. She was fed up with meat, potatoes and gravy. She wanted to serve other types of food and strove for a more talkative and 'cozy' dinner atmosphere. (Notes from the field 19 March 2009).

Dinner? Sure, but first we have to play!

It was about 6 pm and Linda, 35, an unemployed single mother with a university education in environmental science, had spent a good half-hour in the toy store at the shopping centre in the centre of Stockholm with her son Leon, 4, with whom she lived alone in an apartment in a suburb of Stockholm. Despite Linda's initial reluctance to go to the toy store, she was now as committed as Leon was playing with Thomas the train, Rorri the racing car and all their other friends. Linda and Leon were completely absorbed in their own world, looking, pointing, discussing and trying the different products. But they never bought anything. This was a very popular activity after she picked up Leon from the daycare centre. It usually ended with a dinner for about ten euros or more at a café in the shopping centre because if Leon did not eat here it would be too late for him to eat once they reached home. Linda, however, felt that they needed to break the habit with the shopping centre because it was too expensive to eat out every day. Besides, she found it embarrassing to spend so much time in the toy store without buying anything. It was past six o'clock and getting on for time for dinner. Linda knew that the shopping centre closed at seven o'clock and she wanted to get dinner over with before then. She began persuading Leon and promised that they would return to the toy store as soon as they had finished eating. After a bit of disco dancing on one of the toy store's carpets that made sounds as they danced, Linda and Leon went to their usual eating place.

Linda liked this eating place. It served 'hand peeled' shrimp in the salads and 'real' whipped cream with the pancakes and this was what they usually shared: a shrimp salad with 'hand peeled' shrimp, green salad, corn, avocado, cucumber and quinoa along with pancakes, jam and 'real' whipped cream. However, on this particular day Leon did not feel like having pancakes. He was more focused on one of the café's chocolate biscuits. Linda knew a salad would not suffice if they bought a chocolate biscuit instead of the pancakes so she decided to get lasagna instead of the salad. They found a table and sat down. When Linda went to get his apple juice Leon began eating the biscuit. He hardly touched his share of the lasagna despite Linda's repeated attempts to feed him. Linda sighed. They had been in the shopping centre yesterday too. Leon had not been very hungry then either and only Linda had eaten. Instead of eating at the café, Linda brought home a pizza. But she ended up feeding him and putting him to bed too late. Now, once again, Leon had barely eaten anything at all. Besides, there had been 'sugary things before and all that', she remarked. 'I kind of feel like now it's up to me to serve good food and plenty of it. If I don't, it might get out of hand.'

Overall, Linda really struggled with the everyday dinner. She wanted Leon to eat a proper dinner but she also wanted them to spend time together and play together. Linda herself had been brought up by her single mother, an associate professor in art history, who more or less never cooked. Instead, Linda had often warmed up frozen crepes with mushrooms or a slice of pizza in the oven when she was younger and came home from school. Even though dinners had never become a normal part of Linda's everyday life she expressed a longing for them: 'When I got pregnant I thought: "Now I'm going to cook real meatballs" . . . They're so good . . . Because I never got them when I was a kid, I only got frozen ones. And a friend of mine, she had this home-cooked food when I was a kid. It was so good. I love food. My mother also loves food.' (Linda 10 June 2008; notes from the field 26 February 2009.)

QUESTIONS

There are different ways to conceptualize and think about consumption as a way to construct, express and negotiate identity. One way of looking at it is through a practice perspective according to which we express our identity through our activities. Theories of practice explain our behaviour as rooted in routinized patterns of activities that we have learned; a learning that often starts in our early childhood and which therefore is often embedded in our socio-cultural background. A practice can be seen as an interconnected logic of activities linked through *practical understandings* concerning how to act; *procedures* that lay down what is right and wrong; and *engagements* telling us what we are striving for and why this matters. According to Warde (2005) consumption usually occurs in the course of engaging in practices and is something practices entail and require. This approach prompts us to understand consumption through the logic of practices.

1 How do the two examples illustrate our understanding of different aspects of consumer behaviour (e.g. socialization, needs and lifestyles)?

2 How would you explain mothering as a practice in terms of activities and the reasons for these activities, i.e. what do mothers usually do and why? In addition, it is also possible to discuss mothering in terms of its *engagements*, i.e. its goals and why these are important to its practitioners; the *practical understandings* that are required to perform the practice; the set of *procedures* or normative regulations guiding the practice; as well as *things* and their use within the practice (see Warde, 2005: 132–6). For inspiration on mothering as a practice see Ruddick (1995: 13–27).

3 How would you describe Linda's and Marie's mothering? In what ways was consumption used in their mothering; and what role did meal consumption play?

4 What are your own experiences of being mothered as a child? How was consumption used and what role did meal consumption play? Does it differ among fellow members of your class? Why do you think this is the case?

References

Arnould, Eric, J. and Craig J. Thompson (2005), 'Consumer culture theory (CCT): Twenty years of research', *Journal of Consumer Research*, 31(4), 868–82.

Charles, Nickie and Marion Kerr (1988), *Women, food, and families*, Manchester; New York: Manchester University Press.

DeVault, Marjorie, L. (1991), *Feeding the family: The social organization of caring as gendered work*, Chicago: University of Chicago Press.

Hogg, Margaret, Pauline Maclaran, Lydia Martens, Stephanie O'Donohoe and Lorna Stevens, (2011), '(Re)creating Cultural Models of Motherhoods in Contemporary Advertising', *Advertising & Society Review*, 12(2).

Lupton, Deborah (1996), *Food, the body and the self*, London: Sage.

Lury, Celia (1996), *Consumer culture*, Cambridge: Polity Press.

Ruddick, Sara (1995), *Maternal thinking: Toward a politics of peace*, Boston: Beacon Press.

Scott, Linda, M. (2006), 'Editor's introduction: Young Mothers Talk Back', *Advertising & Society Review*, 7(3).

Warde, Alan (2005), 'Consumption and theories of practice', *Journal of Consumer Culture*, 5(2), 131–53.

Firing enthusiasm: Increasing acceptance of cremation and the implications for consumer behaviour

DARACH TURLEY, Dublin City University, Ireland
STEPHANIE O'DONOHOE, University of Edinburgh, Scotland

Some difficult consumer decisions often have to be made at distressing times, when consumers may lack the desire as well as the physical, emotional and financial resources to deal with them as they would normally. The death of a loved one is particularly demanding and traumatic, yet in the midst of their grief bereaved survivors are expected to select an undertaker, arrange a funeral, and oversee the disposal of possessions and property belonging to the deceased. Another decision at this time concerns how to dispose of the dead person's body. In most European countries this is a recent issue. Up to the 1980s, most funerals ended in some form of burial or internment. The precise nature of the burial was typically determined by family circumstance, fame, faith and social standing. However, the overall process was the same; the remains were placed where dust could return to dust at a pace dictated by the laws of nature. Cremation challenged this disposal ritual radically, significantly affecting survivors, the funeral industry and public authorities.

The history of cremation in Europe is a telling example of the 'trickle down' theory of adoption in consumer behaviour. Most members of the British Cremation Society, founded in 1874, hailed from the more educated, avant-garde, unorthodox and privileged strata of society, as did those who joined the French, German and Italian cremation societies established soon after. They questioned prevailing social and religious values relating to disposal of the dead, and had the means to conduct cremations on their own estates or abroad.

Failure to fit comfortably with existing social values is critical for most consumer adoptions, and the introduction of cremation proved to be no exception. The values in question here centred on the prevailing Christian belief in the resurrection of the body. In the second half of the nineteenth century funeral services, sermons, graveyards, headstones and memorial literature were shot through with the metaphor of rest, feeding into the deeply-held Christian belief that the graveyard was merely a temporary resting place, that the bodies of those buried there would somehow rise, refreshed and renewed, on the Last Day. So, it was no surprise that there was a concerted religious backlash to what appeared at the time to be a serious challenge to a core Christian belief. Remains remain. However, if they were not allowed to do so, if bodies were to be incinerated, how could they rise?

Changing social values and the impact of two World Wars, particularly the First World War, changed matters significantly. Europe's battlefields were strewn with millions of military and civilian dead, many of whom could not be retrieved, identified or repatriated. As a result, funerals were often conducted in the absence of any corpse. This forced survivors to decouple both their grief and their hopes for the dead person's future from their mortal remains. In addition to these dramatic events, other social developments helped change people's perceptions of cremation. As the twentieth century progressed, many European countries witnessed a growth in secularism that challenged core religious beliefs including belief in a future bodily resurrection. Wider availability of both electricity and running water fuelled consumers' growing preoccupation with cleanliness and sanitation. For consumers with such a mindset, cremation seemed a more efficient and hygienic option. Rapid urban expansion put pressure on the availability of land for new cemeteries. The search for work often required geographic mobility, and so survivors had to travel further to visit graves. Finally, in the UK the widespread immigration of Hindus, Sikhs and Buddhists – faiths that enjoy a historical and religiously sanctioned tradition of cremating their dead – served to make cremation more visible and to promote it as a viable and acceptable mode of disposal.

The year 1885 saw the opening of the first UK crematorium in Woking, Surrey; three bodies were cremated that year. Early crematoria – both interiors and exteriors – were deliberately constructed to look like churches. The coffin also descended downwards on a lift rather than horizontally on a belt as they do today, in order to resemble the process of burial more closely. By 1914, 0.2 per cent of UK funerals involved a cremation; the current figure is 75 per cent. So, today cremation is by far the most preferred option for dealing with the remains of the deceased in Britain.

There are currently about 250 crematoria in the UK, mostly run by local authorities although a few are operated by private companies. The cost of a typical cremation is £350–400, before adding the fees of the funeral director typically employed by bereaved survivors. Directors seem anxious to promote cremation funerals as essentially the same as a traditional cemetery burial, just with a different ending and their pricing strategy reflects this. While the choice of cremation or burial is the principal disposal decision to be made, some further decisions need to be made once the cremation option has been chosen. First is the choice between a direct and a non-direct cremation. In a direct cremation the remains are removed from where the person died – usually a hospital – and taken straightaway to the crematorium. When survivors are given the ashes they can dispose of them as they wish, with or without incorporating this into some form of service.

A non-direct cremation means that a coffin containing the body is present during the funeral home viewing and/or funeral service and is subsequently taken to a crematorium for incineration. This non-direct option includes a subsidiary option where survivors can choose to either purchase or rent the coffin. Some consumers do not see the point of purchasing an expensive coffin only to have it literally go up in smoke a few days later. Funeral directors can offer these clients the option of 'renting' a coffin between the time of death and final cremation. Recyclable caskets hold an inner cardboard coffin that can slide out the folding back end of the casket at the crematorium. Most funeral directors also offer a range of urns made of wood, metal, marble or stone in which these ashes can be either retained or buried. The main savings of a cremation are the cost of a cemetery gravesite (often up to £5000) and, in the case of a recycled coffin, the price of a coffin that can vary from several hundred to tens of thousands of pounds.

Once the ashes have been returned to the next of kin, the question of what to do with the ashes arises. Sixty per cent of UK mourners choose to take the ashes away with them rather than have them buried or pigeon-holed in a cemetery columbaria. No statistics are available as to where and how these ashes are disposed of; nor indeed whether or not this had been planned for by the deceased. Anecdotal evidence suggests that prime locations for 'scattering of the ashes' are gardens, golf courses, hilltops, former holiday destinations and beaches. Tales of more elaborate if somewhat furtive disposals are not uncommon. According to a recent US newspaper report, attendants watching security monitors at Disneyland noticed a woman dumping a powdery substance from a boat going through the darkened 'Pirates of the Caribbean' cavern. When they confronted her, she told them it was only baby powder, however it later turned out to be the cremated remains of a human being.

However unusual the chosen site(s), disposal of the ashes still represents a new and, for most families, an uncharted area of ritual possibility and creativity. Anthropologists see it as an example of a wider phenomenon called 'double ritual' in the funeral practices of other cultures. In the case of cremation, a funeral service around the time of death can be followed by a second ceremony – the scattering of the ashes – that can take place months or maybe years after the first ritual, giving bereaved survivors more time to decide what they want the disposal to mean and what it says about the deceased.

Scattering the ashes is perceived by most Europeans as a relatively new activity. It is also a secular ritual, created collectively by bereaved families and friends. Understandably survivors want 'to do things properly', but this can be difficult when the ground rules are still quite fluid. This is compounded by the fact that ashes can travel in a way that corpses never could. They can also be divided and apportioned to a number of different people, giving rise to the possibility of multiple rituals at a variety of sites. Common issues that arise include: who should attend the scattering – friends, family or both? Is one occasion more suitable than another? Should anything be said and, if so, by whom? Should the ashes be buried or simply scattered? Who should perform this final act?

As a ritual, scattering ashes should say something about the life and impact of the deceased. However, the persuasive power of this ritual may be compromised if it is carried out in an arbitrary, 'anything goes' fashion or is seen to be too contrived. Of particular importance is what some researchers have called 'using the incorrect idiom of relatedness'; the power of a ritual may suffer if it is not carried out by someone suitably related or close to the deceased – for example, if golfing buddies take over from the family in scattering the ashes over the eighteenth green. These factors may explain the popularity of accounts of scatterings that went awry, of winds that blew the ashes back on attendees, of angry park attendants or green-keepers remonstrating and interrupting the proceedings.

Ritual considerations apart, there are a number of additional features of cremation that seem to make it particularly appealing to bereaved people today. First, it has a certain democratic character. Parodying the American Declaration of Independence, 'all men are cremated equal'. The same ovens are used to incinerate all remains. Ashes also tend not to give rise to some of the more ostentatious headstones and statuary that often adorns graves. Some commentators have also remarked on how cremation suits a generation that has benefited so much from scientific and technological control over nature. In a sense, the technology of cremation cheats nature by destroying the body before its features fade and decay. Cremation also sits well with consumers concerned with their 'green' credentials, since it offers the prospect of recycling coffins and a cheaper, more environmentally friendly funeral overall.

The increasing availability of crematoria has also benefited religious groups for whom cremation is an integral part of their funeral ritual. For example, Hindu families may have the eldest son witness a parent's body being placed in the oven; he can also press the start button thereby fulfilling his *dharma* or sacred duty to light the funeral pyre. In addition, Hindus in Europe can have the ashes of their deceased sent to India for scattering on the Holy River Ganges. Cremations also allow survivors to retain what remains of their loved ones close to them; visits to a cemetery are no longer required. However, this advantage is not without its downside. Survivors who bury ashes in the family garden may find themselves in a quandary should they decide to move house, for example, and having a couple's ashes scattered at a similar location may lack the perceived intimacy of being buried in the same grave. Indeed, ashes do not appear to 'anchor' the dead as does a grave. Research on cemetery behaviour has noted how graves act as physical focal points for a wide range of memorial consumer behaviours. Headstones can be erected, flowers can be placed, plaques can be added, photographs can be mounted, relatives can visit and new family members can be brought and 'introduced' to the deceased.

While cremation is now firmly established as the preferred mode of disposal for the vast majority of Britain's departed, a number of core consumer behaviour and marketing issues remain for the funeral industry. Viewers of *Six Feet Under* will remember that the family running the funeral home were at pains to separate the front stage of their business – reception, viewing rooms, chapel – from its more day-to-day workings in the embalming area downstairs. This distinction between front stage and back stage is critical for many service providers. While the backstage area is, in a sense, 'out of bounds' for customers, understandably they still wonder what precisely goes on there. In traditional funerals this already applied. Mourners wondered what had gone on in that critical interval between the body being collected by the funeral director and the moment when they viewed the deceased dressed and often embalmed for the first time. However, the advent of widespread cremation has added a further, and possibly more critical dimension, to this front stage–back stage divide. Survivors seem to harbour a mixture of curiosity and concern over what exactly happens once the conveyer belt glides the coffin through the Final Curtain after the service. For example, where exactly are the ovens? Precisely when will the cremation take place? Will everything be burned? In a culture that lays so much emphasis on individuality, people want to be assured that the ashes of their loved one will be properly identified and will not be mixed with those of another person. In a word, integrity of the ashes remains a key concern.

The industry's green credentials are also being called into question. Emissions of all descriptions are becoming matters of acute environmental and political concern. Not only do residents feel uncomfortable at having a crematorium located near their homes but public authorities are also anxious that the thousands of vaporized mercury fillings that result do not become an environmental and health hazard. Cremation costs in the UK are set to rise by £100 to finance the installation of new filters to prevent any such toxic emissions. The growth in popularity of 'woodland', all-natural funerals is also impacting on the industry. Cemeteries that allow no engine-driven hearses, no headstones, and only permit biodegradable coffins mark a challenge to the traditional revenue sources of funeral directors. On a broader level, the increasing use of recycled coffins prior to cremation also represents further possible revenue loss.

In the United States, similar developments have prompted funeral homes to diversify. Examples include increased promotion of pre-planned funerals, financial service provision, bereavement counselling, property and downsizing advice as well as monthly gatherings for single survivors who wish to establish or broaden their social horizons. One funeral home has taken this last offering a step further by organizing holidays to a variety of European destinations for their bereaved clientele. Many directors have also sought to widen the range of options available to mourners for retaining the ashes of their loved one. A firm in upstate New York called Eternity Glass (**www.eternityglass.com**) makes fine quality hand-blown, hand-crafted glass sphere urns with a small quantity of cremains preserved inside. Also available are spheres and pendants in which the ash is encased in opaque glass.

QUESTIONS

1 How well do models of consumer decision-making processes account for the choices made by consumers in the immediate aftermath of bereavement? Are there any other life course events that may have a disruptive effect on consumption patterns and practices?

2 The growth in the acceptability of cremation is a notable example of an innovation that succeeds despite being so at odds with people's prevailing mindsets at the outset. Discuss the factors influencing adoption rates for this innovation.

3 Scattering of the dead person's ashes was described above as an emergent consumer ritual, a ritual 'in the making'. Can you think of any other such emergent rituals? Are there any products or services associated with these rituals? What factors might influence the design of such rituals and the degree of satisfaction experienced by key participants?

4 Cremation is now firmly established as the preferred mode of disposal for the vast majority of Britain's departed. Discuss the implications of this for funeral directors.

5 Is there anything funeral directors can do to allay consumer concerns about backstage issues such as maintaining the 'integrity of the cremains'?

Sources and further reading

Cook, E. (2006), 'Saying goodbye our way', *The Guardian*, 14 August, http://www.guardian.co.uk/lifeandstyle/2006/aug/19/familyandrelationships.family

Davies, D. (1997), *Death, ritual and belief: the rhetoric of funerary rites*, London: Cassell.

Jupp, P. (2006), *From dust to ashes: cremation and the British way of death*, Basingstoke: Palgrave Macmillan.

Owen, R. (2008), 'Burial is best – but you can scatter your ashes if you must, rules Vatican', *Times Online*, 11 January, http://www.timesonline.co.uk/tol/news/world/europe/article3168478.ece

Yoshino, K. (2007), 'Woman seen scattering ashes at Disneyland', *Los Angeles Times*, 14 November, http://travel.latimes.com/articles/la-trw-disney14nov14

Part E

CULTURE AND EUROPEAN CONSUMERS

The final part of this book considers consumers as members of a broad cultural system. Chapter 13 starts this part by examining some of the basic building blocks of culture and consumption, and shows how consumer behaviours and culture are constantly interacting with each other. Chapter 14 looks at the production of culture, and how the 'gatekeepers' of culture help shape our sense of fashion and consumer culture. Chapter 15 focuses on the importance of understanding cultural differences throughout Europe, and illustrates the similarities and differences between Europeans, e.g. in terms of religion, ethnicity and access to new technology.

13 CULTURE AND CONSUMER BEHAVIOUR

CHAPTER OBJECTIVES

When you finish reading this chapter you will understand why:

→ A culture is like a society's personality and it shapes our identities as individuals.

→ Culture is the accumulation of shared meanings and traditions.

→ As members of a culture we share beliefs, practices and values, at least to a degree.

→ Myths are stories that express the shared ideals of a culture, and how modern myths are transmitted through the media.

→ We perform rituals every day, in gift-giving as well as many other routines.

→ Graduations, weddings and funerals are modern rites of passage, which require consumption of ritual artifacts.

→ Some goods are perceived to be sacred, while others are perceived to be profane.

→ Collecting is one of the most common ways to provide a certain sacred status to objects.

IT'S THURSDAY NIGHT, 7.30. Sean puts down the phone after speaking with Colum, his study partner in his consumer behaviour class. The weekly night out for the Irish marketing students has begun! Sean has just spent the summer months travelling in Europe. He was always amazed, and delighted, to find a place claiming to be an Irish pub – regardless of how unauthentic the place was, an Irish pub always sold Guinness, a true symbol of Ireland, he reflected. Sean had begun to drink when he started university. Initially, bottled beers straight from the fridge had been his preference. However, now that he's in his third year and a more sophisticated, travelled and rounded person, he feels that those beers were just a little too – well, fashionable. He has thus recently begun to drink Guinness. His dad, uncle and grandad, in fact most of the older men he knows, drink Guinness. That day in consumer behaviour the lecturer had discussed the 'Guinness Time' TV commercial. It featured a young man doing a crazy dance around a settling pint of Guinness. The young man saved his most crazed expression for the point when he took his first sip. The lecturer had pointed out that the objectives of the ad were to associate Guinness with fun – an important reason why young people drink alcohol –

and to encourage them to be patient with the stout, as a good pint takes a number of minutes to settle.[1]

Sean has arranged to meet his friends in the local pub at 8.30. They will order 'three pints of the finest black stuff' and then have their own Guinness ritual. To begin, they watch it being poured and then look for the rising rings of the head – the best indication of a good pint. Once settled, a small top-up, and then ready for action. But they always wait and study their glasses before taking the first mouthful together – what a thing of beauty!

DAMIEN MCLOUGHLIN
University College, Dublin, Ireland

CULTURE AND CONSUMPTION

As we have already seen in the introductory part of this book, consumption choices cannot be understood without considering the cultural context in which they are made: culture is the 'prism' through which people view products and try to make sense of their own and other people's consumer behaviour.

Sean's beer-drinking reflects his desire to associate with and dissociate from (with help from the media and marketers) a certain style, attitude and trendiness. Being an Irishman, his attachment to Guinness has a very different meaning in his world than it would have in, for example, trendy circles in continental cities, where Guinness may be associated with the very fashionability that Sean tries to avoid.

Indeed, it is quite common for cultures to modify symbols identified with other cultures and present these to a new audience. As this occurs, these cultural products undergo a process of **co-optation**, where their original meanings are transformed and often trivialized by outsiders. In this case, an Irish beer was to a large extent divorced from its original connection with the Irish traditional working class or rurality and is now used as a trendy way of consuming 'Irishness' abroad (but without the rural or lower-class aspect).[2]

In Chapter 2, we saw how contemporary society can be regarded as a consumer society or a consumer culture – a culture in which consumption has become a central vehicle for organizing social meanings. This chapter considers culture from a somewhat broader perspective. We will take a look at how some of the characteristics not only of contemporary consumer culture but of all cultures contribute to the shaping of consumer behaviour. Myths, rituals and the sacred are not just features of so-called 'primitive' societies but are basic elements in all cultures. We will take a look at how myths and rituals of the culture in which we live create the meaning of everyday products and how these meanings move through a society to consumers.

This chapter deals mainly with the way very basic cultural values and symbols are expressed in goods and how consumers appropriate these symbols through consumption rituals. The next chapter will then take a closer look at fashion and other change processes in consumer culture. The first part of this chapter reviews what is meant by culture and how cultural priorities are identified and expressed. These social guidelines often take the form of *values*, which have already been discussed in Chapter 6. The second part considers the role of myths and rituals in shaping the cultural meaning of consumer products and consumption activities. The chapter concludes by exploring the concepts of the sacred and the profane and their relevance for consumer behaviour.

Culture, a concept crucial to the understanding of consumer behaviour, may be thought of as the collective memory of a society. Culture is the accumulation of shared meanings, rituals, norms and traditions among the members of an organization or society. It is what defines a human community, its individuals, its social organizations, as well as its economic and political systems. It includes both abstract ideas, such as values and ethics, and the material objects and services, such as cars, clothing, food, art and sports that are produced or valued by a group of people. Thus, individual consumers and groups of consumers are but part of culture, and culture is the overall system within which other systems are organized.

Some of the pioneers in exploring the relationship between consumption and culture were an anthropologist, Mary Douglas, and an economist, Baron Isherwood.[3] They underlined how goods are always used as social markers, not only in the traditional sense of displaying social status (although that is an important feature) but more generally by underlining how uses of goods express particular social relationships (like friendship), particular times (like 'a party'), particular moods (like relaxation), and so on. Most importantly, these marking functions are performed through a variety of daily and not-so-daily consumption rituals. We will take a closer look at consumption rituals later in this chapter. The basic learning from this and other works on consumption and culture is that any consumption activity must be understood in the cultural context in which it is taking place.

Ironically, the effects of culture on consumer behaviour are so powerful and far-reaching that this importance is sometimes difficult to grasp or appreciate.[4] We are surrounded by a lot of practices, from seemingly insignificant behaviours like pressing the start button of our iPod to larger movements like flying to an exotic honeymoon in Tanzania. What is important is that these practices have meaning for us, that we know how to interpret them. Culture is basically this interpretation system which we use to understand all those daily or extraordinary **signifying practices**[5] around us. Culture as a concept is like a fish immersed in water – we do not always appreciate this power until we encounter a different environment, where suddenly many of the assumptions we had taken for granted about the clothes we wear, the food we eat, the way we address others and so on no longer seem to apply. The effect of encountering such differences can be so great that the term 'culture shock' is not an exaggeration. This might be changing, however, since with increased globalization, we encounter other cultures all the times, in the real or the virtual world. And this in turn might make us more reflexive about who we are and what we represent ourselves. Such reflexive culture may challenge the 'water fish swim in' metaphor and make culture just as much an outcome as an antecedent to our consumption.[6]

This does not alter the fact, that the strength of culture often comes as a surprise to marketers (although that might in itself be a little surprising!) But the importance of cultural expectations is often only discovered when they are violated. Several Danish companies are still trying to regain the market shares lost in the Middle East following a Danish newspaper's publication of 12 cartoon drawings of Islam's founding prophet Muhammed (in fact, not all the cartoons actually portrayed the Prophet, but some other person named 'Muhammed'). Not least through the intervention of local Danish Muslim leaders, the cartoons, initially thought of as an attempt to test degrees of freedom of speech, became caught in a violent debate both in Denmark and all over Europe and the Middle East in arguments about respect for religious beliefs and feelings versus the principle of freedom of expression.[7] While we are not taking side in this debate, we use the case to illustrate that sensitivity to cultural issues, whether by journalists or by brand managers, can only come by understanding these underlying dimensions – and that is the goal of this chapter.

A consumer's culture determines the overall priorities they attach to different activities and products. It also determines the success or failure of specific products and services. A product that provides benefits consistent with those desired by members of a culture at a particular time has a much better chance of attaining acceptance in the marketplace. It may be difficult to guess the success or failure of certain products. Some years ago, the American business magazine *Forbes* predicted the imminent bankruptcy of the Danish stereo manufacturer Bang & Olufsen, and advised everybody to sell off their stocks in the company. In addition, they mocked the company's new product as a ghetto blaster, with the difference that the price was $3,000 and not $300. The product was the new 'on-the-wall' stereo with automatic sliding doors – the product was an instant success and the value of Bang & Olufsen stocks multiplied by 40![8] Here was a product that was launched when the time was right – something that *Forbes* overlooked.

The relationship between consumer behaviour and culture is a two-way street. On the one hand, products and services that resonate with the priorities of a culture at any given time have a much better chance of being accepted by consumers. On the other hand, the study of new products and innovations in product design successfully produced by a culture at any point in time provides a window on the dominant cultural ideals of that period. Consider, for example, some products that reflect underlying cultural processes at the time they were introduced:

- Convenience foods and ready-to-eat meals, hinting at changes in family structure and the decline of the full-time housewife.
- Cosmetics like those of The Body Shop, made of natural materials and not tested on animals, which reflected consumers' apprehensions about pollution, waste and animal rights.
- Unisex fragrances, indicating new views on sex roles and a blurring of gender boundaries, as exemplified by Calvin Klein.

Cultural systems

Cultures are organized as open systems of interrelated elements. What this means is that culture is not static. It is continually evolving, synthesizing old ideas with new ones. A cultural system can be said to consist of three interrelated functional areas:[9]

1 *Ecology*: the way in which a system is adapted to its habitat. This area is shaped by the technology used to obtain and distribute resources (for example, industrialized societies *vs* less affluent countries). One example is the Japanese interest in space-saving devices, since living space is often very sparse in Japanese cities.

2 *Social structure*: the way in which orderly social life is maintained. This area includes the domestic and political groups that are dominant within the culture, including for example the importance of the nuclear family *vs* the extended family, different gender roles and degrees of male and female dominance in different areas of life.

3 *Ideology*: the mental characteristics of a people and the way in which they relate to their environment and social groups. This area revolves around the belief that members of a society possess a common **worldview**. They share certain ideas about principles of order and fairness. They also share an **ethos**, or a set of moral and aesthetic principles. In Europe, contemporary Turkey is a good example of a clash of ethos within a culture, where rapid modernization and the construction of a consumer society is enchanting a lot of people but also challenging traditional pious values and thereby provoking people with a different ethos to seek alternative solutions. One consequence is that many Turkish women are confronted with dilemmas concerning respecting a certain piety by wearing a veil (a practice that has gone from stigmatized to more legitimate based on cultural reflexivity on Turkey's 'islamic heritage') and appearing modern, fashionable and seductive at the same time. Fashion veiling is born! Hence, the consumption of the veil becomes inscribed right in the middle of contemporary Turkish cultural politics.[10] Likewise, in a modern society, everybody wants to go on holiday. Thus, the Turkish tourist industry has provided a fancy new hotel industry for faithful Muslims with separate male and female pool and beach areas and entertainment facilities.[11]

How cultures vary

Although every culture is different, a lot of research has aimed at reducing the cultural variation to simpler principles. We have already made reference to the specificity of the Japanese relations with living space. People's culturally formed relationship to space, also called **proxemics**, is one of the fundamental distinctions between different cultures.[12] This is valid both in terms of the public space and the intimate private space immediately surrounding them. Another fundamental distinction between cultures is the relationship with time. It has been suggested that there are **monochronic** (stressing 'one thing at a time and according to schedule' principles) and **polychronic** (stressing 'several things at a time and completion of task') cultural time systems.[13] Which cultural time system do you think you belong to? Notice that when assessing such differences in cultural styles, there may not only be national cultural differences at stake here but also other kinds of cultural distinction such as urban versus rural cultures. This is one of the problems with such grand reductions of cultural differences to a simple scheme. The problem is not that proxemics or time styles are irrelevant, but that they may not be very good descriptors of what distinguishes a particular nation. It should be remembered that everyone is a member of several cultures. You are not only British, or Swedish or . . . , but also a student (which constitutes a particular culture sub-divided into subcultures), with perhaps an upper middle-class background, coming from a relatively small town, etc. As one final example, cultures also differ in their emphasis on individualism *vs* collectivism. In **collectivist cultures**, people subordinate their personal goals to those of a stable in-group. By contrast, consumers in **individualist cultures** attach more importance to personal goals, and people are more likely to change memberships when the demands of the group (e.g. workplace, church, etc.) become too costly. A Dutch researcher on culture, Geert Hofstede, has proposed this and three other dimensions, the relation to differences in social power, handling of uncertainty and risk, and the degree of masculine and feminine values, to account for much of this variability.[14] However, Hofstede's and similar approaches have been much criticized. The four dimensions do not account for the differences in the meaning and the role of the concepts in each culture. That each culture has to cope with problems of power, risk and uncertainty, gender roles and the relationship between the individual and society is obvious. But that the solutions to these problems are reducible to different levels on one and the same scale is dubious, to say the least.

Although we must be able to compare behaviour across cultures by using general concepts, we must do so by initially understanding and analysing every culture, and hence every consumer culture, on the basis of its own premises, an approach known as **ethnoconsumerism**.[15] In Figure 13.1 the principles of an ethnoconsumerist methodology are depicted. Note how central the notions of cultural categories and cultural practices, introduced in Chapter 2 and Chapter 12, are to this approach to studying consumption. To illustrate the contribution of such an approach to the study of consumer behaviour, consider a study of foreign tourist behaviour in Britain, which concluded that a sheer indication of nationality in and by itself was a bad predictor of how tourists coped with the confrontation with the (strange) British culture, whereas an ethnoconsumerist study permitted the researchers to isolate a number of cultural factors and types of behaviour that generated a much richer portrayal of touristic coping behaviour.[16] The point is that whatever consumers do, if we want to understand it fully, we will have to be aware of the cultural background to the activity. Even a simple thing like drinking a cup of coffee does not have the same meaning in different cultures.[17]

Rules for behaviour

Values, as we saw in Chapter 6, are very general principles for judging between good and bad goals, etc. They form the core principles of every culture. From these flow norms, or rules, dictating what is right or wrong, acceptable or unacceptable. Some norms, called *enacted norms*, are explicitly decided upon, such as the rule that a green traffic light means 'go' and a red one means 'stop'. Many norms, however, are much more subtle. These *crescive norms* are embedded in a culture and are only discovered through interaction with other members of that culture. Crescive norms include the following:[18]

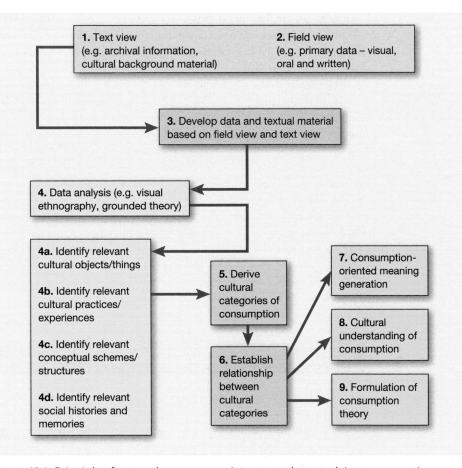

Figure 13.1 Principles for an ethnoconsumerist approach to studying consumption

Source: Laurie Meamber and Alladi Venkatesh, 'Ethnoconsumerist Methodology for Cultural and Cross-Cultural Consumer Research', in R. Elliott and S. Beckmann (eds), *Interpretive Consumer Research* (Copenhagen: Copenhagen Business School Press, 2000): 87–108.

- A **custom** is a norm handed down from the past that controls basic behaviours, such as division of labour in a household or the practice of particular ceremonies. Offering visitors a small thing to eat or drink, such as a cup of coffee or a cup of tea, are in many cultures part of custom, whether the visit is a professional or a private one.

- **Mores** are customs with a strong moral overtone. Mores often involve a taboo, or forbidden behaviour, such as incest or cannibalism. Violation of mores often meets with strong censure from other members of a society. As we saw above, the rise of a highly fashion-conscious and modern Islamic consumer in Turkey (and elsewhere in the Middle East) has led to the construction of a parallel fashion scene, where the mores of displaying the female body parts are not violated.[19]

- **Conventions** are norms regarding the conduct of everyday life. These rules deal with the subtleties of consumer behaviour, including the 'correct' way to furnish one's house, wear one's clothes, host a dinner party, and so on. Consider that the classical races at Royal Ascot recently felt compelled to introduce a stricter dress code, since the hats and clothes on display had become a little too fanciful for the organizers' taste – according to a spokesperson, it was important to obey the formality of the occasion and not dress as on a visit to a nightclub.[20] Sometimes conventions cause cross-cultural problems. For example, the Chinese were grappling with a cultural problem as they prepared for the 2008 Olympics in Beijing: local habits of public spitting and belching were expected to offend many a foreign visitor.[21] But usually it is the visitor who must adapt – to facilitate the respect for cultural conventions, one consultant has developed some 20 apps, one for each country such as China, Turkey and Brazil to be downloaded for a small amount.[22]

All three types of crescive norms may operate to define a culturally appropriate behaviour. For example, mores may tell us what kind of food it is permissible to eat. Note that mores vary across cultures, so eating a dog may be taboo in Europe, while Hindus would shun beef and Muslims avoid pork products. Custom dictates the appropriate hour at which the meal should be served. Conventions tell us how to eat the meal, including such details as the utensils to be used, table etiquette, and even the appropriate apparel to be worn at dinner time.

We often take these conventions for granted, assuming that they are the 'right' things to do (again, until we are exposed to a different culture!). And it is good to remember that much of what we know about these norms is learned *vicariously* (cf. Chapter 7), as we observe the behaviours of others in our peer groups but also actors and actresses in films and TV series, television commercials, print ads and other popular culture media. In the long run, marketers have a great deal to do with influencing consumers' enculturation, which is the process whereby you learn your own society's values, as opposed to acculturation which refers to processes of relating to different cultures.

MAGIC, MYTHS AND RITUALS

Every culture develops stories and practices that help its members to make sense of the world. When we examine these activities in other cultures, they often seem strange or even unfathomable. Yet our *own* cultural practices appear quite normal – even though a visitor may find them equally bizarre. The following section will discuss magic, myths and rituals, three aspects of culture common to all societies, from the ancient to the modern world.

It works like magic!

To appreciate how so-called 'primitive' belief systems which some may consider irrational or superstitious continue to influence our supposedly 'modern', rational society, consider the avid interest of many Western consumers in magic. Marketers of health foods, anti-ageing cosmetics, exercise programmes and gambling casinos often imply that their offerings have 'magical' properties that will ward off sickness, old age, poverty or just plain bad luck. People by the millions carry lucky charms to ward off 'the evil eye', or have 'lucky' clothing or other products which they believe will bring them good fortune. Many of us have a lucky number, that we use on various occasions, such as in sports games (whether we are playing ourselves, betting, or just watching), lotteries, etc. Beliefs in magic structure major consumer events in the West as well as the East. When the calendar hit 7 July 2007 – 7/7/07 – many people in the US scrambled to take advantage of its link to lucky 777. Western culture associates the number seven with good fortune (like the seven sacraments in Roman Catholicism) and US marketers from Wal-Mart to Las Vegas casinos jumped on the bandwagon.[23] Keep in mind that these beliefs are culturecentric so they take on different forms around the world. For example, in China 8 is the luckiest number. The Chinese word for 8 is *ba*, which rhymes with *fa*, the Chinese character for wealth. It is no coincidence that the Summer Olympics in Beijing opened on 8/8/08 at 8.08 pm.

But the magic most prevalent in consumer culture is the magic that pertains to the transformations of our bodies. The health, wellness and beauty industries are replete with suggestions of magical transformations of our bodies, that will help us cleanse our bodily organs, shed excess weight, restore youthful looks, and create a new and more harmonious

Some advertisements borrow heavily from the magical and mythological world of fairy tales. Which one is alluded to here?

M&C Saatchi.

and balanced self. Research has demonstrated the role of magical thinking in the way consumers relate to weight loss programmes[24] and how such weight loss programmes as, for example, Weight Watchers constitute spiritual and therapeutic ways of coping with what is perceived as effects of over-consumption.[25] Note the magic of consumer society – that you can consume (a therapeutic programme) in order to cope with the effects of overconsumption!

Such hopes for a magic transformation lie behind a lot of contemporary consumption pertaining to the self, from the very manifest consumption of cosmetic surgery[26] to the more spiritual consumption of self-enhancement programmes.[27] Often advertisers and consumers construct marketplace mythologies to serve multiple and sometimes competing ideological agendas – this is particularly true in the product categories which consumers use to deal with issues of health, healing and well-being.[28]

An interest in the occult tends to be popular, perhaps even more so when members of a society feel overwhelmed or powerless – magical remedies simplify our lives by giving us 'easy' answers. Marketing efforts are replete with more or less open references to magical practices.[29] And it is not just a matter of fooling consumers: magic is an active part also of our modern lives. Customers at river-rafting trips in America speak about the magical capacities of the river to transform their lives, heal psychological wounds and bring out the best in people.[30] Even a computer is regarded with awe by many consumers as a sort of 'electronic magician', with the ability to solve our problems (or in other cases to make data magically disappear!).[31]

MARKETING OPPORTUNITY

Magic has been the order of the beginning of the twenty-first century. Never before (or at least since the Middle Ages) has the market been so populated with magicians, sorcerers, witches, spirits, druids and other beings of the magical universe. Possibly the single most influential factor here is the marketing genius of – or rather behind – Harry Potter. The completely engineered world of Harry Potter, with the cathedral of magic at Hogwarts, the variety of shops in Diagon Alley, the experience economy of Quidditch, and the plethora of sweets at Honeydukes sweetshop; all of this is based on a very enriching encounter between a society hungry for sorcery and the magic of marketing, if you are to believe one marketing wizard writing under the name of Stephen Brown. The success of the Harry Potter brand is immersed in a contemporary (postmodern?) demand for magic fairy tales and a skilful construction of a complete universe reflecting all of contemporary consumer society's wonderful and not so wonderful consequences of marketplace practices. Can we finally learn the trick? Magic matters! It is marketing for Muggles![32] Is magic a has-been? Check Cartier's French award winning 'Odyssée' 3 min 30 seconds ad from 2012.[33] And fantasy literature is still a big genre for youngsters, so the question might very well be: where might the next marketing magic be coming from?

Myths

Every society possesses a set of myths that define that culture. A **myth** is a story containing symbolic elements that expresses the shared emotions and ideals of a culture. The story may feature some kind of conflict between two opposing forces, and its outcome serves as a moral guide. In this way, a myth reduces anxiety because it provides consumers with guidelines about their world.

An understanding of cultural myths is important to marketers, who in some cases (most likely unconsciously) pattern their strategy along a mythic structure.[34] Consider, for example, the way that a company like McDonald's takes on 'mythical' qualities.[35] The golden arches are a universally recognized symbol, one that is virtually synonymous with American culture. Not only do they signify the possibility for the whole world symbolically to consume a bite of Americana and modernity, but they also offer sanctuary to Americans around the world, who know exactly what to expect once they enter. Basic struggles involving good *vs* evil are played out in the fantasy world created by McDonald's advertising, as when Ronald McDonald confounds the Hamburglar. McDonald's even has a 'seminary' (Hamburger University) where inductees go to learn appropriate behaviours and be initiated into the culture. In short, McDonald's is a kind of mythical utopia representing modernity, leisurely eating and lifestyle, and the American dream – a mythical utopia it shares with other brands such as Disneyland or Disney World.[36]

Corporations often have myths and legends in their history, and some make a deliberate effort to be sure newcomers to the organization learn these. Nike (a name drawn from Greek mythology) designates senior executives as 'corporate storytellers' who explain the company's heritage to the hourly workers at Nike stores.[37] The strongest brands often base their strength on how well they resonate with current mythologies.[38] One example provided is the Jack Daniels that has skilfully used and contributed to the American 'gunfighter myth'.[39] What is this myth about? Consider detective stories in TV and on the big screen – often the hero does not just have to fight the villains, but also his superordinate boss, as the representative of the 'system'. This 'man versus system' is what the gunfighter myth is all about. How many other brands and types of consumption depend on such mythology? A similar mythological narrative of 'the morally good real American' versus 'the morally corrupt and un-American environmentalists', was evoked by consumers of the Hummer brand in order to defend their car choice.[40] Sometimes consumers react against what they see as industry created myths. In Denmark, a country known for its dairy industry, one set of consumers started to react very strongly against what they saw as a 'corporate generated myth' that dairy products are healthy. The conflict escalated to the point where the Danish health authorities, for the first time ever, issued a public warning against following the diet recommendations of this consumer movement, especially for small children.[41] Myths are a battleground!

Of course, one of the most fundamental myths of the Western world is the myth of the 'exotic Other' which is basically different from ourselves, expressed by Kipling in his lines, 'East is East and West is West, and never the twain shall meet'. This is reflected in a lot of consumer behaviour, obviously in the experiences promised by the tourist industry, where myths about destinations are sometimes supported by similar mythologies inherent in, e.g. music, or imagined lifestyles. For example, Hawaii[42] and surf culture[43] in particular have been studied as such mythological universes. We also find this myth, however, in more home-based activities such as in the attraction to and collection of exotic goods such as Oriental carpets.[44]

The functions and structure of myths

Myths serve four interrelated functions in a culture:[45]

1 *Metaphysical*: they help to explain the origins of existence.

2 *Cosmological*: they emphasize that all components of the universe are part of a single picture.

3 *Sociological*: they maintain social order by authorizing a social code to be followed by members of a culture.

4 *Psychological*: they provide models for personal conduct.

Myths can be analysed by examining their underlying structures, a technique pioneered by the anthropologist Claude Lévi-Strauss. Lévi-Strauss noted that many stories involve *binary opposition*, where two opposing ends of some dimension are represented (good *vs* evil, nature *vs* technology). Characters and products often appear in advertisements to be defined by what they *are not* rather than by what they *are* (for example, this is *not* a product for those who feel

This ad for Norwegian trade unions borrows from the Little Red Riding Hood myth. It says: 'There are many advantages in being many.'
Lofavor Norway – Supertanker (SMFB Norway)
Photo: Petrus Olsson, Adamsky.

old, *not* an experience for the frightened, *not* music for the meek, etc.). Such structures have been used to analyse food categories, dividing food into hot *vs* cold, for children, for adults and for old people, for men and for women etc.[46] Myths are often the fundamental element in folk tales where they represent eternal conflicts between, say, good and evil, innocence and guilt, male and female, civility and bestiality.

Recall from the discussion of Freudian theory in Chapter 6 that the ego functions as a kind of 'referee' between the opposing needs of the id and the superego. In a similar fashion, the conflict between mythical opposing forces is sometimes resolved by a *mediating figure*, who can link the opposites by sharing characteristics of each. For example, many myths contain animals that have human abilities (e.g. a talking snake) to bridge the gap between humanity and nature, just as cars (technology) are often given animal names (nature) like Jaguar or Mustang.

Myths are found everywhere in modern popular culture. While we generally equate myths with the ancient Greeks or Romans, modern myths are embodied in many aspects of popular culture, including comic books, films, holidays and even commercials. Sports consumption is replete with myths, for instance myths about 'super-athletes' or 'the eternal no. 2' – or the favourites who always fail – such as the Spanish football team until their victory in the 2008 European championship. Music is also full of myths – myths about the garage band who makes it big, or the myth of the self-destructive artist maintained by many a dead music star.[47]

Comic book superheroes demonstrate how myths can be communicated to consumers of all ages. Indeed, some of these fictional figures represent a **monomyth**, a myth that is common to many cultures.[48] The most prevalent monomyth involves a hero who emerges from the everyday world with supernatural powers and wins a decisive victory over evil forces. He then returns with the power to bestow good things on his fellow men. This basic theme can be found in such classic heroes as Lancelot, Hercules and Ulysses. The success of the Disney movie *Hercules* reminds us that these stories are timeless and appeal to people through the ages.

Comic book heroes are familiar to most consumers, and they are viewed as more credible and effective than celebrity endorsers. Film spin-offs and licensing deals aside, comic books are a multi-million dollar industry. The American version of the monomyth is best epitomized by Superman, a Christ-like figure who renounces worldly temptations and restores harmony to his community. Heroes such as Superman are sometimes used to endow a product, store or service with desirable attributes. This imagery is sometimes borrowed by marketers – PepsiCo tried to enhance its position in the Japanese market by using a figure called 'Pepsiman', a muscle-bound caricature of an American superhero in a skin-tight uniform, to promote the drink. Pepsiman even appears in a Sega game called *Fighting Vipers*.[49]

But there are many other, less obvious, mythological figures surrounding us. For example, the role of Albert Einstein as a mythological figure, and one that is used for giving meaning to and promoting certain consumable objects in films or posters, or in advertisements as a sort of indirect endorsement, has been studied by consumer researchers.[50]

Many blockbuster films and hit TV programmes draw directly on mythic themes. Spiderman draws both on the myth of the superhero as well as the myth of one's eternal fight with one's own negative sides (especially in *Spiderman 3*). So while dramatic special effects or attractive stars certainly do not hurt, a number of these films perhaps owe their success to their presentation of characters and plot structures that follow mythic patterns. Examples of these mythic blockbusters include:[51]

● *The Big Blue*. The sea is the offspring of many myths. Its inaccessibility and depth have always inspired humans to create imagery about this other world. The film depicts the search for a lost symbiosis between man and nature, where the only person with real access to this must give up his human life to become one with the purity and the graciousness of the sea, symbolized by the dolphins.

- *E.T.: The Extraterrestrial.* E.T. represents a familiar myth involving Messianic visitation. The gentle creature from another world visits Earth and performs miracles (e.g. reviving a dying flower). His 'disciples' are local children, who help him combat the forces of modern technology and an unbelieving secular society. The metaphysical function of myth is served by teaching that the humans chosen by God are pure and unselfish. In an inverse format, a similar story is told in the more recent blockbuster *Avatar*.

- *Easy Rider.* This 1969 cult film can be seen as the forerunner of the much-beloved road movie genre that has been among the most popular in recent decades, and which got its definitive feminist version with *Thelma and Louise*. These films feature myths of freedom and rebelliousness against the banalities of daily life (as expressed in one of the theme songs from *Easy Rider*, Steppenwolf's 'Born to be Wild'), which are recycled in a lot of commercial contexts. For instance, in a commercial for Ford's Cougar (another wild animal) model, Dennis Hopper (anno 1998) driving a Cougar raced with himself riding a motorbike in the original *Easy Rider* film.[52]

- *Jaws.* This and films constructed around similar themes draw on myths of the beast, representing the wild, dangerous, untamed nature that is culture's (human beings') enemy. Such myths are known from Christianity and other religious mythologies, such as Norse mythology (the Midgaard Snake, the Fenris Wolf), and have played a central role in the way the Western world has regarded nature over the centuries.

Also more mundane consumer objects can be the subject of mythological narratives. Furthermore, since these are culturally constructed, they change over place and time. Consider, for example, a classic study of the meanings and roles of the Italian scooter in the Italian and British market contexts. Whereas in Italy the scooter was mainly positioned as a

A bag depicting a modern myth object, the scooter.

Photo courtesy of Caroline Penhoat.

539

symbol of the new, modern and liberated Italian woman, epitomized in the Italian superstar actresses of the 1950s, the scooter in Britain became caught in a cultural clash between the more 'masculine' heavy industry and the blue-collar jobs expressed in subcultural terms among the 'rockers' and their motorcycles, and the more white-collar youth subculture of the 'mods', heavily engaged in conspicuous consumption activities. The latter adopted the scooter as their prime symbol and dominant mode of transport.[53] Today, the scooter revived by consumer nostalgia and retro-marketing[54] has become a modern myth object referring to the happy and innocent 'youth' of the youth culture 40 to 50 years ago, as depicted by this bag for sale at London's Portobello Road market in 2008 (see photo on previous page).

Commercials and products as myths

Commercials can be analysed in terms of the underlying cultural themes they represent. Myths of particular places, for example of the lost paradise of Shangri-La, lost but never found somewhere in Tibet, has inspired Westerners captured by Eastern mythology for years. However, the search could be over, since the Chinese Government has now founded an official Shangri-La – a Disneyfied tourist destination based on spiritual and sacred themes.[55] But not only particular places are mythical, also particular times. For example, commercials for various food products ask consumers to 'remember' the mythical good old days when products were wholesome and natural. The mythical theme of the underdog prevailing over the stronger foe (i.e. David and Goliath) has been used by the car rental firm Avis in a now classic campaign where they stated, 'We're only no. 2, we try harder'. Other figures from mythical narratives have been used by advertisers, such as the villain (a brand teasing its competitors), the hero (the brand in control) or the helper (the brand that helps you accomplish something).[56]

This Spanish ad melds modern-day athletes with mythical figures.

Canal/Contrapunto BBDO Agency.

Rituals

A **ritual** is a set of multiple, symbolic behaviours that occur in a fixed sequence and that tend to be repeated periodically.[57] Although bizarre tribal ceremonies, perhaps involving animal or virgin sacrifice, may come to mind when people think of rituals, in reality many contemporary consumer activities are ritualistic. Rituals are traditionally thought of as patterns of behaviour that serve to uphold the social order, but drinking rituals such as Sean's can also be thought of as transgressive and transformative, especially among younger consumers. Hence, drinking as a ritual constitutes a time and space to enter another state of being, i.e. being intoxicated! This relationship to drinking rituals is probably more characteristic of northern European consumers compared to southern Europeans.[58]

MARKETING PITFALL

Consider a ritual that many beer drinkers in the United Kingdom and Ireland hold near and dear to their hearts: the spectacle of a pub bartender 'pulling' the perfect pint of Guinness. According to tradition, the slow pour takes exactly 119.5 seconds as the bartender holds the glass at a 45-degree angle, fills it three-quarters full, lets it settle, and tops it off with its signature creamy head. Guinness wanted to make the pull faster so the bar could serve more drinks on a busy night, so it introduced FastPour, an ultrasound technology that dispenses the dark brew in only 25 seconds. You probably guessed the outcome: the brewer had to scrap the system when drinkers resisted the innovation. Note: Diageo (which owns Guinness) hasn't given up, and it continues to experiment with more efficient techniques in markets where this ritual isn't so inbred. A system it calls GuinnessSurger shows up in Tokyo bars, many of which are too small to accommodate kegs: the bartender pours a pint from a bottle, places the glass on a special plate, and zaps it with ultrasound waves that generate the characteristic head.[59]

A study conducted by the BBDO Worldwide advertising agency illustrates just how crucial rituals are to many brands.[60] It labels brands that we closely link to our rituals **fortress brands** because once they become embedded in our rituals – whether brushing our teeth, drinking a beer, or shaving – we are unlikely to replace them. The study ran in 26 countries, and the researchers found that overall people worldwide practice roughly the same consumer rituals. The study claims that 89 per cent of people repeatedly use the same brand for these sequenced rituals, and three out of four are disappointed or irritated when something disrupts their ritual or their brand of choice is not available. For example, the report identifies one common ritual category it calls *preparing for battle*. For most of us this means getting ready for work. Relevant rituals include brushing teeth, taking a shower or bath, having something to eat or drink, talking to a family member or partner, checking e-mail, shaving, putting on makeup, watching TV or listening to the radio, and reading a newspaper.

Rituals can occur at a variety of levels, as noted in Table 13.1. Some of the rituals described are specifically American, but the US Super Bowl may be compared to the English FA Cup Final or the traditional ski jump competition in Austria on the first day of the new year. Some rituals affirm broad cultural or religious values, like the differences in the ritual of tea drinking in the UK and France. Whereas tea seems a sensuous and mystical drink to the French, the drinking of coffee is regarded as having a more functional purpose. For the British, tea is a daily drink and coffee is seen more as a drink to express oneself.[61]

The ritual of going to a café with a selection of coffee opportunities was unknown outside most of the metropolitan areas of the US until recent times. No longer. The Starbucks Corporation has experienced phenomenal success by turning the coffee break into a cultural event that for many has assumed almost cult-like status. The average Starbucks customer visits 18 times a month, and 10 per cent of the clientele stops by twice a day.[62] Starbucks has

Table 13.1 Types of ritual experience

Primary behaviour source	Ritual type	Examples
Cosmology	Religious	Baptism, meditation, Mass
Cultural values	Rites of passage	Graduation, marriage
	Cultural	Festivals, holidays (Valentine's Day), Super Bowl
Group learning	Civic	Parades, elections, trials
	Group	Business negotiations, office luncheons
	Family	Mealtimes, bedtimes, birthdays, Mother's Day, Christmas
Individual aims and emotions	Personal	Grooming, household rituals

Source: Dennis W. Rook, 'The ritual dimension of consumer behavior', *Journal of Consumer Research*, 12 (December 1985): 251–64. *The Journal of Consumer Research* by AMERICAN ASSOC. FOR PUBLIC OPINION RESEARCH © 1985. Reproduced with permission of UNIVERSITY OF CHICAGO PRESS – Journals.

opened shops in many countries in Europe, re-exporting a new kind of coffee shop culture to places with long traditions for café culture such as France. Thus, several types of places for different 'coffee rituals' may co-exist. One study suggested at least three kinds of coffee shops in the Scandinavian context: the traditional 'Viennese' style where a lot of focus is on the baked goods, the 'starbuckified' modern coffee shop (such as Starbucks but also Baresso, etc.) and the 'local' coffee shop with a less streamlined interior decoration than the modernist ones, and often a devoted clientele of 'alternative-minded' people.[63]

Ritual artefacts

Many businesses owe their livelihoods to their ability to supply **ritual artefacts**, or items used in the performance of rituals, to consumers. Birthday candles, diplomas, specialized foods and beverages (e.g. wedding cakes, ceremonial wine, or even sausages at the stadium), trophies and plaques, band costumes, greetings cards and retirement watches are all used in consumer rituals. In addition, consumers often employ a ritual script, which identifies the artefacts, the sequence in which they are used and who uses them. The proliferation of 'manners and style' books in recent years bears witness to the renewed interest in rituals after the belief of the beat generation that they could abolish ritual behaviour and just act 'normal' and be 'natural'. Of course, such behaviour required a whole new set of rituals . . .

But rituals are not restricted to the special occasions described above. Daily life is full of ritualized behaviour. Wearing a tie on certain occasions can be seen as a ritual, for example. The significance attached to rituals will vary across cultures (Valentine's Day is slowly gaining popularity in several European countries, and in the Middle East),[64] and will often be a mixture of private and public (generally shared) symbolism.[65]

In the model of movement of meaning in the world of goods (see Chapter 2) it is suggested that there are four types of rituals that are central for consumption: possession rituals, exchange rituals, grooming rituals and divestment rituals.[66] Let us begin with considering the first and the last together, since they are logically intertwined: one consumer's divestment can often be linked to another consumer's acquisition of a possession.

Possession and divestment rituals

Whether it is in the form of putting magnets on the refrigerator door, objects hanging from the mirror in the car, stickers and badges put on jackets and bags, consumers often perform various rituals that provide a certain degree of alteration to a newly purchased object. The object is thereby transformed from a mass-produced good to a personalized possession. Possession rituals mark that the object is no longer just any object, it is *my* object. The blank and boring computer screen is personalized through the installation of our background for the desktop, our own set of preferred photos as screensavers and in a multitude of other ways. We personalize the screen and the ringtones of our cellphone. Through these ritualistic inclusions of the mass-produced goods in our own little sphere of being, we are transforming them into objects that are visibly or audibly one's own and also expressions of identity, as we discussed in Chapter 5.

Since we invest personal meanings in our things, we also, oftentimes, invest some efforts in removing the elements of identity when we are getting rid of the things. We call these efforts rituals of disposition. When you move out of your flat, you make sure to clean it of everything that belongs to you, not only because the contract says so, but also because you do not want to allow other people a look into your private life through the personal items or traces left. You may clean it thoroughly, but possibly the new tenant will perform yet another cleaning (another divestment ritual making sure the flat is divested of you) and a possession ritual repainting in order to make sure the flat is now truly theirs. Divestment rituals also occur when cherished possessions are ritualistically transferred from one generation to the next. Such rituals of handing over things to a younger generation can contribute to lower anxieties that the new generations will cherish and protect the family heirloom as well as former generations.

Consequently, rituals of disposition are not only performed in order to remove personalization from consumer objects but, in a way, also to keep it since it confirms, if not the individual, then the family identity. They can also be performed in order to maintain a moral identity. Consider the great efforts some consumers go through in terms of sorting their garbage for maximal recycling. We can consider this sorting behaviour an expression of environmental values, but it is also a ritual that is performed in order to divest the objects 'properly', that is in the morally and socially (and environmentally) correct way. The concept of freecycling also illustrates such a moral approach to divestment;[67] increasingly consumers are willing to share what they no longer need and turning trash for themselves into treasures for other people (see discussion also in Chapter 6).[68] Indeed, consumers can experience the yearning to get rid of some of their possessions as some kind of sacrifice ritual in order to obtain a purer, almost sacred kind of consumer life.[69] We will return to the sacred shortly, but let us add that this idea of divestment as a sacrifice does not only pertain to voluntary simplists and downshifters. A story of ordinary British families found the same kind of sacrifice ritual in the way people related to their leftover food.[70]

Grooming rituals

Whether brushing one's hair 100 strokes a day or talking to oneself in the mirror, virtually all consumers undergo private grooming rituals. These are sequences of behaviours that aid in the transition from the private self to the public self or back again. These rituals serve various purposes, ranging from inspiring confidence before confronting the world to cleansing the body of dirt and other profane materials. Traditionally a female market, the grooming sector for men is a booming business. For example, at the turn of the millennium Unilever opened a new chain of barber shops in the UK that also offer facial treatments and manicures on top of the shaves and beard trims. The adaptation to the male market is almost perfect: the waiting rooms feature PlayStations and personal CD players instead of glossy magazines.[71]

When consumers talk about their grooming rituals, some of the dominant themes that emerge from these stories reflect the almost mystical qualities attributed to grooming products and behaviours. Many people emphasize a before-and-after phenomenon, where the person feels magically transformed after using certain products (similar to the Cinderella myth).[72]

Two sets of binary oppositions that are expressed in personal rituals are *private/public* and *work/leisure*. Many beauty rituals, for instance, reflect a transformation from a natural state to the social world (as when a woman 'puts on her face') or vice versa. In these daily rituals, women reaffirm the value placed by their culture on personal beauty and the quest for eternal youth.[73] This focus is obvious in ads for Oil of Olay beauty cleanser, which proclaim: 'And so your day begins. The Ritual of Oil of Olay.' Similarly, the bath is viewed as a sacred, cleansing time, a way to wash away the sins of the profane world.[74]

Exchange rituals

It would be fair to say that the whole marketplace of exchanging goods, services and information through sharing, buying and selling is one big set of exchange rituals. However, the form of exchange rituals that most ordinary consumers would think of first and foremost is probably giving and receiving gifts. The promotion of appropriate gifts for every conceivable holiday and occasion provides an excellent example of the influence consumer rituals can exert on marketing phenomena and vice versa. In the **gift-giving ritual**, consumers procure the perfect object (artefact), meticulously remove the price tag (symbolically changing the item from a commodity to a unique good), carefully wrap it and deliver it to the recipient.[75]

Gift-giving used to be viewed by researchers primarily as a form of economic exchange, where the giver transfers an item of value to a recipient, who in turn is somehow obliged to reciprocate. However, gift-giving is interpreted increasingly as a symbolic exchange, where the giver is motivated by acknowledging the social bonds between people.[76] These might then be seen as more economic and reciprocal but may also be guided by unselfish factors, such as love or admiration, without expectations of anything in return. Some research indicates that gift-giving evolves as a form of social expression: it is more exchange-oriented (instrumental) in the early stages of a relationship, but becomes more altruistic as the relationship develops.[77] One set of researchers identified multiple ways in which giving a gift can affect a relationship.[78] These are listed in Table 13.2.

Every culture prescribes certain occasions and ceremonies for giving gifts, whether for personal or professional reasons. The giving of birthday presents alone is a major undertaking. Business gifts are an important component in defining professional relationships, and great care is often taken to ensure that the appropriate gifts are purchased.

Table 13.2 Effects of gift-giving on social relationships

Relational effect	Description	Example
Strengthening	Gift-giving improves the quality of a relationship	An unexpected gift such as one given in a romantic situation
Affirmation	Gift-giving validates the positive quality of a relationship	Usually occurs on ritualized occasions such as birthdays
Negligible effect	Gift-giving has a minimal effect on perceptions of relationship quality	Non-formal gift occasions and those where the gift may be perceived as charity or too good for the current state of the relationship
Negative confirmation	Gift-giving validates a negative quality of a relationship between the gift-giver and the receiver	The selection of gift is inappropriate, indicating a lack of knowledge of the receiver. Alternatively the gift is viewed as a method of controlling the receiver
Weakening	Gift-giving harms the quality of the relationship between giver and receiver	When there are 'strings attached' or gift is perceived as a bribe, a sign of disrespect or offensive
Severing	Gift-giving harms the relationship between the giver and the receiver to the extent that the relationship is dissolved	When the gift forms part of a larger problem, such as a threatening relationship. Or when a relationship is severed through the receipt of a 'parting' gift

Source: Adapted from Julie A. Ruth, Cele C. Otnes and Frederic F. Brunel, 'Gift receipt and the reformulation of interpersonal relationships', *Journal of Consumer Research*, 25 (March 1999): 385–402, Table 1: 389.

MULTICULTURAL DIMENSIONS

The importance of gift-giving rituals is underscored by considering Japanese customs, where the wrapping of a gift is as important (if not more so) than the gift itself. The economic value of a gift is secondary to its symbolic meaning.[79] To the Japanese, gifts are viewed as an important aspect of one's duty to others in one's social group. Giving is a moral imperative (known as *giri*).

Highly ritualized gift-giving occurs during the giving of both household/personal gifts and company/professional gifts. Each Japanese has a well-defined set of relatives and friends with whom they share reciprocal gift-giving obligations (*kosai*).[80]

Personal gifts are given on social occasions, such as at funerals, to people who are hospitalized, to mark movements from one stage of life to another (such as weddings, birthdays) and as greetings (when one is meeting a visitor). Company gifts are given to commemorate the anniversary of a corporation's founding or the opening of a new building, as well as being a routine part of doing business, as when rewards are given at trade meetings to announce new products.

Some of the items most desired by Japanese consumers to receive as gifts include gift coupons, beer and soap.[81] In keeping with the Japanese emphasis on saving face, presents are not opened in front of the giver, so that it will not be necessary to hide one's possible disappointment with the present.

Gift giving has long been a cultural trait among the Japanese. In recent years, it has become popular within the context of a westernized Christmas season in Japan.

Gen Nishino/Taxi/Getty Images.

The gift-giving ritual can be broken down into three distinct stages.[82] During *gestation*, the giver is motivated by an event to procure a gift. This event may be either *structural* (i.e. prescribed by the culture, as when people buy Christmas presents), or *emergent* (i.e. the decision is more personal and idiosyncratic). The second stage is *presentation*, or the process of gift exchange. The recipient responds to the gift (either appropriately or not), and the donor evaluates this response.

In the third stage, known as *reformulation*, the bonds between the giver and receiver are adjusted (either looser or tighter) to reflect the new relationship that emerges after the exchange is complete. Negativity can arise if the recipient feels the gift is inappropriate or of inferior quality. The donor may feel the response to the gift was inadequate or insincere or a violation of the reciprocity norm, which obliges people to return the gesture of a gift with one of equal value.[83] Both participants may feel resentful for being 'forced' to participate in the ritual.[84] Indeed, since people may feel fear of becoming either subject to or the cause of a feeling of indebtedness by engaging in gift-giving, some may even 'escape' to the market and sell some of their stuff rather than giving it away, not so much to make money but rather to avoid creating a relationship of indebtedness.[85]

People commonly find (or devise) reasons to give themselves something; they 'treat' themselves. Consumers purchase **self-gifts** as a way to regulate their behaviour. This ritual provides a socially acceptable way of rewarding themselves for good deeds, consoling themselves after negative events or motivating themselves to accomplish some goal.[86] Figure 13.2 is a projective stimulus similar to ones used in research on self-gifting. Consumers are asked to tell a story based on a picture such as this, and their responses are analysed to discover the reasons people view as legitimate for rewarding themselves with self-gifts. For example, one recurring

Figure 13.2 Projective drawing to study the motivations underlying the giving of self-gifts

Source: Based on David G. Mick, Michelle DeMoss and Ronald J. Faber, 'Latent Motivations and Meanings of Self-Gifts: Implications for Retail Management' (research report, Center for Retailing Education and Research, University of Florida, 1990).

story that might emerge is that the woman in the picture had a particularly grueling day at work and needed a pick-me-up in the form of a new fragrance. This theme could then be incorporated into a promotional campaign for a perfume. With the growing evidence of hedonic motives for consumption in recent decades, self-gifts may represent an increasingly important part of the overall consumption pattern.

One final gift-giving ritual that is worth mentioning – since the rise of the internet and its digitalized world has made it much easier and present in our lives – is the idea of sharing; of giving away (in a digital form) what one already possesses, but without losing it oneself. In what may well be the largest gift-giving system in history, the now bygone Napster music sharing community and its successors such as KaZaa and Morpheus have opened a whole new world of consumer exchange rituals with its own specific set of norms for reciprocity and contribution within the online community. For example, people who download files without leaving their files available to others are labelled as 'leeches'.[87] As we all know, this form of gift-giving has not been embraced by all. Copyright holders in the form of music publishers (and musicians) are generally less than amused, so since then we have witnessed what might best be described as a drama between producers protecting their intellectual property rights and consumers underlining their rights to do what they want with their possessions (including online sharing and community building) as long as it is remains a non-commercial activity.[88] These and other moral arguments such as 'fair use' and the fact that buying copies might help other people than the copyright holders make a living are also evoked in order to justify ethical issues in music access.[89] A British study suggests that there are four types of 'pirates', the serious ones actively and quite often seeking out occasions to pirate ('Devils'), the opportunistic ones that will occasionally take a chance on pirating but not very frequently ('Chancers'), pirates who are not actively pirating but accept receiving pirated material ('Receivers'), and the 'Angels' who refrain from any sort of pirating.[90] Which type are you?

Holiday rituals

Holidays are important rituals in both senses of the word. Going on holiday was one of the most widespread rituals and tourism one of the biggest industries of the late twentieth century, and the trend looks set to continue.[91] On holidays consumers step back from their everyday lives and perform ritualistic behaviours unique to those times.[92] For example, going to Disneyland in Paris may mean a ritualized return to the memories of our own dreams of a totally free (of obligations, duties and responsibilities) fantasy land of play.[93] Holiday occasions are filled with ritual artefacts and scripts and are increasingly cast as a time for giving gifts by enterprising marketers. Holidays mean big business to hotels, restaurants, travel agents and so on.

Holidays also exist in terms of special celebratory occasions. For many businesses Christmas is the single most important season. Concerning the holidays of celebrations, most such holidays are based on a myth, and often a real (Guy Fawkes) or imaginary (Cupid on Valentine's Day) character is at the centre of the story. These holidays persist because their basic elements appeal to deep-seated patterns in the functioning of culture.[94]

The Christmas holiday is bursting with myths and rituals, from adventures at the North Pole to those that occur under the mistletoe. One of the most important holiday rituals involves Santa Claus, or an equivalent mythical figure, eagerly awaited by children the world over. Unlike Christ, this person is a champion of materialism. Perhaps it is no coincidence, then, that he appears in stores and shopping centres – secular temples of consumption. Obviously, certain consumers resist the materialism and marketization of Christmas. These 'anti-Christmas' groups may draw upon a counter-mythological figure, like the cynical Christmas-hater Ebenezer Scrooge from Dickens' *A Christmas Carol* as a symbol to flock around online in order to share and reinforce their anti-consumerism Christmas ideals.[95]

Whatever the origins of Santa Claus, the myth surrounding him serves the purpose of socializing children by teaching them to expect a reward when they are good and that members of society get what they deserve. Needless to say, Christmas, Santa Claus and other associated rituals and figures change when they enter into other cultural settings. In the Netherlands he has to compete with Sint Niklaas, who basically is his own doppelgänger, and who even has his own day of celebration on 6 December. In Denmark, Norway and Sweden,

The myth of Santa Claus permeates our culture and marks the biggest consumption ritual in today's world.

ePresence.

Santa Claus competes or is confused with Julenissen (in Sweden, Jultomten), who is a kind of amalgamation between gnomes from ancient pagan beliefs and a contemporary Santa Claus figure. Some of the transformations of Santa Claus in a Japanese context include a figure called 'Uncle Chimney', Santa Claus as a stand-in for the newborn Christ and Santa Claus crucified at the entrance of one department store with the words 'Happy Shopping' written above his head.[96] What does this tell us about the globalization process?

On Valentine's Day, standards regarding sex and love are relaxed or altered as people express feelings that may be hidden during the rest of the year. In addition to cards, a variety of gifts are exchanged (see the opening vignette about Ayşe, Chapter 2), many of which are touted by marketers to represent aphrodisiacs or other sexually related symbols. It seems as if many people in consumer societies are always on the lookout for new rituals to fill their lives. This ritual was once virtually unknown in Scandinavia but is slowly becoming part of their consumption environment.[97] Also, the American ritual of celebrating Halloween is now becoming fashionable in Europe, where the French in particular have adopted it as an occasion for festivities, dancing and the chance to show off new fashions.[98] Also in Denmark, Halloween has become a significant consumer ritual. Between 2005 and 2008 the sales of scary stuff from toy stores has gone up 10 to 20 per cent each year, and the sale of pumpkins (which Danes generally do not eat) has multiplied by 30 between 1999 and 2008.[99] As for many modern rituals, supermarket chains and other commercial agents have played a significant role in spreading these occasions for having a good time but also for boosting sales across borders.

Rites of passage

What does a dance for recently divorced people have in common with 'college initiation cere-monies'? Both are examples of modern **rites of passage**, or special times marked by a change in social status. Every society, both primitive and modern, sets aside times where such changes occur. Some of these changes may occur as a natural part of consumers' lifecycles (puberty or death), while others are more individual in nature (divorce and re-entering the dating market). As we saw with some of the other rituals, there seems to be a renewed interest in transition rites. They are increasingly becoming consumption objects in themselves as well as occasions for consumption. In order to satisfy the 'need' for rituals, not only do we import new ones from abroad, as we have seen, but in times of globalization many cultures also experience a renewed interest in the old rituals that have traditionally framed the cultural identity.[100]

Some marketers attempt to reach consumers on occasions in which their products can enhance a transition from one stage of life to another.[101] A series of Volkswagen ads underlined the role of the car in the freedom of women who were leaving their husbands or boyfriends.

Stages of role transition Much like the metamorphosis of a caterpillar into a butterfly, con-sumers' rites of passage consist of three phases.[102] The first stage, *separation*, occurs when the individual is detached from their original group or status (for example, the first-year university student leaves home). *Liminality* is the middle stage, where the person is literally in between statuses (the new arrival on campus tries to work out what is happening during orientation week). The last stage, *aggregation*, takes place when the person re-enters society after the rite of passage is complete (the student returns home for the Christmas holiday as a 'real university student'). Rites of passage mark many consumer activities, as exemplified by confirmation or other rites of going from the world of the child to the world of the adult. A similar transitional state can be observed when people are prepared for certain occupational roles. For example, athletes and fashion models typically undergo a 'seasoning' process. They are removed from their normal surroundings (athletes are taken to training camps, while young models are often moved to Paris or Milan), indoctrinated into a new subculture and then returned to the real world in their new roles.

The final passage: marketing death The rites of passage associated with death support an entire industry. Death themes are replete in marketing.[103] Survivors must make expensive purchase decisions, often at short notice and driven by emotional and superstitious concerns. Funeral ceremonies help the living to organize their relationships with the deceased, and action tends to be tightly scripted down to the costumes (the ritual black attire, black ribbons for mourners, the body in its best suit) and specific behaviours (sending condolence cards or holding a wake). (However, more and more seem to emphasize a certain personal touch to commemorate the individuality of the deceased.) Mourners 'pay their last respects', and seating during the ceremony is usually dictated by mourners' closeness to the individual. Even the cortège is accorded special status by other motorists, who recognize its separate, sacred nature by not overtaking as it proceeds to the cemetery.[104]

Funeral practices vary across cultures, but they are always rich in symbolism. For example, a study of funeral rituals in Ghana found that the community there determines a person's social value after he has died; this status depends on the type of funeral his family gives him. One of the main purposes of death rituals is to negotiate the social identities of deceased persons. This occurs as mourners treat the corpse with a level of respect that indicates what they think of him. The Asante people who were the subjects of the study do not view death as something to fear but rather as a part of a broader, ongoing process of identity negotiation.[105]

SACRED AND PROFANE CONSUMPTION

As we saw when considering the structure of myths, many types of consumer activity involve the demarcation, or binary opposition, of boundaries, such as good *vs* bad, male *vs* female – or even 'regular' *vs* 'low-fat'. One of the most important of these sets of boundaries is the distinction between the sacred and the profane. **Sacred consumption** involves objects and events that are 'set apart' from normal activities, and are treated with some degree of respect or awe. They may or may not be associated with religion, but most religious items and events tend to be regarded as sacred. **Profane consumption** involves consumer objects and events that are ordinary, everyday objects and events that do not share the 'specialness' of sacred ones. (Note that profane does not mean vulgar or obscene in this context.)

Domains of sacred consumption

Sacred consumption events permeate many aspects of consumers' experiences. We find ways to 'set apart' a variety of places, people and events. In this section, we will consider some examples of ways that 'ordinary' consumption is sometimes not so ordinary after all.

Sacred places

Sacred places have been 'set apart' by a society because they have religious or mystical significance (e.g. Bethlehem, Mecca, Stonehenge) or because they commemorate some aspect of a country's heritage (e.g. the Kremlin, Versailles, the Colosseum in Rome). During 2008, there was quite a debate in Denmark whether to temporarily move the Copenhagen landmark, 'The Little Mermaid', to China for a world exhibit. The marketing people of the Danish tourist industries as well as the export organization thought it would be a scoop to present 'the real thing' to the Chinese visitors at the exhibit, but many Danes felt that it is a degradation of a sacred piece of art and a part of the 'soul' of Copenhagen for a marketing gimmick. The marketers got their way. Remember that in many cases the sacredness of these places is due to the property of contamination – that is, something sacred happened on that spot, so the place itself takes on sacred qualities. There is a plethora of sacred places to be 'consumed' around the world, and we are not only thinking world famous cathedrals. One study investigated consumer behaviour at St Brigid's Holy Well in Ireland. The study reported a plethora of holy but also secular objects left there by pilgrims, often with a little story attached explaining the magical belief in the wish for some kind of transformation, like curing an illness or blessing a relationship or children.[106] Tourism is one of the most common and rapidly spreading forms of consuming the sacred.[107]

Other places are created from the profane world and imbued with sacred qualities. When Ajax, the local football team of Amsterdam, moved from their old stadium, De Meern, to a larger, more modern stadium (De Arena), the turf from the old stadium was carefully lifted from the ground and sold to a local churchyard. The churchyard offers the turf to fans willing to pay a premium price to be buried under authentic Ajax turf!

Even the modern shopping centre can be regarded as a secular 'cathedral of consumption', a special place where community members come to practice shopping rituals.[108] Theme parks are a form of mass-produced fantasy that takes on aspects of sacredness. In particular, the various Disneylands are destinations for pilgrimages from consumers around the globe. Disneyland displays many characteristics of more traditional sacred places, especially for Americans, but Europeans too may consider these parks the quintessence of America. It is even regarded by some as the epitome of child(ish) happiness.[109] A trip to a park is the most common 'last wish' for terminally-ill children.[110]

In many cultures, the home is a particularly sacred place. It represents a crucial distinction between the harsh, external world and consumers' 'inner space'. In northern and western Europe the home is a place where you entertain guests (in southern Europe it is more common to go out), and fortunes are spent each year on interior decorators and home furnishings; the home is thus a central part of consumers' identities.[111] But even here there are vast differences between, for example, the dominant traditionalist style of British homes and the modernist style of Danish homes.[112] Consumers all over the world go to great lengths to create a special environment that allows them to create the quality of homeliness. This effect is created by personalizing the home as much as possible, using such devices as door wreaths, mantel arrangements and a 'memory wall' for family photos.[113] Even public places, like various types of cafés and bars, strive for a home-like atmosphere which shelters customers from the harshness of the outside world.

Sacred people

People themselves can be sacred, when they are idolized and set apart from the masses. Souvenirs, memorabilia and even mundane items touched or used by sacred people take on special meanings and acquire value in their own right. Indeed, many businesses thrive on consumers' desire for products associated with famous people. There is a thriving market for celebrity autographs, and objects once owned by celebrities, whether Princess Diana's gowns or John Lennon's guitars, are often sold at auction for astronomical prices. A store called 'A Star is Worn' sells items donated by celebrities – a black bra autographed by Cher sold for $575. As one observer commented about the store's patrons, 'They want something that belonged to the stars, as if the stars have gone into saint-hood and the people want their shrouds.'[114] More recently, the UK firm of ASOS (As Seen On Screen) has started a thriving online business targeted at 18- to 30-year-olds (primarily female) which offers for sale products that are identical to products that are seen in television shows. The company owners got the idea after reading an article reporting that the broadcasters of *Friends* (the television show) received over 28,000 telephone calls enquiring about a lamp that had appeared in one of the characters' apartments.[115]

MARKETING OPPORTUNITY

There is nothing to boost the popularity of an artist as his or her death – this cynical observation has been made everytime a music celebrity has died and sales of the artist have gone up – in 2012, as we are writing, this was most recently seen in the cases of Amy Winehouse and Whitney Houston. But what about bringing a star back to life?

In spring 2012, rapper Tupac Shakur appeared on stage at the Coachella music festival 15 years after his death following a shooting incident in 1996. Or so it seemed to the audience, who saw the rapper perform and interact (at one point Tupac shouted Coachella!). In fact, what they experienced was a 'hologram', or rather, in fact, a figure made through a digital mirror technique, whose rapping and interacting was sampling and digital loops. A twitter page for the Tupac hologram allegedly gained over 10,000 followers in less than a day. Such popularity is hardly resistible to marketers and to fans of 'sacred stars'. Now there are rumours that Tupac Shakur's hologram will go on tour – and who knows what follows? Maybe we will also see John Lennon back on stage singing a duet with Paul McCartney?[116]

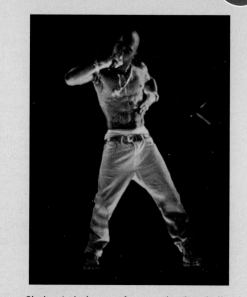

Tupac Shakur in hologram form at the Coachella Music and Arts Festival 2012.

Kevin Winter/Getty Images for Coachella Music and Arts Festival.

Sacred events

Many consumers' activities have taken on a special status. Public events in particular resemble sacred, religious ceremonies, as exemplified by the playing of the national anthems before a game or the reverential lighting of matches and lighters at the end of a rock concert.[117]

For many people, the world of sport is sacred and almost assumes the status of a religion. The roots of modern sports events can be found in ancient religious rites, such as fertility festivals (e.g. the original Olympics).[118] Indeed, it is not uncommon for teams to join in prayer prior to a game. The sports pages are like the Scriptures (and we describe ardent fans as reading them 'religiously'), the stadium is a house of worship, and the fans are members of the congregation. After the first Scottish victory in many years in a football match against England at Wembley Stadium, Scottish fans tore down the goals to bring pieces back home as sacred relics. Indeed, grass from stadiums of important matches, like World Cup finals, has been sold in small portions at large prices.

Devotees engage in group activities, such as tailgate parties (eating and drinking in bars or even the car park prior to the event) and the 'Mexican Wave', where (resembling a revival meeting) participants on cue join the wave-like motion as it makes its way around the stadium. The athletes that fans come to see are godlike; they are reputed to have almost super-human powers (especially football stars in southern Europe and Latin America). Athletes are central figures in a common cultural myth, the hero tale. As exemplified by mythologies of the barefoot Olympic marathon winner (Abebe Bikila from Ethiopia, 1960), or of boxing heroes (legally) fighting their way out of poverty and misery, often the heroes must prove themselves under strenuous circumstances. Victory is achieved only through sheer force of will. Of course, sports heroes are popular endorsers in commercials, but only a few of these sports personalities 'travel' very well, since sports heroes tend to be first and foremost national heroes. However, a few people are known worldwide, at least within the key target market for the ads, so that they can be used in international campaigns.

If sport is one domain that is becoming increasingly sacred (see the section on sacralization below), then the traditionally sacred realm of fine arts is considered by some in danger of desacralization. In a sale of a publishing company of classical music, various representatives voiced the fear that a takeover by one of the giants such as Sony, Polygram or EMI would mean the introduction of a market logic that would destroy its opportunities to continue to sponsor unknown artists and make long-term investments in them. It is argued that classical music is not a product that can be handled by any marketer, but requires special attention and a willingness to accept financial losses in order to secure artistic openness and creativity.[119] Such reactions (as justified as they may be) indicate that artists and managers conceive of themselves as dealing with sacred objects that cannot be subjugated to what is conceived as the profane legitimacy of the market.[120] Indeed, art and marketing is the subject of study for more and more marketing and consumer researchers, for example in considering art as a kind of service.[121] Famous film directors make commercial campaigns and music videos (and music video-makers turn into great film directors), while commercial film-makers celebrate each other with their own sets of prizes for creativity. The great documentary *Exit Through the Gift Shop* by the famous British street artist *Banksy*, of the unfolding of the global street art scene, provides a wonderful example of the intricate relationship between art and marketing in a consumer society.[122] Art and marketing, in short, are becoming increasingly blurred (see the section desacralization below).[123]

Tourism is another example of a sacred, non-ordinary experience of extreme importance to marketers. When people travel on holiday, they occupy sacred time and space. The tourist is continually in search of 'authentic' experiences which differ from their normal world (think of Club Med's motto, 'The antidote to civilization').[124] This travelling experience involves binary oppositions between work and leisure and being 'at home' *vs* 'away'. Norms regarding appropriate behaviour are modified as tourists scramble for illicit experiences they would not dream of engaging in at home.

The desire of travellers to capture these sacred experiences in objects forms the bedrock of the souvenir industry, which may be said to be in the business of selling sacred memories. Whether a personalized matchbook from a wedding or a little piece of the Berlin Wall, souvenirs represent a tangible piece of the consumer's sacred experience.[125]

In addition to personal mementoes, such as ticket stubs saved from a favourite concert, the following are other types of sacred souvenir icons:[126]

- Local products (such as goose liver from Périgord or Scotch whisky).
- Pictorial images (postcards).
- 'Piece of the rock' (seashells, pine cones). Sometimes this can be problematic, however. For example, it is forbidden to bring home corals and seashells from a lot of diving places around the world, in order to prevent tourists from 'tearing down' the coral reef. But temptations are great. Even at Nobel Prize dinners, approximately 100 of the noble guests each year cannot resist bringing home something, typically a coffee spoon, as a souvenir.[127]
- Symbolic shorthand in the form of literal representations of the site (a miniature London double-decker bus, Little Mermaid or Eiffel Tower).
- Markers (Hard Rock Café T-shirts).

Increasingly, we see peculiar blends of the sacred and the secular in tourism and in sacred places promoting themselves. One such case is the town of Glastonbury, England. Being an ancient site for pagan as well as Christian worship, it today profiles itself on an amalgamation of 'serious' New Age beliefs and tongue-in-cheek promotion of experience economy witchcraft à la Harry Potter.[128]

GÜLIZ GER
Bilkent University, Ankara

Given the omnipotent prevalence of consumption in public and private life, I think consumer researchers should, and increasingly are, examining issues of significant social and human impact. An obvious domain is sustainable consumption, from the perspective of both the consumer and the firm. We consumer researchers need to study the firm's decisions and actions as well as those of the consumers since the two inform and are informed by each other. For example, what are the motivators and the conditions for each party to engage in activities that will entail sustainable options? I have been working on collecting success stories of firms acting responsibly and making a difference. My former research on consumer desires and legitimizations of materialism provide important hints for some of the conditions under which consumers will buy into ecologically-friendly consumption.

We live in an era of wars, economic crises and crimes. While we speak about free markets and consumer choice, choices are severely limited, especially (but not solely) for the disadvantaged consumers. The links between such broader issues and consumption and hence the ultimate well-being are also well-worth thinking about and studying.

Politics and religion are some other domains that have a major impact on how consumers think, feel and act, as well as how firms and other market actors operate. Markets are embedded in politics just as much as they are in economics and culture. The interplay of politics and consumption, the lives of persons as consumers and citizens are part and parcel of the field of 'consumer behaviour'. While spirituality may appear to counter consumption, we see that globally, religious fundamentalism is on the rise along with consumption. Be it Islamic fashions, foods and drinks or Christian or Hindu or Buddhist icons and objects consumers negotiate ethics, aesthetics, and politics.

Both today and in the past, consumers and their consumption practices in different parts of the world have been and are constituted by locally-unique forces as well as global forces.

While everyone says we cannot understand the present without understanding the past, only recently consumer researchers have begun to study the historical underpinnings of consumption. Be that recent history of a couple of decades or ancient history of several centuries. The emergence, development and transformation of consumer culture, certain consumption patterns or practices, and/or particular markets in the seventeenth century or the twenty-first century in a particular geography are very informative about the interactions between and among consumers, markets, religions, and the state, nationally and transnationally.

Güliz Ger

From sacred to profane, and back again

Just to make life interesting, in recent times many consumer activities have moved from one sphere to the other. Some things that were formerly regarded as sacred have moved into the realm of the profane, while other, everyday phenomena are now regarded as sacred.[129] Both these processes are relevant to our understanding of contemporary consumer behaviour. A recent study of tea preparation in Turkey illustrates this movement. Although we are more likely to think of thick Turkish coffee, in reality Turks consume more tea per capita than any other country. In this culture people drink tea continuously, like (or instead of) water. Tea is an integral part of daily life; many households and offices boil water for tea in the traditional *çaydanlik* (double teapot) first thing in the morning, and keep it steaming all day so that the beverage is ready at any time. The tea drinking process links to many symbolic meanings – including the traditional glasses, clear to appreciate the tea's colour, and hourglass-shaped like a woman's body – and rituals, such as blending one's own tea, knowing how finely to grind the tea leaves, and how long to steep the tea for optimal flavour. When Lipton introduced the modern tea bag in 1984, Turkey was intent on modernization and soon consumers were buying electric *çaydanlik*, and mugs instead of small, shapely tea glasses. Tea became a symbol of the quick and convenient and the drinking act became more of a fashion statement – it was desacralized. Now, the authors report that many Turkish consumers opt to return to the sacred, traditional rituals as a way to preserve authenticity in the face of rapid societal changes.[130]

Desacralization

Desacralization occurs when a sacred item or symbol is removed from its special place or is duplicated in mass quantities, becoming profane as a result. For example, souvenir reproductions of sacred monuments such as the Leaning Tower of Pisa or the Eiffel Tower, 'pop' artworks of the *Mona Lisa* or adaptations of important symbols such as the Union flag by clothing designers, tend to eliminate their special aspects by turning them into inauthentic commodities, produced mechanically and representing relatively little value.[131]

Religion itself has to some extent been desacralized. Religious symbols, such as stylized crosses or New Age crystals, have moved into the mainstream of fashion jewellery.[132] What used to be deeply religious expressions thus become fashion. In fact, religion itself becomes fashion. We witness an interesting period, where a lot of religions are competing with each other for the consumers' interest. Not all of these are New Age creations based on some sympathetic Asian philosophy. In Iceland and Norway, the ancient Norse viking religion worshipping Thor and Odin is a recognized religious community, and it has asked for recognition in Denmark as well. Even in deeply Catholic Italy, there is a revival of a pagan community of believers in ancient magic and mystery.[133]

MARKETING PITFALL

Big football clubs are global businesses making more money out of the merchandise sold to fans all over the world than out of the sold-out matches at home. However, catering to global fans may come at a price. Already back in 2007, Barcelona started altering its club emblem on jerseys sold in Arab countries such as Saudi Arabia and Algeria. There is a white field with a red cross, and this emblem could be interpreted as a crusader symbol, not very well received among many Arabs, so they removed one arm in the cross, leaving just a red/white striped field on jerseys sold in Arab countries.[134] This move has been confirmed after the club's recent new sponsorship deal with the Qatar Foundation. Also rivals Real Madrid have been through a similar process - while constructing a big sports resort in the UAE, the Sheikh asked the club to remove the Christian cross from the top of the crown in their club emblem. Real Madrid complied in the interest of catering to an increasingly global crowd of fans - and in order to be able to compete with the eternal Catalan rivals for followers in the Middle East.[135]

Religious holidays, particularly Christmas, are regarded by many (and criticized by some) as having been transformed into secular, materialistic occasions devoid of their original sacred significance. Benetton, the Italian clothing manufacturer, has been at the forefront in creating vivid (and often controversial) messages that expose us to our cultural categories and prejudices, but at times they have touched upon the issue of desacralization.[136]

Even the clergy are increasingly adopting secular marketing techniques. Especially in the US, televangelists rely upon the power of television, a secular medium, to convey their messages. The Catholic Church generated a major controversy after it hired a prominent public relations firm to promote its anti-abortion campaign.[137] Nonetheless, many religious groups have taken the secular route, and are now using marketing techniques to increase the number of believers. The question is whether the use of marketing changes the 'product' or 'service' of the churches.[138]

MULTICULTURAL DIMENSIONS

The American 'market for religious belief' with its tele-vangelists and its heavy promotion of various churches and sects is a very exotic experience for many Europeans. The ad below for a Minneapolis church to help recruit worshippers is typical of the American trend towards secular practices being observed by many organized religions. It even uses a pun (on the curing of a head-ache) to pass on the message of salvation.

Sacralization

Sacralization occurs when objects, events and even people take on sacred meaning to a culture or to specific groups within a culture. For example, events like the Cannes Film Festival or Wimbledon and people like Elvis Presley or Princess Diana have become sacralized to some consumers. But the process of sacralization can be used to understand more mundane phenomena than such super-events or popular culture heroes. An interesting study of devoted fans of the Apple corporation and its Macintosh computers concluded that the devotion of the Apple fans was comparable to a religious feeling, portraying Steve Jobs, co-founder and later re-installed CEO of Apple, as a kind of prophet with a message of salvation for the 'chosen few' in a PC-dominated world.[139]

Objectification occurs when sacred qualities are attributed to mundane items. One way that this process can occur is through *contamination*, where objects associated with sacred events or people become sacred in their own right. This explains the desire by many fans for items belonging to, or even touched by, famous people. One standard procedure through which objects become sacralized occurs when they become included in the collection of a museum.

In addition to museum exhibits displaying rare objects, even mundane, inexpensive things may be set apart in private *collections*, where they are transformed from profane items to sacred ones. An item is sacralized as soon as it enters a collection, and it takes on special significance to the collector that, in some cases, may be hard to comprehend by the outsider. **Collecting** refers to the systematic acquisition of a particular object or set of objects, and this widespread activity can be distinguished from hoarding, which is merely unsystematic collecting.[140] Collecting typically involves both rational and emotional components, since collectors are fixed by their objects, but they also carefully organize and exhibit them.[141]

Name an item, and the odds are that a group of collectors are lusting after it. The contents of collections range from various popular culture memorabilia, rare books and autographs, to Barbie dolls, tea bags, lawnmowers and even junk mail.[142] Consumers are often ferociously attached to their collections; this passion is exemplified by the comment made in one study by a woman who collects teddy bears: 'If my house ever burns down, I won't cry over my furniture, I'll cry over the bears.'[143]

Some consumer researchers feel that collectors are motivated to acquire their 'prizes' in order to gratify a high level of materialism in a socially acceptable manner. By systematically

The ad for the Episcopal church discussed in the multicultural dimensions box opposite.

Church Ad Project, 1021 Diffley, Eagen, MN 55123.

amassing a collection, the collector is allowed to 'worship' material objects without feeling guilty or petty. Another perspective is that collecting is an aesthetic experience: for many collectors the pleasure emanates from being involved in creating the collection, rather than from passively admiring the items one has scavenged or bought. Whatever the motivation, hard-core collectors often devote a great deal of time and energy to maintaining and expanding their collections, so for many this activity becomes a central component of their extended selves (see Chapter 5).[144]

MARKETING OPPORTUNITY

Make your brand a collectable, and enhance your exposure and your brand loyalty. Certain products and brands become cult objects for devoted collectors. In the early 1990s, 'Swatch fever' infected many people. The company made more than 500 different models, some of which were special editions designed by artists. Collectors' interest made a formerly mundane product into a rare piece of art (e.g. a 'Jelly Fish' that originally sold for $30 was sold at auction for $17,000). Although thousands of people still collect the watches, the frenzy began to fade by around 1993.[145] Some collectors' items are more stable. One of the corporations exploiting this opportunity to its fullest is the Coca-Cola Company. With the plethora of Coca-Cola collectables, a lot of devoted and often highly specialized collectors have been created all over the world. They appear as 'spokespersons' for the brand when they account for their sometimes fabulous collections in the media, and they create a lot of extra and extremely positive exposure for the brand. As one researcher noted: 'These are brand owners. Coca-Cola is theirs.'[146]

CHAPTER SUMMARY

Now that you have finished reading this chapter you should understand why:

→ A society's *culture* includes its values, ethics and the material objects produced by its people. It is the accumulation of *shared meanings* and traditions among members of a society. A culture can be described in terms of ecology (the way people adapt to their habitat), its social structure and its ideology (including people's moral and aesthetic principles). This chapter describes some aspects of culture and focuses on how cultural meanings are created and transmitted across members of a society.

→ Members of a culture share a system of *beliefs* and *practices*, including *values*. The process of learning the values of one's culture is called enculturation. Each culture can be described by a set of core values. Values can be identified by several methods, though it is often difficult to apply these results directly to marketing campaigns due to their generality.

→ *Myths* are stories containing symbolic elements that express the shared ideals of a culture. Many myths involve some binary opposition, where values are defined in terms of what they are and what they are not (e.g. nature *vs* technology). Modern myths are transmitted through advertising, films and other media.

→ A *ritual* is a set of multiple, symbolic behaviours which occur in a fixed sequence and tend to be repeated periodically. Rituals are related to many consumption activities which occur in popular culture. These include holiday observances, gift-giving and grooming.

→ A *rite of passage* is a special kind of ritual which involves the transition from one role to another. These passages typically entail the need to acquire products and services, called ritual artefacts, to facilitate the transition. Modern rites of passage include graduations, initiation ceremonies, weddings and funerals.

→ Consumer activities can be divided into *sacred* and *profane* domains. Sacred phenomena are 'set apart' from everyday activities or products. People, events or objects can become sacralized. *Objectification* occurs when sacred qualities are ascribed to products or items owned by sacred people. *Sacralization* occurs when formerly sacred objects or activities become part of the everyday, as when 'one-of-a-kind' works of art are reproduced in large quantities. *Desacralization* occurs when objects that previously were considered sacred become commercialized and integrated into popular culture.

→ *Collecting* is one of the most common ways of experiencing sacred consumption in daily life. It is simultaneously one of the domains where consumption and passions are most heavily intertwined.

→ The importance of consumption for understanding social interactions is now so big that we have begun to talk about our own societies as *consumer societies*, indicating that consumption might well be the single most important social activity.

KEY TERMS

Collecting (p. 556)	**Custom** (p. 533)
Collectivist cultures (p. 532)	**Desacralization** (p. 555)
Conventions (p. 533)	**Ethnoconsumerism** (p. 532)
Co-optation (p. 529)	**Ethos** (p. 531)
Culture (p. 529)	**Fortress brands** (p. 541)

CONSUMER BEHAVIOUR CHALLENGE

1 Culture can be thought of as a society's personality. If your culture were a person, could you describe its personality traits?

2 What is the difference between an enacted norm and a crescive norm? Identify the set of crescive norms operating when a man and woman in your culture go out for dinner on a first date. What products and services are affected by these norms?

3 How do the consumer decisions involved in gift-giving differ from other purchase decisions?

4 The chapter argues that not all gift-giving is positive. In what ways can this ritual be unpleasant or negative?

5 Construct a ritual script for a wedding in your culture. How many artefacts can you list that are contained in this script?

6 What are some of the major motivations for the purchase of self-gifts? Discuss some marketing implications of these.

7 Describe the three stages of the rite of passage associated with graduating from university.

8 Identify the ritualized aspects of various kinds of sports that are employed in advertising.

9 Some people have raised objections to the commercial exploitation of cultural figures. For example, in the US many consumers deplored the profits that film-makers and business people made from films such as *Malcolm X* (e.g. by selling a 'Malcolm X' air freshener). Others argued that this commercialization merely helps to educate consumers about what such people stood for, and is inevitable in our society. The 'close-up' portrait of the British royal family in the critically acclaimed movie *The Queen* stirred quite some discussion about how close you should go. What do you think?

10 Interview two or three of your fellow students about collecting, talking about either their own collections or a collection of somebody they know of. Use concepts about the sacred to analyse the responses.

For additional material see the companion website at **www.pearsoned.co.uk/solomon**

NOTES

1. See Dennis W. Rook, 'The ritual dimension of consumer behavior', *Journal of Consumer Research* 12 (December 1985): 251–64; Mary A. Stansfield Tetreault and Robert E. Kleine III, 'Ritual, Ritualized Behavior, and Habit: Refinements and Extensions of the Consumption Ritual Construct', in Marvin Goldberg, Gerald Gorn, and Richard W. Pollay (eds), *Advances in Consumer Research* 17 (Provo, UT: Association for Consumer Research, 1990): 31–8.

2. See for example, A. Fuat Firat, 'Consumer Culture or Culture Consumed', in Janeen A. Costa and G. Bamossy (eds),

Marketing in a Multicultural World: Ethnicity, Nationalism, and Cultural Identity (Thousand Oaks, CA: Sage, 1995): 105–25.

3. Mary Douglas and Baron Isherwood, *The World of Goods*, 2nd edn (London: Routledge, 1996).

4. A classic work on this is, for example, Edward T. Hall, *The Silent Language* (New York: Doubleday, 1959).

5. Paul du Gay, Stuart Hall, Linda Janes, Hugh MacKay and Keith Negus, *Doing Cultural Studies: The Story of the Sony Walkman* (London: Sage, 1997).

6. Søren Askegaard, Dannie Kjeldgaard and Eric J. Arnould, 'Reflexive culture's consequences', in C. Nakata (ed.), *Beyond Hofstede; Culture frameworks for global marketing and management* (Chicago: Palgrave Macmillan, 2009), 101–124.

7. Hans Rask Jensen, 'The Mohammed cartoons controversy and the boycott of Danish products in the Middle East', *European Business Review* 20(3), 2008: 275–89.

8. Personal communication with Jens Bernsen, 29 October 1997.

9. Clifford Geertz, *The Interpretation of Cultures* (New York: Basic Books, 1973); Marvin Harris, *Culture, People and Nature* (New York: Crowell, 1971); John F. Sherry Jr, 'The Cultural Perspective in Consumer Research', in Richard J. Lutz (ed.), *Advances in Consumer Research* 13 (Provo, UT: Association for Consumer Research, 1986): 573–5.

10. Özlem Sandikci and Güliz Ger, 'Veiling in style: How does a stigmatized practice become fashionable?', *Journal of Consumer Research*, 37 (June 2010), 15–36.

11. Güliz Ger and Özlem Sandikci, 'In-Between Modernities and Postmodernities: Theorizing Turkish Consumption-scape', in S. Broniarczyk and K. Nakamoto (eds), *Advances in Consumer Research* 29 (Valdosta, GA: Association for Consumer Research, 2002): 465–70.

12. Edward T. Hall, *The Hidden Dimension* (New York: Doubleday, 1966).

13. Edward T. Hall, *The Dance of Life. The Other Dimension of Time* (New York: Doubleday 1983).

14. Geert Hofstede, *Culture's Consequences* (Beverly Hills, CA: Sage, 1980); see also Laura M. Milner, Dale Fodness and Mark W. Speece, 'Hofstede's Research on Cross-Cultural Work-Related Values: Implications for Consumer Behavior', in W.F. van Raaij and G. Bamossy (eds), *European Advances in Consumer Research* 1 (Provo, UT: Association for Consumer Research, 1993): 70–6.

15. Alladi Venkatesh, 'Ethnoconsumerism: A Proposal for a New Paradigm to Study Cross Cultural Consumer Behavior', in Costa and Bamossy (eds), *Marketing in a Multicultural World*: 26–67.

16. Andrea Davies and James Fitchett, 'Crossing culture: A multi-method enquiry into consumer behaviour and the experience of cultural transition', *Journal of Consumer Behaviour* 3(4) (2006): 315–30.

17. Brad Weiss, 'Coffee Breaks and Coffee Connections: The Lived Experience of a Commodity in Tanzanian and European Worlds', in D. Howes (ed.), *Cross-Cultural Consumption* (London: Routledge, 1996): 93–105.

18. George J. McCall and J.L. Simmons, *Social Psychology: A Sociological Approach* (New York: The Free Press, 1982).

19. Özlem Sandikci and Güliz Ger, 'Constructing and representing the Islamic consumer in Turkey', *Fashion Theory* 11(2/3) (2007): 189–210.

20. http://www.guardian.co.uk/sport/2012/jan/18/royal-ascot-fascinators-hats-dresscode, accessed 2 May 2012.

21. Jim Yardley, 'No Spitting on the Road to Olympic Glory, Beijing Says,' *New York Times Online* (17 April 2007), accessed 17 April 2007.

22. http://www.latimes.com/business/money/la-fi-mo-cultural-faux-pas-20120413,0,6568628.story, accessed 30 April 2012.

23. Laura Petrecca, 'Ad Track: Marketers Bet on lucky 777; That's July 7, 2007', *USA Today Online* (29 May 2007), accessed 29 May 2007.

24. Yannik St. James, Jay M. Handelman and Shirley F. Taylor, 'Magical thinking and consumer coping', *Journal of Consumer Research*, 38 (December 2011): 632–649.

25. Risto Moisio and Mariam Beruchashvili, 'Questing for well-being at Weight Watchers: The role of the spiritual-therapeutic model in a support group', *Journal of Consumer Research*, 36 (February 2010): 857–875.

26. Søren Askegaard, Martine Cardel Gertsen and Roy Langer, 'The body consumed: Reflexivity and cosmetic surgery', *Psychology & Marketing* 19(10) (2002): 793–812.

27. Jennifer Rindfleisch, 'Consuming the self: New age spirituality as "social product" in consumer society', *Consumption, Markets and Culture* 8(4) (2005): 343–60.

28. Craig J. Thompson, 'Marketplace mythology and discourses of power', *Journal of Consumer Research* 31 (June 2004): 162–80. The author formulates the construct of marketplace mythology to explore how cultural myths are used to create marketplace mythologies that serve multiple and often competing ideological agendas. He develops his arguments within the context of the natural health market. While this market is positioned as alternative to mainstream scientific medicine, both practitioners' and consumers' quest for scientific support to validate their holistic healing treatments generate a fundamental paradox. This paper examines the mythic constructions of nature, technology, and science and their relations to both natural health's marketplace mythology of holistic well-being and key competitive forces.

29. Eric Arnould, Cele Otnes and Linda Price, 'Magic in the Marketing Age', in S. Brown, A.M. Doherty and B. Clarke (eds), *Proceedings of the Marketing Illuminations Spectacular* (Belfast: University of Ulster, 1997): 167–78.

30. Eric Arnould and Linda Price, 'River magic: Extraordinary experience and the extended service encounter', *Journal of Consumer Research* 20 (June 1993): 24–45.

31. Molly O'Neill, 'As life gets more complex, magic casts a wider spell', *New York Times* (13 June 1994): A1 (2).

32. Stephen Brown, *Wizard. Harry Potter's Brand Magic* (London: Cyan books, 2005).

33. http://uk.adforum.com/top5/worldwide/276/34472543, accessed 2 May 2012.

34. Douglas B. Holt and Craig J. Thompson, 'Man-of-Action heroes: the pursuit of heroic masculinity in everyday consumption', *Journal of Consumer Research* 31 (September 2004): 425–40.

35. Conrad Phillip Kottak, 'Anthropological Analysis of Mass Enculturation', in Conrad P. Kottak (ed.), *Researching American Culture* (Ann Arbor, MI: University of Michigan Press, 1982): 40–74.

36. Benoît Heilbrunn, 'Brave New Brands. Cultural Branding between Utopia and A-topia', in J. Schroeder and

M-Salzer-Mörling (eds), *Brand Culture* (London: Routledge, 2006): 103–17.

37. Eric Ransdell, 'The Nike Story? Just Tell It!' *Fast Company* (January–February 2000): 44. For example, they recount tales about the coach of the Oregon track team who poured rubber into his family waffle iron to make better shoes for his team – the origin of the Nike waffle sole. The stories emphasize the dedication of runners and coaches to reinforce the importance of teamwork. Rookies even visit the track where the coach worked to be sure they grasp the importance of the Nike legends. And rumour has it that senior Nike executives (including the CEO) have a 'swoosh' tattoo on their backsides.

38. Douglas B. Holt and Douglas Cameron, *Cultural strategy: Using innovative ideologies to build breakthrough brands* (Oxford: Oxford University Press, 2010).

39. Douglas B. Holt, 'Jack Daniels' America. Iconic brands as parasites and proselytizers', *Journal of Consumer Culture*, 6 (3, 2006), 355–377.

40. Marius K. Luedicke, Craig J. Thompson and Markus Giesler, 'Consumer identity work as moral protagonism: How myth and ideology animate a brand-mediated moral conflict', *Journal of Consumer Research*, 36 (April 2010), 1016–1032.

41. Dorthe Brogård kristensen, Heidi Boye and Søren Askegaard, 'Leaving the Milky Way! The formation of a consumer counter mythology', *Journal of Consumer Culture*, 11 (2, 2011), 195–214.

42. Jonathan E. Schroeder and Janet L. Borgerson, 'Packaging Paradise: Consuming Hawaiian Music', in Eric Arnould and Linda Scott (eds), *Advances in Consumer Research* 26 (Provo, UT: Association for Consumer Research, 1999): 46–50.

43. Robin Canniford and Avi Shankar, 'Marketing the Savage: Appropriating Tribal Tropes', in B. Cova, R. Kozinets and A. Shankar (eds), *Consumer Tribes* (London: Butterworth Heinemann, 2007): 35–48.

44. Güliz Ger and Fabian Csaba, 'Flying Carpets: The Production and Consumption of Tradition and Mystique', in S. Hoch and R. Meyer (eds), *Advances in Consumer Research* 27 (Provo, UT: Association for Consumer Research, 2000): 132–7.

45. Joseph Campbell, *Myths, Dreams, and Religion* (New York: E.P. Dutton, 1970).

46. Sidney J. Levy, 'Interpreting consumer mythology: A structural approach to consumer behavior', *Journal of Marketing* 45 (Summer 1981): 49–61.

47. Alan Bradshaw and Morris Holbrook, 'Remembering Chet: Theorizing the mythology of the self-destructive bohemian artist as self-producer and self-consumer in the market for romanticism', *Marketing Theory* 7(2) (2007): 115–36.

48. Jeffrey S. Lang and Patrick Trimble, 'Whatever happened to the man of tomorrow? An examination of the American monomyth and the comic book superhero', *Journal of Popular Culture* 22 (Winter 1988): 157.

49. Yumiko Ono, 'PepsiCo's "American" superhero in Japanese ads is alien to U.S.', *Wall Street Journal Interactive Edition* (23 May 1997).

50. James Fitchett, Douglas Brownlie and Michael Saren, 'On the Cultural Location of Consumption: The Case of Einstein as a Commodity', in *Marketing for an Expanding Europe*, Proceedings of the 25th EMAC Conference (ed.) J. Berács, A. Bauer and J. Simon (Budapest: Budapest University of Economic Sciences, 1996): 435–53; James Fitchett and Michael Saren, 'Consuming Einstein: The Nine Billion Names of the Commodity', in Brown, Doherty and Clarke (eds), *Proceedings of the Marketing Illuminations Spectacular*: 252–63.

51. Elizabeth C. Hirschman, 'Movies as Myths: An Interpretation of Motion Picture Mythology', in Jean Umiker-Sebeok (ed.), *Marketing and Semiotics: New Directions in the Study of Signs for Sale* (Berlin: Mouton de Guyter, 1987): 335–74.

52. *Markedsføring* 1 (1999): 18.

53. Dick Hebdige, 'Object as Image: The Italian Scooter Cycle', in J.B. Schor and D.B. Holt (eds), *The Consumer Society Reader* (New York: The New Press, 2000): 117–54.

54. Stephen Brown, 'Retro-marketing: Yesterday's tomorrows, today', *Marketing Intelligence and Planning* 17(7) (1999): 363–76.

55. Russell W. Belk and Rosa Llamas, 'Paradise lost: The making of Shangri-La'. Videography presented at the Association for Consumer Research European Conference, London: Royal Holloway, June 30–July 3 2010.

56. Benoît Heilbrunn, 'My Brand the Hero? A Semiotic Analysis of the Consumer-Brand Relationship', in M. Lambkin *et al.* (eds), *European Perspectives on Consumer Behaviour* (London: Prentice-Hall, 1998): 370–401.

57. See Rook, 'The ritual dimension of consumer behavior', *op. cit.*; Tetreault and Kleine, 'Ritual, ritualized behavior, and habit', *op. cit.*

58. Kieran Tucker, 'The Value of Ritual Theory for Understanding Alcohol Consumption Behaviours', in K. Ekström and H. Brembeck (eds), *European Advances in Consumer Research* 7 (Duluth, MN: Association for Consumer Research, 2006): 635–640; Emma Banister and Maria Piacenitini, 'Drunk and (Dis)Orderly: The Role of Alcohol in Supporting Liminality' in A.Y. Lee and D. Soman (eds), *Advances in Consumer Research* XXXV (Duluth, MN: Association for Consumer Research, 2008): 311–18.

59. Deborah Ball, 'British Drinkers of Guinness Say They'd Rather Take It Slow', *Wall Street Journal* (22 May 2003), www.wsj.com, accessed 22 May 2003.

60. Karl Greenberg, 'BBDO: Successful Brands Become Hard Habit for Consumers to Break', *Marketing Daily* (14 May 2007), available from http://www.mediapost.com, accessed 14 May 2007.

61. 'The skill of the chase', *Marketing Week* (30 April 1993): 38–40.

62. Bill McDowell, 'Starbucks is ground zero in today's coffee culture', *Advertising Age* (9 December 1996): 1 (2 pp.). For a discussion of the act of coffee drinking as ritual, see Susan Fournier and Julie L. Yao, 'Reviving Brand Loyalty: A Reconceptualization within the Framework of Consumer–Brand Relationships', working paper 96–039, Harvard Business School, 1996.

63. Dannie Kjeldgaard and Jacob Östberg, 'Coffee grounds and the global cup: Glocal consumer culture in Scandinavia', *Consumption, Culture and Markets* 10(2) (2007): 175–88. See also Craig Thompson and Zeynep Arsel, 'The Starbucks brandscape and consumers' (anti-corporate) experiences of glocalization', *Journal of Consumer Research* 31 (December 2004): 631–42.

64. Farnaz Fassisi, 'As authorities frown, Valentine's Day finds place in Iran's heart', *The Wall Street Journal* (12 February 2004), http://online.wsj.com/article/0,,SB107654405884 327601,00.html?mod=home%5Fpage%5Fone%5Fus

65. Robert Grafton Small, 'Consumption and significance: Everyday life in a brand-new second-hand bow tie', *European Journal of Marketing* 27(8) (1993): 38–45.

66. Grant McCracken, *Culture and Consumption* (Bloomington, IN: Indiana University Press, 1988).

67. Michelle R. Nelson, Mark A. Rademacher and Hye-Jin Park, 'Downshifting consumer = upshifting citizen? An examination of a local freecycle community', *ANNALS of the American Academy of Political and Social Science*, 611 (2007): 141–156.

68. Pia A. Albinsson and B. Yasanthi Perera, 'From trash to treasure and beyond: The meaning of voluntary disposition', *Journal of Consumer Behaviour*, 8 (2009): 340–353.

69. Helene Cherrier, 'Disposal and simple living: Exploring the circulation of goods and the development of sacred consumption', *Journal of Consumer Behaviour*, 8 (2009): 327–339.

70. Benedetta Cappellini, 'The sacrifice of re-use: The travels of leftovers and family relations', *Journal of Consumer Behaviour*, 8 (2009), 365–375.

71. 'Lynx to create chain of male grooming stores', *Marketing* (24 August 2000): 5.

72. Dennis W. Rook and Sidney J. Levy, 'Psychosocial Themes in Consumer Grooming Rituals', in Richard P. Bagozzi and Alice M. Tybout (eds), *Advances in Consumer Research* 10 (Provo, UT: Association for Consumer Research, 1983): 329–33.

73. Diane Barthel, *Putting on Appearances: Gender and Attractiveness* (Philadelphia: Temple University Press, 1988).

74. Quoted in *ibid.*

75. Russell W. Belk, Melanie Wallendorf and John Sherry Jr, 'The sacred and the profane in consumer behavior: Theodicy on the odyssey', *Journal of Consumer Research* 16 (June 1989): 1–38.

76. Tina M. Lowrey, Cele C. Otnes and Julie A. Ruth, 'Social influences on dyadic giving over time: A taxonomy from the giver's perspective,' *Journal of Consumer Research* 30 (March 2004): 547–58.

77. Russell W. Belk and Gregory S. Coon, 'Gift giving as agapic love: An alternative to the exchange paradigm based on dating experiences', *Journal of Consumer Research* 20 (December 1993) 3: 393–417.

78. Julie A. Ruth, Cele C. Otnes and Frederic F. Brunel, 'Gift receipt and the reformulation of interpersonal relationships', *Journal of Consumer Research* 25 (March 1999): 385–402.

79. Colin Camerer, 'Gifts as economic signals and social symbols', *American Journal of Sociology* 94 (Supplement 1988): S180–214.

80. Robert T. Green and Dana L. Alden, 'Functional equivalence in cross-cultural consumer behavior: Gift giving in Japan and the United States', *Psychology and Marketing* 5 (Summer 1988): 155–68.

81. Hiroshi Tanaka and Miki Iwamura, 'Gift Selection Strategy of Japanese Seasonal Gift Purchasers: An Explorative Study', paper presented at the Association for Consumer Research, Boston, October 1994.

82. John F. Sherry Jr, 'Gift giving in anthropological perspective', *Journal of Consumer Research* 10 (September 1983): 157–68.

83. Daniel Goleman, 'What's under the tree? Clues to a relationship', *New York Times* (19 December 1989): C1.

84. John F. Sherry Jr, Mary Ann McGrath and Sidney J. Levy, 'The dark side of the gift', *Journal of Business Research* 28(3) (1993): 225–45.

85. Jean-Sebastien Marcoux, 'Escaping the gift economy', *Journal of Consumer Research*, 36 (December 2009): 671–685.

86. David Glen Mick and Michelle DeMoss, 'Self-gifts: Phenomenological insights from four contexts', *Journal of Consumer Research* 17 (December 1990): 327; John F. Sherry Jr, Mary Ann McGrath and Sidney J. Levy, 'Egocentric Consumption: Anatomy of Gifts Given to the Self', in John F. Sherry Jr (ed.), *Contemporary Marketing and Consumer Behavior: An Anthropological Sourcebook* (Thousand Oaks, CA: Sage, 1995).

87. Markus Giesler, 'Consumer gift systems', *Journal of Consumer Research* 33 (September 2006): 283–90.

88. Markus Giesler, 'Conflict and compromise: Drama in marketplace evolution', *Journal of Consumer Research* 34 (April 2008): 739–53.

89. ErciliaGarcia-Alvarez, Jordi Lopez-Sintas and Konstantina Zerva, 'A contextual theory of accessing music: Consumer behavior and ethical arguments', *Consumption, Markets and Culture*, 12 (3, September 2009): 243–264.

90. Antje Cockrill and Mark M.H. Goode, 'DVD pirating intentions, Angels, devils, chancers and receivers', *Journal of Consumer Behaviour*, 11 (2012): 1–10.

91. On tourism as a central part of modern life, see John Urry, *The Tourist Gaze: Leisure and Travel in Contemporary Societies* (London: Sage, 1990), and John Urry, *Consuming Places* (London: Routledge, 1995). Scandinavians (or those who read Swedish) may also consult Tom Odell (ed.), *Nonstop! Turist i upplevelsesindustrialismen* (Lund: Historiska Media, 1999).

92. See, for example, Russell W. Belk, 'Halloween: An Evolving American Consumption Ritual', in Pollay, Gorn and Goldberg (eds), *Advances in Consumer Research* 17: 508–17; Melanie Wallendorf and Eric J. Arnould, 'We gather together: The consumption rituals of Thanksgiving Day', *Journal of Consumer Research* 18 (June 1991): 13–31.

93. Marc Augé, 'Un ethnologue à Euro Disneyland', *Le Monde Diplomatique* (September 1994).

94. Bruno Bettelheim, *The Uses of Enchantment: The Meaning and Importance of Fairy Tales* (New York: Alfred A. Knopf, 1976).

95. Ilona Mikkonen, Johanna Moisander and A. Fuat Firat, 'Cynical identity projects as consumer resistance – the Scrooge as a social critic?', *Consumption, Markets and Culture*, 14 (March 2011): 99–116.

96. Brian Moeran and Lise Skov, 'Cinderella Christmas: Kitsch, Consumerism and Youth in Japan', in D. Miller (ed.), *Unwrapping Christmas* (Oxford: Oxford University Press, 1993): 105–33.

97. *Markedsføring* 1 (1999): 4.

98. Anne Swardson, 'Trick or treat? In Paris, it's dress, dance, eat', *International Herald Tribune* (31 October 1996): 2.

99. http://www.dr.dk/Nyheder/Kultur/2008/10/29/, accessed 1 November 2008.

100. Tuba Ustuner, Güliz Ger and Douglas B. Holt, 'Consuming Ritual: Reframing the Turkish Henna-Night Ceremony', in Hoch and Meyer (eds), *Advances in Consumer Research* 27: 209–14.

101. Michael R. Solomon and Punam Anand, 'Ritual Costumes and Status Transition: The Female Business Suit as Totemic Emblem', in Elizabeth C. Hirschman and Morris Holbrook (eds), *Advances in Consumer Research* 12 (Washington, DC: Association for Consumer Research, 1985): 315–18.

102. Arnold Van Gennep, *The Rites of Passage*, trans. Maika B. Vizedom and Gabrielle L. Caffee (London: Routledge & Kegan Paul, 1960; orig. published 1908); Solomon and Anand, 'Ritual costumes and status transition', *op. cit.*

103. Stephanie O'Donohoe and Darach Turley, 'Dealing with Death: Art, Mortality and the Marketplace', in S. Brown and A. Patterson (eds), *Imagining Marketing, Art, Aesthetics, and the Avant-Garde* (London: Routledge, 2001): 86–106.

104. Walter W. Whitaker III, 'The Contemporary American Funeral Ritual', in Ray B. Browne (ed.), *Rites and Ceremonies in Popular Culture* (Bowling Green, OH: Bowling Green University Popular Press, 1980): 316–25.

105. Samuel K. Bonsu and Russell W. Belk, 'Do not go cheaply into that good night: Death-ritual consumption in Asante, Ghana', *Journal of Consumer Research* 30 (June 2003): 41–55; *cf.* also Stephanie O'Donohoe and Darach Turley, 'Till death do us part? Consumption and the negotiation of relationships following a bereavement', *Advances in Consumer Research* 32(1) (2005): 625–26.

106. Darach Turley, 'Bidding Brigid: Objects of petition and the euphemerized goddess', paper presented at the Association for Consumer Research conference, San Francisco, October 2008.

107. On sacredness in tourism, see, for example, Urry, *The Tourist Gaze* (London: Sage 1990) and Urry, *Consuming Places* (London: Routledge, 1995).

108. Robert V. Kozinets, John F. Sherry Jr, Diana Storm, Adam Duhachek, Krittinee Nuttavuthisit and Benet DeBerry-Spence, 'Ludic agency and retail spectacle', *Journal of Consumer Research* 31 (December 2004): 658–72.

109. Simone Pettigrew, 'Hearts and minds: children's experiences of Disney World', *Consumption, Markets and Culture*, 14 (June 2011): 145–161. See also Shona Bettany and Russell W. Belk 'Disney discourses of self and Other: Animality, primitivity, modernity and postmodernity', *Consumption, Markets and Culture*, 14 (June 2011): 163–176.

110. Kottak, 'Anthropological analysis of mass enculturation', *op. cit.*: 40–74.

111. Gerry Pratt, 'The House as an Expression of Social Worlds', in James S. Duncan (ed.), *Housing and Identity: Cross-Cultural Perspectives* (London: Croom Helm, 1981): 135–79; Michael R. Solomon, 'The role of the surrogate consumer in service delivery', *Service Industries Journal* 7 (July 1987): 292–307.

112. Malene Djursaa and Simon Ulrik Kragh, 'Syntax and Creolization in Cross-Cultural Readings of Rooms', in B. Dubois, T. Lowrey, L.J. Shrum and M. Vanhuele (eds), *European Advances in Consumer Research* 4 (Provo, UT: Association for Consumer Research, 1999): 293–303.

113. Grant McCracken, '"Homeyness": A Cultural Account of One Constellation of Goods and Meanings', in Elizabeth C. Hirschman (ed.), *Interpretive Consumer Research* (Provo, UT: Association for Consumer Research, 1989): 168–84.

114. James Hirsch, 'Taking celebrity worship to new depths', *New York Times* (9 November 1988): C1.

115. Lisa Urquhart, 'A star is worn as on-line retailer grows up', *Financial Times* (22 October 2004), http://news.ft.com/cms/s/341eec5a-23c7-11d9-aee5-00000e2511c8,dwp_uuid=43da3afc-1308-11d9-b869-00000e2511c8.html

116. Russell A. Potter, 'Tupac's posthumous live tour', *New York Times*, 19 April 2012, www.nytimes.com/2012/04/20/opinion/tupac-live-and-onstage, accessed 20 April 2012.

117. Emile Durkheim, *The Elementary Forms of the Religious Life* (New York: Free Press, 1915).

118. Susan Birrell, 'Sports as ritual: Interpretations from Durkheim to Goffman', *Social Forces* 60 (1981) 2: 354–76; Daniel Q. Voigt, 'American Sporting Rituals', in Browne (ed.), *Rites and Ceremonies in Popular Culture*: 125–40.

119. 'Sale of UK publisher of classical music strikes a sour note', *Wall Street Journal Europe* (9 September 1997): 1, 4.

120. Søren Askegaard, 'Marketing, the performing arts, and social change: Beyond the legitimacy crisis', *Consumption, Markets and Culture* 3(1) (1999): 1–25.

121. Simona Botti, 'What Role for Marketing in the Arts? An Analysis of Art Consumption and Artistic Value', in Y. Evrard, W. Hoyer and A. Strazzieri (eds), *Proceedings of the Third International Research Seminar on Marketing Communications and Consumer Behavior* (Aix-en-Provence: IAE, 1999).

122. See also Luca M. Visconti, John F. Sherry Jr, Stefania Borghini and Laurie Anderson, 'Street art, sweet art? Reclaiming the "public" in public space', *Journal of Consumer Research*, 37 (October 2010): 511–529.

123. Brown and Patterson (eds), *Imagining Marketing, Art, Aesthetics, and the Avant-Garde* (London: Routledge, 2000).

124. Urry, *The Tourist Gaze, op. cit.*

125. Belk *et al.*, 'The sacred and the profane in consumer behavior', *op. cit.*

126. Beverly Gordon, 'The souvenir: Messenger of the extra-ordinary', *Journal of Popular Culture* 20 (1986) 3: 135–46.

127. 'Even at the dinner for the Nobel prizes, they steal the spoons', *Wall Street Journal* (7 December 2000): A1, A16.

128. Pauline Maclaran and Linda Scott, 'Spiritual Tourism: Mystical Merchandise and Sacred Shopping in Glastonbury', paper presented at the Association for Consumer Research conference, San Francisco (October 2008).

129. Belk *et al.*, 'The sacred and the profane in consumer behavior', *op. cit.*

130. Güliz Ger and Olga Kravets (2007), 'Rediscovering Sacred Times in the Mundane: Tea Drinking in Turkey', Consuming Routines: Rhythms, Ruptures, and the Temporalities of Consumption, International Workshop, European University Institute, Florence, Italy, 3–5 May; *cf.* also Güliz Ger 'Religion and consumption: The profane sacred', *Advances in Consumer Research* 32(1) (2005): 79–81.

131. Belk *et al.*, 'The sacred and the profane in consumer behavior', *op. cit.*

132. Deborah Hofmann, 'In jewelry, choices sacred and profane, ancient and new', *New York Times* (7 May 1989).

133. Diego Rinallo, 'Living a Magical Life: Sacred Consumption and Spiritual Experience in the Italian Neo-Pagan Community', paper presented at the Association for Consumer Research conference, San Francisco (October 2008).

134. http://www.brusselsjournal.com/node/2775, accessed 2 May 2012.

135. http://www.ciibroadcasting.com/2012/04/10/real-madrid-remove-emblem-cross-for-muslim-fans/, accessed 2 May 2012.

136. Roberto Grandi, 'Benetton's Advertising: A Case History of Postmodern Communication', unpublished manuscript, Center for Modern Culture and Media, University of Bologna, 1994; Shawn Tully, 'Teens: The most global market of all', *Fortune* (16 May 1994): 90–7.

137. Quoted in 'Public relations firm to present anti-abortion effort to bishops', *New York Times* (14 August 1990): A12.

138. Per Østergaard, 'The Broadened Concept of Marketing as a Manifestation of the Postmodern Condition', in *Marketing Theory and Applications*, Proceedings of the AMA Winter Educators Conference 4, R. Varandarajan and B. Jaworski (eds), (Chicago: American Marketing Association, 1993): 234–9.

139. Russell W. Belk and Gülnur Tumbat, 'The cult of Macintosh', *Consumption, Markets and Culture* 8(3) (2005): 205–17.

140. Dan L. Sherrell, Alvin C. Burns and Melodie R. Phillips, 'Fixed Consumption Behavior: The Case of Enduring Acquisition in a Product Category', in Robert L. King (ed.), *Developments in Marketing Science* 14 (1991): 36–40.

141. Russell W. Belk, 'Acquiring, Possessing, and Collecting: Fundamental Processes in Consumer Behavior', in Ronald F. Bushard and Shelby D. Hunt (eds), *Marketing Theory: Philosophy of Science Perspectives* (Chicago: AMA, 1982): 185–90.

142. For an extensive bibliography on collecting, see Russell W. Belk, *Collecting in a Consumer Culture* (London: Routledge, 1995), or Russell W. Belk, Melanie Wallendorf, John F. Sherry Jr and Morris B. Holbrook, 'Collecting in a Consumer Culture', in Russell W. Belk (ed.), *Highways and Buyways* (Provo, UT: Association for Consumer Research, 1991): 178–215. See also Janine Romina Lovatt, 'The People's Show Festival 1994: A Survey', in S. Pearce (ed.), *Experiencing Material Culture in the Western World* (London: Leicester University Press, 1997): 196–254; Werner Muensterberg, *Collecting: An Unruly Passion* (Princeton, NJ: Princeton University Press, 1994); Melanie Wallendorf and Eric J. Arnould, '"My favorite things": A cross-cultural inquiry into object attachment, possessiveness, and social linkage', *Journal of Consumer Research* 14 (March 1988): 531–47. See also Nia Hughes 'Consumption and Collections: the impact of collecting on the construction of identity', unpublished doctoral thesis Lancaster University: July 2008; N Hughes and M.K. Hogg, 'Conceptualizing and exploring couple dyads in the world of collecting', 2006, *Advances in Consumer Research* XXXIII, C. Pechman and L. Price Duluth (eds), MN: Association for Consumer Research 124–130; N. Hughes and M.K. Hogg, 'Problematizing gendered interpretations of collecting behaviour', *Gender, Marketing and Consumer Behavior, Eighth Conference*, Lorna Stevens and Janet Borgerson (eds), Association for Consumer Research, Edinburgh, June 2006.

143. Quoted in Ruth Ann Smith, 'Collecting as Consumption: A Grounded Theory of Collecting Behavior', unpublished manuscript, Virginia Polytechnic Institute and State University, 1994: 14.

144. See Belk, *Collecting in a Consumer Culture, op. cit.*

145. 'A feeding frenzy for Swatches', *New York Times* (29 August 1991): C3; Patricia Leigh Brown, 'Fueling a frenzy: Swatch', *New York Times* (10 May 1992): 1, 9; Mary M. Long and Leon G. Schiffman, 'Swatch fever: An allegory for understanding the paradox of collecting', *Psychology and Marketing* 14 (August 1997) 5: 495–509.

146. Jan Slater, 'Collecting the Real Thing: A Case Study Exploration of Brand Loyalty Enhancement Among Coca-Cola Brand Collectors', in Hoch and Meyer (eds), *Advances in Consumer Research* 27: 202–8.

14 CULTURAL CHANGE PROCESSES

CHAPTER OBJECTIVES

When you finish reading this chapter you will understand why:

→ Styles are like mirrors that reflect underlying cultural conditions.

→ We distinguish between high and low culture, but it is increasingly difficult to do so.

→ Many modern marketers are reality engineers.

→ New products, services and ideas spread through a population, and different types of people are more or less likely to adopt them.

→ Fashion is organized as a system that involves many people, organizations and media.

→ Fashion communicates symbolic meanings of imitation and differentiation to consumers.

→ Fashion follows cycles.

JOOST AND LIEKE have just arrived in Chicago from Amsterdam, and they are checking in to a new hotel EDEN not too far from the Chicago downtown area. Joost is tired after the flight and looks forward to throwing himself on the bed and maybe grabbing a small bottle of something from the minibar, just to wind down. When they arrive in the room, the first thing that catches Joost's attention is a funny kind of thin mattress rolled up in the closet. 'I hope this is not the bed' he thinks to himself, and quickly reassures himself that there are indeed nice big and comfortable beds. He searches – in vain – for the minibar, and finally asks Lieke if she has any idea whether there is one in the room. 'I suppose not', she answers. 'The EDEN hotels are oriented towards wellness, fitness, relaxation for mind and body and healthy eating, so I guess a minibar does not really fit into that concept'. Joost looks very puzzled. 'Did you not see the yoga mattress when we entered the room?' Lieke asks. Joost's reply is prompt – 'Why on earth did you book a hotel room in a fitness centre?' he almost shouts. 'Well, I saw this on the internet – it is a completely new chain and I felt that it might be good to not have to give up my yoga and exercise programmes just because we are away from home – and the food can be so greasy in the United States. I am sure it will do us both good to spend the next week in a healthy environment'. Joost sits down on the bed with a big sigh – 'A "luxury hotel" without a minibar but with yoga mattress and health food – what is the world coming to?', he thinks to himself. Not exactly the kind of arrival he had had in mind . . .[1]

INTRODUCTION

Fashion tattoos. Vuitton handbags. Free-range eggs. Lady Gaga. High-tech furniture. Flash mobs. Postmodern architecture. *Angry Birds*. Personal coaching. Tablets. Hybrid cars. Costa Rican ecotours. Gladiator sandals. We inhabit a world that brims with different styles and possibilities. The food we eat, the cars we drive, the clothes we wear, the places we live and work, the music we listen to – the ebb and flow of popular culture and fashion influences all of them.

Consumers may at times feel overwhelmed by the sheer choice in the marketplace. A person trying to decide on something as routine as what to have for lunch has many hundreds of alternatives from which to choose. Despite this seeming abundance, however, the options available to consumers at any point in time actually represent only a *small fraction* of the total set of possibilities. In this chapter, we shall follow marketers' and cultural gatekeepers' attempts to set their marks on which possibilities get the most attention and which trends and tendencies become victorious in the battle for a place in our minds as consumers. We will take a closer look at the processes of change driving the ever-changing styles of consumption we are presented with. In Chapter 2, we saw how culture and consumption are related through a meaning system, linking culture with consumption through systems of fashion and advertising and through a variety of consumer rituals. In the last chapter, we took a closer look at the rituals, and at some of the cultural mythologies of the advertising system. In this chapter, referring back to Figure 2.1 we will look at how fashions and consumption styles spread within and among societies.

Even though most of the consumers we have been dealing with in this book may live in Western middle-class areas each with their national and local characteristics, they are often able to 'connect' symbolically with millions of other young consumers by relating to styles that originated far away – even though the original meanings of those styles may have little relevance to them. The spread of fashions in consumption is just one example of what happens when the meanings created by some members of a culture are interpreted and produced for mass consumption.

Take the example of rap music. Baggy jeans and outfits featuring gold vinyl skirts, huge gold chains and bejewelled baseball caps, which used to be seen only on the streets of impoverished urban areas, are being adapted by *haute couture* fashion designers for the catwalks of Manhattan and Paris. In addition, a high proportion of people who buy recordings of rap music are white. How did rap music and fashions, which began as forms of expression in the black urban subculture, make it to mainstream America and the rest of the world? A brief chronology is given in Table 14.1.

Table 14.1 The mainstreaming of popular music and fashion

Date	Event
1968	Bronx DJ Kool Herc invents hip-hop.
1973–8	Urban block parties feature break-dancing and graffiti.
1979	A small record company named Sugar Hill becomes the first rap label.
1980	Manhattan art galleries feature graffiti artists.
1981	Blondie's song 'Rapture' hits number one in the charts.
1985	Columbia Records buys the Def Jam label.
1988	MTV begins *Yo! MTV* Raps, featuring Fab 5 Freddy.
1990	Hollywood gets into the act with the hip-hop film *House Party*; Ice-T's rap album is a big hit on college radio stations; amid controversy, white rapper Vanilla Ice hits the big time; NBC launches a new sitcom, *Fresh Prince of Bel Air*.

Table 14.1 (*continued*)

Date	Event
1991	Mattel introduces its Hammer doll (a likeness of the rap star Hammer, formerly known as M.C. Hammer); designer Karl Lagerfeld shows shiny vinyl raincoats and chain belts in his Chanel collection; designer Charlotte Neuville sells gold vinyl suits with matching baseball caps for $800; Isaac Mizrahi features wide-brimmed caps and takeoffs on African medallions; Bloomingdale's launches Anne Klein's rap-inspired clothing line by featuring a rap performance in its Manhattan store.
1992	Rappers start to abandon this look, turning to low-fitting baggy jeans, sometimes worn backwards; white rapper Marky Mark appears in a national campaign wearing Calvin Klein underwear, exposed above his hip-hugging pants; composer Quincy Jones launches *Vibe* magazine and it wins over many white readers.[2]
1993	Hip-hop fashions and slang continue to cross over into mainstream consumer culture. An outdoor ad for Coca-Cola proclaims, 'Get Yours 24-7'. The company is confident that many viewers in its target market will know that the phrase is urban slang for 'always' (24 hours a day, 7 days a week).[3]
1994	The (late) Italian designer Versace pushes oversized overalls favoured by urban youngsters. In one ad, he asks, 'Overalls with an oversize look, something like what rappers and homeboys wear. Why not a sophisticated version?'[4]
1996	Tommy Hilfiger, a designer who was the darling of the preppie set, turns hip-hop. He gives free wardrobes to rap artists such as Grand Puba and Chef Raekwon, and in return finds his name mentioned in rap songs – the ultimate endorsement. The September 1996 issue of *Rolling Stone* features the Fugees; several band members prominently display the Hilfiger logo. In the same year the designer uses rap stars Method Man and Treach of Naughty by Nature as runway models. Hilfiger's new Tommy Girl perfume plays on his name but also is a reference to the New York hip-hop record label Tommy Boy.[5]
1997	Coca-Cola features rapper L.L. Cool J. in a commercial that debuts in the middle of the sitcom *In the House*, a TV show starring the singer.[6]
1998	In their battle with Dockers for an increased share of the khaki market, Gap launches its first global advertising campaign. One of the commercials, 'Khakis Groove', includes a hip-hop dance performance set to music by Bill Mason.[7]
1999	Rapper turned entrepreneur Sean (Puffy) Combs introduces an upscale line of menswear he calls 'urban high fashion'. New companies FUBU, Mecca and Enyce attain financial success in the multibillion-dollar industry.[8] Lauryn Hill and the Fugees sing at a party sponsored by upscale Italian clothier Emporio Armani and she proclaims, 'We just wanna thank Armani for giving a few kids from the ghetto some great suits.'[9]
2000	**360hip-hop.com**, a web-based community dedicated to the hip-hop culture, is launched. In addition to promoting the hip-hop lifestyle, the site allows consumers to purchase clothing and music online while watching video interviews with such artists as Will Smith and Busta Rymes.[10]
2001	Hip-hop dancing becomes the rage among China's youth, who refer to it as *jiew*, or street dancing.[11]
2003	Hip-hop finds its way into toy stores. Toy manufacturers start mimicking the hip-hop practice of using the letter 'Z' instead of the letter 'S' in names. This trend started with the 1991 film *Boyz N The Hood* (a title that was itself borrowed from a 1989 song by the rap group N.W.A.).[12]
2005	The fusion of hip hop and brand culture becomes ever more evident. The global fast-food chain McDonald's offers to pay rappers €4.15 every time a song is played which drops the name of the 'Big-Mac'. Artists who have 'referenced' well-known products include Jay-Z, 50 Cent and Snoop Dogg. Among the happy beneficiaries have been brands such as Courvoisier, Gucci, Dom Perignon, Bentley and Porsche.[13]
2008	Glocal hip hop: hip-hop increasingly disengages from its American roots as artists around the world develop their own localized interpretations, for example aboriginal Australian hip-hop,[14] a Portuguese thriving hip-hop scene based on immigrant populations,[15] and an Islamic hip-hop, and rap with lyrics promoting moralities very different from the original 'booze and girls'.[16]
until 2012	The 'domestication' of hip hop. Some of the outrageousness seems to have gone from the scene. Jay-Z and Beyoncé have become parents, and companies like Rocawear offer hip-hop outfits for the kids.[17]

It's common for mainstream culture to modify symbols from 'cutting-edge' subcultures for a larger audience to consume. As this occurs, these cultural products undergo a process of **co-optation**, where outsiders transform their original meanings. This happened to rap music, which is divorced to a large extent from its original connection with the struggles of young African Americans and is now a mainstream entertainment format.[18] One writer sees the white part of the 'hip-hop nation' as a series of concentric rings. In the centre are those who actually know African Americans and understand their culture. The next ring consists of those who have indirect knowledge of this subculture via friends or relatives but who do not actually rap, spray-paint, or break-dance. Then, there are those a bit further out who simply play hip-hop between other types of music. Finally come the more suburban 'wiggers', who simply try to catch on to the next popular craze.[19] As was mentioned in Table 14.1, these cultural expressions also change when they move from one cultural context to another. Although, on the surface of it, Afro-American and French Arab and African urban and suburban street cultures may look alike, both in terms of musical styles and an affectionate relationship with sneakers, the consumption of the sneaker which in the American context is included in the countercultural statement is more a fashion statement in the French context.[20] The spread of hip-hop fashions and music is only one example of what happens when the marketing system takes a set of subcultural meanings, reinterprets them, and produces them for mass consumption.[21]

Cultural selection

The selection of certain alternatives over others – whether cars, dresses, computers, recording artists, political candidates, religions or even scientific methodologies – is the culmination of a complex filtration process resembling a funnel, as depicted in Figure 14.1. Many possibilities initially compete for adoption, and these are steadily narrowed down as they make their way down the path from conception to consumption in a process of **cultural selection**.

The internet has made the spotting and selection of the various trends and changes in society, the symbol pool, easier. New trend-watching services can be paid for scouring the world for new possibilities in colours, fabrics, designs or combinations. They can access pictures from runways of great fashion shows, look at store decorations from H&M or Zara, or look at photos of cool London/Paris/Amsterdam/Berlin youngsters sporting the latest rebellious twist to the clothing companies' standard offerings. Even though the subscription to these services is costly, many companies think they are well worth their price, because they save in business trips and other types of costly trend-spotting fieldwork.[22]

Web 2.0 has made the communication system for the trends and fashion even more complex, but also more democratic. With the rise of fashion blogs, everyone can become a gatekeeper (see section on cultural gatekeepers below) and promoter for trends and fashions, provided that you are capable of building the necessary trust in your site. One website offers an overview over the most influential blogs based on a fairly explicit and, given all the problems in such a ranking, also fairly reliable methodology.[23] Interestingly, the most influential blog in the spring 2012 version of the ranking – The Sartorialist,[24] consists of street photos of 'ordinary people' from cities like Paris, London, Florence, Milan and New York. Consumers (would like to believe that consumers) have the power . . .

Our tastes and product preferences, then, are obviously not formed in a vacuum. Choices are driven by the images presented to us in mass media, our observations of those around us, and even by our desires to live in the fantasy worlds created by marketers. These options are constantly evolving and changing. A clothing style or type of cuisine that is 'hot' one year may be 'out' the next. Some general characteristics of the evolution of styles and fashions include:

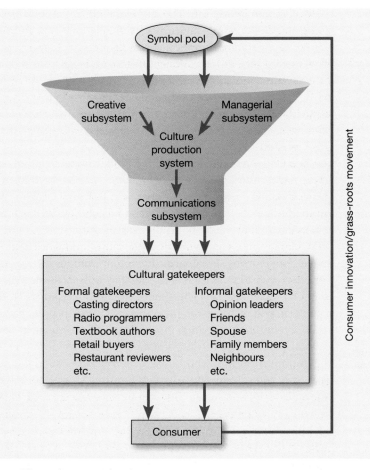

Figure 14.1 The culture production process

Source: Adapted from Michael R. Solomon, 'Building Up and Breaking Down: The Impact of Cultural Sorting on Symbolic Consumption', in J. Sheth and E.C. Hirschman (eds), *Research in Consumer Behavior* (Greenwich, CT: JAI Press, 1988): 325–51.

- Styles are a reflection of more fundamental societal trends (e.g. politics and social conditions).

- A style begins as a risky or unique statement by a relatively small group of people and then spreads as others increasingly become aware of the style and feel confident about trying it.

- Styles usually originate as an interplay between the deliberate inventions of designers and businesspeople and spontaneous actions by ordinary consumers who modify styles to suit their own needs. Designers, manufacturers and merchandisers who can anticipate what consumers want will succeed in the marketplace. In the process, they help to fuel the fire when they encourage distribution of the item.

- These cultural products travel widely, often across countries and even continents.

- Influential people in the media play a significant role in deciding which will succeed.

- Most styles eventually wear out as people continually search for new ways to express themselves and marketers scramble to keep up with these desires.

Culture production systems

No single designer, company or advertising agency is solely responsible for creating popular culture. Every product, whether a hit record, a car or a new fashion, requires the input of many different participants. The set of individuals and organizations responsible for creating and marketing a cultural product is a **cultural production system (CPS)**.[25]

The nature of these systems helps to determine the types of product that eventually emerge from them. Factors such as the number and diversity of competing systems and the amount of innovation versus conformity that is encouraged are important. For example, an analysis of the Country & Western music industry has shown that the hit records it produces tend to be similar to one another during periods when it is dominated by a few large companies, whereas there is more diversity when a greater number of producers are competing within the same market.[26]

The different members of a culture production system may not necessarily be aware of or appreciate the roles played by other members, yet many diverse agents work together to create popular culture.[27] Each member does their best to anticipate which particular images will be most attractive to a consumer market. Of course, those who are able to forecast consumers' tastes consistently will be successful over time.

With the increasing power of bloggers, the boundaries between formal and informal gatekeepers are blurring. It seems as if everyone with an internet connection can assume a self-announced position as gatekeeper, passing judgement on topics as diverse as fashion, music and food to a potentially global audience. And consumers seeking information online seem more than willing to absorb the opinions of 'real' people, peers who seemingly have no financial interest in the products they endorse. As a consequence of this 'democratization' of the cultural production process, formal gatekeepers are losing power and can merely watch as the Justin Biebers and Rebecca Blacks of tomorrow flood the gates, building audiences autonomously and earning fame through YouTube videos, not record companies. Just like everyone with an internet connection can be a gatekeeper, everyone with a videocamera has the potential to be a star.

Components of a CPS

A culture production system has three major subsystems: (1) a *creative subsystem* responsible for generating new symbols and/or products; (2) a *managerial subsystem* responsible for selecting, making tangible, mass-producing and managing the distribution of new symbols and/or products; and (3) a *communications subsystem* responsible for giving meaning to the new product and providing it with a symbolic set of attributes that are communicated to consumers.

A classic example of the three components of a culture production system for a record would be (1) a singer (e.g. Madonna, a creative subsystem); (2) a company (e.g. Atlantic Records, which manufactures and distributes Madonna's records, a managerial subsystem); and (3) the advertising and publicity agencies hired to promote the albums (a communications subsystem). Table 14.2 illustrates some of the many *cultural specialists*, operating in different subsystems, who are required to create a hit CD.

But again, in a YouTube age, there are if not easier than at least more easily accessible ways to stardom. The music industry is under increasing pressure from the digital world. With some decent computer equipment, it is possible to make a home studio and nicely sounding recordings (provided you can play and sing . . . usually!) that you can upload to YouTube yourself – and the rest maybe history. Or so at least was the history of Justin Bieber! iTunes and similar organizations increasingly take the place of the shop owners (how many music shops are left in your area?), and sites like **sellaband.com** provides facilities for hopeful artists to make some splash.

Cultural gatekeepers

Many judges or 'tastemakers' influence the products that are eventually offered to consumers. These judges, or **cultural gatekeepers**, are responsible for filtering the overload of information and materials intended for consumers. Gatekeepers include film, restaurant and car reviewers, interior designers, disc jockeys, retail buyers and magazine editors. Collectively, this set of

Table 14.2 Cultural specialists in the music industry

Specialist	Functions
Songwriter(s)	Compose music and lyrics; must reconcile artistic preferences with estimates of what will succeed in the marketplace
Performer(s)	Interpret music and lyrics; may be formed spontaneously, or may be packaged by an agent to appeal to a predetermined market (e.g. Elton John or Green Day)
Teachers and coaches	Develop and refine performers' talents
Agent	Represent performers to record companies
A&R (artist & repertoire) executive	Acquire artists for the record label
Publicists, image consultants	Create an image for the group that is transmitted to the buying public designers, stylists
Recording technicians, producers	Create a recording to be sold
Marketing executives	Make strategic decisions regarding performer's appearances, ticket pricing, promotional strategies, and so on
Video director	Interpret the song visually to create a music video that will help to promote the record
Music reviewers	Evaluate the merits of a recording for listeners
Disc jockeys, radio programme directors	Decide which records will be given airplay and/or placed in the radio stations' regular rotations
Record shop owner	Decide which of the many records produced will be stocked and/or promoted heavily in the retail environment

agents has been known as the *throughput sector*.[28] Increasingly, however, these 'occupations responsible for the production and legitimation of various images, experiences, identities and lifestyles'[29] are known as **cultural intermediaries**.[30]

Speaking the language of beauty

One study of cultural gatekeepers in the fashion and beauty industry illustrates how some cultural 'products' (in this case, fashion models) are selected and championed over other stylistic possibilities.[31] Editors at such women's magazines as *Cosmopolitan*, *Marie Claire*, *Depêche Mode* and *Elle* play an important role in selecting the specific variations of beauty that will appear in the pages of these 'bibles of fashion'. These images, in turn, will be relied on by millions of readers to decide what 'look' they would like to adopt – and, of course, which particular products and services (such as hairstyles, cosmetics, clothing styles, exercise programmes) they will need to attain these images.

In this study, decision makers at a group of influential magazines identified a small set of 'looks' that characterize many of the diverse fashion models they evaluate on a daily basis – what is more, though each editor was studied independently, overall respondents exhibited a very high level of agreement among themselves regarding what the 'looks' are, what they are called, which are more or less desirable *and* which they expect to be paired with specific product advertisements. This research suggests that cultural gatekeepers tend to rely on the same underlying cultural ideals and priorities when making the selections that in turn get passed down the channel of distribution for consideration by consumers.

We have already encountered numerous examples of the mini revolution we call consumer-generated content; companies today pay attention to everyday people's opinions when they

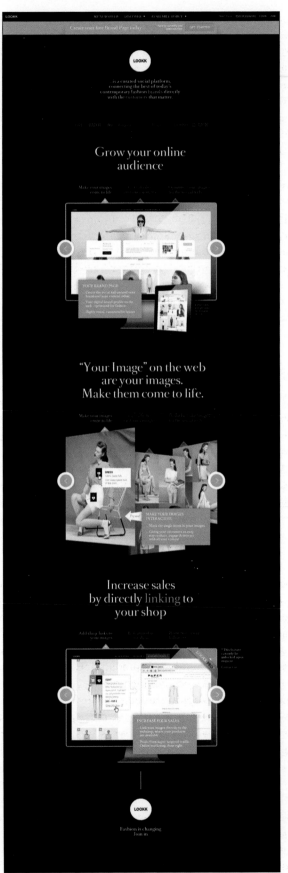

New fashion sites like LOOKK, Fabricly, Threadless and ModCloth illustrate the growing influence that customers and fans play as cultural gatekeepers. They use a crowd sourcing model that empowers buyers to determine what styles they should actually manufacture and sell. Indeed, the fashion site Moda Operandi labels itself a pretailer. It works with an exclusive base of fashionistas to encourage designers to manufacture dress designs that otherwise appeared only on catwalks.

Image from LOOKK.com, courtesy of LOOKK.

design new products, create advertising messages, or improve upon shopping experiences. The rise of social networking changes the basic process of innovation, as the consumer feedback loop in Figure 14.1 grows stronger and stronger. This shift from a top-down to a bottom-up process is a symptom of the transition from *marketerspace* where companies exert total control over the market to *consumerspace*.

Instead, we now live in *consumerspace*, where customers act as partners with companies to decide what the marketplace will offer.[32] This process is becoming more and more common – in terms of your car, your cell phone and a lot of other technology products, basically in a lot of contemporary purchase processes, the consumer contributes to the end-design of the product, thereby taking on the role of the **prosumer**. Even the foods you eat can be prosumed. In a recent study, researchers investigated the so-called community-supported agriculture, where farmers and consumers operate on shared rewards and risks. This system, the researchers underlined, is in a way countercultural to even the organic producers, who have in many cases become too large to be seen as being close to the interests of local consumers. The basic idea is that the consumer can rear their own beef, make sure that animals are living a good life, as well as support local business of high-quality and high-morality food products.[33] It should be added that some consumer researchers prefer to use the term 'working consumer' instead in order to underline that just because the consumer gets a role in the production process, it does not mean that interests of producers and consumer are necessarily harmonious.[34]

High culture and popular culture

Do Beethoven and Adele have anything in common? While both the famous composer and the British singer are associated with music, many would argue that the similarity stops here. We think it doesn't. Culture production systems create many diverse kinds of products, but in terms of how they relate to consumer culture, they might be quite similar. For example, it is not only the followers of Adele and other pop music stars that can be considered from a fan culture perspective and be divided according to their degree of investment and commitment in a particular type of music.[35] Also the audiences for classical music share some of these traits.[36] Some basic distinctions can be offered regarding the characteristics of most cultural products.

Arts and crafts

One distinction can be made between arts and crafts.[37] An **art product** is viewed primarily as an object of aesthetic contemplation without any functional value. A **craft product**, in contrast, is admired because of the beauty with which it performs some function (e.g. a ceramic bowl or hand-carved fishing lures). A piece of art is original, subtle and valuable, and is associated with the elite of society. A craft tends to follow a formula that permits rapid production. According to this framework, elite culture is produced in a purely aesthetic context and is judged by reference to recognized classics. It is high culture – 'serious art'.[38] However, many businesses and consumption practices operate in some grey area in between the two. Consider the tattoo business. Whereas tattooists are basically subject to providing the tattoos the consumers order them to produce, many do consider themselves a certain group of artists and only unwillingly accept to do, for example, brand logo tattoos. They consider it a sell-out to commercial forces where the consumer could have had an artistic expression.[39]

High art *vs* low art

It is not just that these grey areas exist. The whole distinction between high and low culture is not as clear as it may first appear. In addition to the possible class bias that drives such a distinction (i.e. we assume that the rich have culture while the poor do not), high and low culture are blending together in interesting ways. Popular culture reflects the world

At home in the world's great landscapes. ■Elddis

This advertisement demonstrates the adaptation of famous paintings ('high art') to sell products ('low art').

Used with permission of Robson Brown Advertising, Newcastle upon Tyne, England.

around us; these phenomena touch rich and poor. In many places in Europe, advertising is widely appreciated as an art form and the TV/cinema commercials have their own Cannes Festival. In France and the UK certain advertising executives are public figures in their respective countries. For over ten years, Europeans in different countries have paid relatively high entrance fees to watch an all-night programme in a cinema consisting of nothing but television commercials.[40]

The arts are big business. All cultural products that are transmitted by mass media become a part of popular culture.[41] Classical recordings are marketed in much the same way as Top-40 albums,[42] and museums use mass-marketing techniques to sell their wares. The Parisian museums even run a satellite gift shop at the Charles de Gaulle Airport. Remember the discussion of *Banksy* and the relation between street art and marketing in Chapter 13? A multinational team of consumer researchers extended the study of high and low art to the realm of *street art*, where artists create paintings, murals and other pieces in public places. They identified numerous sites where the art became an instrument that was used for 'transactions' between the artists and the people who lived in the area. Although not all reactions were positive, it was common to observe that people's experiences of public spaces were enhanced because the street art created a feeling of empowerment and ownership in formerly barren places.[43]

Marketers often incorporate high art imagery in their promotion of products. They may sponsor artistic events to build public goodwill or feature works of art on shopping bags.[44] When observers from Toyota watched customers in luxury car showrooms, the company found that these consumers tended to view a car as an art object. This theme was then used in an ad for the Lexus with the caption: 'Until now, the only fine arts we supported were sculpture, painting and music.'[45] However, the opposite also happens. Certain companies have taken to the use of consumer-generated snapshots or videos in order to generate a maximum sense of authenticity in their visual communication, *cf.* Jonathan Schroeder's reflections in his 'Consumer behaviour as I see it'. But whether companies are using high art, street art or snapshot aesthetics, everything happens in order to create a visual gimmick that is powerful enough to break through the clutter of our contemporary over-communicating marketplace.

PROFESSOR JONATHAN SCHROEDER
Rochester Institute of Technology

Consumer behaviour as I see it . . .

My interest in consumer behaviour largely focuses on visual consumption – what consumers look at, what they see, and how they make sense of the visual world. The web, among its many influences, has put a premium on understanding visual consumption. By visual consumption, I mean not just visual oriented consumer behaviour such as surfing the internet, watching videos, tourism or window-shopping, but also a methodological framework to investigate the intermingling of consumption, vision and culture, including how visual images are handled by consumer research. Thus, I pay a great deal of attention to identifying what consumers look at, how this is informed by the visual histories of contemporary images, and how those images create meaning and value. Images function within culture, and their interpretive meanings shift over time, across cultures and between consumers. My aims are interpretive rather than positive – to show how images can mean, rather than demonstrate what they mean. Image interpretation remains elusive – never complete, closed, or contained, meant to be contested and debated.

In my research, I am particularly interested in photography – which encompasses still photography, film and video – as a key consumer and information technology. Photography's technical ability to reproduce images makes it a central feature of visual consumption. In many ways, photography dominates how we conceive of people, places and things. However, most consumers receive little photographic training, and few consumer research studies place photography at the centre. Photography just is, apparently, its transparency falsely lulls us into believing no special tools are needed to comprehend its communicative power. We have become so used to photographic representation that it seems inevitable, a natural record of what exists or what has happened. Yet photography is not the truth, it is not a simple record of some reality. I find it useful to think of photography as a consumer behaviour as well as a central information technology. Furthermore, photographs tell us where we have been, who we are, and what we value.

A current research project centres on what I call 'snapshot aesthetics' – the use of snapshots or snapshot-like imagery for strategic communication, by both companies and consumers. Consumers post these images on social networking sites such as Facebook, Myspace, Friendster and bebo. Companies such as Volkswagen, IKEA, American Apparel, Ford Motor Company, Apple and Coca-Cola present snapshot-like images – straightforward, generally unposed photographs of everyday life – in their print, television and internet communications. Many recent ads portray models in classic snapshot poses – out of focus, eyes closed, poorly framed – in contrast to more traditional and historical patterns of formal studio shots or highly posed tableaux. These 'intentional' snapshots are often characterized by 'disruptions' in formal photographic traditions – off lighting, poor focus, blurred images, awkward poses, harsh shadows, and so forth, and may appear less formal, more everyday or 'real' – more 'authentic' to consumers.

I contend that snapshot aesthetics provides an important strategic resource for marketing communication. First, these photographs appear authentic, as if they are beyond the artificially constructed world of typical advertising photography. This visual quality can be harnessed to promote brands as authentic, to invoke the 'average consumer' as a credible product endorser, and to demonstrate how the brand might fit in with the regular consumer's lifestyle. Second, snapshot aesthetics supports a casual image of brands, particularly consumer lifestyle brands. Many brands appeal to less formal consumption – from family dinners to online financial management. Popular fashion brands, in particular, court casual images for their brands and

→

subbrands. Well-known examples include Burberry, Diesel and Sisley – each deploy snapshot-like photographs in high profile branding campaigns for their everyday clothing lines. In this way, photographic style helps articulate market segmentation strategy. For example, Italian designer Giorgio Armani's Collezioni clothing – his most expensive ready-to-wear collection – generally appears in classically composed black-and-white promotional images, whereas the Armani Jeans line – a more recent, entry-level brand – usually features snapshot-like images of sexualized bodies. Moreover, Burberry's successful rebranding from conservative classic to contemporary cool seemed to have benefited greatly from snapshot-like photographs, featuring the likes of supermodels Kate Moss and Stella Tennant. Furthermore, many consumers are busy creating their own ads, which are often in the snapshot style. Websites such as Current TV and YouTube offer consumers a forum to try their hand at brand communication – and occasionally successful specimens are snapped up by brand managers for more conventional broadcast. Other companies sponsor consumer-generated ads, including Converse, MasterCard and Sony.

I argue that the snapshot aesthetic embodies the experience economy by showing consumers in the midst of seemingly real, sometimes exciting, but often mundane experiences. In this way, we can think about snapshot aesthetics as an important visual aspect of documenting, marketing and understanding consumer experience.

View my research on my SSRN author page: **http://ssrn.com/author=348758**

Jonathan Schroeder

Cultural formulae

Mass culture, in contrast, churns out products specifically for a mass market. These products aim to please the average taste of an undifferentiated audience and are predictable because they follow certain patterns. As illustrated in Table 14.3, many popular art forms, such as detective stories or science fiction, generally follow a **cultural formula**, where certain roles and

Table 14.3 Cultural formulae in public art forms

Artform/genre	Classic western	Science fiction	Hard-boiled detective	Family sitcom
Time	1800s	Future	Present	Any time
Location	Edge of civilization	Space	City	Suburbs
Protagonist	Cowboy (lone individual)	Astronaut	Detective	Father (figure)
Heroine	Schoolmistress	Spacegirl	Damsel in distress	Mother (figure)
Villain	Outlaws, killers	Aliens	Killer	Boss, neighbour
Secondary characters	Townsfolk, Indians	Technicians in spacecraft	Police, underworld	Children, dogs
Plot	Restore law and order	Repel aliens	Find killer	Solve problem
Theme	Justice	Triumph of humanity	Pursuit and discovery	Chaos and confusion
Costume	Cowboy hat, boots, etc.	High-tech uniforms	Raincoat	Normal clothes
Locomotion	Horse	Spaceship	Beat-up car	Family estate car
Weaponry	Sixgun, rifle	Rayguns	Pistol, fists	Insults

Source: Arthur A. Berger, *Signs in Contemporary Culture: An Introduction to Semiotics* (New York: Longman, 1984): 86. Copyright © 1984. Reissued 1989 by Sheffield Publishing Company, Salem, WI. Reprinted with permission of the publisher.

props often occur consistently.[46] Computer programs even allow users to 'write' their own romances by systematically varying certain set elements of the story. Romance novels are an extreme case of a cultural formula. The romance novel and other formulae reflect the consumer society by the way consumption events and different brands play a role in the story and in the construction of the different atmospheres described.[47] Subcultures often draw heavily on particular cultural formulae, for example the Goth subculture uses references to the vampire universe to challenge norms about gender identity and sexuality.[48]

Reliance on these formulae also leads to a *recycling* of images, as members of the creative subsystem reach back through time for inspiration. Thus, young people in Britain watch retro channels like Granada Plus and UK Gold broadcasting classic decades-old soaps, and old themes are recycled for new soap series. A few years ago, the hippest cars for the under-30 US consumers were models often identified with the 'grandpa' generation, such as oldsmobiles and buicks from the 1970s and 1980s – the cars were, however, updated with flashy paint and state-of-the-art sound systems.[49] Designers modify styles from Victorian England or colonial Africa, DJs sample sound bits from old songs and combine them in new ways, and Gap runs ads featuring now-dead celebrities including Humphrey Bogart, Gene Kelly and Pablo Picasso dressed in khaki trousers.[50] With easy access to photoshopping and all other kinds of digital software, virtually anyone can 'remix' the past.[51]

Artists and companies in the popular music or film industry may be more guided by ideas of what could make a 'hit' than by any wish for artistic expression. And creators of aesthetic

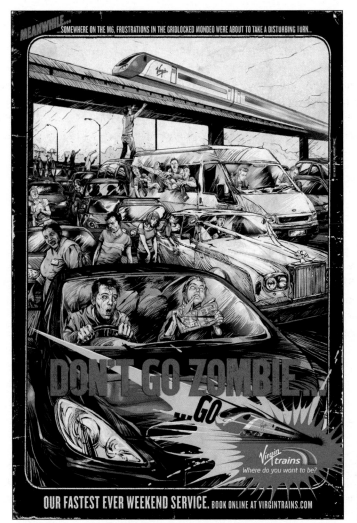

This British advertisement borrows the cultural formula of a horror movie poster.

Source: MCBD and Elvis.

products are increasingly adapting conventional marketing methods to fine-tune their mass-market offerings. In the US, market research is used, for example, to test audience reactions to film concepts. Although testing cannot account for such intangibles as acting quality or cinematography, it can determine if the basic themes of the film strike a responsive chord in the target audience. This type of research is most appropriate for blockbuster films, which usually follow one of the formulae described earlier. In some cases research is combined with publicity, as when the producers of the film *Men in Black*, featuring Will Smith, showed the first 12 minutes of the film to an advance audience and then let them meet the stars to create a pre-release buzz.[52]

Even the content of films is sometimes influenced by this consumer research. Typically, free invitations to pre-screenings are handed out in shopping centres and cinemas. Attendees are asked a few questions about the film, then some are selected to participate in focus groups. Although groups' reactions usually result in only minor editing changes, occasionally more drastic effects result. When initial reaction to the ending of the film *Fatal Attraction* was negative, Paramount Pictures spent an additional $1.3 million to shoot a new one.[53] Of course, this feedback is not always accurate – before the megahit *E.T.: The Extra-Terrestrial* was released, consumer research indicated that no one over the age of four would go to see the film![54]

Reality engineering

The mythical and much beloved Simpsons family debuted in real life as 7-Eleven transformed many of its stores into Kwik-E-Marts to promote the cartoon series' movie. During the promotion customers snapped up Krusty O's cereal, Buzz Cola, and ice Squishees, all products from the show.[55] The Simpsons were also used as an exemplar of particular tribal consumption patterns in one European study.[56] With the increasing importance of such media-becoming-reality and reality televisions' reality-in-the-media, no wonder consumer researchers increasingly look for clues concerning contemporary consumption patterns in the media in addition to looking at consumers.

Like the Simpsons universe, many of the environments in which we find ourselves, whether shopping centres, sports stadiums or theme parks, are composed at least partly of images and characters drawn from products, marketing campaigns or the mass media. **Reality engineering** occurs as elements of popular culture are appropriated by marketers and converted to vehicles for promotional strategies.[57] These elements include sensory and spatial aspects of everyday existence, whether in the form of products appearing in films, scents pumped into offices and shops, advertising hoardings, theme parks, video monitors attached to shopping trolleys, and so on.

The people of Disney Corporation are probably the best worldwide-known reality engineers, through their theme parks in California and Florida, and their newer parks in Japan and Europe. Disneyland-Paris got off to a problematic start when it opened in 1991. Fewer visitors and especially too few clients for the hotel and conference facilities created economic problems. But the conceptualization of the park was changed, made less American and more European, and now the park is drawing huge crowds. Also other consumption facilities and housing areas have been created around it, including a giant shopping centre where one of the streets will be a recreation of a 'typical street' of one of the local villages.[58] Other themed environments like the Asterix park, future parks or artificially created tropical environments are becoming increasingly popular for shorter holidays throughout Europe.

One final recent example of reality engineering: in homage to the famous movie *Casablanca*, a former US diplomat opened a Rick's Café in that Moroccan city. The new Rick's has the same warm atmosphere as the Hollywood original (which was created on a sound stage in Hollywood). Waiters in traditional fez caps and wide-legged pants serve customers at candlelit tables. The owner commented, 'Because there has never been a Rick's Café here, I could be reasonably assured that it would succeed. It was already an institution, and it never even existed. It's not often you get a chance to turn myth into reality.'[59]

The Food Hotel in Germany is completely done in a food theme, from can-shaped furniture to barstools made of beer crates. Each guest room is sponsored by a food brand. A room by the chocolate manufacturer Ferrero recreates the scene of a TV commercial for its Rafaello coconut candies set on a desert island, with palm trees, shells, summer hats, photos of sandy beaches and books about beach holidays. Another room by potato crisp brand, Chio, features a rotating mirrored disco ball and flashing bathroom lights with an integrated sound system.[60]

Thomas Frey/www.epa-photos.com.

MARKETING PITFALL

. . . Or opportunity? . . . Sometimes marketers will engineer fictional realities, for example, through product placement, which we shall discuss next. In the James Bond movie, *Skyfall*, we see the world's favourite agent with a bottle of beer instead of the iconic Vodka Martini – at least in one scene. Heineken has made a product placement agreement with the producers of the new Bond movie worth 45 million dollars. In addition to the product placement, Daniel Craig who is (currently) playing the role of Bond, will appear in Heineken commercials. It will be interesting to see whether this attempt from Heineken to interfere with a very established cultural formula will be beneficial or backfire on the company. As long as they avoid the 'shaken, not stirred' part for the beer scene . . .[61]

Product placement

Reality engineering is accelerating due to the current popularity of product placements by marketers. It is quite common to see real brands prominently displayed or to hear them discussed in films and on television. In many cases, these 'plugs' are no accident. **Product placement** refers to the insertion of specific products and/or the use of brand names in film and TV scripts. Today most major releases are brimming with real products. Directors like to incorporate branded props because they contribute to the film's realism. When Stephen Spielberg made the film *Minority Report* he used such brands as Nokia, Lexus, Pepsi, Guinness, Reebok and American Express to lend familiarity to the plot's futuristic settings. Lexus even created a new sports car model called the Maglev just for the film.[62]

Some researchers claim that product placement can aid in consumer decision-making because the familiarity of these props creates a sense of cultural belonging while generating feelings of emotional security.[63] Another study found that placements consistent with a show's plot do enhance brand attitudes, but incongruent placements that are not consistent with the plot affect brand attitudes *negatively* because they seem out of place.[64] On the other hand, a majority of consumers polled believe the line between advertising and programming is becoming too fuzzy and distracting (though, as might be expected, concerns about this blurring of boundaries rose steadily with the age of respondents).[65] For better or worse products are popping up everywhere. Worldwide product placement in all media was worth $3.5 billion in 2004, a 200 per cent increase from 1994. In the US, there were 117,976 brand occurrences on cable and broadcast networks during the first three months of 2008 alone.[66] By 2011, the most heavy exposure of product placement came through the show *American Idol* – during the month of March 2011, no less than 208 brands appeared in various types of product placement.[67]

MARKETING OPPORTUNITY

Product placement in the news broadcast? The idea may seem strange to most Europeans, but the increased strain on advertising budgets and doubts about standard advertising's effectiveness has introduced product placement in the news. The channel network Fox and McDonald's has made a six-month deal which places two cups of McDonald's frappucinos in front of news anchors Jason Feinberg and Monica Jackson. They do not sip it, however, since it is a fake product with bogus icecubes that don't melt. Unthinkable in Europe? [68]

Product placement has been a Western phenomenon – until recently. In China, product placement is emerging as a new way to get noticed. Most commercials on Chinese state-run TV play back-to-back in ten-minute segments, making it difficult for any one 30-second ad to attract attention. So, enterprising marketers are embedding product messages in the shows instead. A soap opera called *Love Talks* features such products as Maybelline lipstick, Motorola mobile phones and Ponds Vaseline Intensive Care lotion.[69]

In India, the booming Mumbai film industry (known as Bollywood from Mumbai's original name of Bombay, combined with Hollywood) is discovering the potential of films to expose viewers to brand names (Indian cinema attracts huge local audiences, even in villages where television is not available). Coca-Cola paid to have its local soft drink, Thums Up, prominently featured in a Hindi-language remake of the Quentin Tarantino classic *Reservoir Dogs*. Just in case the audience misses the placements, in one scene just before the bullets start to fly a group of slickly dressed gangsters flash each other the thumbs-up sign.[70]

A few further examples to illustrate the power of product placement:

- Although IBM sells a lot more computers, Apples are seen in many more TV shows and films such as *Mission Impossible* and *Independence Day*. Producers like to use the Apple because its image is more hip – you will remember from Chapter 13 that its followers come close to constituting a sect of believers. But Apple will only let that happen if the brand is identified onscreen.[71]

- The hot new thing is product placement in blogs by highly influential young fashion bloggers. Certain fashion and cosmetics companies will send products to influential bloggers for 'testing' in the hope that this will lead to a promotion through the blog. Of course, this practice is risky business since bloggers exist based on their being credible and savvy. Any suspicion that the blog is just another series of ads will be devastating. Still some bloggers make a living out of this . . . The Chinese talent programme *Lycra My Show* is partly funded by Invista, the maker of Lycra fabric, so contestants sing while wearing stretchy Lycra-based clothing. In China Ford produced a *Survivor* clone called *Ford Maverick Beyond Infinity* where 12 contestants on a tropical island hunt for treasure in a Ford Maverick sport utility vehicle, leap onto rafts while wearing Nike clothing, and cool off with Nestlé drinks. Ford's marketing director in China noted, 'We really built the show around the product.'[72]

- Lady Gaga prominently shows off a Virgin Mobile phone, Miracle Whip dressing, and several other brands in her hit video 'Telephone'.[73]

MARKETING PITFALL

Product placement can also be non-intended from the corporate perspective and detrimental too. One little sentence in the blockbuster *Sideways* from 2004 virtually destroyed the American market for Merlot wines, 'If anybody's drinking Merlot, I'm outta here. I am not drinking any f . . . Merlot,' exclaimed the self-designated wine connoisseur Miles in one scene in the movie. This led to a veritable flight from Merlot wines from American consumers and a lot of producers instead tried to sell their Merlot wines overseas – some even removed Merlot from their fields and started to plant other types of grapes.[74] This is a good example that marketers do not own their product or brand – that they are out there as signs in consumer culture and culture producers (consumers or filmmakers or other . . .) can do with them what they want to within the laws of copyright infringement. See also Marius Luedicke's case at the end of Part D.

As gaming goes mass market, marketers turn to **advergaming**, where online games merge with interactive advertisements that let companies target specific types of consumers. Clearly, computer gaming is not what it used to be. Not long ago, the typical players were scruffy teenage boys shooting at TV screens in their basements. But with the online gaming explosion of recent years (the industry rakes in more than €10 billion per year in global revenue), gamers have become a more sophisticated lot and are now more representative of the general population.

The mushrooming popularity of user-generated videos on YouTube and other sites creates a growing market to link ads to these sources as well. This strategy is growing so rapidly that there's even a new (trade marked) term for it. Plinking™ is the act of embedding a product or service link in a video. Why is this new medium so hot?[75]

- Compared to a 30-second TV spot, advertisers can get viewers' attention for a much longer time. Players spend an average of 5 to 7 minutes on an advergame site.

- Physiological measures confirm that players are highly focused and stimulated when they play a game.

- Marketers can tailor the nature of the game and the products in it to the profiles of different users. They can direct strategy games to upscale, educated users, while they gear action games to younger users.

- The format gives advertisers great flexibility, because game makers now ship PC video games with blank spaces in them to insert virtual ads. This allows advertisers to change messages on the fly and pay only for the number of game players that actually see them. Sony Corporation now allows clients to directly insert online ads into PlayStation 3 video games; the in-game ads change over time through a user's internet connection.

- There's great potential to track usage and conduct marketing research. For example, an inaudible audio signal coded into Activision's *Tony Hawk's Underground 2* skating game on PCs alerts a Nielsen monitoring system each time the test game players view Jeep product placements within the game.

Media images significantly influence consumers' perceptions of reality, affecting viewers' notions about such issues as dating behaviour, racial stereotypes and occupational status.[76] Studies of the **cultivation hypothesis**, which relates to media's ability to shape consumers' perceptions of reality, have shown that heavy television viewers tend to over-estimate the degree of affluence in the country, and these effects also extend to such areas as perceptions of the amount of violence in one's culture.[77] Others have underlined the role of media and celebrity spokespersons – in this particular case David Beckham – in shaping children's moral attitudes.[78] Also, the depiction of consumer environments in programmes and advertisements may lead to further marginalization of, for example, unemployed people, who cannot afford to buy into the depicted lifestyle,[79] or to outright addicted consumers, who cannot refrain from constantly buying various goods, although they may not use these at all.

THE DIFFUSION OF INNOVATIONS

New products and styles termed innovations constantly enter the market. An **innovation** is any product or service that is perceived to be new by consumers. These new products or services occur in both consumer and industrial settings. Innovations may take the form of a clothing or fashion accessory style (such as the Croc, the lightweight sandal/shoe), a new manufacturing technique (for example, a new technique now permits the Danish dairy company Thise to produce a completely fat free milk), or a novel way to deliver a service (for example through ordering online and then picking up the goodies at certain pick-up points (see as well the discussion of 'click and collect' in Chapter 3). If an innovation is successful (most are not), it spreads through the population. First it is bought and/or used by only a few people, and then more and more consumers decide to adopt it, until, in some cases, it seems that almost everyone has bought or tried the innovation. Diffusion of innovations refers to the process whereby a new product, service or idea spreads through a population. There is a tendency for technical goods especially to diffuse more rapidly these days. The cell phone, PC and internet all spread much more rapidly than, for example, TV and radio and much more rapidly than the use of, for example, aeroplanes and cars.[80]

MARKETING OPPORTUNITY

Or marketing challenge? One innovation that will be hard to overlook in the coming years is the so-called mobile revolution. Sixty-two per cent of the searches for restaurants on Valentine's Day 2012 in the US were made from mobile apps. Mobile apps drive 50 per cent of the traffic on Facebook and 55 per cent on Twitter, 60 per cent of all smartphone users use their smartphone while watching TV at home, while 58 per cent of tablet owners user theirs for watching TV at home. Nevertheless, 81 per cent of all webshops are not optimized for smartphone or other mobile usage. Apps are all over us (25 billion apps downloaded from the App store as of 2012), but they have to be used wisely and with great care and consideration of how the consumer uses his apps.[81] This is one of the most interesting fields of research in consumer behaviour in the years to come: consumers' patterns of app usage and avoidance of being overwhelmed by their sheer number. As an example of a corporation that has pioneered very clever use of apps, check Volkswagen and their BlueMotion campaign.[82]

Adopting innovations

A consumer's adoption of an innovation may resemble the decision-making sequence discussed in Chapter 9. The person moves through the stages of awareness, information search, evaluation, trial and adoption, although the relative importance of each stage may differ depending on how much is already known about a product,[83] as well as on cultural factors that may affect people's willingness to try new things.[84] A study of 11 European countries found that consumers in individualistic cultures are more innovative than consumers in collective cultures.[85]

One of the more curious large-scale product adoptions in recent history is the victorious introduction of bottled water in modern consumer markets, based on a variety of mythological beliefs about nature, purity, cleansing and health, as well as the increased demand for portable drinks in our highly mobile and efficient society. Notice too, how we have also adopted the American habit of 'coffee-to-go' in Europe. In spite of the fact that numerous studies have demonstrated that in a lot of places there is no particular reason why we should drink bottled water rather than tap water, bottled water has become a symbol of the modern, healthy lifestyle. As the advertisement demonstrates, it has also become associated with particular cultural ways of life – in this case living the Italian way. In fact, as Table 14.4 demonstrates, Italians were the world's leading consumers of bottled water (the Mexicans have since overtaken the Italians, leaving them in second place, **www.worldwater.org**).[86]

However, even within the same culture, not all people adopt an innovation at the same rate. Some do so quite rapidly, and others never do at all. Consumers can be placed into approximate categories based upon the likelihood of adopting an innovation. The categories of adopters, shown in Figure 14.3, can be related to phases of the product lifecycle concept used widely by marketing strategists.

Table 14.4 Global bottled water market: per capita consumption by leading countries 1998–2003(P)

2003 Rank	Countries	Gallons per capita	
		1998	2003(P)
1	Italy	35.9	48.1
2	Mexico	29.2	41.5
3	France	29.5	39.1
4	United Arab Emirates	28.1	38.1
5	Belgium–Luxembourg	30.7	35.1
6	Germany	26.4	33.1
7	Spain	25.1	30.2
8	Switzerland	23.8	25.4
9	Lebanon	16.2	25.3
10	Saudi Arabia	18.9	23.3
11	Cyprus	17.2	22.8
12	Austria	19.8	22.7
13	United States	15.3	22.6
14	Czech Republic	15.4	22.2
15	Portugal	17.2	20.6
	Global average	**3.9**	**6.0**

(P) Preliminary

Source: Beverage Marketing Corporation. Adapted from Richard Wilk, 'Bottled water: The pure commodity in the age of branding' *Journal of Consumer Culture*, vol. 6 no. 3 (2006): 304.

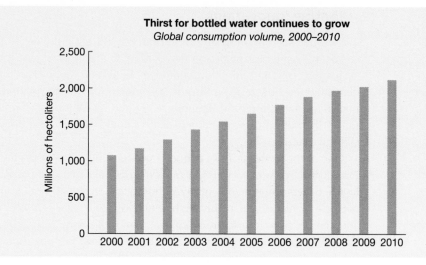

Figure 14.2 Development in consumption of bottled water

Source: http://www.beveragemarketing.com/reportcatalog4a.html

Living the Italian way . . . includes drinking a lot of bottled water!

Pellegrino.

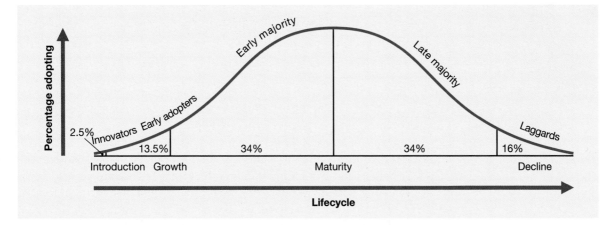

Figure 14.3 Types of adopters

As can be seen in Figure 14.3, roughly one-sixth of the population (innovators and early adopters) is very quick to adopt new products, and one-sixth of the people (laggards) is very slow. The other two-thirds are somewhere in the middle, and these majority adopters represent the mainstream public. In some cases people deliberately wait before adopting an innovation because they assume that its technological qualities will be improved or that its price will fall after it has been on the market.[87] Keep in mind that the proportion of consumers falling into each category is an estimate; the actual size of each depends upon such factors as the complexity of the product, its cost and other product-related factors, and possibly also varies from country to country.

Even though innovators represent only 2.5 per cent of the population, marketers are always interested in identifying them. According to standard theory, these are the brave souls who are always on the lookout for novel developments and will be the first to try a new offering. Just as generalized opinion leaders do not appear to exist, innovators tend to be category-specific. A person who is an innovator in one area may even be a laggard in another (see also the associated discussion about opinion leaders in Chapter 10). For example, someone who prides themselves on being at the cutting edge of fashion may have no conception of new developments in recording technology and stereo equipment.

Despite this qualification, some generalizations can be offered regarding the profile of innovators.[88] Not surprisingly they tend to have more favourable attitudes towards taking risks. They are also, at least in an American context, likely to have higher educational and income levels and to be socially active. However, in a European study of the fashion and clothing market, the same correlation between socio-demographic variables and innovative or early adopting behaviour could not be found.[89] On the other hand, a Spanish study, perhaps not surprisingly, concluded that innovators tend to be younger and, more interestingly, that publicity and advertisement would have the biggest influence on product adoption in the early years of commercialization of a product, whereas word-of-mouth and other non-producer controlled information becomes more important thereafter.[90]

How do we locate innovators? Ad agencies and market research companies are always on the prowl for people who are on top of developing trends. The internet bloggers, already mentioned quite a few times, YouTube, Facebook and other social media are of course an invaluable source. The agency DDB runs a service it calls SignBank, which collects thousands of snippets of information from its 13,000 employees around the world about cultural change in order to advise their clients on what it all means for them.[91]

Early adopters share many of the same characteristics as innovators, but an important difference is their degree of concern for social acceptance, especially with regard to expressive products such as clothing, cosmetics and so on. Generally speaking, an early adopter is receptive to new styles because they are involved in the product category and also place high value on being in fashion. The universality of the dichotomy of innovators and adopters has been challenged by research pertaining to health foods, suggesting that (1) three groups can be distinguished, namely innovators, more-involved adopters and less-involved adopters, and (2) there is not a big difference between the purchase rate of new products between innovators and adopters; rather the difference lies in the kind of innovations tried and the approach to trying new products.[92] Table 14.5 gives a brief description of the different types of consumers and their approach to new product trials.

Innovative companies understand the value of involving their most forward-thinking customers in business decisions before they introduce the final product. More than 650,000 customers tested a beta version of Microsoft Windows 2000. Many were even prepared to pay Microsoft a fee to do this because working with the program would help them understand how it could create value for their own businesses. The value of the research and development investment by customers to Microsoft was more than $500 million.

This approach is more prevalent in high-tech industries that consult their **lead users** about ideas; these are very experienced and knowledgeable customers. Indeed, it is common for these people to propose product improvements – because they have to live with the

Table 14.5 Decision styles of market segments based on adoption, innovation and personal involvement

Adoption decision process stage	Less-involved adopters	Innovators	More-involved adopters
Problem recognition	Passive, reactive	Active	Proactive
Search	Minimal, confined to resolution of minor anomalies caused by current consumption patterns	Superficial but extensively based within and across product class boundaries	Extensive within relevant product category; assiduous exploration of all possible solutions within that framework
Evaluation	Meticulous, rational, slow and cautious; objective appraisal using tried and tested criteria	Quick, impulsive, based on currently accepted criteria; personal and subjective	Careful, confined to considerations raised by the relevant product category: but executed confidently and (for the adopter) briskly within that frame of reference
Decision	Conservative selection within known range of products, continuous innovations preferred	Radical: easily attracted to discontinuously new product class and able to choose quickly within it. Frequent trial, followed by abandonment	Careful selection within a product field that has become familiar through deliberation, vicarious trial, and sound and prudent pre-purchase comparative evaluation
Post-purchase evaluation	Meticulous, tendency to brand loyalty if item performs well	Less loyal; constantly seeking novel experiences through purchase and consumption innovations	Loyal if satisfied but willing to try innovations within the prescribed frame of reference; perhaps tends towards dynamically-continuous

Source: Gordon R. Foxall and Seema Bhate, 'Cognitive style and personal involvement as explicators of innovative purchasing of health food brands', *European Journal of Marketing*, 27(2) (1993): 5–16. Used with permission.

MARKETING OPPORTUNITY

Since around 2006, when a juggler and a lawyer made a big splash, both literally and in the advertising world, through their experiment with producing Geysir-like reactions by adding Mentos to Diet Coke, the world of advertising has put high hopes on overcoming brand scepticism and the lack of credibility in 'classical' advertising through the use of consumer-generated advertising. Other companies that have tried with more, but ever so often less success, to engage consumers/customers in their advertising creation are Master Card, Chevrolet and the Danish State Railroads.[93] There seems to be two major obstacles to whether or not this opportunity will really take off. First of all, companies and agencies are generally quite reluctant to let go of the control of their campaigns. Secondly, there is some evidence that the consumers, although free to have fun with the products that they (supposedly) like and admire, actually are not that interested in being part of a commercial bandwagon.[94]

consequences. According to one estimate, users rather than manufacturers developed 70 per cent of the innovations in the chemical industry![95]

Types of innovations

Innovations can contain a technological level and involve some functional change (for example, car air bags) or be of a more intangible kind, communicating a new social meaning (like a new hairstyle). However, contrary to what much literature states,[96] both are symbolic in the sense that one refers to symbols of technical performance and safety and the other to less tangible symbols, such as courage and individuality. Both types refer to symbols of progress.[97] New products, services and ideas have characteristics that determine the degree to which they will probably diffuse. Innovations that are more novel may be less likely to diffuse, since they require bigger changes in people's lifestyles and thus more effort. On the other hand, most innovations are close to being of the 'me too' kind, and thus do not necessarily possess qualities that would persuade the consumer to shift from existing product types. In any case, it should be noted that in spite of all the good intentions of the marketing concept to ensure that there is a market before the product is developed, the failure rate of new products is as high as ever, if not higher.[98]

Behavioural demands of innovations

Innovations can be categorized in terms of the degree to which they demand changes in behaviour from adopters. Three major types of innovation have been identified, though these three categories are not absolutes. They refer, in a relative sense, to the amount of disruption or change they bring to people's lives.

A **continuous innovation** refers to a modification of an existing product, as when a breakfast cereal is introduced in a sugar-coated version, or Levi's promoted 'shrink-to-fit' jeans. This type of change may be used to set one brand apart from its competitors. The launch of Coke Zero was such a continuous innovation, where the idea was to produce a sugar-free cola targeted to men as opposed to the Diet Coke that was mainly popular among the female segment. This was the idea; however, in many countries, including Denmark, Coke Zero has gained as much popularity among the women as the men.[99] Most product innovations are evolutionary rather than revolutionary. Small changes are made to position the product, add line extensions or merely to alleviate consumer boredom.

Consumers may be lured to the new product, but adoption represents only minor changes in consumption habits, since innovation perhaps adds to the product's convenience or to the range of choices available. A typewriter company, for example, many years ago modified the

587

shape of its product to make it more user friendly. One simple change was the curving of the tops of the keys, a convention that was carried over on today's computer keyboards. One of the reasons for the change was that secretaries with long fingernails had complained about the difficulty of typing on the flat surfaces.

A **dynamically continuous innovation** is a more pronounced change in an existing product, as represented by self-focusing cameras or touch-tone telephones. These innovations have a modest impact on the way people do things, creating some behavioural changes, although the touch-tone telephone is an expression of a larger innovation involving many discontinuous renewals of daily life: the digitalization of communication. When introduced, the IBM electric typewriter, which used a 'golf ball' rather than individual keys, enabled typists to change the typeface of manuscripts simply by replacing one ball with another.

A **discontinuous innovation** creates major changes in the way we live. Major inventions, such as the airplane, the car, the computer and television have radically changed modern lifestyles, although, as can be seen from these examples, major changes normally take some time from the point of introduction. For people in the richer parts of the world, the personal computer has supplanted the typewriter, and it has created the phenomenon of 'telecommuters' by allowing many people to work from their homes. Of course, the cycle continues, as new innovations like new versions of software are constantly being made; dynamically continuous innovations such as the 'mouse' and trackballs compete for adoption, and discontinuous innovations such as streaming video transmitted on cell phones start to appear in stores.

MARKETING OPPORTUNITY

These years, nanotechnology is finding its way to consumer products. Not only can nanotechnology provide hardware so small that it basically becomes invisible without losing processing power, various experiments are also being undertaken with nanocoating of existing consumer objects. Such surface treatment might provide us with car windows that do not fog, paint that does not get scratches, and shirts that do not get stains. Or what about anti-bacteria coated kitchenware and door knobs? Or anti-graffiti paint.[100] Do you have any ideas that would make consumers' lives better through nano-coating?

Prerequisites for successful adoption

Regardless of how much behavioural change is demanded by an innovation, several factors are desirable for a new product to succeed:[101]

- *Compatibility*. The innovation should be compatible with consumers' lifestyles. As an illustration, a manufacturer of personal care products tried unsuccessfully several years ago to introduce a hair remover cream for men as a substitute for razors and shaving cream. This formulation was similar to that used widely by women to remove hair from their legs. Although the product was simple and convenient to use, it failed because men were not interested in a product they perceived to be too feminine and thus threatening to their masculine self-concepts.

- *Trialability*. Since an unknown is accompanied by high perceived risk, people are more likely to adopt an innovation if they can experiment with it prior to making a commitment. To reduce this risk, companies often choose the expensive strategies of distributing free 'trial-size' samples of new products. For example, the Swedish coffee brand Gevalia has distributed free samples targeted especially at young people, because there is some evidence that fewer young people are drinking coffee, and those that do begin later in life.

- *Complexity*. The product should be low in complexity. A product that is easier to understand and use will often be preferred to a competitor. This strategy requires less effort from the consumer, and it also lowers perceived risk. Manufacturers of DVD players, for example, have put a lot of effort into simplifying usage (such as on-screen programming) to encourage adoption.

● *Observability*. An innovation that is easily observable is more likely to spread, since this quality makes it more likely that other potential adopters will become aware of its existence. The rapid proliferation of 'bum bags' (pouches worn around the waist in lieu of wallets or purses) was due to their high visibility. It was easy for others to see the convenience offered.

● *Relative advantage*. Most importantly, the product should offer relative advantage over alternatives. The consumer must believe that its use will provide a benefit other products cannot offer. For example, the success of many environmentally friendly product alternatives may be due to the fact that, once consumers have been convinced about the environmental advantages of the product, it is a clear and easily understandable advantage compared to competing products.

MARKETING OPPORTUNITY

Ever tried the uncertainty of arriving in a new place and worrying about the honesty of taxi drivers? Well, here's an innovation for you. When you click the 'order now' button, a Taxi app developed by the Danish company Click A Taxi will calculate where you are and order a cab from the most reliable local company and keep you updated about the taxi arrival. The app, which combines highly advanced robot technology and ordinary telephone ordering, is already a success in Scandinavia and is supposed to be launched soon in the rest of Europe and USA.[102]

The social context of innovations

One critical but relatively little researched aspect is the importance of the social context of product adoption behaviour.[103] This is linked to the importance of visibility of the product innovation as well as the influence of the reference group which is seen as related to the new product. For example, Western products are admired in many contexts in Asia and Africa, or the marketizing economies of Eastern Europe, for the sole reason of being linked to the status of the Western world, which is seen as 'better', more 'developed' and generally of a higher status.[104] Likewise, in Europe the association of new products with the American way of life will have a significant impact on the adopting behaviour of various groups in society but will differ in different European countries.

Another aspect of the social dimension of innovation is the pitfall of being caught up in too many continuous innovations due to an ever finer market segmentation and customization approach. This may take resources away from more strategic considerations of changing 'the way things are done'.[105] For example, a British bank had created such a complex structure of financial services and accounts, as well as charges attached to these services, that customers began to complain about waiting time and lack of understanding of their own financial affairs. The bank simplified the structure to one account type and a much simpler charge system and successfully made this a unique selling proposition in a market dominated by more complex offerings.[106]

THE FASHION SYSTEM

The **fashion system**[107] consists of all those people and organizations involved in creating symbolic meanings and transferring these meanings to cultural goods. Although people tend to equate fashion with clothing, be it *haute couture* or street wear, it is important to keep in mind that fashion processes affect *all* types of cultural phenomena from the more mundane (what do you think of high fashion nappy bags in unisex style?)[108] to high art, including music, art, architecture and even science (i.e., certain research topics and scientists are 'hot' at any point in time). Even business practices are subject to the fashion process; they evolve and change depending on which management techniques are in vogue, such as total quality management or 'the learning organization'.

Fashion can be thought of as a *code*, or language, that helps us to decipher these meanings.[109] However, fashion seems to be *context-dependent* to a larger extent than language. That is, the same item can be interpreted differently by different consumers and in different situations.[110] In semiotic terms, *cf* Chapter 2, the meaning of many products is *undercoded* – that is, there is no one precise meaning, but rather plenty of room for interpretation among perceivers.

At the outset, it may be helpful to distinguish among some confusing terms. **Fashion** is the process of social diffusion by which a new style is adopted by some group(s) of consumers. In contrast, *a fashion* (or style) refers to a particular combination of attributes. And, to be *in fashion* means that this combination is currently positively evaluated by some reference group. Thus, the term *Danish Modern* refers to particular characteristics of furniture design (i.e. a fashion in interior design); it does not necessarily imply that Danish Modern is a fashion that is currently desired by consumers.[111]

Collective selection

Fashions tend to sweep through countries; it seems that all of a sudden 'everyone' is doing the same thing or wearing the same styles. Some sociologists view fashion as a form of *collective behaviour*, or a wave of social conformity. How do so many people get tuned in to the same phenomenon at once, as happened with hip-hop styles? However, it has also been shown how fashion magazines were helpful in teaching women around the late nineteenth and early twentieth century to conceive of themselves as free and self-determining individuals.[112] We see here again how fashion is a process that links the macro-level cultural changes with micro-level individual behaviour.

Remember that creative subsystems within a culture production system attempt to anticipate the tastes of the buying public. Despite their unique talents, members of this subsystem are also members of mass culture. Like the fashion magazine editors discussed earlier, cultural gatekeepers are drawing from a common set of ideas and symbols, and are influenced by the same cultural phenomena as the eventual consumers of their products.

The process by which certain symbolic alternatives are chosen over others has been termed **collective selection**.[113] As with the creative subsystem, members of the managerial and communications subsystems also seem to develop a common frame of mind. Although products within each category must compete for acceptance in the marketplace, they can usually be characterized by their adherence to a dominant theme or motif – be it the grunge look, sixties nostalgia, Danish Modern or *nouvelle cuisine*.

Behavioural science perspectives on fashion

Fashion is a very complex process which operates on many levels. At one extreme, it is a macro, societal phenomenon affecting many people simultaneously. At the other, it exerts a very personal effect on individual behaviour. A consumer's purchase decisions are often motivated by their desire to be in fashion. Fashion products are aesthetic objects, and their origins are rooted in art and history. For this reason, there are many perspectives on the origin and diffusion of fashion. Although these cannot be described in detail here, some major approaches can be briefly summarized.[114]

Psychological models of fashion

Many psychological factors help to explain why people are motivated to be in fashion. These include conformity, variety-seeking, personal creativity and sexual attraction. For example,

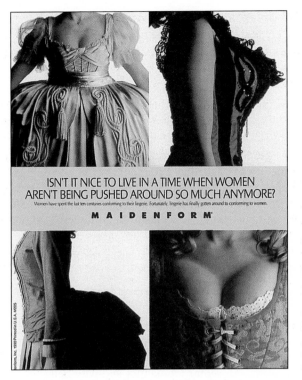

ISN'T IT NICE TO LIVE IN A TIME WHEN WOMEN AREN'T BEING PUSHED AROUND SO MUCH ANYMORE?

Women have spent the last ten centuries conforming to their lingerie. Fortunately, lingerie has finally gotten around to conforming to women.

M A I D E N F O R M

This ad for Maidenform illustrates that fashions have accentuated different parts of the female anatomy throughout history. The underlying premise is, that today (thanks to Maidenform!) we can look 'natural'. What do you think about his underlying premise – aren't women's bodies pushed around anymore?

many consumers seem to have a 'need for uniqueness': they want to be different, but not too different.[115] For this reason, people often conform to the basic outlines of a fashion, but try to improvise and make a personal statement within these guidelines.

One of the earliest theories of fashion proposed that 'shifting **erogenous zones**' accounted for fashion changes. Different parts of the female body are the focus of sexual interest, and clothing styles change to highlight or hide these parts. For example, people in the Victorian era found shoulders exciting, a 'well-turned ankle' was important at the beginning of the twentieth century, while the back was the centre of attention in the 1930s.

While these shifts may be due to boredom, some have speculated that there are deeper reasons for changes in focus; body areas symbolically reflect social values. In medieval times, for example, a rounded belly was desirable. This preference was most likely a reflection of the fact that multiple pregnancies were necessary to maintain population growth in an age when infant mortality was high. Interest in the female leg in the 1920s and 1930s coincided with women's new mobility and independence, while the exposure of breasts in the 1970s signalled a renewed interest in breastfeeding.[116] Breasts were de-emphasized in the 1980s as women concentrated on careers, but some analysts have theorized that a larger bust size is now more popular as women try to combine professional activity with child-rearing. Now, some suggest that the current prevalence of the exposed midriff reflects the premium our society places on fitness.[117] It is important to note that until very recently the study of fashion focused almost exclusively on its impact on women. More recently, consumer researchers have started to focus also on fashion consumers among other groups. First and foremost, men are not exempt from being 'fashion victims', and especially the rise of the 'metrosexual man'[118] has underlined for marketers as well as for researchers the importance of gaining insight into male fashion consumption.

Psychological research suggests that it is possible to distinguish between two different personality types, respectively more or less sensitive to the opinion of their social surroundings (also called high and low self-monitors). The high self-monitors have been demonstrated to stress the brand of a consumer good (specifically clothing) more than low self-monitors, who are on the other hand more positive to functional product attributes.[119]

Economic models of fashion

Economists approach fashion in terms of the model of supply and demand. Items that are in limited supply have high value, while those readily available are less desirable. Rare items command respect and prestige.

Veblen's notion of **conspicuous consumption** proposed that the wealthy consume to display their prosperity, for example by wearing expensive (and at times impractical) clothing. The functioning of conspicuous consumption seems more complex in today's society, since wealthy consumers often engage in *parody display*, where they deliberately adopt formerly low status or inexpensive products, such as jeeps or jeans. On the other hand, new hierarchies develop between generic jeans signalling a traditional, work-oriented, classless or lower-class environment, and designer jeans expressing an urban, upmarket, class-distinctive and more contemporary lifestyle.[120] Other factors also influence the demand curve for fashion-related products. These include a *prestige-exclusivity effect*, where high prices still create high demand, and a *snob effect*, where lower prices actually reduce demand.[121]

Sociological models of fashion

The collective selection model discussed previously is an example of a sociological approach to fashion. This perspective focuses on a subculture's adoption of a fashion (idea, style, etc.) and its subsequent diffusion into society as a whole. This process often begins with youth subcultures such as the hip-hop segment. Another current example is the integration of Goth culture into the mainstream. This fashion started as an expression of rebellion by young outcasts who admired nineteenth-century romantics and who defied conventional styles with their black clothing (often including over-the-top fashion statements such as Count Dracula capes, fishnet stockings, studded collars and black lipstick) and punk music from bands such as Siouxsie & the Banshees and Bauhaus. Today, you can buy vampire-girl lunchboxes, and mall outlets sell tons of clunky cross jewellery and black lace. Hard-core Goths are not amused, but hey, that's fashion for you.[122]

In addition, much attention has been focused on the relationship between product adoption and class structure. The **trickle-down theory**, first proposed in 1904 by Georg Simmel, has been one of the most influential approaches to understanding fashion. It states that there are two conflicting forces that drive fashion change. First, subordinate groups try to adopt the status symbols of the groups above them as they attempt to climb up the ladder of social mobility. Dominant styles thus originate with the upper classes and *trickle down* to those below. However, this is where the second force comes into play: those people in the superordinate groups are constantly looking below them on the ladder to ensure that they are not imitated. They respond to the attempts of lower classes to 'impersonate' them by adopting even *newer* fashions. These two processes create a self-perpetuating cycle of change – the engine that drives fashion.[123]

A contemporary version of conspicuous consumption and the trickle-down effect is the online shopping website ASOS (As Seen On Screen, or As Seen On Star), where consumers can check out styles worn on the big screen, on TV or in other public contexts by celebrities like Kate Middleton, Beyoncé or Lady Gaga. The basic message is: 'Now you too can look like Beyoncé.'[124]

The trickle-down theory was quite useful for understanding the process of fashion changes when applied to a society with a stable class structure, which permitted the easy identification of lower versus upper-class consumers. This task is not so easy in modern times. In contemporary Western society, then, this approach must be modified to account for new developments in mass culture.[125]

● A perspective based on class structure cannot account for the wide range of styles that are simultaneously made available in our society. Modern consumers have a much greater degree of individualized choice than in the past because of advances in technology and distribution. Just as an adolescent is almost instantly aware of the latest style trends by

Some people argue that consumers are at the mercy of fashion designers. One study argued that both consumers and fashion designers feel like victims of each other – designers say that consumer demand and taste is very hard to predict, and consumers say the designers' ever-changing stylistic universes force them into renewing their wardrobe every so often. What do you think?[126]

Courtesy of Diesel S.p.A.

watching reality shows on TV, elite fashion has been largely replaced by mass fashion, since media exposure permits many groups to become aware of a style at the same time. Stores such as Zara and H&M can replenish their inventories in weeks rather than months, and the 'fast-fashion' market has become the fastest growing within the clothing sector.[127]

- Consumers tend to be more influenced by opinion leaders who are similar to them. As a result each social group has its own fashion innovators who determine fashion trends. It is often more accurate to speak of a trickle-across effect, where fashions diffuse horizontally among members of the same social group.[128]

- In times of individualism, standing out is just as important as fitting in. Style reflexivity and confirmation of one's individuality have become crucial parts of the contemporary fashion scene, in particular among youngsters.[129] We try to resolve this paradox, that you have to confirm your individuality at the same time as you want to avoid being an outcast, by making stories for ourselves that we wear, 'what we like to wear' and what 'expresses who we are', rather than what is dictated by fashion.[130] Essentially, as another study demonstrated, fashion consumers are able to follow the Dr Martens slogan: 'We make the shoes, you make the story'.[131]

- Anybody who has been on a skiing holiday will have noticed the subcultural fashions demonstrated among the skiers. In fact, more and more consumption-based subcultures, sailing enthusiasts for instance, adopt their own fashions in order to reinforce their community feeling and distinguish themselves from outsiders.[132]

- Subcultural fashions are also expressed through the variation in ethnic populations. This is not only true in terms of migrants from the Middle East, Asia or Africa but also among different but neighbouring ethnic populations, for example, Russians and Estonians in Estonia, where ethnic and subcultural identity can be expressed through fashion.[133]

● Finally, current fashions often originate with the lower classes and trickle up. Grassroots innovators are typically people who lack prestige in the dominant culture (like urban youth). Since they are less concerned with maintaining the status quo, they are more free to innovate and take risks.[134] Whatever the direction of the trickling, one thing is sure: that fashion is always a complex process of variation, of imitation and differentiation, of adoptions and rejections in relation to one's social surroundings.[135]

This blurring of the origins of fashion has been attributed to the condition of post-modernity when there is no fashion, only fashions, and no rules, only choices,[136] and where the norms and rules can no longer be dictated solely by the haute couture or other cultural gatekeepers but where the individual allows themselves more freedom in creating a personal look by mixing elements from different styles.[137] This obviously has the consequence that the relatively linear models of fashion cycles discussed below become less able to predict actual fashion developments.[138]

A French researcher followed the development in the editorial content of a French fashion magazine since 1945. It turned out that the content became more global and less 'French' over the years, but also that the magazine gradually shifted away from dictating one certain fashion style at each point in time to an approach in the 1990s where several styles were promoted in each issue and consumers were invited to mix and match and create their own personal style independently of high fashion.[139] Swedish retailer H&M has been pioneering the blurring of high and low fashion through their collections in collaboration with, for example, Jimmi Choo and Karl Lagerfeld. A similar blurring of high and low fashion was demonstrated by a prize-winning campaign, where a charity organization used former international top model Renee Toft Simonsen for promoting clothes from their second-hand shops.[140] Neither she nor the agency received any payment for their participation. Some British fashion-hungry women go to *swishing parties*. It is a kind of clothes swapping meeting, where the participants can nibble a little something to eat and sip a glass of wine while checking out the garments brought by other participants. The VISA corporation has stepped in with an organizing principle securing points given for what you hand in, and those can then be used for taking away clothes. This ensures that the swapping does not end up in chaos and free-riding behaviour but becomes a true fashion event. Hence, your access is dependent on bringing a clean, good quality garment, or shoes, that has just spent a little too much time in the wardrobe. This is both economical and environmental, underline the patrons. A total of 900,000 tons of clothing and shoes are thrown away each year in the UK. A swishing party allows people to recycle and embellish themselves at the same time – and it is a cozy event where they meet new friends who are also into fashion.[141]

The fashion system, then, is becoming increasingly complex. Brands may be very significant to consumers and they may be less ashamed to admit that than previously but they are less committed to any one brand over a longer period. The fashion industry is trying to compensate for this by overexposing their brands, putting the brand name very conspicuously all over clothing, bags, accessories, etc. in order to get a maximum of exposure out of the 'catch'.[142] The fashion industry is also exploring the individual styles for new market opportunities and new meanings of fashion goods for wider distribution.[143] Even those trying to rebel against fashion dictates by turning to ugliness as a motif for their choice of 'look' cannot escape. Ugliness in a variety of forms is becoming increasingly fashionable; as one consumer said: 'These shoes were so ugly I just had to have them.'[144] The ugly and disgusting seems to form a specific trend in certain companies' marketing strategies.[145] One cartoon made fun of the fact that the dress of a male hipster could be exactly the same as for a homeless person – except that the hipster's cardigan is branded and the jeans not authentically worn out . . .[146]

Swishing parties are popular among female British fashion consumers.
David Cox.

A 'medical' model of fashion

For years and years, the lowly Hush Puppy was a shoe for nerds. Suddenly – almost overnight – the shoe became a chic fashion statement even though its manufacturer did nothing to promote this image. Why did this style diffuse through the population so quickly? **Meme theory** explains this process with a medical metaphor. A *meme* is an idea or product that enters the consciousness of people over time – examples include tunes, catch-phrases ('You're fired!'), or styles such as the Hush Puppy. In this view, memes spread among consumers in a geometric progression just as a virus starts off in a small way and steadily infects increasing numbers of people until it becomes an epidemic. Memes 'leap' from brain to brain via a process of imitation, as when people find cool pictures or comments on sites like **9gag.com**.

The memes that survive tend to be distinctive and memorable, and the hardiest ones often combine aspects of prior memes. For example, the *Star Wars* movies evoked prior memes relating to the legend of King Arthur, religion, heroic youth and 1930s adventure serials. Indeed, George Lucas studied comparative religion and mythology as he prepared his first draft of the *Star Wars* saga, 'The Story of Mace Windu'.[147]

The diffusion of many products in addition to Hush Puppies seems to follow the same basic path. A few people initially use the product, but change happens in a hurry when the process reaches the moment of critical mass – what one author calls the **tipping point**. For example, Sharp introduced the first low-priced fax machine in 1984 and sold about 80,000 in that year. There was a slow climb in the number of users for the next three years. Then, suddenly, in 1987 enough people had fax machines that it made sense for everyone to have one – Sharp sold a million units. Mobile phones followed a similar trajectory.[148]

Do you remember when you first heard about Twitter? The viral nature of social media allows memes to spread much more rapidly today. For instance, Facebook memes include the popular '25 Things You Didn't Know About Me' and the use of several expressions such as FML ('f##k my life'), while texters often include shorthand phrases like LOL and OMG. In fact, FML made Facebook's Top Ten in its Facebook Memology list for 2009.

Mobile phones have become a fashion statement – and a technological gizmo for showing off among peer groups. This is so obvious for most consumers that it can be used by a completely different company for selling a completely different product.

Courtesy of The Absolut Company.

MARKETING PITFALL

A *knock-off* is a style that has been deliberately copied and modified, often with the intent to sell to a larger or different market. *Haute couture* clothing styles presented by top designers in Paris and elsewhere are commonly 'knocked off' by other designers and sold to the mass market. The web is making it easier than ever for firms to copy these designs – in some cases so quickly that their pirated styles appear in stores at the same time as the originals. Wildcatters such as First View (**http://firstview.com/collection.php?menu=1&clear=1**) have set up websites to show designers' latest creations, sometimes revealing everything from a new collection. Things have become so bad that the House of Chanel requires photographers to sign contracts promising their shots will not be distributed on the internet.[149] But, isn't imitation the sincerest form of flattery?

Cycles of fashion adoption

In 1997, a little digital animal swept across the planet. After enjoying considerable success in Japan in 1996 with about three million units sold, it spread throughout the world during 1997 where the population by the summer had increased to a total of seven million with approximately twice that number in back orders. The Tamagochi, as it was known, was an electronic pet that must be nurtured, played with and taken care of just as a living being. Failure to do so meant that it would weaken and show signs of maltreatment until it eventually dies. That is, in the Japanese version it dies. This unhappy ending did not appeal to Americans who therefore created their own version where it flies off to another planet if not treated well. Needless to say, the Japanese 'authentic' versions quickly became collectors' items (cf the discussion of collections in the previous chapter). Today, many consumers might not know what a Tamagochi is, but anybody with children will know what a Pokémon is.

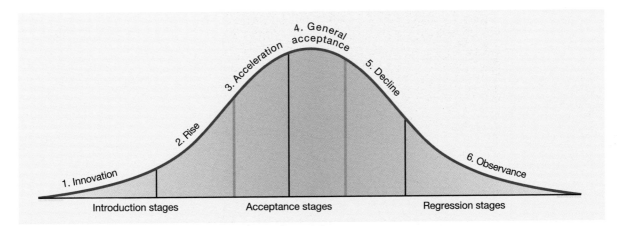

Figure 14.4 A normal fashion cycle

Source: Susan Kaiser, *The Social Psychology of Clothing* (New York: Macmillan, 1985).

The stories of the Tamagochi or the Pokémon – or indeed many other brands – show how quickly a consumer craze can catch on globally. Although the longevity of a particular style can range from a month to a century, fashions tend to flow in a predictable sequence. The **fashion lifecycle** is quite similar to the more familiar product lifecycle. An item or idea progresses through basic stages from birth to death, as shown in Figure 14.4.

Variations in fashion lifecycles

The diffusion process discussed earlier in this chapter is intimately related to the popularity of fashion-related items. To illustrate how this process works, consider how the **fashion acceptance cycle** works in the popular music business. In the *introduction stage*, a song is listened to by a small number of music innovators. It may be played in clubs or on 'cutting-edge' radio stations, which is exactly how 'grunge rock' groups such as Nirvana got their start. During the *acceptance stage*, the song enjoys increased social visibility and acceptance by large segments of the population. A record may get wide airplay on 'Top-40' stations, steadily rising up the charts 'like a bullet'. This process may, of course, be supported or even generated by marketing efforts from the record company.

In the *regression stage*, the item reaches a state of social saturation as it becomes overused, and eventually it sinks into decline and obsolescence as new songs rise to take its place. A hit record may be played once an hour on a Top-40 station for several weeks. At some point, though, people tend to get sick of it and focus their attention on newer releases. The former hit record eventually winds up in the discount rack of your favourite download site. These stages, however, are challenged by the internet where the development may be so rapid, that the stages are hardly distinguishable anymore (remember Justin Bieber's road to fame?). Likewise, retromarketing and retrostyles ensure that not all old stuff goes into oblivion.

Not everybody shares the same musical tastes. Nor, as we discussed above, is everybody necessarily influenced by the same fashion in clothing anymore. As society may become more characterized by lifestyles than by generalizable consumption patterns spreading through social classes as in the class-based fashion models, the social groups in question may consist more of a particular lifestyle than actual social classes. For example, one may distinguish generally between the more risk-prone and the more prudent fashion consumers, and each of these two groups have their own independent fashion cycles that do not necessarily influence the other groups.[150]

Figure 14.5 illustrates that fashions are characterized by slow acceptance at the beginning, which (if the fashion is to 'make it') rapidly accelerate and then taper off. Different classes of

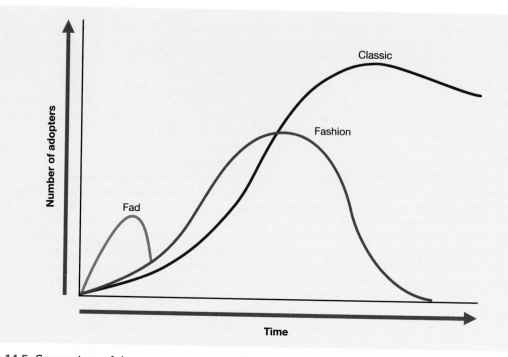

Figure 14.5 Comparison of the acceptance cycle of fads, fashions and classics

Source: Susan Kaiser, *The Social Psychology of Clothing* (New York: Macmillan, 1985).

fashion can be identified by considering the relative length of the fashion acceptance cycle. While many fashions exhibit a moderate cycle, taking several years to work their way through the stages of acceptance and decline, others are extremely long-lived or short-lived.

A **classic** is a fashion with an extremely long acceptance cycle. It is in a sense 'anti-fashion', since it guarantees stability and low risk to the purchaser for a long period of time. Keds sneakers, classic so-called 'tennis shoes' introduced in the US in 1917, have been successful because they appeal to those who are turned off by the high-fashion, trendy appeal of L.A. Gear, Reebok and others. When consumers in focus groups were asked to project what kind of building Keds would be, a common response was a country house with a white picket fence. In other words, the shoes are seen as a stable, classic product. In contrast, Nikes were often described as steel-and-glass skyscrapers, reflecting their more modernistic image.[151]

A **fad** is a very short-lived fashion. Fads are usually adopted by relatively few people. Adopters may all belong to a common subculture, and the fad 'trickles across' members but rarely breaks out of that specific group.[152] Indeed, others are likely to ridicule the fad (which may add fuel to the fire). For example, a pair of researchers recently studied adults who resisted the Harry Potter craze. They found some of these consumers avoid the Hogwarts world because they pride themselves on 'not being taken in'. These adults react negatively to the 'evangelical' enthusiasts who try to convert them to fandom. They recount the resentment of one newlywed on her honeymoon (as related in an essay by her new husband): 'My new page-turning obsession did not go down too well with my new life partner. When on our first night in the Maldives and expecting some form of conjugal rites [she found] herself in second place to a fictional 11-year-old trainee wizard and something called the Sorting Hat.'[153]

Fads are not 'one size fits all' in terms of spread and impact. Figure 14.6 illustrates different types of fads. However, whatever the fad cycle, some key characteristics of fads include:

- The fad is non-utilitarian – that is, it does not perform any explicit purpose function.

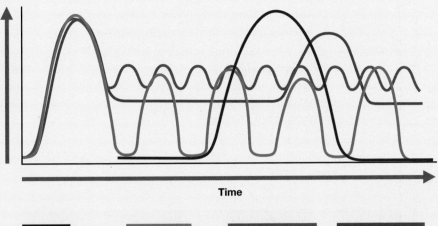

Figure 14.6 The behaviour of fads

- The fad is often adopted on impulse; people do not undergo stages of rational decision-making before joining in.
- The fad diffuses rapidly, gains quick acceptance, and is short-lived.

How to tell whether a fad is 'true', 'cyclical' or one of the other types? For example, experts are discussing whether the current interest in Scandinavian food in the UK is a short-lived fad (since it does not come with the same imagery of a lifestyle to support it as, for example, Mediterraenean food) or it will last longer, based on the new Scandinavian cuisine's striving for what is natural and seasonal.[154] The interest in Scandinavian food has been sparked by the celebration of Scandinavian chefs and restaurants at world competitions, but possibly also due to the media exposure of Scandinavian culture through a set of highly popular TV series, including *The Killing*, *The Bridge* and *Borgen*. Distinguishing beforehand between fads or more lasting tendencies of change is not easy, and many consulting agencies make a living out of being trend-spotters. However, here are a few points that may be helpful in distinguishing short-lived fads from longer-lasting innovations:[155]

- Does it fit with basic lifestyle changes? If a new hairstyle is hard to care for, this innovation will not be consistent with women's increasing time demands. On the other hand, the movement to shorter-term holidays is more likely to last because this innovation makes trip planning easier for harried consumers.
- What are the benefits? The switch to leaner meats and cuts came about because these meats are perceived as healthier, so a real benefit is evident.
- Can it be personalized? Enduring trends tend to accommodate a desire for individuality, whereas styles such as mohawk haircuts or the grunge look are inflexible and do not allow people to express themselves.

- Is it a trend or a side effect? An increased interest in exercise is part of a basic trend towards health consciousness, although the specific form of exercise that is 'in' at any given time will vary (e.g. low-impact aerobics *vs* inline skating).

- What other changes have occurred in the market? Sometimes the popularity of products is influenced by *carry-over effects*. The miniskirt fad in the 1960s brought about a major change in the hosiery market, as sales of tights grew from 10 per cent of this product category to more than 80 per cent in two years. Now, sales of these items are declining due to the casual emphasis in dressing.

- Who has adopted the change? If the innovation is not adopted by working mothers, baby boomers, or some other important market segment, it is not likely to become a trend.

Chapter summary

Now that you have finished reading this chapter you should understand why:

→ The styles prevalent in a culture at any point in time often reflect underlying political and social conditions. The set of agents responsible for creating stylistic alternatives is termed a culture production system. Factors such as the types of people involved in this system and the amount of competition from alternative product forms influence the choices that eventually make their way to the marketplace for consideration by end consumers.

→ Culture is often described in terms of high (or elite) forms and low (or popular) forms. Products of popular culture tend to follow a cultural formula and contain predictable components. On the other hand, these distinctions are blurring in modern society as imagery from 'high art' is increasingly being incorporated into marketing efforts and marketed products (or even marketing products like advertisements) are treated and evaluated as high art.

→ Many modern marketers are reality engineers. Reality engineering occurs when marketers appropriate elements of popular culture to use in their promotional strategies. These elements include sensory and spatial aspects of everyday existence, whether in the form of products that appear in movies, scents pumped into offices and stores, billboards, theme parks, or video monitors attached to shopping carts.

→ The *diffusion of innovations* refers to the process whereby a new product, service or idea spreads through a population. A consumer's decision to adopt a new item depends on their personal characteristics (if they are inclined to try new things) and on the characteristics of the item. Products sometimes stand a better chance of being adopted if they demand relatively little change in behaviour from consumers and are compatible with current practices. They are also more likely to diffuse if they can be tested prior to purchase, if they are not complex, if their use is visible to others, and, most importantly, if they provide a relative advantage vis-à-vis existing products.

→ The fashion system includes everyone involved in the creation and transference of symbolic meanings. Meanings that express common cultural categories (for instance, gender distinctions) are conveyed by many different products. New styles tend to be adopted by many people simultaneously in a process known as collective selection. Perspectives on motivations for adopting new styles include psychological, economic and sociological models of fashion.

→ Fashions tend to follow cycles that resemble the product lifecycle. The two extremes of fashion adoption, classics and fads, can be distinguished in terms of the length of this cycle.

KEY TERMS

Advergaming (p. 581)

Art product (p. 573)

Classic (p. 598)

Collective selection (p. 590)

Conspicuous consumption (p. 592)

Continuous innovation (p. 587)

Co-optation (p. 568)

Craft product (p. 573)

Cultivation hypothesis (p. 582)

Cultural formula (p. 576)

Cultural gatekeepers (p. 570)

Cultural intermediaries (p. 571)

Cultural production system (CPS) (p. 570)

Cultural selection (p. 568)

Discontinuous innovation (p. 588)

Dynamically continuous innovation (p. 588)

Early adopters (p. 585)

Erogenous zones (p. 591)

Fad (p. 598)

Fashion (p. 590)

Fashion acceptance cycle (p. 597)

Fashion lifecycle (p. 597)

Fashion system (p. 589)

Innovation (p. 582)

Lead users (p. 586)

Meme theory (p. 595)

Product placement (p. 580)

Prosumer (p. 573)

Reality engineering (p. 578)

Tipping point (p. 595)

Trickle-down theory (p. 592)

CONSUMER BEHAVIOUR CHALLENGE

1 Construct a 'biography' of a product, tracing its progress from the time it was introduced. How long did it take to diffuse to the mass market? Do the same consumers use the product now as those who first adopted it? What are its future prospects – is it destined for obsolescence? Would you characterize the product as either a classic or a fad?

2 Some consumers complain that they are 'at the mercy' of designers: they are forced to buy whatever styles are in fashion because nothing else is available. Do you agree that there is such a thing as a 'designer conspiracy'?

3 What is the basic difference between a fad, a fashion and a classic? Provide examples of each.

4 What is the difference between an art and a craft? Where would you characterize advertising within this framework?

5 Think about some innovative products that you can remember, but which disappeared. Try to reflect on the reasons why these innovations failed.

6 Then try to remember some successful innovations. What characteristics made them successful? Do the successes and failures fit with the criteria mentioned in this chapter?

7 The marketing opportunity of introducing product placements in, e.g. news programmes, may have some problematic ethical and political side effects? Would you be comfortable with product placement in the news? Why, or why not?

8 The chapter mentions some instances where market research findings influenced artistic decisions, as when a film ending was reshot to accommodate consumers' preferences. Many people would oppose this use of consumer research, claiming that books, films, records or other artistic endeavours should not be designed merely to conform to what people want to read, see or hear. What do you think?

9 Many are claiming a more individualistic style of fashion these years. Discuss whether individualism in style and fashion has actually increased or whether we are being conformist in new ways.

For additional material see the companion website at www.pearsoned.co.uk/solomon

NOTES

1. InterContinental Hotels – owners of the Holiday Inn and Crowne Plaza hotels – revealed their plan to launch a new health and wellness focused hotel chain from 2013. Reacting on the feedback that more and more customers are following the 'wellness trend' and may be afraid to lose their good habits from daily life when travelling. So these hotels, tentatively branded with the name EDEN, should be all about exercise, healthy eating and good sleep. The hotels would supply yoga mats for every room (and possibly omit the minibars) as well as programmes and routines for personal exercise. The brand is to be launched first in the USA but plans are to export it to Europe and Asia after five years of home market consolidation. Christopher Thompson, 'Intercontinental swaps minibars for yoga', *Financial Times*, 28 February 2012, www.ft.com/intl/cms/s/0/9a6bb182-6230-11e1-872e-00144feabdc0, accessed 1 March 2012.

2. Nina Darnton, 'Where the homegirls are', *Newsweek* (17 June 1991): 60; 'The idea chain', *Newsweek* (5 October 1992): 32.

3. Cyndee Miller, 'X marks the lucrative spot, but some advertisers can't hit target', *Marketing News* (2 August 1993): 1.

4. Ad appeared in *Elle* (September 1994).

5. Marc Spiegler, 'Marketing street culture: Bringing hip-hop style to the mainstream', *American Demographics* (November 1996): 23–7; Joshua Levine, 'Badass sells', *Forbes* (21 April 1997): 142–8.

6. Jeff Jensen, 'Hip, wholesome image makes a marketing star of rap's LL Cool J', *Advertising Age* (25 August 1997): 1.

7. Alice Z. Cuneo, 'Gap's 1st global ads confront dockers on a khaki battlefield', *Advertising Age* (20 April 1998): 3–5.

8. Jancee Dunn, 'How hip-hop style bum-rushed the mall', *Rolling Stone* (18 March 1999): 54–9.

9. Quoted in Teri Agins, 'The rare art of "gilt by association": How Armani got stars to be billboards', *The Wall Street Journal Interactive Edition* (14 September 1999).

10. Eryn Brown, 'From rap to retail: Wiring the hip-hop nation', *Fortune* (17 April 2000): 530.

11. Martin Fackler, 'Hip hop invading China', *The Birmingham News* (15 February 2002): D1.

12. Maureen Tkacik, '"Z" zips into the zeitgeist, subbing for "S" in hot slang', *The Wall Street Journal Interactive Edition* (4 January 2003); Maureen Tkacik, 'Slang from the 'hood now sells toyz in target', *The Wall Street Journal Interactive Edition* (30 December 2002).

13. 'Return of the Mac – coming soon' (29 March 2005), http://news.bbc.co.uk/2/hi/business/4389751.stm

14. Arthur, Damien, 'Authenticity and consumption in the Australian hip hop culture', *Qualitative Market Research* 9(2) (2005): 140.

15. http://www.icce.rug.nl/~soundscapes/DATABASES/MIE/Part2_chapter08.shtml; https://sdumail.sdu.dk/exchweb/bin/redir.asp? http://www.icce.rug.nl/~soundscapes/DATABASES/MIE/Part2_chapter08.shtml, accessed 9 April 2009.

16. Danmarks Radio, P1, 5 November 2008.

17. www.rocawear.com/catalog/URW/all_btodviewall, accessed 27 April 2012.

18. Elizabeth M. Blair, 'Commercialization of the rap music youth subculture', *Journal of Popular Culture* 27 (Winter 1993): 21–34; Basil G. Englis, Michael R. Solomon and Anna Olofsson, 'Consumption imagery in music television: A bi-cultural perspective', *Journal of Advertising* 22 (December 1993): 21–34.

19. Marc Spiegler, 'Marketing street culture: Bringing hip-hop style to the mainstream', *American Demographics* (November 1996): 29–34.

20. Janice Brace-Govan and Hélène de Burgh-Woodman, 'Sneakers and street culture: A postcolonial analysis of marginalized cultural consumption', *Consumption, Markets and Culture* 11(2) (2008): 93–112.

21. See, for example, Thomas Frank, *The Conquest of Cool* (Chicago: University of Chicago Press, 1997).

22. Teri Agins, 'To track fickle fashion, apparel firms go online', *The Wall Street Journal* (11 May 2000): B1.

23. www.signature9.com/style-99, accessed 27 April 2012.

24. www.thesartorialist.com

25. Richard A. Peterson, 'The Production of Culture: A Prolegomenon', in Richard A. Peterson (ed.), *The Production of Culture*, Sage Contemporary Social Science Issues (Beverly Hills, CA: Sage, 1976) 33: 7–22.

26. Richard A. Peterson and D.G. Berger, 'Entrepreneurship in organizations: Evidence from the popular music industry', *Administrative Science Quarterly* 16 (1971): 97–107.

27. Elizabeth C. Hirschman, 'Resource exchange in the production and distribution of a motion picture', *Empirical Studies of the Arts* 8 (1990) 1: 31–51; Michael R. Solomon, 'Building Up and Breaking Down: The Impact of Cultural Sorting on Symbolic Consumption', in J. Sheth and E.C. Hirschman (eds), *Research in Consumer Behavior* (Greenwich, CT: JAI Press, 1988): 325–51.

28. See Paul M. Hirsch, 'Processing fads and fashions: An organizational set analysis of cultural industry systems', *American Journal of Sociology* 77 (1972) 4: 639–59; Russell Lynes, *The Tastemakers* (New York: Harper & Brothers, 1954); Michael R. Solomon, 'The missing link: Surrogate consumers in the marketing chain', *Journal of Marketing* 50 (October 1986): 208–19.

29. Jennifer Smith Maguire, 'Provenance and the liminality of production and consumption: The case of wine promoters', *Marketing Theory*, 10 (3, 2010); 269–282.

30. A concept originally introduced by Pierre Bourdieu. See, for example, Paul du Gay, 'Devices and Ddispositions: Pormoting consumption', *Consumption, Market and Culture*, 7 (June 2004): 99–105 and Anne M. Cronin, 'Regimes of mediation: advertising practitioners as cultural intermediaries, *Consumption, Market and Culture*, 7 (December 2004): 349–369.

31. Michael R. Solomon, Richard Ashmore and Laura Longo, 'The beauty match-up hypothesis: Congruence between types of beauty and product images in advertising', *Journal of Advertising* 21 (December 1992): 23–34.

32. Michael R. Solomon, *Conquering Consumerspace: Marketing Strategies for a Branded World* (New York: AMACOM, 2003).

33. Craig J. Thompson and Gökcen Coskuner-Balli, 'Countervailing market responses to corporate co-optation and the ideological recruitment of consumption communities', *Journal of Consumer Research* 34(2) (August 2007): 135–52.

34. Bernard Cova and Daniele Dalli, 'Working consumers: The next step in marketing theory?', *Marketing Theory*, 9 (3, 2009): 315–339. See also Detlev Zwick, Sammy Bonsu and Aron Darmody, 'Putting consumers to work: "Co-creation" and the new marketing govern-mentality', *Journal of Consumer Culture*, 8 (2, 2008): 163-196.

35. Peter Nuttall, 'Insiders, regulars and tourists: Exploring selves and music consumption in adolescence', *Journal of Consumer Behaviour*, 8 (2009): 211-224.

36. Terry O'Sullivan, 'All together now: A symphony orchestra audience as a consuming community', *Consumption, Markets and Culture*, 12 (September 2009): 209–223.

37. Howard S. Becker, 'Arts and crafts', *American Journal of Sociology* 83 (January 1987): 862–89.

38. Herbert J. Gans, 'Popular Culture in America: Social Problem in a Mass Society or Social Asset in a Pluralist Society?' in Howard S. Becker (ed.), *Social Problems: A Modern Approach* (New York: Wiley, 1966).

39. Anders Bengtsson, Jacob Östberg and Dannie Kjeldgaard, 'Prisoners in paradise: Subcultural resistance to the marketization of tattooing', *Consumption, Markets and Culture* 8(3) (2005): 261–74.

40. Peter S. Green, 'Moviegoers devour ads', *Advertising Age* (26 June 1989): 36.

41. Michael R. Real, *Mass-Mediated Culture* (Englewood Cliffs, NJ: Prentice-Hall, 1977).

42. For some websites that show 'Top-40' music sales in Europe and North America, see: http://top40–charts.com/, and http://www.bbc.co.uk/radio1/chart/singles.shtml, accessed 5 August 2005.

43. Luca M. Visconti, John F. Sherry Jr., Stefania Borghini and Laurel Anderson, 'Street Art, Sweet Art? Reclaiming the "Public" in Public Place', *Journal of Consumer Research* Vol. 37, No. 3 (October 2010), pp. 511–529.

44. Annetta Miller, 'Shopping bags imitate art: Seen the sacks? Now visit the museum exhibit', *Newsweek* (23 January 1989): 44.

45. Kim Foltz, 'New species for study: Consumers in action', *New York Times* (18 December 1989): A1.

46. Arthur A. Berger, *Signs in Contemporary Culture: An Introduction to Semiotics* (New York: Longman, 1984).

47. Stephen Brown, 'Psycho shopper: A comparative literary analysis of "the dark side"', in Flemming Hansen (ed.), *European Advances in Consumer Research* 2 (Provo, UT: Association for Consumer Research, 1995): 96–103; Stephen Brown, 'Consumption Behaviour in the Sex'n'Shopping Novels of Judith Krantz: A Post-structuralist Perspective', in J. Lynch and K. Corfman (eds), *Advances in Consumer Research* 23 (Provo, UT: Association for Consumer Research, 1996): 96–103.

48. Christina Goulding and Michael Saren, 'Performing identity: an analysis of gender expression at the Whitby goth festival', *Consumption, Markets and Culture*, 12 (March 2009): 27–46.

49. 'Hip to be Square: Why Young Buyers Covet "Grandpa" Cars', *Wall Street Journal* (9 May 2006): A, p. 1.

50. Randall Frost, 'Staying power: Surviving the limelight', http://www.brandchannel.com/features_effect.asp?pf_id=215#more (accessed 5 August 2005), and Jonathan Guthrie, 'Why using a dead celebrity sells', *Financial Times* (26 April 2005), http://news.ft.com/cms/s/f93e84d2-b675-11d9-aebd-00000e2511c8.html

51. Michiko Kakutani, 'Art is easier the 2d time around', *New York Times* (30 October 1994): E4. See also Stephen Brown, *Retro-Marketing* (London: Routledge, 2001).

52. Nigel Andrews, 'Filming a blockbuster is one thing; striking gold is another', *Financial Times*, accessed via Simon & Schuster College Newslink (20 January 1998).

53. Helene Diamond, 'Lights, camera . . . research!', *Marketing News* (11 September 1989): 10.

54. Nigel Andrews, 'Filming a blockbuster is one thing; striking gold is another', *op. cit.*

55. Nina M. Lentini, 'Doh! Looks Like 7-Eleven Stores May Get Homered', *Marketing Daily* (March 30, 2007), www.mediapost.com, accessed 30 March 2007.

56. Steve Cooper, Damien McLoughlin and Andrew Keating, 'Individual and neo-tribal consumption: Tales from the Simpsons of Springfield', *Journal of Consumer Behaviour* 4(5) (2005): 330–44.

57. Michael R. Solomon and Basil G. Englis, 'Reality engineering: Blurring the boundaries between marketing and popular culture', *Journal of Current Issues and Research in Advertising* 16 (Fall 1994) 2: 1–17.

58. 'Hollywood-sur-brie', *Le Nouvel Observateur* (14 November 1996): 18–19.

59. Nicolas Marmie, 'Casablanca Gets a Rick's', *Montgomery Advertiser* (9 May 2004): 3AA.

60. Jennifer Sokolowsky, 'Germany's Food Hotel: A La Carte Blanche for Brands', *Brand Channel* (25 November 2010), http://www.brandchannel.com/home/post/2010/11/25/Germany-Food-Hotel.aspx, accessed 28 April 2011.

61. www.b.dk/kultur/james-bond-skifter-martini-ud-med-heineken, accessed 28 April 2012.

62. Wayne Friedman, '"Minority report" stars Lexus, Nokia', *Advertising Age* (17 June 2002): 41.

63. Denise E. DeLorme and Leonard N. Reid, 'Moviegoers' experiences and interpretations of brands in films revisited', *Journal of Advertising* 28(2) (1999): 71–90.

64. Cristel Antonia Russell, 'Investigating the effectiveness of product placement in television shows: The role of modality and plot connection congruence on brand memory and attitude', *Journal of Consumer Research* 29 (December 2002): 306–18.

65. Claire Atkinson, 'Ad intrusion up, say consumers', *Advertising Age* (6 January 2003): 1.

66. http://www.marketingcharts.com/television/product-placements-up-6-in-first-quarter-4477/, accessed 29 March 2009.

67. www.adage.com/articlwe/mediaworks/product-placement-hits-high-gear-american-idol, accessed 28 April 2012.

68. John Walsh, 'As seen on screen. Whatever next for product placement', *The Independent*, 24 July 2008, http://www.independent.co.uk/news/media/as-seen-on-screen-whatever-next-for-product-placement-875704.html, accessed on 12 November 2008.

69. Peter Wonacott, 'Chinese TV is an eager medium for (lots of) product placement', *The Wall Street Journal Interactive Edition* (26 January 2000).

70. Gabriel Kahn, 'Product placement booms in new Bollywood films', *The Wall Street Journal Interactive Edition* (30 August 2002).

71. Jennifer Tanaka and Marc Peyser, 'The apples of their eyes', *Newsweek* (30 November 1998): 58.

72. Geoffrey A. Fowler, 'New Star on Chinese TV: Product Placements', *Wall Street Journal Online Edition* (2 June 2004): B1.

73. Joseph Plambeck, 'Product Placement Grows in Music Videos', *New York Times* (5 July 2010), http://www.nytimes.com/2010/07/06/business/media/06adco.html?_r=1&emc=eta1, accessed 28 April 2011.

74. 'Filmreplik ødelagde Merlot i USA', *Berlingske Kultur*, 15 April 2008: 3.

75. Nick Wingfield, 'Sony's PS3 to Get In-Game Ads', *Wall Street Journal* (4 June 2008): B7; Jeffrey Bardzell, Shaowen Bardzell and Tyler Pace, *Player Engagement and In-Game Advertising* (23 November 2008), http://class.classmatandread.net/pp/oto.pdf, accessed 13 September 2011.

76. George Gerbner, Larry Gross, Nancy Signorielli and Michael Morgan, 'Aging with television: Images on television drama and conceptions of social reality', *Journal of Communication* 30 (1980): 37–47.

77. Stephen Fox and William Philber, 'Television viewing and the perception of affluence', *Sociological Quarterly* 19 (1978): 103–12; W. James Potter, 'Three strategies for elaborating the cultivation hypothesis', *Journalism Quarterly* 65 (Winter 1988): 930–9; Gabriel Weimann, 'Images of life in America: The impact of American T.V. in Israel', *International Journal of Intercultural Relations* 8 (1984): 185–97.

78. Patricia Gaya Wicks, Agnes Nairn and Christine Griffin, 'The role of commodified celebrities in children's moral development: The case of David Beckham', *Consumption, Culture and Markets* 10(4) (2007): 401–24.

79. Stephanie O'Donohue, 'On the Outside Looking In: Advertising Experiences Among Young Unemployed Adults', in Flemming Hansen (ed.), *European Advances in Consumer Research* 2 (Provo, UT: Association for Consumer Research): 264–72; Richard Elliott, 'How Do the Unemployed Maintain Their Identity in a Culture of Consumption?' in Hansen (ed.), *European Advances in Consumer Research* 2: 273–6.

80. Adam Therer, 'On measuring technology diffusion rates', techliberation.com/2009/05/28/on-measuring-technology-diffusion-rates, accessed 28 April 2012.

81. Statistics from www.pureoxygenmobile.com, accessed 1 May 2012. Quoted in *Market*, no. 59 (2012).

82. See for example http://www.digitalbuzzblog.com/volkswagen-bluemotion-online-roulette/, accesses 1 May 2012.

83. Susan B. Kaiser, *The Social Psychology of Clothing* (New York: Macmillan, 1985); Thomas S. Robertson, *Innovative Behavior and Communication* (New York: Holt, Rhinehart & Winston, 1971).

84. Eric J. Arnould, 'Toward a broadened theory of preference formation and the diffusion of innovations: Cases from Zinder Province, Niger Republic', *Journal of Consumer Research* 16 (September 1989): 239–67.

85. Jan-Benedict E.M. Steenkamp, Frenkel ter Hofstede and Michel Wedel, 'A cross-national investigation into the individual and national cultural antecedents of consumer innovativeness', *Journal of Marketing* 63(2) (1999): 55–69.

86. Richard Wilk, 'Bottled water: The pure commodity in the age of branding', *Journal of Consumer Culture* 6(3) (2006): 303–25.

87. Susan L. Holak, Donald R. Lehmann and Farena Sultan, 'The role of expectations in the adoption of innovative consumer durables: Some preliminary evidence', *Journal of Retailing* 63 (Fall 1987): 243–59.

88. Hubert Gatignon and Thomas S. Robertson, 'A propositional inventory for new diffusion research', *Journal of Consumer Research* 11 (March 1985): 849–67.

89. Frank Huber, 'Ein konzept zur ermittlung und bearbeitung des frühkaufersegments im bekleidungsmarkt', *Marketing ZFP* 2 (2nd Quarter 1995): 110–21.

90. Eva Martinez, Yolanda Polo and Carlos Flavián, 'The acceptance and diffusion of new consumer durables: Differences between first and last adopters', *Journal of Consumer Marketing* 15(4) (1998): 323–42.

91. Sofie Møller Bjerrisgaard, 'The Global Construction of the Consumer', unpublished PhD project, Dept of Marketing and Management, University of Southern Denmark, Odense, August 2010. See also John A. McCarthy, Martin I. Horn, Mary Kate Szenasy and Jocelyn Feintuch, 'An exploratory study of consumer style: Country differences and international segments', *Journal of Consumer Behaviour* 6(1) (January–February 2007): 48–59.

92. Gordon R. Foxall and Seema Bhate, 'Cognitive style and personal involvement as explicators of innovative purchasing of health food brands', *European Journal of Marketing* 27(2) (1993): 5–16.

93. Adage.com/article/news/ad-age-agency-year-consumer/114132/, accessed 28 April 2012.

94. Stephen Brown, 'O customer where art thou?', *Business Horizons*, 47 (4, 2004): 61–70.

95. Byrnes, Nanette, 'Xeroxs' New Design Team: Customers', *Business Week* (7 May 2007): 72.

96. Elizabeth C. Hirschman, 'Symbolism and Technology as Sources of the Generation of Innovations', in Andrew Mitchell (ed.), *Advances in Consumer Research* 9 (Provo, UT: Association for Consumer Research, 1982): 537–41.

97. Søren Askegaard and A. Fuat Firat, 'Towards a Critique of Material Culture, Consumption and Markets', in Susan M. Pearce (ed.), *Experiencing Material Culture in the Western World* (London: Leicester University Press, 1997): 114–39.

98. Stephen Brown, *Postmodern Marketing* (London: Routledge, 1995).

99. 'Mange kvinder er begyndt at drikke mandecola', *Berlingske Tidende* (19 August 2008), Business: 11.

100. http://www.nanotechproject.org/inventories/consumer/, accessed 7 November 2008.

101. Everett M. Rogers, *Diffusion of Innovations*, 3rd edn (New York: Free Press, 1983).

102. http://markedforing.dk/artikler/dagens-aviser/taxi-app-bliver-milliardforretning?/, accessed 1 May 2012.

103. Robert J. Fisher and Linda L. Price, 'An investigation into the social context of early adoption behavior', *Journal of Consumer Research* 19 (December 1992): 477–86.

104. Güliz Ger and Russell W. Belk, 'I'd like to buy the world a Coke: Consumptionscapes of the "less affluent world"', *Journal of Consumer Policy* 19 (1996): 271–304; Robin A. Coulter, Linda L. Price and Lawrence Feick, 'Rethinking the

origins of involvement and brand commitment: Insights from postsocialist Central Europe', *Journal of Consumer Research* 30 (September 2003): 151–69.

105. W. Chan Kim and Renée Mauborgne, 'Value innovation: The strategic logic of high growth', *Harvard Business Review* (January–February 1997): 103–12.

106. 'Dare to be different', *Marketing* (13 February 1997): 22–3.

107. Roland Barthes, *Système de la mode* (Paris: Seuil, 1967), English: Roland Barthes, *The Language of Fashion* (Oxford: Berg Publishers 2006).

108. 'Diaper bag double take', *Discount Merchandiser* (March 2000).

109. Umberto Eco, *A Theory of Semiotics* (Bloomington, IN: Indiana University Press, 1979).

110. Fred Davis, 'Clothing and Fashion as Communication', in Michael R. Solomon (ed.), *The Psychology of Fashion* (Lexington, MA: Lexington Books, 1985): 15–28.

111. Melanie Wallendorf, 'The Formation of Aesthetic Criteria Through Social Structures and Social Institutions', in Jerry C. Olson (ed.), *Advances in Consumer Research* 7 (Ann Arbor, MI: Association for Consumer Research, 1980): 3–6.

112. Christine Delhaye, 'The development of consumption culture and the individualization of female identity', *Journal of Consumer Culture* 6(1) (2006): 87–115.

113. Herbert Blumer, *Symbolic Interactionism: Perspective and Method* (Englewood Cliffs, NJ: Prentice-Hall, 1969); Howard S. Becker, 'Art as collective action', *American Sociological Review* 39 (December 1973); Richard A. Peterson, 'Revitalizing the culture concept', *Annual Review of Sociology* 5 (1979): 137–66.

114. For more details, see Kaiser, *The Social Psychology of Clothing, op. cit.*; George B. Sproles, 'Behavioral Science Theories of Fashion', in Solomon (ed.), *The Psychology of Fashion, op. cit.*: 55–70.

115. C.R. Snyder and Howard L. Fromkin, *Uniqueness: The Human Pursuit of Difference* (New York: Plenum Press, 1980).

116. Alison Lurie, *The Language of Clothes* (New York: Random House, 1981).

117. Linda Dyett, 'Desperately seeking skin', *Psychology Today* (May/June 1996): 14.

118. Diego Rinallo, 'Producing and Consuming the Metrosexual', in S. Borghini, M.A. McGrath and C. Otnes (eds), *European Advances in Consumer Research*, 2008): 306–08.

119. Susan Auty and Richard Elliott, 'Social Identity and the Meaning of Fashion Brands', in B. Englis and A. Olofsson (eds), *European Advances in Consumer Research* 3 (Provo, UT: Association for Consumer Research, 1998): 1–10.

120. John Fiske, *Understanding Popular Culture* (Boston: Unwin Hyman, 1989): especially 1–21.

121. Harvey Leibenstein, *Beyond Economic Man: A New Foundation for Microeconomics* (Cambridge, MA: Harvard University Press, 1976).

122. Nara Schoenberg, 'Goth Culture Moves into Mainstream', *Montgomery Advertiser* (9 January 2003): 1G.

123. Georg Simmel, 'Fashion', *International Quarterly* 10 (1904): 130–55.

124. www.asos.com, accessed 12 November 2008.

125. Grant D. McCracken, 'The Trickle-Down Theory Rehabilitated', in Solomon (ed.), *The Psychology of Fashion, op. cit.*: 39–54.

126. Søren Askegaard, Deniz Atik and Stefania Borghini, 'The Interplay of Institutional Forces and Consumer Desires in the Moulding of Fashion', in S. Borghini, M.A. McGrath and C. Otnes (eds), *European Advances in Consumer Research* (Duluth, MN: Association for Consumer Research, 2008): 306.

127. 'Fast Fashion in 11 per cent Sales Surge', *Marketing* (20 April 2005): 14.

128. Charles W. King, 'Fashion Adoption: A Rebuttal to the "Trickle-Down" Theory', in Stephen A. Greyser (ed.), *Toward Scientific Marketing* (Chicago: American Marketing Association, 1963): 108–25.

129. Dannie Kjeldgaard, 'The meaning of style? Style reflexivity among Danish high school youths' *Journal of Consumer Behavior*, 8 (2009): 71–83.

130. Terry Newholm and Gillian C. Hopkinson, 'I just tend to wear what I like: Contemporary consumption and the paradoxical construction of individuality', *Marketing Theory*, 9 (2009): 439–462.

131. Gilles Marion and Agnes Nairn, '"We make the shoes, you make the story". Teenage girls' experiences of fashion: Bricolage, tactics and narrative identity', *Consumption, Markets and Culture*, 14 (March 2011): 29–56.

132. Gillian Hogg, Suzanne Horne and David Carmichael, 'Fun, Fashion, or Just Plain Sailing? The Consumption of Clothing in the Sailing Community', in B. Dubois, T. Lowrey, L.J. Shrum and M. Vanhuele (eds), *European Advances in Consumer Research* 4 (Provo, UT: Association for Consumer Research, 1999): 336–40.

133. Triin Vihalemm and Margit Keller, 'Looking Russian or Estonian: Young consumers constructing the ethnic "self" and "other"', *Consumption, Markets and Culture*, 14 (September 2011): 293-309.

134. Alf H. Walle, 'Grassroots innovation', *Marketing Insights* (Summer 1990): 44–51.

135. Patrick Hetzel, 'The Role of Fashion and Design in a Postmodern Society: What Challenges for Firms?' in M.J. Baker (ed.), *Perspectives on Marketing Management* 4 (London: John Wiley & Sons, 1994): 97–118.

136. Stuart and Elizabeth Ewen, cited in Mike Featherstone, *Consumer Culture and Postmodernism* (London: Sage, 1993): 83.

137. Patrick Hetzel, 'The role of fashion and design in a post-modern society: what challenges for firms?' *op. cit.*

138. Anne F. Jensen, 'Acknowledging and Consuming Fashion in the Era after "Good Taste" – From the Beautiful to the Hideous', Doctoral Dissertations from the Faculty of Social Science, no. 40 (Odense: University of Southern Denmark, 1999).

139. Patrick Hetzel, 'A Socio-Semiotic Analysis of the Media/Consumer Relationships in the Production of Fashion Systems: The Case of the "Elle-France" Magazine', in Englis and Olofsson (eds), *European Advances in Consumer Research* 3: 104–7.

140. 'Topmodel i genbrugstøj', *Fyens Stiftstidende, Erhverv* (1 November 2000): 1.

141. http://news.bbc.co.uk/2/hi/uk_news/magazine/7563318.stm and http://www.guardian.co.uk/lifeandstyle/2007/may/18/fashion.ethicalliving, both accessed 12 November 2008.

142. 'Panik i mode-fabrikken', Intervju med Alladi Venkatesh, *Dagens Nyheter* (27 June 2000): B1.

143. Don Slater, *Consumer Culture and Modernity* (Cambridge: Polity Press, 1997).

144. Anne F. Jensen and Søren Askegaard, 'In Pursuit of Ugliness. Searching for a Fashion Concept in the Era After Good Taste', Working Paper in Marketing, no. 17 (Odense: Odense University, 1998).

145. Anonymous, 'FCUK Consumer Research: On Disgust, Revulsion and Other Forms of Offensive Advertising', paper submitted to the 2001 Association for Consumer Research European Conference (Berlin, 20–23 June).

146. Heltnormalt.dk/truthfacts/2012/01/10, accessed 28 April 2012.

147. Robert V. Kozinets, 'Fandoms' menace/pop flows: Exploring the metaphor of entertainment as recombinant/memetic engineering', *Association for Consumer Research* (October 1999). The new science of memetics, which tries to explain how beliefs gain acceptance and predict their progress, was spurred by Richard Dawkins who in the 1970s proposed culture as a Darwinian struggle among 'memes' or mind viruses. See Geoffrey Cowley, 'Viruses of the Mind: How Odd Ideas Survive', *Newsweek* (14 April 1997): 14.

148. Malcolm Gladwell, *The Tipping Point* (New York: Little, Brown and Co., 2000).

149. Robin Givhan, 'Designers caught in a tangled web', *The Washington Post* (5 April 1997): C1 (2 pp.).

150. Anne F. Jensen and Per Østergaard, 'Dressing for Security or Risk? An Exploratory Study of Two Different Ways of Consuming Fashion', in Englis and Olofsson (eds), *European Advances in Consumer Research* 3: 98–103.

151. Anthony Ramirez, 'The pedestrian sneaker makes a comeback', *New York Times* (14 October 1990): F17.

152. B.E. Aguirre, E.L. Quarantelli and Jorge L. Mendoza, 'The collective behavior of fads: The characteristics, effects, and career of streaking', *American Sociological Review* (August 1989): 569.

153. Quoted in Stephen Brown and Anthony Patterson, '"You're a Wizard, Harry!" Consumer responses to the Harry Potter phenomenon', *Advances in Consumer Research* 33 (2006): 155–60.

154. Maddy Savage, 'Scandinavian food: why is it becoming popular in the UK?', *BBC News magazine* 25. February 2012.

155. Martin G. Letscher, 'How to tell fads from trends', *American Demographics* (December 1994): 38–45.

15 CONSUMPTION AND CULTURAL DIFFERENCES

CHAPTER OBJECTIVES

When you finish reading this chapter you will understand why:

→ Our memberships in ethnic, racial and religious subcultures often guide our consumption behaviours.

→ Our identification with microcultures that reflect a shared interest in some organization or activity influences what we buy.

→ Many marketing messages appeal to ethnic and racial identity.

→ Marketers increasingly use religious and spiritual themes when they talk to consumers.

→ The changing nature of the marketplace for euro consumers.

SEVGI, waking early on Saturday morning, braces herself for a long day of errands and chores. As usual, her mother expects her to do the shopping while she is at work, and then prepare the food for the big family get-together tonight. Of course, her older brother would never be asked to do the shopping or help out in the kitchen – these are women's jobs.

Family gatherings make a lot of work, and Sevgi wishes that her mother would use prepared foods once in a while, especially on a Saturday when Sevgi has errands of her own to do. But no, her mother insists on preparing most of her food from scratch; she rarely uses any convenience products, to ensure that the meals she serves are of the highest quality.

Resigned, Sevgi watches TRTint on the family's cable TV while she's getting dressed, and then she heads down to the local newsagent 'De Pijp' to buy a magazine – there are dozens of Turkish magazines and newspapers for sale and she likes to pick up new ones occasionally. Then Sevgi buys the grocery items her mother wants; the Islamic *halal* butcher is a long-time family friend and already has the cuts of lamb prepared for her. The vendors at the open air stalls in the Albert Cuyp Market where she and her mother shop all the time know her, and provide her with choice quality olives and vegetables. One quick stop at the local sweetshop to pick up the family's favourite *drop* (liquorice) and she's almost done. With any luck when she gets back home she will have a little time to download the latest music from Adele. She loves her material, and she'll listen to it whilst she is in the kitchen, chopping, peeling and stirring the vegetables. Sevgi smiles to herself, despite a busy day preparing the house and meal for the family party, she feels that Amsterdam is a great place to live.

607

SUBCULTURES AND CONSUMER IDENTITY

Yes, Sevgi lives in Amsterdam, not Istanbul. However, this consumer vignette could just as easily have taken place in London, Berlin, Stockholm, Marseilles or thousands of other cities throughout Europe. In the mid-1990s there were well over 25 million Europeans who belonged to an ethnic sub-group, and in several European countries such as France, Belgium and Germany, they collectively accounted for around 10 per cent of the total population. In the UK, the ethnic communities were forecast to double in population to over 6 million by the mid 2020s.[1] In 2011 the total population within EU27 was nearing 500 million.[2] During 2008 about 3.8 million people immigrated into one of the EU member states (see Figure 15.1) and at least 2.3 million emigrants are reported to have left one of the EU member states.[3] A sense of the pattern of different types of background of residents (native born, first generation and

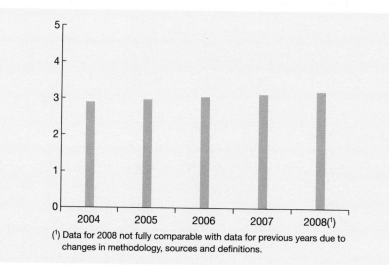

(1) Data for 2008 not fully comparable with data for previous years due to changes in methodology, sources and definitions.

Figure 15.1 Total immigration, EU27 (million)
Source: Eurostat (migr_imm1ctz).

This picture of Star Trek fans (Trekkies) shows the key role played by microcultures in defining the extended self.

Mark Peterson/Corbis.

Table 15.1 Population aged 25–54 of EU27 countries by type of background in 2008

| | Persons with native background | | Second-generation migrants | | | | First-generation migrants | |
| | | | Persons with mixed background | | Persons with foreign background | | | |
	(1000)	%	(1000)	%	(1000)	%	(1000)	%
EU27	**173288.6**	**82.8**	**5982.2**	**2.9**	**4411.2**	**2.1**	**25478.6**	**12.2**
BE	3409.8	77.1	182.5	4.1	177.7	4.0	650.6	14.7
BG	3172.3	99.7	:	:	:	:	:	:
CZ	4272.6	92.8	151.5	3.3	42.8	0.9	136.8	3.0
DK	1942.3	91.1	:	:	:	:	183.1	8.6
DE([1])	26962.3	78.1	494.9	1.4	987.7	2.9	6081.4	17.6
EE	356.1	64.4	49.2	8.9	72.5	13.1	75.3	13.6
IE	1461.5	74.6	44.0	2.2	14.0	0.7	439.8	22.4
EL	4170.3	88.3	33.2	0.7	76.1	0.6	492.1	10.4
ES	17015.0	79.8	200.4	0.9	43.3	0.2	4075.8	19.1
FR	17752.6	73.4	1857.1	7.7	1404.9	5.8	3175.2	13.1
IT	22866.3	88.4	237.8	0.9	16.5	0.1	2752.6	10.6
CY	259.8	75.6	4.4	1.3	:	:	79.6	23.2
LV	677.9	70.8	97.2	10.2	62.4	6.5	119.8	12.5
LT	1312.2	92.0	36.2	2.5	:	:	54.2	3.8
LU	83.1	38.1	16.0	7.3	14.5	6.6	104.9	48.0
HU	4176.9	96.9	27.8	0.6	11.9	0.3	94.3	2.2
MT	158.4	93.6	:	:	:	:	10.9	6.4
NL	5270.8	76.5	398.3	5.8	189.3	2.7	1035.6	15.0
AT	2731.0	74.7	181.2	5.0	70.1	1.9	672.0	18.4
PL	15634.8	96.8	330.8	2.1	134.6	0.8	55.7	0.3
PT	4114.2	88.2	38.6	0.8	20.2	0.4	491.6	10.5
RO	8980.9	99.8	:	:	:	:	17.5	0.2
SI	758.5	83.3	46.3	5.1	23.5	2.6	82.1	9.0
SK	2383.0	97.1	40.0	1.6	9.1	0.4	22.6	0.9
FI	:	:	:	:	:	:	:	:
SE	2647.6	74.2	240.0	6.7	103.1	2.9	576.3	16.2
UK	18851.6	75.6	1253.8	5.0	944.2	3.8	3892.5	15.6
CH	1779.4	53.6	320.0	9.6	187.6	5.7	1032.2	31.1

([1])In case of Germany the country of birth of the parents is approximated by the nationality of the parents.

Source: Eurostat, LFS 2008 ad hoc module (online data code: lfso_08cobsmf); 'A statistical portrait of the first and second generation' 2011 edition, Eurostat: Eurostat statistical books, European Commission, Table 3.1, page 122; http://epp.eurostat.ec.europa.eu/portal/page/portal/product_details/publication?p_product_code=KS-31-10-539, accessed 20 February 2012.

second generation) in the various EU27 countries can be seen in Table 15.1.[4] The areas of emigration from outside the EU into the EU27 for 2009 are shown in Figure 15.2.[5]

Turkish consumers have much in common with members of other racial and ethnic groups who live in Europe. These groups of consumers observe the same national holidays, their expenditures are affected by the country's economic health and they may join together in rooting for their host country's national team in the football World Cup. Nevertheless, while European residency (and in most cases European citizenship) provides the raw material for

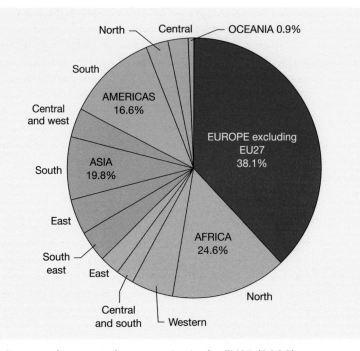

Figure 15.2 Citizens of non-member countries in the EU27 (2009)

Source: Eurostat (migr_pop1ctz).

some consumption decisions, others profoundly affect and are profoundly affected by the enormous variations in the social fabric of the country where they live.

Our group memberships *within* our society-at-large help to define us. A **subculture** is a group whose members share beliefs and common experiences that set them apart from others. Every one of us belongs to many subcultures, depending on our age, race, ethnic background, or place of residence. Sevgi's Turkish heritage exerts a huge influence on her everyday experience and consumption preferences. These memberships can be based on similarities in age (major subcultural consumer groups based on age have already been discussed in Chapter 11), race or ethnic background, place of residence. In contrast to larger, demographically based subcultures, people who are part of a **micro-culture**, freely choose to identify with a lifestyle or aesthetic preference. Whether 'Dead Heads', 'Netizens', or skinheads, each group exhibits its own unique set of norms, vocabulary and product insignias (such as the British Lonsdale sports and fashion clothier, whose sweatshirts signify white racists to many youths in the Netherlands).[6] These micro-cultures or 'communities' can even gel around fictional characters and events, and play a key role in defining the extended self (see Chapter 5). Numerous micro-cultures thrive on their collective worship of mythical and not-so-mythical worlds and characters that range from the music group Phish to Hello Kitty. Many devotees of *Star Trek*, for example, immerse themselves in a make-believe world of starships, phasers and Vulcan mind melds.[7] Our subcultures and micro-cultures often play a key role in defining the extended self (see Chapter 5) and micro-cultures typically command fierce loyalty.

A study of contemporary 'mountain men' in the western United States illustrates the binding influence of a micro-culture on its members. Researchers found that group members shared a strong sense of identity they expressed in weekend retreats, where they reinforced these ties with authentic items as they used *tipis*, buffalo robes, buckskin leggings and beaded moccasins to create a sense of community among fellow mountain men.[8]

Trend trackers find some of the most interesting – and rapidly changing – micro-cultures in Japan, where young women start many trends that eventually make their way around the world.

One is *Onna Otaku* (she-nerds): girls who get their geek on as they stock up on femme-friendly comics, gadgets and action figures instead of makeup and clothes. Another is the growing **cosplay** movement, a form of performance art in which participants wear elaborate costumes that represent a virtual world avatar or other fictional character. These outfits often depict figures from *manga*, *anime* or other forms of graphic novels, but they can also take the form of costumes from movies such as *The Matrix*, *Star Wars*, *Harry Potter* or even *Ace Ventura: Pet Detective* (cosplay cafés in Tokyo feature waitresses who dress as maids). This role-playing subculture appears in various forms in Western culture as well, whether at *anime* or comic conventions, in the popular Goth subculture, or as a form of sexual role-playing (e.g. women who dress in nurse's uniforms).[9]

Ethnic and racial subcultures

Ethnic and religious identity is a significant component of a consumer's self-concept. An **ethnic** or **racial subculture** consists of a self-perpetuating group of consumers who are held together by common cultural and/or genetic ties, and is identified both by its members and by others as being a distinguishable category.[10] In some countries, such as Japan, ethnicity is almost synonymous with the dominant culture, since most citizens claim the same homogeneous cultural ties (although Japan has sizeable minority populations, most notably people of Korean ancestry). In heterogeneous societies like those found in the US and some parts of Europe, many different cultures are represented, and consumers may expend great effort to keep their subcultural identification from being submerged into the mainstream of the dominant society.[11]

Ethnicity and marketing strategies

Although some companies may feel uncomfortable at the notion that people's racial and ethnic differences should be explicitly taken into account when formulating marketing strategies, the reality is that these subcultural memberships are frequently paramount in shaping people's needs and wants. Research indicates, for example, that membership of these groups is often predictive of such consumer variables as level and type of media exposure, food preferences, the wearing of distinctive apparel, political behaviour, leisure activities and even willingness to try new products. However things can also go wrong when borrowing – and in some cases, misinterpreting – ethnically or religiously distinctive symbolism. Consider, for example, the storm of protest from the international Islamic community over a dress in a House of Chanel fashion show. Supermodel Claudia Schiffer wore a strapless evening gown (with a price tag of almost $23,000) that Karl Lagerfeld designed. The dress included Arabic letters that the designer believed spelled out a love poem. Instead, the message was a verse from the Koran, the Muslim holy book. In addition, the word *God* happened to appear over the model's right breast. Both the designer and the model received death threats, and the controversy subsided only after the company burned the dress.

Research evidence indicates that members of minority groups are more likely to find an advertising spokesperson from their own group to be more trustworthy, and this enhanced credibility in turn translates into more positive brand attitudes.[12] In addition, the way marketing messages should be structured depends on subcultural differences in how meanings are communicated. Sociologists make a distinction between *high-context cultures* and *low-context cultures*. In a high-context culture, group members tend to be tightly knit, and they are likely to infer meanings that go beyond the spoken word. Symbols and gestures, rather than words, carry much of the weight of the message. Many minority cultures are high-context and have strong oral traditions, so perceivers will be more sensitive to nuances in advertisements that go beyond the message copy. In contrast, people in **low-context cultures** are more literal, e.g. Anglo-Saxons.[13]

Ethnic and racial stereotypes

Many subcultures have powerful stereotypes the general public associates with them. In these cases outsiders assume that group members possess certain traits. Unfortunately, a communicator can cast the same trait as either positive or negative, depending on his or her biases or intentions. For example, the Scottish stereotype in the United States is largely positive, so we tend to look favourably on their (supposed) frugality. 3M uses Scottish imagery to denote value (e.g. Scotch tape), as does the Scotch Inns, a motel chain that offers inexpensive accommodation.

In the past, marketers used ethnic symbolism as shorthand to convey certain product attributes. However, miscommunications can occur. A 2011 Cadbury advertising campaign that ran in the UK illustrates these sensitivities. A print and billboard ad for Cadbury's Bliss line of Dairy Milk chocolate ran with the tagline, 'move over Naomi, there's a new diva in town'. Many people, including supermodel Naomi Campbell, objected to the racist undertone of the ad; she claimed it 'was in poor taste on a number of levels, not least in the way they likened me to their chocolate bar'. Cadbury defended the ad, arguing that it intended to poke fun at her reputation as a diva and that no link to her skin colour was intended. Although the industry organization that polices England's advertising determined that the message was not racist, the company responded to threats of a global boycott by withdrawing the ad and apologizing to Campbell.[14]

THE ACCULTURATION PROCESS

Acculturation is the process of movement and adaptation to one country's cultural environment by a person from another country.[15] This is a very important issue for marketers because of our increasingly global society. As people move from place to place, they may quickly assimilate to their new homes, or they may resist this blending process and choose to insulate themselves from the mainstream culture. One important way to distinguish between members of a subculture is to consider the extent to which they retain a sense of identification with their country of origin *vs* their host country. As Figure 15.3 shows, many factors affect the nature of this transition process. Individual differences, such as whether the person speaks the host country language, influence how difficult the adjustment will be. This is a very important issue for marketers because of our increasingly global society.

The person's contacts with **acculturation agents** – people and institutions that teach the ways of a culture – are also crucial. Some of these agents are aligned with the *culture of origin* (in Sevgi's case, Turkey). These include family, friends, the mosque, local businesses and Turkish-language media that keep the consumer in touch with their country of origin. Other agents are associated with the *culture of immigration* (in this case, the Netherlands), and help the consumer to learn how to navigate in the new environment. These include state schools and Dutch-language media.

As immigrants adapt to their new surroundings, several processes come into play. *Movement* refers to the factors motivating people to uproot themselves physically from one location and go to another. Although many ethnic members throughout Europe are second generation (born in the country where they live), their parents are more likely to have been the first to arrive in the new country. On arrival, immigrants encounter a need for *translation*. This means attempting to master a set of rules for operating in the new environment, whether learning how to decipher a different currency or understanding the social meanings of unfamiliar clothing styles. This cultural learning leads to a process of *adaptation*, where new consumption patterns are formed. A recent study of Romanian women in Italy and their food consumption practices, for instance, identified the different strategies that they employed 'to negotiate the traditional gender script based on the dominant discourses in their home

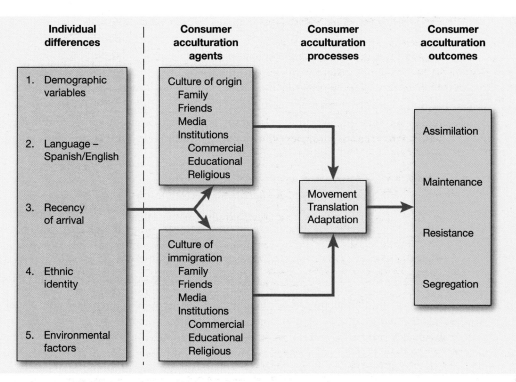

Figure 15.3 A model of consumer acculturation

Source: Adapted from Lisa Peñaloza, '*Atravesando fronteras*/border crossings: A critical ethnographic exploration of the consumer acculturation of Mexican immigrants', *Journal of Consumer Research*, 21 (June 1994): 32–54. Reprinted with the permission of University of Chicago Press.

culture, and the modern woman myth featured in the marketplace representations in the host culture'.[16]

As consumers undergo acculturation, several things happen. Many immigrants undergo (at least to some extent) *assimilation*, where they adopt products, habits and values that are identified with the mainstream culture. At the same time, there is an attempt at *maintenance* of practices associated with the culture of origin. Immigrants stay in touch with people in their country, and many continue to eat ethnic foods and read ethnic newspapers. Their continued identification with their home culture may cause *resistance*, as they resent the pressure to submerge their identities and take on new roles. Finally, immigrants (voluntarily or not) tend to exhibit *segregation*; they are likely to live and shop in places physically separated from the host community. These processes illustrate that ethnicity is a fluid concept and that members of a subculture are constantly recreating its boundaries. Figure 15.3 provides an overview of the processes involved in consumer acculturation.

An *ethnic pluralism* perspective argues that ethnic groups differ from the mainstream in varying degrees, and that adaptation to the larger society occurs selectively. Research evidence argues against the notion that assimilation necessarily involves losing identification with the person's original ethnic group. For example, Sevgi feels comfortable in expressing her 'Turkishness' in a variety of consumption-related ways: the magazines she buys, the TV programmes on the Turkish network she chooses to watch, her choice of ethnically appropriate gifts for events such as weddings and *bayram* (religious holidays).[17] Alternatively, she has no problems at all in expressing consumption behaviours of the mainstream culture – she loves eating *drop* (Dutch liquorice), buys 'Western' music and has her favourite outfits for going out to the cinema and clubs. The best indicator of ethnic assimilation, these researchers argue, is the extent to which members of an ethnic group have social interactions with members of other groups in comparison with their own.[18]

The **progressive learning model** helps us to understand the acculturation process. This perspective assumes that people gradually learn a new culture as they increasingly come in contact with it. Thus, we expect that when people acculturate they will mix the practices of their original culture with those of their new or **host culture**.[19] Research that examines such factors as shopping orientation, the importance people place on various product attributes, media preference and brand loyalty generally supports this pattern.[20] When researchers take into account the intensity of ethnic identification, they find that consumers who retain a strong ethnic identification differ from their more assimilated counterparts in these ways:[21]

- They have a more negative attitude towards business in general (probably caused by frustration as a result of relatively low income levels).
- They are higher users of media that's in their native language.
- They are more brand loyal.
- They are more likely to prefer brands with prestige labels.
- They are more likely to buy brands that specifically advertise to their ethnic group.

The acculturation process embraces all kinds of moves, including those that involve relocating from one place to another within the same country. If you have ever moved (and it is likely you have), you no doubt remember how difficult it was to give up old habits and friends and adapt to what people in your new location do. A recent study of Turkish people who move from the countryside to an urban environment illustrates how people cope with change and unfamiliar circumstances. The authors describe a process of **warming**, which involves transforming objects and places into those that feel cozy, hospitable and authentic. The study's informants described what happened when they tried to turn a cold and unfamiliar house into a home as *güzel* ('beautiful and good', 'modern and warm'). In this context that means incorporating symbols of village life into their new homes by blanketing them with the embroidered, crocheted and lace textiles that people traditionally make by hand for brides' dowries in the villages. The researchers reported that migrants' homes contained far more of these pieces than they would have in their village homes because they used them to adorn the modern appliances they acquired. The dowry textiles symbolize traditional norms and social networks composed of friends and family in the villages, so they link the 'cold' modern objects with the owner's past. Thus, the unfamiliar becomes familiar.[22]

Another group of researchers examined the plight of people who were forced to leave their homes and settle in a foreign country with little planning and few possessions.[23] As 'strangers in a strange land', they must essentially start all over again and completely re-socialize. The authors did an in-depth study of refugees from a number of countries who lived in an Austrian refugee shelter. They found, for example, that teenagers are traumatized by their experience and turn to adaptive consumption strategies to cope. For example, the adolescents (including the boys) all had stuffed animals they used to comfort themselves. And all of the teenage boys wore earrings as a way to create their own community.

A recent ethnographic study of Turkish women squatters has proposed a new model, 'dominated consumer acculturation' (Figure 15.4), in contrast to the model of post-modern consumer acculturation covered by earlier research. The goal of these authors was to identify the role played by particular socio-cultural structures in acculturation by examining Turkish women peasants who were part of the widespread global phenomenon of mass migration of the rural poor into urban areas. In contrast to earlier studies, this research allowed for a more contextual model of acculturation which took account of the variety of acculturation outcomes. This model proposed 'three modes of acculturation structured by this context: migrants reconstitute their village culture in the city, shutting out the dominant ideology; or they collectively pursue the dominant ideology as a myth through ritualized consumption; or they give up on both pursuits, resulting in a shattered identity project.'[24]

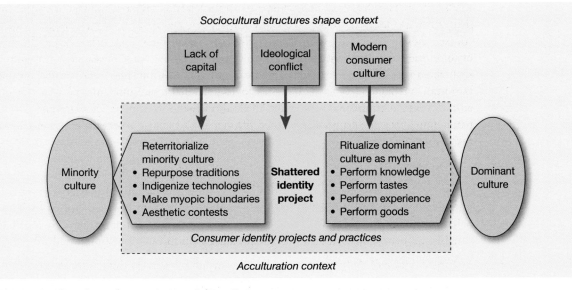

Figure 15.4 Dominated consumer acculturation

Source: Tuba Ustuner and Douglas B. Holt 'Dominated Consumer Acculturation: The Social Construction of Migrant Women's Consumer Identity Projects in a Turkish Squatter' *Journal of Consumer Research*, 34 (June 2007) Figure 2: 53. *The Journal of Consumer Research* by AMERICAN ASSOC. For PUBLIC OPINION RESEARCH. Reproduced with permission of UNIVERSITY OF CHICAGO PRESS.

Religious subcultures

In recent years, we have witnessed an explosion of religion and spirituality in popular culture including the box office success of Mel Gibson's movie *The Passion of the Christ* and the tremendous popularity and controversy surrounding the book *The Da Vinci Code*.[25] You do not have to be active in an organized religion to 'worship' products. A study of a brand community centered on the Apple Newton illustrates how religious themes can spill over into everyday consumption, particularly in the case of 'cult products'. Apple abandoned the Newton PDA years ago, but many avid users still keep the faith. The researchers examined postings in chat rooms devoted to the product. They found that many of the messages have supernatural, religious and magical themes, including the miraculous performance and survival of the brand, as well as the return of the brand creator. The most common postings concerned instances where dead Newton batteries magically come back to life.[26]

Numerous other types of groups serve similar functions for consumers – and indeed, they may be loosely based on religious principles (like the highly successful 12-step programme that guides Alcoholics Anonymous and other addiction support groups). Weight Watchers, the world's largest support group for weight loss, similarly follows a **spiritual-therapeutic model** even though it is a profitable business.[27] One study found that for some people, a brand logo serves the same function that a religious symbol like a crucifix does for others. For people who aren't deeply religious, visible markers of commercial brands are a form of self-expression and a token of self-worth, just like symbolic expressions of one's faith. In another study, a group of college students was primed by being asked to write a short essay on 'what your religion means to you personally', while a control group wrote about how they spend their days. Each group was then sent on an imaginary shopping trip in which they chose between products shown two at a time, national brand versus store brand. Some of the products were forms of self-expression, such as sunglasses, watches and socks. Other products were functional items like bread, batteries and ibuprofen. The group that had been primed to think about religion was less likely to choose branded products for the purpose of self-expression. Another online study found similar results when participants who were high on self-reported measures of religiosity were compared to those who scored low.[28]

THE IMPACT OF RELIGION ON CONSUMPTION

Religion *per se* has not been studied extensively in marketing, possibly because it is seen as a taboo subject. The very low-key or non-existent approach by large multinational or pan-European companies reflects the same sort of caution that these companies have in targeting ethnic groups – companies are having to decide whether religiously or ethnically-tailored programmes foster greater brand loyalty or whether any advantage is outweighed by the risks of misreading the target market and causing offence (as in the example of Cadbury's campaign and Naomi Campbell above). Without question, the most successful companies targeting and serving both ethnic and religious segments are small businesses, whose managers and owners are often members of the group.[29] However, the little evidence that has been accumulated indicates that religious affiliation has the *potential* to be a valuable predictor of consumer behaviour.[30] Religious subcultures have been shown to exert an impact on such consumer variables as personality, attitudes towards sexuality, birth rates and household formation, income and political attitudes.

MARKETING PITFALL

Religious sensibilities vary around the world, and big trouble can result if marketers violate taboo subjects in other cultures. Here are some examples:[31]

- A Lipton ad won the prestigious Gold Lion award in Cannes, but the company had to decline the honour in the face of objections. The ad mocked the Catholic Church as it showed a man standing in the communion line with a bowl of onion dip in his hand.

- An ad for Levi's jeans produced in London shows a young man who buys condoms from a pharmacist and then hides them in the small side pocket of his jeans. When he goes to pick up his date, he discovers that her father is the same pharmacist. The commercial was a hit in the United Kingdom, but people in strongly Catholic Italy and Spain didn't appreciate it at all.

- The French car manufacturer Renault withdrew an ad in a Danish campaign in response to protests from the local Catholic community. It depicted a dialogue during confession between a Catholic priest and a repenting man. The man atones for his sins as he prays *Ave Marias* until he confesses to having scratched the paint of the priest's new Renault – then the priest shouts 'heathen' and orders the man to pay a substantial penalty to the church.

Islamic marketing

Muslims will be more than one-quarter of the Earth's population by 2030, and during that same time period analysts expect the number of US Muslims to more than double. In several European countries, if immigration patterns and Muslims' comparatively higher birth rates continue, experts predict that Muslim populations will exceed 10 per cent of the total.[32] That's a consumer market to take seriously.

Nike committed a legendary error when it released a pair of athletic shoes in 1996 with a logo on the sole that some Muslims believed resembled the Arabic lettering for Allah. Muslims consider the feet unclean, and the company had to recall 800,000 pairs of the shoes globally. Today some companies listen more closely to the needs of this religious subculture. For example, a Malaysian commercial for Sunsilk's Lively Clean & Fresh shampoo depicts a young, smiling woman – but there is not a strand of hair in sight. Her head is completely covered by a *tudung*, the head scarf worn by many Muslim women in that country. Sunsilk's pitch is that it helps remove excess oil from the scalp and hair, a common problem among wearers of *tudungs*.

Mindful of the success of kosher certification, some Muslims recognize that **halal** foods (permissible under the laws of Islam) also may appeal to mainstream consumers. The Islamic Food and Nutrition Council of America certifies halal products with a 'crescent M', much like the circled 'O' of the Orthodox Union, the largest kosher certifier. Both kosher and halal followers are forbidden to eat pork, and both require similar rituals for butchering meat. Religious Jews don't mix milk and meat, nor do they eat shellfish, whereas religious Muslims don't drink alcohol. Neither group eats birds of prey or blood.[33]

Halal as a descriptor is being used for more and more commodities, services and activities, including milk, water, non-prescription medicine, holidays,[34] washing powder, tissues, cosmetics, websites and music. Many major companies are taking steps to reassure consumers that all of their products – not just food – are *halal* by having them officially certified. Colgate-Palmolive claims to be the first international company to have obtained *halal* certification in Malaysia for toothpaste and mouthwash products. Some mouthwashes may contain alcohol, which would be forbidden under *halal* guidelines. Colgate's products now bear the *halal* logo, which also is featured in the company's television commercials. Nokia introduced a phone for the Middle East and North Africa markets that came loaded with an Islamic Organizer with alarms for the five daily prayers, two Islamic e-books and an e-card application that lets people send SMS greeting cards for Ramadan. Ogilvy & Mather recently established a new arm, Ogilvy Noor (Noor means 'light' in Arabic), which the company describes as 'the world's first bespoke Islamic branding practice'. Ogilvy also introduced the Noor index, which rates the appeal of brands to Muslim consumers. The index was formulated on the basis of how consumers ranked more than 30 well-known brands for compliance with *Shariah*, or Islamic law. Lipton tea, owned by Unilever, topped the list, followed by Nestlé. Ogilvy's research shows that young Muslim consumers are different from their Western counterparts; they believe that by staying true to the core values of their religion, they are more likely to achieve success in the modern world.[35] Recent research suggests that 'rather than . . . Muslims becoming "Westernised", . . . Muslim youth is in fact entering a new age of becoming . . . [and] evidence for [this] . . . perspective lies in the increase in visible practice of Islam by Muslim youth – most notably in their dress and the conversations on the internet . . . Muslim youth are consuming commodities that were thought of not to necessarily have any Islamic reference or relevance and they are Islamifying them'.[36] The view of the increasing Islamification of brands is illustrated in Figure 15.5.

Putting together descriptive demographic profiles of Europe's major religious groups is not an exact science. For example, French law prohibits any question on religion in national censuses, although with an estimated 4 to 5 million Muslim inhabitants France undoubtedly has the biggest Islamic community in western Europe. As a faith, Islam is now second only to Roman Catholicism in France.[37] Similar problems with taking a census are found in the UK. Britain's 1.6 million-strong Muslim population is small, but has the fastest growth rate of all religions in the country. The thousand or so existing mosques are likely to be converted warehouses, churches or community halls. The hundreds of new mosques being built feature traditional Islamic domes and minarets – a trend which signals the growing economic vitality of British Muslims, as well as local authorities' growing acceptance of mosques.[38] While Islam is the fastest-growing religion in Europe, it is difficult to generalize about Muslims beyond belief in the teachings of the Koran, identifying holidays and periods of fasting such as Ramadan, and certain dietary restrictions. Coming from more than 120 countries and a variety of ethnic groups (Blacks, Asians, Arabs, Europeans), they are like many groups of consumers in Europe – diverse in their celebrations of consumption habits.

Christianity has dominated the history and cultural development of Europe, and has played an important role in the shaping of the European continent. While the many denominations

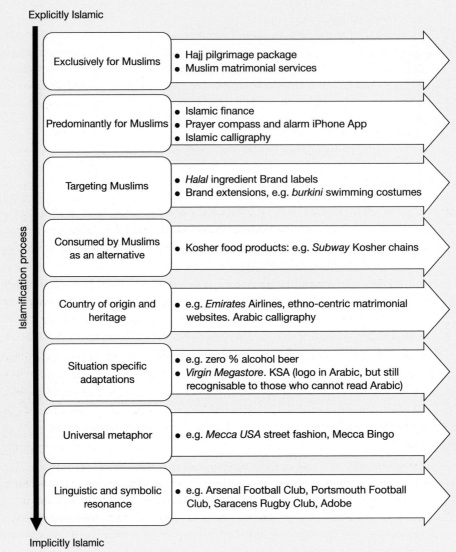

Explicitly Islamic

Islamification process

Implicitly Islamic

Figure 15.5 Classification of Islamic brands (Wilson and Liu 2011:4)

Source: Jonathan Bilal, A.J. Wilson and J. Liu 'The Challenges of Islamic Branding: Navigating Emotions and Halal', Figure 4 Classification of Islamic Brands (p. 34), *Journal of Islamic Marketing* 2 (1), 28–42.

of Christians make it the largest religious grouping in Europe (roughly 600 million), active membership is on the decline, with fewer and fewer adults attending services on any given Sunday.[39] In response to this trend, the Vatican has been involved in a variety of events aimed at developing closer and more active relationships with Europe's youth. Enlisting French fashion designers for World Youth Day, having Bob Dylan perform at a Vatican-sponsored rock concert, and having Easter Mass and information about the Vatican on a website are recent attempts to get youth involved with the church.[40] Divided roughly into the more Protestant north and the predominantly Catholic south, Christianity still makes up the majority religion in Europe in terms of claimed membership. Its major holidays of Easter and Christmas and celebrations such as 'Carnival' (*Faschung* in Germany) are celebrated or observed to such an extent that large industries such as travel and retailing rely on these seasons as the times of the year when they earn the most revenues.

JONATHAN A.J. WILSON
University of Greenwich

Consumer behaviour as I see it . . .

Islam on the radar

In Europe currently, the role of religion to some is a 'hot potato' or even a taboo. Islam is a belief system open to all, regardless of race and nationality. However, recent reports from *Amnesty International* find that its presence in Europe has been met with opposition in some quarters – evoking fear and new forms of racism and nationalism, which often lead to discrimination and exclusion.

In the United Kingdom, *halal* foods and finance products grow in popularity – and not just with Muslims. Cases in practice being fast-food chains and banks offering *halal* (permissible commodities and practices according to Islam). In some of the stores of the sandwich chain *Subway*, they have made all of their products *halal*, by using pork substitutes, such as turkey bacon (as eating pork is prohibited in Islam) – which has been well received.

In stark contrast, many French have been less receptive. Their interpretations have argued that rather than encouraging social cohesion and integration; more *halal* produce sold on home soil poses a threat. A recent article reported how close to one-third of meat in France is in fact slaughtered according to compliance with Islamic law, but is only labelled as such if it is intended for Muslim consumption. The reasons being that commercially, it is easier to produce for any consumer, but not all consumers may wish to consume products branded in the same way.

It is also worth mentioning that *halal* is more than 'meat and money': its definition applies to any commodity and practice. Therefore, as Muslim food, fashion, culture and tourism from countries with Muslim constitutions and heritage – such as Bangladesh, India, Indonesia, Iran, Lebanon, Malaysia, Morocco, Pakistan, Spain and Thailand – are well established, adapted and integrated commodities in Europe, it still remains for marketers and consumers to mediate concerning what blend of overtly labelled Islam is acceptable, and what impact that has on Europe, which is perceived as being secular and/or Christian.

Muslim youth culture

Arguably the most exciting and significant segment in today's global market lies in the hands of Muslim Youth. Advertising and Branding agency *Ogilvy* which has recently formed the subdivision *Ogilvy Noor* (specialising in Islam and Muslims) has estimated that over half of Muslims are under 24 years old and that makes for over 10 per cent of the world's population. The youth market is tough: because how many brands can predict whether they'll be the next cult, or cool thing – especially when tastes change so quickly? If we add into the mix the fact that Muslim youth are balancing adherence to their faith (which is taken from information largely based upon classical texts), with living in the here and now (meaning that some texts have to be brought up to speed with the world today) – then there are plenty of debates to be had.

Amongst the younger generation especially, patterns are being broken up by additional displays of conspicuous consumption – the all-important accessorising and customising. For example, some more orthodox Islamic quarters see women wearing jeans as a departure from Islamic convention; attempting to be Western (the inference being that Western is bad); and imitating men. However, an alternative view would be that jeans are technically comparable with, for example, female Pakistani *shalwar* trousers, or in fact are a →

619

→ step up – as they have more practical uses. Furthermore, whether to wear jeans or not is not the key issue – it's how, when and where. Islamic dress is really about covering and hiding certain body parts and curves. The informed tribes of Muslim Youth social networkers understand this concept, perhaps at times better than their elders – and this basic principle allows youth to experiment. So I would identify key themes around: fashion, customization, personalization and self-mediated collective individualism as appearing to be on the increase. They are encouraging youth to congregate around brand-centric tribes and to associate brands with their faith.[41]

Jonathan A.J. Wilson

GEOGRAPHIC INFLUENCES ON CONSUMPTION

The consumption patterns of different areas of Europe as well as of the different countries (and their regions) have been shaped by unique climates, cultural influences and resources. These differences at the macro, national and regional levels can exert a major impact on consumers' lifestyles, since many of our preferences in foods, entertainment and so on are dictated by local customs and the availability of some diversions rather than others. The lifestyles of people in each part of Europe (e.g. Western Europe, Eastern Europe and Southeastern Europe), as well as in each country and each region differ in a variety of ways, some quite subtle and some quite noticeable, some easy to explain and some not so obvious.[42] Many companies operating in Europe consider Scandinavia (Denmark, Norway and Sweden) or the Benelux (Belgium, the Netherlands and Luxembourg) to be more or less one market due to the perceived similarities between the countries. Similarly, Southeast Europe (SEE) which comprises Albania, Bosnia and Herzegovina, Croatia, former Yugoslav Republic of Macedonia; and Serbia and Montenegro.[43] Eastern Europe, in turn, consists of Belarus, Republic of Moldova, Russian Federation and the Ukraine. That there are relative similarities between these countries is a matter of fact. However, marketers should beware of overestimating the homogeneity of such macro-regions. Portraits of macro-regions can be drawn with rough strokes only with a very big brush. In addition, we should be careful about assuming homogeneity within national borders, because between northern and southern Italy, northern and southern Germany, Paris and Provence, London and Scotland there may be large differences in terms of consumption patterns and lifestyles and, consequently, in marketing and marketing research practices.[44]

EURO-CONSUMERS

There are a number of common trends, but there are also big differences in the local contexts in which these trends are found amongst Euro-consumers, as well as differences in the degree to which the trend is significant in each individual country. A number of trends seem to be valid for consumer markets in the EU.[45] These include:

- a tendency to more unevenly distributed income;
- an increasing number of older people;
- a decrease in household size;
- a growing proportion of immigrants;
- increase in environmental concern and consumption of 'green' products;
- relatively increasing consumption of services compared to durable goods.

Changing nature of the marketplace

One of the most significant trends in the changing nature of the marketplace for consumers across Europe is the increasing convergence of new technology with consumption: whereas there were 247 million internet users in 2006, by the end of 2011 internet penetration in Europe was over 60 per cent, compared with just under 30 per cent worldwide.[46] The internet has an increasing presence in consumer lives both for information search and for purchase (Figure 15.6), although significant barriers remain to buying via the internet (e.g. perceived lack of security of payment systems; issues around privacy and trust; difficulties around delivery, complaints and seeking redress) (Figure 15.7).[47]

However, it is the lack of **e-skills** which restricts opportunities for many consumers. This means that the increasing importance of electronic technology will work to the advantage of those consumers with the requisite level of **digital literacy** and sufficient resources to access computers and the internet. However, Euro-consumers are not currently all equally resourced in terms of either access to computers or the internet (see Table 15.2 and Figure 15.8), or their level of e-skills.

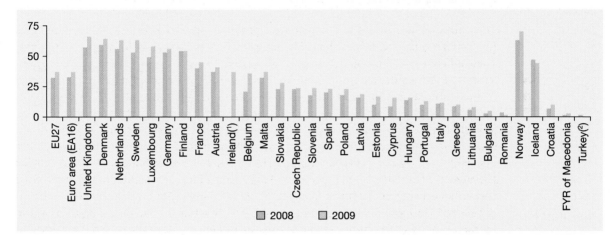

Figure 15.6 Percentage of EU individuals who ordered goods or services over the internet for private use (2009)

([1]) 2008, not available.
([2]) 2007 instead of 2008; 2009, not available.

Data source: Europe in figures: Eurostat Yearbook 2011; Eurostat statistical books ISSN 1681-4789, http://epp.eurostat.ec.europa.eu/cache/ITY_OFFPUB/KS-CD-11-001/EN/KS-CD-11-001-EN.PDF, accessed 21 February 2012

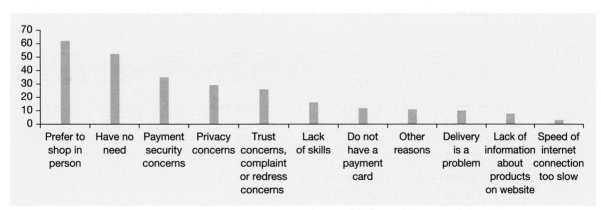

Figure 15.7 Reasons for not using the internet to buy or order goods or services (EU27, 2009([1]))

([1]) During the 12 months prior to the survey.

Data source: Europe in figures: Eurostat Yearbook 2011; Eurostat statistical books ISSN 1681-4789, http://epp.eurostat.ec.europa.eu/cache/ITY_OFFPUB/KS-CD-11-001/EN/KS-CD-11-001-EN.PDF, accessed 21 February 2012.

Table 15.2 Use of ICTs and use of online services (EU27) (% of individuals aged 16–74)

	Computer use			Internet use			Used internet for finding information on goods or services		
	2007	2008	2009	2007	2008	2009	2007	2008	2009
EU27	**63**	**66**	**68**	**57**	**62**	**65**	**47**	**50**	**51**
Euro area (EA16) (¹)	**64**	**66**	**68**	**59**	**63**	**65**	**49**	**52**	**55**
Belgium	70	71	76	67	69	75	55	58	59
Bulgaria	35	40	44	31	35	42	17	22	17
Czech Republic	55	63	64	49	58	60	37	45	50
Denmark	84	86	87	81	84	86	68	73	74
Germany	78	80	81	72	75	77	63	66	69
Estonia	65	66	71	64	66	71	48	53	54
Ireland	62	:	68	57	:	65	44	:	54
Greece	40	44	47	33	38	42	28	31	33
Spain	57	61	63	52	57	60	42	46	47
France	69	71	72	64	68	69	55	57	60
Italy	43	46	49	38	42	46	27	30	33
Cyprus	47	47	53	38	39	48	32	32	39
Latvia	58	63	65	55	61	64	39	49	50
Lithuania	52	56	60	49	53	58	36	37	44
Luxembourg	80	83	88	78	81	86	68	69	75
Hungary	58	63	63	52	59	59	43	49	48
Malta	48	51	60	45	49	58	34	42	48
Netherlands	87	88	90	84	87	89	76	76	79
Austria	73	76	75	67	71	72	47	51	54
Poland	52	55	59	44	49	56	27	33	29
Portugal	46	46	51	40	42	46	33	34	40
Romania	34	35	42	24	29	33	12	17	12
Slovenia	58	60	65	53	56	62	47	48	49
Slovakia	64	72	74	56	66	70	39	49	50
Finland	81	84	84	79	83	82	68	73	73
Sweden	88	89	91	80	88	90	70	75	77
United Kingdom	78	80	84	72	76	82	62	64	64
Iceland	91	92	93	90	91	93	78	78	80
Norway	90	90	91	85	89	91	76	80	83
Croatia	:	:	:	:	:	:	30	33	33
FYR of Macedonia	:	50	55	:	42	50	:	22	26
Turkey	30	:	:	27	:	:	11	:	:
Serbia	41	:	49	30	:	38	19	:	22

(¹) 2007 and 2008: EA15 instead of EA16.

Source: Eurostat (isoc_ci_cfp_cu, isoc_ci_ifp_iu and isoc_ci_ac_i) *Europe in figures: Eurostat Yearbook 2011*; Eurostat statistical books ISSN 1681-4789, http://epp.eurostat.ec.europa.eu/cache/ITY_OFFPUB/KS-CD-11-001/EN/KS-CD-11-001-EN.PDF, accessed 21 February 2012 Table 7.20 p. 358.

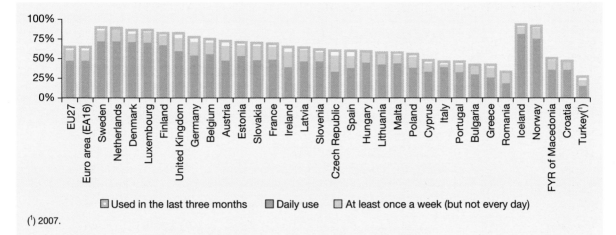

Figure 15.8 **Frequency of internet use 2009** (% of individuals aged 16–74)

Data source: Europe in figures: Eurostat Yearbook 2011; Eurostat statistical books ISSN 1681-4789, http://epp.eurostat.ec.europa.eu/cache/ ITY_OFFPUB/KS-CD-11-001/EN/KS-CD-11-001-EN.PDF, accessed 21 February 2012.

MARKETING OPPORTUNITY?

How skilled are Europeans in using computers and the internet?

One of the most remarkable developments over the past ten years has probably been the way in which the internet – previously known only to a small circle of scientists and university students – has infiltrated, and become an important part of, our everyday lives. The internet is not only changing our way of communicating with friends, relatives and colleagues, but also our way of working and shopping. Many traditional services are slowly being replaced by their electronic or online counterparts: banking, ticket sales, travel and holiday information, contacts with public administration, etc. This rapid growth faces a barrier, however; namely the capability of citizens or the labour force to understand and use the applications or, more generally, their ability to use Information and Communication Technologies (ICT).

E-skills at a glance

Graph 1 (Figure 15.9) shows the skill levels of different sub-groups of the EU:

- A first observation is that 37 per cent have no computer skills whatsoever, while only 22 per cent seem to be acquainted with a wide range of computer activities.

- As expected, educational level is an important factor: while only 11 per cent of people with a higher education have no basic e-skills, this applies to more than 60 per cent of people not educated beyond lower secondary level.

- As regards age, more than 3 out of 4 people over 65 years of age have no computer skills at all, but even among young people aged 16 to 24, about 10 per cent appear to have no basic e-skills.

Digital literacy is a problem for a large part of the population

Digital literacy involves the confident and critical use of ICT for work, leisure and communication . . . These basic ICT e-skills cover a wide range of activities from basic skills in computer to internet. As seen in Graph 1, a considerable proportion of European citizens have no computer skills at all. The fact that 37 per cent of the population lack basic computer skills is not so surprising when considering Graph 2 (Figure 15.10), which shows that in 2010 more than 50 per cent of residents in Romania, Greece and Turkey had never accessed the internet; and over 40 per cent had not accessed the internet in Buglaria, Portugal, Cyprus, Croatia and the FYRoM (Former Yugoslav Republic of Macedonia). This was in comparison with Luxembourg, Denmark, Sweden, Norway, Iceland and The Netherlands where only 10 per cent of the population (aged 16–74) or less had not accessed the internet during 2010. It is clear that a lack of internet access (and the associated skills) will prevent people in some countries from participating fully in the information society.[48]

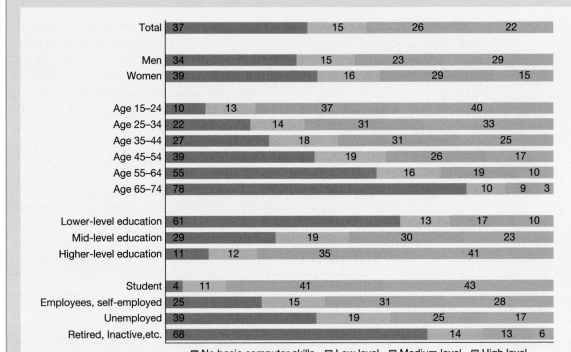

Figure 15.9 Individuals' level of basic computer skills (2005), EU25

(as a percentage of the total number of individuals aged 16 to 74)

Source: http://epp.eurostat.ec.europa.eu/cache/ITY_OFFPUB/KS-NP-06-017/EN/KS-NP-06-017-EN.PDF, accessed 12 August 2008.

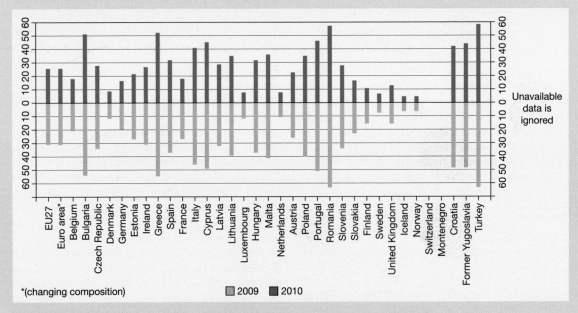

Figure 15.10 Individuals not using the internet (2009 [green] *vs* 2010 [blue])

(as a percentage of the total number of individuals aged 16 to 74)

Source of data: Eurostat statistics on information society http://epp.eurostat.ec.europa.eu/portal/page/portal/information_society/ introduction, accessed 21 February 2012; graph: http://epp.eurostat.ec.europa.eu/tgm/graphDownload.do?tab=graph&language=en&plugi n=1&pcode=tin00093, accessed 21 February 2012. MET Hyperlink to the graph: http://epp.eurostat.ec.europa.eu/tgm/graph.do?pcode= tin00093&language=en. Short description: individuals who never used the internet – whether at home, at work or from anywhere else and whether for private or professional purposes. Code: tin00093.

Euro-consumers' advertising preferences and European regulations

Finally, another important distinction to recognize amongst various groups of European consumers is that different countries are accustomed to different forms of advertising. Unlike the Anglo-Saxon advertising culture, for instance, comparative advertising is banned in most Latin and Germanic countries in Europe. In many cases, advertising content is regulated by the government. For example, tobacco advertising in Denmark is not allowed to depict young people, and Swedish tobacco advertising targeted at end-users must not show any people at all. The European Commission in Brussels has taken initiatives to impose even stricter controls on advertising, introducing among other things a total ban on tobacco advertising in Europe.

Differences among European countries are not just restricted to the legal questions. There are also differences concerning attitudes to advertising, as well as which type of television advertising spots and print ads will work best in various European countries. A comparative study of French and German TV spots revealed a distinct profile of the ads in these two countries. French TV ads tended to have less product information, to have a less direct way of communicating about socially sensitive topics, to rely more on non-verbal and implicit communication types and to present women in a more seductive and sexually alluring manner.[49] The same differences concerning the general image of French communication as seductive and imaginative *vs* a more factual and sober German style were confirmed when looking at other types of communication such as television news programmes and news magazines. Another study of all ads sent out on a couple of channels in each country confirmed this difference, stressing the more frequent use of puns and the more rapid and personalized rhythm of the French ads, although no difference in information level was found.[50] Surprisingly, in the latter study not one single common ad was sampled in Germany and France. It seems that the use of pan-European advertising is still limited.

One possible explanation for this difference may be due to the distinction between **low-context** and **high-context cultures**.[51] In a high-context culture, messages tend to be more implicit and built into the communication context, whereas communication in low-context cultures tends to be more explicit, specific and direct. France, according to this perspective of classifying culture, is relatively high-context compared with Germany, which belongs among

The ad for Cravendale Milk illustrates the use of humour in an advertising message.
The Advertising Archives.

the most low-context cultures in the world. The British, for example, have a more favourable attitude to advertising than either the French or the Germans. They tend to think of advertising as a humorous and entertaining part of daily life, and have fewer concerns about its manipulative capacities.[52] Indeed, the British ads may be funnier. One study found a relatively big difference between the degree to which humour is used in televised advertising. Humour was used in 88.8 per cent of British ads compared to 74.5 per cent in France and only 61 per cent in Germany. And in a sample of internationally used ads, the share of humorous ads dropped to 32.2 per cent.[53] It seems that humour is still a very national thing. Or maybe there are other explanations? These findings are supported by another source which concluded that, relative to Americans, the British tended to regard advertising as a form of entertainment. Compared with the US, British television commercials also contained less information.[54] One advertising executive stated outright that from watching a sample reel of German and British car ads respectively, it would be evident that the German ones would be much more rational and the British ones much more emotional.[55]

Not only do attitudes about ads vary across Europe, the same can be said for preferences for media. For example, in France outdoor posters are a highly developed and popular medium for creative campaigns. Cinema advertising is also enjoyable to the French. In the UK, adverts in daily newspapers are more important compared with other European countries, and in Germany the radio medium is more important than elsewhere.[56] But the use of various media is difficult to compare among countries due to variations in the regulation of media use: interrupting programmes with advertising is not permitted in Scandinavian countries, for example, and is not practised on German public TV channels. The variations could be explained by different factors such as relative familiarity with the product concept (in Italy), the small size of the product in relation to local competitors (the Netherlands), popularity of English-style humour (Germany) and the prevailing advertising style in the country (France). It is probably safe to conclude that, although there are often certain similarities in the way ads are understood across cultures, the readership tends to focus on different themes in different countries.[57]

CHAPTER SUMMARY

Now that you have finished reading this chapter you should understand why:

→ Our memberships in ethnic, racial and religious subcultures often play a big role in guiding our consumption behaviours.

→ Consumers identify with many groups that share common characteristics and identities. Subcultures are large groups that exist within a society, and membership in them often gives marketers a valuable clue about individuals' consumption decisions. A person's ethnic origins, racial identity, and religious background often are major components of his or her identity. However, the growing numbers of people who claim multi-ethnic backgrounds are beginning to blur the traditional distinctions drawn among these subcultures.

→ Additional influences come from our identification with microcultures that reflect a shared interest in some organization or activity.

→ Micro-cultures are communities of consumers who participate in or otherwise identify with specific art forms, popular culture movements and hobbies.

→ Many marketing messages appeal to ethnic and racial identity.

→ Recently, several minority groups have caught the attention of marketers as their economic power has grown. Segmenting consumers by their *ethnicity* can be effective, but care must be taken not to rely on inaccurate (and sometimes offensive) ethnic stereotypes.

→ Marketers increasingly use religious and spiritual themes when they talk to consumers.

→ The quest for spirituality influences demand in product categories including books, music and cinema. Although the impact of religious identification on consumer behaviour is not clear, some differences among religious subcultures do emerge. Marketers need to consider the sensibilities of believers carefully when they use religious symbolism to appeal to members of different denominations.

→ The changing nature of the marketplace for Euro-consumers.

→ Given that we, as consumers, must take part in many activities that reflect our local cultures, Euro-consumers as an overall segment are very difficult to identify.

→ Varying levels of resources (e.g. digital literacy; e-skills; access to computers and the internet) mean that some Euro-consumers have greater opportunities to benefit from the convergence of consumption and the new electronic technologies than others.

→ Because a consumer's culture exerts such a big influence on their consumption, marketers must learn as much as possible about differences in cultural norms and preferences. Marketing and advertising strategies must be tailored to each culture, rather than standardized across cultures in the European marketplace.

KEY TERMS

Acculturation (p. 612)
Acculturation agents (p. 612)
Cosplay (p. 611)
Digital literacy (p. 621)
E-skills (p. 621)
Ethnic subculture (p. 611)
Halal (p. 617)
High-context culture (p. 625)

Host culture (p. 614)
Low-context culture (p. 611)
Micro-culture (p. 610)
Progressive learning model (p. 614)
Racial subculture (p. 611)
Spiritual-therapeutic model (p. 615)
Subculture (p. 610)
Warming (p. 614)

CONSUMER BEHAVIOUR CHALLENGE

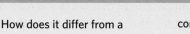

1 What is a subculture? How does it differ from a microculture?

2 What is acculturation? Who are acculturation agents?

3 Describe the processes involved when a person assimilates to a new host culture.

4 Describe the progressive learning model and discuss why this perspective is important when marketing to subcultures.

5 How do religious subcultures affect consumption decisions?

6 Locate current examples of marketing stimuli that depend on an ethnic or religious stereotype to communicate a message. How effective are these appeals?

7 If you have access to foreign TV channels, try to compare the advertising in the ones from your own country with the foreign ones. Are the styles different? Are the predominant products different? Is the use of a certain style of advertisement for a certain type of product similar or dissimilar?

8 Locate one or more consumers (perhaps family members) who have emigrated from another country. Interview them about how they adapted to their host culture. In particular, what changes did they make in their consumption practices over time?

→ **9** Religious symbolism is being used increasingly in advertising, even though some people object to this practice. For example, the French fashion house Marithe and François Girbaud used a poster of well-dressed women posed in a version of Leonardo da Vinci's *The Last Supper*: the poster was banned in Milan.[58] In another example, a French Volkswagen ad for the relaunch of the Golf showed a modern version of *The Last Supper* with the tag line, 'Let us rejoice, my friends, for a new Golf has been born'.[59] A group of clergy in France sued the company and the ad had to be removed from 10,000 hoardings. One of the bishops involved in the suit said, 'Advertising experts have told us that ads aim for the sacred in order to shock, because using sex does not work any more.' Do you agree? Should religion be used to market products? Do you find this strategy effective or offensive? When and where is this appropriate, if at all?

10 Work in small groups. Assume the role of market researchers who have to report to a FMCG brand manager from a multinational who is about to undertake a product launch into a new geographic area within Europe. Draw up a list of key characteristics of European consumers that you would need to know in order to market to them. Visit the EU stats website **http://epp.eurostat.ec. europa.eu/portal/page/portal/statistics/themes**, identify, collect and analyse relevant data, and present (with your interpretation and recommendations) this information in a usable and accessible form to the brand manager.

For additional material see the companion website at www.pearsoned.co.uk/solomon

NOTES

1. Demographic Statistics 1997: Population and Social Conditions Series (Luxembourg: Office for Official Publications of the European Communities, 1997); 'Colour Blind', *Marketing Week* (21 June 1996): 38–40.

2. *Europe in figures: Eurostat Yearbook 2011*; Eurostat statistical books ISSN 1681-4789, p. 109, http://epp.eurostat.ec.europa.eu/cache/ITY_OFFPUB/KS-CD-11-001/EN/KS-CD-11-001-EN.PDF, accessed 20 February 2012.

3. *Europe in figures: Eurostat Yearbook 2011*; Eurostat statistical books ISSN 1681-4789, p. 149, http://epp.eurostat.ec.europa.eu/cache/ITY_OFFPUB/KS-CD-11-001/EN/KS-CD-11-001-EN.PDF, accessed 20 February 2012.

4. '*A statistical portrait of the first and second generation*', 2011 edition, Eurostat: Eurostat statistical books, European Commission, Table 3.1, page 122, http://epp.eurostat.ec.europa.eu/portal/page/portal/product_details/publication?p_product_code=KS-31-10-539, accessed 20 February 2012.

5. *Europe in figures: Eurostat Yearbook 2011*; Eurostat statistical books ISSN 1681-4789, p. 154, http://epp.eurostat.ec.europa.eu/cache/ITY_OFFPUB/KS-CD-11-001/EN/KS-CD-11-001-EN.PDF, accessed 20 February 2012.

6. 'Groningerdiscothekenverbiedenomstredenkleding (Groningen disco forbids controversial clothing), *De Telegraaf* (11 January 2005), http://www2.telegraaf.nl/binnenland/17132161/Groninger_discotheken_verbieden_omstreden_kleding.html. See also: http://www.humanityinaction.org/knowledgebase/219-lonsdale-gone-racism-solved-lonsdale-youth-and-the-police

7. Erik Davis, 'tlhInganHolDajatlh'a?' (Do You Speak Klingon?)', *Utne Reader* (March/April 1994): 122–29; additional material provided by personal communication, Prof. Robert V. Kozinets, Northwestern University, October 1997;

and adapted from Philip Kotler, Gary Armstrong, Peggy H. Cunningham and Robert Warren, *Principles of Marketing*, 3rd Canadian edn (Scarborough, Ontario: Prentice Hall Canada, 1997): 96.

8. Russell W. Belk and Janeen Arnold Costa, 'The Mountain Man Myth: A Contemporary Consuming Fantasy', *Journal of Consumer Research* 25 (1998): 218–40.

9. 'Cosplay', www.cosplay.com, accessed 20 June 2011; www.acparadise.com, accessed 20 June 2011; Lisa Katayama, 'Anatomy of a Nerd; Japanese Schoolgirl Watch', *Wired* (March 2006), www.wired.com/wired/archive/14.03/play.html?pg=3, accessed 6 October 2007.

10. See Frederik Barth, *Ethnic Groups and Boundaries: The Social Organization of Culture Difference* (London: Allen & Unwin, 1969); D. Bell, 'Ethnicity and Social Change', in N. Glazer and D.P. Moynihan (eds), *Ethnicity: Theory and Experience* (Cambridge, MA: Harvard University Press, 1975): 141–74; D.L. Horowitz, 'Ethnic Identity', in *ibid*.: 109–40; J. Kotkin, *Tribes* (New York: Random House, 1993); Venkatesh, 'Ethnoconsumerism', *op. cit.*; Michel Laroche, Annamma Joy, Michael Hui and Chankon Kim, 'An Examination of Ethnicity Measures: Convergent Validity and Cross-Cultural Equivalence', in Rebecca H. Holman and Michael R. Solomon (eds), *Advances in Consumer Research* 18 (Provo, UT: Association for Consumer Research, 1991): 150–7; Melanie Wallendorf and Michael Reilly, 'Ethnic migration, assimilation, and consumption', *Journal of Consumer Research* 10 (December 1983): 292–302; Milton J. Yinger, 'Ethnicity', *Annual Review of Sociology* 11 (1985): 151–80.

11. For a detailed picture of immigrants to the EU27 from within EU27 states and outside of EU27 states see Eurostat, particularly *Europe in figures: Eurostat Yearbook 2011*; Eurostat

statistical books ISSN 1681-4789, http://epp.eurostat.ec. europa.eu/cache/ITY_OFFPUB/KS-CD-11-001/EN/KS-CD-11-001-EN.PDF, accessed 20 February 2012; and *A statistical portrait of the first and second generation*, 2011 edition, Eurostat: Eurostat statistical books, European Commission, http://epp.eurostat.ec.europa.eu/portal/page/portal/product_details/publication?p_product_code=KS-31-10-539, accessed 20 February 2012.

12. Rohit Desphandé and Douglas M. Stayman, 'A tale of two cities: distinctiveness theory and advertising effectiveness', *Journal of Marketing Research* 31 (February 1994): 57–64; Stephen Riggins, 'The Media Imperative: Ethnic Minority Survival in the Age of Mass Communication', in S.H. Riggins (ed.), *Ethnic Minority Media: An International Perspective* (London: Sage, 1992): 1–22.

13. Steve Rabin, 'How to Sell across Cultures', *American Demographics* (March 1994): 56–57.

14. Adam Sherwin, 'ASA Says Cadbury Was Not Racist When It Compared Campbell to Chocolate Bar', *The Independent* (21 June 2011), http://www.independent.co.uk/news/media/advertising/asa-says-cadbury-was-not-racist-when-it-compared-campbell-to-chocolate-bar-2300278.html, accessed 22 June 2011.

15. See Lisa Peñaloza, '*AtravesandoFronteras*/Border Crossings: A Critical Ethnographic Exploration of the Consumer Acculturation of Mexican Immigrants', *Journal of Consumer Research* 21 (June 1994): 32–54; Lisa Peñaloza and Mary C. Gilly, 'Marketer Acculturation: The Changer and the Changed', *Journal of Marketing* 63 (July 1999): 84–104; Carol Kaufman-Scarborough, 'Eat Bitter Food and Give Birth to a Girl; Eat Sweet Things and Give Birth to a Cavalryman: Multicultural Health Care Issues for Consumer Behavior', *Advances in Consumer Research* 32, no. 1 (2005): 226–69; Søren Askegaard, Eric J. Arnould and Dannie Kjeldgaard, 'Postassimilationist Ethnic Consumer Research: Qualifications and Extensions', *Journal of Consumer Research* 32, no. 1 (2005): 160.

16. Zuzanna Chytkova and Dannie Kjeldgaard, 'Migrant women's identity formation and the marketplace: between constraint and creativity' in Alan Bradshaw, Chris Hackley and Pauline Maclaran (eds), *European Association for Consumer Research Conference* 2010 RHUL, page p. 26.

17. Gokcen Coskuner and Ozlem Sandikci, 'New Clothing: Meanings and Practices', in Barbara E. Kahn and Mary Frances Luce (eds), *Advances in Consumer Research* 31 (Valdosta, GA: Association for Consumer Research, 2004): 285–90.

18. A. Fuat Firat, 'Consumer Culture or Culture Consumed?' in Costa and Bamossy (eds), *Marketing in a Multicultural World*: 105–25; Michael Laroche, Chankon Kim, Michael K. Hui and Annamma Joy, 'An empirical study of multidimensional ethnic change: The case of the French Canadians in Quebec', *Journal of Cross-Cultural Psychology* 27(1) (January 1996): 114–31.

19. Melanie Wallendorf and Michael Reilly, 'Ethnic migration, assimilation, and consumption', *Journal of Consumer Research* 10 (December 1983): 292–302.

20. Ronald J. Faber, Thomas C. O'Guinn and John A. McCarty, 'Ethnicity, acculturation and the importance of product attributes', *Psychology & Marketing* 4 (Summer 1987): 121–34; Humberto Valencia, 'Developing an Index to Measure Hispanicness', in Elizabeth C. Hirschman and Morris B. Holbrook (eds), *Advances in Consumer Research* 12 (Provo, Utah: Association for Consumer Research, 1985): 118–21.

21. Rohit Deshpande, Wayne D. Hoyer and Naveen Donthu, 'The intensity of ethnic affiliation: A study of the sociology of hispanic consumption', *Journal of Consumer Research* 13 (September 1986): 214–20.

22. Ger, Güliz, 'Warming: Making the new familiar and moral', *Journal of European Ethnology* (special issue of the journal *Ethnologia Europea*), Richard Wilk and Orvar Lofgren (eds) 35(1–2) (2005): 19–22.

23. Elisabeth Kriechbaum-Vitellozzi and Robert Kreuzbauer, 'Poverty consumption: Consumer behavior of refugees in industrialized countries', *Advances in Consumer Research* 33(1) (2006); *cf.* also L. Wamwara-Mbugua, T. Wakiuru, Bettina Cornwell, and Gregory Boller, 'Triple acculturation: The role of African Americans in the consumer acculturation of Kenyan immigrants', *Advances in Consumer Research* 33(1) (2006).

24. Tuba Ustuner and Douglas B. Holt, 'Dominated consumer acculturation: The social construction of poor migrant women's consumer identity projects in a Turkish squatter', *Journal of Consumer Research* 34 (June 2007): 41.

25. Dan Brown, *The Da Vinci Code* (New York: Doubleday, 2003).

26. Albert M. Muñiz Jr and Hope Jensen Schau, 'Religiosity in the abandoned Apple Newton brand community', *Journal of Consumer Research* 31 (March 2005): 737–47.

27. Risto Moisio and Mariam Beruchashvili (2010), 'Questing for Well-Being at Weight Watchers: The Role of the Spiritual-Therapeutic Model in a Support Group', *Journal of Consumer Research* 36, no. 5 (2010): 857–75.

28. Ron Shachar, Tülin Erdem, Keisha M. Cutright and Gavan J. Fitzsimons, 'Brands: The Opiate of the Non-Religious Masses?', *Marketing Science* 30, no. 1 (January–February 2011): 92–111.

29. Elizabeth C. Hirschman, 'Religious Affiliation and Consumption Processes: An Initial Paradigm', in *Research in Marketing* (Greenwich, CT: JAI Press, 1983): 131–70.

30. See, for example, Nejet Delener, 'The effects of religious factors on perceived risk in durable goods purchase decisions', *Journal of ConsumerMarketing* 7 (Summer 1990): 27–38.

31. Karlene Lukovitz, 'Pepsi Co Pulls Controversial Video Entry from Site', *Marketing Daily* (5 January 2011), http://www.mediapost.com/publications/?fa=Articles.showArticle&art_aid=142406&nid=122346, accessed 25 April 2011; Jack Neff, 'Dip Ad Stirs Church Ire', *Advertising Age* (2 July 2001): 8; G. Burton, 'Oh, My Heck! Beer Billboard Gets the Boot', *Salt Lake Tribune* (6 November 2001); 'Religion Reshapes Realities for U.S. Restaurants in Middle East', *Nation's Restaurant News* 32 (16 February 1998); Sarah Ellison, 'Sexy-Ad Reel Shows What Tickles in Tokyo Can Fade Fast in France', *Wall Street Journal* (31 March 2000), www.wsj.com, accessed 31 March 2000; Claudia Penteado, 'Brazilian Ad Irks Church', *Advertising Age* (23 March 2000): 11; 'Burger King Will Alter Ad That Has Offended Muslims', *Wall Street Journal* (15 March 2000), www.wsj.com, accessed 15 March 2000.

32. Cathy Lynn Grossman, 'Number of U.S. Muslims to Double', *USA Today* (27 January 2011), http://www.usatoday.com/news/religion/2011-01-27-1Amuslim27_ST_N.htm, accessed 22 June 2011.

33. Barry Newman, 'Halal Meets Kosher in Health-Food Aisle', *Wall Street Journal* (5 May 2006): B1; Louise Story, 'Rewriting the Ad for Muslim-Americans', *New York Times Online* (28 April 2007), www.nytimes.com, accessed 28 April 2007.

34. E.g. Touzani and Hirshman study 'the celebration of Ramadan in France among North African émigrés . . . [exploring

particularly] . . . how they transfer their religious rituals during Ramadan to this cultural setting', Mourad Touzani and Elizabeth Hirschman, 'Minority Religious Rituals in the Past Colonial World: Ramadan in France' in Alan Bradshaw, Chris Hackley and Pauline Maclaran (eds), *European Association for Consumer Research Conference* 2010 RHUL, page p. 9.

35. Liz Gooch, 'Advertisers Seek to Speak to Muslim Consumers', *New York Times* (11 August 2010), http://www.nytimes.com/2010/08/12/business/media/12branding.html?pagewanted=1&_r=1&ref=media, accessed 25 April 2011.

36. Jonathan Bilal, A.J. Wilson, 'Muslim Youth Culture: A New Wave of Hip Hop Grunge', *The Halal Journal*, World Halal Forum 2012 Special Edition 32–38, www.halaljournal.com, p. 34; see also Jonathan Bilal, A.J. Wilson and J. Liu, 'The challenges of Islamic Branding: Navigating Emotions and Halal', *Journal of Islamic Marketing* 2 (1) 28–42.

37. 'The Muslims in France: Rejecting their ancestors the Gauls', *The Economist* (16 November 1996): 113–14.

38. Clare Garner, 'Builders answer Islam's growing call to prayer', *The Independent* (4 February 1997): 7.

39. Madeline Bunting, 'Churchgoing bottoms out', *The Guardian* (10 August 1996): 2; 'Catholic Church loses mass appeal', *The Guardian* (30 January 1996): 4; 'België is nietlanger-katholiek (Belgium is no longer Catholic)', *Trouw* (19 September 1996); Madeline Bunting, 'Revolving door throws doubt on evangelical churches' revival', *The Guardian* (28 August 1996); for a comprehensive website on the world's religions and their populations, see: http://www.adherents.com/Religions_By_Adherents.html.

40. Amy Barrett, 'John Paul II to share stage with marketers', *Wall Street Journal Europe* (19 August 1997): 4; see also www.mix.it/rai/papa

41. For further reading on Islamic marketing and lifestyles (e.g. music) see: Wilson, J.A.J. (2012), 'The new wave of trans-formational Islamic Marketing – reflections and definitions', *Journal of Islamic Marketing*, vol. 3 Iss. 1, pp. 5–11; Wilson, J.A.J. (2011), 'New-School Brand Creation and Creativity – lessons from Hip-Hop and the Global Branded Generation', *Journal of Brand Management*, vol. 19 Issue 2, Oct/Nov, pp. 91–111; Wilson, J.A.J. and Liu, J. (2011), 'The Challenges of Islamic Branding: navigating Emotions and Halal', *Journal of Islamic Marketing*, vol. 2 Iss. 1, pp. 28–42; Wilson, J.A.J and Liu, J. (2010), 'Shaping the Halal into a brand?', *Journal of Islamic Marketing*, vol. 1 Iss. 2, pp. 107–123; Wilson, J.A.J. and Liu, J. (2009), 'The Polytheism of Branding: Evaluating brands through their Worship', in Nafees, L., Krishnan, O. and Gore, T. (eds), *Brand Research*, Macmillan Publishers India Ltd, New Delhi, pp. 207–229.

42. The EU website is an excellent source of information about different geographical, social, demographic and economic aspects of life in Europe: see *Europe in Figures: Eurostat Yearbook 2011*, Eurostat statistical books ISSN 1681-4789, http://epp.eurostat.ec.europa.eu/cache/ITY_OFFPUB/KS-CD-11-001/EN/KS-CD-11-001-EN.PDF, accessed 20 February 2012, e.g. population structure by major age groups (Table 2.5, p. 118); and EU-27 population pyramids 1990 v. 2009 (Figure 2.3).

43. European Environment Agency, 'Sustainable consumption and production in South East Europe and Eastern Europe, Caucasus and Central Asia: Joint UNEP-EEA report on the opportunities and lessons learned', Copenhagen and Geneva EEA Report 3/2007.

44. 'Going it alone', *Marketing News* (11 September 2000).

45. Peter S.H. Leeflang and W. Fred van Raaij, 'The changing consumer in the European Union: A "Meta-Analysis"', *International Journal of Research in Marketing* 12(5) (1995): 373–87.

46. http://www.internetworldstats.com/stats4.htm, accessed April 19 2012; see also: https://www.cia.gov/library/publications/the-world-factbook/geos/ee.html

47. 'The Consumer Markets Scoreboard: Monitoring Consumer Outcomes in the Single Market', COM (2008) 31, European Communities, Luxembourg, 2008: 50; see also Russ Belk and Rosa Llamas (eds), 'The Routledge Companion to the Digital Consumer' Psychology Press, Taylor Francis Group, London 2012, http://www.psypress.com/the-routledge-companion-to-the-digital-consumer-9780415679923

48. Source of Data: Eurostat statistics on information society, http://epp.eurostat.ec.europa.eu/portal/page/portal/information_society/introduction, accessed 21 February 2012; graph: http://epp.eurostat.ec.europa.eu/tgm/graphDownload.do?tab=graph&language=en&plugin=1&pcode=tin00093 accessed 21 February 2012, MET Hyperlink to the graph: http://epp.eurostat.ec.europa.eu/tgm/graph.do?pcode=tin00093&language=en, short description: Individuals who never used the Internet – whether at home, at work or from anywhere else and whether for private or professional purposes. Code: tin00093.

49. Michael Schroeder, 'Germany – France: Different Advertising Styles – Different Communication Concepts', in W.F. van Raaij and G. Bamossy (eds), *European Advances in Consumer Research* 1 (Provo, UT: Association for Consumer Research, 1993): 77–83.

50. Björn Walliser and Fabienne Moreau, 'Comparaison du style français et allemand de la publicité télévisée', *Cahiers du CESAG* 98 1/11 (1998).

51. Edward T. Hall, *Beyond Culture* (New York: Doubleday, 1976).

52. Hans Heyder, Karl Georg Musiol and Klaus Peters, 'Advertising in Europe – attitudes towards advertising in certain key East and West European countries', *Marketing and Research Today* (March 1992): 58–68.

53. Ullrich Appelbaum and Chris Halliburton, 'How to develop international advertising campaigns that work: The example of the European food and beverage sector', *International Journal of Advertising* 12(3) (1993): 223–41.

54. Marc G. Weinberger and Harlan E. Spotts, 'A situational view of information content in TV advertising in the U.S. and U.K.', *Journal of Marketing* 53 (January 1989): 89–94; see also Abhilasha Mehta, 'Global markets and standardized advertising: Is it happening? An analysis of common brands in USA and UK', in *Proceedings of the 1992 Conference of the American Academy of Advertising* (1992): 170.

55. 'Abroadminded', *Marketing* (24 April 1997): 20–1.

56. Heyder, Musiol and Peters, 'Advertising in Europe', *op. cit.*

57. Eduardo Camargo, 'The Measurement of Meaning: Sherlock Holmes in Pursuit of the Marlboro Man', in Umiker-Sebeok (ed.), *Marketing and Semiotics*: 463–83.

58. Sophie Arie, 'Supper is off: Milan bans Da Vinci parody', *The Guardian* (4 February 2005): 15.

59. Claudia Penteado, 'Brazilian ad irks Church', *Advertising Age* (23 March 2000): 11.

Commercialization of rituals: Ramadan celebrations in Turkey

ÖZLEM SANDIKCI AND ŞAHVER ÖMERAKI, Bilkent University, Turkey

Each year, during the ninth month of the lunar calendar, Muslims perform their religious obligation of Ramadan fasting. For a whole month, from sunrise to sunset, adult Muslims whose health permits abstain from food, drink and sexual activity. The sunset prayer announces the end of fasting and the beginning of post-sunset dinner (*iftar*) which is followed by special night prayers. Many Muslims consider Ramadan as the most significant of the ritual duties. Ramadan signifies a time for reflection and spiritual discipline, for expressing gratitude for God's guidance and forgiveness of past sins, for acknowledgment of human dependence on God, as well as remembering and responding to the needs of the poor and hungry.

However, across the Muslim world, there are several signs that Ramadan, a time of fasting, prayer and reflection, is changing from a religious month to a holiday marked by consumption. The spirit of capitalism is felt in practices ranging from the marketing of specialty items (e.g. fasting calendars and lanterns) emblazoned with company logos to luxurious Ramadan feasts promoted by restaurants and hotels, the Ramadan greeting cards, and the Ramadan sweepstakes. It appears that Ramadan is taking on the commercial trappings of Christmas and Hanukah and becoming an increasingly commercialized ritual.

Similar developments are visible in Turkey. Ramadan celebrations now take place more in the public space – especially in retail environments – and in a visibly consumption-oriented manner. For instance, five-star hotels offer lavish Ramadan feasts, Ramadan festivals take place in high-traffic historical sites, and shopping malls transform themselves into Ramadan themed environments offering a variety of shopping and entertainment experiences. Underlying such changes are both state agencies and private companies who cooperate with each other to revive interest in the public celebrations of Ramadan and attract visitors. More and more, Ramadan looks like other Western-originated holiday rituals such as New Year, St Valentine's Day and Mother's and Father's Days that are already celebrated in Turkey but almost exclusively as holidays of consumption.

There are three important contexts where new consumption-oriented forms of Ramadan celebrations take place: Ramadan festivals organized by the municipalities, shopping malls, and hotels and restaurants. In each of these contexts theming operates as the key marketing instrument to attract visitors and educate them on how to celebrate Ramadan away from home. Retailers in these settings use several cultural motifs in order to invoke the Ottoman past and seek to create environments that look like old Ottoman streets and neighbourhoods. The Ottoman theming invokes nostalgia for a bygone age and offers a new interpretation of many forgotten rituals.

Municipalities in Istanbul, Ankara and other big cities organize Ramadan festivals. In the 1992 local elections the Islamist party took over the governance of many municipalities in Turkey including Istanbul. The very first Ramadan festival was organized by Istanbul municipality in the same year. Soon festivals spread to different neighborhoods in Istanbul and other cities. Although there are some variations across the festivals conducted at different locations, what these festivals commonly involve are a wide selection of food and ample opportunities for shopping and entertainment. Municipalities promote the festivals as an attempt to revive the spirit of 'old' Ramadans by constructing temporary consumption spaces that foster participation of different segments of society in these collective celebrations. As no entrance fee is charged, even people with limited incomes can visit the festival areas. However, in order to participate in the joy of the festivals one needs to spend money, i.e. on food and certain entertainment activities. Religious and tourist areas transform into big marketplaces, packed with several stands selling food and beverages as well as all kinds of paraphernalia. On each day of the Ramadan month, thousands of consumers crowd the festival places and wait until the time that the daily fasting will be over. After the call of the prayer that announces the end of the fast, entertainment begins. The activities include religious panels addressing different aspects of Ramadan and Islam as well as artistic performances. The performances mostly include traditional art forms, such as *karagöz* (traditional shadow show) and *meddah* (an earlier form of stand-up shows), which were very popular during the time of the Ottoman Empire but had been long forgotten in the modern era. On the other hand, for those interested in shopping, the stands, which are built in the form of traditional Ottoman houses, offer a wide range of selections from religious objects, such as Qurans and spiritual books, to electronic appliances and Chinese-made decorative ornaments. Moreover, several local and global companies promote their products by distributing samples and other promotional materials. For example, one year Unilever distributed bowls of its newly launched instant soup and cups of Lipton brand flavoured teas. Retailers also indulge themselves in the same spirit by wearing the attire of the Ottoman era. Taken as a whole, municipalities, by creating these festive consumption spaces, make Ramadan an attractive event for companies, retailers, residents and tourists. In the meantime, the municipality also profits as it collects rents from companies and retailers participating in the event.

Shopping malls become another site for the revival of the Ramadan ritual. During the holy month, shopping malls turn into festive places themed with Ottoman symbols. For example, during Ramadan the interior of a shopping mall was once decorated with lively coloured *fezzes*, which were initially used by the Ottoman soldiers and then were adopted as an everyday hat by Ottoman men. Corridors were also decorated by lanterns, which connote the lanterns used to light the streets in the Ottoman Empire. Similar to the festivals organized by municipalities, the malls after *iftar* provide live music, shadow shows, and plays for children. Traditional coffee houses with their stools and small tables are also placed in most of the malls, offering a nostalgic place to relax and drink coffee or tea after the feast. Additionally, small stands are located all over the mall, which sell nostalgic candies and beverages (e.g. candy floss or cotton candy; toffee apple; cotton halva [rather like candy floss or cotton candy]). Shopping malls, similar to the municipality festivals, seek to re-construct the spirit of the publicly-celebrated Ramadan experience, an experience that had lost its public appeal during the making of the modern Turkish republic. The Ottoman theming allows consumers to experience the collective but forgotten past through fantasy, similar to the role of Disney's Main Street in US culture.

Restaurants, from fast-food chains like McDonald's to luxurious five-star hotels, offer different *iftar* menus in a variety of price ranges. The most conspicuous consumption of *iftar* feasts occurs in five-star hotels and restaurants, which use advertising to try and create an alternative 'elite spirit' of Ramadan. The market offers to its elite Muslim followers the ability to experience the sacredness of the month in an exclusive environment. However, rather than being available to everyone, luxurious hotels and restaurants re-produce differences in class positions, as *iftar* dinners cost $30 or more per person. The Ramadan feasts at the five-star hotels and up-scale restaurants include a plethora of dishes, starters, main dishes and sweets, which reflect the abundance of choices presented to the modern consumer. Consumers partake of their *iftar* dinners either in set menus or in American-style buffets. The choice of dinner menus is not limited to a single fixed menu. Rather, hotels and restaurants offered at least four different menus in order to cater for their customers' tastes. In addition, individuals can create their own customized menus. The food offered usually includes a combination of the rich cuisine of the Ottoman Empire and a variety of options from amongst Turkish and World cuisines (e.g. Mexican, Italian and Greek cuisine). The consumer is not limited to the local tastes of his/her country; rather, food acquires a global taste. The choice of food dishes and also the presentation of the food combine to create an elite feast. The food is often served on copper dishes, which used to be the tableware in the Ottoman Empire. Live traditional Turkish music is also performed throughout the feast. In some of the restaurants, even *Whirling Dervish* performances are carried out. Some restaurants have revived traditions that were long forgotten, such as '*Diş Kirası*'. During the Ottoman times, when a family invited visitors for the *iftar* feast, the hosts also gave small gifts to their guests. Modernizing this ritual, an up-scale restaurant offers gifts like silver cigarette cases and amber rosaries to its patrons. Through their sophisticated decorations, selection of dishes and entertainment activities, the up-scale restaurants and five-star hotels have all attempted to create a simulation of the elite Ramadan celebrations of the sultans in the Ottoman palace.

Western holidays like Christmas, Valentine's Day and Hallowe'en rather than displacing traditional local holidays, might have acted to revive and modify existing local rituals. The commercialization of ritual is attained through two processes that complement each other in order to revive and spread the ritual. On the one hand, at the symbolic level, there are distinctive characteristics that differentiate the ritual of Ramadan from other holidays and provide a unique experience for consumers. Different forms of post-sunset *iftar* feasts and celebrations, together with the use of the symbols from the Ottoman Ramadan festivals, encourage a local heterogeneity. On the other hand, rituals are still developed and embellished with the needs of the profit-oriented industries in mind. The global consumerist ideology facilitates and strengthens the consumption of 'sacralized' commodities in the form of products, services, places and experiences, and offer consumers a new occasion for shopping and leisure. Ramadan turns into a commercialized ritual, combining a variety of symbols connoting religious values and beliefs as well as markers of the global consumption ethos. Theming, which underlies all three contexts operate as a major instrument of commercialization.

Local municipalities and the market forge close ties for the revival of Ramadan. Municipalities transform religious and historical places into temporary commercial markets. While the local government profits from organizing the sites, retailers profit by finding another channel through which to market their products. However, what underlies this cooperation is not only the profit motive, but also the state's political ambitions. The Islamist party, which controls the governance of major cities as well as the country, emphasizes both the religious and Ottoman values for the contemporary Turkish identity and takes advantage of any incidence that can be converted into some form of cultural and religious propaganda.

On the other hand, social structures also create a restricted experience of the ritual for many individuals. For example, the luxurious feasts in five-star hotels and restaurants and certain forms of entertainment in the municipality festivals, which require payment of a cover fee, limit accessibility. Rather than acting as a ritual that emphasizes ultimate unity and equality of all believers before God, Ramadan festivals reinforce and reproduce accepted social hierarchies.

QUESTIONS

1 Which agents play a role in the transformation of Ramadan celebrations? What are their motives?

2 What is the role of globalization in the revival and execution of Ramadan rituals?

3 How might social class affect the execution of the ritual?

4 What are the possible positive and negative effects of the commercialization of rituals?

Acculturating to diversity: the changed meaning of consumer acculturation in globalization

JULIE EMONTSPOOL, University of Southern Denmark, Denmark

The usual understanding of migration assumes transitions from so-called developing countries to prosperous Western societies by migrants in search of a better life. While these transitions represent a major share of migratory movements, our global world has seen a diversification in the origins of migrants. The International Organization for Migration states, for instance, that instead of concentrating on a few countries, migration nowadays involves all countries of the world (International Organization for Migration (IOM)).

This globalization of migratory movements runs parallel to a diversification of migrants' educational and professional profiles due to the increasing number of global organizations. More and more companies are requiring their employees to be mobile or to have had previous international experience. Researchers and marketers interested in migrant adaptation therefore need to take this turn into account and rethink some elements of our current understanding of (and theories about) consumer acculturation.

Miguel, a middle class migrant in Belgium

Miguel is one of these new migrants. Twenty-nine years old, he has lived in Brussels for three years, following his Erasmus-funded studies in Vienna when he was a university student, and two years of work experience in Dublin. He works as an IT specialist for an international company that offers worldwide support in informatics. Fearing loneliness in this foreign city, he moved into a shared apartment situated in *Matongé*, a slowly gentrifying African neighbourhood. As his flatmates are Italian and German, Miguel lives in a very multicultural setting.

After the first months of settling in, he decided to attend weekly French lessons, in order to be able to immerse himself in the Belgian environment. Unfortunately his plan did not work out as he had expected. His daily interactions during and after work still took place mainly in English; many of his friends were foreigners just like himself. To remedy this problem, an acquaintance advised him to go to one of the many salsa bars in Brussels, which is a very popular way of meeting people. After a few salsa lessons, he started dancing and met several Belgians. But Miguel was amazed to discover that getting to know Belgium and

its inhabitants involved adaptation to several different cultures at once; many of the people he encountered were immigrants from Latin America, and several of his new Belgian friends were of Moroccan and Congolese descent. So what does adaptation mean in the Belgium setting?

Miguel's food consumption echoes this slightly unexpected twist in his adaptation. After Miguel left Spain, his mother started sending him monthly parcels of Spanish products: sausage, marinated seafood, or biscuits. She was very concerned that he would not feel at home in his new city. Although he enjoys these products, he has asked her to stop sending them. He still bakes tortilla from time to time, and eats other Spanish products, but his everyday consumption could rather be described as *food creolization* (James, 1999, p. 90). With his flatmates, he regularly has dinner at one of the street restaurants below his apartment, ordering Congolese *Chicken Moambé* with fried plantain bananas. At home, Miguel cooks mainly South East Asian or Chinese cuisine because it is good and quickly prepared, but he also integrates the widely available Brussel sprouts and Belgian endives into his menus, and does not hesitate to prepare tapas which reflect Lebanese culinary influences.

A new view of migration

Miguel's example is not exceptional in Brussels, nor is it limited to this city. Global cities tend to be home to a wide mix of cultures, drawn either from earlier colonial links, or from labour migration or from the presence of international companies and institutions. The focus of these global cities lies in international connections rather than national interests, so that they thereby become magnets for global travellers of all kinds (Sassen, 2001).

This diversification of cultural influences exists in urban contexts across countries and continents. In Brussels, for instance, national statistics show that there are migrants from more or less every country in the world (Department of Federal Immigration Belgium, 2008). Multiple labour migration waves, first from southern Europe, then from North Africa and Eastern Europe, have diversified the ethnic landscape in Belgium and added to the original immigration which was the result of the country's colonial past in the Congo (Morelli, 2004).

Within the European Union, the Maastricht and Amsterdam Treaties (1993 and 1997) along with the multiplication of education programmes allowing for university students to spend a semester abroad, have increased intra-EU migration of professionals (Recchi and Nebe, 2003). In Brussels in particular, European institutions such as the European Parliament and the European Commission, the NATO headquarters, European or regional headquarters of multiple multinationals (General Electric, IBM, Toyota or Microsoft) and multiple NGOS attract large numbers of migrants (Investing in Belgium, 2010). Politicians, journalists, diplomats, lobbyists and international expatriates, all live in Brussels and need to acculturate to their new environment. Alongside low-skilled immigrants and professional elites active in high-level positions, today's migratory environments also include many different types of migrants, who move between European states (Fassmann, 2009).

Many of these migrants cluster in the capital city, meaning that the foreign population in Brussels originates from all parts of the world, and is a mixture of labour migration groups and groups from other backgrounds. This leads to a conception of Brussels' inhabitants as what the local dialect calls *Zinneke* (Website of the Zinneke Parade 2010). Initially this term referred to both the city's river and its stray dogs, but now the word has developed over time into a representation of the city's cosmopolitan and multicultural identity, a feature characteristic of global cities all over the world.

Consequently, a large number of people from wide and diverse backgrounds and origins interact in a multicultural context, impacting the meaning of adaptation in unfamiliar consumer cultural environments (Peñaloza, 1994).

Implications for consumer acculturation

Consumer researchers study the adaptation of people arriving in a new country in terms of acculturation. This adaptation is a two-way movement; both the migrants and the host society change as a result of cultural contact (Redfield, Linton and Herskovits, 1936). The diversity of cultures interacting in today's European societies therefore changes our understanding of consumer acculturation as defined by Peñaloza (1994), and suggests multiple cultural influences both within the consumption environment and on migrants' identity.

Peñaloza's (1994) description of the acculturation proposes four outcomes; assimilation, maintenance, resistance and segregation. In her model, migrants can assimilate some elements of the host culture, maintain some other elements of home culture, resist the acculturation pressures of home and host culture at times, and live in segregated areas of town.

In global cities, these outcomes need to be altered in order to take account of the diversity of migrants and cultural contexts:

- Assimilation to the local consumer cultural environment means that migrants adapt to the host culture's broad variety of cultures, and not only to what might be considered as authentic Belgian consumption habits. Miguel for instance enjoys Congolese and Maghrebi (North African) food, which is part of the local product environment in Belgium, but that is not representative of the original Belgian culture.

- Maintaining cultural consumption habits from your home culture can also mean different things as a result of globalization. Pieter, one of Miguel's friends, is Dutch. While Pieter does not feel the need to follow traditional Dutch consumption behaviour now that he lives in Brussels, he does not want to relinquish the Indonesian cuisine which has been a major influence on the restaurant landscape in the Netherlands. Unfortunately, this type of cuisine is less common in Belgium, which means Pieter has to bring Indonesian products back with him from his trips to the Netherlands, and thereby he successfully recreates his Indonesian-influenced consumption habits in Brussels.

- While the diversification of cultural influences leads many migrants and locals to become more open and more cosmopolitan in their consumption habits, resistance or segregation issues remain. Migrants can resist Belgian consumption habits: endives and horse meat do not generate enthusiasm among all migrants, a discomfort that was similarly experienced by US citizens living in France (Usunier, 1999). But this resistance can also relate to specific global or foreign cultural influences. Many British migrants, for instance, resist Indian cuisine in Brussels; they think it's bland and tasteless in comparison with the 'real' Indian cuisine to be found in the UK. Other migrants are disappointed by some global products sold in the host environment. They expected these global products to be the same all over the world, but local adaptations of global products can lead to confusion amongst the migrants.

- Spatial and cultural segregation of some ethnic groups remains a feature in many countries. This tendency is not limited to disadvantaged migrant populations; many cities have seen the emergence of expatriate *enclaves* (Lauring and Selmer, 2009). In Brussels, some migrants active in high positions in the European institutions cluster on the outskirts of Brussels around British or Scandinavian schools for their children. Cities with high numbers of migrants active in international organizations therefore also see segregation of migrants who might welcome the opportunity to assimilate to the local environment. The consequences for consumption behaviour are that many of these migrants buy in speciality shops that import products from foreign countries. Their knowledge of the local market is relatively limited, and their expenses high, as the shops adapt the price levels to the supposedly higher incomes of these migrants.

In conclusion, consumer acculturation processes involve a multiplicity of influences, not only from the home and host cultures, but also from the diversity of environments in global cities like Brussels. The study of ethnic consumption behaviour needs thus to take account of multiple borders. Consumer researchers and marketers alike have to consider diversity in the study of migrant consumption behaviour, and move away from considering home and host consumption environments as culturally homogenous, and rather focus on how identity and consumption shift as migrants experience migration and adaptation.

QUESTIONS

1 How would you describe Miguel's culture?

2 Who or what are the acculturation agents that influence the adaptation of his consumption behaviour?

3 What changes in our understanding of acculturation processes does Miguel's case suggest to you? How does the idea of moving from home to host country change in the context of an increasingly globalized environment?

4 Do you observe the same trends in your city or in your country? What are the similarities and differences?

References

Department of Federal Immigration Belgium (2008), 'La Population Étrangère En Belgique', website of the Department of Federal Immigration Belgium, http://www.dofi.fgov.be/fr/statistieken/statistiques_etrangers/Stat_ETRANGERS.htm

Fassmann, Heinz (2009), 'European Migration: Historical Overview and Statistical Problems', in *Statistics and Reality: Concepts and Measurements of Migration in Europe*, by Heinz Fassmann, Ursula Reeger and Wiebke Sievers, 21–44, Amsterdam University Press.

International Organization for Migration (IOM), 'International Organization for Migration – Facts & Figures', http://www.iom.int/jahia/Jahia/about-migration/facts-and-figures/lang/en.

Investing in Belgium (2010), 'Corporate Headquarters – Investing in Belgium – Business.belgium.be', http://business.belgium.be/en/investing_in_belgium/key_sectors/hqs/

James, Allison (1999), 'Cooking the Books. Global or Local Identities in Contemporary British Food Cultures', in *Cross-cultural Consumption. Global Markets Local Realities*, Routledge, London.

Lauring, J. and J. Selmer (2009), 'Expatriate Compound Living: An Ethnographic Field Study', *The International Journal of Human Resource Management*, 20(7): 1451–1467.

Morelli, Anne (ed.) (2004), *Histoire Des Étrangers Et De L'immigration En Belgique: De La Préhistoire À Nos Jours*, 2e édition, Bruxelles: Couleur livres.

Peñaloza, Lisa (1994), 'Atravesando Fronteras/border Crossings: A Critical Ethnographic Exploration of the Consumer Acculturation of Mexican Immigrants', *Journal of Consumer Research*, 21(1) (June): 32.

Recchi, E. and T.M. Nebe (2003), 'Migration and Political Identity in the European Union: Research Issues and Theoretical Premises', *Florenz: PIONEUR Working Paper*.

Redfield, R., R. Linton and M.J. Herskovits (1936), 'Memorandum for the Study of Acculturation', *American Anthropologist*, 38(1): 149–152.

Sassen, S. (2001), *The Global City: New York, London, Tokyo*, Princeton Univ Press.

Usunier, Jean-Claude (1999), 'Food Consumption and the Expatriation Experience: A Study of American Expatriates in France', *European Advances in Consumer Research*, 4: 177–196.

Website of the Zinneke Parade (2010), 'Website of the Zinneke Parade', *Zinneke Parade*, http://www.zinneke.org/rubrique2.html

Volunteers as co-creators of cultural events: the case of the Midnight Sun Film Festival in Sodankylä, Lapland

ANU VALTONEN AND MINNI HAANPÄÄ, University of Lapland, Finland

Cultural events play a vital role in the contemporary economy. They offer experiences for customers; attract tourists; sustain cultural heritage; play a part in the creation of destinations; and generate various economic benefits. The execution of these events commonly depends on the work of the volunteers. Volunteers are, in this sense, important co-creators of events. Moreover, they are distinct co-creators as they are situated in between the producers and the consumers. Precisely for this reason, they provide an illuminating example of how the roles of marketplace actors are becoming increasingly blurred. This theme is at the centre of many recent theorizations. Volunteers also enable us to better understand the communal aspects of cultural events. As earlier studies have cogently shown, the community that emerges around cultural events is a significant part of the consuming experience. Think of, for instance, how consumers create a sense of togetherness through communal practices in time-limited events such as Burning Man (Kozinets, 2002).

The cultural event that we focus on in this case is the Midnight Sun Film Festival. The annual week-long festival takes place in the small municipality of Sodankylä, in Finnish Lapland. It was founded by the famous Finnish film directors, the Kaurismäki brothers, in 1986, and it is now recognized worldwide. Each year the festival attracts about 25,000 visitors and about 200 volunteers work at the event. During the festival movies are screened for 24 hours a day. All together there are around 140 movies and other events such as director interviews that take place during the festival. It is worth noting that the current leader of the festival started his career as a volunteer. Now, let us ask one woman to tell us her story as a volunteer.

'I decided to volunteer again for the Sodankylä film festival. I get excited just sending in an application form: would they accept me or not? Yes, great, I have been accepted. The organization tells me that the workload will be six hours per day, food and accommodation will be provided, and I will have free access to see films when I am not working. I am asked to take with me a sleeping bag, toiletries for personal hygiene and protection against everything (rain, sunshine, mosquitos, etc.). It is as if I am going to take part in an adults' scout camp! And that is what fascinates me. To gain new experiences, meet new people, have access to a whole new world, and perhaps, even to a new career. The thrill of the unknown, but in an easy and safe way. And also a way to save money: why pay for accommodation, food and films when you can get them for free?

In the middle of June, I arrive at Sodankylä, Lapland, after a long journey including hitchhiking in trucks and cars. On arrival, they give me a badge. Now, I am a volunteer! I am one of *us*. We are going to be in the same boat for a whole week. Some of the other volunteers I know from earlier years, but most of them are unfamiliar to me. There are students, taxi drivers, secretaries; those who are passionate about films and those who are passionate about volunteering; younger and older ones; people from all over the country, mostly from the southern cities, some also from abroad. Only local people seem to be missing.

We work here in order to create the festival. We take care of the ticket sales, clean the rooms in the summer hotel, serve the lunches, sell beer, guard the area at night, take care of the film sessions, and those of us who have advanced up the volunteers' career ladder are allowed to take care of the back stage and VIP guests. We sometimes feel that the event is disorganized and too many things are left undone, we feel tired after some sleepless nights, and we try to achieve a balance between work and fun. And in this way, we get more out of the festival.

As one of us says at the end of the week "Being a volunteer is much more than being a mere film tourist. The experience is much deeper." As a volunteer I feel that I belong to the film community. I am more of an "insider", and not an "outsider". I would not even consider going to a festival except as a volunteer. It offers so many possibilities for meeting new people, for gaining new experiences, for learning new things. I have offered my small input to the festivals and I have received so much more in return'.

Link to the festival: **http://www.msfilmfestival.fi**

Cultural events in Finland

- 1.9 million audience at the member events and festivals of Finland Festivals (head association for almost hundred Finnish cultural events)
- Audience is mainly domestic
- Organized during the summer season
- Mainly organized by associations
- Have long traditions
- Duration usually between 3 to 14 days
- Most common budget between 100,000–299,000 EUR
- About two year-round workers per festival (full or part-time)
- Number of volunteers in all events and festivals organized in 2008 was approximately 4800 persons, compared to the number of year-round staff of 157 persons

Sources: Pasanen and Hakola, 2009; Finland Festivals, 2008.

QUESTIONS

1 Reflect on your own experiences of being a volunteer, or being a customer in events based upon the work of volunteers. Share your views in groups.

2 Compare the categories of volunteers, producers and consumers. What kinds of distinctions and similarities can you identify?

3 Take the viewpoint of volunteers and describe the participatory communal activity of the event – make comparisons with the study of Kozinets (2002).

4 How could event managers appropriate (or use) the volunteer's insights in developing the event?

References

Kozinets, R. (2002), 'Can Consumers Escape the Market? Emancipatory Illuminations from Burning Man', *Journal of Consumer Research*, 29 (June), 20–38.

Pasanen, K. and Hakola, E.-M. (2009), Suomalaisten kulttuuritapahtumien matkailullinen merkittävyys ja kansainvälinen potentiaali. MEK: A:166. Matkailun edistämiskeskus, Helsinki. (The importance of Finnish cultural events for tourism.)

Finland Festivals (2008) Festivaalien taloudellisia avainlukuja – Finland Festivalsin jäsenfestivaalien taloustietoja vuodelta 2008, from: http://www.festivals.fi/resource/files/festivaalien-taloudellisia-avainlukuja-2008.pdf. (Key Economic Figures of Members of Festivals of Finland.)

Majority consumers' resistance to ethnic marketing:
lessons learned from Austria's MPreis customers*

MARIUS K. LUEDICKE, University of Innsbruck, Austria

In autumn 2008, our company ran an advertisement in a Turkish magazine that we subsequently displayed in our supermarkets in Telfs. It was a one-page ad. We placed the ad in return for displaying the magazine in our stores. The magazine was displayed on a stand that was hidden away somewhere at the back of the store where few people took much notice of it. But then the national evening news on TV aired a short report about the Turkish magazine and it started an uproar. We received hundreds of e-mails from customers, some with vehement criticisms. Most threatened never to patronize our stores again unless we removed the Turkish magazines, and many passionately expressed their feelings of disappointment with Mpreis.

Manager at MPreis headquarters, Interview 2010

What was going on in the Austrian market town of Telfs on this day in autumn 2008? Why did local MPreis customers react so passionately against the company's attempt to better serve the Turkish community in the small town? What spurred this backlash? And how did MPreis respond to it?

To gain some sense of perspective about the issues, let us just step back a moment and consider the broader socio-historical context of this incident. From 1960 onwards, about 63 million immigrants have entered the European Union, making immigration one of the top drivers of socio-cultural change, not only in metropolitan cities like Vienna, but also in rather rural market towns like Telfs. For local companies, the influx of immigrants opened up a variety of opportunities. For instance, companies in the food sector began to cater for immigrants' religiously motivated needs by selling halal meats or kosher foods; and companies in the telecom sector began to offer special telephone plans for immigrants who wished to call their families back in their home countries. Such 'ethnic marketing' initiatives allowed companies to turn immigrant citizens into new customer segments and thus to grow their sales and profits.

But companies could also benefit from immigrants as employees. Between 1961 and 1971, for instance, Austrian

companies recruited more than 16,000 men from the Turkish countryside to support the thriving local Austrian factories with their skilled labour. Without these 'guest workers', Austrian industry would have been unable to meet the rapidly growing international demand for its produce and, thus, unable to leverage the region's economic wealth. In the late 1980s, many of the Turkish guest workers decided to stay in Austria and bring their families in, rather than returning to their home country. Fifty years on, more than 110,000 Turkish citizens live in Austria, working in a broad range of occupations and thus contributing their share to the gross domestic product.

MPreis, the target of the above consumer campaign, is an Austrian supermarket that has served customers in the province of Tyrol since 1920. The company is highly respected and liked for its regional rootedness, its ecological and social responsibility, and its internationally admired store and product innovations. In its home market Tyrol, MPreis is the largest food retail company with 150,000 customers per day, 5,200 employees, 660 million euros annual revenue, and about 20 per cent regionally sourced products. The founder was Therese Mölk and her sons and grandsons presently manage the company and are widely respected as diligent, regionally rooted entrepreneurs who have build the company responsibly and consistently in the interest of the local community. Owing to a shortage of qualified local sales personnel, MPreis has recently begun to recruit more and more staff members from the ranks of second and third generation Turkish immigrants. The company's employees with Turkish backgrounds are born in Tirol, speak the local idiom fluently, and are widely recognized by local customers as friendly and competent.

In view of this widely accepted multicultural approach, MPreis' decision to advertise in a Turkish language magazine and display the magazine in their stores does not appear particularly risky. So why did it still cause such an outburst of passionate feelings from among some local customers?

It is well-known among acculturation researchers that immigration not only induces a need for adjustment among immigrant citizens, but also among members of the local majority population. Acculturation theorists maintain that

*This case offers some food for thought that links to the discussion in Chapter 15 on ethnic and religious subcultures.

local majority consumers, like immigrants, choose from among four different 'acculturation strategies' that each define a different ideal role for immigrants to play in the local society. Majority citizens who decide to welcome immigrants as enrichments to their socio-cultural fabric pursue a 'multiculturalism' strategy. Majority citizens who expect immigrants to abandon their original culture and to assimilate to the local culture subscribe to a 'melting pot' or 'pressure cooker' strategy. Majority citizens who, by themselves denying access to the newcomers, leave immigrants no choice but to pursue their original cultural ways at a distance from the mainstream pursue a 'segregation' strategy. And majority consumers who proactively exclude immigrants from their local culture advance their ideal of 'exclusion'.

Immigrant consumers, by entering a foreign market sphere that is already endowed with longstanding traditions, habits and interactive rules, inevitably alter the existing socio-cultural configuration of their new home place. One feature of this existing configuration may be that majority consumers have already built emotionally resonant relationships with their local brands. This relationship often includes implicit rules about who is a legitimate relationship partner, and who is not. Such a definition about legitimate and illegitimate customers evolves over time and is influenced by multiple factors, including the local economic situation, as well as historical relationships, cultural distance, or power (im-) balances between immigrants and majority consumers.

Against this backdrop it is probably not surprising to find that some fraction of local consumers do not experience positive feelings when their relationship partner is opened up to a new consumer segment that they deem to be illegitimate. Under certain conditions, such as those in Telfs, these consumers may experience negative feelings and even feel betrayed when a brand such as MPreis violates their implicit relationship rules and threatens their sense of trust in the relationship.

Using the theoretical notions of acculturation and consumer-brand relationships, we are now in a position to be able to analyse the incident, and also better understand the motivations behind the following e-mail that MPreis customer Anton [pseudonym] sent the company:

Ladies and Gentlemen,

With regard to the TV broadcast yesterday I would like to inform you – even though you are most likely not interested in this (because you care more about our Turkish fellow citizens now) – that I and my entire family (even though this won't have much of an impact) will avoid MPreis stores in the future.

It must be a joke that rather than expecting immigrants to integrate, you actually help them not to adapt [by publishing] in the Turkish magazine. Nothing against foreigners, that is not my intention, but everywhere on the planet one has to conform, so why not here? I don't think that I will ever find a German magazine in a Turkish supermarket.

Best and final greetings, Anton

This e-mail vividly documents the author's sense of disappointment and relationship betrayal. Before the ad was published in the Turkish magazine, Anton's writing implies, MPreis was predominantly (or entirely) interested in serving Tyrolean consumers. The company appeared to be closely aligned to the expectations of local customers that immigrants need to fit in and 'integrate' into the local culture (or leave). The theoretical term for what Anton expects from immigrants is not 'integration' but 'assimilation', which results when a Turkish immigrant abandons her home cultural roots in favour of fully adopting Austrian culture. When seen from the majority citizen perspective, his expectation reflects a 'pressure cooker' acculturation strategy.

In the past, Anton's loyal brand relationship partner MPreis has clearly (yet not necessarily deliberately) followed such a pressure cooker acculturation strategy. The company opened its ranks to Turkish employees, which eliminates segregation and exclusion as strategies and is indicative of the absence of an underlying racist attitude. But since MPreis only recruited immigrants who were able to behave and speak like locals, they did not pursue a truly integrative 'multiculturalism' strategy. From the perspective of consumers such as Anton there is nothing wrong with employing Turkish staff as long as they abandon (or hide) their original cultural values and practices.

The appearance of the Turkish magazine in MPreis stores suggested an unexpected (and unexplained) turn in MPreis's acculturation strategy. For consumers like Anton, allowing original Turkish cultural influences to enter the MPreis stores violated the relationship contract that they felt had been established among the local relationship partners. MPreis seemed to no longer pursue a pressure cooker strategy, but had turned towards a multiculturalism strategy that Anton passionately rejects. In the MPreis stores, Turkish citizens now no longer had 'to conform' to local culture, as Anton bemoans, but were explicitly recognized and treated as an equally appreciated customer group with their own cultural influences, including a foreign language that is incomprehensible to most (if not all) local consumers.

This shift from pressure cooker to multiculturalism strategy felt for Anton like a relationship betrayal. He thus draws on the well-known cultural template of the 'cuckold' when formulating his email response. He first states that he will drop the partner ('I would like to inform you . . . that I and my entire family . . . will avoid MPreis stores in the future'). Then he explains that he does so because he feels less appreciated as a consumer now ('because you care more about our Turkish fellow citizens now') and that

MPreis, firstly has betrayed their implicit agreement ('it must be a joke') that local citizens and companies have the right to expect immigrants to integrate; and secondly, should not be seen to be helping immigrants not to adapt. In terms of the larger socio-cultural environment in Telfs, the Turkish language magazine – that Anton cannot read – reinforces a local feeling of shifts in socio-cultural power relations. Through their action, MPreis seem to have advanced these dynamic shifts, rather than hindered them.

We can learn three important lessons from MPreis and their segment of integration-critical customers:

1 Consumers seem to presume that companies deliberately pursue a particular acculturation strategy, even if they do not.
2 The company's acculturation strategy is part of the brand's meaning and thus part of what motivates consumers to engage with the company, or discourages them from doing so.
3 If company practices that have traditionally manifested such a strategy (deliberately or not) change, consumers can feel betrayed and incited to punish the disloyal partner by withdrawing their euros from their stores.

And how did MPreis respond? On the same day the backlash hit the stores, the company removed the Turkish magazines from its displays. The marketing manager made clear that the company did not deliberately plan this change, but had only wanted to connect better with their valued Turkish employees. They did not expect or intend to offend anyone.

QUESTIONS FOR DISCUSSION

Immerse yourself into the role of MPreis' head of marketing:

1 Why did the Turkish language magazine in the supermarket cause such a backlash?
2 How would you respond to the consumer criticism? And why?
3 How important are local history, power and language issues in this context?
4 Assume your goal is to support integration and multiculturalism in the town, how would you go about it? What options do marketers have to foster integration?

And more generally, reflecting on your own experiences:

5 Would a similar backlash occur in your own neighborhood as well?
6 If so, why? And if not, why not?

GLOSSARY

80/20 rule The rule of thumb (or heuristic) whereby only 20% of a product's users account for 80% of the volume of that product that a company sells (p. 226)

Abandoned products Grocery items that shoppers buy but never use (p. 232)

ABC model of attitudes A multidimensional perspective stating that attitudes are jointly defined by affect, behaviour and cognition (p. 295)

Absolute threshold The minimum amount of stimulation that can be detected by a sensory channel (p. 131)

Accommodative purchase decision The process to achieve agreement among a group whose members have different preferences or priorities (p. 454)

Acculturation The process of learning the beliefs and behaviours endorsed by another culture (pp. 211, 612)

Acculturation agents Friends, family, local businesses and other reference groups which facilitate the learning of cultural norms (p. 612)

Achieved status A status that is based on merit. In other words, a status that reflects one's skills, which has been obtained through one's activities and accomplishments, and as such the status is earned and chosen. To be a top athlete or a professor is an achieved status (p. 488)

Activation models of memory Approaches to memory stressing different levels of processing that occur and activate some aspects of memory rather than others, depending on the nature of the processing task (p. 275)

Activity stores A retailing concept that lets consumers participate in the production of the products or services being sold in the store (p. 85)

Actual self A person's realistic appraisal of his or her qualities (p. 153)

Adaptation The process that occurs when a sensation becomes so familiar that it is no longer the focus of attention (p. 136)

Advergaming Online games merged with interactive advertisements that let companies target specific types of consumers (p. 581)

Affect The way a consumer feels about an attitude object (pp. 191, 294)

Affluenza A term used to describe what some critics see as the negative side effects for consumers' mental and physical health of an excessive focus on consumption; and the underlying assumption of an inverse relationship between happiness and concern with material goods (p. 51)

Age cohort A group of consumers of the same approximate age who have undergone similar experiences (p. 461)

Agentic goals Goals that stress self-assertion and mastery and are associated with males (p. 162)

AIOs (Activities, Interests and Opinions) The psychographic variables used by researchers in grouping consumers (p. 225)

Anchoring A concept in behavioural economics that refers to a number that people use as a standard for future judgements (p. 347)

Androgyny The possession of both masculine and feminine traits (p. 164)

Animism Cultural practices whereby inanimate objects are given qualities that make them somehow alive (p. 203)

Anti-brand communities Groups of consumers who share a common disdain for a celebrity, store or brand (p. 406)

Anti-consumption The actions taken by consumers involving the deliberate defacement or mutilation of products (p. 51)

Appeal The basis of the persuasive message in an advertisement which can be linked to a range of emotions (e.g. fear) and message types (e.g. humour) (p. 317)

Approach–approach conflict A person must choose between two desirable alternatives (p. 191)

Approach–avoidance conflict A person desires a goal but wishes to avoid it at the same time (p. 192)

Archetypes A universally shared idea or behaviour pattern, central to Carl Jung's conception of personality; archetypes involve themes – such as birth, death, or the devil – that appear frequently in myths, stories and dreams (p. 200)

Art product A creation viewed primarily as an object of aesthetic contemplation without any functional value (p. 573)

Ascribed status Status that one has inherited through birth or which is assigned to one later in life. It is not chosen but given to you. To be a prince or to be born into a wealthy family is an ascribed status. Also such phenomena as gender prejudice are based on ascribed status where certain characteristics of 'being a woman' can be ascribed to you (p. 488)

Aspirational reference group High-profile athletes and celebrities used in marketing efforts to promote a product (p. 403)

Asynchronous interactions Digital marketing efforts which don't require all participants to respond immediately, like when you email a friend and get an answer the next day (p. 15)

Atmospherics The use of space and physical features in store design to evoke certain effects in buyers (p. 85)

Attention The assignment of cognitive capacity to selected stimuli (pp. 121, 134)

Attitude A lasting, general evaluation of people (including oneself), objects or issues (p. 292)

Attitude object (A$_o$) Anything towards which one has an attitude (p. 292)

Attitude towards the act of buying (A$_{act}$) The perceived consequences of a purchase (p. 309)

Attitude towards the advertisement (A$_{ad}$) A predisposition to respond favourably to a particular advertising stimulus during an exposure situation (p. 298)

Augmented reality This term refers to media that combine a physical layer with a digital layer to create a combined experience. If you've ever watched a 3D movie with those clunky glasses, you've experienced one form of augmented reality (p. 132)

Autocratic decisions Purchase decisions that are made exclusively by one spouse (p. 455)

Avatar Manifestation of a Hindu deity in superhuman or animal form. In the computing world it has come to mean a cyberspace presence represented by a character that you can move around inside a visual, graphical world (p. 154)

Avoidance reference groups Reference groups which a consumer specifically chooses not to be associated with via his/her consumption choices (p. 405)

Avoidance–avoidance conflict Occurs when we may face a choice between two undesirable alternatives (p. 193)

B2C e-commerce Businesses selling to consumers through electronic marketing (p. 14)

Balance theory Considers relations among elements a person might perceive as belonging together and people's tendency to change relations among elements in order to make them consistent or balanced (p. 303)

Behavioural economics The study of the behavioural determinants of economic decisions (pp. 346, 479)

Behavioural influence perspective The view that consumer decisions are learned responses to environmental cues (p. 336)

Behavioural learning theories The perspectives on learning that assume that learning takes place as the result of responses to external events (p. 261)

Behavioural targeting The appearance and personality a person takes on as an avatar in a computer-mediated environment like Second Life (p. 230)

Being space A retail environment that resembles a residential living room where customers are encouraged to congregate (p. 82)

Blissful ignorance effect States that people who have details about a product before they buy it do not expect to be as happy with it as do those who got only ambiguous information (p. 351)

Body cathexis A person's feelings about aspects of his or her body (p. 169)

Body image A consumer's subjective evaluation of his or her physical appearance (p. 169)

Boomerang kids Children or dependents who find themselves needing to return to their parents/guardians home, primarily for financial reasons (p. 464)

Bounded rationality A concept in behavioural economics that states since we rarely have the resources (especially the time) to weigh every possible factor into a decision, we settle for a solution that is just good enough (p. 345)

Brand The name associated by a manufacturer with their product in order to distinguish their product from similar products in the marketplace; it can often also be a trademark (p. 38)

Brand advocates Consumers who supply product reviews online (p. 363)

Brand communities A set of consumers who share a set of social relationships based on usage or interest in a product (pp. 38, 406)

Brand equity A brand that has strong positive associations and consequently commands a lot of loyalty (p. 268)

Brand-fests Usually organized by companies to promote and celebrate their brands; and often used to encourage the development of brand communities in order to build brand loyalty and reinforce group membership (pp. 406, 434)

Brand loyalty A pattern of repeat product purchases accompanied by an underlying positive attitude towards the brand (p. 370)

Brand personality A set of traits people attribute to a product as if it were a person (p. 202)

Buzz Word of mouth that is viewed as authentic and generated by customers (p. 316)

C2C e-commerce Consumer-to-consumer activity through the internet (p. 14)

Capital Following Bourdieu, capital involves a variety of resources (e.g. economic, cultural and social) that can be used as assets in various contexts (p. 506)

Carbon footprint The impact human activities have on the environment in terms of the amount of greenhouse gases they produce; measured in units of carbon dioxide (p. 222)

Category exemplars Brands that are particularly relevant examples of a broader classification (p. 358)

Classic A fashion with an extremely long acceptance cycle (p. 598)

Classical conditioning The learning that occurs when a stimulus eliciting a response is paired with another stimulus which initially does not elicit a response on its own but will cause a similar response over time because of its association with the first stimulus (p. 262)

Co-consumers Other patrons in a consumer setting (p. 67)

Coercive power Influencing a person by social or physical intimidation (p. 399)

Cognition The beliefs a consumer has about an attitude object (p. 295)

Cognitive development The ability to comprehend concepts of increasing complexity as a person ages (p. 460)

Cognitive learning The learning that occurs as a result of internal mental processes (p. 266)

Cognitive processing style A predisposition to process information. Some of us tend to have a *rational system of cognition* that processes information analytically and sequentially using roles of logic, while others rely on an *experiential system of cognition* that processes information more holistically and in parallel (p. 335)

Cohesiveness The degree to which members of a group are attracted to each other and how much each values their membership in this group (p. 405)

Collecting The accumulation of rare or mundane and inexpensive objects, which transforms profane items into sacred ones (p. 556)

Collective selection The process whereby certain symbolic alternatives tend to be chosen jointly in preference to others by members of a group (p. 590)

Collective value creation The process whereby brand community members work together to develop better ways to use and customize products (p. 406)

Collectivist culture A cultural orientation which encourages people to subordinate their personal goals to those of a stable in-group (p. 532)

Communal goals Goals that stress affiliation and the fostering of harmonious relations and are associated with females (p. 162)

Communities of practice Groups of people engaged in some mutual endeavour or activity (p. 407)

Community In a digital context, a group of people who engage in supportive and sociable relationships with others who share one or more common interests (p. 429)

Comparative influence The process whereby a reference group influences decisions about specific brands or activities (p. 403)

Compensatory decision rules Allow information about attributes of competing products to be averaged; poor standing on one attribute may be offset by good standing on another (p. 372)

Compulsive buying A physiological and/or psychological dependency on products or services. The act of shopping can be an addictive experience for some consumers (p. 50)

Computer-mediated environments (CMEs) A term that refers to the creation of alternative realities/fanciful worlds via the use of computers (p. 154)

Conformity A change in beliefs or actions as a reaction to real or perceived group pressure (p. 410)

Conscientious consumerism A new value that combines a focus on personal health with a concern for global health (p. 222)

Consensual purchase decision A decision in which the group agrees on the desired purchase and differs only in terms of how it will be achieved (p. 454)

Consideration set The products a consumer actually deliberates about choosing (p. 355)

Conspicuous consumption The purchase and prominent display of luxury goods as evidence of the consumer's ability to afford them (pp. 503, 592)

Consumer behaviour The processes involved when individuals or groups select, purchase, use or dispose of products, services, ideas or experiences to satisfy needs or desires (p. 3)

Consumer confidence The state of mind of consumers relative to their optimism or pessimism about economic decisions; people tend to make more discretionary purchases when their confidence in the economy is high (p. 484)

Consumer culture The relationship between market forces, consumption processes and the key characteristics of what is normally understood to be 'a culture' (p. 34)

Consumer-generated content (CGC) A hallmark of Web 2.0; everyday people voice their opinions about products, brands and companies on blogs, podcasts and social networking sites and film their own commercials which they post on websites (p. 207)

Consumer hyperchoice A condition where the large number of available options forces us to make repeated choices that drain psychological energy and diminish our ability to make smart decisions (p. 333)

Consumer policy Concern of public bodies (including many national and international agencies) to oversee consumer-related activities for the welfare of consumers, e.g. health and safety issues around the consumption of legal and illegal substances such as alcohol, cigarettes and drugs; sustainability issues and the environment (p. 17)

Consumer satisfaction/dissatisfaction (CS/D) The overall attitude a person has about a product after it has been purchased (p. 89)

Consumer socialization The process by which people acquire skills that enable them to function in the marketplace (p. 458)

Consumer society A society where the social life is organized less around our identities as producers or workers in the production system, and more according to our roles as consumers in the consumption system (p. 26)

Consumer tribe Group of people who share a lifestyle and who can identify with each other because of a shared allegiance to an activity or a product (p. 406)

Consumption communities Consumption communities are groups of people who share the consumption of a brand or product (p. 4)

Continuous innovation A product change or new product that requires relatively little adaptation in the consumer's behaviour (p. 587)

Conventions Norms regarding the conduct of everyday life (p. 533)

Co-optation A cultural process where the original meaning of a product or other symbol associated with a subculture is modified by members of mainstream culture (pp. 529, 568)

Core values Common general values held by a culture (p. 210)

Corporate paradox The more involved a company appears to be in the dissemination of news about its products, the less credible it becomes (p. 316)

Corporate social responsibility (CSR) CSR addresses two kinds of responsibility: companies' commercial responsibility to run their businesses successfully and their social responsibilities to their local communities and wider society (p. 54)

Cosmopolitanism A cultural value that emphasizes being open to the world and striving for diverse experiences (p. 221)

Cosplay A form of performance art in which participants wear elaborate costumes that represent a virtual world avatar or other fictional character (p. 611)

Country of origin Original country from which a product is produced. Can be an important piece of information in the decision-making process (p. 365)

Craft product A creation valued because of the beauty with which it performs some function; this type of product tends to follow a formula that permits rapid production; it is easier to understand than an art product (p. 573)

Cultivation hypothesis A perspective emphasizing media's ability to distort consumers' perceptions of reality (p. 582)

Cultural categories The grouping of ideas and values that reflect the basic ways members of society characterize the world (p. 36)

Cultural formula Where certain roles and props often occur consistently in many popular art forms, such as detective stories or science fiction (p. 576)

Cultural gatekeepers Individuals who are responsible for determining the types of message and symbolism to which members of mass culture are exposed (p. 570)

Cultural intermediaries Cultural agents that mediate information between high culture and popular mass culture (p. 571)

Cultural production system (CPS) The set of individuals or organizations responsible for creating and marketing a cultural product (p. 570)

Cultural selection The process where some alternatives are selected in preference to those selected by cultural gatekeepers (p. 568)

Culture The values, ethics, rituals, traditions, material objects and services produced or valued by members of society (p. 529)

Culture of participation A belief in democracy, the ability to freely interact with other people, companies and organization, open access to venues that allows users to share content from simple comments to reviews, ratings, photos, stories, and more, and the power to build on the content of others from your own unique point of view (p. 15)

Custom A norm that is derived from a traditional way of doing something (p. 533)

Cyberbullying When one or more people post malicious comments online about someone else in a coordinated effort to harass them (p. 426)

Cybercrime Illegal activities undertaken on the internet and can include risks of identity theft and data loss to consumers (p. 231)

Cybermediary Intermediary that helps to filter and organize online market information so that consumers can identify and evaluate alternatives more efficiently (p. 362)

Cyberplace An online social community (p. 429)

Cyberspace Refers to the virtual world created by the internet where individuals can engage in a variety of activities including the buying and selling of goods and services; and also games playing (p. 76)

Database marketing Involves tracking consumers' buying habits and crafting products and information tailored to people's wants and needs (p. 13)

Decision polarization The process whereby individuals' choices tend to become more extreme (polarized), in either a conservative or risky direction, following group discussion of alternatives (p. 408)

De-individuation The process whereby individual identities are submerged within a group, reducing inhibitions against socially inappropriate behaviour (p. 408)

Democracy In a social media context, a term that refers to rule by the people; community leaders are appointed or elected based on their demonstrated ability to add value to the group (p. 431)

Demographics The observable measurements of a population's characteristics, such as birth rates, age distribution or income (p. 9)

Desacralization The process that occurs when a sacred item or symbol is removed or is duplicated in mass quantities and as a result becomes profane (p. 555)

Determinant attributes The attributes actually used to differentiate among choices (p. 360)

Differential threshold The ability of a sensory system to detect changes or differences among stimuli (p. 131)

Digital literacy Involves a set of requisite IT skills, at a sufficient level of capability, in order to be able to access, navigate and use the internet; and thus enable individuals to participate fully in the information society of the twenty-first century (p. 621)

Digital native Consumers grew up 'wired' in a highly networked, always-on world where digital technology had always existed (p. 14)

Digital virtual consumption Purchases of virtual goods for use in online games and social communities (p. 434)

Discontinuous innovation A product change or new product that requires a significant amount of adaptation of behaviour by the adopter (p. 588)

Discretionary income The money available to an individual or household over and above that required for maintaining a standard of living (p. 482)

Dissociative reference groups Reference groups with which a consumer does not want to be linked; and therefore the consumer usually avoids products and services (or brand imagery) linked to these groups (p. 405)

Distinction A term used by French sociologist Pierre Bourdieu for establishing a class system based on consumer tastes (p. 507)

Divestment rituals The steps people take to gradually distance themselves from things they treasure so that they can sell them or give them away (p. 237)

Doppelgänger brand image A brand image which looks like the original, but is in fact a critique of it (p. 202)

Downshifting Reducing reliance on possessions and learning to get by with less (p. 220)

Drive The desire to satisfy a biological need in order to reduce physiological arousal (p. 187)

Drive theory Focuses on the desire to satisfy a biological need in order to reduce physiological arousal (p. 188)

Dynamically continuous innovation A product change or new product that requires a moderate amount of adaptation of behaviour by the adopter (p. 588)

Early adopters People receptive to new styles because they are involved in the product category and place high value on being fashionable (p. 585)

Economics of information A branch of microeconomic theory that studies how information affects an *economy* and economic decisions. Information has special characteristics. It is easy to create but hard to trust. It is easy to spread but hard to control. It influences many decisions (p. 22)

Ego The system that mediates between the id and the superego in the mind (p. 197)

Elaborated codes The ways of expressing and interpreting meanings that are complex and depend on a sophisticated worldview; they tend to be used by the middle and upper classes (p. 498)

Elaboration likelihood model (ELM) The approach that one of two routes to persuasion (central *vs* peripheral) will be followed, depending on the personal relevance of a message; the route taken determines the relative importance of message contents *vs* other characteristics, such as source attractiveness (p. 322)

Electronic recommendation agent A software tool that tries to understand a human decision maker's multiattribute preferences for a product category by asking the user to communicate his or her preferences. Based on that data, the software then recommends a list of alternatives sorted by the degree that they fit with the person's preferences (p. 362)

Emic perspective An approach to studying cultures that stresses the unique aspects of each culture (p. 43)

Encoding The process in which information from short-term memory is entered into long-term memory in recognizable form (p. 272)

Enculturation The process of learning the beliefs and behaviours endorsed by one's own culture (p. 211)

Erogenous zones Areas of the body considered by members of a culture to be foci of sexual attractiveness (p. 591)

E-skills Abilities specifically associated with the electronic world, e.g. internet, web, online retail sites and social media; and could include *inter alia* abilities to surf the net; navigate around websites; search for and buy goods and services online; use basic software programs such as word-processing and spreadsheets; and undertake key word searches of databases in electronic formats (p. 621)

Ethical consumer A consumer often taking ethical, environmental, social and/or political issues into consideration when making purchase and consumption decisions (p. 51)

Ethnic subculture A self-perpetuating group of consumers held together by common cultural ties (p. 611)

Ethnocentrism The belief in the superiority of one's own country's practices and products (p. 365)

Ethnoconsumerism The understanding and analysis of each culture, including consumer culture, on the basis of its own premises (p. 532)

Ethos A set of moral, aesthetic and evaluative principles (p. 531)

Etic perspective An approach to studying culture that stresses the commonalities across cultures (p. 43)

Evaluative criteria The dimensions used by consumers to compare competing product alternatives (p. 359)

Evoked set Those products already in memory plus those prominent in the retail environment that are actively considered during a consumer's choice process (pp. 275, 355)

Exchange The process whereby two or more organizations or people give and receive something of value (p. 6)

Exchange theory The perspective that every interaction involves an exchange of value (p. 89)

Expectancy disconfirmation model The perspective that consumers form beliefs about product performance based on prior experience with the product and/or communications about the product that imply a certain level of quality; their actual satisfaction depends on the degree to which performance is consistent with these expectations (p. 91)

Expectancy theory The perspective that behaviour is largely 'pulled' by expectations of achieving desirable 'outcomes' or positive incentives, rather than 'pushed' from within (p. 189)

Experience economy A marketplace structure where not just the product or some additional services are provided for the consumer but a complete consumption experience (p. 39)

Experiential perspective An approach stressing the gestalt or totality of the product or service experience, focusing on consumers' affective responses in the marketplace (p. 336)

Expert power Authority derived from possessing a specific knowledge or skill (p. 398)

Exposure An initial stage of perception where some sensations come within range of consumers' sensory receptors (p. 121)

Extended family Traditional family structure where several generations and/or relatives such as aunts, uncles and cousins live together (p. 448)

Extended problem-solving An elaborate decision-making process often initiated by a motive that's fairly central to the self-concept and accompanied by perceived risk; the consumer tries to collect as much information as possible and carefully weighs product alternatives (p. 338)

Extended self The definition of self created by the external objects with which one surrounds oneself (p. 160)

Extinction The process whereby learned connections between a stimulus and response are eroded so that the response is no longer reinforced (p. 263)

Fad A short-lived fashion (p. 598)

Family financial officer (FFO) The family member who is in charge of making financial decisions (p. 455)

Family household A housing unit containing at least two people who are related by blood or marriage (p. 449)

Family lifecycle (FLC) A classification scheme that segments consumers in terms of changes in income and family composition and the changes in demands placed on this income (p. 453)

Fashion The process of social diffusion by which a new style is adopted by a group or groups of consumers (p. 590)

Fashion acceptance cycle The diffusion process of a style through three stages: introduction, acceptance and regression (p. 597)

Fashion lifecycle The 'career' or stages in the life of a fashion as it progresses from launch to obsolescence (p. 597)

Fashion system Those people or organizations involved in creating symbolic meanings and transferring these meanings to cultural goods (p. 589)

Feature bloat Another term for feature creep, denoting the increasing complexity of products and the associated difficulties of comprehension for consumers in learning how to use the products (p. 358)

Feature creep Trend towards an increasing number of options a product offers that make it more difficult for consumers to decide among competitors (p. 358)

Feature fatigue Another term for feature creep, denoting the increasing complexity of products and the associated difficulties of comprehension for consumers in learning how to use the products (p. 358)

Fertility rate A rate determined by the number of births per year per 1,000 women of child-bearing age (p. 449)

Figure-ground principle The gestalt principle whereby one part of a stimulus configuration dominates a situation while other aspects recede into the background (p. 139)

Flaming A violation of digital etiquette to express when a post is written in all capital letters (p. 432)

Flashmobs A group of people who converge on a physical location to perform some act 'spontaneously' and then disperse (p. 207)

Flows Exchanges of resources, information, or influence among members of an online social network (p. 430)

Flow state Situation in which consumers are truly involved with a product, an ad, or a website (p. 205)

Folksonomy An online posting system where users categorize entries themselves rather than relying upon a pre-established set of labels (p. 429)

Foot-in-the-door technique Based on the observation that a consumer is more likely to comply with a request if he or she has first agreed to comply with a smaller request (p. 302)

Fortress brands Brands that consumers closely link to rituals; this makes it unlikely they will be replaced (p. 541)

Framing A concept in behavioural economics that the way a problem is posed to consumers (especially in terms of gains or losses) influences the decision they make (p. 346)

Freecycling The practice of giving away useful but unwanted goods to keep them out of landfills (p. 236)

Freegans A takeoff on *vegans*, who shun all animal products; anti-consumerists who live off discards as a political statement against corporations and materialism (p. 236)

Frequency marketing A marketing technique that reinforces regular purchasers by giving them prizes with values that increase along with the amount purchased (p. 270)

Freudian theory Viennese psychologist Sigmund Freud (1856–1939) was one of the founders of psychoanalysis and conceptualized the mind as being structured in three parts (id, ego and superego) (p. 197)

Functional theory of attitudes A pragmatic approach that focuses on how attitudes facilitate social behaviour; attitudes exist because they serve some function for the person (p. 293)

Game-based marketing A strategy that involves integrating brand communications in the context of an online group activity (p. 340)

Game platform An online interface that allows users to engage in games and other social activities with members of a community (p. 339)

Generation X (Gen-Xers or baby busters) The cohort of consumers aged 18–29, who were profoundly affected by the economic recession of the early 1990s (p. 464)

Genre In the context of social gaming, the method of play such as simulation, action, and role-playing (p. 340)

Gestalt psychology A school of thought that maintains people derive meaning from the totality of a set of stimuli rather than from an individual stimulus (p. 138)

Gift-giving ritual The events involved in the selection, presentation, acceptance and interpretation of a gift (p. 544)

Global consumer culture A culture in which people around the world are united through their common devotion to brand name consumer goods, movie stars, celebrities and leisure activities (p. 13)

Globalization The process whereby geographical distance is decreasing in importance for the constitution of the social world. Instead, the social world is structured by how groups and societies are positioned in relation to global flows of people, money, technology, mediated information and ideas (p. 43)

Glocalization The basic principle that the flows that constitute globalization (see above) are always adopted into local cultures (p. 49)

Goal A consumer's desired end-state (p. 187)

Greenwashing Inflated claims about a product's environmental benefits. A play on the word 'whitewash', but employed here to describe activities of firms which seek to create the perception that they are conscientious about the potential environmental impact of their activities and thus that they are environmentally friendly, although it is unclear how far the espoused environmental values feed through into actual company policy (p. 223)

Grey market Term used to describe the phenomenon of a fast-growing segment of consumers aged 62 or older (p. 468)

Guerrilla marketing Promotional strategies that use unconventional locations and intensive word-of-mouth campaigns (p. 426)

Habitual decision-making The consumption choices that are made out of habit, without additional information search or deliberation among products (p. 341)

Habitus Systems of classification of phenomena adopted from our socialization processes (p. 506)

Halal Food and other products whose usage is permissible according to the laws of Islam (p. 617)

Hedonic adaptation In order to maintain a fairly stable level of happiness we tend to become used to positive and negative events in our lives (p. 221)

Hedonic consumption The multisensory, fantasy and emotional aspects of consumers' interactions with products (p. 124)

Heuristics The mental rules of thumb that lead to a speedy decision (p. 364)

Hierarchy of effects A fixed sequence of steps that occurs during attitude formation; this sequence varies depending on such factors as the consumer's level of involvement with the attitude object (p. 295)

Hierarchy of needs Psychologist Abraham Maslow developed a system whereby needs were ranked in ascending order of importance starting with the lower order needs (physiological, i.e. requirements for water, sleep and food), through safety, belongingness, ego needs and culminating in individuals' desire for self-actualization (p. 194)

High-context culture Group members tend to be tightly knit and messages and meanings are implicit and built into the communication context (p. 625)

Highlighting effect The order in which consumers learn about brands determines the strength of association between these brands and their attributes (p. 278)

Homeostasis The state of being where the body is in physiological balance; goal-oriented behaviour attempts to reduce or eliminate an unpleasant motivational state and returns to a balanced one (p. 188)

Home shopping parties A selling format where a company representative makes a sales presentation to a group of people who gather at the home of a friend or acquaintance (p. 409)

Homogamy The tendency for individuals to marry others similar to themselves (p. 486)

Homophily The degree to which a pair of individuals is similar in terms of education, social status and beliefs (p. 413)

Horizontal revolution Horizontal revolution is characterized in part by the prevalence of social media. Social media are the online means of communication, conveyance, collaboration, and cultivation among interconnected and interdependent networks of people, communities, and organizations enhanced by technological capabilities and mobility (p. 14)

Host culture A new culture to which a person must acculturate (p. 614)

Hype Corporate propaganda planted by companies to create product sensation – dismissed as inauthentic by customers (p. 316)

Hyperopia The medical term for people who have far-sighted vision; describes people who are so obsessed with preparing for the future that they can't enjoy the present (p. 348)

Hyperreality A phenomenon associated with modern advertising in which what is initially stimulation or hype becomes real (pp. 40, 142)

Icon A sign that resembles the product in some culturally meaningful way (p. 140)

Id The system oriented towards immediate gratification (p. 197)

Ideal self One's personality is composed of the *real self* and the *ideal self*. Your real self is who you actually are, while your ideal self is the person you want to be. The ideal self is an idealized version of yourself created out of what you have learned from your life experiences, the demands of society, and what you admire in your role models (p. 153)

Identificational membership reference group A group that has a significant effect on an individual's aspirations such that the individual forms an attitude towards the group and seeks to conform to the group's expectations and to join it (p. 405)

Impression management The process by which consumers work hard to 'manage' what others think of us by strategically choosing clothing and other cues that will put us in a good light (p. 153)

Impulse buying A process that occurs when the consumer experiences a sudden urge to purchase an item that he or she cannot resist (p. 87)

Incidental brand exposure Where consumers are influenced by brand stimuli they don't realize they have experienced such as unplanned exposure to brand logos (p. 350)

Incidental similarity Points of commonality between a buyer and a seller such as a shared birthday (p. 89)

Index A sign that is connected to a product because they share some property (p. 140)

Individualism Personal value orientation that encourages people to attach more importance to personal goals than to group goals; values such as personal enjoyment and freedom are stressed (p. 216)

Individualist culture A cultural orientation that encourages people to attach more importance to personal goals than to group goals; values such as personal enjoyment and freedom are stressed (p. 532)

Inertia The process whereby purchase decisions are made out of habit because the consumer lacks the motivation to consider alternatives (pp. 205, 370)

Influence impressions Brand-specific mentions on social media posts (p. 421)

Influence network A two-way dialogue between participants in a social network and opinion leaders (p. 415)

Influentials Within the two-step model of communication, these people were generally regarded as having the greatest amount of impact on fellow consumers in trying to sway the outcome of the consumer decision or attitude (e.g. to the brand; to the advertising message) (p. 415)

Information cascades An online communication process where one piece of information triggers a sequence of interactions (p. 415)

Information power Power given simply because one knows something others would like to know (p. 398)

Information search The process whereby a consumer searches for appropriate information to make a reasonable decision (p. 332)

Informational social influence The conformity that occurs because the group's behaviour is taken as evidence about reality (p. 409)

Innovation A product or style that is perceived as new by consumers (p. 582)

Innovative communicators Opinion leaders who are also early purchasers (p. 415)

Instrumental values Those goals that are endorsed because they are needed to achieve desired end-states or terminal values (p. 215)

Intelligent agents Software programs that learn from past user behaviour in order to recommend new purchases (p. 362)

Interactions In a social media context, behaviour-based ties between participants such as talking with each other, attending an event together, or working together (p. 430)

Interactive mobile marketing Real-time promotional campaigns targeted to consumers' cell phones (p. 208)

Interference A process whereby additional learned information displaces earlier information resulting in memory loss for the item learned previously (p. 279)

Interpretant The meaning derived from a symbol (p. 140)

Interpretation The process whereby meanings are assigned to stimuli (p. 121)

Interpretivism A research perspective that produces a 'thick' description of a consumer's subjective experiences and stresses the importance of the individual's social construction of reality (p. 25)

Involvement The motivation to process product-related information (p. 204)

JND (just noticeable difference) The minimum change in a stimulus that can be detected by a perceiver (p. 131)

Kin network system The rituals intended to maintain ties among family members, both immediate and extended (p. 456)

Knowledge structures Organized systems of concepts relating to brands, stores and other concepts (pp. 275, 356)

Laddering A technique for uncovering consumers' associations between specific attributes and general consequences (p. 217)

Lateral cycling A process where already purchased objects are sold to others or exchanged for other items (p. 235)

Latitudes of acceptance and rejection Formed around an attitude standard; ideas that fall within a latitude will be favourably received, while those falling outside this zone will not (p. 302)

Lead users Involved, experienced customers (usually corporate customers) who are very knowledgeable about the field (p. 586)

Learning A relatively permanent change in a behaviour as a result of experience (p. 261)

Legitimate power Influence over others due to a position conferred by a society or organization (p. 398)

Lifestyle A set of shared values or tastes exhibited by a group of consumers especially as these are reflected in consumption patterns (p. 223)

Lifestyle marketing perspective A perspective that recognizes that people are increasingly conscious that we sort ourselves and each other into groups on the basis of the things we/they like to do and how we/they spend our/their disposable income (p. 227)

Limited problem-solving A problem-solving process in which consumers are not motivated to search for information or evaluate rigorously each alternative; instead they use simple decision rules to arrive at a purchase decision (p. 340)

List of Values (LOV) scale A scale developed to isolate values with more direct marketing applications. Identifies consumer segments based on the values members endorse and relates each value to differences in consumption behaviours (p. 216)

LOHAS An acronym for 'lifestyles of health and sustainability'; a consumer segment that worries about the environment, wants products to be produced in a sustainable way, and who spend money to advance what they see as their personal development and potential (p. 222)

Long-term memory The system that allows us to retain information for a long period (p. 275)

Long tail Rather than the conventional approach of many companies to marketing which is to sell a lot of one product to most customers, here the notion is that companies should pursue 'the long tail', i.e. a strategy of selling a large variety of products to a smaller number of customers to achieve the same level of business, so that there is a shift from mass markets to many, many niche markets (p. 362)

Looking-glass self The process of imagining the reaction of others towards oneself (p. 156)

Low-context culture Messages tend to be more explicit, specific and direct (p. 611)

Low-literate consumer People who read at a very low level; tend to avoid situations where they will have to reveal their inability to master basic consumption decisions such as ordering from a menu (p. 352)

Lurkers Passive members of an online community who do not contribute to interactions (p. 432)

Market beliefs The specific beliefs of decision rules pertaining to marketplace phenomena (p. 365)

Market maven A person who often serves as a source of information about marketplace activities (p. 416)

Market segmentation Strategies targeting a brand only to specific groups rather than to everybody (p. 8)

Masculinism Study devoted to the male image and the cultural meanings of masculinity (p. 166)

Mass customization The personalization of products and services for individual customers at a mass-production price (p. 206)

Mass connectors Highly influential members of social media networks (p. 421)

Materialism The importance consumers attach to worldly possessions (p. 219)

Maximising A decision strategy that seeks to deliver the best possible result (p. 345)

Meaning The fundamental of unit of human society. All cultures are systems of meaning. As sociologists Nisbet and Perrin (1970) formulated it: The symbol is to the social world what the atom is to the physical world and the cell is to the biological world (*The Social Bond*, 1970) (p. 35)

Means–end chain model Assumes that people link very specific product attributes (indirectly) to terminal values such as freedom or safety (p. 217)

MECCAs (Means-end Conceptualization of the Components of Advertising Strategy) A research approach in which researchers generate a map depicting relationships between functional product or service attributes and terminal values and then use this information to develop advertising strategy (p. 217)

Media democratization In a social media context, members of social communities, not traditional media publishers like magazines or newspaper companies, control the creation, delivery, and popularity of content (p. 431)

Media multiplexity In a social media context, when flows of communication go in many directions at any point in time and often on multiple platforms (p. 430)

Meetups Members of an online network arrange to meet in a physical location (p. 430)

Membership reference group Ordinary people whose consumption activities provide informational social influence (p. 409)

Meme theory A perspective that uses a medical metaphor to explain how an idea or product enters the consciousness of people over time, much like a virus (p. 595)

Memory A process of acquiring information and storing it over time (p. 272)

Mental accounting Principle that states that decisions are influenced by the way a problem is posed (p. 346)

Mental budgets Consumers' pre-set expectations of how much they intend to spend on a shopping trip (p. 86)

Mere exposure phenomenon The tendency to like persons or things if we see them more often (p. 405)

Metrosexual A straight, urban male who exhibits strong interests and knowledge regarding product categories such as fashion, home design, gourmet cooking, and personal care that run counter to the traditional male sex role (p. 166)

Micro-culture Groups that form around a strong shared identification with an activity or art form (p. 610)

Microloans Small sums – typically less than $100 – banks lend to entrepreneurs in developing countries (p. 500)

Milieu In the context of social gaming, the visual nature of the game such as science fiction, fantasy, horror and retro (p. 339)

MMOGS (massive multiplayer online games) Social games where large numbers of people in different physical locations participate (p. 434)

MMORPGs (massively multiplayer online role playing games) Online role-playing games that typically involve thousands of players (pp. 340, 434)

Mobile shopping apps Smartphone applications that retailers provide to guide shoppers in stores and malls (p. 86)

Mode In the context of social gaming, the way players experience the game world (p. 339)

Momentum effect An accelerating diffusion of a message in social media due to the contributions of influential members (p. 422)

Monochronic A cultural relation to time that stresses its linearity and attach importance to engaging in one task at a time. Time is conceived mechanically, as in a clockwork (p. 532)

Monomyth A myth with basic characteristics that are found in many cultures (p. 538)

Mores Norms with strong moral overtones (p. 533)

Motivation An internal state that activates goal-oriented behaviour (p. 187)

Motivational research A qualitative research approach based on psychoanalytical (Freudian) interpretations with a heavy emphasis on unconscious motives for consumption (p. 198)

Multi-attribute attitude models Those models that assume that a consumer's attitude (evaluation) of an attitude object depends on the beliefs he or she has about several or many attributes of the object; the use of a multiattribute model implies that an attitude towards a product or brand can be predicted by identifying these specific beliefs and combining them to derive a measure of the consumer's overall attitude (p. 305)

Multitasking The best performance by an individual of appearing to handle more than one task at the same time. The term is derived from computer multitasking. An example of multitasking is taking phone calls while typing an email. Some believe that multitasking can result in time wasted due to human context switching and apparently causing more errors due to insufficient attention (p. 135)

Myth A story containing symbolic elements which expresses the shared emotion and ideals of a culture (p. 536)

Name-letter effect All things being equal we like others who share our names or even initials better than those who don't (p. 403)

Narrative transportation The result of a highly involving message where people become immersed in the storyline (p. 206)

Need A basic biological motive (p. 187)

Negative reinforcement The process whereby a negative reward weakens responses to stimuli so that inappropriate behaviour is avoided in the future (p. 264)

Negative word-of-mouth The passing on of negative experiences involved with products or services by consumers to other potential customers to influence others' choices (pp. 422, 424)

Network units Members of a social network (p. 429)

Neuromarketing A new technique that uses a brain scanning device called functional magnetic resonance imaging (fMRI), that tracks blood flow as people perform mental tasks. Scientists know that specific regions of the brain light up in these scans to show increased blood flow when a person recognizes a face, hears a song, makes a decision, senses deception, and so on. Now they are trying to harness this technology to measure consumers' reactions to movie trailers, choices about automobiles, the appeal of a pretty face, and loyalty to specific brands (p. 360)

Neuroscience Study of the brain via experimental methods to assess the different types and levels of reactions to various forms of marketing stimuli (e.g. advertisements) (p. 361)

Nodes Members of a social network connected to others via one or more shared relationships (p. 429)

Non-compensatory decision rules A set of simple rules used to evaluate competing alternatives; a brand with a low standing on one relevant attribute is eliminated from the consumer's choice set (p. 371)

Normative influence The process in which a reference group helps to set and enforce basic standards of conduct (p. 403)

Normative social influence The conformity that occurs when a person alters his or her behaviour to meet the expectations of a person or group (p. 410)

Norms The informal rules that govern what is right and wrong (p. 410)

Nostalgia A bittersweet emotion when the past is viewed with sadness and longing; many 'classic' products appeal to consumers' memories of their younger days (p. 280)

Nuclear family A contemporary living arrangement composed of a married couple and their children (p. 448)

Object A semiotic term, the product that is the focus of the message (p. 140)

Object sociality The extent to which an object (text, image, video) is shared among members of online social networks (p. 430)

Observational learning The process in which people learn by watching the actions of others and noting the reinforcements they receive for their behaviours (p. 267)

Open rates The percentage of people who open an e-mail message from a marketer (p. 68)

Operant conditioning The process by which the individual learns to perform behaviours that produce positive outcomes and to avoid those that yield negative outcomes (p. 264)

Opinion leaders Those people who are knowledgeable about products and who are frequently able to influence others' attitudes or behaviours with regard to a product category (p. 413)

Opinion seekers Usually opinion leaders who are also involved in a product category and actively search for information (p. 415)

Paradigm A widely accepted view or model of phenomena being studied. The perspective that regards people as rational information processors is currently the dominant paradigm, though this approach is now being challenged by a new wave of research that emphasizes the frequently subjective nature of consumer decision-making (p. 25)

Parental yielding The process that occurs when a parental decision-maker is influenced by a child's product request (p. 457)

Parody display The deliberate avoidance of widely used status symbols, whereby the person seeks status by mocking it (p. 506)

Passion-centric Members of a social network share an intense interest in some topic (p. 430)

Pastiche The playful and ironic mixing of existing categories and styles (p. 41)

Perceived age How old a person feels rather than his or her chronological age (p. 470)

Perceived risk The belief that use of a product has potentially negative consequences, either physical or social (p. 351)

Perception The process by which stimuli are selected, organized or interpreted (p. 121)

Perceptual defence People see what they want to see – and don't see what they don't want to see. If a stimulus is threatening to us we may not process it – or we may distort its meaning so that it is more acceptable. For example, a heavy smoker may block out images of cancer-scarred lungs because these vivid reminders hit too close to home (p. 136)

Perceptual map A research tool used to understand how a brand is positioned in consumers' minds relative to competitors (p. 123)

Perceptual selection The process in which people attend to only a small portion of the stimuli to which they are exposed (p. 135)

Perceptual vigilance Stimuli that consumers attend to because it relates to their current needs (p. 135)

Personality A person's unique psychological makeup, which consistently influences the way the person responds to his or her environment (pp. 185, 199)

Personality traits Identifiable characteristics that define a person (p. 200)

Persuasion An active attempt to change attitudes (p. 313)

Pluralism The coexistence of various styles, truths and fashions (p. 40)

Point-of-purchase stimuli (POP) The promotional materials that are deployed in shops or other outlets to influence consumers, decisions at the time products are purchased (p. 87)

Polychronic A cultural relation to time that stresses its circularity and allows for engaging in multiple tasks at a time. Time is conceived organically, as in natural cycles (life, seasons, . . .) (p. 532)

Popular culture The music, films, sports, books, celebrities and other forms of entertainment consumed by the mass market (p. 34)

Pop-up stores Temporary locations that allow a company to test new brands without a huge financial commitment (p. 83)

Positive reinforcement The process whereby rewards provided by the environment strengthen responses to stimuli (p. 264)

Positivism A research perspective that relies on the principles of the 'scientific method' and assumes that a single reality exists; events in the world can be objectively measured; and the causes of behaviour can be identified, manipulated and predicted (p. 25)

Postmodernism A theory that questions the search for universal truths and values and the existence of objective knowledge (p. 40)

Potlatch A Kwakiutl Indian feast at which the host displays his wealth and gives extravagant gifts (p. 503)

Power users Opinion leaders in online networks (p. 421)

Practice theory A theoretical framework that stresses, how much of human behaviour is inscribed in routines that we have picked up over time through our socialization. As such, it is heavily based on our social backgrounds and our learned skills and tastes (see Distinction) (p. 509)

Presence The effect that people experience when they interact with a computer-mediated environment (p. 431)

Pretailer An e-commerce site that provides exclusive styles by prodding manufacturers to produce catwalk pieces they wouldn't otherwise make to sell in stores (p. 78)

Priming The process in which certain properties of a stimulus are more likely to evoke a schema than others (p. 137)

Principle of closure Implies that consumers tend to perceive an incomplete picture as complete (p. 138)

Principle of cognitive consistency The belief that consumers value harmony among their thoughts, feelings and behaviours and that they are motivated to maintain uniformity among these elements (p. 300)

Principle of least interest The person who is least committed to staying in a relationship has the most power (p. 411)

Principle of similarity The gestalt principle that describes how consumers tend to group objects that share similar physical characteristics (p. 139)

Problem recognition The process that occurs whenever the consumer sees a significant difference between his or her current state and some desired or ideal state; this recognition initiates the decision-making process (p. 341)

Productivity orientation A continual striving to use time constructively (p. 190)

Product placement The process of obtaining exposure for a product by arranging for it to be inserted into a film, television programme or some other medium (p. 580)

Product signal Communicates an underlying quality of a product through the use of aspects that are only visible in the ad (p. 364)

Profane consumption The process of consuming objects and events that are ordinary or of the everyday world (p. 550)

Progressive learning model The perspective that people gradually learn a new culture as they increasingly come in contact with it; consumers assimilate into a new culture, mixing practices from their old and new environments to create a hybrid culture (p. 614)

Propinquity As physical distance between people decreases and opportunities for interaction increase, they are more likely to form relationships (p. 405)

Prospect theory A descriptive model of how people make choices (p. 348)

Prosumer A consumer that reflects the tendency to blur production and consumption processes as in tailor-made solutions, consumer involvement in production and assembling processes, etc. (p. 573)

Proxemics The study of the social construction of personalized space. How close or distant can you stand, sit, etc. to family, friends, strangers. Proxemics often cause cross-cultural discomfort as 'comfortable distance' from strangers is not defined in the same way across cultures (p. 532)

Psychographics The use of psychological, sociological and anthropological factors to construct market segments (pp. 9, 223, 224)

Psychology of Loss Aversion (PLA) A concept from economics that argues that, when making decisions, individuals tend to have a stronger preference to avoid losses rather than to acquire gains (p. 348)

Psychophysics The science that focuses on how the physical environment is integrated into the consumer's subjective experience (p. 131)

Punishment The process or outcome that occurs when a response is followed by unpleasant events (p. 264)

Purchase momentum Initial impulses to buy in order to satisfy our needs increase the likelihood that we will buy even more (p. 335)

Queuing theory The mathematical study of waiting lines (p. 71)

Racial subculture A self-perpetuating group held together by ties of common culture and/or genetics, identified by its members and others as a distinguishable category (p. 611)

Rational perspective A view of the consumer as a careful, analytical decision-maker who tries to maximize utility in purchase decisions (p. 334)

Reactance A boomerang effect that may occur when consumers are threatened with a loss of freedom of choice; they respond by doing the opposite of the behaviour advocated in a persuasive message (p. 412)

Reader-response theory A theory that stresses the role of an interpreting reader in the constitution of human communication. It is thus critical of the idea, that the sender's intended meaning can be used to define, what a communication is (or should be) about (p. 314)

Reality engineering The process whereby elements of popular culture are appropriated by marketers and become integrated into marketing strategies (e.g. product placement) (p. 578)

Reclaimers Businesses which seek to rescue and recycle items of potential historical interest or collectable value, e.g. architectural features of houses undergoing demolition such as fireplaces, doors, windows (p. 235)

Reference group An actual or imaginary individual or group which has a significant effect on an individual's evaluations, aspirations or behaviour (p. 395)

Referent power The power of prominent people to affect others' consumption behaviours by virtue of product endorsements, distinctive fashion statements or championing causes (p. 398)

Relationship marketing The strategic perspective that stresses the long-term, human side of buyer/seller interactions (p. 12)

Reputation economy A reward system based on recognition of one's expertise by others who read online product reviews (p. 363)

Response bias A form of contamination in survey research where some factor, such as the desire to make a good impression on the experimenter, leads respondents to modify their true answers (p. 284)

Restricted codes The ways of expressing and interpreting meanings that focus on the content of objects and tend to be used by the working class (p. 497)

Retail theming Strategy where stores create imaginative environments that transport shoppers to fantasy worlds or provide other kinds of stimulation (p. 82)

Retrieval The process whereby desired information is accessed from long-term memory (p. 272)

Reward power A person or group with the means to provide positive reinforcement (p. 398)

RFID (response frequency identification device) tag A small plastic tag that holds a computer chip capable of storing a small amount of information, along with an antenna that lets the device communicate with a computer network. These devices are being implanted in a wide range of products to enable marketers to track inventory more efficiently (p. 14)

Risk society A term coined by German sociologist to describe a situation, where modernity and scientific progress is no longer perceived to increasingly reduce risk but, on the contrary, is perceived to increasingly produce risks (global warming, nuclear waste, . . .) (p. 51)

Risky shift Group members show a greater willingness to consider riskier alternatives following group discussions than they would if each member made his or her own decision without prior discussion (p. 408)

Rites of passage Sacred times marked by a change in social status (p. 549)

Ritual A set of multiple, symbolic behaviours that occur in fixed sequence and that tend to be repeated periodically (p. 541)

Ritual artefacts Items or consumer goods used in the performance of rituals (p. 542)

Role theory The perspective that much of consumer behaviour resembles action in a play (p. 6)

Rumour A word-of-mouth campaign to promote one product and criticize its competitors (p. 424)

Sacralization A process that occurs when ordinary objects, events or people take on sacred meaning to a culture or to specific groups within a culture (p. 556)

Sacred consumption The process of consuming objects and events that are set apart from normal life and treated with some degree of respect or awe (p. 550)

Satisficing A decision strategy that aims to yield an adequate solution rather than the best solution in order to reduce the costs of the decision-making process (p. 345)

Savings rate The amount of money saved for later use influenced by consumers' pessimism or optimism about their personal circumstances and perceptions of the economy (p. 484)

Schema An organized collection of beliefs and feelings represented in a cognitive category (pp. 122, 276)

Search engines Software (such as Google) that helps consumers access information based upon their specific requests (p. 344)

Self-concept The attitude a person holds to him- or herself (p. 151)

Self-gifts The products or services bought by consumers for their own use as a reward or consolation (p. 546)

Self-image congruence models The approaches based on the prediction that products will be chosen when their attributes match some aspect of the self (p. 159)

Self-perception theory An alternative explanation of dissonance effects; it assumes that people use observations of their own behaviour to infer their attitudes towards an object (p. 302)

Semiotics A field of study that examines the correspondence between a sign and the meaning(s) it conveys (p. 140)

Sensation The immediate response of sensory receptors to such basic stimuli as light, colour and sound (p. 121)

Sensory marketing Sensory marketing occurs where companies pay extra attention to the impact of sensations on our product experiences (p. 124)

Sensory memory The temporary storage of information received from the senses (p. 274)

Sensory overload Sensory overload occurs where consumers are exposed to far more information than they can process (p. 134)

Sentiment analysis A process (sometimes also called *opinion mining*) that scours the social media universe to collect and analyse the words people use when they describe a specific product or company (p. 191)

Sex-typed traits Characteristics that are stereotypically associated with one sex or another (p. 163)

Sharing sites E-commerce sites that allow users to share, exchange and rent goods in a local setting (p. 235)

Shopping orientation A consumer's general attitudes and motivations regarding the act of shopping (p. 74)

Short-term memory The system that allows us to retain information for a short period (p. 274)

Sign The sensory imagery that represents the intended meanings of the object (p. 140)

Signifying practices Practices that have meaning to individuals, who know how to interpret them, thanks to the understanding of culture as the interpreting system (p. 530)

Sisyphus effect Decision-makers who are so thorough they don't even rely on their past experiences to guide their current choice. Instead they start almost from scratch to research options for each unique decision situation (p. 345)

Social class The overall rank of people in society; people who are grouped within the same social class are approximately equal in terms of their social standing, occupations and lifestyles (p. 485)

Social comparison theory The perspective that people compare their outcomes with others as a way to increase the stability of their own self-evaluation, especially when physical evidence is unavailable (p. 411)

Social game A multi-player, competitive, goal-oriented activity with defined rules of engagement and online connectivity among a community of players (pp. 208, 339)

Social graphs Social networks; relationships among members of online communities (p. 430)

Social hierarchy A ranking of social desirability in terms of consumers' access to such resources as money, education and luxury goods (p. 479)

Social judgement theory The perspective that people assimilate new information about attitude objects in the light of what they already know or feel; the initial attitude as a frame of reference and new information are categorized in terms of this standard (p. 302)

Social loafing The tendency for people not to devote as much to a task when their contribution is part of a larger group effort (p. 408)

Social marketing The promotion of causes and ideas (social products), such as energy conservation, charities and population control (p. 18)

Social media Social media are the online means of communication, conveyance, collaboration, and cultivation among interconnected and interdependent networks of people, communities and organizations enhanced by technological capabilities and mobility (p. 14)

Social mobility The movement of individuals from one social class to another (p. 491)

Social network A group of people who connect with one another online due to some shared interest or affiliation (p. 429)

Social networking A growing practice whereby websites let members post information about themselves and make contact with others who share similar interests and opinions or who want to make business contacts (p. 430)

Social object theory Proposes that social networks will be more powerful communities if there is a way to activate relationships among people and objects within them (p. 430)

Social power The capacity of one person to alter the actions or outcome of another (p. 398)

Social stratification The process in a social system by which scarce and valuable resources are distributed unequally to status positions which become more or less permanently ranked in terms of the share of valuable resources each receives (p. 488)

Sociometric methods The techniques for measuring group dynamics that involve tracing of communication patterns in and among groups (p. 419)

Source attractiveness The dimensions of a communicator which increase his or her persuasiveness; these include expertise and attractiveness (p. 315)

Source credibility A communication source's perceived expertise, objectivity or trustworthiness (p. 315)

Spacing effect The tendency to recall printed material to a greater extent when the advertiser repeats the target item periodically rather than presenting it over and over at the same time (p. 277)

Spectacles A marketing message that takes the form of a public performance (p. 207)

Spiritual–therapeutic model Organizations that encourage behavioural changes such as weight loss that are loosely based on religious principles (p. 615)

Stage of cognitive development Segmentation of children by age or their ability to comprehend concepts of increasing complexity (p. 460)

Status crystallization The extent to which different indicators of a person's status are consistent with one another (p. 492)

Status symbols Products that are purchased and displayed to signal membership in a desirable social class (p. 479)

Stereotype An example regarded as typical of a particular group of people (p. 366)

Stimulus discrimination The process that occurs when behaviour caused by two stimuli is different as when consumers learn to differentiate a brand from its competitors (p. 264)

Stimulus generalization The process that occurs when the behaviour caused by a reaction to one stimulus occurs in the presence of other, similar stimuli (p. 263)

Storage The process that occurs when knowledge entered in long-term memory is integrated with what is already in memory and 'warehoused' until needed (p. 272)

Store gestalt Consumers' global evaluation of a store (p. 85)

Store image The 'personality' of a shop composed of attributes such as location, merchandise suitability and the knowledge and congeniality of the sales staff (p. 85)

Subculture A group whose members share beliefs and common experiences that set them apart from the members of the main culture (p. 610)

Subliminal perception Subliminal perception refers to a stimulus below the level of the consumer's awareness (p. 133)

Superego The system that internalizes society's rules and that works to prevent the id from seeking selfish gratification (p. 197)

Surrogate consumer A professional who is retained to evaluate and/or make purchases on behalf of a consumer (p. 417)

Symbol A sign that is related to a product through either conventional or agreed-on associations (p. 140)

Symbolic interactionism A sociological approach stressing that relationships with people play a large part in forming the self; people live in a symbolic environment and the meaning attached to any situation or object is determined by a person's interpretation of those symbols (p. 156)

Symbolic self-completion theory The perspective that people who have an incomplete self-definition in some context will compensate by acquiring symbols associated with a desired social identity (p. 158)

Synchronous interactions Digital interactions that occur in real-time like when you text back-and-forth with a friend (p. 15)

Syncratic decisions Purchase decisions that are made jointly by spouses (p. 455)

Taste culture A group of consumers who share aesthetic and intellectual preferences (p. 497)

Terminal values End-states desired by members of a culture (p. 215)

Theory of cognitive dissonance Theory based on the premise that people have a need for order and consistency in their lives and that a state of tension is created when beliefs or behaviours conflict with one another (p. 192)

Theory of planned behaviour A theory about the link between attitudes and behaviour. The concept was proposed by Icek Ajzen to improve on the predictive power of the theory of reasoned action by including perceived behavioural control. It is one of the most predictive persuasion theories. It has been applied to studies of the relations among beliefs, attitudes, behavioural intentions and behaviours in various fields such as advertising, public relations, advertising campaigns and healthcare. The theory states that attitude towards behaviour, subjective norms and perceived behavioural control, together shape an individual's behavioural intentions and behaviours (p. 308)

Theory of reasoned action A version of the Fishbein multi-attitude theory that considers such factors as social pressure and the attitude towards the act of buying a product rather than attitudes towards just the product itself (p. 308)

Theory of trying States that the criterion of behaviour in the reasoned action model of attitude measurement should be replaced with *trying* to reach a goal (p. 311)

Ties Connections between members of a social network (p. 429)

Tie strength The nature and potency of the bond between members of a social network (p. 420)

Time poverty A feeling of having less time available than is required to meet the demands of everyday living (p. 69)

Time style Determined by an individual's priorities, it incorporates such dimensions as economic time, past or future orientation, time submissiveness and time anxiety (p. 68)

Tipping point Moment of critical mass (p. 595)

Torn self Where individuals struggle between retaining their original authentic culture while still enjoying the cultural freedoms offered by the Western society in which they live (p. 154)

Trade dress Colour combinations come to be so strongly associated with a corporation that they become known as the company's trade dress, and the company may even be granted exclusive use of these colours (p. 126)

Transactional advertising An advertising message in a social game that rewards players if they respond to a request (p. 208)

Transitional economies Countries that are in the process of transforming their economic system from a controlled, centralized system to a free market one (p. 49)

Tribal marketing strategy Linking a product's identity to an activity-based 'tribe' such as basketball players (p. 407)

Trickle-down theory The perspective that fashions spread as a result of status symbols associated with the upper classes trickling down to the other social classes as these consumers try to emulate those with higher status (p. 592)

Two-step flow model of influence Proposes that a small group of *influencers* disseminate information since they can modify the opinions of a large number of other people (p. 415)

U-commerce The use of ubiquitous networks that will slowly but surely become a part of us, such as wearable computers or customized advertisements beamed to us on our mobile phones (p. 13)

Underground economy Secondary markets (such as flea markets) where transactions are not officially recorded (p. 235)

Unplanned buying When a shopper buys merchandise she did not intend to purchase, often because she recognizes a new need while in the store (p. 87)

User-generated content User-generated content occurs where everyday people voice their opinions about products, brands and companies on blogs, podcasts and social networking sites such as Facebook and Twitter, and even film their own commercials that thousands view on sites such as YouTube. Probably the biggest marketing phenomenon of this decade (p. 15)

Uses and gratifications theory Argues that consumers are an active, goal-directed audience who draw on mass media as a resource to satisfy needs (p. 314)

Value A belief that some condition is preferable to its opposite (p. 209)

Value system A culture's ranking of the relative importance of values (p. 211)

Values and Lifestyles (VALS) A psychographic segmentation system used to categorize consumers into clusters (p. 218)

Variety amnesia A condition where people consume products to the point where they no longer enjoy them (p. 346)

Variety seeking The desire to choose new alternatives over more familiar ones (p. 346)

Viral marketing The strategy of getting customers to sell a product on behalf of the company that creates it (p. 428)

Virtual goods Digital items that people buy and sell online (p. 434)

Virtual identities The appearance and personality a person takes on as an avatar in a computer-mediated environment like Second Life (p. 154)

Virtual water footprint Represents how much total water is required to produce a product, taking account of the use of water resources throughout the production process (p. 222)

Virtual worlds Immersive 3-D virtual, i.e. online and web-based, environments such as Second Life (p. 434)

Want The particular form of consumption chosen to satisfy a need (p. 187)

Warming Process of transforming new objects and places into those that feel cozy, hospitable and authentic (p. 614)

Web Internet exchange system that has evolved from its original roots as a form of one-way transmission from producers to consumers to a social, interactive medium (Web 2.0) (p. 195)

Web 2.0 The rebirth of the internet as a social, interactive medium from its original roots as a form of one-way transmission from producers to consumers (p. 15)

Weber's Law The principle that the stronger the initial stimulus, the greater its change must be for it to be noticed (p. 131)

Wisdom of crowds A perspective that argues under the right circumstances, groups are smarter than the smartest people in them; implies that large numbers of consumers can predict successful products (p. 432)

Word-of-mouth communication (WOM) The information transmitted by individual consumers on an informal basis (p. 422)

Word–phrase dictionary In sentiment analysis, a library that codes data so that the program can scan the text to identify whether the words in the dictionary appear (p. 191)

Worldview The ideas shared by members of a culture about principles of order and fairness (p. 531)

Zipf's Law Pattern that describes the tendency for the most robust effect to be far more powerful than others in its class; applies to consumer behaviour in terms of buyers' overwhelming preferences for the market leader in a product category (p. 368)

INDEX OF PERSONAL NAMES

INDEX OF COMPANIES AND PRODUCTS

SUBJECT INDEX